Street by Street

GREATER MANCHESTER

ALTRINCHAM, ASHTON-UNDER-LYNE, BRAMHALL, GLOSSOP, HAZEL GROVE, HYDE, LITTLEBOROUGH, MIDDLETON, PRESTWICH, SALE, SALFORD, STALYBRIDGE, STRETFORD, WILMSLOW

Enlarged Areas Bolton, Bury, Oldham, Rochdale, Stockport, Wigan

2nd edition August 2003
© Automobile Association Developments Limited 2003

Original edition printed May 2001

Ordnance Survey® This product includes map data licensed from Ordnance Survey ® with the permission of the Controller of Her Majesty's Stationery Office.
© Crown copyright 2003.
All rights reserved. Licence No: 399221.

Published by AA Publishing (a trading name of Automobile Association Developments Limited, whose registered office is Millstream, Maidenhead Road, Windsor, Berkshire SL4 5GD. Registered number 1878835).

Mapping produced by the Cartography Department of The Automobile Association. (A1709)

A CIP Catalogue record for this book is available from the British Library.

Printed in Italy by Printer Trento srl.

Ref: MX044z

Key to map pages	ii-iii
Key to map symbols	iv–1
Enlarged map pages	2-15
Main map pages	16-131
Index – towns & villages	132–133
Index – streets	134-195
Index – featured places	195-203
Acknowledgements	204

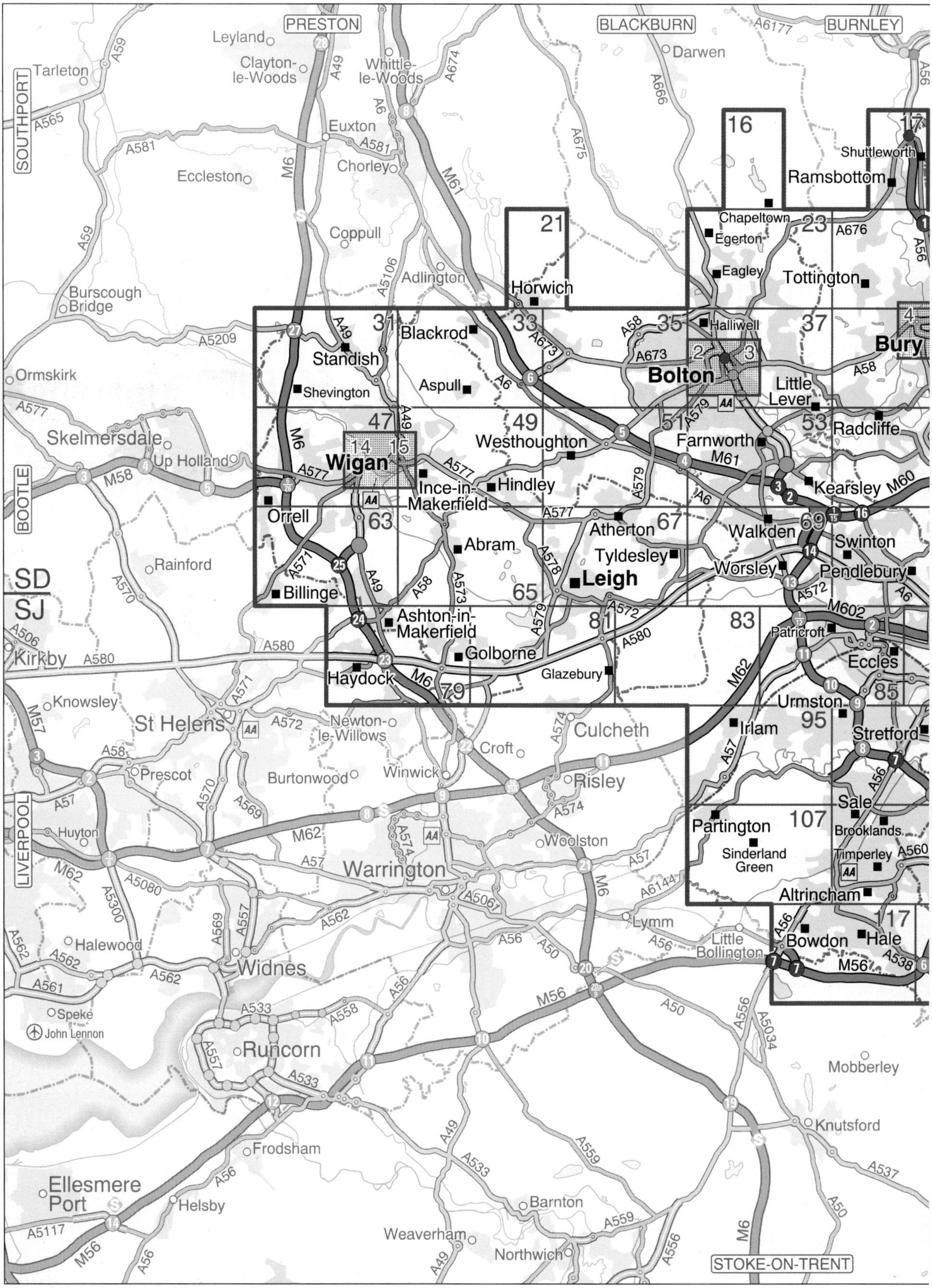

PRESTON BLACKBURN BURNLEY

Tarleton Leyland Clayton-le-Woods Whittle-le-Woods Darwen

SOUTHPORT A565 A581 Euxton Chorley A675 A666 A6177 A56

Eccleston Coppull 16 Shuttleworth Ramsbottom

Adlington 21 Chapeltown 23 A676 Tottington

Burscough Bridge A5209 Horwich Egerton Eagley 37 Bury

Ormskirk 31 Blackrod 33 35 Halliwell A58

Standish Aspull A6 Bolton Little Lever 53 Radcliffe

Skelmersdale Shevington 47 49 Westhoughton 51 Farnworth Kearsley A60

Up Holland 14 15 Wigan Hindley Atherton 67 Walkden Swinton Pendlebury

Orrell Ince-in-Makerfield 63 Abram Tyldesley Worsley Eccles

Rainford Billinge 65 Leigh 81 83 Patricroft 85

Kirkby Ashton-in-Makerfield Golborne Glazebury Urmston 95 Stretford

Knowsley Haydock 79 Culcheth Irlam Sale Brooklands

St Helens Newton-le-Willows Croft Risley Partington 107 Timperley A560

Prescot Burtonwood Winwick Woolston Sinderland Green Altrincham

Liverpool Huyton Warrington Lymm 117 Bowdon Hale M56

Halewood Widnes Little Bollington

Speke John Lennon Runcorn

Frodsham Mobberley Knutsford

Ellesmere Port Helsby Barnton Weaverham Northwich STOKE-ON-TRENT

SD / SJ BOOTLE

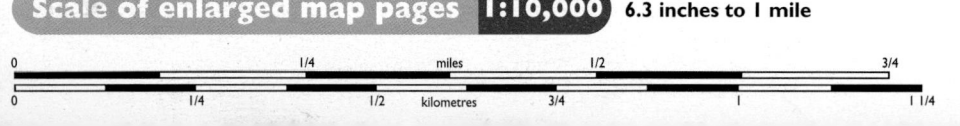

Scale of enlarged map pages 1:10,000 6.3 inches to 1 mile

miles 0 1/4 1/2 3/4

kilometres 0 1/4 1/2 3/4 1 1 1/4

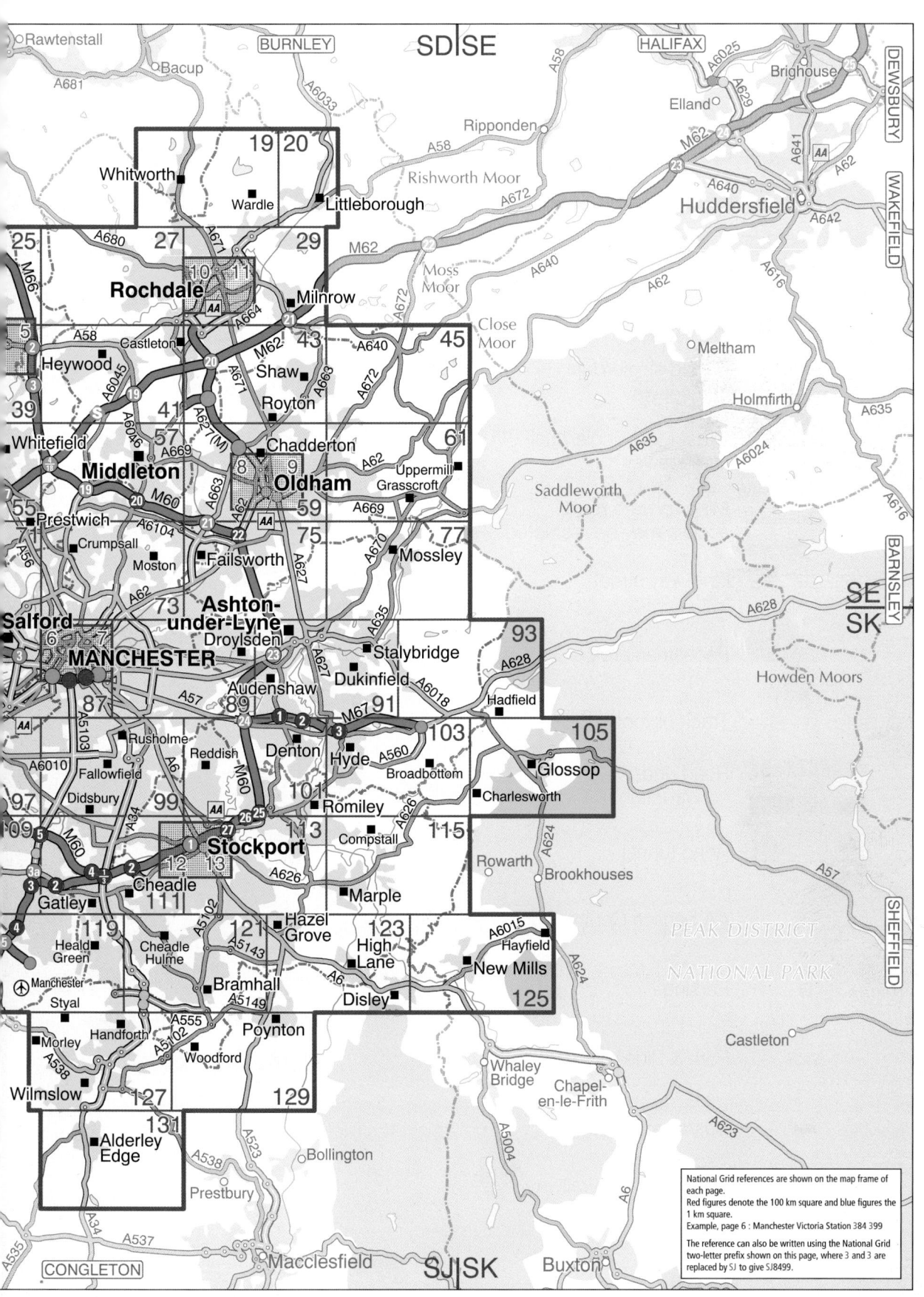

National Grid references are shown on the map frame of each page.
Red figures denote the 100 km square and blue figures the 1 km square.
Example, page 6 : Manchester Victoria Station 384 399

The reference can also be written using the National Grid two-letter prefix shown on this page, where 3 and 3 are replaced by SJ to give SJ8499.

3.6 inches to 1 mile **Scale of main map pages 1:17,500**

Junction 9	Motorway & junction	⊖	Light railway & station
Services	Motorway service area	++++++++++	Preserved private railway
	Primary road single/dual carriageway	LC	Level crossing
Services	Primary road service area	•—•—•—•—	Tramway
	A road single/dual carriageway	- - - - - - -	Ferry route
	B road single/dual carriageway	....	Airport runway
	Other road single/dual carriageway	— · — · — ·	County, administrative boundary
	Minor/private road, access may be restricted	▾▾▾▾▾▾▾▾	Mounds
← ←	One-way street	93	Page continuation 1:17,500
	Pedestrian area	7	Page continuation to enlarged scale 1:10,000
============	Track or footpath		River/canal, lake
▪▪▪▪▪▪▪▪	Road under construction		Aqueduct, lock, weir
[- - = =]	Road tunnel	465 ▲ Winter Hill	Peak (with height in metres)
AA	AA Service Centre		Beach
P	Parking		Woodland
P+🚌	Park & Ride		Park
🚌	Bus/coach station		Cemetery
	Railway & main railway station		Built-up area
	Railway & minor railway station		Featured building
⊖	Underground station	⊓⊓⊓⊓	City wall

A&E	Hospital with 24-hour A&E department
PO	Post Office
	Public library
i	Tourist Information Centre
i	Seasonal Tourist Information Centre
	Petrol station, 24 hour — Major suppliers only
†	Church/chapel
	Public toilets
	Toilet with disabled facilities
PH	Public house — AA recommended
	Restaurant — AA inspected
Madeira Hotel	Hotel — AA inspected
	Theatre or performing arts centre
	Cinema
	Golf course
▲	Camping — AA inspected
	Caravan site — AA inspected
	Camping & caravan site — AA inspected
	Theme park
	Abbey, cathedral or priory
	Castle
	Historic house or building
Wakehurst Place NT	National Trust property
M	Museum or art gallery
	Roman antiquity
	Ancient site, battlefield or monument
	Industrial interest
	Garden
	Garden Centre — Garden Centre Association Member
	Garden Centre — Wyevale Garden Centre
	Arboretum
	Farm or animal centre
	Zoological or wildlife collection
	Bird collection
	Nature reserve
	Aquarium
V	Visitor or heritage centre
	Country park
	Cave
	Windmill
	Distillery, brewery or vineyard

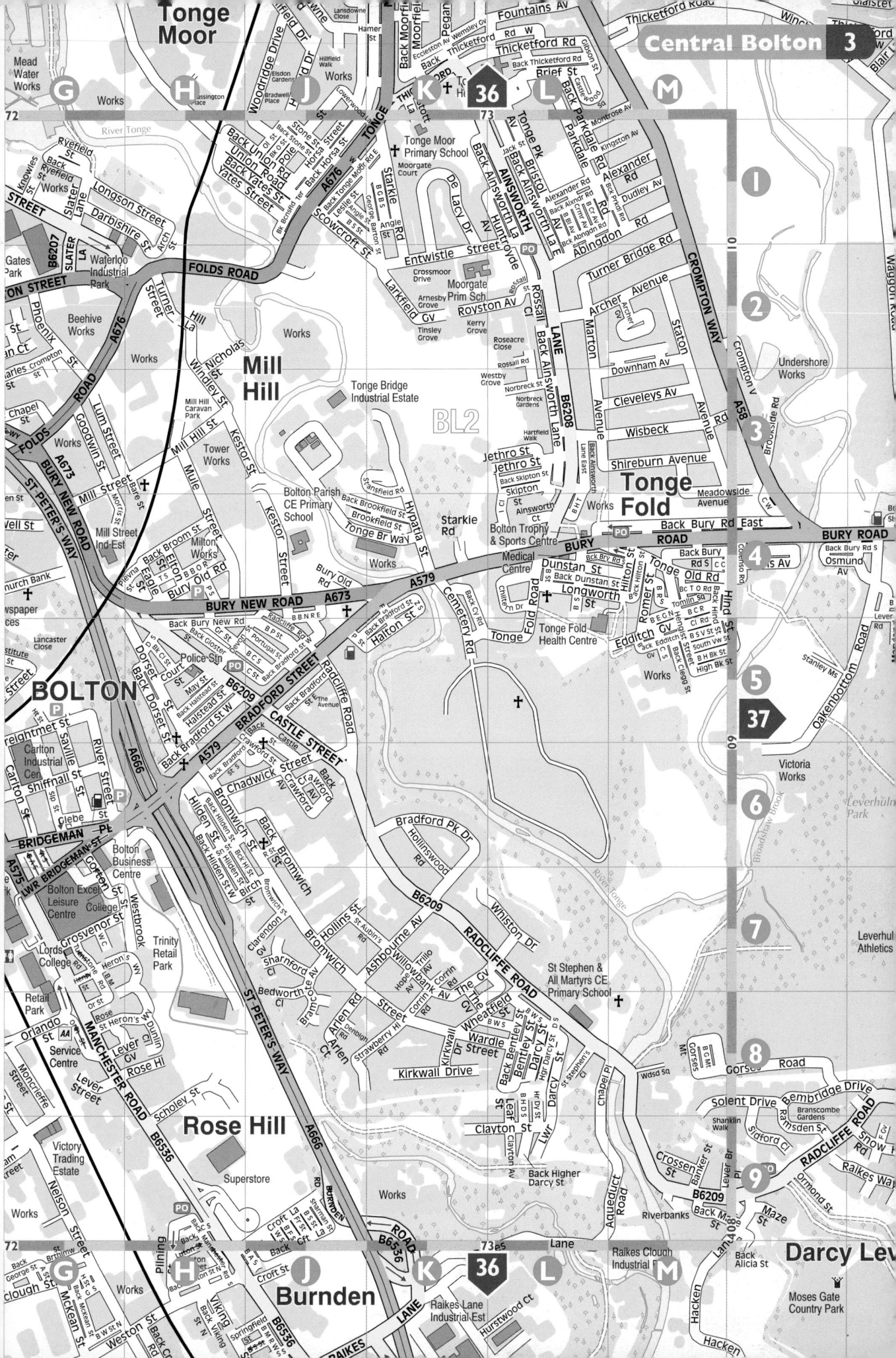

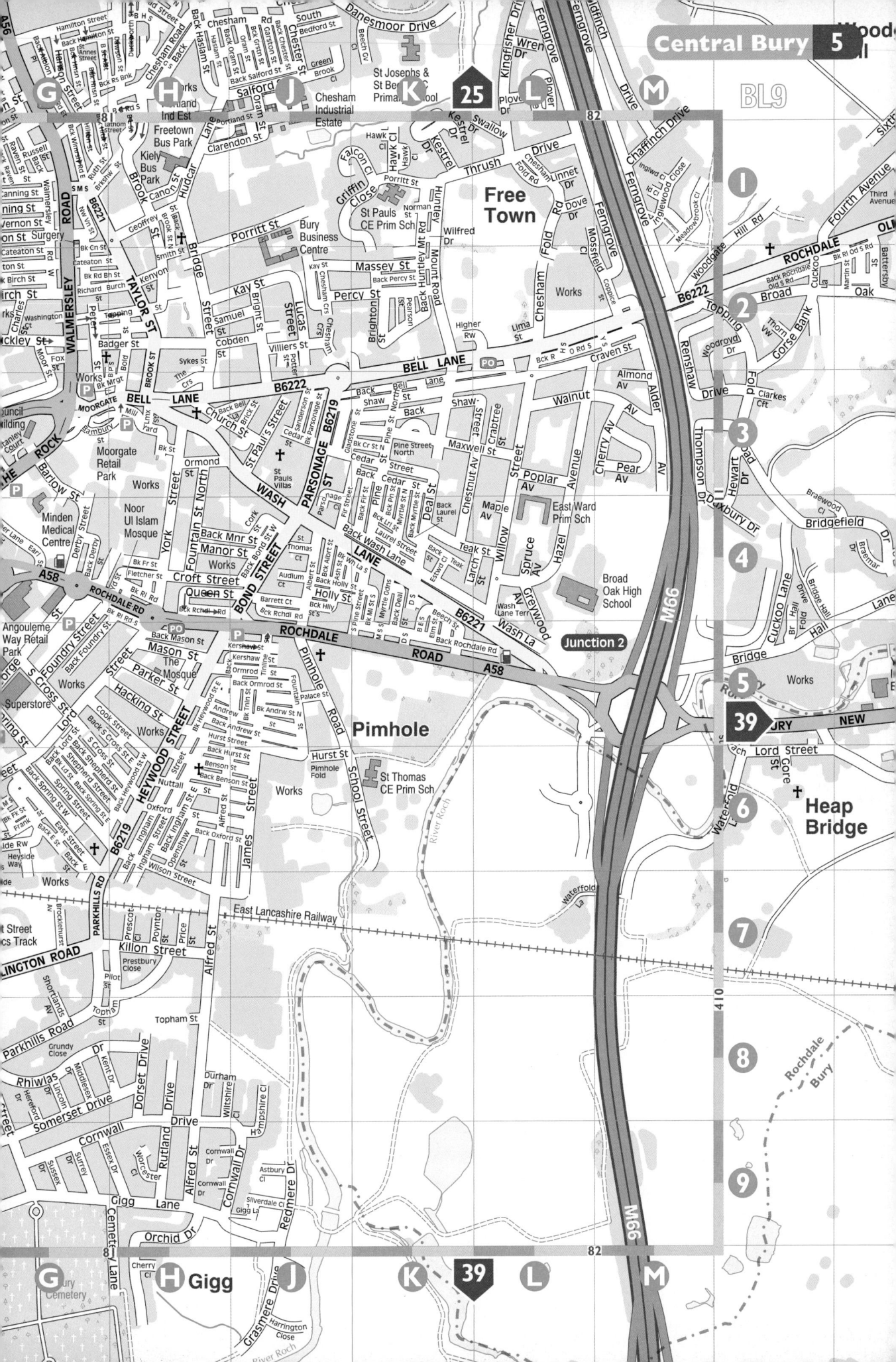

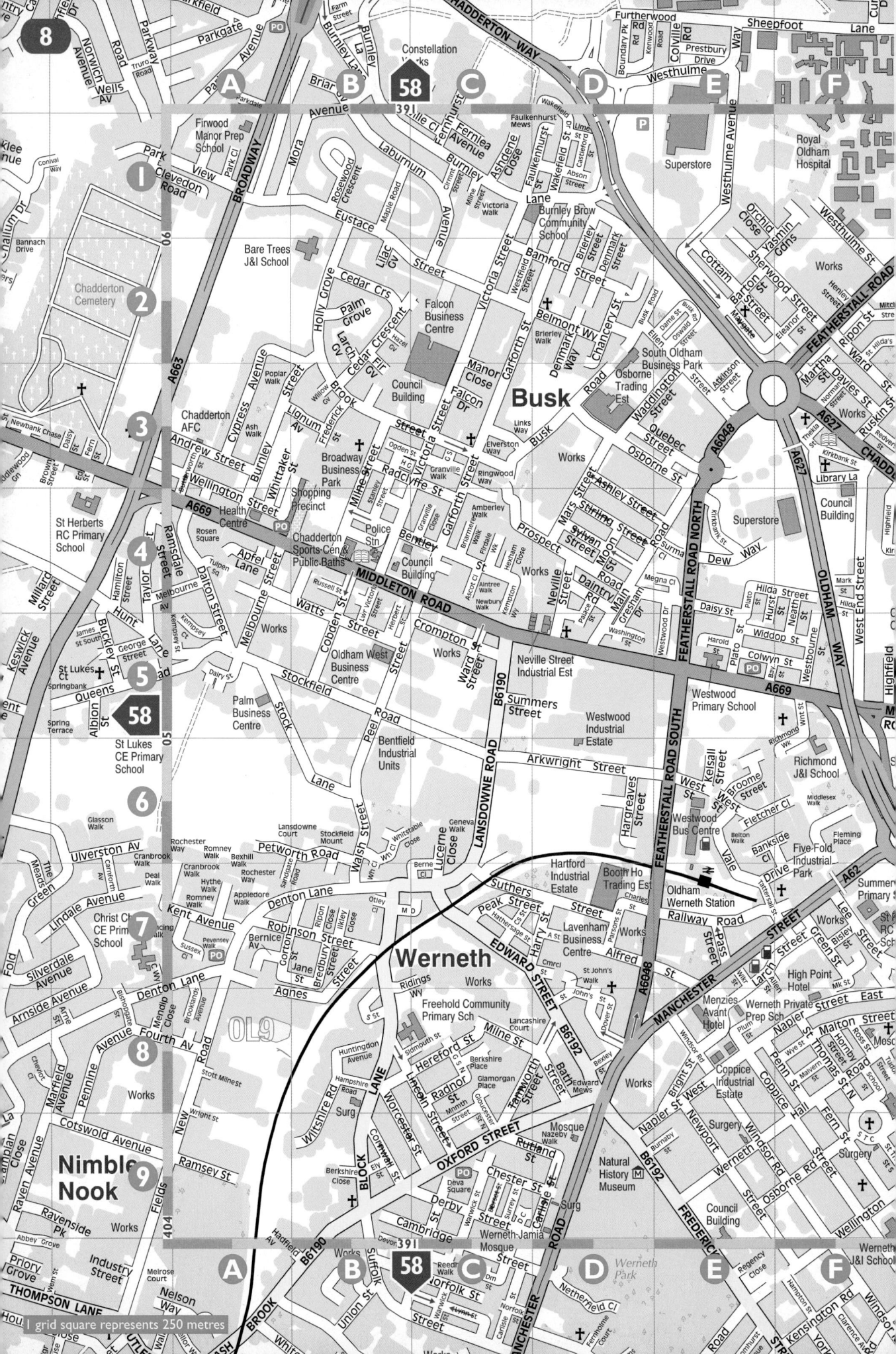

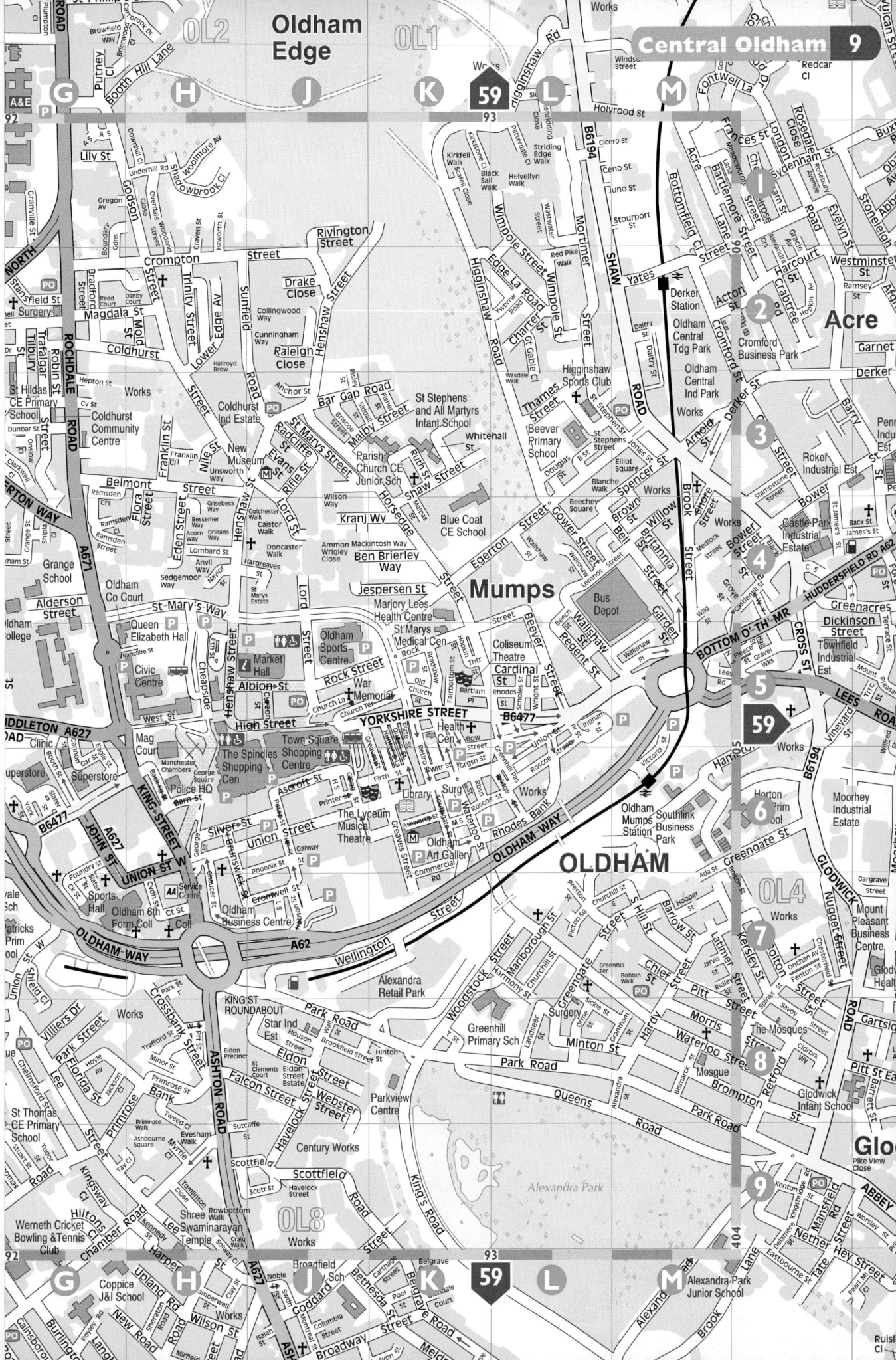

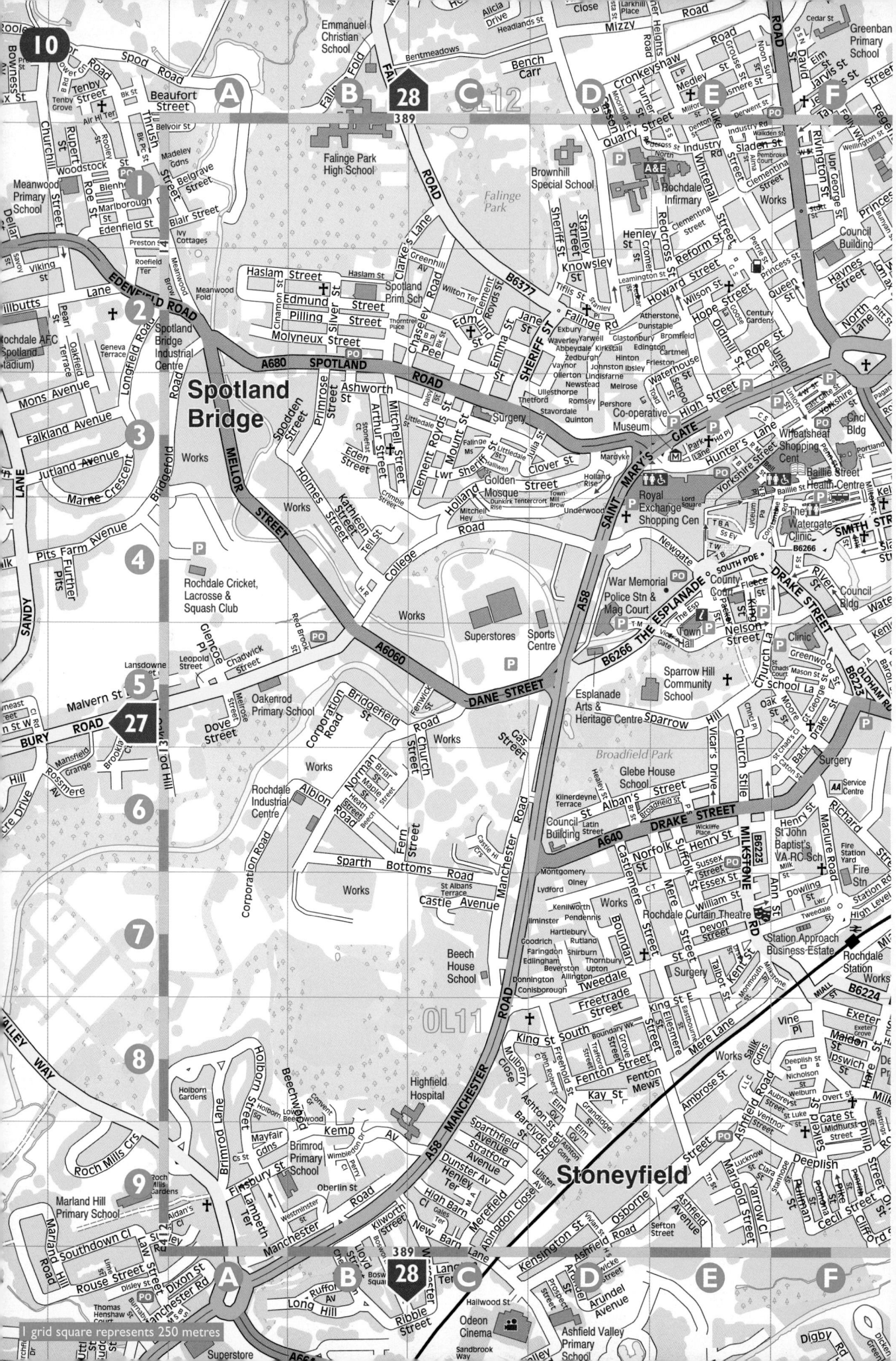

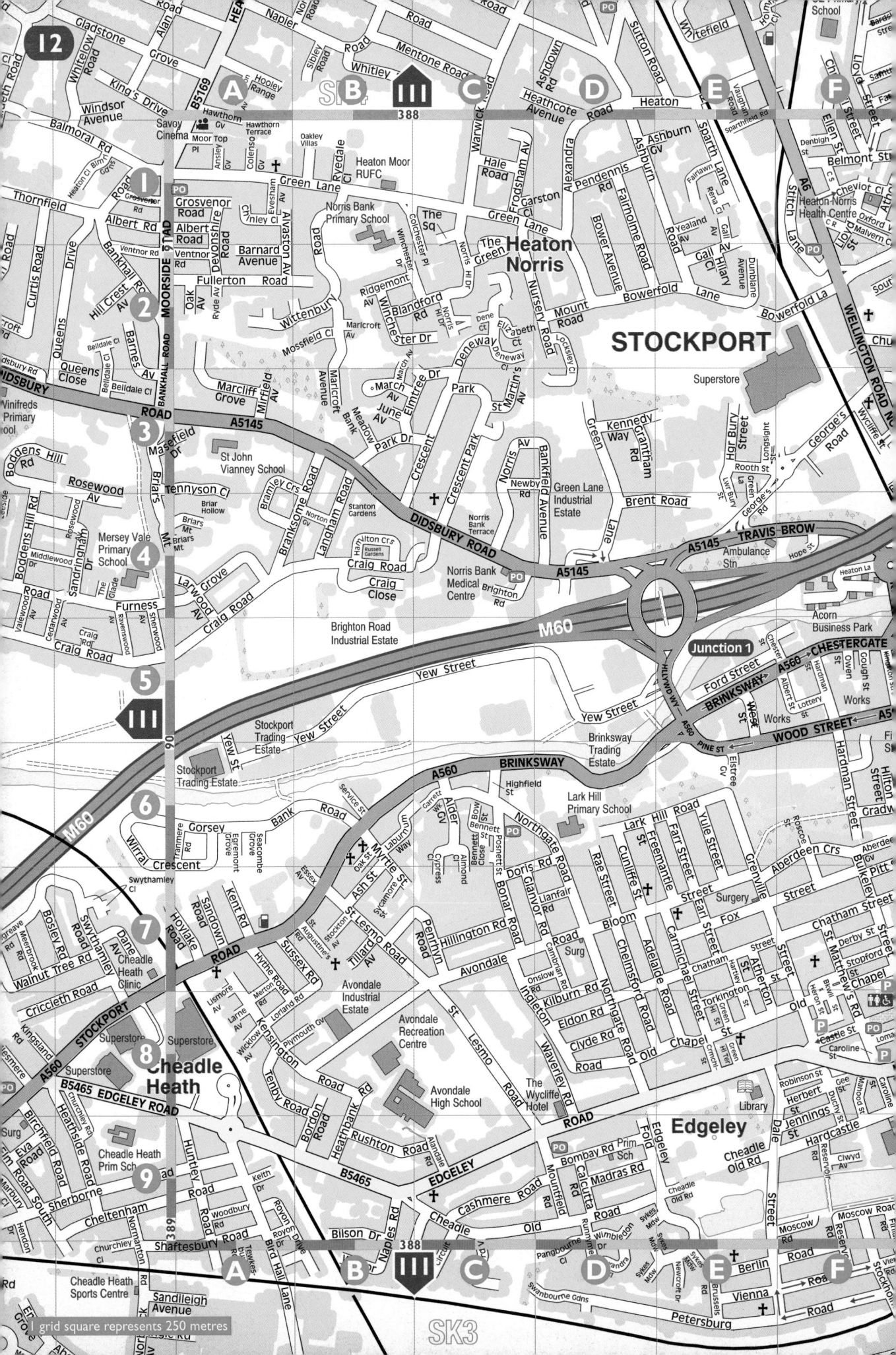

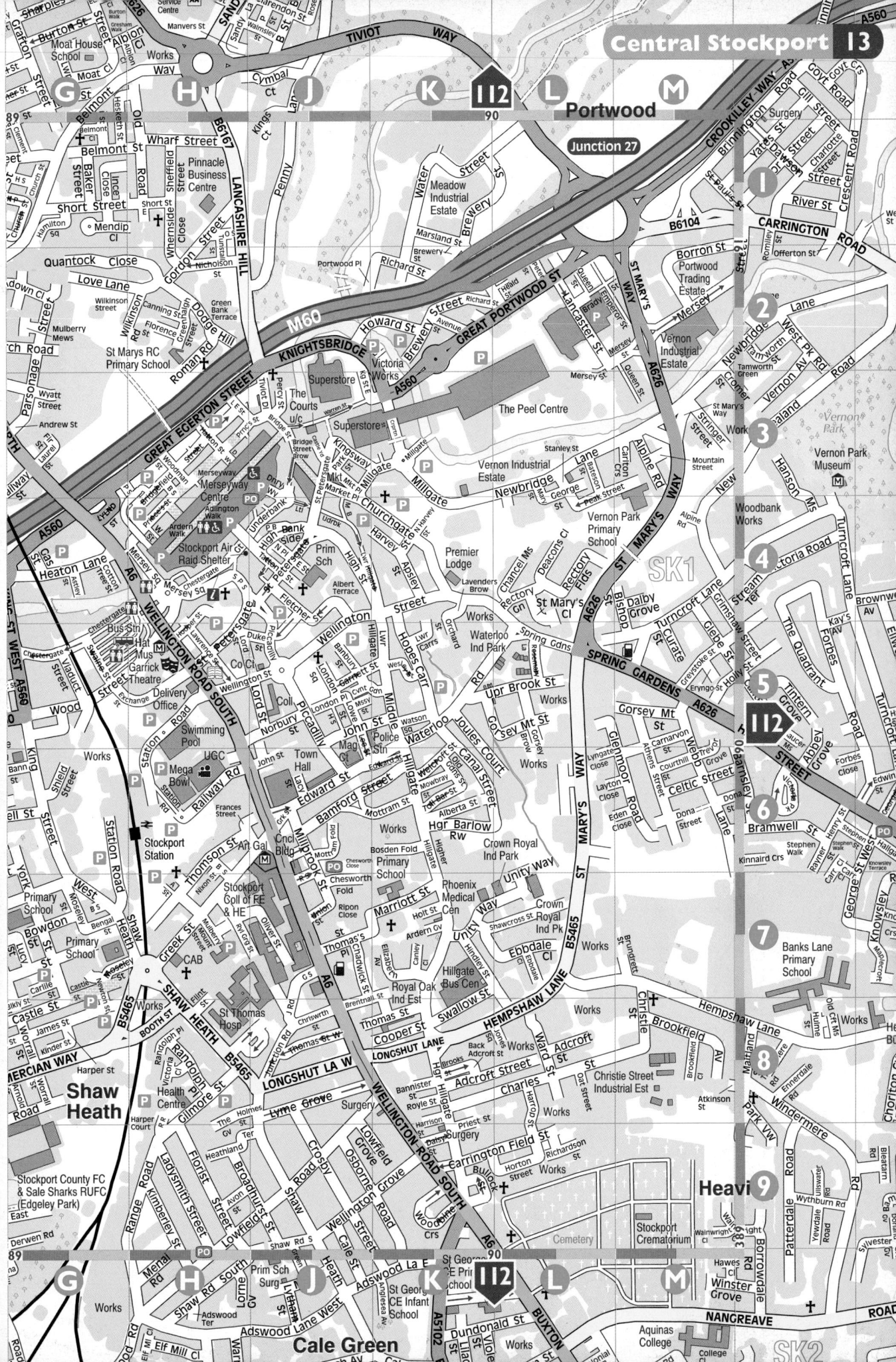

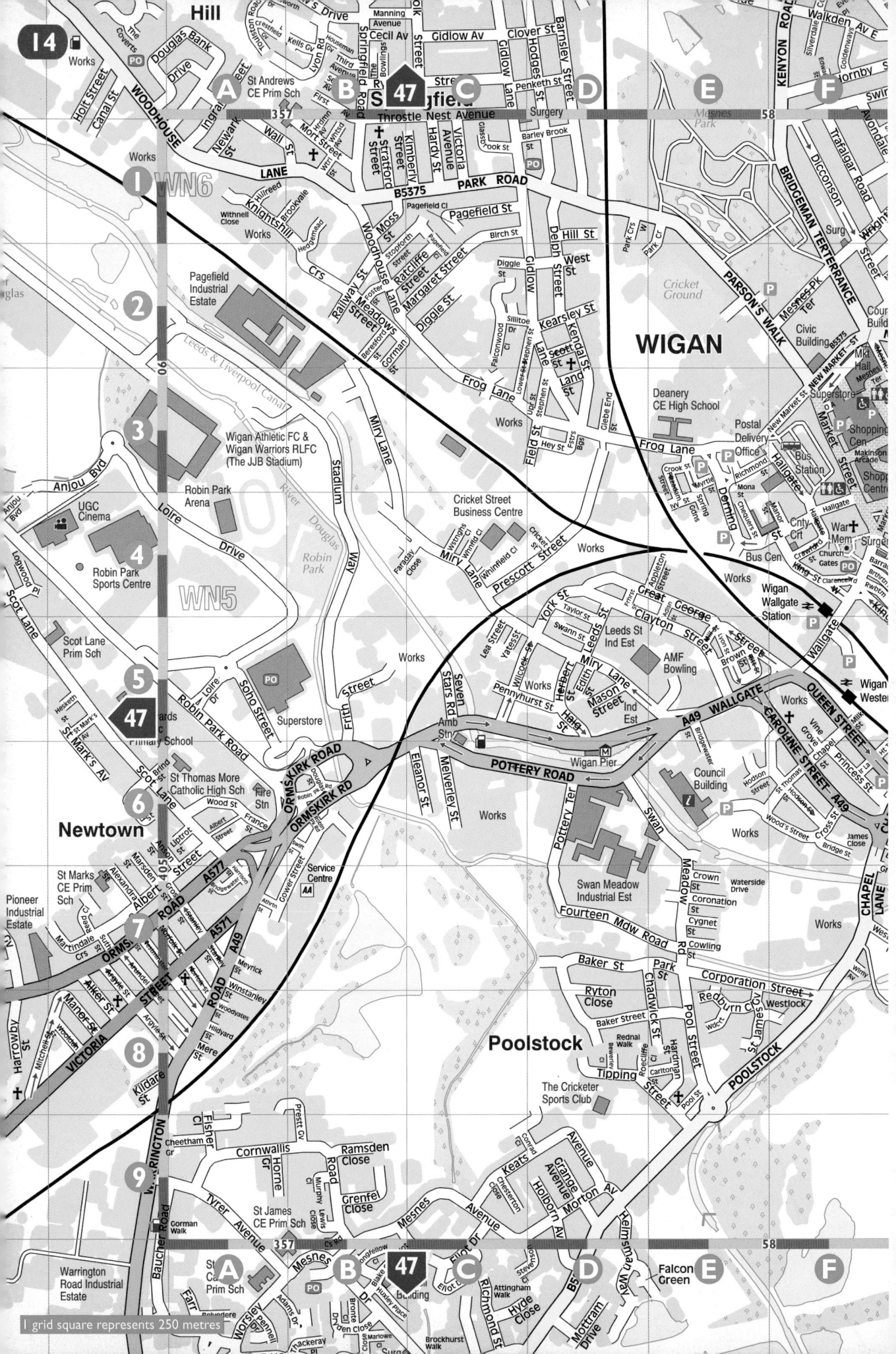

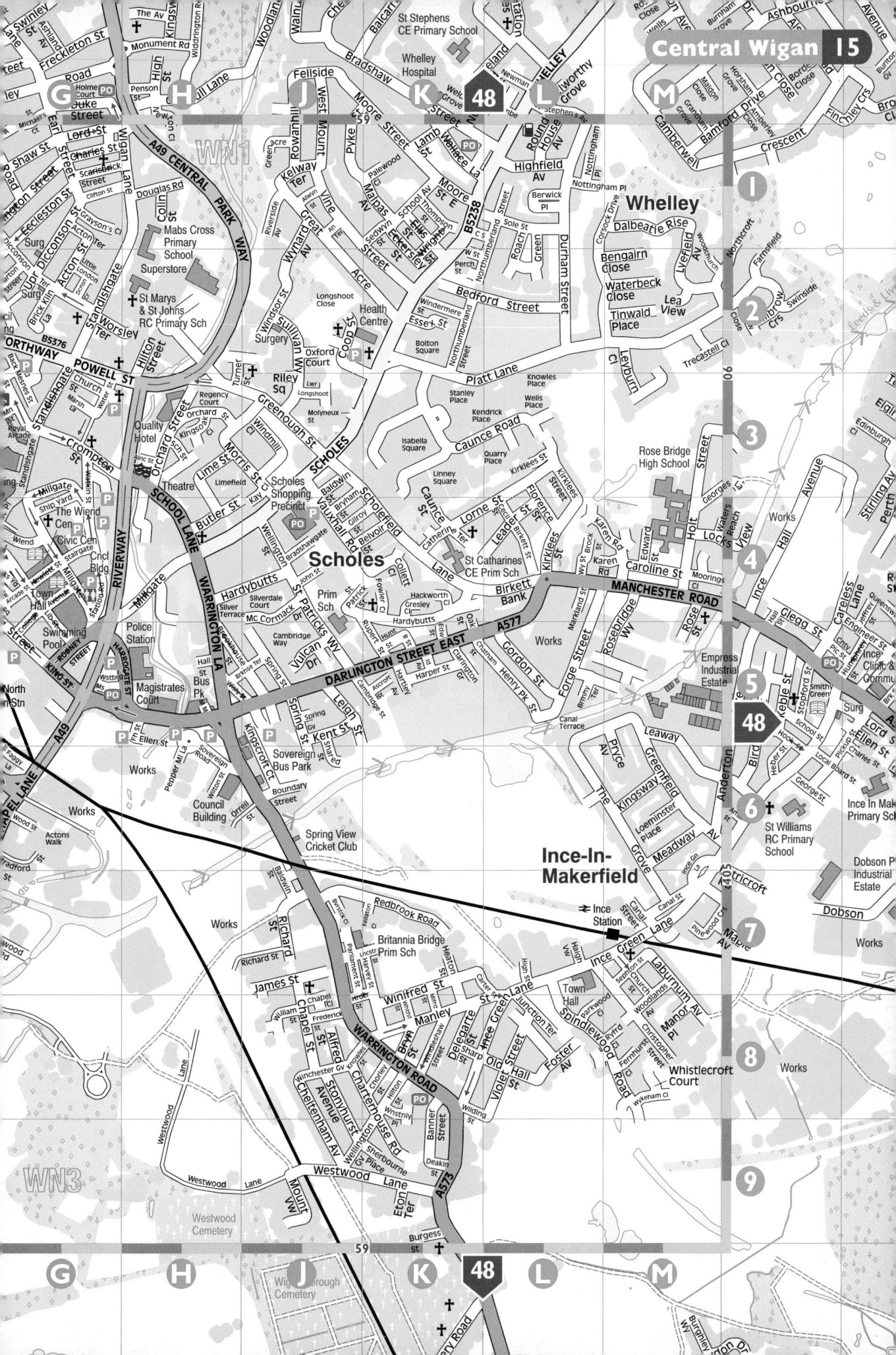

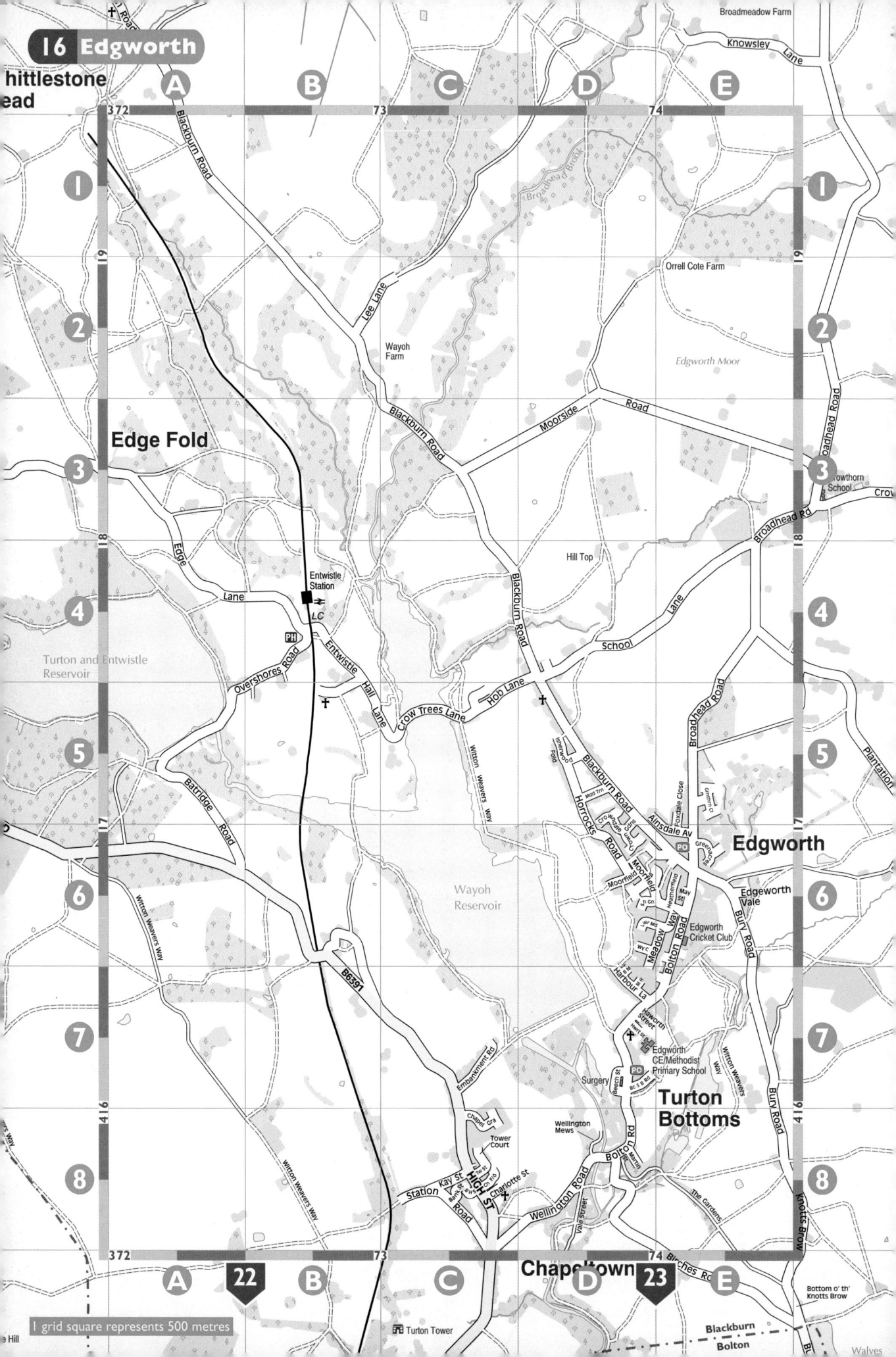

Broadmeadow Farm

Knowsley Lane

hittlestone
ead

A 372 **B** 73 **C** **D** 74 **E**

Broadhead Brook

Orrell Cote Farm

Lee Lane

Wayoh
Farm

Edgworth Moor

Edge Fold

Blackburn Road

oadhead Road

Moorside Road

owthorn
School

Crow

Broadhead Rd

Hill Top

Entwistle
Station

LC

PH

Edge Lane

Overshores Road

Entwistle Hall Lane

Crow Trees Lane

Hob Lane

Blackburn Road

School Lane

**Turton and Entwistle
Reservoir**

Witton Weavers Way

Sherwood Road

Blackburn Road

Plantation

Batridge Road

Blackwood

Ainsdale Av

PO

Gree

Edgworth

Horrocks Road

Mdo Trm

Con

Moorfield

Edgeworth
Vale

Bury Road

**Wayoh
Reservoir**

Mav
St

Heatherfield

Meadow Way

Bolton Road

Edgworth
Cricket Club

Witton Weavers Way

Harbour La

Haworth Street

Witton Weavers Way

Bury Road

Embankment Rd

B6391

Edgworth
CE/Methodist
Primary School

Surgery

Beech St

PO

**Turton
Bottoms**

Chapel Gra

Wellington
Mews

Tower
Court

Station Road

Kay St

Bank St

HIGH ST

Charlotte St

Bolton Rd

Bolton Road

Wellington Road

Vale Street

The Gardens

Knotts Brow

Chapeltown

A 372 **22** **B** 73 **C** **D** 74 **23** Birches Rd **E**

Turton Tower

Bottom o' th'
Knotts Brow

**Blackburn
Bolton**

Walves

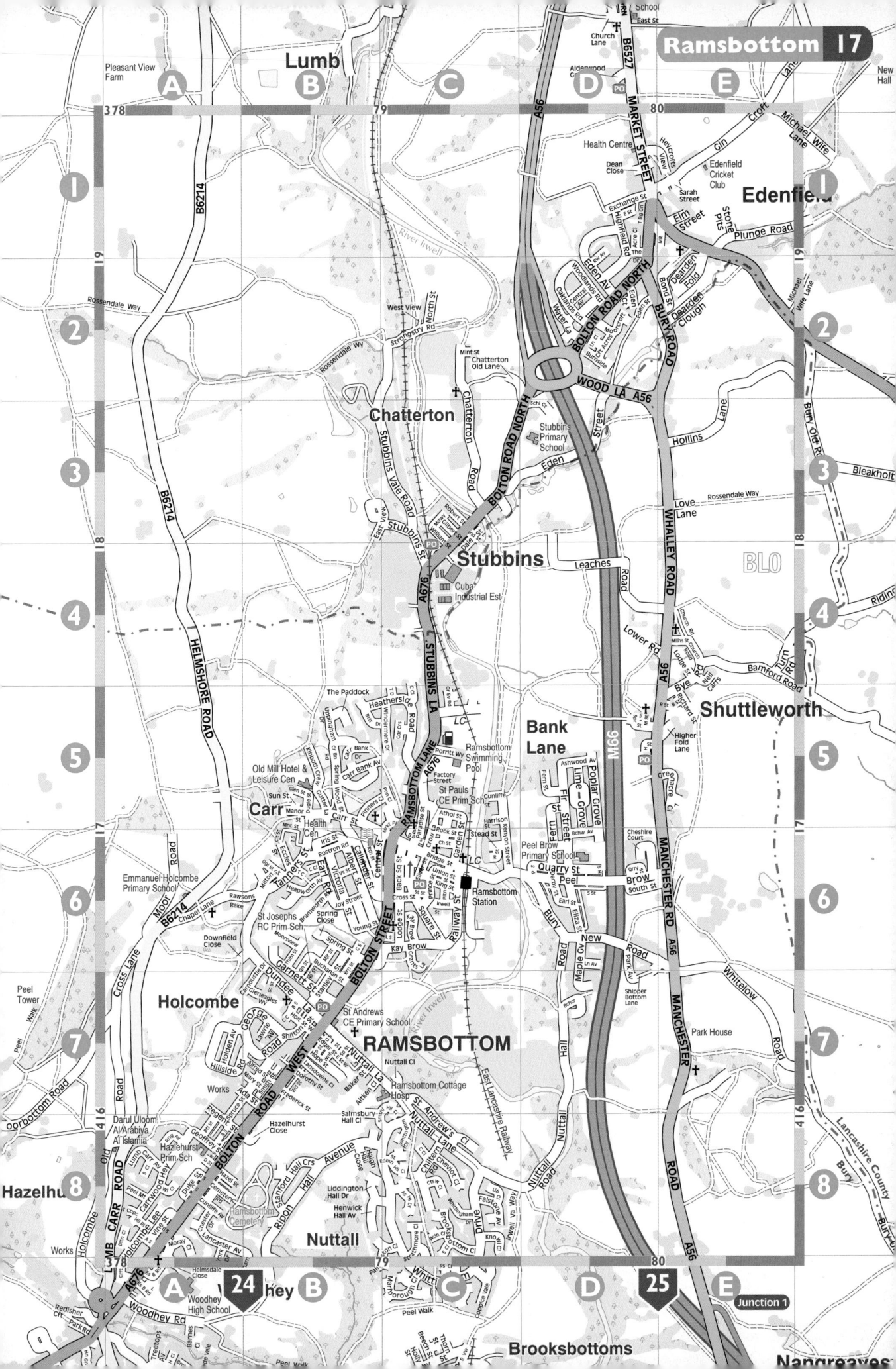

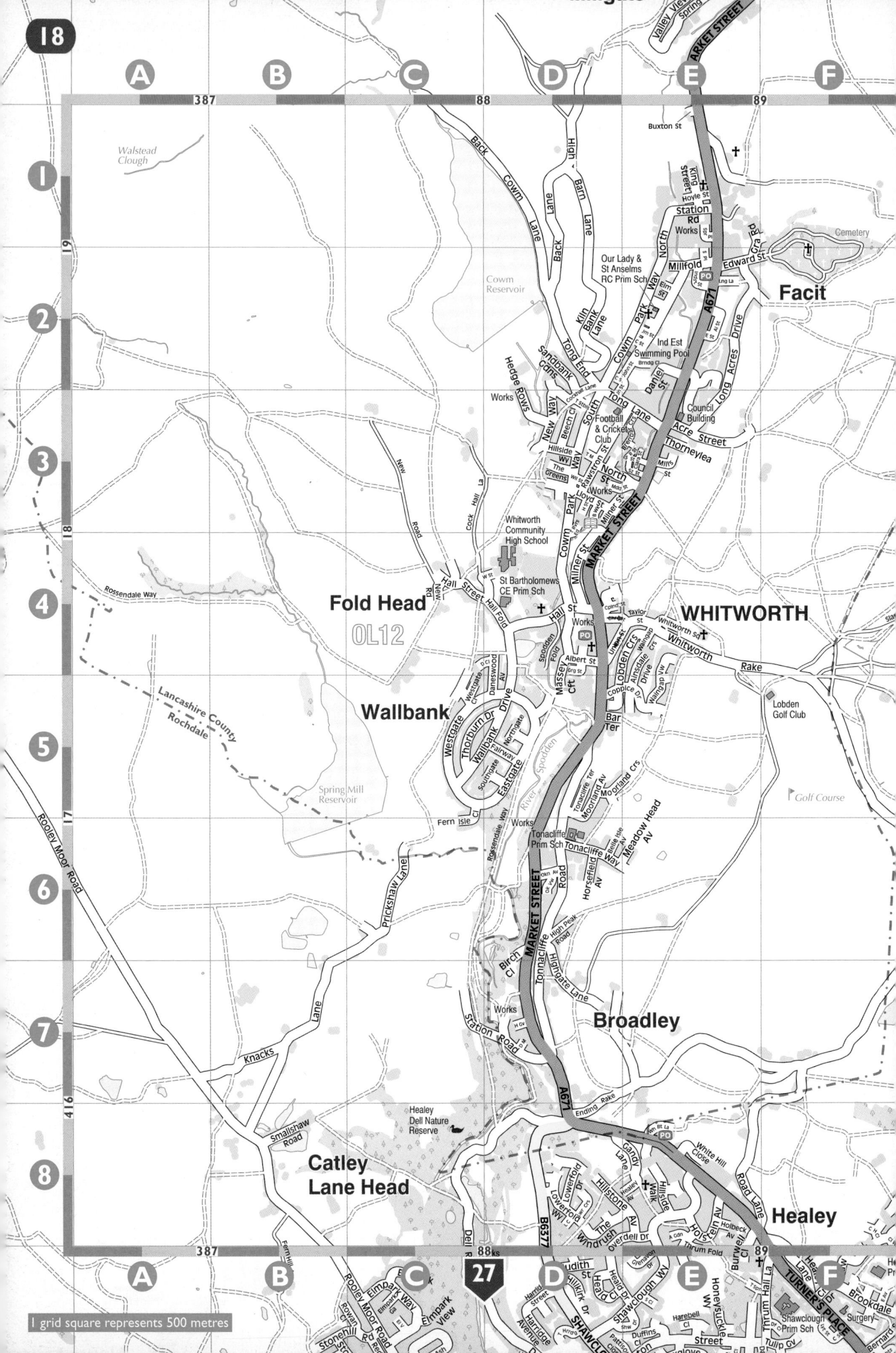

G   H   J   K   L   M

90   91   92

Calderdale
Rochdale

I

2

Shore Moor

Turn
Slack
Clough

3

Watergove
Reservoir

4

20

Barn Field Lane   Lower House Lane   Ramsden Lane

Bent La   Gib   Clough House Lane

Alderbank   Wardle Fold   Bank Lane   Moor Gate Lane   5

Knowl Syke St   Chapel St   Wardle Road   Wheatcroft   Close   Shore Hall   Higher Shore Road

Hard Lane   Gate   St James CE Primary School   Alpine Drive   Pennine   Crossfield Rd   Bank Barn Lane   Middle Wood Lane   Cote Lane   Edmunds

Clough Street   Combrook Close   Heath Road   Fern St   Holly   Hibson Cl   Overdale Drive   Shaftesbury   Woodend Lane   Pedler Brow Lane   Shore Fold   Sh

Hey Bottom Lane   Rydings Lane   East St   Newhouse Close   Lane   Almond Close   6   Brookfield   Chester

Dirty Leech   Limers Ga   Hey Bottom La   Rydings Lane   Lawflat   Elm Grove   Watermouse Close   Birch   Birch Road   Wardle   Starring

Dewhirst Road   Wardle Road   Wardle High Sch   Rochdale Healthcare   7   Starri   Way   Oliver

Ring Lows Lane   Hurstead   Meadow   Gloucester Avenue   St Andrew's VC CE Prim Sch   Arm Road   Cemetery   New Road   New Street   Dearn

Syke Lane   Ring Lows Lane   Rydings Road   Rydings Special Sch   Spinners Gdns   Queens Avenue   Works   Birch Road   Green   Birch Avenue   Union Rd   New Road

Wainga Rise   Syke   Great Howarth   Kings Gv   Gt Howarth   Ashbrook Hey Lane   Steps Meadow   Oakcliffe Road   Thimble Cl   The Thimbles   Old Road   Stubley   8   Stubley Mill

Wood Hey Gv   Newark Rd   Norton Rd   Buckley   Rydings Road   Edge   Hollowspell   Greensnook   Frances Street   A58   Smithybridge   Rose Avenue

G   H   J   28   K   L   M

Burnley   Greengate   Dearnl

90   91   92

Kentmere Prim Sch   Buckley   Louise   Wheelwright Drive   Tarnside Cl   Yea Fold   Eafield Road

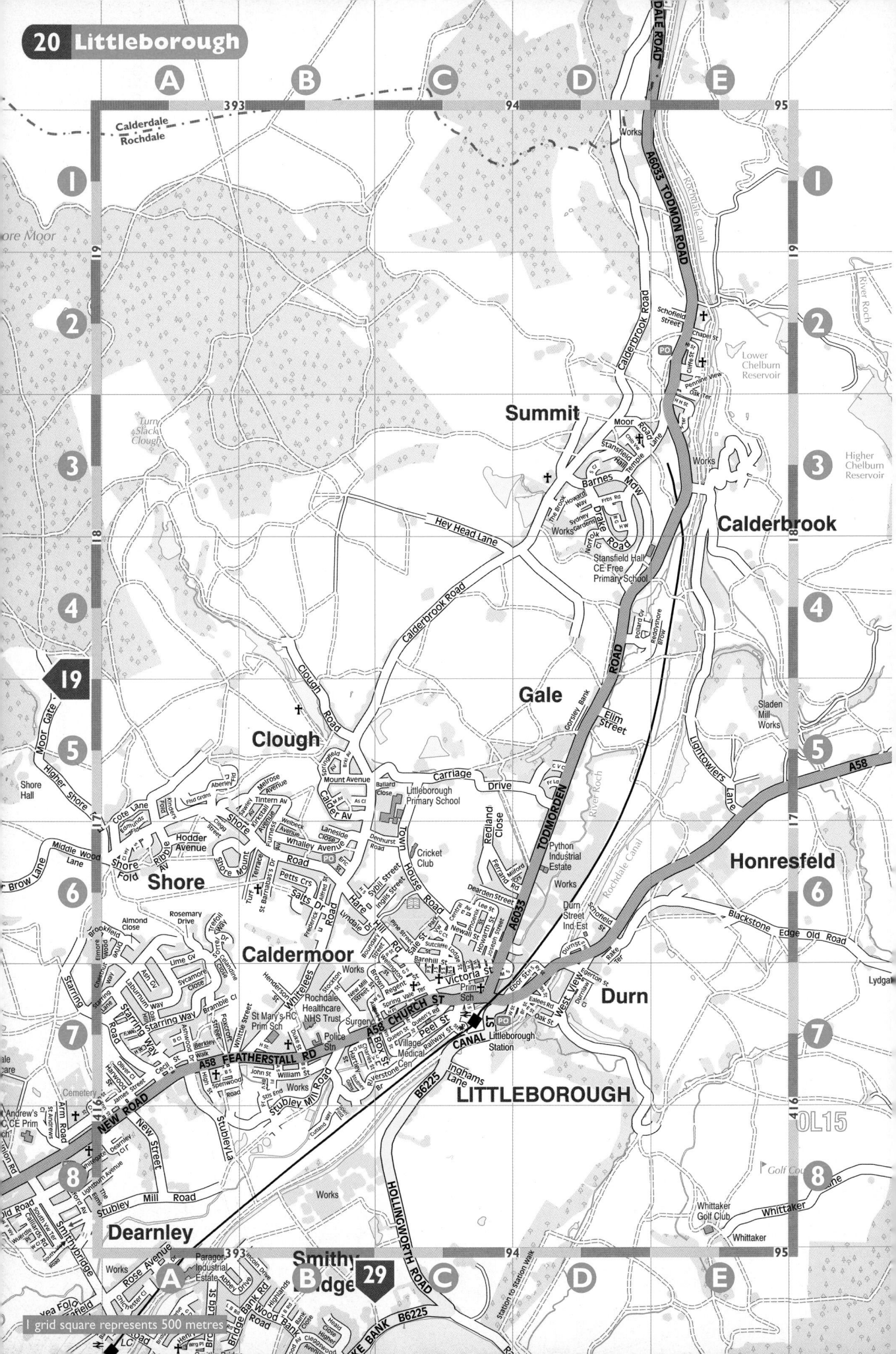

A   B   C   D   E

393   94   95

Calderdale
Rochdale

ore Moor

Turn
Slack
Clough

Summit

Lower
Chelburn
Reservoir

Higher
Chelburn
Reservoir

Calderbrook

Hey Head Lane

Stansfield Hall
CE Free
Primary School

Clough Road

Gale

Honresfeld

19

Clough

Carriage
Drive

Littleborough
Primary School

Shore
Hall

Higher Shore

Mount Avenue

Calder Av

Redland
Close

Python
Industrial
Estate

Sladen
Mill
Works

Middle Wood
Lane

Brow Lane

Hodder
Avenue

Shore
Fold

Shore

Whalley Avenue

Laneside
Close

Dearden Street

Durn
Street
Ind Est

Blackstone

Edge Old Road

Rosemary
Drive

Caldermoor

Cricket
Club

Town
House Road

Victoria St

Durn

Lydga

Starring

Starring Way

Starring Way

St Mary's RC
Prim Sch

Rochdale
Healthcare
NHS Trust
Surgery

CHURCH ST

West View

Police
Stn

A58 FEATHERSTALL RD

A58

Village
Medical
Cen

Littleborough
Station

LITTLEBOROUGH

B6225

New Road

New Street

Stubley Mill Road

Andrew's
CCE Prim
ch

Cemetery

Hollingworth Road

Golf Co

Dearnley

Whittaker
Golf Club

Whittaker

Smithy
Bridge   29

Rose Avenue

Paragon
Industrial
Estate

393   94   95

Smithybridge

B6225

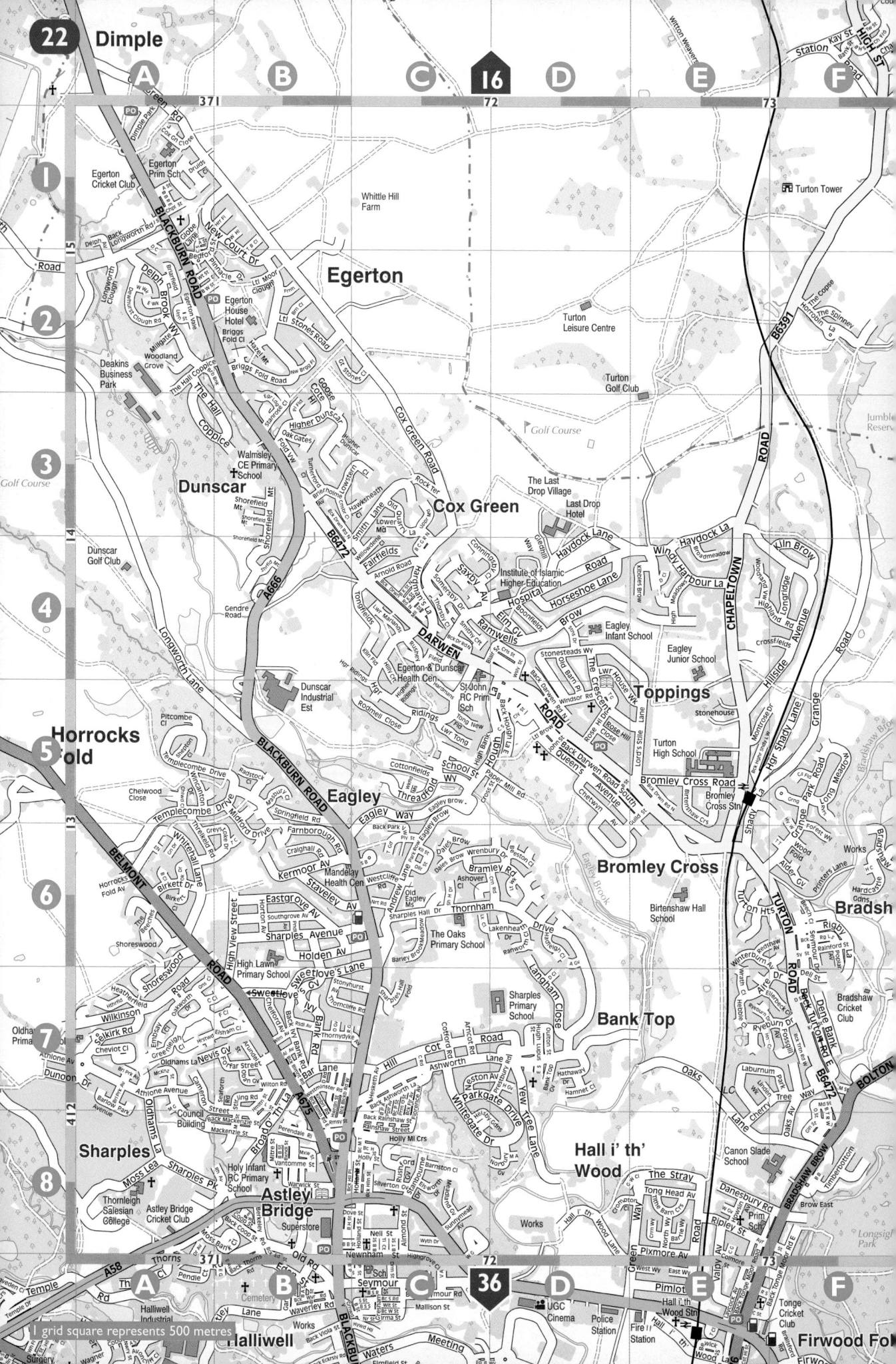

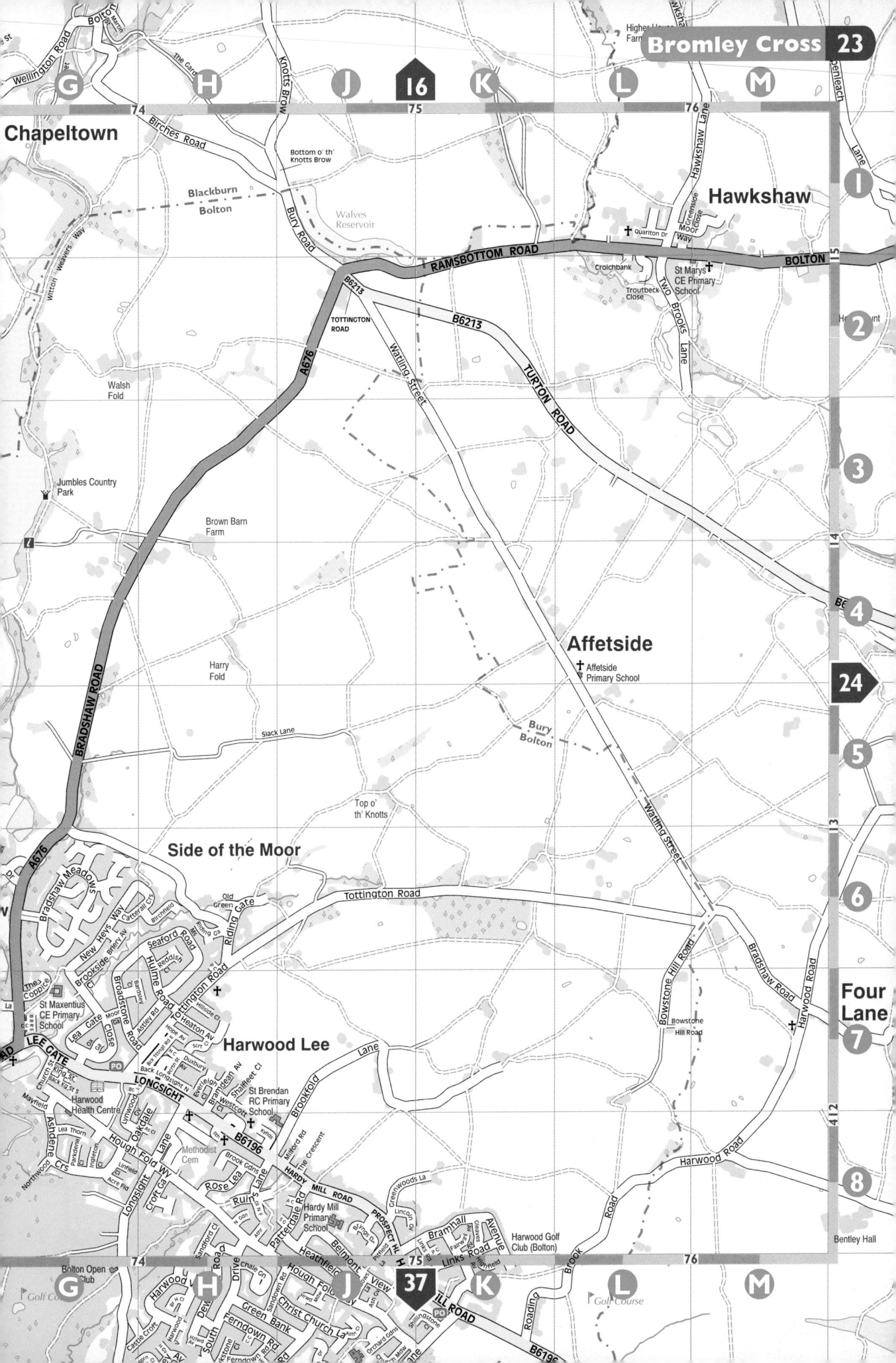

Chapeltown

Hawkshaw

Affetside

Side of the Moor

Harwood Lee

Four Lane

Walves Reservoir

Jumbles Country Park

Blackburn
Bolton

Bottom o' th' Knotts Brow

Birches Road

Knotts Brow

Bury Road

RAMSBOTTOM ROAD

BOLTON

Quariton Dr

St Marys CE Primary School

Croichbank

Troutbeck Close

Greenside Moor Way

Hawkshaw Lane

Two Brooks Lane

B6213

TOTTINGTON ROAD

B6213

Watling Street

A676

TURTON ROAD

Walsh Fold

Brown Barn Farm

Harry Fold

BRADSHAW ROAD

Slack Lane

Top o' th' Knotts

Affetside Primary School

Bury Bolton

Watling Street

Bowstone Hill Road

Bowstone Hill Road

Bradshaw Road

Harwood Road

A676

Bradshaw Meadows

New Heys Way

Catterall Crs

Old Green Gate

Riding Gate

Tottington Road

Brookside

Seaford Road

Hulme Road

Tottington Road

Reddish

St Maxentius CE Primary School

The Coppice

Lea Gate

LEE GATE

Harwood Health Centre

LONGSIGHT

Heaton Av

Astley Rd

Hope Av

Duxbury

St Brendan RC Primary School

Lane

Brookfold Lane

Hough Fold Wy

Oakdale

Lynwood

Methodist Cem

B6196

Rose Lea

Longsight Lane

Patterdale Rd

The Crescent

Milford Rd

HARDY MILL ROAD

Hardy Mill Primary School

Greenwoods La

Lincoln Cl

PROSPECT H

Heathfield

Belmont

Bramhall

Links Road

Avenue

Harwood Golf Club (Bolton)

Harwood Road

Brook

Bentley Hall

Golf Course

Bolton Open Golf Club

Harwood

Christ Church La

Green Bank

Ferndown Rd

South

MILL ROAD

Roading

Golf Course

B6196

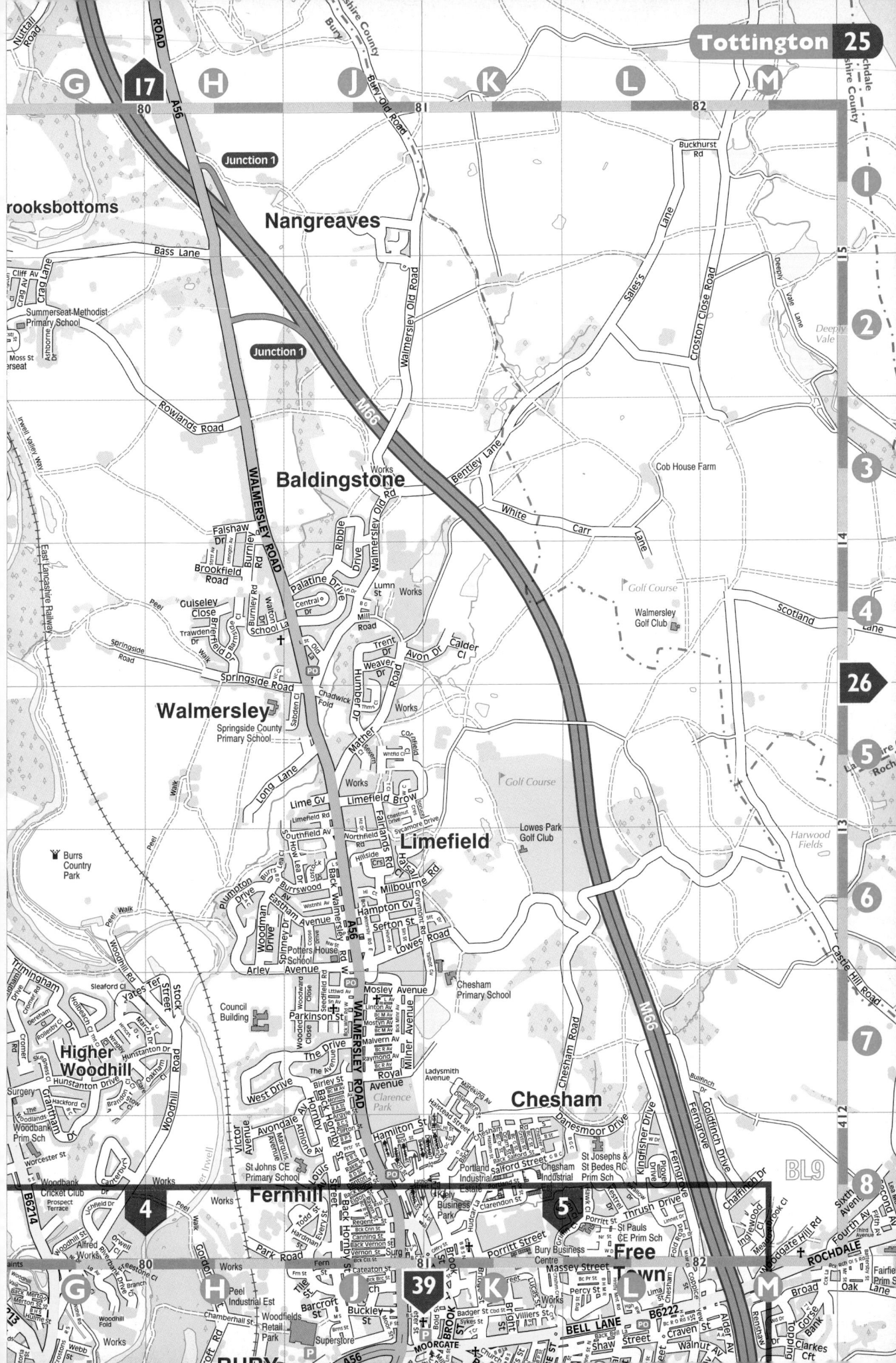

G **17** H J K L M

80 A56

Brooksbottoms

Nuttall Road

Crag Lane

Cliff Av

Ber L

Summerseat-Methodist
Primary School

Ashborne Rd

Moss St
Summerseat

Bass Lane

Junction 1

Nangreaves

Bury Old Road

Shire County

81

Deeply Vale Lane

Buckhurst Rd

Croston Close Road

5 I

Sales's Lane

82

Rochdale
Shire County

Deeply Vale 2

Rowlands Road

Junction 1

M66

Bentley Lane

Cob House Farm

White Carr Lane

3

Scotland Lane 4

WALMERSLEY ROAD

Baldingstone

Works
Rd

Falshaw Dr

Lumgin Av

Burnley Rd

Brookfield Road

Ribble Drive

Palatine Drive

Central Dr

Walmersley Old Road

Lumn St

Mill Road

Works

Guiseley Close

Trawden Dr

Brierfields Dr

Burnley Rd

School Lane

PO

Trent Dr

Weaver Dr

Avon Dr

Calder Cl

Golf Course

Walmersley
Golf Club

26

Springside Road

Springside Road

Humber Dm

Chadwick Fold

Works

Walmersley

Springside County
Primary School

East Lancashire Railway

Irwell Valley Way

Peel

springside Road

Walk

Mather St

Sabden Cl

Cofield

Wntfld

Golf Course

Lowes Park
Golf Club

Harwood
Fields

5 Shire
Rochd

Castle Hill Road

Long Lane

Lime Gv

Limefield Rd

Southfield Av

Northfield Rd

Hillside Crs

Limefield Brow

Falhands Rd

Chestnut Av

Sycamore Drive

Limefield

6

Burrs Country
Park

Peel Walk

Plumpton Drive

Burrswood Av

Eastham Av

Woodman Drive

Spinney Dr

Potters House
School

Back Walmersley Rd

Wistnni Av

Milbourne Rd

Hampton Gv

Sefton St

Hasel Rd

Sfn

Lowes
Road

M66

4

Woodhill Rd

Stock Street

Council
Building

Parkinson St

Woodward
Close

Seedfield Rd

Arley Avenue

Mosley Avenue

Linton Av

Chesham
Primary School

Chesham Road

B

Higher
Woodhill

Hunstanton Dr

Hunstanton Drive

Surgery

The Woodlands

Grantham

Worcester St

Hackford Cl

Branson St

The Drive

The Avenue

West Drive

Birley St

Avondale Avenue

Marquis St

Athlone St

WALMERSLEY ROAD

Hamilton St

PO

Victor Avenue

Louis St

Halstead Street

Hudley St

Milner Avenue

Royal Avenue

Clarence
Park

Ladysmith Avenue

Danesmoor Drive

Chesham

St Josephs &
St Bedes RC
Prim Sch

Kingfisher Drive

Goldfinch Drive

Ferngrove

Bullfinch Dr

412

7

B6214

Woodbank
Cricket Club

Prospect
Terrace

Schofield Dr

Woodhill Rd

Alfred
Works

Carter Cl

Peel Walk

Works

Park Road

St Johns CE
Primary School

Fernhill

80

Hardman St

Back Hornby St

Todd St

Canning St

Back Vernon St

Vernon St

81

Bold St

Regent St

Kay Business Park

Clarendon St

5

Portland
Industrial
Estate

Salford Street

Chesham
Industrial

Porrit St

St Pauls
CE Prim Sch

Thrush Drive

Inglewood Cl

Chaffinch Dr

BL9

8

Woodhill Fold

Chamberhall St

The St

Peel

Peel Industrial Est

Barcroft St

Buckley St

Ferns St

Woodfields
Retail Park

Superstore

P

39

MOORGATE

BROOK ST

Badger St

Sykes St

Right St

Porritt Street

Cateaton St

Bury Business
Centre

Massey Street

Percy St

Chesham

Sixth Avenue

ROCHDALE

Moorgate Hill Rd

Second Av

Third Avenue

Fourth Av

Fairfield
Prim Sch

Oak

**Free
Town**

Broad
St

Clarkes
Cft

BELL LANE

B6222

Craven St

Walnut Av

Shaw

Church St

PO

Renshaw

Coplow

Topping St

Webb St

Croston St

Works

G H J **39** K L M

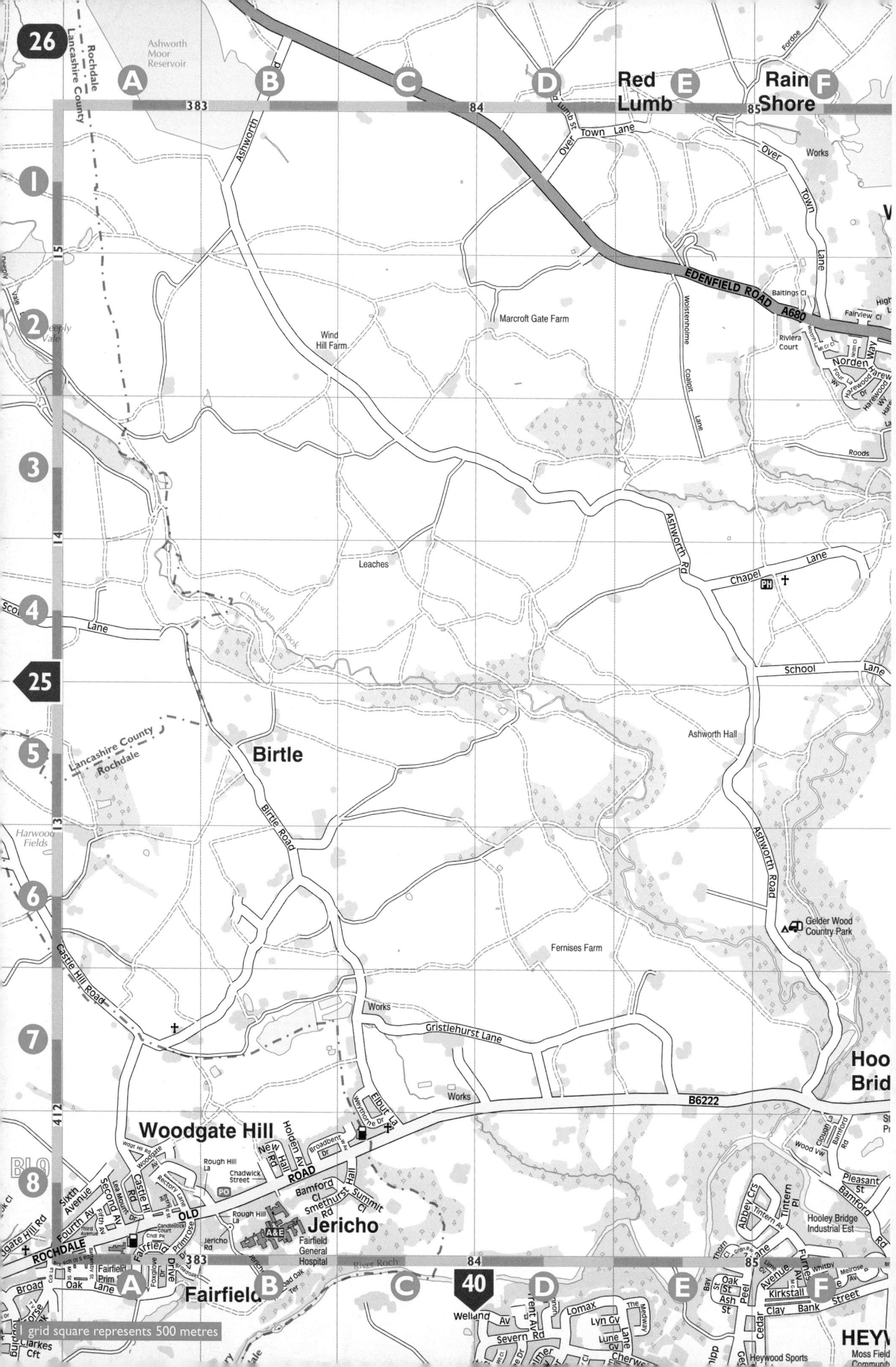

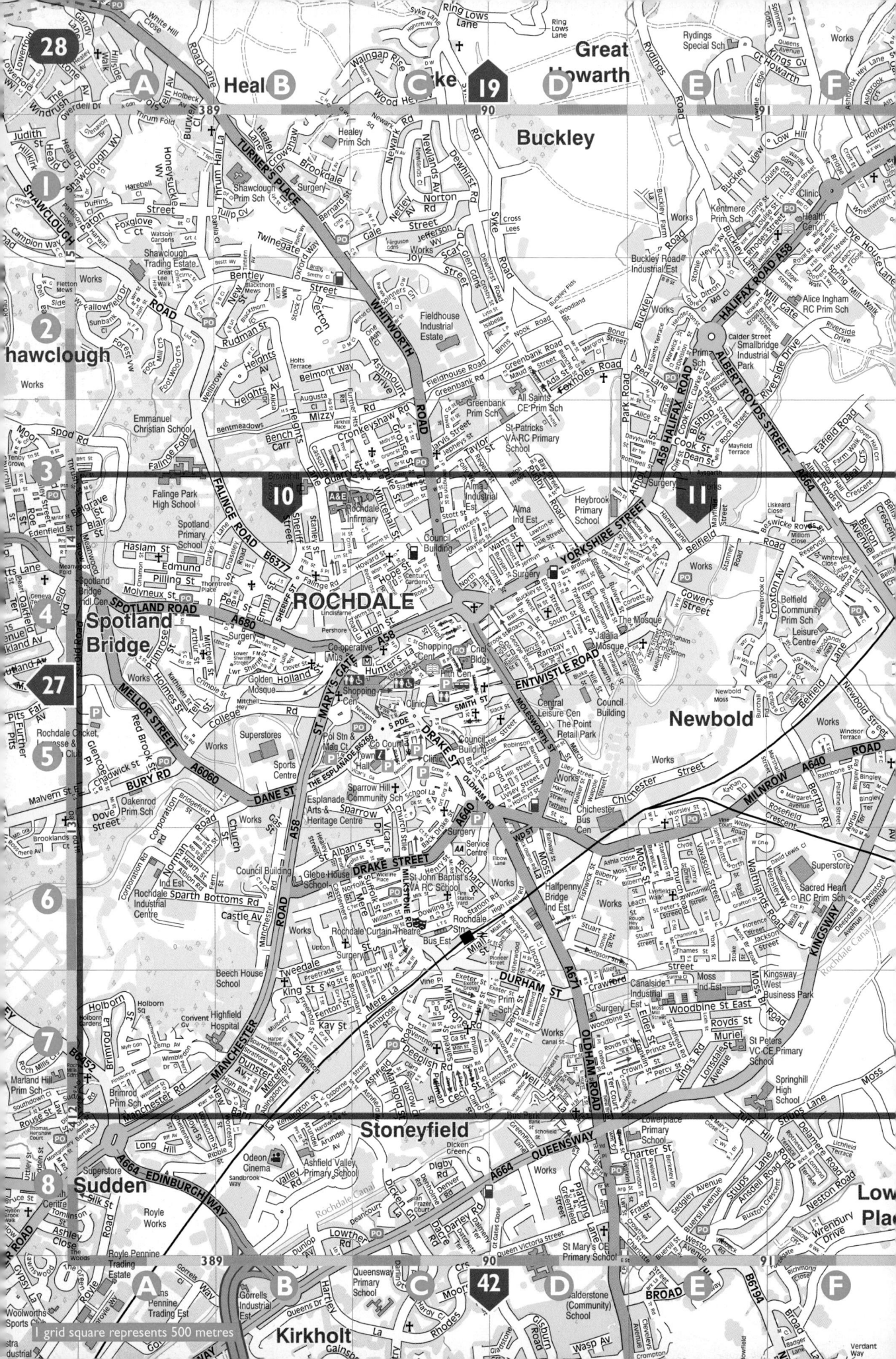

Adlington
Hall Farm

A · B · C · D · E · F

359 · 60 · 61

Blackrod

CHORLEY ROAD

BLACKROD BROW

Aberdeen
Farm

Crowshaw
Farm

Nightingale R
Thirlmere Rd
Harrison Crs
Ainse Road
Clifton Dr
Hill Lane
BLACK HORSE ST
Folds
Surgery
Council
Building
Vicarage Rd W

Blundell Lane

Little
Scotland

Scotland

Blackrod Church
School

Worthington
Lakes
(Reserv)

Wigan
Golf Club

Ariey Lane

Bolton
Wigan

Bolton
Wigan

Copperas Lane

Sibberings
Farm

Half Acre

Golf Course

Tucker's Hill Brow

Tucker's
Hill Farm

Ariey Lane

Pennington La
Pennington Lane

Toddington Lane

Freezeland Far

RED ROCK LANE B5239 SCHOOL LANE

Red
Rock

Willoughbys

Meadow Pit Lane

B5239

31

MEADOW PIT LANE

RILEY LANE

Gorses
Farm

Winstanleys

St Davids
CE Prim Sch

Haigh

Stanley

Pendlebury Lane

School Lane

Copperas Lane

Church St
Henley Street
Victoria Cl
B5239

HAIGH ROAD

Gorses Dr
Stancliffe Grove
Ratcliffe Road
Parklands Dr
Ashfield Drive
Stanley Road

Sennicar Lane

Leeds & Liverpool Canal

Haigh Hall Country Park

New Road

St Mary's Road
St John's St
St Elizabeth's St
St David's Crescent
Cricl Bdg
Lindsay Ter
Holly Rd
Brayford

Our Lady
RC Prim
Sch
Aspull
Clinic

Wigan
RUFC

Sennicar Lane

Douglas Valley
Business Park

WN1

Wingates Road

Crawford Avenue
Balcarres Road

Manor Cv

Woods Road

Crawford St

The A

Brock Mill Lane
Leyland St

Woodfield
Primary Sch

Hall Lane

Higher Lane

WIGAN ROAD

Mill La

Bel-Air Hotel

Works

B5376
Tenny
Grove
Milton St

Marylebone Pl

A · B · C · 48 · D · E · F

359 · 60 · 61

High St
Southern's Fold
B5238 Woodfield
St Bridge St

1 grid square represents 500 metres

HORWICH

CHURCH STREET

Scot Lane End

Hilton House

Cooper Turning

ASPULL

Four Gates

Junction 6

Scot Lane Industrial Estate

Scot Lane End CE Prim Sch

Blackrod Primary School

Blackrod Station

Park Hall Farm

Red Moss

Horwich Business Park

Horwich Leisure Centre

Bolton West Service Area

Comfort Inn

Cemetery

Greenbarn Way

Hillside Avenue

Bolton Sports Arena

Bolton Running Track

Horwich Parkway

Express by Holiday Inn

Reebok Museum

Paragon Business Park

Brinsop Hall

Dodd Lane Industrial Estate

M61

A6

A6027

B5408

B5408

B5238

B5239

A673

STATION ROAD

MANCHESTER ROAD

BLACKROD BY-PASS ROAD

CHORLEY ROAD

CHORLEY NEW ROAD

SCOT LANE

BOLTON ROAD

DICCONSON LANE

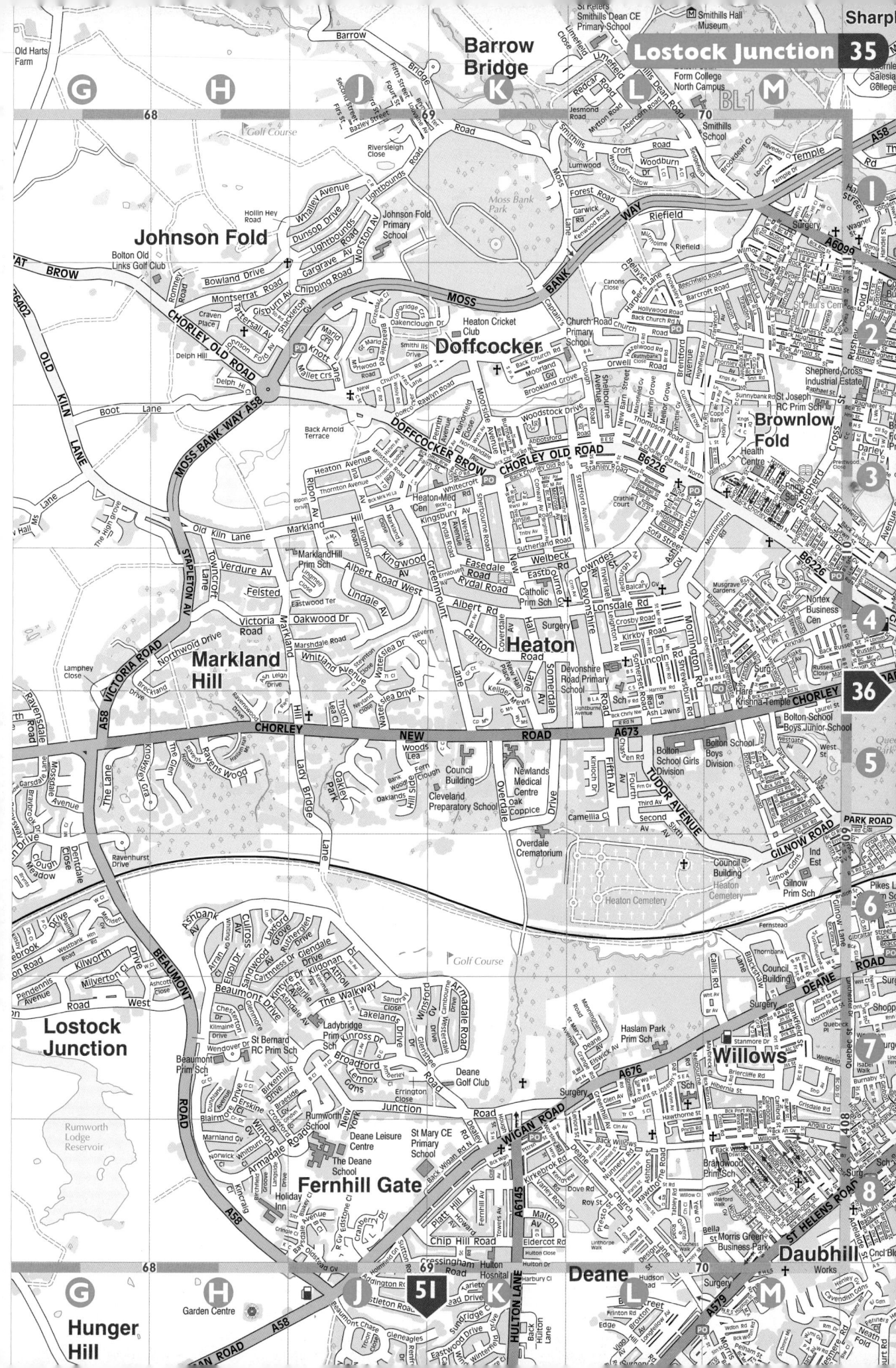

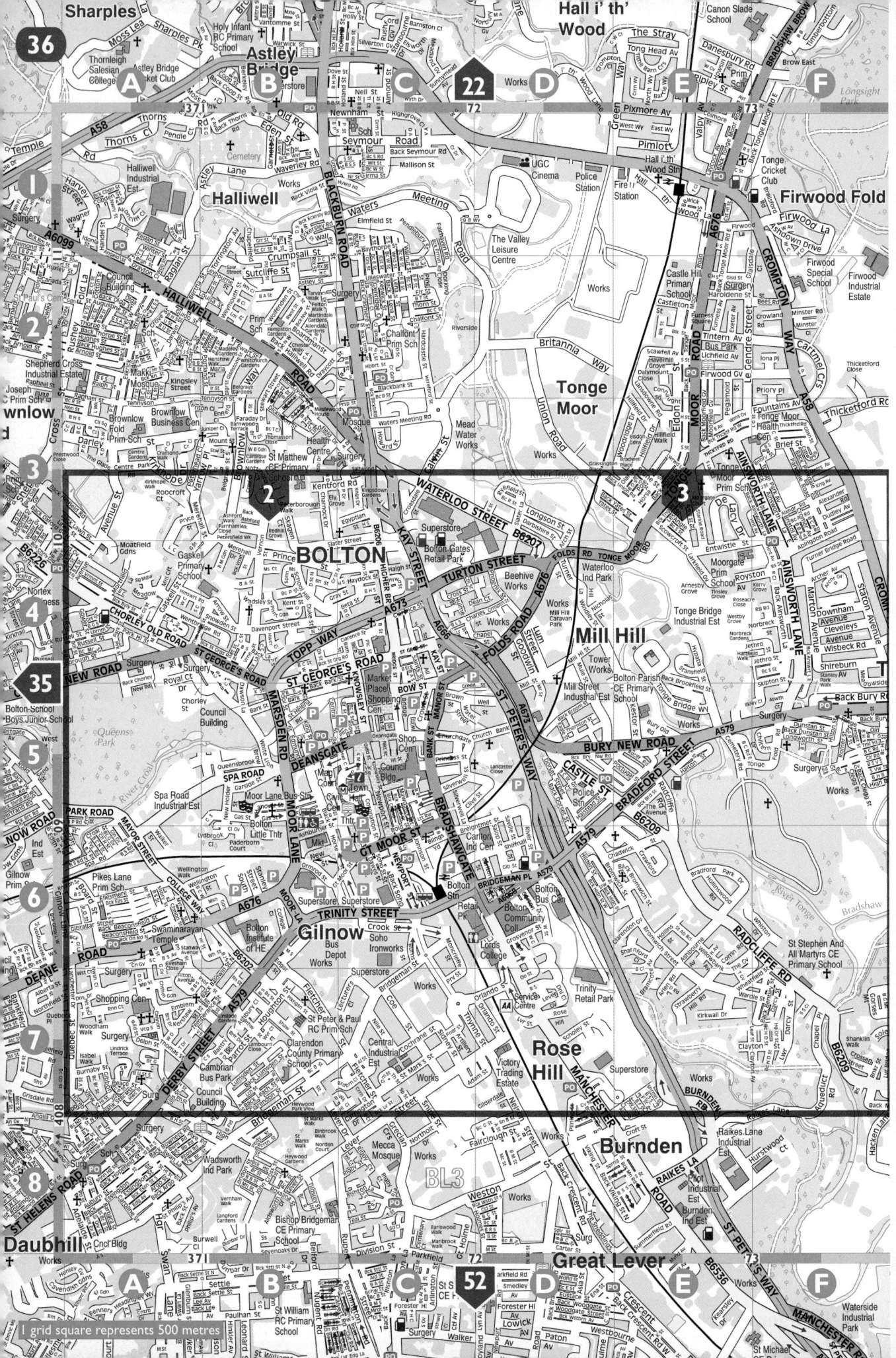

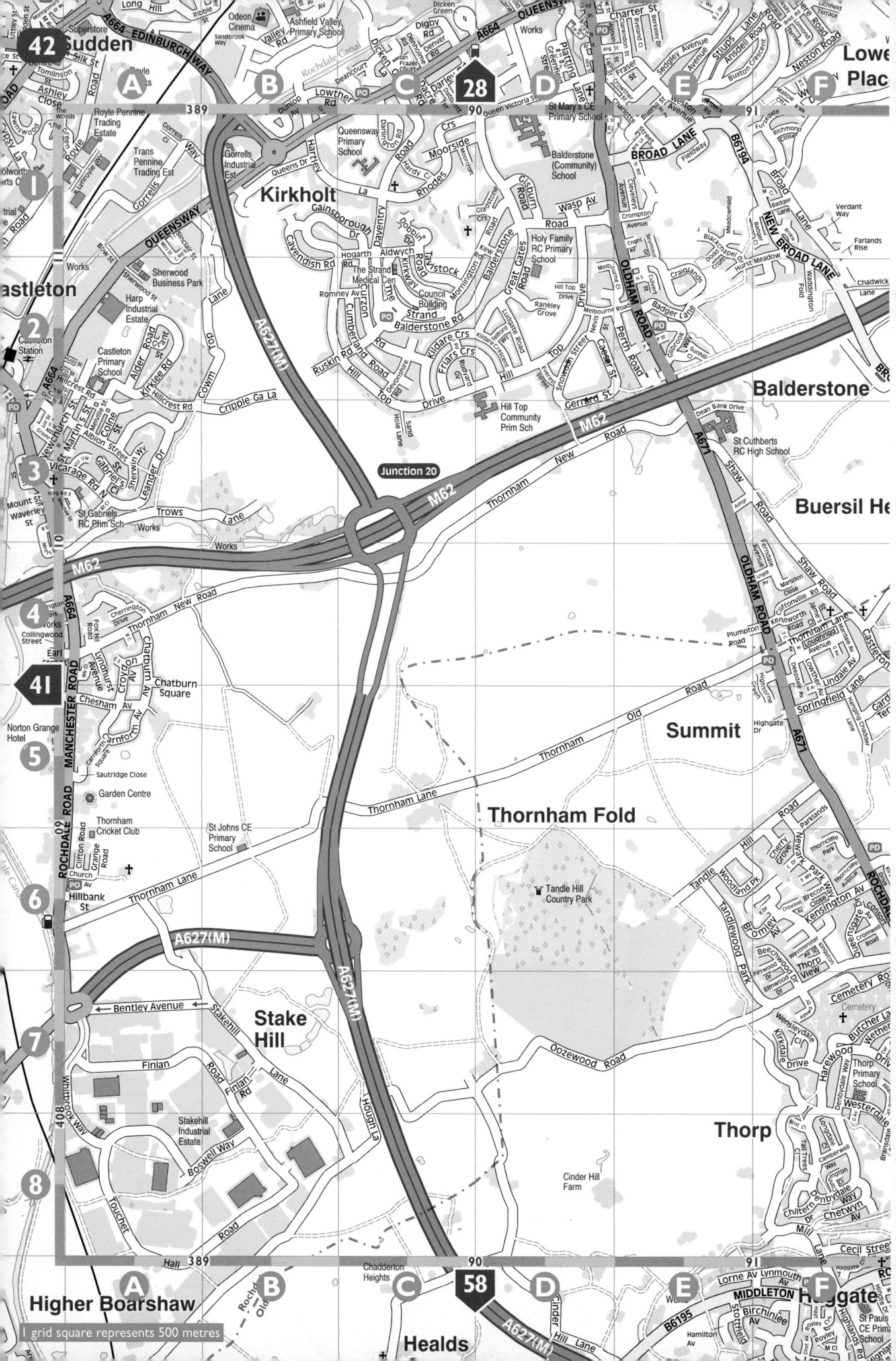

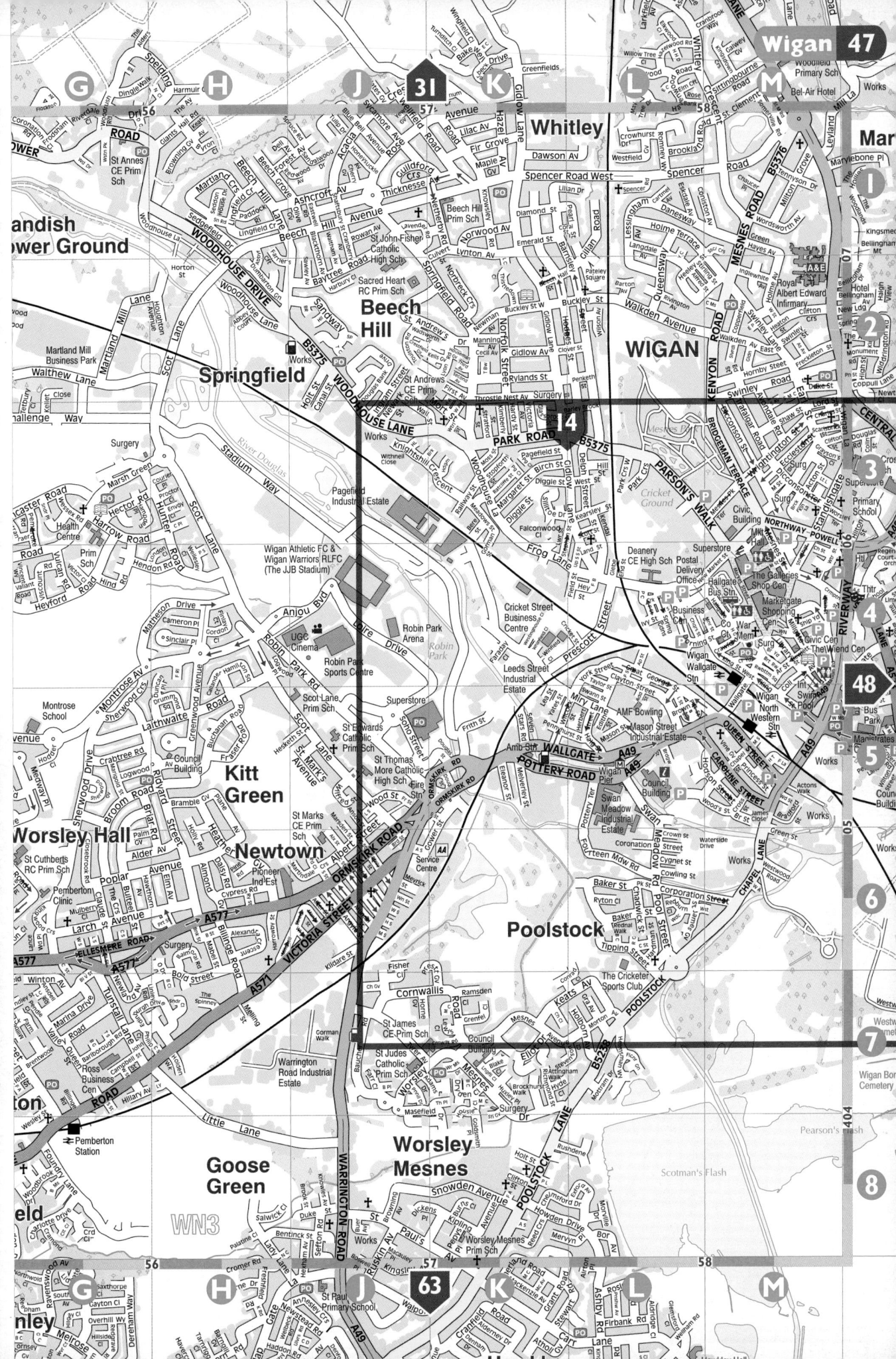

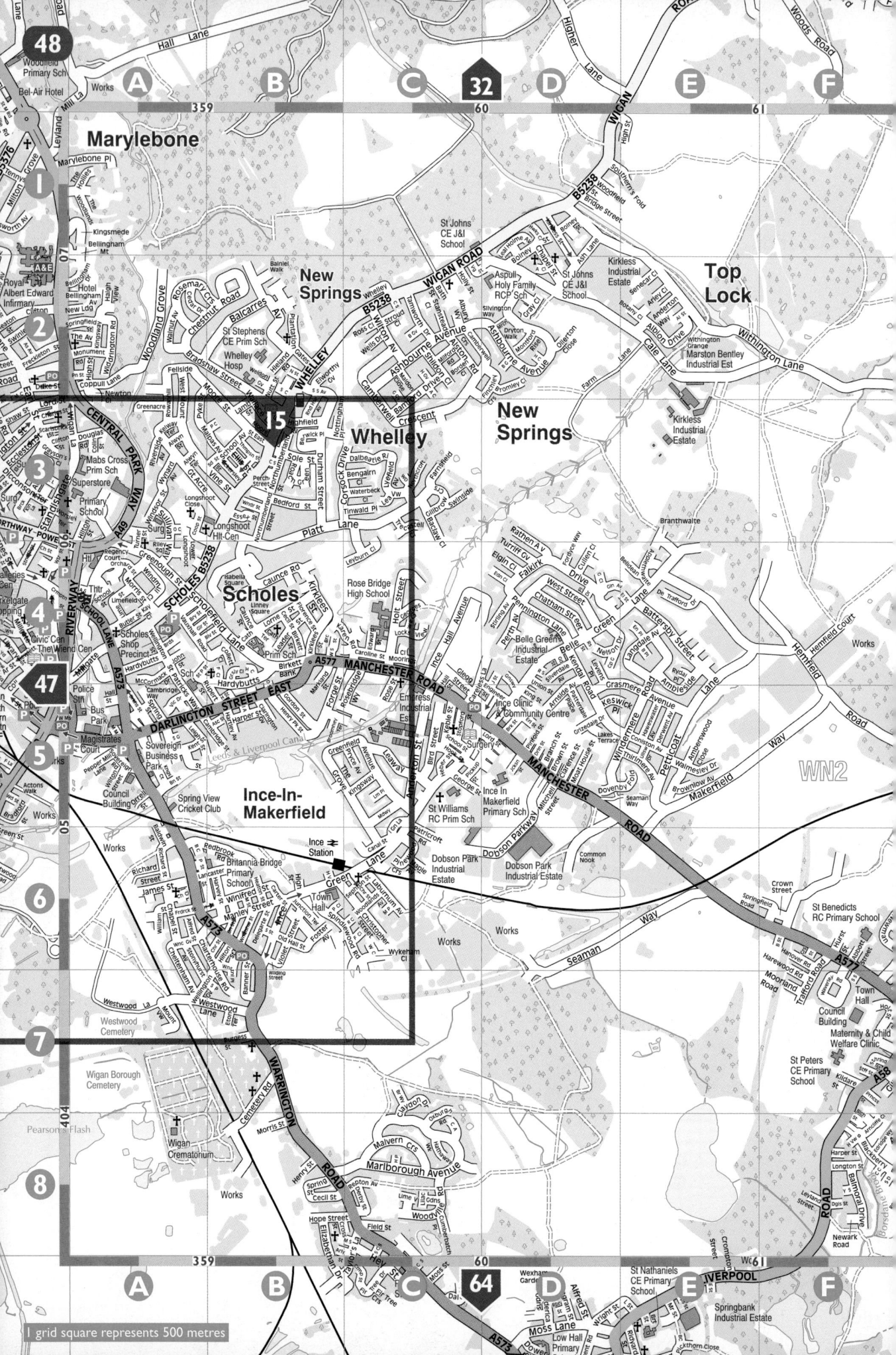

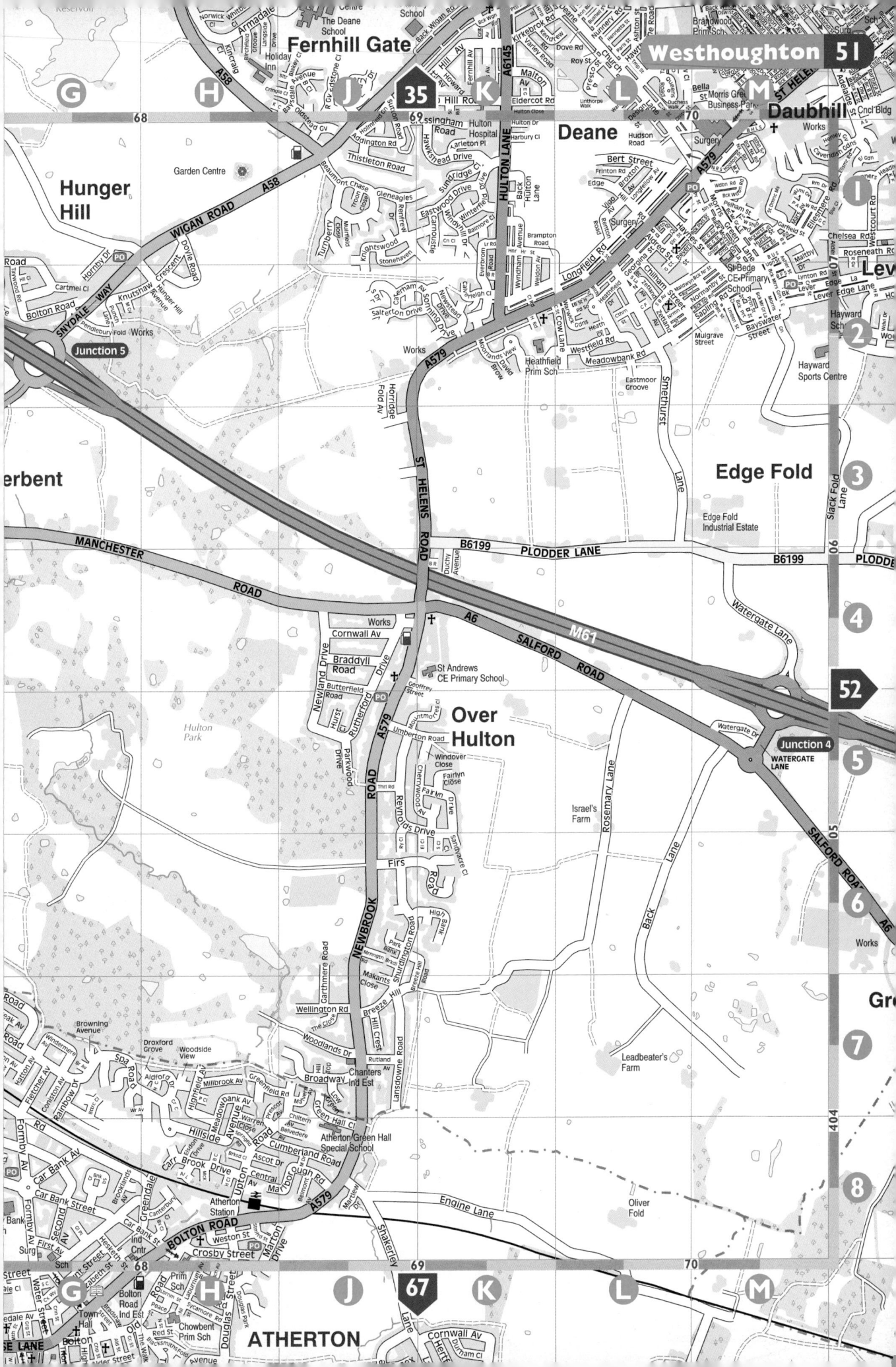

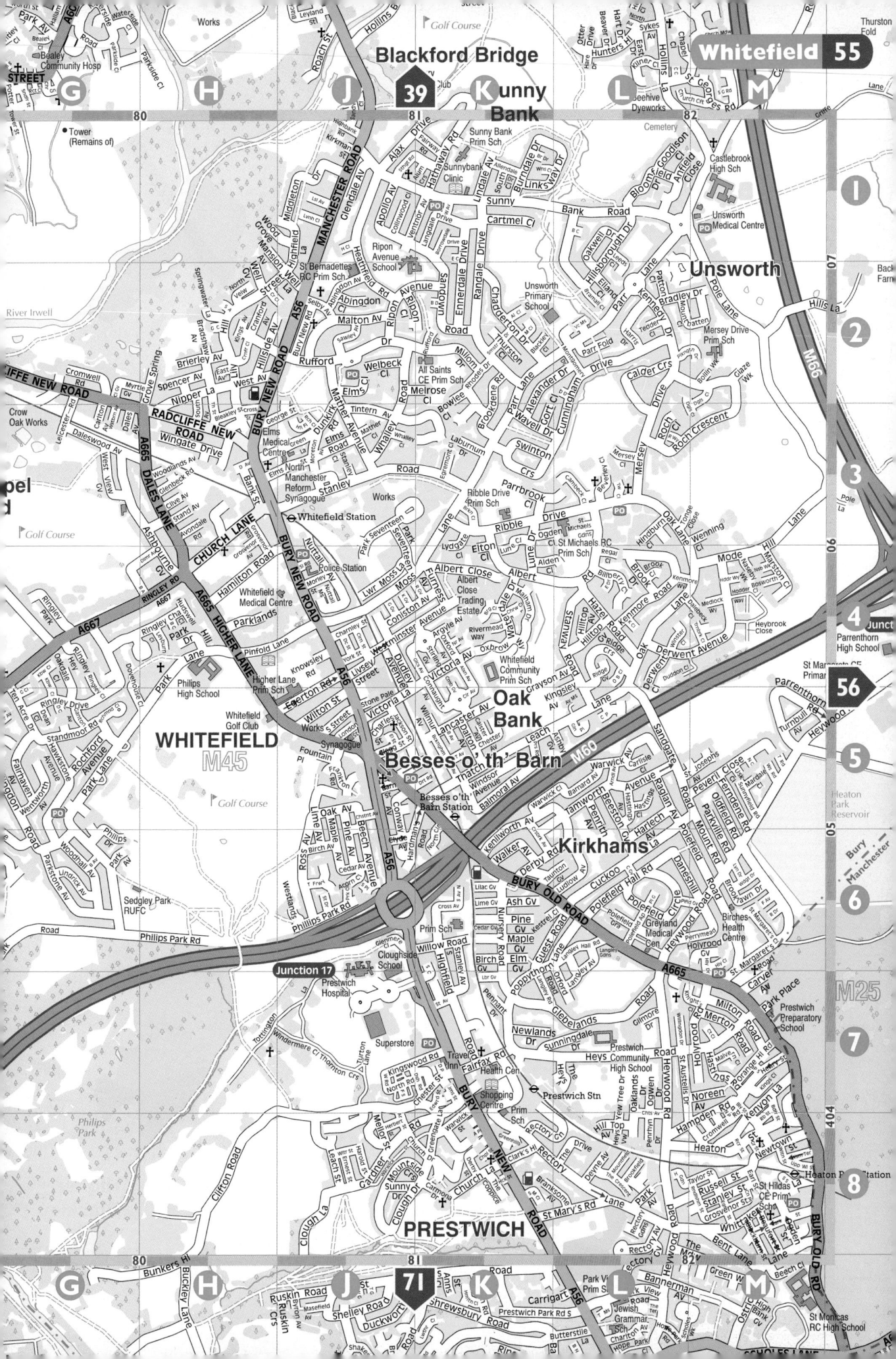

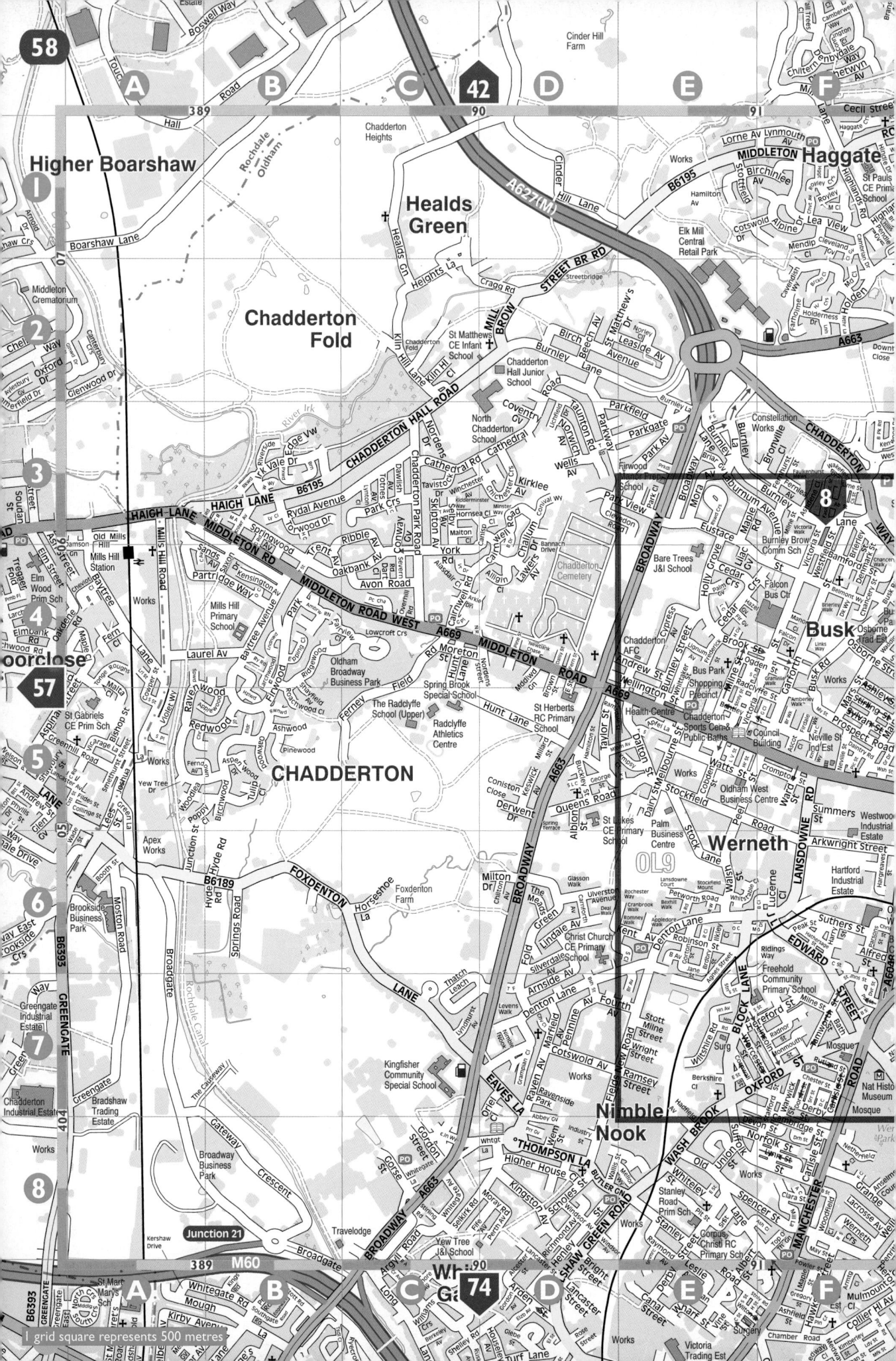

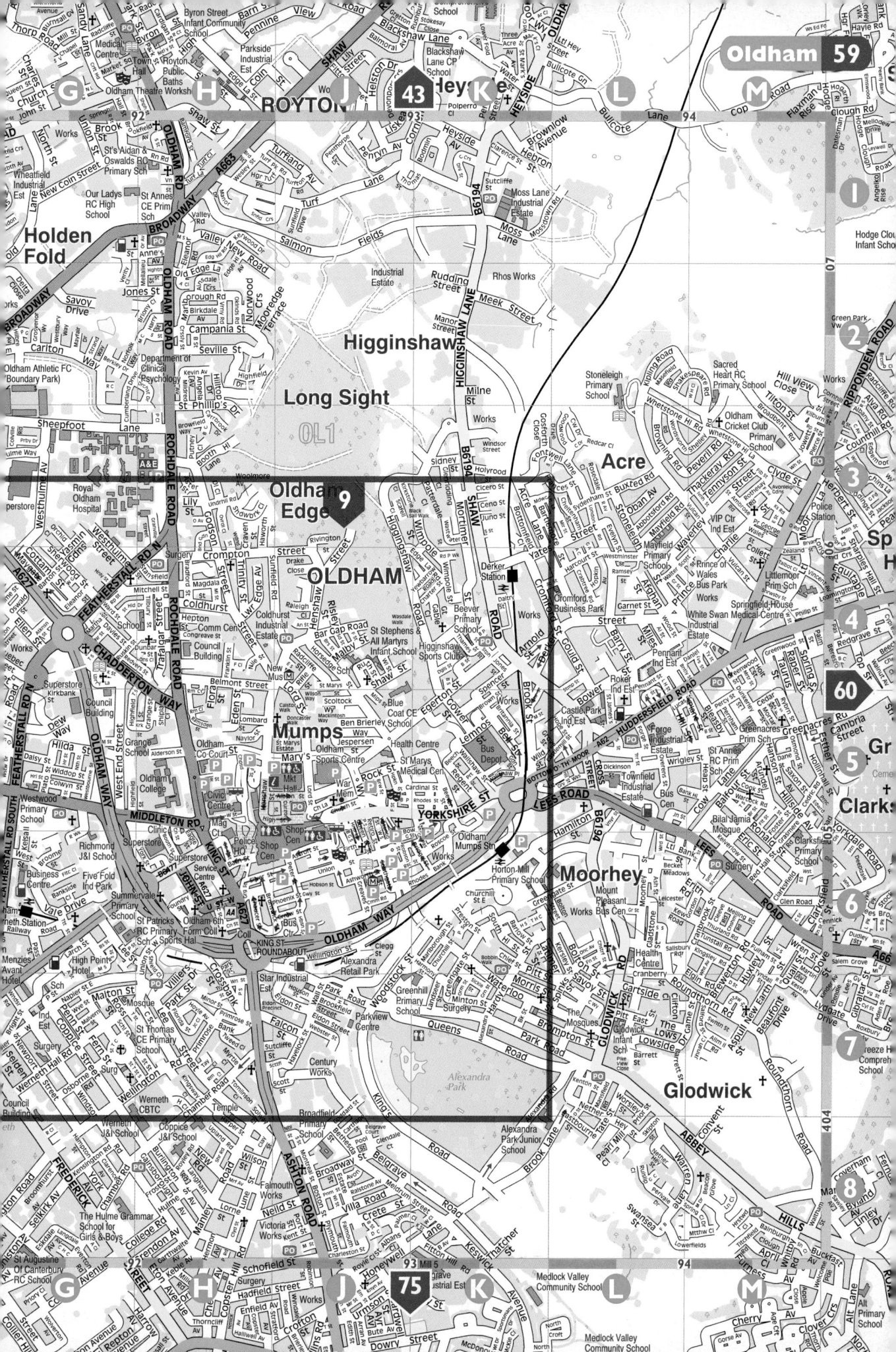

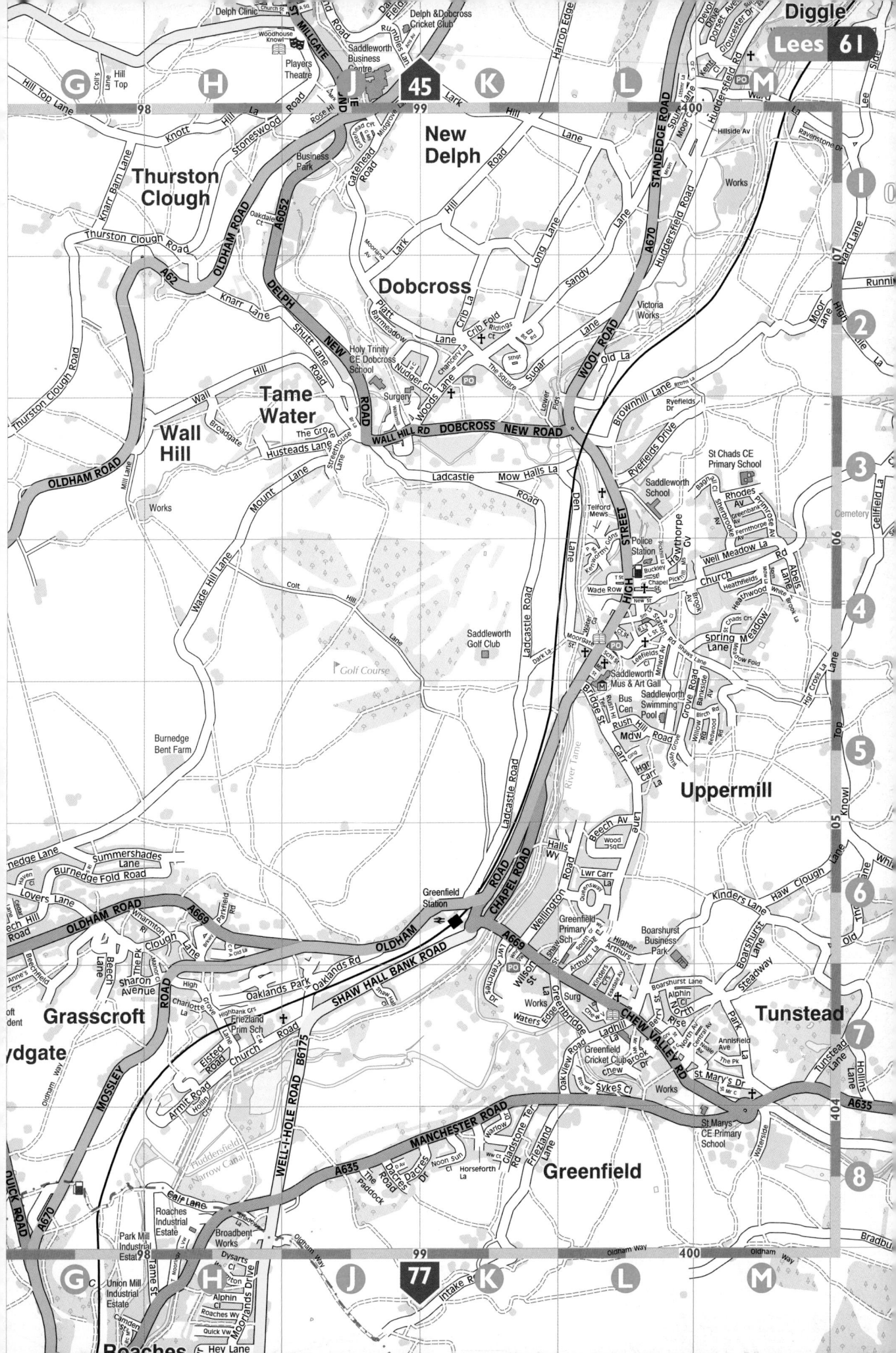

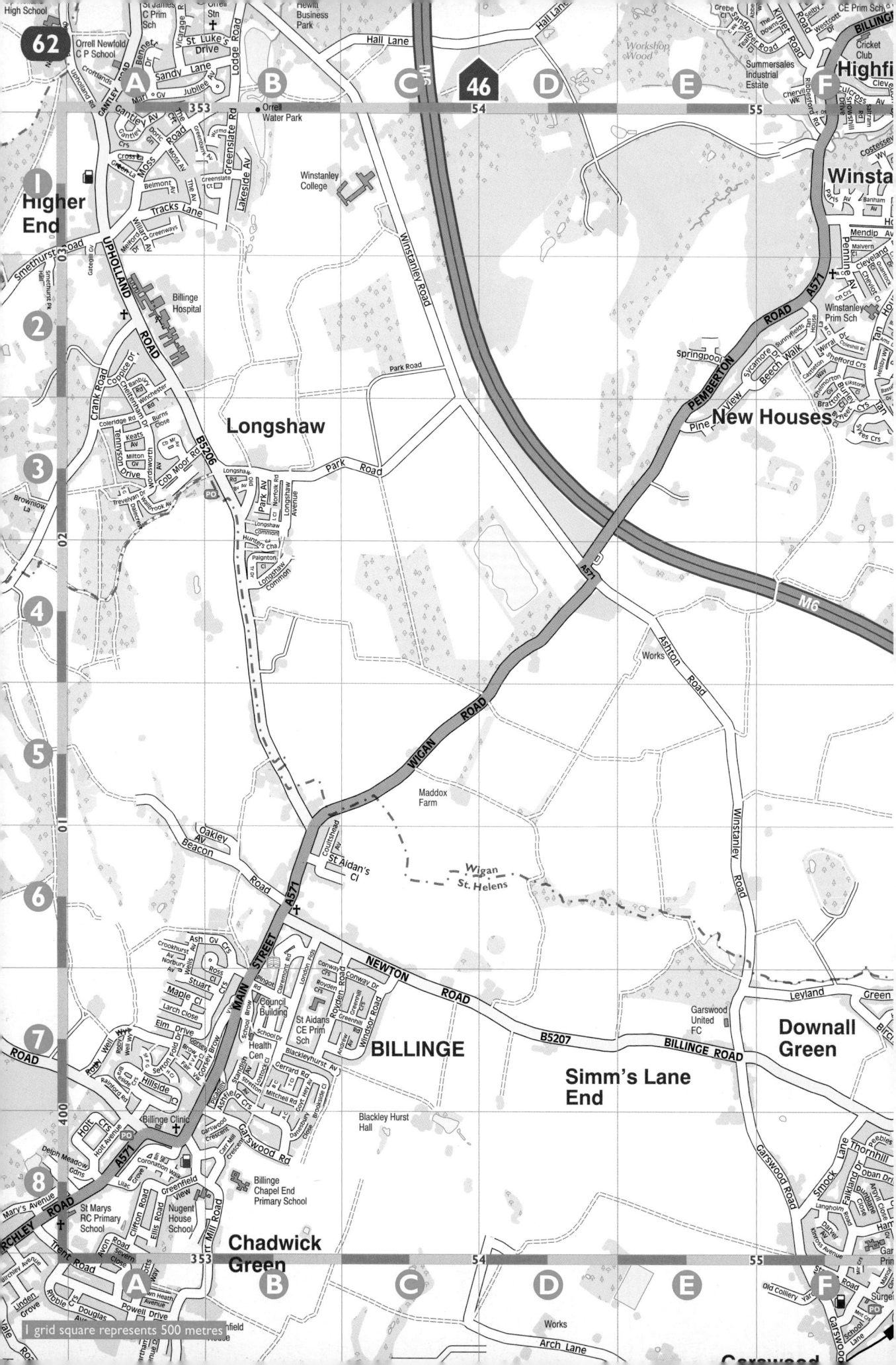

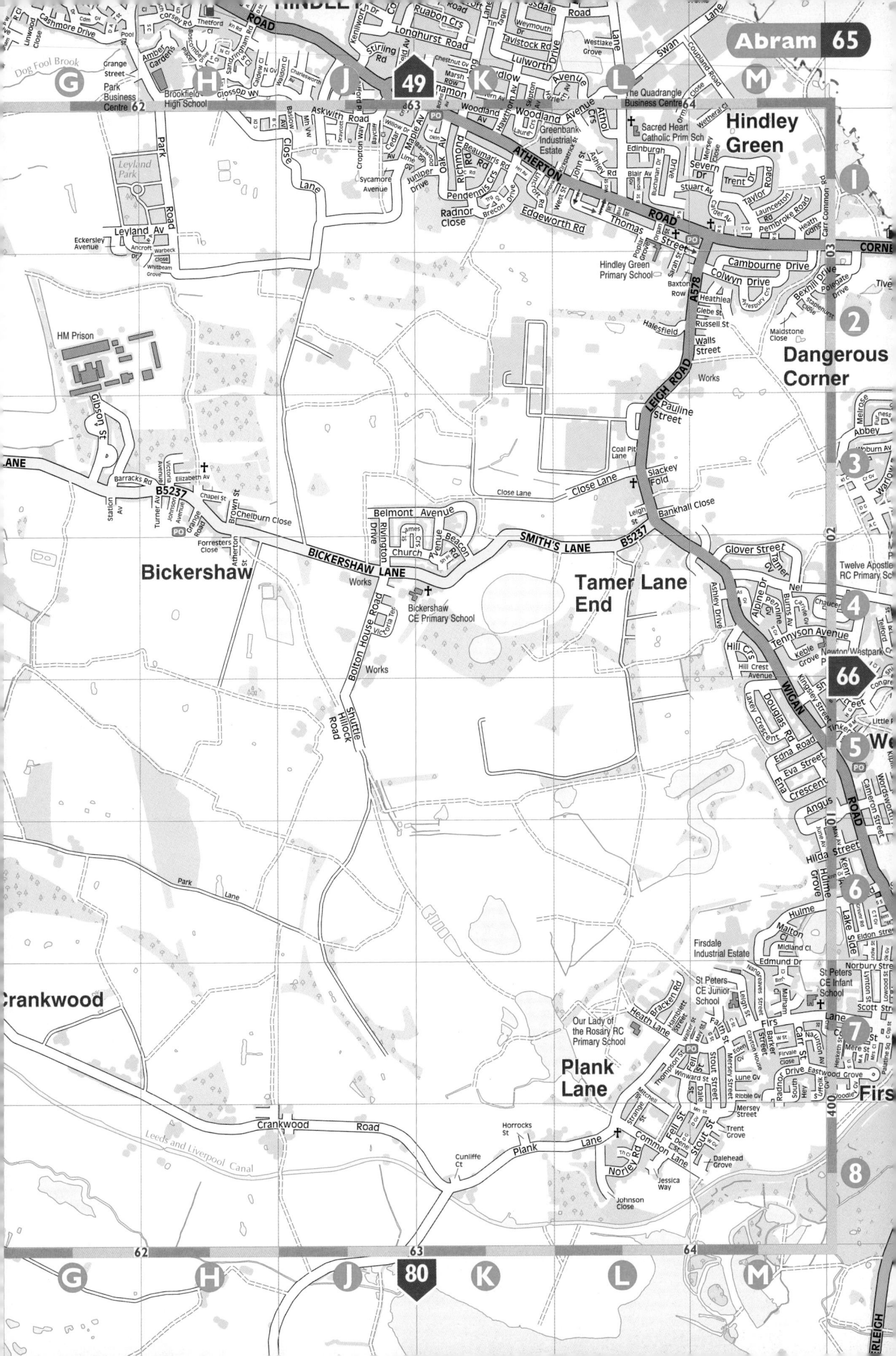

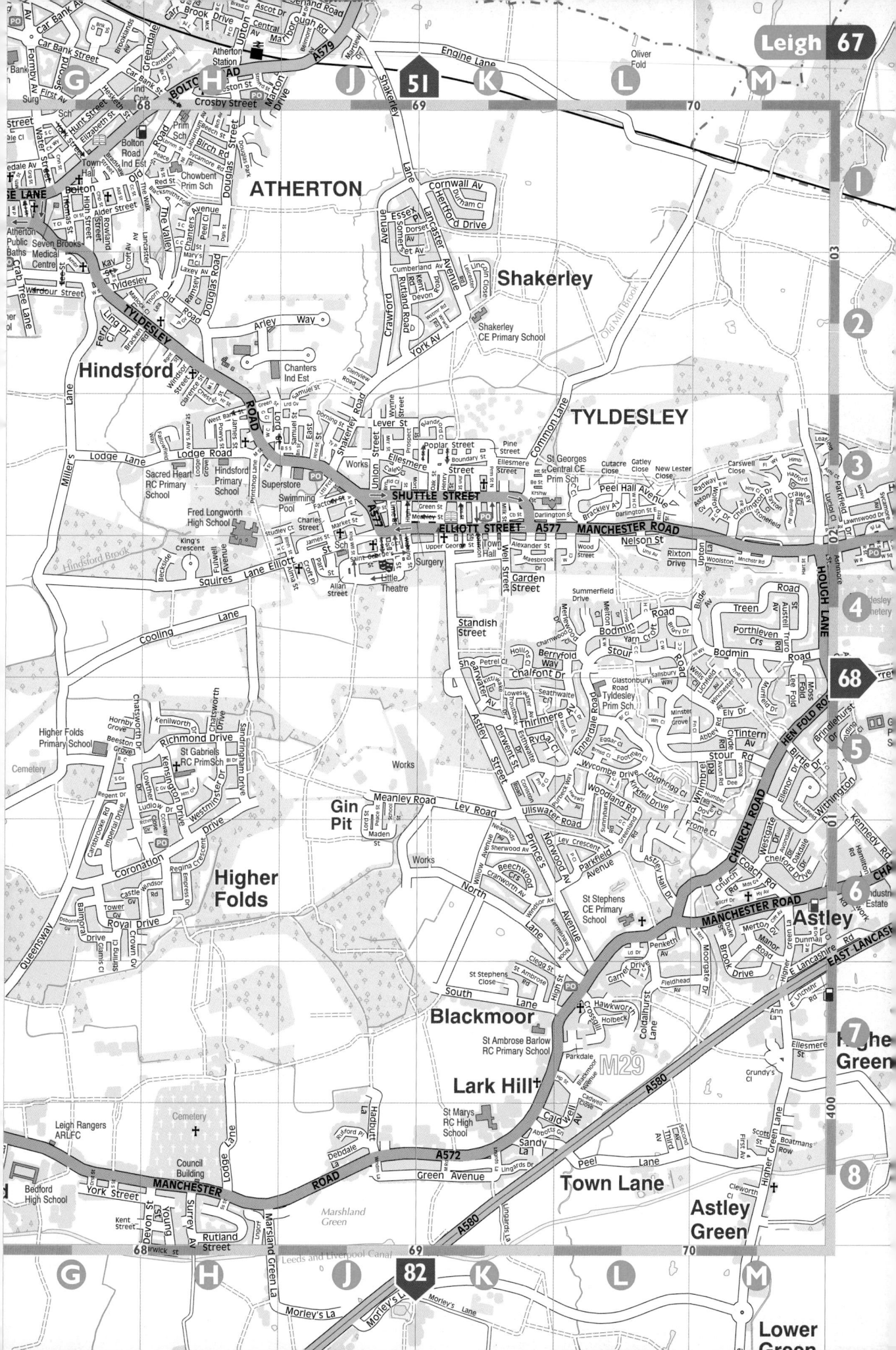

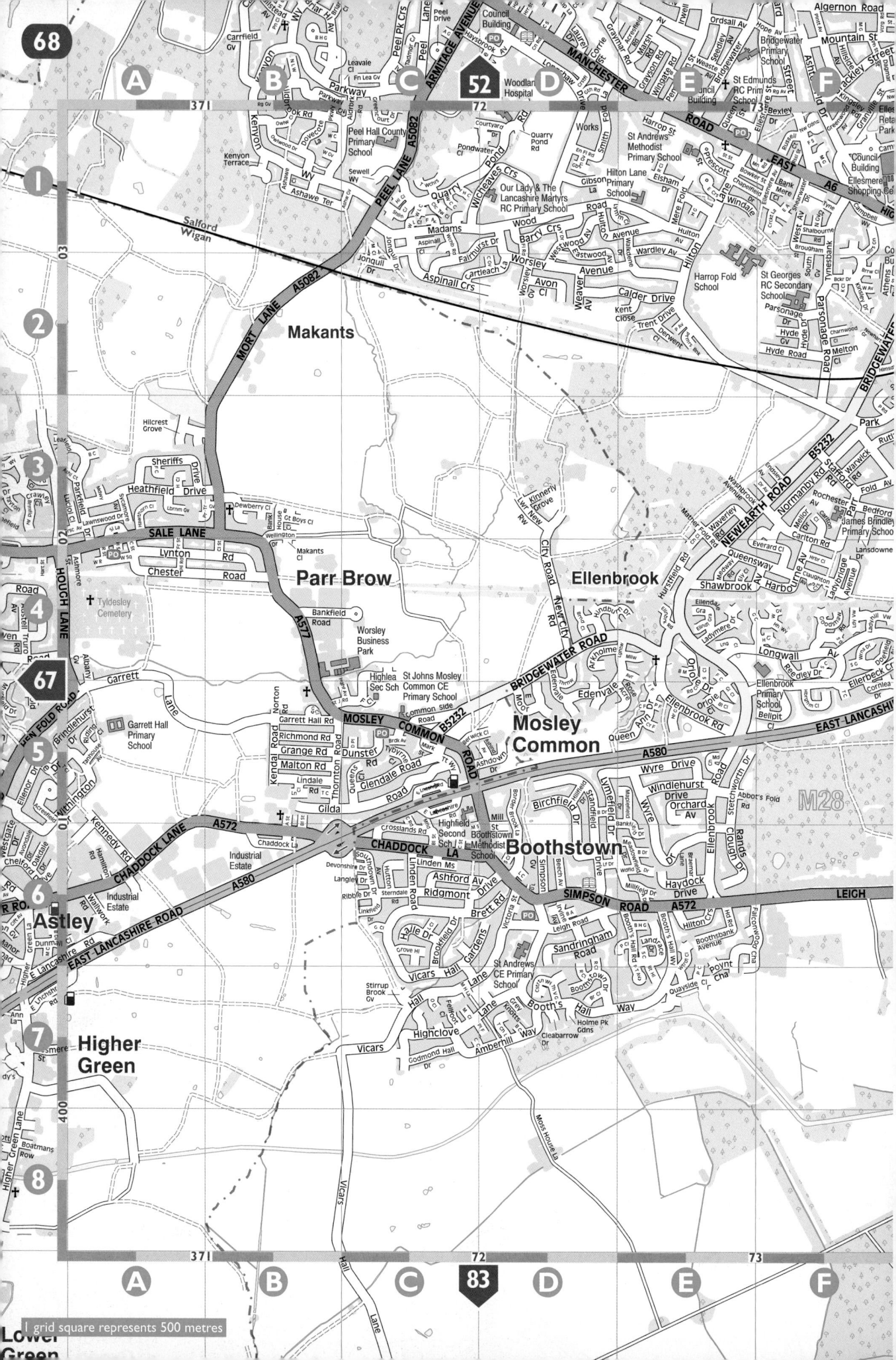

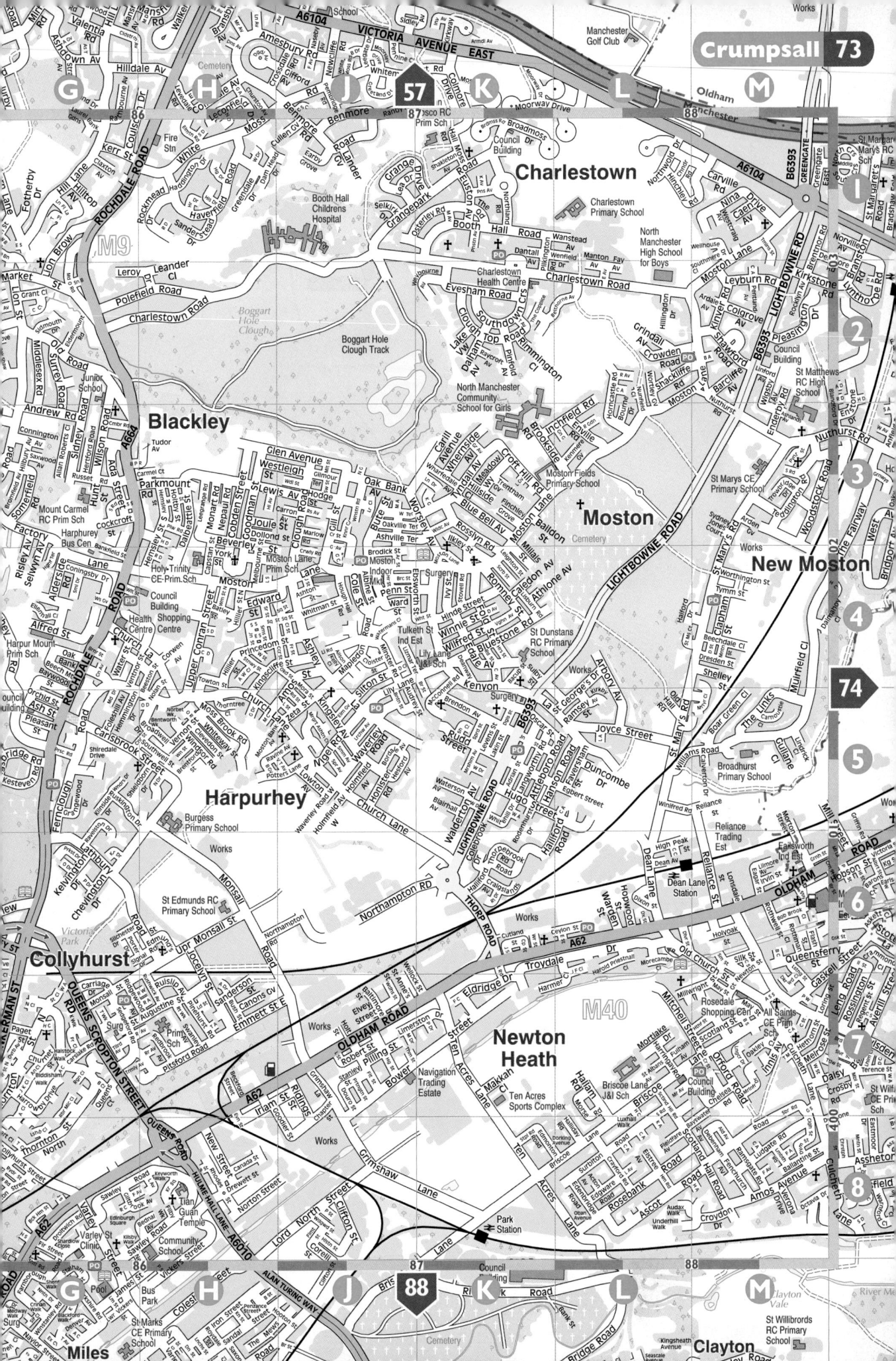

G H J **57** K L M

I

Charlestown

Blackley

Moston

New Moston

2

3

4

74

5

Harpurhey

6

Collyhurst

Newton Heath

M40

7

8

G H J **88** K L M

Miles

Clayton

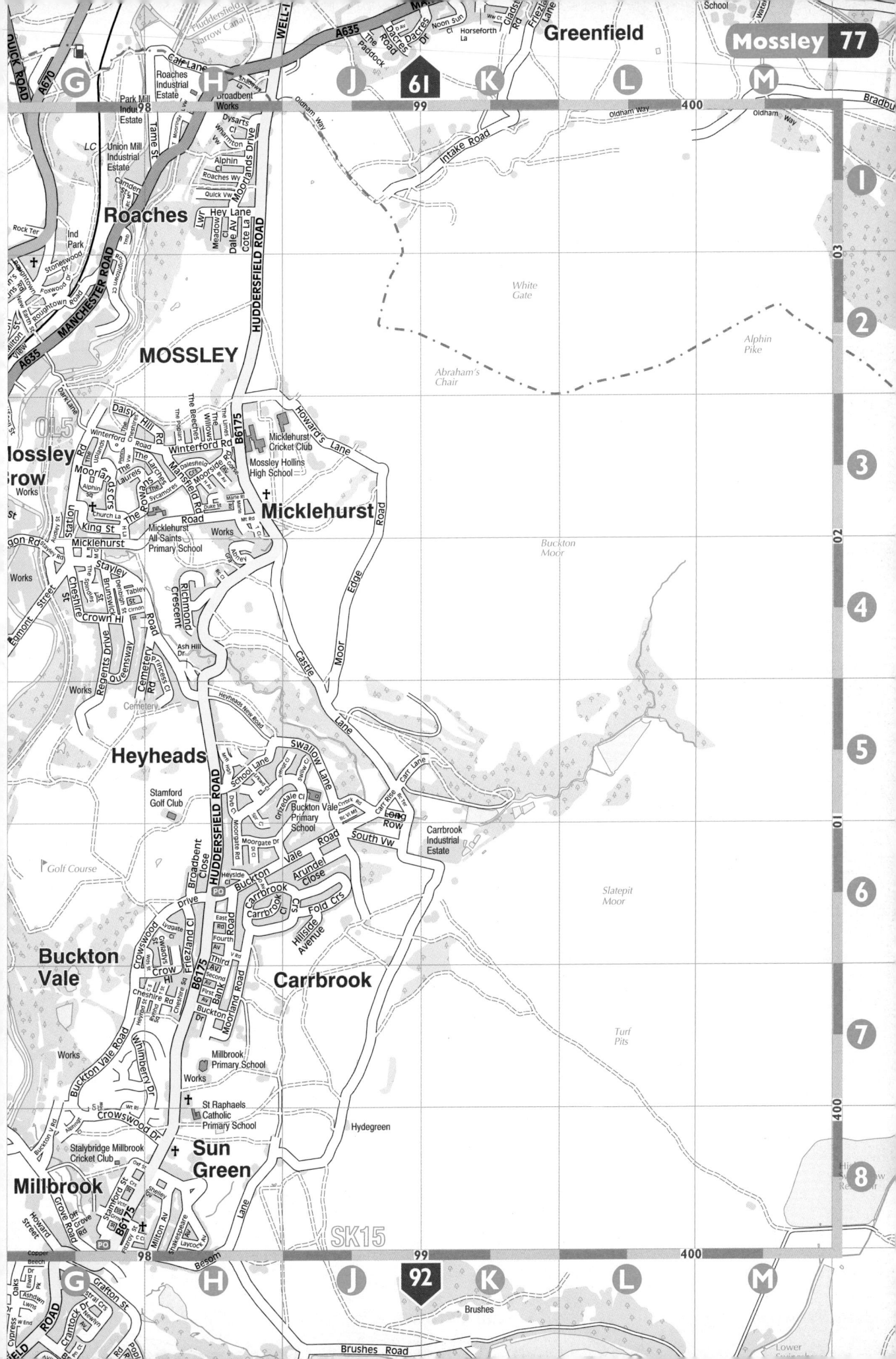

Greenfield

MOSSLEY

Roaches

Micklehurst

Mossley Brow

Heyheads

Buckton Vale

Carrbrook

Millbrook

Sun Green

White Gate

Abraham's Chair

Alphin Pike

Buckton Moor

Slatepit Moor

Turf Pits

SK15

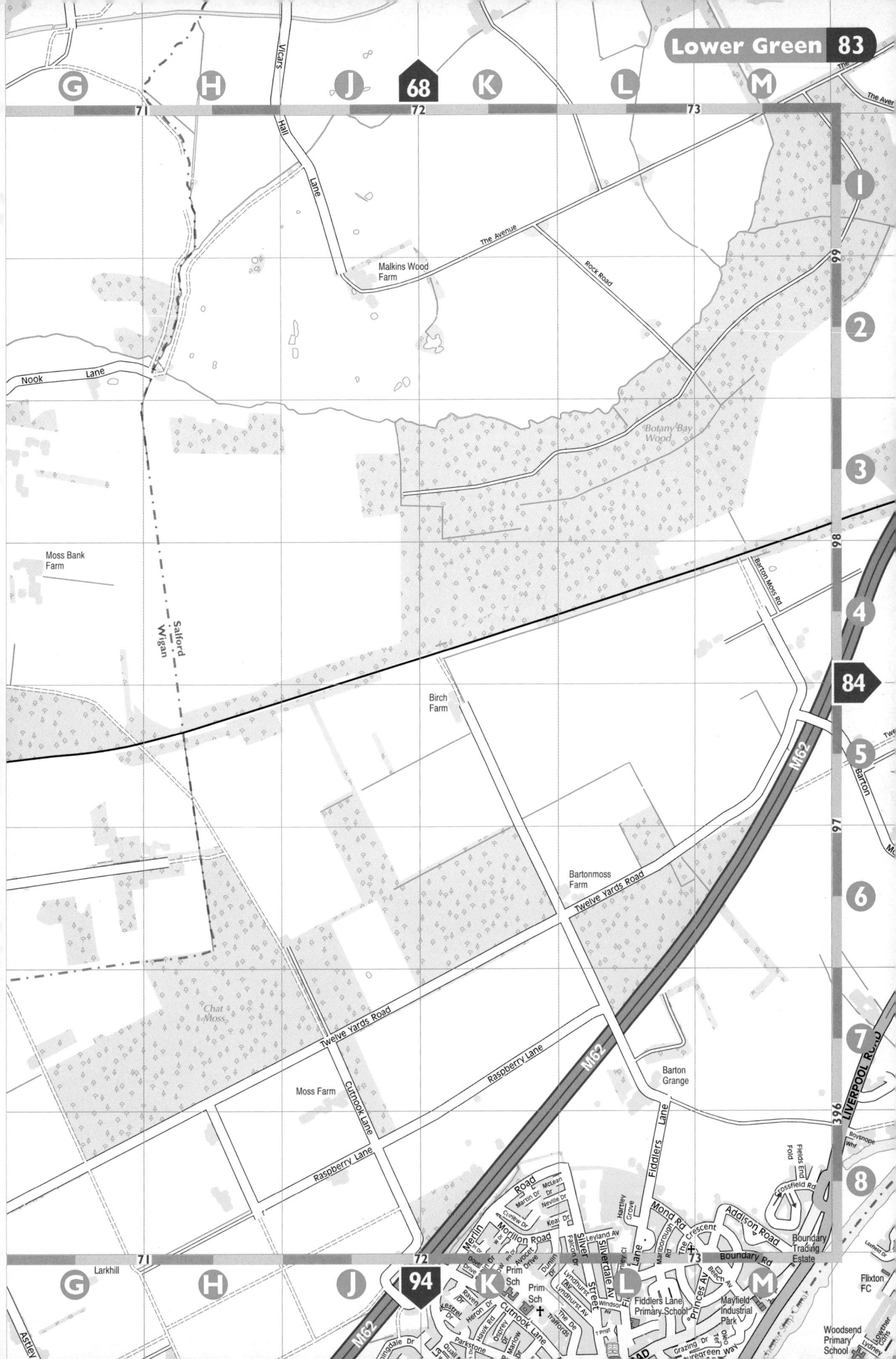

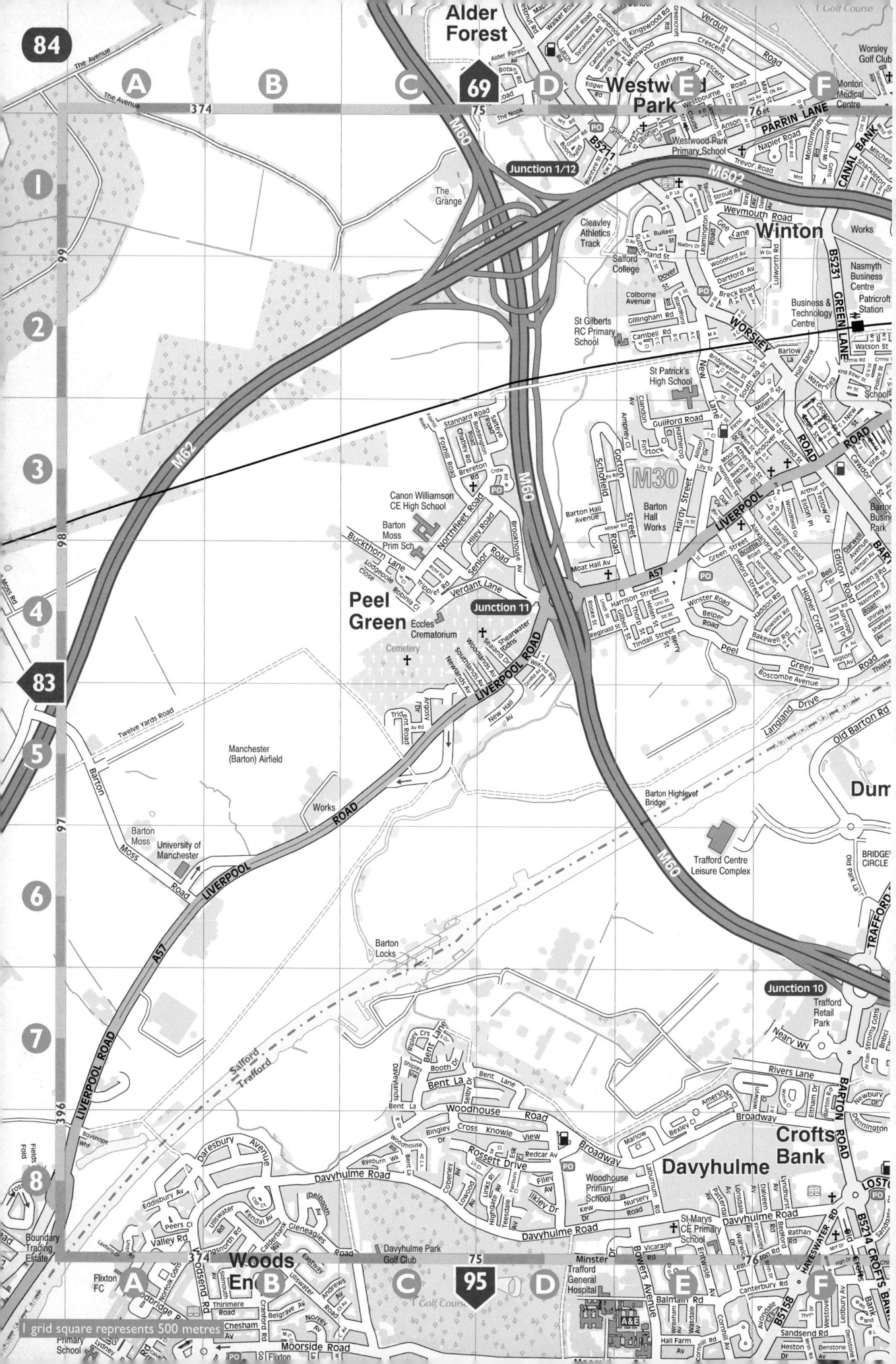

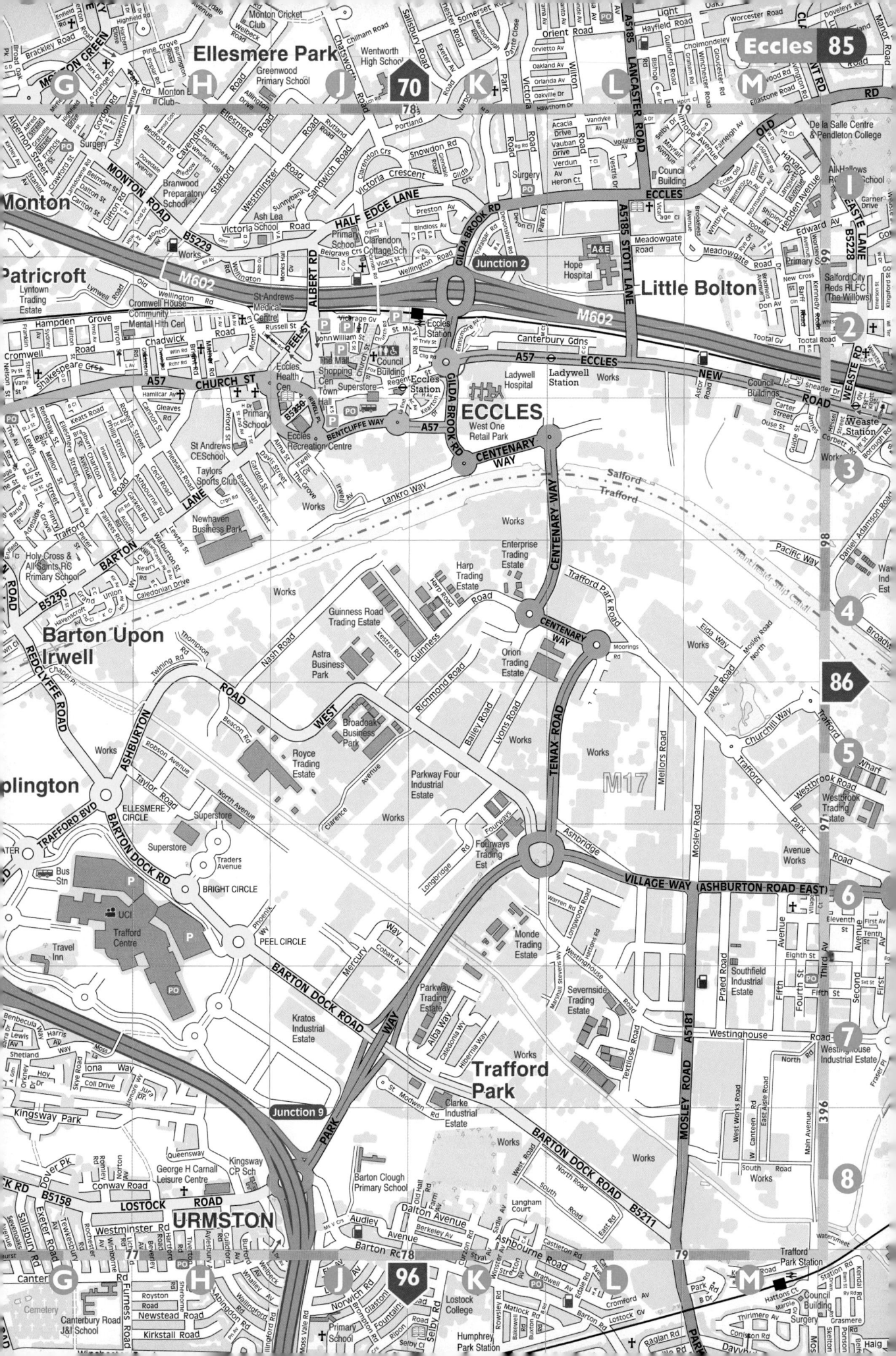

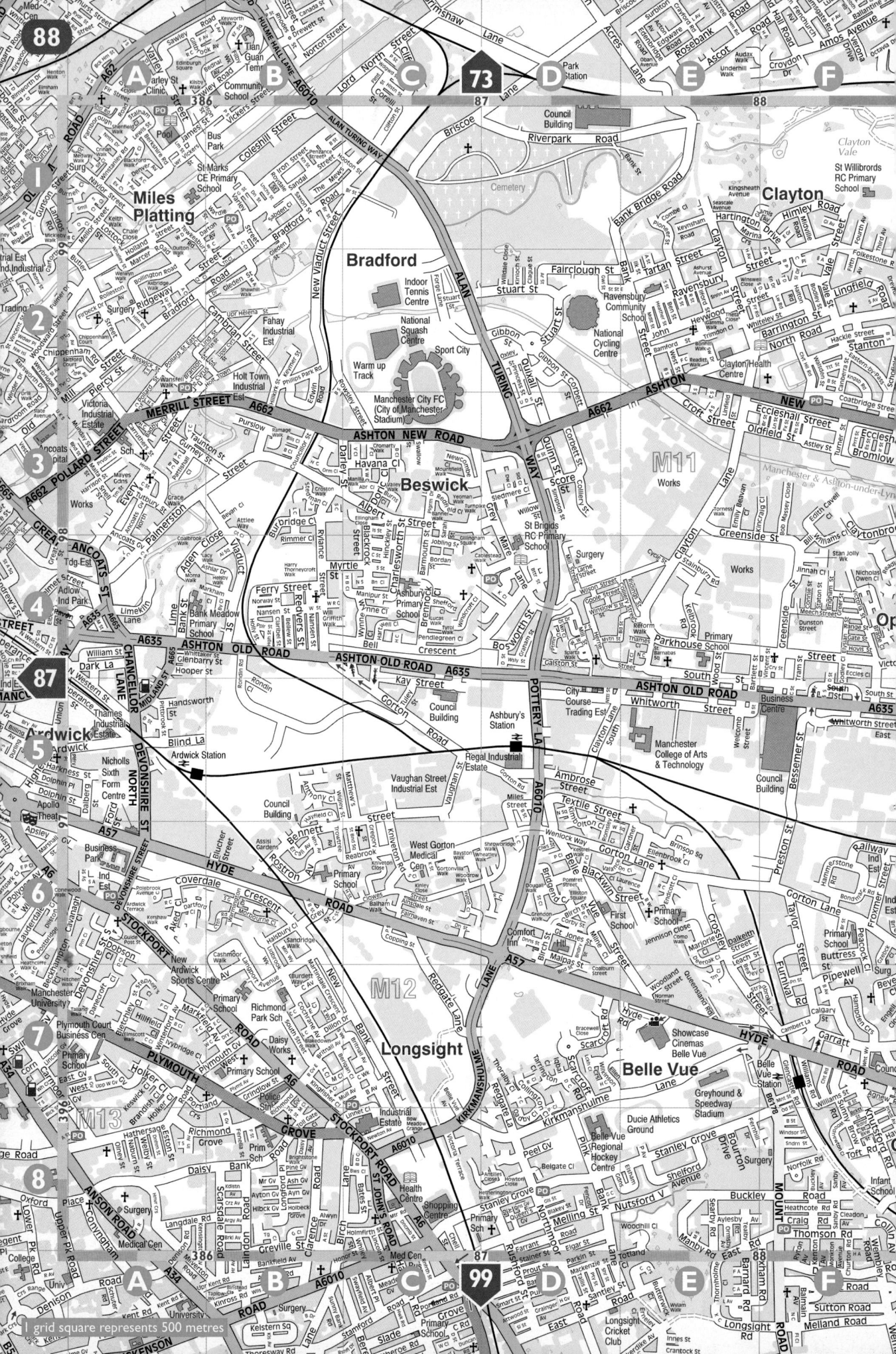

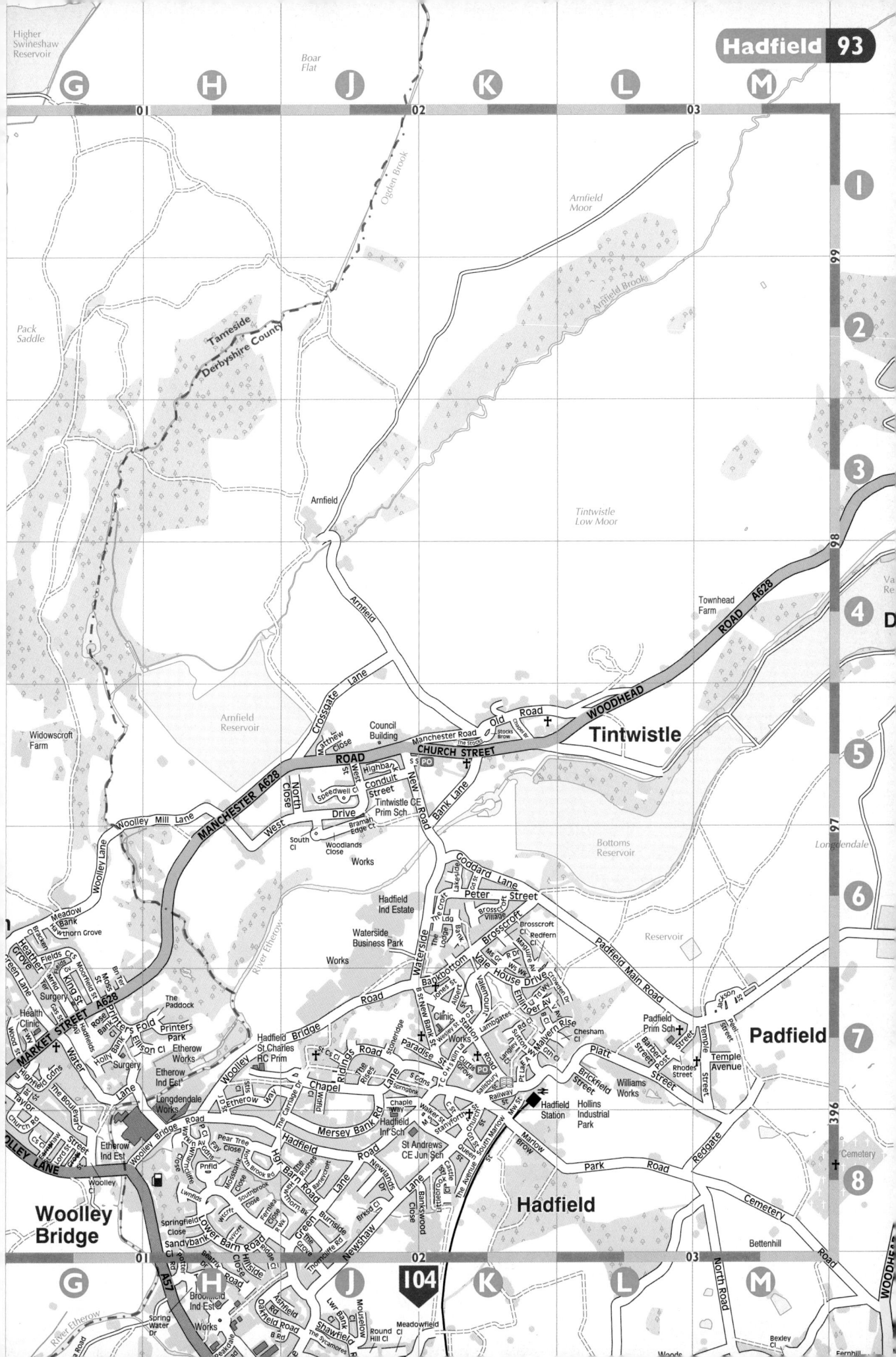

G H J K L M

Higher Swineshaw Reservoir

Boar Flat

Ogden Brook

Arnfield Moor

Arnfield Brook

Pack Saddle

Tameside
Derbyshire County

Arnfield

Tintwistle Low Moor

Townhead Farm

WOODHEAD ROAD A628

Widowscroft Farm

Arnfield Reservoir

Crossgate Lane

Arnfield Lane

Council Building
Matthew Close
The Stocks
Manchester Road
Stocks Brow
Old Road
Tintwistle

CHURCH STREET
ROAD
PO
Highbank
North Close
West
Speedwell Cl
Conduit Street
New Road
Bank Lane
Tintwistle CE Prim Sch

Woolley Mill Lane
MANCHESTER A628
West Drive
Braman Edge Ct
South Cl
Woodlands Close
Works

Bottoms Reservoir

Longdendale

Hadfield Ind Estate

Goddard Lane
The Croft
Peter Street
Brosscroft Village
Reservoir

Waterside Business Park
Works
The Lodge
Brosscroft
Brosscroft Cl
Redfern
Padfield Main Road

Meadow Bank
Wthorn Grove
Heather Bank
Green Lane
Fields Crs
King St
Moss St
Bankbottom
Jones St
Vale House Drive
Valemount
Enholder Av
Clinic

Padfield Prim Sch

Padfield

Surgery
The Paddock
Printers Fold
Printers Park
Hadfield Bridge
St Charles RC Prim
Etherow Works
Paradise St
Stoneridge
Lambgates
Mavern Rise
Chesham Cl
Platt
Barber Street
Post Street
Rhodes Street
Williams Works

Temple Avenue

Health Clinic
MARKET STREET A628
Water Lane
Surgery
Holly Bank
Ellison Cl
Etherow Ind Est
Longdendale Works
Chapel
Woolley
Ridings Road
The River
PO
Salisbury
Brickfield Street
Williams Works

River Etherow

The Boulevard
Taylor
Highfield Gdns
Church'n Rd
Woolley Bridge Road
Etherow Ind Est
Pear Tree Close
Pnfld
Chaple Way
Hadfield Inf Sch
St Andrews CE Jun Sch
Walker St
Stanford
Queen St
South Marlow St
Railway St
Marlow Brow
Hadfield Station
Hollins Industrial Park

WOOLLEY LANE
Woolley Bridge
Springfield Close
Lwrnfds
Sandybank
Hadfield
High Barn Road
Mersey Bank Road
Newlands Dr
Bankswood Close
Newshaw Lane
St Gdns
Littleton
Park Road
Redgate

Hadfield

Woolley Bridge

Lower Barn Road
Hillside Road
Green Lane
Meadowfield

Cemetery
Cemetery Road
Bettenhill

A57
Broomfield Ind Est
Spring Water Dr
Works
Ashfield Road
Oakfield Road
The Sycamores
Round Hill Cl
Woods
Bexley Cl
WOODHEAD

North Road

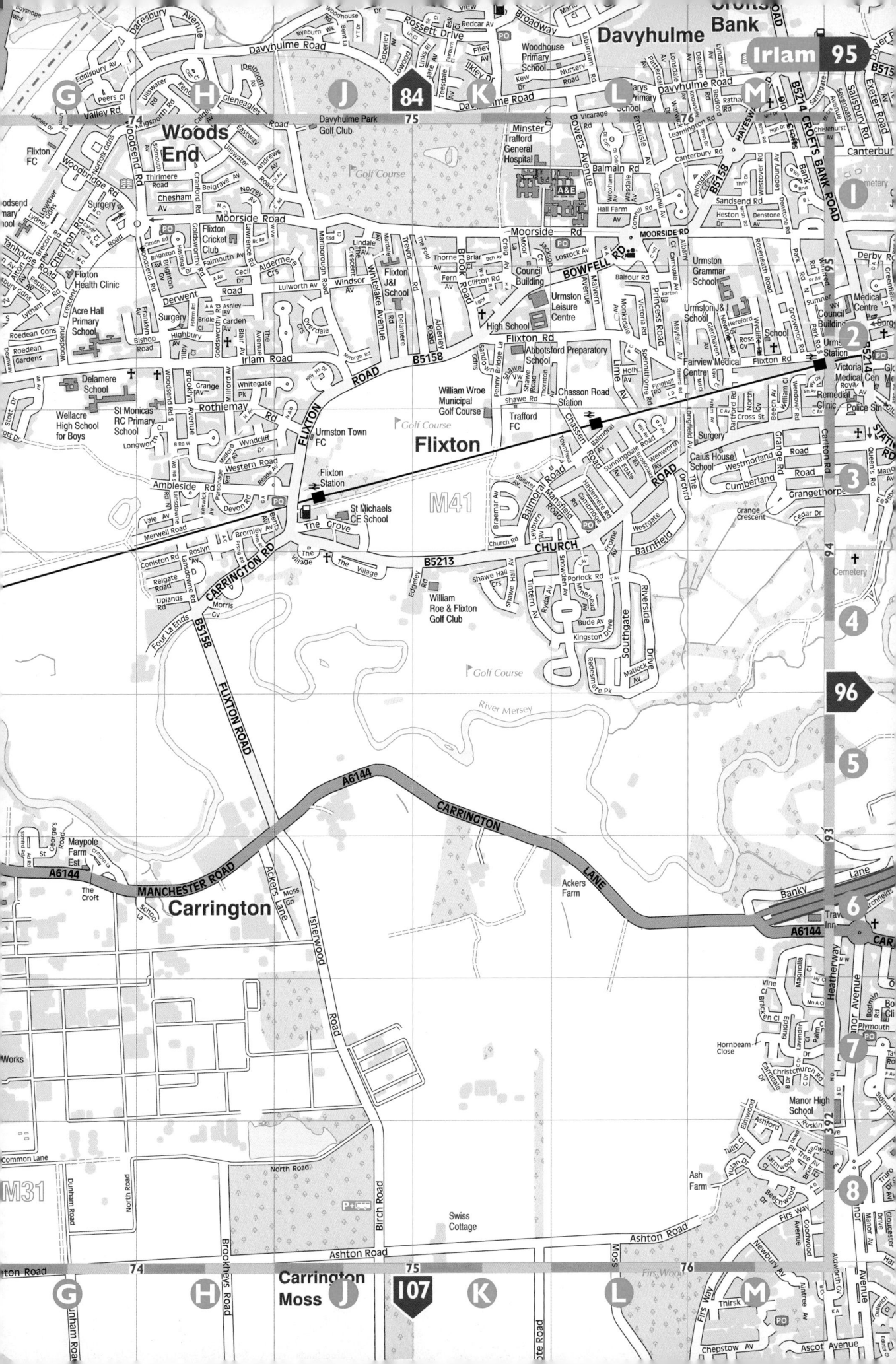

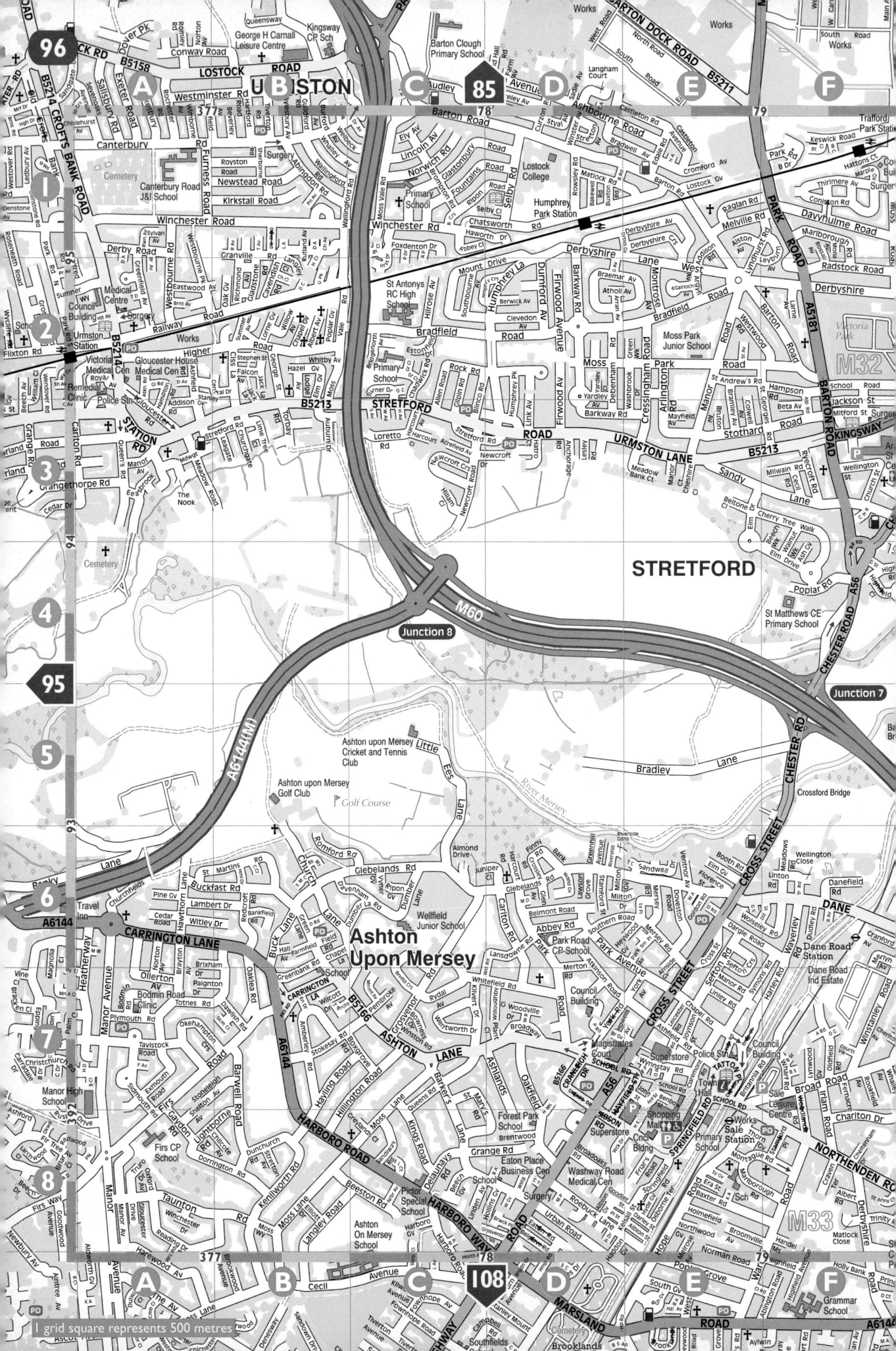

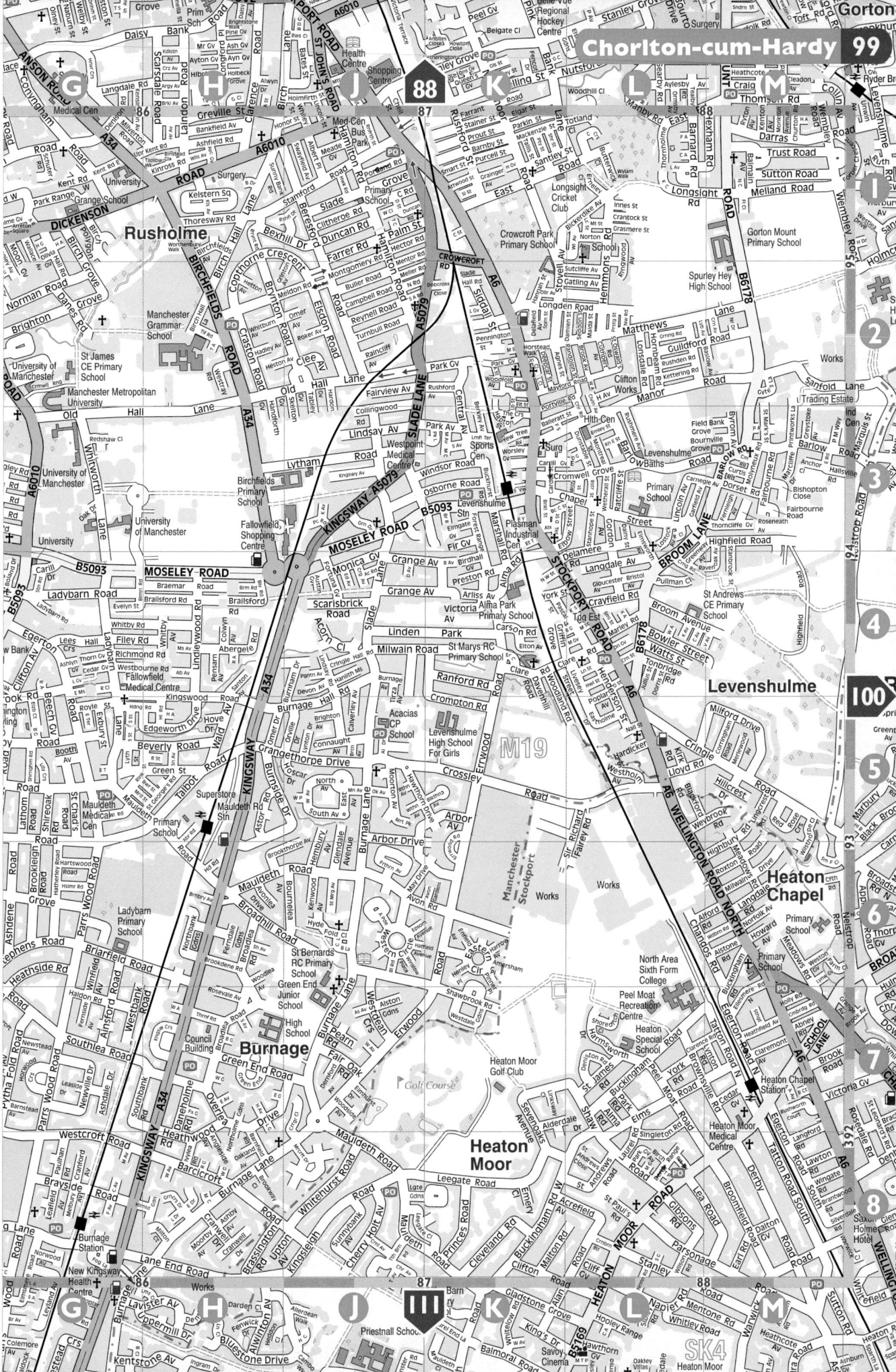

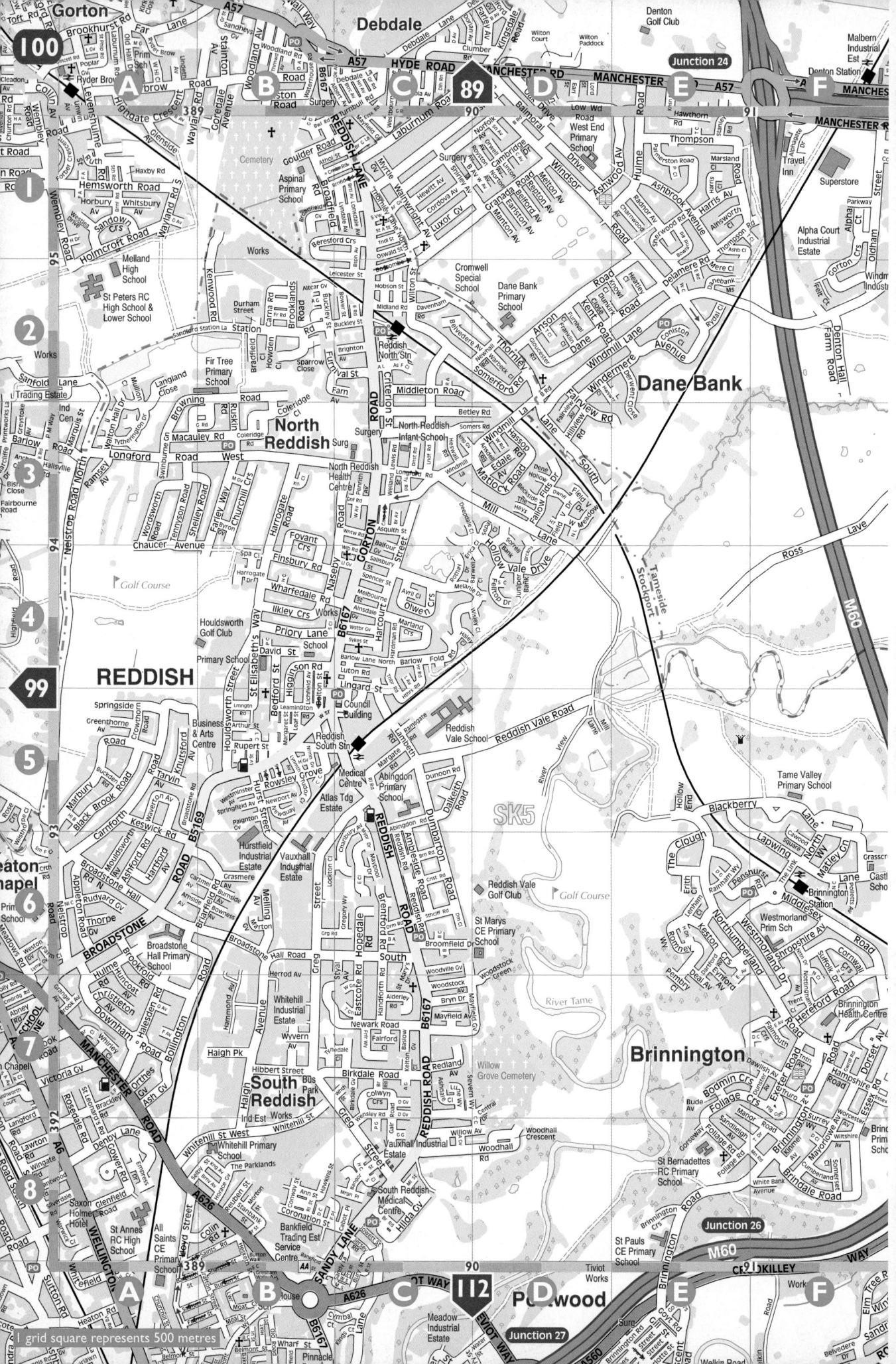

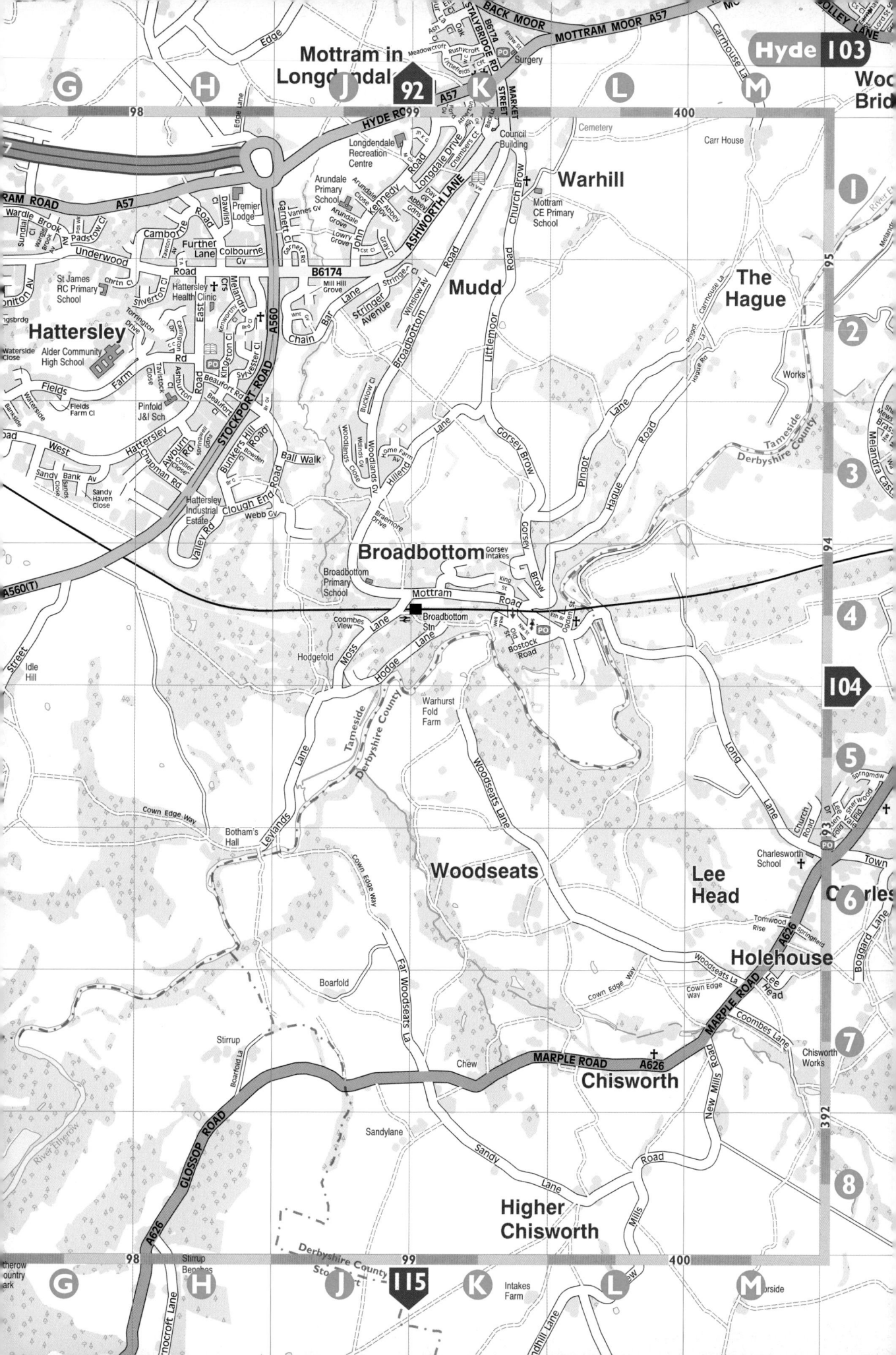

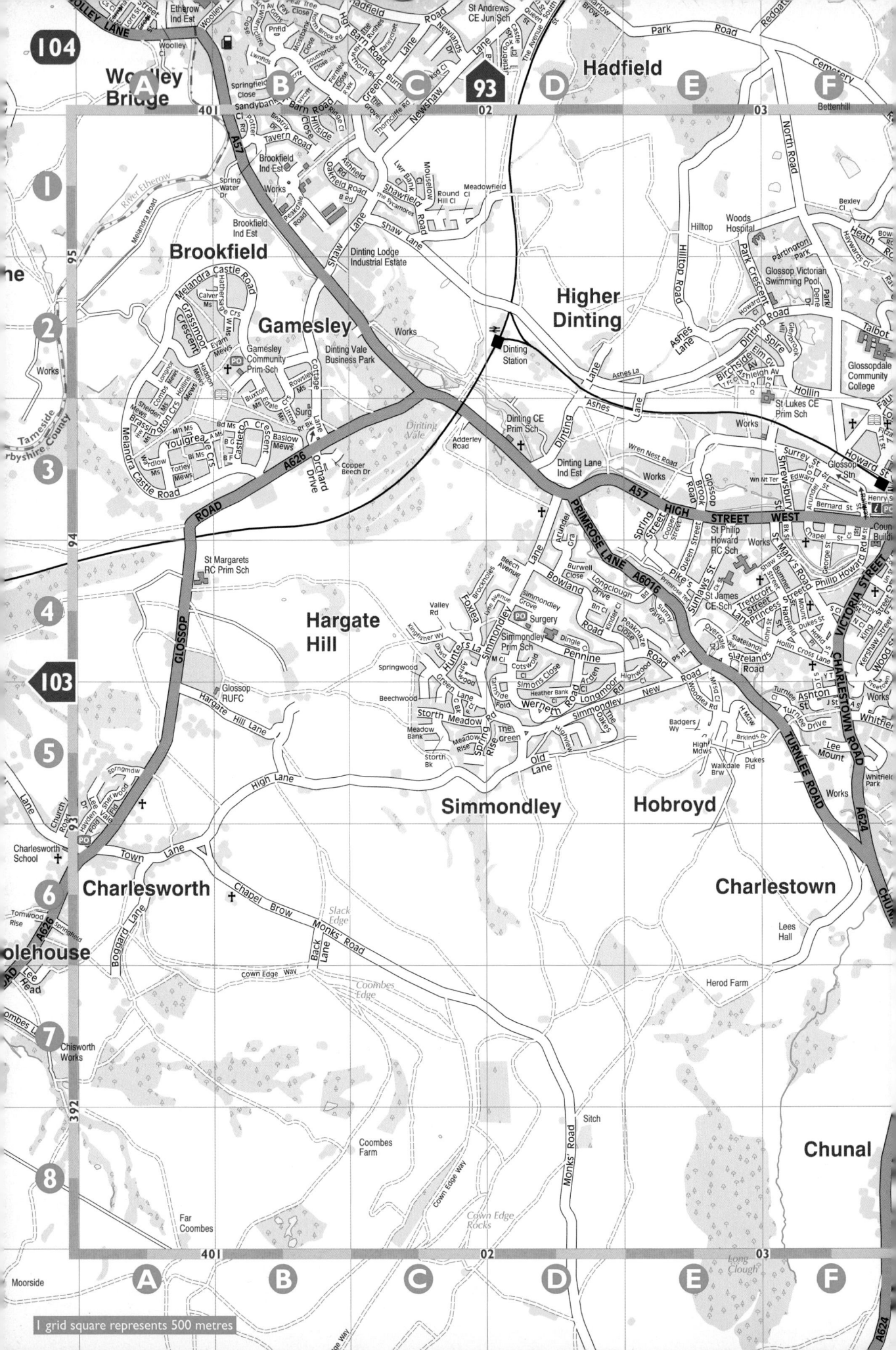

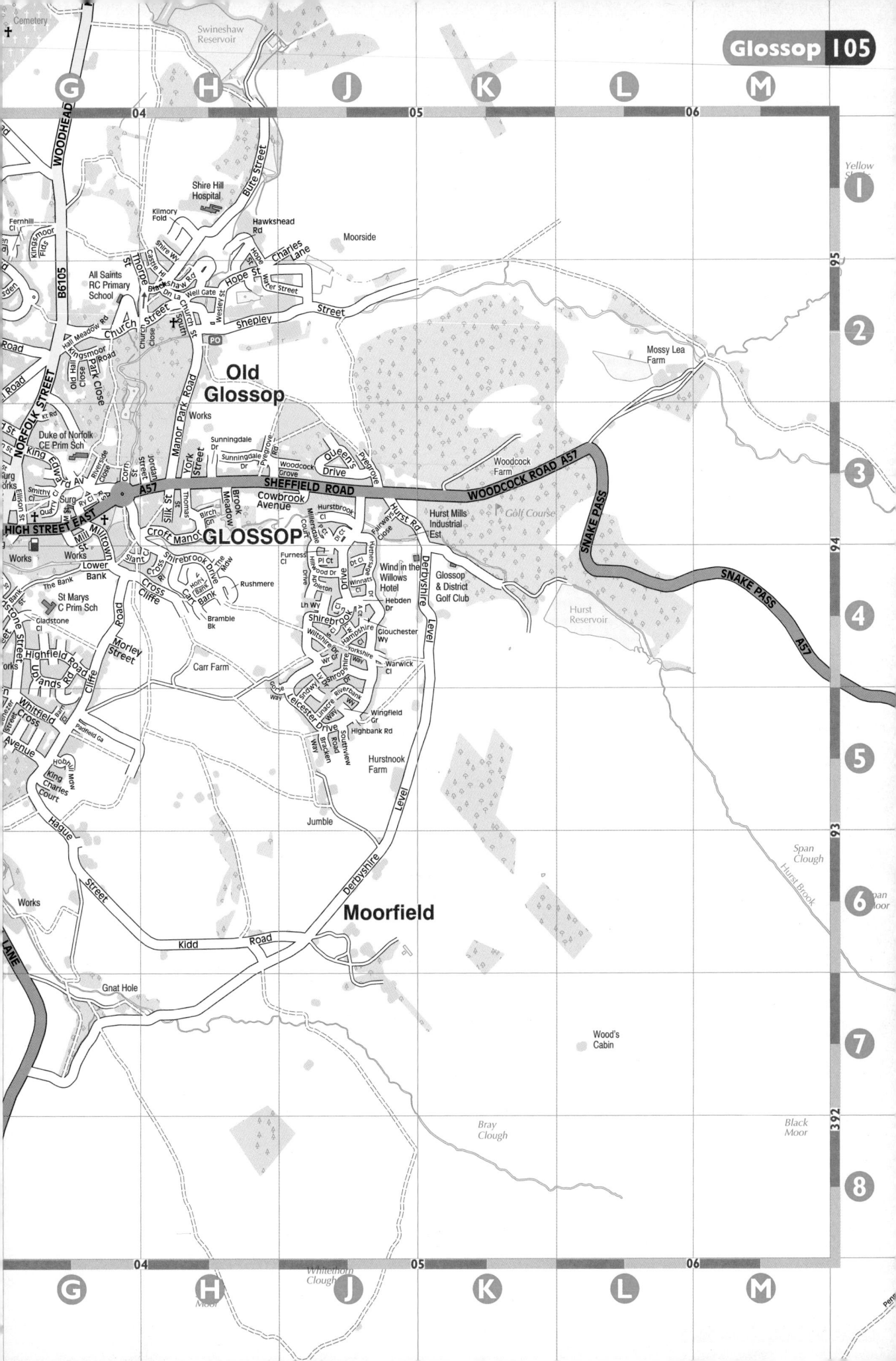

Cemetery

Swineshaw Reservoir

WOODHEAD

G   H   J   K   L   M

Yellow Slacks

Shire Hill Hospital

Kilmory Fold

Hawkshead Rd

Moorside

Fernhill Cl

Kingsmoor Flats

All Saints RC Primary School

Charles Lane

Hope St

Water Street

Shepley Street

Mossy Lea Farm

Old Glossop

B6105

Duke of Norfolk CE Prim Sch

King Edward Av

NORFOLK STREET

Manor Park Road

Works

Queen's Drive

Sunningdale Dr

Sunningdale Dr

Woodcock Grove

Pyegrove

Woodcock Farm

Woodcock Road A57

SHEFFIELD ROAD

SNAKE PASS

Cowbrook Avenue

A57

Golf Course

HIGH STREET EAST

Mill St

Works

Croft Manor

GLOSSOP

Hurstbrook Cl

Hurst Mills Industrial Est

SNAKE PASS A57

The Bank

Lower Bank

Shirebrook Drive

Cross Cliffe

Carr Bank

Rushmere

Bramble Bk

Furness Cl

Pl Ct

Appleton

Wind in the Willows Hotel

Hebden Dr

Glossop & District Golf Club

Hurst Reservoir

St Marys C Prim Sch

Gladstone Cl

Morley Street

Highfield Road

Uplands

Carr Farm

Shirebrook

Wiltshire Cl

Hillwood Dr

Winnats Cl

Hampshire Way

Yorkshire

Glouchester Wy

Warwick Cl

Whitfield Cross Avenue

Padfield Ga

King Charles Court

Hobh

Leicester Drive

Shropshire

Gorse Way

Unacre Way

Southview

Bracken Way

Riverbank Wy

Wingfield Gr

Highbank Rd

Derbyshire Level

Hurstnook Farm

Hague Street

Jumble

Moorfield

Works

LANE

Gnat Hole

Kidd Road

Derbyshire Level

Span Clough

Hurst Brook

Span Moor

Wood's Cabin

Bray Clough

Black Moor

Whitethorn Clough

Moor

Pen

G   H   J   K   L   M

I 2 3 4 5 6 7 8

04   05   06

95 94 93 392

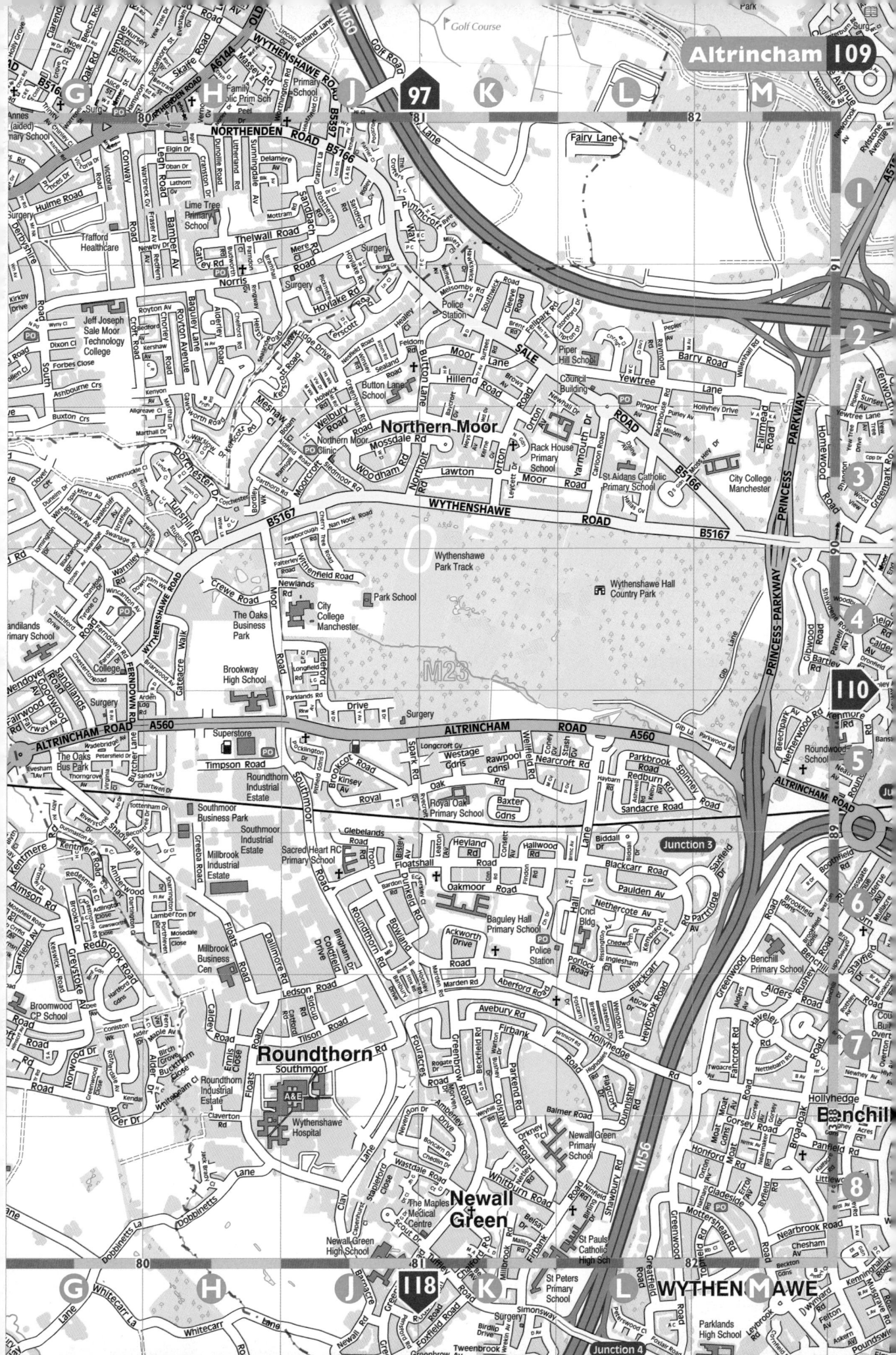

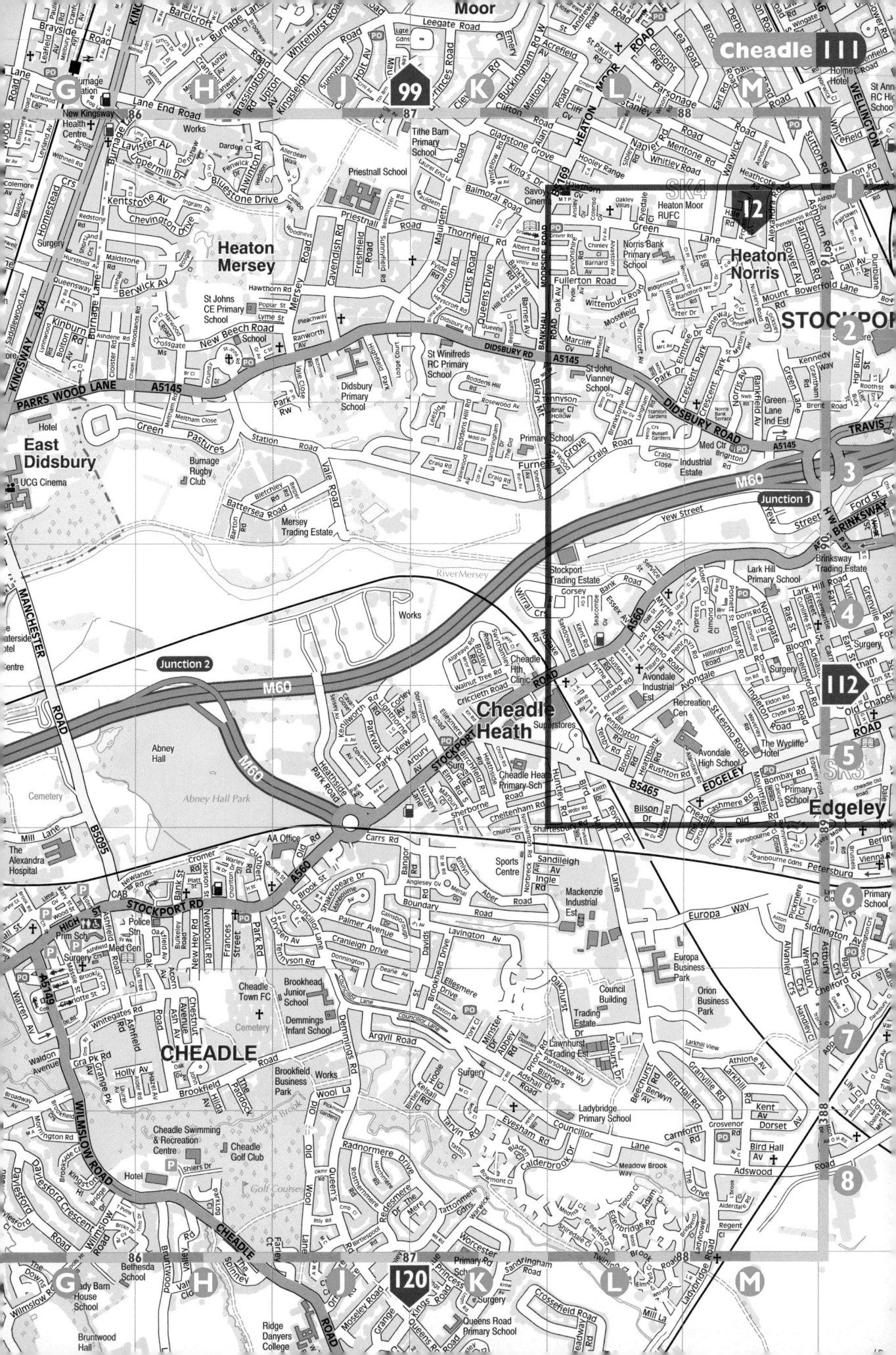

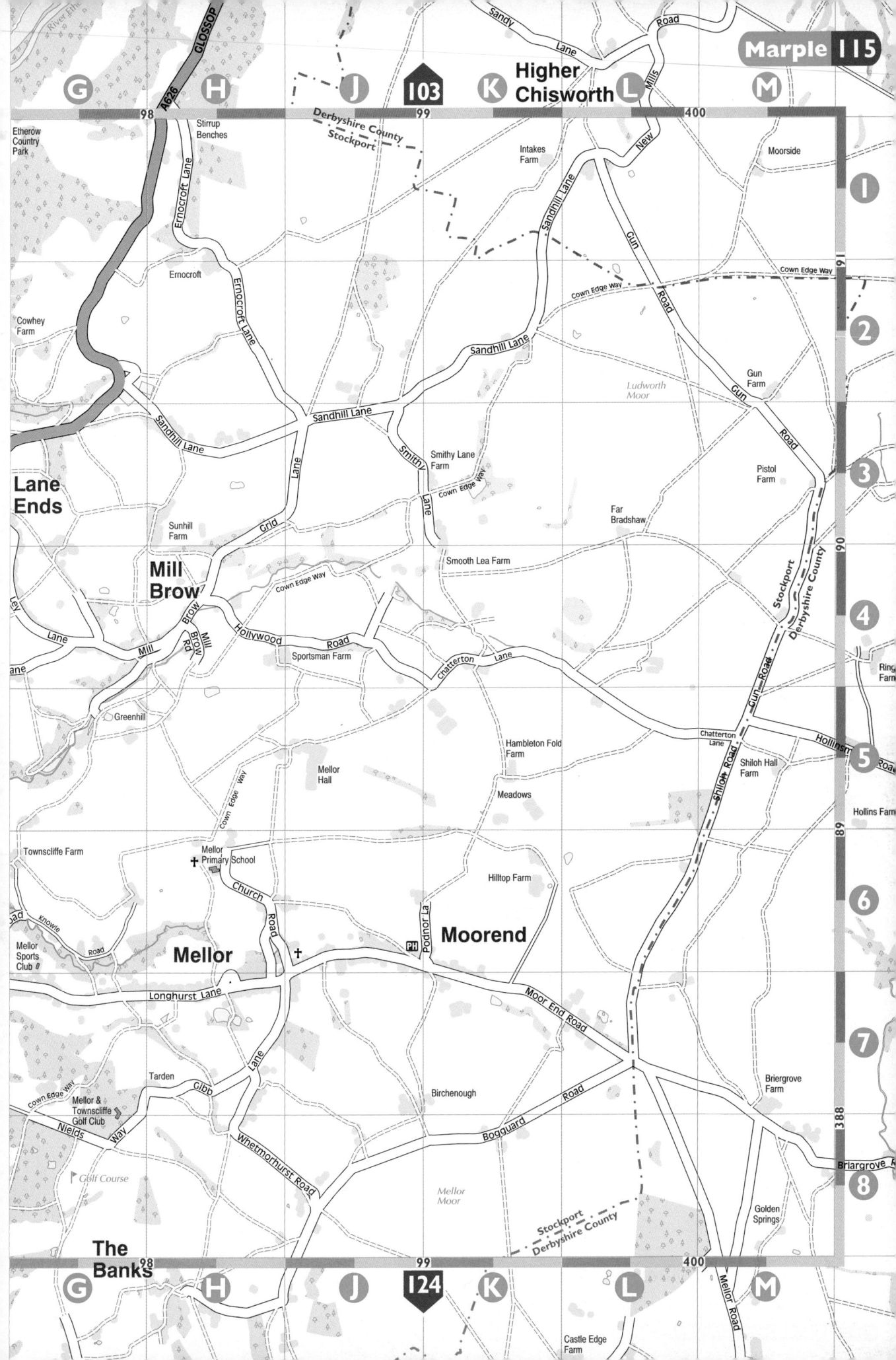

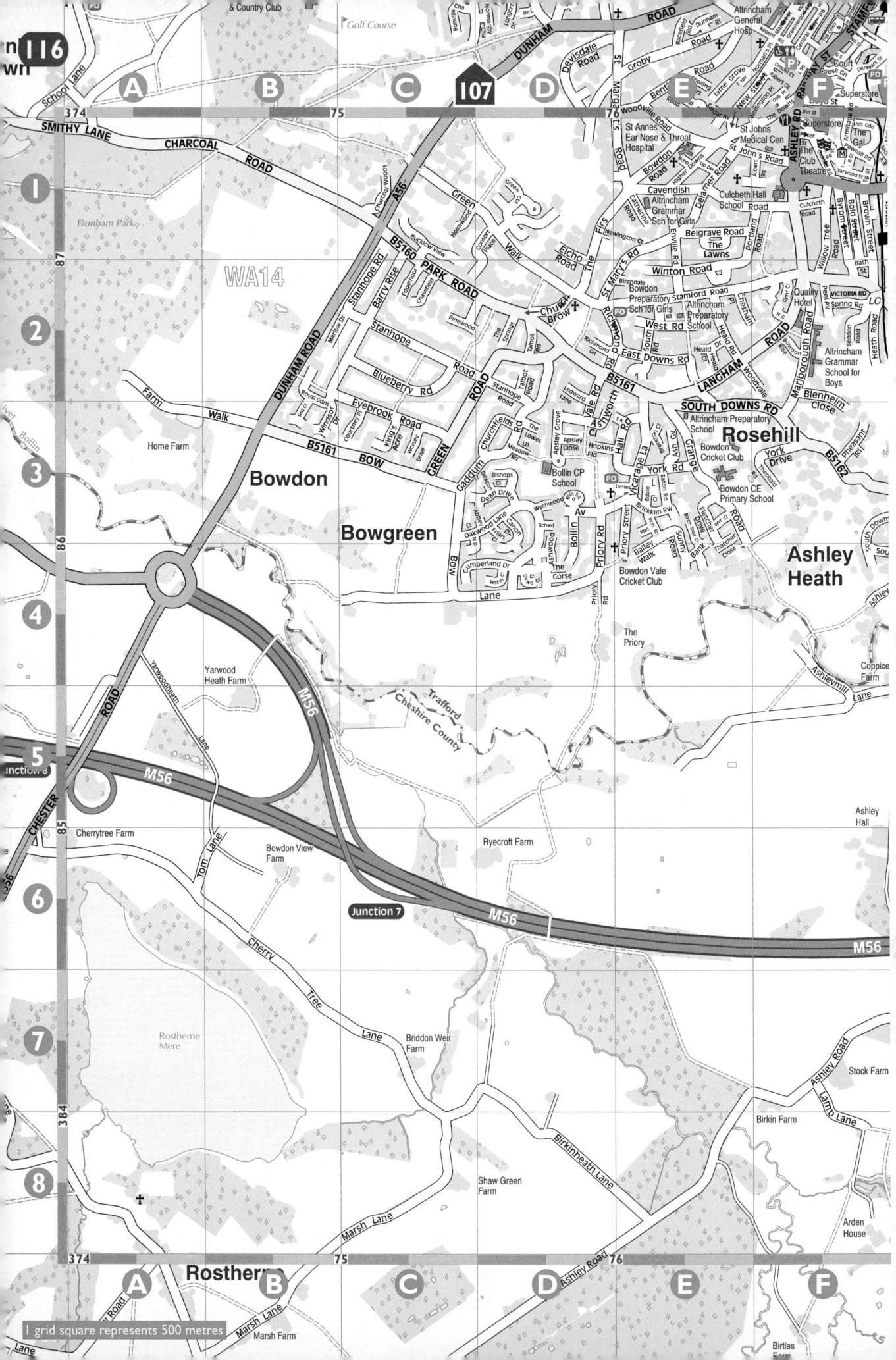

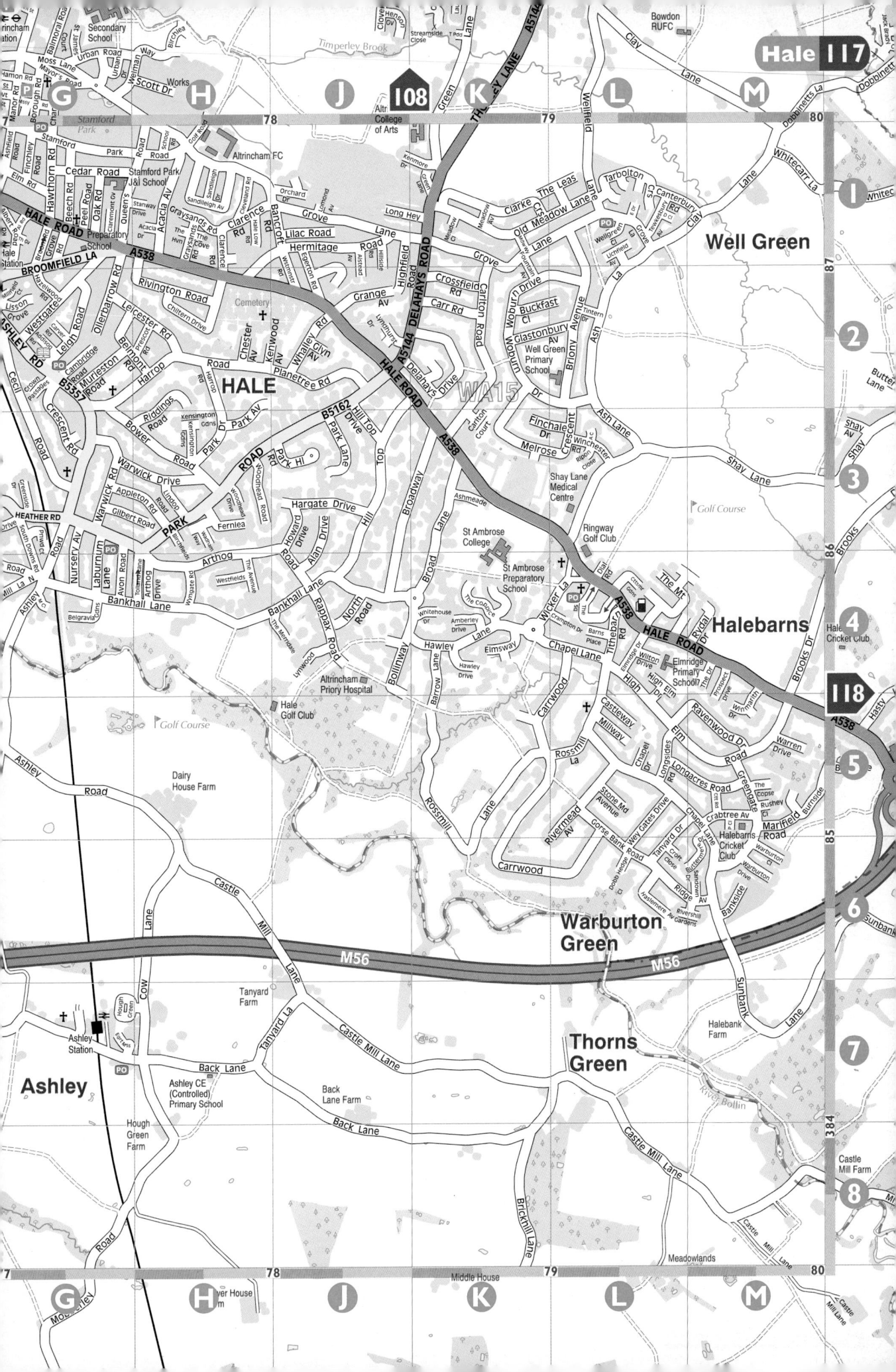

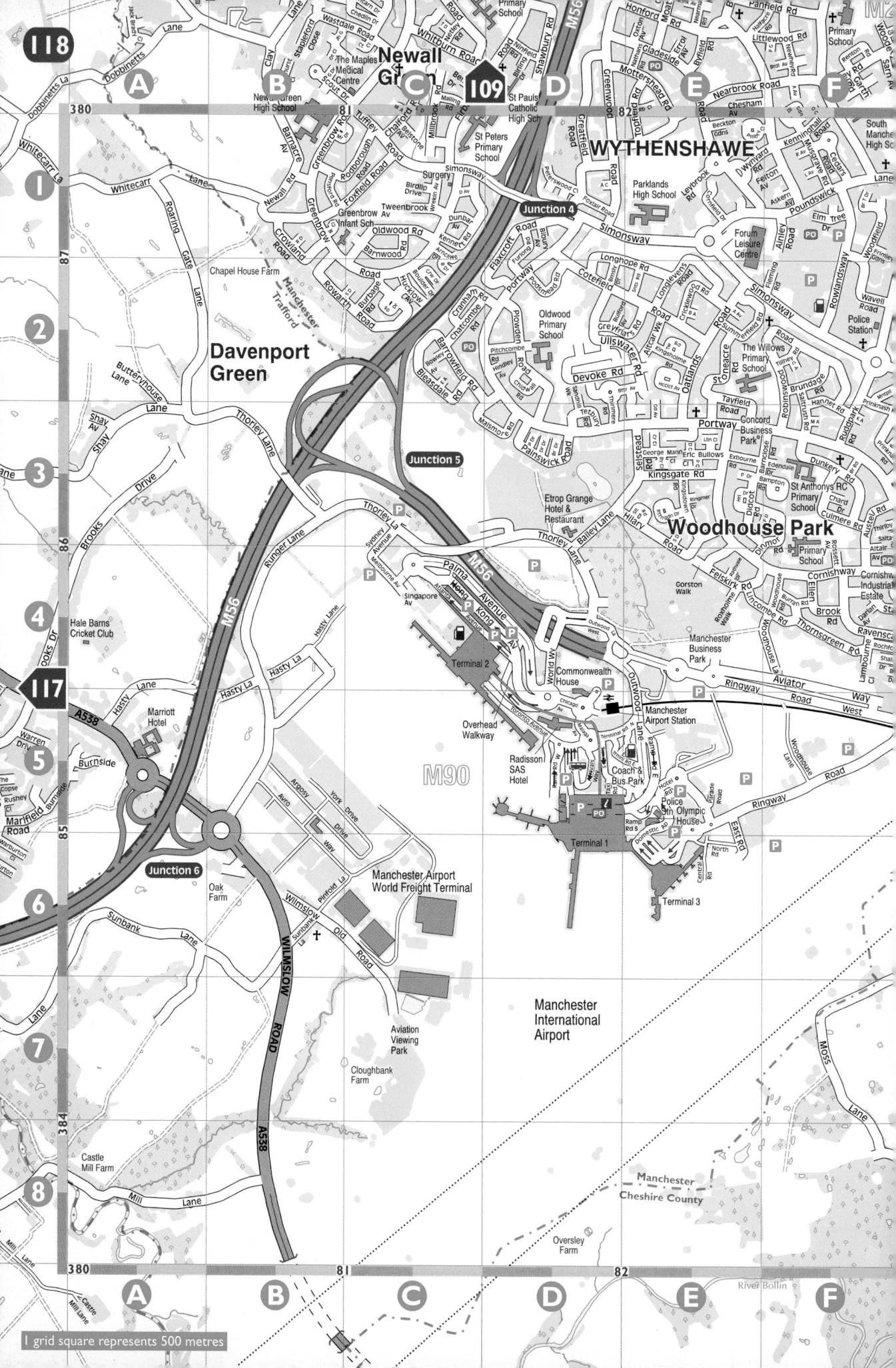

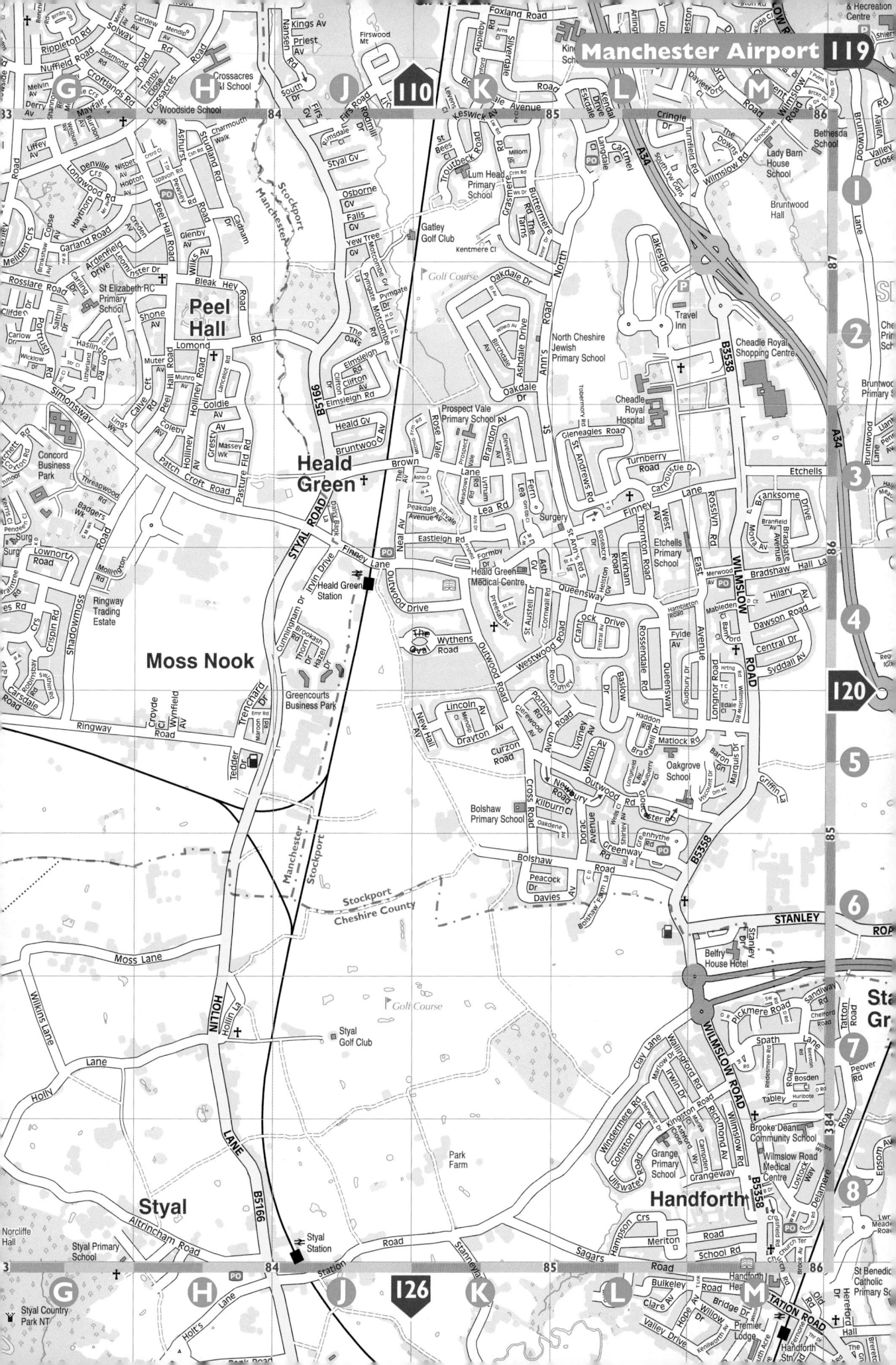

Hall

Road

Aspenshaw Road

Thornsett Primary School

Wethercotes

Sitch Lane

Cliff

Swallow

House

Lane

Lea Rd

Market Street

Fairy Bank Rd
Highfield Rd
Cote Lane

Council Building

Hayfield Primary School

River Sett

Wood Gdns

Chandre

Bowden Cl
Howardon

PO
Bank
Surg

Thornsett

Sycamore Road
Quarry Road
Spinnerbottom
PO

Birch Vale Industrial Estate

Station Rd

Works

Birch Hall Cl

NEW

MILLS

ROAD

Station Rd
Church St Fr Br

Wood la

PH

Vicarage La

Spring vale

Kinder Road

Thornsett Trading Estate

Works

Works

Lantern Pike View

Sett Valley Trail

Thornsett

Thornsett

Cemetery

Morland Road

A6015

St John Street

Meadows
Highway

The Birches
The Oaks

Surg

Ridge Top Lane

Highgate Road

A6 CHAPEL

Valley Road

Thornsett

Birch Vale

Hayfield

ow
eighton

HAYFIELD ROAD

Over Lee Farm

Ridge Top

Barnsfold Farm

ersett Lane

Cold Harbour Farm

Over Hill Road

Ollersett

Far Phoside

Pingot Road

Works

Moor Lodge

Piece Farm

Hills Farm

Laneside Road

Shedyard Farm

Over Hill Road

New Allotments

Beardwood Farm

Gowhole

Ladypit Road

ss Vale Station

ey

The Haugh

Cloughhead

Throstle

Cracken Edge

A624

A6015

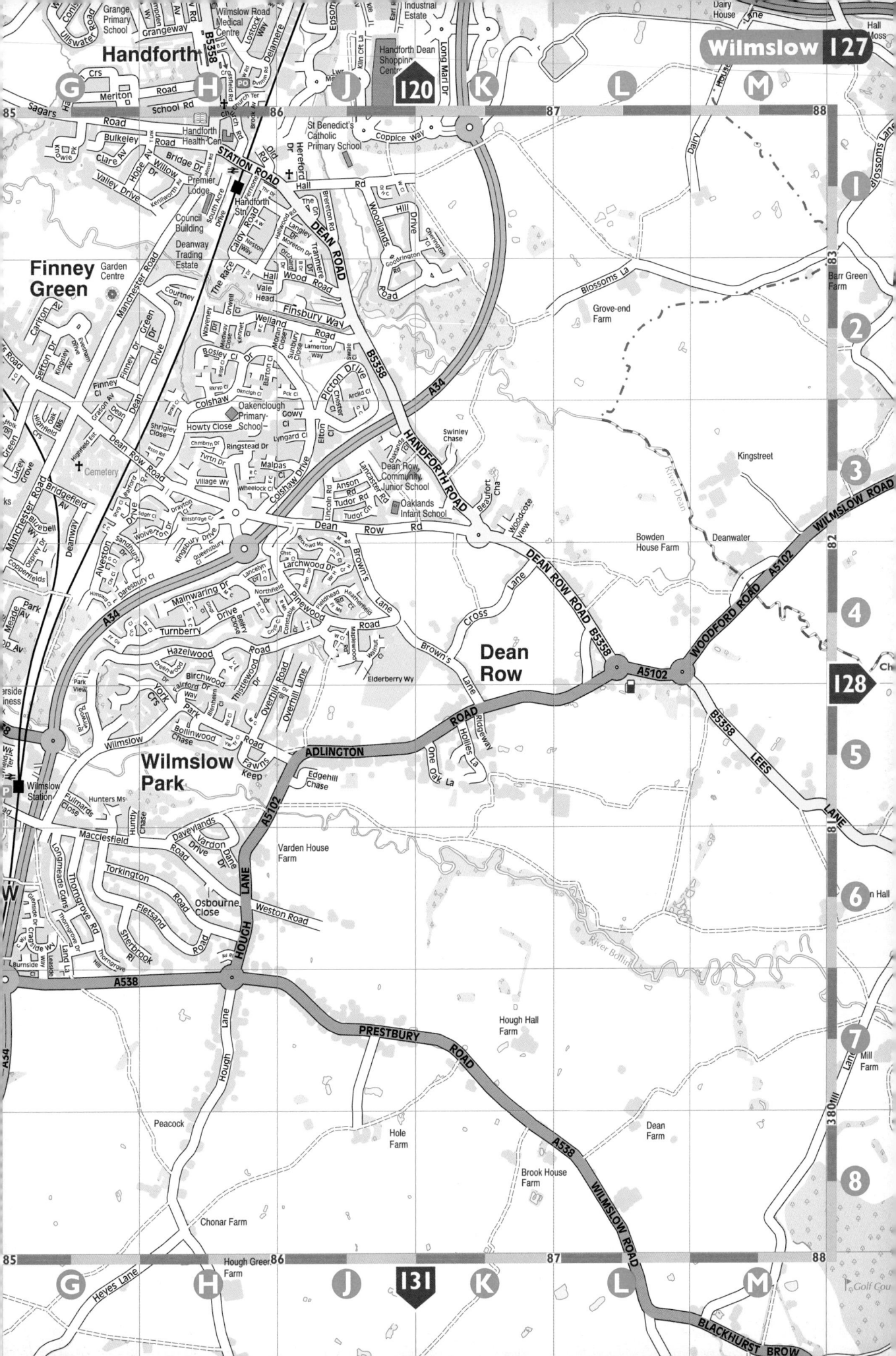

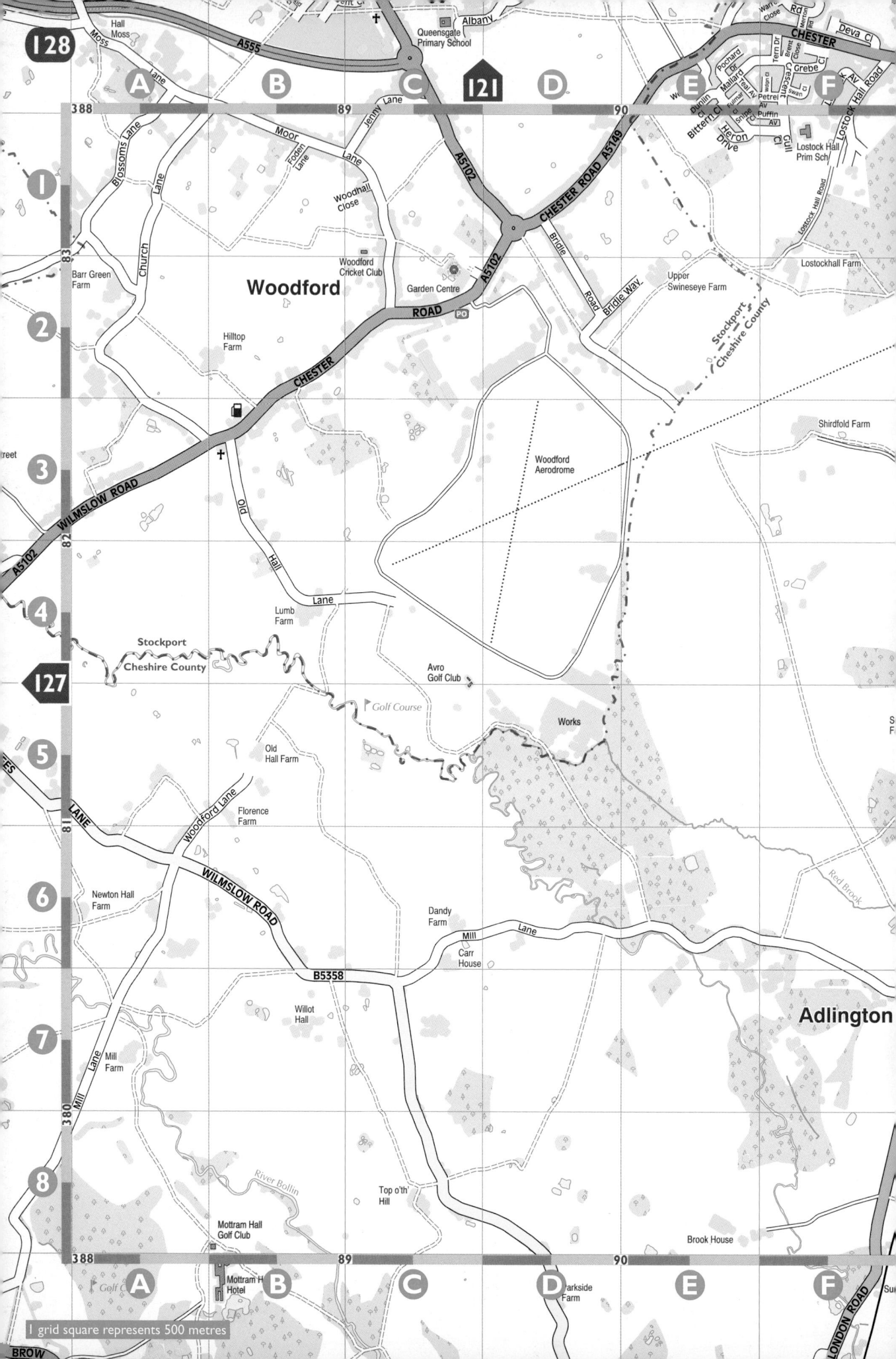

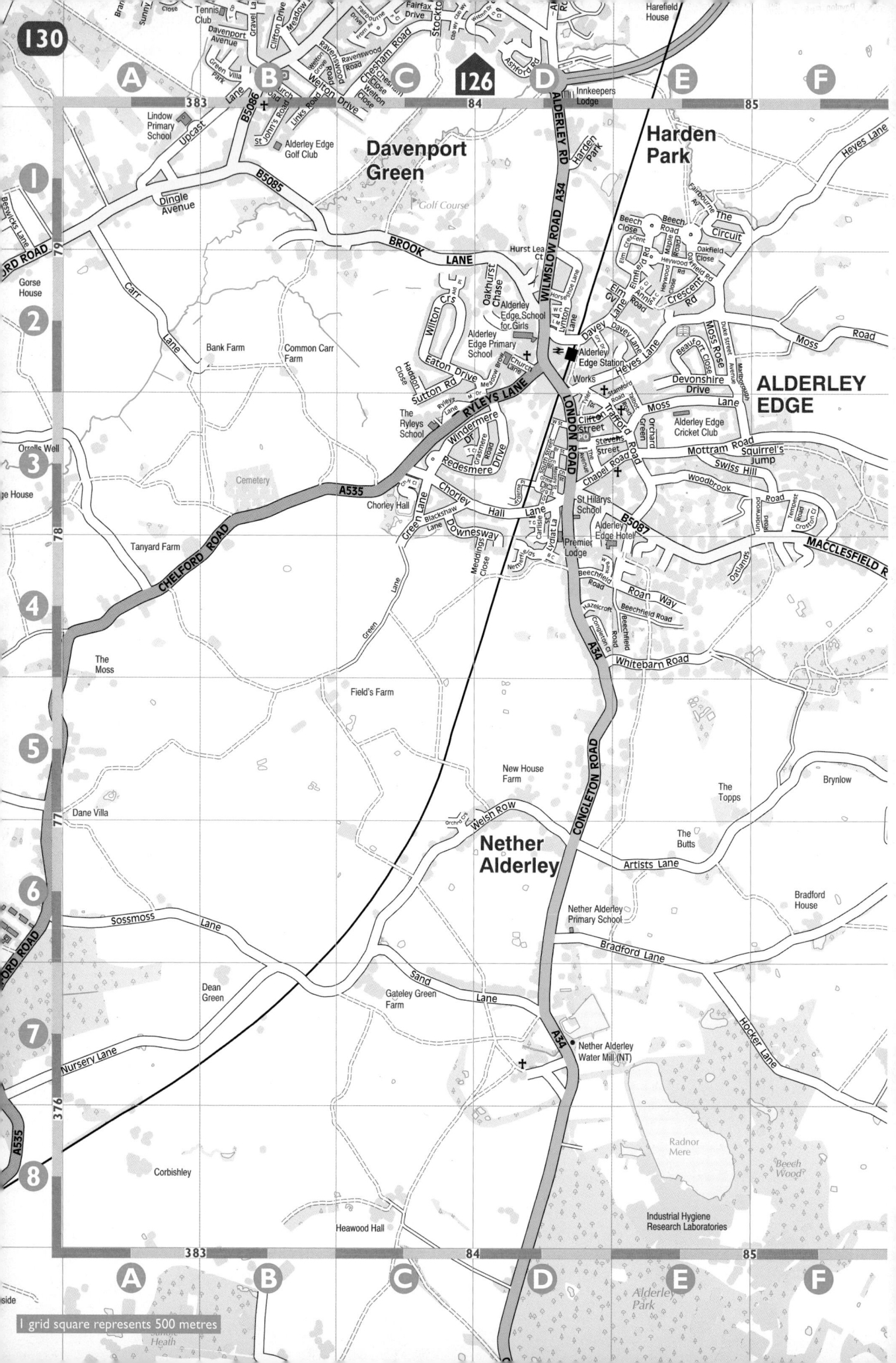

Mottram Hall
Golf Club

Mottram Hall
Hotel

G Farm

Brook House
Farm

127

WILMS ROAD

Hough Green
Farm

Brook Farm

Hough Lane

Higher House
Farm

Lower House

Alderley Road

Mottram Road

Hough

The Crescent

PO

Rushton
Fold

Wilmslow

Moss Lane

Old Road

BLACKHURST BROW

Golf Course

Smithy

Lane

Mottram Cross

Mottram
St Andrew
Primary School

Priest Lane

Lane

Legh
Hall

WILMSLOW ROAD

Findlow
Farm

**Mottram
St Andrew**

Oak Road

Alderley
Edge

Clock House
Farm

Danielhill

Allen's Farm

Pool Lane

Hunter's Pool
Farm

Hill
Top

The Wizard

Edge House
Farm

Adder's
Moss

Oak Road

Hunters

Greendale

Artists Lane

Bradford Lane

MACCLESFIELD ROAD

Finlow

Lane

Hill

Mount Farm

Prestbury
Road

School Lane

Festival

Ashbrook
Road

Hare Hill
(NT)

Oak Road

Withinlee
Farm

Withinlee Road

Holm W

Finlow Hill
Farm

Prestbury
Road

Hayman's
Farm

Slade Lane

B5087

Greenhouse Road

Chelford Road

Harebarrow
Farm

MACCLESFIELD ROAD

Higher House
Farm

Vardentown

Birtles Lane

Hocker Lane

Acton Farm

Shawcross

Hocker Lane

Yewtree

Wrigley Lane

Fittontown
Farm

River

Abbey Hey	89	J7
Abram	64	F4
Acre	59	L3
Adlington	128	F7
Adswood	112	A7
Affetside	23	L4
Ainsworth	38	A3
Alder Forest	69	J8
Alderley Edge	130	F2
Alkrington Garden Village	57	H7
Alt	76	A1
Alt Hill	75	M4
Altrincham	108	C7
Ancoats	7	L4
Arden Park	101	G8
Ashley	117	G7
Ashley Heath	116	F4
Ashton-in-Makerfield	79	G1
Ashton-under-Lyne	90	C1
Ashton Upon Mersey	96	C6
Aspull	33	G7
Aspull Common	80	E3
Astley	67	M6
Astley Bridge	22	B8
Astley Green	67	M8
Atherton	67	H1
Audenshaw	90	B5
Austerlands	60	E4
Backbower	102	B4
Bagslate Moor	27	J4
Balderstone	42	E2
Baldingstone	25	H3
Bamford	27	G5
Bamfurlong	64	B4
Bank Lane	17	D5
The Banks	115	C8
Bank Top	22	D7
Bardsley	75	K3
Barton Upon Irwell	85	G4
Bedford	66	F8
Beech Hill	47	J2
Belfield	29	G5
Belle Vue	88	E7
Benchill	109	M8
Bentgate	29	K8
Besses o' th' Barn	55	J5
Beswick	88	C3
Bickershaw	65	H4
Billinge	62	C7
Birch	40	F8
Birch Vale	125	J2
Birtle	26	B5
Blackford Bridge	39	J8
Black Lane	38	C6
Blackley	73	H3
Blackmoor	67	K7
Blackrod	32	F1
Bleak Hey Nook	45	M5
Boar's Head	31	K6
Bolholt	24	D8
Bolton	3	G5
Booth Green	129	J5
Boothstown	68	D6
Bottom o' th' Moor	34	B1
Bowdon	116	B3
Bowgreen	116	C3
Bowlee	56	D3
Bradford	88	C2
Bradley Fold	37	L5
Bradshaw	22	F6
Bramhall	120	F7
Bramhall Moor	121	K2
Bramhall Park	120	E3
Bredbury	113	H1
Bredbury Green	113	K2
Breightmet	37	K4
Brinnington	100	E7
Broadbottom	103	J4
Broadfield	40	E3
Broadhalgh	27	J5
Broadheath	107	M5
Broadley	18	D7
Broadoak Park	69	M7
Bromley Cross	22	D6
Brook Bottom	76	D2
Brook Bottom	124	A3
Brookfield	104	A2
Brooklands	108	E2
Brooksbottoms	24	F1
Broughton Park	72	A3
Brownlow Fold	35	M3
Brunswick	87	L6
Brushes	92	B1
Bryn	63	J6
Bryn Gates	64	C5
Buckley	28	D1
Buckton Vale	77	G6
Buersil Head	42	F3
Burnage	99	H7
Burnden	36	D8
Burnedge	43	H3
Bury	4	D3
Busk	8	C3
Calderbrook	20	L3
Caldermoor	20	B6
Cale Green	112	C6
Captain Fold	41	H1
Carr	17	B5
Carrbrook	77	H7
Carr Green	106	C6
Carrington	95	K4
Carrington Moss	107	J1
Castle Hill	101	H5
Castleton	41	M2
Catley Lane Head	18	B8
Chadderton	58	B5
Chadderton Fold	58	B2
Chadkirk	113	L4
Chadwick Green	62	B8
Chapel Field	54	F3
Chapeltown	23	G1
Charlestown	71	L8
Charlestown	73	K1

Charlestown	104	E6
Charlesworth	104	A6
Chatterton	17	B3
Cheadle	111	H7
Cheadle Heath	111	K5
Cheadle Hulme	120	C4
Cheetham Hill	72	E6
Chequerbent	50	F3
Cherry Tree	114	C2
Chesham	25	K7
Chew Moor	34	F8
Chisworth	103	L7
Chorlton-cum-Hardy	98	A5
Chunal	104	F8
Cinder Hill	54	A4
Clarksfield	60	A5
Clayton	88	F1
Cliff	125	K1
Clifton	70	B1
Clifton Green	70	E2
Clifton Junction	70	F1
Clough	20	B5
Clough	44	A6
Collyhurst	73	G6
Compstall	114	D1
Cooper Turning	33	L7
Copley	91	M2
Copster Hill	75	H2
Cox Green	22	C3
Crankwood	64	F7
Crimble	27	J8
Crofts Bank	84	F8
Crompton Fold	43	M3
Crooke	46	F1
Crowhill	75	J8
Crumpsall	72	C3
Cutgate	27	K4
Daisy Hill	50	D6
Daisy Nook	74	F7
Dale	45	J7
Dales Brow	70	A6
Dane Bank	100	E2
Danebank	124	A7
Dangerous Corner	65	M2
Darcy Lever	37	G7
Darn Hill	40	C3
Daubhill	35	M8
Davenport	112	B8
Davenport Green	118	B2
Davenport Green	130	C1
Davyhulme	84	E8
Deane	51	L1
Dean Row	127	K4
Dearnley	20	A8
Debdale	89	J8
Delph	45	H8
Denshaw	45	G2
Denton	101	J1
Didsbury	110	E1
Diggle	45	M8
Disley	123	K6
Dobcross	61	J2
Doffcocker	35	K2
Dog Hill	44	B5
Dover	64	E6
Downall Green	62	F7
Droylsden	89	H3
Dukinfield	90	F5
Dumplington	84	F5
Dunham Town	107	G8
Dunham Woodhouses	106	E8
Dunscar	22	A3
Durn	20	D7
Eagley	22	B5
East Didsbury	111	G3
Eccles	85	K3
Edenfield	17	E1
Edge Fold	16	A3
Edge Fold	51	M3
Edge Green	79	J1
Edgeley	12	E9
Edgworth	16	E6
Egerton	22	B2
Ellenbrook	68	D4
Ellesmere Park	70	B8
Elton	38	E2
Facit	18	F2
Failsworth	74	B5
Fairfield	89	K5
Fallowfield	98	E4
Far Moor	46	B7
Farnworth	52	F4
Fern Bank	91	L3
Fernhill	4	E1
Fernhill Gate	35	J8
Finney Green	127	G2
Firgrove	29	G6
Firs Lane	66	A7
Firswood	97	L1
Firwood Fold	36	F1
Fishpool	4	C8
Fitton Hill	75	K2
Flixton	95	K3
Flowery Field	91	G8
Foggbrook	113	J5
Fold Head	18	B4
Fold Green	33	M8
Four Lane Ends	24	A7
Fowley Common	81	L7
Free Town	5	L1
Fullwood	44	A7
Fulshaw Park	126	E7
Gale	20	D5
Gamesley	104	B2
Gathurst	46	C1
Gatley	110	D8
Gee Cross	102	B5
Gigg	39	K5
Gillbent	120	B6
Gilnow	2	B6
Gin Pit	67	J5
Glazebury	81	L6

Glodwick	59	L7
Glossop	105	H3
Godley	102	B1
Godley Hill	102	E1
Golborne	79	L5
Goose Green	47	H8
Gorse Hill	97	H1
Gorton	88	F8
Cowhole	125	G8
Grains Bar	44	D6
Grasscroft	61	G7
Gravel Hole	43	G5
Great Howarth	19	H8
Great Lever	52	D1
Great Moor	112	F6
Greave	102	A8
Greenacres	60	A5
Greendale	131	M5
Greenfield	61	K8
Greengate	29	G1
Greenheys	52	A7
Greenmount	24	B2
Greenside	89	L1
Grotton	60	E7
Guide Bridge	90	B3
Hadfield	93	K8
Hag Fold	50	E7
Haggate	58	F1
Hague Bar	124	B4
The Hague	103	M2
Haigh	32	E5
Hale	117	H2
Halebarns	117	M4
Halfway Houses	37	M6
Hall i' th' Wood	22	D8
Halliwell	36	B1
Handforth	119	L8
Harden Park	130	E1
Hargate Hill	104	B4
Harper Green	52	E3
Harpurhey	73	H5
Hart Common	49	L5
Hartshead Green	76	E5
Hartshead Pike	76	C3
Harwood	37	K1
Harwood Lee	23	H7
Heady Hill	40	D2
Heald Green	119	J3
Healds Green	58	C1
Healey	18	F8
Heatley	106	A7
Heaton	35	K4
Heaton Chapel	99	M6
Heaton Mersey	111	H1
Heaton Moor	99	K8
Heaton Norris	12	C2
Heaviley	13	M9
Heyheads	77	G5
Heyrod	76	E8
Heyside	43	K8
Heywood	40	F1
Higginshaw	59	J2
High Crompton	43	H5
Higher Blackley	56	F8
Higher Boarshaw	57	M1
Higher Broughton	72	A6
Higher Chisworth	103	K8
Higher Dinting	104	D2
Higher Disley	123	M7
Higher Folds	67	H6
Higher Green	68	A7
Higher Poynton	129	M2
Higher Woodhill	25	G7
Highfield	46	F8
Highfield	52	C5
High Lane	123	G5
Hill Top	53	C8
Hilton House	33	K6
Hilton Park	71	K2
Hindley	49	H8
Hindley Green	65	M1
Hindsford	67	G2
Hobroyd	104	E5
Hockley	129	L1
Holcombe	17	A7
Holcombe Brook	24	C1
Holden Fold	59	C1
Holehouse	103	M6
Hollingworth	92	F6
Hollins	39	L7
Hollins	52	A4
Hollinwood	74	D3
Holts	60	B8
Honresfeld	20	E6
Hooley Bridge	26	F7
Hooley Brow	27	G8
Hooley Hill	90	B5
Hope Green	129	H3
Horwich	21	B8
Hough	131	G3
Howe Bridge	66	E3
Hulme	87	H6
Hunger Hill	30	C1
Hunger Hill	51	G1
Hurst	90	D3
Hurstead	19	K8
Hyde	102	A1
Ince-in-Makerfield	15	L6
Irlam	94	C3
Irlams o' th' Height	70	F7
Jericho	26	B8

Johnson Fold	35	G1
Jubilee	43	L2
Kearsley	53	L6
Kenyon	80	D8
Kersal	71	L3
Kingston	101	L1
Kirkhams	55	L6
Kirkholt	42	B1
Kirklees	24	E5
Kitt Green	47	H5
Kitt's Moss	120	F7
Knott Lanes	75	J5
Lacey Green	126	F3
Lady House	29	H8
Lamberhead Green	46	D7
Land Gate	63	K5
Landslow Green	92	E5
Lane Ends	115	G3
Lane Ends	124	A8
Lane Head	80	C6
Langley	56	F1
Lark Hill	67	K7
Lately Common	81	M3
Lee Head	103	M6
Lees	60	B6
Leigh	66	F7
Levenshulme	99	M4
Lever-Edge	52	A2
Ley Hey Park	114	B5
Lilford	66	D6
Limefield	25	J6
Limehurst	75	K6
Lime Side	75	G3
Linfitts	45	G7
Linnyshaw	69	H1
Little Bolton	85	L2
Littleborough	20	C7
Little Clegg	29	H2
Little Hulton	52	C8
Little Lever	37	L8
Little Moor	113	G4
Littlemoss	74	F8
Little Scotland	32	D2
Longshaw	62	B3
Long Sight	59	J2
Longsight	88	C7
Lostock	34	B6
Lostock Junction	35	G7
Low Compton	43	H6
Lower Bredbury	112	F2
Lower Green	82	F1
Lower Kersal	71	K6
Lower Place	28	F8
Low Leighton	124	F4
Lowton	80	A4
Lowton Common	80	D4
Lowton Heath	79	M6
Lowton St Mary's	80	D5
Luzley	76	K6
Luzley Brook	43	J7
Lydgate	60	F7
Makants	68	B2
Manchester	6	B7
Markland Hill	35	H4
Marland	27	L7
Marple	114	B6
Marple Bridge	114	E5
Marpleridge	123	H2
Marsh Green	46	F3
Marylebone	48	A1
Matley	92	C6
Mellor	115	H6
Micklehurst	77	H3
Middleton	57	G3
Middlewood	122	D7
Midway	129	H2
Miles Platting	88	A1
Millbrook	77	G8
Mill Brow	115	H4
Mill Hill	3	H3
Milnrow	29	K6
Monton	85	G1
Moorclose	57	M4
Moorend	115	K6
Moorfield	105	J6
Moorhey	59	L6
Moorside	60	B1
Moorside	70	A5
Morley	126	A3
Moses Gate	52	F2
Mosley Common	68	D5
Mossbrow	106	A5
Mossley	77	G2
Mossley Brow	76	F3
Moss Nook	119	H4
Moss Side	87	J8
Moston	73	L3
Mottram in Longdendale	92	C3
Mottram Rise	92	M6
Mottram St Andrew	131	K3
Mudd	103	K2
Mumps	9	K4
Nangreaves	25	H1
Nether Alderley	130	D6
Newall Green	109	K8
Newbold	11	L4
New Boston	78	C6
New Bury	52	D5
New Delph	61	K1
Newhey	43	J1
New Houses	62	E3
New Mills	124	D4
New Moston	73	M4
New Springs	48	B2
Newton	91	H7
Newton Heath	73	K7
Newton Wood	90	D6
Newtown	47	H6
Newtown	70	B3
Newtown	124	D7
Nimble Nook	58	D8
Nob End	53	K2
Norbury Moor	122	A3

Norden	27	G3
Northenden	110	A4
Northern Moor	109	J3
North Reddish	100	B3
Nuttall	17	B8
Oak Bank	55	K5
Offerton	113	H5
Offerton Green	113	K6
Old Boston	78	E5
Oldfield Brow	107	L7
Old Glossop	105	H2
Oldham	9	L6
Old Tame	44	E4
Old Trafford	86	E7
Openshaw	88	F4
Ordsall	86	E5
Orrell	46	D5
Orrell Post	46	B5
Outwood	54	D4
Over Hulton	51	K5
Padfield	93	M7
Park Bridge	75	M2
Parr Brow	68	B4
Partington	106	C2
Patricroft	84	F2
Peel Green	84	C4
Peel Hall	119	H2
Pemberton	46	F7
Pendlebury	70	F5
Pendleton	86	D1
Pennington	81	G1
Pennington Green	49	H2
Pickley Green	66	B3
Pimhole	5	K5
Pitses	76	A1
Plank Lane	65	L7
Platt Bridge	64	E2
Pocket Nook	80	F4
Poolstock	14	C8
Portwood	112	D1
Pownall Park	126	D4
Poynton	122	B8
Prestolee	53	L4
Prestwich	55	J8
Quick	60	F8
Quick Edge	76	E1
Radcliffe	38	D8
Rainsough	71	K3
Rakewood	29	M3
Ramsbottom	17	B7
Reddish	100	A4
Red Rock	32	A4
Redvales	39	H6
Rhodes	56	E5
Ridge Hill	76	C8
Ringley	54	A5
Roaches	77	G1
Rochdale	11	H4
Roebuck Low	60	D2
Roe Cross	92	C7
Roe Green	69	K4
Romiley	114	A2
Rose Hill	3	H9
Rosehill	116	E3
Roundthorn	109	H7
Royton	43	H8
Rusholme	99	G1
Sale	108	B1
Salford	86	C3
Salford Quays	86	B5
Scholes	15	J4
Scot Lane End	33	H5
Scouthead	60	E3
Sedgley Park	71	M2
Seedley	86	B1
Shakerley	67	K2
Sharples	22	A8
Sharston	110	C7
Shaw	43	K4
Shawclough	27	M2
Shawfield	27	J2
Shaw Heath	13	G8
Shaw Side	43	L7
Shevington	30	D7
Shevington Moor	30	D2
Shevington Vale	30	C4
Sholver	44	A8
Shore	20	A6
Shuttleworth	17	E5
Side of the Moor	23	H6
Simister	56	B4
Simmondley	104	C5
Simm's Lane End	62	D7
Sinderland Green	107	G3
Skellorn Green	129	H4
Slackcote	44	E5
Slattocks	41	M6
Smallbridge	29	G1
Smallshaw	75	M6
Smithy Bridge	29	K1
Smithy Green	120	D4
South Reddish	100	B7
Spotland Bridge	10	A3
Springfield	47	H2
Springhead	60	D6
Spring Hill	60	A3
Stake Hill	42	B7
Stalybridge	91	H3
Stand	54	F4
Standish	31	J3
Standish Lower Ground	46	F1
Stanley Green	120	A1
Stanycliffe	57	L1
Starling	38	D2
Stepping Hill	113	G8
St George's	86	F6
Stockport	12	D2
Stoneclough	53	L5
Stoneyfield	10	D9
Stoneyfield	28	C8
Strangeways	72	C8
Stretford	96	F4
Strines	123	L3

Stubbins 17 C4	Tintwistle 93 L5	Uppermill 61 L5	Westleigh 66 A5	Woodhey 24 D1
Stubshaw Cross 64 A7	Tonge Fold 3 M3	Urmston 85 H8	Westwood Park 69 K8	Woodhouse Park 118 E3
Styal 119 H8	Tonge Moor 36 D2	Walkden 53 C8	Whalley Range 98 B2	Woodhouses 74 D6
Sudden 27 M8	Tontine 46 A6	Wallbank 18 C5	Whelley 15 M1	Woodhouses 107 L2
Summerseat 24 E3	Top Lock 48 E2	Wall Hill 61 H3	Whitefield 55 H5	Woodlands 91 L5
Summit 20 C3	Top of Hebers 41 H8	Wallsuches 21 E8	White Gate 74 C1	Wood Lanes 129 L4
Summit 40 C2	Top o' th' Meadows 60 C4	Walmersley 25 H5	Whitley 47 K1	Woodley 101 M7
Summit 42 E5	Toppings 22 E5	Walshaw 24 B8	Whitworth 18 E4	Wood Road 24 F3
Sun Green 77 H8	Torkington 122 D2	Warburton Green 117 L6	Wigan 14 D2	Woodseats 103 K6
Sunny Bank 39 K8	Tottington 24 B6	Wardle 19 L6	Wilderswood 21 D6	Woods End 95 H1
Swinton 70 A4	Town Green 64 A8	Wardley 69 M3	Willows 35 M7	Woods Moor 121 K1
Swinton Park 70 E6	Town Lane 67 L8	Wardsend 129 L3	Wilmslow 126 F6	Woolfold 24 D8
Syke 19 G8	Town of Lowton 79 K7	Warhill 103 L1	Wilmslow Park 127 H5	Woolley Bridge 93 G8
Tamer Lane End 65 L4	Trafford Park 85 K7	Waterloo 75 J7	Windlehurst 123 G3	Worsley 69 J5
Tame Water 61 H3	Trub 41 M5	Watersheddings 60 A3	Wingates 50 A1	Worsley Hall 46 F6
Taunton 75 H7	Tunshill 29 M5	Water's Nook 50 E4	Winstanley 62 F1	Worsley Mesnes 47 J8
Thornham Fold 42 D5	Tunstead 61 M7	Weaste 86 B3	Winstanleys 31 M5	Wythenshawe 118 D1
Thornsett 125 G2	Turf Hill 29 G8	Well Green 117 M1	Winton 84 F1	Yew Tree 91 H5
Thorns Green 117 L7	Turton Bottoms 16 E7	Werneth 8 B7	Wolstenholme 26 F1	
Thorp 42 E8	Twiss Green 81 H7	Werneth Low 102 C7	Woodend 123 L4	
Thurston Clough 61 G1	Tyldesley 67 L3	West Didsbury 98 B7	Woodford 128 B2	
Timperley 108 D5	Unsworth 55 L2	Westhoughton 50 A3	Woodgate Hill 26 A8	

USING THE STREET INDEX

Street names are listed alphabetically. Each street name is followed by its postal town or area locality, the Postcode District, the page number, and the reference to the square in which the name is found.

Standard index entries are shown as follows:

Abberley Dr *NEWH/MOS* M40 ......**74** A2

Street names and selected addresses not shown on the map due to scale restrictions are shown in the index with an asterisk:

Abbeyfield Sq *OP/CLY* * M11........**88** E4

GENERAL ABBREVIATIONS

ACC	ACCESS	CTYD	COURTYARD	HLS	HILLS	MWY	MOTORWAY	SE	SOUTH EAST
ALY	ALLEY	CUTT	CUTTINGS	HO	HOUSE	N	NORTH	SER	SERVICE AREA
AP	APPROACH	CV	COVE	HOL	HOLLOW	NE	NORTH EAST	SH	SHORE
AR	ARCADE	CYN	CANYON	HOSP	HOSPITAL	NW	NORTH WEST	SHOP	SHOPPING
ASS	ASSOCIATION	DEPT	DEPARTMENT	HRB	HARBOUR	O/P	OVERPASS	SKWY	SKYWAY
AV	AVENUE	DL	DALE	HTH	HEATH	OFF	OFFICE	SMT	SUMMIT
BCH	BEACH	DM	DAM	HTS	HEIGHTS	ORCH	ORCHARD	SOC	SOCIETY
BLDS	BUILDINGS	DR	DRIVE	HVN	HAVEN	OV	OVAL	SP	SPUR
BND	BEND	DRO	DROVE	HWY	HIGHWAY	PAL	PALACE	SPR	SPRING
BNK	BANK	DRY	DRIVEWAY	IMP	IMPERIAL	PAS	PASSAGE	SQ	SQUARE
BR	BRIDGE	DWGS	DWELLINGS	IN	INLET	PAV	PAVILION	ST	STREET
BRK	BROOK	E	EAST	IND EST	INDUSTRIAL ESTATE	PDE	PARADE	STN	STATION
BTM	BOTTOM	EMB	EMBANKMENT	INF	INFIRMARY	PH	PUBLIC HOUSE	STR	STREAM
BUS	BUSINESS	EMBY	EMBASSY	INFO	INFORMATION	PK	PARK	STRD	STRAND
BVD	BOULEVARD	ESP	ESPLANADE	INT	INTERCHANGE	PKWY	PARKWAY	SW	SOUTH WEST
BY	BYPASS	EST	ESTATE	IS	ISLAND	PL	PLACE	TDG	TRADING
CATH	CATHEDRAL	EX	EXCHANGE	JCT	JUNCTION	PLN	PLAIN	TER	TERRACE
CEM	CEMETERY	EXPY	EXPRESSWAY	JTY	JETTY	PLNS	PLAINS	THWY	THROUGHWAY
CEN	CENTRE	EXT	EXTENSION	KG	KING	PLZ	PLAZA	TNL	TUNNEL
CFT	CROFT	F/O	FLYOVER	KNL	KNOLL	POL	POLICE STATION	TOLL	TOLLWAY
CH	CHURCH	FC	FOOTBALL CLUB	L	LAKE	PR	PRINCE	TPK	TURNPIKE
CHA	CHASE	FK	FORK	LA	LANE	PREC	PRECINCT	TR	TRACK
CHYD	CHURCHYARD	FLD	FIELD	LDG	LODGE	PREP	PREPARATORY	TRL	TRAIL
CIR	CIRCLE	FLDS	FIELDS	LGT	LIGHT	PRIM	PRIMARY	TWR	TOWER
CIRC	CIRCUS	FLS	FALLS	LK	LOCK	PROM	PROMENADE	U/P	UNDERPASS
CL	CLOSE	FLS	FLATS	LKS	LAKES	PRS	PRINCESS	UNI	UNIVERSITY
CLFS	CLIFFS	FM	FARM	LNDG	LANDING	PRT	PORT	UPR	UPPER
CMP	CAMP	FT	FORT	LTL	LITTLE	PT	POINT	V	VALE
CNR	CORNER	FWY	FREEWAY	LWR	LOWER	PTH	PATH	VA	VALLEY
CO	COUNTY	FY	FERRY	MAG	MAGISTRATE	PZ	PIAZZA	VIAD	VIADUCT
COLL	COLLEGE	GA	GATE	MAN	MANSIONS	QD	QUADRANT	VIL	VILLA
COM	COMMON	GAL	GALLERY	MD	MEAD	QU	QUEEN	VIS	VISTA
COMM	COMMISSION	GDN	GARDEN	MDW	MEADOWS	QY	QUAY	VLG	VILLAGE
CON	CONVENT	GDNS	GARDENS	MEM	MEMORIAL	R	RIVER	VLS	VILLAS
COT	COTTAGE	GLD	GLADE	MKT	MARKET	RBT	ROUNDABOUT	VW	VIEW
COTS	COTTAGES	GLN	GLEN	MKTS	MARKETS	RD	ROAD	W	WEST
CP	CAPE	GN	GREEN	ML	MALL	RDG	RIDGE	WD	WOOD
CPS	COPSE	GND	GROUND	ML	MILL	REP	REPUBLIC	WHF	WHARF
CR	CREEK	GRA	GRANGE	MNR	MANOR	RES	RESERVOIR	WK	WALK
CREM	CREMATORIUM	GRG	GARAGE	MS	MEWS	RFC	RUGBY FOOTBALL CLUB	WKS	WALKS
CRS	CRESCENT	GT	GREAT	MSN	MISSION	RI	RISE	WLS	WELLS
CSWY	CAUSEWAY	GTWY	GATEWAY	MT	MOUNT	RP	RAMP	WY	WAY
CT	COURT	GV	GROVE	MTN	MOUNTAIN	RW	ROW	YD	YARD
CTRL	CENTRAL	HGR	HIGHER	MTS	MOUNTAINS	S	SOUTH	YHA	YOUTH HOSTEL
CTS	COURTS	HL	HILL	MUS	MUSEUM	SCH	SCHOOL		

POSTCODE TOWNS AND AREA ABBREVIATIONS

AIMK	Ashton-in-Makerfield	CHLY/EC	Chorley/Eccleston	HTNM	Heaton Moor	OLDE	Oldham east	STRET	Stretford
ALT	Altrincham	CHLYE	Chorley east/	HULME	Hulme	OLDS	Oldham south	SWIN	Swinton
ANC	Ancoats		Adlington/Whittle-le-Woods	HYDE	Hyde	OLDTF/WHR	Old Trafford/	TOD	Todmorden
ATH	Atherton	CMANE	Central Manchester east	IRL	Irlam		Whalley Range	TOT/BURYW	Tottington/Bury west
AUL	Ashton-under-Lyne	CMANW	Central Manchester west	KNUT	Knutsford	OP/CLY	Openshaw/Clayton	TRPK	Trafford Park
AULW	Ashton-under-Lyne west	CSLFD	Central Salford	LEIGH	Leigh	ORD	Ordsall	TYLD	Tyldesley
BKLY	Blackley	DID/WITH	Didsbury/Withington	LHULT	Little Hulton	PART	Partington	UPML	Uppermill
BNG/LEV	Burnage/Levenshulme	DROY	Droylsden	LIT	Littleborough	POY/DIS	Poynton/Disley	URM	Urmston
BOL	Bolton	DTN/ASHW	Denton/Audenshaw	LYMM	Lymm	PWCH	Prestwich	WALK	Walkden
BOLE	Bolton east	DUK	Dukinfield	MANAIR	Manchester Airport	RAD	Radcliffe	WGN	Wigan
BOLS/LL	Bolton south/Little Lever	DWN	Darwen	MCFLDN	Macclesfield north	RAMS	Ramsbottom	WGNE/HIN	Wigan east/Hindley
BRAM/HZG	Bramhall/Hazel Grove	ECC	Eccles	MDTN	Middleton (Gtr. Man)	RDSH	Reddish	WGNNW/ST	Wigan northwest/Standish
BRO	Broughton	EDGW/EG	Edgeworth/Egerton	MILN	Milnrow	RNFD/HAY	Rainford/Haydock	WGNS/IIMK	Wigan south/
BRUN/LGST	Brunswick/Longsight	EDGY/DAV	Edgeley/Davenport	MOSL	Mossley	ROCH	Rochdale		Ince-in-Makerfield
BURY	Bury	FAIL	Failsworth	MPL/ROM	Marple/Romiley	ROY/SHW	Royton/Shaw	WGNW/BIL/OR	Wigan west/Billinge/
CCHDY	Chorlton-cum-Hardy	FWTH	Farnworth	NEWH/MOS	Newton Heath/Moston	RUSH/FAL	Rusholme/Fallowfield		Orrell
CHAD	Chadderton	GLSP	Glossop	NEWLW	Newton-le-Willows	SALE	Sale	WGTN/LGST	West Gorton/Longsight
CHD/CHDH	Cheadle/	GOL/RIS/CUL	Golborne/Risley/Culcheth	NM/HAY	New Mills/Hayfield	SALQ	Salford Quays	WHIT	Whitworth
	Cheadle Hulme	GTN	Gorton	NTHM/RTH	Northern Moor/	SKEL	Skelmersdale	WHTF	Whitefield
CHF/WBR	Chapel-en-le-Frith/Whaley	HALE/TIMP	Hale/Timperley		Roundthorn	SLFD	Salford	WHTN	Westhoughton
	Bridge	HEY	Heywood	OFTN	Offerton	STKP	Stockport	WILM/AE	Wilmslow/Alderley Edge
CHH	Cheetham Hill	HOR/BR	Horwich/Blackrod	OLD	Oldham	STLY	Stalybridge	WYTH/NTH	Wythenshawe/Northenden

1

3rd St *WGNE/HIN* WN2 ....**64** B5
4th St *WGNE/HIN* WN2 ....**64** C5

A

Abberley Dr *NEWH/MOS* M40 ...**74** A2
Abberley Wy *WGNS/IIMK* WN3 ...**46** E8
Abberton Rd *DID/WITH* M20 .....**98** D6
Abbey Cl *ALT* WA14 ....**116** C3
  RAD M26 ....**36** B8
  STRET M32 ....**96** C1
Abbey Ct *RAD* M26 ....**38** B8
  WGNNW/ST WN6 ....**47** H2
Abbey Crs *HEY* OL10 ....**26** E8
Abbey Dl *WGNNW/ST* WN6 ......**30** A5
Abbeydale *WHIT* OL12 ....**10** D2
Abbeydale Cl *AUL* OL6 ....**76** B6
Abbey Dr *LIT* OL15 ....**29** J1
  SWIN M27 ....**70** B4
  TOT/BURYW BL8 ....**38** D3
  WGNE/BIL/O WN5 ....**46** B6
Abbeyfields *WCNNW/ST* WN6 ...**47** H2
Abbeyfield Sq *OP/CLY* * M11 ...**88** E4
Abbey Gdns *HYDE* SK14 ....**103** J1
Abbey Gv *CHAD* OL9 ....**58** D8
  ECC M30 ....**85** H2
  HYDE SK14 ....**103** J1
  STKP SK1 ....**112** E4
Abbey Hey La *GTN* M18 ....**89** H6
Abbey Hills Rd *OLDS* OL8 ......**59** L8
Abbey La *LEIGH* WN7 ....**66** A3
Abbey Lawn *OLDTF/WHR* M16 ..**97** L1
Abbeyway North
  RNFD/HAY WA11 ....**78** D5
Abbeyway South
  RNFD/HAY WA11 ....**78** D6
Abbeywood Av * *WN18* M18 ....**89** H8
Abbingdon Wy *LEIGH* WN7 .....**66** A3
Abbot Cft *WHTN* BL5 ....**50** C6
Abbotsbury Cl *POY/DIS* SK12 ..**121** M1
Abbots Cl *SALE* M33 ....**97** G7
Abbotsfield Cl *URM* * M41 ......**95** G1
Abbot's Fold Rd *WALK* M28 ....**68** E5
Abbotsford Dr *GOL/RIS/CU* WA3 ..**80** A3
Abbotsford Dr *MDTN* M24 ......**41** G8
Abbotsford Gv *ALT* WA14 .....**108** B4
Abbotsford Rd *BOL* BL1 ....**35** K3
  CCHDY M21 ....**97** L2
  OLD OL1 ....**59** L3
Abbotside Cl *OLDTF/WHR* M16 ..**98** A1
Abbotsleigh Dr *BRAM/HZG* SK7 ..**121** H2
Abbotts Gn *TYLD* M29 ....**67** K8
Abbott St *BOLS/LL* BL3 ....**2** C9
  HOR/BR BL6 ....**21** B8
  ROCH OL11 ....**41** L1
  WGNE/HIN WN2 ....**48** F6
Abden St *RAD* M26 ....**54** D1
Abels La *UPML* OL3 ....**61** M4
Aber Av *OFTN* SK2 ....**112** F8
Abercarn Cl *CHH* M8 ....**72** D5
Abercorn Rd *BOL* BL1 ....**35** L1
Abercorn St *OLDE* * OL4 ....**60** A6
Abercrombie Ct *SALE* M33 .....**97** G7
Aberdeen Wk
  BRUN/LGST * M13 ....**87** L6
Aberdeen Crs *EDGY/DAV* SK3 ..**12** E7
Aberdeen Gdns *WHIT* OL12 ....**18** E8
Aberdeen Gv *EDGY/DAV* SK3 ..**12** F6
Aberdeen St *BRUN/LGST* M13 ..**87** L7
Aberford Rd *NTHM/RTH* M23 ..**109** K7
Abergele Rd *RUSH/FAL* M14 ...**99** H4
Abergele St *OFTN* SK2 ....**112** C6
Aberley Fold *LIT* OL15 ....**20** A5
Abernant Cl *OP/CLY* M11 ....**88** C3
Abernethy St *HOR/BR* BL6 .....**34** A2
Aber Rd *CHD/CHDH* SK8 ......**111** K6
Abersoch Av *RUSH/FAL* M14 ...**99** H4
Abingdon Av *WHIT* M45 ....**55** J2
Abingdon Cl *CHAD* * OL9 ....**58** E8
  ROCH OL11 ....**28** B8
  WHIT M45 ....**55** J2
Abingdon Rd *BOLE* BL2 ....**3** L2
  BRAM/HZG SK7 ....**121** G3
  RDSH SK5 ....**100** C5
  URM M41 ....**96** B1
Abingdon St *AUL* OL6 ....**91** G2
  CMANE M1 ....**7** G6
Abinger Rd *AIMK* WN4 ....**63** G8
Abington Dr *WGNE/HIN* WN2 ..**64** D3
Abington Rd *SALE* M33 ....**108** F1
Abney Gra *MOSL* OL5 ....**77** H4
Abney Rd *HTNM* SK4 ....**99** M7
  MOSL OL5 ....**76** F4
Aboukir St *MILN* OL16 ....**11** H5
Abraham St *HOR/BR* BL6 ....**21** B8
Abram Cl *RUSH/FAL* M14 ......**98** D3
Abram St *SLFD* M6 ....**71** J6
Absalom Dr *CHH* M8 ....**72** C4
Abson St *OLD* OL1 ....**9** M7
Acacia Av *CHD/CHDH* SK8 ...**120** C2
  DTN/ASHW M34 ....**101** K1
  HALE/TIMP WA15 ....**117** H1
  SWIN M27 ....**70** B6
  WILM/AE SK9 ....**126** D3
Acacia Crs *WGNNW/ST* WN6 ..**47** J1
  SLFD M6 ....**85** L1
Acacia Dr *HALE/TIMP* WA15 ..**117** H1
Acacia Gv *RDSH* SK5 ....**100** C8
Acacia Rd *OLDS* OL8 ....**75** G3
The Acacias *URM* * M41 ....**96** A4
Acacia St *NEWLW* WA12 ....**78** C8
Academy Wk *HULME* * M15 ....**87** H7
Ace Ml *CHAD* * OL9 ....**58** C8
Acer Cl *HYDE* SK14 ....**102** D2
  ROCH OL11 ....**27** G3
Acheson St *GTN* M18 ....**89** G7
Ackers La *PART* M31 ....**95** H6
Ackers St *BRUN/LGST* M13 ....**87** L7
Ackhurst La *WGNW/BIL/O* WN5 ..**46** C2
Ack La East *BRAM/HZG* SK7 ..**120** F6
  BRAM/HZG SK7 ....**121** H3
Ack La West *CHD/CHDH* SK8 ..**120** D5

Ackroyd Av *GTN* M18 ....**89** K6
Ackroyd St *OP/CLY* M11 ....**89** H5
Ackworth Rd *SWIN* M27 ....**70** B3
Acme Dr *SWIN* M27 ....**70** E4
Acomb St *BRUN/LGST* M13 ....**87** L7
  HYDE SK14 ....**102** B4
Acorn Av *CHD/CHDH* SK8 ....**111** H6
  LEIGH WN7 ....**81** J1
  WHIT M45 ....**55** J6
Acorn Ct *LEIGH* WN7 ....**81** L1
Acorn St *OLDE* OL4 ....**60** B6
Acorn Wy *OLD* OL1 ....**78** E2
A ct *AIMK* WN4 ....**78** E2
Acre Barn *ROY/SHW* OL2 ......**43** H4
Acre Fld *BOLE* BL2 ....**23** G8
Acrefield *SALE* M33 ....**108** D1
Acrefield Av *HTNM* SK4 ....**99** K8
  URM M41 ....**96** C3
Acre La *CHD/CHDH* SK8 ......**120** D6
  OLD OL1 ....**9** M1
Acresbrook *STLY* SK15 ....**91** M5
Acres Ct *WYTH/NTH* M22 ....**110** A8
Acresdale *HOR/BR* BL6 ....**34** F6
Acresfield *TYLD* M29 ....**67** M5
Acresfield Cl *HOR/BR* * BL6 ...**32** F1
  OLDS OL8 ....**59** G8
Acresfield Rd
  HALE/TIMP WA15 ....**108** D4
  HYDE SK14 ....**91** J7
  LHULT M38 ....**52** E8
  MDTN M24 ....**57** M1
  RNFD/HAY WA11 ....**78** B5
  SALE M33 ....**96** D6
  TYLD M29 ....**67** M5
  UPML OL3 ....**45** H7
Acres La *STLY* SK15 ....**91** L3
Acres Rd *CCHDY* M21 ....**97** K4
  CHD/CHDH * SK8 ....**110** D7
Acres St *CHAD* OL9 ....**74** E2
  DTN/ASHW M34 ....**101** H1
  GLSP SK13 ....**104** F5
  MPL/ROM SK6 ....**113** L2
  RAD M26 ....**54** E1
  WHIT OL12 ....**18** E3
Acreswood Av *WGNE/HIN* WN2 ..**49** K8
Acre Top Rd *BKLY* M9 ....**56** E7
Acreville Gv *GOL/RIS/CU* WA3 ..**81** M5
Acton Av *NEWH/MOS* M40 ....**73** L8
Acton St *OLD* OL1 ....**9** M2
  WGN WN1 ....**15** C2
  WGN WN1 ....**11** G1
Actons Wk *WGNS/IIMK* WN3 ..**15** C6
Acton Ter *WGN* WN1 ....**15** C1
Adair St *CMANE* M1 ....**7** M6
  ROCH OL11 ....**41** L2
Adam Cl *CHD/CHDH* SK8 ....**111** L8
Adams Av *CHAD* M21 ....**97** L6
Adams Cl *POY/DIS* SK12 .....**129** J2
Adams Dr *WGNS/IIMK* WN3 ...**47** J7
Adamson Gdns *DID/WITH* M20 ..**110** C1
Adamson Rd *ECC* M30 ....**84** F4
Adamson St *AIMK* WN4 ....**78** D1
Adamson Wk *RUSH/FAL* * M14 ..**98** E1
Adam St *AUL* OL6 ....**90** F1
  BOLS/LL BL3 ....**2** F9
  OLDS OL8 ....**75** J2
Ada St *BKLY* M9 ....**73** C3
  OLDE OL4 ....**9** M7
  RAMS BL0 ....**17** A7
  WHIT OL12 ....**28** D2
Adcroft St *STKP* SK1 ....**13** L8
Addenbrook Rd *CHH* M8 ....**72** B7
Adderley Rd *GLSP* SK13 ......**104** C3
Addington Rd *BOLS/LL* BL3 ....**51** J1
Addington St *ANC* M4 ....**7** J2
Addison Av *AUL* OL6 ....**91** G1
Addison Cl *BRUN/LGST* M13 ..**87** M6
Addison Crs *OLDTF/WHR* M16 ..**86** E8
Addison Dr *MDTN* M24 ....**57** M1
Addison Rd *HALE/TIMP* WA15 ..**117** G2
  IRL M44 ....**83** M8
  PART M31 ....**95** G6
  STRET M32 ....**96** E2
  URM M41 ....**96** A3
Addison St *WGNS/IIMK* WN3 ..**14** E5
Adelaide Rd *BRAM/HZG* SK7 ..**121** G6
  EDGY/DAV SK3 ....**12** D7
Adelaide St *BOLS/LL* BL3 ....**36** A8
  CHH M8 ....**72** C7
  ECC M30 ....**85** G3
  HEY OL10 ....**41** G2
  MDTN M24 ....**57** K4
  RAMS BL0 ....**17** K4
  SWIN M27 ....**70** A5
Adelaide St East *HEY* OL10 ...**41** G2
Adeline St *ANC* M4 ....**87** K1
Adelphi Dr *LHULT* M38 ....**52** E7
Adelphi Gv *LHULT* M38 ....**52** E7
Adelphi St *CSLFD* M3 ....**6** A1
  RAD M26 ....**38** C7
  WGNNW/ST WN6 ....**31** H1
Aden Cl *WGN/LGST* M12 ......**88** A4
Aden St *OLDE* OL4 ....**60** A7
  WHIT * OL12 ....**28** D3
Adisham Dr *BOL* BL1 ....**36** C3
Adlington Cl *HALE/TIMP* WA15 ..**109** C6
  POY/DIS SK12 ....**129** K2
  TOT/BURYW BL8 ....**38** D3
Adlington Dr *STRET* M32 ....**86** C8
Adlington Pk *MCFLDN* SK10 ..**129** C3
Adlington Rd *WILM/AE* SK9 ...**127** J5
Adlington St *BOLS/LL* BL3 ......**52** A1
  OLDE OL4 ....**9** M1
Adlington Wk *STKP* SK1 ....**13** H4
Adrian Rd *BOL* BL1 ....**35** M2
Adrian St *NEWH/MOS* M40 ....**73** K5
Adrian Ter *MILN* OL16 ....**11** M6
Adria Rd *DID/WITH* M20 ......**110** F1
Adscombe St *OLDTF/WHR* M16 ..**87** H8
Adshall Rd *CHD/CHDH* SK8 ..**111** K7
Adshead Cl *WYTH/NTH* M22 ..**118** E2
Adstock Wk *NEWH/MOS* M40 ..**7** L1
Adstone Cl *ANC* M4 ....**88** A3
Adswood Cl *OLDE* OL4 ....**60** A3
Adswood Gv *EDGY/DAV* SK3 ..**112** A6
Adswood La East *OFTN* SK2 ..**112** C6
Adswood La West
  EDGY/DAV SK3 ....**112** B6
Adswood Old Hall Rd
  CHD/CHDH SK8 ....**112** A8
Adswood Rd *CHD/CHDH* SK8 ..**111** M8
Adswood St *NEWH/MOS* M40 ..**88** B2
Adswood Ter *EDGY/DAV* SK3 ..**112** B6
Adwell Cl *GOL/RIS/CU* WA3 ...**80** D4
Aegean Cl *BRO* M7 ....**71** M7
Aegean Rd *ALT* WA14 ....**107** K6
Affetside Dr *TOT/BURYW* BL8 ..**38** B2
Affleck Av *RAD* M26 ....**53** K4

Afghan St *OLD* OL1 ....**59** L4
Age Cft *OLDS* OL8 ....**75** M1
Agecroft Rd *MPL/ROM* SK6 ..**113** K3
  SWIN M27 ....**71** K2
Agecroft Rd East *PWCH* M25 ..**71** K2
Agecroft Rd West *PWCH* M25 ..**71** J2
Agincourt St *HEY* OL10 ....**40** E2
Agnes Cl *CHAD* OL9 ....**58** F8
Agnes St *BNG/LEV* M19 ....**99** K2
  BRO M7 ....**72** C5
  CHAD OL9 ....**8** A8
Agnew Pl *SLFD* M6 ....**71** K8
Agnew Rd *GTN* M18 ....**88** F7
Aigburth Gv *RDSH* SK5 ....**100** B2
Ailsa Cl *NEWH/MOS* M40 ......**73** G7
Aimson Rd *HALE/TIMP* WA15 ..**109** G6
Aimson Rd West
  HALE/TIMP WA15 ....**108** F6
Ainley Rd *WYTH/NTH* M22 ...**118** F1
Ainley Wd *DUK* SK16 ....**91** J3
  UPML OL3 ....**45** H7
Ainsbrook Av *UPML* OL3 ......**45** J8
Ainscoughs Ct *LEIGH* WN7 ...**66** B8
Ainscow Av *HOR/BR* BL6 ......**34** B3
Ainsdale Av *ATH* M46 ....**50** F8
  EDGW/EG BL7 ....**16** D5
  PWCH M25 ....**72** A3
  TOT/BURYW BL8 ....**38** E2
Ainsdale Cl *BRAM/HZG* SK7 ..**121** J5
  OLDS OL8 ....**59** G8
Ainsdale Crs *ROY/SHW* OL2 ..**59** H2
Ainsdale Dr *CHD/CHDH* SK8 ..**119** K3
  SALE M33 ....**108** A3
  WHIT OL12 ....**18** E5
Ainsdale Gv *RDSH* SK5 ....**100** C4
Ainsdale Rd *BOLS/LL* BL3 ......**52** B2
  WGTN/LGST M12 ....**88** C6
Ainse Rd *HOR/BR* BL6 ....**32** E1
Ainsford Rd *DID/WITH* M20 ...**99** G7
Ainsley Gv *WALK* M28 ....**69** G2
Ainslie Rd *BOL* BL1 ....**35** K3
Ainsty Rd *RUSH/FAL* M14 .....**87** K8
Ainsworth Av *HOR/BR* BL6 ....**34** B5
Ainsworth Cl *DTN/ASHW* M34 ..**100** F1
Ainsworth Ct *BOLE* BL2 ....**3** L4
Ainsworth Hall Rd *BOLE* BL2 ..**37** L5
Ainsworth La *BOLE* BL2 ....**3** L1
Ainsworth Rd *BOLS/LL* BL3 ....**53** K1
  RAD M26 ....**38** C7
  TOT/BURYW BL8 ....**38** D2
Ainsworth St *BOL* BL1 ....**35** M2
  MILN OL16 ....**11** G7
Aintree Av *SALE* M33 ....**107** M1
Aintree Cl *BRAM/HZG* SK7 ...**122** B2
Aintree Dr *ROCH* OL11 ....**27** H4
Aintree Rd *BOLS/LL* BL3 ....**53** K2
Aintree St *OP/CLY* M11 ....**88** E3
Aintree Wk *CHAD* OL9 ....**8** C4
Airedale Cl *CHD/CHDH* SK8 ..**110** F6
Airedale Ct *ALT* * WA14 ......**108** B7
Aire Dr *BOLE* BL2 ....**22** E7
Aireworth St *WHTN* BL5 ....**50** B1
Air Hill Ter *WHIT* * OL12 ....**27** M3
Airton Cl *NEWH/MOS* M40 .....**87** M1
Airton Pl *WGNS/IIMK* WN3 ....**63** L1
Aitken Cl *RAMS* BL0 ....**17** B7
Aitken St *BNG/LEV* * M19 .....**99** M3
  RAMS BL0 ....**17** B7
Ajax Dr *BURY* BL9 ....**55** J1
Ajax St *RAMS* BL0 ....**17** B7
  ROCH OL11 ....**41** L1
Aked Cl *WGTN/LGST* M12 .....**88** A6
Akesmoor Dr *STKP* SK2 ......**112** F6
Alamein Dr *MPL/ROM* SK6 ...**114** B2
Alan Av *FAIL* M35 ....**74** C7
Alanbrooke Wk *HULME* * M15 ..**87** H7
Alandale Av *DTN/ASHW* M34 ..**90** B5
Alandale Rd *EDGY/DAV* SK3 ..**12** C9
Alan Dr *HALE/TIMP* WA15 ....**117** J4
  MPL/ROM SK6 ....**114** B6
Alan Rd *DID/WITH* M20 ....**98** F6
  HTNM SK4 ....**111** K1
Alan St *BOL* BL1 ....**36** K1
Alan Turing Wy
  NEWH/MOS M40 ....**88** B1
Alasdair Cl *CHAD* OL9 ....**58** D4
Alba Cl *ECC* M30 ....**85** G3
Alban St *BRO* M7 ....**72** A7
Albany Av *OP/CLY* M11 ....**89** J5
Albany Ct *URM* M41 ....**95** L1
Albany Gv *TYLD* M29 ....**68** A4
Albany Rd *BRAM/HZG* SK7 ..**121** G8
  CCHDY M21 ....**97** L3
  ECC M30 ....**84** E1
  WILM/AE SK9 ....**126** D7
Albany St *MDTN* M24 ....**57** L5
  OLDE OL4 ....**60** A3
  ROCH OL11 ....**11** H9
Albany Wy *SLFD* M6 ....**86** D1
Alba Wy *STRET* M32 ....**85** K7
Albemarle Av *DID/WITH* M20 ..**98** D6
Albemarle Rd *CCHDY* M21 ....**97** K4
Albemarle St *AUL* OL6 ....**90** F1
  RUSH/FAL M14 ....**87** K8
Albemarle Ter *AUL* * OL6 ......**90** F1
Alberbury Av *NTHM/RTH* M23 ..**109** G5
Albermarle Rd *SWIN* M27 .....**70** B5
Alberta St *BOLS/LL* BL3 ....**35** M7
  STKP SK1 ....**13** K6
Albert Av *DUK* SK16 ....**90** F6
  GTN M18 ....**89** H8
  PWCH M25 ....**71** M8
  ROY/SHW OL2 ....**43** K7
  URM M41 ....**96** B3
  WALK M28 ....**52** F7
Albert Cl *CHD/CHDH* SK8 ....**120** C2
  WHTF M45 ....**55** K4
Albert Colliery Est
  WGNE/HIN * WN2 ....**65** J4
Albert Gdns *NEWH/MOS* M40 ..**74** A7
Albert Gv *FWTH* BL4 ....**53** G4
  WGTN/LGST M12 ....**88** D8
Albert Hill St *DID/WITH* * M20 ..**110** F1
Alberton Cl *WGNE/HIN* WN2 ..**32** F6
Albert Park Rd *BRO* M7 ....**71** M7
Albert Pl *ALT* WA14 ....**99** J1
Albert Rd *BOL* BL1 ....**35** K4
  CHD/CHDH SK8 ....**120** C2
  ECC M30 ....**85** J2
  FWTH BL4 ....**52** F3
  HALE/TIMP WA15 ....**117** G1
  HTNM SK4 ....**12** A1
  HYDE SK14 ....**102** A2
  SALE M33 ....**96** F8
  WHTF M45 ....**55** K4
  WILM/AE SK9 ....**126** E6

Albert Rd East
  HALE/TIMP WA15 ....**117** G1
Albert Rd West *BOL* BL1 ....**35** J4
  MILN OL16 ....**28** E2
Albert Royds St *MILN* OL16 ...**11** L7
  MILN OL16 ....**11** L7
Albert Sq *ALT* WA14 ....**116** F1
  CMANW M2 ....**6** F5
  STLY SK15 ....**91** J3
Albert St *AIMK* WN4 ....**78** E1
  BOLS/LL * BL3 ....**53** L1
  BRAM/HZG SK7 ....**121** M1
  BURY BL9 ....**5** J4
  DROY M43 ....**89** L3
  HTNM * SK4 ....**101** J1
  EDGW/EG BL7 ....**16** D1
  EDGY/DAV SK3 ....**12** F5
  FWTH BL4 ....**53** G5
  GLSP SK13 ....**93** K7
  HEY OL10 ....**40** E2
  HOR/BR BL6 ....**21** B8
  HYDE SK14 ....**102** C1
  IRL M44 ....**94** B6
  LIT OL15 ....**20** B7
  MDTN M24 ....**57** L5
  MILN OL16 ....**29** J7
  OLDE OL4 ....**60** B7
  OLDS OL8 ....**74** E3
  OLDTF/WHR * M16 ....**86** F6
  OP/CLY M11 ....**88** C3
  PWCH * M25 ....**55** M7
  RAMS BL0 ....**17** B6
  ROY/SHW OL2 ....**43** G8
  ROY/SHW OL2 ....**43** K5
  WGNE/HIN WN2 ....**49** G7
  WGNW/BIL/O WN5 ....**14** A6
  WGNW/BIL/O WN5 ....**47** J6
  WHIT OL12 ....**18** D4
Albert St West *FAIL* M35 ......**74** A6
Albine St *NEWH/MOS* M40 .....**73** J4
Albion Cl *HTNM* SK4 ....**112** B1
Albion Close Gdns
  ROY/SHW OL2 ....**43** J8
Albion Dr *DROY* M43 ....**89** K2
  WGNE/HIN WN2 ....**48** E2
Albion Fold *DROY* M43 ....**89** K2
Albion Gdns *STLY* SK15 ....**91** L2
Albion Gv *SALE* M33 ....**96** D8
Albion Pk *GOL/RIS/CU* * WA3 ..**81** M6
Albion Pl *BRAM/HZG* * SK7 ..**121** M1
  BRO M7 ....**71** M7
  ORD M5 ....**86** F2
  PWCH M25 ....**55** K8
Albion Rd *NM/HAY* SK22 ....**124** E5
  ROCH OL11 ....**10** B6
  RUSH/FAL M14 ....**98** F3
Albion St *AUL* OL6 ....**90** F1
  BOLS/LL * BL3 ....**2** E9
  CHAD OL9 ....**58** D6
  CMANE M1 ....**6** F7
  FAIL M35 ....**74** B5
  FWTH BL4 ....**53** K6
  LEIGH WN7 ....**66** C8
  LIT OL15 ....**20** B7
  OLD OL1 ....**9** H5
  OLDTF/WHR M16 ....**87** Q8
  RAD M26 ....**54** E3
  SALE M33 ....**96** E6
  STLY SK15 ....**91** L2
  SWIN M27 ....**70** D4
  WGNE/HIN WN2 ....**48** E2
  WGNE/HIN WN2 ....**64** D2
  WHTN BL5 ....**50** B1
Albion Wy *ORD* M5 ....**86** E5
Albury Dr *BNG/LEV* M19 .....**111** G2
  WHIT OL12 ....**27** J2
Albury Wy *WGNE/HIN* WN2 ...**48** C2
Albyns Av *CHH* M8 ....**72** D5
Alcester Av *EDGY/DAV* SK3 ..**111** M8
Alcester Cl *MDTN* M24 ....**57** L6
  TOT/BURYW BL8 ....**38** E1
  SALE M33 ....**108** C2
Alcester Rd *CHD/CHDH* SK8 ..**110** E8
  SALE M33 ....**108** C2
  WILM/AE SK9 ....**126** D7
Alcester St *OLD* OL1 ....**74** D1
Aldborough Cl *DID/WITH* M20 ..**98** E6
Aldbourne Cl *NEWH/MOS* M40 ..**73** G7
Aldbury Ter *BOL* * BL1 ....**36** A3
Aldcliffe *GOL/RIS/CU* WA3 ....**80** C5
Aldcroft St *GTN* * M18 ....**89** G2
Alden Cl *WHTF* M45 ....**55** K4
Alder Av *AIMK* WN4 ....**63** J7
  BURY BL9 ....**5** M3
  POY/DIS SK12 ....**129** K5
  WGNW/BIL/O WN5 ....**47** G6
  WGNW/BIL/O * WN5 ....**62** A7
Alderbank *HOR/BR* BL6 ....**33** J1
  WHIT OL12 ....**19** K5
Alderbank Cl *FWTH* BL4 ....**53** J6
Alderbrook Rd *LHULT* M38 ....**68** C1
Alder Cl *AUL* OL6 ....**75** L5
  LEIGH WN7 ....**81** J2
Alder Ct *CHH* * M8 ....**72** C3
Aldercroft Av *BOLE* BL2 ....**37** G3
  WYTH/NTH M22 ....**118** E2
Alderdale Dr *DROY* M43 ......**89** G2
  HTNM SK4 ....**99** K7
  MPL/ROM SK6 ....**123** C5
Alderdale Gv *WILM/AE* SK9 ..**126** C7
Alderdale Rd *CHD/CHDH* SK8 ..**111** M8
Alder Dr *HALE/TIMP* WA15 ..**109** H7
  STLY SK15 ....**91** M1
  SWIN M27 ....**69** M3
Alderfield Rd *CCHDY* M21 .....**97** J3
Alderfield St *ATH* M46 ....**67** G1
Alder Forest Av *ECC* M30 .....**69** K8
Aldergate Gv *AUL* OL6 ....**76** C7
Aldergien Rd *CHH* M8 ....**72** C6
Alder Gv *BOLE* BL2 ....**22** F6
  DTN/ASHW M34 ....**101** K1
  EDGY/DAV SK3 ....**12** C6
  STRET M32 ....**97** H2
Alder La *OLDS* OL8 ....**75** G2
  WGNE/HIN WN2 ....**49** L7
Alder Lee Cl *WGNS/IIMK* WN3 ..**63** C2
Alderley Av *BOL* BL1 ....**22** B7
  GOL/RIS/CU WA3 ....**80** A5
  POY/DIS SK12 ....**129** K2
Alderley Cl *BRAM/HZG* SK7 ..**122** B4
  POY/DIS SK12 ....**129** K2
Alderley La *LEIGH* WN7 ....**81** L2
Alderley Ldg *WILM/AE* SK9 ..**126** E7
Alderley Rd *MCFLDN* SK10 ..**131** J2
  RDSH SK5 ....**100** C2
  SALE M33 ....**109** H2
  URM M41 ....**95** K2
  WGNE/HIN WN2 ....**49** K7
  WILM/AE SK9 ....**126** E6
  WILM/AE SK9 ....**126** E6

Alderley St *AUL* OL6 ....**76** A7
Alderman Foley Dr *WHIT* OL12 ..**27** K2
Alderman Sq *WGTN/LGST* M12 ..**88** B4
Aldermary Rd *CCHDY* M21 ....**98** A5
Aldermaston Gv *BKLY* M9 .....**56** E6
Aldermere Crs *URM* M41 ......**95** H2
Alderminster Av *LHULT* M38 ..**52** D7
Aldermoor Cl *OP/CLY* M11 ....**88** F4
Alderney Dr *WGNS/IIMK* WN3 ..**63** K1
Alder Rd *CHD/CHDH* SK8 ....**111** C7
  FAIL M35 ....**74** C7
  GOL/RIS/CU WA3 ....**80** C4
  MDTN M24 ....**57** M2
  ROCH OL11 ....**42** A2
The Alders *WGNNW/ST* WN6 ..**31** C8
Alders Av *WYTH/NTH* M22 ...**109** M7
Alders Ct *OLDS* OL8 ....**75** K4
Aldersgate *NM/HAY* SK22 ....**124** C4
Aldersgate Rd *CHD/CHDH* SK8 ..**120** E7
  OFTN SK2 ....**112** E6
Aldersgreen Av *MPL/ROM* SK6 ..**123** H5
Alders Green Rd
  WGNE/HIN WN2 ....**49** K7
Alderside Rd *BKLY* M9 ....**73** G4
Aldersley Av *BKLY* M9 ....**56** E8
Alderson St *CHAD* OL9 ....**9** G4
  SLFD M6 ....**71** K8
Alders Rd *POY/DIS* SK12 ....**123** J5
  WYTH/NTH M22 ....**109** M7
Alder St *ATH* M46 ....**67** G1
  BOLS/LL BL3 ....**52** C1
  ECC M30 ....**69** K8
  SLFD M6 ....**86** C2
Aldersyde St *BOLS/LL* BL3 ....**52** A1
Alderton Dr *AIMK* WN4 ....**78** D1
  WHTN BL5 ....**50** B6
Alderue Av *WYTH/NTH* M22 ..**110** A6
Alderwood Fold *OLDE* OL4 ....**60** C8
Aldfield Rd *NTHM/RTH* M23 ..**109** H3
Aldford Dr *ATH* M46 ....**51** H7
Aldford Gv *BOLE* BL2 ....**37** L7
Aldford Pl *WILM/AE* SK9 ....**130** C2
Aldford Wy *WGNNW/ST* WN6 ..**31** H4
Aldham Av *NEWH/MOS* M40 ..**73** M8
Aldred Cl *CHH* M8 ....**72** E6
Aldred St *BOLS/LL* BL3 ....**51** L1
  FAIL M35 ....**74** B5
  LEIGH WN7 ....**66** B4
  ORD M5 ....**86** E2
  WGNE/HIN WN2 ....**49** G8
Aldridge Cl *WGNS/IIMK* WN3 ..**63** L1
Aldsworth Dr *BOLS/LL* BL3 ...**36** B8
  NEWH/MOS M40 ....**73** H7
Aldwick Av *DID/WITH* M20 ...**110** F1
Aldwinians Cl *DTN/ASHW* M34 ..**90** B7
Aldworth Gv *SALE* M33 ....**96** A8
Aldwych *ROCH* OL11 ....**42** C1
Aldwych Av *RUSH/FAL* M14 ...**98** E1
Aldwyn Cl *DTN/ASHW* M34 ...**90** B7
Aldwyn Crs *BRAM/HZG* SK7 ..**121** L2
Aldwyn Park Rd
  DTN/ASHW M34 ....**89** M5
Alexander Av *FAIL* M35 ....**74** D4
Alexander Briant Ct
  FWTH * BL4 ....**52** F5
Alexander Dr *BURY* BL9 ....**55** K3
  HALE/TIMP WA15 ....**108** D4
  MILN OL16 ....**29** H6
Alexander Gdns *BRO* M7 .....**72** A8
Alexander Rd *BOLE* BL2 ....**3** L1
Alexander St *ROCH* OL11 ......**41** L2
  RUSH/FAL M14 ....**98** C2
  WHTF M45 ....**55** K4
Alexandra Cl *EDGY/DAV* SK3 ..**111** M6
Alexandra Ct *URM* M41 ....**95** L3
Alexandra Crs *OLD* OL1 ....**59** L4
  WGNW/BIL/O WN5 ....**47** H6
Alexandra Dr *BNG/LEV* M19 ..**99** J5
Alexandra Gv *IRL* M44 ....**94** C4
Alexandra Ms *OLDS* * OL8 .....**9** M9
Alexandra Rd *AIMK* WN4 ......**63** L8
  AUL OL6 ....**75** L8
  DTN/ASHW M34 ....**90** B4
  ECC M30 ....**84** E3
  HOR/BR BL6 ....**34** B4
  HTNM SK4 ....**12** D1
  OLDS OL8 ....**59** K8
  OLDTF/WHR M16 ....**87** H8
  RAD M26 ....**53** K4
  SALE M33 ....**109** C1
  WALK M28 ....**52** F7
Alexandra Rd South
  OLDTF/WHR M16 ....**98** B1
Alexandra St *AUL* OL6 ....**76** A8
  BOLS/LL BL3 ....**36** A8
  BRO * M7 ....**87** G1
  FWTH BL4 ....**53** G5
  HEY OL10 ....**41** H4
  HYDE SK14 ....**101** M3
  OLDS OL8 ....**9** M8
  WGNE/HIN WN2 ....**64** D4
  WGNW/BIL/O WN5 ....**47** J6
Alexandra Ter *BNG/LEV* M19 ..**99** K3
  OLDE OL4 ....**60** B1
Alexandria Dr *WHTN* BL5 ......**50** E4
Alford Av *DID/WITH* M20 ......**98** D4
Alford Cl *BOLE* BL2 ....**37** L7
Alford Rd *HTNM* SK4 ....**99** L6
Alford St *CHAD* OL9 ....**74** E2
Alfred Av *WALK* M28 ....**69** K5
Alfred James Cl *NEWH/MOS* M40 ..**7** M1
Alfred St *GOL/RIS/CU* WA3 ....**80** A4
  RNFD/HAY WA11 ....**78** B5
Alfred St *AUL* * OL6 ....**76** A8
  BKLY M9 ....**73** G4
  BOLS/LL * BL3 ....**36** A8
  BURY BL9 ....**5** K7
  CHAD OL9 ....**8** D7
  ECC M30 ....**85** G1
  EDGW/EG BL7 ....**22** A1
  FAIL M35 ....**53** C2
  FWTH BL4 ....**53** J4
  HYDE SK14 ....**101** M3
  IRL M44 ....**94** B4
  LIT OL15 ....**20** B6
  RAMS BL0 ....**17** B7
  ROY/SHW OL2 ....**43** K5
  TYLD M29 ....**67** J3
  WALK M28 ....**69** J1
  WGN WN1 ....**47** L2
  WGNE/HIN WN2 ....**64** D1
  WGNS/IIMK WN3 ....**15** J8
  WHIT OL12 ....**18** E2
Alfreton Av *DTN/ASHW* M34 ..**101** K4

Alfreton Rd OFTN SK2 113 G6
Alfriston Dr NTHM/RTH M23 109 K2
Alger Ms AUL OL6 76 A8
Algernon Rd WALK M28 52 F8
Algernon St ECC M30 85 G1
SWIN M27 70 A4
WGNE/HIN WN2 49 G7
WGNS/IIMK WN3 47 K8
Alger St AUL OL6 76 A8
Algreave Rd EDGY/DAV SK3 111 K4
Alice Ingham Ct WHIT OL12 27 L3
Alice St BOLS/LL BL3 35 M7
HYDE SK14 102 B5
SALE M33 97 G8
SWIN M27 70 E4
WHIT OL12 28 E3
Alicia Dr WHIT OL12 28 B2
Alison Kelly Cl BKLY M9 73 J4
Alison St ROY/SHW OL2 43 K4
RUSH/FAL M14 98 C1
Alker Rd NEWH/MOS * M40 88 A1
Alker St WGNW/BIL/O WN5 47 J6
Alkrington Cl BURY BL9 55 K2
Alkrington Gn MDTN M24 57 J6
Alkrington Hall Rd North
MDTN M24 57 J5
Alkrington Hall Rd South
MDTN M24 57 H6
Alkrington Park Rd MDTN M24 57 H5
Allama Iqbal Rd OLDE OL4 59 M7
Allandale ALT WA14 107 L8
Allandale Dr ROY/SHW OL2 42 F7
Allandale Rd BNG/LEV * M19 99 J3
Allan Roberts Cl BKLY M9 73 G3
Allanson Rd WYTH/NTH M22 110 B3
Allan St TYLD M29 67 J4
Alldis Cl WGTN/LGST M12 88 B7
Alldis St OFTN SK2 112 E7
Allen Av GOL/RIS/CU WA3 81 M8
HYDE SK14 102 C4
Allenby Gv WHTN BL5 50 A5
Allenby Rd IRL M44 94 A8
SWIN M27 69 M6
Allenby St ATH M46 66 E2
ROY/SHW OL2 43 K5
Allen Cl ROY/SHW OL2 43 K6
Allendale Dr BURY BL9 55 K1
Allendale Gdns BOL BL1 36 B2
Allen Dale Wk CSLFD M3 6 A2
Allen Rd URM M41 96 C3
Allen St BOLS/LL BL3 53 K1
MILN OL16 11 H8
OLDS OL8 8 E7
RAD M26 54 B1
TOT/BURYW BL8 4 A3
Allerby Wy GOL/RIS/CU WA3 80 B4
Allerdean Wk HTNM SK4 111 J1
Allerford St OLDTF/WHR M16 87 H8
Allerton Cl WHTN BL5 50 D3
Allerton Wk BRUN/LGST * M13 87 L6
Allesley Cl WHTN BL5 50 D3
Allesley Dr CHH M8 72 C7
Allgreave Cl SALE M33 109 G3
Alliance St WGN WN1 15 H3
Alligin Cl CHAD OL9 58 D4
Allingham St BRUN/LGST M13 88 B8
Allington ROCH OL11 10 D7
Allington Dr ECC M30 70 B8
Alliott Wk HULME M15 87 H7
Allison Gv ECC M30 84 E3
Allison St CHH M8 72 C7
Allotment Rd IRL M44 94 A6
All Saint's Cl ROY/SHW OL2 43 G7
All Saints Ct STRET * M32 96 E2
All Saints Gv WGNE/HIN WN2 49 H7
All Saints Pl TOT/BURYW BL8 4 A2
All Saints' Rd HTNM SK4 112 A1
All Saints' St BOL BL1 2 F3
NEWH/MOS M40 73 M7
All Saints Ter WHIT OL12 28 E2
Allscott Wy AIMK WN4 78 F1
Allsopp St BOL BL1 2 E7
Allwood St ORD M5 6 A5
Alma Gv WGNS/IIMK WN3 63 H2
Alma La WILM/AE SK9 126 E6
Alma Rd BNG/LEV M19 99 K4
BRAM/HZG SK7 122 C4
HTNM SK4 99 L7
SALE M33 108 B2
WHTN BL5 50 C4
Alma St ATH M46 66 F1
BOLS/LL BL3 35 M8
BOLS/LL BL3 53 L1
ECC M30 85 J3
FWTH * BL4 53 L7
LEIGH WN7 66 B4
RAD M26 38 C7
STLY SK15 91 L2
TYLD M29 67 J4
WHIT OL12 10 E1
Alminstone Cl NEWH/MOS M40 74 A8
Almond Av BURY BL9 5 M3
Almond Brook Rd
WGNNW/ST WN6 30 E2
Almond Cl EDGY/DAV SK3 12 C6
FAIL M35 74 C6
LIT OL15 20 A6
SLFD M6 86 D2
Almond Crs WGNNW/ST WN6 31 J5
Almond Dr SALE M33 96 C6
Almond Gv BOL * BL1 36 C1
WGNW/BIL/O WN5 47 H6
Almond Rd OLDE OL4 60 A3
Almond St BOL BL1 22 C8
FWTH BL4 52 F4
NEWH/MOS * M40 72 E8
Almond Tree Rd
CHD/CHDH SK8 120 C3
Almond Wy HYDE SK14 102 D2
Alms Hill Rd CHH M8 72 D5
Alness Rd OLDTF/WHR M16 98 B2
Alnwick Cl WGNE/HIN WN2 33 G7
Alnwick Dr BURY BL9 39 J7
Alnwick Rd BKLY M9 57 G7
Alpha Ct DTN/ASHW M34 100 F1
Alphagate Dr DTN/ASHW M34 100 F1
Alpha Pl HULME * M15 6 D8
Alpha Rd STRET M32 96 F2
Alpha St OP/CLY M11 89 H5
SLFD M6 86 C1
Alpha St West SLFD M6 86 B1
Alphin Cl MOSL OL5 77 H1
UPML OL3 61 L7
Alphingate Cl STLY SK15 77 G8
Alphin Sq MOSL OL5 77 G3
Alphonsus St OLDTF/WHR M16 86 F8
Alpine Dr LEIGH WN7 65 M4
MILN OL16 29 K5
ROY/SHW OL2 58 F1
WHIT OL12 19 K6
Alpine Rd STKP SK1 13 M4
Alpine St OP/CLY M11 88 E2
Alport Av OLDTF/WHR * M16 97 M2
Alresford Rd MDTN M24 57 J7
SLFD M6 71 G7
Alsager Cl CCHDY M21 97 L6
Alsfeld Wy NM/HAY SK22 124 C4
Alsop Av BRO * M7 71 L5
Alstead Av HALE/TIMP WA15 117 J1
Alston Av ROY/SHW OL2 43 L4
SALE M33 108 C1
STRET M32 96 E1
Alston Cl BRAM/HZG * SK7 121 J3
Alstone Dr ALT WA14 107 K6
Alstone Rd HTNM SK4 99 M6
Alston Gdns BNG/LEV M19 99 J7
Alston Lea ATH M46 51 H8
Alston Rd GTN M18 89 H7
WGNE/HIN WN2 48 C2
Alston St BOLS/LL * BL3 52 B1
TOT/BURYW * BL8 24 F8
Altair Av WYTH/NTH M22 118 F4
Altair Pl BRO M7 71 M8
Altcar Gv RDSH SK5 100 B2
Altcar Wk WYTH/NTH M22 118 E2
Alt Cl LEIGH WN7 66 A7
Alt Fold Dr OLDS OL8 76 A1
Alt Gv AUL OL6 75 L6
Altham Cl BURY BL9 39 G5
Alt Hill La AUL OL6 75 L4
AUL OL6 75 M3
Alt La AUL OL6 75 M2
OLDS OL8 76 A1
Alton Av URM M41 95 G2
Alton Cl AIMK WN4 63 K8
AUL OL6 75 M5
BURY BL9 39 K7
Alton Rd WILM/AE SK9 126 D4
Alton Sq OP/CLY M11 89 H5
Alton St OLDS OL8 75 J1
Altrincham Rd NTHM/RTH M23 109 H5
WILM/AE SK9 126 A2
WYTH/NTH M22 110 A6
Altrincham St CMANE M1 7 J7
Alum Crs BURY BL9 55 K1
Alvanley Cl SALE M33 108 E3
WGNW/BIL/O WN5 46 E3
Alvanley Crs EDGY/DAV SK3 111 M6
Alvan Sq OP/CLY * M11 89 H5
Alva Rd OLDE OL4 60 A2
Alvaston Av HTNM SK4 12 A1
Alvaston Rd GTN M18 89 H8
Alveley Av DID/WITH M20 98 F7
Alverstone Rd DID/WITH M20 98 F6
Alveston Dr WILM/AE SK9 127 G4
Alvington Gv BRAM/HZG SK7 121 J3
Alwin Rd ROY/SHW OL2 43 K4
Alwinton Av HTNM SK4 111 H1
Alworth Rd BKLY M9 57 G7
Alwyn Cl LEIGH WN7 81 J3
Alwyn Dr BRUN/LGST M13 88 B8
Alwyn St WGN WN1 15 J1
Alwyn Ter WGN WN1 15 J1
Amar St WGNE/HIN * WN2 48 C5
Amathyst Cl WGNE/HIN WN2 48 D2
Ambassador Pl
HALE/TIMP * WA15 108 B7
Amber Gdns DUK * SK16 90 E4
WGNE/HIN WN2 49 H8
Ambergate ATH M46 67 G2
Amber Gv WHTN BL5 50 C2
Amberhill Wy WALK M28 68 C7
Amberley Cl BOLS/LL BL3 35 J7
WGNE/HIN WN2 48 C2
Amberley Dr HALE/TIMP WA15 117 K4
IRL M44 94 D3
NTHM/RTH M23 109 K7
Amberley Rd SALE M33 96 B7
Amberley Wk CHAD OL9 8 C4
Amber St ANC M4 7 H2
Amberswood Cl
WGNE/HIN WN2 48 E5
Amberwood CHAD OL9 58 B4
Amberwood Dr
NTHM/RTH M23 109 G6
Amblecote Dr East LHULT M38 52 D6
Amblecote Dr West LHULT M38 52 D6
Ambleside STLY SK15 91 K1
WGNE/HIN WN2 48 E4
WGNW/BIL/O WN5 46 F5
Ambleside Av AULW OL7 75 J8
HALE/TIMP WA15 108 F7
Ambleside Cl BOLE BL2 23 J8
MDTN M24 57 H3
Ambleside Rd RDSH SK5 100 C6
URM M41 95 H3
Ambrose Av LEIGH WN7 66 B3
Ambrose Ct WYTH/NTH * M22 110 A3
Ambrose Dr DID/WITH M20 98 A8
Ambrose St ROCH OL11 10 E8
WGTN/LGST M12 88 D5
Ambush St OP/CLY M11 89 J5
Amelia St DTN/ASHW M34 90 C8
HYDE SK14 102 B2
Amersham Cl URM M41 84 E7
Amersham Pl BNG/LEV M19 99 K6
Amersham St ORD M5 86 C3
Amesbury Dr WGNS/IIMK WN3 62 F2
Amesbury Gv RDSH SK5 100 C7
Amesbury Rd BKLY M9 57 H8
Amherst Rd DID/WITH M20 98 F5
Amis Gv GOL/RIS/CU WA3 80 B4
Amlwch Av OFTN SK2 113 G6
Ammons Wy UPML OL3 45 J7
Ammon Wrigley Cl OLD OL1 9 J4
Amory St WGTN/LGST M12 7 L7
Amos Av NEWH/MOS M40 73 M8
Amos St BKLY M9 73 J5
SLFD M6 86 B2
Ampney Cl ECC M30 84 E3
Amwell St CHH M8 72 E5
Amy St MDTN M24 57 L3
WHIT OL12 27 L3
Anaconda Dr CSLFD M3 6 C1
Anchorage Quay SALQ M50 86 D4
Anchorage Rd URM M41 96 D3
Anchor Cl BNG/LEV M19 99 M3
Anchor Ct CHH * M8 72 C3
Anchor La FWTH BL4 52 C5
Anchorside Cl CCHDY M21 97 L5
Anchor St OLD OL1 9 J3
Ancoats Gv ANC M4 88 A3
Ancoats Gv North ANC M4 88 A3
Ancoats St OLDE OL4 60 B6
Ancroft Dr WGNE/HIN WN2 65 G1
Ancroft St HULME M15 87 H6
Anderton Cl TOT/BURYW BL8 38 C3
Anderton Ct HOR/BR * BL6 21 A7
Anderton Gv AUL OL6 76 B7
Anderton La CHLYE PR6 33 H1
Anderton St WGNE/HIN WN2 48 C5
Anderton Wy WGNE/HIN WN2 48 E2
WILM/AE SK9 127 H1
Andoc Av ECC M30 85 J3
Andover Av MDTN M24 57 L7
Andover Crs WGNS/IIMK WN3 62 F2
Andover Rd RNFD/HAY WA11 78 B4
Andover St ECC M30 84 F3
Andre St OP/CLY * M11 88 F2
Andrew Av WGNW/BIL/O WN5 62 B7
Andrew Cl RAD M26 54 F3
TOT/BURYW BL8 24 C3
Andrew La BOL BL1 22 C6
MPL/ROM SK6 123 G3
Andrew Rd BKLY M9 73 G3
Andrews Av URM M41 95 H1
Andrew St AUL * OL6 76 A7
BURY BL9 5 H5
CHAD OL9 58 D4
FAIL M35 74 B4
HTNM SK4 13 G3
HYDE SK14 102 C1
MDTN M24 57 M5
MOSL OL5 76 F4
Anerley Rd DID/WITH M20 98 E8
Anfield Cl BURY BL9 55 L1
Anfield Rd BOLS/LL BL3 52 B2
CHD/CHDH SK8 120 B2
NEWH/MOS M40 74 A3
SALE M33 96 F7
Angela Av ROY/SHW OL2 59 H2
Angela St HULME M15 6 B9
Angel Cl DUK SK16 90 E5
Angelko Ri OLD OL1 60 A1
Angelo St BOL BL1 36 A1
Angel St ANC M4 7 H1
BRAM/HZG SK7 121 M1
DTN/ASHW M34 90 D8
Anglers Rest IRL M44 94 B7
Anglesea Av OFTN SK2 112 C6
Anglesey Cl AULW OL7 75 J6
Anglesey Dr POY/DIS SK12 122 A6
Anglesey Gv CHD/CHDH SK8 111 J6
Anglesey Rd AULW OL7 75 J6
Anglesey Water POY/DIS SK12 122 A6
Angleside Av BNG/LEV M19 99 H8
Angle St BOLE BL2 3 K1
Anglia Gv BOLS/LL BL3 35 M8
Angora Dr CSLFD M3 6 A1
Angouleme Wy BURY BL9 4 E6
Angus Av HEY OL10 40 D3
LEIGH WN7 65 M6
Anita St ANC M4 7 K2
Anjou Bvd WGNW/BIL/O WN5 47 H4
Annable Rd DROY M43 89 L3
GTN M18 89 H6
IRL M44 94 C4
MPL/ROM SK6 113 G1
Annald Sq DROY M43 89 K4
Annan Gv AIMK WN4 64 B7
Annan St DTN/ASHW * M34 90 C8
Annecy Cl TOT/BURYW BL8 24 E8
Anne Line Cl ROCH * OL11 11 G9
Anne Nuttall Rd HULME M15 6 B9
Annersley Av ROY/SHW OL2 43 K6
Annesley Crs WGNS/IIMK WN3 63 J1
Annesley Rd NEWH/MOS M40 74 A3
Anne St DUK SK16 91 G4
Annette Av NEWLW WA12 78 D7
Annie St RAMS BL0 17 A8
SLFD M6 86 B2
Annis Cl WILM/AE SK9 130 E2
Annisdale Cl ECC M30 84 E2
Annisfield Av UPML OL3 61 M7
Annis Rd BOLS/LL BL3 35 L8
WILM/AE SK9 130 E2
Ann La TYLD M29 67 M7
Ann Sq OLDE OL4 60 A4
Ann St AULW OL7 90 C4
DTN/ASHW M34 101 H1
FWTH BL4 53 H5
HEY OL10 41 G1
HYDE SK14 101 M1
LEIGH WN7 66 B4
RDSH SK5 100 B8
ROCH OL11 10 E7
Anscombe Cl NEWH/MOS M40 88 A1
Ansdell Av CCHDY M21 97 L5
Ansdell Dr DROY M43 89 H2
Ansdell Rd HOR/BR BL6 21 C8
MILN OL16 28 E8
RDSH SK5 100 D3
WGNW/BIL/O WN5 47 G7
Ansdell St CHH M8 72 D5
Ansell Cl GTN M18 89 G6
Anselms Ct OLDS OL8 58 F8
Ansford Av WGNE/HIN WN2 64 E4
Ansleigh Av CHH M8 72 D3
Ansley Gv HTNM SK4 12 A1
Anslow Cl NEWH/MOS M40 73 G7
Anson Av SWIN M27 70 B6
Anson Cl BRAM/HZG SK7 121 M3
Anson Pl WGNW/BIL/O WN5 46 F4
Anson Rd DTN/ASHW M34 100 D2
POY/DIS SK12 129 M1
RUSH/FAL M14 88 A8
SWIN M27 70 B6
WILM/AE SK9 127 J3
Anson St BOL BL1 36 C1
ECC M30 84 E1
WGNW/BIL/O WN5 47 J5
Answell Av CHH M8 72 D2
Antares Av BRO M7 87 G1
Anthony Cl WGTN/LGST M12 88 B5
Anthony St MOSL OL5 76 E3
Anthorn Rd WGNS/IIMK WN3 63 H1
Antilles Cl WGTN/LGST M12 88 D8
Antler Ct AIMK WN4 63 L6
Antrim Cl BNG/LEV M19 111 G2
WGNS/IIMK WN3 62 F2
Anvil Cl WGNW/BIL/O WN5 46 A7
Anvil Wy OLD OL1 9 H4
Anyon Vls HOR/BR * BL6 21 B8
Apethorn La HYDE SK14 101 M4
Apfel La CHAD OL9 8 A4
Apollo Av BURY BL9 55 J1
Apperley Gra ECC M30 70 B8
Appian Wy BRO M7 72 B7
Appleby Av HALE/TIMP WA15 108 F7
HYDE SK14 90 F7
Appleby Cl EDGY/DAV SK3 112 A7
TOT/BURYW BL8 38 C2
Appleby Gdns BOLE * BL2 3 H1
Appleby Rd CHD/CHDH SK8 110 E8
Apple Cl OLDS OL8 75 M1
Apple Dell Av GOL/RIS/CU WA3 79 M4
Appledore Dr BOLE BL2 37 J2
NTHM/RTH M23 109 G5
Appledore Wk CHAD OL9 8 A7
Appleford Dr CHH M8 72 E6
Apple St HYDE SK14 102 F5
Applethwaite WGNE/HIN WN2 48 E4
Appleton Dr GLSP SK13 105 J4
Appleton Gv SALE M33 108 B2
Appleton Rd HALE/TIMP WA15 117 G3
HTNM SK4 100 A6
Appleton St WGNS/IIMK WN3 14 E4
Apple Tree Ct ORD M5 86 D2
Apple Tree Rd NM/HAY SK22 124 E2
Apple Wy MDTN M24 57 L6
Applewood CHAD OL9 58 A5
April Cl OLDS OL8 59 M8
Apsley Cl ALT WA14 116 D3
Apsley Gv ALT WA14 116 D3
WGTN/LGST M12 87 M6
Apsley Rd DTN/ASHW M34 90 C8
Apsley St STKP SK1 13 K4
Aquarius La SLFD * M6 71 M8
Aquarius St HULME M15 87 K7
Aqueduct Rd BOLS/LL BL3 3 M9
Aragon Dr HEY OL10 40 F2
Aragon Wy MPL/ROM SK6 114 B6
Arbor Av BNG/LEV M19 99 K5
Arbor Dr BNG/LEV M19 99 J5
Arbor Gv DROY M43 89 J1
LHULT M38 52 B8
Arbory Av NEWH/MOS M40 73 L4
Arbory Cl LEIGH WN7 66 F7
Arbour Cl BURY BL9 25 H6
SLFD M6 86 C1
Arbour La WGNNW/ST WN6 30 E3
Arbour Rd OLDE OL4 60 B8
Arbroath St OP/CLY M11 89 G3
Arbury Av EDGY/DAV SK3 111 J5
The Arcades AUL * OL6 90 E1
Arcade St WGN WN1 15 G4
Arcadia Av SALE M33 108 D3
Archer Av BOLE BL2 3 L2
Archer Gv BOLE BL2 3 M2
Archer Pk MDTN M24 57 H4
Archer Pl STRET M32 96 C2
Archer St LEIGH WN7 81 L2
MOSL OL5 76 F2
OFTN SK2 112 F7
OP/CLY M11 88 D2
WALK M28 68 B6
Archie St ORD M5 86 D5
Arch St BOL BL1 3 H2
Archway HULME M15 87 J7
Arclid Cl WILM/AE SK9 127 J2
Arcon Cl MILN OL16 29 H6
Arcon Dr OLDTF/WHR M16 98 B1
Arcon Pl ALT WA14 107 K6
Ardale Av NEWH/MOS M40 73 M2
Ardcombe Av BKLY M9 56 F7
Ardeen Wk BRUN/LGST * M13 87 M6
Arden Av MDTN M24 57 L7
Arden Cl AUL OL6 76 C6
BURY BL9 4 D8
GLSP SK13 104 D5
Arden Ct BRAM/HZG SK7 120 F3
Ardenfield DTN/ASHW M34 101 K5
Ardenfield Dr WYTH/NTH M22 119 G2
Arden Gv NEWH/MOS M40 73 M3
Arden Lodge Rd
NTHM/RTH M23 109 G5
Arden Rd MPL/ROM SK6 101 H5
Ardens Cl SWIN M27 70 A2
Arden St CHAD OL9 74 D1
NM/HAY SK22 124 E5
Ardent Wy BRO M7 71 L3
Arderne Pl WILM/AE SK9 130 D3
Arderne Rd HALE/TIMP WA15 108 D4
Ardern Gv STKP SK1 13 K7
Ardern Rd CHH M8 72 C3
Ardern Wk STKP SK1 13 H4
Ardley Rd HOR/BR BL6 21 C8
Ardwick Gn North
WGTN/LGST M12 7 L8
Ardwick Gn South
BRUN/LGST M13 7 L8
Ardwick Ter WGTN/LGST M12 88 A6
Argo St BOLS/LL BL3 36 A8
Argosy Dr ECC M30 84 C5
MANAIR M90 118 B5
Argus St OLDS OL8 74 F2
Argyle Av RUSH/FAL M14 88 B8
WALK M28 52 F7
WHTF M45 55 K4
Argyle Crs HEY OL10 40 E3
Argyle St ATH M46 66 F2
BRAM/HZG SK7 122 A2
BURY BL9 25 J8
DROY M43 89 K3
GTN M18 89 G7
HEY OL10 40 C3
OLD OL1 59 L4
ROCH OL11 28 D8
SWIN M27 70 B5
WGNE/HIN WN2 49 H7
WGNW/BIL/O WN5 47 J6
Argyll Av STRET M32 96 E2
Argyll Cl AIMK WN4 62 F8
FAIL M35 74 E5
Argyll Park Rd FAIL M35 74 E5
Argyll Rd CHAD OL9 74 C1
CHD/CHDH SK8 111 J7
Argyll St AUL OL6 91 H1
MOSL OL5 76 F3
Arkendale Cl FAIL * M35 74 F5
Arkholme WALK M28 68 D4
Arkle Av CHD/CHDH SK8 120 A8
Arkle Dr CHAD OL9 58 C4
Arkley Wk BRUN/LGST M13 87 L6
Ark St BNG/LEV M19 99 K2
Arkwright Cl BOL BL1 35 M3
Arkwright Dr MPL/ROM SK6 114 D6
Arkwright Rd MPL/ROM SK6 114 D6
Arkwright St CHAD OL9 8 C6
HOR/BR BL6 33 M2
Arlen Ct BOLE BL2 3 J8
Arlen Rd BOLE BL2 3 J8
Arlen Wy HEY * OL10 40 E2
Arley Av BURY BL9 25 H7
DID/WITH M20 98 C7
Arley Cl ALT WA14 108 A4
DUK SK16 91 G6
WGNE/HIN WN2 48 E2
Arley Dr ROY/SHW OL2 43 M4
SALE M33 108 D2
Arley Gv EDGY/DAV SK3 112 A8
Arley La CHLY/EC PR7 32 C2
WGN WN1 32 A3
Arley Mere Cl CHD/CHDH SK8 120 B1
Arley Moss Wk BRUN/LGST * M13 7 K9
Arley St RAD M26 54 E3
WGNS/IIMK WN3 48 B8
Arley Wy ATH M46 67 H2
Arlies Cl STLY SK15 76 D8
Arlies La STLY SK15 76 E7
Arlies St AUL OL6 76 A8
Arlington Av DTN/ASHW M34 101 K2
PWCH M25 71 L2
SWIN M27 70 A6
Arlington Cl BURY BL9 24 F2
Arlington Crs WILM/AE SK9 126 C7
Arlington Dr GOL/RIS/CU WA3 80 F4
OFTN SK2 121 J1
POY/DIS SK12 129 H1
Arlington Rd CHD/CHDH SK8 110 F8
STRET M32 96 E3
Arlington St AUL OL6 90 F1
BOLS/LL BL3 52 C1
CHH M8 72 C3
CSLFD M3 6 B1
Arlington Wy WILM/AE SK9 126 C7
Arliss Av BNG/LEV M19 99 K4
Armadale Av BKLY M9 57 K8
Armadale Cl EDGY/DAV SK3 112 B8
Armadale Rd DUK SK16 90 F4
HOR/BR * BL6 35 H7
Armdale Ri OLDE OL4 60 B3
Armentieres STLY SK15 91 K3
Armitage Av LHULT M38 52 D8
Armitage Cl HYDE SK14 102 B4
MDTN M24 57 G5
OLDS OL8 74 F1
Armitage Gv LHULT M38 52 C8
Armitage Rd ALT WA14 116 F1
Armitage St ECC M30 84 F3
Armit Rd OLDE OL4 61 H8
Armitstead St WGNE/HIN WN2 49 G8
Armour Pl BKLY M9 72 F2
Armoury Bank AIMK WN4 78 E1
Armoury St EDGY/DAV SK3 13 H7
Arm Rd WHIT OL12 19 M7
Armstrong Hurst Cl WHIT OL12 28 E1
Armstrong St HOR/BR BL6 33 M2
WGNE/HIN * WN2 48 D1
Arncliffe Cl WGNE/HIN WN2 48 F8
Arncliffe Dr NTHM/RTH M23 118 C1
Arncliffe Ri OLDE OL4 44 D8
Arncot Rd BOL BL1 22 C7
Arncott Cl ROY/SHW OL2 43 K8
Arne Cl OFTN SK2 113 K7
Arnesby Av SALE M33 97 H6
Arnesby Gv BOLE BL2 3 K2
Arne St CHAD * OL9 58 D7
Arnfield Dr WALK M28 68 E6
Arnfield La GLSP SK13 93 J4
Arnfield Rd DID/WITH M20 98 F6
EDGY/DAV SK3 112 A7
Arnold Av HEY OL10 41 H5
HYDE SK14 102 C5
Arnold Cl DUK SK16 91 K5
Arnold Dr DROY M43 89 K3
MDTN M24 57 M1
Arnold Rd EDGW/EG BL7 22 C4
HYDE SK14 102 C5
OLDTF/WHR M16 98 B3
Arnold St AUL OL6 75 M8
BOL BL1 35 M2
EDGY/DAV SK3 13 G8
OLD OL1 9 M3
Arnott Crs HULME M15 87 J7
Arnside Av BRAM/HZG SK7 121 L2
CHAD OL9 58 D7
HTNM SK4 100 A6
WGNE/HIN WN2 48 D5
Arnside Cl CHD/CHDH SK8 110 E8
MPL/ROM SK6 123 G4
ROY/SHW OL2 44 A5
Arnside Dr HYDE SK14 90 F8
ROCH OL11 27 H7
SLFD M6 85 L1
Arnside Gv BOLE BL2 37 H4
SALE M33 96 E7
Arnside Rd WGNE/HIN WN2 49 K7
WGNW/BIL/O WN5 46 D4
Arnside St RUSH/FAL M14 98 E2
Arran Av OLDS OL8 75 J1
SALE M33 108 F1
STRET M32 96 D2
Arran Cl BOLS/LL BL3 35 H6
Arrandale Ct URM * M41 96 A1
Arran Gdns URM M41 85 G7
Arran Gv RAD M26 38 B7
Arran Rd DUK SK16 90 F5
Arran St BRO M7 72 A6
NEWH/MOS M40 73 J4
Arras Gv RDSH SK5 100 C1
Arreton Sq RUSH/FAL M14 99 G1
Arrivals Wy MANAIR M90 118 D5
Arrowfield Rd CCHDY M21 98 A6
Arrowhill Rd RAD M26 38 C4
Arrowsmith Rd
RNFD/HAY WA11 78 C5
Arrow St BOL BL1 2 C2
BRO M7 72 A7
LEIGH WN7 81 L1
Arthington St MILN OL16 11 J3
Arthog Dr HALE/TIMP WA15 117 H4
Arthog Rd DID/WITH M20 110 F2
HALE/TIMP WA15 117 H4
Arthur Av WALK M28 52 F7
Arthur La BOLE BL2 37 K1
Arthur Rd OLDTF/WHR M16 97 M1
Arthurs La UPML OL3 61 L7
Arthur St BOLS/LL BL3 53 K1
ECC M30 84 F3
FWTH BL4 53 G4
HEY * OL10 41 G2
HYDE SK14 101 M3
LEIGH WN7 66 B8
PWCH M25 55 J8
RDSH SK5 100 B5
ROY/SHW OL2 43 K5
SWIN M27 70 A5
TOT/BURYW BL8 4 A5
WALK M28 69 G3
WGNE/HIN WN2 49 H7
WHIT OL12 10 B3
Artillery Pl WYTH/NTH * M22 110 C8
Artillery St BOLS/LL BL3 2 F8
CSLFD M3 6 D6
Artists La MCFLDN SK10 130 E6
Arundale WHTN BL5 50 C2
Arundale Av OLDTF/WHR M16 98 B3
Arundale Cl HYDE SK14 103 J1
Arundale Gv HYDE SK14 103 J1
Arundel Av BRAM/HZG SK7 121 M4
ROCH OL11 28 B8
URM M41 94 F3
WHTF M45 55 L5
Arundel Cl HALE/TIMP WA15 117 L3
STLY SK15 77 J6
TOT/BURYW BL8 24 F6
Arundel Gv LEIGH WN7 66 C6
Arundel Gra GLSP SK13 104 D4
Arundel Gv OFTN SK2 112 E8

Arundel Rd CHD/CHDH SK8 120 C6
Arundel St AUL OL6 91 H1
BOL BL1 22 B7
GLSP SK13 104 F3
HULME M15 6 B8
MOSL OL5 76 E3
OLDE OL4 59 M5
ROCH OL11 28 B8
SWIN M27 69 M3
WGNE/HIN WN2 49 H7
WGNW/BIL/O WN5 47 J6
Asby Cl MDTN M24 57 G2
Ascension Rd BRO M7 72 A8
Ascot Av SALE M33 107 M1
STRET M32 97 J1
Ascot Cl CHAD OL9 8 C4
ROCH OL11 27 H4
Ascot Dr ATH M46 51 H8
BRAM/HZG SK7 122 C2
URM M41 94 F2
Ascot Mdw BURY BL9 4 D8
Ascot Pde BNG/LEV M19 99 J6
Ascot Rd BOLS/LL BL3 53 J1
NEWH/MOS M40 73 L8
Ascroft St OLD OL1 9 J6
WGN WN1 15 K5
Asgard Dr ORD M5 86 F4
Asgard Gv ORD M5 86 F4
Ash Av ALT WA14 107 K7
CHD/CHDH SK8 111 H7
IRL M44 94 A7
Ashawe Cl LHULT M38 68 B1
Ashawe Gv LHULT M38 68 C1
Ashawe Ter LHULT M38 68 B1
Ashbank Av BOLS/LL BL3 35 H6
Ashbee St BOL BL1 36 B1
Ashberry Cl WILM/AE SK9 127 H4
Ashborne Dr BURY BL9 25 G2
Ashbourne Av BOLE BL2 3 K7
CHD/CHDH SK8 111 J6
MDTN M24 57 M1
URM M41 95 H2
WGNE/HIN WN2 48 D2
WGNE/HIN WN2 49 J7
Ashbourne Cl LEIGH WN7 66 A3
WHIT OL12 19 L6
Ashbourne Ct GLSP SK13 105 J4
Ashbourne Crs SALE M33 109 G2
Ashbourne Dr AUL OL6 76 C6
MPL/ROM SK6 123 G6
Ashbourne Gv BRO M7 72 B5
WALK M28 69 H4
WHTF M45 55 H3
Ashbourne Rd BRAM/HZG SK7 122 B4
DTN/ASHW M34 101 H2
ECC M30 85 H3
SLFD M6 70 F7
STRET M32 85 K8
Ashbourne Sq OLDS OL8 9 H9
Ashbourne St ROCH OL11 27 H3
Ashbridge TRPK M17 85 L6
Ashbridge Rd FAIL M35 74 E6
Ashbrook Av DTN/ASHW M34 100 E1
Ashbrook Cl CHD/CHDH SK8 119 K3
DTN/ASHW M34 100 E1
Ashbrook Crs WHIT OL12 19 K8
Ashbrook Farm Cl RDSH SK5 100 C2
Ashbrook Hey La WHIT OL12 19 K8
Ashbrook La RDSH SK5 100 C2
Ashbrook Rd MCFLDN SK10 131 J6
Ashbrook St OP/CLY M11 89 K5
Ashburn Av BNG/LEV M19 99 J7
Ashburner St BOL BL1 2 D6
Ashburn Gv HTNM SK4 12 D1
Ashburn Rd HTNM SK4 12 D1
Ashburton Cl HYDE SK14 103 H2
Ashburton Rd EDGY/DAV SK3 112 B8
Ashburton Rd West URM M41 85 G5
Ashbury Cl BOLS/LL BL3 2 C8
Ashbury Dr RNFD/HAY WA11 78 A5
Ashbury Pl NEWH/MOS * M40 73 H8
Ashby Av BNG/LEV M19 99 H8
Ashby Cl BOLS/LL BL3 52 E1
Ashby Gv LEIGH WN7 65 M4
WHTF M45 55 K5
Ashby Rd WGNS/IIMK WN3 63 L1
Ash Cl AUL OL6 76 A7
HYDE SK14 92 D8
OFTN SK2 112 F7
WGNNW/ST WN6 30 A5
WHIT OL12 19 K8
Ashcombe Dr BOLE BL2 37 K6
RAD M26 38 A7
Ashcott Av WYTH/NTH M22 110 A8
Ashcott Cl HOR/BR BL6 35 G7
Ashcroft WILM/AE SK9 126 D7
Ashcroft Av SLFD M6 71 H8
WGNNW/ST WN6 47 J1
Ashcroft St WGNE/HIN WN2 49 H8
Ashdale Av BOLS/LL BL3 35 H7
Ashdale Cl RDSH SK5 100 C7
Ashdale Crs DROY M43 89 J3
Ashdale Dr CHD/CHDH SK8 119 K2
DID/WITH M20 99 G7
Ashdale Rd WGNE/HIN WN2 49 J7
WGNS/IIMK WN3 63 K2
Ashdene AUL OL6 90 F2
Ashdene Cl CHAD OL9 8 C1
Ashdene Crs BOLE BL2 23 G8
Ashdene Ri OLD OL1 44 A8
Ashdene Rd DID/WITH M20 99 G6
HTNM SK4 111 G2
WILM/AE SK9 126 D7
Ashdown Av BKLY M9 57 G8
MPL/ROM SK6 101 M7
Ashdown Dr BOLE BL2 36 F1
SWIN M27 70 D6
WALK M28 68 C5
Ashdowne Lawns STLY SK15 92 A1
Ashdown Gv BKLY M9 57 G8
Ashdown Rd HTNM SK4 111 M1
Ashdown Ter BKLY M9 57 G8
Ashdown Wy ROY/SHW OL2 43 H4
Ash Dr SWIN M27 69 M2
Asher St BOLS/LL BL3 51 M1
Ashes Cl STLY SK15 91 M4
Ashes Dr BOLE BL2 37 J4
Ashes La GLSP SK13 104 D3
MILN OL16 29 H5
OLDE OL4 60 C6
STLY SK15 91 M4
Ashfield DTN/ASHW M34 90 D7
Ashfield Av ATH M46 50 F8
ROCH OL11 10 E9
WGNE/HIN WN2 49 J8
Ashfield Cl SLFD M6 86 B1
Ashfield Crs CHD/CHDH SK8 111 G6
OLDE OL4 60 C6
WGNW/BIL/O WN5 62 B7
Ashfield Dr NEWH/MOS M40 74 A8
WGNE/HIN WN2 32 F7
Ashfield Gv BOL BL1 22 D6
EDGY/DAV * SK3 112 C8
GTN * M18 89 J8
IRL M44 94 B6
MPL/ROM SK6 114 E3
Ashfield House Gdns
WGNNW/ST WN6 31 J4
Ashfield La MILN OL16 29 J8
Ashfield Park Dr
WGNNW/ST WN6 31 J4
Ashfield Rd BRUN/LGST M13 99 H1
CHD/CHDH SK8 111 G6
EDGY/DAV SK3 112 C8
GLSP SK13 104 B1
HALE/TIMP WA15 117 G1
ROCH OL11 10 D9
SALE M33 96 E7
URM M41 96 A2
Ashfield Sq DROY M43 89 J3
Ashfield St OLDS OL8 74 F1
Ashford SALE M33 95 M8
Ashford Av ECC M30 84 F4
RDSH * SK5 100 C2
SWIN M27 69 M6
WALK M28 68 C6
Ashford Cl BOLE BL2 23 H8
OLDE * OL4 60 A3
TOT/BURYW BL8 38 E3
WILM/AE SK9 119 L8
Ashford Ms GLSP SK13 104 A3
Ashford Ri WGN WN1 31 L8
Ashford Rd DID/WITH M20 98 D5
HTNM SK4 100 A6
WILM/AE SK9 126 E8
Ashford St HEY OL10 40 C2
Ashford Wk BOL BL1 2 C1
CHAD * OL9 58 D6
Ashgate Av WYTH/NTH M22 110 B8
Ashgrove MILN OL16 42 E3
Ash Gv ALT WA14 116 E3
BOL BL1 35 L4
BOLE BL2 37 J1
CHD/CHDH SK8 119 K4
DROY M43 89 K4
HALE/TIMP WA15 108 C5
HTNM SK4 100 A7
LIT OL15 20 A7
MILN OL16 43 K1
MPL/ROM SK6 114 B7
OLDE OL4 60 D5
PWCH M25 55 K6
RAMS BL0 24 C1
ROY/SHW OL2 43 G6
RUSH/FAL M14 88 B8
STLY SK15 91 J2
STRET M32 96 F4
SWIN M27 70 A7
TOT/BURYW BL8 24 D7
WALK M28 69 H3
WGNNW/ST WN6 31 J4
WGNW/BIL/O WN5 46 C6
WHTN BL5 50 B5
Ash Grove Crs
WGNW/BIL/O WN5 62 A6
Ash Hill Dr MOSL OL5 77 H4
Ashia Cl MILN OL16 11 H6
Ashill Wk CSLFD M3 6 D6
Ashington Cl BOL BL1 35 L1
WGNW/BIL/O WN5 46 E3
Ashington Dr TOT/BURYW BL8 38 C2
Ashkirk St GTN M18 89 G7
Ashland Av AIMK WN4 63 K8
WGN WN1 47 M2
Ashlands SALE M33 96 D7
Ashlands Av NEWH/MOS M40 73 M3
SWIN M27 69 M6
WALK M28 68 D5
Ashlands Dr DTN/ASHW M34 90 B6
Ashlands Rd HALE/TIMP WA15 108 C3
Ash La HALE/TIMP WA15 117 L3
WGNE/HIN WN2 48 D2
Ashlar Dr WGTN/LGST M12 88 A4
Ash Lawns BOL BL1 35 L5
Ashlea Dl BKLY M9 72 F2
Ashlea Gv OLDE OL4 60 E6
Ashleigh Av GLSP SK13 104 E2
Ashleigh Cl ROY/SHW OL2 59 H2
Ash Leigh Dr BOL BL1 35 H4
Ashleigh Rd HALE/TIMP WA15 108 E4
Ashley Av BOLE BL2 37 G4
OLDTF/WHR M16 87 G8
SWIN M27 70 A6
URM M41 95 H2
Ashley Cl ROCH OL11 27 M8
Ashley Court Dr
NEWH/MOS M40 74 C3
Ashley Crs SWIN M27 70 A5
Ashley Dr BRAM/HZG SK7 120 E6
LEIGH WN7 65 M4
SALE M33 108 B2
SWIN M27 70 A6
Ashley Gdns HYDE SK14 102 B3
MPL/ROM SK6 122 F4
Ashley La BKLY M9 73 J4
Ashley Ms HYDE SK14 102 B3
WHTF M45 55 L5
Ashleymill La ALT WA14 116 F4
Ashley Mill La North ALT WA14 116 F4
Ashley Rd ALT WA14 116 F1
DROY M43 89 H2
OFTN SK2 112 D7
WGNE/HIN WN2 65 L1
WILM/AE SK9 126 F3
Ashley St CHAD OL9 8 D3
HYDE SK14 91 H8
SLFD M6 86 B2
Ashling Ct TYLD M29 67 M3
Ashlor St BURY BL9 4 D7
Ashlyn Gv RUSH/FAL M14 99 G4
Ashlynne AUL OL6 90 F1
Ashmeade HALE/TIMP WA15 117 K3
Ashmond Rd OLDE OL4 60 C6
Ashmoor Rd WYTH/NTH M22 118 F3
Ashmore Av EDGY/DAV SK3 111 J5
Ashmore St TYLD M29 68 A4
Ashmount Dr WHIT OL12 28 C2
Ashness Cl HOR/BR BL6 33 J1
Ashness Dr BOLE BL2 37 H3
BRAM/HZG SK7 121 H4
MDTN M24 57 G1
Ashover Av WGTN/LGST * M12 88 C6
Ashover Cl BOL BL1 22 C6
Ashover St STRET M32 97 H1
Ashridge Cl HOR/BR BL6 34 F6
Ashridge Dr DUK SK16 90 E5
ECC M30 84 F4
Ashridge Wy WGNW/BIL/O WN5 46 E4
Ash Rd DROY M43 89 J2
DTN/ASHW M34 89 K8
FWTH BL4 53 J7
PART M31 106 A1
POY/DIS SK12 129 K1
RNFD/HAY WA11 78 B5
Ash Sq OLDE OL4 60 A4
Ashstead Rd SALE M33 108 F3
Ash St BKLY M9 73 G5
BOLE BL2 3 G6
BRAM/HZG SK7 121 M1
BURY BL9 5 J4
DTN/ASHW M34 90 A5
EDGY/DAV SK3 12 B7
FAIL M35 74 B4
GOL/RIS/CU WA3 79 L2
HEY OL10 40 E1
MDTN M24 57 M3
OLDE OL4 59 L6
ROCH OL11 41 M2
SLFD M6 86 C2
TYLD M29 67 K3
Ashton Av ALT WA14 108 B6
Ashton Crs CHAD OL9 74 D1
Ashton Field Dr LHULT M38 52 F8
Ashton Gallery WGN * WN1 14 F3
Ashton Gdns ROCH OL11 10 D9
Ashton Heath AIMK WN4 78 F2
Ashton Hill La DROY M43 89 K4
Ashton La MDTN M24 57 K4
SALE M33 96 C7
Ashton New Rd OP/CLY M11 88 D3
Ashton Old Rd OP/CLY M11 88 B4
Ashton Pl BRAM/HZG SK7 122 B3
Ashton Rd BKLY M9 57 G7
DROY M43 89 K3
DTN/ASHW M34 90 B7
FAIL M35 74 F6
GOL/RIS/CU WA3 79 J2
HYDE SK14 91 G6
MPL/ROM SK6 101 H6
NEWLW WA12 78 F6
OLDS OL8 9 H8
PART M31 106 F1
WGNW/BIL/O WN5 62 E4
Ashton Rd East FAIL M35 74 C4
Ashton Rd West FAIL M35 74 B5
Ashton St BKLY M9 73 J4
BOLS/LL BL3 35 L8
BOLS/LL BL3 53 L1
CHAD OL9 74 C1
DUK SK16 90 D6
GLSP SK13 104 F5
HEY OL10 40 F2
MPL/ROM SK6 101 M6
ROCH OL11 10 C8
Ash Tree Av DROY M43 89 J2
Ash Tree Dr DUK SK16 91 J5
Ash Tree Rd CHH M8 72 D3
HYDE SK14 91 L7
Ashurst Av OP/CLY M11 88 E2
Ashurst Cl BOLE BL2 37 J1
HYDE SK14 102 D3
Ashurst Dr EDGY/DAV SK3 111 L7
Ashurst Rd WGNNW/ST WN6 30 D2
WYTH/NTH M22 119 H1
Ashville Ter NEWH/MOS M40 73 J3
Ash Wk CHAD OL9 8 A3
MDTN M24 57 J6
Ashway AUL * OL6 90 D1
Ashway Clough North
OFTN * SK2 113 G7
Ashway Clough South
OFTN * SK2 113 G7
Ashwell Av GOL/RIS/CU WA3 80 A3
Ashwell Rd NTHM/RTH M23 109 L5
Ashwell St BOLE * BL2 36 E1
Ashwood ALT WA14 116 D4
CHAD OL9 58 B5
GLSP SK13 104 C4
RAD M26 53 L5
Ashwood Av AIMK WN4 78 D2
DID/WITH M20 98 B8
DTN/ASHW M34 100 D1
GOL/RIS/CU WA3 80 A4
RAMS BL0 17 D5
SALE M33 108 B1
WALK M28 52 F7
WGNE/HIN WN2 64 F5
Ashwood Crs MPL/ROM SK6 114 C5
Ashwood Dr LIT OL15 20 A7
ROY/SHW OL2 42 F7
TOT/BURYW BL8 24 E6
Ashwood Rd POY/DIS * SK12 123 M6
Ashworth Av BOLS/LL BL3 53 M1
DTN/ASHW M34 90 B5
URM M41 95 H2
Ashworth Cl ALT WA14 116 D3
CHAD OL9 58 E8
LIT OL15 20 B5
Ashworth La BOL BL1 22 C7
HYDE SK14 103 J1
Ashworth Ms HEY OL10 40 D2
Ashworth Rd ROCH OL11 26 B1
ROCH OL11 26 E3
Ashworth St CHH M8 72 B7
DTN/ASHW M34 90 B8
FAIL M35 74 A6
FWTH BL4 52 F4
HEY OL10 41 G4
OLD OL1 9 K6
RAD M26 38 F8
TOT/BURYW BL8 4 A3
WGNE/HIN WN2 49 H1
WHIT OL12 10 B3
Asia St BOLS/LL BL3 52 D1
Askern Av WYTH/NTH M22 118 F1
Askett Cl NEWH/MOS M40 74 A6
Askwith Rd WGNE/HIN WN2 65 J1
Aspell Cl MDTN M24 57 J4
Aspen Cl HALE/TIMP WA15 109 H7
WHTN BL5 50 C2
Aspen Gdns WHIT * OL12 27 K3
Aspen Gn DTN/ASHW M34 101 K2
The Aspens CHD/CHDH * SK8 110 D6
Aspenshaw Rd NM/HAY SK22 125 G1
Aspen Wk WGNNW/ST * WN6 47 K1
Aspen Wy MPL/ROM SK6 123 J5
Aspenwood AIMK WN4 78 D2
Aspen Wd HYDE SK14 102 C1
Aspenwood Cl MPL/ROM SK6 114 B5
Aspen Wood Dr CHAD OL9 58 B5
Aspenwood Dr CHH M8 72 F3
SALE M33 95 M8
Aspinall Cl WALK M28 68 C1
Aspinall Crs WALK M28 68 C2
Aspinall Rd WGNNW/ST WN6 30 E3
Aspinall St HEY OL10 41 H2
HOR/BR BL6 34 A3
MDTN M24 57 M5
RUSH/FAL M14 98 F1
WGNE/HIN WN2 64 D2
Aspinall Wy HOR/BR BL6 33 M4
Aspin La ANC M4 7 H1
Aspland Rd HYDE SK14 102 C5
Aspull Common LEIGH WN7 80 F3
Aspull St OLDE OL4 59 M7
Asquith Av DUK SK16 90 F6
Asquith St RDSH SK5 100 C3
Assheton Av DTN/ASHW M34 89 M3
Assheton Cl AUL OL6 90 E1
Assheton Crs NEWH/MOS M40 74 A8
Assheton Rd NEWH/MOS M40 74 A8
ROY/SHW OL2 43 J5
Assheton St MDTN M24 57 K2
Assheton Wy MDTN M24 57 K4
Assisi Gdns WGTN/LGST M12 88 B6
Assumpton Rd MDTN M24 57 G1
Astan Av DROY M43 89 G1
Astbury Av DTN/ASHW M34 90 A3
Astbury Cl BURY BL9 5 J9
GOL/RIS/CU WA3 80 E4
HALE/TIMP * WA15 108 B6
OLDE OL4 60 C6
Astbury Crs EDGY/DAV SK3 112 A6
Astbury St RAD M26 54 E3
Aster Av FWTH BL4 52 D3
Aster Rd RNFD/HAY WA11 78 C6
Aster St OLD OL1 9 G1
Astley Cl ROY/SHW OL2 43 J5
Astley Ct IRL M44 94 B4
Astley Gdns DUK SK16 90 E4
Astley Gv STLY SK15 91 J1
Astley Hall Dr RAMS BL0 17 C8
TYLD M29 67 L6
Astley La BOL BL1 36 B1
Astley Rd BOLE BL2 23 H7
IRL M44 82 F7
STLY SK15 91 J2
Astley St BOL BL1 36 B2
DUK SK16 90 D5
HTNM SK4 13 G4
LEIGH WN7 66 E8
OP/CLY M11 88 F3
STLY SK15 91 K4
TYLD M29 67 K5
Aston Av RUSH/FAL M14 98 C2
Aston Cl EDGY/DAV SK3 111 M6
Aston Gv TYLD M29 67 M3
Astor Rd BNG/LEV M19 99 H5
SALQ M50 85 M3
Atcham Gv BKLY M9 56 E6
Athenian Gdns BRO M7 71 M7
Athens Dr WALK M28 68 F2
Athens St STKP SK1 13 M5
Athens Wy OLDE OL4 60 B6
Atherfield BOLE BL2 23 H8
Atherleigh Gv LEIGH WN7 66 C5
Atherleigh Wy LEIGH WN7 66 C4
LEIGH WN7 81 G1
Atherley Gv NEWH/MOS M40 74 C2
Atherstone WHIT OL12 10 D2
Atherstone Av CHH M8 72 C2
Atherstone Cl TOT/BURYW BL8 24 F8
Atherton Av HYDE SK14 103 K1
Atherton Cl FAIL M35 74 E7
Atherton Gv HYDE SK14 92 D8
Atherton La IRL M44 94 B7
Atherton Rd WGNE/HIN WN2 49 G7
Atherton Sq WGN * WN1 14 F3
Atherton St CSLFD M3 6 C6
ECC M30 84 E3
EDGY/DAV SK3 12 E7
OLDE OL4 60 B7
WGNE/HIN WN2 65 H4
WGNW/BIL/O WN5 14 A7
Athertons Yd WGN * WN1 31 M8
Athlone Av BOL BL1 22 A7
BURY BL9 25 J8
CHD/CHDH SK8 111 M7
NEWH/MOS M40 73 K4
Athol Cl NEWLW WA12 78 C8
Athol Crs WGNE/HIN WN2 49 L8
Athole St ORD M5 86 C3
Atholl Av STRET M32 96 D2
Atholl Cl BOLS/LL BL3 35 J6
Atholl Dr HEY OL10 40 D4
Atholl Gv WGNS/IIMK WN3 63 K1
Athol Rd BRAM/HZG SK7 120 F7
OLDTF/WHR M16 98 B3
Athol St AUL OL6 90 F1
ECC M30 84 E3
GTN M18 100 B1
HTNM SK4 12 F1
RAMS BL0 17 C5
WHIT OL12 28 E3
Atkinson Av BOLS/LL BL3 52 E1
Atkinson Rd SALE M33 96 D6
URM M41 96 A2
Atkinson St CHAD OL9 8 E3
CSLFD M3 6 D5
OFTN SK2 13 M8
ROCH OL11 41 M2
WGNE/HIN WN2 64 E4
Atkin St WALK M28 69 G2
Atlanta Av MANAIR M90 118 C4
Atlantic St ALT WA14 107 K6
Atlas Pk WYTH/NTH * M22 119 H3
Atlas St AULW OL7 75 K8
DUK * SK16 91 G4
Atlow Dr NTHM/RTH M23 109 L7
Attenbury's La ALT WA14 108 B4
Attenburys Park Est
ALT * WA14 108 B4
Attercliffe Rd CCHDY M21 97 K5
Attewell St OP/CLY * M11 88 D4
Attingham Wk WGNS/IIMK WN3 47 K7
Attleboro Rd NEWH/MOS M40 73 K5
Attlee Av GOL/RIS/CU WA3 81 L8
Attlee Wy WGTN/LGST M12 88 B3
Attwood Rd HALE/TIMP WA15 108 E7
Attwood St WGTN/LGST M12 99 K1
Atwood Rd DID/WITH M20 110 F1
Atwood St CMANE M1 7 G7
Auberson Rd BOLS/LL BL3 52 A1
Aubrey Rd DID/WITH M20 99 H6
Aubrey St ORD M5 86 D5
ROCH OL11 10 E8
Auburn Av HYDE SK14 102 B4
MPL/ROM SK6 101 H8
Auburn Dr URM M41 96 B3
Auburn Rd DTN/ASHW M34 101 G2
OLDTF/WHR M16 86 E8
Auburn St BOLS/LL BL3 36 A8
CMANE M1 7 J6
Auckland Dr SLFD M6 71 K7
Auckland Rd BNG/LEV M19 99 J4
Audax Wk NEWH/MOS M40 73 L8
Auden Cl OP/CLY M11 89 G3
Audenshaw Hall Gv
DTN/ASHW M34 89 L5
Audenshaw Rd DTN/ASHW M34 89 M5
Audlem Cl NEWH/MOS M40 88 A2
Audley Av STRET M32 85 J8
Audley Rd BNG/LEV * M19 99 L2
Audley St AUL OL6 91 H2
MOSL OL5 77 G4
Audlum Ct BURY BL9 5 J4
Audrey Av GTN M18 89 H7
Audrey St BKLY M9 73 J4
Aughton Cl WGNW/BIL/O WN5 62 B8
Aughton St WGNE/HIN WN2 48 F8
Augusta Cl WHIT OL12 28 B3
Augusta St WHIT OL12 28 B2
Augustine Webster Cl BKLY M9 73 H4
Augustus St BOLS/LL BL3 36 D8
CSLFD M3 72 D8
Augustus Wy OLDTF/WHR M16 87 G8
Austell Rd WYTH/NTH M22 118 F3
Austen Av BURY BL9 39 J6
Austen Rd ECC M30 85 G3
Austin Av AIMK WN4 63 H8
Austin Dr DID/WITH M20 98 F8
Austin Gv BNG/LEV M19 99 J4
Austin's La HOR/BR BL6 34 C3
Austin St LEIGH * WN7 66 A7
Autumn St BRUN/LGST M13 87 M8
Avalon Cl TOT/BURYW BL8 24 C5
Avalon Dr DID/WITH M20 110 F4
Avebury Cl CHH M8 72 C6
GOL/RIS/CU WA3 80 B4
HOR/BR BL6 34 C3
Avebury Rd NTHM/RTH M23 109 K7
Avens Rd PART M31 106 C1
The Avenue BOLE BL2 3 J5
BRO M7 71 M7
BURY BL9 25 J7
CHD/CHDH SK8 119 J3
ECC M30 85 G3
GLSP SK13 93 K8
HALE/TIMP WA15 117 H4
LEIGH WN7 66 C6
MPL/ROM SK6 113 G1
NEWLW WA12 78 F8
ROY/SHW OL2 43 K6
SALE M33 108 A1
URM M41 95 H2
WALK M28 69 G8
WALK M28 69 H5
WALK M28 83 K1
WGN WN1 48 A2
WGNNW/ST WN6 31 H8
WGNW/BIL/O WN5 62 A1
WHTN BL5 50 C3
WILM/AE SK9 130 D3
Avenue St BOL BL1 2 A2
STKP SK1 13 K2
Averham Cl AIMK WN4 78 E3
Averhill WALK M28 68 E4
Averill St NEWH/MOS M40 74 A7
Averon Ri OLD OL1 44 A8
Aveson Av CCHDY M21 97 L6
Avian Dr RUSH/FAL M14 98 E4
Aviary Rd WALK M28 69 H6
Aviator Wy WYTH/NTH M22 118 F4
Aviemore Cl AIMK WN4 63 G8
RAMS BL0 24 D2
Avis St ROY/SHW OL2 43 K5
Avocet Cl LEIGH WN7 66 D6
NEWLW WA12 78 F8
Avocet Dr ALT WA14 107 L4
IRL M44 94 D1
Avonbrook Dr NEWH/MOS M40 74 C2
Avoncliff Cl BOL BL1 36 A1
Avon Cl MILN OL16 29 K6
MPL/ROM SK6 114 B7
WALK M28 68 D2
Avoncourt Dr DID/WITH M20 98 D8
Avondale SWIN M27 70 D2
Avondale Av BRAM/HZG SK7 122 B2
BURY BL9 25 H8
Avondale Crs URM M41 95 M1
Avondale Dr RAMS BL0 24 C2
SLFD M6 70 E7
TYLD M29 67 M6
Avondale Ri WILM/AE SK9 127 H6
Avondale Rd BRAM/HZG SK7 122 B2
EDGY/DAV SK3 12 C7
FWTH BL4 52 C4
STRET M32 86 B8
WGN WN1 47 M2
WHTF M45 55 H3
Avondale St BOL BL1 35 M3
CHH M8 72 D5
WGNNW/ST WN6 31 H2
Avon Dr BURY BL9 25 J4
Avon Gdns BNG/LEV M19 99 K6
Avonhead Cl HOR/BR BL6 33 J1
Avonlea Dr BNG/LEV M19 99 H6
Avonlea Rd DROY M43 89 H2
SALE M33 108 A3
Avonleigh Gdns OLD OL1 59 M3
Avon Rd AIMK WN4 64 B7
BNG/LEV M19 99 J6
CHAD OL9 58 C4
CHD/CHDH SK8 119 K5
FWTH BL4 53 L7
HALE/TIMP WA15 117 G4
HEY OL10 40 D2
ROY/SHW OL2 43 L4
TYLD M29 67 M5
WGNW/BIL/O WN5 46 F5
Avon St BOL BL1 35 L3
EDGY/DAV SK3 13 H9
LEIGH WN7 66 E8
OLDS OL8 59 J8
Avril Cl RDSH SK5 100 C4
Avro Cl RUSH/FAL M14 98 E3
Avroe Rd ECC M30 84 C5
Avro Wy MANAIR M90 118 B5
Awburn Rd HYDE SK14 103 H3
Axbridge Wk NEWH/MOS M40 88 A2
Axeholme Ct HOR/BR BL6 33 J1
Axford Cl CHH M8 72 C6
Axon Sq OLDTF/WHR M16 87 J8
Aycliffe Av CCHDY M21 98 A7
Aycliffe Gv BRUN/LGST M13 99 H1
Aye Bridge Rd GOL/RIS/CU WA3 64 E7
Aylesbury Av DTN/ASHW M34 101 J3
URM M41 85 H8
Aylesbury Cl ORD M5 86 D3
Aylesbury Crs WGNE/HIN WN2 65 M2
Aylesbury Gv MDTN M24 57 M2
Aylesby Av GTN M18 88 E8
Aylesford Rd RUSH/FAL M14 99 G1
Aylesford Wk BOL * BL1 2 D1
Aylsham Cl MPL/ROM SK6 101 J7
Aylsham Ms SWIN M27 70 A7
Aylwin Dr SALE M33 108 E1
Ayr Av OLDS OL8 75 J1
Ayr Cl BRAM/HZG SK7 122 C2
Ayrefield Gv WGNNW/ST WN6 30 A6

Ayres Rd OLDTF/WHR M16 86 F8
Ayr Gv HEY OL10 40 D4
Ayrshire Rd BRO M7 71 K6
Ayr St BOLE BL2 22 E8
Ayrton Gv LHULT M38 52 D7
Aysgarth MILN OL16 28 E3
Aysgarth Av CHD/CHDH SK8 110 F6
GTN M18 89 H6
MPL/ROM SK6 102 A8
Aysgarth Cl SALE M33 108 A1
Ayshford Cl ALT WA14 107 L6
Ayton Gv RUSH/FAL M14 88 B8
Aytoun St CMANE M1 7 H5
Azalea Av GTN M18 89 G6

B

Babbacombe Gv BKLY M9 56 E7
Babbacombe Rd OFTN SK2 112 F6
Back Abingdon Rd BOLE BL2 3 L2
Back Acton St CMANE * M1 7 J6
Back Adcroft St STKP SK1 13 K8
Back Adrian Rd BOL BL1 35 M2
Back Adrian Rd East BOL * BL1 35 M2
Back Ainscow St BOL BL1 2 C2
Back Ainsworth La BOLE BL2 3 K1
Back Ainsworth La East
BOLE BL2 3 L1
Back Ainsworth Rd North
TOT/BURYW BL8 38 F2
Back Ainsworth Rd South
TOT/BURYW BL8 38 F2
Back Ainsworth St BOL * BL1 36 A2
Back Albert St BURY BL9 5 J4
Back Albion Pl BURY BL9 25 J8
Back Alder St BOLS/LL BL3 52 C1
Back Alexander Rd BOLE BL2 3 L1
Back Alexandra St BOLS/LL BL3 35 M8
Back Alfred St BOLS/LL * BL3 36 E8
Back Alice St BOLS/LL * BL3 35 M7
BOLS/LL BL3 53 L1
Back Alicia St BOLS/LL * BL3 37 G8
Back All Saints' St BOL * BL1 2 F3
Back Alston St BOLS/LL BL3 52 B1
Back Andrew St BURY BL9 5 H5
Back Andrew St North BURY BL9 5 J5
Back Anglia Gv BOLS/LL BL3 35 M8
Back Annis Rd BOLS/LL * BL3 35 L8
Back Anson St BOL * BL1 36 C1
Back Apple Ter BOL * BL1 36 A2
Back Argo St BOLS/LL BL3 36 A8
Back Argyle St BURY BL9 25 J7
Back Arlington St BOLS/LL BL3 52 C1
Back Arnold St BOL BL1 35 M2
Back Arnold Ter BOL BL1 35 J3
Back Ashbee St BOL BL1 36 B1
Back Ashford Wk BOL BL1 2 C1
Back Ashley St ANC M4 7 J1
Back Ash St BOLE BL2 3 G6
BURY * BL9 5 J4
Back Ashton St BOLS/LL * BL3 35 L8
Back Ashworth La BOL BL1 22 C7
Back Ashworth St
TOT/BURYW BL8 4 A3
Back Astley St BOL BL1 36 B2
Back Auburn St BOLS/LL * BL3 36 A8
Back Augustus St BOLS/LL * BL3 36 D8
Back Augustus St West
BOLS/LL * BL3 36 D8
Back Avenue St BOL BL1 2 A2
Back Avondale St BOL * BL1 35 M3
Back Baldwin St BOLS/LL BL3 2 C8
Back Baldwin St North
BOLS/LL BL3 2 C8
Back Balloon St ANC * M4 7 G2
Back Banbury St BOLE BL2 36 F3
Back Bankfield St BOLS/LL BL3 35 M7
Back Bank St CHH M8 72 D8
Back Bantry St BOLS/LL BL3 2 C9
Back Barbara St BOLS/LL BL3 36 A8
Back Bark St BOL BL1 2 D4
Back Bashall St BOL BL1 35 M4
Back Battenberg Rd BOL * BL1 35 M4
Back Baxendale St BOL BL1 22 B8
Back Bayley St BOL BL1 2 A2
Back Baythorpe St BOL * BL1 36 C2
Back Baytorpe St North
BOL * BL1 36 C1
Back Beaconsfield St
BOLS/LL BL3 2 A7
Back Beaconsfield Ter BOLE BL2 3 J1
Back Beatrice Rd BOL BL1 35 M3
Back Bedford St BOL BL1 2 A3
Back Beech St BOL BL1 36 C2
Back Beechwood St
BOLS/LL BL3 52 C1
Back Belbeck St
TOT/BURYW BL8 38 F2
Back Bell La BURY BL9 5 H3
Back Belmont Rd BOL BL1 22 B7
Back Belmont Rd East BOL BL1 22 B7
Back Bennett's La BOL BL1 35 M2
Back Bennett's La East BOL BL1 35 M2
Back Benson St BURY BL9 5 H6
Back Bentinck St BOL BL1 35 L3
Back Bentley St BOLE BL2 3 L8
Back Bertrand Rd BOL BL1 35 M5
Back Beverley Rd BOL BL1 35 M4
Back Birch St BURY BL9 5 G2
Back Birley St BOL BL1 22 B8
Back Blackbank St BOL BL1 36 C3
Back Blackburn Rd BOL BL1 36 C2
Back Blackburn Rd East
EDGW/EG BL7 22 A1
Back Blackburn Rd West
BOL BL1 22 B8
BOL * BL1 22 B8
BOL * BL1 36 B1
EDGW/EG * BL7 22 B4
Back Blackburn St BOL BL1 36 C1
Back Blackwood St
BOLS/LL BL3 36 D8
Back Bolton Rd North
TOT/BURYW BL8 38 F3
Back Bolton Rd South
TOT/BURYW BL8 4 A5
Back Bolton St BOL BL1 36 C2
Back Bolton St South BURY BL9 4 D4
Back Bond St West BURY BL9 5 J4
Back Boundary St BOL BL1 36 A2
Back Bowen St BOL * BL1 35 L3
Backbower La HYDE SK14 102 C4
Back Bowness Rd BOLS/LL BL3 36 A8
Back Bradford Rd BOLS/LL BL3 36 D8
BOLS/LL BL3 52 D1
Back Bradford Rd West
BOLS/LL BL3 52 D1
Back Bradford St BOLE BL2 3 K5
Back Bradford St East BOLE BL2 3 J5
Back Bradford St South
BOLE BL2 3 H6
Back Bradford St West BOLE BL2 3 H6
Back Bradshaw BOLE BL2 22 F8
Back Bradshaw Brow West
BOLE * BL2 22 F8
Back Bradshawgate BOL BL1 2 F5
Back Bradshaw Rd East
BOLE BL2 23 G7
Back Bradshaw St MILN OL16 11 H2
Back Brandon St BOLS/LL BL3 36 A8
Back Brandon St North
BOLS/LL BL3 36 A8
Back Brandon St West
BOLS/LL * BL3 36 A8
Back Brandwood St
BOLS/LL BL3 35 M8
Back Bridgeman St
BOLS/LL BL3 36 A8
Back Bridge St BOL BL1 2 E3
CSLFD M3 6 E4
NM/HAY SK22 124 E3
RAMS BL0 17 C6
Back Brierley St BURY BL9 4 E8
Back Brierley St South BURY BL9 4 E9
Back Brigade St BOL BL1 35 M5
Back Brindley St BOL BL1 22 C8
Back Brink's Pl BOL * BL1 2 C4
Back Bristol Av BOLE BL2 3 L1
Back Bristol St BOLS/LL BL3 2 B7
Back Broach St BOLS/LL BL3 36 B8
Back Broad O' Th' La BOL * BL1 22 B8
Back Broad St BURY BL9 4 E5
Back Bromwich St BOLE BL2 3 J6
Back Brookfield St BOLE BL2 3 J4
Back Brook St North BURY BL9 5 H1
Back Broom St BOLE BL2 3 H4
Back Bryce St BOLS/LL BL3 2 D9
Back Burnaby St BOLS/LL BL3 2 A9
Back Burnham Av BOL BL1 35 K3
Back Bury New Rd BOLE BL2 3 H5
Back Bury New Rd East
BOLE BL2 3 J5
Back Bury Old Rd BOLE BL2 3 H4
Back Bury Rd BOLE BL2 37 H5
Back Bury Rd East BOLE BL2 3 M4
Back Bury Rd South BOLE BL2 3 M4
BOLE BL2 37 G5
Back Bushell St BOLS/LL * BL3 35 L8
Back Byrom St TOT/BURYW BL8 24 E8
Back Byrom St South
TOT/BURYW * BL8 24 E8
Back Calder Rd BOLS/LL BL3 52 B1
Back Caledonia St BOLS/LL BL3 35 M7
Back Calvert Rd BOLS/LL BL3 52 C1
Back Cambridge St AULW * OL7 90 C3
Back Camp St BRO * M7 72 A7
Back Canada St BOL * BL1 35 M2
HOR/BR BL6 33 L1
Back Canning St BURY BL9 4 F1
Back Carter St BOLS/LL BL3 36 D8
Back Castle St BOLE BL2 3 H5
Back Cateaton St BURY BL9 4 F2
Back Cecilia St BOLS/LL BL3 36 D8
Back Cecil St BOLE BL2 3 J5
Back Cedar St BURY BL9 5 K3
Back Cedar St North BURY BL9 5 K3
Back Cemetery Rd East
BOLE BL2 3 K4
Back Cestrian St BOLS/LL * BL3 52 C1
Back Chalfont St BOL BL1 36 C2
Back Chapel St BNG/LEV M19 99 K3
BRAM/HZG * SK7 122 A1
HOR/BR * BL6 33 M1
TOT/BURYW BL8 24 C5
WHIT * OL12 19 K5
Back Chapman St BOL BL1 35 L3
Back Charles Holden St BOL BL1 2 A6
Back Chaucer St BOL BL1 36 A3
Back Cheapside BOL BL1 2 E5
Back Chesham Rd North
BURY * BL9 25 K8
Back Chesham Rd South
BURY BL9 25 K8
Back Chester St BURY BL9 25 K8
Back China La CMANE M1 7 J5
Back Chorley New Rd BOL BL1 2 A3
Back Chorley New Rd North
BOL BL1 35 M5
Back Chorley Old Rd BOL BL1 35 K3
Back Chorley Old Rd North
BOL BL1 35 K3
Back Chorley Old Rd South
BOL BL1 35 K3
Back Chorley St BOL BL1 2 C4
Back Chorley St East BOL * BL1 2 C3
Back Church Av BOLS/LL BL3 35 M8
Back Church Rd BOL BL1 35 K2
Back Church Rd North BOL BL1 35 L2
Back Church St BOL BL1 2 D3
BOLS/LL BL3 53 K1
Back Clarendon Rd BOLE BL2 3 M4
Back Clarke St BOL * BL1 35 M4
Back Clay St East
EDGW/EG * BL7 22 D5
Back Clay St West
EDGW/EG * BL7 22 D5
Back Clegg's Bldgs BOL * BL1 2 C3
Back Clegg St BOLE BL2 3 M5
Back Clifton St BURY BL9 25 J8
Back Cloister St BOL * BL1 35 M2
Back Clyde St BOL BL1 36 B2
Back Cobden St BOL BL1 36 A1
Back Colenso Rd BOLE * BL2 37 G5
Back College Land CSLFD * M3 6 E4
Back College Wy BOLS/LL BL3 2 B6
Back Columbia Rd BOL * BL1 35 M4
Back Common St WHTN BL5 49 L5
Back Coniston St BOL * BL1 36 C1
Back Coop St BOL BL1 22 B8
Back Cornall St TOT/BURYW BL8 38 F1
Back Corson St FWTH BL4 53 G2
Back Cottam St TOT/BURYW BL8 4 A2
Back Cotton St BOL BL1 36 A2
Back Cowm La WHIT OL12 18 C1
Back Cox Green Rd North
EDGW/EG BL7 22 C4
Back Crawford Av BOLE BL2 3 J6
Back Crawford St BOLE * BL2 3 J6
Back Crescent Av BOL BL1 2 B3
Back Crescent Rd BOLS/LL BL3 36 D8
Back Crescent Rd West
BOLS/LL BL3 52 D1
Back Croft La BOLS/LL BL3 36 E8
Back Cromer Av BOLE BL2 3 L1
Back Cross La NEWLW WA12 78 E8
Back Crostons Rd
TOT/BURYW BL8 4 B3
Back Croston St BOLS/LL BL3 35 M8
Back Crown St HOR/BR BL6 21 A8
Back Crumpsall St North
BOL BL1 36 B1
Back Cundey St BOL * BL1 35 M3
Back Curzon Rd BOL BL1 35 M5
Back Cyril St BOLS/LL * BL3 3 H9
Back Daisy St BOLS/LL BL3 35 M8
Back Darley St FWTH BL4 53 H4
Back Darwen Rd North
EDGW/EG BL7 22 B3
EDGW/EG BL7 22 D4
Back Darwen Rd South
EDGW/EG BL7 22 D5
Back Darwin St BOL * BL1 36 A2
Back Deal St BOLS/LL * BL3 52 C1
BURY BL9 5 K5
Back Deane Church La
BOLS/LL * BL3 35 L8
Back Deane Church La West
BOLS/LL * BL3 35 L8
Back Deane Rd BOLS/LL BL3 35 M7
Back Deane Rd North
BOLS/LL BL3 2 A7
Back Delamere St South
BURY * BL9 25 K7
Back Denton St BURY BL9 25 J8
Back Derby St BOLS/LL BL3 2 C8
BURY BL9 5 G4
Back Design St BOLS/LL * BL3 35 L8
Back Devonshire Rd BOL BL1 35 K3
Back Devon St North BURY BL9 4 E8
Back Devon St South BURY BL9 4 F9
Back Dijon St BOLS/LL BL3 35 M8
Back Dijon St North
BOLS/LL BL3 35 M8
Back Dobie St BOLS/LL * BL3 36 D8
Back Doffcocker Brow BOL BL1 35 J3
Back Dorset St BOLE BL2 3 H5
Back Dougill St BOL BL1 35 L3
Back Dougill St South BOL BL1 35 L3
Back Drake St MILN OL16 10 F6
Back Drummond St BOL * BL1 22 B8
Back Ducie Av BOL BL1 35 M5
Back Duckworth St BURY BL9 25 K8
Back Duncan St BRO M7 71 M5
HOR/BR * BL6 33 M1
Back Dunstan St BOLE BL2 3 L4
Back Durham St ROCH OL11 11 G8
Back Duxbury St BOL * BL1 36 A2
Back Earnshaw St
BOLS/LL * BL3 51 M1
Back Eastbank St BOL BL1 36 C1
Back East St BURY BL9 5 G6
Back Eckersley Rd BOL BL1 36 B1
Back Edditch Gv BOLE BL2 3 M5
Back Edditch Gv North BOLE BL2 3 M5
Back Eden St BOL BL1 22 B8
Back Edgmont Av
BOLS/LL * BL3 36 A8
Back Eldon St BURY BL9 4 F1
Back Elgin St BOL BL1 36 A2
Back Ellesmere Rd BOLS/LL BL3 51 M1
Back Ellesmere St BOLS/LL BL3 2 A7
Back Elm St BURY BL9 5 K5
Back Elmwood Gv BOL * BL1 35 M4
Back Elmwood Gv West
BOL * BL1 35 M4
Back Elsworth St CSLFD M3 87 K1
Back Emmett St HOR/BR BL6 33 L1
Back Empire Rd BOLE BL2 37 G4
Back Empress St BOL BL1 35 L3
Back Ena St BOLS/LL * BL3 52 D1
Back Ernest St BOL BL1 2 A6
Back Eskrick St BOL * BL1 36 A2
Back Eskrick St East BOL * BL1 36 A2
Back Eskrick St South BOL BL1 36 A2
Back Eskrick St West BOL BL1 36 A2
Back Essingdon St BOLS/LL BL3 36 A8
Back Essingdon St South
BOLS/LL BL3 36 A8
Back Eustace St BOLS/LL BL3 52 D1
Back Euxton St BOLS/LL BL3 36 A8
Back Everton St North
BOL * BL1 36 C2
Back Ewart St BOL * BL1 36 B2
Back Fairhaven Rd BOL BL1 36 C1
Back Fair St BOLS/LL BL3 51 M2
Back Fenton St
TOT/BURYW BL8 38 F1
Back Fern St East BOLS/LL BL3 35 M6
Back Fir St BURY BL9 5 K4
Back Fletcher St BURY BL9 5 H4
RAD * M26 53 L5
Back Fletcher St South
BOLS/LL BL3 2 E9
Back Flora St BOLS/LL * BL3 36 B8
Back Florence Av BOL BL1 22 C8
Back Fortune St BOLS/LL BL3 3 J9
Back Foundry St BURY BL9 5 G5
Back Frances St BOL BL1 36 A2
Back Frank St BOL * BL1 36 A3
BURY BL9 5 G6
Back Fylde St FWTH BL4 53 G2
Back Gainsborough Av
BOLS/LL BL3 51 M1
Back Garside Gv BOL * BL1 35 M2
Back Garston St BURY BL9 25 K8
Back Gaskell St BOL BL1 2 B3
Back Gaskell St East BOL * BL1 2 B3
Back Gaythorne St BOL * BL1 36 C1
Back George Barton St BOLE BL2 3 K1
Back George St BOLS/LL BL3 36 D8
CMANE M1 7 G5
HOR/BR BL6 33 M1
Back Georgiana St West
BURY BL9 4 F6
Back Gibraltar St BOLS/LL BL3 2 A7
Back Gibraltar St South
BOLS/LL * BL3 2 A7
Back Gigg La BURY BL9 4 F9
Back Gilmour St MDTN M24 57 K4
Back Gilnow Gv BOL BL1 2 A6
Back Gilnow La BOLS/LL BL3 2 A7
Back Gilnow La West
BOLS/LL BL3 35 M6
Back Gilnow Rd BOL BL1 35 M6
Back Glen Av BOLS/LL * BL3 35 L7
Back Glenboro Av
TOT/BURYW BL8 38 E2
Back Glen Bott St BOL * BL1 36 A2
Back Gloster St BOLE BL2 3 H5
Back Goldsmith St BOLS/LL BL3 36 A8
Back Goodlad St
TOT/BURYW BL8 24 E8
Back Gordon Av BOLS/LL BL3 35 M7
Back Gorses Mt BOLE BL2 3 M8
Back Grafton St BOL BL1 2 A3
Back Grantham Cl BOL * BL1 36 B3
Back Grasmere St BOL BL1 36 C2
Back Greaves St OLD * OL1 9 K6
Back Greenhalgh St
BOLS/LL * BL3 53 K1
Back Greenland Rd BOLS/LL BL3 52 C1
Back Green La BOLS/LL BL3 52 E2
Back Green La South
BOLS/LL BL3 52 C1
Back Green St MDTN M24 57 L3
Back Gregory Av BOLE BL2 37 H4
Back Grendon St BOLS/LL BL3 51 M1
Back Gresham St BOL * BL1 36 C1
Back Grosvenor St STLY SK15 91 K3
Back Grove St BOL BL1 36 A2
Back Hadwin St BOL BL1 2 E1
Back Halliwell La CHH * M8 72 C5
Back Halliwell Rd BOL BL1 36 B2
Back Halliwell Rd South
BOL * BL1 36 A2
Back Halstead St BOLE BL2 3 H5
BURY BL9 25 K8
Back Hamilton St BRO * M7 72 A6
BURY BL9 25 J8
Back Hampson St
NEWH/MOS M40 73 G8
Back Hanson St BURY BL9 25 J8
Back Hargreaves St BOL BL1 36 B2
Back Harper's La South
BOL * BL1 35 L2
Back Hartington Rd BOL * BL1 35 M4
Back Hart St WHTN BL5 49 L5
Back Harvey St
TOT/BURYW BL8 38 F1
Back Haslam St BURY * BL9 25 K8
Back Haslam Ter BOLE BL2 3 L4
Back Hatfield Rd BOL BL1 35 M3
Back Hawthorne Rd
BOLS/LL * BL3 35 L8
Back Hawthorne Rd East
BOLS/LL * BL3 35 L7
Back Hawthorn Rd West
BOLS/LL * BL3 35 L7
Back Haydn St BOL BL1 36 A2
Back Haydock St BOL BL1 2 E2
Back Hayward St
TOT/BURYW BL8 4 A2
Back Hengist St BOLE * BL2 3 M4
Back Hennon St BOL BL1 36 A3
Back Henrietta St BOLS/LL * BL3 35 L8
Back Henry Lee St BOLS/LL BL3 51 M1
Back Heywood St East
BURY BL9 5 H5
Back Heywood St West
BURY BL9 5 H6
Back High Bank St BOLE BL2 3 M5
Back Higher Darcy St
BOLS/LL BL3 3 L9
Back Higher Shady La West
EDGW/EG BL7 22 E5
Back Higher Swan La
BOLS/LL BL3 52 A1
Back Higher Swan La West
BOLS/LL BL3 52 A1
Back High St BOLS/LL BL3 36 A8
EDGW/EG BL7 16 C8
Back High St South
BOLS/LL BL3 36 B8
Back High St West
BOLS/LL * BL3 36 B8
Back Hilden St BOLE BL2 3 H6
Back Hilden St West BOLE BL2 3 H6
Back Hilton St BOLE BL2 3 M4
BRO M7 72 A5
BURY * BL9 25 L8
Back Hind St BOLE BL2 3 M4
Back Holland St BOL BL1 22 C8
Back Holland St East BOL * BL1 22 C8
Back Holly Pl BOL BL1 22 B8
Back Holly St BOL BL1 22 C8
BURY BL9 5 J4
Back Holly St South BURY BL9 5 J4
Back Hopefield St BOLS/LL BL3 36 A8
Back Hope St BRO M7 72 A5
OLD OL1 59 L5
Back Horbury St
TOT/BURYW BL8 38 F2
Back Horeb St East
BOLS/LL * BL3 2 A9
Back Hornby St BURY BL9 25 J7
Back Hornby St East BURY BL9 4 F2
Back Hornby St West BURY * BL9 4 F2
Back Horne St North BURY BL9 4 E8
Back Horne St South BURY BL9 4 E9
Back Horsa St BOLE BL2 3 J1
Back Horsa St North BOLE * BL2 3 J1
Back Hotel St BOL * BL1 2 E4
Back Hough La East
EDGW/EG BL7 22 D5
Back Howarden St BOL * BL1 22 B7
Back Howcroft St
BOLS/LL * BL3 36 A8
Back Howe St BRO M7 71 M5
Back Hughes St BOL BL1 35 M2
Back Hulbert St
TOT/BURYW * BL8 38 F3
Back Hulme St ORD M5 86 F3
TOT/BURYW BL8 4 B2
Back Hulton La BOLS/LL * BL3 35 K8
Back Hulton La South
BOLS/LL * BL3 51 K2
Back Hulton La West
BOLS/LL * BL3 35 K8
Back Huntley Mount Rd
BURY BL9 5 K2
Back Hurst St BOLS/LL BL3 51 M1
BURY BL9 5 H6
Back Huxley St BOL BL1 35 M2
Back Ingham St BURY BL9 5 H6
Back Ingham St East BURY BL9 5 H6
Back Irlam St BOL BL1 36 B1
Back Irlam St North BOL * BL1 36 B1
Back Ivy Bank Rd BOL BL1 22 B7
Back Ivy Rd BOL BL1 35 M3
Back Ivy Rd West BOL * BL1 35 M2
Back James St BOLS/LL BL3 53 L1
Back Jauncey St BOLS/LL BL3 35 M7
Back John Brown St BOL * BL1 2 B3
Back John Cross St
BOLS/LL * BL3 36 B8
Back Johnson St BOL * BL1 2 F6
Back John St BOLS/LL BL3 2 C7
Back Junction St CMANE M1 7 K4
Back Keighley St BOL BL1 35 M2
Back Kendal Rd BOL BL1 35 M4
Back Kershaw St BURY BL9 5 J5
Back Kingholm Gdns BOL * BL1 36 A3
Back Kingsley St BOL BL1 36 A2
Back King St BOL BL1 2 D4
CHAD OL9 9 H6
Back King St North
EDGW/EG BL7 22 C4
Back King St South BOLE BL2 23 G7
Back Knight St TOT/BURYW BL8 38 F2
Back Knowl St STLY SK15 91 L2
Back Knowsley Rd BOL * BL1 35 L2
Back Knowsley St BOL BL1 2 E4
BURY BL9 4 E5
Back Kylemore Av
BOLS/LL * BL3 35 L7
Back La ALT WA14 106 E7
AUL OL6 76 D2
AULW OL7 75 G7
BOL BL1 2 C3
GLSP SK13 104 B6
HALE/TIMP WA15 117 H7
HYDE SK14 103 K1
OLDE OL4 60 F3
WGNNW/ST WN6 30 B4
WHIT OL12 18 D2
WHTN BL5 51 L6
Back Lark St BOL BL1 2 F3
Back Latham St BOL BL1 36 C2
Back Lathom St BURY BL9 25 K8
Back Laurel St BURY BL9 5 K4
Back Lawn St BOL BL1 35 M3
Back Leachfield St BOL BL1 36 A1
Back Leach St BOLS/LL BL3 2 C9
Back Lee Av BOLS/LL BL3 52 A1
Back Lee St UPML OL3 61 L4
Back Lena St BOL BL1 36 C2
Back Lenora St BOLS/LL * BL3 35 L7
Back Lever Edge La
BOLS/LL BL3 51 M2
Back Lever Edge La South
BOLS/LL BL3 52 B1
Back Lever St BOLS/LL BL3 2 F9
BOLS/LL BL3 36 B8
Back Lever St North
BOLS/LL BL3 37 K8
Back Lever St South
BOLS/LL * BL3 36 B8
Back Lightburne Av BOL BL1 35 L5
Back Lilly St BOL BL1 2 A2
Back Lincoln Rd BOL * BL1 35 M4
Back Lindley St BOLS/LL * BL3 53 L1
Back Linton Av BURY BL9 25 J7
Back Longden St BOL BL1 35 M4
Back Longfield Rd
BOLS/LL * BL3 51 L1
Back Long La BOLE BL2 37 H5
Back Longsight North BOLE BL2 23 H7
Back Longsight South
BOLE BL2 23 G7
Back Longworth Rd
EDGW/EG BL7 22 A1
Back Lonsdale St
TOT/BURYW BL8 4 A4
Back Lord St BOLS/LL BL3 53 L1
BURY BL9 5 G6
Back Loxham St BOLS/LL BL3 53 G2
Back Lumsden St BOLS/LL BL3 2 C9
Back Luton St BOLS/LL BL3 36 D8
Back Lytton St BOL BL1 36 A3
Back Mackenzie St BOL BL1 22 A8
Back Malvern Av BOL BL1 35 K3
BURY BL9 25 J7
Back Manchester Old Rd
BURY BL9 4 D7
Back Manchester Rd BOLE BL2 3 G7
BOLS/LL BL3 52 F2
BURY BL9 4 D5
Back Manchester Rd East
BOLE * BL2 3 G8
Back Manchester Rd South
BOLS/LL BL3 3 H9
Back Manchester Rd West
BOLS/LL BL3 36 E8
Back Manchester St
HEY * OL10 41 H3
Back Manor St BURY BL9 5 H4
Back Maple St BOLS/LL * BL3 2 B8
Back Marion St South
BOLS/LL * BL3 52 F2
Back Market St BOLS/LL BL3 53 L1
BURY BL9 4 E5
LEIGH WN7 66 C7
NEWLW WA12 78 D8
RAD M26 53 L5
WGNE/HIN * WN2 49 G7
Back Market St West BURY BL9 4 E4
Back Markland Hill La BOL BL1 35 J3
Back Markland Hill La East
BOL * BL1 35 J3
Back Markland Hill La West
BOL * BL1 35 J3
Back Marlborough St BOL BL1 2 A3
Back Marsh Fold La BOL * BL1 35 M4
Back Mary St BOLS/LL * BL3 2 B8
Back Mason St BURY BL9 5 H5
Back Massie St
CHD/CHDH * SK8 111 G6
Back Mawdsley St BOL BL1 2 E5
Back Maxwell St BOL * BL1 22 B8
Back Maybank St BOLS/LL BL3 2 A9
Back Mayfield Av BOLS/LL BL3 52 E1
Back Mayor St BOL BL1 2 A6
TOT/BURYW BL8 4 A2
Back Maze St BOLS/LL BL3 3 M9
Back McDonna St BOL BL1 35 M1
Back McKean St BOLS/LL BL3 36 D8
Back McKean St North
BOLS/LL * BL3 36 D8
Back Melbourne Rd
BOLS/LL BL3 35 M7
Back Melbourne St STLY SK15 91 K2
Back Mellor Gv BOL * BL1 35 L3
Back Mellor Gv West BOL * BL1 35 L3
Back Melrose Av BOL BL1 35 K3
Back Melville St BOLS/LL BL3 52 D1
Back Mercia St BOLS/LL BL3 35 M7
Back Meredith St BOLS/LL BL3 52 C1
Back Mere Gdns BOL BL1 2 C2
Back Merlin Gv BOL * BL1 35 L3
Back Merton St TOT/BURYW BL8 4 B2
Back Mesnes St WGN WN1 15 G2
Back Methwold St
BOLS/LL * BL3 35 M8
Back Milford Rd BOLS/LL BL3 52 B1
Back Miller St BOL * BL1 22 B8
Back Millet St BURY BL9 4 C5
Back Mill St North
EDGW/EG * BL7 22 C4
Back Mill St South
EDGW/EG * BL7 22 C4
Back Milner Av BURY BL9 25 J7
Back Minorca St BOLS/LL * BL3 36 B8
Back Monmouth Av BURY BL9 25 J7
Back Moor HYDE SK14 92 D8
Back Moorfield Gv BOLE BL2 36 E3
Back Moorgate BURY BL9 5 G3
Back Mornington Rd East
BOL BL1 35 M4

Back Morris Green La BOLS/LL BL3.....51 M2
Back Morris Green La East BOLS/LL BL3.....51 M2
Back Moss Ter BOL BL1.....2 E3
Back Mostyn Av BURY BL9.....25 J7
Back Mowbray St BOL * BL1.....35 L3
Back Murton Ter BOL * BL1.....22 C8
Back Musgrave Rd BOL.....35 M4
Back Musgrave Rd North BOL BL1.....35 M4
Back Myrtle St BURY BL9.....5 K4
Back Myrtle St South BURY BL9.....5 K5
Back Nebo St BOLS/LL BL3.....36 A8
Back Nelson St HOR/BR * BL6.....34 A1
Back Nelson St North BURY BL9.....4 F8
Back Nelson St South BURY BL9.....4 F8
Back Nevada St BOL BL1.....36 B3
Back Newbold St TOT/BURYW BL8.....38 F2
Back New George St TOT/BURYW BL8.....4 A3
Back Newhall La BOL BL1.....35 K3
Back Newport Rd BOLS/LL * BL3.....36 D8
Back Newport St BOL BL1.....2 E6
Back Newton St BOL BL1.....36 B2
Back Nixon Rd BOLS/LL BL3.....51 M1
Back Normanby St BOLS/LL BL3.....51 M2
Back Norris St BOLS/LL * BL3.....53 K1
Back Northern Gv BOL BL1.....35 M3
Back Norwood Gv BOL BL1.....35 M4
Back Nunnery Rd BOLS/LL.....35 L8
Back Nut St BOL * BL1.....36 A2
Back Oak St RAD M26.....54 F3
Back Olaf St BOLE BL2.....3 L1
Back Oldham Rd MILN OL16.....11 G6
Back Oldham St BOLS/LL BL3.....2 A7
Back Olga St BOL BL1.....36 A2
Back Olga St North BOL * BL1.....36 A2
Back Olive Bank TOT/BURYW BL8.....24 E8
Back Oram St BURY BL9.....25 K8
Back Oriel St BOLS/LL BL3.....35 M7
Back Ormrod St BURY BL9.....5 J5
Back Osborne Gv BOL BL1.....35 M3
Back O' Th' Low Rd OLDE OL4.....60 C4
Back Oxford Gv North BOL BL1.....35 M3
Back Oxford St BURY BL9.....5 H6
Back Packer St BOL BL1.....2 B3
Back Palace St BOL BL1.....2 E3
Back Palm St BOL BL1.....36 B1
Back Parkdale Rd BOLE BL2.....3 L1
Back Parkfield Rd BOLS/LL BL3.....52 D1
Back Parkhills Rd North BURY BL9.....4 E8
Back Parkhills Rd South BURY BL9.....4 F9
Back Parkinson St BOLS/LL * BL3.....35 M7
Back Park Rd BOL BL1.....2 A5
BOL BL1.....35 M5
Back Park St BOL BL1.....2 A3
Back Park Vw EDGW/EG BL7.....22 C6
Back Park View Rd BOLS/LL * BL3.....35 M8
Back Parsonage St BURY BL9.....5 J3
Backparsons La BURY BL9.....4 F4
Back Partington St BOLS/LL BL3.....51 M2
Back Patience St WHIT * OL12.....27 M3
Back Patterson St BOLS/LL * BL3.....35 K8
Back Peabody St BOLS/LL * BL3.....36 B8
Back Peace St BOLS/LL * BL3.....2 A9
Back Pedder St BOL BL1.....35 M3
Back Peers St TOT/BURYW BL8.....4 A5
Back Penarth Rd BOLS/LL BL3.....35 M7
Back Pennington Rd BOLS/LL * BL3.....52 B1
Back Percy St BURY BL9.....5 K2
Back Peter St BURY BL9.....5 H3
Back Peveril St BOLS/LL * BL3.....51 L1
BOLS/LL BL3.....35 M1
Back Phoenix St BURY BL9.....4 D5
Back Piccadilly CMANE M1.....7 H4
Back Pikes La West BOLS/LL BL3.....35 M7
Back Pine St BOL BL1.....36 C2
BURY BL9.....5 K4
Back Pleasant St BOL BL1.....2 D2
Back Pool Fold CMANW * M2.....6 F4
Back Poplar Av BOL BL1.....35 J8
Back Porter St BURY BL9.....25 J8
Back Portland St AUL OL6.....90 D2
Back Portugal St BOLE BL2.....3 J5
Back Preston St BOLS/LL BL3.....52 C1
Back Primrose St BOL * BL1.....22 C8
Back Primula St BOL BL1.....22 C8
Back Proctor St TOT/BURYW BL8.....38 F3
Back Progress St BOL * BL1.....36 C3
Back Quay St CSLFD M3.....6 C5
Back Quebec St BOLS/LL BL3.....2 A9
Back Queensgate BOL BL1.....35 M4
Back Queen St BOL * BL1.....2 D5
Back Radcliffe Rd East BOLE * BL2.....3 J4
Back Raimond St BOL BL1.....35 M1
Back Rainshaw St BOL BL1.....22 C8
Back Rake St BURY BL9.....25 J8
Back Randal St BOLS/LL * BL3.....35 M8
Back Range St BOLS/LL BL3.....36 A8
Back Raphael St BOL BL1.....36 A3
Back Raven St BURY BL9.....5 G1
Back Rawlinson St HOR/BR * BL6.....21 B8
Back Rawson Rd BOL BL1.....35 M3
Back Rawson Rd North BOL BL1.....35 M3
Back Raymond Av BURY BL9.....25 J7
Back Red Bank ANC M4.....87 K1
Back Redhill Gv BOL BL1.....2 C2
Back Regent St BURY BL9.....4 F1
Back Ribblesdale Rd BOLS/LL BL3.....36 A8
Back Richard Burch St BURY BL9.....5 G2
Back Richelieu St BOLS/LL BL3.....36 D8
Back Rigby La North BOLE * BL2.....22 F6
Back Rigby La South BOLE * BL2.....22 F6
Back Rishton La BOLS/LL BL3.....52 C1
Back Rishton La East BOLS/LL BL3.....52 C1
Back Rochdale Old North Rd BURY.....5 M2
Back Rochdale Old Rd South BURY BL9.....5 L2
Back Rochdale Rd BURY BL9.....5 H4
Back Rochdale Rd South BURY BL9.....5 G4
Back Rock Av BOL BL1.....35 M1
Back Roland Rd BOLS/LL BL3.....35 M7
Back Roman Rd BRO M7.....72 B6

Back Romer St BOLE BL2.....3 M4
Back Rosamond St BOLS/LL BL3.....35 M8
Back Roscow Av BOLE BL2.....37 H4
Back Rose Bank BOL * BL9.....25 J8
Back Roseberry St BOLS/LL * BL3.....35 M8
Back Rossini St BOL BL1.....36 A1
Back Rw WHIT * OL12.....18 C6
Back Rowena St BOLS/LL * BL3.....52 F2
Back Rowland St BOLS/LL BL3.....51 L1
Back Roxalina St BOLS/LL BL3.....36 B8
Back Royal Av BURY BL9.....25 J7
Back Royds St MILN OL16.....11 H9
Back Rudolph St BOLS/LL BL3.....52 C1
Back Rumworth St BOLS/LL BL3.....36 A8
Back Rushton Rd BOL * BL1.....35 L3
Back Russell Cl BOL * BL1.....35 M4
Back Russell St BOL BL1.....35 M4
Back Rutland St BOL BL1.....35 M3
Back Ryefield St BOL BL1.....3 G1
Back St Anne's St BURY BL9.....25 J8
Back St Ann St BOL BL1.....36 B3
Back St Augustine St BOL BL1.....36 A2
Back St George's Rd ANC M4.....7 J1
BOL BL1.....2 D3
Back St George's Rd North BOL BL1.....2 B3
Back St Helens Rd BOLS/LL * BL3.....36 A8
Back St Helens Rd South BOLS/LL BL3.....51 L2
Back St James's St OLD * OL1.....59 L5
Back St Mark's La CHH * M8.....72 C4
Back St Mary's Pl BURY * BL9.....4 D5
Back St Philip's Av BOLS/LL BL3.....35 L8
Back St Thomas St East BOL * BL1.....36 A2
Back Salford LEIGH * WN7.....66 C7
Back Salford St BURY BL9.....25 K8
Back Salisbury St BOLS/LL BL3.....2 B6
Back Salisbury Ter BOLE BL2.....37 G5
Back Sandon St BOLS/LL * BL3.....36 A8
Back Sandon St West BOLS/LL * BL3.....36 A8
Back Sandy Bank Rd EDGW/EG BL7.....16 D7
Back Sankey St BURY BL9.....4 D5
Back Sapling Rd BOLS/LL BL3.....51 M1
Back Sapling Rd South BOLS/LL * BL3.....51 M2
Back Scholes St TOT/BURYW BL8.....4 A3
Back Scott St OLDS * OL8.....9 H9
Back Scowcroft St BOLE BL2.....3 J1
Back Settle St BOLS/LL BL3.....52 B1
Back Settle St North BOLS/LL BL3.....52 B1
Back Seymour Rd BOL BL1.....36 C1
Back Shakerley La ATH * M46.....67 J3
Back Sharman St BOLS/LL BL3.....3 J9
Back Shaw-street BURY BL9.....5 K3
Back Shepherd St BURY BL9.....5 G5
Back Sherwood St BOL BL1.....36 C1
Back Shipton St BOL BL1.....35 L3
Back Short St ATH M46.....67 H3
Back Shuttle St BOLS/LL BL3.....2 C7
Back Silverdale Rd BOL BL1.....35 M5
Back Silver St BURY BL9.....4 E5
Back Skipton St BOLE BL2.....3 J1
Back Smethurst La BOLS/LL BL3.....51 L2
Back Smethurst La West BOLS/LL * BL3.....51 L2
Back Sofa St BOL BL1.....35 L3
Back Soho St BOL BL1.....3 G1
Back Somerset Rd BOL BL1.....35 L5
Back Somerville St BOL * BL1.....35 M1
Back South Cross St East BURY BL9.....5 G5
Back Southfield St BOLS/LL BL3.....36 E8
Back South Pde CSLFD M3.....6 E4
Back South St BOLS/LL BL3.....52 B1
Back South View St BOLE BL2.....3 M5
Back Spa Rd BOLS/LL BL3.....2 A6
Back Spa Rd North BOL BL1.....2 A6
Back Spa Rd West BOL * BL1.....2 A6
Back Spear St CMANE * M1.....7 J3
Back Springfield St BOLS/LL BL3.....36 D8
Back Spring Gdns BOL BL1.....2 D5
MDTN M24.....57 K2
Back Spring St East BURY BL9.....5 C6
Back Spring St West BURY BL9.....5 C6
Back Square St RAMS BL0.....17 C6
Back Stainsbury St BOLS/LL BL3.....35 M8
Back Stanley St RAMS * BL0.....17 B7
Back Stephen St TOT/BURYW BL8.....38 F2
Back Stewart St BOL BL1.....36 B3
Back Stone St BOLE BL2.....3 J1
Back Sunlight Rd BOL BL1.....35 M5
Back Sunning Hill St BOLS/LL * BL3.....36 A8
Back Sunnyside Rd BOL BL1.....35 M2
Back Swan La BOLS/LL * BL3.....36 A8
Back Talbot St BOL BL1.....22 C8
Back Tavistock Rd BOL BL1.....2 A6
Back Teak St BURY BL9.....5 K4
Back Tenterden St BURY BL9.....4 D5
Back Tenterden St BURY BL9.....4 C5
Back Thicketford Rd BOLE * BL2.....36 F3
Back Thicketford Rd West BOLE BL2.....36 E3
Back Thomasson Cl BOL BL1.....36 B3
Back Thomas St ANC * M4.....7 H3
Back Thorns Rd BOL BL1.....36 C2
Back Thorn St BOL BL1.....36 C2
Back Thorpe St BOL BL1.....36 A2
Back Thurnham St BOLS/LL * BL3.....51 M1
Back Tinline St BURY BL9.....5 J5
Back Tonge Moor Rd BOLE BL2.....36 E2
Back Tonge Moor Rd East BOLE BL2.....3 J1
BOLE BL2.....36 E2
Back Tonge Old Rd BOLE BL2.....3 M4
Back Tottington Rd TOT/BURYW BL8.....24 E8
Back Tottington Rd East BURY.....23 H7
Back Tottington Rd North TOT/BURYW BL8.....4 A2
Back Tottington Rd South TOT/BURYW BL8.....4 A2
Back Tudor St BOLS/LL * BL3.....35 M8
Back Turner St ANC * M4.....7 H3
Back Turton Rd East BOLE BL2.....22 F7
Back Turton Rd West BOLE BL2.....22 F7
Back Uganda St BOLS/LL BL3.....51 M1
Back Ulleswater St BOL BL1.....36 C2
Back Union St BOLE BL2.....3 H1
NM/HAY SK22.....124 E5

Back Unsworth St South BOLS/LL BL3.....2 B9
Back Uttley St BOL BL1.....36 C1
Back Venice St BOL BL1.....35 M8
Back Vernon St BOL BL1.....2 C3
BURY BL9.....5 G1
Back Vernon St South BOL * BL1.....2 C3
Back Vickerman St BOL BL1.....36 A2
Back Victoria Gv BOL BL1.....35 M3
Back Victoria Gv North BOL BL1.....35 M3
Back Victory St East BOL BL1.....35 M4
Back View BOLS/LL BL3.....2 A9
Back Viking St North BOLS/LL BL3.....36 D8
Back Vincent St BOL BL1.....2 A6
Back Vine St BOLS/LL BL3.....35 M6
Back Viola St BOL BL1.....36 B1
Back Waldeck St BOL BL1.....35 M4
Back Walmersley Rd East BURY BL9.....5 G1
Back Walmersley Rd West BURY BL9.....5 G1
WGN WN1.....15 J3
WGNE/HIN WN2.....65 L3
WGNS/IIMK WN3.....15 J6
WGNW/BIL/O WN5.....46 E7
Back Walnut St BOL BL1.....36 C1
Back Walshaw Rd North TOT/BURYW BL8.....4 A3
Back Walshaw Rd South TOT/BURYW BL8.....38 F1
Back Wapping St BOL * BL1.....36 A2
Back Wardle St BOLE BL2.....3 K8
Back Wash La BURY BL9.....5 J4
Back Wash La South BURY BL9.....5 J4
Back Water St EDGW/EG BL7.....22 A2
STKP * SK1.....13 K2
Back Waverley Rd BOL BL1.....36 B1
Back Webster St BOLS/LL * BL3.....36 E8
Back Wellington Rd South BOL * BL1.....4 E8
Back Wells St BURY BL9.....4 D7
Back Westbourne Av BOLS/LL BL3.....52 D1
Back Weston St North BOLS/LL * BL3.....36 D8
Back Weston St South BOLS/LL BL3.....36 C8
Back Westwood Rd BOL * BL1.....35 M4
Back Wheatfield St BOLE BL2.....3 L8
Back Whittle Gv BOL * BL1.....35 L3
Back Whittle St TOT/BURYW BL8.....4 A2
Back Wigan Rd BOLS/LL BL3.....35 K8
Back Wigan Rd North BOLS/LL BL3.....35 K8
Back Wigan Rd South BOLS/LL * BL3.....35 L7
Back Willows BOLS/LL BL3.....35 L8
Back Willows La BOLS/LL BL3.....35 M8
Back Willows La North BOLS/LL BL3.....35 M8
Back Willows La South BOLS/LL * BL3.....35 M8
Back Wilmot St BOL * BL1.....35 M1
Back Wilton St BOL BL1.....36 C1
Back Windermere St BOL BL1.....36 C1
Back Windsor Gv BOL BL1.....35 M3
Back Wolfenden St BOL * BL1.....36 B2
Back Woodbine Rd BOLS/LL BL3.....51 M1
Back Woodfield St BOLS/LL * BL3.....52 D1
Back Woodgate St BOLS/LL BL3.....52 D1
Back Wood St HOR/BR BL6.....33 M1
MILN OL16.....29 K6
TOT/BURYW BL8.....24 D3
Back Worcester St BOL BL1.....36 B3
Back Wordsworth St BOL BL1.....36 A2
Back Worsel St BOLS/LL BL3.....35 M8
Back Worsel St North BOLS/LL * BL3.....35 M8
Back Wright St HOR/BR BL6.....21 B8
Back Wynne St BOL BL1.....36 B2
Back Yates St BOLE BL2.....3 H1
Baclaw Cl WGN WN1.....48 C3
Bacon Av DTN/ASHW M34.....101 K5
Bacup St NEWH/MOS M40.....73 M4
Badbury Cl RNFD/HAY WA11.....78 A5
Badby Cl M4.....88 A3
Badder St BOL BL1.....2 C3
Bader Dr HEY OL10.....41 G5
Badger Cl MILN OL16.....42 F1
Badger Edge La OLDE OL4.....60 F1
Badger La MILN OL16.....42 E2
Badger St BURY BL9.....5 G2
Badgers Wk WYTH/NTH M22.....119 G3
Badgers Wy GLSP SK13.....104 E5
Bag La ATH M46.....50 E8
Bagnall Cl UPML OL3.....61 M9
WHIT OL12.....27 J2
Bagot St OP/CLY M11.....88 D2
SWIN M27.....69 M3
Bagshaw La WGNE/HIN WN2.....49 L2
Bagshaw St HYDE SK14.....91 G7
Bagslate Moor La ROCH OL11.....27 J4
Bagslate Moor Rd ROCH OL11.....27 J5
Bagstock Av POY/DIS SK12.....129 J2
Baguley Crs EDGY/DAV SK3.....112 A6
Baguley Dr WHTF M45.....55 K2
Baguley La SALE M33.....109 H2
Baguley Rd SALE M33.....97 H8
Baguley St DROY M43.....89 L3
Bahama Cl RNFD/HAY WA11.....78 A4
Bahama Rd RNFD/HAY WA11.....78 A4
Baildon Rd ROCH OL11.....27 L3
Baildon St NEWH/MOS M40.....73 K3
Bailey Fold BOLS/LL BL3.....50 E4
Bailey La BOLE * BL2.....37 H3
MANAIR M90.....118 D3
PART M31.....94 C8
Bailey Rd TRPK M17.....85 K5
Bailey St OP/CLY * M11.....9 L5
OP/CLY M11.....89 G3
PWCH M25.....55 M7
Bailey Wk ALT WA14.....116 E4
Baillie St MILN OL16.....10 F3
RAD M26.....39 H7
Baillie St East MILN OL16.....11 G3
The Bails BRO M7.....71 M6
Bainbridge Av GOL/RIS/CU WA3.....80 B4
Bainbridge Cl WGTN/LGST * M12.....88 A6
Bainburgh Clough OLDS OL8.....59 M8
Baines Av IRL M44.....94 C3
Baines St BOL BL1.....35 L4
Bain St SWIN M27.....70 C5
Baird St CMANE M1.....7 K6
Baitings Cl WHIT OL12.....26 F2
Baker St FWTH BL4.....53 G5
STLY SK15.....91 L3
WGNS/IIMK WN3.....14 D8
DTN/ASHW M34.....101 K4
Bakewell Dr WGNNW/ST WN6.....31 K8
Bakewell Rd BRAM/HZG SK7.....122 A4
DROY M43.....84 E4
ECC M30.....84 C3
STRET M32.....96 D1
Bakewell St EDGY/DAV SK3.....12 F7
GTN M18.....88 F8
Bala Cl ORD M5.....86 D2
Balcarres Av WGN WN1.....48 B2
Balcarres Rd WGNE/HIN WN2.....32 E8
Balcary Gv BOL BL1.....35 L4
Balcombe Cl TOT/BURYW BL8.....24 E5
Balderstone Rd ROCH OL11.....42 D2
Baldock Rd DID/WITH M20.....111 G1
Baldrine Dr WGNE/HIN WN2.....49 L7
Baldwin Rd BNG/LEV M19.....99 J6
Baldwin St BOLS/LL BL3.....2 C8
WGN WN1.....15 J3
WGNE/HIN WN2.....65 L3
WGNS/IIMK WN3.....15 J6
WGNW/BIL/O WN5.....46 E7
Bale St CMANW M2.....6 F6
Balfour Gv RDSH SK5.....100 C3
Balfour Rd ALT WA14.....108 A5
URM M41.....95 L2
WHIT OL12.....27 M3
Balfour St CHH M8.....72 D4
OLDE OL4.....59 M5
ROY/SHW OL2.....43 L4
SLFD M6.....71 J6
Balham Wk WGTN/LGST M12.....88 C6
Balkan St RAD M26.....54 A4
Ballantine St NEWH/MOS M40.....73 M8
Ballantyne Wy GOL/RIS/CU WA3.....80 B4
Ballard Cl LIT OL15.....20 C5
Ballard Wy ROY/SHW OL2.....43 H5
Ballater Av URM M41.....95 K3
Ballater Cl HEY OL10.....40 D3
Ballbrook Av DID/WITH M20.....98 D7
Balleratt St BNG/LEV M19.....99 K3
Balliol Cl MPL/ROM SK6.....101 M8
Balliol St CHH M8.....72 D4
SWIN M27.....70 B4
Balliol Wy AIMK WN4.....63 J8
Balloon St ANC M4.....7 G2
Ball St MILN OL16.....11 G3
Ball Wk HYDE SK14.....103 J3
Balmain Av GTN M18.....99 M1
Balmain Rd URM M41.....95 L1
Balmer Rd NTHM/RTH M23.....109 K7
Balmfield St CHH M8.....72 D7
Balmford St HULME * M15.....6 B8
Balmoral Av BOLS/LL BL3.....53 K1
CHD/CHDH SK8.....120 C2
DTN/ASHW M34.....90 A5
GOL/RIS/CU WA3.....80 A3
HYDE SK14.....102 B4
ROCH OL11.....27 L4
ROY/SHW OL2.....43 J8
STRET M32.....97 G1
URM M41.....95 J3
WHTF M45.....55 K5
Balmoral Cl BURY BL9.....39 K7
HOR/BR BL6.....34 A2
MILN OL16.....29 K6
TOT/BURYW BL8.....24 D3
Balmoral Dr AULW OL7.....75 H7
Balmoral Gdns HTNM SK4.....111 K1
Balmoral Gra PWCH M25.....72 B1
Balmoral Gv BRAM/HZG SK7.....122 B1
Balmoral Rd AIMK WN4.....63 K8
FWTH BL4.....52 F5
HALE/TIMP WA15.....108 B8
HTNM SK4.....111 K1
RUSH/FAL M14.....99 G4
SWIN M27.....70 D2
URM M41.....95 K3
WGNW/BIL/O WN5.....47 H6
Balmoral St GTN M18.....88 F8
Balmoral Wy WILM/AE SK9.....126 E6
Balmore Cl BOLS/LL BL3.....51 K1
Balm St RAMS BL0.....17 B7
Balniel Wk WGN WN1.....48 B2
Balsam Cl BRUN/LGST M13.....7 K9
Balshaw Av IRL M44.....94 C2
Balshaw Cl BOLS/LL BL3.....35 M7
Balshaw Ct IRL M44.....94 D2
Baltic Rd ALT WA14.....107 K6
Baltic St SLFD M6.....86 B2
Baltimore St NEWH/MOS M40.....73 J7
Bamber Av SALE M33.....109 H1
Bamber Cft WHTN BL5.....50 B1
Bamber St BKLY M9.....57 G7
Bamber Wk BOLS/LL * BL3.....2 C8
Bamburgh Cl RAD M26.....37 M7
Bamburgh Dr AULW OL7.....75 H7
Bamburgh Pl AIMK WN4.....63 K7
Bamford Av DTN/ASHW M34.....101 J4
MDTN M24.....57 K2
Bamford Cl BURY BL9.....26 B8
CHD/CHDH SK8.....119 M4
Bamford Ct ROCH OL11.....27 L6
Bamford Dr WGNE/HIN WN2.....15 M1
Bamford Fold GLSP SK13.....104 B3
Bamford Gdns HALE/TIMP WA15.....109 G1
Bamford Gn GLSP SK13.....104 B3
Bamford Gv AUL OL6.....76 C6
Bamford Ms GLSP SK13.....104 B3
Bamford Rd DID/WITH M20.....110 D1
HEY OL10.....40 E1
RAMS BL0.....17 E4
Bamford St CHAD OL9.....8 C2
LIT OL15.....20 A7
OP/CLY M11.....89 G2
ROY/SHW OL2.....43 H8
STKP SK1.....13 K7
Bamford Wy ROCH OL11.....27 J6
Bampton Av WYTH/NTH M22.....118 E3
Bampton Cl OFTN SK2.....112 E5
WHTN BL5.....50 B3
Bampton Rd WYTH/NTH M22.....118 D3
Banbury Cl OLDE OL4.....60 A6
Banbury Dr ALT WA14.....108 A4
Banbury Ms SWIN M27.....70 A3
Banbury Rd FAIL M35.....74 B8
MDTN M24.....57 J7
NTHM/RTH M23.....109 J7
WGNW/BIL/O WN5.....62 A2
Banbury St BOLE BL2.....3 J5
STKP SK1.....13 J5
Bancroft Av CHD/CHDH SK8.....120 C6
Bancroft Cl MPL/ROM SK6.....113 H1
Bancroft Fold HYDE SK14.....91 L7
Bancroft Rd HALE/TIMP WA15.....117 J1
SWIN M27.....70 B3
Banff Gv HEY OL10.....40 D3
Banff Rd RUSH/FAL M14.....87 M8
Bangor Fold LEIGH WN7.....66 A4
Bangor St CHD/CHDH SK8.....111 J6
Bangor St AUL OL6.....91 H2
BOL BL1.....2 D2
HULME * M15.....87 G7
MILN * OL16.....11 J7
RDSH SK5.....100 C8
Banham Av WGNS/IIMK WN3.....62 F1
The Bank GLSP SK13.....93 M5
Bank Av WGNW/BIL/O WN5.....46 A7
Bank Barn La WHIT OL12.....19 L5
Bankbottom GLSP SK13.....93 K7
Bank Bridge Rd OP/CLY M11.....88 D1
Bankbrook WGNNW/ST WN6.....31 G8
Bank Buildings WGNE/HIN * WN2.....64 D2
Bank Cl LIT OL15.....29 K1
Banker St BOLS/LL BL3.....3 M9
Bankes Av WGNW/BIL/O WN5.....46 A7
Bankfield HYDE SK14.....91 G7
Bank Fid WHTN BL5.....50 C4
Bankfield Av BRUN/LGST M13.....99 H1
DROY M43.....89 K2
HTNM SK4.....12 D3
IRL M44.....94 A7
Bankfield Cl BOLE BL2.....37 M3
Bankfield Dr OLDS OL8.....75 L2
WALK M28.....68 D6
Bankfield La ROCH OL11.....27 H4
Bankfield Rd CHD/CHDH SK8.....120 B3
FWTH BL4.....53 C5
MPL/ROM SK6.....101 J2
SALE M33.....96 B6
TYLD M29.....68 A4
Bank Field St RAD M26.....54 A5
Bankfield St BKLY M9.....73 C3
BOLS/LL BL3.....35 M8
RDSH SK5.....100 C8
Bank Gv LHULT M38.....52 C6
Bank Hall HYDE * SK14.....38 D2
Bankhall Cl WGNE/HIN WN2.....65 L3
Bankhall La HALE/TIMP WA15.....117 G4
Bankhall Rd HTNM SK4.....111 K2
Bank Hey WHTN * BL5.....50 C4
Bankhirst Cl CHH M8.....59 L5
Bank House Cl TYLD M29.....68 B3
Bank House Rd BKLY M9.....56 F8
Bankhouse Rd TOT/BURYW BL8.....24 E8
Banklands Cl IRL M44.....94 A7
Bank La GLSP SK13.....93 K5
LHULT M38.....52 C6
SLFD M6.....71 H6
WHIT OL12.....19 M1
Bankley St BNG/LEV M19.....99 K3
Bank Meadow HOR/BR BL6.....21 C1
Bank Mellor Rd NM/HAY SK22.....124 E5
Bank Mere Cl WALK M28.....68 F7
Bankmill Cl BRUN/LGST M13.....7 K9
Bank Pas GOL/RIS/CU * WA3.....79 K3
Bank Pl CSLFD M3.....6 C3
Bank Rd CHH M8.....72 D2
MPL/ROM SK6.....113 K1
STLY SK15.....77 H7
Banks Ct LEIGH WN7.....66 A7
Banks Cft HEY OL10.....41 G5
Bankside HALE/TIMP WA15.....117 M6
HYDE SK14.....105 G3
Bank Side WHTN BL5.....50 C4
Bankside Av AIMK WN4.....63 K4
RAD M26.....38 D3
UPML OL3.....61 M5
Bankside Cl CHAD OL9.....8 E6
MPL/ROM SK6.....114 E3
WILM/AE SK9.....127 H3
Bankside Ct HTNM * SK4.....111 K2
Bankside Rd DID/WITH M20.....110 E5
Banks La STKP SK1.....112 E4
Bank Stanway Av BOLS/LL BL3.....2 B7
Bank St AULW OL7.....90 E2
BOL BL1.....2 C4
BRO M7.....72 C4
BURY BL9.....4 D5
CHD/CHDH SK8.....111 H6
CSLFD M3.....6 A3
DROY M43.....89 J4
DTN/ASHW M34.....101 L4
EDGW/EG BL7.....22 E2
FWTH BL4.....53 G4
GLSP SK13.....93 J7
GLSP SK13.....105 G4
GOL/RIS/CU WA3.....79 K3
HEY OL10.....41 H4
HYDE SK14.....102 A1
MPL/ROM SK6.....113 K1
NM/HAY SK22.....125 M2
OLDE OL4.....60 A6
OP/CLY M11.....88 D2
RAD M26.....38 E5
RAMS BL0.....17 E5
ROCH OL11.....28 B3
SALE M33.....96 F7
TOT/BURYW BL8.....24 C8
WGNE/HIN WN2.....64 D1
WGNW/BIL/O WN5.....47 H6
WHTF M45.....55 H3
Bankswood Cl GLSP SK13.....93 K8
Bank Top AUL OL6.....90 F2
HEY OL10.....40 E1
Bank Top Gv BOL BL1.....22 D7
Bank Top Pk OLDE OL4.....60 A6
Bank Top St HEY OL10.....40 E1
Bank Wd BOL BL1.....35 J5
Bankwood WGNNW/ST WN6.....30 B6
Banky La SALE M33.....95 M6
Bannach Dr CHAD OL9.....58 D4
Bannatyne Cl NEWH/MOS M40.....74 B3
Bannerman Av PWCH M25.....71 L3
Bannerman Rd DROY M43.....89 L3
Bannerman St WGNE/HIN WN2.....15 K3
WGNS/IIMK WN3.....15 K3
Bannister Dr CHD/CHDH SK8.....111 H4
Bannister St BOLE BL2.....37 H2
OFTN SK2.....13 K8
Bannister Wy WGNS/IIMK WN3.....62 F1

Bann St *EDGY/DAV* SK3 .....13 G6
Banstead Av *WYTH/NTH* M22 .....110 A5
Bantry Av *BKLY* M9 .....72 E1
Bantry St *BOLS/LL* BL3 .....2 C9
Baptist St *ANC* M4 .....7 J1
Barathea Rd *BOLS/LL* BL3 .....41 K1
Barbara Rd *BOLS/LL* BL3 .....51 F1
Barbara St *BOL* BL2 .....36 A8
Barbeck Rd *NEWH/MOS* M40 .....88 B1
Barberry Bank *EDGW/EG* BL7 .....22 A2
Barberry Cl *ALT* WA14 .....107 L4
Barber St *GLSP* SK13 .....93 L7
OP/CLY * M11 .....89 H5
Barbican St *WGTN/LGST* M20 .....98 E5
Barbon Wk *ANC* M4 .....7 L3
Barbrook Cl *WGNNW/ST* WN6 .....30 E2
Barbury Cl *LEIGH* WN7 .....66 C5
Barchester Av *BOLE* BL2 .....37 H3
Barcheston Rd *CHD/CHDH* SK8 .....110 F8
Barcicroft Rd *BNG/LEV* M19 .....99 H8
Barclay Rd *POY/DIS* SK12 .....129 J2
Barclays Av *SLFD* M6 .....71 G6
Barclyde St *ROCH* OL11 .....10 C8
STRET M32 .....96 C1
Barcombe Cl *OLDE* OL4 .....60 A2
Barcroft Rd *BOL* BL1 .....35 L2
Barcroft St *BURY* BL9 .....4 F2
Bardale Gv *AIMK* WN4 .....78 D1
Bardell Cl *POY/DIS* SK12 .....129 H2
Bardney Av *GOL/RIS/CU* WA3 .....79 J3
Bardon Cl *BOL* * BL1 .....36 A3
Bardon Rd *NTHM/RTH* M23 .....109 J6
Bardsea Rd *WYTH/NTH* M22 .....118 F3
Bardsley Av *FAIL* M35 .....74 C5
Bardsley Cl *BOLE* BL2 .....23 G7
HYDE SK14 .....103 H2
Bardsley Gate Av *STLY* SK15 .....92 B6
Bardsley St *CHAD* OL9 .....74 C1
HTNM SK4 .....112 A1
MDTN * M24 .....57 K3
NEWH/MOS M40 .....74 A7
OLDE OL4 .....60 A4
OLDE * OL4 .....60 B7
Bardsley Vale Av *OLDS* OL8 .....75 K4
Bardwell Av *WHTN* BL5 .....50 A4
Barehill St *LIT* OL15 .....20 C6
Bare St *BOL* * BL1 .....3 H3
Barff Rd *ORD* M5 .....85 M2
Barfold Cl *OFTN* SK2 .....113 F4
Barfoot Br *SALE* M33 .....96 F5
Barford Dr *GOL/RIS/CU* WA3 .....79 K4
WILM/AE SK9 .....127 G3
Barford Gv *HOR/BR* BL6 .....34 C3
Bar Gap Rd *OLD* OL1 .....9 K2
Barkan Wy *SWIN* M27 .....70 E4
Barker Rd *MPL/ROM* SK6 .....113 J1
Barker's La *SALE* M33 .....96 C7
Barker St *BURY* BL9 .....4 D7
CSLFD M3 .....72 C8
HEY OL10 .....40 E3
LEIGH WN7 .....65 M7
Barke St *MILN* OL16 .....29 H1
Barking St *NEWH/MOS* M40 .....88 B1
Bark St *BOL* BL1 .....2 D4
FWTH BL4 .....53 L7
Bark St East *BOL* BL1 .....2 E5
Bark Wk *HULME* M15 .....87 J6
Barkway Rd *STRET* M32 .....96 D3
Barkwell La *MOSL* OL5 .....76 E3
Bar La *BOL* BL1 .....22 B7
Barlborough Rd
WGNNW/ST WN5 .....47 G7
Barlea Av *NEWH/MOS* M40 .....74 A3
Barley Brook Meadow *BOL* BL1 .....22 C6
Barley Brook St
WGNNW/ST WN6 .....14 C1
Barleycorn Cl *SALE* M33 .....109 J1
Barley Cft *CHD/CHDH* SK8 .....120 B4
Barleycroft *GLSP* SK13 .....93 J8
Barley Croft Rd *HYDE* SK14 .....91 H6
Barleycroft St *OLDTF/WHR* M16 .....87 J8
Barley Dr *BRAM/HZG* SK7 .....121 G5
Barleyfield Wk *MDTN* M24 .....57 H3
Barley Hall St *HEY* OL10 .....41 H1
Barlow Ct *WALK* * M28 .....69 H1
Barlow Crs *MPL/ROM* SK6 .....114 C8
Barlow Fold *BURY* BL9 .....39 J7
Barlow Fold Cl *BURY* BL9 .....39 H7
Barlow Fold Rd *MPL/ROM* SK6 .....114 A1
RDSH SK5 .....100 C5
Barlow Hall Rd *CCHDY* M21 .....97 M7
Barlow La *ECC* M30 .....84 F2
Barlow La North *RDSH* SK5 .....100 C5
Barlow Moor Cl *WHIT* OL12 .....27 H2
Barlow Moor Ct *DID/WITH* M20 .....98 C8
Barlow Moor Rd *CCHDY* M21 .....97 L5
DID/WITH M20 .....98 B8
Barlow Park Av *BOL* BL1 .....22 A7
Barlow Pl *BRUN/LGST* M13 .....7 L9
Barlow Rd *ALT* WA14 .....107 L4
BNG/LEV M19 .....99 M3
DUK SK16 .....91 G4
ORD M5 .....86 F3
STRET M32 .....86 C8
WILM/AE SK9 .....126 F3
Barlow's La South
BRAM/HZG SK7 .....121 L1
Barlow St *BURY* BL9 .....5 G3
ECC M30 .....85 G3
HEY OL10 .....40 F2
HOR/BR BL6 .....33 M2
MILN OL16 .....11 G4
OLDE OL4 .....9 M7
RAD M26 .....54 E1
WALK M28 .....53 G8
Barlow Wood Dr
MPL/ROM SK6 .....123 K1
Barmeadow *UPML* OL3 .....61 J2
Barmhouse Cl *HYDE* SK14 .....102 D1
Barmhouse La *HYDE* SK14 .....102 D1
Barmhouse Ms *HYDE* SK14 .....102 D1
Barmouth St *OP/CLY* M11 .....88 C4
Barmouth Wk *OLDS* OL8 .....74 E2
Barnaby Rd *POY/DIS* SK12 .....129 H2
Barnabys St *WHTN* BL5 .....50 A1
Barn Acre *HOR/BR* BL6 .....33 H3
Barnacre Av *BOLE* BL2 .....37 J5
NTHM/RTH M23 .....118 B1
Barnard Av *HTNM* SK4 .....12 A1
WHTF M45 .....55 L5
Barnard Cl *AULW* OL7 .....75 J8
Barnard Rd *GTN* M18 .....99 L1
Barnard St *BOLE* * BL2 .....3 L3
Barnbrook St *BURY* BL9 .....5 H5
Barnby St *WGTN/LGST* M12 .....99 L1
Barn Cl *GLSP* SK13 .....105 G5

URM M41 .....94 F2
Barnclose Rd *WYTH/NTH* M22 .....118 F3
Barn Ct *BOLE* * BL2 .....36 F2
Barn Cft *HOR/BR* BL6 .....34 C1
Barncroft Gdns
WYTH/NTH * M22 .....109 M7
Barncroft Rd *FWTH* BL4 .....53 G4
Barnes Av *HTNM* SK4 .....111 K2
Barnes Cl *FWTH* BL4 .....53 G4
Barnes Mdw *LIT* OL15 .....20 D3
Barnes St *NEWH/MOS* M40 .....73 M7
Barneswell St *NEWH/MOS* M40 .....73 M7
Barnet Rd *BOL* * BL1 .....35 L2
Barnett Av *DID/WITH* M20 .....98 E6
Barnett Dr *CSLFD* M3 .....6 B2
Barnfield *URM* M41 .....95 L4
Barnfield Av *MPL/ROM* SK6 .....114 A1
Barnfield Cl *EDGW/EG* BL7 .....86 C3
ORD M5 .....86 C3
RAD M26 .....54 B1
TYLD M29 .....67 J3
Barnfield Crs *SALE* M33 .....96 C7
Barnfield Dr *WALK* M28 .....68 A6
WHTN BL5 .....50 D3
Barn Field La *WHIT* OL12 .....19 H5
Barnfield Ri *ROY/SHW* OL2 .....43 K3
Barnfield Rd *BNG/LEV* M19 .....99 H8
HYDE SK14 .....91 L7
SWIN M27 .....70 A2
Barnfield Rd East
EDGY/DAV SK3 .....112 C8
Barnfield Rd West
EDGY/DAV SK3 .....112 A8
Barnfield St *DTN/ASHW* M34 .....90 A8
HEY OL10 .....41 H2
WHIT OL12 .....28 C2
Barn Fold *OLDE* OL4 .....60 B7
Barngate Dr *MOSL* OL5 .....76 F4
Barngate Rd *CHD/CHDH* SK8 .....110 D6
Barngill Gv *WGNS/IIMK* WN3 .....63 H1
Barn Gv *DTN/ASHW* M34 .....90 A5
Barnham Cl *GOL/RIS/CU* WA3 .....79 K4
Barn Hl *WHTN* BL5 .....50 B3
Barnhill Av *PWCH* M25 .....71 L2
Barnhill Dr *PWCH* M25 .....71 L2
Barnhill Rd *PWCH* M25 .....71 K1
Barnhill St *RUSH/FAL* M14 .....87 J8
Barn Hill Ter *WHTN* BL5 .....50 B3
Barn La *GOL/RIS/CU* WA3 .....79 J5
Barnley Cl *IRL* M44 .....94 C1
Barn Meadow *EDGW/EG* BL7 .....16 D7
Barnsdale Cl *BOLE* BL2 .....37 M3
Barnsdale Dr *CHH* M8 .....72 D6
Barnside Av *WALK* M28 .....69 H4
Barnside Cl *BURY* BL9 .....25 H4
Barnside Wy *FAIL* M35 .....74 F5
Barns La *LYMM* WA13 .....106 C3
Barnsley St *STKP* SK1 .....13 M6
Barns Pl *HALE/TIMP* WA15 .....117 L4
Barnstable Dr *NEWH/MOS* M40 .....72 F6
Barnstead Av *DID/WITH* M20 .....99 G7
Barnston Av *RUSH/FAL* M14 .....98 E2
Barnston Cl *BOL* BL1 .....22 C8
Barn St *BOL* BL1 .....2 D5
OLD OL1 .....9 H6
WHTF M45 .....55 J5
Barnton Cl *GOL/RIS/CU* WA3 .....80 A5
Barnview Dr *IRL* M44 .....94 D3
Barnwell Av *GOL/RIS/CU* WA3 .....89 L8
Barnwell Cl *DTN/ASHW* M34 .....90 B7
Barnwood Cl *BOL* * BL1 .....36 B3
Barnwood Dr *BOL* BL1 .....36 B3
Barnwood Rd *NTHM/RTH* M23 .....118 F3
Barnwood Ter *BOL* BL1 .....36 B3
Baroness Gv *BOL* M7 .....71 M8
Baron Fold Crs *LHULT* M38 .....52 C7
Baron Fold Gv *LHULT* M38 .....52 C7
Baron Fold Rd *LHULT* * M38 .....52 C7
Baron Gn *CHD/CHDH* SK8 .....119 M5
Baron Rd *HYDE* SK14 .....102 C5
Barons Ct *FAIL* M35 .....74 A6
Baron St *BURY* BL9 .....4 C6
MILN OL16 .....10 F5
Barrack Hl *MPL/ROM* SK6 .....113 M1
Barrack Hill Cl *MPL/ROM* SK6 .....113 K1
Barrack Sq *WGN* * WN1 .....15 G4
Barrack St *HULME* M15 .....6 A9
Barracks Yd *WGN* WN1 .....14 F4
Barra Dr *URM* M41 .....85 G3
Barrass St *OP/CLY* M11 .....89 G5
Barratt Gdns *MDTN* M24 .....57 G1
Barrett Av *FWTH* BL4 .....53 J5
Barrett Ct *BURY* BL9 .....5 J4
Barrett St *OLDE* OL4 .....59 L1
Barrfield Rd *SLFD* M6 .....71 H8
Barr Hill Av *SLFD* M6 .....71 H7
Barrhill Cl *HULME* M15 .....87 G6
Barrie St *LEIGH* WN7 .....66 A4
Barrie Wy *BOL* BL1 .....22 E8
Barrington Av *CHD/CHDH* SK8 .....120 C2
DROY M43 .....89 J3
Barrington Rd *ALT* WA14 .....108 A6
Barrington St *OP/CLY* M11 .....88 F2
Barrisdale Cl *BOLS/LL* BL3 .....35 J7
Barrow Bridge Rd *WGN* WN1 .....31 L3
Barrowcroft Cl *WGN* WN1 .....31 L3
Barrowdale Rd
GOL/RIS/CU WA3 .....79 L4
Barrowfield Rd
WYTH/NTH M22 .....118 C2
Barrowfields *MDTN* M24 .....57 K2
Barrow Hill Rd *CHH* M8 .....72 C7
Barrow La *HALE/TIMP* WA15 .....117 K5
Barrow Meadow
CHD/CHDH SK8 .....120 A4
Barrows Ct *BOL* BL1 .....2 E6
Barrowshaw Cl *WALK* M28 .....68 F2
Barrow St *AIMK* WN4 .....64 A7
CSLFD M3 .....6 B7
Barrs Fold Cl *WHTN* BL5 .....50 A1
Barrs Fold Rd *WHTN* BL5 .....50 A1
Barrule Av *BRAM/HZG* SK7 .....122 A3
Barry Crs *WALK* M28 .....68 D1
Barry Lawson Cl *CHH* * M8 .....72 C5
Barry Ri *ALT* WA14 .....116 C2
Barry Rd *NTHM/RTH* M23 .....109 L2
RDSH SK5 .....100 C2
Barry St *OLD* OL1 .....59 L4
Barsham Dr *BOLS/LL* BL3 .....2 B8
Bar St *WGNE/HIN* WN2 .....64 D3
Bar Ter *WHIT* OL12 .....18 D1

Bartlam Pl *OLD* OL1 .....9 K5
Bartlemore St *OLD* OL1 .....9 M1
Bartlett Rd *ROY/SHW* OL2 .....43 K6
Bartlett St *OP/CLY* M11 .....88 E5
Bartley Rd *WYTH/NTH* M22 .....109 M4
Barton Av *URM* M41 .....95 L2
WGN WN1 .....47 L2
Barton Cl *WILM/AE* SK9 .....127 H2
Barton Clough
WGNW/BIL/O WN5 .....85 B7
Barton Dock Rd *URM* M41 .....85 G5
Barton Fold *HYDE* SK14 .....102 A3
Barton Hall Av *ECC* M30 .....84 D3
Barton Highlevel Br *ECC* M30 .....84 E5
Barton La *ECC* M30 .....85 J3
Barton Moss Rd *ECC* M30 .....83 M4
Barton Rd *ECC* M30 .....84 E5
FWTH BL4 .....52 E5
HTNM SK4 .....111 H3
HYDE SK14 .....90 F7
MDTN M24 .....57 J4
STRET M32 .....96 E2
SWIN M27 .....70 D5
URM M41 .....84 F8
WALK M28 .....69 J7
Barton St *CSLFD* M3 .....6 D7
FWTH BL4 .....53 H5
GOL/RIS/CU WA3 .....79 K4
OLD OL1 .....8 E2
WGNE/HIN WN2 .....64 E1
WGNE/HIN WN2 .....46 E7
Barway Rd *CCHDY* M21 .....97 J3
Barwell Cl *GOL/RIS/CU* WA3 .....79 M3
RDSH SK5 .....100 F4
Barwell Rd *SALE* M33 .....96 B7
Barwell Sq *FWTH* BL4 .....52 E2
Barwick Pl *SALE* M33 .....96 B8
Basechurch Wk
WGTN/LGST * M12 .....88 C6
Basford Rd *OLDTF/WHR* M16 .....97 L1
Bashall St *BOL* BL1 .....35 M4
Basil Ct *MILN* OL16 .....11 K6
Basildon Cl *BRUN/LGST* M13 .....88 A7
Basil St *BOLS/LL* BL3 .....2 C8
HTNM SK4 .....12 F1
MILN OL16 .....11 K6
RUSH/FAL * M14 .....98 F1
Basle Cl *BRAM/HZG* SK7 .....121 G1
Baslow Av *BNG/LEV* M19 .....99 J2
WGNE/HIN WN2 .....49 J8
Baslow Dr *BRAM/HZG* SK7 .....122 B4
CHD/CHDH SK8 .....119 L4
Baslow Ms *GLSP* SK13 .....104 B3
Baslow Rd *DROY* M43 .....89 H1
DTN/ASHW M34 .....101 J4
STRET M32 .....96 D1
Baslow St *OP/CLY* M11 .....88 B3
Basset Av *SLFD* M6 .....71 M7
Bassett Gv *WGNS/IIMK* WN3 .....62 F2
Bassett Wy *WHIT* OL12 .....28 B2
Bass La *BURY* BL9 .....25 H1
Bass St *BOLE* BL2 .....3 L4
DUK SK16 .....90 E4
Basswood Gn *WGNE/HIN* WN2 .....65 K1
Basten Dr *BOL* M7 .....72 A6
Batchelor Cl *CCHDY* M21 .....98 B5
Bateman St *HOR/BR* BL6 .....34 A2
Batemill Rd *NM/HAY* SK22 .....124 F2
Bates Cl *ROCH* OL11 .....42 A3
Bateson St *STKP* SK1 .....13 L3
Bateson Wy *OLDS* * OL8 .....9 J8
Bates St *BRUN/LGST* M13 .....88 C8
DUK SK16 .....90 F4
Bath Cl *BRAM/HZG* SK7 .....122 C2
Bath Crs *CHD/CHDH* SK8 .....120 D6
OLDTF/WHR M16 .....86 F7
Batheaston Gv *LEIGH* WN7 .....66 A5
Bath St *ALT* WA14 .....116 F2
AIM M46 .....66 D1
BOL BL1 .....2 D8
CHAD OL9 .....8 D8
WGNE/HIN WN2 .....48 C2
WHIT OL12 .....11 H1
Batley St *BKLY* M9 .....73 H4
Batridge Rd *EDGW/EG* BL7 .....16 A5
Battenberg Rd *BOL* * BL1 .....35 M4
Battersbay Gv *BRAM/HZG* SK7 .....122 A2
Battersby Ct *OFTN* * SK2 .....113 H6
Battersby St *BURY* BL9 .....26 A8
LEIGH WN7 .....66 E8
OP/CLY * M11 .....89 H5
ROCH OL11 .....27 L6
WGNE/HIN WN2 .....49 K1
Battersea Rd *HTNM* SK4 .....111 H3
Batty St *CHH* M8 .....72 F7
Baucher Rd *WGNS/IIMK* WN3 .....47 J7
The Baum *MILN* OL16 .....10 E3
Baverstock Cl *WGNS/IIMK* WN3 .....15 J7
Baxendale St *BOL* BL1 .....22 B8
Baxter Gdns *NTHM/RTH* M23 .....109 K5
Baxter Rd *SALE* M33 .....96 E8
Baxter's Rw *WGNE/HIN* WN2 .....65 L2
Baxter St *OLDS* OL8 .....74 E2
Baybutt St *RAD* * M26 .....54 F1
Baycliff Cl *WGNE/HIN* WN2 .....65 J1
Baycroft Gv *NTHM/RTH* M23 .....109 K3
Baydon Av *CHH* M8 .....72 C6
Bayfield Gv *NEWH/MOS* * M40 .....73 K3
Bayley Ct *BOL* BL1 .....2 A2
Bayley St *STLY* SK15 .....91 H2
Baysdale Av *BOLS/LL* BL3 .....35 J8
Bayston Wk *WGTN/LGST* M12 .....88 C6
Bay St *CHAD* OL9 .....8 E5
HEY OL10 .....40 E1
WHIT OL12 .....11 H1
Bayswater Av *NEWH/MOS* M40 .....73 L8
Bayswater St *BOLS/LL* BL3 .....51 M2
Baythorpe St *BOL* BL1 .....36 C1
Baytree Av *CHAD* OL9 .....58 B4
DTN/ASHW M34 .....90 A8
Baytree Dr *MPL/ROM* SK6 .....101 J8
Baytree Gv *RAMS* BL0 .....24 E2
Baytree La *MDTN* M24 .....58 A4
Baytree Rd *WGNNW/ST* WN6 .....47 J2
Baytree Wk *WHIT* OL12 .....18 D5
Baywood St *BKLY* M9 .....73 G4
Bazaar St *SLFD* M6 .....71 K8
Bazley Rd *WYTH/NTH* M22 .....110 A3
Bazley St *BOL* BL1 .....3 K9
Beacomfold *MPL/ROM* SK6 .....114 E1
Beacon Dr *NTHM/RTH* M23 .....118 C2
Beacon Dr *NTHM/RTH* M23 .....118 C2
Beacon Hl *WGNW/BIL/O* WN5 .....62 A5
Beacon Rd *MPL/ROM* SK6 .....113 K3

TRPK M17 .....85 H5
WGNE/HIN WN2 .....65 K4
WGNW/ST WN6 .....30 E1
WGNW/BIL/O WN5 .....62 A6
Beacons Vw *WGNNW/ST* WN6 .....30 A5
Beaconsfield *RUSH/FAL* * M14 .....98 F5
Beaconsfield Rd *ALT* WA14 .....108 A5
Beaconsfield St *BOLS/LL* BL3 .....2 A7
Beaconsfield Ter *STLY* SK15 .....77 J5
Beacon Vw *MPL/ROM* SK6 .....114 C4
Beadham Dr *BKLY* M9 .....56 D7
Beaford Cl *WGNW/BIL/O* WN5 .....46 E7
Beaford Dr *WYTH/NTH* M22 .....118 F4
Bealbank Cl *MILN* OL16 .....43 K1
Beal Cl *HTNM* SK4 .....111 G1
Beal Crs *MILN* OL16 .....11 H1
Bealcroft Cl *MILN* OL16 .....29 H5
Beal Dr *WGNE/HIN* WN2 .....64 D2
Beale Gv *CCHDY* M21 .....97 L4
Bealey Av *RAD* M26 .....39 H7
Bealey Cl *GTN* M18 .....88 E6
RAD M26 .....39 G8
Bealey Dr *BURY* BL9 .....39 G5
Beal La *ROY/SHW* OL2 .....43 M6
Beaminster Rd *HTNM* SK4 .....111 J1
Beaminster Wk
BRUN/LGST M13 .....87 M7
Beamish Cl *BRUN/LGST* M13 .....87 M6
Beamsley Dr *WYTH/NTH* M22 .....118 D2
Beanfields *WALK* M28 .....69 J7
Bean Leach Av *OFTN* SK2 .....113 J6
Bean Leach Dr *OFTN* SK2 .....113 J6
Bean Leach Rd *BRAM/HZG* SK7 .....113 H6
Beard Crs *NM/HAY* SK22 .....124 F4
Beard Rd *GTN* * M18 .....88 F8
Beardsmore Dr
GOL/RIS/CU WA3 .....80 A4
Beard St *DROY* M43 .....89 J3
ROY/SHW OL2 .....59 H1
Beardwood Rd *BKLY* M9 .....57 G8
Bearswood Cl *HYDE* SK14 .....102 C3
Beathwaite Dr *BRAM/HZG* SK7 .....120 E8
Beatrice Av *CHD/CHDH* SK8 .....120 B2
GTN M18 .....89 J8
Beatrice Rd *BOL* BL1 .....35 M4
WALK M28 .....69 L5
Beatrice St *DTN/ASHW* M34 .....101 H1
FWTH BL4 .....53 L7
ROCH * OL11 .....10 A5
SWIN M27 .....70 A3
Beatrice Wignall St *DROY* * M43 .....89 K4
Beatrix Dr *GLSP* SK13 .....104 B1
Beatson Wk *ANC* M4 .....7 L4
Beattock Cl *HULME* * M15 .....6 B9
Beattock St *HULME* M15 .....6 B9
Beatty Dr *WHTN* BL5 .....50 B3
Beauchamp St *AUL* OL6 .....90 F1
Beaufont Dr *OLDE* OL4 .....59 M7
Beaufort Av *DID/WITH* M20 .....98 C7
SALE M33 .....108 F2
SWIN M27 .....70 A5
Beaufort Cha *WILM/AE* SK9 .....127 K3
Beaufort Cl *HYDE* SK14 .....103 F1
SALE M33 .....108 F1
Beaufort Rd *AUL* OL6 .....91 G1
HYDE SK14 .....103 H2
OFTN SK2 .....113 G6
SALE M33 .....108 F1
Beaufort St *CSLFD* M3 .....6 C7
ECC M30 .....84 E1
PWCH M25 .....55 M8
WGNE/HIN * WN2 .....49 C7
WGNW/BIL/O WN5 .....47 H6
WHIT OL12 .....28 A3
Beauly Cl *RAMS* BL0 .....24 D2
Beaumaris Cl *LEIGH* WN7 .....65 M7
Beaumaris Crs *BRAM/HZG* SK7 .....121 L4
Beaumaris Rd *WGNE/HIN* WN2 .....65 K1
Beaumonds Wy *ROCH* OL11 .....27 J6
Beaumont Av *HOR/BR* BL6 .....33 G4
Beaumont Cha *BOLS/LL* BL3 .....51 J1
Beaumont Cl *LIT* OL15 .....20 A7
Beaumont Gv
WGNW/BIL/O WN5 .....46 E4
Beaumont Rd *CCHDY* M21 .....97 L5
HOR/BR BL6 .....21 B8
HOR/BR BL6 .....35 H6
Beaumont St *AUL* OL6 .....90 F1
Beauvale Dr *OFTN* SK2 .....112 F5
Beaverbrook Av
GOL/RIS/CU WA3 .....81 L8
Beaver Ct *AIMK* WN4 .....63 H6
Beaver Dr *BURY* BL9 .....39 G8
Beaver Rd *DID/WITH* M20 .....110 E1
Beaver St *CMANE* M1 .....7 G7
Bebbington Cl *SALE* M33 .....109 J2
Bebbington St *OP/CLY* * M11 .....88 F3
Beccles Rd *SALE* M33 .....108 E3
Beckenham Cl *BURY* BL9 .....38 E3
Beckenham Rd *CHH* M8 .....72 D5
Becket Av *BRO* M7 .....72 B6
Becket Mdw *OLDE* OL4 .....59 L4
Beckett Av *GTN* M18 .....88 F8
OLDE OL4 .....60 B5
Beckfield Rd *NTHM/RTH* M23 .....109 K7
Beckfoot Dr *BRUN/LGST* M13 .....99 H1
Beckford St *NEWH/MOS* M40 .....73 H7
Beck Gv *ROY/SHW* OL2 .....44 A4
WALK M28 .....69 H3
Beckhampton Cl
BRUN/LGST M13 .....87 M7
Beckley Av *PWCH* M25 .....71 K2
Beckley Cl *ROY/SHW* OL2 .....43 K8
Beckside *RDSH* SK5 .....100 C5
Beck St *CSLFD* M3 .....6 C3
OP/CLY * M11 .....89 H5
Beckton Gdns *WYTH/NTH* M22 .....118 E1
Beckwith *WGNE/HIN* WN2 .....64 E1
Becontree Av *DTN/ASHW* M34 .....90 A7
Becontree Dr *NTHM/RTH* M23 .....109 G6
Bedells La *WILM/AE* SK9 .....126 E6
Bede St *BOL* BL1 .....35 M2
Bedford Av *HYDE* SK14 .....102 B1
OLDTF/WHR M16 .....98 A2
ROY/SHW OL2 .....43 J5
SALE M33 .....109 G2
SWIN * M27 .....70 B5
WALK M28 .....53 G8
Bedford Dr *ATH* M46 .....66 D3
HALE/TIMP WA15 .....117 G4
Bedford Pl *AIMK* WN4 .....63 K7
Bedford Rd *ECC* M30 .....85 H1
OLDTF/WHR M16 .....97 K2
URM M41 .....84 F8
Bedford St *BOL* BL1 .....2 A3
BURY BL9 .....25 K8
EDGW/EG BL7 .....22 A2
HEY OL10 .....41 H2

LEIGH * WN7 .....66 D7
PWCH M25 .....55 M7
RDSH SK5 .....100 B5
WGN WN1 .....15 K2
WGNW/BIL/O * WN5 .....46 F7
Bedlam Gn *BURY* BL9 .....4 F4
Bednal Av *NEWH/MOS* M40 .....73 M8
Bedwell St *OLDTF/WHR* M16 .....98 C1
Beech Av *ATH* M46 .....67 H1
BOLS/LL BL3 .....53 L2
BRAM/HZG SK7 .....122 A2
CHAD OL9 .....58 D2
CHD/CHDH SK8 .....110 E7
DROY M43 .....89 J3
DTN/ASHW M34 .....90 A8
EDGY/DAV SK3 .....112 C6
FWTH BL4 .....53 L7
GLSP SK13 .....104 D4
GOL/RIS/CU WA3 .....80 C5
HOR/BR BL6 .....34 B3
IRL M44 .....94 F1
MPL/ROM SK6 .....114 A6
NM/HAY SK22 .....124 F3
OLDE OL4 .....60 A4
RAD M26 .....54 C4
RNFD/HAY WA11 .....78 C5
SLFD M6 .....71 H8
UPML OL3 .....61 L6
URM M41 .....95 M3
WHTF M45 .....55 J5
WYTH/NTH M22 .....110 A4
Beech Cl *BOLE* BL2 .....22 F6
PWCH M25 .....71 M1
WHIT OL12 .....18 D3
Beech Cottages *WILM/AE* * SK9 .....130 D4
Beech Ct *WILM/AE* * SK9 .....127 H6
Beech Crs *LEIGH* WN7 .....81 H1
POY/DIS SK12 .....122 A8
WGNW/ST WN6 .....31 H4
Beechcroft *PWCH* M25 .....71 M2
Beechcroft Av *BOLE* BL2 .....37 H6
Beechcroft Cl *NEWH/MOS* M40 .....88 A1
Beechcroft Gv *BOLE* BL2 .....37 H6
Beechdale Cl *NEWH/MOS* M40 .....73 M4
Beech Dr *LEIGH* WN7 .....81 J2
The Beeches *ATH* * M46 .....67 G1
BOL BL1 .....22 A6
DID/WITH M20 .....98 C8
MOSL OL5 .....77 H2
Beeches Ms *DID/WITH* M20 .....98 C8
Beechey Sq *OLD* * OL1 .....9 L4
Beechfield *ALT* WA14 .....116 E1
SALE M33 .....108 C2
Beechfield Av *LHULT* M38 .....52 D7
RAD M26 .....54 F3
URM M41 .....95 K1
WGNE/HIN WN2 .....49 K8
WILM/AE SK9 .....126 C7
Beechfield Cl *OLDE* OL4 .....60 C6
ROCH OL11 .....27 H6
Beechfield Dr *BURY* BL9 .....39 H5
LEIGH WN7 .....81 J1
Beechfield Ms *HYDE* * SK14 .....102 F1
Beechfield Rd *BOL* BL1 .....35 L2
CHD/CHDH SK8 .....120 D4
EDGY/DAV SK3 .....112 C8
GLSP SK13 .....104 B1
MILN OL16 .....29 H7
SWIN M27 .....70 B7
Beechfield St *CHH* M8 .....72 D6
Beech Gv *AULW* OL7 .....90 C3
LEIGH WN7 .....81 H2
LHULT M38 .....52 E1
RUSH/FAL M14 .....99 G4
SALE M33 .....96 C8
SLFD M6 .....71 H8
STLY SK15 .....91 J4
TOT/BURYW BL8 .....24 D3
WGNE/HIN WN2 .....64 F5
WGNNW/ST WN6 .....47 H1
WILM/AE SK9 .....126 E6
Beech Grove Cl *BURY* BL9 .....25 L8
Beech Hall St *WGNNW/ST* WN6 .....47 K2
Beech Hill Av *WGNNW/ST* WN6 .....47 K1
Beech Hill La *WGNNW/ST* WN6 .....47 L1
Beech Hill Rd *OLDE* OL4 .....60 F6
Beech Hurst Cl
OLDTF/WHR * M16 .....98 A1
Beech La *MPL/ROM* SK6 .....113 M2
OLDE OL4 .....61 G6
WILM/AE SK9 .....126 E6
Beech Ms *CCHDY* M21 .....97 K4
OFTN SK2 .....112 D7
Beech Mt *AULW* OL7 .....75 K6
BKLY M9 .....73 G4
Beechpark Av *WYTH/NTH* M22 .....109 M5
Beech Rd *CCHDY* M21 .....97 L4
CHD/CHDH SK8 .....120 D3
EDGY/DAV SK3 .....112 B6
GOL/RIS/CU WA3 .....79 K3
HALE/TIMP WA15 .....117 C1
MPL/ROM SK6 .....123 H5
SALE M33 .....97 G8
WGNE/HIN WN2 .....130 E1
Beech St *ATH* M46 .....67 H1
BOL BL1 .....36 C2
BURY BL9 .....5 K4
ECC M30 .....84 E3
EDGW/EG BL7 .....16 D7
FAIL M35 .....74 B4
HYDE SK14 .....102 A1
MDTN * M24 .....57 J4
MILN OL16 .....29 K8
OLD OL1 .....9 L5
RAD M26 .....54 F3
RAMS BL0 .....24 F1
ROCH OL11 .....10 B6
SWIN M27 .....70 C5
Beech Tree Av *WGNNW/ST* WN6 .....30 A4
Beech Tree Houses
WGNE/HIN WN2 .....49 K8
Beechurst Rd *CHD/CHDH* SK8 .....111 H4
Beech Vw *HYDE* SK14 .....102 D2
Beech Wk *LEIGH* WN7 .....81 H7
MDTN M24 .....57 J6
STRET M32 .....96 F4
WGNS/IIMK WN3 .....62 F2
Beechway *MPL/ROM* SK6 .....123 H5
WILM/AE SK9 .....126 D7
Beechwood *ALT* WA14 .....116 D3
GLSP SK13 .....104 C5
ROCH OL11 .....10 A8

ROY/SHW OL2 44 A4
Beechwood Av AIMK WN4 78 D2
CCHDY M21 97 M4
LIT OL15 29 K1
MPL/ROM SK6 113 M2
NEWLW WA12 79 G8
RAMS BL0 17 D6
STLY SK15 76 F8
URM M41 95 H1
WGNNW/ST WN6 30 C7
Beechwood Ct TOT/BURYW BL8 24 D7
Beechwood Crs TYLD M29 67 K6
WGNW/BIL/O WN5 46 B6
Beechwood Dr HYDE SK14 102 C3
MOSL OL5 76 F2
MPL/ROM SK6 114 D6
ROY/SHW OL2 42 F6
SALE M33 95 M8
WALK M28 69 L6
WILM/AE * SK9 127 J4
Beechwood Gv BKLY M9 73 H5
CHD/CHDH SK8 120 C4
Beechwood La
GOL/RIS/CU WA3 81 G8
Beechwood Rd OLDS OL8 75 J2
PWCH M25 72 A1
Beechwood St BOLS/LL BL3 52 C1
Beede St OP/CLY M11 88 E4
Beedon Av BOLS/LL BL3 37 K8
Bee Fold La ATH M46 66 E2
Beehive Gn WHTN BL5 50 E3
Beehive St OLDS OL8 75 J1
Beeley St HYDE SK14 102 B2
SLFD M6 71 L7
Beenham Cl SALE M33 107 M1
Beeston Av BRO M7 71 L6
HALE/TIMP WA15 108 C6
Beeston Cl BOL BL1 22 D6
Beeston Gv EDGY/DAV SK3 112 B7
LEIGH WN7 67 G5
WHTF M45 55 L5
Beeston Rd SALE M33 96 B8
WILM/AE SK9 119 M7
Beeston St BKLY M9 73 H5
Beeth St OP/CLY M11 89 G6
Beeton Gv BRUN/LGST M13 88 B8
Beever St OLD OL1 9 L4
OLDTF/WHR M16 86 F7
Begley Cl MPL/ROM SK6 113 J3
Begonia Av FWTH BL4 52 D3
Beilby Rd RNFD/HAY WA11 78 C5
Belayse Cl BOL BL1 35 L1
Belbeck St TOT/BURYW BL8 38 F2
Belbeck St South
TOT/BURYW BL8 4 A5
Belcroft Cl WYTH/NTH M22 110 B4
Belcroft Dr LHULT M38 52 B6
Belcroft Gv LHULT * M38 52 B7
Belding Av NEWH/MOS M40 74 C3
Beldon Rd BKLY M9 56 E8
Belfairs Cl AULW OL7 75 L6
Belfield Cl MILN OL16 11 M2
Belfield La MILN OL16 11 L4
MILN OL16 29 G5
Belfield Mill La MILN OL16 29 G4
Belfield Old Rd MILN OL16 11 L2
Belfield Rd DID/WITH M20 110 E1
MILN OL16 11 K2
PWCH M25 72 B1
Belford Av DTN/ASHW M34 100 D1
Belford Dr BOLS/LL BL3 36 B8
Belford Rd STRET M32 97 G1
Belfort Dr ORD M5 86 E4
Belfry Cl WILM/AE SK9 127 H4
Belfry Crs WGNNW/ST WN6 31 J2
Belgate Cl WGTN/LGST M12 88 D8
Belgium St ROCH OL11 27 H5
Belgrave Av FAIL M35 74 E4
MPL/ROM SK6 114 C6
OLDS OL8 59 K8
URM M41 95 H1
Belgrave Cl LEIGH WN7 80 F4
WGNS/IIMK WN3 63 G1
Belgrave Ct OLDS OL8 59 J8
Belgrave Crs ECC M30 85 J1
HOR/BR BL6 34 A1
OFTN SK2 112 D8
Belgrave Dr RAD M26 38 D8
Belgrave Gdns BOL BL1 36 B2
Belgrave Rd ALT WA14 116 E1
IRL M44 94 A7
NEWH/MOS M40 74 B3
OLDS OL8 59 J8
SALE M33 96 D8
Belgrave St ATH M46 66 D1
BOL BL1 36 B2
HEY OL10 40 F3
RAD M26 38 D8
WHIT OL12 10 A1
Belgrave St South BOL BL1 2 C1
Belgravia Gdns CCHDY M21 97 K4
HALE/TIMP WA15 117 G4
Belgravia Ms ROY/SHW OL2 43 M5
Belhaven Rd CHH M8 72 C2
Bellairs St BOLS/LL BL3 51 M1
Bellamy Dr LEIGH WN7 66 E7
Bella St BOLS/LL BL3 35 M8
Bell Clough Rd DROY M43 89 L1
Bell Crs OP/CLY M11 88 C4
Belldale Cl HTNM SK4 111 K2
Belldean WGNE/HIN WN2 48 D4
Belle Green La WGNE/HIN WN2 48 D4
Belle Isle Av WHIT OL12 18 D6
Bellerby Cl WHTF M45 55 H4
Belleville Av WYTH/NTH M22 119 G4
Belle Vue Av WGTN/LGST M12 88 C7
Belle Vue St WGNW/BIL/O WN5 47 G7
WGTN/LGST M12 88 D6
Belle Vue Ter BURY BL9 4 D6
Bellew St OP/CLY M11 88 B4
Bellfield Av CHD/CHDH SK8 120 D3
OLDS OL8 75 J2
Bellhill Gdns SLFD M6 86 C1
Bellingham Av WGN WN1 47 M2
Bellingham Cl ROY/SHW OL2 43 L4
TOT/BURYW BL8 38 C2
Bellingham Dr WGN WN1 47 M2
Bellingham Mt WGN WN1 48 A1
Bellis Cl WGTN/LGST M12 88 B3
Bell La BURY BL9 5 H3
MILN OL16 29 L5
WGNW/BIL/O WN5 46 E4
Bell Meadow Dr ROCH OL11 27 J7
Bellott St CHH M8 72 D6
Bellott Wk OLD * OL1 9 H2
Bellpit Cl WALK M28 68 F5
Bells Croft Av
NEWH/MOS * M40 73 L5
Bellshill Crs MILN OL16 11 M1
Bell St DROY M43 89 L2
LEIGH WN7 66 A3
MILN OL16 10 E3
OLD OL1 9 M4
WGNE/HIN WN2 49 H6
Bell Ter ECC M30 84 F4
Bellwood WHTN BL5 49 M5
Belmont Av ATH M46 51 J8
DTN/ASHW M34 90 A8
FWTH BL4 54 A7
GOL/RIS/CU WA3 79 M3
OLDE OL4 60 C5
SLFD M6 85 K1
WGNE/HIN WN2 65 J3
WGNW/BIL/O WN5 62 A1
Belmont Cl HTNM SK4 13 G1
Belmont Dr MPL/ROM SK6 114 E3
TOT/BURYW BL8 38 D3
WGNE/HIN WN2 32 F7
Belmont Rd BOL BL1 22 A6
BRAM/HZG SK7 121 G7
CHD/CHDH SK8 110 E6
HALE/TIMP WA15 117 G2
HOR/BR BL6 21 C3
RAD M26 54 D3
SALE M33 96 D6
WGNE/HIN WN2 49 J7
Belmont St ECC M30 85 G1
HTNM SK4 12 F1
OLD OL1 9 G3
OLDE OL4 60 B7
ORD M5 86 A3
Belmont Ter PART * M31 95 G6
Belmont Vw BOLE BL2 23 J8
Belmont Wk BRUN/LGST * M13 87 M6
Belmont Wy CHAD OL9 8 D2
HTNM SK4 13 G1
WHIT OL12 28 B2
Belper Rd ECC M30 84 E4
HTNM SK4 111 J3
Belroy Ct PWCH * M25 71 L1
Belsay Cl AULW OL7 75 H7
Belsay Dr NTHM/RTH M23 109 K8
Belsfield Ter AUL * OL6 75 M4
Belstone Av NTHM/RTH M23 118 C1
Belstone Cl BRAM/HZG SK7 121 H2
Belthorne Av BKLY M9 73 K2
Belton Av MILN OL16 11 M1
Beltone Cl STRET M32 96 E3
Belton Wk CHAD OL9 8 E6
Belvedere Av ATH M46 51 J8
RDSH SK5 100 C2
TOT/BURYW BL8 24 D3
Belvedere Cl LEIGH WN7 67 G5
Belvedere Ct PWCH * M25 71 K1
Belvedere Dr DUK SK16 91 H4
MPL/ROM SK6 112 F1
Belvedere Pl WGNS/IIMK WN3 47 J7
Belvedere Ri OLD OL1 60 A1
Belvedere Rd AIMK WN4 78 F1
NEWLW WA12 78 E8
RUSH/FAL M14 99 H4
SLFD M6 86 D1
Belvedere St SLFD * M6 86 E1
Belvoir Av BNG/LEV * M19 99 K2
BRAM/HZG SK7 122 A4
Belvoir Mdw MILN OL16 19 M8
Belvoir St BOLE BL2 3 L4
WGN WN1 15 J4
WHIT OL12 10 A1
Belvor Av DTN/ASHW M34 90 B5
Belwood Rd CCHDY M21 97 K5
Bembridge Cl RUSH/FAL M14 98 F1
Bembridge Cl WGNS/IIMK WN3 63 H2
Bembridge Dr BOLS/LL BL3 37 G7
Bembridge Rd DTN/ASHW M34 101 L4
Bempton Cl OFTN SK2 113 K7
Bemrose Av ALT WA14 107 M6
Bemsley Pl ORD * M5 86 D4
Benbecula Wy URM M41 85 G7
Benbow Av WGTN/LGST M12 88 C7
Benbow St SALE M33 96 E7
Ben Brierley Wy OLD OL1 9 J4
Bench Carr WHIT OL12 28 B3
Benchill Court Rd
WYTH/NTH M22 110 B8
Benchill Dr WYTH/NTH M22 110 A7
Benchill Rd WYTH/NTH M22 109 M6
Bendall St OP/CLY M11 89 H4
Ben Davies Ct MPL/ROM * SK6 113 M2
Bendemeer URM M41 95 M1
Bendix St ANC M4 7 J2
Benedict Cl BRO M7 71 M7
Benedict Dr DUK SK16 90 F6
Benfield Av NEWH/MOS M40 73 M2
Benfield St HEY OL10 41 G2
Benfleet Cl WGTN/LGST * M12 88 D6
Bengairn Cl WGN WN1 15 L2
Bengal La AUL OL6 75 M8
Bengal St ANC M4 7 K2
EDGY/DAV SK3 13 G7
LEIGH WN7 66 C7
Benjamin Fold AIMK WN4 63 L7
Benmore Cl HEY OL10 40 D2
Benmore Rd BKLY M9 57 J8
Bennet St RAD M26 38 A8
Bennett Cl EDGY/DAV SK3 12 C6
Bennett Dr BRO M7 72 B6
WGNW/BIL/O WN5 46 A8
Bennett Rd CHH M8 72 C3
Bennett's La BOL BL1 35 M2
Bennett St AULW OL7 90 C3
EDGY/DAV SK3 12 C6
HYDE SK14 90 F7
HYDE SK14 93 G7
STLY * SK15 91 K3
STRET * M32 96 F3
WGTN/LGST M12 88 B6
Benny La DROY M43 90 A1
Benson Cl BRO M7 72 B7
Benson St BURY BL9 5 H6
EDGW/EG * BL7 16 E7
Ben St OP/CLY M11 88 E2
Bentcliffe Wy ECC M30 85 J3
Bentfield Crs MILN OL16 29 K8
Bent Fold Dr BURY * BL9 55 K3
Bentgate Cl MILN OL16 29 K8
Bentgate St MILN OL16 43 K1
Bentham Cl TOT/BURYW BL8 38 B1
Bentham Pl WGNNW/ST WN6 31 J2
Bentham Rd WGNNW/ST WN6 31 H3
Bent Hill St BOLS/LL * BL3 35 K8
Bentinck Cl ALT * WA14 107 M8
Bentinck Rd ALT WA14 107 M8
Bentinck St AULW OL7 90 E2
BOL BL1 35 L3
FWTH BL4 52 F3
HULME M15 6 A9
WGNS/IIMK WN3 47 H8
WHIT OL12 27 M3
Bent La CHH M8 72 C5
PWCH M25 55 M8
Bent Lanes URM M41 84 C8
Bentley Av MDTN M24 42 A7
Bentley Cl RAD M26 38 F8
Bentley Ct FWTH BL4 53 G3
Bentley Fold TOT/BURYW BL8 24 C8
Bentley Fold Cottages
TOT/BURYW * BL8 24 C8
Bentley Hall Rd
TOT/BURYW BL8 24 A8
Bentley La BURY BL9 25 K3
Bentley Ms WHIT * OL12 28 B2
Bentley Rd BRO M7 72 B4
CCHDY M21 97 K3
DTN/ASHW M34 101 J1
Bentley St BOLE BL2 3 L8
CHAD OL9 8 B4
FWTH BL4 53 G3
OLD OL1 59 L4
WHIT OL12 28 B2
Bentmeadows WHIT OL12 28 B3
Benton Dr MPL/ROM SK6 114 F4
Benton St BKLY M9 73 J5
Bents Av MPL/ROM SK6 113 J1
URM M41 95 H3
Bents Farm Cl LIT * OL15 20 A7
Bentside Rd POY/DIS SK12 123 M7
Bent Spur Rd FWTH BL4 53 K7
Bent St CHH M8 72 D7
FWTH BL4 53 H5
Bentworth Cl WHTN BL5 50 C6
Bentworth Wk BKLY M9 73 H5
Beresford Av BOLS/LL BL3 35 M7
Beresford Crs OLDE OL4 60 A4
RDSH SK5 100 B1
Beresford Rd BRUN/LGST M13 99 J1
STRET M32 86 B8
Beresford St FAIL M35 74 B5
MILN OL16 29 L8
OLDE OL4 60 A4
RUSH/FAL M14 98 C1
WGNNW/ST WN6 14 B2
Berigan Cl WGTN/LGST M12 88 B7
Berisford Cl HALE/TIMP WA15 108 B5
Berkeley Av CHAD OL9 74 C1
RUSH/FAL M14 88 B8
STRET M32 85 K8
WGNS/IIMK WN3 63 G2
Berkeley Cl HYDE SK14 102 A3
LEIGH WN7 80 F4
OFTN SK2 112 F4
Berkeley Crs HYDE SK14 102 A3
RAD M26 37 M7
Berkeley Dr MILN OL16 28 E8
Berkeley Rd BOL BL1 22 B8
BRAM/HZG SK7 122 B1
Berkeley St AUL OL6 90 D1
Berkley Av BNG/LEV M19 99 K2
Berkley Dr ROY/SHW OL2 59 G2
Berkley St ROY/SHW OL2 43 G7
Berkley Wk LIT OL15 20 A7
Berkshire Cl CHAD OL9 8 B9
Berkshire Ct BURY BL9 39 J5
Berkshire Pl CHAD OL9 8 C8
Berkshire Rd NEWH/MOS M40 88 A1
Berlin Rd EDGY/DAV SK3 112 A6
Berlin St BOLS/LL BL3 35 M6
Bermondsay St ORD M5 86 E4
Bernard Gv BOL BL1 35 M2
Bernard St BKLY M9 73 G4
GLSP SK13 104 F3
WHIT OL12 28 B1
Berne Av HOR/BR BL6 33 K1
Berne Cl BRAM/HZG SK7 112 B8
CHAD OL9 8 C7
Bernice Av CHAD OL9 8 A7
Bernice St BOL BL1 35 M2
Berriedale Cl OLDTF/WHR * M16 98 A2
Berrie Gv BNG/LEV M19 99 K4
Berrington Gv AIMK WN4 78 D1
Berry Brow NEWH/MOS M40 74 A8
Berry Cl WILM/AE SK9 126 E7
Berrycroft La MPL/ROM SK6 113 K1
Berryfold Wy TYLD M29 67 K4
Berry St CMANE M1 7 K7
ECC M30 84 E4
STLY SK15 91 M4
SWIN M27 70 C2
UPML OL3 61 L7
Bertha Rd MILN OL16 11 L5
Bertha St BOL BL1 36 A2
OP/CLY M11 88 E5
ROY/SHW OL2 43 L7
Bertie St ROCH OL11 27 M8
Bertram St SALE M33 97 H8
WGTN/LGST * M12 88 D6
Bertrand Rd BOL BL1 35 M5
Bert St BOLS/LL BL3 51 L1
Berwick Av HTNM SK4 111 G2
URM M41 96 D2
WHTF M45 55 K5
Berwick Cl HEY OL10 40 D3
WALK M28 68 C5
Berwick Pl WGN WN1 15 L1
Berwick St MILN OL16 11 J6
Berwyn Av BKLY M9 56 F7
CHD/CHDH SK8 111 L7
MDTN M24 57 M4
Berwyn Cl HOR/BR BL6 21 C7
OLDS OL8 75 H1
Beryl Av TOT/BURYW BL8 24 C5
Beryl St BOL BL1 36 C1
Besom La STLY SK15 92 B1
Bessemer Rd IRL M44 94 C6
Bessemer St OP/CLY M11 88 F5
Bessemer Wy OLD OL1 9 H4
Bessie's Well Pl
WGNNW/ST * WN6 31 J4
Bessybrook Cl HOR/BR BL6 34 F6
Beswick Dr FAIL M35 74 D6
Beswicke Royds St MILN OL16 11 K1
Beswicke St LIT OL15 20 D7
WHIT OL12 10 C2
Beswick Rw ANC M4 7 G2
Beswick St ANC M4 88 A2
DROY M43 89 L3
Beta Av STRET M32 96 F3
Beta St BOL BL1 2 D2
Bethany La MILN OL16 29 M8
Bethel Av FAIL M35 74 B5
Bethel Gn LIT * OL15 20 D3
Bethel St HEY OL10 40 F2
Bethersden Rd WGN WN1 31 L7
Bethesda St OLDS OL8 59 J8
Bethnall Dr RUSH/FAL M14 98 D4
Betjeman Pl ROY/SHW OL2 44 A5
Betleymere Rd CHD/CHDH SK8 111 J8
Betley Rd RDSH SK5 100 C3
Betley St CMANE M1 7 L6
HEY * OL10 40 F3
RAD M26 38 F8
Betnor Av STKP SK1 112 E3
Betony Cl WHIT OL12 28 A1
Bettison Av LEIGH WN7 81 M1
Bettwood Dr CHH M8 72 C2
Betula Gv BRO M7 72 A6
Betula Ms ROCH OL11 27 G3
Beulah Av WGNW/BIL/O WN5 62 A8
Bevan Cl WGTN/LGST M12 88 B3
Bevendon Sq BRO M7 72 B6
Beveridge St RUSH/FAL M14 98 D1
Beverley Av DTN/ASHW M34 101 K2
LEIGH WN7 66 D7
URM M41 85 H8
WGNW/BIL/O WN5 62 B3
Beverley Cl WHTF M45 55 L3
Beverley Pl MILN * OL16 11 G3
Beverley Rd BOL BL1 35 M4
BOLS/LL BL3 53 J1
OFTN SK2 112 F4
SWIN M27 70 F5
WGNW/BIL/O WN5 46 E4
Beverley St BKLY M9 73 H3
Beverley Wk OLDS * OL8 9 H9
Beverly Cl AUL OL6 75 L6
Beverly Rd RUSH/FAL M14 99 G5
Beverston ROCH OL11 10 D7
Beverston Dr BRO M7 72 B6
Bevill Sq CSLFD M3 6 C2
Bevin Av GOL/RIS/CU WA3 81 L8
Bevington St AIMK WN4 63 J7
Bevis Gn BURY BL9 25 J4
Bewerley Cl WGNS/IIMK WN3 14 D8
Bewick St BOLE BL2 36 E1
Bewley Gv LEIGH WN7 66 D6
Bewley St OLDS OL8 75 G2
Bexhill Av HALE/TIMP WA15 108 C6
Bexhill Cl BOLS/LL BL3 53 M1
Bexhill Dr BRUN/LGST M13 99 H1
WGNE/HIN WN2 65 M2
Bexhill Rd EDGY/DAV SK3 112 B8
Bexhill Wk CHAD OL9 8 A6
Bexington Rd OLDTF/WHR M16 98 A1
Bexley Cl GLSP SK13 104 F1
URM M41 84 E8
Bexley Dr LHULT M38 68 F1
TOT/BURYW BL8 38 E3
Bexley Sq CSLFD M3 6 B3
Bexley St CHAD OL9 8 D8
WGNE/HIN WN2 65 L1
Beyer Cl GTN M18 88 F7
Bibby La BNG/LEV M19 99 J6
Bibby St BURY BL9 39 J7
HYDE * SK14 91 G7
Bibury Av WYTH/NTH M22 118 D1
Bickerdike Av WGTN/LGST M12 99 L1
Bickershaw Dr WALK M28 68 F2
Bickershaw La WGNE/HIN WN2 64 F3
Bickerstaffe Cl ROY/SHW OL2 43 K7
Bickerton Rd BRAM/HZG SK7 121 J3
Bickerton Rd ALT WA14 107 L7
Bickley Gv TYLD M29 67 M6
Biddall Dr NTHM/RTH M23 109 L6
Biddisham Wk NEWH/MOS M40 73 G7
Biddulph Av OFTN SK2 112 F7
Bideford Dr BOLE BL2 37 K6
NTHM/RTH M23 109 J5
Bideford Rd OFTN SK2 112 F3
ROCH OL11 41 L1
Bidford Cl TYLD M29 67 M3
Bidston Cl ROY/SHW OL2 44 A6
TOT/BURYW BL8 38 C2
Bidston Dr WILM/AE SK9 127 J2
Big Fold HOR/BR * BL6 33 G2
Bignor St CHH M8 72 D6
Bilbao St BOL BL1 35 M4
Bilberry St MILN OL16 11 H6
Bilbrook St ANC M4 87 L1
Billberry Cl WHTF M45 55 L4
Billing Av WGTN/LGST M12 7 L8
Billinge Ar WGN * WN1 14 F3
Billinge Cl BOL BL1 2 E2
Billinge Rd AIMK WN4 62 E7
WGNW/BIL/O WN5 47 G7
Billington Av NEWLW WA12 78 E6
Billington Rd SWIN M27 71 H4
Bill Williams Cl OP/CLY M11 88 F4
Billy La SWIN M27 70 C2
Bilson Dr EDGY/DAV SK3 12 B9
Binbrook Wk BOLS/LL BL3 36 B8
Bindloss Av ECC M30 85 K1
Bingham Dr NTHM/RTH M23 109 J6
Bingham St SWIN M27 70 C4
Bingley Cl OP/CLY M11 88 C4
Bingley Dr URM M41 84 C8
Bingley Rd MILN OL16 11 M5
Bingley Sq MILN OL16 11 M5
Bingley St FWTH BL4 53 G5
Bingley Ter MILN OL16 11 M5
Binns Nook Rd WHIT OL12 28 D2
Binns Pl CMANE M1 7 K4
Binns St STLY SK15 91 H3
Binsley Cl IRL M44 94 D3
Binstead Cl RUSH/FAL M14 99 H4
Birchacre Gv RUSH/FAL M14 99 G5
Birchall Av GOL/RIS/CU WA3 81 G8
Birchall Cl DUK SK16 91 G6
Birchall Gn MPL/ROM SK6 101 J7
Birch Av FAIL M35 74 C6
HTNM SK4 99 L8
IRL M44 94 A7
MDTN M24 57 K5
MPL/ROM SK6 114 A2
OLD OL1 58 D2
OLDS OL8 75 G2
OLDTF/WHR M16 86 D8
SALE M33 108 E1
SLFD M6 71 H8
TOT/BURYW BL8 24 D7
WGNNW/ST WN6 31 J4
WHIT OL12 19 L8
WHTF M45 55 J6
WHTN BL5 50 C5
WILM/AE SK9 126 D6
Birch Cl WHIT OL12 18 D7
Birch Crs MILN OL16 43 K1
NEWLW WA12 78 C8
Birchdale ALT WA14 116 E2
Birchdale Av CHD/CHDH SK8 119 K2
Birch Dr BRAM/HZG SK7 121 L2
OLDE OL4 60 B7
SWIN M27 70 E4
Birchell Wy HULME M15 87 J6
Birchenall St NEWH/MOS M40 73 J4
Birchenlea St CHAD OL9 74 D1
The Birches NM/HAY SK22 125 L2
SALE M33 96 B7
Birches Rd EDGW/EG BL7 23 H1
Birchfield BOLE BL2 23 H6
Birchfield Av ATH M46 50 E8
HEY OL10 40 B3
Birchfield Dr ROCH OL11 27 M7
WALK M28 68 D5
Birchfield Gv BOLS/LL BL3 35 H8
Birchfield Ms HYDE * SK14 102 A2
Birchfield Rd EDGY/DAV SK3 111 K5
Birchfields HALE/TIMP WA15 117 H3
OLDE OL4 60 C8
Birchfields Av BRUN/LGST M13 99 H1
Birchfields Rd BRUN/LGST M13 99 H1
Birchfold Cl LHULT M38 52 E8
Birchgate Wk BOLS/LL BL3 2 D9
Birch Gn GLSP SK13 105 H3
Birch Gv AIMK WN4 62 F7
DTN/ASHW M34 90 C6
DTN/ASHW M34 101 H1
HALE/TIMP WA15 109 H7
PWCH M25 55 K6
RAMS BL0 24 D1
RUSH/FAL M14 99 G1
Birch Hall Cl NM/HAY SK22 125 J2
OLDE OL4 60 B8
Birch Hall La BRUN/LGST M13 99 H2
Birch Hey Cl WHIT OL12 19 K8
Birch Hill Crs WHIT OL12 19 M8
Birch Hill La WHIT OL12 19 L6
Birchington Rd DID/WITH M20 98 D4
Birchinlee Av ROY/SHW OL2 58 E1
Birchin Pl ANC * M4 7 H4
Birch La BRUN/LGST M13 88 B8
DUK SK16 91 G4
Birchlea HALE/TIMP WA15 108 C8
Birch-Lea Cl BURY BL9 39 J5
Birchleaf Gv ORD M5 85 M2
Birch Mt WHIT OL12 19 M8
Birch Polygon RUSH/FAL M14 99 G1
Birch Rd ATH M46 67 H1
CHD/CHDH SK8 110 D7
CHH M8 72 E3
FWTH BL4 53 J6
LEIGH WN7 66 C5
MDTN M24 57 M2
PART M31 106 A1
PART M31 107 J1
POY/DIS SK12 129 K2
RNFD/HAY WA11 78 B5
SWIN M27 70 A7
UPML OL3 61 M5
WALK M28 69 H3
WGNE/HIN WN2 64 E5
WHIT OL12 19 K6
Birchside Av GLSP SK13 104 E2
Birch St AULW OL7 90 C3
BOLE BL2 3 H7
BURY BL9 5 G2
DROY * M43 89 L4
HEY OL10 41 G3
RAD M26 39 H7
STLY SK15 76 F7
TYLD * M29 67 K3
WGNE/HIN WN2 49 G7
WGNNW/ST WN6 14 C1
WGTN/LGST M12 88 D6
WHIT OL12 19 K6
Birch Ter HYDE * SK14 101 M2
Birch Tree Av BRAM/HZG SK7 122 C3
Birch Tree Cl ALT WA14 116 E3
Birch Tree Dr WYTH/NTH M22 118 F1
Birch Tree Rd GOL/RIS/CU WA3 80 C4
Birchvale Av MPL/ROM SK6 114 A1
Birchvale Cl HULME M15 6 C9
Birchway BRAM/HZG SK7 120 F5
MPL/ROM SK6 123 H5
Birchwood CHAD OL9 58 B5
Birchwood Cl LEIGH WN7 81 J1
WGNS/IIMK WN3 62 F3
Birchwood Dr WILM/AE SK9 127 H4
Birchwood Rd MDTN M24 57 M4
Birchwood Wy DUK * SK16 91 G6
Bird Hall Av CHD/CHDH SK8 111 M8
Birdhall Gv BNG/LEV M19 99 K4
Bird Hall La EDGY/DAV SK3 111 L6
Bird Hall Rd CHD/CHDH SK8 111 L7
Birdlip Dr NTHM/RTH M23 118 C1
Bird St WGNE/HIN WN2 48 C5
Birkby Dr MDTN M24 57 H2
Birkdale Av ATH M46 50 F7
ROY/SHW OL2 59 H2
WHTF M45 55 G6
Birkdale Cl BRAM/HZG SK7 121 H5
HEY OL10 41 G4
HYDE SK14 91 H7
Birkdale Dr SALE M33 108 B2
TOT/BURYW BL8 38 E2
Birkdale Gdns BOLS/LL BL3 2 B9
Birkdale Gv ECC M30 85 J2
RDSH SK5 100 C7
Birkdale Pl SALE * M33 96 C6
Birkdale Rd MILN OL16 28 F8
RDSH SK5 100 C7
Birkdale St CHH M8 72 D5
Birkenhills Dr BOLS/LL BL3 35 H7
Birkett Bank WGN WN1 15 L4
Birkett Cl BOL BL1 22 A6
Birkett Dr BOL BL1 22 A6
Birkett St WGN WN1 15 L4
Birkinbrook Cl WHTF M45 55 K3
Birkinheath La ALT WA14 116 D8
Birks Av OLDE OL4 60 C4
Birks Dr TOT/BURYW BL8 24 E6
Birkside Cl WGNS/IIMK WN3 63 K3
Birkworth Ct OFTN SK2 113 G6
Birley Cl HALE/TIMP WA15 108 C5
WGNNW/ST WN6 30 C4
Birley Pk DID/WITH M20 110 C1
Birley St BURY BL9 25 J7
LEIGH WN7 66 D6
NEWLW WA12 79 G8
WHIT OL12 28 D3
Birling Dr NTHM/RTH M23 109 L8
Birnham Gv HEY OL10 40 D3
Birshaw Cl ROY/SHW OL2 43 L7
Birtenshaw Crs EDGW/EG BL7 22 E5
Birtle Dr TYLD M29 67 M5
Birtle Rd BURY BL9 26 B5
Birtles Av RDSH SK5 100 C1
Birtles Cl CHD/CHDH SK8 111 J7
DUK SK16 91 G6
Birtlespool Rd CHD/CHDH SK8 111 J8
Birtley Wk NEWH/MOS * M40 7 M1
Birt St NEWH/MOS M40 73 G8
Birwood Rd CHH M8 72 E2
Biscay Cl OP/CLY M11 88 C3
Bishopbridge Cl BOLS/LL BL3 36 C8
Bishop Cl OLDTF/WHR M16 87 H8
Bishopdale Cl ROY/SHW OL2 43 G7
Bishopgate St CHAD OL9 58 D7
Bishop Marshall Cl
NEWH/MOS * M40 73 G7

Bishop Marshall Wy
MDTN M24 .....41 G8
Bishop Reeves Rd
RNFD/HAY WA11 .....78 B5
URM M41 .....95 C2
Bishops Cl ALT WA14 .....116 D3
AULW OL6 .....75 K7
BOLS/LL BL3 .....52 D2
CHD/CHDH SK8 .....111 K7
Bishopsgate CMANW M2 .....6 F6
Bishopsgate Wk MILN OL16 .....28 F8
Bishops Ms SALE M33 .....96 B6
Bishops Meadow MDTN M24.....57 G1
Bishop's Rd BOLS/LL BL3 .....52 D2
Bishop St MDTN M24 .....58 A5
MILN OL16 .....11 H3
STKP SK1 .....13 L4
Bishopton Cl BNG/LEV M19 .....99 M3
Bisley Av NTHM/RTH M23 .....109 J6
Bisley St OLDS OL8 .....8 F7
Bismarck St OLDS OL8 .....9 M8
Bispham Av BOLE BL2 .....37 J5
RDSH SK5 .....100 C2
Bispham Cl TOT/BURYW BL8 .....38 C3
Bispham Dr AIMK WN4 .....63 J7
Bispham Gv BRO M7 .....72 B5
Bispham St BOLE * BL2 .....3 L2
Bittern Cl POY/DIS SK12 .....128 E1
ROCH OL11 .....27 J5
Bittern Dr DROY M43 .....89M1
Blackbank St BOL BL1 .....36 C2
Blackberry Cl ALT WA14 .....107 L4
Blackberry Rd WGNE/HIN WN2 .....48 F8
Blackberry La RDSH SK5 .....100 C3
Black Brook WALK M28 .....100 A5
Blackburn Cl GOL/RIS/CU WA3 .....80 C4
Blackburn Gdns DID/WITH M20.....98 D8
Blackburn Pl ORD M5 .....86 F3
Blackburn Rd BOL BL1 .....36 B1
EDGW/EG BL7 .....22 A1
Blackburn St CSLFD M3 .....6 A1
OLDTF/WHR M16 .....86 F7
PWCH M25 .....55M8
RAD M26 .....54 D1
Blackcap Cl WALK M28 .....68 E5
Blackcarr Rd NTHM/RTH M23 .....109 L7
Blackchapel Dr MILN OL16 .....43 C7
Blackcroft Cl SWIN M27 .....70 B4
Blackdown Gv OLDS OL8 .....75 H1
Blackett St CMANE * M1 .....88 A4
Blackfield La BRO M7 .....71M4
Blackfields M7 .....72 A4
Blackford Rd BNG/LEV M19 .....99 L5
Blackford Wk NEWH/MOS M40.....88 A1
Blackfriars Rd CSLFD M3 .....6 C1
Blackfriars St CSLFD M3 .....6 E3
Blackhill Cl BRUN/LGST M13.....7 K9
Blackhorse Av HOR/BR * BL6.....32 F2
Blackhorse Cl HOR/BR BL6.....32 F1
Black Horse St BOL BL1 .....2 D5
FWTH BL4 .....53 H5
HOR/BR BL6 .....32 F1
Blackhurst Brow
MCFLDN SK10 .....131 H4
Blackledge Cl
WGNW/BIL/O WN5 .....46 B7
Blackledge St BOLS/LL BL3.....35M8
Blackley Cl BURY BL9 .....55 K2
Blackleyhurst Av
WGNW/BIL/O WN5 .....62 B7
Blackley New Rd BKLY M9 .....72 C1
Blackley Park Rd BKLY M9 .....73 G3
Blackley St MDTN M24 .....56 E5
OLDTF/WHR M16 .....86 F7
Blacklock St CSLFD M3 .....72 C8
Blackmoor Av TYLD M29 .....67 L7
Black Moss Cl RAD * M26 .....54 A1
Black Moss Rd ALT WA14 .....107 H5
Blackpits Rd ROCH OL11 .....27 G3
Blackpool St OP/CLY M11 .....88 F2
Blackrock St OP/CLY M11 .....88 C3
Blackrod By-Pass Rd
HOR/BR BL6 .....33 J4
Blackrod Dr TOT/BURYW BL8.....38 C3
Black Sail Wk OLD OL1 .....9 K1
Blackshaw La BOLS/LL BL3.....35M6
ROY/SHW OL2 .....43 J8
WILM/AE SK9 .....130 C3
Blackshaw Rd GLSP SK13 .....105 H2
Blackshaw St EDGY/DAV SK3 .....13 H6
Blacksmith La ROCH OL11 .....27 L8
Blacksmiths Fold ATH M46 .....67 H1
Blackstock St BRUN/LGST M13.....87M8
Blackstone Av MILN OL16.....11M2
Blackstone Edge Old Rd
LIT OL15 .....20 E6
Blackstone Rd STKP SK2 .....113 G7
Blackthorn Av BNG/LEV M19 .....99 K5
WGNNW/ST WN6 .....47 J1
Blackthorn Cl WHIT OL12 .....28 B2
Blackthorne Rd BOL BL1 .....35 K3
Blackthorne Dr SALE M33 .....108 A2
Blackthorne Rd HYDE SK14 .....102 B6
Blackthorn Ms WHIT OL12 .....28 B2
Blackthorn Rd OLDS OL8 .....74 F4
Blackwin St WGTN/LGST M12.....88 D6
Blackwood Dr NTHM/RTH M23 .....109 G4
Blackwood St BOLS/LL BL3 .....36 D8
Bladen Cl CHD/CHDH SK8 .....111 K8
Bladon St CMANE * M1 .....7 J8
Blair Av LHULT M38 .....52 E8
URM M41 .....95 H2
WGNE/HIN WN2 .....65 L1
Blair Cl BRAM/HZG SK7 .....121 L4
ROY/SHW OL2 .....43 L5
SALE M33 .....107M3
Blairhall Av NEWH/MOS M40 .....73 K4
Blair La BOLE BL2 .....37 G3
Blairmore Dr BOLS/LL BL3 .....35 H8
Blair Rd OLDTF/WHR M16 .....98 B3
Blair St EDGW/EG BL7 .....22 C4
FWTH BL4 .....53 K6
OLDTF/WHR M16 .....87 G7
WHIT OL12 .....10 A1
Blake Cl WGNS/IIMK WN3 .....47 K7
Blakedown Wk
WGTN/LGST * M12.....88 B7
Blake Dr OFTN SK2 .....113 H6
Blake Gdns BOL BL1 .....36 A2
Blakelock St ROY/SHW OL2 .....43 K5
Blakemere Av SALE M33.....109 H1
Blakemore Wk
WGTN/LGST * M12.....88 B3
Blake St BOL BL1 .....36 A2
EDGW/EG BL7 .....22 D5

MILN OL16 .....11 H3
Blakeswell Cl URM M41 .....95 G1
Blakey St BOLS/LL BL3 .....35 J8
Blakey St WGTN/LGST M12.....88 D8
Blanchard St HULME M15 .....87 H7
Blanche St WHIT OL12 .....28 D2
Blanche Wk OLD OL1 .....9 L3
Bland Cl FAIL M35 .....74 B5
Blandford Av WALK M28 .....69 J4
Blandford Cl TOT/BURYW BL8 .....25 G7
TYLD M29 .....67 K3
Blandford Dr NEWH/MOS M40 .....74 A7
Blandford Ri HOR/BR BL6 .....34 D3
Blandford Rd ECC M30 .....84 E2
HTNM SK4 .....12 B2
SLFD M6 .....71 L7
Blandford St AUL OL6 .....90 D1
STKP SK1 .....15 J1
Bland Rd PWCH M25 .....71 L2
Bland St OLDTF/WHR * M16 .....87 H8
Blanefield Cl CCHDY M21 .....98 B5
Blantyre Av WALK M28 .....69 H2
Blantyre Rd SWIN M27 .....70 E6
Blantyre St ECC M30 .....84 D1
HULME M15 .....6 B8
SWIN M27 .....70 A4
WGNE/HIN WN2 .....49 H6
Blanwood Dr CHH M8 .....72 E5
Blaydon Cl WGNE/HIN WN2 .....33 G7
Blazemoss Bank OFTN SK2.....113 G7
Bleach St WGNE/HIN WN2 .....49 J7
Bleackley St TOT/BURYW BL8 .....24 F8
Bleak Hey Nook La UPML OL3.....45M4
Bleak Hey Rd WYTH/NTH M22 .....119 H2
Bleakledge Gn WGNE/HIN WN2.....49 J5
Bleakledge Gv WGNE/HIN WN2.....49 H6
Bleak St WHTF M45 .....55 H3
Bleasby St OLDE OL4 .....59M5
Bleasdale Cl HOR/BR BL6 .....34 C4
Bleasdale Rd BOL BL1 .....35 J2
NEWLW WA12 .....78 E8
WYTH/NTH M22 .....118 C2
Bleasefell Cha WALK M28 .....68 D7
Bleatarn Rd STKP SK1 .....112 E5
Bledlow Cl ECC M30 .....85 H1
Blenheim Av OLDTF/WHR M16 .....98 A2
Blenheim Cl ALT WA14 .....116 C2
BURY BL9 .....5 H2
GLSP SK13 .....93 K7
HEY OL10 .....41 H2
POY/DIS SK12 .....122 B8
WILM/AE SK9 .....127 H5
Blenheim Dr LEIGH WN7 .....67 H5
Blenheim Rd AIMK WN4 .....79 G2
BOLE BL2 .....37 H5
OLDTF/WHR M16 .....97 K1
WGNW/BIL/O WN5 .....46 F4
Blenheim St OLDE OL4 .....60 A3
TYLD M29 .....67 J4
WHIT * OL12 .....27M3
Blenheim av OLD OL1 .....60 A1
Blenmar Cl RAD M26 .....38 F7
Bletchley Cl BRUN/LGST M13.....88 A7
Bletchley Rd HTNM SK4 .....111 H3
Blethyn St BOLS/LL BL3 .....51 L2
Blewberry Cl LEIGH WN7 .....66 C5
Bligh Rd WHTF BL5 .....50 B3
Blinco Rd URM M41 .....96 C3
Blind La WGTN/LGST M12 .....88 A5
Blindsill Rd FWTH BL4 .....52 E5
Blissford Cl WGNE/HIN WN2.....49 G8
Blisworth Av ECC M30 .....85 H4
Blisworth Cl ANC M4 .....88 A3
Block La CHAD OL9 .....8 B9
Blodwell St SLFD M6 .....86 C2
Blomley St ROCH OL11 .....41M2
WALK M28 .....68 E1
Bloomfield Rd FWTH BL4 .....53 G6
Bloomfield St BOL BL1 .....36 B1
Bloomsbury Gv
HALE/TIMP WA15 .....108 D2
Bloomsbury La
HALE/TIMP WA15 .....108 D6
Bloom St CMANE M1 .....7 H6
CSLFD M3 .....6 D2
EDGY/DAV SK3 .....12 D7
RAMS BL0 .....17 A8
Blossom Pl MILN * OL16 .....10 E3
Blossom Rd PART M31 .....106 B2
Blossoms Hey CHD/CHDH SK8.....120 A3
Blossoms La BRAM/HZG SK7 .....127 L2
Blossoms St OFTN * SK2 .....13 K9
Blossom St ANC M4 .....7 K3
CSLFD M3 .....6 C4
TYLD M29 .....67 K3
Blucher St AULW OL7 .....75 K6
ORD M5 .....86 F3
WGTN/LGST M12 .....88 B5
Blue Bell Av RNFD/HAY WA11.....78 B5
WGNNW/ST WN6 .....31 J8
Bluebell Av NEWH/MOS M40 .....73 K5
Bluebell Cl HYDE SK14 .....91 J7
Bluebell Dr ROCH OL11 .....41 L1
Bluebell Gv CHD/CHDH SK8 .....111 G8
Bluebell Wy WILM/AE SK9 .....127 G3
Blueberry Dr ROY/SHW OL2.....44 A5
Blueberry Rd ALT WA14 .....116 C2
Blueberry's ROY/SHW OL2 .....44 D3
Blue Ribbon Wk SWIN M27 .....70 D3
Bluestone Dr DTN/ASHW M34 .....100 D2
NEWH/MOS M40 .....73 J4
Bluestone Rd DTN/ASHW M34.....100 D2
NEWH/MOS M40 .....73 J4
Blundell La HOR/BR BL6 .....32 D2
Blundell Ms WGNS/IIMK WN3.....47 G8
Blundell St BOL BL1 .....2 D4
Blundering La STLY SK15 .....92 A6
Blunn St OLDS OL8 .....59 J8
Blyborough Cl SLFD M6 .....71 H8
Blyth Av LIT * OL15 .....29 J1
Blythe Av BRAM/HZG SK7.....120 E6
Blyton St HULME M15 .....87 L7
Boad St STKP SK1 .....7 K6
Boardale Dr MDTN M24 .....57 H3
Boardman Cl BOL BL1 .....36 B2
Boardman Fold Cl MDTN M24 .....57 H2
Boardman Fold Rd MDTN M24 .....57 J2
Boardman La MDTN M24 .....56 E4
Boardman Rd CHH M8 .....72 C2
Boardman St BOL BL1 .....36 B2
ECC M30 .....85 H3

Board St AUL OL6 .....76 A8
BOLS/LL BL3 .....2 E7
Boarfold La GLSP SK13 .....103 H7
Boar Green Cl NEWH/MOS M40.....73M5
Boarshaw Clough MDTN M24 .....57 L2
Boarshaw Clough Wy
MDTN M24 .....57 L2
Boarshaw Crs MDTN M24.....57M2
Boarshaw La MDTN M24 .....58 A1
Boarshaw Rd MDTN M24 .....57 K3
Boars Head Av WGNNW/ST WN6.....31 K5
Boarshurst La UPML OL3 .....61M7
Boat La IRL M44 .....94 E2
WYTH/NTH M22 .....110 D3
Boardmans Rw TYLD M29 .....67M8
Bobbin Wk ANC * M4 .....7 L4
OLDE OL4 .....9M7
Bob Brook Cl FAIL M35 .....73M6
Bob Massey Cl OP/CLY M11 .....88 F4
Bob's La IRL M44 .....94 A8
Boddens Hill Rd HTNM SK4 .....111 K3
Bodden St GOL/RIS/CU WA3 .....80 D5
Boddington Rd ECC M30 .....84 C3
Bodiam Rd TOT/BURYW BL8 .....24 C3
Bodley St OP/CLY M11 .....88 F2
Bodmin Cl ROY/SHW OL2 .....59 K1
Bodmin Crs RDSH SK5 .....100 E7
Bodmin Dr BRAM/HZG SK7 .....121 G5
WGNE/HIN WN2 .....64 D3
Bodmin Rd SALE M33 .....96 A7
TYLD M29 .....67M4
Boggard La GLSP SK13 .....104 A7
Bogguard Rd MPL/ROM SK6 .....115 K8
Bognor Rd EDGY/DAV SK3 .....112 B8
Bolam Cl NTHM/RTH M23 .....109 J3
Boland Dr RUSH/FAL M14 .....99 G4
Bolderod Pl OLD * OL1 .....9 G2
Bolderstone Pl OFTN SK2.....113 H8
Bolderwood Dr WGNE/HIN WN2.....49 G8
Bold St ALT WA14 .....116 F1
BOL BL1 .....2 E6
BURY BL9 .....5 H2
HULME M15 .....87 H7
LEIGH WN7 .....66 C7
SWIN M27 .....70 C2
WGNW/BIL/O WN5 .....47 H7
Bolesworth Cl CCHDY M21 .....97 J4
Boleyn Ct HEY OL10.....40 F4
Bolholt Ter TOT/BURYW BL8 .....24 E8
Bolivia St ORD M5 .....85M2
Bollin Av ALT WA14 .....116 D4
Bollin Cl FWTH BL4 .....53 K6
Bollin Ct HULME M15.....87 G6
Bollin Dr ALT WA14 .....108 B4
SALE M33 .....108 E2
Bollings Yd BOL * BL1 .....2 F6
Bollington Rd HTNM SK4 .....100 A7
NEWH/MOS M40 .....88 A2
Bollington St AULW OL7 .....90 D3
Bollin Hi WILM/AE SK9 .....126 F4
Bollin Sq ALT WA14 .....116 D3
Bollin Wk WHTF M45 .....55M2
WILM/AE SK9 .....126 F5
Bollinway HALE/TIMP WA15 .....117 J4
Bollinwood Cha WILM/AE SK9 .....127 H5
Bolney St WGNE/HIN WN2 .....48 D2
Bolshaw Farm La
CHD/CHDH SK8 .....119 K6
Bolshaw Rd CHD/CHDH SK8.....119 K6
Bolton Cl BNG/LEV M19 .....111 G2
CHD/CHDH SK8.....120 D6
Bolton Ct GOL/RIS/CU WA3 .....80 E4
POY/DIS SK12 .....121M8
PWCH M25 .....71 J2
Bolton House Rd
WGNE/HIN WN2 .....65 J5
Bolton Old Rd ATH M46 .....67 G1
Bolton Rd AIMK WN4.....64 B7
ATH M46 .....51 J8
BOLE BL2 .....22 F7
EDGW/EG BL7 .....16 D8
FWTH BL4 .....53 C2
FWTH BL4 .....53 J5
RAD M26 .....38 A8
ROCH OL11 .....27 K8
SLFD M6 .....71 G7
SWIN M27 .....70 D3
TOT/BURYW BL8 .....23M2
TOT/BURYW BL8 .....38 D4
WALK M28 .....53 G8
WGNE/HIN WN2 .....32 F7
WHTN BL5 .....50 C4
Bolton Rd North RAMS BL0 .....17 C3
Bolton Rd West RAMS BL0 .....17 A8
Bolton Sq WGN WN1 .....15 K2
Bolton St AIMK WN4 .....63 C7
BURY BL9 .....5 J4
CSLFD M3 .....6 C4
OLDE OL4 .....59 L6
RAD M26 .....54 C1
RAMS BL0 .....17 B7
RDSH SK5 .....100 B5
TOT/BURYW BL8 .....8 B4
Bombay Rd EDGY/DAV SK3 .....12 C6
WGNW/BIL/O WN5 .....46 F4
Bombay St AUL OL6 .....76 A8
CMANE M1 .....7 H7
Bonar Cl EDGY/DAV * SK3 .....12 C6
Bonar Rd EDGY/DAV SK3 .....12 C7
Boncarn Dr NTHM/RTH M23 .....109 K8
Bonchurch Wk WGTN/LGST M12.....88 E6
Bond Cl HOR/BR BL6 .....33M1
Bondmark Rd GTN M18 .....88 F6
Bond Sq BRO * M7 .....72 B6
Bond St ATH M46 .....67 J3
BURY BL9 .....5 J4
DTN/ASHW M34 .....101 J1
LEIGH WN7 .....66 C7
RAMS BL0 .....17 E2
STLY SK15 .....91 K1
WGTN/LGST M12 .....7 L7
WHIT OL12 .....28 D2
Bongham Wk OP/CLY M11 .....88 D7
Bonhill Wk OP/CLY M11 .....88 D7
Bonington Ri MPL/ROM SK6 .....114 E4
Bonis Crs OFTN SK2 .....112 F8
Bonny Brow St MDTN M24 .....56 F5
Bonnywell Rd LEIGH WN7 .....81 J1
Bonsall Av WYTH/NTH M22 .....110 D8
Bonsall St HULME M15 .....87 J6
Bonscale Crs MDTN M24 .....57 H1
Bonville Cha ALT WA14 .....107 K8
Bonville Rd ALT WA14 .....107 K7
Boodle St AUL OL6 .....75 L8
AULW OL7 .....90 E1
Boond St ANC M4 .....88 A3

CSLFD M3 .....6 D2
Boonfields EDGW/EG BL7 .....22 D4
Booth Av RUSH/FAL M14 .....99 G5
Booth Bridge Cl MDTN * M24 .....56 F5
Boothby Rd SWIN M27 .....70 B3
Boothby St OFTN SK2 .....112 F8
Booth Cl STLY SK15 .....91 J3
TOT/BURYW BL8 .....24 D7
Booth Dr URM M41 .....84 C7
Boothcote DTN/ASHW M34 .....90 A6
Boothfield ECC M30 .....84 D1
Boothfield Rd WYTH/NTH M22.....109 M6
Boothfields TOT/BURYW BL8 .....4 A3
Booth Hall Dr TOT/BURYW BL8 .....24 C7
Booth Hall Rd BKLY M9 .....73 K1
Booth Hill La OLD OL1 .....58 F4
Booth Rd ALT WA14 .....107M8
BOLS/LL BL3 .....53 L2
DTN/ASHW M34 .....89 K5
OLDTF/WHR M16 .....97M1
SALE M33 .....96 E6
WILM/AE SK9 .....126 E3
Boothroyden Rd BKLY M9 .....56 F6
Boothroyden Rd WYTH/NTH M22 .....109M6
Boothsbank Av WALK M28 .....68 E6
Booth's Brow Rd AIMK WN4 .....63 G6
Booth's Hall Gv WALK M28 .....68 E5
Booth's Hall Gv WALK M28 .....68 E5
Booth's Hall Rd WALK M28 .....68 E5
Booth's Hall Wy WALK M28 .....68 E5
Boothstown Dr WALK M28 .....68 D7
Booth St AUL * OL6 .....90 E2
BOL BL1 .....35M1
CHAD OL9 .....9 G6
CSLFD M3 .....6 E3
DTN/ASHW M34 .....90 C7
EDGY/DAV SK3 .....13 H8
FAIL M35 .....74 B5
HYDE SK14 .....92 F8
HYDE SK14 .....102 B3
MDTN M24 .....58 A6
OLDE OL4 .....60 B6
STLY SK15 .....91 J4
TOT/BURYW BL8 .....24 C7
Booth St East BRUN/LGST M13 .....87 L6
Booth St West HULME M15 .....87 K6
Booth Ter
WYTH/NTH * M22 .....119 H6
Boothwood Rd SWIN M27 .....54 A8
Bootle St CMANW M2 .....6 F5
Bor Av WGNS/IIMK WN3 .....47 L8
Bordale Av BKLY M9 .....73 J5
Bordan St OP/CLY M11 .....88 C4
Border Brook La WALK M28 .....68 D5
Border Wy BURY BL9 .....39 K6
Bordley Wk NTHM/RTH M23 .....109 H3
Bordon Rd EDGY/DAV SK3 .....12 B9
Boringdon Cl NEWH/MOS * M40.....73 K4
Borland Av NEWH/MOS M40 .....74 A3
Borough Av RAD M26 .....39 G7
SWIN M27 .....70 D3
Borough Rd HALE/TIMP WA15.....108 B8
SALQ M50 .....86 A3
Borough St STLY SK15 .....91 K3
The Borrans WALK * M28 .....68 C7
Borron Rd NEWLW WA12 .....78 E7
Borron St STKP SK1 .....13M2
Borrowdale Av BOL BL1 .....35 K4
CHD/CHDH SK8 .....110 B8
Borrowdale Crs AULW OL7 .....75 J8
DID/WITH M20 .....98 B8
Borrowdale Dr BURY BL9 .....55 K1
ROCH OL11 .....27 L8
Borrowdale Rd MDTN M24 .....57 H2
OFTN SK2 .....112 E5
WGNW/BIL/O * WN5 .....46 E5
Borsdane Av WGNE/HIN WN2 .....49 H8
Borsden St SWIN M27 .....70 A3
Borth Av OFTN SK2 .....112 F5
Borwell St GTN M18.....89 G6
Boscobel Rd BOLS/LL BL3 .....52 E2
Boscombe Av ECC M30 .....84 F4
Boscombe Dr BRAM/HZG SK7 .....121 G6
Boscombe Pl WGNE/HIN WN2 .....49 H8
Boscombe St RDSH SK5 .....100 C2
RUSH/FAL M14 .....98 E2
Boscow Rd BOLS/LL BL3 .....53 K2
Bosden Av BRAM/HZG SK7 .....122 A1
Bosden Cl WILM/AE SK9 .....119M7
Bosden Fold STKP SK1 .....13 J6
Bosdenfold Rd BRAM/HZG SK7 .....122 A1
Bosden Hall Rd BRAM/HZG SK7.....122 A1
Bosdin Rd East URM * M41 .....95 H3
Bosdin Rd West URM M41 .....95 H3
Bosley Av DID/WITH M20 .....98 A3
Bosley Cl WILM/AE SK9 .....127 H2
Bosley Dr POY/DIS SK12 .....129 L1
Bosley Rd EDGY/DAV SK3 .....111 K4
Bossall Av BKLY M9 .....57 H8
Bossington Cl OFTN SK2 .....112 F4
Bostock Rd HYDE SK14 .....103 K4
Bostock Wk BRUN/LGST M13.....7 K9
Boston Cl BRAM/HZG SK7 .....120 F5
FAIL M35 .....74 C3
GOL/RIS/CU WA3 .....81 J8
Boston Ct SALQ M50 .....86 B4
Boston Gv LEIGH WN7 .....66 B3
Boston St BOL * BL1 .....36 B2
HULME M15 .....87 J7
HYDE SK14 .....102 B1
OLDS OL8 .....59 J8
Botanical Av OLDTF/WHR M16 .....86 D7
Botany La HEY OL10 .....40 E1
WGNE/HIN WN2 .....48 D2
Botany Rd ECC M30 .....69 K8
MPL/ROM SK6 .....101 K6
Botesworth Gn MILN OL16 .....29 K7
Botham Cl HULME M15 .....87 K7
Bothwell Rd NEWH/MOS M40 .....7M1
Bottesford Av DID/WITH M20.....98 C7
Bottomfield Cl OLD OL1 .....9M1
Bottom O' Th' Knotts Brow
EDGW/EG BL7 .....23 J1
Bottom O' Th' Moor BOLE BL2.....37 G2
HOR/BR BL6 .....34 C1
OLDE OL4 .....9M5
Bottom St HYDE SK14 .....102 C1
Boughey St LEIGH WN7 .....66 B7
Boulden Dr TOT/BURYW BL8.....24 F7

Boulder Dr NTHM/RTH M23 .....118 C2
Boulderstone Rd STLY SK15 .....76 F6
The Boulevard BRAM/HZG SK7 .....122 A2
STLY SK15 .....93 G7
Boundary Dr BOLE BL2 .....37 K7
Boundary Gdns BOL * BL1 .....36 A3
OLD OL1 .....9 G2
Boundary Gv SALE M33 .....109 J2
Boundary La HULME M15 .....87 K6
WGNNW/ST WN6 .....30 D1
Boundary Park Rd OLD OL1 .....58 F3
Boundary Rd CHD/CHDH SK8 .....111 J6
IRL M44 .....94 F1
SWIN M27 .....70 C4
Boundary St BOL BL1 .....36 A2
BOLE BL2 .....37 L7
LEIGH WN7 .....66 E8
LIT OL15 .....20 B6
ROCH OL11 .....10 D7
TYLD M29 .....67 K3
WGN WN1 .....15 J6
WGTN/LGST M12 .....88 D7
Boundary St East CMANE * M1 .....7 H9
Boundary St West HULME M15.....87 K6
Boundary Ter
WYTH/NTH * M22 .....119 H6
Boundry Gn WGNE/HIN WN2 .....33 H4
Bourdon St NEWH/MOS M40.....88 A1
Bourget St BRO M7 .....72 C4
Bournbrook Av LHULT M38 .....52 D6
Bourne Av GOL/RIS/CU WA3 .....80 A4
SWIN M27 .....70 C5
Bourne Dr NEWH/MOS M40 .....73 J3
Bournelea Av BNG/LEV M19 .....99 J6
Bourne Rd ROY/SHW OL2 .....43 K4
Bourne St CHAD OL9 .....74 D2
HTNM SK4 .....100 B8
WILM/AE SK9 .....126 D6
Bourneville Dr TOT/BURYW BL8 .....38 D2
Bournville Av HTNM SK4 .....100 B8
Bournville Gv BNG/LEV M19 .....99 L3
Bourton Cl TOT/BURYW BL8.....38 C1
Bourton Ct TYLD M29 .....68 A3
Bourton Dr GTN M18 .....88 A8
Bowden Cl GOL/RIS/CU WA3 .....81 J8
HYDE SK14 .....103 H3
LEIGH WN7 .....81M2
NM/HAY SK22 .....125 L1
ROCH OL11 .....42 A4
Bowden Crs NM/HAY SK22.....124 F4
Bowden La MPL/ROM SK6 .....114 B5
Bowden Rd GLSP SK13 .....104 F1
SWIN M27 .....70 D5
Bowden St BOLS/LL BL3 .....2 F6
BRAM/HZG SK7 .....122 A1
DTN/ASHW M34 .....101 H1
Bowdon Av RUSH/FAL M14 .....98 C3
Bowdon Ri ALT WA14 .....116 F2
Bowdon Rd ALT WA14 .....116 E1
Bowdon St EDGY/DAV SK3 .....13 C7
Bowen Cl BRAM/HZG SK7 .....121 H7
Bowen St BOL BL1 .....35 L3
Bower Av BRAM/HZG SK7 .....121M3
HTNM SK4 .....12 D1
WHIT SK12 .....19 L8
Bower Ct HYDE SK14 .....91 K7
Bowerfield Av BRAM/HZG SK7 .....121M4
Bowerfield Crs BRAM/HZG SK7 .....122 A4
Bowerfold La HTNM SK4 .....12 C1
Bower Gv STLY SK15 .....92 A4
Bower La HALE/TIMP WA15.....117 C3
Bowers Av URM M41 .....84 E8
Bowers St RUSH/FAL M14 .....99 G5
Bower St BRO * M7 .....72 B5
BURY BL9 .....5M2
NEWH/MOS M40 .....73 J7
OLD OL1 .....9M4
RDSH SK5 .....100 C4
Bower Ter DROY M43 .....89M1
Bowery Av CHD/CHDH SK8 .....120 B6
Bowes Cl TOT/BURYW BL8 .....24 E7
Bowes St RUSH/FAL M14 .....98 C3
Bowfell Dr MPL/ROM SK6 .....123 G4
Bowfell Gv BKLY M9 .....72 E1
Bowfell Rd URM M41 .....95 L2
Bowgreave Av BOLE BL2 .....37 J5
Bow Green Rd ALT WA14 .....116 C3
Bowgreen Wk HULME M15 .....87 G6
Bowker Av DTN/ASHW M34 .....101 K4
Bowker Bank Av CHH M8 .....72 C2
Bowker Cl ROCH OL11 .....27 H3
Bowkers Rw BOL BL1 .....2 F5
Bowker St BRO M7 .....72 A6
HYDE SK14 .....102 B1
RAD M26 .....54 D1
WALK M28 .....68 E1
Bowlacre Rd HYDE SK14 .....102 A6
Bowland Av AIMK WN4 .....63 L8
GOL/RIS/CU WA3 .....79M3
GTN M18 .....89 K8
Bowland Cl AUL OL6 .....75M5
OFTN SK2 .....113 H7
ROY/SHW OL2 .....43 L5
TOT/BURYW BL8 .....38 B1
Bowland Dr BOL BL1 .....35 H2
Bowland Gv MILN OL16 .....29 J8
Bowland Rd DTN/ASHW M34 .....100 F1
GLSP SK13 .....105 L7
MPL/ROM SK6 .....101 L7
NTHM/RTH M23 .....109 J6
Bow La ALT WA14 .....116 C4
CMANW M2 .....6 F5
HEY OL10 .....40 F2
Bowlee Cl BNG/LEV M19 .....99 L4
ROY/SHW OL2 .....43 L5
Bowler St BNG/LEV M19 .....99 L4
ROY/SHW OL2 .....43 L5
Bowlers Wk WHIT OL12 .....28 C2
Bowley Av WYTH/NTH M22.....118 C2
The Bowling Gn RAMS BL0 .....17 D1
Bowling Green St HEY OL10 .....41 G2
HYDE SK14 .....101M2
Bowling Green Wy ROCH OL11 .....12 B1
Bowling Rd GTN M18 .....100 B1
The Bowlings WGNNW/ST WN6.....47 K2
Bowling St CHAD OL9 .....74 E2
Bowman Crs AUL OL6 .....91 G1
Bow Meadow Gra
WGTN/LGST M12 .....88 C8
Bowmont Cl CHD/CHDH SK8 .....111 K8
Bowness Av CHD/CHDH SK8.....120 D3
HTNM SK4 .....100 B6
IRL M44 .....94 A8
WHIT OL12 .....27M3
Bowness Dr SALE M33 .....96 C7

Bowness Pl *WGNE/HIN* WN2 ....48 E4
Bowness Rd *AULW* OL7 ....75 J8
  BOLS/LL BL3 ....36 A8
  BOLS/LL BL3 ....37 J8
  MDTN M24 ....57 G3
Bowness St *OP/CLY* M11 ....89 J5
Bowring St *BRO* M7 ....71 M7
Bow Rd *LEIGH* WN7 ....81 L1
Bowscale Cl *BRUN/LGST* M13 ....88 C8
Bowstone Hill Rd *BOLE* BL2 ......23 L7
Bow St *BOL* BL1 ....2 E4
  CMANW M1 ....2 E5
  DUK SK16 ....90 F2
  EDGY/DAV SK3 ....12 C6
  OLD OL1 ....9 K5
  ROCH OL11 ....42 A1
Boxgrove Rd *SALE* M33 ....96 B7
Boxhill Dr *NTHM/RTH* M23 ....109 K3
Box St *LIT* OL15 ....20 B7
  RAMS * BLO 17 D6
Boxtree Av *GTN* M18 ....100 A1
Boyd Cl *WGNNW/ST* WN6 ....31 J4
Boydell St *LEIGH* WN7 ....66 C6
Boyd St *WGTN/LGST* M12 ....88 D5
Boyer St *OLDTF/WHR* M16 ......86 E7
Boyle St *BOL* BL1 ....35 K3
  CHH M8 ....72 E6
Boysnope Whf *ECC* M30 ....84 A8
Brabant Rd *CHD/CHDH* SK8 ....120 D2
Brabazon Pl *WGNW/BIL/O* WN5 ..46 F4
Brabham Cl *WGTN* M21 ....97 L4
Brabham Ms *SWIN* M27 ....69 M5
Brabyns Av *MPL/ROM* SK6 .....114 A1
Brabyns Brow *MPL/ROM* SK6 ...114 D5
Brabyns Rd *HYDE* SK14 ....102 B5
Bracadale Dr *EDGY/DAV* SK3 ...112 B8
Bracewell Cl *WGTN/LGST* M12 ...88 D7
Bracken Av *WALK* M28 ....69 H1
Bracken Cl *BOL* BL1 ....22 A6
  DROY M43 ....89 M2
  HEY OL10 ....41 G4
  HYDE SK14 ....93 G6
  MPL/ROM SK6 ....114 F5
  OLDE OL4 ....60 A4
  SALE M33 ....95 M7
Bracken Dr *NTHM/RTH* M23 ....109 L7
Brackenhurst Av *MOSL* OL5 .....77 H3
Bracken Lea *WHTN* BL5 ....50 C7
Bracken Lea Fold *WHIT* OL12 ....27 L2
Brackenlea Pl *EDGY/DAV* SK3 ..112 A7
Bracken Rd *AUL* OL6 ....67 C2
  LEIGH WN7 ....65 L7
Brackenside *RDSH* SK5 ....100 D4
Bracken Wy *GLSP* SK13 ....105 J5
Brackenwood Cl *ROY/SHW* OL2 ...58 F2
Brackenwood Dr
  CHD/CHDH SK8 ....111 G8
Brackenwood Ms
  WILM/AE SK9 ....127 J5
Brackley Av *HULME* M15 ....6 A9
  IRL M44 ....94 A6
  TYLD M29 ....67 L3
Brackley Dr *MDTN* M24 ....57 K7
Brackley Ldg *ECC* * M30 ....85 J1
Brackley Rd *ECC* M30 ....70 A8
  HTNM SK4 ....100 A1
  WHTN BL5 ....51 K4
Brackley Sq *OLD* * OL1 ....9 M3
  OLD * OL1 ....9 L3
  WALK M28 ....52 F8
Bracondale Av *BOL* BL1 ....35 L2
Bradbourne Cl *BOLS/LL* BL3 ......2 D9
Bradburn Cl *ECC* M30 ....85 G5
Bradburn Rd *IRL* M44 ....94 B5
Bradburn St *ECC* M30 ....85 G3
Bradburn Wk *CHH* M8 ....72 C4
Bradbury Av *ALT* WA14 ....107 K7
Bradbury St *AULW* * OL7 ....75 K8
  HYDE SK14 ....102 B3
  RAD M26 ....54 D2
Bradda Mt *BRAM/HZG* SK7 .....121 H2
Braddan Av *SALE* M33 ....108 F1
Bradden Cl *ORD* M5 ....86 D3
Braddocks Cl *WHIT* OL12 ....19 L8
Braddon Av *URM* M41 ....96 A1
Braddon Rd *MPL/ROM* SK6 ....101 K7
Braddon St *OP/CLY* M11 ....88 F3
Braddyll Rd *WHTN* BL5 ....51 J4
Brade Cl *OP/CLY* M11 ....88 F4
Bradfield Av *SLFD* M6 ....85 M2
Bradfield Cl *RDSH* SK5 ....100 B2
Bradfield Rd *URM* M41 ....96 C2
  BOLS/LL BL3 ....52 E1
Bradford Crs *BOLS/LL* * BL3 .....36 D8
Bradford La *MCFLDN* SK10 ....130 D6
Bradford Park Dr *BOLE* BL2 ......3 K6
Bradford Rd *BOLS/LL* BL3 ....52 D2
  ECC M30 ....70 B8
  NEWH/MOS M40 ....88 B1
Bradford St *BOLE* BL2 ....3 H5
  FWTH BL4 ....53 G5
  OLD OL1 ....9 G2
  WGNS/IIMK WN3 ....14 F6
Bradford Ter *BOLE* BL9 ....4 C7
Bradgate Av *CHD/CHDH* SK8 ...119 M3
Bradgate Rd *NTHM/RTH* M22 ...110 B4
Bradgate Rd *ALT* WA14 ....107 K7
  SALE M33 ....108 E2
Bradgate St *AULW* OL7 ....90 D1
Bradgreen Rd *ECC* M30 ....84 D4
Bradley Av *BRO* M7 ....71 L5
Bradley Cl *HALE/TIMP* WA15 ...108 B5
Bradley Dr *BURY* BL9 ....24 F5
Bradley Fold *STLY* SK15 ....91 L2
Bradley Fold Rd *BOLE* BL2 ......37 L6
Bradley Green Rd *HYDE* SK14 ...91 J6
Bradley La *BOLS/LL* BL3 ....37 L7
  MILN OL16 ....29 L8
  STRET M32 ....96 E5
  WGNNW/ST WN6 ....31 J2
Bradleys Count *CMANE* * M1 ......7 J4
Bradley Smithy La *WHIT* OL12 ...28 B2
Bradley St *CMANE* M1 ....7 J3
  MILN OL16 ....29 L8
Bradney Cl *BKLY* M9 ....56 E8
Bradnor Rd *WYTH/NTH* M22 ...110 A5
Bradshaw Av *DID/WITH* M20 ....98 E5
  NEWH/MOS M40 ....74 B7
  WHTF M45 ....55 H2
Bradshaw Brow *BOLE* BL2 ......22 F8
  BOLE BL2 ....36 E1
Bradshaw Cl *WGNNW/ST* WN6 ...31 G3
Bradshaw Crs *MPL/ROM* SK6 ...114 D5
Bradshaw Fold Av
  NEWH/MOS M40 ....74 A1
  LEIGH WN7 ....66 C7
Bradshawgate *BOL* BL1 ....2 F5
  LEIGH WN7 ....66 C7

  WGN WN1 ....15 J4
Bradshaw Hall Dr *BOLE* BL2 ....22 F6
Bradshaw Hall Fold *BOLE* * BL2 ..23 G6
Bradshaw Hall La
  CHD/CHDH SK8 ....119 M4
Bradshaw La *STRET* M32 ....97 G4
Bradshaw Mdw *BOLE* BL2 ......23 G6
Bradshaw Rd *BOLE* BL2 ....23 G5
  MPL/ROM SK6 ....114 C5
  TOT/BURYW BL8 ....23 M6
Bradshaw St *ANC* * M4 ....7 G2
  ATH M46 ....67 G1
  BRO M7 ....72 B6
  FWTH BL4 ....53 G5
  HEY OL10 ....41 H2
  OLD OL1 ....9 K5
  RAD M26 ....54 C1
  WGN WN1 ....48 A2
  WGNW/BIL/O WN5 ......46 D6
Bradshaw St North *BRO* M7 .....72 A5
Bradstock Rd *OLDTF/WHR* M16 ..98 B1
Bradstone Rd *CHH* M8 ....72 C7
Bradwell Av *DID/WITH* M20 .....98 C6
  STRET M32 ....96 D1
Bradwell Dr *CHD/CHDH* SK8 ....119 L5
Bradwell Pl *BOLE* BL2 ....36 E3
  GOL/RIS/CU WA3 ....80 B5
Bradwen Av *CHH* M8 ....72 D3
Bradwen Cl *HYDE* SK14 ....102 B5
Brady St *HOR/BR* BL6 ....21 A7
  STKP SK1 ....13 L2
Braeburn Ct *LEIGH* WN7 ....66 A7
Braemar Av *STRET* M32 ....96 D2
  URM M41 ....95 K3
Braemar Dr *BRAM/HZG* SK7 ...122 B1
  RUSH/FAL M14 ....99 H4
Braemore Cl *ROY/SHW* OL2 .....43 H4
  WGNS/IIMK WN3 ....62 F2
Braemore Dr *HYDE* SK14 ....103 J3
Brae Side *OLDS* OL8 ....75 H2
Braeside *STRET* * M32 ....96 D3
Braeside Cl *OFTN* SK2 ....113 J7
Braeside Gv *BOLS/LL* BL3 ....35 H7
Braewood Cl *BURY* BL9 ....39 M1
Bragenham St *GTN* M18 ....88 F7
Braidhaven *WGNNW/ST* WN6 ...30 B5
Brailsford Rd *BOLE* BL2 ....36 F1
  RUSH/FAL M14 ....99 H4
Braintree Rd *WYTH/NTH* M22 ...119 G4
Braithwaite Rd
  GOL/RIS/CU WA3 ....80 A3
  MDTN M24 ....41 G8
Brakehouse Cl *MILN* OL16 ......29 H6
Brakenhurst Dr *BRO* * M7 ....72 C6
Brakesmere Gv *LHULT* M38 .....52 C8
Braley St *CMANE* * M1 ....7 K8
Bramall Edge Ct *GLSP* SK13 .....93 J6
Bramall Cl *BURY* BL9 ....55 L2
Bramall St *HYDE* SK14 ....91 G8
Bramble Av *OLDE* OL4 ....60 A3
  ORD M5 ....86 F5
Bramble Bank *GLSP* SK13 ......105 H4
Bramble Cl *LIT* OL15 ....20 A7
Bramble Cft *WHTN* BL5 ....50 D1
Brambling Cl *DTN/ASHW* M34 ...89 M2
  OFTN SK2 ....113 K8
Brambling Dr *WHTN* BL5 ....50 A6
Brambling Wy *GOL/RIS/CU* WA3 ..80 B5
Bramcote Av *BOLE* BL2 ....37 J3
  NTHM/RTH M23 ....109 L6
Bramdean Av *BOLE* BL2 ....23 H7
Bramfield Wk *HULME* M15 ....6 B9
Bramhall Cl *DUK* SK16 ....91 G6
  HALE/TIMP WA15 ......108 C6
  MILN OL16 ....29 H6
  SALE M33 ....109 H1
Bramhall La South
  BRAM/HZG SK7 ....121 G2
  OFTN SK2 ....112 C6
Bramhall Moor La
  BRAM/HZG SK7 ....121 K3
Bramhall Park Rd
  BRAM/HZG SK7 ....120 E3
Bramhall Rd *BOLS/LL* BL3 ....52 E1
  GTN * M18 ....89 H7
Bramham Rd *MPL/ROM* SK6 ...114 C8
Bramley Av *BNG/LEV* M19 ......99 K4
  STRET M32 ....96 E2
Bramley Cl *BRAM/HZG* SK7 ....121 G6
  SWIN M27 ....69 M6
Bramley Crs *HTNM* SK4 ....12 A4
Bramley Dr *BRAM/HZG* SK7 ...121 G6
  TOT/BURYW BL8 ....24 F5
Bramley Meade *BRO* M7 ....72 B5
Bramley Rd *BOL* BL1 ....22 C6
  BRAM/HZG SK7 ....121 G6
  ROCH OL11 ....27 H4
Bramley St *BRO* M7 ....72 B7
Brammay Dr *TOT/BURYW* BL8 ...24 B7
Brampton Cl *WGNE/HIN* WN2 ...64 C3
Brampton Rd *BOLS/LL* BL3 .....51 K1
  BRAM/HZG SK7 ....121 H2
Brampton St *ATH* * M46 ....67 G1
Bramway *BRAM/HZG* SK7 .....120 E5
  MPL/ROM SK6 ....114 B5
Bramwell Dr *BRUN/LGST* M13 ...87 M6
Bramwell St *STKP* SK1 ....112 E4
Bramworth Av *RAMS* BLO 17 B6
Brancaster Dr *GOL/RIS/CU* WA3 ..80 D5
Brancaster Rd *CMANE* M1 ....7 H8
Branch Rd *LIT* OL15 ....29 H3
Branch St *WGNE/HIN* WN2 ......48 D5
Branch Wy *RNFD/HAY* WA11 ....78 A4
Brancker St *WHTN* BL5 ....51 H4
Brandish Cl *BRUN/LGST* M13 ...88 A4
Brandle Av *TOT/BURYW* BL8 ....24 F6
Brandlehow Dr *MDTN* M24 ......56 F2
Brandlesholme Rd
  TOT/BURYW BL8 ....24 F6
Brandon Av *CHD/CHDH* SK8 ...119 K3
  DTN/ASHW M34 ....100 C3
  ECC M30 ....70 D8
  WYTH/NTH M22 ....109 M4
Brandon Brow *OLD* * OL1 ....9 H2
Brandon Rd *TOT/BURYW* BL8 ...25 G2
  WILM/AE SK9 ....127 H1

Brandon Crs *ROY/SHW* OL2 .....43 K4
Brandon Rd *SLFD* M6 ....86 A1
Brandon St *BOLS/LL* BL3 ....36 A8
  MILN OL16 ....29 H6
Brandram Rd *PWCH* * M25 ......55 L8
Brandreth Pl *WGNNW/ST* WN6 ..31 J3
Brandsby Gdns *ORD* M5 ....86 D4
Brandwood *OLD* OL1 ....58 B3
Brandwood Av *CCHDY* M21 .....98 A8
Brandwood Cl *WALK* M28 ....68 A2
Brandwood St *BOLS/LL* BL3 .....35 M8
Branfield Av *CHD/CHDH* SK8 ...119 M3
Branksome Av *PWCH* M25 ....55 K8
Branksome Dr *BKLY* M9 ....56 E6
  CHD/CHDH SK8 ....119 M5
  SLFD M6 ....70 D7
Branksome Rd *HTNM* SK4 ......12 A4
Brannach Dr *CHAD* OL9 ....58 D4
Bransby Av *BKLY* M9 ....57 H8
Branscombe Dr *SALE* M33 ......95 M7
Branscombe Gdns
  BOLS/LL * BL3 ....37 G7
Bransdale Av *ROY/SHW* OL2 .....42 F8
Bransdale Cl *BOLS/LL* BL3 ....35 J8
Bransdale Dr *AIMK* WN4 ....79 G1
Bransfield Cl *WGNS/IIMK* WN3 ...63 K1
Bransford Cl *AIMK* WN4 ....78 F2
Bransford Rd *OP/CLY* M11 ......89 G4
  URM M41 ....95 M1
Branson Cl *GOL/RIS/CU* WA3 ....79 K2
Branson St *NEWH/MOS* M40 ....88 A2
Branston Rd *NEWH/MOS* M40 ...74 A2
Brantfell Gv *BOLE* BL2 ....37 J4
Branthwaite *WGNE/HIN* WN2 ...48 E3
Brantingham Rd *CCHDY* M21 ....97 L3
Brantwood Cl *ROY/SHW* OL2 ....42 F8
Brantwood Dr *BOLE* BL2 ....37 J4
Brantwood Rd *BRO* M7 ....72 A4
  HTNM SK4 ....99 M8
Brantwood Ter *BKLY* * M9 ....73 J5
Brassey St *AUL* OL6 ....75 L8
  MDTN M24 ....57 K3
Brassica Cl *ECC* M30 ....69 K8
Brassington Av *ORD* M5 ....86 E4
Brassington Crs *CLSP* SK13 ....104 A3
Brassington Rd *HTNM* SK4 ......99 J8
Brathay Cl *BOLE* BL2 ....37 J3
Bratton Cl *WGNS/IIMK* WN3 ....62 F3
Bratton Wk *BRUN/LGST* * M13 ..88 A6
Brattray Dr *MDTN* M24 ....57 H1
Braunston Cl *ECC* M30 ....85 H4
Bray Av *ECC* M30 ....84 C1
Braybrook Dr *BOL* BL1 ....35 G5
Bray Cl *CHD/CHDH* SK8 ....120 A2
Brayford Dr *WGNE/HIN* WN2 ...32 F7
Brayford Rd *WYTH/NTH* M22 ...110 F3
Brayshaw Cl *HEY* OL10 ....40 E3
Brayside Rd *DID/WITH* M20 .....98 E5
Braystan Gdns *CHD/CHDH* SK8 .110 E6
Brayston Fold *MDTN* M24 ......56 F4
Brayton Av *DID/WITH* M20 .....110 F2
  SALE M33 ....95 G1
Brayton Ct *WGNE/HIN* WN2 ....49 G6
Brazennose St *CSLFD* M3 ....6 E5
Brazil St *CMANE* M1 ....7 H7
Brazley Av *BOLS/LL* BL3 ....52 D1
  HOR/BR BL6 ....34 B3
Bread St *GTN* M18 ....89 H6
Breaktemper *WHTN* BL5 ....50 B3
Breaston Av *LEIGH* WN7 ....81 L1
Breckland Cl *STLY* SK15 ....92 A2
Breckland Dr *BOL* BL1 ....35 G4
Breckles Pl *BOLS/LL* * BL3 ....2 B8
Breck Rd *ECC* M30 ....84 E2
  CHD/CHDH SK8 ....120 A3
  DTN/ASHW M34 ....101 J3
  URM M41 ....95 G1
Brecon Cl *POY/DIS* SK12 ......121 B8
  ROY/SHW OL2 ....42 F6
  WGNE/HIN WN2 ....64 C2
Brecon Crs *AUL* OL6 ....75 L6
Brecon Dr *BURY* BL9 ....39 H5
  WGNE/HIN WN2 ....65 K1
Brecon Wk *OLDS* * OL8 ....74 E2
Bredbury Dr *FWTH* BL4 ....53 H4
Bredbury Gn *MPL/ROM* SK6 ...113 K3
Bredbury Park Wy
  MPL/ROM SK6 ....101 H7
Bredbury St *CHAD* OL9 ....9 G7
  HYDE * SK14 ....91 G7
Breeze Hi *ATH* M46 ....71 L2
  WGNNW/ST WN6 ....31 L5
Breeze Hill Rd *ATH* M46 ....71 L5
  OLDE OL4 ....60 A7
Breeze Mt *PWCH* M25 ....71 L2
Breightmet Dr *BOLE* BL2 ....37 H5
Breightmet Fold La *BOLE* BL2 ...37 J5
  BOLE BL2 ....37 J5
Breightmet St *BOLE* BL2 ....3 J5
Brellafield Dr *ROY/SHW* OL2 ....43 J3
Brenbar Crs *WHIT* OL12 ....18 E3
Brenchley Dr *NTHM/RTH* M23 ..109 K3
Brencon Av *WHIT* OL12 ....108 F3
Brendall Cl *OFTN* SK2 ....113 K7
Brendon Av *NEWH/MOS* M40 ...73 K5
  RDSH SK5 ....100 C6
Brendon Cl *GLSP* SK13 ....104 D4
Brendon Dr *DTN/ASHW* M34 ...90 A3
Brendon Hills *ROY/SHW* OL2 ....58 F1
Brennan Cl *HULME* M15 ....87 K7
Brennan Ct *OLDS* OL8 ....74 E2
Brennock Cl *OP/CLY* M11 ......88 C4
Brentbridge Rd *RUSH/FAL* M14 ..98 E4
Brent Cl *BOLE* BL2 ....37 L7
  POY/DIS SK12 ....121 K8
Brentfield Av *CHH* M8 ....72 C6
Brentford Av *BOL* BL1 ....35 L2
Brentford Rd *RDSH* SK5 ....100 C6
Brentford St *BKLY* M9 ....73 H5
Brent Moor Rd *BRAM/HZG* SK7 ..121 J1
Brentnall St *STKP* SK1 ....13 J8
Brentnor Rd *NEWH/MOS* M40 ..73 M2
Brenton Av *SALE* M33 ....96 D8
Brent Rd *HTNM* SK4 ....12 C4
  NTHM/RTH M23 ....109 K2
Brentwood *SALE* M33 ....86 B1
  WGNW/BIL/O WN5 ......47 G7
Brentwood Av *ALT* WA14 .....108 B5
  IRL M44 ....94 A6
  URM M41 ....96 A2
  WALK M28 ....69 J6
Brentwood Cl *LIT* OL15 ....29 J1
  OLDTF/WHR M16 ....98 C1
  RDSH SK5 ....101 G4
  STLY SK15 ....91 M2

Brentwood Ct *PWCH* M25 ....71 J1
Brentwood Crs *ALT* WA14 .....108 B6
  ECC M30 ....70 A8
  FWTH BL4 ....52 E2
Brentwood Dr *SWIN* M27 ....70 A6
Brereton Cl *ALT* WA14 ....116 B3
Brereton Dr *WALK* M28 ....69 J5
Brereton Gv *IRL* M44 ....94 B6
Brereton Rd *ECC* M30 ....84 C3
  WILM/AE SK9 ....127 J1
Breslyn St *CSLFD* M3 ....6 F1
Bretherton Rw *WGN* WN1 ......14 F4
Bretherton St *WGNE/HIN* WN2 ..48 F6
Brethren's Ct *DROY* M43 ....89 K4
Bretland Gdns *HYDE* SK14 ....103 H3
Brettargh St *SLFD* M6 ....71 K8
Brett Rd *WALK* M28 ....68 C6
Brett St *WYTH/NTH* M22 ......110 B3
Brewer's Gn *BRAM/HZG* SK7 ...121 M1
Brewer St *CMANE* M1 ....7 J4
Brewerton Rd *OLDE* OL4 ....59 M7
Brewery La *LEIGH* WN7 ....66 D7
  STKP SK1 ....13 K2
Brewster St *BKLY* * M9 ....73 G4
  MDTN M24 ....57 K2
Brian Av *DROY* M43 ....89 M1
Brian Redhead Ct *HULME* M15 ...6 C9
Brian Rd *FWTH* BL4 ....52 D2
Brian St *ROCH* OL11 ....41 L2
Briarcre Ter *AUL* * OL6 ....75 M4
  OLDE OL4 ....60 A3
Briar Cl *AIMK* WN4 ....63 K8
  SALE M33 ....95 K1
  URM M41 ....95 K1
  WGNE/HIN WN2 ....49 G8
  WHIT OL12 ....27 K3
Briar Crs *WYTH/NTH* M22 .....110 B7
Briarcroft Dr *ATH* M46 ....66 D3
Briardene *DTN/ASHW* * M34 ....90 D7
Briardene Gdns
  WYTH/NTH M22 ....110 B8
Briarfield *EDGW/EG* BL7 ....22 A2
Briarfield Rd *CHD/CHDH* SK8 ..120 D1
  DID/WITH M20 ....99 G6
  FWTH BL4 ....52 D3
  HALE/TIMP WA15 ......108 F6
  HTNM SK4 ....100 B6
  UPML OL3 ....61 K2
  WALK M28 ....69 J5
Briar Gv *CHAD* OL9 ....58 E3
  LEIGH WN7 ....66 B4
  MPL/ROM SK6 ....101 K7
Briar Hill Av *LHULT* M38 ....52 B8
Briar Hill Cl *LHULT* M38 ....52 B8
Briar Hill Gv *LHULT* M38 ....52 B8
Briar Hill Wy *SLFD* * M6 ....86 D1
Briar Hollow *HTNM* SK4 ....12 A4
Briarlands Av *SALE* M33 ....108 C2
Briarlands Cl *BRAM/HZG* SK7 ..120 F6
Briarlea Gdns *BNG/LEV* M19 ....99 H7
Briarley Gdns *MPL/ROM* SK6 ..101 M6
Briarly *WGNNW/ST* WN6 ....31 K5
Briarmere Wk *CHAD* OL9 ....8 C4
Briar Rd *GOL/RIS/CU* WA3 ......79 L4
  WGNW/BIL/O WN5 ......47 G5
Briars Mt *HTNM* SK4 ....111 K2
Briars Pk *CHD/CHDH* SK8 .....120 E3
Briarstead Cl *BRAM/HZG* SK7 ..120 F5
Briar St *BOLE* * BL2 ....37 G5
  ROCH OL11 ....10 B6
Briarwood *WILM/AE* SK9 ......127 G5
Briarwood Av *DROY* M43 ....89 H1
  NTHM/RTH M23 ....109 G4
Briarwood Cha *CHD/CHDH* SK8 .120 D3
Briarwood Crs *MPL/ROM* SK6 ..114 C8
Briary Dr *TYLD* M29 ....67 L4
Brice St *DUK* SK16 ....90 F4
Brickbridge Rd *MPL/ROM* SK6 ..114 D5
Brickfield St *GLSP* SK13 ....93 L7
  MILN OL16 ....29 K4
Brickhill La *HALE/TIMP* WA15 ..117 K8
Brick Houses *GLSP* * SK13 .....103 J7
Brick Kiln La *WGN* WN1 ....15 G2
Brickkiln Rw *ALT* WA14 ....116 E3
Brickley St *CSLFD* M3 ....87 K1
Brick St *ANC* * M4 ....7 J3
  BURY BL9 ....5 J3
Bridcam St *CHH* M8 ....72 D7
Briddon St *CSLFD* M3 ....87 J1
Brideoake St *LEIGH* WN7 ......66 E8
  OLDE OL4 ....60 B4
Brideoak St *CHH* M8 ....72 D6
Bridestowe Av *HYDE* SK14 ....102 F1
Bridge Av *MPL/ROM* SK6 ......101 K7
Bridge Bank Rd *LIT* OL15 ....29 J1
Bridge Cl *PART* M31 ....106 D1
  RAD M26 ....54 E2
Bridgecrest Ct
  CHD/CHDH * SK8 ......120 E2
Bridgecroft St *WGNE/HIN* WN2 ..49 H6
Bridge Dr *CHD/CHDH* SK8 .....111 G8
  WILM/AE SK9 ....127 G5
Bridgefield Crs *OLDE* OL4 ......60 C6
Bridgefield Dr *BURY* BL9 ....39 M2
Bridgefield St *RAD* M26 ....54 E1
  ROCH OL11 ....10 B5
  STKP SK1 ....13 H4
Bridgefold Rd *ROCH* OL11 .....27 M5
Bridgefoot Cl *WALK* M28 ....68 D7
Bridge Gv *HALE/TIMP* WA15 ...108 C5
Bridge Hall Dr *BURY* BL9 ....39 M2
Bridge Hall Fold *BURY* BL9 .....39 M2
Bridge Hall La *BURY* BL9 ....39 M2
Bridge La *BRAM/HZG* SK7 .....121 H2
Bridgelea Ms *DID/WITH* M20 ....98 E6
Bridgelea Rd *DID/WITH* M20 ....98 E5
Bridgeman Pl *BOLE* BL2 ....3 K6
Bridgeman St *BOLS/LL* BL3 .....36 B8
  FWTH BL4 ....53 G3
Bridgeman Ter *WGN* WN1 ......14 F1
Bridgemere Cl *RAD* M26 ....38 C7
Bridgend Cl *CHD/CHDH* SK8 ...111 L8
  WGTN/LGST M12 ....88 B5
Bridgenorth Av *URM* M41 ......96 C2
Bridgenorth Dr *LIT* OL15 ....29 J1
Bridge Rd *BURY* BL9 ....4 C6
  HALE/TIMP WA15 ......108 F5
Bridges Av *BURY* BL9 ....39 G6
Bridges Ct *BOL* BL1 ....2 A6
Bridge's St *ATH* M46 ....66 E2
Bridge St *BOL* BL1 ....2 E5
  BURY BL9 ....5 H3
  CSLFD M3 ....6 D3
  DROY M43 ....89 L3
  DUK SK16 ....90 D6

  BL4 ....53 H3
Gol/RIS/CU* WA3 ....79 K5
  HEY OL10 ....40 E2
  HOR/BR BL6 ....21 C8
  MDTN * M24 ....57 K4
  MILN OL16 ....29 J4
  NEWLW WA12 ....79 K5
  NM/HAY SK22 ....124 E3
  OLD OL1 ....9 L6
  OLDE OL4 ....60 C6
  RAD M26 ....53 L4
  RAMS BLO 17 C6
  ROCH OL11 ....41 M3
  ROY/SHW * OL2 ....43 M4
  STKP SK1 ....13 J3
  STLY SK15 ....91 J3
  SWIN M27 ....70 B6
  UPML OL3 ....61 L5
  WGNE/HIN WN2 ....48 D1
  WGNS/IIMK WN3 ....14 F6
  WHIT OL12 ....18 D3
  WHIT * OL12 ....28 F1
Bridge St Brow *STKP* SK1 ......13 J3
Bridgewater Cir *TRPK* M17 .....84 F6
Bridgewater Pl *ANC* M4 ....7 G4
Bridgewater Rd *ALT* WA14 ....108 A5
  SWIN M27 ....70 E5
  WALK M28 ....68 D5
Bridgewater St *BOL* BL1 ....2 A6
  CSLFD M3 ....6 A6
  CSLFD M3 ....87 H1
  ECC M30 ....84 E2
  FWTH BL4 ....53 G4
  LHULT M38 ....52 C8
  OLD OL1 ....9 L3
  SALE M33 ....96 F1
  STRET * M32 ....97 H2
  WGNE/HIN WN2 ....14 G6
  WGNS/IIMK WN3 ....14 E5
  WGNW/BIL/O WN5 ......47 G5
Bridgewater Viad *HULME* M15 ...6 D8
Bridgewater Wy
  OLDTF/WHR M16 ....86 E7
Bridgfield Cl *GTN* M18 ....123 C5
Bridgnorth Rd *BKLY* M9 ....72 D1
Bridle Cl *DROY* M43 ....89 M1
  URM M41 ....96 A2
Bridle Fold *RAD* M26 ....38 D8
Bridle Rd *BRAM/HZG* SK7 ......128 D1
  PWCH M25 ....56 A5
Bridle Wy *BRAM/HZG* SK7 .....128 D2
Bridleway *NM/HAY* SK22 .....124 F3
Bridlington Av *SLFD* * M6 ....85 J1
Bridlington Cl *NEWH/MOS* M40 ..73 M6
Bridport Av *NEWH/MOS* M40 ...74 A4
Bridson La *BOLE* BL2 ....37 G3
Bridson St *OLDE* OL4 ....59 M5
  SLFD M6 ....86 B3
Brief St *BOLE* BL2 ....36 F3
Brien Av *ALT* WA14 ....108 A6
Briercliffe Cl *GTN* M18 ....88 F6
Briercliffe Rd *BOLS/LL* BL3 .....35 M7
Brierfield Av *ATH* M46 ....50 F8
Brierfield Dr *BURY* BL9 ....25 H4
Brierholme Av *EDGW/EG* BL7 ...22 B3
Brierley Av *FAIL* M35 ....74 D5
  WHTF M45 ....55 H2
Brierley Cl *AUL* OL6 ....76 C6
  DTN/ASHW M34 ....101 H2
Brierley Dr *MDTN* M24 ....57 K5
Brierley Rd East *SWIN* M27 .....70 B3
Brierley Rd West *SWIN* M27 ....70 B3
Brierley St *BURY* BL9 ....4 B8
  CHAD OL9 ....8 D2
  DUK * SK16 ....91 G3
  HEY OL10 ....41 G2
  OLDS OL8 ....75 J1
Brierley Wk *CHAD* OL9 ....8 D2
Brierton Dr *WYTH/NTH* M22 ...118 D3
Brierwood Cl *OLD* OL1 ....59 H3
Briery Av *BOLE* BL2 ....23 G6
Brigade Dr *STRET* M32 ....96 F1
Brigade St *BOL* BL1 ....35 M5
Brigadier Cl *DID/WITH* M20 .....98 E6
Brigantine Cl *ORD* M5 ....86 D4
Briggs Cl *SALE* M33 ....107 M3
Briggs Fold Cl *EDGW/EG* BL7 ...22 B2
Briggs Fold Rd *EDGW/EG* BL7 ...22 B2
Briggs Rd *STRET* * M32 ....86 C8
  LEIGH WN7 ....66 B5
Brigham St *OP/CLY* M11 ....88 F4
Bright Cir *URM* M41 ....85 H6
Brightman St *WGNE/HIN* WN2 ..89 G6
Brighton Av *BNG/LEV* M19 .....99 J5
  BOL BL1 ....35 K3
  BRO M7 ....72 B6
  RDSH SK5 ....100 C2
  URM M41 ....95 H1
Brighton Gv *HYDE* SK14 ......102 B3
  RUSH/FAL M14 ....99 G2
  SALE M33 ....95 M2
Brighton Pl *BRUN/LGST* M13 ...87 L6
Brighton Range *GTN* * M18 .....89 J8
Brighton Rd *HTNM* SK4 ....12 C4
  OLDE OL4 ....60 C3
Brighton St *ANC* M4 ....87 K1
  BURY BL9 ....5 K2
Bright Rd *ECC* M30 ....84 D2
Brightstone Wk *RUSH/FAL* M14 ..88 B8
Bright St *AUL* OL6 ....91 G2
  BURY BL9 ....5 J2
  DROY M43 ....89 L3
  LEIGH WN7 ....66 B5
  MILN OL16 ....10 E8
  OLDS OL8 ....8 B8
  RAD M26 ....38 F8
Brightwater Cl *WHTF* M45 .....55 K4
Brightwell Wk *ANC* M4 ....7 J2
Brignall Gv *GOL/RIS/CU* WA3 ...80 A3
Brigstock Av *GTN* M18 ....88 F7
Brimelow St *MPL/ROM* SK6 ...112 F1
Brimfield Av *TYLD* M29 ....67 M3
Brimmy Croft La *UPML* OL3 ....45 H4
Brimrod La *ROCH* OL11 ....10 A9
Brimscombe Av
  WYTH/NTH M22 ....118 C3
Brindale Rd *RDSH* SK5 ....100 F8
Brindle Cl *SLFD* M6 ....71 J8
Brindle Heath Rd *SLFD* M6 .....71 J8
Brindlehurst Dr *TYLD* M29 .....67 M5
Brindle St *TYLD* M29 ....67 K3
  WGNE/HIN WN2 ....49 J5
Brindley Av *BKLY* M9 ....56 E7
  MPL/ROM SK6 ....114 C7
  SALE M33 ....107 K1

WALK M28 68 D6
Brindley Cl ATH M46 66 D2
FWTH BL4 52 E4
Brindley Rd OLDTF/WHR M16 86 E7
Brindley St ECC M30 84 E1
HOR/BR * BL6 33 M2
SWIN M27 70 C2
WALK M28 68 C6
WALK M28 69 G2
WGNW/BIL/O WN5 46 F7
Brinell Dr IRL M44 94 C7
Brinkburn Rd BRAM/HZG SK7 122 C1
Brinklow Cl OP/CLY M11 89 H5
Brinkshaw Av WYTH/NTH M22 119 G2
Brinks La BOLE BL2 37 K5
Brinks Rw HOR/BR * BL6 21 D7
Brinksway BOL BL1 34 F5
EDGY/DAV SK3 12 C6
Brinnington Crs RDSH SK5 100 E8
Brinnington Rd STKP SK1 13 M1
Brinsop Hall La WHTN BL5 33 K7
Brinsop Sq GTN M18 88 E6
Brinsworth Dr CHH M8 72 D6
Briony Av HALE/TIMP WA15 117 L2
Briony Cl ROY/SHW OL2 59 H2
Brisbane Cl BRAM/HZG SK7 121 H7
Brisbane St HULME M15 87 L7
Briscoe La NEWH/MOS M40 73 L7
Briscoe St OLD OL1 9 J3
Bristle Hall Wy WHTN BL5 50 C2
Bristle St HULME M15 87 K6
Bristol Av AUL OL6 75 L5
BNG/LEV M19 99 L4
BOLE BL2 3 L1
Bristol St BRO M7 72 B5
Bristowe St OP/CLY M11 89 G1
Britain St BURY BL9 39 H6
Britannia Av ROY/SHW OL2 43 M6
Britannia Cl RAD M26 54 D1
Britannia Rd SALE M33 96 E7
WGNW/BIL/O WN5 46 F4
Britannia St AULW OL7 90 C4
HEY OL10 40 E2
OLD OL1 9 M4
SLFD M6 71 K6
Britannia Wy BOL BL1 36 D2
Britnall Av WGTN/LGST M12 88 B7
Briton St MILN OL16 11 H2
ROY/SHW OL2 59 H2
Brixham Av CHD/CHDH SK8 120 B5
Brixham Dr SALE M33 96 A6
Brixham Rd OLDTF/WHR M16 86 E8
Brixham Wk BRAM/HZG SK7 121 G5
BRUN/LGST M13 87 M7
Brixton Av DID/WITH M20 98 D6
Broach St BOLS/LL BL3 36 B8
Broadacre STLY SK15 92 B6
WGNNW/ST WN6 30 D2
Broad Acre WHIT OL12 27 H2
Broadbent Av AUL OL6 75 M6
DUK SK16 91 G4
Broadbent Cl ROY/SHW OL2 43 J7
STLY SK15 77 H6
Broadbent Dr BURY BL9 26 B8
Broadbent Gv HYDE SK14 103 H3
Broadbent Rd OLD OL1 59 M3
Broadbent St HYDE SK14 91 G8
SWIN M27 70 A5
Broadbottom Rd HYDE SK14 103 J2
Broadcarr La MOSL OL5 76 D3
Broadfield Cl DTN/ASHW M34 101 K2
Broadfield Dr LIT OL15 29 J1
Broadfield Gv RDSH SK5 100 B1
Broadfield Rd GTN M18 100 B1
RUSH/FAL M14 98 D1
Broadfield Stile MILN OL16 10 D6
Broadfield St HEY OL10 40 E3
MILN OL16 10 D6
Broadford Rd BOLS/LL BL3 35 J7
Broadgate MDTN M24 58 A6
UPML OL3 61 H3
Broadgate Meadow
SWIN * M27 70 C5
Broadgreen Gdns FWTH * BL4 53 G2
Broadhalgh Av ROCH OL11 27 K5
Broadhalgh Rd ROCH OL11 27 K6
Broadhead Rd EDGW/EG BL7 16 E5
Broadheath Cl WHTN BL5 50 D3
Broad Hey MPL/ROM SK6 114 A1
Broadhey Vw NM/HAY SK22 124 D3
Broad Hill Cl BRAM/HZG SK7 121 J2
Broadhill Rd BNG/LEV M19 99 H6
STLY SK15 76 D8
Broadhurst DTN/ASHW M34 90 D7
Broadhurst Av SWIN M27 70 C1
Broadhurst Ct BOLS/LL BL3 36 A8
Broadhurst Gv AUL OL6 75 M6
Broadhurst St BOLS/LL * BL3 36 A8
EDGY/DAV SK3 13 H9
Broad Ing WHIT * OL12 27 L3
Broadlands WGNNW/ST WN6 30 E6
Broadlands Rd SWIN M27 69 M6
Broad La HALE/TIMP WA15 117 K4
MILN OL16 42 F1
UPML OL3 45 H5
Broad Lea URM M41 95 M1
Broadlea Gv WHIT OL12 27 M2
Broadlea Rd BNG/LEV M19 99 H6
Broadley Av GOL/RIS/CU WA3 79 M5
WYTH/NTH M22 110 A8
Broadmeadow EDGW/EG BL7 22 E4
Broadmeadow Av
OLDTF/WHR M16 98 C3
Broadmoss Dr BKLY M9 73 K1
Broadmoss Rd BKLY M9 73 K1
Broadmount Ter CHAD * OL9 58 E8
Broadoak Av WALK M28 68 C5
WYTH/NTH M22 109 M7
Broadoak Crs AUL OL6 75 L7
Broad Oak Crs OLDS OL8 75 K2
Broadoak Dr WYTH/NTH M22 110 A7
Broad Oak La BURY BL9 39 M1
DID/WITH M20 110 F4
Broad Oak Pk ECC M30 70 A8
WALK M28 69 L6
Broad Oak Rd FWTH BL4 52 D2
Broadoak Rd AUL OL6 75 L7
BRAM/HZG SK7 121 H2
ROCH OL11 27 H6
WYTH/NTH M22 109 M8
Broadoaks BURY BL9 40 A1
Broadoaks Rd SALE M33 96 D8
URM M41 95 L3
Broad Oak Ter BURY BL9 40 B1
Broad O' Th' La BOL BL1 22 B8
WGNNW/ST WN6 30 D6
Broadriding Rd
WGNNW/ST WN6 30 B6
Broad Rd SALE M33 96 F7
Broad Shaw La MILN OL16 43 G2
Broadstone Av OLDE OL4 44 C8
Broadstone Cl PWCH M25 71 K1
WHIT OL12 27 K3
Broadstone Hall Rd North
HTNM SK4 100 A6
Broadstone Hall Rd South
HTNM SK4 100 B6
Broadstone Rd BOLE BL2 23 G7
HTNM SK4 100 A6
Broad St BURY BL9 4 E5
MDTN M24 56 F5
SWIN M27 71 G6
Broad Wk WHTN BL5 50 B5
WILM/AE SK9 126 D4
The Broadway MPL/ROM SK6 101 H8
Broadway ATH M46 51 J7
BRAM/HZG SK7 121 H2
CHAD OL9 8 A1
CHD/CHDH SK8 110 F8
DROY M43 89 K4
FAIL M35 74 A4
FWTH BL4 52 D2
HALE/TIMP WA15 117 J3
HOR/BR BL6 34 A1
HYDE SK14 90 E7
IRL M44 94 D3
OFTN SK2 112 F5
PART M31 94 D8
ROY/SHW OL2 59 G2
SALE M33 96 D7
SALQ M50 86 B4
URM M41 84 D8
WALK M28 69 G3
WGNE/HIN WN2 49 K7
WILM/AE SK9 126 F6
Broadway Av CHD/CHDH SK8 111 G7
Broadway Cl URM M41 84 F8
Broadway North DROY M43 89 K4
Broadway St OLDS OL8 59 J8
Broadwell Dr BKLY M9 73 H5
LEIGH WN7 81 H3
Broadwood HOR/BR BL6 34 F5
Broadwood Cl MPL/ROM SK6 123 H5
Brocade Cl CSLFD M3 6 A1
Broche Cl ROCH OL11 41 L1
Brock Av BOLE BL2 37 J5
Brock Cl OP/CLY M11 89 G5
Brock Dr CHD/CHDH SK8 120 C4
Brockenhurst Dr BOLE BL2 37 J1
Brockford Dr BKLY M9 57 H7
Brockholes GLSP SK13 104 C4
Brockhurst Wk
WGNS/IIMK WN3 47 K7
Brocklebank Rd MILN OL16 29 G5
RUSH/FAL M14 98 F4
Brocklehurst Av BURY BL9 5 G7
Brocklehurst St BKLY M9 73 K4
Brockley Av RUSH/FAL M14 98 E2
Brock Mill La WGN WN1 31 M7
Brock Pl WGNE/HIN WN2 64 C2
Brockstedes Av AIMK WN4 63 H6
Brock St CMANE * M1 7 K4
WGN WN1 15 L4
Brockway MILN OL16 42 F1
Brocstedes Rd AIMK WN4 63 G5
Brodick Dr BOLE BL2 37 J6
Brodick St NEWH/MOS M40 73 J4
Brodie Cl ECC M30 84 E2
Brogan St GTN M18 89 G7
Brogden Av GOL/RIS/CU WA3 81 H8
Brogden Dr CHD/CHDH SK8 110 E7
Brogden Gv SALE M33 108 D1
Bromborough Av
DID/WITH M20 98 D4
Bromfield WHIT OL12 10 E2
Bromfield Av BKLY M9 73 G3
Bromleigh Av CHD/CHDH SK8 110 E6
Bromley Av GOL/RIS/CU WA3 80 A5
ROY/SHW OL2 42 E6
URM M41 95 H3
Bromley Cl WGNE/HIN WN2 48 D2
Bromley Crs AUL OL6 75 L6
Bromley Cross Rd
EDGW/EG BL7 22 E5
Bromley Dr LEIGH WN7 66 A4
Bromley Rd SALE M33 108 F2
Bromley St ANC M4 87 L1
CHAD OL9 74 D2
DTN/ASHW * M34 101 J1
Bromlow St OP/CLY M11 88 F3
Brompton Av FAIL M35 74 E4
Brompton Rd HTNM SK4 111 K2
RUSH/FAL M14 98 E2
STRET M32 96 C1
Brompton St OLDE OL4 9 M8
Bromsgrove Av ECC M30 84 E2
Bromshill Dr BRO M7 72 B6
Bromwich St BOLE BL2 3 H6
Brondgate Meadow SWIN M27 70 C6
Bronington Cl WYTH/NTH M22 110 B5
Bronte Av BURY BL9 39 J6
Bronte Cl BOL BL1 36 A3
OLD OL1 44 A8
WGNS/IIMK WN3 47 K7
WHIT OL12 27 K2
Bronte St HULME M15 87 K7
Bronville Cl CHAD OL9 8 C1
The Brook LIT OL15 20 D3
Brookash Rd WYTH/NTH M22 119 J4
Brook Av BNG/LEV M19 99 L2
DROY * M43 89 K3
HALE/TIMP WA15 108 B6
HTNM SK4 100 A7
ROY/SHW OL2 43 L4
SWIN M27 70 C5
UPML OL3 61 L4
WILM/AE SK9 127 H1
Brook Bank BOLE * BL2 37 G1
Brookbank Cl MDTN M24 57 L5
Brook Bottom Rd
NM/HAY SK22 124 B3
RAD M26 38 C6
Brookburn Rd CCHDY M21 97 K5
Brook Cl HALE/TIMP WA15 108 B6
WHTF M45 55 L4
Brook Cnr WHTN BL5 50 D1
Brookcot Rd NTHM/RTH M23 109 J5
Brookcroft Av WYTH/NTH M22 110 A7
Brookcroft Rd WYTH/NTH M22 110 A7
Brookdale ATH M46 51 J6
WHIT OL12 28 B1
Brookdale Av DTN/ASHW M34 90 B5
MPL/ROM SK6 114 D8
NEWH/MOS M40 74 A8
Brookdale Cl BOL BL1 36 C2
MPL/ROM SK6 113 J1
Brookdale Pk LHULT * M38 52 E6
Brookdale Ri BRAM/HZG SK7 121 H2
Brookdale Rd BRAM/HZG SK7 121 H3
CHD/CHDH SK8 110 C7
WGNE/HIN WN2 49 J7
Brookdale St FAIL M35 74 A5
Brookdean Cl BOL BL1 35 M1
Brookdene Rd BNG/LEV M19 99 H6
BURY BL9 55 K3
Brook Dr MPL/ROM SK6 114 C8
TYLD M29 67 M6
WHTF M45 55 L4
Brooke Dr WILM/AE SK9 119 M8
Brookes St MDTN M24 57 L2
Brooke Wy WILM/AE * SK9 119 M8
Brook Farm Cl PART M31 106 B3
Brookfield PWCH M25 55 L8
ROY/SHW OL2 43 K3
Brookfield Av BOLE BL2 37 M3
CCHDY M21 97 M5
HALE/TIMP WA15 108 C5
MPL/ROM SK6 101 K8
POY/DIS SK12 129 G1
ROY/SHW OL2 59 G1
SLFD M6 85 M1
STKP SK1 13 M8
URM M41 95 K2
Brookfield Cl STKP SK1 13 M8
Brookfield Crs CHD/CHDH SK8 111 G7
Brookfield Dr
HALE/TIMP WA15 108 D5
LIT OL15 19 M6
SWIN M27 70 B3
WALK M28 68 C6
Brookfield Gdns
WYTH/NTH M22 109 M6
Brookfield Gv AUL OL6 91 G2
Brookfield Rd BURY BL9 25 H4
CHD/CHDH SK8 111 H7
CHH M8 72 D3
ECC M30 69 L8
GOL/RIS/CU WA3 80 F8
WGNNW/ST WN6 30 E2
Brookfields
WGNW/BIL/O * WN5 46 E7
Brookfield St BOLE BL2 3 J4
LEIGH WN7 66 D6
OLDS OL8 9 J8
Brookfold FAIL M35 74 B4
Brookfold La BOLE BL2 23 J8
Brook Fold La HYDE SK14 102 D3
Brookfold Rd HTNM SK4 100 A6
Brook Gdns BOLE BL2 23 H8
HEY OL10 40 F2
Brook Green La GTN M18 100 C1
Brook Gv IRL M44 94 D2
Brookhead Av DID/WITH * M20 98 C5
Brookhead Dr CHD/CHDH SK8 111 K7
Brookhey Av BOLS/LL BL3 52 C1
Brook Hey Cl WHIT OL12 19 L8
Brookheys Rd PART M31 95 H8
Brookhill Cl UPML OL3 45 M7
Brookhill St NEWH/MOS M40 88 B1
Brookhouse Av ECC M30 84 D3
FWTH BL4 52 F6
Brook House Cl BOLE BL2 37 H1
TOT/BURYW BL8 24 B4
Brookhouse St WGN WN1 15 H5
Brookhouse Ter WGN WN1 15 H5
Brookhurst La LHULT M38 52 B6
Brookhurst Rd GTN M18 89 G8
Brookland Av DTN/ASHW M34 101 G2
FWTH BL4 52 F5
WGNE/HIN WN2 49 G6
Brookland Gv BOL BL1 35 K2
Brookland Rd WGN WN1 47 L1
The Brooklands HEY OL10 40 F2
Brooklands HOR/BR BL6 33 M1
Brooklands Av AIMK WN4 79 G2
ATH M46 51 G8
CHAD OL9 8 A8
DID/WITH M20 98 D6
LEIGH WN7 81 H1
Brooklands Cl HTNM SK4 100 A7
IRL M44 94 C2
MOSL OL5 76 E2
Brooklands Ct ROCH OL11 27 M6
Brooklands Crs SALE M33 108 E1
Brooklands Dr DROY M43 89 M1
GLSP SK13 104 E5
OLDE OL4 60 E6
WGNW/BIL/O WN5 46 A7
Brooklands Pde OLDE * OL4 60 E6
Brooklands Rd BRAM/HZG SK7 122 A3
NTHM/RTH M23 108 F4
PWCH M25 72 B2
RAMS BL0 24 C2
RDSH SK5 100 B2
SALE M33 108 E2
SWIN M27 70 A6
Brooklands Station Ap
SALE M33 108 D1
Brooklands St ROY/SHW OL2 43 G7
Brookland St MILN * OL16 42 E1
Brook La BURY BL9 39 K7
HALE/TIMP WA15 108 B6
MILN OL16 42 E1
OLDE OL4 60 B6
OLDS OL8 59 K8
UPML OL3 61 J3
WGNW/BIL/O WN5 46 D7
WILM/AE SK9 130 C1
Brooklawn Dr DID/WITH M20 98 E8
PWCH M25 55 M6
Brookledge La MCFLDN SK10 129 G7
Brookleigh Rd DID/WITH M20 99 G6
Brooklet Cl OLDE OL4 60 D7
Brooklyn Av LIT OL15 20 B5
MILN OL16 19 L8
OLDTF/WHR M16 97 L2
URM M41 95 H2
Brooklyn Crs CHD/CHDH SK8 111 G7
Brook Lynn Av GOL/RIS/CU WA3 80 C3
Brooklyn Rd CHD/CHDH SK8 111 G7
OFTN SK2 112 F6
Brooklyn St BOL BL1 36 B3
OLD * OL1 59 M3
Brook Meadow GLSP SK13 105 H3
WHTN * BL5 50 D4
Brook Rd CHD/CHDH SK8 111 G6
HTNM SK4 99 M7
RUSH/FAL M14 98 F5
URM M41 95 K1
Brooks Av BRAM/HZG SK7 121 M1
HYDE SK14 102 B3
RAD M26 38 C6
Brooksbottom Cl RAMS BL0 17 C8
Brooks Dr FAIL M35 74 B6
HALE/TIMP WA15 109 G6
HALE/TIMP WA15 117 M4
Brooks End ROCH OL11 27 H3
Brookshaw St BURY BL9 5 G1
OP/CLY M11 88 D3
Brooks Houses LEIGH WN7 66 B4
Brookside GLSP SK13 104 E4
OLDE OL4 60 A6
WGNS/IIMK * WN3 47 K7
Brookside Av AIMK WN4 63 J4
DROY M43 89 M1
FWTH BL4 52 F5
OFTN SK2 113 H6
OLDE OL4 60 E6
POY/DIS SK12 129 J1
Brookside Cl ATH M46 51 H8
BOLE BL2 23 G7
CHD/CHDH SK8 111 G8
GLSP SK13 93 J8
HYDE SK14 102 D1
RAMS BL0 24 D1
WGNW/BIL/O WN5 62 B8
Brookside Crs MDTN M24 57 M6
TOT/BURYW BL8 24 C4
WALK M28 69 H1
Brookside Dr HYDE SK14 102 D1
PWCH M25 72 A3
Brookside La MPL/ROM SK6 123 G5
Brookside Rd BOLE BL2 37 G4
CHD/CHDH SK8 110 D6
NEWH/MOS M40 73 K3
SALE M33 108 D2
WGN WN1 31 L3
Brooksmouth TOT/BURYW BL8 4 B5
Brook's Pl WHIT OL12 10 C2
Brook's Rd OLDTF/WHR M16 97 M1
Brooks St STKP SK1 13 K8
Brookstone Cl CCHDY M21 98 A6
Brook St AIMK WN4 78 F2
ATH M46 66 E1
BOL BL1 2 E4
BRAM/HZG SK7 122 A2
BURY BL9 5 H1
CHAD OL9 8 B3
CHD/CHDH SK8 111 J6
CMANE M1 7 H8
FAIL M35 74 A6
FWTH BL4 53 H3
GLSP SK13 104 F3
GOL/RIS/CU WA3 79 K5
GOL/RIS/CU WA3 80 D3
HYDE SK14 102 B1
LIT OL15 20 D7
OLD OL1 9 M3
RAD M26 53 K5
RAD M26 54 E1
ROY/SHW OL2 59 G1
SALE M33 96 F7
SLFD M6 71 L8
SWIN M27 70 A4
WGNE/HIN WN2 48 D5
WGNS/IIMK WN3 47 J8
WHIT OL12 19 K6
WHTN * BL5 50 C3
Brook St East AUL OL6 90 D2
Brook St West AULW OL7 90 D2
Brookthorn Cl OFTN SK2 113 J7
Brookthorpe Av BNG/LEV M19 99 H6
Brookthorpe Rd
TOT/BURYW BL8 38 D1
Brookvale WGNNW/ST WN6 14 A1
Brookview WGNE/HIN WN2 49 G8
Brookwater Cl TOT/BURYW BL8 24 C6
Brookway HALE/TIMP WA15 108 C6
OLDE OL4 60 B7
OLDE OL4 61 H6
Brookway Cl BNG/LEV M19 99 H8
Brookwood Av CHH M8 72 F4
SALE M33 108 B1
Brookwood Cl DTN/ASHW M34 101 K5
Brooky Moor EDGW/EG * BL7 16 E6
Broom Av BNG/LEV M19 99 L4
BRO M7 72 B4
LEIGH WN7 66 B5
RDSH SK5 100 C6
Broome Gv FAIL M35 74 C6
Broomehouse Av IRL M44 94 B4
Broome St CHAD OL9 8 E6
Broomfield SWIN M27 71 G6
Broomfield Cl BOLE BL2 37 M4
RDSH SK5 100 C6
WILM/AE * SK9 127 J4
Broomfield Crs EDGY/DAV SK3 112 D8
MDTN M24 57 G3
Broomfield Dr CHH M8 72 C5
RDSH SK5 100 C6
Broomfield La
HALE/TIMP WA15 117 G2
Broomfield Pl WGNNW/ST WN6 31 H3
Broomfield Rd BOLS/LL BL3 35 M7
HTNM SK4 99 M8
WGNNW/ST WN6 31 H3
Broomfields DTN/ASHW M34 90 D7
Broomfield Sq ROCH * OL11 10 E8
Broomfield Ter MILN OL16 29 L8
WGN * WN1 15 L5
Broomflat Cl WGNNW/ST WN6 31 H3
Broomgrove La DTN/ASHW M34 90 D8
Broomhall Rd BKLY M9 56 D7
SWIN M27 71 G6
Broomhey Av WGN WN1 31 M7
Broomhey Ter WGNE/HIN WN2 15 L5
Broomhill Dr BRAM/HZG SK7 120 F3
Broomholme WGNNW/ST WN6 30 A5
Broomhurst Av OLDS OL8 59 G8
Broom La BNG/LEV M19 99 L4
BRO M7 72 A4
Broom Rd HALE/TIMP WA15 117 G1
PART M31 106 C2
WGNW/BIL/O WN5 47 G5
Broomstair Rd DTN/ASHW M34 90 C6
Broom St MILN OL16 29 L8
SWIN M27 70 C5
TOT/BURYW BL8 4 B4
Broomville Av SALE M33 96 E8
Broom Wy WHTN BL5 50 D2
Broomwood Rd
HALE/TIMP WA15 108 F7
Broomwood Wk HULME * M15 87 J6
Broseley Av DID/WITH M20 111 G1
GOL/RIS/CU WA3 81 G8
Broseley La GOL/RIS/CU WA3 81 G7
Broseley Rd OLDTF/WHR M16 97 K2
Brosscroft GLSP SK13 93 K6
Brosscroft Cl GLSP SK13 93 K6
Brosscroft Village GLSP SK13 93 K6
Brotherdale Cl ROY/SHW OL2 43 G7
Brotherod Hall Rd WHIT OL12 27 M2
Brotherton Cl HULME M15 6 A9
Brotherton Dr CSLFD M3 6 B2
Brotherton Wy NEWLW WA12 78 E8
Brougham St STLY SK15 91 J3
WALK M28 68 F1
Brough Cl WGNE/HIN WN2 65 H1
Broughton Av GOL/RIS/CU WA3 80 A5
LHULT M38 52 D8
Broughton Cl MDTN M24 57 G2
Broughton La BRO M7 72 A7
Broughton Rd MCFLDN SK10 129 G7
RDSH SK5 100 C8
SLFD M6 86 D1
Broughton Rd East SLFD M6 71 L8
Broughton St BOL BL1 36 A2
CHH M8 72 C7
CHH M8 72 D8
Broughville Dr DID/WITH M20 110 F4
Brow Av MDTN M24 57 L6
Brow East BOLE BL2 22 F8
Browfield Av ORD M5 86 E5
Browfield Wy OLD OL1 59 H3
Browmere Dr DID/WITH M20 98 C8
Brownacre St DID/WITH M20 98 E6
Brown Bank Rd LIT OL15 29 J1
Browncross St CSLFD M3 6 C4
Brown Edge Rd OLDE OL4 60 B8
Brownhill Dr OLDE OL4 60 D5
Brownhill La UPML OL3 61 L3
Brownhills Cl TOT/BURYW BL8 24 D7
Brownhills Ct CCHDY * M21 97 L4
Brownhill St OP/CLY * M11 88 D4
Browning Av ATH M46 51 G7
DROY M43 89 K3
WGNS/IIMK WN3 47 J8
Browning Cl BOL BL1 36 A3
Browning Gv WGNNW/ST WN6 47 H1
Browning Rd MDTN M24 57 L2
OLD OL1 59 L3
RDSH SK5 100 A3
SWIN M27 70 B4
Browning St CSLFD M3 6 B3
HULME M15 87 G6
LEIGH WN7 66 A6
Brown La CHD/CHDH SK8 119 J3
Brownlea Av DUK SK16 90 F5
Brownley Court Rd
WYTH/NTH M22 110 A7
Brownley Rd WYTH/NTH M22 110 B7
Brown Lodge St LIT OL15 29 J1
Brownlow Av ROY/SHW OL2 59 K1
WGNE/HIN WN2 48 E5
Brownlow Cl POY/DIS SK12 129 J2
Brownlow Rd HOR/BR BL6 21 B8
Brownlow Wy BOL BL1 2 C1
Brownmere WGNNW/ST WN6 47 J2
Brownside Cl MILN OL16 28 F1
Brown's La WILM/AE SK9 127 J4
Brownslow Wk
BRUN/LGST * M13 7 K9
Browns Rd BOLE BL2 37 L6
Brown St ALT WA14 116 F1
BOL BL1 2 F4
CHAD OL9 58 D5
CMANW M2 7 G4
CSLFD M3 6 D3
FAIL M35 74 B5
HEY OL10 40 F1
HOR/BR BL6 33 G2
LIT OL15 20 B7
MDTN M24 57 K2
OLD OL1 9 M4
RAD M26 38 C6
RAMS BL0 17 B7
SLFD M6 86 C3
STKP SK1 13 H3
TYLD * M29 67 J5
WGNE/HIN WN2 48 D5
WGNE/HIN WN2 65 H3
WGNS/IIMK WN3 14 E5
WILM/AE SK9 130 D3
Brown St North LEIGH WN7 66 D7
Brown St South LEIGH WN7 66 D8
Brownsville Rd HTNM SK4 99 L7
Brownville Gv DUK SK16 91 H5
Brownwood Av STKP SK1 112 E3
Brownwood Cl SALE M33 108 F3
Brows Av NTHM/RTH M23 109 K2
Brow St ROCH OL11 28 D8
Broxton Av BOLS/LL BL3 51 L1
WGNW/BIL/O WN5 46 C5
Broxton St NEWH/MOS M40 88 C1
Broxwood Cl GTN * M18 89 G7
Bruce St ROCH OL11 27 M8
Brundage Rd WYTH/NTH M22 118 F2
Brundrett Pl SALE M33 96 C8
Brundrett's Rd CCHDY M21 97 L4
Brundrett St STKP SK1 13 M7
Brunel Av ORD M5 86 E3
Brunel Cl STRET M32 97 H2
Brunel St BOL BL1 36 A1
HOR/BR BL6 33 M2
Brunet Wk WGTN/LGST * M12 88 C6
Brunstead Cl NTHM/RTH M23 109 G6
Brunswick Av HOR/BR BL6 34 A2
Brunswick Ct BOL BL1 2 D3
Brunswick Rd ALT WA14 108 A5
DID/WITH M20 98 F6
NEWLW WA12 78 C8
Brunswick Sq OLD * OL1 9 J6
Brunswick St BRUN/LGST M13 87 M6
BURY BL9 4 F2
DUK SK16 90 F4
HEY OL10 40 F2
LEIGH WN7 66 D8
MILN OL16 11 H2
MOSL OL5 77 G4
OLD OL1 9 H6
ROY/SHW OL2 43 L5
STRET M32 96 F4
Brunton Rd RDSH SK5 100 C6
Brunt St RUSH/FAL M14 98 E1
Bruntwood Av CHD/CHDH SK8 119 J3
Bruntwood La CHD/CHDH SK8 111 H8
Brushes Av STLY SK15 92 A1
Brushes Rd STLY SK15 92 A1
Brussels Rd EDGY/DAV SK3 112 A6
Bruton Av STRET M32 96 E3
Bryan Rd CCHDY M21 97 L2
Bryan St OLDE OL4 59 M3
Bryant Cl BRUN/LGST M13 87 M7
Bryantsfield BOL BL1 35 G6
Bryce St HYDE SK14 91 G8
Brydges Rd MPL/ROM SK6 114 B7
Brydon Av WGTN/LGST M12 7 M8
Brydon Cl SLFD M6 86 C2
Bryham St WGN WN1 15 J4
Bryndale Gv SALE M33 108 C3
Brynden Av DID/WITH M20 98 F7
Bryn Dr RDSH SK5 100 C7
Brynford Av BKLY M9 56 D7
Bryn Gates La AIMK WN4 63 M4
Bryngs Dr BOLE BL2 23 J8
Brynhall Cl RAD M26 38 B7
Brynheys Cl LHULT M38 52 D7
Brynn St WGNE/HIN WN2 64 C5
Brynorme Rd CHH M8 72 D2
Bryn Rd AIMK WN4 63 K6

Bryn Rd South *AIMK* WN4 .....63 M8
Bryn St *AIMK* WN4 .....78 E1
　WGNS/IIMK WN3 .....15 K8
Brynton Rd *BRUN/LGST* M13 .....99 H1
Bryn Wk *BOL* BL2 .....2 E2
Bryone Dr *OFTN* SK2 .....112 E7
Bryony Cl *WGNW/BIL/O* WN5 .....46 A7
　WYTH/NTH M22 .....118 E3
Buchanan Dr *WGNE/HIN* WN2 .....65 L1
Buchanan Rd
　WGNW/BIL/O WN5 .....47 H5
Buchanan St *LEIGH* WN7 .....66 B7
　RAMS BL0 .....17 B6
　SWIN M27 .....70 C3
Buchan St *OP/CLY* M11 .....88 E2
Buckden Rd *HTNM* SK4 .....100 A5
Buckfast Av *OLDS* OL8 .....59M8
　RNFD/HAY WA11 .....78 C5
Buckfast Cl *CCHDY* M21 .....97 L3
　CHD/CHDH SK8 .....120 D5
　HALE/TIMP WA15 .....117 K2
　POY/DIS SK12 .....121M7
Buckfast Rd *MDTN* M24 .....41 J8
　SALE M33 .....96 A6
Buckfield Av *OLDS* OL8 .....86 E5
Buckhurst Rd *BNG/LEV* M19 .....99 K3
　BURY BL9 .....25 L1
Buckingham Av *HOR/BR* BL6 .....34 B2
　ORD M5 .....86 A2
　WHTF M45 .....55 K5
Buckingham Cl
　WGNW/BIL/O WN5 .....47 H7
Buckingham Dr *DUK* SK16 .....91 J5
　TOT/BURYW BL8 .....38 E4
Buckingham Park Cl
　ROY/SHW OL2 .....43 L4
Buckingham Rd *ALT* WA14 .....108 C3
　CCHDY M21 .....97 L3
　CHD/CHDH SK8 .....120 B2
　DROY M43 .....89 H3
　HTNM SK4 .....99 L7
　POY/DIS SK12 .....121M8
　PWCH * M25 .....71 L2
　STLY SK15 .....91 K1
　STRET M32 .....86 C7
　SWIN M27 .....70 D2
　WILM/AE SK9 .....126 D6
Buckingham Rd West
　HTNM SK4 .....99 K8
Buckingham St *MILN* OL16 .....11 H2
　OFTN * SK2 .....112 D6
　ORD M5 .....86 C3
Buckingham Wy
　HALE/TIMP WA15 .....108 D6
Buckland Av *BKLY* M9 .....72 D1
Buckland Cl *WGNW/BIL/O* WN5 .....46 E3
Buckland Gv *HYDE* SK14 .....102 A4
Buckland Rd *SLFD* M6 .....71 G8
Buck La *SALE* M33 .....96 B6
Buckley Av *CCHDY* M21 .....88 F8
Buckley Brook St *WHIT* OL12 .....28 E2
Buckley Cha *MILN* OL16 .....29 H7
Buckley Cl *HYDE* SK14 .....102 B5
Buckley Dr *MPL/ROM* SK6 .....113 K3
　UPML OL3 .....44 F3
Buckley Farm La *WHIT* OL12 .....28 E1
Buckley Flds *WHIT* OL12 .....28 D2
Buckley Hill La *WHIT* OL12 .....29 H7
Buckley La *FWTH* BL4 .....52 F5
　PWCH M25 .....71 H1
　WHIT OL12 .....28 E1
Buckley Rd *GTN* M18 .....88 E8
　WHIT OL12 .....28 E2
Buckley Sq *FWTH* BL4 .....52 F6
Buckley St *BRO* M7 .....72 A8
　BURY BL9 .....5 G2
　CHAD OL9 .....58 D5
　DTN/ASHW M34 .....90 A5
　HEY OL10 .....41 G1
　MILN OL16 .....11 G2
　OLDE OL4 .....60 B7
　OP/CLY M11 .....89 K1
　RDSH SK5 .....100 B2
　ROY/SHW OL2 .....43M5
　STLY SK15 .....91 J4
　UPML OL3 .....61 K2
　WGNNW/ST WN6 .....47 K2
Buckley St West
　WGNNW/ST WN6 .....47 K2
Buckley Vw *WHIT* OL12 .....28 E1
Bucklow Av *PART* M31 .....94 C8
　RUSH/FAL M14 .....98 E3
Bucklow Cl *HYDE* SK14 .....103 J3
　OLDE OL4 .....60 B1
Bucklow Dr *WYTH/NTH* M22 .....110 B4
Bucklow Vw *ALT* WA14 .....116 C1
Buckstones Rd *OLD* OL1 .....44 B6
　ROY/SHW OL2 .....43M3
Buck St *LEIGH* WN7 .....66 C8
Buckthorn Cl *CCHDY* M21 .....98 A6
　WHTN BL5 .....50 C2
Buckthorn La *ECC* M30 .....84 C3
Buckton Cl *UPML* OL3 .....45M7
Buckton Dr *STLY* SK15 .....77 H7
Buckton Vale Ms *STLY* SK15 .....77 J5
Buckton Vale Rd *STLY* SK15 .....77 G8
Buckwood Cl *BRAM/HZG* SK7 .....122 C1
Buddleia Gv *BRO* M7 .....72 A6
Bude Av *RDSH* SK5 .....100 E7
　TYLD M29 .....67M4
　URM M41 .....95 L4
Bude Cl *BRAM/HZG* SK7 .....121 H5
Budsworth Av *DID/WITH* M20 .....98 E5
Budworth Rd *SALE* M33 .....109 H1
Buer Av *WGNS/IIMK* WN3 .....47 J8
Buersil Av *MILN* OL16 .....28 E8
Buersil St *MILN* OL16 .....11 K8
Buerton Av *BKLY* M9 .....56 D7
Bugle St *CMANE* * M1 .....6 D7
Buile Dr *BKLY* M9 .....57 J8
Buile Hill Av *LHULT* M38 .....52 E8
Buile Hill Dr *ORD* M5 .....86 A1
Buile Hill Gv *LHULT* M38 .....52 E7
Buile St *BRO* M7 .....72 B5
Bulford Av *WYTH/NTH* M22 .....118 D2
Bulkeley Rd *CHD/CHDH* SK8 .....111 H6
　POY/DIS SK12 .....129 J1
　WILM/AE SK9 .....127 G1
Bulkeley St *EDGY/DAV* SK3 .....12 C1
Bullcote Gn *ROY/SHW* OL2 .....43 K8
Bullcote La *ROY/SHW* OL2 .....43 L8
Bullcroft Dr *TYLD* M29 .....67M6
Buller Ms *TOT/BURYW* BL8 .....38 E3
Buller Rd *BRUN/LGST* M13 .....99 J2
Buller St *BOLS/LL* BL3 .....52 F2
　DROY M43 .....89 L4
　OLDE OL4 .....60 A4
　TOT/BURYW BL8 .....38 E3

Bullfinch Dr *BURY* BL9 .....25 L7
Bull Hill Crs *RAD* M26 .....54 E4
Bullock St *OFTN* SK2 .....13 K9
Bullows Rd *LHULT* M38 .....52 C6
Bulteel St *BOLS/LL* BL3 .....51M2
　ECC M30 .....84 E1
　WALK M28 .....68 B6
　WGNW/BIL/O WN5 .....47 G6
Bulwer St *MILN* OL16 .....11 H2
The Bungalows
　BRAM/HZG * SK7 .....113 J8
　NM/HAY * SK22 .....124 E3
Bunkers Hl *PWCH* M25 .....71 H1
Bunkers Hill Rd *HYDE* SK14 .....103 H3
Bunkershill Rd *MPL/ROM* SK6 .....113 L3
Bunsen St *CMANE* * M1 .....7 J4
Bunting Cl *GOL/RIS/CU* WA3 .....80 B4
Bunting Ms *WALK* M28 .....68 E4
Bunyan Cl *OLD* OL1 .....44 A8
Bunyan St *WHIT* OL12 .....11 K2
Bunyard St *CHH* M8 .....72 E6
Burbage Rd *NTHM/RTH* M23 .....118 C2
Burbridge Cl *OP/CLY* M11 .....88 B4
Burchall Fld *MILN* OL16 .....11 K4
Burdale Dr *SLFD* M6 .....70 E8
Burder St *OLDS* OL8 .....74 F2
Burdett Av *ROCH* OL11 .....27 J3
Burdett Wy *WGNS/IIMK* * M12 .....88 B7
Burdith Av *RUSH/FAL* M14 .....98 D2
Burdon Av *WYTH/NTH* M22 .....110 B8
Burford Av *BRAM/HZG* SK7 .....120 E7
　OLDTF/WHR M16 .....98 A2
　URM M41 .....85 H8
Burford Crs *WILM/AE* SK9 .....126 C7
Burford Dr *BOLS/LL* BL3 .....2 C8
　OLDTF/WHR M16 .....98 A2
　SWIN M27 .....70 B2
Burford Gv *SALE* M33 .....108 B3
Burford Rd *OLDTF/WHR* M16 .....98 A2
Burgess Av *AUL* OL6 .....75M7
Burgess Dr *FAIL* M35 .....74 C5
Burgess St *WGNS/IIMK* WN3 .....15 K3
Burghley Av *OLDE* OL4 .....60 A6
Burghley Cl *BOLS/LL* BL3 .....37 L7
　STLY SK15 .....91 K2
Burghley Dr *BOLS/LL* BL3 .....37 L7
Burghley Wy *WGNS/IIMK* WN3 .....48 C7
Burgin Wk *NEWH/MOS* M40 .....72 F8
Burgundy Dr *TOT/BURYW* M24 .....24 C5
Burke St *BOL* BL1 .....36 A2
Burkitt St *HYDE* SK14 .....102 B2
Burland Cl *BRO* M7 .....72 A7
Burland St *WGNW/BIL/O* WN5 .....47 J3
Burleigh Cl *BRAM/HZG* SK7 .....121 J3
Burleigh Ms *CCHDY* M21 .....97 L6
Burleigh Rd *STRET* M32 .....86 B8
Burleigh St *BRUN/LGST* M13 .....87 L7
Burlescombe Cl *ALT* WA14 .....107 L6
Burley Av *GOL/RIS/CU* WA3 .....80 A3
Burley Ct *HTNM* * SK4 .....12 C2
Burley Crs *WGNS/IIMK* WN3 .....48 C7
Burlington Av *OLDS* OL8 .....59 H8
Burlington Cl *HTNM* SK4 .....111 H2
Burlington Dr *EDGY/DAV* SK3 .....112 C8
Burlington Gdns
　EDGY/DAV SK3 .....112 C8
Burlington Ms *EDGY/DAV* SK3 .....112 C8
Burlington Rd *ALT* WA14 .....108 A7
　DID/WITH M20 .....98 F5
　ECC M30 .....70 B8
Burlington St *AULW* OL7 .....90 C2
　HULME M15 .....87 K7
　ROCH OL11 .....28 D8
　WGNE/HIN WN2 .....49 H7
Burlton Gv *WGNE/HIN* WN2 .....48 D2
Burman St *OP/CLY* M11 .....89 J5
Burnaby St *BOLS/LL* BL3 .....2 A9
　OLDS OL8 .....8 D9
　ROCH OL11 .....27M8
Burnage Av *BNG/LEV* M19 .....99 J4
Burnage Hall Rd *BNG/LEV* M19 .....99 H5
Burnage La *BNG/LEV* M19 .....99 J7
　HTNM SK4 .....99 L7
Burnage Range *BNG/LEV* M19 .....99 K3
Burnaston Gv
　WGNW/BIL/O WN5 .....47 G7
Burnbray Av *BNG/LEV* M19 .....99 H6
Burndale Dr *BURY* BL9 .....55 K1
Burnden Rd *BOLS/LL* BL3 .....3 K9
Burnden Wy *HOR/BR* BL6 .....33M4
Burnedge Cl *WHIT* OL12 .....18 E2
Burnedge Fold Rd *OLDE* OL4 .....61 G6
Burnedge La *OLDE* OL4 .....60 F6
Burnell Cl *NEWH/MOS* M40 .....7M1
Burnedge La *OLDE* OL4 .....60 F6
Burnet Cl *MILN* OL16 .....28 F8
　TYLD M29 .....67 L5
Burnett Av *ORD* M5 .....86 E4
Burnett Cl *NEWH/MOS* M40 .....73 G7
Burnfell *GOL/RIS/CU* WA3 .....80 B5
Burnfield Rd *GTN* M18 .....100 A1
Burnham Av *BOL* BL1 .....35 K3
　RDSH SK5 .....100 C3
Burnham Cl *CHD/CHDH* SK8 .....120 D2
　GOL/RIS/CU WA3 .....81 H8
Burnham Dr *BNG/LEV* M19 .....99 J5
　URM M41 .....95M1
Burnham Gv *WGNE/HIN* WN2 .....48 D2
Burnham Rd *DTN/ASHW* M34 .....100 D1
Burnhill Ct *WGNNW/ST* * WN6 .....31 H4
Burnley La *CHAD* OL9 .....8 C1
Burnley Rd *BURY* BL9 .....25 H4
　LEIGH WN7 .....70 A3
Burnley St *CHAD* OL9 .....8 A3
　FAIL M35 .....74 D5
Burnmoor Rd *BOLE* BL2 .....37 J4
Burnsall Av *GOL/RIS/CU* WA3 .....80 C4
　WHTF M45 .....55 G4
Burnsall Gv *ROY/SHW* OL2 .....43 G8
Burns Av *ATH* M46 .....51 G7
　BURY BL9 .....39 J6
　CHD/CHDH SK8 .....111 J6
　LEIGH WN7 .....65M4
　SWIN M27 .....70 A3
Burns Cl *AIMK* WN4 .....63 J6
　OLD OL1 .....9 J6
　OP/CLY M11 .....88 C3
　WGNS/IIMK WN3 .....47 K8
　WGNW/BIL/O WN5 .....62 A3
Burns Fold *DUK* SK16 .....91 K5
Burns Gdns *PWCH* * M25 .....71 J1
Burnsgv *DROY* M43 .....89 K2
Burnside *GLSP* SK13 .....93 J8
　HALE/TIMP WA15 .....117M5
　RAMS BL0 .....17 D2
　ROY/SHW OL2 .....44 A4
　STLY SK15 .....92 A5
Burnside Av *HTNM* SK4 .....100 B6
　SLFD M6 .....70 D7

Burnside Cl *HEY* OL10 .....41 G3
　MPL/ROM SK6 .....113 J1
　RAD M26 .....38 C5
　STLY SK15 .....92 A5
　TYLD M29 .....67 L5
　WILM/AE SK9 .....127 G6
Burnside Dr *BNG/LEV* M19 .....99 H5
Burnside Rd *BOL* BL1 .....35 L2
　CHD/CHDH SK8 .....110 D7
　WGNE/HIN WN2 .....64 E3
Burns Rd *DTN/ASHW* M34 .....101 K5
　LHULT M38 .....52 E7
　WGNE/HIN WN2 .....64 E3
Burns St *BOLS/LL* BL3 .....2 F7
　HEY OL10 .....41 G3
Burnthorp Av *NEWH/MOS* M40 .....72 E1
Burnthorpe Cl *ROCH* OL11 .....27 H6
Burnvale *WGNS/IIMK* WN3 .....63 G2
Burran Rd *WYTH/NTH* M22 .....118 F4
Burrington Dr *LEIGH* WN7 .....66 A5
Burrows Av *CCHDY* M21 .....97 L6
Burrs Cl *TOT/BURYW* BL8 .....24 F6
Burrs Lea Cl *BURY* BL9 .....25 H6
Burrswood Av *BURY* BL9 .....25 H6
Burrswood Dr *BURY* BL9 .....25 H6
Bursar Cl *NEWLW* WA12 .....79 G8
Burslem Av *DID/WITH* M20 .....98 D4
Burstead St *GTN* M18 .....89 H6
Burstock St *ANC* M4 .....87 L1
Burston St *GTN* M18 .....88 F6
Burton Av *DID/WITH* M20 .....98 E6
　HALE/TIMP WA15 .....108 D3
　TOT/BURYW BL8 .....4 A5
Burton Dr *POY/DIS* SK12 .....121M8
Burton Gv *WALK* M28 .....69M4
Burton Rd *DID/WITH* M20 .....98 C8
Burton St *HTNM* SK4 .....112 B1
　MDTN M24 .....57 J4
　NEWH/MOS M40 .....72 E8
　OLDE OL4 .....60 B6
Burton Wk *CSLFD* M3 .....6 B2
　HTNM SK4 .....100 B8
Burtonwood Ct *MDTN* M24 .....57 J3
Burtree St *WGTN/LGST* * M12 .....88 D6
Burwell Cl *BOLS/LL* BL3 .....36 A8
　GLSP SK13 .....104 D4
　LEIGH WN7 .....66 D8
　WHIT OL12 .....28 A1
Burwell Gv *NTHM/RTH* M23 .....109 J5
Bury & Bolton Rd *RAD* M26 .....38 A5
Bury & Rochdale Old Rd
　HEY OL10 .....26 E7
Bury Av *OLDTF/WHR* M16 .....97M2
Bury New Rd *BOL* BL1 .....3 G3
　BOLE BL2 .....37 L5
　BRO M7 .....72 A5
　HEY OL10 .....40 A2
　PWCH M25 .....55 K7
　RAMS BL0 .....17 E6
　WHTF M45 .....55 H5
Bury Old Rd *BOLE* BL2 .....3 H4
　BOLE BL2 .....37 K3
　HEY OL10 .....40 B3
　PWCH M25 .....55 K6
Bury Pl *OP/CLY* M11 .....88 F2
Bury Rd *BOLE* BL2 .....37 H5
　EDGW/EG BL7 .....16 E6
　EDGW/EG BL7 .....23 J1
　RAD M26 .....38 E8
　RAMS BL0 .....17 D2
　ROCH OL11 .....27 J6
　TOT/BURYW BL8 .....24 C6
Bury St *CSLFD* M3 .....6 D2
　HEY OL10 .....40 E2
　MOSL OL5 .....76 F4
　RAD M26 .....38 F8
　RDSH SK5 .....112 C1
Bushell St *BOLS/LL* BL3 .....35 L8
Bushey Dr *NTHM/RTH* M23 .....109 K7
Busheyfield Cl *HYDE* SK14 .....91 G7
Bush St *NEWH/MOS* M40 .....73 H7
Busk Rd *CHAD* OL9 .....8 D3
Busk Wk *CHAD* * OL9 .....8 D2
Butcher La *BURY* BL9 .....4 F4
　NTHM/RTH M23 .....109 J5
　ROY/SHW OL2 .....42 F7
Butcher St *AIMK* WN4 .....78 E2
Bute Av *OLDS* OL8 .....75 J1
Bute Cl *BOL* BL1 .....35 L3
　GLSP SK13 .....105 H1
　NEWH/MOS M40 .....73 J3
　ORD M5 .....86 A3
Butler Gn *CHAD* OL9 .....58 D8
Butler La *NEWH/MOS* M40 .....7M1
Butler St *ANC* M4 .....7M2
　RAMS BL0 .....17 A8
　WGN WN1 .....15 H4
Butley St *BRAM/HZG* SK7 .....113 H8
Butman St *GTN* M18 .....89 J6
Buttercup Cl *TOT/BURYW* BL8 .....24 C3
Buttercup Cl *ATH* M46 .....51 C7
Buttercup Dr *EDGY/DAV* SK3 .....112 A8
　OLDE OL4 .....60 B2
　ROCH OL11 .....41 L1
Butterfield Cl *CHD/CHDH* SK8 .....120 D3
Butterfield Rd *WHTN* BL5 .....51 J4
Butterhouse La *UPML* OL3 .....61 L2
Butter La *CSLFD* * M3 .....6 E4
Butterley Cl *DUK* SK16 .....91 J5
Buttermere Av *AULW* OL7 .....75 J8
　CHD/CHDH SK8 .....119 K1
　FWTH BL4 .....52 B4
　OLDE OL4 .....60 A1
　PART M31 .....106 B1
　MDTN M24 .....57 H3
Buttermere Cl *BOLS/LL* BL3 .....37 J8
　STRET M32 .....96 F1
Buttermere Dr
　HALE/TIMP WA15 .....117 L6
　MDTN M24 .....57 H2
　RAMS BL0 .....17 B5
Buttermere Gv *ROY/SHW* OL2 .....43 G5
Buttermere Rd *AULW* OL7 .....75 J8
　CHD/CHDH SK8 .....119 K1
　FWTH BL4 .....52 B4
　OLDE OL4 .....60 A1
　PART M31 .....106 B1
Buttermill Cl *IRL* M44 .....94 E4
Butterstile Av *PWCH* M25 .....71 J3
Butterstile La *PWCH* M25 .....71 H3
Butterwick Cl *WGTN/LGST* M12 .....99 L1
Butterworth Fld *HOR/BR* BL6 .....33 J1
Butterworth Hall *MILN* OL16 .....29 K7
Butterworth La *CHAD* OL9 .....74 B1
Butterworth St *CHAD* OL9 .....8 A4
　LIT OL15 .....20 C4
　MDTN M24 .....57M5
　OLDE OL4 .....59M5
　OP/CLY M11 .....88 D4
Butterworth Wy *UPML* OL3 .....61 L7

Butteryhouse La
　HALE/TIMP WA15 .....118 A2
Butt Hill Av *PWCH* M25 .....71 L1
Butt Hill Dr *PWCH* M25 .....71 L1
Butt Hill Rd *PWCH* M25 .....71 L1
Butt La *OLDE* OL4 .....60 E8
Button Hole *ROY/SHW* OL2 .....44 A5
Button La *NTHM/RTH* M23 .....109 J2
Buttress St *GTN* M18 .....88 F6
The Butts *MILN* OL16 .....10 E4
The Butts Av *MILN* OL16 .....10 E4
Butts Av *LEIGH* WN7 .....81 L1
Butts *LEIGH* WN7 .....81 K1
Buxted Rd *OLD* OL1 .....59 L3
Buxton Av *AUL* OL6 .....76 C6
　DID/WITH M20 .....98 C6
Buxton Cl *ATH* M46 .....51 H8
Buxton Crs *MILN* OL16 .....28 E8
　SALE M33 .....109 G3
Buxton La *DROY* M43 .....89 H4
　MPL/ROM SK6 .....114 B7
Buxton Ms *GLSP* SK13 .....104 B3
Buxton Old Rd *POY/DIS* SK12 .....123M6
Buxton Pl *OLDS* * OL8 .....9 H9
Buxton Rd *BRAM/HZG* SK7 .....122 B3
　NM/HAY SK22 .....124 D6
　OFTN SK2 .....112 F8
　STRET M32 .....96 D1
Buxton St *BRAM/HZG* SK7 .....121M1
　CHD/CHDH SK8 .....110 D1
　CMANE M1 .....7 K7
　HEY OL10 .....41 G5
　TOT/BURYW BL8 .....4 A5
　WHIT OL12 .....18 E1
Buxton Ter *HYDE* SK14 .....93 G6
Bye Rd *RAMS* BL0 .....17 E5
Byfield Rd *WYTH/NTH* M22 .....109M8
Byfleet Cl *WGNS/IIMK* WN3 .....62 F3
Byland Av *CHD/CHDH* SK8 .....120 D6
　OLDE OL4 .....60 A8
Byland Cl *BOL* BL1 .....36 B2
Bylands Cl *POY/DIS* * SK12 .....121M8
Bylands Fold *DUK* SK16 .....91 G6
Byley Ri *WGNNW/ST* WN6 .....31 H4
Byng Av *IRL* M44 .....94 E6
Byng St *FWTH* BL4 .....53 G4
　HEY OL10 .....41 H4
Byrcland Cl *WGTN/LGST* M12 .....88 B4
Byre Cl *SALE* M33 .....109 K1
Byrness Cl *NEWH/MOS* M40 .....51 H8
Byrom Av *BNG/LEV* M19 .....99M3
Byrom Dr *GOL/RIS/CU* WA3 .....80 C2
Byrom St *ALT* WA14 .....116 F1
　CSLFD M3 .....6 D6
　OLDTF/WHR M16 .....87 G8
　ORD M5 .....86 D4
　TOT/BURYW BL8 .....24 E8
Byron Av *DROY* M43 .....89 K2
　PWCH M25 .....71 J1
　RAD M26 .....38 A8
　SWIN M27 .....70 B4
　WGNE/HIN WN2 .....49 G7
Byron Cl *WGNE/HIN* WN2 .....64 E4
　WGNNW/ST WN6 .....47 H1
Byron Dr *CHD/CHDH* SK8 .....111 J6
Byron Gv *LEIGH* WN7 .....66 B5
　RDSH SK5 .....100 B3
Byron Rd *DTN/ASHW* M34 .....101 J4
　MDTN M24 .....57 J2
　STRET M32 .....97 H1
　TOT/BURYW BL8 .....24 C2
Byron's Dr *HALE/TIMP* WA15 .....108 D6
Byron St *ECC* M30 .....85 G2
　LEIGH WN7 .....66 C6
　OLDS OL8 .....74 E2
　ROY/SHW OL2 .....43 G8
Byron Wk *FWTH* BL4 .....52 E6
Byrth Rd *OLDS* OL8 .....75 J4

C

Cabin La *OLDE* OL4 .....60 D1
Cablestead Wk *OP/CLY* M11 .....88 D1
Cable St *ANC* M4 .....7 H2
　BOL BL1 .....2 F2
　CSLFD M3 .....6 D2
Cabot Pl *RDSH* SK5 .....100 D3
Cabot St *BRUN/LGST* * M13 .....87 L6
Caddington Rd *CCHDY* M21 .....97M4
Cadishead Wy *IRL* M44 .....94 D5
Cadman Gv *WGNE/HIN* WN2 .....49 G8
Cadnam Dr *WYTH/NTH* M22 .....119 H1
Cadogan Dr *WGNS/IIMK* WN3 .....63 G2
Cadogan Pl *BRO* * M7 .....72 B3
Cadogan St *RUSH/FAL* M14 .....87 K6
Cadum Wk *BRUN/LGST* M13 .....87M6
Caen Av *NEWH/MOS* M40 .....73M1
Caernarvon Cl *TOT/BURYW* BL8 .....24 C3
Caernarvon Rd *BRAM/HZG* SK7 .....121 J5
Caernarvon Rd *WGNE/HIN* WN2 .....65 K1
Caesar St *ROCH* OL11 .....42 D2
Cairn Dr *ROCH* OL11 .....27 H1
Cairn St *OLD* OL1 .....9 J4
Cairngorm Dr *BOLS/LL* BL3 .....35 H7
Cairns Pl *AUL* OL6 .....76 A7
Cairn Wk *OP/CLY* * M11 .....88 C3
Cairnwell Rd *CHAD* OL9 .....58 D4
Caister Av *WHTF* M45 .....55 G5
Caister Cl *URM* M41 .....94 F3
Caistor Cl *OLDTF/WHR* M16 .....98 A2
Caistor St *STKP* SK1 .....112 E1
Caistor Wk *OLD* OL1 .....9 J4
Caithness Cl *NTHM/RTH* M23 .....109 K8
Caithness Dr *BOLS/LL* BL3 .....35 H7
Caithness Rd *HEY* OL10 .....27 H7
Cakebread St *WGTN/LGST* M12 .....7 L8
Calbourne Crs *WGTN/LGST* M12 .....99 L1
Calcutta Rd *EDGY/DAV* SK3 .....12 D9
Caldbeck Av *BOL* BL1 .....35 J3
　SALE M33 .....97 L2
Caldbeck Cl *AIMK* WN4 .....63 L8
Caldbeck Dr *FWTH* BL4 .....52 B5
　MDTN M24 .....57 H3
Caldecott Rd *BKLY* M9 .....56 D7
Calder Av *IRL* M44 .....94 C3
　LIT OL15 .....20 B5
　WGNE/HIN WN2 .....65M1
　WYTH/NTH M22 .....110 A2
Calderbank Av *URM* M41 .....95 H1
Calderbank St
　WGNW/BIL/O WN5 .....47 H7
Calderbrook Dr
　CHD/CHDH SK8 .....111 K8
Calderbrook Rd *LIT* OL15 .....20 C4
Calderbrook Wy *OLDE* OL4 .....59 L7
Calder Cl *BURY* BL9 .....25 K4
　POY/DIS SK12 .....129 H2
　RDSH SK5 .....100 C7

Calder Ct *URM* M41 .....84 B8
Calder Crs *WHTF* M45 .....55 L2
Calder Dr *FWTH* BL4 .....53 L7
　SWIN M28 .....80 D3
　WALK M28 .....68 D2
Calder Gv *ROY/SHW* OL2 .....43 K4
Calder Pl *WGNW/BIL/O* WN5 .....46 F5
Calder Rd *BOLS/LL* BL3 .....52 B1
Caldershaw La *WHIT* OL12 .....27 K2
Caldershaw Rd *WHIT* OL12 .....27 K3
Calder St *MILN* OL16 .....11 J5
　ORD M5 .....6 A7
Caldervale Av *CCHDY* M21 .....97M8
Calderwood Cl *TOT/BURYW* BL8 .....24 C6
Caldey Cl *WGNE/HIN* WN2 .....49 H8
Caldey Rd *NTHM/RTH* M23 .....109 H7
Caldford Cl *WGNE/HIN* WN2 .....32 F6
Caldon Cl *ECC* M30 .....85 G4
Caldwell Av *TYLD* M29 .....67 L7
Caldwell Cl *TYLD* M29 .....67 L7
Caldwell St *WHTN* BL5 .....50 F2
Caldy Dr *RAMS* BL0 .....24 D1
Caldy Rd *SLFD* M6 .....71 G8
　WILM/AE SK9 .....127 H1
Caleb Cl *TYLD* M29 .....67 J3
Caledon Av *NEWH/MOS* M40 .....73 K4
Caledonian Dr *ECC* M30 .....85 H4
Caledonia St *BOLS/LL* BL3 .....35M7
　RAD M26 .....38 F8
Caledonia Wy *STRET* M32 .....85 K7
Cale Gn *EDGY/DAV* SK3 .....112 C6
Cale La *WGNE/HIN* WN2 .....48 E2
Cale Rd *NM/HAY* SK22 .....124 F4
Cale St *OFTN* SK2 .....13 J9
　CMANE M1 .....7 G7
Calf Hey *LIT* OL15 .....20 A6
Calf Hey Cl *RAD* M26 .....54 A1
Calf Hey North *ROCH* OL11 .....28 D8
Calf Hey Rd *ROY/SHW* OL2 .....44 A4
Calf Hey South *ROCH* OL11 .....28 D8
Calf La *OLDE* OL4 .....61 H8
Calgarth Dr *MDTN* M24 .....57 G1
Calgary St *GTN* M18 .....89 H8
Calico Cl *CSLFD* M3 .....6 A1
Calico La *CHF/WBR* SK23 .....124 F3
Calico Wood Av
　WGNNW/ST WN6 .....30 C6
Callaghan Wk *HEY* OL10 .....40 F3
Calland Av *HYDE* SK14 .....91 J4
Callander Ct *WGNW/BIL/O* WN5 .....47 H5
Callender St *RAMS* BL0 .....17 B6
Calliards Rd *MILN* OL16 .....19M8
Callingdon Rd *CCHDY* M21 .....98 A7
Callington Cl *HYDE* SK14 .....103 H2
Callington Dr *HYDE* SK14 .....103 H2
Callis Rd *BOLS/LL* BL3 .....35M6
Callum Wk *BRUN/LGST* * M13 .....87M6
Calluna Ms *DID/WITH* * M20 .....98 D8
Calow Dr *LEIGH* WN7 .....81M1
Caltha St *RAMS* BL0 .....17 B6
Calthorpe Av *BKLY* M9 .....72 F5
Calton Av *BRO* M7 .....71 K5
Calton Cl *WGNS/IIMK* WN3 .....47 G8
Calve Croft Rd *WYTH/NTH* M22 .....119 G3
Calveley Wk *WGNNW/ST* WN6 .....31 H4
Calver Av *ECC* M30 .....84 B8
Calver Cl *URM* M41 .....95 G1
Calverhall Wy *URM* WN4 .....78 D1
Calver Hey Cl *WHTN* BL5 .....50 F2
Calverleigh Cl *BOLS/LL* BL3 .....51 K2
Calverley Av *BNG/LEV* M19 .....99 J5
Calverley Cl *WILM/AE* SK9 .....127 G4
Calverley Wy *WHIT* OL12 .....18 F8
Calverly Rd *CHD/CHDH* SK8 .....111 K7
Calver Ms *GLSP* SK13 .....104 A2
Calverton Dr *NEWH/MOS* M40 .....73M5
Calvert Rd *BOLS/LL* BL3 .....52 B1
Calvert St *ORD* M5 .....86 A2
Calvine Wk *NEWH/MOS* * M40 .....87M1
Calvin St *BOL* BL1 .....2 F1
Cambeck Cl *WHTF* M45 .....55 L3
Cambell Rd *ECC* M30 .....84 E2
Camberley Cl *BRAM/HZG* SK7 .....121 J5
　TOT/BURYW BL8 .....24 D7
Camberley Dr *ROCH* OL11 .....27 J6
Cambert La *GTN* M18 .....88 F7
　WGNE/HIN WN2 .....48 C2
Camberwell Crs
　WGNE/HIN WN2 .....49 G3
Camberwell Dr *AULW* OL7 .....75 K6
Camberwell St *CHH* * M8 .....72 D8
　OLDS * OL8 .....59 H8
Camborne Rd *HYDE* SK14 .....103 H1
Camborne St *RUSH/FAL* M14 .....98 E2
Cambourne Dr *BOLS/LL* BL3 .....35 K7
Cambo Wk *HTNM* SK4 .....111 J1
Cambrai Crs *ECC* M30 .....69 K8
Cambrian Crs *WGNS/IIMK* WN3 .....62 F7
　ROY/SHW OL2 .....58 F7
Cambrian Rd *EDGY/DAV* SK3 .....12 D7
Cambrian St *NEWH/MOS* M40 .....88 B2
Cambria Sq *BOLS/LL* * BL3 .....35M7
Cambria St *BOLS/LL* BL3 .....35M7
　OLDE OL4 .....60 A8
Cambridge Av *OLDTF/WHR* M16 .....97M2
　ROCH OL11 .....27 H8
　WILM/AE SK9 .....126 D5
Cambridge Cl *FWTH* BL4 .....52 A3
　SALE M33 .....108 A1
Cambridge Dr *BOLS/LL* BL3 .....37 L8
　DTN/ASHW M34 .....100 D1
　MPL/ROM SK6 .....101M7
Cambridge Gv *ECC* M30 .....85 J2
　WHTF M45 .....55 K4
Cambridge Rd *BKLY* M9 .....73 G3
　CHD/CHDH SK8 .....110 E6
　FAIL M35 .....74 C7
　HALE/TIMP WA15 .....117 G2
　HOR/BR BL6 .....34 C4
　HTNM SK4 .....99M7
　URM M41 .....95 J7
　WGNW/BIL/O WN5 .....46 B4
Cambridge St *ATH* M46 .....66 F2
　AULW OL7 .....90 C3
　BRO M7 .....72 B8
　DROY OL9 .....90 F3
　DUK SK16 .....90 F8
　HULME M15 .....6 F8
　OFTN SK2 .....112 D6
　STLY SK15 .....91 K2
Cambridge Wy *WGN* WN1 .....15 J3
Camden Av *NEWH/MOS* M40 .....73M8
Camden Cl *BOLE* BL2 .....37M3
Camden St *MOSL* OL5 .....77 G1

Camelford Cl HULME * M15 87 K6
Camelia Rd BKLY M9 72 F5
Camellia Cl BOL BL1 35 L5
Camelot Cl NEWLW WA12 78 C8
Cameron Ct ROY/SHW OL2 43 G6
Cameron Pl WGNW/BIL/O WN5 47 H4
Cameron St BOL BL1 22 A7
CMANE * M1 6 E7
LEIGH WN7 66 A5
TOT/BURYW BL8 4 A4
Camm St WGNE/HIN WN2 64 D4
Campania St ROY/SHW OL2 59 H2
Campbell Cl TOT/BURYW BL8 24 B8
Campbell Ct FWTH BL4 52 F2
Campbell Rd BOLS/LL BL3 51 K2
BRUN/LGST M13 99 J2
SALE M33 108 C1
SWIN M27 70 B6
Campbell St FWTH BL4 52 E3
RDSH SK5 100 C3
WGNW/BIL/O WN5 47 G7
WHIT * OL12 28 B2
Campbell Wy WALK M28 68 F1
Campden Wy WILM/AE SK9 119 M8
Campion Gv AIMK WN4 63 J8
Campion Wy WHIT OL12 27 M1
Camp Rd AIMK WN4 78 B1
Camp St AUL OL6 90 E1
BRO M7 71 M8
CSLFD M3 6 D6
TOT/BURYW BL8 38 F1
Camrose Gdns BOL BL1 36 B3
Camrose Wk BRUN/LGST * M13 88 A7
Cams Acre Cl RAD M26 54 B1
Cams La RAD M26 54 B2
Canaan GOL/RIS/CU WA3 80 F4
Canada St BOL BL1 35 M2
HOR/BR BL6 33 L1
NEWH/MOS M40 73 H8
OFTN SK2 112 D6
Canal Bank ECC M30 84 F1
Canal Bridge La OP/CLY M11 89 H3
Canal Cottages Yd ANC * M4 7 M5
Canal Rd ALT WA14 108 B5
Canal Side ECC M30 84 F1
Canal St CHAD OL9 74 E1
CMANE M1 7 H6
DROY M43 89 K3
HEY OL10 41 H4
HYDE SK14 101 M1
LIT OL15 20 C7
MPL/ROM SK6 114 D6
ORD * M5 86 F3
ROCH OL11 11 H9
STKP SK1 13 K6
STLY * SK15 91 K3
WGNE/HIN WN2 15 M7
WGNNW/ST WN6 47 J3
Canal Ter WGNE/HIN WN2 15 L5
Canberra Rd BRAM/HZG SK7 121 G7
WGNW/BIL/O WN5 46 F3
Canberra St OP/CLY M11 88 F2
Candahar St BOLS/LL BL3 52 D1
Candleford Pl OFTN SK2 113 H8
Candleford Rd DID/WITH * M20 98 E6
Candlestick Ct BURY BL9 26 A8
Candlestick Pk BURY BL9 26 A8
Candy La MCFLDN SK10 129 G4
Canisp Cl CHAD OL9 58 D4
Canley Cl STKP SK1 13 K7
Canmore Cl BOLS/LL BL3 51 K1
Cannel Fold WALK M28 68 E5
Canning Dr BOL BL1 36 B2
Canning St BOL * BL1 36 B2
BURY BL9 4 F1
HTNM SK4 13 H2
Cannon Gv BOLS/LL BL3 2 A8
Cannon St ANC M4 7 G3
ATH M46 67 G1
BOLS/LL BL3 2 B8
CHAD OL9 9 G5
CSLFD M3 6 A2
ECC M30 85 H3
HYDE SK14 92 F7
RAD M26 38 C7
RAMS BL0 17 A8
Cannon St North BOLS/LL * BL3 2 B7
Cann St TOT/BURYW BL8 24 A4
Canon Cl WGNNW/ST WN6 31 J2
Canon Dr ALT WA14 116 D3
Canon Flynn Ct MILN OL16 11 M4
Canon Green Dr CSLFD M3 6 C1
Canons Cl BOL BL1 35 L2
Canons Gv NEWH/MOS M40 73 H7
Canonsleigh Cl CHH M8 72 B7
Canon St BURY BL9 5 H1
MILN OL16 28 E2
Canonsway SWIN M27 70 B5
Canon Tighe Ct CHAD * OL9 58 D5
Canon Wilson Cl
RNFD/HAY WA11 78 A6
Cansfield Gv AIMK WN4 63 K8
Canterbury Av GOL/RIS/CU WA3 80 A3
Canterbury Cl ATH M46 51 H8
DUK SK16 91 G6
ROCH OL11 27 K5
Canterbury Crs MDTN M24 58 A2
Canterbury Dr PWCH M25 71 M2
TOT/BURYW BL8 25 G8
Canterbury Gdns ORD M5 85 K2
Canterbury Gv BOLS/LL BL3 52 A1
Canterbury Pk DID/WITH M20 110 C1
Canterbury Rd
HALE/TIMP WA15 117 L1
STKP SK1 112 E3
URM M41 95 L1
Canterbury St AUL OL6 75 L8
Canterfield Cl DROY M43 90 A2
Cantrell St OP/CLY M11 88 E3
Canute Rd STRET M32 97 H1
Canute St BOLE BL2 36 F3
RAD M26 54 B1
SLFD * M6 86 E2
Capella Wk BRO M7 71 M8
Capenhurst Cl NTHM/RTH M23 109 J8
Capesthorne Cl BRAM/HZG SK7 122 B4
Capesthorne Dr ROY/SHW OL2 43 J5
Capesthorne Rd
BRAM/HZG SK7 122 B4
DUK SK16 91 G6
HALE/TIMP WA15 109 G6
MPL/ROM SK6 123 G5
WILM/AE SK9 126 C7
Cape St DID/WITH M20 98 F5
Capital Rd OP/CLY M11 89 J5
Capps St WGNE/HIN WN2 64 E1
Capricorn Wy SLFD * M6 71 M8
Capstan St BKLY M9 73 H4
Capstone Dr MPL/ROM SK6 114 B6
Captain Clarke Rd HYDE SK14 90 E7
Captain Fold HEY * OL10 41 H2
Captain Fold Rd LHULT M38 52 C7
Captain Lees Gdns WHTN BL5 50 D4
Captain Lees Rd WHTN BL5 50 D4
Captain's Clough Rd BOL BL1 35 K2
Captain's La AIMK WN4 78 F1
Captain St HOR/BR BL6 21 B8
Capton Cl BRAM/HZG SK7 121 J2
Carawood Cl WGNNW/ST WN6 30 A5
Car Bank Av ATH M46 51 G8
Car Bank Sq ATH M46 51 G8
Car Bank St ATH M46 50 E8
Carberry Rd GTN M18 89 H7
Carden Av SWIN M27 70 A5
URM M41 95 H2
Carder Cl SWIN M27 70 C5
Carders Cl LEIGH WN7 66 B8
Carder Av WYTH/NTH M22 110 B8
Cardiff Cl OLDS OL8 74 E2
Cardiff St BRO M7 72 B5
Cardigan Dr BURY BL9 39 H5
Cardigan Rd OLDS OL8 74 E2
Cardigan St ROY/SHW OL2 43 H8
SLFD * M6 86 B3
WHIT OL12 28 B1
Cardinal Ms MDTN M24 57 G2
Cardinal St CHH M8 72 E6
OLD OL1 9 L5
Carding Gv CSLFD M3 6 C1
Cardroom Rd ANC M4 7 L4
Cardus St BNG/LEV M19 99 K3
Cardwell Gdns BOL * BL1 36 B2
Cardwell Rd ECC M30 84 D3
Cardwell St OLDS OL8 75 J1
Careless La WGNE/HIN WN2 48 C5
Carey Cl BRO * M7 72 A8
WGNS/IIMK WN3 63 G2
Carey Wk HULME M15 87 J7
Carfax Fold WHIT OL12 27 L2
Carfax St GTN M18 89 G7
Carill Av NEWH/MOS M40 73 K3
Carill Dr RUSH/FAL M14 99 G4
Carina Pl BRO M7 71 M8
Carisbrook Av URM M41 95 M3
WHTF M45 55 K5
Carisbrook Dr SWIN M27 70 D6
Carisbrooke Av BRAM/HZG SK7 121 M3
Carisbrooke Dr BOL BL1 36 C1
Carisbrooke Rd LEIGH WN7 67 G6
Carisbrook St BKLY M9 73 G5
Carlburn St OP/CLY M11 89 G2
Carleton Rd POY/DIS SK12 122 E8
Carley Gv BKLY M9 56 E8
Carlford Gv PWCH M25 71 J1
Carlile St EDGY/DAV SK3 13 G7
Carlin Ga HALE/TIMP WA15 108 D6
Carling Dr WYTH/NTH M22 119 G2
Carlingford Cl EDGY/DAV SK3 112 B7
Carlisle Cl BOLS/LL BL3 53 K2
MPL/ROM SK6 113 K3
WHTF M45 55 L5
Carlisle Crs AUL OL6 75 M5
Carlisle Dr ALT WA14 108 B4
IRL M44 94 D2
Carlisle St CHAD OL9 58 F8
EDGW/EG BL7 22 D4
SWIN M27 70 C2
WGNE/HIN * WN2 49 H6
WGNW/BIL/O WN5 47 G6
WHIT OL12 28 B1
WILM/AE SK9 130 D4
Carloon Rd NTHM/RTH M23 109 L3
Carlow Dr WYTH/NTH M22 119 G2
Carl St BOL * BL1 36 A2
Carlton Av BOLS/LL BL3 35 K8
BRAM/HZG SK7 120 F7
CHD/CHDH SK8 120 B1
MPL/ROM SK6 114 A1
OLDE OL4 60 A3
PWCH M25 72 B2
WHTF M45 55 G3
WILM/AE SK9 127 G2
Carlton Cl BOLE BL2 37 H1
HOR/BR BL6 33 G2
WALK M28 68 F3
Carlton Ct HALE/TIMP WA15 117 K3
Carlton Crs STKP SK1 13 M3
Carlton Dr CHD/CHDH SK8 110 D6
PWCH M25 72 B2
Carlton Gv HOR/BR BL6 34 A3
WGNE/HIN WN2 65 J1
Carlton Pl BRAM/HZG * SK7 122 B3
FWTH * BL4 53 G3
Carlton Range GTN * M18 89 J8
Carlton Rd AUL OL6 75 M7
BOL BL1 35 K4
GOL/RIS/CU WA3 80 A3
HALE/TIMP WA15 117 K2
HTNM SK4 111 K2
HYDE SK14 102 D1
OLDTF/WHR M16 98 A1
SALE M33 96 D6
SLFD M6 71 H8
URM M41 95 M3
WALK M28 68 F3
Carlton St BOLE BL2 3 G6
BURY BL9 4 F9
ECC M30 85 G1
FWTH BL4 53 G3
OLDTF/WHR M16 86 F8
WGNS/IIMK WN3 14 E8
Carlton Wy ROY/SHW OL2 59 G2
Carlyle Cl CHH M8 72 D6
Carlyle Gv LEIGH WN7 65 M4
Carlyle St BURY BL9 4 C4
Carlyn Av SALE M33 97 G7
Carmel Av ORD M5 86 F5
Carmel Cl ORD M5 86 F4
Carmel Ct BKLY M9 73 G3
Carmel Ms WILM/AE SK9 126 F2
Carmenna Dr BRAM/HZG SK7 121 H5
Carmichael Ct PART M31 106 B1
Carmichael St EDGY/DAV SK3 12 E8
Carmine Fold MDTN M24 57 J2
Carmona Dr PWCH M25 55 K8
Carmoor Rd BRUN/LGST M13 87 M7
Carnaby St BKLY M9 73 J3
Carna Rd RDSH SK5 100 B2
Carnarvon St BRO * M7 72 B5
CSLFD M3 87 J1
OLDS OL8 74 E2
STKP SK1 13 M6
Carnation Rd FWTH BL4 52 D3
OLDE OL4 60 B8
Carnegie Av BNG/LEV M19 99 L3
Carnegie Cl SALE M33 108 A1
Carnegie Dr AIMK WN4 63 K7
Carnforth Av CHAD OL9 58 D6
ROCH OL11 42 A5
WGNE/HIN WN2 49 K7
Carnforth Dr SALE M33 108 D1
TOT/BURYW BL8 24 D2
Carnforth Rd CHD/CHDH SK8 111 L8
HTNM SK4 99 M6
Carnforth Sq ROCH OL11 42 A5
Carnforth St RUSH/FAL M14 98 E1
Carnoustie BOLS/LL BL3 51 K1
Carnoustie Cl NEWH/MOS M40 73 M5
WILM/AE SK9 127 H4
Carnoustie Dr CHD/CHDH SK8 119 L3
RAMS BL0 17 A7
Carnwood Cl NEWH/MOS M40 74 A8
Caroline Dr ANC M4 7 L4
Caroline St AUL OL6 90 F1
BOLS/LL BL3 36 A8
BRO M7 72 B8
EDGY/DAV SK3 12 F8
IRL M44 94 B4
STLY SK15 91 K3
WGN WN1 15 M4
WGNS/IIMK WN3 14 E5
Carpenters La ANC M4 7 H3
Carpenters Wk DROY M43 89 J4
Carpenters Wy MILN OL16 28 E8
Carradale Dr SALE M33 95 M7
Carradon Dr WGNNW/ST WN6 31 H3
Carr Av PWCH M25 71 J2
Carr Bank GLSP SK13 105 H4
Carr Bank Av CHH M8 72 C1
RAMS BL0 17 B5
Carr Bank Dr RAMS BL0 17 B5
Carr Bank Rd RAMS BL0 17 B5
Carrbrook Cl STLY SK15 77 H6
Carrbrook Crs STLY SK15 77 H6
Carr Brook Dr ATH M46 51 H8
Carrbrook Dr OLD OL1 59 H3
Carrbrook Rd STLY SK15 77 J5
Carrbrook Ter RAD M26 38 F8
Carr Brow MPL/ROM SK6 123 J5
Carr Cl STKP SK1 112 E4
Carr Common Rd
WGNE/HIN WN2 66 A1
Carrfield Av EDGY/DAV SK3 112 D8
HALE/TIMP WA15 109 G7
LHULT M38 52 B8
Carrfield Gv LHULT M38 52 B8
Carr Fold RAMS * BL0 17 B5
Carrgate Rd DTN/ASHW M34 101 L1
Carrgreen Cl BNG/LEV M19 99 J7
Carrgreen La LYMM WA13 106 C6
Carrhill Quarry Cl MOSL OL5 76 F2
Carrhill Rd MOSL OL5 76 F2
Carrhill Ter MOSL * OL5 76 F2
Carrhouse La HYDE SK14 92 F8
Carr House Rd OLDE OL4 60 C5
Carriage Dr LIT OL15 20 C5
NEWH/MOS M40 73 G7
The Carriage Dr GLSP SK13 93 H8
The Carriages ALT * WA14 107 M8
Carriage St OLDTF/WHR M16 87 G7
Carrick Gdns MDTN M24 41 J8
Carrie St BOL BL1 35 L4
Carrigart PWCH M25 71 K1
Carrill Gv East BNG/LEV M19 99 K3
Carrington Cl MILN OL16 29 G1
Carrington Dr BOLS/LL BL3 36 C8
Carrington Field St OFTN SK2 13 K9
Carrington Gv LEIGH * WN7 66 C5
Carrington La SALE M33 96 A6
SALE M33 96 B7
Carrington Rd RUSH/FAL M14 98 F4
STKP SK1 112 E1
URM M41 95 H4
Carrington St CHAD OL9 74 E1
LEIGH WN7 66 C5
SWIN M27 70 E3
Carrington Ter SWIN * M27 70 D3
Carr La LEIGH WN7 81 H4
MILN OL16 29 M6
STLY SK15 77 J5
UPML OL3 45 M7
UPML OL3 61 L4
WGNS/IIMK WN3 63 K1
WILM/AE SK9 130 A2
Carr Mill Crs WGNW/BIL/O WN5 62 B8
Carr Mill Ms WILM/AE * SK9 126 F3
Carron Av BKLY M9 73 H3
Carron Gv BOLE BL2 37 J5
Carr Ri STLY SK15 77 J5
Carr Rd HALE/TIMP WA15 117 K2
HOR/BR BL6 21 B7
IRL M44 94 E2
Carrsfield Rd WYTH/NTH M22 110 B6
Carrslea Cl RAD M26 38 B7
Carrs Rd CHD/CHDH SK8 111 J6
Carr St AUL OL6 76 A7
LEIGH WN7 65 M7
RAMS BL0 17 B5
SWIN M27 70 A5
WGNE/HIN WN2 49 G6
Carrsvale Av URM M41 95 L1
Carrswood Rd NTHM/RTH M23 108 F4
Carruthers Cl HEY OL10 41 J1
Carruthers St ANC M4 88 A3
Carr Vw NM/HAY * SK22 124 F7
Carrwood HALE/TIMP WA15 117 K5
Carrwood Av BRAM/HZG SK7 121 G4
Carrwood Hey RAMS BL0 17 A8
Carr Wood Rd BRAM/HZG SK7 120 F3
Carrwood Rd WILM/AE SK9 126 D4
Carsdale Rd WYTH/NTH M22 119 G5
Carslake Av BOL BL1 35 M4
Carslake Rd NEWH/MOS M40 73 G7
Carson Rd BNG/LEV M19 99 K4
Carstairs Av EDGY/DAV SK3 112 D8
Carstairs Cl CHH M8 72 C5
Car St WGNE/HIN WN2 64 D3
Carswell Cl TYLD M29 67 M3
Carter Cl DTN/ASHW * M34 101 J2
Carter Pl HYDE * SK14 91 G7
Carter St BOLS/LL BL3 36 D8
BRO * M7 72 A7
FWTH * BL4 53 H5
HYDE SK14 91 G7
MOSL OL5 76 F4
SALQ M50 85 M3
STLY SK15 91 L2
WGNS/IIMK WN3 15 K7
Carthage St OLDS OL8 59 J8
Cartleach Gv WALK M28 68 C2
Cartleach La WALK M28 68 C2
Cartmel WHIT OL12 10 E2
Cartmel Av HTNM SK4 100 A6
MILN OL16 29 J8
WGN WN1 47 L1
Cartmel Cl BOLS/LL BL3 51 G2
BRAM/HZG SK7 121 L1
BURY BL9 55 K1
CHD/CHDH SK8 119 L1
OLDS OL8 75 G1
Cartmel Crs BOLE BL2 36 F2
CHAD OL9 74 C2
Cartmel Dr HALE/TIMP WA15 109 G6
Cartmel Gv WALK M28 69 L5
Cartridge Cl WYTH/NTH M22 119 H1
Cartridge St HEY OL10 40 F2
Cartwright Gv LEIGH WN7 66 A3
Cartwright Rd CCHDY M21 97 J4
Cartwright St DTN/ASHW M34 90 C6
HYDE SK14 91 K7
Carver Av PWCH M25 55 M7
Carver Cl OLDTF/WHR M16 86 E7
Carver Dr MPL/ROM SK6 114 B7
Carver Rd HALE/TIMP WA15 117 G2
MPL/ROM SK6 114 B7
Carver St OLDTF/WHR M16 86 E7
Carver Wk HULME * M15 87 J7
Carville Rd BKLY M9 73 M1
Carwood Gv HOR/BR BL6 34 A3
Cascade Dr CHH M8 72 B7
Case Rd RNFD/HAY WA11 78 A6
Cash Gate Ct OLDS * OL8 75 G1
Cashmere Rd EDGY/DAV SK3 12 C9
Cashmoor Wk WGTN/LGST M12 88 B6
Cashmore Dr WGNE/HIN WN2 49 G8
Caspian Rd ALT WA14 107 K6
Cass Av ORD M5 86 D4
Cassidy Cl ANC M4 7 K2
Cassidy Gdns MDTN M24 41 G8
Casson Ga WHIT OL12 28 B3
Casson St FAIL M35 74 C5
Casterton Wy WALK M28 68 D7
Castle Av DTN/ASHW M34 101 H2
ROCH OL11 10 C7
Castlebrook Cl BURY BL9 39 L8
Castle Cl DROY M43 89 L2
Castle Ct AUL OL6 75 L5
Castle Crs HOR/BR BL6 21 C7
Castle Cft BOLE BL2 37 G1
Castlecroft Av HOR/BR BL6 33 G2
Castlecroft Rd BURY BL9 4 D4
Castledene Av SLFD M6 86 B1
Castle Edge Rd NM/HAY SK22 124 C2
Castle Farm La OFTN SK2 112 F7
Castlefield Av BRO M7 72 B4
Castlefield Br ORD M5 6 A6
Castleford Cl BOL * BL1 2 B2
Castleford St OLD OL1 8 D1
Castle Gv LEIGH WN7 67 G6
RAMS BL0 24 D2
Castle Hall Cl STLY SK15 91 L3
Castle Hall Ct STLY * SK15 91 K3
Castle Hall Vw STLY SK15 91 K3
Castle Hl GLSP SK13 105 H1
NEWLW WA12 79 H8
Castle Hill Crs ROCH OL11 10 C6
Castle Hill Pk MPL/ROM * SK6 101 J6
WGNE/HIN WN2 49 J5
Castle Hill Rd BURY BL9 25 M6
BURY BL9 26 A8
PWCH M25 72 A2
WGNE/HIN WN2 49 H6
Castle Hill St BOLE BL2 36 E2
Castle La MOSL OL5 77 J4
Castlemere Cl WGNS/IIMK WN3 63 G3
Castlemere Dr ROY/SHW OL2 44 A4
Castlemere Rd BKLY M9 72 F1
Castlemere St ROCH OL11 10 D6
Castlemere Ter ROCH OL11 10 D7
Castle Mill La HALE/TIMP WA15 117 H6
Castlemill St OLD OL1 59 L5
Castlemoor Av BRO M7 71 L4
Castle Quay HULME M15 6 C8
Castlerea Cl ECC M30 85 G4
Castlerigg Dr MDTN M24 56 F2
ROY/SHW OL2 42 F6
Castle Ri WGNE/HIN WN2 49 H7
Castle Rd BURY BL9 39 M8
Castle Shaw Rd OFTN SK2 113 G7
Castle St BOLE BL2 3 J5
BURY BL9 4 E4
BURY BL9 24 F2
CSLFD M3 6 C7
ECC M30 85 J2
EDGY/DAV SK3 13 G8
FWTH * BL4 53 G5
GLSP SK13 93 K8
HYDE SK14 102 C1
MDTN M24 58 A5
STLY SK15 91 K3
TYLD M29 67 J3
WGNE/HIN WN2 49 H6
Castleton Av STRET M32 96 E1
Castleton Crs GLSP SK13 104 B3
Castleton Dr MPL/ROM SK6 123 H6
Castleton Gv AUL OL6 76 C6
Castleton Rd BRAM/HZG SK7 122 A3
BRO M7 72 B3
ROY/SHW OL2 42 F4
STRET M32 85 K8
Castleton Rd South ROCH OL11 42 A2
Castleton St ALT WA14 107 M5
BOLE BL2 36 E2
CHAD OL9 8 C7
Castleton Wk OP/CLY * M11 88 C3
Castleton Wy WGNS/IIMK WN3 62 F2
Castleway HALE/TIMP WA15 117 L5
ROCH OL11 41 L2
SLFD M6 71 H8
Castle Wy SWIN M27 70 D2
Castleway WGNE/HIN WN2 49 J7
Castlewood Gdns OFTN SK2 112 F7
Castlewood Rd BRO M7 71 J4
Castlewood Sq BOLE BL2 36 F3
Castle Yd STKP SK1 13 J3
Catchdale Cl BKLY M9 56 F7
Catches Cl ROCH OL11 27 L4
Catches La ROCH OL11 27 L3
Cateaton St BURY BL9 4 F2
CSLFD M3 6 F3
Caterham Av BOLS/LL BL3 51 J2
Caterham St ANC M4 88 A3
Catfield Wk HULME * M15 6 B9
Catford Rd NTHM/RTH M23 109 J7
Cathedral Ap CSLFD M3 6 F2
Cathedral Cl DUK SK16 91 G6
Cathedral Gdns CSLFD M3 6 F2
Cathedral Gates CSLFD * M3 6 F3
Cathedral Rd CHAD OL9 58 D3
Cathedral St ANC M4 6 F3
Catherine Houses HTNM * SK4 111 J2
Catherine Rd ALT WA14 116 E1
CHH M8 72 B3
MPL/ROM SK6 113 J3
SWIN M27 69 M5
Catherine St BOLS/LL BL3 51 L2
BRAM/HZG SK7 113 H8
BURY BL9 39 H6
ECC M30 84 D1
HYDE SK14 102 A1
LEIGH WN7 66 C6
OLDE OL4 60 B6
OP/CLY M11 89 H5
Catherine St East HOR/BR BL6 21 B7
Catherine St West HOR/BR BL6 21 A7
Catherine Ter WGN WN1 15 K4
Catherston Cl
OLDTF/WHR M16 98 B1
Cathrine St East
DTN/ASHW M34 101 G1
Cathrine St West
DTN/ASHW M34 101 G1
Catlow La ANC * M4 7 H3
Catlow St BRO M7 72 B8
Caton Cl BURY BL9 4 D9
Caton Dr ATH M46 66 D4
Caton St MILN OL16 10 F6
Cato St RAMS * BL0 17 A8
Catterall Crs BOLE BL2 23 G6
Catterick Av DID/WITH M20 110 F1
SALE M33 107 M2
Catterick Dr BOLS/LL BL3 53 K1
Catterick Rd DID/WITH M20 110 F1
Catterwood Dr MPL/ROM SK6 114 E2
Cattlin Wy OLDS OL8 74 F2
Caunce Av GOL/RIS/CU WA3 79 K5
Caunce Rd WGN WN1 15 K3
Caunce St WGN WN1 15 K3
The Causeway ALT WA14 108 A8
CHAD OL9 58 A7
Causewood Cl OLDE OL4 44 B8
Causey Dr MDTN M24 57 G1
Cavanagh Cl BRUN/LGST M13 88 A6
Cavan Cl EDGY/DAV SK3 111 J5
Cavell St CMANE * M1 7 J4
Cavell Wy SLFD M6 86 D3
Cavendish Av DID/WITH M20 98 C6
SWIN M27 70 F1
Cavendish Dr WGNS/IIMK WN3 63 G2
Cavendish Gdns BOLS/LL BL3 51 M1
Cavendish Gv ECC M30 85 H1
Cavendish Ms WILM/AE SK9 126 E7
Cavendish Pl AUL * OL6 90 D1
Cavendish Rd ALT WA14 116 E1
BRAM/HZG SK7 121 M3
BRO M7 72 A3
DID/WITH M20 98 C6
ECC M30 85 H1
HTNM SK4 111 J2
ROCH OL11 42 B1
STRET M32 86 B8
URM M41 96 B1
WALK M28 69 L6
Cavendish St AUL OL6 90 D1
CHAD OL9 9 H7
HULME M15 7 H9
LEIGH WN7 66 C5
Cavendish Wy ROY/SHW OL2 58 F2
Cavenham Gv BOL BL1 35 M4
Caversham Dr BKLY M9 73 H4
Cawdor Av FWTH BL4 52 E2
Cawdor Ct FWTH BL4 52 F2
Cawdor Pl HALE/TIMP WA15 108 F6
Cawdor Rd RUSH/FAL M14 98 F3
Cawdor St ECC M30 84 F3
FWTH BL4 52 E2
HULME M15 6 A9
LEIGH WN7 66 C8
SWIN M27 70 A4
WALK M28 69 H2
WGNE/HIN WN2 49 H7
WGNW/BIL/O WN5 47 J6
Cawley Av GOL/RIS/CU WA3 81 H8
PWCH M25 71 J2
Cawley La MCFLDN SK10 129 J5
Cawley Ter BKLY * M9 56 D7
Cawood Sq RDSH SK5 100 F6
Cawston Wk CHH M8 72 D6
Caxton Cl WGNS/IIMK WN3 63 J2
Caxton Rd RUSH/FAL M14 98 E3
Caxton St CSLFD * M3 6 D3
HEY OL10 41 G2
ROCH OL11 41 M2
Caxton Wy ORD M5 86 E3
Caygill St CSLFD M3 6 D2
Cayley St MILN OL16 11 J5
Caythorpe St RUSH/FAL M14 98 D1
Cayton St WGTN/LGST M12 99 K1
C' Ct AIMK WN4 78 E2
The Ceal MPL/ROM SK6 114 E2
Cecil Av SALE M33 108 B1
WGNNW/ST WN6 47 K2
Cecil Dr URM M41 95 H2
Cecil Gv GTN M18 89 G8
Cecilia St BOLS/LL BL3 36 D8
Cecil Rd BKLY M9 57 G8
ECC M30 85 H3
HALE/TIMP WA15 117 G2
STRET M32 96 F3
Cecil St BOLE BL2 3 J5
BRUN/LGST M13 87 L7
BURY BL9 4 F6
DUK SK16 90 E4
EDGY/DAV * SK3 13 G8
LEIGH WN7 66 D8
LIT OL15 20 A7
MOSL OL5 76 F4
ROCH OL11 10 F9
ROY/SHW OL2 42 F8
STLY SK15 91 L3
WALK M28 69 G1
WGN WN1 15 L4
WGNS/IIMK WN3 48 B8
Cedar Av ALT WA14 107 M8
ATH M46 50 E8
AUL OL6 76 A7
BOLS/LL BL3 53 L2
BRAM/HZG SK7 122 A2
GOL/RIS/CU WA3 80 C5
HEY OL10 40 F1
HOR/BR BL6 34 B3
STLY SK15 91 M1
WGNE/HIN WN2 65 J1
WGNNW/ST WN6 31 J4
WHTF M45 55 J6
Cedar Bank Cl MILN OL16 29 G5
Cedar Cl GLSP SK13 104 E2
POY/DIS SK12 129 J1
Cedar Ct HALE/TIMP * WA15 108 E7
Cedar Crs CHAD OL9 8 B3
RAMS BL0 17 C5
Cedar Dr DROY M43 89 L2
SWIN M27 54 A8
URM M41 95 M3
WGN WN1 48 A2
Cedar Gv AIMK WN4 63 G7
DTN/ASHW M34 101 H1
DUK SK16 91 J4
FWTH BL4 52 E4
HTNM SK4 99 M7

PWCH M25 ....55 K6
RNFD/HAY WA11 ....78 B5
ROY/SHW OL2 ....43 G6
ROY/SHW OL2 ....43 L6
RUSH/FAL M14 ....99 C4
WGNW/BIL/O WN5 ....83 B5
WHTN BL5 ....50 B5
Cedar La MILN OL16 ....43 K1
OLDE OL4 ....61 G6
Cedar Lawn CHD/CHDH * SK8 ...120 C2
Cedar Ct AULW OL7 ....75 K7
Cedar Pl BRO M7 ....71 M8
Cedar Rd CHD/CHDH SK8 ...110 D7
FAIL M35 ....74 C6
HALE/TIMP WA15 ....117 G5
LEIGH WN7 ....66 B4
MDTN M24 ....57 M4
MPL/ROM SK6 ....114 B8
OFTN SK2 ....112 E8
PART M31 ....106 B1
SALE M33 ....96 A6
Cedars Rd WYTH/NTH M22 ...118 F1
Cedar St AUL OL6 ....76 A8
BURY BL9 ....5 J3
HYDE SK14 ....91 G7
OLDE OL4 ....59M5
WHIT OL12 ....28 C3
Cedar Vw AUL * OL6 ....76 A8
Cedarwood Av HTNM SK4 ...111 K3
Cedar Wood Ct BOL * BL1 ...35 J4
Cedric Rd CHH M8 ....72 B2
OLDE OL4 ....59M5
Cedric St ORD M5 ....86 A2
Celandine Cl LIT OL15 ....20 C1
Celandine Wk WGNS/IIMK WN3 ...46 E8
Celia St CHH M8 ....72 F4
Cellini Sq BOL BL1 ....36 A3
Celtic St STKP SK1 ....13 M6
Cemetery La BURY BL9 ....5 K8
Cemetery Rd BOLE BL2 ....3 K4
DROY M43 ....89 J3
DTN/ASHW M34 ....90 C6
DTN/ASHW M34 ....101 J3
FAIL M35 ....74 C6
FWTH BL4 ....53 J3
GLSP SK13 ....93M8
MOSL OL5 ....77 G5
ORD M5 ....86 B3
RAD M26 ....38 C8
RAMS BL0 ....17 A8
ROY/SHW OL2 ....42 F7
SWIN M27 ....70 B3
WGNS/IIMK WN3 ....8 D1
Cemetery Rd North SWIN M27 ...70 B2
Cemetery St MDTN M24 ....57 K3
WHTN BL5 ....50 B3
Cennick Cl OLDE OL4 ....59M6
Ceno St OLD OL1 ....9 L1
Centaur Cl SWIN M27 ....70 C2
Centenary Ct BOLS/LL BL3 ...36 C8
Centenary Wy SALQ M50 .....85 K3
Central Av ATH M46 ....51 H8
BNG/LEV M19 ....99 K2
BURY BL9 ....39 G5
FWTH BL4 ....52 D4
LEIGH * WN7 ....81M1
LIT OL15 ....20 C6
RAMS BL0 ....17 D2
SALE M33 ....108 A3
SLFD M6 ....71 H6
SWIN M27 ....71 C2
UPML * OL3 ....61 L7
UPML OL3 ....61M7
WALK M28 ....52 F7
Central Dr BRAM/HZG SK7 ...120 F2
BURY BL9 ....25 J4
CHD/CHDH SK8 ....119M4
CHH M8 ....72 E5
MPL/ROM SK6 ....113M1
RDSH SK5 ....100 D7
SWIN M27 ....70 B5
URM M41 ....96 A2
WGNNW/ST WN6 ....30 E6
WHTN BL5 ....50 B3
Central Flats WGNE/HIN * WN2 ...48 C5
Central Park Est TRPK * M17 ...85M6
Central Park Wy WGN WN1 ...15 H1
Central Rd DID/WITH M20 ...98 D7
MANAIR M90 ....118 E6
PART M31 ....106 C1
Central St BOL BL1 ....2 D4
CMANW M2 ....6 F5
RAMS BL0 ....17 B6
Central Wy ALT WA14 ....108 A4
Centre Ct LEIGH WN7 ....80 E3
Centre Gdns BOL BL1 ....36 A3
Centre Park Rd BOL BL1 ....2 A1
Centre Vale CI LIT OL15 ....20 D5
Centurion Gv BRO M7 ....72 B7
Century Gdns WHIT OL12 .....10 E2
Century Ldg FWTH BL4 ....52 F4
Cestrian St BOLS/LL BL3 .....52 C1
Ceylon St NEWH/MOS M40 ...73 K6
OLDE OL4 ....60 A7
Chadbury Cl HOR/BR BL6 .....50 F1
Chadderton Dr BURY BL9 .....55 K2
Chadderton Fold OLD OL1 .....58 C3
Chadderton Hall Rd CHAD OL9 ...58 C3
Chadderton Park Rd CHAD OL9 ...58 C3
Chadderton St ANC M4 ....7 J2
Chadderton Wy OP/CLY * M11 ...8 F3
OLD OL1 ....58 F3
Chaddesley Wk OP/CLY * M11 ...88 D4
Chaddock La TYLD M29 ....68 A6
WALK M28 ....68 D7
The Chaddock Level WALK M28 ...68 D7
Chadkirk Rd MPL/ROM SK6 ...113 L3
Chadvil Rd CHD/CHDH SK8 ...110 F7
Chadwell Rd OFTN SK2 ....113 H5
Chadwick Cl MILN OL16 ....29 K7
RUSH/FAL * M14 ....98 E1
WILM/AE SK9 ....127 G3
Chadwick Fold BURY BL9 .....25 J5
Chadwick Hall Rd ROCH OL11 ...27 L6
Chadwick La HEY OL10 ....41 K2
MILN OL16 ....42 F2
URM M41 ....96 C2
Chadwick St AUL OL6 ....91 H2
BOLE BL2 ....3 H6
BOLS/LL BL3 ....53 L1
BURY BL9 ....26 B8
GLSP SK13 ....104 E4
LEIGH WN7 ....66 C6
MILN OL16 ....29 J4
MPL/ROM SK6 ....114 C7
ROCH OL11 ....10 A5
STKP SK1 ....13 J7
SWIN M27 ....70 C4
WGNE/HIN WN2 ....49 H6

WGNS/IIMK WN3 ....14 D7
Chaffinch Cl DROY M43 ....89M1
OLDE OL4 ....60 A8
WYTH/NTH M22 ....110 C7
Chaffinch Dr BURY BL9 ....55M1
Chaffinch Gv STLY * SK15 ...77 H5
Chain Bar La HYDE SK14 .....103 J2
Chain Rd BKLY M9 ....57 G7
Chain St CMANE M1 ....7 G5
Chalbury Ct WGNE/HIN * WN2 ...49 G8
Chalcombe Gra
WGNN/LGST * M12 ....88 C8
Chale Cl NEWH/MOS M40 ....88 A1
Chale Dr MDTN M24 ....57M6
Chale Gn BOLE BL2 ....37 H1
Chalfont Av URM * M41 ....96 B2
Chalfont Cl OLDS * OL8 ....59 L8
Chalfont Dr CHH M8 ....72 D5
TYLD M29 ....67 K5
WALK M28 ....69 H4
Chalfont St BOL BL1 ....36 C2
Chalford Rd NTHM/RTH M23 ...118 C1
Challenge Wy
WGNW/BIL/O WN5 ....46 F3
Challenor Sq WGTN/LGST * M12 ...88 D6
Challum Dr CHAD OL9 ....58 D4
Chamber Hall Cl OLDS OL8 ...59 G8
Chamberhall St BURY BL9 .....4 E2
Chamber Rd OLDS OL8 ....4 E2
Chamber House Dr ROCH OL11 ...41 L1
Chamberlain Dr WILM/AE SK9 ...127 H3
Chamberlain Rd STLY SK15 ...76 F7
Chamberlain St BOLS/LL BL3 ...2 E7
Chamber Rd OLDS OL8 ....74 F1
ROY/SHW OL2 ....43 K5
Chambers Ct HYDE SK14 .....103 K1
Chambers Field Ct ORD M5 ...86 D3
Champness Hall MILN * OL16 ...10 F5
Chancel Av ORD M5 ....86 F4
Chancel Cl DUK SK16 ....90 F4
Chancel La WILM/AE SK9 ...126 F4
Chancellor La WGTN/LGST M12 ...88 A4
Chancel Ms STKP SK1 ....13 L4
Chancel Pl CMANE * M1 ....7 H5
MILN OL16 ....10 E5
Chancery Cl TYLD M29 ....67 L4
Chancery La BOL BL1 ....2 F5
CMANW M2 ....6 F5
ROY/SHW * OL2 ....43M5
UPML OL3 ....61 K2
Chancery St CHAD OL9 ....8 D2
OLDE OL4 ....59M6
Chancery Wk CHAD * OL9 ......8 D1
Chandler Wy GOL/RIS/CU WA3 ...80 B4
Chandley St CHD/CHDH * SK8 ...111 G6
Chandos Gv ORD M5 ....86 A2
Chandos Rd CCHDY M21 ......97M3
HTNM SK4 ....99 L6
PWCH M25 ....71 L2
Chandos Rd South CCHDY M21 ...97M3
Chandos St ROY/SHW OL2 ...43M5
Change Wy CSLFD M3 ....6 C1
Channing Cl MILN OL16 ....11 K7
Channing Sq MILN OL16 ....11 J7
Channing St MILN OL16 ....11 J7
The Chanters WALK M28 ....68 F5
Chanters Av ATH M46 ....67 H1
Chantlers Av TOT/BURYW BL8 ...38 D3
Chantry Cl POY/DIS SK12 ....124 A7
RDSH SK5 ....100 B5
WHTN BL5 ....50 C7
Chantry Fold POY/DIS SK12 ...124 A6
Chantry Rd POY/DIS SK12 ...123M6
Chantry Wk AIMK WN4 ....63 J7
Chapel Aly BOL * BL1 ....2 F4
Chapel Brow GLSP SK13 ....93 K5
GLSP SK13 ....104 B6
Chapel Cl BURY BL9 ....39 L8
DUK SK16 ....90 F4
WGNS/IIMK WN3 ....15 J8
Chapel Ct ALT WA14 ....108 A8
Chapel Cft ROY/SHW OL2 .....43 G8
Chapel Dr AUL OL6 ....76 B7
HALE/TIMP WA15 ....117 L5
Chapelfield Rd M26 ....54 F3
Chapelfield Cl STLY SK15 .....77 G8
Chapelfield Dr WALK M28 .....68 E1
Chapel Field Rd
DTN/ASHW M34 ....101 J1
Chapelfield Rd WGTN/LGST M12 ...7M7
Chapel Flds WGNE/HIN WN2 ...16 C8
Chapel Fields La
WGNE/HIN WN2 ....49 H7
Chapelfield St BOL BL1 ....36 B1
Chapel Gdns TOT/BURYW * BL8 ...24 B3
Chapel Ga MILN OL16 ....29 J6
Chapel Gra EDGW/EG BL7 ....16 C8
Chapel Gn DTN/ASHW M34 ...101 J1
Chapel Green Rd WGNE/HIN WN2 ...48 M6
Chapel Gv URM M41 ....96 B2
Chapel HI LIT OL15 ....20 C6
Chapelhill Dr BKLY M9 ....72 F1
Chapel La BKLY M9 ....72 E1
GLSP SK13 ....93 J7
HALE/TIMP WA15 ....117 K4
PART M31 ....106 C1
ROCH OL11 ....26 E4
ROY/SHW OL2 ....43 G8
SALE M33 ....96 B6
TOT/BURYW BL8 ....17 A6
WGNS/IIMK WN3 ....14 F7
WILM/AE SK9 ....126 D6
Chapel Meadow WALK M28 ...68 E5
Chapel Pl AIMK * WN4 ....78 E1
BOLS/LL BL3 ....3 L8
URM M41 ....85 G4
Chapel Rd IRL M44 ....94 D2
OLDS OL8 ....74 F1
PWCH M25 ....71 J3
SALE M33 ....96 E7
SWIN M27 ....69M5
UPML OL3 ....61 K6
WILM/AE SK9 ....130 D3
WYTH/NTH M22 ....110 A4
Chapelstead WHTN BL5 ....50 C7
Chapel St AIMK WN4 ....78 E1
ATH M46 ....67 G1
AUL OL6 ....90 F1
BNG/LEV M19 ....99 K3
BOL BL1 ....3 G3
BOLS/LL * BL3 ....53 K1
BRAM/HZG SK7 ....122 A1
BURY BL9 ....4 F4
CHAD OL9 ....8 A3
CHD/CHDH SK8 ....111 G7
CSLFD M3 ....6 C3
DROY M43 ....89 K3
DUK SK16 ....90 F4
ECC M30 ....84 F3
EDGW/EG BL7 ....22 A1
FWTH * BL4 ....53 H4
GLSP SK13 ....104 F3

HEY * OL10 ....41 G2
HOR/BR BL6 ....33 G2
HOR/BR BL6 ....33M1
HTNM SK4 ....111 G2
HYDE SK14 ....102 A3
LEIGH WN7 ....66 D8
LIT OL15 ....20 E2
MDTN * M24 ....56 F5
MDTN M24 ....57 J4
MOSL OL5 ....76 E3
NM/HAY SK22 ....124 D6
OLDE OL4 ....60 B6
PWCH M25 ....55 K8
RNFD/HAY WA11 ....78 B6
ROCH OL11 ....28 D8
ROY/SHW OL2 ....43 G8
STLY SK15 ....91 K2
SWIN M27 ....70 D3
TOT/BURYW BL8 ....24 C5
TYLD * M29 ....67 K3
UPML OL3 ....61 L4
WALK M28 ....52 F6
WGNE/HIN WN2 ....48 D1
WGNE/HIN WN2 ....49 G7
WGNE/HIN WN2 ....64 D2
WGNE/HIN WN2 ....65 H3
WGNS/IIMK WN3 ....14 F6
WGNS/IIMK WN3 ....15 J8
WGNW/BIL/O WN5 ....46 E7
WHIT OL12 ....19 K5
WILM/AE SK9 ....130 D3
Chapeltown Rd EDGW/EG BL7 ...22 E4
RAD M26 ....54 D3
Chapeltown St CMANE M1 ......7 L6
Chapel Vw DUK SK16 ....90 F4
Chapel Wks CHD/CHDH SK8 ...120 C6
CMANE M1 ....6 F4
Chapelway Gdns ROY/SHW OL2 ...43 G6
Chaplin Cl SLFD M6 ....71 H8
Chapman Ms GTN * M18 ....89 C7
Chapman Rd HYDE SK14 .....103 H3
Chapman St BOL BL1 ....35 L3
GTN M18 ....89 G6
Chappell Rd DROY M43 ....89 K2
Chappeltown Rd RAD M26 .....54 C3
Chapter St NEWH/MOS M40 ...73 J8
Charcoal Rd ALT WA14 ....116 A1
Charcoal Woods ALT WA14 ...116 C1
Chard Av WYTH/NTH M22 ...118 F3
Chardin Av MPL/ROM SK6 ...114 F4
Chard St RAD M26 ....54 D1
Charfield St NEWH/MOS M40 ...74 A7
Charges St AULW OL7 ....90 C3
Chariot St OP/CLY M11 ....89 G4
Charity St LEIGH WN7 ....65M7
Charlbury Av PWCH M25 ......72 A1
RDSH SK5 ....100 C6
Charlbury Wy ROY/SHW OL2 ...43 K7
Charlecote Rd POY/DIS SK12 ...122 B8
Charles Av DTN/ASHW M34 ...89 M1
MPL/ROM SK6 ....113M5
Charles Ct BOL * BL1 ....2 F3
Charles Halle Rd HULME M15 ...87 K7
Charles Holden St BOL BL1 .....2 A4
Charles La GLSP SK13 ....105 H2
MILN OL16 ....29 K7
Charles Ms MILN * OL16 ....29 K7
Charles Morris Cl FAIL M35 ...74 E4
Charles Shaw Cl OLDE OL4 ...60 A5
Charles St AULW OL7 ....90 E2
BOL BL1 ....2 F3
BRAM/HZG SK7 ....121M1
BURY BL9 ....5 G2
CHAD OL9 ....8 D7
CMANE M1 ....7 G8
CMANE M1 ....7 H7
DROY * M43 ....89 H3
DTN/ASHW M34 ....90 C7
EDGW/EG BL7 ....22 A2
FWTH BL4 ....53 H3
GLSP SK13 ....104 F3
GOL/RIS/CU WA3 ....79 K3
HEY OL10 ....41 H4
IRL M44 ....94 B6
LEIGH WN7 ....66 C6
LIT OL15 ....20 B7
ROY/SHW OL2 ....43 G8
SLFD M6 ....71 J8
STKP SK1 ....13 L8
SWIN M27 ....70 A3
TYLD M29 ....67 K3
WGN WN1 ....15 G1
WGNE/HIN WN2 ....49 H5
WHIT OL12 ....18 E2
WHTF M45 ....55 J5
Charleston Cl SALE M33 ......108 A2
Charleston Sq URM M41 ....95 L1
Charleston St OLDS OL8 ....59 J8
Charlestown Rd BKLY M9 .....72 C2
GLSP SK13 ....104 F4
Charlestown Rd East
OFTN SK2 ....121 J1
Charlestown Rd West
EDGY/DAV SK3 ....121 H1
Charles Whittaker St WHIT OL12 ...27 J3
Charlesworth Av BOLS/LL BL3 ...52 E2
DTN/ASHW M34 ....101 J4
WGNE/HIN WN2 ....49 J8
Charlesworth St OFTN SK2 ...18 J8
OP/CLY M11 ....88 C4
Charley Av BRO M7 ....72 A8
Charlock Av WHTN BL5 ....50 A6
Charlock Cl LEIGH WN7 ....81 J1
Charlock Sq ALT WA14 ....107 L4
Charlotte Dr WGNS/IIMK WN3 ...47 G8
Charlotte La OLDE OL4 ....61 H7
Charlotte St BOL BL1 ....36 B2
CHD/CHDH SK8 ....111 G7
CMANW * M2 ....7 G5
EDGW/EG BL7 ....16 B7
RAMS * BL0 ....17 B7
ROCH OL11 ....28 B8
STKP SK1 ....112 E1
Charlton Av ECC M30 ....85 C3
HYDE SK14 ....91 K8
PWCH M25 ....71 L1
Charlton Cl AIMK WN4 ....63 K7
Charlton Dr SALE M33 ....96 F8
SWIN M27 ....70 A2
Charlton Pl CMANE M1 ....7 K5
Charlton Rd BNG/LEV M19 ...99 L2
Charminster Dr CHH M8 ....72 D7
Charmouth Wk
WYTH/NTH M22 ....119 H1
Charnley Cl NEWH/MOS M40 ...88 B1
Charnley St WHTF M45 ....55 J4
Charnock Dr BOL BL1 ....36 C1

Charnock St WGNE/HIN WN2 ...64 E3
Charnville Rd CHD/CHDH SK8 ...110 C8
Charnwood Av
DTN/ASHW M34 ....100 E1
Charnwood Cl AUL OL6 ....75M5
ROY/SHW OL2 ....43 H4
TYLD M29 ....67 K4
WALK M28 ....68 F2
Charnwood Crs
BRAM/HZG SK7 ....121M4
Charnwood Rd BKLY M9 ....57 G7
MPL/ROM SK6 ....101M7
Charter Av RAD M26 ....54 C7
Charter Cl SALE M33 ....108 A1
Charterhouse Rd
WGNS/IIMK WN3 ....15 J3
Charter Rd HALE/TIMP WA15 ...108 B8
Charter Dr CSLFD M3 ....87 J1
MILN OL16 ....28 D8
OLD OL1 ....9 L2
Chartwell Cl SLFD M6 ....86 C2
Chartwell Dr NTHM/RTH M23 ...109 C5
The Chase WALK M28 ....69 K7
Chase Briar Wd
CHD/CHDH * SK8 ....120 D3
Chasefield Rd ALT WA14 .....116 C2
Chaseley Rd SLFD M6 ....71 H8
WHIT OL12 ....10 C2
Chasewood BNG/LEV * M19 ...99 K3
Chassen Av URM * M41 ....95 K2
Chassen Ct URM * M41 ....95 L3
Chassen Rd BOL BL1 ....35 L5
URM M41 ....95 L3
Chataway Rd CHH M8 ....72 E4
Chatburn Av GOL/RIS/CU WA3 ...79M3
ROCH OL11 ....42 A4
Chatburn Gdns HEY OL10 .....40 C7
Chatburn Rd BOL BL1 ....35 J1
CCHDY M21 ....97M4
Chatcombe Rd
WYTH/NTH M22 ....118 C2
Chatfield Rd CCHDY M21 ......97 L4
Chatford Cl BRO M7 ....72 B8
Chatham Ct DID/WITH * M20 ...98 D6
Chatham Gdns BOLS/LL BL3 ...2 E5
Chatham Gv DID/WITH M20 ...98 D6
Chatham Pl BOLS/LL * BL3 .....2 E5
Chatham Rd GTN * M18 ......100 B1
OLDTF/WHR M16 ....97 L1
Chatham St CMANE M1 ....7 J5
EDGY/DAV SK3 ....12 E7
HYDE SK14 ....102 A5
LEIGH WN7 ....66 A5
WGN WN1 ....15 K5
WGNE/HIN WN2 ....48 D4
Chatley Rd ECC M30 ....84 C3
Chatley St CSLFD M3 ....72 C8
Chatswood Av OFTN SK2 ....112 C6
Chatsworth Av
GOL/RIS/CU WA3 ....81 J3
PWCH M25 ....55 L8
WGNS/IIMK WN3 ....48 C8
Chatsworth Cl AIMK WN4 .....63 J8
BURY BL9 ....39 K7
DROY M43 ....89 G1
HALE/TIMP WA15 ....108 F7
ROY/SHW OL2 ....43M4
URM M41 ....96 B2
Chatsworth Dr LEIGH WN7 ...67 H5
Chatsworth Gv
OLDTF/WHR M16 ....98 A2
Chatsworth Ms BRAM/HZG SK7 ...120 F2
Chatsworth Rd BRAM/HZG SK7 ...122 B3
DROY M43 ....89 H1
ECC M30 ....70 C8
GTN M18 ....88 F7
MPL/ROM SK6 ....125 H6
RAD M26 ....38 B7
STRET M32 ....96 C1
SWIN M27 ....69 L7
WILM/AE SK9 ....126 C8
Chatsworth St OLDE OL4 ......59M7
WGNW/BIL/O WN5 ....46 F7
WHIT OL12 ....28 B1
Chatteris Cl WGNE/HIN WN2 ...49 H8
Chatterton Cl DID/WITH M20 ...98 F6
Chatterton La MPL/ROM SK6 ...115 K4
MPL/ROM SK6 ....115M5
Chatterton Old La RAMS BL0 ...17 C2
Chatterton Rd RAMS BL0 .....17 C2
Chattock Cl OLDTF/WHR M16 ...98 B1
Chatton Cl TOT/BURYW BL8 ...38 C2
Chatwood Rd NEWH/MOS M40 ...74 A2
Chaucer Av DROY M43 ....89 K3
DTN/ASHW M34 ....101 K5
RDSH SK5 ....100 A4
Chaucer Gv LEIGH WN7 ....65M4
Chaucer Ms STKP SK1 ....112 E1
Chaucer Pl WGN WN1 ....47M1
WGNE/HIN WN2 ....64 E3
Chaucer Ri DUK SK16 ....91 K5
Chaucer Rd MDTN M24 ....57 L2
Chaucer St BOL BL1 ....36 A3
OLD OL1 ....9 H6
ROCH OL11 ....41M2
ROY/SHW OL2 ....43 G8
Chaucer Wk BRUN/LGST * M13 ...87M6
Chauncy Rd NEWH/MOS M40 ...74 B4
Chaytor Av NEWH/MOS M40 ...73 L5
Cheadle Av BRO M7 ....71 K5
Cheadle Old Rd EDGY/DAV SK3 ...12 C9
EDGY/DAV SK3 ....12 E9
Cheadle Pl CHD/CHDH * SK8 ...111 L7
Cheadle Rd CHD/CHDH SK8 ...111 H8
Cheadle Sq BOL BL1 ....2 C5
Cheadle St OP/CLY M11 ....89 G4
Cheadle Wd CHD/CHDH SK8 ...120 A8
Cheam Rd HALE/TIMP WA15 ...108 C4
Cheapside CMANW M2 ....6 F4
HYDE SK14 ....102 B1
Cheapside OLD OL1 ....9 H5
Cheapside Sq BOL * BL1 ....2 C5
Cheddar St GTN M18 ....89 C7
Chedlee Dr CHD/CHDH SK8 ...120 A3
Chedlin Dr NTHM/RTH M23 ...109 K8
Chedworth Crs LHULT M38 ...52 D6
Chedworth Gv BOLS/LL * BL3 ...2 C8
Cheeryble St DROY M43 ....89 J4
Cheesden Fold Rd HYDE SK14 ...102 A4
Cheetham Gv WGNS/IIMK WN3 ...14 A9
Cheetham HI ROY/SHW OL2 ...43 G8
Cheetham Hill Rd ANC M4 ......7 G1
CHH M8 ....72 D7
DUK SK16 ....91 G6
Cheetham Pl MPL/ROM SK6 ...101 J4
Cheetham Rd SWIN M27 ......70 D5
The Cheethams HOR/BR BL6 ...33 H4

Cheetham St FAIL M35 ....74 D4
MDTN M24 ....57 J4
MILN OL16 ....10 E3
NEWH/MOS * M40 ....73 H7
OLD * OL1 ....59 L5
RAD M26 ....38 F8
ROY/SHW OL2 ....43M6
Cheetwood St CHH M8 ....72 C7
Cheetwood St CHH M8 ....72 C7
Chelbourne Dr OLDS * OL8 ...74 E2
Chelburn Ct WGNE/HIN WN2 ...65 H3
Chelburn Vw LIT OL15 ....20 D3
Chelford Av BOL BL1 ....22 B7
GOL/RIS/CU WA3 ....80 A5
Chelford Cl HALE/TIMP WA15 ...108 B6
MDTN M24 ....57M2
WGNS/IIMK WN3 ....63 J2
TYLD M29 ....67M6
Chelford Dr SWIN M27 ....70 B2
Chelford Gv EDGY/DAV SK3 ...111M7
Chelford Gv MCFLDN SK10 ...131 L7
OLDTF/WHR M16 ....97M1
SALE M33 ....109 H1
WIN/AE SK9 ....119M7
Chellow Dene MOSL OL5 ......76 A3
Chell St WGTN/LGST M12 .....88 C8
Chelmarsh Av AIMK WN4 .....78 F1
Chelmer Cl WHTN BL5 ....50 C3
Chelmer Gv HEY OL10 ....40 D1
Chelmorton Gv
WGNS/IIMK WN3 ....62 F2
Chelmsford Av NEWH/MOS M40 ...73 L8
Chelmsford Dr WGNS/IIMK WN3 ...47 K8
Chelmsford Rd EDGY/DAV SK3 ...12 D7
EDGY/DAV SK3 ....12 D8
OLDS OL8 ....59 J8
Chelsea Av RAD M26 ....38 A8
Chelsea Cl ROY/SHW OL2 ....43 L5
Chelsea Ct WHTN * BL5 ....50 A7
Chelsea Rd BOLS/LL BL3 .....51M1
NEWH/MOS M40 ....94 F3
Chelsea St BURY BL9 ....39 J7
ROCH OL11 ....10 A9
Chelsfield Gv CCHDY M21 .....98 A1
Chelston Av NEWH/MOS M40 ...74 A2
Chelston Dr CHD/CHDH SK8 ...119 L6
Cheltenham Av
WGNS/IIMK WN3 ....15 J8
Cheltenham Crs BRO M7 ......72 B4
Cheltenham Dr NEWLW WA12 ...79 J3
SALE M33 ....96 F8
WGNW/BIL/O WN5 ....62 A2
Cheltenham Gn MDTN M24 ...57 K6
Cheltenham Rd CCHDY M21 ...97 L2
EDGY/DAV SK3 ....111 K5
MDTN M24 ....57 K6
Cheltenham St OLD OL1 ....59 L3
ROCH OL11 ....18 A5
SLFD M6 ....71 K8
WGNE/HIN WN2 ....48 C2
Chelwood Cl BOL BL1 ....22 A5
Chelwood Dr DROY M43 ....89 J2
Chelwood Ms HOR/BR * BL6 ...34 E5
Chelwood Pk RNFD/HAY WA11 ...78 E7
Chendre Cl NM/HAY SK22 ...125 L1
Chendre Rd BKLY M9 ....73 L1
Cheney Cl OP/CLY * M11 ......89 G5
Chepstow Av SALE M33 ......107M1
Chepstow Cl ROCH OL11 ......27 J4
Chepstow Dr BRAM/HZG SK7 ...122 C2
OLD OL1 ....59 L3
Chepstow Gv LEIGH WN7 .....67 H5
Chepstow Rd CCHDY M21 .....97 K3
OLD OL1 ....70 D2
Chepstow St CMANE M1 ....6 F7
Chepstow St South CMANE * M1 ...6 F7
Chequers Rd CCHDY M21 .....97 L4
Chequers St WGN WN1 ....14 E4
Cherington Cl NTHM/RTH M23 ...109 J1
Cherington Dr TYLD M29 ......67M3
Cherington Rd CHD/CHDH SK8 ...110 F8
Cheriton Av SALE M33 ....96 F7
Cheriton Cl HYDE SK14 ....103 C2
Cheriton Dr BOLE BL2 ....37 H6
Cheriton Ri OFTN SK2 ....113 K6
Cheriton Rd URM M41 ....96 A1
Cherrington Dr ROCH OL11 ...42 A4
Cherry Av AUL OL6 ....76 D8
BURY BL9 ....5M3
OLDS OL8 ....75M1
Cherrybrook Dr
WGNS/IIMK WN3 ....63 G3
Cherry Cl BURY BL9 ....39 K5
NEWLW WA12 ....78 C8
OFTN SK2 ....113 H5
Cherrycroft MPL/ROM SK6 ...114 B3
Cherry Dr SWIN M27 ....70 C4
Cherry Gv LEIGH WN7 ....66 C4
ROCH OL11 ....27 K4
ROY/SHW OL2 ....42 F6
STLY SK15 ....91 K4
WGNW/BIL/O WN6 ....47 J1
Cherry Hall Dr ROY/SHW * OL2 ...43 H5
Cherry Hinton OLD * OL1 ....8 E2
Cherry Holt Av HTNM SK4 .....99 J8
Cherry La LIT OL15 ....44 E1
SALE M33 ....107M2
Cherry Orchard Cl
BRAM/HZG SK7 ....120 F3
Cherry St PWCH * M25 ....55M7
Cherryton Wk BRUN/LGST M13 ...87M6
Cherry Tree Av FWTH BL4 ....52 C4
POY/DIS SK12 ....129 K1
Cherry Tree Cl
HALE/TIMP WA15 ....108 E7
MPL/ROM SK6 ....114 B2
WILM/AE SK9 ....127 J4
Cherry Tree Ct OFTN SK2 ....112 F8
Cherry Tree Dr BRAM/HZG SK7 ...122 C2
Cherry Tree Gv LEIGH WN7 ...66 A6
ATH M46 ....67 G2
Cherry Tree La ALT WA14 ....116 B6
MPL/ROM SK6 ....114 B2
OFTN SK2 ....112 F7
TOT/BURYW BL8 ....38 C5
Cherry Tree Rd CHD/CHDH SK8 ...120 B3
GOL/RIS/CU WA3 ....80 C4
NTHM/RTH M23 ....109 J3
Cherry Tree Wk STRET M32 ...96 E3
Cherry Wk CHD/CHDH SK8 ...120 B4
Cherrywood CHAD OL9 ....58 A5
Cherrywood Av WHTN BL5 ...51 K5
Cherry Wood Cl WALK M28 ...68 C4
Chertsey Cl GTN M18 ....89 H7
ROY/SHW OL2 ....43 L4
Chervil Cl RUSH/FAL M14 ......98 E3
Chervil Wk WGNS/IIMK WN3 ...46 F3

Chervil Cl RUSH/FAL M14 ....98 F4
Cherwell Av HEY OL10 ....40 D1
Cherwell Cl CHD/CHDH SK8 ...120 C5
  OLDS OL8 ....74 F3
  WGNE/HIN WN2 ....32 F6
  WHTF M45 ....55 K4
Cherwell Rd WHTN BL5 ....50 C2
Chesham Av BOL BL1 ....36 B2
  ROCH OL11 ....42 A5
  URM M41 ....95 H1
  WYTH/NTH M22 ....109 M8
Chesham Cl GLSP SK13 ....93 L7
  WILM/AE SK9 ....126 D8
Chesham Crs BURY BL9 ....5 J2
Chesham Fold Rd BURY BL9 ....5 L2
Chesham Pl ALT WA14 ....116 E2
Chesham Rd BURY BL9 ....25 L7
  ECC * M30 ....84 F4
  OLDE OL4 ....59 M6
  WILM/AE SK9 ....126 D8
Cheshire Cl STRET M32 ....96 E3
Cheshire Ct RAMS BL0 ....17 D6
Cheshire Ring Canal Wk
  ALT WA14 ....107 H7
  MCFLDN SK10 ....129 L6
  MPL/ROM SK6 ....101 L6
  MPL/ROM SK6 ....114 C4
Cheshire Rd PART M31 ....106 A2
  STLY SK15 ....77 G7
The Cheshires MOSL OL5 ....77 G3
Cheshire Sq STLY SK15 ....77 G3
Cheshire St MOSL OL5 ....77 G4
Chesney Av CHAD OL9 ....74 B2
Chesshyre Av ANC * M4 ....88 A3
Chessington Ri SWIN M27 ....70 D1
Chester Av BOLS/LL BL3 ....37 L8
  DUK SK16 ....91 H5
  GOL/RIS/CU WA3 ....80 A4
  HALE/TIMP WA15 ....117 H2
  ROCH OL11 ....27 K6
  SALE M33 ....107 L3
  STLY SK15 ....92 A1
  URM M41 ....96 B3
  WHTF M45 ....55 K5
Chester Cl BOLS/LL BL3 ....37 L8
  IRL M44 ....94 A7
  WILM/AE SK9 ....127 J2
Chester Dr AIMK WN4 ....79 G2
  RAMS BL0 ....17 A8
Chesterfield Gv AUL OL6 ....91 G1
Chesterfield St OLDE OL4 ....59 L6
Chestergate EDGY/DAV SK3 ....13 G5
  STKP SK1 ....13 H4
Chester Rd BRAM/HZG SK7 ...121 M5
  BRAM/HZG SK7 ....128 B2
  HULME M15 ....6 A9
  OLDTF/WHR M16 ....86 F7
  POY/DIS SK12 ....121 K8
  STRET M32 ....86 B8
  STRET M32 ....96 F4
  TYLD M29 ....68 A4
Chester St ATH M46 ....67 H2
  BURY BL9 ....25 K8
  CHAD OL9 ....8 C9
  DTN/ASHW M34 ....101 J2
  EDGY/DAV SK3 ....12 E5
  HULME M15 ....6 F9
  LEIGH WN7 ....66 C7
  PWCH M25 ....55 K7
  SWIN M27 ....70 B5
Chesterton Cl WGNS/IIMK WN3 ...14 C9
Chesterton Dr BOLS/LL BL3 ....35 H7
Chesterton Gv DROY M43 ....89 K2
Chesterton Rd NTHM/RTH M23 ...109 G4
Chester Wk BOL BL1 ....36 B2
Chestnut Av ATH * M46 ....50 F8
  BURY BL9 ....5 K4
  CCHDY M21 ....97 L4
  CHD/CHDH SK8 ....111 H7
  DROY M43 ....89 H1
  IRL M44 ....94 A7
  LEIGH WN7 ....81 H1
  TOT/BURYW BL8 ....24 D7
  WALK M28 ....69 G2
  WHTF M45 ....55 J5
Chestnut Cl BOLS/LL BL3 ....35 L8
  NM/HAY SK22 ....125 G3
  OLDE OL4 ....60 A4
  STLY SK15 ....91 K4
  WILM/AE SK9 ....127 J4
Chestnut Crs OLDS OL8 ....75 K2
Chestnut Dr BURY BL9 ....25 J5
  LEIGH WN7 ....81 J1
  POY/DIS SK12 ....129 K1
  SALE M33 ....108 A3
  WHTN BL5 ....50 C5
Chestnut Gdns
  DTN/ASHW M34 ....101 H2
  HEY OL10 ....40 F3
Chestnut Gv AIMK WN4 ....64 A8
  FAIL M35 ....74 C6
  GOL/RIS/CU WA3 ....80 C4
  RAD M26 ....54 C4
  WGNE/HIN WN2 ....49 K8
Chestnut La LEIGH WN7 ....81 J2
Chestnut Rd ECC M30 ....69 K8
  WGN WN1 ....48 A2
Chestnut St CHAD OL9 ....74 D1
Chestnut Wy LIT OL15 ....19 M7
Chesworth Cl STKP SK1 ....13 J6
Chesworth Fold STKP SK1 ....13 J7
Chetham Cl ORD * M5 ....86 E5
Chetwode Av AIMK WN4 ....78 E2
Chetwyn Av EDGW/EG BL7 ....22 D5
  ROY/SHW OL2 ....42 F8
Chetwynd Av URM M41 ....95 M3
Chetwynd Cl SALE M33 ....96 B6
Chevassut St HULME M15 ....87 H6
Chevington Dr BKLY M9 ....73 G6
  HTNM SK4 ....111 J1
Cheviot Av CHD/CHDH SK8 ...120 D2
  OLDS OL8 ....75 H1
  ROY/SHW OL2 ....58 F1
Cheviot Cl BOL BL1 ....22 F1
  CHAD OL9 ....58 D7
  HOR/BR BL6 ....21 C7
  HTNM SK4 ....12 F1
  MDTN M24 ....58 A4
  MILN OL16 ....29 K5
  RAMS BL0 ....17 C8
  SLFD M6 ....86 B1
  TOT/BURYW BL8 ....38 D1
  WGNS/IIMK WN3 ....62 F2
Cheviot Rd BRAM/HZG SK7 ...121 K3
Cheviots Rd ROY/SHW OL2 ....43 K4
Cheviot St CSLFD M3 ....87 J1
Chevithorne Cl ALT WA14 ....107 L7

Chevril Cl HULME M15 ....87 K6
Chevron Cl ROCH OL11 ....41 L1
  SLFD M6 ....86 E2
Chevron Pl ALT WA14 ....108 A5
Chew Brook Dr UPML OL3 ....61 L7
Chew Moor La WHTN BL5 ....50 D2
Chew V DUK SK16 ....91 J5
  UPML OL3 ....61 L7
Chew Valley Rd UPML OL3 ....61 L7
Chicago Av MANAIR M90 ...118 D5
Chichester Av HM M46 ....66 D2
Chichester Cl LIT OL15 ....29 J1
  SALE M33 ....108 A1
Chichester Crs CHAD OL9 ....58 D3
Chichester Rd HULME M15 ....87 H7
  MPL/ROM SK6 ....113 M2
Chichester Rd South
  HULME * M15 ....87 H7
Chichester St MILN OL16 ....11 J5
Chidlow Av DID/WITH M20 ....98 D5
Chidwall Rd WYTH/NTH M22 ...118 D2
Chief St OLDE OL4 ....9 M7
Chiffon Wy CSLFD M3 ....6 A1
Chigwell Cl WYTH/NTH M22 ...110 B7
Chilcote Av SALE M33 ....96 A8
Childwall Cl BOLS/LL BL3 ....52 D2
Chilgrove Av HOR/BR BL6 ....33 C3
Chilham Rd ECC M30 ....69 H2
  WALK M28 ....69 H2
Chilham St BOLS/LL BL3 ....51 L2
  SWIN M27 ....70 B6
  WGNW/BIL/O WN5 ....46 D6
Chillingham Dr LEIGH WN7 ....66 E8
Chilmark Dr NTHM/RTH M23 ...109 K6
Chiltern Av ATH M46 ....51 J7
  URM M41 ....95 J1
Chiltern Cl AIMK WN4 ....78 F2
  BRAM/HZG SK7 ....121 K3
  HOR/BR BL6 ....21 C7
  RAMS BL0 ....17 C8
  ROY/SHW OL2 ....43 J4
  WALK M28 ....69 H4
Chiltern Dr BOLE BL2 ....3 L4
  HALE/TIMP WA15 ....117 H2
  OFTN SK2 ....112 D8
  ROY/SHW OL2 ....42 F8
  SWIN M27 ....70 C6
  TOT/BURYW BL8 ....24 E8
  WGNS/IIMK WN3 ....62 F1
Chiltern Gdns SALE M33 ....108 F4
Chiltern Rd GOL/RIS/CU WA3 ...81 H8
  RAMS BL0 ....17 C8
Chiltern Wy TYLD M29 ....67 L4
Chilton Av CHAD OL9 ....58 D6
Chilton Cl LEIGH WN7 ....66 C5
Chilton Dr MDTN M24 ....57 M5
Chilworth St RUSH/FAL M14 ...98 E2
Chime Bank CHH M8 ....72 F6
Chimes Rd AIMK WN4 ....63 J6
China La CMANE M1 ....7 J5
Chingford Wk
  BRUN/LGST * M13 ....88 C8
Chinley Av NEWH/MOS M40 ...73 K4
  STRET M32 ....85 K8
Chinley Cl BRAM/HZG SK7 ...121 C1
  HTNM SK4 ....12 A1
  SALE M33 ....109 G1
Chinley St SLFD M6 ....71 L7
Chinnor Cl LEIGH WN7 ....65 K7
Chinwell Vw BNG/LEV * M19 ...99 K3
Chip Hill Rd BOLS/LL BL3 ....35 K8
Chippendale Pl AUL OL6 ....76 B7
Chippenham Av OFTN SK2 ....112 F5
Chippenham Ct ANC M4 ....88 A2
Chippenham Rd ANC M4 ....7 M3
Chipping Fold MILN OL16 ....29 J7
Chipping Rd BOL BL1 ....22 F1
Chipstead Av WGTN/LGST M12 ...88 B7
Chirmside St TOT/BURYW BL8 ...38 E3
Chirton Cl RNFD/HAY WA11 ...78 A5
Chisacre Dr WGNNW/ST WN6 ...30 A5
Chiseldon Av WYTH/NTH M22 ...119 G2
Chiselhurst St CHH M8 ....72 D5
Chisholm Cl WGNNW/ST WN6 ...30 A5
Chisholme Cl TOT/BURYW BL8 ...24 C2
Chisholm St OP/CLY M11 ....89 G5
Chisledon Av CHH * M8 ....72 C6
Chisledon Ct RNFD/HAY WA11 ...78 A5
Chislehurst Av URM M41 ....95 M1
Chislehurst Cl TOT/BURYW BL8 ...38 E3
Chiswell St NEWH/BIL/O WN5 ...46 F7
Chiswick Dr BOLS/LL BL3 ....37 L7
Chiswick Rd DID/WITH M20 ...110 F1
Chisworth Cl BRAM/HZG SK7 ...121 C1
  LEIGH WN7 ....66 B5
Chisworth St BOLE BL2 ....36 E1
Choir St BRO M7 ....72 B8
Chokeberry Cl ALT WA14 ....107 L4
Cholmondeley Av ALT * WA14 ...108 A5
Cholmondeley Rd SLFD M6 ....70 E8
Chomlea Mnr SLFD * M6 ....70 F8
Choral Gv BRO M7 ....72 A7
Chorley Gv TOT/BURYW BL8 ...38 C3
Chorley Hall Cl WILM/AE SK9 ...130 C3
Chorley Hall La WILM/AE SK9 ...130 C3
Chorley New Rd HOR/BR BL6 ...33 L1
  HOR/BR BL6 ....34 C4
Chorley Old Rd BOL BL1 ....35 H2
  HOR/BR BL6 ....34 B1
Chorley Rd HOR/BR BL6 ....32 F1
  SALE M33 ....109 H2
  SWIN M27 ....70 A3
  WGN WN1 ....31 L3
  WGNNW/ST WN6 ....31 L6
  WHTN BL5 ....33 J6
  WHTN BL5 ....33 M8
  WHTN BL5 ....50 B1
Chorley St BOL * BL1 ....2 C3
  STRET M32 ....86 C8
  WGNS/IIMK WN3 ....15 K8
Chorley Wood Av
  BNG/LEV * M19 ....99 J6
Chorlton Dr CHD/CHDH SK8 ...111 H6
Chorlton Fold ECC M30 ....70 A7
Chorlton Gv STKP SK1 ....13 L5
Chorlton Pl CCHDY M21 ....97 L5
Chorlton Rd HULME M15 ....6 B9
  OLDTF/WHR M16 ....87 G7
Chorlton St CMANE M1 ....7 H5
  OLDTF/WHR M16 ....86 F7
Chorlton Ter BRUN/LGST * M13 ...87 L7
Chowbent Cl ATH M46 ....67 H1
Chretien Rd WYTH/NTH M22 ...110 A2
Christ Church Cl BOLE * BL2 ...37 J2
Christchurch La BOLE BL2 ....37 J1
Christchurch Rd SALE M33 ....95 M7
Christie Cl STRET M32 ....97 H5
Christie St STKP SK1 ....13 M7
Christine St ROY/SHW OL2 ....43 J4

Christleton WGNNW/ST WN6 ...30 E6
Christleton Av HTNM SK4 ...100 A7
Christopher Acre ROCH OL11 ...27 H3
Christopher St NEWH/MOS M40 ...74 A8
  ORD M5 ....86 D3
Chronnell Dr BOLE BL2 ....37 H4
  WGNS/IIMK WN3 ....15 M8
Chudleigh Cl ALT WA14 ....107 L6
Chudleigh Rd CHH M8 ....72 D2
Chulsey Gate La HOR/BR BL6 ...34 B8
Chulsey St BOLS/LL BL3 ....51 L1
Chunal La GLSP SK13 ....104 F6
Church Av BOLS/LL BL3 ....35 M8
  DTN/ASHW M34 ....101 K4
  HYDE SK14 ....102 C4
  MDTN M24 ....42 A6
  NEWH/MOS M40 ....73 M7
  OLDE OL4 ....60 D7
  RAMS BL0 ....54 E2
  ROCH OL11 ....10 C5
  ROY/SHW OL2 ....43 C8
  STLY SK15 ....91 K2
  STRET M32 ....96 F3
  SWIN M27 ....70 B4
  SWIN M27 ....70 E4
  TOT/BURYW BL8 ....24 C7
  UPML OL3 ....45 H8
  WGN WN1 ....15 C3
  WGNE/HIN WN2 ....32 E6
  WGNE/HIN WN2 ....49 G7
  WGNNW/ST WN6 ....31 H3
  WGNS/IIMK WN3 ....15 M7
  WGNW/BIL/O WN5 ....46 A7
  WGNW/BIL/O WN5 ....46 E6
  WHIT OL12 ....18 D4
  WHTN BL5 ....50 B3
  WILM/AE SK9 ....126 F5
Church Bank BOL BL1 ....2 F4
Churchbank STLY SK15 ....92 A2
Church Brow ALT WA14 ....116 D2
  HYDE SK14 ....102 A3
  HYDE SK14 ....103 K1
Church Cl GLSP SK13 ....105 L2
  RAD M26 ....53 L4
  RAMS BL0 ....17 B7
Church Ct BURY * BL9 ....5 H3
  DUK SK16 ....90 E3
Church Cft BURY BL9 ....39 L8
Church Dr PWCH M25 ....55 J8
  WGNW/BIL/O WN5 ....46 A7
Church Flds ALT WA14 ....116 D3
  DTN/ASHW M34 ....90 B5
  SALE M33 ....96 A6
Churchfield Wk OP/CLY * M11 ...88 D4
Churchgate BOL BL1 ....2 F4
  STKP SK1 ....13 J4
  URM M41 ....96 B3
Churchgate Buildings
  CMANE * M1 ....7 L6
Church Gates WGN WN1 ....14 F4
Church Gn RAD M26 ....39 G8
  SLFD M6 ....86 C1
Church Gv BRAM/HZG SK7 ...122 A2
  WGN * WN1 ....15 K4
Churchill Av BOLE BL2 ....38 A3
  GOL/RIS/CU WA3 ....81 L8
Churchill Cl HEY OL10 ....41 H4
Churchill Crs MPL/ROM SK6 ...114 A5
  RDSH SK5 ....100 B5
Churchill Rd ALT WA14 ....108 A5
Churchill St BOLE * BL2 ....3 M4
  HTNM SK4 ....112 A1
  OLDE OL4 ....9 L7
  WHIT OL12 ....27 M3
Churchill St East OLDE OL4 ....9 L7
Churchill Wy SLFD M6 ....86 D2
  TRPK M17 ....85 M5
Churchlands La
  WGNNW/ST WN6 ....31 J3
Church La BKLY M9 ....73 G4
  BNG/LEV M19 ....99 J6
  BRAM/HZG SK7 ....128 A2
  BRO M7 ....71 L3
  GOL/RIS/CU WA3 ....80 A5
  MILN OL16 ....10 E5
  MOSL OL5 ....77 G3
  MPL/ROM SK6 ....113 M2
  MPL/ROM SK6 ....114 C6
  NM/HAY SK22 ....124 E4
  OLD OL1 ....9 J5
  PWCH M25 ....55 K8
  SALE M33 ....96 B6
  WGNNW/ST WN6 ....30 D6
  WHTF M45 ....55 H4
  WHTN BL5 ....50 B1
  WILM/AE SK9 ....130 D2
Churchley Cl EDGY/DAV SK3 ...111 K6
Churchley Rd EDGY/DAV SK3 ...111 K5
Church Mdw BOLE BL2 ....37 J1
Church Meadow BURY BL9 ....39 L7
  HYDE SK14 ....101 M1
  OLDE OL4 ....61 H7
Church Ms DTN/ASHW M34 ...101 H1
Church Rd BOL BL1 ....110 D7
  CHD/CHDH SK8 ....110 D7
  CHD/CHDH SK8 ....120 D5
  ECC M30 ....85 J2
  FWTH BL4 ....53 H4
  GLSP SK13 ....103 M6
  HTNM SK4 ....12 F2
  HYDE SK14 ....93 G8
  MDTN M24 ....58 A5
  MILN OL16 ....11 J6
  MPL/ROM SK6 ....115 H6
  NM/HAY SK22 ....124 E5
  OLDE OL4 ....61 H7
  RAD M26 ....53 K4
  RAMS BL0 ....17 E4
  RNFD/HAY WA11 ....78 B6
  ROY/SHW OL2 ....43 L6
  SALE M33 ....97 G8
  TYLD M29 ....67 M6
  UPML OL3 ....61 M4
  URM * M41 ....95 K4
  WALK M28 ....69 G1
  WGNE/HIN WN2 ....64 E1
  WILM/AE SK9 ....126 C8
  WILM/AE SK9 ....127 H1
  WYTH/NTH M22 ....110 A3
Church Rd East SALE M33 ....97 G8
Church Rd West SALE M33 ....96 F8
Churchside FWTH BL4 ....52 E5
Churchside Cl BKLY M9 ....73 G2
Church Stile MILN OL16 ....10 E5
Churchston Av BRAM/HZG SK7 ...121 J2
Church St ALT WA14 ....108 A7
  ANC M4 ....7 H3
  AUL OL6 ....90 E2
  BOLE BL2 ....23 G7
  BOLE BL2 ....37 M3
  BOLS/LL BL3 ....53 J1
  BURY BL9 ....5 H5
  CHD/CHDH SK8 ....111 G6
  DROY M43 ....89 K3
  DTN/ASHW * M34 ....90 C5
  DUK SK16 ....91 G4
  ECC M30 ....85 H2
  FAIL M35 ....74 B5
  FWTH BL4 ....53 H5
  GLSP SK13 ....93 J5
  GLSP SK13 ....93 K8

  GLSP SK13 ....105 G2
  GOL/RIS/CU WA3 ....79 L3
  HEY OL10 ....41 G2
  HOR/BR BL6 ....32 F2
  HOR/BR BL6 ....33 M1
  HTNM SK4 ....13 C1
  HYDE SK14 ....102 A3
  LEIGH WN7 ....66 C7
  LIT OL15 ....20 C7
  MDTN * M24 ....57 K2
  MILN OL16 ....29 C1
  MILN OL16 ....29 L8
  MPL/ROM SK6 ....101 K7
  MPL/ROM * SK6 ....114 C7
  NEWLW WA12 ....79 H8
  NM/HAY SK22 ....125 M2
  OLDE OL4 ....60 D7
  RAD M26 ....54 E2
  RAMS BL0 ....17 C6
  ROCH OL11 ....10 C5
  ROY/SHW OL2 ....43 C8
  STLY SK15 ....91 K2
  STRET M32 ....96 F3
  SWIN M27 ....70 B4
  SWIN M27 ....70 E4
  TOT/BURYW BL8 ....24 C7
  UPML OL3 ....45 H8
  WGN WN1 ....15 G3
  WGNE/HIN WN2 ....32 E6
  WGNE/HIN WN2 ....49 G7
  WGNNW/ST WN6 ....31 H3
  WGNS/IIMK WN3 ....15 M7
  WGNW/BIL/O WN5 ....46 A7
  WGNW/BIL/O WN5 ....46 E6
  WHIT OL12 ....18 D4
  WHTN BL5 ....50 B3
  WILM/AE SK9 ....126 F5
Church St East OLDE OL4 ....60 B4
  RAD M26 ....54 F1
Church St South GLSP SK13 ....105 H2
Church St West RAD M26 ....54 E1
Church Ter MILN OL16 ....29 K7
  OLD OL1 ....9 J5
  SALE * M33 ....96 D6
  WILM/AE SK9 ....119 M8
Churchtown Av BOLE BL2 ....37 J5
  HYDE SK14 ....102 A3
  IRL M44 ....94 D2
  WHIT OL12 ....27 H2
Church Vw HYDE SK14 ....102 A1
  MILN OL16 ....28 E8
  MOSL OL5 ....77 G4
  RDSH * SK5 ....112 C1
  WHTF M45 ....55 J4
Churchward Sq HOR/BR BL6 ...33 M2
Churchwood Rd
  DID/WITH M20 ....110 E1
Churnet St NEWH/MOS M40 ...73 G7
Churnett Cl WHTN BL5 ....50 C2
Churston Av BKLY M9 ....57 H8
Churton Av SALE M33 ....108 B1
Churton Gv WGNNW/ST WN6 ...30 E2
Churton Rd GTN M18 ....99 M1
Churwell Av HTNM SK4 ....99 J8
Cicero St BKLY M9 ....73 H4
Cinamon St WHIT OL12 ....10 A2
Cinder Hl BURY * BL9 ....25 L6
Cinder Hill La OLD OL1 ....58 D1
Cinder St ANC * M4 ....7 L2
Cinnabar Dr MDTN M24 ....57 J2
Cinnamon Av WGNE/HIN WN2 ...49 K8
Cipher St ANC M4 ....7 L1
Circle South TRPK M17 ....86 B6
The Circuit CHD/CHDH SK8 ...120 C5
  DID/WITH M20 ....98 E7
  EDGY/DAV SK3 ....111 M6
  WILM/AE SK9 ....130 E1
Circular Rd DID/WITH M20 ....98 E7
  DTN/ASHW M34 ....101 H3
  PWCH M25 ....71 L2
Circus St CMANE * M1 ....7 J5
Cirencester Cl LHULT M38 ....52 D6
Ciss La URM M41 ....96 B2
Citrus Wy SLFD M6 ....86 B1
City Av DTN/ASHW M34 ....101 K4
City Gdns DTN/ASHW * M34 ...101 K2
City Rd HULME M15 ....87 G6
  WALK M28 ....68 D4
  WGNW/BIL/O WN5 ....46 E5
City Rd East HULME M15 ....6 E9
City Wk SWIN M27 ....70 E4
Civic Centre BOL * BL1 ....2 E5
Clacton Wk BRUN/LGST * M13 ...87 M6
Clague St OP/CLY M11 ....88 D2
Claife Av NEWH/MOS M40 ....73 L2
Clammerclough Rd FWTH BL4 ...53 J4
Clandon Av ECC M30 ....84 E2
Clanwood Cl WGNS/IIMK WN3 ...63 H2
Clapgate MPL/ROM SK6 ....113 K3
Clap Gate La WGNS/IIMK WN3 ...63 H1
Clapgate Rd ROCH OL11 ....27 H5
Clapham St NEWH/MOS M40 ...73 M4
Clara Gorton Ct MILN OL16 ....11 K6
Clara St CHAD OL9 ....58 F8
  ROCH OL11 ....10 E9
  WHIT OL12 ....18 E3
Clare Av WILM/AE SK9 ....127 G1
Clare Cl TOT/BURYW BL8 ....25 G7
Claremont Av ALT WA14 ....108 A4
  DID/WITH M20 ....98 D7
  HTNM SK4 ....99 M7
  MPL/ROM SK6 ....113 M6
  WGNE/HIN WN2 ....49 J7
Claremont Ct BOL * BL1 ....36 B5
Claremont Dr ALT WA14 ....108 A4
  LHULT M38 ....52 E7
Claremont Gdns AUL OL6 ....76 B7
Claremont Gv DID/WITH M20 ...110 D1
  HALE/TIMP WA15 ....117 G1
Claremont Range GTN * M18 ...89 J3
Claremont Rd CHD/CHDH SK8 ...120 C4
  GOL/RIS/CU WA3 ....81 G8
  MILN OL16 ....29 H7
  OFTN SK2 ....112 E8
  ROCH OL11 ....27 M5
  RUSH/FAL M14 ....98 E1
  SALE M33 ....96 E1
  SLFD M6 ....70 F8
  WGNW/BIL/O WN5 ....62 B7
Claremont St AUL OL6 ....76 A8
  CHAD OL9 ....8 C1
  FAIL M35 ....74 C5
  OLDS OL8 ....75 J2
  SLFD M6 ....70 F6
Clarence Ar AUL * OL6 ....90 E2
Clarence Av OLDS OL8 ....59 G8
  TRPK M17 ....85 J6
  WHTF M45 ....55 K5

Clarence Ct BOL * BL1 ....2 C3
  WILM/AE SK9 ....126 E6
Clarence Rd AUL OL6 ....75 M8
  BRUN/LGST M13 ....99 H3
  HALE/TIMP WA15 ....117 H1
  HTNM SK4 ....99 J7
  SWIN M27 ....69 M5
Clarence St AIMK WN4 ....63 J8
  ATH M46 ....67 H3
  BOL BL1 ....2 E3
  BRO M7 ....72 A8
  CMANW * M2 ....6 F5
  FWTH BL4 ....53 H5
  GOL/RIS/CU WA3 ....79 K3
  HYDE SK14 ....91 H8
  LEIGH WN7 ....66 E8
  NEWLW WA12 ....78 C8
  ROY/SHW OL2 ....59 K1
  STLY SK15 ....91 H3
  WGNE/HIN WN2 ....48 D5
  WHIT OL12 ....28 A2
Clarence Yd WGN WN1 ....14 F4
Clarendon Av
  HALE/TIMP WA15 ....108 B7
  HTNM SK4 ....111 K1
  SALE M33 ....97 G7
Clarendon Crs ECC M30 ....85 J1
  SALE M33 ....97 G7
Clarendon Gv BOLE BL2 ....3 J7
Clarendon Pl HYDE SK14 ....102 B2
Clarendon Rd BOLE BL2 ....3 M5
  BRAM/HZG SK7 ....122 B1
  DTN/ASHW M34 ....89 K5
  ECC M30 ....85 J1
  HYDE SK14 ....101 L2
  IRL M44 ....94 B5
  OLDTF/WHR M16 ....97 M2
  SALE M33 ....97 G8
  SWIN M27 ....70 C4
  URM M41 ....95 H1
Clarendon Rd West CCHDY M21 ...97 L2
Clarendon St BOLS/LL BL3 ....2 C9
  DUK SK16 ....90 D4
  HULME M15 ....6 F9
  HULME M15 ....87 J6
  HYDE SK14 ....102 A1
  MILN OL16 ....28 E8
  MOSL OL5 ....77 G4
  RDSH * SK5 ....112 C1
  WHTF M45 ....55 J4
Clare Rd BNG/LEV M19 ....99 K4
  RDSH * SK5 ....100 C8
Clare St CMANE M1 ....7 K8
  DTN/ASHW M34 ....90 B8
  ORD * M5 ....86 F3
Claribel St OP/CLY M11 ....88 B4
Claridge Rd CCHDY M21 ....97 K3
Clarington Gv WGN WN1 ....15 K5
Clarion St ANC M4 ....7 L1
Clark Av GTN M18 ....89 H7
  ORD M5 ....86 E5
Clarke Av GOL/RIS/CU WA3 ...81 J8
  ORD M5 ....86 E5
Clarke Brow MDTN M24 ....57 K3
Clarke Crs HALE/TIMP WA15 ...117 K1
  LHULT M38 ....52 A6
Clarkes Cft BURY BL9 ....39 M1
Clarke's La WHIT OL12 ....10 B3
Clarke St AULW * OL7 ....90 C4
  BOL BL1 ....35 M4
  HEY OL10 ....41 G2
  LEIGH WN7 ....66 B8
  MILN OL16 ....28 E2
Clarksfield Rd OLDE OL4 ....59 M6
Clarksfield St OLDE OL4 ....59 M6
Clark's HI PWCH M25 ....55 K8
Clarkson Cl DTN/ASHW M34 ...101 G2
  MDTN M24 ....57 K5
Clark Wy HYDE SK14 ....102 A4
Clarkwell Cl OLD OL1 ....9 G3
Claude Av SWIN M27 ....70 A4
Claude Rd CCHDY M21 ....97 K5
Claude St CHH M8 ....72 D3
  ECC M30 ....69 L8
  SWIN M27 ....70 A4
Claudia Sq STLY SK15 ....77 H7
Claughton Av BOLE BL2 ....37 J5
  WALK M28 ....69 G5
Claughton Rd TOT/BURYW BL8 ...24 C8
Claverton Rd NTHM/RTH M23 ...109 H8
Claxton Av BKLY M9 ....73 G1
Clay Bank DROY M43 ....89 H3
Claybank Dr TOT/BURYW BL8 ...24 B5
Clay Bank St HEY OL10 ....40 F1
Claybar Dr ECC M30 ....85 H7
Claybridge Cl
  WGNW/BIL/O WN5 ....46 E3
Claybrook Wk OP/CLY * M11 ...88 D3
Clayburn Rd HULME M15 ....87 H6
Claycourt Av ECC M30 ....69 L8
Claydon Dr BOLS/LL BL3 ....37 L7
  WGNS/IIMK WN3 ....48 C8
Clayfield Dr ROCH OL11 ....27 J4
Claygate Dr BKLY M9 ....57 G7
Clayhill Gv GOL/RIS/CU WA3 ...80 E4
Claylands Cl WILM/AE SK9 ....93 G8
Clay La HALE/TIMP WA15 ....108 F8
  NTHM/RTH M23 ....109 J8
  ROCH OL11 ....27 H4
  WILM/AE SK9 ....119 J7
  WILM/AE SK9 ....126 A8
Claymere Av ROCH OL11 ....27 H4
Claymore St BOLS/LL * BL3 ...52 C1
  GTN M18 ....89 H6
Claypool Rd HOR/BR BL6 ....34 B5
Clay St EDGW/EG BL7 ....20 A7
  LIT OL15 ....29 H8
Clayton Av BOLS/LL BL3 ....3 L9
  DID/WITH M20 ....110 E1
  GOL/RIS/CU WA3 ....80 E4
Claytonbrook Rd OP/CLY M11 ...88 F1
Clayton Cl HULME M15 ....87 H7
  TOT/BURYW BL8 ....38 C3
Clayton Hall Rd OP/CLY M11 ...88 F2
Clayton House LEIGH WN7 ....65 M7
Clayton La OP/CLY M11 ....88 E4
Clayton La South OP/CLY M11 ...88 D5
Claytons Cl OLDE OL4 ....59 H8
Clayton St BOLS/LL BL3 ....3 L9
  CHAD OL9 ....90 A4
  DTN/ASHW M34 ....101 J2
  DUK SK16 ....91 G4
  FAIL * M35 ....74 B5
  OP/CLY M11 ....88 E1
  WGNS/IIMK WN3 ....14 D4
  WHIT OL12 ....28 E2
Cleabarrow Dr WALK M28 ....68 D7
Cleadon Av GTN M18 ....88 F8
Cleadon Dr South
  TOT/BURYW BL8 ....24 F7
Cleavley St ECC M30 ....84 E2

Clee Av BRUN/LGST M13 99 J2
Cleethorpes Av BKLY M9 72 E1
Cleeve Rd NTHM/RTH M23 109 K2
OLDE OL4 59 M6
Cleeve Wy CHD/CHDH SK8 120 D6
Clegg Hall Rd MILN OL16 29 G2
Clegg Pl AUL OL6 76 A8
Clegg's Buildings BOL * BL1 2 C3
Clegg's La LHULT M38 52 D7
Clegg St BOLE BL2 3 M5
DROY * M43 89 J3
LIT OL15 20 A5
MILN OL16 29 K7
MPL/ROM SK6 113 J1
OLD OL1 9 J6
OLDE OL4 60 D6
TYLD M29 67 K6
WHIT OL12 18 D2
WHTF M45 55 J5
Cleggswood Av LIT OL15 29 K1
Clelland St FWTH BL4 53 H5
Clement Av ATH M46 66 D2
Clement Ct MILN OL16 11 K6
Clementina St WHIT OL12 10 E1
Clementine Cl SLFD M6 86 E2
Clement Rd MPL/ROM SK6 114 E5
Clement Royds St WHIT OL12 10 C3
Clement Stott Cl BKLY M9 57 J8
Clement St BRO M7 72 A8
HTNM SK4 13 G1
Cleminson St CSLFD M3 6 B3
Clemshaw Cl HEY OL10 40 F3
Clerewood Av CHD/CHDH SK8 119 K5
Clerke St BURY BL9 4 F4
Clevedon Av URM M41 96 D2
Clevedon Dr WGNS/IIMK WN3 46 F8
Clevedon Rd CHAD OL9 58 D3
Clevedon St BKLY M9 73 H5
Cleveland Av BNG/LEV M19 99 L2
HYDE * SK14 101 M2
SLFD M6 85 M1
WGNS/IIMK WN3 62 F2
Cleveland Cl RAMS BL0 24 F1
Cleveland Dr AIMK WN4 63 M8
GOL/RIS/CU WA3 80 A4
MILN OL16 29 K6
Cleveland Gdns BOLS/LL BL3 35 L8
Cleveland Gv ROY/SHW OL2 58 F2
Cleveland Rd CHH M8 72 E2
HALE/TIMP WA15 117 H1
HTNM SK4 99 K8
Cleveland St BOLS/LL * BL3 35 L8
Cleveleys Av BOLE BL2 3 M3
BURY BL9 4 D9
CCHDY M21 97 M5
CHD/CHDH SK8 119 K3
MILN OL16 42 E1
Cleveleys Gv BRO M7 72 B5
Cleves Ct HEY OL10 40 F3
Clevlands Cl ROY/SHW OL2 43 K4
Cleworth Cl TYLD M29 67 M8
Cleworth Rd MDTN M24 57 J2
Cleworth St HULME * M15 6 A9
Cleworth Wk HULME M15 6 A9
Clibran St CHH M8 72 E6
Clifden Dr WYTH/NTH M22 119 G2
Cliff Av BRO M7 71 M6
BURY BL9 25 G2
TOT/BURYW BL8 24 B5
Cliff Crs BRO M7 72 A5
Cliff Dl STLY SK15 91 J4
Cliffdale Dr CHH M8 72 D3
Cliffe Rd GLSP SK13 105 G5
Cliffe St LIT OL15 20 E2
Cliff Gv HTNM SK4 99 L8
Cliff Hill Rd ROY/SHW OL2 43 M3
Cliffmere Cl CHD/CHDH SK8 120 B1
Clifford Av DTN/ASHW M34 90 B7
HALE/TIMP WA15 108 D6
Clifford Rd BOLS/LL * BL3 51 K2
POY/DIS SK12 121 L8
WILM/AE SK9 126 D6
Clifford St ECC M30 84 E4
LEIGH WN7 66 E8
ROCH OL11 10 F9
SWIN M27 70 E4
Cliff Rd WILM/AE SK9 126 F4
Cliff Side WILM/AE SK9 126 F4
Cliff St MILN OL16 28 E3
Clifton Av CHD/CHDH SK8 119 J2
ECC M30 85 G1
HALE/TIMP WA15 108 B7
OLDE * OL4 59 L7
RUSH/FAL M14 99 G4
TYLD M29 67 M6
Clifton Cl HEY OL10 40 F3
OLDE OL4 59 L7
OLDTF/WHR M16 87 G7
Clifton Ct FWTH BL4 52 E2
Clifton Crs ROY/SHW OL2 59 K1
WGN WN1 47 M2
Clifton Dr CHD/CHDH SK8 110 C7
CHD/CHDH SK8 119 J2
HOR/BR BL6 32 E1
MPL/ROM SK6 114 C5
SWIN M27 70 A2
WILM/AE SK9 126 C8
Clifton Gv OLDTF/WHR M16 87 G7
SWIN M27 69 M2
Clifton Holmes UPML OL3 45 H7
Clifton House Rd SWIN M27 54 B7
Cliftonmill Mdw
GOL/RIS/CU WA3 79 J4
Clifton Park Rd OFTN SK2 112 D7
Clifton Pl PWCH * M25 55 K7
Clifton Rd AIMK WN4 63 J6
CCHDY M21 97 M4
ECC M30 85 G1
HTNM SK4 99 K8
LEIGH WN7 81 H2
MDTN M24 42 A6
PWCH M25 55 H8
SALE M33 108 E1
URM M41 95 K2
WGNW/BIL/O WN5 62 A8
Clifton St AUL OL6 90 D1
BOL BL1 2 C3
BURY BL9 25 J8
FAIL M35 74 D3
FWTH BL4 53 J5
LEIGH WN7 66 A7
MILN OL16 29 J6
NEWH/MOS M40 73 J8
OLDTF/WHR M16 87 G7
ROCH * OL11 11 G9
TYLD M29 68 B4
WGN WN1 15 G1
WGNS/IIMK WN3 47 K8
WILM/AE SK9 130 D3
Clifton Vw SWIN M27 54 B8
Cliftonville Dr SLFD M6 70 E6
Cliftonville Rd MILN OL16 42 F4
Clinton Av RUSH/FAL M14 98 D2
Clinton Gdns RUSH/FAL M14 98 D2
Clinton St AUL * OL6 76 A8
Clinton Wk OLDE * OL4 9 L7
Clippers Quay SALQ M50 86 D6
Clipsley Crs OLDE OL4 44 C8
Cliston Wk BRAM/HZG SK7 121 J2
Clitheroe Cl HEY OL10 41 G1
Clitheroe Dr TOT/BURYW BL8 38 C2
Clitheroe Rd BRUN/LGST M13 99 J1
Clito St BKLY M9 73 J4
Clive Av WHTF M45 55 H3
Clivedale Pl BOL BL1 2 F5
Clively Av SWIN M27 70 E3
Clive Rd FAIL M35 74 B5
WHTN BL5 50 B6
Clive St ANC M4 7 J1
AULW OL7 75 K7
BOLE BL2 2 F5
OLDS OL8 75 G2
Clivia Gv BRO * M7 72 A6
Cloak St CMANE M1 7 H8
Clock House Av DROY M43 89 H1
Clockhouse Ms DROY * M43 89 H1
Clock St CHAD OL9 74 E2
Clock Tower Cl HYDE SK14 102 B3
WALK M28 68 C1
Cloister Av LEIGH WN7 66 A3
Cloister Cl DUK SK16 90 F6
Cloister Rd HTNM SK4 111 G2
The Cloisters CHD/CHDH SK8 111 K7
MILN OL16 28 E3
SALE M33 97 G8
WHTN BL5 50 B7
Cloister St BKLY M9 73 J4
BOL BL1 35 M2
Clopton Wk HULME M15 87 H6
Close St WGNE/HIN WN2 49 J6
The Close ALT WA14 107 M7
ATH M46 51 J7
BOLE BL2 36 E1
MDTN M24 57 L1
MPL/ROM SK6 114 D3
STLY SK15 76 C8
STLY SK15 91 J1
TOT/BURYW BL8 24 F6
Closebrook Rd
WGNW/BIL/O WN5 47 G6
Close La WGNE/HIN WN2 65 J1
WGNE/HIN WN2 65 L3
Closes Farm BOLS/LL BL3 51 L2
Clothorn Rd DID/WITH M20 98 E8
Cloudstock Gv LHULT M38 52 B7
The Clough AIMK WN4 63 G8
BOL * BL1 35 H4
RDSH SK5 100 E6
Clough Av MPL/ROM SK6 114 F6
SALE M33 108 A3
WHTN BL5 50 C4
WILM/AE SK9 126 F2
Clough Bank BKLY * M9 73 G2
Cloughbank RAD M26 53 M5
Clough Dr PWCH M25 55 J8
Clough End Rd HYDE SK14 103 H3
Cloughfield Av ORD M5 86 E4
Cloughfold RAD M26 53 L5
Clough Fold WHTN BL5 50 C4
Clough Fold Rd HYDE SK14 101 M3
Clough Ga HYDE * SK14 102 C4
OLDS OL8 75 G2
Clough Gv AIMK WN4 63 J7
WHTF M45 55 G2
Clough House Dr LEIGH WN7 66 E7
Clough House La WHIT OL12 19 J6
Clough La HEY OL10 26 F8
OLDE OL4 61 H6
PWCH M25 55 J8
Clough Meadow BOL BL1 35 G6
MPL/ROM SK6 101 M7
Clough Meadow Rd RAD M26 54 B1
Clough Park Av OLDE OL4 61 H6
Clough Rd BKLY M9 73 J4
DROY M43 89 L2
FAIL M35 74 D5
LIT OL15 20 B4
MDTN M24 57 K2
ROY/SHW OL2 44 A6
Cloughs Av CHAD OL9 58 A4
Clough Side MPL/ROM SK6 114 F5
Cloughside POY/DIS SK12 124 A6
Clough St FWTH BL4 53 J5
MDTN M24 57 L2
NEWH/MOS M40 73 M8
RAD M26 54 F3
WHIT OL12 19 K6
Clough Ter LIT * OL15 20 B5
Clough Top Rd BKLY M9 73 K2
Cloughwood Crs
WGNNW/ST WN6 30 A5
Clovelly Av LEIGH WN7 66 C4
OLDS OL8 74 F2
Clovelly Rd CCHDY M21 97 M4
OFTN SK2 112 F4
SWIN M27 69 M5
Clovelly St NEWH/MOS * M40 74 A7
ROCH OL11 41 L1
Clover Av EDGY/DAV SK3 112 A7
Cloverbank Av BNG/LEV M19 99 G8
Clover Crs OLDS OL8 75 M1
Clover Cft SALE M33 109 G3
Cloverdale Dr AIMK WN4 78 F2
Cloverdale Sq BOL BL1 35 K3
Clover Hall Crs MILN OL16 11 M1
Cloverley Dr HALE/TIMP WA15 108 D8
Clover Rd HALE/TIMP WA15 108 D7
MPL/ROM SK6 114 B1
Clover St WGNNW/ST WN6 47 K2
WHIT OL12 10 D3
Clover Vw MILN * OL16 11 K3
Clowes St CHAD OL9 74 D2
CSLFD M3 6 D3
WGTN/LGST M12 88 D6
Club St OP/CLY M11 89 J5
Clumber Cl POY/DIS SK12 129 J1
Clumber Rd GTN M18 89 J8
POY/DIS SK12 129 J1
Clunton Av BOLS/LL BL3 35 L8
Clutha Rd EDGY/DAV SK3 112 C8
Clwyd Av EDGY/DAV SK3 12 F9
Clyde Av WHTF M45 55 J6
Clyde Ct MILN OL16 11 J6
Clyde Rd DID/WITH M20 98 C8
EDGY/DAV SK3 12 D8
RAD M26 38 C7
TYLD M29 67 M5
Clydesdale St OLDS OL8 59 H8
Clyde St AULW OL7 90 C3
BOL * BL1 36 B2
LEIGH * WN7 66 E8
OLD OL1 59 M3
Clyde Ter RAD * M26 38 C7
Clyne St STRET M32 86 C7
Coach House Dr
WGNNW/ST WN6 30 E6
Coach La ROCH OL11 27 H7
Coach Rd HYDE SK14 92 F7
TYLD M29 67 M6
Coach St ATH M46 67 G1
Coalbrook Wk WGTN/LGST M12 88 A4
Coalburn St WGTN/LGST M12 88 D7
Coal Pit La LEIGH WN7 66 B4
OLDS OL8 75 G5
WGNE/HIN WN2 65 L3
Coalshaw Green Rd CHAD OL9 74 D1
Coatbridge St OP/CLY M11 88 F3
Cobalt Av URM M41 85 J6
Cobb Cl CHH M8 72 B1
Cobbett's Wy WILM/AE SK9 126 D8
Cobble Bank BKLY M9 72 F1
Cobden St AUL * OL6 91 G2
BKLY M9 73 H3
BOL BL1 36 A1
BURY BL9 5 H2
CHAD OL9 8 B5
EDGW/EG * BL7 22 A2
HEY OL10 41 G3
NEWLW WA12 79 G8
OLDE OL4 60 A3
RAD M26 38 C6
SLFD M6 71 J8
TYLD M29 67 K3
Coberley Av URM M41 84 C8
Cob Hall Rd STRET M32 96 F3
Cobham Av BOLS/LL BL3 52 A1
NEWH/MOS M40 73 M2
Coblers Hl UPML * OL3 45 J7
Cob Moor Av WGNW/BIL/O WN5 62 A3
Cob Moor Rd WGNW/BIL/O WN5 62 A3
Cobourg St CMANE M1 7 J6
Coburg Av BRO M7 72 A8
Cochrane Av WGTN/LGST M12 88 B7
Cochrane St BOLS/LL BL3 2 F9
Cock Brow HYDE SK14 102 F5
Cock Clod St RAD M26 54 F1
Cockcroft St BKLY M9 73 G3
Cockerell Springs BOLE * BL2 3 G6
Cocker Hl STLY SK15 91 L2
Cocker Mill La ROY/SHW OL2 43 J7
Cockers La STLY SK15 92 A4
Cocker St LHULT M38 52 D8
Cockey Moor Rd BOLE BL2 38 A3
Cock Hall La WHIT OL12 18 C3
Cockhall La WHIT OL12 18 D3
Coconut Gv SLFD * M6 86 E2
Codale Dr BOLE BL2 37 J3
Coddington Av OP/CLY M11 89 H4
Code La WHTN BL5 33 L8
Coe St BOLS/LL BL3 2 E8
Coghlan Cl OP/CLY * M11 88 E2
Coin St ROY/SHW OL2 43 H8
Colborne Av ECC M30 84 E2
MPL/ROM SK6 113 L2
RDSH * SK5 100 C1
Colbourne Av CHH M8 72 C3
Colbourne Gv HYDE SK14 103 H1
Colburn Cl WGNS/IIMK WN3 63 K2
Colby Rd WGNS/IIMK WN3 63 L1
Colchester Av BOLE BL2 37 H4
Colchester Cl NTHM/RTH M23 109 H3
Colchester Dr FWTH BL4 52 D3
Colchester Pl HTNM SK4 12 B1
Colchester Wk OLD OL1 9 J4
Colclough Cl NEWH/MOS M40 73 L6
Coldalhurst La TYLD M29 67 M7
Coldfield Dr NTHM/RTH M23 109 J6
Cold Greave Cl MILN OL16 29 M8
Coldhurst St OLD OL1 9 G2
Coldstone Dr AIMK WN4 63 G8
Coldstream Av BKLY M9 57 G8
Cole Av NEWLW WA12 78 F8
Colebrook Dr NEWH/MOS M40 73 K6
Colebrook Rd
HALE/TIMP WA15 108 D6
Coleby Av OLDTF/WHR M16 86 F8
WYTH/NTH M22 119 H3
Coleclough Pl GOL/RIS/CU WA3 81 J8
Coledale Dr MDTN M24 56 F2
Coleford Gv BOL BL1 2 C6
Colemore Av DID/WITH M20 111 G1
Colenso Ct BOLE BL2 3 M4
Colenso Gv HTNM SK4 12 A1
Colenso Rd BOLE BL2 37 G5
Colenso St OLDS OL8 75 G1
Coleport Cl CHD/CHDH SK8 120 C3
Coleridge Av MDTN M24 57 M1
RAD M26 54 B1
WGNW/BIL/O WN5 46 D6
Coleridge Cl RDSH SK5 100 B3
Coleridge Rd LIT OL15 29 J2
OLD OL1 44 B8
OLDTF/WHR M16 97 M1
RDSH SK5 100 B3
TOT/BURYW BL8 24 C2
WGNW/BIL/O WN5 62 A3
Colerne Wy WGNS/IIMK WN3 63 G2
Colesbourne Cl LHULT M38 52 D6
Coleshill Ri WGNS/IIMK WN3 62 F2
Coleshill St NEWH/MOS M40 88 B1
Cole St BKLY M9 73 J4
Colgate Crs RUSH/FAL M14 98 E4
Colgate La ORD M5 86 D6
Colgrove Av NEWH/MOS M40 73 M2
Colina Dr CHH M8 72 B7
Colindale Av BKLY M9 57 H8
Colindale Cl BOLS/LL * BL3 35 M7
Colin Murphy Rd HULME M15 6 B9
Colin Rd HTNM SK4 100 B8
Colin St WGN WN1 15 H1
Colinton Cl BOL BL1 36 A3
Colinwood Cl BURY BL9 55 J1
Collard St ATH M46 50 E8
Coll Dr URM M41 85 G7
College Av OLDS OL8 75 G1
WGN WN1 15 G5
College Cl BOLS/LL BL3 2 D7
OFTN SK2 112 D6
WILM/AE SK9 126 C4
College Dr OLDTF/WHR M16 97 M2
College Rd ECC M30 85 K2
OLDS OL8 59 G8
OLDTF/WHR M16 98 A2
WHIT OL12 10 B4
College St LEIGH WN7 66 D7
College Wy BOLS/LL BL3 2 B6
Collen Crs TOT/BURYW BL8 24 E6
Collett Cl WGN WN1 15 K4
Collett St OLD OL1 59 M4
Colley St MILN OL16 11 H1
STRET M32 86 C7
Collie Av SLFD M6 71 M7
Collier Av MILN OL16 29 J5
Collier Cl HYDE SK14 103 H3
Collier Hl OLDS OL8 75 G1
Collier Hill Av OLDS OL8 74 F1
Colliers Cl LEIGH WN7 81 H1
Collier St CSLFD M3 6 D2
CSLFD M3 6 D7
GLSP SK13 104 F4
SLFD M6 71 J6
SWIN M27 70 B5
WGNE/HIN WN2 49 G6
Colliery La ATH M46 50 C8
Colliery St OP/CLY M11 88 D3
Collin Av GTN M18 88 F8
Collingburn Av ORD M5 86 E5
Colling Cl IRL M44 94 D3
Collinge Av MDTN M24 57 M4
Collinge St HEY OL10 40 F2
MDTN M24 58 A5
ROY/SHW * OL2 43 L5
TOT/BURYW BL8 24 E8
WGNE/HIN WN2 64 D2
Collingham St CHH M8 72 D8
Colling St RAMS * BL0 17 B7
Collington Cl WGTN/LGST M12 88 D7
Collingwood Av DROY M43 89 H1
Collingwood Cl POY/DIS SK12 129 L1
Collingwood Dr SWIN M27 70 D5
Collingwood Rd BNG/LEV M19 99 J3
Collingwood St ROCH OL11 41 M4
WGNNW/ST WN6 31 H3
Collingwood Wy OLD OL1 9 J2
WHTN BL5 50 B3
Collins La WHTN BL5 50 C6
Collins St TOT/BURYW BL8 24 C8
Collisdene Rd
WGNW/BIL/O WN5 46 A6
Collop Dr HEY OL10 41 H5
Coll's La UPML OL3 45 G8
Collyhurst Av WALK M28 69 H2
Collyhurst Rd NEWH/MOS M40 72 F7
Collyhurst St NEWH/MOS M40 72 F8
Colman Gdns ORD M5 86 E5
Colmore Dr BKLY M9 57 K8
Colmore Gv BOLE BL2 22 E8
Colmore St BOLE BL2 36 E1
Colnbrook WGNNW/ST WN6 30 E3
Colne St ROCH OL11 42 A3
Colonial Rd OFTN SK2 112 D6
Colshaw Dr WILM/AE SK9 127 H3
Colshaw Rd NTHM/RTH M23 109 K7
Colson Dr MDTN M24 57 J5
Colt Hill La UPML OL3 61 J4
Coltsfoot Cl LEIGH WN7 66 E7
Coltsfoot Dr ALT WA14 107 L4
Columbia Av GTN M18 89 J8
Columbia Rd BOL BL1 35 M4
Columbia St OLDS * OL8 59 J8
Columbine Cl WHIT OL12 27 M1
Columbine St OP/CLY M11 89 G5
Colville Dr TOT/BURYW BL8 38 E3
Colville Gv HALE/TIMP WA15 108 D6
SALE M33 108 B3
Colville Rd OLD OL1 59 G3
Colwell Av STRET M32 96 E3
Colwick Av ALT WA14 108 B6
Colwith Av BOLE BL2 37 H3
Colwyn Av MDTN M24 57 K6
RUSH/FAL M14 99 H4
Colwyn Crs RDSH SK5 100 C7
Colwyn Dr WGNE/HIN WN2 65 M2
Colwyn Gv ATH M46 50 F7
Colwyn Rd BRAM/HZG SK7 121 H4
CHD/CHDH SK8 120 A3
SWIN M27 69 M6
Colwyn St AULW OL7 75 K6
CHAD OL9 8 E5
ROCH OL11 41 L2
SLFD M6 86 C1
Combe Cl OP/CLY M11 88 E1
Combermere Av DID/WITH M20 98 D5
Combermere Cl
CHD/CHDH SK8 111 J8
TYLD M29 67 L3
Combermere St DUK SK16 90 F3
Combs Cl NM/HAY SK22 124 C4
Combs Ms GLSP SK13 104 A3
Comer Ter SALE M33 96 D8
Comet Rd WGNW/BIL/O WN5 46 F4
Comet St CMANE M1 7 K5
Commercial Av CHD/CHDH SK8 120 A7
Commercial Brow HYDE SK14 91 H8
Commercial Rd BRAM/HZG SK7 121 M1
OLD OL1 9 K7
Commercial St CHAD OL9 8 D7
HULME M15 6 D8
HYDE SK14 102 B1
Commodore Pl
WGNW/BIL/O WN5 47 H3
Common La GOL/RIS/CU WA3 81 G8
LEIGH WN7 65 L8
PART M31 94 E7
PART M31 94 F8
TYLD M29 67 K3
Common Nook WGNE/HIN WN2 48 D6
Common Side Rd WALK M28 68 C5
Common St WHTN BL5 49 L5
Como St BOLS/LL * BL3 35 M8
Como Wk GTN M18 88 E6
Compass St OP/CLY M11 88 F5
Compstall Av RUSH/FAL M14 98 E3
Compstall Gv GTN * M18 89 H6
Compstall Mills Est
MPL/ROM * SK6 114 E2
Compstall Rd MPL/ROM SK6 114 A2
Compton Cl URM M41 94 F3
Compton Dr NTHM/RTH * M23 118 C2
Compton Wy MDTN M24 57 M5
ROY/SHW OL2 43 L6
Comus St ORD M5 86 F4
Concert La CMANW M2 7 G5
Concord Av WGNS/IIMK WN3 63 L1
Concord Pl SLFD M6 71 K7
Condor Cl DROY * M43 89 M1
Condor Pl SLFD M6 71 K7
Condor Wk BRUN/LGST * M13 87 L6
Conduit St AUL OL6 90 F2
GLSP SK13 93 J5
OLD OL1 60 A1
Conewood Wk BRUN/LGST M13 87 M6
Coney Gv NTHM/RTH M23 109 K5
Coneymead STLY SK15 76 D8
Congleton Cl WILM/AE SK9 130 D4
Congleton Rd MCFLDN SK10 130 D6
Congou St CMANE M1 7 L6
Congreave St OLD OL1 9 G3
Congresbury Rd LEIGH WN7 66 A5
Coningsby Dr BKLY M9 73 G4
Conisber Cl EDGW/EG BL7 22 B3
Conisborough ROCH OL11 10 C7
Conisborough Pl WHTF M45 55 L5
Coniston BOL * BL1 36 C1
Coniston Av AIMK WN4 63 L8
ATH M46 51 G7
BKLY M9 73 G4
FWTH BL4 52 B5
HYDE SK14 90 F8
LHULT M38 52 D8
OLDS OL8 75 G1
SALE M33 108 F2
WGN WN1 47 L1
WGNE/HIN WN2 48 E5
WGNW/BIL/O WN5 46 C4
WHTF M45 55 J4
Coniston Cl BOLS/LL BL3 37 K8
CHAD OL9 58 D5
DTN/ASHW M34 100 E2
RAMS BL0 17 C5
Coniston Dr BURY BL9 39 H5
MDTN M24 57 H2
STLY SK15 91 K1
WGNE/HIN WN2 64 E4
WILM/AE SK9 119 L8
Coniston Gv AULW OL7 75 K8
HEY OL10 41 G4
LHULT M38 52 D8
ROY/SHW OL2 43 G6
Coniston Park Dr
WGNNW/ST WN6 31 K5
Coniston Rd CHD/CHDH SK8 110 E6
HOR/BR BL6 33 G1
MPL/ROM SK6 122 F4
PART M31 94 B8
RDSH SK5 100 C6
STRET M32 96 F1
SWIN M27 70 C6
TYLD M29 67 K5
URM M41 95 H4
WGNE/HIN WN2 49 H8
Coniston St LEIGH WN7 66 B7
NEWH/MOS M40 73 M7
SLFD M6 71 L8
Coniston Wk HALE/TIMP WA15 109 G7
Conival Wy CHAD OL9 58 D3
Conmere Sq HULME M15 6 F9
Connaught Av BNG/LEV M19 99 J5
ROCH OL11 42 E1
WHTF M45 55 K4
Connaught Cl WILM/AE SK9 127 G4
Connaught Sq BOLE BL2 36 E2
Connaught St CHAD OL9 9 H7
TOT/BURYW BL8 38 E3
Connel Cl BOLE BL2 37 J6
Connell Rd NTHM/RTH M23 109 K6
Connell Wy HEY * OL10 41 J1
Connery Crs AUL OL6 76 A6
Connie St OP/CLY M11 88 F4
Conningsby Cl EDGW/EG BL7 22 C4
Connington Av BKLY M9 73 G3
Connington Cl ROY/SHW OL2 42 F8
Connor Wy CHD/CHDH SK8 110 C8
Conrad Cl OLD OL1 44 B8
WGNS/IIMK WN3 14 C9
Conran St BKLY M9 73 G5
Consett Av NTHM/RTH M23 109 K6
Consort Av ROY/SHW OL2 42 F6
Consort Cl DUK SK16 90 F6
Consort Pl ALT WA14 116 D1
Constable Cl BOL BL1 36 A3
Constable Dr MPL/ROM SK6 114 E4
WILM/AE SK9 127 J4
Constable St GTN M18 89 H6
Constance Gdns SLFD M6 86 C3
Constance Rd BOLS/LL BL3 35 M7
PART M31 106 C1
Constance St HULME * M15 6 D8
Constantia St WGNS/IIMK WN3 64 C1
Constantine Rd MILN OL16 10 E4
Constantine St OLDE OL4 60 A6
Consul St WYTH/NTH M22 110 B3
Convamore Rd BRAM/HZG SK7 120 F6
Convent Gv ROCH OL11 10 B8
Convent St OLDS OL8 59 M8
Conway Av BOL BL1 35 K3
IRL M44 94 C4
SWIN M27 70 E1
WHTF M45 55 J5
Conway Cl HEY OL10 40 D1
LEIGH WN7 67 H5
MDTN M24 57 K5
OLDTF/WHR * M16 97 K1
RAMS BL0 17 B6
Conway Crs RAMS BL0 24 C2
WGNW/BIL/O WN5 62 B6
Conway Dr BRAM/HZG SK7 121 L3
BURY BL9 40 A2
HALE/TIMP WA15 108 F6
STLY SK15 91 K1
WGNE/HIN WN2 33 G8
WGNW/BIL/O WN5 62 C7
Conway Gv CHAD OL9 58 C4
Conway Rd AIMK WN4 64 B7
CHD/CHDH SK8 120 A2
SALE M33 109 G1
URM M41 85 G8
WGNE/HIN WN2 49 J8
Conway St FWTH BL4 53 G5
RDSH SK5 100 B8
WGNW/BIL/O WN5 46 F7
Conyngham Rd RUSH/FAL M14 88 A8
Cook Av RNFD/HAY WA11 78 B5
Cooke St AIMK WN4 63 J6
BRAM/HZG SK7 121 M1
DTN/ASHW M34 101 J1
FAIL M35 74 C4
FWTH BL4 53 H5
HOR/BR BL6 21 D8
HYDE SK14 91 J7
Cook St BURY BL9 5 G5
CSLFD M3 6 C3
DTN/ASHW M34 90 C6
ECC M30 84 F2
EDGY/DAV * SK3 13 G5
LEIGH WN7 66 C7
MILN OL16 28 E3
OLDE OL4 59 M5
WGNE/HIN WN2 64 D3
Cook Ter MILN OL16 28 E3
Cooling La TYLD M29 67 G4
Coomassie St HEY OL10 40 F2
RAD M26 54 D1
SLFD * M6 86 C1
Coombe Cl TYLD M29 67 L4
Coombes Av HYDE SK14 102 C3
MPL/ROM SK6 114 C7
Coombes La GLSP SK13 103 M7
Coombes St OFTN SK2 112 E7
Coombes Vw HYDE SK14 103 J4

Co-operation St FAIL M35 74 C3
Co-operative St
BRAM/HZG SK7 122 A1
LEIGH WN7 66 A7
LHULT * M38 52 B7
OLDE OL4 60 C6
ROY/SHW * OL2 43 L5
SLFD * M6 86 C2
UPML * OL3 61 L4
Cooper Fold MDTN M24 41 K8
Cooper La BKLY M9 57 G7
MDTN M24 57 J1
Coopers Gln WGNE/HIN WN2 48 D4
Cooper St BRAM/HZG SK7 122 B1
BURY BL9 4 E4
CMANW M2 6 F5
DROY * M43 89 H3
DUK SK16 90 E3
GLSP SK13 104 E4
HOR/BR BL6 21 B8
OLDE OL4 60 D5
STKP SK1 13 K8
STRET M32 97 G3
WHIT OL12 19 L8
Coopers Wk MILN OL16 28 F2
Cooper Ter MILN OL16 11 J2
Coop St ANC * M4 7 J2
BOL BL1 22 B8
WGN WN1 15 J2
Copage Dr MPL/ROM SK6 101 K8
Cope Bank BOL BL1 35 M3
Cope Bank West BOL * BL1 35 L2
Cope Cl OP/CLY * M11 89 H5
Copeland Av SWIN M27 70 F3
Copeland Cl MDTN M24 56 F3
Copeland Dr WGNNW/ST WN6 31 J2
Copeland Ms BOL BL1 35 K5
Copeland St HYDE SK14 91 G7
Copeman Cl BRUN/LGST M13 87 M6
Copenhagen Sq MILN * OL16 11 H3
Copenhagen St MILN OL16 11 H3
NEWH/MOS M40 73 K6
Copesthorne Cl WGNE/HIN WN2 32 F6
Copgrove Rd CCHDY M21 97 L5
Copley Av STLY SK15 91 M2
Copley Park Ms STLY SK15 91 M2
Copley Rd CCHDY M21 97 K2
Copley St ROY/SHW * OL2 43 L4
Coplow Dl WGNE/HIN WN2 65 H1
Copperas Cl WGNNW/ST WN6 30 D5
Copperas La DROY M43 89 H4
HOR/BR BL6 32 E3
WGNE/HIN WN2 32 D6
Copperas St ANC M4 7 H3
Copperbeech Cl
WYTH/NTH M22 110 B3
Copper Beech Dr GLSP SK13 104 B3
STLY SK15 92 A1
Copperbeech Dr
WGNNW/ST WN6 31 L5
Copper Beech Mnr
GLSP * SK13 104 B3
Copperfield WGN WN1 47 M2
Copperfield Rd CHD/CHDH SK8 120 D7
POY/DIS SK12 129 H2
Copperfields HOR/BR BL6 50 E1
WILM/AE SK9 127 G4
Copper La WHTF M45 54 E5
The Coppice BKLY M9 73 K2
BOLE BL2 23 G7
HALE/TIMP WA15 117 K4
PWCH M25 55 K8
RAMS BL0 17 A8
SWIN M27 69 M7
WALK M28 69 J4
Coppice Av POY/DIS SK12 123 J6
SALE M33 108 A2
Coppice Cl MPL/ROM SK6 101 L8
Coppice Dr WGNS/IIMK WN3 63 J1
WGNW/BIL/O WN5 62 A2
WHIT OL12 18 D5
WYTH/NTH M22 110 A3
Coppice La POY/DIS SK12 123 J6
Coppice Rd POY/DIS SK12 129 M1
Coppice St BURY BL9 5 M2
OLDS OL8 8 E8
Coppice V RAMS BL0 24 F1
Coppice Wk DTN/ASHW M34 101 G2
Coppice Wy WILM/AE SK9 127 J1
Copping St WGTN/LGST M12 88 C6
The Coppins WILM/AE SK9 126 C8
Coppleridge Dr CHH M8 72 D2
Copplestone Dr SALE M33 95 M7
Coppull La WGN WN1 48 A2
Cop Rd ROY/SHW OL2 43 M8
The Copse EDGW/EG BL7 22 F2
HALE/TIMP WA15 117 M5
MPL/ROM SK6 114 F4
NEWLW WA12 78 D8
WGNW/BIL/O WN5 46 D6
Copse Av WYTH/NTH M22 119 G1
Copse Dr BURY BL9 25 J6
Copson St DID/WITH M20 98 E5
Copster Av OLDS OL8 75 H1
Copster Hill Rd OLDS OL8 75 H1
Copster Pl OLDS OL8 75 H1
Copthall La CHH M8 72 C4
Copthorne Cl HEY OL10 41 G4
Copthorne Crs BRUN/LGST M13 99 H2
Copthorne Dr BOLE BL2 37 H6
Copthorn Wk TOT/BURYW BL8 24 C7
Coptrod Head Cl WHIT OL12 18 F8
Coral Av CHD/CHDH SK8 120 C3
Coral Gv LEIGH WN7 66 B8
Coralin Wy AIMK WN4 63 J5
Coral Rd CHD/CHDH SK8 120 C3
Coral St BRUN/LGST M13 7 L9
WGNNW/ST WN6 47 K1
Coram St GTN M18 89 J6
Corbar Rd OFTN SK2 112 D7
Corbett St MILN OL16 11 H2
OP/CLY M11 88 D3
Corbett Wy UPML OL3 44 F3
Corbrook Rd CHAD OL9 58 B3
Corby St WGTN/LGST M12 88 D6
Corcoran Dr MPL/ROM SK6 114 C2
Corda Av WYTH/NTH M22 110 A4
Cordingley Av DROY M43 89 J4
Cordova Av DTN/ASHW M34 100 C1
Corelli St NEWH/MOS M40 73 J8
Corfe Cl URM M41 94 F3
WGNE/HIN WN2 33 G7
Corfe Crs BRAM/HZG SK7 121 M3
Corhampton Crs ATH M46 51 H7
Corinthian Av BRO M7 71 M7
Corkland Cl AUL OL6 91 G2
Corkland Rd CCHDY M21 97 L4
Corkland St AUL OL6 91 H2
Corks La POY/DIS SK12 124 A7
Cork St BURY BL9 5 J4
WGTN/LGST M12 88 A4
Corley Av EDGY/DAV SK3 111 J5
Corley Wk OP/CLY * M11 88 C3
Cormallen Gv FAIL M35 74 D5
Cornall St TOT/BURYW BL8 38 F1
Cornbrook Arches HULME M15 86 F5
Cornbrook Cl WHIT OL12 19 K6
WHTN BL5 50 A6
Cornbrook Gv OLDTF/WHR M16 87 G7
Cornbrook Park Rd HULME M15 86 F6
Cornbrook Rd HULME * M15 86 F5
Cornbrook St OLDTF/WHR M16 87 G7
Cornbrook Wy OLDTF/WHR M16 87 G7
Corn Cl BRUN/LGST M13 87 M7
Cornelian Gv AIMK WN4 63 J7
Cornell St ANC M4 7 K2
Corner Cft WILM/AE SK9 126 E8
Cornergate WHTN BL5 50 B7
Corner La WGNE/HIN WN2 66 A2
Cornet St BRO M7 72 A7
Cornfield STLY SK15 92 B5
Cornfield Cl BURY BL9 25 J5
SALE * M33 109 J1
Cornfield Dr WYTH/NTH M22 118 E1
Cornfield Rd MPL/ROM SK6 114 B1
Cornfield St MILN OL16 29 J7
Cornford Av GTN M18 99 L1
Corn Hey Rd SALE M33 107 M2
Cornhill Av URM M41 95 L1
Corn Hill La DTN/ASHW M34 89 K7
Cornhill Rd URM M41 95 L1
Cornhill St OLD OL1 59 M2
Cornish Wy ROY/SHW OL2 59 J1
Cornishway WYTH/NTH M22 118 F4
Cornlea Dr WALK M28 68 F5
Corn Mill Cl WHIT OL12 19 K8
Corn Mill La STLY SK15 91 L3
Corn St FAIL M35 73 M6
GLSP SK13 105 G3
LEIGH WN7 66 A7
OLDE * OL4 9 M5
Cornwall Av BNG/LEV M19 99 L4
TYLD M29 67 K1
WHTN BL5 51 J4
Cornwall Cl MPL/ROM SK6 123 G5
Cornwall Crs RDSH SK5 100 F6
UPML OL3 45 L8
WGN WN1 31 L3
Cornwall Dr BURY BL9 5 H9
WGNE/HIN WN2 49 J6
Cornwallis Rd WGNS/IIMK WN3 14 A9
Cornwall Pl WGNW/BIL/O WN5 46 F6
Cornwall Rd CHD/CHDH SK8 119 K4
DROY M43 89 K1
IRL M44 94 A7
Cornwall St CHAD OL9 8 B9
ECC M30 84 F3
OP/CLY M11 89 G5
Cornwell Cl WILM/AE SK9 127 H4
Corona Av HYDE SK14 102 B1
OLDS OL8 75 G1
Coronation Av ATH M46 50 F7
DUK SK16 91 J5
GOL/RIS/CU WA3 81 M5
HEY OL10 41 H4
HYDE SK14 102 B3
Coronation Dr LEIGH WN7 67 G6
RNFD/HAY WA11 78 D5
Coronation Gdns RAD M26 38 B8
Coronation Rd AUL OL6 75 M6
DROY M43 89 J1
FAIL M35 74 B7
RAD M26 38 B8
WGNNW/ST WN6 47 G1
Coronation Sq WGTN/LGST M12 7 M7
Coronation St AIMK WN4 63 G6
BOL BL1 2 E5
DTN/ASHW M34 100 F1
OP/CLY * M11 88 F4
ORD M5 86 E4
RDSH SK5 100 B8
SWIN M27 70 D3
WGNS/IIMK WN3 14 E7
Coronation Wk
WGNW/BIL/O WN5 62 A8
Corporation Rd DTN/ASHW M34 90 A7
ROCH OL11 10 A7
Corporation St ANC M4 7 G1
BOL BL1 2 E4
CMANW M2 6 F4
HYDE * SK14 102 A2
MDTN M24 57 K4
STKP SK1 13 K3
STLY SK15 91 K3
WGNS/IIMK WN3 14 E7
Corran Cl ECC M30 84 E2
Corranstone Cl HOR/BR BL6 33 L1
Correction Brow POY/DIS SK12 122 E6
Corrie Cl DTN/ASHW M34 101 J3
Corrie Crs FWTH BL4 54 A8
Corrie Dr FWTH BL4 54 A8
Corrie Rd SWIN M27 70 D1
Corrie St LHULT M38 52 D8
Corrie Wy MPL/ROM SK6 101 H7
Corrigan St GTN M18 89 H6
Corringham Rd BNG/LEV M19 99 M5
Corring Wy BOL BL1 22 E8
Corrin Rd BOLE BL2 3 K8
Corriss Av BKLY M9 56 D7
Corry St HEY OL10 41 H2
Corsey Rd WGNE/HIN WN2 49 H8
Corsock Dr WGN WN1 15 L1
Corson St FWTH BL4 53 G2
Corston Gv HOR/BR BL6 33 G3
Corwen Av BKLY M9 73 H4
Corwen Cl OLDS OL8 74 E2
Cosgate Cl WGNW/BIL/O WN5 46 B7
Cosgrove Crs FAIL M35 74 B7
Cosgrove Rd FAIL M35 74 B7
Cosham Rd WYTH/NTH M22 119 H1
Costessey Wy WGNS/IIMK WN3 62 F1
Costobadie Cl HYDE SK14 103 J1
Cosworth Cl LEIGH WN7 66 E8
Cotaline Cl ROCH OL11 41 L1
Cotefield Av BOLS/LL BL3 52 C1
Cotefield Cl MPL/ROM * SK6 114 C7
Cotefield Rd WYTH/NTH M22 118 D2
Cote Green La MPL/ROM SK6 114 E3
Cote Green Rd MPL/ROM SK6 114 E3
Cote La LIT OL15 20 A6
MOSL OL5 77 H1
NM/HAY SK22 125 M1
UPML OL3 45 L5
Cotford Rd BOL BL1 22 C7
Cotham St CSLFD M3 87 J1
Cotman Dr MPL/ROM SK6 114 F4
Cotswold Av BRAM/HZG SK7 121 K3
CHAD OL9 58 D7
GOL/RIS/CU WA3 80 A6
ROY/SHW OL2 43 J4
URM M41 95 J1
WGNW/BIL/O WN5 46 E7
Cotswold Cl GLSP SK13 104 D4
PWCH M25 55 M7
RAMS BL0 17 C8
Cotswold Crs MILN OL16 29 K5
TOT/BURYW BL8 38 E1
Cotswold Dr HOR/BR BL6 21 C7
ROY/SHW OL2 58 E1
SLFD M6 86 C1
Cotswold Rd HTNM SK4 12 F1
Cottage Cft BOLE BL2 23 G7
Cottage Gdns MPL/ROM SK6 113 G1
Cottage Gv WILM/AE SK9 126 C7
Cottage La GLSP SK13 104 B2
The Cottages OLDE * OL4 60 C5
Cottam Crs MPL/ROM SK6 114 E5
Cottam Gv SWIN M27 70 D5
Cottam St OLD OL1 8 E2
TOT/BURYW BL8 4 A2
Cottenham La BRO M7 72 B8
Cottenham St BRUN/LGST M13 87 L6
Cotterdale Cl OLDTF/WHR * M16 98 A1
Cotteril Cl SALE M33 108 F3
Cotterill St SLFD M6 86 D2
Cotter St WGTN/LGST M12 7 L8
Cottesmore Dr CHH M8 72 F4
Cottesmore Gdns
HALE/TIMP WA15 117 L4
Cottesmore Wy
GOL/RIS/CU WA3 79 L3
Cottingham Dr AUL OL6 75 M8
Cottingham Rd
WGTN/LGST M12 88 B6
Cottingley Cl BOL BL1 22 A7
Cotton Cl HYDE SK14 102 B3
Cottonfield Rd DID/WITH M20 98 F6
Cottonfields EDGW/EG BL7 22 C5
Cotton Fold MILN OL16 11 L7
Cotton Hl DID/WITH M20 98 F7
Cotton La DID/WITH M20 98 F6
Cotton St ANC M4 7 K3
BOL BL1 36 A2
LEIGH WN7 66 A7
Cotton St East AUL OL6 90 D2
Cotton St West AULW OL7 90 D2
Cotton Tree Cl OLDE OL4 60 A4
Cotton Tree St HTNM SK4 13 G4
Cottonwood Dr SALE M33 95 M7
Cottrell Rd HALE/TIMP WA15 117 M5
Coucill Sq FWTH BL4 53 H4
Coulsden Dr BKLY M9 73 G1
Coulthart St AUL OL6 90 E1
Coulthurst St RAMS BL0 17 B6
Coultshead Av
WGNW/BIL/O WN5 62 B6
Council Av AIMK WN4 78 E1
Councillor La CHD/CHDH SK8 111 J7
Councillor St OP/CLY M11 88 B3
Countess Av CHD/CHDH SK8 120 A7
Countess Gv BRO M7 72 A7
Countess La RAD M26 38 A7
Countess Pl PWCH M25 55 M8
Countess Rd DID/WITH M20 110 E1
Countess St AUL OL6 91 G2
OFTN SK2 112 D7
Counthill Dr CHH M8 72 B2
Counthill Rd OLDE OL4 60 A3
Counting House Rd
POY/DIS SK12 124 A7
Count St MILN OL16 11 H9
County Av AUL OL6 76 B8
County Police St
WGNE/HIN WN2 48 C3
County Rd WALK M28 52 D8
County St CMANW M2 6 F5
OLDS OL8 74 F2
Coupes Gn WHTN BL5 50 B6
Coupland Cl OLDE OL4 44 C8
Coupland Rd WGNE/HIN WN2 49 L8
Coupland St HULME M15 87 K7
WHIT OL12 18 D4
Courier Pl WGNW/BIL/O WN5 47 H3
Courier St GTN M18 89 H6
Course Vw OLDE OL4 76 B1
Court Dr NEWH/MOS M40 74 B8
Courtfield Av BKLY * M9 57 G8
Courthill St STKP SK1 13 M6
Courtney Gn WILM/AE SK9 127 H2
Courtney Pl ALT WA14 116 C3
Court St BOLE BL2 3 H5
UPML OL3 61 L4
Courts Vw SALE M33 96 F7
The Courtyard BOL * BL1 36 C3
HEY * OL10 41 J3
HYDE * SK14 93 G7
Courtyard Dr WALK M28 68 C1
Cousin Flds BOLE BL2 22 F5
The Cove HALE/TIMP WA15 117 H1
Covell Rd POY/DIS SK12 121 M7
Covent Gdn STKP SK1 13 J5
Coventry Av EDGY/DAV SK3 111 J5
Coventry Gv CHAD OL9 58 D3
Coventry Rd RAD M26 38 C7
Coventry St ROCH * OL11 10 F7
Coverdale Av BOL BL1 35 K4
ROY/SHW OL2 42 F7
Coverdale Cl HEY OL10 40 F3
Coverdale Crs WGTN/LGST M12 88 A6
Coverdale Rd WHTN BL5 50 A4
Coverham Av OLDE OL4 60 A8
Coverhill Rd OLDE OL4 60 E7
Covert Rd OLDE OL4 76 B1
WYTH/NTH M22 110 B7
The Coverts WGNNW/ST WN6 47 J2
Covington Pl WILM/AE SK9 126 F6
Cowan St NEWH/MOS M40 88 A2
Cowbrook Av GLSP SK13 105 H3
Cowburn Dr NM/HAY SK22 124 E3
Cowburn St CSLFD M3 87 J1
HEY OL10 41 H3
LEIGH WN7 66 A7
WGNE/HIN WN2 49 J5
Cowdals Rd HOR/BR BL6 34 E8
Cowesby St RUSH/FAL M14 98 D1
Cowhill La AUL OL6 90 F1
Cowie St ROY/SHW OL2 43 L4
Cow La BOLS/LL BL3 51 L2
BRAM/HZG SK7 113 G8
FAIL M35 74 B5
HALE/TIMP WA15 117 H7
OLDE OL4 59 M5
ORD M5 86 F3
SALE M33 97 H6
Cow Lees WHTN BL5 50 D3
Cowley Rd BOL BL1 22 C7
Cowley St NEWH/MOS M40 73 M6
Cowling St BRO M7 71 J4
WGNS/IIMK WN3 14 E7
Cowlishaw ROY/SHW OL2 43 K7
Cowlishaw La ROY/SHW OL2 43 K7
Cowlishaw Rd HYDE SK14 102 C7
Cowm Park Wy North
WHIT OL12 18 D2
Cowm Park Wy South
WHIT OL12 18 D4
Cowm Top La ROCH OL11 42 B2
Cown Edge Wy GLSP SK13 115 M2
HYDE SK14 102 A6
HYDE SK14 103 H5
MPL/ROM SK6 114 F8
OFTN SK2 113 K8
Cowper St AUL OL6 90 F1
LEIGH WN7 66 A7
MDTN M24 58 A5
Coxfield WGNNW/ST WN6 30 A5
Coxton Rd WYTH/NTH M22 119 G3
Cox Wy ATH M46 67 G1
Crabbe St ANC M4 87 K1
Crab La BKLY M9 56 E8
Crabtree Av HALE/TIMP WA15 117 M5
POY/DIS SK12 124 A7
Crab Tree La ATH M46 67 G2
Crabtree La OP/CLY M11 89 G3
Crabtree Rd OLD OL1 59 L4
WGNW/BIL/O WN5 47 G5
Crabtree St BURY BL9 5 L3
Craddock Rd SALE M33 108 F2
Craddock St MOSL OL5 76 F3
Cradley Av OP/CLY M11 89 G4
Crag Av BURY BL9 25 G2
Cragg Fold BURY * BL9 25 G2
Cragg Rd OLD OL1 58 D2
Cragie St CHH M8 72 C7
Crag La BURY BL9 25 G2
Cragside Wy WILM/AE SK9 127 G6
Craig Av TOT/BURYW BL8 38 E3
URM M41 95 K1
Craig Cl HTNM SK4 12 B4
Craighall Av BNG/LEV M19 99 J4
Craighall Rd BOL BL1 22 B6
Craiglands MILN OL16 42 E2
Craigmore Av DID/WITH M20 98 A8
Craignair Ct SWIN * M27 70 F4
Craig Rd GTN M18 88 F8
HTNM SK4 111 K3
Craigslands Av NEWH/MOS M40 73 K6
Craig Wk OLDS OL8 9 H9
Craigweil Av DID/WITH M20 110 F1
Craigwell Rd PWCH M25 72 A2
Cramer St NEWH/MOS * M40 73 J7
Crammond Cl NEWH/MOS M40 74 A6
Cramond Cl BOL BL1 36 A3
WGNS/IIMK WN3 47 G8
Cramond Wk BOL BL1 36 A3
Crampton Dr HALE/TIMP WA15 117 L4
Crampton La PART M31 95 G6
Cranage Rd BNG/LEV M19 99 L4
Cranark Cl BOL BL1 35 K5
Cranberry Av WGNNW/ST WN6 47 J1
Cranberry Cl ALT WA14 107 L4
Cranberry Dr BOLS/LL BL3 35 J8
Cranberry Rd PART M31 106 C1
Cranberry St OLDE OL4 59 L7
Cranborne Cl HOR/BR BL6 34 C3
WGNNW/ST WN6 31 G3
Cranbourne Av CHD/CHDH SK8 120 D2
Cranbourne Cl
HALE/TIMP WA15 108 D6
Cranbourne Rd AULW OL7 75 K8
AULW OL7 75 L7
CCHDY M21 97 L4
HTNM SK4 99 L8
OLDTF/WHR M16 86 F8
ROCH OL11 27 H6
Cranbourne St ORD M5 86 F3
Cranbourne Ter AUL OL6 75 L7
Cranbrook Av AIMK WN4 63 K8
Cranbrook Dr PWCH M25 71 M2
Cranbrook Gdns AULW * OL7 75 L8
Cranbrook Rd ECC M30 69 K8
GTN M18 100 B1
Cranbrook St AULW OL7 75 K8
OLDE OL4 59 M6
RAD M26 38 F7
Cranbrook Wk CHAD OL9 8 A7
Cranbrook Wy WGN WN1 31 L8
Cranby St WGNE/HIN WN2 49 G7
Crandon Dr DID/WITH M20 110 F4
Cranesbill Cl WYTH/NTH M22 118 E3
Crane St BOLS/LL * BL3 51 L1
WGTN/LGST M12 7 M7
Cranfield Cl NEWH/MOS M40 88 A2
Cranfield Rd HOR/BR BL6 34 A5
WGNS/IIMK WN3 63 K1
Cranford Av DID/WITH M20 99 G8
SALE M33 96 F6
STRET M32 97 J1
WHTF M45 55 H2
Cranford Cl SLFD M6 70 E6
WHTF M45 55 H2
Cranford Dr IRL M44 94 C1
Cranford Gdns MPL/ROM SK6 114 C5
URM * M41 95 H1
Cranford Rd URM M41 95 H1
WILM/AE SK9 126 E3
Cranford St BOLS/LL BL3 51 M2
Cranham Av GOL/RIS/CU WA3 80 B5
Cranham Cl TOT/BURYW BL8 38 E1
Cranham Close Crs LHULT * M38 52 D6
Cranham Rd WYTH/NTH M22 118 C2
Crankwood Rd WGNE/HIN WN2 64 E6
WGNE/HIN WN2 65 H8
Cranleigh WGNNW/ST WN6 31 J4
Cranleigh Av HTNM SK4 99 J8
Cranleigh Cl HOR/BR BL6 33 G3
OLDE OL4 60 A3
Cranleigh Dr BRAM/HZG SK7 122 C4
CHD/CHDH SK8 111 J6
SALE M33 96 D7
SALE M33 108 F3
TYLD M29 67 L4
WALK M28 69 H4
Cranlington Dr CHH M8 72 C6
Cranmer Ct HEY OL10 40 F3
Cranmere Av BNG/LEV M19 99 M2
Cranmere Dr SALE M33 108 A2
Cranmer Rd DID/WITH M20 98 E8
Cranshaw St TYLD M29 68 A4
Cranstal Dr WGNE/HIN WN2 49 K7
Cranston Dr DID/WITH M20 110 E4
SALE M33 109 H1
Cranston Gv CHD/CHDH SK8 110 C7
Cranswick St RUSH/FAL M14 98 D1
Crantock Dr CHD/CHDH SK8 119 L4
STLY SK15 92 A1
Crantock St WGTN/LGST M12 99 L1
Cranwell Av GOL/RIS/CU WA3 81 J8
Cranwell Dr BNG/LEV M19 99 H8
Cranworth Av TYLD M29 67 K6
Cranworth St STLY SK15 91 L3
Craston Rd BRUN/LGST M13 99 H2
Crathie Ct BOL BL1 35 L3
Craven Av GOL/RIS/CU WA3 80 B5
ORD M5 86 E4
Craven Ct ALT * WA14 107 M5
Craven Dr ALT WA14 107 M4
ORD M5 86 D6
Craven Gdns ROCH * OL11 10 D8
Cravenhurst Av
NEWH/MOS M40 73 L8
Craven Pl BOL BL1 35 H2
OP/CLY M11 88 F2
Craven Rd ALT WA14 107 M5
RDSH * SK5 100 C6
Craven St AUL * OL6 76 A7
BURY BL9 5 L2
OLD OL1 9 H2
ORD M5 86 F3
Craven St East HOR/BR BL6 34 A2
Craven Ter SALE M33 96 F8
Cravenwood Rd CHH M8 72 D4
Crawford Av BOLE BL2 3 J6
TYLD M29 67 J2
WALK M28 69 J4
WGNE/HIN WN2 32 F7
Crawford Pl WGN * WN1 48 A1
Crawford St AUL OL6 91 G2
BOLE BL2 3 H5
ECC M30 85 G1
MILN OL16 11 H8
NEWH/MOS * M40 73 M7
WGN WN1 14 F4
WGNE/HIN WN2 32 F8
Crawley Av ECC M30 85 K1
WYTH/NTH M22 118 F1
Crawley Cl TYLD M29 67 M3
Crawley Gv OFTN SK2 112 E6
Crawley Wy CHAD * OL9 58 D6
The Cray MILN OL16 29 H6
Craydon St OP/CLY M11 88 F4
Crayfield Rd BNG/LEV M19 99 L4
Crayford Rd NEWH/MOS M40 73 L8
Cray Wk BRUN/LGST M13 7 J9
Creaton Wy MDTN M24 41 G8
Creden Av WYTH/NTH M22 119 G1
Crediton Cl ALT WA14 107 L6
HULME M15 87 J6
Crediton Dr BOLE BL2 37 K5
WGNE/HIN WN2 64 D3
Cresbury St WGTN/LGST * M12 88 A5
The Crescent ALT WA14 107 K7
BNG/LEV M19 99 K3
BOLE BL2 23 J8
BOLS/LL BL3 53 L2
BURY BL9 5 H3
CHD/CHDH SK8 111 G6
DROY M43 89 J3
EDGW/EG BL7 22 D4
EDGY/DAV SK3 112 D8
HALE/TIMP WA15 108 C5
HOR/BR BL6 34 A3
IRL M44 94 E1
MCFLDN SK10 131 K2
MDTN M24 57 H4
MOSL OL5 76 E3
MPL/ROM SK6 101 G8
NM/HAY SK22 124 D4
PWCH M25 55 L8
RAD M26 38 A7
ROY/SHW OL2 43 K6
STLY SK15 92 A6
URM M41 95 J1
WGNE/HIN * WN2 48 E5
WGNW/BIL/O WN5 47 G6
WHIT * OL12 18 D4
WHTN BL5 50 B5
Crescent ORD M5 6 A3
Crescent Av AIMK WN4 63 K8
BOL BL1 2 B3
CHH * M8 72 D4
FWTH BL4 52 F6
PWCH M25 71 L2
SWIN M27 70 E4
Crescent Cl DUK SK16 90 F3
EDGY/DAV SK3 112 D7
Crescent Dr CHH M8 72 E4
LHULT M38 52 E7
Crescent Fold HYDE * SK14 103 J4
Crescent Gv BNG/LEV * M19 99 K3
PWCH M25 71 L2
Crescent Pk HTNM SK4 12 C4
Crescent Range RUSH/FAL M14 98 F1
Crescent Rd ALT WA14 107 K6
BOLS/LL BL3 52 E1
CHAD OL9 74 B2
CHD/CHDH SK8 110 F6
CHH M8 72 D4
DUK SK16 90 F3
FWTH BL4 53 J6
HALE/TIMP WA15 117 G2
HOR/BR BL6 34 B4
ROCH OL11 27 L8
STKP SK1 112 E1
WILM/AE SK9 130 E2
Crescent St CHH M8 72 F4
Crescent Wy EDGY/DAV SK3 112 D7
Cressell Pk WGNNW/ST WN6 30 D2
Cressfield Wy CCHDY M21 98 A5
Cressingham Rd BOLS/LL BL3 51 J1
STRET M32 96 E3
Cressington Cl SLFD * M6 86 B2
Cresswell Av NM/HAY SK22 124 E4
Cresswell Gv DID/WITH M20 98 D7
Cresswell St NM/HAY SK22 124 E4
The Crest DROY M43 89 K5
Crestfield Gv WGNNW/ST WN6 47 J2
Crestfold WALK M28 52 D8
Crest St CSLFD M3 6 F1
Crestwood Av WGNS/IIMK WN3 63 H1
Creswick Cl WGNE/HIN WN2 48 F8
Crete St OLDS OL8 59 J8
Crewe Rd NTHM/RTH M23 109 H4
Crib Fold UPML OL3 61 K2
Crib La UPML OL3 61 K2
Criccieth Av WGNE/HIN WN2 33 G7
Criccieth Rd EDGY/DAV SK3 111 K5
Criccieth St OLDTF/WHR M16 87 J8
Cricketers Wy WHTN BL5 50 B4
Cricketfield La WALK M28 68 F1
Cricket's La AUL OL6 90 F1
Cricket St BOLS/LL BL3 2 B9
DTN/ASHW * M34 90 D8
WGNNW/ST WN6 14 D4
Cricket Vw MILN OL16 29 J7
Cricklewood Rd
WYTH/NTH M22 118 E2
Crimble La HEY OL10 27 H7
Crimbles St OLDE OL4 60 B4
Crimble St WHIT OL12 10 B3

Crime La OLDS OL8 75 G5
Crimsworth Av
OLDTF/WHR M16 97 L2
Crinan Wk NEWH/MOS M40 88 A1
Cringlebarrow Cl WALK M28 68 C7
Cringle Cl BOLS/LL BL3 35 H8
Cringle Dr CHD/CHDH SK8 110 F8
Cringleford Wk
WGTN/LGST M12 88 C7
Cringle Hall Rd BNG/LEV M19 99 J4
Cringle Rd BNG/LEV M19 99 L5
Crippen St ATH M46 66 D3
Cripple Ga WGNNW/ST WN6 30 C2
Cripple Gate La ROCH OL11 42 B3
Crispin Rd WYTH/NTH M22 119 G4
Critchley Cl HYDE SK14 102 C3
Criterion St RDSH SK5 100 C2
Croal Av WGNE/HIN WN2 64 D2
Croal St BOL BL1 2 A6
Croasdale Dr ROY/SHW OL2 43 H7
Croasdale St BOL BL1 2 E1
Crocus Dr ROY/SHW OL2 43 K7
The Croft BURY BL9 39 K6
GLSP SK13 93 K6
HYDE SK14 92 D8
OLDS OL8 75 H2
PART M31 95 G6
WGNW/BIL/O WN5 46 A8
Croft Acres RAMS BL0 17 D2
Croft Av ATH M46 67 G2
GOL/RIS/CU WA3 79 J2
PWCH M25 56 C4
WGNW/BIL/O WN5 46 A7
Croft Bank BRO * M7 71 M7
GTN M18 89 H7
Croft Brow OLDS OL8 75 J2
Croft Cl HALE/TIMP WA15 117 L6
Croft Dr TOT/BURYW BL8 24 B6
The Crofters SALE M33 109 J1
Crofters Brook RAD M26 38 F8
Crofters Gn WILM/AE SK9 126 D6
Crofters Wk BOLE BL2 22 F6
Croft Ga BOLE BL2 23 H8
Croft Gates Rd MDTN M24 57 G5
Croft Gv LHULT M38 52 C7
Croft Head ROY/SHW OL2 43 G8
Croft Head Dr MILN OL16 29 J5
Croft Hill Rd NEWH/MOS M40 73 K3
Croftlands RAMS BL0 24 D1
WGNW/BIL/O WN5 46 A8
Croftlands Rd WYTH/NTH M22 110 B8
Croft La BOLS/LL BL3 3 J9
BURY BL9 39 K7
RAD M26 38 F8
Croftleigh Cl WHTF M45 55 H2
Croft Mnr GLSP SK13 105 H3
Crofton Av HALE/TIMP WA15 108 D4
Crofton St OLDS OL8 75 J1
OLDTF/WHR M16 87 G8
RUSH/FAL M14 98 E1
Croft Pl TYLD M29 67 J4
Croft Rd CHD/CHDH SK8 120 D1
SALE M33 109 H2
WILM/AE SK9 126 C8
Crofts Bank Rd URM M41 84 F8
Croftside Av WALK M28 69 H1
Croftside Cl WALK M28 69 H1
Croftside Gv WALK M28 69 H1
Croftside Wy WILM/AE SK9 127 G6
Croft St BOLS/LL BL3 36 E8
BRO M7 71 M7
BURY BL9 5 H4
FAIL M35 74 D3
GOL/RIS/CU * WA3 79 K4
HYDE SK14 102 A2
LHULT M38 52 C7
OP/CLY M11 88 E3
STLY SK15 91 L2
WHIT OL12 28 F1
WHTN BL5 50 B1
Croftwood Sq
WGNW/BIL/O WN5 46 F2
Croichbank TOT/BURYW BL8 23 L2
Cromar Rd BRAM/HZG SK7 122 B1
Cromarty Av CHAD OL9 74 C1
Cromarty Wk OP/CLY M11 88 C3
Crombie Av WYTH/NTH M22 110 A4
Crombouke Dr LEIGH WN7 66 B3
Crombouke Fold WALK M28 68 E5
Cromdale Av BOL BL1 35 L4
BRAM/HZG SK7 122 B1
Cromedale Crs WGNNW/ST WN6 31 K5
Cromer Av BOLE BL2 3 L1
DID/WITH M20 98 E6
DTN/ASHW M34 100 D1
Cromer Dr ATH M46 66 D2
Cromer Rd CHD/CHDH SK8 111 H6
SALE M33 108 F1
TOT/BURYW BL8 25 G7
WGNS/IIMK WN3 63 H1
Cromer St MDTN M24 57 K3
OP/CLY * M11 89 G3
ROY/SHW * OL2 43 L5
STKP SK1 13 M3
WHIT OL12 10 D1
Cromford Av STRET M32 96 E1
Cromford Cl BOL BL1 2 C1
Cromford Dr WGNW/BIL/O WN5 46 E7
Cromford Gdns BOL BL1 36 C2
Cromford St OLD OL1 9 M2
Cromhurst St CHH M8 72 D3
Cromley Rd MPL/ROM SK6 123 G5
OFTN SK2 121 J1
Crompton Av BOLE BL2 37 H4
ROCH OL11 42 E1
Crompton Circuit ROY/SHW OL2 44 D2
Crompton Cl BOL BL1 22 D8
MPL/ROM SK6 114 C5
RAD M26 54 E4
Crompton Pl BOL * BL1 2 F5
RAD M26 54 E1
Crompton Rd BNG/LEV M19 99 K5
HOR/BR BL6 34 C4
RAD M26 53 K4
Crompton St AUL OL6 76 B8
BOL BL1 3 G3
BURY BL9 4 E4
CHAD OL9 8 C5
FWTH BL4 53 H5
OLD OL1 9 H2
ROY/SHW OL2 43 L5
ROY/SHW * OL2 59 H1
SWIN M27 70 B4
WALK M28 69 J2
WGN WN1 15 G3
WGNE/HIN WN2 48 E8
WGNS/IIMK WN3 64 C1
Crompton V BOLE BL2 37 G4
Cromwell Av CHD/CHDH SK8 110 D6
MPL/ROM SK6 113 M5
OLDTF/WHR M16 97 M2
Cromwell Cl NEWLW WA12 78 D8
Cromwell Gv BNG/LEV M19 99 K3
BRO M7 71 M7
Cromwell Range RUSH/FAL M14 99 G2
Cromwell Rd BRAM/HZG SK7 120 F6
ECC M30 84 F2
IRL M44 94 B5
MPL/ROM SK6 101 G6
PWCH M25 55 M8
ROY/SHW OL2 42 F6
SLFD M6 71 K8
SLFD M6 71 L7
STRET M32 97 H3
SWIN M27 70 B3
WHTF M45 55 G2
Cromwell St BOLS/LL BL3 2 B6
HEY OL10 41 G3
HTNM SK4 12 F1
OLD OL1 9 J7
Crondall St RUSH/FAL M14 98 D1
Cronkeyshaw Rd WHIT OL12 28 B3
Cronshaw St BNG/LEV M19 99 L4
Crookall St AIMK WN4 63 M8
Crooke Rd WGNNW/ST WN6 46 F1
Crookhill Dr CHH M8 72 C5
Crookhurst Av
WGNW/BIL/O WN5 62 A6
Crookilley Wy MPL/ROM SK6 101 G7
STKP SK1 13 M1
Crook St BOLS/LL BL3 2 E7
HYDE SK14 102 A2
MILN OL16 11 G3
WGN WN1 14 E3
WGNE/HIN * WN2 49 G8
Croom Wk NEWH/MOS * M40 88 A2
Cropton Wy WGNE/HIN WN2 65 J1
Crosby Av WALK M28 69 J2
Crosby Rd BOL BL1 35 L4
NEWH/MOS M40 74 A7
RAD M26 38 B5
SLFD * M6 71 G7
Crosby St ATH M46 51 H8
OFTN SK2 13 J9
WHIT OL12 28 C2
Crosfield Av BURY BL9 24 F2
Crosfield Gv GTN M18 89 G8
The Cross GLSP SK13 93 K7
TOT/BURYW * BL8 24 C6
Crossacres Rd WYTH/NTH M22 110 C8
Cross Av PWCH M25 55 K6
Crossbank Av OLDE OL4 60 C5
Crossbank Cl BRUN/LGST M13 88 A7
Crossbank St CHAD OL9 9 G7
Crossbridge Rd HYDE SK14 102 D2
Crossbrook Wy MILN OL16 29 K7
Crossby Cl MDTN M24 57 J7
Cross Cliffe GLSP SK13 105 H4
Crosscliffe St OLDTF/WHR M16 87 J8
Crossdale Rd BKLY M9 57 H8
BOLE BL2 37 J4
WGNE/HIN WN2 49 J7
Crossefield Rd CHD/CHDH SK8 120 C1
Crossen St BOLS/LL BL3 3 M9
Crossfell Av BKLY M9 56 E7
Crossfield Cl DTN/ASHW M34 101 K2
Cross Field Cl ROY/SHW OL2 43 M3
Crossfield Cl STLY SK15 91 K3
WHIT OL12 19 K5
Crossfield Dr RAD M26 54 B1
SWIN M27 70 B3
WALK M28 69 J5
Crossfield Gv MPL/ROM SK6 114 E3
OFTN SK2 112 E8
Crossfield Pl ROCH OL11 11 G9
Crossfield Rd ECC M30 83 M8
HALE/TIMP WA15 117 K2
WHIT OL12 19 K6
WILM/AE SK9 119 M8
Crossfields EDGW/EG BL7 22 E4
Crossfield St BURY BL9 39 J8
Crossford Br SALE M33 96 F5
Crossford Cl WGNS/IIMK WN3 47 G8
Crossford Ct SALE * M33 96 E6
Crossford Dr BOLS/LL BL3 35 H7
Crossford St STRET M32 97 G2
Crossgate Av WYTH/NTH M22 110 A6
Crossgate La GLSP SK13 93 J5
Crossgate Ms HTNM SK4 111 H2
Crossgates Rd MILN OL16 29 J5
Crossgill TYLD M29 67 L7
Cross Glebe St AUL * OL6 90 F1
Cross Gv HALE/TIMP WA15 108 C4
Crosshill St OLDTF/WHR M16 87 J8
Cross Keys St ANC M4 7 J2
Cross Knowle Vw URM M41 84 C8
Crossland Rd CCHDY M21 97 K4
DROY M43 89 K2
Crosslands PWCH M25 71 K1
Crosslands Rd WALK M28 68 C6
Cross La DROY M43 75 G8
GTN M18 89 G7
MPL/ROM SK6 114 B7
ORD M5 86 D3
RAD M26 38 F8
TOT/BURYW BL8 17 A7
WGNW/BIL/O WN5 62 A1
WILM/AE SK9 127 K4
Cross La East PART M31 106 C2
Cross La West PART M31 106 B2
Cross Lees WHIT OL12 28 D1
Crossley Ct ANC M4 88 A3
Crossley Crs AUL OL6 76 A6
Crossley Rd BNG/LEV M19 99 K5
SALE M33 96 D6
Crossley St BOLS/LL BL3 37 K8
GTN M18 88 E6
MILN OL16 29 H6
ROY/SHW OL2 43 M5
ROY/SHW OL2 59 H2
STLY SK15 91 J2
Crossmead Dr BKLY M9 57 H7
Crossmeadow Cl ROCH OL11 27 K4
Crossmoor Crs MPL/ROM SK6 113 M2
Crossmoor Dr BOLE BL2 3 K2
Crossmoor Gv MPL/ROM SK6 113 M2
Cross Ormrod St BOLS/LL BL3 2 A7
Cross Ri GLSP SK13 105 H4
Cross Rd CCHDY M21 97 L5
CHD/CHDH SK8 119 K5
Cross St ALT WA14 108 A8
ATH M46 50 E8
AUL OL6 76 A7
AUL OL6 90 D2
BOL BL1 2 F2
BOLS/LL BL3 53 L1
BURY BL9 4 F4
CSLFD M3 6 D3
DTN/ASHW M34 90 B7
EDGW/EG BL7 22 C5
FWTH BL4 53 G3
FWTH BL4 53 L7
GLSP SK13 93 K7
GLSP SK13 104 F3
GOL/RIS/CU WA3 79 K5
HEY OL10 41 H3
HYDE SK14 93 G8
HYDE SK14 102 A2
LEIGH WN7 66 D8
MDTN M24 57 J4
MILN OL16 29 G5
MOSL * OL5 76 F2
NM/HAY * SK22 124 E4
OLDE OL4 59 L5
OLDE * OL4 60 B6
OLDE OL4 60 D6
OLDTF/WHR M16 87 G7
RAMS BL0 17 C6
ROCH OL11 41 M2
SALE M33 96 E6
STLY SK15 77 G8
STRET M32 97 G2
SWIN M27 71 G2
TYLD * M29 67 J4
URM M41 95 M3
WALK M28 69 M5
WGNE/HIN WN2 49 G7
WGNNW/ST WN6 31 H3
WGNS/IIMK WN3 14 F6
WGNS/IIMK WN3 48 B8
WGNW/BIL/O * WN5 46 E6
WHTF M45 55 H3
Crosswaite Rd OFTN SK2 113 G6
Crossway BRAM/HZG SK7 121 G7
DID/WITH M20 110 E1
OFTN SK2 112 D8
Crossway Cl AIMK WN4 64 B7
Crossways OLDS OL8 75 K3
Croston Cl WILM/AE SK9 130 F3
Croston Close Rd BURY BL9 25 L2
Crostons Rd TOT/BURYW BL8 4 B3
Croston St BOLS/LL BL3 35 M8
WGNE/HIN WN2 48 F6
Croston Wk OP/CLY M11 88 B3
Croton St HTNM SK4 111 H2
Croughton Cl OP/CLY * M11 89 G5
Crowborough Cl HOR/BR BL6 34 C3
Crowborough Wk HULME M15 87 J7
Crowcroft Rd BRUN/LGST M13 99 K1
Crowden Dr GLSP SK13 93 K7
Crowden Rd NEWH/MOS M40 73 L2
Crow Hl STLY SK15 77 H7
Crow Hl North MDTN M24 57 J6
Crowhill Rd AULW OL7 75 J8
Crow Hl South MDTN M24 57 J6
Crow Hill Vw OLDE OL4 60 C8
Crowhurst Dr WGN WN1 47 L1
Crowland Gdns CHD/CHDH SK8 120 D6
Crowland Rd BOLE BL2 36 F2
NTHM/RTH M23 118 B1
Crow La RAMS BL0 17 C6
Crow La East NEWLW WA12 78 F8
Crow La West NEWLW WA12 78 E8
Crowley La OLDE OL4 60 A3
Crowley Rd BKLY M9 73 J4
HALE/TIMP WA15 108 E6
Crown Ct BRAM/HZG SK7 121 M1
Crowndale EDGW/EG BL7 16 D5
Crowneast St ROCH OL11 27 M5
Crown Fields Cl NEWLW WA12 78 E7
Crown Gdns EDGW/EG BL7 16 D6
MILN OL16 11 H9
NEWLW WA12 78 E8
Crowngreen Rd ECC M30 85 H3
Crown Gv LEIGH WN7 67 G6
Crown Hl MOSL OL5 77 G4
Crownhill Dr DROY M43 89 K2
Crown La ANC M4 7 H1
HOR/BR BL6 33 J1
Crown Park Dr NEWLW WA12 78 E8
Crown Passages
HALE/TIMP WA15 117 G2
Crown Point Av
NEWH/MOS * M40 73 M7
Crown Rd HEY OL10 40 E2
Crown Sq CSLFD M3 6 D5
Crown St ATH M46 66 F1
AUL OL6 90 E2
BOL BL1 2 F4
CSLFD M3 6 D2
DTN/ASHW M34 90 B8
FAIL M35 74 C4
HULME M15 6 C8
MILN OL16 11 J9
MPL/ROM * SK6 101 J8
MPL/ROM SK6 123 H1
NEWH/MOS M40 73 M7
ROY/SHW * OL2 43 L5
WGNE/HIN WN2 48 F6
WGNS/IIMK WN3 14 E7
Crow Orchard Rd
WGNNW/ST WN6 30 D2
Crowsdale Pl OFTN SK2 113 H8
Crowshaw Dr WHIT OL12 28 B1
Crow's Nest BOLS/LL BL3 37 J7
Crowswood Dr STLY SK15 77 G7
Crowther Av ORD M5 86 D4
Crowther Dr WGNS/IIMK WN3 63 H3
Crowther St GTN M18 89 G7
LIT OL15 19 M8
MILN OL16 29 J8
Crowthorn Dr NTHM/RTH M23 118 C2
Crowthorn Rd AULW OL7 90 C3
HTNM SK4 100 A5
Crowton Av SALE M33 108 A2
Crow Trees La EDGW/EG BL7 16 C5
Crow Wood Rd
GOL/RIS/CU WA3 80 A3
Croxdale Cl AULW OL7 75 H7
Croxton Av MILN OL16 11 K3
Croxton Cl MPL/ROM SK6 114 B7
SALE M33 108 A2
Croyde Cl BOLE BL2 37 J1
WYTH/NTH M22 119 H5
Croydon Av LEIGH WN7 66 C4
ROCH OL11 42 A5
ROY/SHW OL2 42 F6
Croydon Dr NEWH/MOS M40 73 M8
Croydon Sq ROCH OL11 42 A4
Crummock Cl BOLS/LL BL3 53 J1
Crummock Dr MDTN M24 57 H1
WGNS/IIMK WN3 63 J1
Crummock Rd CHD/CHDH SK8 119 K1
FWTH BL4 52 B5
Crumpsall La CHH M8 72 C3
Crumpsall St BOL BL1 36 B2
Crumpsall V BKLY M9 72 F2
Crumpsall Wy CHH M8 72 E3
Crundale Rd BOL BL1 22 C6
Cruttenden Rd OFTN SK2 112 F8
Cryer St DROY M43 74 F8
Cuba St MDTN M24 57 M4
Cubley Rd BRO M7 72 B4
Cuckoo Gv PWCH M25 55 L6
Cuckoo La BURY BL9 39 M2
PWCH M25 55 L6
Cuddington Av DID/WITH M20 98 D4
Cuddington Crs EDGY/DAV SK3 112 A6
Cudworth Rd BKLY M9 56 D7
Culand St WGTN/LGST M12 88 B6
Culbert Av DID/WITH M20 110 F1
Culchetch Av MPL/ROM SK6 114 C6
Culcheth Av WGNE/HIN WN2 64 E3
Culcheth Hall Dr GOL/RIS/CU WA3 81 J8
Culcheth La NEWH/MOS M40 73 M7
Culcheth Rd ALT WA14 116 F1
Culcross Av WGNS/IIMK WN3 46 F8
Culford Cl WGTN/LGST M12 88 B7
Culham Cl BOL * BL1 36 A2
Cullen Cl WGNE/HIN WN2 48 D4
Cullen Gv BKLY M9 73 H1
Cullercoats Wk
WGTN/LGST * M12 99 L1
Culmere Rd WYTH/NTH M22 118 F3
Culraven WGNE/HIN * WN2 32 E5
Culross Av BOLS/LL BL3 35 H6
NEWH/MOS M40 74 B3
Culvercliff Wk CSLFD M3 6 D6
Culver Rd EDGY/DAV SK3 112 A7
Culvert St MILN OL16 42 E2
OLDE OL4 60 B3
WGNNW/ST WN6 47 K2
Culverwell Dr ORD M5 86 E2
Culzean Cl LEIGH WN7 66 E8
Cumberbatch Pl
WGNS/IIMK WN3 48 C8
Cumber Cl WILM/AE SK9 126 B8
Cumber Dr WILM/AE SK9 126 B8
Cumberland Av DUK SK16 91 H4
HEY OL10 40 D2
RDSH SK5 100 F8
SWIN M27 70 C2
TYLD M29 67 J2
Cumberland Cl BURY BL9 39 H6
Cumberland Dr ALT WA14 116 C4
OLD OL1 59 G3
Cumberland Gv AULW OL7 75 L8
Cumberland Rd ATH M46 51 G7
BKLY * M9 73 G3
PART M31 106 A2
ROCH OL11 42 C2
SALE M33 108 F2
URM M41 95 M3
Cumberland St BRO M7 72 A8
STLY SK15 91 J2
WGN WN1 15 K1
Cumber La WILM/AE SK9 126 B8
Cumbrae Gdns ORD M5 86 B3
Cumbrae Rd BNG/LEV M19 99 M3
Cumbrian Cl BRUN/LGST * M13 87 M6
ROY/SHW OL2 43 J4
WGNE/HIN WN2 64 E2
Cumbria Wk SLFD M6 71 L8
Cummings St OLDS OL8 74 F2
Cunard Cl BRUN/LGST M13 87 M6
Cuncliffe Dr ROY/SHW OL2 44 A5
SALE M33 108 F1
Cundey St BOL * BL1 35 M3
Cundiff Rd CCHDY M21 97 L6
Cundy St HYDE SK14 91 H8
Cunliffe Av NEWLW WA12 78 E7
RAMS BL0 17 A8
Cunliffe Brow BOL BL1 35 L2
Cunliffe Ct LEIGH WN7 65 K8
Cunliffe St EDGY/DAV SK3 12 D6
HYDE SK14 90 F8
LEIGH WN7 65 M7
RAMS BL0 17 C5
Cunningham Dr BURY BL9 55 L3
WYTH/NTH M22 119 J4
Cunningham Rd WHTN BL5 49 M5
Cunningham Wy OLD OL1 9 J2
Curate St STKP SK1 13 M5
Curlew Cl GOL/RIS/CU WA3 80 A4
ROCH OL11 27 J5
Curlew Dr IRL M44 83 K8
Curlew Rd OLDE OL4 60 B8
Currier La AUL OL6 90 F2
Curteis St HOR/BR BL6 21 B8
Curtels Cl WALK M28 69 M5
Curtis Gv GLSP SK13 93 K7
Curtis Rd BNG/LEV M19 99 M3
HTNM SK4 111 K2
Curtis St BOLS/LL BL3 51 M2
WGNW/BIL/O WN5 47 G6
Curzon Av RUSH/FAL M14 88 B8
Curzon Dr HALE/TIMP WA15 108 E6
Curzon Gn OFTN SK2 113 G4
Curzon Ms WILM/AE SK9 126 E6
Curzon Rd AUL OL6 75 M8
BOL BL1 35 M5
BRO M7 72 A5
CHD/CHDH SK8 119 K5
OFTN SK2 113 G5
POY/DIS SK12 129 J2
ROCH OL11 42 C2
SALE M33 96 E7
STRET M32 96 D1
Curzon St MOSL OL5 76 F3
OLD OL1 9 J5
Cutacre Cl TYLD M29 67 L3
Cutgate Cl NTHM/RTH M23 109 H3
Cutgate Rd WHIT OL12 27 L3
Cuthbert Av BNG/LEV M19 99 M2
Cuthbert Rd CHD/CHDH SK8 111 H6
Cuthbert St BOLS/LL BL3 51 K2
WGNW/BIL/O WN5 47 G6
Cutland St NEWH/MOS M40 73 K6
Cutland Wy LIT OL15 20 B8
Cut La WHIT OL12 27 J3
Cutler Hill Rd FAIL M35 74 F5
Cutnook La IRL M44 83 J7
Cutter Cl ORD M5 86 D4
Cycle St OP/CLY M11 88 E4
Cyclone St OP/CLY M11 88 C4
Cygnet St WGNS/IIMK WN3 14 E7
Cygnus Av BRO M7 86 F1
Cymbal Ct RDSH SK5 112 B1
Cynthia Dr MPL/ROM SK6 114 C7
Cypress Av CHAD OL9 8 A3
Cypress Cl EDGY/DAV SK3 12 C6
Cypress Gdns MILN OL16 29 G5
Cypress Gv DTN/ASHW M34 101 K1
FWTH * BL4 53 J5
Cypress Oaks STLY SK15 92 A1
Cypress Rd DROY M43 89 K1
ECC M30 69 K8
OLDE OL4 60 A4
WGNW/BIL/O WN5 47 H6
Cypress St MDTN M24 57 M4
Cypress Wy MPL/ROM SK6 123 J5
Cyprus Cl OLDE OL4 60 A7
ORD M5 86 C3
Cyprus St STRET M32 97 G2
Cyril St BOLS/LL BL3 3 H9
ROY/SHW OL2 43 M5
RUSH/FAL M14 98 E1
Cyrus St NEWH/MOS M40 88 A2

D

Daccamill Dr SWIN M27 70 C6
Dacre Av OLDTF/WHR M16 97 L2
Dacre Cl MDTN M24 56 E3
Dacre Rd ROCH OL11 28 C8
Dacres Av UPML OL3 61 J8
Dacres Dr UPML OL3 61 J8
Dacres Rd UPML OL3 61 J8
Daffodil Cl WHIT OL12 28 B1
Daffodil Rd FWTH BL4 52 D3
Daffodil St BOL BL1 22 C7
Dagenham Rd RUSH/FAL * M14 98 F1
Dagmar St WALK M28 52 F8
Dagnall Av CCHDY M21 97 L6
Dahlia Cl WHIT OL12 28 A1
Daimler St CHH M8 72 D6
Dain Cl DUK SK16 91 G4
Daine Av NTHM/RTH M23 109 L3
Dainton St WGTN/LGST M12 88 A5
Daintry Cl HULME M15 87 J6
Daintry Rd CHAD OL9 8 D4
Dairydale Cl IRL M44 94 E1
Dairyground Rd
BRAM/HZG SK7 121 G5
Dairyhouse La ALT WA14 107 L5
Dairy House La BRAM/HZG SK7 127 M1
Dairy House Rd
CHD/CHDH SK8 120 D7
Dairy St CHAD OL9 8 A5
Daisy Av BRUN/LGST M13 88 B8
FWTH BL4 52 D3
Daisy Bank NEWH/MOS M40 73 M7
Daisy Bank Av SLFD M6 70 F6
Daisybank Cl WGNE/HIN WN2 49 G7
Daisy Bank La WYTH/NTH M22 119 J3
Daisy Bank Rd RUSH/FAL M14 88 A8
Daisyfield HOR/BR * BL6 34 A3
Daisyfield Cl WYTH/NTH M22 118 E3
Daisyfield Ct TOT/BURYW BL8 38 F3
Daisy Hall Dr WHTN BL5 50 B7
Daisyhill Cl SALE M33 97 H8
Daisyhill Ct WHTN BL5 50 C7
Daisy Hill Rd MOSL OL5 77 G3
Daisy Ms EDGY/DAV SK3 112 A8
Daisy Rd WGNW/BIL/O WN5 47 H6
Daisy St BOLS/LL BL3 35 M8
CHAD OL9 8 E4
CHAD OL9 58 D4
OFTN SK2 13 K9
TOT/BURYW BL8 4 A5
WHIT OL12 10 C3
Daisy Wy MPL/ROM SK6 123 H5
Dakerwood Cl NEWH/MOS M40 73 M7
Dakins Rd LEIGH WN7 81 L2
Dakley St OP/CLY M11 88 F5
Dakota Av SALQ M50 86 B4
Dakota South SALQ M50 86 C4
Dalbeattie Ri WGN WN1 15 M1
Dalbeattie St BKLY M9 73 H4
Dalberg St WGTN/LGST M12 88 A5
Dalbury Dr NEWH/MOS M40 72 F7
Dalby Av SWIN M27 70 B5
Dalby Gv STKP SK1 13 M4
Dalby Rd WGNE/HIN WN2 49 L7
Dale Av BRAM/HZG SK7 121 H4
ECC M30 84 F1
MOSL OL5 77 H1
Dalebank ATH M46 50 F7
Dalebank Ms SWIN * M27 54 A7
Dalebeck Cl WHTF M45 55 L4
Dale Brook Av DUK SK16 91 G6
Dalebrook Ct HTNM * SK4 12 D4
Dalebrook Rd SALE M33 108 F3
Dalecrest WGNW/BIL/O WN5 62 A3
Dale Flds UPML OL3 45 J8
Daleford Sq BRUN/LGST * M13 7 K9
Dalegarth Av HOR/BR BL6 34 F5
Dale Gv AULW OL7 75 K7
HALE/TIMP WA15 108 C5
IRL M44 94 B6
LEIGH WN7 65 M8
Dalehead Dr ROY/SHW OL2 44 A5
Dalehead Gv LEIGH WN7 65 M8
Dale La UPML OL3 45 J7
Dale Lee WHTN BL5 50 D4
Dale Rd GOL/RIS/CU WA3 79 K5
MDTN M24 57 L2
MPL/ROM SK6 114 B5
NM/HAY SK22 124 E5
Dales Av CHH M8 72 C2
WHTF M45 55 G3
Dales Brow BOL BL1 22 C6
SWIN * M27 70 A6
Dales Brow Av AULW OL7 75 K7
Dalesfield Crs MOSL OL5 77 H3
Dalesford Cl LEIGH WN7 80 F4
Dales Gv WALK M28 69 J3
Daleside Av AIMK WN4 63 K4
Dales La WHTF M45 55 H3
Dalesman Cl BKLY M9 73 J4
Dalesman Dr OLD OL1 60 A1
Dalesman Wk HULME * M15 87 J6
Dales Park Dr SWIN * M27 70 A6
Dale St ANC M4 7 H4
EDGY/DAV SK3 12 E9
FWTH * BL4 53 H3
LEIGH WN7 65 M7
MDTN M24 57 L5
MILN OL16 11 L4
RAD M26 54 D2
RAMS BL0 17 C4
ROY/SHW OL2 43 L6
STLY SK15 91 J3
SWIN M27 70 B6
TOT/BURYW BL8 24 F8
WGNS/IIMK WN3 64 C1
WHTN BL5 50 C7
Dale St East HOR/BR BL6 34 A3
Dale St West AULW OL7 90 D2
HOR/BR BL6 34 A2
Daleswood Av WHTF M45 55 G3
Dale Vw DTN/ASHW M34 101 K5
HYDE SK14 102 A4
LIT OL15 21 J2
NEWLW WA12 79 H8
Dalham Av BKLY M9 73 K2
Dalkeith Gv BOLS/LL BL3 35 J7
Dalkeith Rd RDSH SK5 100 C5

WGNE/HIN WN2 ....49 K7
Dalkeith St GTN M18 ....88 E6
Dallas St SALQ M50 ....86 B4
Dalley Av BRO M7 ....72 A8
Dallimore Rd NTHM/RTH M23 ...109 H6
Dalmain Cl CHH M8 ....72 C6
Dalmeny Ter ROCH OL11 ....28 C8
Dalmorton Rd CCHDY M21 ....98 A4
Dalny St BNG/LEV M19 ....99 L3
Dalston Av FAIL M35 ....74 E4
Dalston Dr BRAM/HZG SK7 ....120 E7
DID/WITH M20 ....110 F2
Dalston Gv WGNS/IIMK WN3 ....63 G1
Dalton Av MILN OL16 ....29 C5
RUSH/FAL M14 ....98 D2
STRET M32 ....85 J8
WHTF M45 ....55 K5
Dalton Cl MILN OL16 ....29 C5
RAMS BL0 ....17 A8
WGNW/BIL/O WN5 ....46 E5
Dalton Dr SWIN M27 ....71 G5
WGNS/IIMK WN3 ....63 H1
Dalton Fold WHTN BL5 ....50 C4
Dalton Gdns URM M41 ....95 L1
Dalton Gv AIMK WN4 ....63 K8
HTNM SK4 ....99 M8
Dalton Rd BKLY M9 ....57 G7
MDTN M24 ....56 E5
Dalton St ANC M4 ....87 L1
CHAD OL9 ....8 A4
ECC M30 ....85 G1
FAIL M35 ....74 B4
OLD * OL1 ....59 L5
SALE M33 ....96 F6
TOT/BURYW BL8 ....38 E2
Daltry St OLD OL1 ....9M2
Dalveen Av URM M41 ....84 F8
Dalveen Dr HALE/TIMP WA15 .....108 C5
Dalymount Cl BOLE BL2 ....36 E2
Damask Av CSLFD M3 ....6 A2
Dame Hollow CHD/CHDH SK8 ...119M5
Damery Ct BRAM/HZG SK7 ....121 C4
Dameral Cl CHH * M8 ....72 D6
Damery Rd BRAM/HZG SK7 ....121 C4
Dame St CHAD OL9 ....8 E2
Dam Head Dr BKLY M9 ....73 H1
Damian Dr NEWLW WA12 ....78 D7
Damien St BNG/LEV M19 ....99 L2
Dam La GOL/RIS/CU WA3 ....79 J1
Dams Head Fold WHTN BL5 ....50 C3
Damson Gn MDTN M24 ....57M4
Dan Bank MPL/ROM SK6 ....113 M6
Danby Cl HYDE SK14 ....91 J8
Danby Ct OLD OL1 ....9 C2
Danby Pl HYDE SK14 ....91 J8
Danby Rd BOLS/LL BL3 ....52 B1
HYDE SK14 ....91 J8
Dane Av EDGY/DAV * SK3 ....111 K4
PART M31 ....94 C8
Dane Bank MDTN M24 ....57 L4
Dane Bank Dr POY/DIS SK12 ....123 M6
Danebank Ms DTN/ASHW M34 ....100 D8
Danebank Wk BRUN/LGST * M13 ..7 K9
Danebridge Cl FWTH * BL4 ....53 H4
Danebury Cl WGNE/HIN * WN2 .....49 G8
Dane Cl BRAM/HZG SK7 ....120 F2
Danecroft Cl BRUN/LGST M13 ....88 A7
Dane Dr WILM/AE SK9 ....127 H6
Danefield Ct CHD/CHDH SK8 ....119 M4
Danefield Rd SALE M33 ....96 F6
Dane Hill Cl POY/DIS SK12 ....123 M7
Daneholme Rd BNG/LEV M19 ....99 H7
Dane Ms SALE * M33 ....96 E6
SALE M33 ....96 F6
Danes Av WGNE/HIN WN2 ....49 H6
Danes Brook Cl WGNE/HIN WN2 ..49 H6
Danesbury Cl
WGNW/BIL/O WN5 ....46 B3
Danesbury Ri CHD/CHDH SK8 .....111 G7
Danesbury Rd BOL BL1 ....22 E8
Danes Gn WGNE/HIN WN2 ....49 H5
Daneshill PWCH M25 ....55 L6
Danesmoor Dr BURY BL9 ....25 K8
Danesmoor Rd DID/WITH M20 ....98 D7
Danes Rd RUSH/FAL M14 ....99 G2
OLDE M15 ....59M5
OP/CLY M11 ....89 H5
ROCH OL11 ....10 C5
Danesway PWCH M25 ....72 A2
SWIN M27 ....70 F6
WGN WN1 ....47 L1
Daneswood Av BKLY * M9 ....57 J8
WHIT OL12 ....18 C4
Daneswood Cl WHIT OL12 ....18 C4
Danett Cl WGTN/LGST M12 ....88 D6
Danforth Gv BNG/LEV M19 ....99 L4
Daniel Adamson Rd PART M31 ....106 A1
Daniel Adamson Rd SALQ M50 .....86 A4
Daniel Fold WHIT OL12 ....27 L2
Daniel's La STKP * SK1 ....13 J3
Daniel St BRAM/HZG SK7 ....122 A2
HEY * OL10 ....40 E2
OLD OL1 ....59 L4
ROY/SHW OL2 ....59 K1
WHIT OL12 ....18 E3
Danisher La OLDS OL8 ....75 K5
Dannywood Cl HYDE SK14 ....101 M4
Danson St NEWH/MOS M40 ....88 B1
Dantall Av BKLY M9 ....73 K1
Dante Cl SLFD M6 ....70 D8
Danty St DUK * SK16 ....90 E3
Dantzic St ANC M4 ....7 H1
Dantzic St ANC M4 ....87 L1
Danwood Cl HYDE SK14 ....101 L3
Darbishire St BOL BL1 ....3 G1
Darby La WGNE/HIN WN2 ....49 G6
Darby Rd IRL M44 ....94 D6
Darbyshire Cl BOL BL1 ....35 M4
Darbyshire St RAD M26 ....54 D1
Darcy St BOLE BL2 ....3 L8
Darden Cl HTNM SK4 ....111 H1
Darell Wk CHH M8 ....72 E6
Daresbury Av URM M41 ....84 A8
Daresbury Cl EDGY/DAV SK3 ......111 K4
SALE M33 ....109 J1
WILM/AE SK9 ....127 M3
Daresbury Rd CCHDY M21 ....97 J3
Daresbury St CHH M8 ....72 D4
Dargai St OP/CLY M11 ....89 G3
Dargle Rd SALE M33 ....96 E6
Darian Av WYTH/NTH M22 ....118 F4
Daric Cl WGNE/HIN WN7 ....80 F3
Dark La MOSL OL5 ....77 G2
OLDE OL4 ....45 H6
UPML OL3 ....61 K4
WGTN/LGST M12 ....88 A4
Darley Av CCHDY M21 ....97M6

CHD/CHDH SK8 ....110 E7
ECC M30 ....84 F4
FWTH BL4 ....53 H3
Darley Gv FWTH BL4 ....53 H3
Darley Rd BRAM/HZG SK7 ....122 B5
OLDTF/WHR M16 ....97M1
ROCH OL11 ....28 C8
WGNS/IIMK WN3 ....63 L1
Darley St BOL BL1 ....36 A3
FWTH BL4 ....53 H4
HOR/BR BL6 ....21 J7
OP/CLY M11 ....89 G5
SALE M33 ....96 E8
STRET M32 ....86 A8
Darley Ter BOL * BL1 ....36 A3
Darlington Cl TOT/BURYW BL8 .....24 E8
Darlington Rd DID/WITH M20 ....98 D6
ROCH OL11 ....42 C1
Darlington St TYLD M29 ....67 K3
WGNE/HIN WN2 ....48 D5
Darlington St East TYLD M29 ....67 L3
WGN WN1 ....15 J5
Darliston Av BKLY M9 ....56 F7
Darnall Av DID/WITH M20 ....98 D4
Darnbrook Dr WYTH/NTH M22 ...118 F3
Darncombe Cl OLDTF/WHR M16 ...87 J8
Darnhall St WGNS/IIMK * WN3 .....48 C8
Darnley Av WALK M28 ....68 F3
Darnley St OLDTF/WHR M16 ....87 G8
Darnton Gdns AUL OL6 ....91 H1
Darnton Rd AUL OL6 ....91 H1
Darran Av WGNS/IIMK WN3 ....63 J1
Darras Rd GTN M18 ....99M1
Dart Cl CHAD OL9 ....58 C4
Dartford Av ECC M30 ....84 C2
RDSH SK5 ....100 E6
Dartford Cl WGTN/LGST M12 ....88 A6
Dartford Rd URM M41 ....95M3
Dartington Cl BRAM/HZG SK7 ....121 H1
NTHM/RTH M23 ....109 G6
Dartmouth Cl OLDS OL8 ....59 J8
Dartmouth Crs OLDS OL8 ....75 K7
Dartmouth Rd CCHDY M21 ....97M4
WHTF M45 ....55 K5
Dartnall Cl POY/DIS SK12 ....123 J6
Darton Av NEWH/MOS M40 ....88 A1
Darvel Av AIMK WN4 ....63 J7
Darvel Cl BOLE BL2 ....37 J6
Darwell Av ECC M30 ....84 F4
Darwen Rd EDGW/EG BL7 ....22 C4
Darwen St OLDTF/WHR M16 ....86 F7
Darwin Gv BRAM/HZG SK7 ....121 G6
Darwin St AULW OL7 ....90 D2
BOL BL1 ....36 A2
HYDE SK14 ....91 K7
OLDE OL4 ....59M7
Dashwood Av PWCH M25 ....55 J7
Datchet Ter ROCH OL11 ....28 C8
Dauntesy Av SWIN * M27 ....71 G5
Davehall Av WILM/AE SK9 ....126 E5
Davenfield Gv DID/WITH M20 .....110 E1
Davenfield Rd DID/WITH M20 .....110 E1
Davenham Rd RDSH SK5 ....100 C2
SALE M33 ....96 B6
WILM/AE SK9 ....119M8
Davenhill Rd BNG/LEV M19 ....99 K4
Davenport Av DID/WITH M20 ....98 E5
WILM/AE SK9 ....126 C3
Davenport Dr MPL/ROM SK6 ....101 L6
Davenport Fold Rd BOLE * BL2 ....23 K8
Davenport Gdns BOL BL1 ....2 D3
Davenport Park Rd OFTN SK2 .....112 D7
Davenport St BRAM/HZG SK7 .....121 M1
BOL BL1 ....2 C3
DROY * M43 ....89 H3
DTN/ASHW M34 ....90 B4
Daventry Rd CCHDY M21 ....98 A4
Davey La WILM/AE SK9 ....130 D2
David Brow BOLS/LL BL3 ....51 K2
David Cl DTN/ASHW * M34 ....101 K3
David Lewis Cl MILN OL16 ....11 L6
David's Farm Cl MDTN M24 ....57 L6
Davids La OLDE OL4 ....60 C5
Davidson Dr MDTN M24 ....57 L6
David's Rd DROY M43 ....89 H2
David St DTN/ASHW M34 ....101 K3
RDSH SK5 ....100 B4
TOT/BURYW * BL8 ....24 F8
TOT/BURYW BL8 ....38 F1
WHIT OL12 ....28 C3
David St North WHIT * OL12 ....28 C3
NEWLW WA12 ....78 F8
Davies Av CHD/CHDH SK8 ....119 K6
Davies Rd MPL/ROM SK6 ....113 G6
PART M31 ....106 C1
Davies Sq RUSH/FAL M14 ....87 K8
Davies St AULW OL7 ....90 C3
FWTH BL4 ....53 K5
OLD OL1 ....8 F3
WGNE/HIN WN2 ....64 D2
Davis St ECC M30 ....85 H3
Davy Av SWIN M27 ....71 C2
Davyhulme Rd STRET M32 ....96 F1
URM M41 ....84 B8
Davyhulme Rd East STRET M32 ....97 G1
Davyhulme St WHIT OL12 ....28 C5
Davy St NEWH/MOS * M40 ....72 D2
Dawber St AIMK WN4 ....64 A8
Dawes St BOL BL1 ....2 E1
Dawley Cl AIMK WN4 ....78 D1
Dawlish Av CHAD OL9 ....58 C3
CHD/CHDH SK8 ....120 B4
DROY M43 ....89 H2
RDSH SK5 ....100 C2
Dawlish Cl BRAM/HZG SK7 ....121 G5
HYDE SK14 ....103 H1
Dawlish Rd CCHDY M21 ....97M4
SALE M33 ....96 B7
Dawlish Wy GOL/RIS/CU WA3 ....79 J3
Dawnay St OP/CLY * M11 ....88 E5
Dawn St ROY/SHW * OL2 ....43 L6
Dawnwood Sq
WGNW/BIL/O WN5 ....46 F2
Dawson Av WGNNW/ST WN6 ....47 K1
Dawson La BOL * BL1 ....2 D4
Dawson Rd ALT WA14 ....108 A5
CHD/CHDH SK8 ....119M4
Dawson St ATH * M46 ....66 F1
BURY BL9 ....25 K8
CSLFD M3 ....6 D2
HEY OL10 ....40 B4
HYDE SK14 ....102 B3
OLDE * OL4 ....60 A6
OLDE * OL4 ....60 B7
STKP SK1 ....112 E1
SWIN M27 ....70 D4

Day Dr FAIL M35 ....74 C6
Day Gv HYDE SK14 ....103 K1
Daylesford Cl CHD/CHDH SK8 .....110 F8
Daylesford Crs CHD/CHDH SK8 ...111 G8
Daylesford Rd CHD/CHDH SK8 ....111 G8
Deacon Cl ALT WA14 ....116 D3
Deacons Cl STKP SK1 ....13 L4
Deacons Crs TOT/BURYW BL8 ......24 D7
Deacon Dr SLFD M6 ....71 G6
Deakin St WGNS/IIMK WN3 ....15 K9
Deal Av RDSH SK5 ....100 E6
Deal Cl NEWH/MOS M40 ....74 A7
Dealey Rd BOLS/LL BL3 ....35 K8
Deal St BOLS/LL BL3 ....52 C1
BURY BL9 ....5 K5
CSLFD * M3 ....6 D3
HYDE SK14 ....102 B2
SALE M33 ....96 C8
Dean Av NEWH/MOS M40 ....73 L6
OLDTF/WHR M16 ....97 L1
Deanbank Av BNG/LEV M19 ....99 J4
Dean Bank Dr MILN OL16 ....42 E3
Dean Brook Cl
NEWH/MOS * M40 ....73 L5
Dean Cl FWTH BL4 ....52 C4
PART M31 ....94 C8
RAMS BL0 ....17 D1
WHTF M45 ....55 H5
WILM/AE SK9 ....127 C3
Dean Ct BOL BL1 ....2 F2
GOL/RIS/CU WA3 ....79 K5
HULME * M15 ....87 G6
Deancourt ROCH OL11 ....28 B8
Dean Crs WGNW/BIL/O WN5 ....46 E4
Dean Dr ALT WA14 ....116 D3
WILM/AE SK9 ....127 C3
Deane Av ALT WA14 ....116 C4
CHD/CHDH SK8 ....111 J7
HALE/TIMP WA15 ....108 B5
Deane Church La BOLS/LL BL3 .....35 L8
Deane Rd BOLS/LL BL3 ....35M7
Deanery Wy STKP SK1 ....13 H3
Deane Wk BOLS/LL BL3 ....2 C7
Dean Head LIT * OL15 ....20 D1
Dean La BRAM/HZG SK7 ....122 A4
NEWH/MOS M40 ....73 L6
Dean Meadow NEWLW WA12 ....78 F8
Dean Moor Rd BRAM/HZG SK7 ...121 J2
Dean Rd CSLFD M3 ....6 D1
GOL/RIS/CU WA3 ....79 K5
GTN M18 ....89 H8
IRL M44 ....94 B6
WILM/AE SK9 ....127 J1
Dean Row Rd WILM/AE SK9 ....127 C3
Deanscourt Av SWIN M27 ....70 B5
Deansgate BOL BL1 ....2 D5
CSLFD M3 ....6 D6
Deansgate La
HALE/TIMP WA15 ....108 B5
Deanshut Rd OLDS OL8 ....75 K2
Deanswood Dr BKLY M9 ....56 D7
Deanwater Cl BRUN/LGST * M13 ..7 K9
Deanwater Ct
CHD/CHDH * SK8 ....119M5
STRET * M32 ....96 F4
Deanway NEWH/MOS M40 ....73 K4
URM M41 ....95 C2
WILM/AE SK9 ....127 C4
Dean Wood Av
WGNW/BIL/O WN5 ....46 B3
Dearden Av LHULT M38 ....52 D7
Dearden Clough RAMS BL0 ....17 E2
Dearden Fold RAMS BL0 ....17 E2
TOT/BURYW * BL8 ....38 F3
Deardens St TOT/BURYW BL8 ......38 F3
Dearden St BOLS/LL BL3 ....37 K8
HULME M15 ....87 H6
LIT OL15 ....20 C6
STLY * SK15 ....91 K2
Dearmans Pl CSLFD M3 ....6 D3
Dearne Dr STRET M32 ....97 H2
Dearnley Cl LIT OL15 ....20 M4
Debdale La GTN M18 ....89 J8
TYLD M29 ....67 J8
Deben Cl WGNNW/ST WN6 ....31 C3
Debenham Av NEWH/MOS M40 ....73M8
Debenham Ct FWTH * BL4 ....53 C5
Debenham Rd STRET M32 ....96 D3
Dee Av HALE/TIMP WA15 ....109 C7
Dee Dr FWTH BL4 ....53 K7
Deepcar St BNG/LEV M19 ....99 K2
Deepdale LEIGH WN7 ....81M1
OLDE OL4 ....60 A6
Deepdale Av DID/WITH M20 ....98 D4
MILN OL16 ....11M7
ROY/SHW OL2 ....42 F4
Deepdale Dr SWIN M27 ....71 G5
Deepdale Rd BOLE BL2 ....37 J3
Deeping Av OLDTF/WHR M16 ....98 A2
Deep La LIT OL15 ....29 L4
Deeplish Rd ROCH OL11 ....10 F9
Deeplish St ROCH OL11 ....10 F8
Deeply Vale La BURY BL9 ....25 M2
Deeracre Av OFTN SK2 ....112 F6
Deerfold Cl GTN * M18 ....89 G7
Deerhurst Dr CHH M8 ....72 C6
Dee Rd TYLD M29 ....67M5
Deeroak Cl GTN M18 ....88 E6
Deerpark Rd OLDTF/WHR M16 .....98 B3
Deer St CMANE M1 ....7 L6
Defence St BOLS/LL BL3 ....2 B7
Defiance St ATH M46 ....66 F1
Deganwy Gv RDSH SK5 ....100 C7
Delacourt Rd RUSH/FAL M14 ....98 D4
De Lacy Dr BOLE BL2 ....3 K1
Delafield Av WGTN/LGST M12 ....99 K2
Delaford Av WALK M28 ....69 H5
Delaford Cl EDGY/DAV SK3 ....112 B8
Delahays Dr HALE/TIMP WA15 ....117 J2
Delahays Range GTN M18 ....89 J3
Delahays Rd HALE/TIMP WA15 ...117 J2
Delaine Rd DID/WITH M20 ....98 F2
Delamere Av GOL/RIS/CU WA3 .....80 A6
ROY/SHW OL2 ....44 A4
SALE M33 ....109 H1
SLFD M6 ....70 F6
STRET M32 ....97 C2
SWIN M27 ....70 D4

WHTF M45 ....55 H4
Delamere Cl BRAM/HZG SK7 ......122 C1
MPL/ROM SK6 ....101 M7
STLY SK15 ....77 H6
Delamere Dr BNG/LEV M19 ....99 K4
BRAM/HZG SK7 ....122 C1
CHD/CHDH SK8 ....110 E7
MILN OL16 ....28 F8
OFTN SK2 ....112 E8
URM M41 ....95 J2
WILM/AE SK9 ....119M8
Delamere Gdns AUL OL6 ....90 E2
BURY BL9 ....25 K7
OLDS OL8 ....59 L8
OP/CLY M11 ....89 J5
Delamer Rd ALT WA14 ....116 C1
Delaunays Rd CHH M8 ....72 E2
SALE M33 ....96 C8
Delbooth Av URM M41 ....84 B8
Delegarte St WGNS/IIMK WN3 .....15 K8
Delfhaven Ct WGNNW/ST WN6 .....31 K5
Delfur Rd BRAM/HZG SK7 ....121 H5
Delhi Rd IRL M44 ....94 C4
The Dell ALT WA14 ....116 B3
Dellar St WHIT OL12 ....27M3
Dell Av SWIN M27 ....71 G5
WGNNW/ST WN6 ....47 H1
Dellcot Cl PWCH M25 ....72 A2
SLFD M6 ....70 E7
Dellcot La WALK M28 ....69 J7
Dell Gdns WHIT OL12 ....27 L2
Dellhide Cl OLDE OL4 ....60 D6
Dell Meadow WHIT OL12 ....18 D7
Dell Side MPL/ROM SK6 ....113 H1
Dellside Cl AIMK WN4 ....63 G6
Dellside Gv WALK M28 ....69 H1
Dell Side Wy WHIT OL12 ....27M2
Dell St BOLE BL2 ....22 F7
The Delph WALK * M28 ....69 J6
Delph Av EDGW/EG BL7 ....22 A1
Delph Brook Wy EDGW/EG BL7 ...22 A2
Delph Gv LEIGH WN7 ....66 A3
Delph Hill BOL BL1 ....35 H2
Delph Hill Cl BOL BL1 ....35 H2
Delphi Av WALK M28 ....69 G2
Delph La BOLE BL2 ....22 F7
UPML OL3 ....45 J7
Delph New Rd UPML OL3 ....61 H2
Delph Rd UPML OL3 ....44 F5
Delphside Cl WGNW/BIL/O WN5 ...46 A7
Delph St BOLS/LL BL3 ....2 B9
MILN OL16 ....29 J6
WGNNW/ST WN6 ....14 D1
Delside Av NEWH/MOS M40 ....73 K4
Delta Cl ROY/SHW OL2 ....59 G2
Delta Rd DTN/ASHW M34 ....90 A7
Delvino Wk HULME M15 ....87 K8
Delwood Gdns WYTH/NTH M22 ..118 B5
De-Massey Cl MPL/ROM * SK6 ...101 L6
Demesne Cl STLY SK15 ....91M3
Demesne Crs STLY SK15 ....91M3
Demesne Dr STLY SK15 ....91M3
Demesne Rd OLDTF/WHR M16 .....98 B2
Demmings Rd CHD/CHDH SK8 ...111 J7
Dempsey Dr BURY BL9 ....55 L2
Denbigh Cl BRAM/HZG SK7 ....121 L4
Denbigh Dr ROY/SHW OL2 ....43 J6
Denbigh Gv ATH M46 ....50 F7
Denbigh Pl SLFD M6 ....86 D3
Denbigh Rd BOLE BL2 ....3 J8
DTN/ASHW M34 ....101 J3
SWIN M27 ....70 D2
Denbigh St HTNM SK4 ....12 F1
OLDS OL8 ....75 C5
OLDS * OL8 ....75 J1
Denbigh Wk HULME M15 ....87 H7
Denbury Dr ALT WA14 ....107 L8
Denbury Gn BRAM/HZG SK7 ....121 J2
Denbydale Wy ROY/SHW OL2 ....42 F7
Denby La HTNM SK4 ....100 A8
Denby Rd DUK SK16 ....90 F5
Dencombe St BRUN/LGST M13 ....88 C8
Dene Av NEWLW WA12 ....78 C8
Dene Bank BOLE BL2 ....22 F7
Dene Brow DTN/ASHW M34 ....101 L4
Dene Ct HTNM SK4 ....12 C2
Dene Dr MDTN M24 ....56 C5
Denefield Av MPL/ROM SK6 ....114 E3
Deneford Rd DID/WITH M20 ....110 B2
Dene Gv LEIGH WN7 ....65 L8
Dene Hollow RDSH SK5 ....100 D3
Dene Pk DID/WITH M20 ....110 D2
Deneside Crs BRAM/HZG SK7 .....122 A3
Dene St MDTN M24 ....57 G2
LEIGH WN7 ....65 L8
Deneway HTNM SK4 ....12 C2
MPL/ROM SK6 ....123 H5
Deneway Ms HTNM SK4 ....12 C2
Denewell Cl BRUN/LGST M13 ....88 A7
Denewood Ct WILM/AE SK9 ....119 G8
Denham Cl BOL BL1 ....23 J1
Denham Dr BRAM/HZG SK7 ....120 F5
IRL M44 ....94 D3
WGNS/IIMK WN3 ....63 K1
Denham St BRUN/LGST M13 ....88 A7
Den Hill Dr OLDE OL4 ....60 C6
Denhill Rd HULME M15 ....87 J8
Denholme Rd ROCH OL11 ....28 C8
Denhurst Rd LIT OL15 ....20 B6
Denis Av OLDTF/WHR M16 ....98 B2
Denison Rd BRAM/HZG SK7 ....122 A4
RUSH/FAL M14 ....98 F1
Denison St RUSH/FAL M14 ....98 F1
Denmark Rd ALT WA14 ....108 A8
CHAD OL9 ....8 D2
MILN OL16 ....11 H2
OLDE OL4 ....60 A8
Denmark Wy CHAD OL9 ....8 D3
Dennington Dr URM M41 ....84 F8
Dennison Av DID/WITH M20 ....110 A8
Dennison Rd CHD/CHDH SK8 .....120 C4
Denshaw Av DTN/ASHW M34 ....90 A7
Denshaw Cl BNG/LEV M19 ....111 H1

Denshaw Rd UPML OL3 ....44 F7
Densmead Wk NEWH/MOS M40 .....7M1
Densmore St FAIL * M35 ....74 B5
Denson Rd HALE/TIMP WA15 .....108 C4
Denstone Av ECC M30 ....85 H1
SALE M33 ....108 B1
URM M41 ....95M1
Denstone Crs BOLE BL2 ....37 G2
Denstone Rd RDSH SK5 ....100 C3
SLFD M6 ....71 G7
URM M41 ....95M1
Dentdale Cl BOL BL1 ....35 G6
Denton Gv WGNW/BIL/O WN5 .....46 E4
Denton Hall Farm Rd
DTN/ASHW M34 ....100 F2
Denton La CHAD OL9 ....58 D7
Denton Rd BOLE BL2 ....37 L6
DTN/ASHW M34 ....90 B7
Denton St BURY BL9 ....4 F1
HEY OL10 ....40 F3
WHIT OL10 ....10 E1
Denver Av NEWH/MOS M40 ....88 A1
Denver Dr HALE/TIMP WA15 ......108 D6
Denver Rd ROCH OL11 ....28 C8
Denville Crs WYTH/NTH M22 ......119 G1
Denzell Gdns ALT * WA14 ....116 C1
Depleach Rd CHD/CHDH SK8 ......111 C2
Deptford Av NTHM/RTH M23 ......118 C1
De Quincey Rd ALT WA14 ....108 A3
Deramore Cl AUL OL6 ....91 H1
Deramore St RUSH/FAL M14 ....98 E1
Derby Av SLFD M6 ....86 B2
CCHDY M21 ....98 A1
GOL/RIS/CU WA3 ....79M3
HTNM SK4 ....99M8
NM/HAY SK22 ....124 F3
RAD M26 ....53 K4
RUSH/FAL M14 ....98 F5
SLFD M6 ....86 B2
URM M41 ....96 A1
WHTF M45 ....55 K5
Derbyshire Av STRET M32 ....96 E1
Derbyshire Crs STRET M32 ....96 E1
Derbyshire La STRET M32 ....96 D1
Derbyshire La West URM M41 ......96 C1
Derbyshire Level GLSP SK13 ....105 J6
Derbyshire Rd NEWH/MOS M40 ...74 A8
PART M31 ....106 A2
POY/DIS SK12 ....122 F7
SALE M33 ....96 F8
WGNS/IIMK WN3 ....63 G3
Derbyshire Rd South
SALE M33 ....109 G1
Derbyshire Rw BOL * BL1 ....36 B1
Derby Cl OP/CLY M11 ....88 F5
Derby St ALT WA14 ....108 B7
ATH M46 ....50 F8
AULW OL7 ....75 K7
BOLS/LL BL3 ....2 E5
BURY BL9 ....5 G4
CHAD OL9 ....8 C9
CHAD OL9 ....74 E1
CHH M8 ....72 B7
DTN/ASHW M34 ....90 A8
EDGY/DAV SK3 ....12 F7
FAIL * M35 ....74 D3
GLSP SK13 ....104 F4
HEY OL10 ....40 E2
HOR/BR BL6 ....34 A3
LEIGH WN7 ....66 D8
MOSL * OL5 ....77 G4
MPL/ROM SK6 ....113 G6
PWCH M25 ....55 K8
RAMS BL0 ....17 D6
ROCH OL11 ....11 G8
WGNS/IIMK WN3 ....48 C8
WHTN BL5 ....50 C3
Design St BOLS/LL BL3 ....51 L1
Desmond Rd WYTH/NTH M22 ....110 B8
Desmond St ATH M46 ....66 D2
De Trafford Dr WGNE/HIN WN2 .....4M8
The De Traffords IRL M44 ....94 D1
Dettingen St SLFD M6 ....71 H6
Deva Cl BRAM/HZG SK7 ....121M3
POY/DIS SK12 ....121 K8
Deva Sq CHAD OL9 ....8 C9

Devas St HULME M15 ....87 L7
Deverill Av GTN M18 ....89 J8
Devine Cl CSLFD M3 ....6 A2
　ROY/SHW OL2 ....43 G6
Devisdale Gra ALT * WA14 ....116 D1
Devisdale Rd ALT WA14 ....107 L8
Devoke Av WALK M28 ....69 H2
Devoke Gv FWTH BL4 ....52 B4
Devoke Rd WYTH/NTH M22 ....118 D2
Devon Av BNG/LEV M19 ....99 J4
　WHTF M45 ....55 H3
Devon Cl BOLS/LL BL3 ....37 L8
　RDSH SK5 ....100 F8
　ROY/SHW OL2 ....43 J5
　SLFD M6 ....85 K1
　WGNE/HIN WN2 ....33 G7
　WGNW/BIL/O WN5 ....46 F6
Devon Dr BOLE BL2 ....37 M3
　UPML OL3 ....45 M8
　WGN WN1 ....31 L3
Devonport Crs ROY/SHW OL2 ....43 J8
Devon Rd DROY M43 ....89 K1
　FAIL M35 ....74 B6
　PART M31 ....106 B2
　TYLD M29 ....67 J2
　URM M41 ....95 H3
Devonshire Cl HEY OL10 ....40 D2
　URM M41 ....96 B2
Devonshire Dr WALK M28 ....68 B6
　WILM/AE SK9 ....130 E2
Devonshire Park Rd OFTN SK2 ....112 D7
Devonshire Pl PWCH M25 ....55 K7
Devonshire Rd ALT WA14 ....107 M6
　ATH M46 ....35 L4
　BOL BL1 ....35 L4
　BRAM/HZG SK7 ....122 B4
　CCHDY M21 ....97 M4
　ECC M30 ....85 H2
　HTNM SK4 ....12 A2
　ROCH OL11 ....42 C2
　SLFD M6 ....85 K1
　WALK M28 ....52 F6
Devonshire St BRO M7 ....72 B6
　WGTN/LGST M12 ....88 A6
Devonshire St East
　NEWH/MOS * M40 ....74 A7
Devonshire St North
　WGTN/LGST M12 ....88 A6
Devonshire St South
　BRUN/LGST M13 ....88 A7
Devon St BOLE BL2 ....3 H5
　BURY BL9 ....4 E8
　CHAD OL9 ....58 E8
　FWTH BL4 ....53 G2
　LEIGH WN7 ....67 H8
　ROCH OL11 ....10 E7
　SWIN M27 ....70 C2
　WGNE/HIN WN2 ....49 H7
Devon Wy OLDS OL8 ....74 F2
Dewar Cl OP/CLY M11 ....88 D3
Dewberry Cl TYLD M29 ....68 B3
Dewes Av SWIN M27 ....70 E2
Dewey St OP/CLY M11 ....89 G5
Dewhirst Rd WHIT OL12 ....19 G7
Dewhirst Wy WHIT OL12 ....19 G8
Dewhurst Clough Rd
　EDGW/EG BL7 ....22 A2
Dewhurst Ct EDGW/EG BL7 ....22 A1
Dewhurst Rd BOLE BL2 ....37 H1
Dewhurst St CHH M8 ....72 C8
　HEY * OL10 ....41 H2
Dewint Av MPL/ROM SK6 ....114 E4
Dew Meadow Cl WHIT OL12 ....28 B2
Dewsnap Cl DUK * SK16 ....90 F6
Dewsnap La DUK SK16 ....90 F6
　HYDE SK14 ....92 D6
Dew Wy CHAD OL9 ....8 E4
Dexter Rd BKLY M9 ....56 D7
　RUSH/FAL M14 ....87 M8
Deyne Av PWCH M25 ....55 L8
　RUSH/FAL M14 ....87 M8
Deyne St SLFD M6 ....86 B2
Dial Ct FWTH * BL4 ....53 G4
Dial Park Rd OFTN SK2 ....113 G8
Dial Rd HALE/TIMP WA15 ....117 L4
　OFTN SK2 ....112 F7
Dialstone La OFTN SK2 ....112 F5
Diamond St AUL OL6 ....76 A8
　LEIGH WN7 ....66 B8
　OFTN SK2 ....112 D6
　WGNNW/ST WN6 ....47 K1
Diamond Ter MPL/ROM SK6 ....123 H1
Diane Rd AIMK WN4 ....64 A7
Dicconson Crs WGN WN1 ....15 G2
Dicconson La WHTN BL5 ....33 L8
Dicconson Ter WGN WN1 ....14 F1
Dicken Gn ROCH OL11 ....28 C8
Dicken Green La ROCH OL11 ....28 C8
Dickens Cl CHD/CHDH SK8 ....120 D7
Dickens Dr WGNE/HIN WN2 ....64 E4
Dickens La POY/DIS SK12 ....129 J1
Dickenson Rd RUSH/FAL M14 ....99 G1
Dickenson St WGNE/HIN WN2 ....49 H8
Dickens Pl WGNS/IIMK WN3 ....47 J8
Dickens Rd ECC M30 ....85 G3
Dickens St HEY * OL10 ....40 F7
　OLD OL1 ....44 B8
Dickinson Cl BOL * BL1 ....36 B3
Dickinson St BOL BL1 ....36 B3
　CMANE M1 ....7 G6
　CSLFD M3 ....87 H1
　OLDE OL4 ....59 L5
Dickson St West HOR/BR BL6 ....21 A8
Didcot Rd WYTH/NTH M22 ....118 E3
Didley Sq WGTN/LGST * M12 ....88 D6
Didsbury Gv WGNE/HIN WN2 ....49 G7
Didsbury Pk DID/WITH M20 ....110 E2
Didsbury Rd HTNM SK4 ....12 B4
Digby Rd ROCH OL11 ....28 C8
Dig Gate La MILN OL16 ....43 H1
Diggles La ROCH OL11 ....27 H6
Diggle St ROY/SHW OL2 ....43 L6
　WGNNW/ST WN6 ....14 C2
Diglands Av NM/HAY SK22 ....124 F3
Dijon St BOLS/LL BL3 ....35 M8
Dilham Ct BOL * BL1 ....35 M4
Dillmoss Wk HULME * M15 ....87 G6
Dillon Dr WGTN/LGST M12 ....88 B7
Dilston Ct BRUN/LGST M13 ....87 M6
The Dingle BRAM/HZG SK7 ....120 B6
　HYDE SK14 ....102 B6
Dingle Av WILM/AE SK9 ....130 A1
Dingle Bank Rd
　BRAM/HZG SK7 ....120 F2
Dingle Cl GLSP SK13 ....104 D4
　MPL/ROM SK6 ....114 A2
Dingle Dr DROY M43 ....89 L1
Dingle Gv CHD/CHDH SK8 ....110 C6
Dingle Rd MDTN M24 ....57 H6
Dingle Ter AUL OL6 ....75 L2
Dingle Wk BOL BL1 ....2 E2
　WGNNW/ST WN6 ....31 G8
Dinmor Rd WYTH/NTH M22 ....118 E4
Dinnington Dr CHH M8 ....72 C6
Dinorwic Cl CHH M8 ....72 D2
Dinsdale Dr BOLS/LL BL3 ....2 A8
Dinting Av DID/WITH M20 ....98 D5
Dinting La GLSP SK13 ....104 D3
Dinting Rd GLSP SK13 ....104 E2
Dinton St HULME M15 ....86 F5
Dirty La OLDE OL4 ....60 E3
　UPML OL3 ....45 L4
Dirty Leech WHIT OL12 ....19 G6
Discovery Dr HTNM * SK4 ....99 M7
Disley Av DID/WITH M20 ....98 C6
Disley St ROCH OL11 ....27 M8
Distaff Rd POY/DIS SK12 ....121 K8
Ditton Mead Cl WHIT OL12 ....28 C2
Division St BOLS/LL BL3 ....52 C1
　WHIT OL12 ....28 E2
Dixey St HOR/BR BL6 ....33 K1
Dixon Av BRO M7 ....72 A6
　NEWLW WA12 ....78 F7
Dixon Cl RNFD/HAY WA11 ....78 D4
　SALE M33 ....109 G2
Dixon Closes ROCH OL11 ....27 H5
Dixon Dr SWIN M27 ....54 B8
　WGNNW/ST WN6 ....30 D7
Dixon Green Dr FWTH BL4 ....52 F4
Dixon Rd DTN/ASHW M34 ....101 L3
Dixon St AUL OL6 ....76 A8
　HOR/BR BL6 ....33 L1
　IRL M44 ....94 B4
　MDTN M24 ....57 K2
　NEWH/MOS M40 ....73 L6
　OLDE OL4 ....60 B4
　ROCH OL11 ....27 M8
　SLFD M6 ....85 K1
　WHTN BL5 ....50 B1
Dobb Brow Rd WHTN BL5 ....50 A5
Dobb Hedge Cl
　HALE/TIMP WA15 ....117 L6
Dobbin Dr ROCH OL11 ....42 C1
Dobbinetts La
　HALE/TIMP WA15 ....117M1
　WYTH/NTH M23 ....109 H8
Dobcross Cl BRUN/LGST M13 ....99 K2
Dobcross New Rd UPML OL3 ....61 K3
Dobhill St FWTH BL4 ....53 G4
Dobroyd St CHH M8 ....72 D4
Dobson Cl BRUN/LGST M13 ....88 A6
　WGNNW/ST WN6 ....30 B2
Dobson Pkwy WGNE/HIN WN2 ....48 D6
Dobson Rd BOL BL1 ....35 M5
Dobson St BOL BL1 ....36 A2
Doctor Fold La HEY OL10 ....40 E6
Doctor La OLDE OL4 ....60 F3
Doctors La BURY BL9 ....4 C4
Doctor's Nook LEIGH WN7 ....66 C7
Dodd Cft MILN OL16 ....42 E2
Doddington La ORD M5 ....86 D4
Doddington Wk
　DTN/ASHW * M34 ....101 H3
Dodd La WHTN BL5 ....49 H1
Dodd's Farm La
　WGNE/HIN WN2 ....49 H1
Dodd St ORD M5 ....86 A2
Dodge Fold OFTN SK2 ....113 H6
Dodge Hl HTNM SK4 ....13 H2
Dodgson St MILN OL16 ....11 H7
Dodhurst Rd WGNE/HIN WN2 ....49 J6
Dodworth Cl HULME M15 ....87 J6
Doe Brow SWIN M27 ....54 B8
Doefield Av WALK M28 ....68 F4
Doeford Cl GOL/RIS/CU WA3 ....81 H7
Doe Hey Gv FWTH BL4 ....52 E2
Doe Hey Rd BOLS/LL BL3 ....52 E2
Doffcocker Brow BOL BL1 ....35 J3
Doffcocker La BOL BL1 ....35 J3
Dogford Rd ROY/SHW OL2 ....43 G7
Dolbey St ORD M5 ....86 B3
Dolefield CSLFD M3 ....6 D5
D'Olivera Ct MDTN M24 ....57 H5
Dollond St BKLY M9 ....73 H3
Dolphin Pl WGTN/LGST M12 ....7M9
Dolphin St WGTN/LGST M12 ....7M9
Doman St BOLS/LL BL3 ....52 A1
Dombey Rd POY/DIS SK12 ....129 H2
The Dome ALT * WA14 ....108 A8
Domett St BKLY M9 ....72 F2
Dominic Cl NTHM/RTH M23 ....109 H5
Donald Av HYDE SK14 ....102 C5
Donald St CMANE * M1 ....7 H7
Dona St STKP SK1 ....13M6
Don Av SLFD M6 ....85M2
Doncaster Av DID/WITH M20 ....98 D5
Doncaster Cl BOLS/LL BL3 ....53 J1
Doncaster Wk OLD OL1 ....9 J4
Donhead Wk BRUN/LGST * M13 ....87M6
Donkey La WILM/AE SK9 ....126 E7
Donleigh St NEWH/MOS M40 ....74 A6
Donnington Rd ROCH OL11 ....10 C7
Donnington Av CHD/CHDH SK8 ....111 J7
Donnington Cl LEIGH WN7 ....81 G3
Donnington Gdns WALK * M28 ....69 G1
Donnington Rd GTN M18 ....89 H7
　RAD M26 ....37M7
Donnison St WGTN/LGST M12 ....88 D6
Donovan Av NEWH/MOS M40 ....72 F8
Don St BOLS/LL BL3 ....52 A1
　MDTN M24 ....57M3
Doodson Av IRL M44 ....94 C2
Doodson Sq FWTH BL4 ....53 G4
Dooley La MPL/ROM SK6 ....113 L5
Dootson St WGNE/HIN WN2 ....49 M6
　WGNE/HIN WN2 ....64 D3
Dorac Av CHD/CHDH SK8 ....119 L6
Dora St RAMS BL0 ....17 A8
Dorchester Av BOLE BL2 ....37 J3
　DTN/ASHW M34 ....101 J3
　PWCH M25 ....71M2
　URM M41 ....96 C1
Dorchester Cl
　HALE/TIMP WA15 ....117 L1
　WILM/AE SK9 ....127 H4
Dorchester Ct CHD/CHDH SK8 ....120 D3
　SALE M33 ....108 F2
Dorchester Dr NTHM/RTH M23 ....109 H5
　ROY/SHW OL2 ....59 G2
Dorchester Rd BRAM/HZG SK7 ....121 K3
　SWIN M27 ....70 C6
Dorclyn Av URM M41 ....96 A2
Dorfield Cl MPL/ROM SK6 ....113 H1
Doric Av MPL/ROM SK6 ....113 G1
Doric Cl OP/CLY M11 ....88 C3
Doric Gn WGNW/BIL/O WN5 ....62 A1
Doris Av BOLE BL2 ....37 G5
Doris St EDGY/DAV SK3 ....12 C7
Doris St MDTN M24 ....57 K2
Dorket Gv WHTN BL5 ....50 A6
Dorking Av NEWH/MOS M40 ....73 K8
Dorking Cl BOL BL1 ....36 C2
　STKP SK1 ....112 E5
Dorlan Av GTN M18 ....89 J8
Dorland Gv OFTN SK2 ....112 E5
Dorman St OP/CLY M11 ....89 G5
Dormer St BOL BL1 ....36 C1
Dorney St GTN M18 ....89 G7
Dorning Rd SWIN M27 ....70 D5
Dorning St ATH M46 ....67 J3
　ECC M30 ....85 G3
　FWTH BL4 ....53 J4
　HOR/BR BL6 ....33 H5
　LEIGH * WN7 ....66 B7
　TOT/BURYW BL8 ....24 E8
　WGN WN1 ....14 E3
Dorothy Gv LEIGH WN7 ....66 B8
Dorothy Rd BRAM/HZG SK7 ....122 B1
Dorothy St BRO M7 ....72 C5
　RAMS BL0 ....17 B7
Dorrington Rd EDGY/DAV SK3 ....111 K5
　SALE M33 ....96 A8
Dorris St BNG/LEV M19 ....99 L4
　BOLS/LL * BL3 ....51M1
Dorrit Cl POY/DIS SK12 ....129 J2
Dorset Av BRAM/HZG SK7 ....120 F5
　CHD/CHDH SK8 ....111M8
　DTN/ASHW M34 ....89M4
　FWTH BL4 ....52 F4
　RDSH SK5 ....100 F7
　ROY/SHW OL2 ....43 J5
　RUSH/FAL M14 ....98 D2
　TYLD M29 ....67 J1
　UPML OL3 ....45M8
Dorset Cl FWTH BL4 ....52 F4
　HEY OL10 ....40 D3
　WGNW/BIL/O WN5 ....46 F6
Dorset Dr BURY BL9 ....5 H8
Dorset Rd ALT WA14 ....107 L8
　ATH M46 ....50 F8
　BNG/LEV M19 ....99M3
　DROY M43 ....89 J1
　IRL M44 ....94 A6
　WGN WN1 ....31 L3
Dorset St AUL OL6 ....91 G2
　BOLE BL2 ....3 H5
　CHAD OL9 ....8 C9
　LEIGH WN7 ....67 G8
　ROCH OL11 ....10 E7
　STRET M32 ....97 G3
　SWIN M27 ....70 C2
　WGNE/HIN WN2 ....49 H6
Dorsey St ANC * M4 ....7 J3
Dorstone Cl NEWH/MOS M40 ....73M8
Dorwood Av BKLY M9 ....56 F7
Dotterel Cl LEIGH WN7 ....66 D6
Dougall Wk WGTN/LGST M12 ....88 D6
Doughty Av ECC M30 ....85 J1
Douglas Cl BOLS/LL BL3 ....35 L5
Douglas Av HOR/BR BL6 ....21 C7
　STRET M32 ....97 G1
　TOT/BURYW BL8 ....38 E2
Douglas Dr WGNNW/ST WN6 ....30 C7
　WGNW/BIL/O WN5 ....46 B5
Douglas Gn SLFD M6 ....71 K7
Douglas Pk ATH M46 ....67 H1
Douglas Rd ATH M46 ....67 H7
　BRAM/HZG SK7 ....122 A1
　EDGY/DAV SK3 ....112 B8
　LEIGH WN7 ....65M5
　SWIN M27 ....69M5
　WGN WN1 ....15 H1
　WGNNW/ST WN6 ....30 E2
Douglas St ATH M46 ....67 H1
　AUL OL6 ....91 G1
　BOL * BL1 ....22 B7
　BRO M7 ....72 A6
　FAIL M35 ....74 D5
　HYDE SK14 ....102 B2
　NEWH/MOS M40 ....73 K5
　OLD OL1 ....9 L3
　RAMS BL0 ....17 B6
　SWIN M27 ....70 D5
　WGNE/HIN WN2 ....48 F8
　WGNW/BIL/O WN5 ....14 B6
Doulton St NEWH/MOS M40 ....73M4
Dounby Av ECC M30 ....84 E1
Douro St NEWH/MOS M40 ....73 J7
Douthwaite Dr MPL/ROM SK6 ....114 B3
Dove Bank Rd BOLS/LL BL3 ....37 J8
Dovebrook Cl STLY SK15 ....77 H5
Dovecote DROY M43 ....90 A1
Dovecote Cl EDGW/EG BL7 ....22 E4
Dovecote La LHULT M38 ....68 B1
Dovecote Ms CCHDY M21 ....97 K4
Dovedale Av DID/WITH M20 ....98 D5
　DROY M43 ....89 H2
　ECC M30 ....85 H1
　PWCH M25 ....72 A1
　URM M41 ....96 A2
Dovedale Cl MPL/ROM SK6 ....123 G5
Dovedale Ct GLSP SK13 ....105 J3
Dovedale Crs AIMK WN4 ....63 K4
Dovedale Dr WGNNW/ST WN6 ....31 G2
　WHIT OL12 ....19 L6
Dovedale Rd AIMK WN4 ....63 K4
　BOLE BL2 ....37 J2
　OFTN SK2 ....113 G5
Dovedale St FAIL M35 ....74 B5
Dove Dr BURY BL9 ....5 L1
　IRL M44 ....94 D1
Dovehouse Cl WHTF M45 ....55 G4
Doveleys Rd SLFD M6 ....71 H7
Dovenby Fold WGNE/HIN WN2 ....48 D5
Dover Cl TOT/BURYW BL8 ....24 D3
Dovercourt Av HTNM * SK4 ....111 J1
Dover Gv BOLS/LL BL3 ....2 B1
Doveridge Gdns SLFD M6 ....86 C1
Dove Rd BOLS/LL BL3 ....35 L8
Dover Pk URM M41 ....85 G8
Dover Rd SWIN M27 ....70 D2
Dover St BRUN/LGST M13 ....87 L6
　CHAD OL9 ....8 A2
　ECC M30 ....84 E2
　FWTH BL4 ....52 F2
　MILN * OL16 ....28 E2
　RDSH * SK5 ....100 B5
Dovestone Crs DUK SK16 ....91 J5
Dovestone Wk
　NEWH/MOS * M40 ....74 B3
Doveston Rd SALE M33 ....96 E6
Dove St BOL BL1 ....22 B8
　GOL/RIS/CU WA3 ....79 K2
　OLDE OL4 ....59M6
　ROCH OL11 ....10 A5
Dovey Cl TYLD M29 ....67M5
Dower St WGNE/HIN WN2 ....64 D1
Dow Fold TOT/BURYW BL8 ....38 C1
Dow La TOT/BURYW BL8 ....38 C1
Dowland Cl NTHM/RTH * M23 ....109 J2
Dowling Cl WGNNW/ST WN6 ....47 L1
Dowling St ROCH OL11 ....10 F7
Downall Green Rd AIMK WN4 ....63 H6
Downes Wy WYTH/NTH M22 ....110 B6
Downfield Cl TOT/BURYW BL8 ....17 A6
Downgreen Rd BOLE BL2 ....37 H1
Downham Av BOL BL2 ....3 M5
Downham Cha
　HALE/TIMP WA15 ....108 E6
Downham Cl ROY/SHW OL2 ....58 F2
Downham Crs PWCH M25 ....72 B1
Downham Gdns PWCH M25 ....72 B1
Downham Rd HEY OL10 ....40 D2
　HTNM SK4 ....100 A7
Downham Wk NTHM/RTH M23 ....109 G4
Downhill Cl OLD OL1 ....9 H1
Downing Cl AULW OL7 ....75 J6
　WGNE/HIN WN2 ....64 D3
Downing St AULW OL7 ....75 J6
　CMANE M1 ....7 K8
　LEIGH * WN7 ....66 C7
Downley Cl WHIT OL12 ....27 K2
Downley Dr ANC M4 ....7M3
The Downs ALT WA14 ....116 F1
　CHD/CHDH SK8 ....119M1
　MDTN M24 ....57 L6
　PWCH M25 ....71 K1
　WGNS/IIMK WN3 ....46 F8
Downs Dr ALT WA14 ....108 A3
Downshaw Rd AULW OL7 ....75 K6
Downton Av WGNE/HIN WN2 ....49 G8
Dowry Rd OLDE OL4 ....60 B6
Dowry St OLDS OL8 ....75 J1
Dowson Rd HYDE SK14 ....102 B4
Dowson St BOLE BL2 ....3 H5
Dow St HYDE SK14 ....91 G7
Doyle Av MPL/ROM SK6 ....113 G1
Doyle Cl OLD OL1 ....44 B8
Doyle Rd BOLS/LL BL3 ....51 H1
Drake Av FWTH BL4 ....53 G6
　IRL M44 ....94 B6
Drake Cl OLD OL1 ....9 J2
Drake Ct RDSH SK5 ....100 B8
Drake Hall WHTN BL5 ....50 A7
Drake Rd ALT WA14 ....107 L4
Drake St ATH M46 ....66 F2
　MILN OL16 ....10 E4
　ROCH OL11 ....10 E6
Draycott Cl WGNE/HIN WN2 ....65 J1
Draycott St BOL BL1 ....36 B2
Draycott St East BOL BL1 ....36 C2
Drayfields DROY M43 ....90 A2
Drayford Cl NTHM/RTH M23 ....109 J2
Drayton Av CHD/CHDH SK8 ....119 K5
Drayton Cl BOL BL1 ....36 A2
　SALE M33 ....108 A2
　WILM/AE SK9 ....127 H3
Drayton Gv HALE/TIMP WA15 ....108 D8
Drayton Wk OLDTF/WHR M16 ....86 F7
Dresden St NEWH/MOS M40 ....73M4
Drewett St NEWH/MOS M40 ....73 H6
Dreyfus Av OP/CLY M11 ....88 F2
Driffield St ECC M30 ....84 F4
　RUSH/FAL M14 ....98 D1
Drill Wk ANC M4 ....7M4
Drinkwater Rd PWCH M25 ....71 J3
Driscoll St BRUN/LGST M13 ....99 J1
The Drive BRO M7 ....71M3
　BURY BL9 ....25 J7
　CHD/CHDH SK8 ....111M8
　DID/WITH M20 ....110 F1
　HALE/TIMP WA15 ....117M4
　LEIGH WN7 ....81 J1
　MPL/ROM SK6 ....114 B6
　PWCH M25 ....55 L8
　RAMS BL0 ....17 D1
　RDSH SK5 ....100 F8
　SALE M33 ....108 B3
　WHTN * BL5 ....50 A7
Droitwich Rd NEWH/MOS M40 ....73M8
Dronfield Rd SLFD M6 ....71 G8
　WYTH/NTH M22 ....110 A4
Droughts La PWCH M25 ....56 A4
Droxford Gv ATH M46 ....51 H7
Droylsden Rd DTN/ASHW M34 ....89 L3
　NEWH/MOS M40 ....74 A7
Druids Cl EDGW/EG BL7 ....22 E4
Druid St AIMK WN4 ....63 H5
Drummer's La AIMK WN4 ....78 F2
Drummond Sq
　WGNNW/ST WN6 ....47 H5
Drummond St BOL * BL1 ....22 B8
Drummond Wy LEIGH WN7 ....66 E7
Drury La CHAD OL9 ....74 D1
Drury St BNG/LEV M19 ....99 K3
Dryad Cl SWIN M27 ....70 C2
Drybrook Cl BRUN/LGST M13 ....88 B7
Dryburgh Av BOL BL1 ....36 A1
Dryden Av AIMK WN4 ....63 J5
　CHD/CHDH SK8 ....111 K6
　SWIN M27 ....70 A5
Dryden Cl DUK SK16 ....91 L5
　MPL/ROM SK6 ....114 C8
　WGNS/IIMK WN3 ....47 K7
Dryden Rd OLDTF/WHR M16 ....97M1
Dryden St BRUN/LGST M13 ....87M6
Dryfield La HOR/BR BL6 ....21 A7
Dryhurst Dr POY/DIS SK12 ....123M6
Dryhurst La POY/DIS SK12 ....123M6
Dryhurst Wk HULME M15 ....87 K6
Drymoss OLDS OL8 ....75 J3
Dryton Wk WGNE/HIN WN2 ....48 D2
Drywood Av WALK M28 ....69 K7
Ducal St ANC M4 ....7 J2
Duchess Park Cl ROY/SHW OL2 ....43 K4
Duchess Rd CHH M8 ....72 E4
Duchess St ROY/SHW OL2 ....43 K4
　WGNW/BIL/O WN5 ....35 L8
Duchy Av WALK M28 ....69 L4
　WHTN BL5 ....51 K4
Duchy Bank SLFD M6 ....71 G6
Duchy Rd SLFD M6 ....71 G6
Duchy St EDGY/DAV SK3 ....12 F8
　SLFD M6 ....86 C1
Ducie Av BOL BL1 ....35M5
Ducie Gv HULME M15 ....87 L7
Ducie St CMANE M1 ....7 K5
　OLDS OL8 ....75 J4
　RAD M26 ....38 C7
　WHTF M45 ....55 J4
Duckshaw La FWTH BL4 ....52 F4
Dudworth Rd PWCH M25 ....71 J1
　ROY/SHW OL2 ....43M5
Duddon Av BOLE BL2 ....37 J3
Duddon Cl WHTF M45 ....55 J4
Duddon Dr WGNNW/ST WN6 ....31 J5
　WHTF M45 ....55 J4
Dudley Av BOLE BL2 ....37M3
　WHTF M45 ....55 J4
Dudley Cl HULME M15 ....87 H7
　IRL M44 ....94 A8
　OLDTF/WHR M16 ....98 A1
　SALE M33 ....70 C3
　SWIN M27 ....70 C3
Dudley Rd HALE/TIMP WA15 ....108 E5
　CHH M8 ....72 C6
　DTN/ASHW M34 ....84 F3
　ECC M30 ....60 A6
　SALE M33 ....96 E6
Dudley St AIMK WN4 ....63 K7
Dudlow Wk HULME * M15 ....87 G6
Duerden St BOLS/LL * BL3 ....51 K2
Duffield Ct MDTN * M24 ....57 J7
Duffield Gdns MDTN M24 ....57 J7
Duffield Rd MDTN M24 ....57 J7
　SLFD M6 ....71 G7
Duffins Cl WHIT OL12 ....28 A1
Dugdale Av BKLY M9 ....57 H8
Dugie St RAMS BL0 ....17 B5
Duke Av CHD/CHDH SK8 ....120 B6
　GOL/RIS/CU WA3 ....81M5
Duke Ct OLDTF/WHR M16 ....87 G7
Dukefield St WYTH/NTH M22 ....110 B4
Duke Pl CSLFD M3 ....6 C7
Duke Rd BOLE BL2 ....37 J3
　HYDE SK14 ....91 J7
Dukes Fold GLSP SK13 ....104 E5
Dukes Platting AUL OL6 ....76 C7
Dukes St GLSP SK13 ....104 F4
Duke St AIMK WN4 ....78 F1
　AUL * OL6 ....90 C2
　BOL BL1 ....2 D3
　BRO M7 ....72 A7
　CSLFD M3 ....6 C7
　DTN/ASHW M34 ....101 H1
　ECC M30 ....69M8
　FAIL M35 ....74 D4
　GOL/RIS/CU WA3 ....79 K3
　HEY OL10 ....40 E2
　LEIGH WN7 ....66 B8
　LHULT M38 ....52 D7
　LIT OL15 ....20 D3
　MOSL OL5 ....77 H3
　RAD M26 ....54 E2
　RAMS BL0 ....17 A8
　ROY/SHW OL2 ....43M6
　STKP SK1 ....13 H5
　STLY SK15 ....91 J3
　TYLD M29 ....67M6
　WALK M28 ....69 K2
　WGN WN1 ....47M2
　WGNE/HIN WN2 ....64 D1
　WGNS/IIMK WN3 ....47 J8
　WHIT OL12 ....28 C3
　WILM/AE SK9 ....130 E2
Duke St North BOL BL1 ....2 D2
Dukinfield Rd HYDE SK14 ....90 D7
Dukinfield St LEIGH * WN7 ....66 D7
Dulford Wk BRUN/LGST * M13 ....87M7
Dulgar St OP/CLY * M11 ....88 E4
Dulverton Gdns BOLS/LL * BL3 ....53 L2
Dulverton St NEWH/MOS M40 ....73 L6
Dulwich Cl SALE M33 ....108 A1
Dulwich St ANC M4 ....87 L1
Dumbarton Cl RDSH SK5 ....100 C6
Dumbarton Dr HEY OL10 ....40 C4
Dumbarton Gn
　WGNNW/ST WN6 ....47 H2
Dumbarton Rd RDSH SK5 ....100 C5
Dumbell St SWIN M27 ....70 C2
Dumers La RAD M26 ....39 G8
Dumfries Av UPML OL3 ....44 F2
Dumfries Dr UPML OL3 ....44 F2
Dumfries Hollow HEY OL10 ....41 G5
Dunbar Av NTHM/RTH M23 ....118 C1
Dunbar Dr BOLS/LL BL3 ....52 B1
Dunbar Gv HEY OL10 ....40 C4
Dunbar St OLD OL1 ....9 G3
Dunblane Av BOLS/LL BL3 ....35 H7
　HTNM SK4 ....12 E2
Dunblane Cl AIMK WN4 ....62 F8
Duncan Av NEWLW WA12 ....78 F7
Duncan Pl WGNW/BIL/O WN5 ....47 H5
Duncan Rd BRUN/LGST M13 ....99 J1
Duncan St BRO M7 ....71M6
　DUK SK16 ....90 M6
　HOR/BR BL6 ....33M1
　ORD M5 ....6 C9
Dunchurch Cl HOR/BR BL6 ....35 G6
Dunchurch Rd SALE M33 ....96 B8
Dun Cl CSLFD M3 ....6 A3
Duncombe Dr NEWH/MOS M40 ....73 L5
Duncombe Rd BOLS/LL BL3 ....52 B2
Duncote Gv ROY/SHW OL2 ....58 F8
Dundee Cl HEY OL10 ....40 C3
Dundee La RAMS BL0 ....17 B6
Dundonald Rd CHD/CHDH SK8 ....120 C5
　DID/WITH M20 ....110 F1
Dundonald St OFTN SK2 ....112 C6
Dundraw Cl MDTN M24 ....56 E3
Dundrennan Cl POY/DIS SK12 ....121M7
Dunecroft DTN/ASHW * M34 ....90 B8
Dunedin Dr SLFD M6 ....71 J7
Dunedin Rd TOT/BURYW BL8 ....24 C2
Dunelm Dr NTHM/RTH M23 ....109 J3
Dunham Av GOL/RIS/CU WA3 ....79 J3
Dunham Cl WHTN BL5 ....50 A7
Dunham Gv ALT WA14 ....107 L8
Dunham Lawn ALT WA14 ....107 L8
Dunham Ms ALT * WA14 ....116 B3
Dunham Ri ALT WA14 ....107M8
Dunham Rd ALT WA14 ....107 L8
　ALT WA14 ....116 B2
　DUK SK16 ....91 G6
　LYMM WA13 ....106 B5
　PART M31 ....95 G8
　WILM/AE SK9 ....119M7
Dunham St HULME M15 ....87 H6
　OLDE OL4 ....60 B4

Dunkeld Rd *NTHM/RTH* M23 .....109 J6
Dunkerley Av *FAIL* M35 .....74 C5
Dunkerley St *AULW* OL7 .....75 K7
  OLDE OL4 .....59 M4
  ROY/SHW * OL2 .....43 C8
Dunkery Rd *WYTH/NTH* M22 .....118 F3
Dunkirk Cl *DTN/ASHW* M34 .....100 D2
Dunkirk La *HYDE* SK14 .....90 E8
Dunkirk Ri *WHIT* OL12 .....10 C4
Dunkirk Rd *WHTF* M45 .....55 J3
Dunkirk St *DROY* M43 .....89 L3
Dunley Cl *RUSH/FAL* M14 .....88 D7
Dunlin Cl *BOLE* BL2 .....3 H8
  OFTN SK2 .....113 K7
  POY/DIS SK12 .....121 J8
  ROCH OL11 .....27 J5
Dunlin Dr *IRL* M44 .....94 D1
Dunlin Gv *LEIGH* WN7 .....66 E7
Dunlop Av *ROCH* OL11 .....42 B1
Dunlop St *CSLFD* * M3 .....6 E4
Dunmail Cl *TYLD* M29 .....67 M6
Dunmail Dr *MDTN* M24 .....57 H1
Dunmaston Av
  NTHM/RTH M23 .....109 J5
Dunmore Rd *CHD/CHDH* SK8 .....110 E6
Dunmow Ct *ROY/SHW* * OL2 .....113 H7
Dunne La *GLSP* SK13 .....105 H2
Dunnisher Rd *NTHM/RTH* M23 .....109 L8
Dunnock Cl *OFTN* SK2 .....113 J7
Dunnollie Rd *SALE* M33 .....109 H1
Dunoon Cl *HEY* OL10 .....40 D3
Dunoon Rd *RDSH* SK5 .....100 C5
  WGNE/HIN WN2 .....33 G7
Dunrobin Cl *HEY* OL10 .....40 D4
Dunscar Cl *WHTF* M45 .....55 H5
Dunscore Rd *WGNS/IIMK* WN3 .....63 H1
Dunsdale Dr *AIMK* WN4 .....78 F1
Dunsfold Dr *NTHM/RTH* M23 .....109 C4
Dunsley Av *NEWH/MOS* M40 .....74 A2
Dunsmore Cl *OLDTF/WHR* M16 .....87 C8
Dunsop Dr *BOL* BL1 .....35 J1
Dunstable *WHIT* OL12 .....10 D2
Dunstable St *BNG/LEV* M19 .....99 L3
Dunstall Rd *WYTH/NTH* M22 .....110 B7
Dunstan St *BOLE* BL2 .....3 L4
  DTN/ASHW M34 .....90 B5
Dunster Av *BKLY* M9 .....57 H8
  RDSH SK5 .....100 F7
  ROCH OL11 .....10 C9
  SWIN M27 .....70 E2
Dunster Cl *BRAM/HZG* SK7 .....121 L3
  WGNE/HIN WN2 .....64 D3
Dunster Dr *URM* M41 .....94 F3
Dunster Pl *WALK* M28 .....68 C5
Dunster Rd *WALK* M28 .....68 C5
Dunsters Av *TOT/BURYW* BL8 .....24 F7
Dunston St *OP/CLY* M11 .....88 E2
Dunton Gn *RDSH* SK5 .....100 E6
Dunvegan Rd *BRAM/HZG* SK7 .....122 B3
Dunwood Av *ROY/SHW* OL2 .....43 M4
Dunwood Park Cts
  ROY/SHW OL2 .....43 M3
Dunwoods Park Cts
  ROY/SHW OL2 .....43 M3
Dunworth St *RUSH/FAL* M14 .....98 E1
Durant St *ANC* * M4 .....7 J1
Durban Cl *ROY/SHW* OL2 .....43 K6
Durban Rd *BOL* BL1 .....22 B7
Durban St *ATH* M46 .....66 D2
  AULW OL7 .....90 B3
  OLDS OL8 .....74 F1
  ROCH OL11 .....41 M2
Durden Ms *ROY/SHW* OL2 .....43 L6
Durham Av *URM* M41 .....96 B1
Durham Cl *BOLS/LL* BL3 .....37 L8
  DUK SK16 .....91 G6
  MPL/ROM SK6 .....113 K3
  TYLD M29 .....67 K1
Durham Crs *FAIL* M35 .....74 D6
Durham Dr *AUL* OL6 .....76 A4
  BURY BL9 .....5 H8
  RAMS BL0 .....24 D1
Durham Rd *SLFD* M6 .....70 F7
  WGNE/HIN WN2 .....49 H7
Durham St *BKLY* * M9 .....73 H5
  BOL BL1 .....36 C2
  CHAD OL9 .....58 F8
  DROY M43 .....89 K4
  RAD M26 .....38 F7
  RDSH SK5 .....100 B2
  ROCH OL11 .....10 F8
  WGN WN1 .....15 L1
Durley Av *CHH* M8 .....72 E5
  HALE/TIMP WA15 .....108 C5
Durling St *WGTN/LGST* M12 .....7 M9
Durnford Av *URM* M41 .....96 D2
Durnford Cl *WHIT* OL12 .....27 C2
Durnford St *MDTN* M24 .....57 J3
Durnlaw Cl *LIT* OL15 .....20 D7
Durn St *LIT* OL15 .....20 D6
Durrell Wy *GOL/RIS/CU* WA3 .....80 B4
Dursley Dr *AIMK* WN4 .....64 A8
Dutton Gv *LEIGH* WN7 .....81 M2
Dutton St *CSLFD* M3 .....87 J1
Duty St *BOL* BL1 .....36 B1
Duxbury Av *BOLE* BL2 .....23 H7
  BOLS/LL BL3 .....37 K7
Duxbury Dr *BURY* BL9 .....5 M4
Duxbury St *BOL* BL1 .....36 A2
Dyche St *ANC* M4 .....7 H2
Dye House La *MILN* OL16 .....28 F1
  NM/HAY SK22 .....124 E4
Dye La *MPL/ROM* SK6 .....113 L2
Dyers Ct *LIT* * OL15 .....20 B6
Dyer St *GOL/RIS/CU* WA3 .....79 J4
  OP/CLY M11 .....88 D4
  ORD M5 .....86 F5
Dymchurch Av *RAD* M26 .....53 M5
Dymchurch St *NEWH/MOS* M40 .....73 M8
Dysarts Cl *MOSL* OL5 .....77 H1
Dysart St *AUL* OL6 .....91 G2
  OFTN SK2 .....112 F7
Dyserth Gv *RDSH* SK5 .....100 C7
Dyson Cl *FWTH* BL4 .....53 G4
Dyson Gv *OLDE* * OL4 .....60 C5
Dyson St *FWTH* * BL4 .....53 G4
  MOSL * OL5 .....76 E2
Dystelegh Rd *POY/DIS* SK12 .....123 M6

E

Eades St *SLFD* M6 .....86 D1
Eadington St *CHH* M8 .....72 D3
Eafield Av *MILN* OL16 .....29 J5
Eafield Cl *MILN* OL16 .....29 J5
Eafield Rd *MILN* OL16 .....28 F3

MILN OL16 .....29 H1
Eagar St *NEWH/MOS* M40 .....73 M6
Eagle Dr *SLFD* M6 .....71 K7
Eagle Mill Ct *UPML* * OL3 .....45 J7
Eagle St *BOLE* BL2 .....3 H4
  CHAD OL9 .....9 G5
  ROCH * OL11 .....11 G5
Eagley Brook Wy *BOL* BL1 .....36 C1
Eagley Brow *BOL* BL1 .....22 C6
Eagley Dr *TOT/BURYW* BL8 .....38 D3
Eagley Wy *EDGW/EG* BL7 .....22 C6
Ealand Cha *HOR/BR* BL6 .....33 J1
Ealees Rd *LIT* OL15 .....20 D7
Ealing Av *RUSH/FAL* M14 .....98 E2
Ealinger Wy *SWIN* M27 .....70 C2
Ealing Pl *BNG/LEV* * M19 .....99 K6
Eames Av *RAD* M26 .....53 K4
Earby Gv *BKLY* M9 .....73 J1
Earle Rd *BRAM/HZG* SK7 .....121 G2
Earlesfield Cl *SALE* M33 .....108 A2
Earle St *AULW* OL7 .....90 C3
Earl Rd *CHD/CHDH* SK8 .....120 A7
  HTNM SK4 .....99 M8
  RAMS BL0 .....17 B6
Earlston Av *DTN/ASHW* M34 .....100 D1
Earl St *ATH* M46 .....66 F2
  BRO M7 .....72 A8
  BURY BL9 .....5 G4
  DTN/ASHW M34 .....89 K8
  EDGY/DAV SK3 .....12 E7
  HEY OL10 .....40 F2
  MOSL OL5 .....76 E3
  PWCH M25 .....55 M8
  RAMS BL0 .....17 D6
  ROCH OL11 .....41 M4
  WGN WN1 .....47 M2
  WGNE/HIN WN2 .....48 D5
Earls Wy *FAIL* M35 .....74 A6
Earlswood Wk *BOLS/LL* BL3 .....36 C8
Earl Wk *WGTN/LGST* * M12 .....88 C7
Early Bank *STLY* SK15 .....91 M5
Early Bank Rd *HYDE* SK14 .....91 L6
  WHIT OL12 .....28 B1
Earnshaw Av *AULW* * OL7 .....75 J7
Earnshaw St *BOLS/LL* * BL3 .....51 M1
  HYDE SK14 .....93 G8
Easby Cl *CHD/CHDH* SK8 .....120 D6
  POY/DIS SK12 .....121 M7
Easby Rd *MDTN* M24 .....57 J1
Easedale Cl *URM* M41 .....95 J1
Easedale Rd *BOL* BL1 .....35 K4
East Aisle Rd *TRPK* M17 .....85 M8
East Av *BNG/LEV* M19 .....99 J5
  CHD/CHDH SK8 .....119 M4
  GOL/RIS/CU WA3 .....79 M3
  LEIGH WN7 .....81 M1
  STLY SK15 .....91 L8
  WHTF M45 .....55 H7
Eastbank St *BOL* BL1 .....36 C2
East Bond St *LEIGH* WN7 .....66 D7
Eastbourne Gv *BOL* BL1 .....35 K4
Eastbourne St *OLDS* OL8 .....59 L7
  ROCH OL11 .....10 E8
East Bridgewater St *LEIGH* 66 D8
Eastbrook Av *RAD* M26 .....38 F8
Eastburn Av *NEWH/MOS* M40 .....87 M1
East Central Dr *SWIN* M27 .....70 E5
Eastchurch Cl *FWTH* BL4 .....53 C5
Eastcombe Av *BRO* M7 .....71 L5
Eastcote Rd *RDSH* SK5 .....100 C7
Eastdale Pl *ALT* * WA14 .....108 A5
East Downs Rd *ALT* WA14 .....116 E2
  CHD/CHDH SK8 .....120 B2
East Dr *BURY* BL9 .....39 L8
  MPL/ROM SK6 .....123 H1
  SLFD M6 .....71 H7
  SWIN M27 .....70 E5
Easterdale *OLDE* OL4 .....59 M6
Eastern Av *SWIN* M27 .....71 G1
Eastern By-Pass *OP/CLY* M11 .....88 F2
Eastern Cir *BNG/LEV* M19 .....99 K6
Eastfield *SLFD* M6 .....71 H8
Eastfield Av *MDTN* M24 .....57 K5
  NEWH/MOS M40 .....88 B1
Eastfields *RAD* M26 .....38 B7
Eastford Sq *NEWH/MOS* M40 .....72 E8
Eastgarth *WGNE/HIN* WN2 .....64 E2
Eastgate *WHIT* OL12 .....18 D5
Eastgate St *AULW* OL7 .....90 D3
East Gate St *MILN* OL16 .....10 F5
East Gra *OP/CLY* M11 .....88 F1
East Gv *BRUN/LGST* M13 .....87 M7
Eastgrove Av *BOL* BL1 .....22 D6
Eastham Av *BURY* BL9 .....25 H6
  RUSH/FAL M14 .....98 E3
Eastham Wy *LHULT* M38 .....52 E7
Easthaven Av *OP/CLY* M11 .....88 F3
East Hill St *OLDE* * OL4 .....9 M7
Easthope Cl *DID/WITH* M20 .....98 E5
East Lancashire Rd
  GOL/RIS/CU WA3 .....79 L6
  RNFD/HAY WA11 .....78 A4
  TYLD M29 .....67 M7
  WALK M28 .....68 C5
Eastlands *BKLY* M9 .....57 G7
East Lea *DTN/ASHW* M34 .....101 K1
Eastleigh Av *BRO* M7 .....72 B4
Eastleigh Crs *LEIGH* WN7 .....81 L1
Eastleigh Dr *NEWH/MOS* M40 .....88 A1
Eastleigh Rd *CHD/CHDH* SK8 .....119 K3
  PWCH M25 .....72 B1
East Lynn Dr *WALK* M28 .....69 K2
East Meade *BOLS/LL* BL3 .....52 B2
  CCHDY M21 .....97 L5
  PWCH M25 .....72 A2
  SWIN M27 .....70 B2
East Moor *WALK* M28 .....68 D5
Eastmoor Dr *NEWH/MOS* M40 .....74 A8
Eastmoor Gv *WHTN* BL5 .....51 L2
East Mt *WGNW/BIL/O* WN5 .....46 C6
East Newton St *ANC* * M4 .....7 M1
Easton Cl *MDTN* M24 .....57 M5
Easton Dr *CHD/CHDH* SK8 .....111 K7
Easton Rd *DROY* M43 .....89 H2
East Ordsall La *ORD* M5 .....6 A5
Eastover *MPL/ROM* SK6 .....113 K4
East Park Cl *BRUN/LGST* M13 .....87 M6
Eastpark Cl *BRUN/LGST* M13 .....87 M6
East Philip St *CSLFD* M3 .....87 H1
East Rd *BOL* BL1 .....22 B8
  MANAIR M90 .....118 E5
  STLY SK15 .....77 H6
  STRET M32 .....85 L8
  WGTN/LGST M12 .....99 K1
Eastry Av *RDSH* SK5 .....100 E7
East St *AIMK* WN4 .....64 A8
  ATH M46 .....67 J3

  AUL OL6 .....76 A8
  BOLS/LL BL3 .....5 G6
  DTN/ASHW M34 .....90 C6
  LIT OL15 .....20 D7
  MILN OL16 .....11 G2
  MILN OL16 .....29 G5
  RAD M26 .....54 E1
  WGNE/HIN WN2 .....65 L1
  WHIT OL12 .....19 K6
East V *MPL/ROM* SK6 .....114 D7
Eastville Gdns *BNG/LEV* M19 .....99 H7
East Vw *MDTN* M24 .....57 J4
  RAMS BL0 .....17 B3
  RAMS BL0 .....24 F1
East Wk *EDGW/EG* BL7 .....22 A2
Eastward Av *WILM/AE* SK9 .....126 D6
East Wy *BOL* BL1 .....36 E1
Eastway *MDTN* M24 .....57 J3
  ROY/SHW OL2 .....43 L6
  SALE M33 .....108 C3
  URM M41 .....95 H1
Eastwell Rd *AIMK* WN4 .....78 D1
Eastwood Av *DROY* M43 .....89 H3
  NEWH/MOS M40 .....74 A2
  WALK M28 .....96 A2
  WALK M28 .....68 D1
Eastwood Cl *BURY* BL9 .....5 K4
Eastwood Dr *BOLS/LL* BL3 .....51 K1
Eastwood Gv *LEIGH* WN7 .....65 M7
Eastwood Rd *NEWH/MOS* M40 .....74 C3
Eastwood St *DTN/ASHW* M34 .....90 A5
  WALK M28 .....20 C7
Eastwood Ter *BOL* BL1 .....35 J4
Eatock Rd *WGNE/HIN* WN2 .....64 E1
Eatock Wy *WHTN* BL5 .....50 A6
Eaton Cl *CHD/CHDH* SK8 .....120 B1
  DUK SK16 .....90 F6
  POY/DIS SK12 .....129 L1
Eaton Dr *AULW* OL7 .....75 J8
  HALE/TIMP WA15 .....108 D4
  WILM/AE SK9 .....130 C2
Eaton Rd *ALT* WA14 .....116 E3
  CHH M8 .....72 C3
  SALE M33 .....96 D8
Eaton St *WGNE/HIN* WN2 .....49 H6
Eaves Knoll Rd *NM/HAY* SK22 .....124 C5
Eaves La *CHAD* OL9 .....58 D7
Ebbdale Cl *STKP* SK1 .....13 H5
Ebberstone St *RUSH/FAL* M14 .....98 D2
Ebden St *CMANE* * M1 .....7 J7
Ebenezer St *GLSP* SK13 .....104 F5
  HULME M15 .....6 F9
Ebor Cl *ROY/SHW* OL2 .....43 K4
Ebor Rd *WYTH/NTH* * M22 .....110 B8
Ebor St *LIT* OL15 .....20 D7
Ebsworth St *NEWH/MOS* M40 .....73 J4
Ebury St *RAD* M26 .....38 C8
Eccles Bridge Rd *MPL/ROM* SK6 .....114 C7
Eccles Cl *OP/CLY* M11 .....88 E3
Eccleshall St *OP/CLY* M11 .....88 E3
Eccles New Rd *ORD* M5 .....86 D2
Eccles Old Rd *SLFD* M6 .....85 M1
Eccles Rd *SWIN* M27 .....70 C6
  WGNW/BIL/O WN5 .....17 B6
Eccleston Av *BOLE* BL2 .....36 E3
  SWIN M27 .....70 A6
Eccleston Cl *TOT/BURYW* BL8 .....38 D3
Eccleston Pl *BRO* * M7 .....72 A4
Eccleston Rd *EDGY/DAV* SK3 .....112 B8
Eccleston St *FAIL* * M35 .....74 D4
  WGN WN1 .....15 G1
Eccups La *WILM/AE* SK9 .....126 A4
Echo St *CMANE* M1 .....7 J7
Eckersall Rd *WGNE/HIN* WN2 .....65 G1
Eckersley Cl *NTHM/RTH* M23 .....109 J6
Eckersley Fold La *ATH* M46 .....66 D3
Eckersley Rd *BOL* BL1 .....36 B1
Eckersley St *BOLS/LL* BL3 .....35 M8
  WGN WN1 .....15 K1
Eckford St *CHH* M8 .....72 E6
Eclipse Cl *MILN* OL16 .....11 L4
Edale Av *DTN/ASHW* M34 .....90 A5
  DTN/ASHW M34 .....101 J4
  NEWH/MOS M40 .....73 K4
  RDSH SK5 .....100 D3
  URM M41 .....95 J3
Edale Cl *ALT* WA14 .....116 E3
  ATH M46 .....66 F1
  BRAM/HZG SK7 .....122 A3
  CHD/CHDH SK8 .....119 M5
  IRL M44 .....94 D5
Edale Crs *GLSP* SK13 .....104 B3
Edale Dr *WGNNW/ST* WN6 .....31 H2
Edale Gv *AUL* OL6 .....76 D6
  SALE M33 .....108 B2
Edale Rd *BOLS/LL* * BL3 .....35 K8
  FWTH BL4 .....52 F5
  LEIGH WN7 .....66 E8
  STRET M32 .....96 E1
Edale St *SLFD* M6 .....71 L7
Edbrook Wk *BRUN/LGST* * M13 .....88 A7
Eddie Colman Cl
  NEWH/MOS * M40 .....73 L7
Eddisbury Av *DID/WITH* M20 .....98 C4
  URM M41 .....84 A8
Eddisford Dr *GOL/RIS/CU* WA3 .....81 G7
Edditch Gv *BOLE* BL2 .....3 M5
Eddleston St *AIMK* WN4 .....63 J6
Eddystone Cl *ORD* M5 .....87 G2
Eden Av *BOL* BL1 .....36 B1
  GOL/RIS/CU WA3 .....81 M8
  MPL/ROM SK6 .....123 G5
  RAMS BL0 .....17 D2
Eden Bank *LEIGH* WN7 .....66 E6
Edenbridge Dr *RAD* M26 .....53 L5
Edenbridge Rd *CHD/CHDH* SK8 .....111 L8
  NEWH/MOS M40 .....73 L8
Eden Cl *HEY* OL10 .....40 D1
  HULME M15 .....87 J6
  STKP SK1 .....13 L6
  WILM/AE SK9 .....127 G7
Eden Ct *RAMS* BL0 .....17 D2
Edendale Dr *WYTH/NTH* M22 .....118 F3
Enfield La *WALK* M28 .....69 J8
Enfield Rd *PWCH* M25 .....72 B1
  ROCH OL11 .....27 K5
  ROCH OL11 .....27 K3
Enfield St *WHIT* OL12 .....19 K6
Eden Gv *BOL* BL1 .....36 B1
Edenhall Av *BNG/LEV* M19 .....99 J4
Edenhurst Dr
  HALE/TIMP WA15 .....108 E7
Edenhurst Rd *OFTN* SK2 .....112 E6
Eden Pl *CHD/CHDH* SK8 .....111 G6
Eden St *WGNNW/ST* WN6 .....31 K8
Edensor Dr *HALE/TIMP* WA15 .....117 L1
Eden St *BOL* BL1 .....36 B1

  BURY BL9 .....4 F3
  OLD OL1 .....9 G2
  RAMS BL0 .....17 D3
  WHIT OL12 .....19 L8
Edenvale *WALK* M28 .....68 D5
Eden Wy *ROY/SHW* OL2 .....43 K4
Edgar St *BOLS/LL* BL3 .....2 D7
  MILN OL16 .....28 F2
  RAMS BL0 .....17 B7
Edgar St West *RAMS* BL0 .....17 B7
Edgbaston Dr *OLDTF/WHR* M16 .....97 K1
Edgedale Av *BNG/LEV* M19 .....99 H7
Edgefield Av *BKLY* M9 .....57 H8
Edge Fold *FWTH* BL4 .....51 M3
Edge Fold Crs *WALK* M28 .....69 G4
Edge Fold Rd *WALK* M28 .....69 G3
Edge Gn *WALK* * M28 .....68 F4
Edge Green La *GOL/RIS/CU* WA3 .....79 J2
Edge Green Rd
  GOL/RIS/CU WA3 .....79 J3
Edge Green St *AIMK* WN4 .....64 A8
Edge Hall Rd *WGNW/BIL/O* WN5 .....46 B8
Edge Hill Av *ROY/SHW* OL2 .....59 H2
Edgehill Cha *WILM/AE* SK9 .....127 J5
Edgehill Cl *SLFD* M6 .....86 C2
  ROY/SHW OL2 .....59 H1
Edgehill Rd *SLFD* M6 .....85 M1
Edgehill St *ANC* * M4 .....7 H3
Edge La *EDGW/EG* BL7 .....16 A4
  HYDE SK14 .....92 B8
  OP/CLY M11 .....89 G2
  STRET M32 .....97 H3
Edge Lane Rd *OLD* OL1 .....9 K2
Edge Lane St *ROY/SHW* OL2 .....43 H8
Edgeley Fold *EDGY/DAV* SK3 .....12 D9
Edgeley Rd *EDGY/DAV* SK3 .....12 C5
  URM M41 .....95 K4
Edgemoor *ALT* WA14 .....116 C2
Edgemoor Cl *OLDE* OL4 .....60 A3
  RAD M26 .....38 B7
Edgemoor Dr *ROCH* OL11 .....27 J7
Edgerley Pl *AIMK* WN4 .....78 D1
Edgerton Rd *GOL/RIS/CU* WA3 .....80 B4
Edge St *ANC* M4 .....7 H3
Edge Vw *OLD* OL1 .....58 B3
Edgeware Av *PWCH* M25 .....56 C8
Edgeware Gv *WGNS/IIMK* WN3 .....63 C1
Edgeware Rd *CHAD* OL9 .....74 B1
  ECC M30 .....69 K8
Edgewater *ORD* M5 .....86 A2
Edgeway *WILM/AE* SK9 .....126 F7
Edgeway Rd *WGNS/IIMK* WN3 .....30 D7
Edgeworth Av *BOLE* BL2 .....38 A3
Edgeworth Dr *RUSH/FAL* M14 .....99 H5
Edgeworth Rd *GOL/RIS/CU* WA3 .....79 J3
  WGNE/HIN WN2 .....65 K1
Edgeworth V *EDGW/EG* BL7 .....16 E6
Edgmont Av *BOLS/LL* BL3 .....36 A8
Edgware Rd *NEWH/MOS* M40 .....73 L8
Edgworth Cl *HEY* OL10 .....40 D2
Edgworth Dr *TOT/BURYW* BL8 .....38 D3
Edilom Rd *CHH* M8 .....72 A6
Edinburgh Cl *CHD/CHDH* SK8 .....111 J6
  WGNE/HIN WN2 .....48 B7
Edinburgh Dr *MPL/ROM* SK6 .....101 M8
  WGNE/HIN WN2 .....65 L1
  WGNW/BIL/O WN5 .....47 G7
Edinburgh Rd *BOLS/LL* BL3 .....53 K2
Edinburgh Sq *NEWH/MOS* M40 .....73 C8
Edinburgh Wy *ROCH* OL11 .....28 A8
Edington *WHIT* OL12 .....10 D2
Edison Rd *ECC* M30 .....84 F4
Edison St *WGTN/LGST* * M12 .....7 M7
Edison St *OP/CLY* M11 .....89 H5
Edith Av *RUSH/FAL* M14 .....98 D2
Edith Cavell Cl *OP/CLY* M11 .....88 F3
Edith St *BOL* BL1 .....35 M6
  FWTH BL4 .....53 C5
  OLDS OL8 .....75 J1
  WGNS/IIMK WN3 .....14 D5
Edlin Cl *WGTN/LGST* M12 .....7 K6
Edlingham *ROCH* OL11 .....10 C7
Edmonds St *MDTN* M24 .....57 L3
Edmonton Rd *EDGY/DAV* SK3 .....112 D8
  NEWH/MOS M40 .....73 K8
Edmund Cl *HTNM* SK4 .....112 B1
Edmund Dr *LEIGH* WN7 .....65 M7
Edmunds Ct *BOLS/LL* BL3 .....2 B7
Edmunds Fold *LIT* OL15 .....20 A6
Edmund St *CSLFD* * M3 .....6 C3
  DROY M43 .....89 K4
  FAIL * M35 .....74 C4
  RAD * M26 .....38 F8
  ROY/SHW OL2 .....43 M5
  SLFD M6 .....71 H7
  WHIT OL12 .....10 C2
Edna Rd *LEIGH* WN7 .....65 M5
Edna St *HYDE* SK14 .....102 A2
Edridge Wy *WGNE/HIN* WN2 .....48 F8
Edson Rd *CHH* M8 .....72 C1
Edstone Cl *BOLS/LL* BL3 .....36 D8
Edward Av *CCHDY* M21 .....97 J5
  GOL/RIS/CU WA3 .....79 H2
  SLFD M6 .....85 M1
Edward Charlton Rd
  OLDTF/WHR M16 .....97 L2
Edward Ct *ALT* WA14 .....107 L5
Edward Dr *AIMK* WN4 .....63 L8
Edward Ms *CHAD* OL9 .....8 D8
Edward Rd *BKLY* M9 .....57 G7
  ROY/SHW OL2 .....43 K6
Edwards Cl *MPL/ROM* SK6 .....114 B7
Edwards Dr *WHTF* M45 .....55 L4
Edward St *AUL* OL6 .....91 H2
  BKLY M9 .....73 H4
  BOLS/LL BL3 .....2 A8
  BRO M7 .....72 B8
  BURY BL9 .....5 H6
  CHAD OL9 .....8 D5
  CHAD OL9 .....58 D5
  DROY * M43 .....89 K4
  DTN/ASHW M34 .....90 A5
  DTN/ASHW M34 .....90 C8
  DUK SK16 .....90 F6
  FWTH BL4 .....52 E2
  GLSP SK13 .....104 F3
  HOR/BR BL6 .....33 K1
  HYDE SK14 .....101 M1
  LEIGH WN7 .....66 D8
  MDTN M24 .....57 L2
  MILN OL16 .....11 J8
  MPL/ROM SK6 .....114 D3
  PWCH M25 .....71 M2
  RAD M26 .....53 L4
  RAD M26 .....54 E2
  SALE M33 .....97 H8
  STKP SK1 .....13 J6

  WGN WN1 .....15 M4
  WGN WN1 .....47 M2
  WHIT OL12 .....18 E2
  WHIT OL12 .....19 L8
  WHTN BL5 .....50 B8
Edwards Wy *MPL/ROM* SK6 .....114 B7
Edwin Rd *OP/CLY* M11 .....88 B3
Edwin St *BURY* BL9 .....4 F5
  WGN WN1 .....15 K5
Eeasbrook *URM* M41 .....96 A3
Egbert St *NEWH/MOS* M40 .....73 L5
Egerton Ct *WALK* * M28 .....69 K4
Egerton Crs *DID/WITH* * M20 .....98 E5
Egerton Dr *SALE* M33 .....96 E7
Egerton Gv *WALK* M28 .....69 C1
Egerton Ldg *EDGW/EG* BL7 .....22 B3
Egerton Ms *DROY* * M43 .....89 K4
  RUSH/FAL M14 .....99 C4
Egerton Moss
  HALE/TIMP WA15 .....117 C7
Egerton Pk *WALK* M28 .....69 L5
Egerton Pl *ROY/SHW* OL2 .....43 K6
Egerton Rd *ECC* M30 .....70 A8
  EDGY/DAV SK3 .....112 D8
  HALE/TIMP WA15 .....117 J1
  RUSH/FAL M14 .....99 C4
  WALK M28 .....69 L5
  WHTF M45 .....55 J5
  WILM/AE SK9 .....126 F4
Egerton Rd North *CCHDY* M21 .....97 M3
  HTNM SK4 .....99 M7
Egerton Rd South *CCHDY* M21 .....97 M4
  HTNM SK4 .....99 M7
Egerton St *AUL* OL6 .....90 F1
  CSLFD M3 .....6 B8
  DROY M43 .....89 L3
  DTN/ASHW M34 .....90 A7
  ECC M30 .....84 C2
  FWTH BL4 .....52 F3
  HEY OL10 .....40 F3
  HULME M15 .....6 B8
  LIT OL15 .....20 D7
  MDTN * M24 .....56 F5
  MOSL OL5 .....76 F2
  OLD OL1 .....9 K4
  PWCH M25 .....55 M8
  WGNE/HIN WN2 .....64 E5
Egerton V *EDGW/EG* BL7 .....22 A2
Eggar Ct *TYLD* M29 .....67 L5
Eggington St *NEWH/MOS* M40 .....72 F7
Egham Ct *BOLE* * BL2 .....3 J1
Egham St *CHH* M8 .....72 D4
Egmont St *MOSL* OL5 .....77 C4
  SLFD M6 .....71 H6
Egremont Av *DID/WITH* M20 .....98 D5
Egremont Cl *WHTF* M45 .....55 K3
Egremont Ct *BRO* * M7 .....71 M4
Egremont Gv *EDGY/DAV* SK3 .....12 A6
Egremont Rd *MILN* OL16 .....29 H8
Egret Dr *IRL* * M44 .....94 D1
Egyptian St *BOL* BL1 .....2 E1
Egypt La *PWCH* M25 .....56 A3
Ehlinger Av *GLSP* SK13 .....93 K7
Eida Wy *TRPK* M17 .....85 M4
Eight Acre *WHTF* M45 .....54 F5
Eighth Av *OLDS* OL8 .....75 G3
Eighth St *TRPK* M17 .....85 M6
Eileen Gv *RUSH/FAL* M14 .....98 F2
Eileen Gv West *RUSH/FAL* M14 .....98 E2
Elaine Av *BKLY* M9 .....73 L2
Elaine Cl *AIMK* WN4 .....64 A7
Elbe St *WGTN/LGST* * M12 .....7 M7
Elbow La *ROCH* OL11 .....11 G6
Elbow St *BNG/LEV* M19 .....99 K3
Elbut La *BURY* BL9 .....26 C7
Elcho Ct *ALT* * WA14 .....116 D2
Elcho Rd *ALT* WA14 .....116 D1
Elcombe Av *GOL/RIS/CU* WA3 .....80 B5
Elcot Cl *NEWH/MOS* * M40 .....72 F7
  WGN WN1 .....15 L8
Elderberry Cl *UPML* OL3 .....45 M7
Elderberry Wy *WILM/AE* SK9 .....127 J4
Elder Cl *OFTN* SK2 .....113 C4
Eldercot Gv *BOLS/LL* BL3 .....35 K8
Eldercot Rd *BOLS/LL* BL3 .....35 K8
Eldercroft Rd
  HALE/TIMP WA15 .....108 F7
Elderfield Dr *MPL/ROM* SK6 .....101 J8
Elder Gv *NEWH/MOS* M40 .....74 C2
Eldermount Rd *BKLY* M9 .....73 C2
Elder Rd *OLDE* OL4 .....60 B6
Elder St *MILN* OL16 .....11 J8
Elderwood *CHAD* OL9 .....58 B5
Eldon Cl *DTN/ASHW* M34 .....90 B5
Eldon Gdns *AIMK* WN4 .....63 K6
Eldon Pl *ECC* M30 .....84 F3
Eldon Prec *OLDS* OL8 .....9 H8
Eldon Rd *EDGY/DAV* SK3 .....12 D4
  IRL M44 .....94 D2
Eldon St *BOLE* BL2 .....36 E3
  BURY BL9 .....4 F1
  LEIGH WN7 .....66 A6
  OLDS OL8 .....9 J8
Eldon Street Est *OLDS* OL8 .....9 J8
Eldridge Dr *NEWH/MOS* M40 .....73 K7
Eleanor Rd *CCHDY* M21 .....97 J5
  ROY/SHW OL2 .....59 H2
Eleanor St *BOL* BL1 .....22 D7
  OLD OL1 .....8 F2
  WGNS/IIMK WN3 .....14 C5
Electo St *OP/CLY* M11 .....89 H5
Elevator Rd *TRPK* M17 .....86 B6
Eleventh St *TRPK* M17 .....86 A6
Elf Mill Cl *EDGY/DAV* SK3 .....112 B6
Elford Gv *GTN* M18 .....89 K8
Elgar St *WGTN/LGST* M12 .....99 K1
Elgin Av *AIMK* WN4 .....64 C8
  DID/WITH * M20 .....111 G1
Elgin Cl *WGNE/HIN* WN2 .....48 D4
Elgin Dr *SALE* M33 .....109 H1
Elgin Rd *DUK* SK16 .....90 F6
  OLDE OL4 .....59 L6
Elgin St *AULW* OL7 .....75 K8
  BOL BL1 .....35 M2
  STLY SK15 .....91 L3
Elgol Cl *EDGY/DAV* SK3 .....112 C7
Elgol Dr *BOLS/LL* BL3 .....35 H7
Elham Cl *RAD* M26 .....53 M5
Elim St *LIT* OL15 .....20 D5
Eliot Dr *WGNS/IIMK* WN3 .....47 K7
Eliot Rd *ECC* M30 .....85 C3
Eli St *CHAD* OL9 .....74 D1
Eliza Ann St *ECC* M30 .....84 F3
  NEWH/MOS M40 .....72 F8
Elizabethan Dr *WGNS/IIMK* WN3 .....48 B3
Elizabethan Wy *MILN* OL16 .....29 H6
Elizabeth Av *CHAD* OL9 .....74 D1
  DTN/ASHW M34 .....90 B7

POY/DIS SK12 .....123 M7
ROY/SHW OL2 .....58 F1
STKP SK1 .....13 K7
WGNE/HIN WN2 .....65 H3
Elizabeth Cl STRET M32 .....97 G2
Elizabeth St SK4 .....12 C2
RUSH/FAL M14 .....99 G5
Elizabeth Gv ROY/SHW OL2 .....43 L6
Elizabeth Rd PART M31 .....94 C8
RNFD/HAY WA11 .....78 B5
Elizabeth Slinger Rd
DID/WITH M20 .....98 B8
Elizabeth St ATH M46 .....67 G1
AUL OL6 .....75 L8
CHH M8 .....72 C6
DTN/ASHW M34 .....101 G1
HEY OL10 .....40 F2
HYDE SK14 .....102 A1
LEIGH WN7 .....81 L1
RAD M26 .....54 D1
RAMS * BL0 .....17 D1
ROCH OL11 .....41 M1
SWIN M27 .....70 C3
WGNE/HIN WN2 .....48 D4
WHTF M45 .....55 J5
Eliza St HULME M15 .....87 H6
RAMS BL0 .....17 D6
Elkanagh Gdns SLFD M6 .....86 C1
Elkstone Av LHULT M38 .....52 D6
Elkstone Cl WGNS/IIMK WN3 .....62 F2
Elkwood Cl WGN WN1 .....31 L8
Ellanby Cl RUSH/FAL M14 .....98 E1
Elland Cl BURY BL9 .....55 L2
WHTN BL5 .....50 A1
Ellastone Dr URM * M41 .....96 A2
Ellastone Rd SLFD M6 .....70 F8
Ellbourne Rd BKLY M9 .....73 J2
Ellenbrook Cl WGTN/LGST M12 .....88 E6
Ellenbrook Rd WALK M28 .....68 C5
Ellen Brook Rd
WYTH/NTH M22 .....118 F4
Ellendale Gra WALK M28 .....68 E4
Ellen Gv FWTH BL4 .....53 M8
Ellenhall Cl BKLY M9 .....73 G4
Ellenor Dr TYLD M29 .....67 M5
Ellenroad Ap MILN OL16 .....29 K8
Ellenroad St MILN OL16 .....29 K8
Ellenrod Dr WHIT OL12 .....27 K2
Ellenrod La WHIT OL12 .....27 K2
Ellenshaw Cl WHIT OL12 .....27 K2
Ellen St BOL BL1 .....35 M1
CHAD OL9 .....8 D2
DROY M43 .....89 L4
HTNM SK4 .....112 A1
WGN WN1 .....15 H5
Ellen Wilkinson Crs
WGTN/LGST M12 .....88 D7
Elleray Cl BOLS/LL BL3 .....53 M1
Elleray Rd MDTN M24 .....57 J7
SLFD M6 .....71 G7
Ellerbeck Cl BOLE BL2 .....22 E7
Ellerbeck Crs WALK M28 .....68 F5
Ellerby Av SWIN M27 .....70 D1
Ellerscroft * SK22 .....125 G3
Ellesmere Av AUL OL6 .....75 M5
ECC M30 .....85 H2
MPL/ROM SK6 .....114 C6
WALK M28 .....68 F1
Ellesmere Cir URM M41 .....85 G5
Ellesmere Cl DUK SK16 .....91 H5
Ellesmere Dr CHD/CHDH SK8 .....111 K7
Ellesmere Gdns BOLS/LL BL3 .....52 A1
Ellesmere Rd AIMK WN4 .....63 J7
ALT WA14 .....108 A6
BOLS/LL BL3 .....51 M1
CCHDY M21 .....97 M3
ECC M30 .....70 B8
EDGY/DAV SK3 .....111 K5
GOL/RIS/CU WA3 .....79 L3
WGNW/BIL/O WN5 .....47 G6
Ellesmere Rd North HTNM SK4 .....99 M7
Ellesmere Rd South CCHDY M21 .....97 M4
Ellesmere St BOLS/LL BL3 .....2 A7
ECC M30 .....85 G3
FAIL M35 .....74 C4
FWTH BL4 .....53 C4
HULME M15 .....6 A9
LEIGH WN7 .....66 C8
LHULT M38 .....68 F1
ROCH OL11 .....10 E8
SWIN M27 .....70 A5
SWIN M27 .....70 D3
TYLD M29 .....67 K3
TYLD M29 .....67 M7
Ellesmere Ter RUSH/FAL M14 .....99 G5
Ellingham Cl OP/CLY M11 .....88 C3
Elliot Sq OLD OL1 .....9 M3
Elliot St BOL BL1 .....35 M1
OLDE OL4 .....60 B6
Elliott Av GOL/RIS/CU WA3 .....79 L3
HYDE SK14 .....91 G7
Elliott Dr SALE M33 .....96 B8
WGNE/HIN WN2 .....49 G5
Elliott St FWTH BL4 .....52 F5
TYLD M29 .....67 H4
WHIT OL12 .....11 G2
Ellis Crs WALK M28 .....68 E1
Ellis Dr CHH M8 .....72 E1
Ellis Fold WHIT OL12 .....27 H2
Ellis La MDTN M24 .....56 E4
Ellison Cl HYDE SK14 .....93 G7
Ellison St GLSP SK13 .....105 G3
Ellis Rd WGNW/BIL/O WN5 .....62 A8
Ellis St BOLS/LL BL3 .....2 B9
BRO M7 .....87 H6
HULME M15 .....87 H6
HYDE SK14 .....102 C2
TOT/BURYW BL8 .....38 E2
WGN WN1 .....15 K1
Elliston Sq WGTN/LGST M12 .....88 D7
Ellonby Ri HOR/BR BL6 .....34 F7
Ellor St SLFD M6 .....86 C1
Ellwood Rd STKP SK1 .....112 E3
Elly Clough ROY/SHW * OL2 .....58 F1
Elm Av AIMK WN4 .....63 G2
GOL/RIS/CU WA3 .....79 K3
RAD M26 .....54 C4
WGNNW/ST WN6 .....31 J4
WGNW/BIL/O WN5 .....47 H6
Elmbank AV DID/WITH M20 .....98 B8
Elmbank Rd MDTN M24 .....57 M4
Elmbridge Wk HULME * M15 .....87 K6
Elm Cl HYDE SK14 .....92 D8
POY/DIS SK12 .....129 K1
Elm Crs WALK M28 .....69 K5
WILM/AE SK9 .....130 E2
Elm Cft WGN WN1 .....31 L8
Elmdale Av CHD/CHDH SK8 .....119 K2
Elmdale Wk HULME * M15 .....87 K6
Elm Dr DTN/ASHW M34 .....90 A7

STRET M32 .....96 E3
WGNW/BIL/O WN5 .....62 A7
Elmfield WGNNW/ST WN6 .....30 E6
Elmfield Av ATH M46 .....50 E8
WYTH/NTH M22 .....110 B4
Elmfield Dr MPL/ROM SK6 .....114 B6
Elmfield Rd DTN/ASHW M34 .....89 M4
EDGY/DAV SK3 .....112 C7
WGN WN1 .....31 L7
WILM/AE SK9 .....130 E2
Elmfield St BOL BL1 .....36 C2
CHH M8 .....72 D6
Elmgate Gv BNG/LEV M19 .....99 K3
Elm Gv AUL OL6 .....75 M7
DID/WITH M20 .....110 E1
DROY M43 .....89 J8
EDGW/EG BL7 .....22 D4
FWTH BL4 .....52 E4
GLSP SK13 .....104 E2
HYDE SK14 .....102 C2
MILN OL16 .....43 K1
OLDE OL4 .....60 B8
PWCH M25 .....55 K6
ROCH OL11 .....10 D9
SALE M33 .....96 E6
URM M41 .....96 B2
WALK M28 .....69 L3
WHIT OL12 .....19 K7
WILM/AE SK9 .....130 E2
Elm Gv BOL * BL1 .....2 D1
Elmham Wk NEWH/MOS M40 .....72 F8
Elmhow Gv WGNS/IIMK WN3 .....63 K2
Elmhurst Dr BNG/LEV M19 .....99 J7
Elmley Cl OFTN SK2 .....113 K7
Elmore Wd LIT OL15 .....19 M6
Elmpark Ga WHIT OL12 .....27 L1
Elmpark Gv WHIT OL12 .....27 L1
Elmpark V WHIT OL12 .....27 L1
Elmpark Vw WHIT OL12 .....27 L1
Elmpark Wy WHIT OL12 .....27 L1
Elm Rd BOLS/LL BL3 .....53 L2
CHD/CHDH SK8 .....110 D7
DID/WITH M20 .....98 D8
FWTH BL4 .....53 J7
HALE/TIMP WA15 .....117 G1
HTNM SK4 .....99 H5
OLDS OL8 .....75 G3
RNFD/HAY * WA11 .....78 B5
WGNE/HIN WN2 .....64 F5
WHTN BL5 .....50 B5
Elm Rd South EDGY/DAV SK3 .....111 K5
The Elms GOL/RIS/CU WA3 .....80 C5
LIT OL15 .....19 M8
MOSL * OL5 .....76 E3
Elmsbury Wk AIMK WN4 .....63 J7
Elms Cl WHTF M45 .....55 J7
Elmscott Wk BRUN/LGST M13 .....88 A7
Elmsdale Av BKLY M9 .....57 G7
Elmsfield Av ROCH OL11 .....27 H3
Elmsleigh Rd CHD/CHDH SK8 .....119 J3
Elmsmere Rd DID/WITH M20 .....111 G1
Elmsworth Av BNG/LEV M19 .....99 L3
Elms Rd HTNM SK4 .....99 L7
STLY SK15 .....92 A1
WHTF M45 .....55 J3
Elms St WHTF M45 .....55 H3
Elmstead Av DID/WITH M20 .....98 D6
Elmstone Cl CHD/CHDH SK8 .....120 D1
Elmstone Gv BOL * BL1 .....2 E1
Elm St BURY BL9 .....5 K5
ECC M30 .....85 G3
FAIL M35 .....74 C4
FWTH BL4 .....53 C3
HEY OL10 .....41 G2
LEIGH WN7 .....81 J1
MDTN M24 .....57 M4
MPL/ROM SK6 .....101 J8
RAMS * BL0 .....17 D6
RAMS BL0 .....17 E1
SWIN M27 .....70 B3
TYLD * M29 .....67 K3
WGNE/HIN WN2 .....64 D2
WHIT OL12 .....18 E2
WHIT OL12 .....28 C3
Elmsway BRAM/HZG SK7 .....120 E5
HALE/TIMP WA15 .....117 K4
MPL/ROM SK6 .....123 C6
Elmswood OLD OL1 .....44 A8
Elmswood Av RUSH/FAL M14 .....98 C2
Elmswood Dr HYDE * SK14 .....102 B5
Elmsworth Av BNG/LEV M19 .....99 L3
Elmwood Gv BKLY M9 .....73 J5
BOL * BL1 .....35 M4
Elmwood OLD OL1 .....44 A8
Elmwood Av AIMK WN4 .....78 D2
Elmwood Cl WHTN BL5 .....51 K6
Elmwood Dr ROY/SHW OL2 .....42 F7
Elmwood Gv BKLY M9 .....73 J5
Elinup Av WGNNW/ST WN6 .....30 E6
Elsa Rd BNG/LEV M19 .....99 M3
Elsdon Dr ATH M46 .....51 H8
GTN M18 .....89 G6
Elsdon Gdns BOLE BL2 .....36 E3
Elsdon Rd BRUN/LGST M13 .....99 J2
Elsfield Cl BOL * BL1 .....36 A2
Elsham Cl BOL BL1 .....22 B7
Elsham Dr WALK M28 .....68 E1
Elsham Gdns GTN M18 .....88 E8
Elsie St BKLY M9 .....73 H4
FWTH BL4 .....52 F4
RAMS * BL0 .....17 A8
Elsinore Av IRL M44 .....94 C3
Elsinore Cl FAIL M35 .....74 E5
Elsinore Rd OLDTF/WHR M16 .....86 F4
Elsinore St BOLE BL2 .....36 E1
Elsma Rd NEWH/MOS M40 .....74 B8
Elsmore Rd RUSH/FAL M14 .....98 C3
Elson St TOT/BURYW BL8 .....24 E8
Elstead Gv AIMK WN4 .....63 G8
Elsted Rd OLDE OL4 .....61 H7
Elston Av NEWLW WA12 .....78 A3
Elstree Av NEWH/MOS M40 .....73 L8
Elstree Gv EDGY/DAV SK3 .....12 B7
Elswick Av BOLS/LL BL3 .....35 L7
BRAM/HZG SK7 .....121 C5
CCHDY M21 .....97 L4
Elsworth Dr BOL BL1 .....22 C8
Elsworth St CSLFD M3 .....87 H5
Eltham Av OFTN * SK2 .....112 F7
Eltham Cl AIMK WN4 .....79 G1

Eltham Dr URM M41 .....84 F8
Eltham St BNG/LEV M19 .....99 K2
Elton Av BNG/LEV M19 .....99 K4
Elton Cl GOL/RIS/CU WA3 .....80 B5
WHTF M45 .....55 K4
WILM/AE SK9 .....127 J3
Elton Dr BRAM/HZG SK7 .....121 M4
Elton Rd SALE M33 .....108 A2
Elton St BOLE BL2 .....3 H4
BRO M7 .....87 G1
ROCH OL11 .....41 M3
STRET M32 .....86 C7
Elton's Yd BRO M7 .....87 G1
Elton Vale Rd TOT/BURYW BL8 .....38 E2
Elvate Crs CHH M8 .....72 B7
Elverdon Cl HULME M15 .....87 H7
Elverston St WYTH/NTH M22 .....110 B3
Elverston Wy CHAD OL9 .....8 C3
Elvey St NEWH/MOS M40 .....73 J7
Elvington Cr WGNW/BIL/O WN5 .....46 E3
Elvington Crs WALK M28 .....68 F4
Elway Rd AIMK WN4 .....78 F1
Elwick Cl OLDTF/WHR M16 .....98 C1
Elworthy Gv WGN WN1 .....48 B2
Elwyn Av WYTH/NTH M22 .....110 A5
Ely Av STRET M32 .....96 C1
Ely Cl WALK M28 .....68 E4
Ely Crs FAIL M35 .....74 C7
Ely Dr TOT/BURYW BL8 .....4 C1
TYLD M29 .....67 M5
Ely Gv BOL * BL1 .....2 D1
Elysian St OP/CLY M11 .....88 F4
Elyst Chad OL9 .....8 B9
Ember St OP/CLY M11 .....89 G2
Emblem St BOLS/LL BL3 .....2 B8
Embleton Cl BOLE BL2 .....37 H3
Embsay Cl BOL BL1 .....22 A7
Emerald Av LEIGH WN7 .....66 B8
Emerald Rd WYTH/NTH M22 .....119 H5
Emerald St BOL BL1 .....36 C1
DTN/ASHW M34 .....101 H1
WGNNW/ST WN6 .....47 K1
Emerson Av ECC M30 .....85 K1
Emerson Dr MDTN M24 .....57 J3
Emerson St ORD M5 .....86 A2
Emery Av CCHDY M21 .....97 M6
Emery Cl ALT WA14 .....108 A5
HTNM SK4 .....99 K8
Emily Beavan Cl OP/CLY M11 .....88 E3
Emily Pl DROY M43 .....89 J3
Emley St BNG/LEV M19 .....99 L3
Emlyn Gv CHD/CHDH SK8 .....111 K6
Emlyn St FWTH BL4 .....52 F3
SWIN M27 .....70 A4
WALK M28 .....69 G1
WGNE/HIN WN2 .....48 F7
Emmanuel Cl BOLS/LL * BL3 .....2 B8
Emmanuel Pl BOLS/LL BL3 .....2 B8
Emma St OLDS OL8 .....75 J1
WHIT OL12 .....10 C2
Emmett St HOR/BR BL6 .....33 L1
Emmett St East
NEWH/MOS M40 .....73 H7
Emmott Cl HEY OL10 .....40 F2
Emmott Wy OLD OL1 .....9 H3
Emperor St STKP SK1 .....13 L2
Empire Rd BOLE BL2 .....37 G4
DUK SK16 .....90 F6
Empire St CSLFD M3 .....6 D1
Empress Av MPL/ROM SK6 .....114 C7
Empress Dr HTNM SK4 .....100 A8
LEIGH WN7 .....67 H6
Empress St BOL * BL1 .....35 L3
CHH M8 .....72 C4
OLDTF/WHR M16 .....86 F6
Emsworth Dr SALE M33 .....108 F3
Ena Crs LEIGH WN7 .....65 M5
Ena St BOLS/LL BL3 .....52 D1
OLD OL1 .....59 M3
Enbridge St ORD M5 .....86 D4
Encombe Pl CSLFD M3 .....6 A3
Endcott Cl GTN M18 .....88 E6
Enderby Rd NEWH/MOS M40 .....73 M3
Ending Rake WHIT OL12 .....18 D8
Endon Dr OLDTF/WHR M16 .....98 C4
Endon St BOL BL1 .....35 L3
Endsleigh Rd DID/WITH M20 .....98 F6
Endsley Av WALK M28 .....68 F3
Energy St NEWH/MOS * M40 .....88 B1
Enfield Av BNG/LEV M19 .....99 K6
OLDS OL8 .....75 H1
Enfield Cl BOL BL1 .....36 B3
BURY BL9 .....39 J7
ECC M30 .....85 G4
ROCH OL11 .....27 H3
Enfield Dr OP/CLY M11 .....88 F2
Enfield Gv LEIGH WN7 .....66 D7
Enfield Rd ECC M30 .....70 A8
Enfield Rd HYDE * SK14 .....102 B5
WALK M28 .....68 F7
WGNW/BIL/O WN5 .....46 F7
Enfield St WGNE/HIN WN2 .....49 H7
Enford Av WYTH/NTH M22 .....118 C2
Engell Cl GTN M18 .....88 F7
Engine Cl WGNE/HIN WN2 .....48 B8
Engine Fold Rd WALK M28 .....68 D1
Engine La TYLD M29 .....51 K8
Engine St CHAD OL9 .....58 B8
Engledene BOL BL1 .....22 A6
English St LEIGH WN7 .....66 D8
Enid Cl BRO M7 .....72 A7
Enid Pl WGNE/HIN WN2 .....64 C4
Ennerdale Av AIMK WN4 .....63 L7
BOLE BL2 .....37 J3
CCHDY M21 .....98 A8
ROY/SHW OL2 .....42 F5
SWIN M27 .....70 C6
Ennerdale Cl BOLS/LL BL3 .....53 J1
BURY BL9 .....55 K2
CHD/CHDH SK8 .....119 K1
HALE/TIMP WA15 .....108 D5
SALE M33 .....96 B7
Ennerdale Dr BURY BL9 .....55 K2
CHD/CHDH SK8 .....119 K1
HALE/TIMP WA15 .....108 D5
SALE M33 .....96 B7
Ennerdale Gdns AULW OL7 .....75 J7
Ennerdale Gv AULW OL7 .....75 J7
FWTH BL4 .....52 B4
Ennerdale Pl WGNE/HIN WN2 .....48 E4
Ennerdale Rd LEIGH WN7 .....66 B8
MDTN M24 .....57 H2
MPL/ROM SK6 .....101 L8
PART M31 .....106 B1
ROCH OL11 .....27 L8
STKP SK1 .....112 E5
TYLD M29 .....67 L5
WGNE/HIN WN2 .....49 H7
Ennerdale Ter STLY SK15 .....91 K1
Ennis Cl NTHM/RTH M23 .....109 H7
Ennismore Av ECC M30 .....85 K3
Ensor Wy NM/HAY SK22 .....124 E5

Enstone Dr NEWH/MOS M40 .....74 A3
Enstone Wy TYLD M29 .....67 M3
Enterprise Pk HOR/BR BL6 .....33 M4
Entwisle Av URM M41 .....84 E8
Entwisle Rd MILN OL16 .....11 G3
Entwisle Rw FWTH BL4 .....53 G4
MILN OL16 .....29 H6
SWIN M27 .....70 A3
Entwistle Gv LEIGH WN7 .....81 L4
Entwistle Hall La EDGW/EG BL7 .....16 B4
Entwistle St BOLE BL2 .....3 K2
MILN OL16 .....11 G3
SWIN M27 .....70 B4
Enver Rd CHH M8 .....72 E4
Enville Rd ALT WA14 .....116 E1
NEWH/MOS M40 .....73 J3
SLFD M6 .....71 H6
Enville St AUL OL6 .....90 F1
BKLY M9 .....73 G1
DTN/ASHW M34 .....90 B5
Envoy Cl WGNW/BIL/O WN5 .....47 H3
Epping Cl AUL OL6 .....75 M5
CHAD OL9 .....58 B4
Epping Dr SALE M33 .....95 M7
Epping Rd DTN/ASHW M34 .....100 E2
Epping St HULME M15 .....87 J6
Eppleworth Ri SWIN M27 .....70 D1
Epsley Cl HULME M15 .....87 K6
Epsom Av BNG/LEV M19 .....99 J6
SALE M33 .....107 M2
WILM/AE SK9 .....120 A8
Epsom Cl BRAM/HZG SK7 .....122 B2
ROCH OL11 .....27 H4
Epsom Dr WGNE/HIN WN2 .....64 C5
Epworth St CMANE M1 .....7 M5
Equitable St MILN OL16 .....29 J1
OLDE OL4 .....60 A4
Ercall Av WGTN/LGST M12 .....88 B6
Erica Av OLDE OL4 .....44 C8
Erica Cl RDSH SK5 .....100 C4
Erica Dr BNG/LEV M19 .....99 H8
Eric Brook Cl RUSH/FAL M14 .....98 D1
Eric Bullows Cl
WYTH/NTH M22 .....118 E3
Eric St LIT OL15 .....20 B6
OLDE OL4 .....59 M6
Erin St OP/CLY * M11 .....89 H5
Erith Cl RDSH SK5 .....100 E6
Erith Rd OLDE OL4 .....59 L6
Erlesmere Av DTN/ASHW M34 .....90 B8
Erlesmere Cl OLDE OL4 .....44 C8
Erlington Av OLDTF/WHR M16 .....97 L1
Ermen Rd ECC M30 .....84 F4
Ermington Dr CHH M8 .....72 C6
Erneley Cl WGTN/LGST M12 .....99 L1
Ernest St BOL BL1 .....2 A5
CHD/CHDH SK8 .....110 F6
OFTN SK2 .....112 D6
PWCH M25 .....55 J8
Ernest Ter WHIT OL12 .....28 E3
Ernlouen Av BOL BL1 .....35 K4
Ernocroft Gv GTN * M18 .....89 H6
Ernocroft La MPL/ROM SK6 .....115 H1
Ernocroft Rd MPL/ROM SK6 .....114 E3
Erradale Crs WGNS/IIMK WN3 .....63 G2
Errington Cl OFTN SK2 .....113 H6
Errington Cl BOLS/LL BL3 .....35 J7
Errington Dr BRO M7 .....72 A8
Errol Av BKLY M9 .....56 D7
WYTH/NTH M22 .....109 M8
Errwood Crs BNG/LEV M19 .....99 K4
Errwood Rd BNG/LEV M19 .....99 K6
Erskine Cl BOLS/LL BL3 .....35 H7
Erskine Pl WGNE/HIN WN2 .....64 E3
Erskine Rd BKLY M9 .....57 H7
PART M31 .....106 C1
Erskine St HULME M15 .....87 G6
MPL/ROM SK6 .....114 E2
Erwin St NEWH/MOS M40 .....73 L6
Erwood Rd HTNM SK4 .....99 J7
Eryngo St STKP SK1 .....13 M5
Esher Dr SALE M33 .....108 E4
Esk Cl URM M41 .....84 D8
Eskdale CHD/CHDH SK8 .....110 F8
Eskdale Av BOLE BL2 .....22 A4
BRAM/HZG SK7 .....120 F2
DID/WITH M20 .....98 D5
HOR/BR BL6 .....33 H5
MPL/ROM SK6 .....101 J2
OLDS OL8 .....59 G8
ROCH OL11 .....27 L8
ROY/SHW OL2 .....43 G5
WGN WN1 .....47 L1
Eskdale Dr HALE/TIMP WA15 .....108 F5
MDTN M24 .....57 J1
Eskdale Gv FWTH BL4 .....52 C4
Eskdale Ms UPML * OL3 .....61 L7
Eskdale Rd AIMK WN4 .....63 J7
WGNE/HIN WN2 .....49 H7
Eskrick St BOL BL1 .....36 A2
Eskrigge Cl BRO M7 .....72 C4
Esmond Rd CHH M8 .....72 D5
Esmont Dr MDTN M24 .....57 H1
The Esplanade MILN OL16 .....10 D5
Essex Av DID/WITH M20 .....98 B8
DROY M43 .....89 K1
EDGY/DAV SK3 .....12 B7
HEY OL10 .....40 B3
Essex Cl FAIL M35 .....74 C7
ROY/SHW OL2 .....43 J5
Essex Dr BURY BL9 .....5 G9
Essex Pl TYLD M29 .....67 J1
Essex Rd GTN M18 .....100 C1
RDSH SK5 .....100 F7
WGN WN1 .....31 L4
Essex St CMANW M2 .....6 F5
HOR/BR BL6 .....34 A3
ROCH OL11 .....10 E7
WGN WN1 .....15 K2
Essex Wy HULME M15 .....87 G7
Essingdon St BOLS/LL BL3 .....36 A8
Estate St OLDS OL8 .....59 J8
Estate St South OLDS * OL8 .....59 J8
Est Bank Rd RAMS BL0 .....24 D1
Esther St OLDE OL4 .....59 M5
Esthwaite Dr TYLD M29 .....67 K5
Estonfield Dr URM M41 .....96 C2
Eston St BRUN/LGST M13 .....88 A8
Eswick St OP/CLY M11 .....88 F3
Etchells Rd CHD/CHDH SK8 .....119 M3
Etchells St STKP SK1 .....13 J4
Ethel Av BKLY M9 .....57 G7
SWIN M27 .....70 B4
Ethel Ct MILN OL16 .....11 K6
Ethel St BOLS/LL BL3 .....2 A7

OLDS OL8 .....75 J1
WHIT OL12 .....18 E2
Ethel Ter BNG/LEV M19 .....99 K3
Etherley Cl IRL M44 .....94 D2
Etherow Av MPL/ROM SK6 .....114 E2
NEWH/MOS M40 .....74 C7
Etherow Brow HYDE SK14 .....103 L4
Etherow Wy GLSP SK13 .....93 H7
Etherstone St CHH M8 .....72 F4
NEWH/MOS * M40 .....66 B8
Eton Av OLDS OL8 .....75 H1
Eton Cl OLDTF/WHR M16 .....87 G7
ROCH OL11 .....27 L6
Eton Ct OLDTF/WHR * M16 .....87 G7
NEWH/MOS M40 .....73 J3
Eton Hill Rd RAD M26 .....38 F7
Eton St LEIGH WN7 .....81 J1
Eton Ter WGNS/IIMK WN3 .....15 K9
Eton Wy WGNW/BIL/O WN5 .....46 C4
Eton Wy North RAD M26 .....38 F7
Eton Wy South RAD M26 .....38 F7
Etruria Cl BRUN/LGST M13 .....88 B7
Ettington Cl TOT/BURYW BL8 .....38 D1
Ettrick Cl OP/CLY M11 .....89 G5
Euclid Cl OP/CLY M11 .....88 D3
Europa Ga TRPK M17 .....86 A7
Europa Wy CHD/CHDH SK8 .....111 M6
RDSH SK5 .....53 K5
TRPK M17 .....86 A7
Eustace St BOLS/LL BL3 .....52 D1
CHAD OL9 .....8 B1
Euston Av MPL M9 .....73 K1
Euxton Cl TOT/BURYW BL8 .....38 C4
Evan Cl DID/WITH M20 .....110 D1
Evans Cl DID/WITH M20 .....110 D1
RNFD/HAY WA11 .....78 B5
Evans Rd ECC M30 .....84 D3
Evans St AUL OL6 .....75 G8
CSLFD M3 .....6 D1
MDTN M24 .....57 L4
OLD OL1 .....9 J3
Evanstone Cl HOR/BR BL6 .....33 L1
IRL M44 .....94 E5
Eva Rd EDGY/DAV SK3 .....111 K5
Eva St LEIGH WN7 .....81 M5
RUSH/FAL M14 .....98 F1
WHIT OL12 .....28 D2
Evelyn St RUSH/FAL M14 .....99 G4
Evening St FAIL M35 .....74 C4
Evenley Cl GTN * M18 .....89 H6
Everard Cl WALK M28 .....68 E6
Everard St ORD M5 .....86 E5
Everbrom Rd BOLS/LL BL3 .....51 K2
Everdingen Av AULW OL7 .....75 L7
Everest Cl HYDE SK14 .....91 K8
Everest Pl WGN WN1 .....47 M2
Everest Rd ATH M46 .....91 K8
HYDE SK14 .....91 K8
Everglade OLDS OL8 .....75 K3
Everleigh Cl BOLE BL2 .....23 H7
Everleigh Dr CHH M8 .....72 C6
Eversden Ct BRO * M7 .....72 B2
Eversley Rd DID/WITH M20 .....110 D1
Everton Rd OLDS OL8 .....59 G8
RDSH SK5 .....100 C2
Everton St ANC M4 .....70 B4
SWIN M27 .....70 B4
Every St ANC M4 .....7 L2
BURY BL9 .....4 F1
RAMS * BL0 .....17 D6
Evesham Av DID/WITH M20 .....98 B7
LEIGH WN7 .....81 G3
NTHM/RTH M23 .....109 G5
Evesham Cl BOLS/LL BL3 .....2 B7
LEIGH WN7 .....81 G3
MDTN M24 .....57 L7
Evesham Dr FWTH * BL4 .....52 E2
Evesham Drive WILM/AE SK9 .....127 G2
Evesham Gdns MDTN * M24 .....57 K7
Evesham Gv AUL OL6 .....75 M5
SALE M33 .....97 H8
Evesham Rd BKLY M9 .....73 K2
CHD/CHDH SK8 .....111 K8
MDTN M24 .....57 K7
Evesham Wk BOLS/LL BL3 .....2 B7
MDTN M24 .....57 L7
OLDS * M24 .....3 H9
Eveside Cl CHD/CHDH * SK8 .....111 L8
Eve St OLDS OL8 .....75 J3
Ewan Cl GTN M18 .....89 G6
Ewart Av ORD M5 .....86 D3
Ewart St BOL BL1 .....36 B2
Ewhurst Av SWIN M27 .....70 A6
Ewing Cl CHH M8 .....72 D3
Ewood OLDS OL8 .....75 K4
Ewood Dr TOT/BURYW BL8 .....38 C4
Exbourne Rd WYTH/NTH M22 .....118 E3
Exbury WHIT OL12 .....10 D1
Exbury St RUSH/FAL M14 .....99 G5
Excalibur Wy IRL M44 .....94 C3
Excelsior Ter MILN OL16 .....29 J1
Exchange Quay ORD M5 .....86 D6
Exchange Sq CSLFD M3 .....6 F3
Exchange St BOL * BL1 .....2 E5
CMANW * M2 .....6 F4
EDGY/DAV SK3 .....13 G5
OLDE * OL4 .....9 G6
RAMS BL0 .....17 D1
Exeter Av BOLE BL2 .....36 E2
DTN/ASHW M34 .....101 J3
ECC M30 .....70 D8
FWTH BL4 .....52 C3
RAD M26 .....38 A7
Exeter Cl CHD/CHDH SK8 .....120 B4
DUK SK16 .....91 C6
Exeter Dr AUL OL6 .....76 A5
WGNE/HIN WN2 .....33 G7
Exeter Gv ROCH OL11 .....10 F8
Exeter Rd RDSH SK5 .....100 F7
URM M41 .....85 G8
WGNE/HIN WN2 .....33 G7
Exeter St ROCH OL11 .....10 F8
SLFD M6 .....86 B2
Exford Av WGNS/IIMK WN3 .....47 L8
Exford Cl NEWH/MOS M40 .....88 A1
RDSH SK5 .....100 C3
Exford Dr BOLE BL2 .....37 K6
Exit Rd West MANAIR * M90 .....118 D3
Exmoor Cl AUL OL6 .....75 M5
Exmouth Av RDSH SK5 .....100 F7
Exmouth Pl ROCH OL11 .....42 D1
Exmouth Rd SALE M33 .....96 A7
Exmouth Sq ROCH OL11 .....42 D1
Exmouth St ROCH OL11 .....42 D1
Exmouth Wk OLDTF/WHR M16 .....87 K6
Eyam Gv OFTN SK2 .....113 C8
Eyam Ms GLSP SK13 .....104 C3

Eyam Rd BRAM/HZG SK7 122 A4
Eyebrook Rd ALT WA14 116 C3
Eyet St LEIGH WN7 66 B7
Eynford Av RDSH SK5 100 E6
Eyre St HULME M15 87 K7

F

Faber St ANC M4 87 K1
Factory Brow HOR/BR BL6 33 G1
  MDTN M24 56 F5
Factory Fold WGNE/HIN * WN2 48 D5
Factory Hl HOR/BR BL6 21 D8
Factory La BKLY M9 73 G3
  ORD * M5 6 A4
  POY/DIS SK12 124 A5
Factory St MDTN M24 57 J4
  RAD M26 54 E1
  RAMS BL0 17 C5
  TYLD M29 67 J3
Factory St East ATH M46 66 F1
Factory St West ATH M46 66 F1
Faggy La WGNS/IIMK WN3 15 G6
Failsworth Rd FAIL M35 74 E5
Fair Acres BOLE BL2 37 H1
Fairacres WGNNW/ST WN6 30 E3
Fairacres Rd MPL/ROM SK6 123 G4
Fairbairn St HOR/BR BL6 33 L2
Fairbank Dr MDTN M24 57 G2
Fairbottom St OLD OL1 9 K5
Fairbourne Av WGNS/IIMK WN3 47 K8
  WILM/AE SK9 126 D8
Fairbourne Cl WILM/AE SK9 126 D8
Fairbourne Dr
  HALE/TIMP WA15 108 E3
  WILM/AE SK9 126 D8
Fairbourne Rd BNG/LEV M19 99 M3
  DTN/ASHW M34 101 H2
Fairbrook Dr SLFD M6 86 B2
Fairbrother St ORD M5 86 F5
Fairburn Cl URM M41 84 D8
Fairclough St BOLS/LL BL3 36 C8
  OP/CLY M11 88 D2
  WGN WN1 15 H5
  WGNE/HIN WN2 49 G6
Fairfax Av DID/WITH M20 98 E8
  HALE/TIMP WA15 108 D6
Fairfax Cl MPL/ROM SK6 114 A5
Fairfax Dr LIT OL15 29 J1
  WILM/AE SK9 126 D8
Fairfax Rd PWCH M25 55 K7
Fairfield Av CHD/CHDH SK8 120 B2
  DROY M43 89 K4
  MPL/ROM SK6 101 K8
  WGNE/HIN WN2 64 D2
  WGNW/BIL/O WN5 47 G7
Fairfield Dr BURY BL9 40 A1
Fairfield Rd DROY M43 89 K4
  FWTH BL4 52 F5
  HALE/TIMP WA15 108 F7
  MDTN M24 57 H3
  OP/CLY M11 89 H5
Fairfields EDGW/EG BL7 22 C4
  OLDS OL8 75 H2
Fairfield Sq DROY M43 89 K4
Fairfield St CMANE M1 7 K7
  SLFD M6 71 G7
  WGNW/BIL/O WN5 46 F7
Fairford Cl RDSH SK5 100 C7
Fairford Dr BOLS/LL BL3 2 C9
Fairford Wy RDSH SK5 100 C7
  WILM/AE SK9 127 H5
Fairhaven Av CCHDY M21 97 L5
  WHTF M45 55 G5
  WHTN BL5 50 E4
Fairhaven Cl BRAM/HZG SK7 121 H4
Fairhaven Rd BOL BL1 36 C1
Fairhaven St WGTN/LGST M12 88 C6
Fairhills Rd IRL M44 94 D4
Fairholme Av AIMK WN4 63 L8
  URM M41 95 M2
Fairholme Rd DID/WITH M20 98 F6
  HTNM SK4 12 D1
Fairhope Av SLFD M6 70 E8
Fairhurst Av WGNNW/ST WN6 31 G1
Fairhurst Dr WALK M28 68 C2
Fairhurst St LEIGH WN7 66 B7
  WGNS/IIMK WN3 14 D4
Fairisle Cl OP/CLY M11 88 C3
Fairlands Rd BURY BL9 25 J5
  SALE M33 108 C2
Fairlands St ROCH OL11 42 E2
Fairlawn HTNM SK4 12 E1
Fairlawn Cl RUSH/FAL M14 87 K8
Fairlea DTN/ASHW M34 101 K2
Fairlea Av DID/WITH M20 110 F2
Fairlee Av DTN/ASHW M34 89 M3
Fairleigh Av SLFD M6 85 M1
Fairless Rd ECC M30 85 G3
Fairlie Av BOLS/LL BL3 35 J7
Fairlie Dr HALE/TIMP WA15 108 E4
Fairlyn Cl WHTN BL5 51 K5
Fairlyn Dr WHTN BL5 51 K5
Fairman St OLDTF/WHR M16 98 C1
Fairmead Rd NTHM/RTH M23 109 M3
Fairmile Dr DID/WITH M20 110 F4
Fairmount Av BOLE BL2 37 H4
Fairmount Rd SWIN M27 69 L6
Fairoak Ct BOLS/LL BL3 2 A8
Fair Oak Rd BNG/LEV M19 99 J7
Fairstead Cl WHTN BL5 50 A4
Fairstead Wk OP/CLY M11 89 J5
Fair St BOLS/LL * BL3 51 M2
  CMANE M1 7 L5
  SWIN M27 70 D3
Fair Vw WGNW/BIL/O WN5 62 A7
Fairview Av BNG/LEV M19 99 J2
  DTN/ASHW M34 100 D3
Fair View Av WGNW/BIL/O WN5 62 A7
Fairview Cl AIMK WN4 63 L8
  CHAD OL9 58 B4
  MPL/ROM SK6 114 C5
  WHIT OL12 26 F2
Fairview Dr MPL/ROM SK6 114 C5
Fairview Rd DTN/ASHW M34 100 D2
  HALE/TIMP WA15 108 F7
The Fairway NEWH/MOS M40 74 A4
  OFTN SK2 113 G5
Fairway BRAM/HZG SK7 120 F6
  CHD/CHDH SK8 110 E8
  DROY M43 89 K4
  PWCH M25 72 A2
Fair Wy ROCH OL11 41 L3
Fairway SWIN M27 70 F5
  WHIT OL12 18 D5
Fairway Av BOLE BL2 23 K8
  NTHM/RTH M23 109 G5
Fairway Crs ROY/SHW OL2 43 G6
Fairway Dr SALE M33 108 B2
Fairway Rd BURY BL9 55 K1
  OLDE OL4 60 B8
The Fairways AIMK WN4 78 A2
  WHTF M45 55 J6
  WHTN BL5 50 B4
Fairways HOR/BR BL6 33 M1
Fairways Cl GLSP SK13 105 J3
Fairwood Rd NTHM/RTH M23 109 G5
Fairy Bank Crs NM/HAY SK22 125 M1
Fairy Bank Rd NM/HAY SK22 125 M1
Fairy La CHH M8 72 B7
  SALE M33 97 J8
  SALE M33 109 L1
Fairy St TOT/BURYW BL8 4 A5
Fairywell Cl WILM/AE SK9 127 H3
Fairywell Dr SALE M33 108 D3
Fairywell Rd HALE/TIMP WA15 108 E5
Faith St BOL BL1 35 J3
  LEIGH WN7 65 M7
Falcon Av URM M41 96 B2
Falcon Cl BURY BL9 5 J1
  LEIGH WN7 66 E7
  NM/HAY SK22 124 F4
  WHIT OL12 27 G2
Falcon Crs SWIN M27 70 E2
Falcon Dr CHAD OL9 8 C3
  IRL M44 83 L8
  LHULT M38 52 D7
  MDTN M24 57 H1
Falconers Gn WGNS/IIMK WN3 47 L7
Falcon St OLDS OL8 9 H8
Falconwood Cha WALK M28 68 E6
Falconwood Cl WGNNW/ST WN6 14 C2
Falfield Dr CHH M8 72 E7
Falinge Fold WHIT OL12 28 A3
Falinge Ms WHIT OL12 10 C3
Falinge Rd WHIT OL12 10 D2
Falkirk Dr BOLE BL2 37 J6
  WGNE/HIN WN2 48 D4
Falkirk Gv WGNW/BIL/O WN5 46 F4
Falkirk St OLDE OL4 59 M5
Falkland Av NEWH/MOS M40 73 G8
  ROCH OL11 27 M4
Falkland Cl OLDE OL4 44 B8
Falkland Dr AIMK WN4 62 F8
Falkland Rd BOLE BL2 37 K5
Fall Birch Rd HOR/BR BL6 34 C4
Fallons Rd WALK M28 69 M3
Fallow Cl WHTN BL5 50 B2
Fallowfield Av ORD M5 86 E4
Fallowfield Dr WHIT OL12 28 A2
Fallow Fields Dr RDSH SK5 100 D3
Fallowfield Wy ATH M46 67 H3
The Fallows CHAD OL9 58 D7
Falls Gv CHD/CHDH SK8 119 J1
Falmer Cl TOT/BURYW BL8 24 F6
Falmer Dr WYTH/NTH M22 118 F3
Falmer St GTN M18 89 J6
Falmouth Av SALE M33 96 A7
  URM M41 95 H1
Falmouth Crs RDSH SK5 100 F7
Falmouth Rd IRL M44 94 E2
Falmouth St NEWH/MOS M40 73 J8
  OLDS OL8 59 J8
  ROCH * OL11 11 G7
Falsgrave Cl NEWH/MOS M40 73 K7
Falshaw Dr BURY BL9 25 H3
Falstaff Ms MPL/ROM SK6 113 K1
Falston Av NEWH/MOS M40 74 A2
Falstone Av RAMS BL0 17 C8
Falstone Cl WGNS/IIMK WN3 63 G2
Falterley Rd NTHM/RTH M23 109 H4
Fancroft Rd WYTH/NTH M22 109 M7
Faraday Av CHH M8 72 D6
  SWIN M27 71 G2
Faraday Cl WGNNW/ST WN6 14 B4
Faraday Dr BOL BL1 36 B3
Faraday Ri WHIT OL12 27 L3
Faraday St CMANE M1 7 J4
Farcroft Av RAD M26 38 F7
Farcroft Cl NTHM/RTH M23 109 J4
Far Cromwell Rd
  MPL/ROM SK6 101 G6
Fardale ROY/SHW OL2 43 L6
Farden Dr NTHM/RTH M23 109 G4
Fardon Cl WGNS/IIMK WN3 63 J1
Farefield Av GOL/RIS/CU WA3 79 J2
Farewell Cl ROCH OL11 41 M2
Far Hey Cl RAD M26 54 B1
Farholme ROY/SHW OL2 58 F2
Faringdon ROCH OL11 10 C7
Faringdon Wk BOLS/LL BL3 2 C8
Farland Pl BOLS/LL BL3 35 J7
Farlands Dr DID/WITH M20 110 E5
Farlands Ri MILN OL16 42 F1
Far La GTN M18 89 G8
Farley Av GTN M18 89 K8
Farley Ct CHD/CHDH SK8 111 J8
Farley Rd SALE M33 108 F2
Farley Wy RDSH SK5 100 B3
Farliegh Cl WHTN BL5 50 D2
Farman St BOLS/LL * BL3 52 A1
Farm Av STRET M32 85 K8
Farm Cl HTNM SK4 99 M6
  TOT/BURYW BL8 24 C6
Farmers Cl NTHM/RTH M23 109 K2
Farmer St HTNM SK4 112 A1
Farmfield SALE M33 96 B6
Farm Hl PWCH * M25 55 K7
Farmlands Wk OLD OL1 43 M8
Farm La HYDE SK14 102 A4
  POY/DIS SK12 123 J6
  PWCH M25 56 B4
  WALK M28 69 J7
  WGNE/HIN WN2 48 D2
Farm Meadow Rd
  WGNW/BIL/O WN5 46 B7
Farm Rd OLDS OL8 74 F4
Farmside Av IRL M44 94 D1
Farmstead Cl FAIL M35 74 F6
Farm St CHAD OL9 58 E3
  FAIL M35 74 A6
  HEY OL10 41 H4
Farm Wk ALT WA14 116 A2
  LIT OL15 20 A7
  MILN OL16 28 F3
Farmway MDTN M24 57 J5
Farm Yd BNG/LEV M19 99 K3
Farn Av RDSH SK5 100 B2
Farnborough Av OLDE OL4 60 A6
Farnborough Rd BOL BL1 22 B6
  NEWH/MOS M40 88 A1
Farndale Gv AIMK WN4 78 F2
Farndale Sq LHULT M38 68 F1
Farndon Av BRAM/HZG SK7 113 J8
Farndon Cl SALE M33 109 H1
Farndon Dr HALE/TIMP WA15 108 D6
Farndon Rd RDSH SK5 100 B2
Farnham Av BKLY M9 57 G7
Farnham Cl BOL * BL1 2 C1
  CHD/CHDH SK8 120 C5
  LEIGH WN7 66 C6
Farnham Dr IRL M44 94 D3
Farnley Cl WHIT OL12 27 J2
Farnley St WGTN/LGST * M12 88 D6
Farnsfield WGN WN1 48 C3
Farnsworth Cl AULW OL7 75 L7
Farnworth Dr RUSH/FAL M14 98 F2
Farnworth St BOLS/LL * BL3 35 M8
  HEY OL10 40 F2
  LEIGH * WN7 66 E8
Farrand Rd OLDS OL8 74 E2
Farrant Rd WGTN/LGST M12 99 K1
Farrar Rd DROY M43 89 J4
Farr Cl WGNS/IIMK WN3 47 J7
Farrell St CSLFD M3 87 H1
  WGNW/BIL/O WN5 46 F7
Farrer Rd BRUN/LGST M13 99 J2
Far Ridings MPL/ROM SK6 114 A1
Farrier Cl SALE M33 109 J1
Farrier's Cft WGNNW/ST WN6 47 H1
Farriers La ROCH OL11 27 L8
Farringdon St SLFD * M6 86 B1
Farrowdale Av ROY/SHW OL2 43 L6
Farrow St ROY/SHW OL2 43 L6
Farrow St East ROY/SHW OL2 43 L6
Farr St EDGY/DAV SK3 12 E6
Farwood Cl OLDTF/WHR M16 86 F7
Far Woodseats La GLSP SK13 103 J6
Fastnet St OP/CLY M11 88 D4
Faulkenhurst Ms OLD OL1 8 C1
Faulkenhurst St CHAD OL9 8 C1
Faulkner Dr HALE/TIMP WA15 108 E8
Faulkner Rd STRET M32 97 H2
Faulkner St BOLS/LL BL3 2 D9
  CMANE M1 7 G6
  MILN OL16 10 F4
Fauvel Rd GLSP SK13 104 F3
Faversham Brow OLD * OL1 9 H2
Faversham St NEWH/MOS M40 73 L5
Fawborough Rd
  NTHM/RTH M23 109 J3
Fawcetts Fold WHTN BL5 34 B8
Fawcett St BOLE BL2 3 K4
Fawley Av HYDE SK14 102 A3
Fawley Gv WYTH/NTH M22 110 A8
Fawns Keep STLY SK15 92 B6
  WILM/AE SK9 127 H5
Fay Av BKLY M9 73 L2
Fay Gdns GLSP SK13 93 H8
Faywood Dr MPL/ROM SK6 114 D6
Fearney Side BOLS/LL BL3 53 J1
Fearnham Cl LEIGH WN7 81 H3
Fearnhead Av HOR/BR BL6 21 B7
Fearnhead St BOLS/LL BL3 35 M8
Fearn St HEY OL10 40 F2
Featherstall Brook Vie LIT OL15 20 B7
Featherstall Rd LIT OL15 20 A7
Featherstall Rd North OLD OL1 8 F2
Featherstall Rd South CHAD OL9 8 E7
Federation St ANC M4 7 G2
  PWCH M25 55 J7
Feldom Rd NTHM/RTH M23 109 J2
Fellbridge Cl WHTN BL5 50 D3
Fellbrigg Cl GTN M18 99 M1
Fellfoot Cl WALK M28 68 C7
Fellpark Rd NTHM/RTH M23 109 K2
Fells Gv WALK M28 69 J3
Fellside BOLE BL2 37 K1
  WGN WN1 48 A2
Fellside Cl TOT/BURYW * BL8 24 C3
Fellside Gdns LIT OL15 20 A5
Fellside Gn STLY SK15 91 K1
Fell St LEIGH WN7 65 L8
  TOT/BURYW BL8 38 F2
Felltop Dr RDSH SK5 100 D4
Felskirk Rd WYTH/NTH M22 118 E4
Felsted BOL BL1 35 H4
Felt Ct DTN/ASHW M34 100 F2
Felthorpe Dr CHH M8 72 C6
Felton Av WYTH/NTH M22 118 E1
Felton Cl BURY BL9 39 K7
Felton Wk BOL BL1 36 B2
Fencegate Av HTNM SK4 100 A7
Fence St OFTN SK2 113 G8
Fenchurch Av NEWH/MOS M40 73 M8
Fencot Dr WGTN/LGST M12 88 D8
Fenella St BRUN/LGST M13 88 B8
Fenham Cl NEWH/MOS * M40 72 F7
Fenmore Av GTN M18 99 L1
Fennel St ANC M4 6 F2
Fenners Cl BOLS/LL BL3 52 A1
Fenney St BRO M7 72 A7
Fenney St East BRO M7 72 B6
Fenn St HULME M15 87 H6
Fenside Rd WYTH/NTH M22 110 B7
Fenton Av OFTN SK2 112 F8
Fenton Ms ROCH OL11 10 D8
Fenton St OLDE OL4 59 L6
  ROCH OL11 10 D8
  ROY/SHW OL2 43 L7
  TOT/BURYW BL8 38 F1
Fenwick Cl WHTN BL5 50 C6
Fenwick Dr HTNM SK4 111 H1
Fenwick St HULME M15 87 K6
  ROCH OL11 10 C5
Ferdinand St NEWH/MOS * M40 73 G8
Fereday St WALK M28 52 F8
Ferguson Gdns WHIT OL12 28 C1
Ferguson Ri WGNW/BIL/O WN5 47 H4
Ferguson Wy OLDE OL4 60 A3
Fernacre SALE M33 96 F7
Fernally St HYDE SK14 102 B1
Fern Av URM M41 95 K2
Fern Bank NEWH/MOS * M40 73 M5
Fernbank RAD * M26 54 D4
Fern Bank STLY SK15 91 M4
Fern Bank Cl STLY SK15 91 M4
Fern Bank Dr NTHM/RTH M23 109 H5
Fern Bank St HYDE SK14 102 B4
Fernbray Av BNG/LEV M19 99 G8
Fernbray Rd WGNE/HIN WN2 49 J6
Fernbrook Cl BRUN/LGST M13 88 A7
Fern Cl ATH M46 67 G2
  MDTN M24 58 A4
  MPL/ROM SK6 114 C6
  OLDE OL4 60 C6
  WGNNW/ST WN6 30 D6
Fern Clough BOL BL1 35 J5
Fernclough Rd BKLY M9 73 G6
Fern Crs STLY SK15 91 M4
Ferndale Av MILN OL16 42 F3
  OFTN SK2 112 E8
  WHTF M45 54 F5
Ferndale Cl OLDE OL4 60 A8
Ferndale Gdns BNG/LEV M19 99 H6
Ferndale Rd SALE M33 108 E2
Fern Dene WHIT OL12 27 L2
Ferndene Rd DID/WITH M20 98 E7
  WHTF M45 55 M5
Ferndown Av BRAM/HZG SK7 121 L3
  CHAD OL9 58 A5
Ferndown Dr IRL M44 94 D1
Ferndown Rd BOLE BL2 37 H1
  NTHM/RTH M23 109 G4
Ferney Field Rd CHAD OL9 58 C5
Ferngate Dr DID/WITH M20 98 E6
Ferngrove BURY BL9 5 M1
Fernhill MPL/ROM SK6 114 E6
Fernhill Av BOLS/LL BL3 35 K8
Fernhill Cl GLSP SK13 105 G1
Fernhill Dr GTN M18 88 E8
Fern Hill La WHIT OL12 18 B8
Fernhills EDGW/EG BL7 22 B2
Fernhill St BURY BL9 4 F2
Fernholme Ct OLDS OL8 58 F8
Fernhurst Cl WGNS/IIMK WN3 15 M8
Fernhurst Rd DID/WITH M20 98 F7
Fernhurst St CHAD OL9 8 C1
Fernie St ANC * M4 87 K1
Fernilee Cl NM/HAY SK22 124 E3
Fern Isle Cl WHIT OL12 18 C6
Fern Lea CHD/CHDH SK8 119 K3
Fernlea HALE/TIMP WA15 117 H3
Fernlea Av OLD OL1 8 C1
Fernlea Cl GLSP SK13 93 H8
  WHIT OL12 27 L2
Fernlea Crs SWIN M27 70 B5
Fernlea Gv AIMK WN4 63 G7
Fern Lea Gv LHULT M38 52 C8
Fernleigh HOR/BR * BL6 34 A3
Fernleigh Av BNG/LEV M19 99 M3
Fernleigh Dr OLDTF/WHR * M16 86 F7
Fernley Av DTN/ASHW M34 101 K2
Fernley Rd OFTN SK2 112 E6
Fernone WILM/AE SK9 127 H1
Ferns Gv BOL BL1 35 L5
Fernside RAD M26 53 L6
Fernside Av DID/WITH M20 99 G7
Fernside Gv WALK * M28 53 H8
  WGNS/IIMK WN3 63 G3
Fernside Wy WHIT OL12 27 K3
Fernstead BOLS/LL BL3 35 M6
Fernstone Cl HOR/BR BL6 33 K1
Fern St BOLS/LL BL3 35 M6
  BURY BL9 4 F2
  CHAD OL9 58 D4
  CHH M8 72 D8
  FWTH BL4 53 H3
  OLDS OL8 8 F8
  RAMS BL0 17 D6
  ROCH OL11 10 B6
  WHIT OL12 19 K6
Fernthorpe Av UPML OL3 61 M3
Fern Vw HALE/TIMP WA15 109 H7
Fernview Dr RAMS BL0 24 D3
Fernwood MPL/ROM SK6 114 F5
Fernwood Av GTN M18 100 A1
Fernwood Gv WILM/AE SK9 127 G4
Ferrand Ldg LIT OL15 20 D5
Ferrand Rd LIT OL15 20 C6
Ferrer St AIMK WN4 63 J6
Ferring Wk CHAD * OL9 8 A7
Ferris St OP/CLY M11 89 G4
Ferrous Wy IRL M44 94 C6
Ferryhill Rd IRL M44 94 D2
Ferry Rd IRL M44 94 E2
Ferry St OP/CLY M11 88 B4
Festival Dr MCFLDN SK10 131 J6
Fettler Cl SWIN M27 70 B5
Fewston Cl BOL BL1 22 B7
Fiddlers La IRL M44 83 L8
Field Bank Gv BNG/LEV M19 99 L3
Field Cl BRAM/HZG SK7 120 F8
  MPL/ROM SK6 114 A7
Fieldcroft ROCH OL11 27 L5
Fielden Av CCHDY M21 97 L3
Fielden Rd DID/WITH M20 98 C7
Fielders Wy SWIN M27 54 B8
Fieldfare Av NEWH/MOS M40 73 L8
Fieldfare Cl GOL/RIS/CU WA3 80 A4
Fieldfare Wy AULW OL7 75 K5
Fieldhead Av ROCH OL11 27 K5
  TOT/BURYW BL8 38 D3
  TYLD M29 67 L7
Fieldhead Ms WILM/AE SK9 127 J4
Fieldhead Rd WILM/AE SK9 127 J4
Field House La MPL/ROM SK6 114 D6
Fieldhouse Rd WHIT OL12 28 C2
Fielding Av POY/DIS SK12 129 J2
Fielding St ECC M30 84 F3
  MDTN M24 57 K2
Field La AUL OL6 76 A7
Field Pl DID/WITH * M20 110 E1
Field Rd MILN OL16 29 G5
  SALE M33 96 B6
The Fields WGNE/HIN WN2 32 F8
  WGNNW/ST WN6 31 J4
Fields Crs HYDE SK14 93 G6
Fieldsend Cl STLY SK15 92 A4
Fieldsend Dr LEIGH WN7 80 F4
Fields End Fold ECC M30 83 M8
Fields Farm Cl HYDE SK14 103 G3
Fields Farm Rd HYDE SK14 103 G2
Fields Gv HYDE SK14 93 G7
Fields New Rd CHAD OL9 58 D7
Field St DROY M43 89 J4
  FAIL M35 74 B5
  GTN M18 89 H6
  HYDE SK14 91 G7
  MPL/ROM SK6 113 J1
  ROCH OL11 28 D8
  SLFD M6 86 C2
  WGNE/HIN WN2 49 H8
  WGNNW/ST WN6 14 D3
  WGNS/IIMK WN3 48 C8
Fieldsway OLDS OL8 75 H2
Field Vale Dr RDSH SK5 100 D3
Fieldvale Rd SALE M33 108 B3
Field View Wk OLDTF/WHR M16 98 C2
Field Wk HALE/TIMP * WA15 117 K1
Fieldway MILN OL16 42 E1
  WGNE/HIN WN2 64 E2
Fife Av CHAD OL9 58 C8
Fifield Cl OLDS OL8 75 K1
Fifth Av BOL BL1 35 L5
  BURY BL9 26 A8
  DUK SK16 90 D4
  OLDS OL8 74 F2
  OP/CLY M11 88 F2
  TRPK M17 85 M7
Fifth St TRPK M17 85 M7
Filbert St OLD OL1 59 M3
Filby Wk NEWH/MOS M40 73 H8
Fildes St MDTN M24 58 A5
Filey Av OLDTF/WHR M16 98 A2
  URM M41 84 D8
Filey Dr SLFD M6 71 G6
Filey Rd OFTN SK2 112 F5
  RUSH/FAL M14 99 G4
Filey St MILN OL16 28 F2
Filton Av BOLS/LL * BL3 2 B8
Finance St LIT OL15 19 M7
Finborough Cl OLDTF/WHR M16 87 H8
Finchale Dr HALE/TIMP WA15 117 K3
Finch Av FWTH BL4 52 C5
Finchdale Gdns
  GOL/RIS/CU WA3 80 E4
Finchley Av NEWH/MOS M40 73 M8
Finchley Cl TOT/BURYW BL8 38 E3
Finchley Crs WGNE/HIN WN2 48 D3
Finchley Gv NEWH/MOS M40 73 K3
Finchley Rd HALE/TIMP WA15 117 G1
  RUSH/FAL M14 98 E4
Finch Mill Av WGNNW/ST WN6 30 A5
Finchwood Rd WYTH/NTH M22 110 B7
Findon Rd NTHM/RTH M23 109 K6
Finghall Rd URM M41 95 L2
Finishing Wk ANC M4 7 M4
Finland Rd EDGY/DAV SK3 12 F9
Finlan Rd MDTN M24 42 B7
Finlay Ct WGNW/BIL/O WN5 47 H4
Finlay St FWTH * BL4 53 G4
Finlow Hill La MCFLDN SK10 131 G6
Finney Cl WILM/AE SK9 127 G2
Finney Dr CCHDY M21 97 K5
  WILM/AE SK9 127 G2
Finney Gv RNFD/HAY WA11 78 B6
Finney La WYTH/NTH M22 119 J4
Finney St BOLS/LL * BL3 36 C8
Finningley Rd BKLY M9 56 E6
Finny Bank Rd SALE M33 96 D6
Finsbury Av NEWH/MOS M40 73 M8
Finsbury Rd RDSH SK5 100 B4
Finsbury St ROCH OL11 10 A9
Finsbury Wy WILM/AE SK9 127 J2
Finstock Cl ECC M30 84 E3
Fintry Gv ECC M30 85 G3
Fir Av BRAM/HZG SK7 121 G4
Firbank Rd NTHM/RTH M23 118 C1
Fir Bank Rd ROY/SHW OL2 43 G6
Firbank Rd WGNS/IIMK WN3 63 L1
Firbarn Cl MILN OL16 29 G5
Firbeck Dr ANC M4 88 A2
Fir Cl POY/DIS SK12 129 J1
Fircroft WGNNW/ST WN6 30 D2
Fircroft Rd OLDS OL8 75 K2
Firdale Av NEWH/MOS M40 74 B3
Firdale Wk CHAD OL9 8 C4
Firecrest Cl WALK M28 68 E4
Firefly Cl CSLFD M3 6 A4
Fire Station Sq ORD * M5 86 F2
Fire Station Yd ROCH OL11 10 F6
Firethorn Av BNG/LEV M19 99 J6
Firethorn Cl WHTN BL5 50 C2
Firethorn Dr HYDE SK14 102 D2
Firfield Gv WALK M28 69 J1
Fir Gv BNG/LEV M19 99 K3
  CHAD OL9 8 B2
  WGNNW/ST WN6 47 K1
Firgrove Av MILN OL16 29 G4
Firgrove Gdns MILN OL16 29 G4
Fir La ROY/SHW OL2 43 G6
Fir Rd BRAM/HZG SK7 121 G4
  DTN/ASHW M34 101 K1
  FWTH BL4 52 E4
  MPL/ROM SK6 114 B8
  SWIN M27 70 B6
The Firs ALT WA14 116 D2
Firs Av AUL OL6 75 L8
  FAIL M35 74 B5
  OLDTF/WHR M16 97 L2
Firsby Av MPL/ROM SK6 101 J8
Firsby St BNG/LEV M19 99 K3
Firs Cottages WGNE/HIN * WN2 49 G3
Firs Gv CHD/CHDH SK8 110 D8
Firs La LEIGH WN7 65 M7
Firs Park Crs WGNE/HIN WN2 49 G3
Firs Rd CHD/CHDH SK8 119 J1
  SALE M33 96 A8
  WHTN BL5 51 J6
First Av ATH M46 51 G8
  MCFLDN SK10 129 H3
  OLDS OL8 75 G2
  OP/CLY M11 89 G2
  STLY SK15 77 H7
  SWIN M27 70 A7
  TOT/BURYW BL8 24 C6
  TRPK M17 86 A7
  TYLD M29 67 M8
  WGNE/HIN WN2 49 G7
  WGNNW/ST WN6 47 K2
Fir St BOL BL1 36 C2
  BURY BL9 5 J4
  ECC M30 85 G3
  FAIL M35 74 B5
  HEY OL10 41 H3
  HTNM SK4 13 G3
  NEWH/MOS M40 73 G8
  OLDTF/WHR * M16 86 F8
  RAD M26 54 E2
  RAMS BL0 17 D5
  ROY/SHW OL2 43 G7
  SLFD M6 86 C2
Firs Wy SALE M33 107 M1
Firswood Dr HYDE SK14 102 D1
  ROY/SHW OL2 42 F7
  SWIN M27 70 B6
Firswood Mt CHD/CHDH SK8 110 D8
Firth St OLD OL1 9 K6
Fir Tree Av GOL/RIS/CU WA3 80 C4
  OLDS OL8 75 K2
  SALE M33 95 M8
  WALK M28 68 E6
Fir Tree Cl DUK SK16 91 J5
Fir Tree Crs DUK SK16 91 J4
  WGNS/IIMK WN3 64 C1
Fir Tree Dr HYDE SK14 91 H7
  WGNS/IIMK WN3 64 C1
Fir Tree La DUK SK16 91 J5
Fir Tree St WGNS/IIMK * WN3 48 C8
Firvale Av CHD/CHDH SK8 119 K3
Firvale Cl LEIGH WN7 65 M7
Firwood Av FWTH BL4 52 F6
  URM M41 96 D3
Firwood Cl OFTN SK2 112 F4
Firwood Crs RAD M26 54 E3
Firwood Gv AIMK WN4 78 C2
  BOLE BL2 36 E2
Firwood La BOLE BL2 36 E1
Firwood Pk CHAD OL9 58 B5
Fishbourne Sq RUSH/FAL * M14 98 F1
Fisher Av WGNE/HIN WN2 64 F5
Fisher Cl WGNS/IIMK WN3 14 A9
Fisher Dr WGNW/BIL/O WN5 46 B6
Fisherfield WHIT OL12 27 J3
Fishermore Rd URM M41 95 H2
Fishers Br NM/HAY SK22 125 M2
Fisher St OLD OL1 9 K3

Fishwick St *MILN* OL16 ....11 H7
Fistral Av *CHD/CHDH* SK8 ....119 L4
Fistral Crs *STLY* SK15 ....92 A1
Fitton Av *CCHDY* M21 ....97 L6
Fitton Crs *SWIN* M27 ....70 C1
Fitton Hill Rd *OLDS* OL8 ....59 K8
Fitton St *MILN* OL16 ....11 K7
  ROY/SHW OL2 ....43 J5
Fitzadam St *WGN* WN1 ....14 E3
Fitzalan St *GLSP* SK13 ....104 F3
Fitzgeorge St *NEWH/MOS* M40 ..72 F7
Fitzgerald Cl *PWCH* M25 ....71 J2
Fitzgerald Wy *SLFD* * M6 ....86 C1
Fitzhugh St *BOL* * BL1 ....22 D7
Fitzroy St *AULW* OL7 ....90 C3
  DROY M43 ....89 L4
  STLY SK15 ....92 A1
Fitzwarren St *SLFD* M6 ....86 C2
Fitzwilliam St *BRO* M7 ....72 A8
Five Quarters *RAD* M26 ....38 B7
Flagcroft Dr *NTHM/RTH* M23....109 L7
Flagg Wood Av *MPL/ROM* SK6 ..114 A5
Flag Rw *ANC* * M4 ....87 L1
Flagship Av *ORD* * M5 ....86 E4
Flake La *ROY/SHW* OL2 ....43 G8
Flamborough Wk
  RUSH/FAL * M14 ....98 E1
Flamingo Cl *WGTN/LGST* M12 ..88 D6
Flamstead Av
  NTHM/RTH M23 ....109 H6
Flannel St *MILN* OL16 ....11 G2
Flapper Fold La *ATH* M46 ....50 F8
Flashfields *PWCH* M25 ....71 J3
Flash St *NEWH/MOS* M40 ....73 M6
Flatley Cl *HULME* M15 ....87 K6
Flavian Wk *OP/CLY* * M11 ....88 E4
Flaxcroft Rd *WYTH/NTH* M22 ...118 D2
Flaxfield Av *STLY* SK15 ....92 A2
Flaxman Ri *OLD* 43 M8
Flaxpool Cl *OLDTF/WHR* M16 ...87 H8
Flax St *CSLFD* M3 ....6 B1
  RAMS * BL0 ....17 A8
Fleece St *MILN* OL16 ....10 E4
  OLDE * OL4 ....59 L5
Fleeson St *RUSH/FAL* M14 ......98 F1
Fleet Av *AUL* OL6 ....90 D2
Fleet St *GTN* M18 ....89 J6
  HOR/BR BL6 ....34 A1
  HYDE SK14 ....91 H8
  OLDE OL4 ....59 J6
  WGNW/BIL/O WN5 ....46 E6
Fleetwood Dr *NEWLW* WA12 ....78 E8
Fleetwood Rd *WALK* M28 ....68 D1
Fleming Dr *AIMK* WN4 ....64 A8
Fleming Rd *WYTH/NTH* M22 ....118 F2
Flemish Rd *HYDE* SK14 ....101 L2
Fletcher Av *ATH* M46 ....51 C7
  SWIN M27 ....70 D1
Fletcher Cl *OLDS* OL8 ....8 E6
  HEY OL10 ....41 C3
Fletcher Dr *ALT* WA14 ....116 E3
  POY/DIS SK12 ....123 H6
Fletcher Fold Rd *BURY* BL9 .....39 J6
Fletcher Sq *CMANE* * M1 ....7 L5
Fletcher St *ATH* * M46 ....66 F1
  BOLS/LL BL3 ....2 D8
  BOLS/LL BL3 ....53 L1
  BURY BL9 ....5 H4
  FWTH BL4 ....53 G4
  NEWH/MOS M40 ....73 J7
  RAD M26 ....38 F8
  ROCH OL11 ....11 H9
  STKP SK1 ....13 J4
Fletsand Rd *WILM/AE* SK9 .....127 C6
Fletton Cl *WHIT* OL12 ....28 B2
Fletton Ms *WHIT* OL12 ....27 M2
Flint Cl *BRAM/HZG* SK7 ....121 L3
  OP/CLY * M11 ....88 E2
Flint St *DROY* M43 ....89 L2
  EDGY/DAV SK3 ....13 H8
  OLD * OL1 ....59 M4
Flitcroft Ct *BOLS/LL* * BL3 ....36 C8
Flixton Rd *PART* M31 ....95 H4
  URM M41 ....95 M4
Floatshall Rd *NTHM/RTH* M23 .109 J6
Floats Rd *NTHM/RTH* M23 .....109 H7
Flockton Av *WGNNW/ST* WN6 ...31 C8
Flora Rd *AIMK* WN4 ....78 E2
  BKLY M9 ....72 F1
  BOLS/LL * BL3 ....36 A8
  OLD OL1 ....9 H4
Florence Av *BOL* BL1 ....22 C8
Florence Ct *EDGY/DAV* * SK3 ...12 B9
Florence Park Ct *DID/WITH* M20 .98 F8
Florence Steet *MILN* OL16 ....11 K7
Florence St *BOLS/LL* * BL3 ....36 A8
  DROY M43 ....89 L4
  ECC M30 ....84 E3
  FAIL M35 ....74 C4
  HTNM SK4 ....13 H2
  SALE M33 ....96 E6
  WGN WN1 ....15 L3
Florence Wy *HYDE* SK14 ....93 C7
Florida St *OLDS* OL8 ....9 C8
Florin Gdns *SLFD* M6 ....86 C1
Florist St *EDGY/DAV* SK3 ....13 H9
Flowery Bank *OLDS* OL8 ....59 L8
Flowery Fld *OFTN* SK2 ....121 J1
Flowery Field Gn *HYDE* SK14 ...90 F8
Floyd Av *CCHDY* M21 ....97 M6
Floyer Rd *BKLY* M9 ....57 H8
Foden La *BNG/LEV* * BRAM/HZG* SK7 .128 B1
Fog La *BNG/LEV* M19 ....99 C8
The Fold *BKLY* M9 ....73 C1
  URM M41 ....95 K1
Fold Av *DROY* M43 ....89 L5
Fold Crs *STLY* SK15 ....77 J6
Fold Gdns *WHIT* OL12 ....27 L1
Fold Gn *CHAD* OL9 ....58 D6
Fold Ms *BRAM/HZG* SK7 ....122 A1
Fold Rd *RAD* M26 ....53 M5
Folds *HOR/BR* BL6 ....32 F1
Folds Rd *BOL* BL1 ....3 C3
Fold St *BOL* * BL1 ....2 F5
  BURY BL9 ....4 C4
  GOL/RIS/CU WA3 ....79 C3
  HEY OL10 ....41 H1
  NEWH/MOS M40 ....73 K4
  OLDS OL8 ....9 C6
Fold Vw *EDGW/EG* BL7 ....22 B3
  OLDE OL4 ....75 K2
Foleshill Av *BKLY* M9 ....72 F1
Foley Gdns *HEY* OL10 ....41 H5
Foley St *WGNE/HIN* WN2 ....49 C7
Foliage Crs *RDSH* SK5 ....100 E7
Foliage Rd *RDSH* SK5 ....100 E8
Folkestone Rd East
  OP/CLY M11 ....89 C2

Folkestone Rd West
  OP/CLY M11 ....88 F2
Follows St *GTN* M18 ....89 G6
Folly La *SWIN* M27 ....70 A7
Folly Wk *WHIT* OL12 ....28 C3
Fonthill Gv *SALE* M33 ....108 C3
Fontwell Cl *OLDTF/WHR* M16 ...97 M1
Fontwell La *OLD* OL1 ....59 K3
Fontwell Rd *BOLS/LL* BL3 ....53 K2
Fooley Cl *DROY* M43 ....89 H4
Footman Cl *TYLD* M29 ....67 L5
Foot Mill Crs *WHIT* OL12 ....28 A2
Foot Wood Crs *WHIT* OL12 ....28 A2
Forber Crs *GTN* M18 ....99 M1
Forbes Cl *SALE* M33 ....109 G2
  STKP SK1 ....112 E4
  WGNE/HIN WN2 ....49 H5
Forbes Pk *BRAM/HZG* SK7 .....120 F5
Forbes Rd *STKP* SK1 ....112 E3
Forbes St *MPL/ROM* SK6 ....101 J8
Fordbank Rd *DID/WITH* M20 ...110 D2
Ford Gv *HYDE* SK14 ....92 D8
Fordham Gv *BOL* BL1 ....35 M4
Fordland Cl *GOL/RIS/CU* WA3 ...80 B3
Ford La *SLFD* M6 ....71 K8
  WYTH/NTH M22 ....110 B3
Ford Ldg *DID/WITH* M20 ....110 E2
Ford's Barn *HZG* SK7 ....120 F6
Ford St *CSLFD* M3 ....6 B3
  DUK SK16 ....90 F6
  EDGY/DAV SK3 ....12 E5
  RAD M26 ....53 K4
  WGTN/LGST M12 ....88 A6
Fordyce Wy *WGNE/HIN* WN2 ....48 D4
Foreland Cl *NEWH/MOS* M40 ...73 G7
Forest Cl *DUK* SK16 ....90 F6
Forest Ct *URM* M41 ....95 G1
Forest Dr *HALE/TIMP* WA15 ...108 C6
  SALE M33 ....108 B2
  WGNNW/ST WN6 ....30 D2
  WHTN BL5 ....50 D8
Forester Hill Av *BOLS/LL* BL3 ...52 D1
Forester Hill Cl *BOLS/LL* BL3 ....52 C1
Forest Gdns *PART* M31 ....106 A1
Forest Range *BNG/LEV* M19 .....99 K3
Forest Rd *BOL* BL1 ....35 L1
Forest St *AUL* OL6 ....75 M8
  ECC M30 ....85 J2
  OLDS OL8 ....75 J1
Forest Vw *WHIT* OL12 ....28 A2
Forest Wy *BOLE* BL2 ....22 F6
Forfar St *BOL* BL1 ....22 B7
Forge La *OP/CLY* M11 ....88 E2
Forge St *OLDE* OL4 ....59 L5
  WGNE/HIN WN2 ....15 L5
Formby Av *ATH* M46 ....51 C8
  CCHDY M21 ....98 A5
Formby Dr *CHD/CHDH* SK8 ....119 K4
Formby Rd *SLFD* M6 ....71 H7
Forres Gv *WHTN* BL5 ....62 F8
Forrester Dr *ROY/SHW* OL2 .....44 A4
  STLY SK15 ....91 M5
Forresters Cl *WGNE/HIN* WN2 ...65 H4
Forrester St *WALK* M28 ....68 C7
Forrest Rd *DTN/ASHW* M34 ....101 L3
Forshaw Av *GTN* M18 ....89 J6
Forshaw St *DTN/ASHW* M34 ....90 A8
Forster St *GOL/RIS/CU* WA3 .....79 K3
Forsyth St *WHIT* OL12 ....27 H2
Fortescue Rd *OFTN* SK2 ....113 C5
Forth Pl *RAD* M26 ....38 C7
Forth Rd *RAD* M26 ....38 C7
Forth St *LEIGH* WN7 ....66 F8
Forton Av *BOLE* BL2 ....37 H5
Forton Rd *WGNS/IIMK* WN3 ....63 J2
Fortran Cl *SLFD* M6 ....86 D3
Fortrose Av *BKLY* M9 ....72 E1
Fortuna Gv *BNG/LEV* M19 ....99 J4
Fortune St *BOLS/LL* BL3 ....3 J9
Fortyacre Dr *MPL/ROM* SK6 ...113 H1
Forum Gv *BRO* M7 ....72 B7
Fosbrook Av *DID/WITH* M20 .....98 F8
Foscarn Dr *NTHM/RTH* M23 ...109 L7
Fossgill Av *BOLE* BL2 ....22 F7
Foster Av *WGNS/IIMK* WN3 .....15 L8
Foster Ct *BURY* * BL9 ....26 A8
Foster La *BOLE* BL2 ....37 J3
Fosters Buildings
  WGNNW/ST WN6 ....14 D3
Foster St *DTN/ASHW* M34 ......101 J1
  OLDE OL4 ....59 M6
  RAD M26 ....54 C1
  WGNNW/ST WN6 ....14 B2
Fotherby Dr *BKLY* M9 ....73 C1
Fotherby Pl *WGNS/IIMK* WN3 ...63 K1
Foulds Av *TOT/BURYW* BL8 ......32 B7
Foundry La *ANC* M4 ....7 J3
  WGNS/IIMK WN3 ....47 C8
Foundry St *BOLS/LL* BL3 ....2 F8
  BOLS/LL BL3 ....53 K1
  BURY BL9 ....5 C5
  CHAD OL9 ....90 F4
  DUK SK16 ....90 F4
  HEY OL10 ....40 F2
  LEIGH WN7 ....66 E8
  RAD M26 ....54 D1
  WGNE/HIN WN2 ....49 G7
Fountain Av
  HALE/TIMP WA15 ....117 K4
Fountain Pk *WHTN* BL5 ....49 M7
Fountains Av *BOLE* BL2 ....36 F3
  RNFD/HAY WA11 ....78 C5
Fountains Cl *TYLD* M29 ....67 M5
Fountains Rd *CHD/CHDH* SK8 .120 D6
  STRET M32 ....96 C1
Fountain St *AUL* OL6 ....76 B8
  BURY BL9 ....5 J5
  CMANW M2 ....7 C5
  ECC M30 ....85 G4
  HYDE SK14 ....102 C1
  MDTN M24 ....57 J4
  OLD OL1 ....9 H5
  TOT/BURYW BL8 ....4 A5
Fountains St North *BURY* BL9 ...5 H4
Fountains Wk *CHAD* * OL9 ....58 D7
  DUK SK16 ....90 F4
  GOL/RIS/CU WA3 ....80 E4
Fouracres Rd *NTHM/RTH* M23 ..109 J7
Four Lane Ends *URM* M41 ....95 H4
Four Lanes *HYDE* SK14 ....92 D8
Four Lanes Wy *ROCH* OL11 .....26 F2
Fourmarts Rd
  WGNW/BIL/O WN5 ....46 E2
Four Stalls End *LIT* OL15 ....20 B8
Fountain Meadows Rd *
  WGNS/IIMK WN3 ....14 D7

Fourth Av *BOL* BL1 ....35 L5
  BURY BL9 ....25 M8
  CHAD OL9 ....58 D7
  OLDS OL8 ....74 F2
  OP/CLY M11 ....88 F1
  STLY SK15 ....77 H6
  SWIN M27 ....70 A7
Fourth St *TRPK* M17 ....85 M7
Fourways *TRPK* M17 ....85 K6
Four Yards *CMANW* M2 ....6 F5
Fovant Crs *RDSH* SK5 ....100 B3
Fowler Av *GTN* M18 ....89 J5
Fowler Cl *WGN* WN1 ....15 K4
Fowler St *OLDS* OL8 ....74 F1
Fowley Common La
  GOL/RIS/CU WA3 ....81 L7
Fownhope Av *SALE* M33 ....108 C1
Fownhope Rd *SALE* M33 ....108 C1
Foxall Cl *MDTN* M24 ....56 F5
Foxall St *MDTN* M24 ....56 F5
Foxbank St *BRUN/LGST* M13 ...88 B8
Fox Bench Cl *CHD/CHDH* SK8 .128 E6
Foxbench Wk *CCHDY* M21 ....98 A6
Fox Cl *HALE/TIMP* WA15 ....108 C6
Foxcroft St *LIT* OL15 ....20 A7
Foxdale Cl *EDGW/EG* BL7 ....16 E6
Foxdale St *OP/CLY* M11 ....88 F7
Foxdene Gv *WGNS/IIMK* WN3 ...63 H2
Foxdenton Dr *STRET* M32 ....96 C1
Foxdenton La *MDTN* M24 ....58 B6
Foxendale Wk *BOLS/LL* * BL3 .....2 E9
Foxfield Cl *TOT/BURYW* BL8 ....24 E7
Foxfield Dr *OLDS* OL8 ....74 F3
Foxfield Gv *WGNNW/ST* WN6 ...30 E6
Foxfield Rd *NTHM/RTH* M23 ..118 C1
Foxfold Cl *WALK* M28 ....68 C5
Foxglove Cl *WHIT* OL12 ....28 A1
Foxglove Dr *ALT* WA14 ....107 M4
  BURY BL9 ....40 A1
Foxglove St *STLY* SK15 ....91 J1
Foxhall La *WHTN* M15 ....108 B6
  HALE/TIMP WA15 ....108 B6
Foxham Dr *BRO* M7 ....72 B6
Foxhill *ALT* WA14 ....107 K7
Fox Hl *ROY/SHW* OL2 ....43 H4
Foxhill Cha *OFTN* SK2 ....113 K7
Foxhill Dr *STLY* SK15 ....91 M4
Foxhill Rd *ECC* M30 ....84 C3
Fox Hill Rd *ROCH* OL11 ....42 A4
Foxholes Rd *HOR/BR* BL6 ....21 D8
  HYDE SK14 ....102 A4
  WHIT OL12 ....28 D2
Foxlair Rd *WYTH/NTH* M22 ....118 D1
Foxland Rd *CHD/CHDH* SK8 ...110 E8
Foxlea *GLSP* SK13 ....104 C4
Foxley Gv *BOLS/LL* BL3 ....2 B6
Fox Park Rd *OLDS* OL8 ....74 F3
Fox Platt Rd *MOSL* * OL5 ....76 E3
Fox Platt Ter *MOSL* OL5 ....76 F4
Fox St *BURY* BL9 ....5 C2
  ECC M30 ....85 J2
  EDGY/DAV SK3 ....12 E7
  HEY OL10 ....40 F2
  HOR/BR BL6 ....33 M2
  MILN OL16 ....11 J2
  MILN OL16 ....29 H6
  OLDS OL8 ....74 F2
Foxton St *MDTN* M24 ....56 F5
Foxwood Cl *WGNW/BIL/O* WN5 .46 B7
Foxwood Dr *MOSL* OL5 ....77 C2
Foxwood Gdns *BNG/LEV* M19 ..99 H1
Foynes Cl *NEWH/MOS* * M40 ...73 G7
Foy St *AIMK* WN4 ....78 E1
Framingham Rd *SALE* M33 .....108 E2
Framley Rd *CCHDY* M21 ....98 C5
Frampton Cl *MDTN* M24 ....57 L5
Fram St *BKLY* M9 ....73 J4
  SLFD * M6 ....86 B2
Frances Av *CHD/CHDH* SK8 ...110 D6
Frances Pl *ATH* M46 ....66 D2
Frances St *BOL* BL1 ....36 A2
  BRUN/LGST M13 ....87 L6
  CHD/CHDH SK8 ....111 H6
  DTN/ASHW M34 ....101 L4
  EDGY/DAV SK3 ....13 H6
  HYDE SK14 ....101 M1
  IRL M44 ....94 B7
  MILN OL16 ....29 G1
  OLD OL1 ....59 K3
Frances St West *HYDE* SK14 ..101 L1
France St *WGNE/HIN* WN2 ......49 G6
  WGNW/BIL/O WN5 ....14 A6
  WHTN BL5 ....50 B6
Francis Av *ECC* M30 ....85 H2
  WALK M28 ....69 J2
Francis Rd *DID/WITH* M20 ....98 F7
  IRL M44 ....94 C4
Francis St *CSLFD* M3 ....87 J1
  ECC M30 ....85 G1
  FAIL M35 ....74 C5
  FWTH BL4 ....52 F3
  LEIGH WN7 ....66 B5
  TYLD M29 ....68 A4
  WGNE/HIN WN2 ....49 G7
Frankby Cl *SWIN* * M27 ....70 F5
Frankford Av *BOL* * BL1 ....35 M2
Frankford Sq *BOL* * BL1 ....35 M2
Frankland Cl *OP/CLY* M11 ....88 E1
Franklin Cl *DTN/ASHW* M34 ...100 D2
  OLD OL1 ....9 H3
Franklin Rd *DROY* M43 ....89 K3
Franklin St *ECC* M30 ....85 H2
  MILN OL16 ....11 J9
  OLD OL1 ....9 H3
Franklyn Av *URM* M41 ....95 H2
Franklyn Rd *GTN* M18 ....89 H6
Frank Perkins Wy *IRL* M44 ......94 C5
Frank St *BOL* BL1 ....36 A3
  BURY BL9 ....5 J6
  FAIL M35 ....74 B5
  HYDE SK14 ....102 B2
  SLFD M6 ....71 J8
Frankton Rd *WHTF* M45 ....55 J5
Franton Rd *OP/CLY* M11 ....88 E2
Fraser Av *SALE* M33 ....108 B3
Fraser Pl *TRPK* M17 ....86 A7
Fraser Rd *CHH* M8 ....72 C3
  WGNW/BIL/O WN5 ....47 H5
Fraser St *AUL* OL6 ....90 F1
  MILN OL16 ....28 E8
  ROY/SHW OL2 ....43 K4
  SWIN M27 ....70 D3
Frawley Av *NEWLW* WA12 ....78 E7
Frecheville Ct *BURY* BL9 ....4 D7
Freckleton Av *CCHDY* M21 ......97 M8
Freckleton Dr *TOT/BURYW* BL8 .38 C4
Freckleton St *WGN* WN1 ....47 M2

Frederica Gdns *WGNE/HIN* WN2 .64 D1
Frederick Av *ROY/SHW* * OL2 ...43 K7
Frederick Rd *SLFD* M6 ....71 J8
Frederick St *AIMK* WN4 ....63 K7
  AUL OL6 ....91 H2
  CHAD OL9 ....8 B3
  CSLFD M3 ....6 C3
  DTN/ASHW M34 ....90 C7
  FWTH BL4 ....53 G4
  LIT OL15 ....20 B6
  OLDS OL8 ....8 E9
  RAMS BL0 ....17 B7
  WGNE/HIN WN2 ....49 G7
  WGNS/IIMK WN3 ....15 J8
Frederick Ter *BKLY* * M9 ....73 G3
Frederic St *WGN* * WN1 ....15 L4
Fred Tilson Cl *RUSH/FAL* M14 ...98 D1
Freehold St *ROCH* OL11 ....10 D8
Freelands *TYLD* M29 ....67 M3
Freeman Av *AUL* OL6 ....91 G1
Freeman Rd *DUK* SK16 ....90 F6
Freeman Sq *HULME* * M15 ....87 K6
Freemantle St *EDGY/DAV* SK3 .12 D6
Freesia Av *WALK* M28 ....68 C1
Freestone Cl *TOT/BURYW* BL8 ...4 C2
Freetown *RUSH/FAL* M14 ....87 K8
Freetown GLSP SK13 ....104 F5
Freetown Cl *RUSH/FAL* M14 ....87 K8
Freetrade St *ROCH* OL11 ....10 D8
Fremantle Av *GTN* M18 ....100 A1
French Av *OLD* OL1 ....59 M3
  STLY SK15 ....91 M3
French Barn La *BKLY* M9 ....72 F1
French Gv *BOLS/LL* BL3 ....37 G7
French St *AUL* OL6 ....76 A3
  STLY SK15 ....91 M3
Frenchwood Ct
  WGNE/HIN WN2 ....32 F8
Fresca Rd *OLD* OL1 ....44 A8
Fresh Cl *GLSP* SK13 ....104 C5
Freshfield *CHD/CHDH* SK8 .....119 K3
Freshfield Av *ATH* M46 ....50 F8
  BOLS/LL BL3 ....52 A2
  HYDE SK14 ....102 A3
  PWCH M25 ....55 M8
Freshfield Cl *FAIL* M35 ....74 D6
  MPL/ROM SK6 ....114 E3
Freshfield Gv *BOLS/LL* BL3 ......52 C2
Freshfield Rd *HTNM* SK4 ....111 J2
  WGNE/HIN WN2 ....49 J7
  WGNS/IIMK WN3 ....63 H1
Freshfields *RAD* M26 ....38 A7
Freshpool Wy *WYTH/NTH* M22 .110 B6
Freshwater Dr *DTN/ASHW* M34 .101 L4
Freshwater St *GTN* M18 ....89 H6
Fresnel Cl *HYDE* SK14 ....91 K8
Frewland Av *EDGY/DAV* SK3 ...112 C9
Freya Gv *ORD* M5 ....86 F4
Friarmere Rd *UPML* OL3 ....45 H7
Friars Cl *ALT* WA14 ....116 D3
  TYLD M29 ....68 A3
  WILM/AE SK9 ....126 C4
Friars Crs *ROCH* OL11 ....42 C2
Friar's Rd *SALE* M33 ....96 E8
Friendship Av *GTN* * M18 ....89 H8
Frieston Wk *WHIT* OL12 ....10 D2
Frieston Rd *ALT* WA14 ....108 B3
Friezland Cl *STLY* SK15 ....77 H7
Friezland La *UPML* OL3 ....61 K8
Frimley Gdns *WYTH/NTH* M22 .118 F1
Frinton Av *NEWH/MOS* * M40 ...74 A1
Frinton Cl *SALE* M33 ....108 C3
Frinton Rd *BOLS/LL* BL3 ....51 L1
Frith Rd *DID/WITH* M20 ....98 F7
Frith St *WGNNW/ST* WN6 ....14 B5
Frobisher Cl *BRUN/LGST* M13 ..88 A7
Frobisher Pl *RDSH* SK5 ....100 B8
Frobisher Rd *LIT* OL15 ....20 D3
Frodesley Wk
  WGTN/LGST * M12 ....88 C6
Frodsham Av *HTNM* SK4 ....12 C1
Frodsham Cl *WGNNW/ST* WN6 .47 G1
Frodsham Rd *SALE* M33 ....109 H2
Frodsham St *RUSH/FAL* * M14 ..98 E1
Frog La *WGNNW/ST* WN6 ....14 C3
Frogley St *BOLE* * BL2 ....36 E1
Frogmore Av *HYDE* SK14 ....102 B5
Frome Av *OFTN* SK2 ....112 F7
  URM M41 ....95 L4
Frome Cl *TYLD* M29 ....67 L6
Frome Dr *CHH* M8 ....72 E5
Frome St *OLDE* OL4 ....59 M6
Frostlands Rd *OLDTF/WHR* M16 .87 H8
Frostlands St
  OLDTF/WHR * M16 ....98 B1
Frost St *ANC* * M4 ....88 A3
  OLDS OL8 ....59 H8
Froxmer St *GTN* M18 ....88 F6
Fryent Cl *HOR/BR* BL6 ....33 C2
Fulbeck Av *WGNS/IIMK* WN3 ...63 K2
Fulbrook Dr *CHD/CHDH* SK8 ..120 C6
Fulbrook Wy *TYLD* M29 ....67 M3
Fulford St *OLDTF/WHR* M16 .....86 F8
Fulham Av *NEWH/MOS* M40 ....73 J7
Fulham St *OLDE* OL4 ....59 M6
Fullerton Rd *HTNM* SK4 ....12 A2
Full Pot La *ROCH* OL11 ....27 H4
Fulmar Cl *POY/DIS* SK12 ....121 J8
  WHTN BL5 ....50 A6
Fulmar Dr *OFTN* SK2 ....113 J7
  SALE M33 ....107 M2
Fulmards Cl *WILM/AE* SK9 .....127 G5
Fulmer Gdns *ROCH* OL11 ....27 J5
Fulmer Dr *ANC* M4 ....7 M2
Fulmere Ct *SWIN* M27 ....70 A6
Fulneck Sq *DROY* M43 ....89 K4
Fulshaw Av *WILM/AE* SK9 ......126 E6
Fulshaw Ct *WILM/AE* SK9 ......126 E7
Fulshaw Pk *WILM/AE* SK9 ......126 E8
Fulshaw Pk South
  WILM/AE SK9 ....126 E8
Fulstone Ms *OFTN* SK2 ....112 E6
Fulwell Av *TYLD* M29 ....67 H4
Fulwood Av *BKLY* M9 ....57 J8
Fulwood Cl *TOT/BURYW* BL8 ...38 C5
Fulwood Rd *GOL/RIS/CU* WA3 ..80 B6
Furbarn La *ROCH* OL11 ....27 G5
Furbarn Rd *ROCH* OL11 ....27 H5
Furlong Cl *WGNE/HIN* WN2 .....64 C5
Furlong Rd *WYTH/NTH* M22 ...118 D2
Furnace St *DUK* SK16 ....90 E3
  HYDE SK14 ....90 F8
Furness Av *AULW* OL7 ....75 J7
  BOLE BL2 ....37 G1
  HEY OL10 ....26 E8
  LIT OL15 ....20 E5
  OLDS OL8 ....59 M8
  WHTF M45 ....55 K4
Furness Cl *GLSP* SK13 ....105 J4
  MILN OL16 ....29 H6

  POY/DIS SK12 ....121 L8
Furness Crs *LEIGH* WN7 ....66 A3
Furness Gv *HTNM* SK4 ....111 K3
Furness Lodge Cl
  CHF/WBR SK23 ....124 F8
Furness Quay *SALQ* M50 ....86 D5
Furness Rd *BOL* BL1 ....35 L5
  CHD/CHDH SK8 ....120 E6
  MDTN M24 ....57 J1
  RUSH/FAL M14 ....98 F3
  URM M41 ....96 A1
Furness Sq *BOLE* BL2 ....36 E2
Furnival Cl *DTN/ASHW* M34 ...100 D2
Furnival Rd *GTN* M18 ....88 F6
Furnival St *LEIGH* WN7 ....66 C5
  RDSH SK5 ....100 B2
Furrow Dr *ECC* M30 ....69 L8
Further Fld *ROCH* OL11 ....27 G3
Further Hey Cl *OLDE* OL4 ....60 B5
Further La *HYDE* SK14 ....103 H1
Further Pits *ROCH* OL11 ....27 M5
Furtherwood Rd *OLD* OL1 ....58 F2
Furze Av *WHTN* BL5 ....50 C5
Furzegate *MILN* OL16 ....42 F1
Furze La *OLDE* OL4 ....60 A3
Fushia Gv *BRO* M7 ....86 F4
Futura Pk *HOR/BR* BL6 ....33 M4
Fylde Av *BOLE* BL2 ....36 E3
  CHD/CHDH SK8 ....119 L4
Fylde Rd *HTNM* SK4 ....111 K2
Fylde St *FWTH* BL4 ....53 G2
Fylde St East *FWTH* BL4 ....53 C2

G

Gable Av *WILM/AE* SK9 ....126 E5
Gable Dr *MDTN* M24 ....57 H3
The Gables *SALE* * M33 ....97 H7
Gable St *BOLE* * M33 ....23 G7
  OP/CLY M11 ....88 D2
The Gabriels *ROY/SHW* OL2 .....43 J5
Gabriels Ter *MDTN* M24 ....57 M5
Gadbury Av *ATH* M46 ....66 E1
Gaddum Rd *ALT* WA14 ....116 C3
  DID/WITH M20 ....110 F1
Gadwall Cl *WALK* M28 ....69 G4
Gail Av *HTNM* SK4 ....12 E2
Gail Cl *FAIL* M35 ....74 B7
  WILM/AE SK9 ....130 E2
Gainford Av *CHD/CHDH* SK8 ...110 A4
Gainford Gdns *NEWH/MOS* M40 .73 L3
Gainford Rd *RDSH* SK5 ....100 C3
Gainford Wk *BOLS/LL* * BL3 .....36 B8
Gainsborough Av *BOLS/LL* BL3 .51 M1
  DID/WITH * M20 ....98 F7
  MPL/ROM SK6 ....114 E4
  OLDS OL8 ....59 H8
  STRET * M32 ....97 J1
Gainsborough Cl
  WGNS/IIMK WN3 ....63 G1
  WILM/AE SK9 ....127 H4
Gainsborough Dr
  CHD/CHDH SK8 ....111 J6
  ROCH OL11 ....42 B1
Gainsborough Rd *CHAD* OL9 ...58 B4
  DTN/ASHW M34 ....90 A3
  RAMS BL0 ....24 D3
Gainsborough St *BRO* M7 ....72 B5
Gairloch Av *STRET* M32 ....96 E2
Gair Rd *RDSH* SK5 ....100 C8
Gair St *HYDE* SK14 ....91 G8
Gaitskell Cl *WGTN/LGST* M12 ...88 B3
Galbraith Rd *DID/WITH* M20 ...110 F1
Galbraith St *CMANE* * M1 ....7 H7
Galbraith Wy *ROCH* OL11 ....27 H4
Gale Dr *MDTN* M24 ....57 G2
Gale Rd *PWCH* M25 ....71 K7
Gale St *HEY* OL10 ....40 E2
  WHIT OL12 ....28 C1
Galgate Cl *HULME* M15 ....6 B9
  TOT/BURYW BL8 ....38 C3
Galindo St *BOLE* BL2 ....60 A4
Galland St *OLDE* OL4 ....60 A5
Galloway Cl *BOLS/LL* BL3 ....35 H7
  HEY OL10 ....40 C3
Galloway Dr *SWIN* M27 ....54 C8
Galloway Rd *SWIN* * M27 ....70 A6
Gallowsclough Rd *STLY* SK15 ...92 B4
Galston St *OP/CLY* M11 ....88 D4
Galsworthy Av *CHH* M8 ....72 D7
Galvin Rd *BKLY* M9 ....72 E1
Galway St *OLD* OL1 ....9 J6
Galwey Gv *WGN* WN1 ....31 M8
Gambleside Cl *WALK* M28 ....68 E4
Gamble St *LEIGH* WN7 ....66 D8
Gambrel Bank Rd *AUL* OL6 ......75 L6
Gambrel Gvl *AUL* OL6 ....75 L6
Game St *OLDE* OL4 ....59 M7
Gamma Wk *OP/CLY* M11 ....88 E2
Gandy La *WHIT* OL12 ....18 D8
Gantley Av *WGNW/BIL/O* WN5 ..46 A8
Gantley Crs *WGNW/BIL/O* WN5 .62 A1
Gantley Rd *WGNW/BIL/O* WN5 .62 A1
Gantock Wk *RUSH/FAL* M14 .....98 F1
Ganton Av *WHTF* M45 ....55 G5
Garbrook Av *BKLY* M9 ....56 C5
Garden Av *DROY* M43 ....89 L2
  STRET M32 ....97 G2
Garden City *RAMS* BL0 ....24 C8
Garden Cl *LIT* OL15 ....29 J2
Garden La *ALT* WA14 ....108 A7
  CSLFD M3 ....6 E4
  CSLFD M3 ....6 E4
  MILN OL16 ....11 G3
  WALK M28 ....68 D6
Garden Ms *AUL* * OL6 ....91 G2
Garden Rw *HEY* OL10 ....26 E8
The Gardens *BOL* BL1 ....22 C6
  EDGW/EG BL7 ....22 D4
Garden St *DTN/ASHW* M34 ......90 C6
  ECC M30 ....85 H3
  FWTH BL4 ....53 H4
  HYDE SK14 ....91 H8
  MILN OL16 ....29 L8
  OFTN * SK2 ....112 F7
  OLD OL1 ....9 K4
  RAMS BL0 ....24 B8
  TYLD M29 ....67 K4
Garden Ter *ROY/SHW* OL2 ....42 F5
Garden Wk *AUL* OL6 ....75 M8
Garden Wall Cl *ORD* M5 ....86 F4
Garden Wy *LIT* OL15 ....21 G5
Gardner Rd *PWCH* M25 ....55 M8
Gardner St *SLFD* M6 ....71 K8
  WGTN/LGST M12 ....88 B2

Garfield Av BNG/LEV M19 99 L3
Garfield Cl ROCH OL11 27 H4
Garfield Gv BOLS/LL BL3 2 B7
Garfield St BOLS/LL BL3 51 M1
STKP * SK1 13 L2
Garforth Av ANC M4 7 M2
Garforth St CHAD OL9 8 C4
Gargrave Av BOL BL1 35 J2
Gargrave St BRO M7 71 J4
OLDE OL4 59 L6
Garland Rd WYTH/NTH M22 119 G1
Garlick St CHAD OL9 9 G6
GTN M18 89 G7
HYDE * SK14 102 C1
Garnant Cl BKLY M9 73 J4
Garner Av HALE/TIMP WA15 108 D3
Garner Cl ALT WA14 116 F2
Garner Dr ECC * M30 84 F1
SLFD M6 86 A1
TYLD M29 67 L7
Garner's La EDGY/DAV SK3 112 C7
Garnet St OLD OL1 59 L4
Garnett Cl HYDE SK14 103 J1
Garnett Rd HYDE SK14 103 J1
Garnett St BOL BL1 36 B1
RAMS BL0 17 B6
STKP SK1 13 J5
Garratt Wy GTN M18 88 F7
Garret Gv ROY/SHW OL2 43 M5
Garrett Hall Rd WALK M28 68 B5
Garrett La TYLD M29 68 A5
Garrett Wk EDGY/DAV SK3 12 C6
Garrick Gdns WYTH/NTH M22 110 A8
Garsdale La BOL BL1 35 G5
Garside Av GOL/RIS/CU WA3 80 A5
Garside Gv BOL BL1 35 M2
WGNS/IIMK WN3 63 H2
Garside Hey Rd
TOT/BURYW BL8 24 E6
Garside St BOL BL1 2 C5
DTN/ASHW * M34 101 J2
HYDE SK14 102 B3
Garstang Av BOLE BL2 37 H6
Garstang Dr TOT/BURYW BL8 38 C3
Garston Av ATH M46 50 E7
Garston Cl HTNM SK4 12 C1
LEIGH WN7 66 B3
Garston St BURY BL9 25 K8
Garswood Crs
WGNW/BIL/O WN5 62 A8
Garswood Dr TOT/BURYW BL8 24 E6
Garswood Rd BOLS/LL BL3 52 B2
RUSH/FAL M14 98 C2
WGNW/BIL/O WN5 62 B8
Garswood St AIMK WN4 78 E1
The Garth ORD M5 86 A2
Garth Av HALE/TIMP WA15 108 B6
Garthland Rd BRAM/HZG SK7 122 B1
Garthmere Rd ATH M46 51 J7
Garthorne Cl OLDTF/WHR M16 87 G8
Garthorp Rd NTHM/RTH M23 109 H3
Garth Rd MPL/ROM SK6 114 D6
OFTN SK2 112 F5
WYTH/NTH M22 110 A8
Garthwaite Av OLDS OL8 75 H1
Garton Dr GOL/RIS/CU WA3 80 B3
Gartside St AULW * OL7 90 B3
CSLFD M3 6 D5
OLDE OL4 59 L7
UPML * OL3 45 H8
Garwick Rd BOL BL1 35 L1
Garwood St HULME M15 6 D9
Gascoyne St RUSH/FAL M14 98 E1
Gaskell Cl LIT * OL15 20 B6
Gaskell Ri OLD OL1 44 B7
Gaskell Rd ALT WA14 108 A6
ECC M30 85 G3
Gaskell St BOL BL1 2 B3
DUK * SK16 90 E3
NEWH/MOS M40 73 M7
SWIN M27 70 C2
WGNE/HIN WN2 49 H5
Gaskill St HEY OL10 40 D2
Gas St AUL OL6 90 E1
BOL BL1 2 C5
FWTH BL4 53 G3
HEY OL10 41 G2
HTNM SK4 13 G4
HYDE SK14 93 G7
ROCH OL11 10 C5
WGNE/HIN WN2 64 E2
Gatcombe Sq RUSH/FAL M14 98 F1
Gateacre Wk NTHM/RTH M23 109 H5
Gate Field Cl RAD M26 54 B1
Gategill Gv WGNW/BIL/O WN5 62 A2
Gatehead Cft UPML OL3 61 J1
Gatehead Ms UPML OL3 61 J1
Gatehead Rd UPML OL3 61 J1
Gatehouse LIT * OL15 20 E6
Gatehouse Rd WALK M28 52 D8
Gate Keeper Fold AULW OL7 75 K5
Gatesgarth Rd MDTN M24 56 F2
Gateshead Cl RUSH/FAL M14 87 L8
Gate St DUK SK16 90 D6
OP/CLY M11 88 F4
ROCH OL11 10 F9
Gateway Crs CHAD OL9 58 B8
Gateway Rd GTN * M18 88 F6
The Gateways SWIN M27 70 C3
Gathill Cl CHD/CHDH SK8 120 B3
Gathurst Hall
WGNNW/ST * WN6 46 C1
Gathurst La WGNNW/ST WN6 30 C7
Gathurst Rd WGNW/BIL/O WN5 46 B4
Gathurst St GTN M18 89 H6
Gatley Av RUSH/FAL M14 98 D3
Gatley Brow OLD * OL1 9 H2
Gatley Cl TYLD M29 67 L3
Gatley Gn CHD/CHDH SK8 110 D7
Gatley Rd CHD/CHDH SK8 110 F7
SALE M33 109 H1
Gatling Av WGTN/LGST M12 99 K2
Gatwick Av NTHM/RTH M23 109 L6
Gavin Av ORD M5 86 D3
Gawsworth Av DID/WITH M20 110 F3
Gawsworth Cl BRAM/HZG SK7 121 G7
EDGY/DAV SK3 112 A7
GLSP SK13 93 K7
HALE/TIMP WA15 109 G6
POY/DIS SK12 129 K2
ROY/SHW OL2 43 M5
Gawsworth Ms CHD/CHDH SK8 110 E7
Gawsworth Rd
GOL/RIS/CU WA3 79 J3
SALE M33 109 H2
Gawthorne Cl BRAM/HZG SK7 121 L2
Gawthorpe Cl BURY BL9 39 K7
Gaydon Rd SALE M33 96 A8
Gaynor Av RNFD/HAY WA11 78 C5
Gaythorne St BOL BL1 36 C1
Gaythorn St ORD M5 86 F3
Gayton Cl WGNS/IIMK WN3 63 G1
Gee Cross Fold HYDE SK14 102 B5
Gee La ECC M30 84 E1
Gee St EDGY/DAV SK3 12 F8
Geinsbury Cl OLDS OL8 59 L8
Gellert Pl WHTN BL5 50 B6
Gellert Rd WHTN BL5 50 B6
Gemini Rd SLFD M6 71 M8
Gencoyne Dr BOL BL1 22 A6
Gendre Rd EDGW/EG BL7 22 B4
Geneva Rd BRAM/HZG SK7 120 F1
Geneva Ter ROCH OL11 27 M4
Geneva Wk CHAD OL9 8 C6
Genista Gv BRO * M7 72 A6
Geoffrey St BURY BL9 5 H1
RAMS BL0 17 A8
WHTN BL5 51 J4
George Barton St BOLE BL2 3 J1
George La MPL/ROM SK6 101 K8
George Leigh St ANC M4 7 K3
George Mann Cl
WYTH/NTH M22 118 E3
George Richards Wy ALT WA14 107 L5
George Rd RAMS BL0 17 B7
George's La HOR/BR BL6 21 D5
WGN WN1 15 M4
George Sq OLD OL1 9 H6
George's Rd HTNM SK4 12 E4
SALE M33 108 E1
George's Rd West
POY/DIS SK12 129 H1
George's Ter WGNW/BIL/O WN5 46 A7
George St AIMK WN4 63 M8
ATH M46 67 G1
AUL OL6 90 F1
BURY BL9 5 G5
CHAD OL9 58 D5
CMANE M1 7 G6
DTN/ASHW M34 101 K1
ECC M30 84 F3
FAIL M35 74 C4
FWTH BL4 52 E5
GLSP SK13 104 F4
HEY OL10 40 E1
HOR/BR BL6 33 M1
IRL M44 94 E1
LIT * OL15 20 C7
MILN OL16 11 G2
MILN OL16 29 G1
MOSL OL5 76 F3
MPL/ROM SK6 114 E2
NEWLW * WA12 78 D8
OLD OL1 9 H6
PWCH M25 71 L3
RAD M26 54 C1
ROY/SHW OL2 43 M3
STKP SK1 13 L4
STLY SK15 91 K2
URM M41 96 B2
WGNE/HIN WN2 48 C5
WGNE/HIN WN2 49 H8
WHIT OL12 18 D4
WHTF M45 55 H3
WHTN BL5 50 C4
WILM/AE SK9 130 D3
George St East STKP SK1 112 E4
George St North BRO M7 72 C4
George St South BRO M7 72 B4
George St West STKP SK1 112 E4
Georgette Dr CSLFD M3 6 D1
Georgiana St BURY BL9 4 F6
FWTH BL4 52 E3
Georgina Ct BOLS/LL BL3 51 L2
Georgina St BOLS/LL BL3 51 L2
Gerald Av CHH M8 72 D4
Gerald Rd SLFD M6 71 K7
Gerard St AIMK WN4 78 E1
Germain Cl BKLY M9 56 F7
Gerrard Av HALE/TIMP WA15 108 D4
Gerrard Cl WGNE/HIN WN2 49 G2
Gerrard Rd WGNW/BIL/O WN5 62 B7
Gerrards Cl IRL M44 94 D2
Gerrards Gdns HYDE SK14 102 B5
Gerrards Hollow HYDE SK14 102 A5
Gerrard St FWTH BL4 53 H4
LEIGH * WN7 66 C7
ROCH OL11 42 D3
SLFD M6 86 D1
STLY SK15 91 L3
WHTN BL5 50 B3
Gerrards Wd HYDE SK14 102 A5
Gertrude Cl ORD M5 86 D4
Gervis Cl NEWH/MOS * M40 73 G7
Ghyll Gv WALK M28 69 H2
Giants Hall Rd WGNNW/ST WN6 47 H1
Gibb La MPL/ROM SK6 115 H7
Gibbon Av WYTH/NTH M22 118 F2
Gibbon's Rd AIMK WN4 78 A2
Gibbon St BOLS/LL BL3 2 A9
OP/CLY M11 88 D2
Gibb Rd WALK M28 69 L5
Gibbs St CSLFD M3 6 A4
Gib La NTHM/RTH M23 109 L5
Gibraltar La DTN/ASHW M34 101 L4
Gibraltar St BOLS/LL BL3 2 A7
OLDE OL4 60 A7
Gibsmere Cl HALE/TIMP WA15 109 G6
Gibson Av GTN M18 89 J5
Gibson Gv WALK M28 68 D1
Gibson La WALK M28 68 D1
Gibson Pl ANC M4 87 K1
Gibsons Rd HTNM SK4 99 L8
Gibson St BOLE BL2 36 F3
MILN OL16 11 M2
OLDE * OL4 59 M6
WGNE/HIN WN2 65 G2
Gibson Wy ALT WA14 107 M4
Gibwood Rd WYTH/NTH M22 109 M4
Gidlow Av WGNNW/ST WN6 47 K2
Gidlow La WGNNW/ST WN6 14 C2
WGNNW/ST WN6 31 K8
Gidlow St GTN M18 89 H6
WGNE/HIN WN2 48 D4
Gifford Av BKLY M9 57 J8
Gifford Pl WGNE/HIN WN2 49 J8
Gigg La BURY BL9 5 J9
Gilbertbank MPL/ROM SK6 101 K8
Gilbert Rd HALE/TIMP WA15 117 G3
Gilbert St ECC M30 84 E4
HULME M15 6 D8
ORD * M5 86 C3
RAMS BL0 17 C3
WALK M28 68 F3
WGNE/HIN WN2 48 F7
Gilbrook Wy MILN OL16 42 E2
Gilchrist Rd IRL M44 94 B6
Gilda Brook Rd ECC M30 85 K2
Gilda Crs ECC M30 85 K1
Gilda Rd WALK M28 68 B5
Gildenhall FAIL M35 74 D5
Gilderdale Cl ROY/SHW OL2 43 L4
Gilderdale St BOLS/LL BL3 36 C8
Gildersdale Dr BKLY M9 56 E6
Gildridge Rd OLDTF/WHR M16 98 B3
Gilesgate RUSH/FAL M14 98 F1
Giles St WGTN/LGST M12 88 D8
Gillan Rd WGNNW/ST WN6 47 L2
Gill Av WGNNW/ST WN6 30 E6
Gillbent Rd CHD/CHDH SK8 120 C6
Gillbrook Rd DID/WITH M20 110 E2
Gillbrow Crs WGN WN1 48 C3
Gillemere Gv ROY/SHW OL2 43 M5
Gillers Gn WALK M28 68 F2
Gillford Av BKLY M9 73 J4
Gillingham Rd ECC M30 84 E2
Gillingham Sq OP/CLY M11 88 C4
Gill St BKLY M9 73 J3
STKP SK1 112 E1
Gillwood Dr MPL/ROM SK6 113 J3
Gilman Cl BKLY * M9 72 F2
Gilman St BKLY M9 72 F2
Gilmerton Dr NEWH/MOS * M40 73 M7
Gilmore Dr PWCH M25 55 L7
Gilmore St EDGY/DAV SK3 13 H8
Gilmour St MDTN M24 57 K4
Gilmour Ter BKLY M9 73 J3
Gilnow Gdns BOL BL1 35 M6
Gilnow Gv BOL BL1 2 A6
Gilnow La BOLS/LL BL3 35 M6
Gilnow Rd BOL BL1 35 M6
Gilpin Pl WGNE/HIN WN2 64 C2
Gilpin Rd URM M41 96 C3
Gilroy St WGN WN1 15 J4
Giltbrook Av NEWH/MOS M40 73 G8
Gilwell Dr NTHM/RTH M23 109 J8
Gilwood Gv MDTN M24 41 J8
Gin Croft La RAMS BL0 17 E1
Gingham Brow HOR/BR BL6 21 D8
Gingham Pk RAD M26 38 B7
Gipsy La OFTN SK2 112 F6
Girton Av AIMK WN4 63 J8
Girton St BOLE * BL2 37 G5
BRO M7 72 B8
Girvan Av NEWH/MOS M40 74 A2
Girvan Cl BOLS/LL BL3 51 M1
Girvan Crs AIMK WN4 62 F8
Gisborn Dr SLFD M6 71 J7
Gisburn Av BOL BL1 35 H2
GOL/RIS/CU WA3 79 J2
Gisburn Dr TOT/BURYW BL8 38 B1
Gisburne Av NEWH/MOS M40 74 A2
Gisburn Rd ROCH OL11 42 D1
Givendale Dr CHH M8 72 D2
Givvons Fold OLDE OL4 60 A3
Glabyn Av HOR/BR BL6 34 C4
Gladden Hey Dr
WGNS/IIMK WN3 63 G3
The Glade BOL BL1 36 A3
HTNM SK4 111 K3
WGNNW/ST WN6 30 E6
Glade Brow OLDE * OL4 60 D6
Gladeside Rd WYTH/NTH M22 109 M8
Glade St BOL BL1 35 M5
Gladewood Cl WILM/AE SK9 127 G4
Gladstone Cl BOL * BL1 36 B2
GLSP SK13 105 G4
Gladstone Ct HULME M15 87 H8
Gladstone Crs ROCH OL11 42 D1
Gladstone Gv HTNM SK4 111 K1
Gladstone Ms HTNM * SK4 13 H1
Gladstone Pl FWTH BL4 52 F3
Gladstone Rd ALT WA14 108 A6
ECC M30 85 H2
FWTH BL4 52 F3
URM M41 96 B2
Gladstone St BOL BL1 36 B2
BURY BL9 5 J3
GLSP SK13 93 K8
GLSP SK13 104 F4
OFTN SK2 112 F8
OLDE OL4 59 L6
SWIN M27 70 D4
WHTN BL5 50 B3
Gladstone Terrace Rd
UPML OL3 61 K8
Gladstone Wy NEWLW WA12 78 E8
Gladwyn Av DID/WITH M20 98 B8
Gladys St FWTH BL4 53 G2
Glaisdale OLDE OL4 60 A6
Glaisdale Cl AIMK WN4 78 F1
BOLE BL2 36 E2
Glaisdale St BOLE BL2 36 E2
Glaister La BOLE BL2 37 G3
Glamis Av HEY OL10 41 H5
OP/CLY M11 88 E1
STRET M32 96 D2
Glamis Cl LEIGH WN7 67 G6
Glamorgan Pl CHAD OL9 8 C8
Glandon Dr CHD/CHDH SK8 120 E5
Glanford Av BKLY M9 72 D1
Glanvor Rd EDGY/DAV SK3 12 C7
Glassbrook St WGNNW/ST WN6 14 C1
Glasshouse St ANC M4 7 L1
Glasson Wk CHAD OL9 58 D6
Glass St FWTH * BL4 53 H5
Glastonbury WHIT OL12 10 D2
Glastonbury Av
CHD/CHDH SK8 120 E6
GOL/RIS/CU WA3 80 E4
HALE/TIMP WA15 117 K2
Glastonbury Dr POY/DIS SK12 121 M7
Glastonbury Rd STRET M32 96 C1
TYLD M29 67 L5
Glaswen Gv RDSH SK5 100 C8
Glazebrook Cl HEY OL10 40 F3
Glazebury Dr NTHM/RTH M23 109 L7
WHTN BL5 50 C2
Glazedale Av ROY/SHW OL2 42 F8
Glaze Wk WHTF M45 55 M2
Gleaves Av BOLE BL2 23 K8
Gleaves Rd ECC M30 85 H3
Gleave St BOL * BL1 2 F3
SALE M33 96 E6
Glebe Av AIMK WN4 78 E2
Glebe Cl WGNNW/ST WN6 31 H3
Glebe End St WGNNW/ST WN6 14 D3
Glebelands Rd NTHM/RTH M23 109 J6
PWCH M25 55 K7
SALE M33 96 D6
Glebe La OLD OL1 60 B1
Glebe Rd URM M41 96 A2
WGNNW/ST WN6 31 J4
Glebe St BOLE BL2 3 G6
CHAD OL9 74 D1
LEIGH WN7 66 C6
RAD M26 54 E1
ROY/SHW OL2 43 L5
STKP SK1 13 M5
WGNE/HIN WN2 65 M2
WHTN BL5 50 B3
Gleden St NEWH/MOS M40 88 B2
Gledhall St STLY SK15 91 J2
Gledhill Av ORD M5 86 D5
Gledhill Cl ROY/SHW OL2 43 K3
Gledhill St DID/WITH M20 98 E5
Gledhill Wy EDGW/EG BL7 22 D3
Glegg St WGNE/HIN WN2 48 C4
Glemsford Cl NEWH/MOS * M40 73 L6
WGNS/IIMK WN3 63 L1
The Glen BOL BL1 35 H5
MDTN M24 57 L6
Glenacre Gdns GTN M18 100 B1
Glenart ECC M30 85 H1
Glen Av BKLY M9 73 H3
BOLS/LL BL3 35 L7
FWTH BL4 53 L6
SALE M33 96 D6
SWIN M27 70 A4
WALK M28 69 K4
Glenavon Dr ROY/SHW OL2 43 J4
WHIT OL12 28 A1
Glenbarry Cl BRUN/LGST M13 87 L6
Glenbarry St WGTN/LGST M12 88 A4
Glenbeck Cl HOR/BR BL6 34 A3
Glenbeck Rd WHTF M45 55 H3
Glenboro Av TOT/BURYW BL8 38 E2
Glen Bott St BOL BL1 36 A2
Glenbourne Pk BRAM/HZG SK7 120 F7
Glenbranter Av WGNE/HIN WN2 48 D4
Glenbrook Gdns FWTH BL4 53 G2
Glenbrook Hl GLSP SK13 104 F2
Glenbrook Rd BKLY M9 56 D7
Glenburn St BOLS/LL BL3 52 A1
Glenby Av WYTH/NTH M22 119 H1
Glencar WHTN BL5 50 A5
Glencastle Rd GTN M18 88 F7
Glencoe Cl HEY OL10 40 B3
Glencoe Dr BOLE BL2 37 J6
SALE M33 107 M2
Glencoe Pl ROCH OL11 10 A5
Glencoe St OLDS * OL8 74 F2
Glen Cottages BOL * BL1 35 H2
Glencross Av CCHDY M21 97 K2
Glendale SWIN M27 70 E3
Glendale Av AIMK WN4 63 M8
BNG/LEV M19 99 J6
BURY BL9 55 J1
Glendale Ct OLDS OL8 59 J8
Glendale Dr BOLS/LL BL3 35 J6
Glendale Rd ECC M30 85 K1
WALK M28 68 C5
Glendene Av BRAM/HZG SK7 120 F7
DROY M43 89 M1
Glenden Foot WHIT OL12 28 A2
Glendevon Cl BOLS/LL BL3 35 H8
WGNE/HIN WN2 48 D4
Glendevon Pl WHTF M45 55 L5
Glendinning St SLFD M6 86 B2
Glendon Ct OLD OL1 44 B8
Glendon Crs AUL OL6 75 L5
Glendore ORD M5 85 M2
Glendower Dr NEWH/MOS M40 72 F7
Glen Dr WGNNW/ST WN6 30 B4
Gleneagles BOLS/LL BL3 51 J1
Gleneagles Av HEY OL10 41 G4
Gleneagles Cl BRAM/HZG SK7 121 J5
WILM/AE SK9 127 H4
Gleneagles Rd CHD/CHDH SK8 119 L3
URM M41 84 B8
Gleneagles Wy RAMS BL0 17 B7
Glenfield ALT WA14 107 L8
Glenfield Cl OLDE OL4 60 A6
Glenfield Dr POY/DIS SK12 129 H1
Glenfield Rd HTNM SK4 100 A8
Glenfield Sq FWTH BL4 52 E2
Glenfyne Rd SLFD M6 71 G7
Glen Gdns WHIT OL12 28 C1
Glengarth UPML OL3 61 L5
Glengarth Dr HOR/BR BL6 34 F6
Glen Gv MDTN M24 57 M6
ROY/SHW OL2 43 G7
Glenhaven Av URM M41 95 M2
Glenholme Rd BRAM/HZG SK7 120 F5
Glenhurst Rd BNG/LEV * M19 99 H7
Glenilla Av WALK M28 69 H5
Glenlea Dr DID/WITH M20 110 E4
Glenmaye Gv WGNE/HIN WN2 49 K7
Glenmere Cl WHTF M45 55 J6
Glenmere Rd DID/WITH M20 110 F4
Glenmoor Rd STKP SK1 13 L5
Glenmore Av DID/WITH M20 98 B8
FWTH BL4 52 D2
Glenmore Cl BOLS/LL BL3 35 H7
ROCH OL11 27 H7
Glenmore Dr CHH M8 72 E5
FAIL M35 74 E4
Glenmore Gv DUK SK16 90 F4
Glenmore Rd RAMS BL0 24 C2
Glenmore St BURY BL9 4 D6
Glenolden St OP/CLY M11 89 G2
Glenpark LEIGH WN7 66 D6
Glenridding Cl OLD OL1 59 K3
Glenridge Cl BOL BL1 36 C2
Glen Ri HALE/TIMP WA15 108 D7
Glen Rd OLDE OL4 59 M6
Glen Royd WHIT OL12 27 M3
Glensdale Dr NEWH/MOS M40 74 B3
Glenshee Dr BOLS/LL BL3 35 J7
Glenside Av GTN M18 100 A1
Glenside Dr BOLS/LL BL3 52 C2
MPL/ROM SK6 101 L7
WILM/AE SK9 127 G6
Glenside Gdns FAIL M35 74 D5
Glenside Gv WALK M28 53 H8
Glen St RAMS BL0 17 B5
SALQ M50 86 D5
Glenthorn Av BKLY M9 57 G6
Glenthorne St BOL BL1 36 B3
Glenthorn Gv SALE M33 108 E1
Glentrool Ms BOL BL1 35 K5
Glent Vw STLY SK15 76 D8
Glenvale Cl RAD M26 54 E1
Glen Vw ROY/SHW OL2 43 G7
Glenview Rd TYLD M29 67 J2
Glenville Wy DTN/ASHW M34 101 K2
Glenwood Av HYDE SK14 91 G7
Glenwood Cl RAD M26 54 E2
Glenwood Dr BKLY M9 73 H5
MDTN M24 57 M2
Glenwood Gv OFTN SK2 121 K1
Glenwyn Av BKLY M9 57 H8
Globe Cl OLDTF/WHR M16 87 G7
Globe La DUK SK16 90 E5
EDGW/EG BL7 22 A1
Globe Sq DUK SK16 90 D5
Glodwick Rd OLDE OL4 59 L7
Glossop Brook Rd GLSP SK13 104 E3
Glossop Rd GLSP SK13 103 H8
GLSP SK13 104 A4
MPL/ROM SK6 114 F3
Glossop Wy WGNE/HIN WN2 49 H8
Gloster St BOLE BL2 3 H5
Gloucester Av BNG/LEV M19 99 L4
GOL/RIS/CU WA3 79 L3
HEY OL10 40 F5
HOR/BR BL6 34 A2
MPL/ROM SK6 114 C6
WHIT OL12 19 L8
WHTF M45 55 J4
Gloucester Cl AUL OL6 76 A4
Gloucester Crs WGNE/HIN WN2 49 H6
Gloucester Dr SALE M33 96 A8
UPML OL3 45 M8
Gloucester Pl ATH M46 51 G8
SLFD M6 86 D1
Gloucester Ri DUK SK16 91 K5
Gloucester Rd CHD/CHDH SK8 119 L5
DROY M43 89 K1
DTN/ASHW M34 100 D2
HYDE SK14 102 B4
MDTN M24 57 K6
POY/DIS SK12 121 M8
SLFD M6 70 F8
URM M41 96 A3
WGNW/BIL/O WN5 46 F6
Gloucester St ATH M46 66 F1
CMANE M1 6 F8
ORD M5 86 F4
SLFD M6 71 K8
Gloucester St North CHAD OL9 8 C8
Gloucester Wy GLSP SK13 105 J4
Glover Centre MOSL * OL5 77 G4
Glover Dr HYDE SK14 102 B2
Glover St HOR/BR BL6 21 B8
LEIGH WN7 65 M4
Glyn Av HALE/TIMP WA15 117 J2
Glynne St FWTH BL4 52 F4
Glynrene Dr SWIN M27 69 M2
Glynwood Pk FWTH BL4 52 F3
Goats Gate Ter WHTF * M45 55 G2
Godbert Av CCHDY M21 97 M7
Goddard La GLSP SK13 93 K6
Goddard St OLDS OL8 59 J8
Godfrey Av DROY M43 89 G1
Godfrey Range GTN M18 89 J8
Godfrey Rd SLFD M6 70 F7
Godlee Dr SWIN M27 70 B5
Godley Cl OP/CLY M11 88 F5
Godley Hill Rd HYDE SK14 102 E1
Godley St HYDE SK14 91 J8
Godmond Hall Dr WALK M28 68 C7
Godson St OLD OL1 9 G1
Godward Rd NM/HAY SK22 124 D4
Godwin St GTN M18 89 H6
Golborne Av DID/WITH M20 98 C5
Golborne Dale Rd NEWLW WA12 79 K8
Golborne Gallery WGN * WN1 14 F3
Golborne Pl WGN * WN1 15 K3
Golborne Rd AIMK WN4 64 A8
GOL/RIS/CU WA3 79 M4
Golborne St NEWLW WA12 79 H8
Goldbourne Dr ROY/SHW OL2 43 L4
Goldbrook Cl HEY OL10 41 H3
Goldcrest Cl WALK M28 68 E5
WYTH/NTH M22 110 C7
Goldenhill Av OP/CLY M11 88 F1
Golden St ECC M30 85 G3
ROY/SHW OL2 44 B4
Goldenways WGN WN1 47 M2
Goldfinch Dr BURY BL9 25 M7
Goldfinch Wy DROY M43 89 M1
Goldie Av WYTH/NTH M22 119 H3
Goldrill Av BOLE BL2 37 J4
Goldrill Gdns BOLE BL2 37 J4
Goldsmith Av OLD OL1 44 B8
ORD M5 86 A2
Goldsmith Pl WGNS/IIMK WN3 47 K8
Goldsmith Rd RDSH SK5 100 A3
Goldsmith St BOLS/LL BL3 36 A8
Gold St CMANE * M1 7 H5
Goldsworthy Rd URM M41 95 H2
Goldsworthy Rd URM M41 95 H1
Golf Rd HALE/TIMP WA15 117 H1
SALE M33 97 J8
Golfview Dr ECC M30 70 A8
Gooch St HOR/BR BL6 33 L2
Goodacre HYDE SK14 91 L6
Gooden St HEY OL10 41 H3
Goodiers Dr ORD M5 86 D4
Goodier St NEWH/MOS M40 73 H7
SALE M33 96 D8
Goodier Vw HYDE SK14 91 J7
Goodison Cl BURY BL9 55 L1
Goodlad St TOT/BURYW BL8 24 E8
Goodman St BKLY M9 73 H3
Goodrich ROCH OL11 10 C7
Goodridge Av WYTH/NTH M22 118 E2
Goodrington Rd WILM/AE SK9 127 J2
Goodshaw Rd WALK M28 68 F4
Good Shepherd Cl MILN OL16 11 H3
Goodwill Cl SWIN M27 70 C5
Goodwin Sq BKLY * M9 73 G5
Goodwin St BOL BL1 3 G3
Goodwood Av NTHM/RTH M23 109 G4
SALE M33 95 M8
Goodwood Cl BOLS/LL BL3 53 J1
Goodwood Crs
HALE/TIMP WA15 108 F6
Goodwood Dr OLD OL1 59 L3
SWIN M27 70 E5
Goodwood Rd MPL/ROM SK6 114 B7
Goole St OP/CLY M11 88 D4
Goose Cote Hl EDGW/EG BL7 22 B2
Goose Gn ALT WA14 108 A8
Goose La WHIT OL12 10 E2
Goosetrey Cl WILM/AE SK9 127 J3
Goostrey Av DID/WITH M20 98 C4
Gordon Av AIMK WN4 63 H8
BNG/LEV M19 99 L3
BOLS/LL BL3 35 M7
BRAM/HZG SK7 121 M1
CHAD OL9 74 D1
OLDE OL4 59 M6
RNFD/HAY WA11 78 C5
Gordon Cl WGNW/BIL/O WN5 47 H4
Gordon Ct LIT OL15 20 C6
Gordon Pl DID/WITH M20 98 E7
Gordon Rd ECC M30 85 G1
SALE M33 96 E6
SWIN M27 69 M6
Gordonstoun Crs
WGNW/BIL/O WN5 46 C5
Gordon St AUL * OL6 76 A8
BRO M7 72 A8
BURY BL9 4 D1
CHAD OL9 58 C8
GTN M18 89 H6
HTNM SK4 13 H2
HYDE SK14 102 B2

LEIGH WN7 66 C6
MILN OL16 43 L1
OLDE OL4 60 D6
OLDTF/WHR M16 87 G8
ROCH * OL11 11 H9
ROY/SHW OL2 43 M5
STLY SK15 91 L3
WGN WN1 15 L5
Gordon Ter BKLY * M9 73 H4
Gordon Wy HEY OL10 40 C3
Gore Av FAIL M35 74 E5
ORD M5 86 A2
Gorebrook Ct WGTN/LGST M12 88 D8
Gore Crs ORD M5 86 A1
Goredale Av GTN M18 100 B1
Gore Dr SLFD M6 86 A1
Gorelan Rd GTN * M18 89 G7
Gore St BURY BL9 39 M3
CMANE M1 7 J5
CSLFD M3 6 C4
SLFD M6 86 D1
WGNW/BIL/O WN5 46 E6
Goring Av GTN M18 89 G6
Gorman St WGNNW/ST WN6 14 B3
Gorman Wk WGNS/IIMK WN3 14 A9
Gorrells Wy ROCH OL11 42 A1
Gorrels Cl ROCH OL11 42 A1
Gorrel St ROCH OL11 11 H9
The Gorse ALT WA14 116 D4
Gorse Av DROY M43 89 M2
MOSL OL5 77 H3
MPL/ROM SK6 114 B6
OLDS OL8 75 M1
STRET M32 97 J1
Gorse Bank BURY BL9 39 M1
Gorse Bank Rd
HALE/TIMP WA15 117 L5
Gorse Crs STRET M32 97 J1
Gorse Dr LHULT M38 52 C6
STRET M32 97 J1
Gorsefield Dr SWIN M27 70 C5
Gorsefield Hey WILM/AE SK9 127 J4
Gorse Hall Cl DUK * SK16 91 J5
Gorse Hall Dr STLY SK15 91 J3
Gorse Hall Rd DUK SK16 91 H5
Gorselands CHD/CHDH SK8 120 D7
Gorse La STRET M32 97 J1
Gorse Rd MILN OL16 29 J6
SWIN M27 70 B6
WALK M28 69 H2
Gorses Dr WGNE/HIN WN2 32 F6
Gorses Mt BOLE BL2 3 M8
Gorse Sq PART M31 106 A1
Gorses Rd BOLS/LL BL3 3 M8
Gorse St CHAD OL9 58 C8
STRET M32 97 H1
Gorse Wy GLSP SK13 105 H4
Gorseway RDSH SK5 100 E8
Gorsey Av WYTH/NTH M22 109 M8
Gorsey Bank Rd EDGY/DAV SK3 12 A6
Gorsey Brow HYDE SK14 103 K3
MPL/ROM SK6 113 K2
STKP SK1 13 L5
WGNW/BIL/O WN5 62 A7
Gorsey Brow Cl
WGNW/BIL/O WN5 62 A7
Gorsey Clough Wk
TOT/BURYW BL8 24 C7
Gorsey Dr WYTH/NTH M22 109 M8
Gorseyfields DROY M43 89 K4
Gorsey Hey WHTN BL5 50 B5
Gorsey Hill St HEY OL10 41 G3
Gorsey Intakes HYDE SK14 103 K4
Gorsey La ALT WA14 107 L7
AUL OL6 76 C6
LYMM WA13 106 D6
Gorsey Mount St STKP SK1 13 K5
STKP SK1 13 M5
Gorsey Rd WILM/AE SK9 126 D5
WYTH/NTH M22 109 M8
Gorsey Wy AUL OL6 76 B6
Gorsley Bank LIT OL15 20 D5
Gorston Wk WYTH/NTH M22 118 E4
Gort Cl BURY BL9 55 K3
Gorton Crs DTN/ASHW M34 100 F2
Gorton Gv WALK M28 52 F7
Gorton La WGTN/LGST M12 88 D6
Gorton Rd OP/CLY M11 88 C5
RDSH SK5 100 C4
Gorton St AULW OL7 90 C3
BOLE BL2 3 G6
CHAD OL9 8 A7
CSLFD * M3 6 E2
ECC M30 84 D3
FWTH BL4 52 E5
HEY OL10 41 H2
NEWH/MOS M40 72 F8
Gortonvilla Wk WGTN/LGST M12 88 C6
Gosforth Cl OLD OL1 59 K3
TOT/BURYW BL8 24 F7
Goshen La BURY BL9 39 J6
Gosport Sq BRO M7 72 A7
Goss Hall St OLDE * OL4 59 M6
Gotha Wk BRUN/LGST * M13 87 M6
Gotherage Cl MPL/ROM SK6 114 B2
Gotherage La MPL/ROM SK6 114 B2
Gothic Cl MPL/ROM SK6 114 C2
Gough St EDGY/DAV SK3 12 F5
HEY * OL10 41 H2
Goulden Rd DID/WITH M20 98 D7
Goulden St ANC M4 7 J2
SLFD M6 86 B2
Goulder Rd GTN M18 100 B1
Gould St ANC M4 87 L1
DTN/ASHW M34 101 H1
OLD OL1 59 L4
Gourham Dr CHD/CHDH SK8 120 B2
Govan St WYTH/NTH M22 110 B3
Gowan Dr MDTN M24 57 G2
Gowanlock's St BOL BL1 36 B2
Gowan Rd OLDTF/WHR M16 98 B3
Gower Av BRAM/HZG SK7 121 L1
Gowerdale Rd RDSH SK5 100 F7
Gower Rd HTNM SK4 100 A8
HYDE SK14 102 A3
Gowers St MILN OL16 11 J2
Gower St AUL * OL6 90 F1
BOL BL1 2 A3
FWTH BL4 52 F3
OLD OL1 9 L4
SWIN M27 70 D3
WGNW/BIL/O WN5 14 A7
Gowran Pk OLDE OL4 60 A6
Gowy Cl WILM/AE SK9 127 J3
Goyt Av MPL/ROM SK6 114 C8
Goyt Crs MPL/ROM SK6 113 J1
STKP SK1 112 E1
Goyt Hey Av WGNW/BIL/O WN5 62 B8
Goyt Rd MPL/ROM SK6 114 C8
NM/HAY SK22 124 E6
POY/DIS SK12 123 M7
STKP SK1 112 E1
Goyt Valley Rd MPL/ROM SK6 113 J2
Goyt Vw NM/HAY SK22 124 D6
Goyt Wy MPL/ROM SK6 114 C3
MPL/ROM SK6 114 E7
NM/HAY SK22 124 E6
Grace St HOR/BR BL6 21 B8
LEIGH WN7 65 M7
WHIT OL12 28 D2
Grace Wk ANC M4 88 A3
Gracie Av OLD OL1 59 L3
Gradwell St EDGY/DAV SK3 12 F6
Grafton Av ECC M30 70 D8
Grafton Ct MILN OL16 11 K7
The Graftons ALT * WA14 108 A8
Grafton St ALT WA14 108 A8
ATH M46 66 D3
AUL OL6 91 G2
BOL BL1 2 A3
BRUN/LGST M13 87 L7
BURY BL9 4 F9
FAIL M35 74 C4
HTNM SK4 112 B1
MILN OL16 11 K7
OLD OL1 44 B8
STLY SK15 92 A1
Graham Dr POY/DIS SK12 123 L5
Graham Rd SLFD M6 70 F8
STKP SK1 112 E4
Graham St AULW OL7 90 C3
BOL * BL1 2 E2
OP/CLY M11 88 D4
WGNE/HIN WN2 64 D3
Grainger Av WGTN/LGST M12 99 K1
Grains Rd ROY/SHW OL2 43 M5
UPML OL3 44 E7
Grain Vw ORD * M5 86 D4
Gralam Cl SALE M33 109 H3
Grammar School Rd OLDS OL8 74 E1
Grampian Cl CHAD OL9 58 D7
Grampian Wy GOL/RIS/CU WA3 80 A3
ROY/SHW OL2 43 K4
Granada Ms OLDTF/WHR * M16 98 B3
Granada Rd DTN/ASHW M34 100 D1
Granary La WALK M28 69 J8
Granary Wy SALE M33 108 C2
Granby Rd CHD/CHDH SK8 120 D4
HALE/TIMP WA15 108 D3
OFTN SK2 112 E7
STRET M32 97 H3
SWIN M27 69 M5
Granby Rw CMANE M1 7 H7
Granby St CHAD OL9 74 D2
TOT/BURYW BL8 24 C8
Grandale St RUSH/FAL * M14 98 F1
Grand Central Sq
EDGY/DAV * SK3 13 H6
Grandidge St ROCH OL11 10 D8
Grand Union Wy ECC M30 85 G4
Granford Cl ALT * WA14 108 A5
The Grange HYDE SK14 102 C3
OLD * OL1 59 L4
RUSH/FAL M14 98 F1
WHTN BL5 49 M4
Grange Av BNG/LEV M19 99 J4
BOLS/LL BL3 53 M1
CHD/CHDH SK8 120 B1
ECC M30 70 A8
HALE/TIMP WA15 108 E5
HALE/TIMP WA15 117 J2
HTNM SK4 99 M7
MILN OL16 29 J8
OLDS OL8 58 F8
STRET M32 97 G2
SWIN M27 70 A2
URM M41 95 H2
WGNS/IIMK WN3 14 D9
WGNW/BIL/O WN5 46 E5
Grange Cl GOL/RIS/CU WA3 79 M6
HYDE SK14 102 C3
Grange Ct OLDS * OL8 58 F8
Grange Crs URM M41 95 M3
Grange Dr BKLY M9 73 J1
ECC M30 70 A8
Grangeforth Rd CHH M8 72 C4
Grange Gv WHTF M45 55 J4
Grange La DID/WITH M20 110 E2
UPML OL3 45 J6
Grange Park Av AUL OL6 76 C6
CHD/CHDH SK8 111 G7
WILM/AE SK9 126 E4
Grangepark Rd BKLY M9 73 J1
Grange Park Rd BOLE BL2 22 F6
CHD/CHDH SK8 111 G7
Grange Pl IRL M44 94 A7
Grange Rd AIMK WN4 63 J6
ALT WA14 116 E3
BOLE BL2 22 F5
BOLS/LL BL3 35 L7
BRAM/HZG SK7 121 H1
CCHDY M21 97 K2
ECC M30 69 J8
FWTH BL4 52 D3
HALE/TIMP WA15 108 E5
HYDE SK14 102 C3
MDTN M24 42 A6
RNFD/HAY WA11 78 A7
SALE M33 96 C8
TOT/BURYW BL8 38 E2
URM M41 95 M3
WALK M28 68 B5
WGNE/HIN WN2 65 H3
WHIT OL12 18 E2
Grange Rd North HYDE SK14 102 C2
Grange Rd South HYDE SK14 102 C3
Grange St CHAD OL9 9 G4
FAIL M35 74 A6
LEIGH WN7 81 H1
SLFD M6 86 B2
WGNE/HIN WN2 49 G8
Grangethorpe Dr BNG/LEV M19 99 H5
Grangethorpe Rd
RUSH/FAL M14 98 F2
URM M41 95 M3
Grange Va RNFD/HAY WA11 78 A6
Grangeway WILM/AE SK9 119 M8
Grangewood BOLE BL2 22 F5
Grangewood Dr BKLY M9 73 G5
Granite St OLD OL1 59 L4
Gransden Dr CHH M8 72 F6
Granshaw St NEWH/MOS M40 88 B1
Gransmoor Av OP/CLY M11 89 J5
Gransmoor Rd OP/CLY M11 89 J5
Grantchester Pl FWTH BL4 52 C3
Grantchester Wy BOLE BL2 37 J6
Grant Cl BKLY M9 73 G2
Grantham Cl BOL * BL1 36 B3
Grantham Dr TOT/BURYW BL8 25 G7
Grantham Gv WGNE/HIN WN2 48 C2
Grantham Rd HTNM SK4 12 D3
Grantham St OLDE OL4 9 M8
Grantley St AIMK WN4 63 K7
Grant Rd WGNS/IIMK WN3 63 K1
Grants La RAMS BL0 17 C6
Grant St FWTH BL4 52 E2
ROCH OL11 42 A2
Grantwood AIMK WN4 63 K7
Granville Av BRO M7 72 B4
Granville Cl CHAD OL9 8 C4
Granville Ct MILN OL16 43 L1
Granville Gdns DID/WITH M20 110 D2
Granville Rd BOLS/LL BL3 51 M1
CHD/CHDH SK8 111 M7
DTN/ASHW M34 89 L3
HALE/TIMP WA15 108 F6
RUSH/FAL M14 98 F4
URM M41 96 B1
WILM/AE SK9 126 D7
Granville St AUL OL6 91 G2
CHAD OL9 8 C3
ECC M30 85 G1
FWTH BL4 53 G3
LEIGH WN7 66 C5
OLD OL1 9 G1
WALK M28 68 F1
WGNE/HIN * WN2 49 H7
Granville Wk CHAD OL9 8 C3
Grasmere Av BOLS/LL BL3 37 K8
FWTH BL4 52 C5
HEY OL10 41 G4
HTNM SK4 100 B6
SWIN M27 69 M2
URM M41 95 H3
WGNE/HIN WN2 48 D5
WGNE/HIN WN2 49 H8
WGNW/BIL/O WN5 46 C4
WHTF M45 54 F5
Grasmere Cl STLY SK15 76 D8
Grasmere Crs BRAM/HZG SK7 121 G4
ECC M30 69 L8
MPL/ROM SK6 123 G3
Grasmere Dr AIMK WN4 63 L7
BURY BL9 39 K5
Grasmere Gv AULW OL7 75 J8
Grasmere Rd CHD/CHDH SK8 119 K1
HALE/TIMP WA15 108 F6
OLDE OL4 59 M6
PART M31 106 B1
ROY/SHW OL2 43 G6
SALE M33 108 F2
STRET M32 97 G1
SWIN M27 70 C6
WGNW/BIL/O WN5 46 F5
WILM/AE SK9 130 D3
Grasmere St BOL BL1 36 C2
LEIGH WN7 66 B7
WGTN/LGST M12 99 L1
WHIT OL12 28 C3
Grasmere Ter WGNE/HIN WN2 64 E4
Grasmere Wk MDTN M24 57 J2
Grason Av WILM/AE SK9 127 G3
Grasscroft RDSH SK5 100 F6
Grasscroft Cl RUSH/FAL M14 98 C2
Grasscroft Rd STLY SK15 91 K3
WGNE/HIN WN2 49 K8
Grassfield Av BRO M7 71 M6
Grassholme Dr OFTN SK2 113 K7
Grassingham Gdns SLFD M6 86 C1
Grassington Av
NEWH/MOS M40 73 K3
Grassington Ct TOT/BURYW BL8 24 B8
Grassington Dr HEY OL10 40 A3
Grassington Pl BOL BL1 36 D3
Grass Md DTN/ASHW M34 101 K4
Grassmoor Crs GLSP SK13 104 A2
Gratrix Av ORD M5 86 E5
Gratrix La SALE M33 109 J1
Gratrix St GTN M18 89 H8
Gratten Ct WALK M28 52 F8
Gravel Bank Rd MPL/ROM SK6 101 L6
Gravel La CSLFD M3 6 E2
WILM/AE SK9 126 C8
Gravel Wks OLDE OL4 59 L5
Gravenmoor Dr BRO M7 72 B6
Grave Oak La GOL/RIS/CU WA3 81 L3
Graver La NEWH/MOS M40 74 A7
Gray Av RNFD/HAY WA11 78 A6
Gray Cl HYDE SK14 103 J1
WGNE/HIN WN2 48 D2
Graymar Rd LHULT M38 52 D8
Graymarsh Dr POY/DIS SK12 129 J2
Graysands Rd
HALE/TIMP WA15 117 H1
Grayson Av WHTF M45 55 K5
Grayson Rd LHULT M38 52 E8
Grayson's Cl WGN WN1 15 G1
Grayson Wy UPML OL3 61 L6
Gray St BOL BL1 2 D2
Gray St North BOL BL1 2 D2
Graythorpe Wk ORD * M5 86 D3
Graythorp Wk RUSH/FAL M14 98 E1
Graythwaite Rd BOL BL1 35 J2
Grazing Dr IRL M44 94 E1
Greame St OLDTF/WHR M16 98 C1
Great Acre WGN WN1 15 J1
Great Ancoats St ANC M4 7 J3
Great Bank Rd WHTN BL5 50 A2
Great Bent Cl WHIT OL12 19 L8
Great Boys Cl TYLD M29 68 B3
Great Bridgewater St
CMANW M2 6 E7
Great Cheetham St East
BRO M7 72 B6
Great Cheetham St West
BRO M7 71 M7
Great Clowes St BRO M7 71 M6
Great Delph RNFD/HAY WA11 78 A5
Great Ducie St CHH M8 72 C8
CSLFD M3 6 F1
Great Eaves Rd RAMS BL0 17 C5
Great Egerton St STKP SK1 13 H3
Greatfield Rd WYTH/NTH M22 109 L8
Great Flatt WHIT OL12 27 L3
Great Gable Cl OLD OL1 9 J2
Great Gates Cl ROCH OL11 28 D8
Great Gates Rd ROCH OL11 42 D2
Great George St CSLFD M3 6 A3
MILN * OL16 10 E6
WGNS/IIMK WN3 14 D4
Great Heaton Cl MDTN * M24 56 F5
Great Holme BOLS/LL BL3 52 C1
Great Howarth WHIT OL12 19 J8
Great Jackson St HULME M15 6 C8
Great John St CSLFD M3 6 C6
Great Jones St WGTN/LGST M12 88 D6
Great Lee WHIT OL12 28 A1
Great Lee Wk WHIT OL12 28 A2
Great Marlborough St
CMANE M1 6 F7
Great Marld Cl BOL BL1 35 J2
Great Meadow ROY/SHW OL2 43 J3
Great Moor St BOL BL1 2 E6
OFTN SK2 112 E7
Great Moss Rd TYLD M29 82 F2
Great Newton St
NEWH/MOS M40 73 M7
Great Norbury St HYDE SK14 102 A2
Great Portwood St STKP SK1 13 K2
Great Southern St
RUSH/FAL M14 98 E1
Great Stone Cl RAD * M26 54 A1
Great Stone Rd STRET M32 86 C8
Great Stones Cl EDGW/EG BL7 22 B2
Great St CMANE M1 7 M6
Great Underbank STKP SK1 13 H4
Great Western St
OLDTF/WHR M16 87 H8
Greave MPL/ROM SK6 102 A8
Greave Av ROCH OL11 27 L4
Greave Fold MPL/ROM SK6 101 M8
Greave Rd STKP SK1 112 F4
Greaves Av FAIL M35 74 B6
Greaves Cl WGNNW/ST WN6 30 C4
Greaves Rd WILM/AE SK9 126 C5
Greaves St MOSL OL5 76 E2
OLD OL1 9 K6
OLDE OL4 60 C6
ROY/SHW * OL2 43 M5
Greave St ROY/SHW OL2 43 M5
Grebe Cl POY/DIS SK12 121 K8
WGNS/IIMK WN3 46 E8
Grecian Crs BOLS/LL BL3 36 C8
Grecian St BRO M7 71 M7
Grecian St North BRO M7 71 M6
Grecian Ter BRO * M7 71 M7
Gredle Cl URM M41 96 C2
Greeba Rd NTHM/RTH M23 109 H6
Greek St CMANE M1 7 J9
EDGY/DAV SK3 13 H7
The Green CHD/CHDH SK8 120 B4
GLSP SK13 104 D5
HTNM SK4 12 C2
MPL/ROM SK6 123 J1
OLDS OL8 75 K1
ROCH OL11 41 M1
SWIN M27 70 E2
TOT/BURYW BL8 24 C3
WALK M28 69 J7
WGNW/BIL/O WN5 46 E6
WILM/AE SK9 127 J1
Greenacre WGN WN1 15 J1
Green Acre WHTN BL5 50 C5
Greenacre Cl RAMS BL0 17 E5
Greenacre La WALK M28 69 J8
Green Acre Pk BOL * BL1 36 C3
Greenacres EDGW/EG BL7 16 E6
Greenacres Cl GOL/RIS/CU WA3 80 E4
Greenacres Dr BNG/LEV M19 99 H8
Greenacres Rd OLDE OL4 59 M5
Greenall St AIMK WN4 63 L7
Green Av BOLS/LL BL3 52 E1
LHULT M38 52 B7
SWIN M27 70 C5
TYLD M29 67 K8
Green Bank BOLE BL2 37 H1
GLSP SK13 104 C5
Greenbank WGNE/HIN WN2 64 E5
WGNE/HIN WN2 65 K1
Greenbank Av CHD/CHDH SK8 110 D7
HTNM SK4 111 H2
SWIN * M27 70 A6
UPML OL3 61 M3
WGNW/BIL/O WN5 62 A1
Greenbank Crs MPL/ROM SK6 114 C7
Greenbank Dr LIT OL15 29 J1
Greenbank Rd BOLS/LL BL3 35 L7
CHD/CHDH * SK8 110 D6
MPL/ROM SK6 114 E3
RAD M26 38 C7
SALE M33 96 B7
SLFD M6 86 B1
WHIT OL12 28 D2
Green Bank Ter HTNM SK4 13 H2
Greenbank Ter MDTN M24 57 M3
Greenbarn Wy HOR/BR BL6 33 G3
Greenbeech Cl MPL/ROM SK6 114 B5
Green Booth Cl DUK SK16 91 J5
Greenbooth Rd WHIT OL12 27 G1
Green Bridge Cl ROCH * OL11 28 C8
Greenbridge La UPML OL3 61 K7
Green Brook Cl BURY BL9 25 K8
Greenbrook St BURY BL9 25 K8
Greenbrow Rd
NTHM/RTH M23 118 B1
Greenburn Dr BOLE BL2 37 H2
Green Cl ATH M46 67 H3
CHD/CHDH SK8 110 D6
Green Common La WHTN BL5 50 E6
Green Ct GOL/RIS/CU WA3 80 E3
Greencourt Dr LHULT M38 52 C8
Green Cts ALT WA14 116 D1
Green Cft MPL/ROM SK6 114 A1
Greencroft Meadow
ROY/SHW OL2 43 J7
Greencroft Rd ECC M30 69 L8
Greendale ATH M46 51 H8
Greendale Crs LEIGH WN7 66 F8
Greendale Dr BKLY M9 73 H1
Greendale Gv DTN/ASHW M34 101 L4
Green Dr BNG/LEV M19 99 J3
HALE/TIMP WA15 108 D5
HOR/BR BL6 34 F5
WILM/AE SK9 127 H2
Green End BNG/LEV M19 99 H7
DTN/ASHW M34 101 L4
Green End Rd BNG/LEV M19 99 H7
Greenfield Av ECC M30 84 D5
URM M41 96 A2
WGNE/HIN WN2 15 M6
Greenfield Cl EDGY/DAV SK3 112 B6
HALE/TIMP WA15 108 F6
NM/HAY SK22 124 C4
TOT/BURYW BL8 38 D3
WHTN BL5 50 D3
Greenfield Ct HEY OL10 41 G3
Greenfield La MILN OL16 29 G1
ROCH OL11 28 D8
ROY/SHW OL2 43 L6
Greenfield Rd ATH M46 51 H7
Greenfields WGNNW/ST WN6 31 K8
Greenfields Cl NEWLW WA12 78 F8
WGNE/HIN WN2 49 J6
Greenfields Crs AIMK WN4 63 L8
Greenfield St DTN/ASHW M34 90 A5
GLSP SK13 93 K6
HYDE SK14 102 A2
ROCH OL11 28 D8
Greenfield Vw
WGNW/BIL/O WN5 62 A8
Green Fold GTN M18 89 J6
Greenfold Av FWTH BL4 52 E5
Green Fold La WHTN BL5 50 B5
Greenfold Wy LEIGH WN7 81 K1
Greenford Cl CHD/CHDH SK8 111 L8
WGNW/BIL/O WN5 46 A6
Greenford Rd CHH M8 72 D5
Green Gables Cl
CHD/CHDH SK8 119 K3
Greengate CSLFD M3 6 E2
HALE/TIMP WA15 117 M5
HYDE SK14 102 A4
MDTN M24 57 M7
Greengate Cl WHIT OL12 19 L8
Greengate East
NEWH/MOS M40 73 M1
Greengate La BOLE BL2 37 J4
PWCH M25 55 K8
Greengate Rd DTN/ASHW M34 90 D8
Greengate St OLDE OL4 9 L8
Greengate West CSLFD M3 6 C1
Green Grove Bank MILN OL16 28 F1
Greenhalgh Moss La
TOT/BURYW BL8 24 E7
Greenhalgh St FAIL M35 73 M6
HTNM SK4 13 H2
Greenhalgh Wk ANC M4 7 L3
Green Hall Cl ATH M46 51 J7
Green Hall Ms WILM/AE SK9 126 F6
Greenham Rd NTHM/RTH M23 109 J2
Greenhaven Cl WALK M28 69 J1
Green Hayes Av WGN WN1 47 M1
Greenhey WGNW/BIL/O WN5 46 D5
Greenheys BOLE BL2 37 H1
DROY M43 89 K2
Greenheys Crs TOT/BURYW BL8 24 B3
Greenheys La HULME M15 87 J7
Greenheys La West HULME M15 87 J7
Greenheys Rd LHULT M38 52 B6
Greenhill PWCH M25 55 K8
Greenhill Av BOLS/LL BL3 35 L7
FWTH BL4 52 F5
ROY/SHW OL2 43 H3
SALE M33 96 D6
WHIT OL12 10 C2
Greenhill Crs WGNW/BIL/O WN5 62 C7
Greenhill Pas OLD OL1 9 L5
Green Hill Rd HYDE SK14 102 C1
Greenhill Rd CHH M8 72 D5
HALE/TIMP WA15 108 F6
MDTN M24 57 M5
TOT/BURYW BL8 38 D3
WGNW/BIL/O WN5 62 B7
Green Hill St EDGY/DAV SK3 12 E8
Green Hill Ter EDGY/DAV SK3 12 E8
Greenhill Ter OLDE OL4 9 L7
Greenhill Wk POY/DIS SK12 123 M6
Green Hollow STLY SK15 77 G8
Greenholm Cl NEWH/MOS M40 74 A3
Greenhow St DROY M43 89 J4
Greenhurst Crs OLDS OL8 75 K2
Greenhurst La AUL OL6 76 B6
Greenhurst Rd AUL OL6 76 A5
Greenhythe Rd CHD/CHDH SK8 119 L6
Greening Rd BNG/LEV M19 99 L2
Greenland Av WGNNW/ST WN6 31 J4
Greenland Cl TYLD M29 67 L6
Greenland Rd BOLS/LL BL3 52 C2
TYLD M29 67 L6
Greenland St CHH M8 72 C5
SLFD * M6 86 B2
Green La AUL OL6 75 L7
BOLS/LL BL3 52 C1
BRAM/HZG SK7 121 M1
ECC M30 84 F2
FAIL M35 74 B8
FWTH BL4 53 K5
GLSP SK13 93 J8
GLSP SK13 104 C4
GOL/RIS/CU WA3 80 D2
GTN M18 89 G6
HALE/TIMP WA15 108 E8
HEY OL10 41 H2
HEY * OL10 41 H4
HOR/BR BL6 21 B7
HTNM SK4 12 A1
HTNM SK4 12 E3
HYDE SK14 92 F6
HYDE SK14 102 D3
IRL M44 94 A7
LEIGH WN7 66 F7
MDTN M24 57 L3
MDTN M24 58 A5
MPL/ROM SK6 113 L3
OLDE OL4 60 D2
OLDS OL8 75 H2
POY/DIS SK12 122 E8
POY/DIS SK12 123 M7
SALE M33 96 B6
WGNE/HIN WN2 49 L7
WGNNW/ST WN6 31 H4
WGNW/BIL/O WN5 62 A1
WHIT * OL12 10 D2
WHTF M45 55 J3
WILM/AE SK9 126 F5
WILM/AE SK9 130 C4
Green La North
HALE/TIMP WA15 108 E8
Greenlea Av GTN M18 100 A1
Greenleach La WALK M28 69 J4
Greenlea Cl WGNW/BIL/O WN5 46 A7
Greenleaf Cl WALK M28 68 C6
Greenleas HOR/BR BL6 34 F6
Greenlees St WHIT OL12 10 E2
Greenleigh Cl BOL BL1 22 A7
Green Meadow WHIT OL12 19 L8
Green Mdw MPL/ROM SK6 114 C5
WHTN BL5 50 A5
Green Meadows Dr
MPL/ROM SK6 114 C5
Green Meadows Wk
WYTH/NTH M22 119 G3
Greenmount Cl TOT/BURYW BL8 24 C2
Greenmount Ct BOL BL1 35 K4
Greenmount Dr HEY OL10 41 J5
TOT/BURYW BL8 24 C1
Greenmount La BOL BL1 35 J4
Greenmount Pk FWTH BL4 53 K6
Greenoak RAD M26 53 M5
Greenoak Dr SALE M33 108 F3
WALK M28 52 F7
Greenock Cl BOLS/LL BL3 35 H7
Greenough St ATH M46 66 D3
WGN WN1 15 J3
Greenpark Cl TOT/BURYW BL8 24 B3
Greenpark Rd WYTH/NTH M22 110 A3
Green Park Vw OLD * OL1 59 L4
OLD OL1 60 A2
Green Pastures HTNM SK4 111 H3
Green Pine Rd HOR/BR BL6 34 A5

Greenrigg Cl WGNNW/ST WN6 31 J5
Green Rd PART M31 106 B1
Greenroyd Av BOLE BL2 37 H2
Greenroyde ROCH * OL11 10 C9
The Greens WHIT OL12 18 D3
Greenshall La POY/DIS SK12 124 B6
Greenshank Cl LEIGH WN7 66 E7
NEWLW WA12 78 F8
ROCH * OL11 27 J5
Greenside WALK M28 69 K7
Greenside Av FWTH BL4 53 J6
OLDE OL4 60 A2
Greenside Cl DUK SK16 91 K4
TOT/BURYW BL8 23 L1
Greenside Crs DROY M43 89 J1
Greenside Dr HALE/TIMP WA15 117 G3
IRL M44 94 C3
TOT/BURYW BL8 24 B4
Greenside La DROY M43 89 H1
Greenside Pl DTN/ASHW * M34 101 K4
Greenside St BOLE BL2 37 M3
OP/CLY M11 88 E3
Greenside Wy MDTN M24 57 M7
Greenslate Ct
WGNW/BIL/O WN5 62 A1
Green & Slater Homes
HTNM * SK4 111 K1
Greenslate Rd
WGNW/BIL/O WN5 62 B1
Greensmith Wy WHTN BL5 50 B2
Greenson Dr MDTN M24 57 H5
Greenstead Av CHH M8 72 D4
Greenstone Av HOR/BR BL6 33 K1
Greenstone Dr SLFD M6 71 J7
Green St ATH M46 67 H3
BOL BL1 2 F4
ECC M30 84 E4
EDGY/DAV SK3 112 C6
FWTH BL4 52 F3
HYDE SK14 102 B3
MDTN M24 57 L3
OLDS OL8 8 F7
RAD M26 54 D1
RAMS * BL0 17 E1
RUSH/FAL M14 99 H5
STRET M32 96 F4
TOT/BURYW BL8 24 C8
TYLD M29 67 K3
WGNE/HIN WN2 64 E2
WGNS/IIMK WN3 14 F7
WILM/AE SK9 130 D3
Greensward Cl WGNNW/ST WN6 30 E3
Greenthorne Av HTNM SK4 100 A5
Greenthorne Cl EDGW/EG BL7 16 E5
Green Tree Gdns
MPL/ROM SK6 113 L2
Greenvale ROCH OL11 27 G4
WGNNW/ST WN6 30 C8
Greenvale Dr CHD/CHDH SK8 110 F6
Greenview Dr DID/WITH M20 110 F4
ROCH OL11 27 J4
Green Villa Pk WILM/AE SK9 126 C8
Green Wk ALT WA14 116 C1
CHD/CHDH SK8 110 D6
HALE/TIMP WA15 108 C5
OLDTF/WHR M16 97 M2
STRET M32 96 E2
Green Wks PWCH M25 71 M1
Greenwatch Cl ECC M30 84 F3
Green Wy BOL BL1 36 E1
ROCH OL11 41 L3
Greenway AIMK WN4 63 K8
ALT WA14 107 K7
BRAM/HZG SK7 120 F6
HOR/BR BL6 34 C1
HYDE SK14 102 A3
MDTN M24 57 H7
MPL/ROM SK6 114 B3
ROY/SHW OL2 43 J3
WILM/AE SK9 126 E6
WYTH/NTH M22 110 B4
Greenway Av BNG/LEV M19 99 L4
Green Way Cl BOL BL1 22 D8
Greenway Cl SALE M33 108 A1
TOT/BURYW BL8 38 E1
Greenway Dr MOSL OL5 76 F2
Greenway Rd CHD/CHDH SK8 119 L6
HALE/TIMP WA15 108 C4
Greenways AULW OL7 75 J6
LEIGH WN7 66 D6
NEWH/MOS M40 74 A3
WGNNW/ST WN6 31 K6
WGNW/BIL/O WN5 62 A1
Greenwich Cl NEWH/MOS M40 74 A8
ROCH OL11 27 J6
Greenwood Av AUL OL6 75 M6
LHULT M38 68 F1
OFTN SK2 112 F6
SWIN M27 70 E3
WGNW/BIL/O WN5 47 H5
Greenwood Cl
HALE/TIMP WA15 109 G7
WALK M28 68 B5
Greenwood Dr WILM/AE SK9 127 H4
Greenwood La HOR/BR BL6 34 B3
Greenwood Rd
WGNNW/ST WN6 31 H2
WYTH/NTH M22 109 L8
Greenwoods La BOLE BL2 23 J8
Greenwood St ALT WA14 108 A8
FWTH BL4 53 G4
LIT OL15 20 C7
MILN OL16 10 F5
OLDE OL4 59 M4
OLDS * OL8 75 J3
SLFD M6 71 J8
Greenwood V BOL BL1 36 B1
Greenwood V South BOL * BL1 36 C1
Greer St OP/CLY M11 88 F4
Greetland Dr BKLY M9 57 J8
Gregge St HEY OL10 41 H3
Greg Ms WILM/AE SK9 126 F2
Gregory Av ATH M46 50 F7
BOLE BL2 37 H4
MPL/ROM SK6 113 L3
Gregory St OLDS OL8 74 F1
WGNE/HIN * WN2 48 F6
WGNE/HIN WN2 49 K5
WGTN/LGST M12 88 C6
Gregory Wy RDSH SK5 100 C6
Gregson Fld BOLS/LL BL3 36 B8
Gregson Rd RDSH SK5 100 B6
Gregson St OLD OL1 9 K6
Greg St RDSH SK5 100 B6
Greiley Wk RUSH/FAL M14 98 E1
Grenaby Av WGNE/HIN WN2 49 K7
Grendale Av BRAM/HZG SK7 122 A3
STKP SK1 112 E3
Grendon Av OLDS OL8 75 H1
Grendon St BOLS/LL BL3 51 M1
Grendon Wk WGTN/LGST M12 88 D6
Grenfel Cl WGNS/IIMK WN3 14 B9
Grenfell Rd DID/WITH M20 110 D1
Grenham Av HULME M15 87 G6
Grenville Rd BRAM/HZG SK7 121 L1
Grenville St DUK SK16 90 F4
EDGY/DAV SK3 12 E6
STLY SK15 77 G8
Gresford Cl CCHDY M21 97 K4
Gresham Cl WHTF M45 55 G5
Gresham Dr CHAD OL9 8 D5
Gresham St BOL BL1 36 C1
DTN/ASHW M34 90 C8
Gresham Wk HTNM SK4 112 B1
Gresley Av HOR/BR BL6 33 M1
Gresley Cl WGN WN1 15 K4
Gresty Av WYTH/NTH M22 119 H3
Greswell St DTN/ASHW M34 90 B8
Greta Av CHD/CHDH SK8 119 L6
Gretna Rd ATH M46 66 D3
Greton Cl BRUN/LGST M13 88 B8
Gretton Cl ROY/SHW OL2 43 J8
Greville St BRUN/LGST M13 99 H1
Grey Cl MPL/ROM SK6 101 K8
Greyfriars AIMK WN4 78 C1
Greyfriars Rd WYTH/NTH M22 118 D2
Greyhound Dr SLFD M6 71 L7
Greyhound Rd MCFLDN SK10 131 L7
Grey Knotts WALK M28 68 D7
Greylag Crs WALK M28 69 G4
Greylands Cl SALE M33 96 B8
Greylands Rd DID/WITH M20 110 F4
Grey Mare La OP/CLY M11 88 D3
Greymont Rd BURY BL9 25 J6
Grey Rd AIMK WN4 63 K8
ALT WA14 107 M7
Greystoke Av BNG/LEV M19 99 M3
HALE/TIMP WA15 109 G6
SALE M33 108 E1
Greystoke Crs WHTF M45 55 H2
Greystoke Dr BOL BL1 22 A6
MDTN M24 57 G2
WILM/AE SK9 130 D2
Greystoke La FAIL M35 74 A6
Greystoke St STKP SK1 13 M5
Greystone Av OLDTF/WHR M16 98 C4
WGNE/HIN WN2 32 F7
Grey St AUL OL6 90 F2
DTN/ASHW M34 101 G1
MDTN M24 57 J3
PWCH M25 55 M8
STLY SK15 91 M3
WGTN/LGST M12 88 B6
Greyswood Av CHH M8 72 C6
Greytown Cl SLFD M6 71 J7
Greywood Av BURY BL9 5 L4
Grid La MPL/ROM SK6 115 H3
Grierson St BOL BL1 36 B1
OLDTF/WHR M16 87 H8
Griffe La BURY BL9 39 M8
Griffin Cl BURY BL9 5 J1
NM/HAY SK22 124 E6
Griffin Ct CSLFD * M3 6 C3
Griffin Gv BNG/LEV M19 99 K4
Griffin La CHD/CHDH SK8 119 M5
Griffin Rd FAIL M35 74 A5
Griffin St BRO M7 71 M6
Griffiths Cl BRO * M7 72 A8
Griffiths St NEWH/MOS M40 73 M7
Grimes St WHIT OL12 27 J3
Grime St RAMS BL0 17 A8
Grimscott Cl BKLY * M9 73 J3
Grimshaw Av FAIL M35 74 D4
Grimshaw Cl MPL/ROM SK6 101 K8
Grimshaw La MDTN M24 57 L5
NEWH/MOS M40 73 J7
Grimshaw St FAIL * M35 74 B4
GOL/RIS/CU WA3 79 K3
STKP SK1 13 M4
Grimstead Cl NTHM/RTH M23 109 H6
Grindall Av BKLY M9 73 L2
Grindley Av CCHDY M21 97 M8
Grindlow St BRUN/LGST M13 88 B7
Grindon Av BRO M7 71 K5
Grindrod St RAD M26 38 D8
Grindsbrook Rd RAD M26 38 C5
Grinton Av BRUN/LGST M13 99 H2
Grisdale Dr MDTN M24 57 H2
Grisdale Rd BOLS/LL BL3 35 M7
Grisebeck Wy OLD OL1 9 H4
Grisedale Av ROY/SHW OL2 42 F4
Grisedale Rd ROCH OL11 27 L8
Gristlehurst La BURY BL9 26 C7
Grizebeck Cl GTN M18 88 F6
Grizedale Cl BOL BL1 35 J2
STLY SK15 77 H5
Grizedale Dr WGNE/HIN WN2 48 D5
Grizedale Rd MPL/ROM SK6 101 L8
Groby Rd ALT WA14 107 M8
CCHDY M21 97 L4
DTN/ASHW M34 90 B5
Groby Rd North
DTN/ASHW M34 90 A4
Groby St OLDS OL8 75 J1
STLY SK15 91 M3
Groom St CMANE * M1 7 J9
Grosvenor Av GOL/RIS/CU WA3 80 A4
WHTF M45 55 H4
Grosvenor Cl WALK M28 52 F7
WILM/AE SK9 126 E8
Grosvenor Ct AULW OL7 90 D3
CHD/CHDH SK8 111 G6
Grosvenor Crs HYDE SK14 101 M3
Grosvenor Dr POY/DIS SK12 129 G1
WALK M28 52 F7
Grosvenor Gdns BRO M7 72 A8
STLY * SK15 91 K3
WYTH/NTH M22 110 B6
Grosvenor Pl AULW * OL7 90 D3
Grosvenor Rd ALT WA14 108 B6
CHD/CHDH SK8 111 M8
ECC M30 84 D1
HTNM SK4 12 A1
HTNM SK4 111 K1
HYDE SK14 102 A3
LEIGH WN7 66 A6
MPL/ROM SK6 114 C5
OLDTF/WHR M16 98 A2
SALE M33 96 C7
SWIN M27 70 E5
URM M41 95 M2
WALK M28 52 F7
WHTF M45 55 H3
Grosvenor Sq BRO M7 72 A8
SALE M33 96 C8
Grosvenor St AULW OL7 90 D3
BOLE BL2 3 G7
BOLS/LL BL3 37 K8
BRAM/HZG SK7 121 M1
BURY BL9 4 F8
CMANE M1 7 H9
DTN/ASHW M34 90 A8
FWTH BL4 53 J4
HEY OL10 40 E3
PWCH M25 55 M8
RAD M26 38 C8
ROCH OL11 41 M3
STKP SK1 13 J7
STLY SK15 91 K3
STRET M32 97 G2
SWIN M27 70 C2
WGNE/HIN WN2 49 G7
WGNW/BIL/O WN5 47 J6
Grosvenor Wy ROY/SHW OL2 59 G2
Grotton Hollow OLDE OL4 60 E6
Grotton Mdw OLDE OL4 60 E7
Grouse St WHIT OL12 28 C3
The Grove ALT * WA14 108 A7
BOLE BL2 3 K8
BOLS/LL BL3 53 L1
CHD/CHDH SK8 120 C6
DID/WITH M20 110 E3
ECC M30 85 J3
EDGY/DAV SK3 13 H9
GLSP SK13 93 J8
GOL/RIS/CU WA3 80 A3
ROY/SHW OL2 43 K6
SALE M33 108 E1
UPML OL3 61 J3
URM M41 95 J3
WGNE/HIN WN2 15 L6
Grove Av FAIL M35 74 B7
WILM/AE SK9 126 E5
Grove Cl RUSH/FAL M14 98 F1
Grove Ct BRAM/HZG * SK7 122 A1
SALE M33 97 G8
Grove Hl WALK M28 68 C6
Grovehurst SWIN M27 69 L6
Grove La CHD/CHDH SK8 120 C6
DID/WITH M20 110 E2
HALE/TIMP WA15 108 D6
HALE/TIMP WA15 117 K1
WGNNW/ST WN6 31 J4
Grove Ms WALK * M28 69 G1
Grove Pl WGNNW/ST WN6 31 J4
Grove Rd HALE/TIMP WA15 117 G1
MDTN M24 57 L2
STLY SK15 77 G8
UPML OL3 61 L5
Grove Spring WHTF M45 55 H2
Grove St AIMK WN4 63 K8
AULW OL7 75 H7
BOL BL1 36 A2
BRAM/HZG * SK7 122 A1
BRO M7 72 B7
DROY M43 89 J4
DUK SK16 91 G3
FWTH BL4 53 H4
HEY OL10 41 H2
LEIGH WN7 66 E8
NM/HAY SK22 124 D5
OLD OL1 9 M4
ROCH OL11 10 D8
UPML OL3 61 L7
WILM/AE * SK9 126 F5
Grove Wy WILM/AE SK9 126 F5
Grovewood Cl AULW OL7 75 H7
Grovewood Dr WGNNW/ST WN6 30 B5
Grundey St BRAM/HZG SK7 122 A2
Grundy Av PWCH M25 71 H2
Grundy Cl BURY BL9 5 G8
Grundy La BURY BL9 4 E9
Grundy Rd FWTH BL4 53 H5
Grundy's Cl TYLD M29 67 M7
Grundy St BOLS/LL BL3 36 A8
GOL/RIS/CU WA3 79 K5
HEY OL10 41 H4
HTNM SK4 111 H2
WALK M28 69 J1
WHTN BL5 50 B3
Guardian Ms
NTHM/RTH * M23 108 F3
Guernsey Cl BNG/LEV * M19 99 K6
Guest Rd PWCH M25 55 K6
Guest St LEIGH WN7 66 D7
Guide La DTN/ASHW M34 90 B4
Guide Post Sq
BRUN/LGST * M13 88 A6
Guide Post St BRUN/LGST M13 88 A6
Guide St SALQ M50 85 M3
Guido St BOL BL1 36 A2
FAIL M35 74 B5
Guild Av WALK M28 69 G2
Guildford Av CHD/CHDH SK8 120 C6
Guildford Cl STKP SK1 112 E5
Guildford Crs WGNNW/ST WN6 47 J1
Guildford Dr AUL OL6 75 M5
Guildford Gv MDTN M24 57 M1
Guildford Rd BNG/LEV M19 99 L2
BOL BL1 35 L2
DUK SK16 91 K5
SLFD M6 70 E8
URM M41 85 H8
Guildford St MILN * OL16 11 G5
Guildhall Cl HULME M15 87 K7
Guild St EDGW/EG BL7 22 E6
Guilford Rd ECC M30 84 E3
Guinness Rd TRPK M17 85 K4
Guiseley Cl BURY BL9 25 H4
Gullane Cl NEWH/MOS M40 73 M5
Gull Cl POY/DIS SK12 128 F1
Gulvain Pl CHAD OL9 58 C4
Gun Rd MPL/ROM SK6 115 L1
Gunson St NEWH/MOS M40 7 M1
Gun St ANC M4 7 K3
Gunters Av WHTN BL5 50 B6
Gurner Av ORD M5 86 E5
Gurney St ANC M4 88 A3
Gutter La RAMS BL0 17 B5
Guy Fawkes St ORD M5 86 E5
Guy St BRO M7 72 C5
Guywood La MPL/ROM SK6 101 M8
Gwelo St OP/CLY M11 88 D2
Gwenbury Av STKP SK1 112 E3
Gwendor Av CHH M8 72 C1
Gwladys St STLY SK15 77 H6
Gylden Cl HYDE SK14 91 L6
Gypsy La OFTN SK2 113 G6
ROCH OL11 41 M1
Gyte's La BNG/LEV M19 99 M2

H

Habergham Cl WALK M28 68 F5
Hackberry Cl ALT WA14 107 L4
Hacken Bridge Rd BOLS/LL BL3 37 G8
Hacken La BOLS/LL BL3 36 F8
Hackford Cl BOL BL1 35 M4
TOT/BURYW BL8 25 G7
Hacking St BRO M7 72 B6
BURY BL9 5 H5
PWCH M25 55 K8
Hackle St OP/CLY M11 88 F2
Hackleton Cl ANC M4 88 A3
Hackness Rd CCHDY M21 97 J4
Hackney Av NEWH/MOS M40 73 M8
Hackney Cl RAD M26 38 D7
Hackworth Cl WGN WN1 15 K4
Hadbutt La TYLD M29 67 J8
Haddington Dr BKLY M9 73 H1
Haddon Av NEWH/MOS M40 74 B3
Haddon Cl BURY BL9 39 K7
MPL/ROM SK6 123 G6
WILM/AE SK9 130 C2
Haddon Gv HALE/TIMP WA15 108 C5
RDSH SK5 100 B5
SALE M33 108 D1
Haddon Hall Rd DROY M43 89 H2
Haddon Ms GLSP SK13 104 A2
Haddon Rd BRAM/HZG SK7 122 A3
CCHDY M21 98 A7
CHD/CHDH SK8 119 L5
ECC M30 84 F4
GOL/RIS/CU WA3 80 A3
SWIN M27 69 M7
WGNS/IIMK WN3 63 H1
Haddon St ROCH OL11 28 B8
SLFD M6 71 L7
STRET M32 86 A8
Haddon Wy ROY/SHW OL2 43 M4
Hadfield Av CHAD OL9 8 A9
Hadfield Crs AUL OL6 76 B7
Hadfield Pl GLSP SK13 104 F4
Hadfield Rd GLSP SK13 93 J8
Hadfields Av HYDE SK14 93 G7
Hadfield Sq GLSP SK13 104 F4
Hadfield St BRO M7 72 B6
DUK SK16 90 D5
GLSP SK13 104 F4
OLDS OL8 75 H1
OLDTF/WHR M16 86 F6
Hadleigh Cl BOL BL1 22 D6
Hadley Av BRUN/LGST M13 99 H2
Hadley Cl CHD/CHDH SK8 120 B3
Hadley St SLFD M6 71 L7
Hadlow Gn RDSH SK5 100 E6
Hadlow Wk NEWH/MOS * M40 88 B1
Hadwin St BOL BL1 2 E1
Hafton Rd BRO M7 71 L6
Hag Bank La POY/DIS SK12 123 M5
Haggate ROY/SHW OL2 58 F1
Haggate Crs ROY/SHW OL2 58 F1
Hagley Rd ORD M5 86 D6
The Hags BURY BL9 39 K7
Haguebar Rd NM/HAY SK22 124 B4
Hague Bush Cl
GOL/RIS/CU * WA3 80 B3
Hague Fold Rd NM/HAY SK22 124 B4
Hague Rd DID/WITH M20 98 D7
HYDE SK14 103 L3
Hague St AUL OL6 75 M8
GLSP SK13 105 G5
NEWH/MOS M40 73 J7
OLDE OL4 60 B4
Haig Ct TOT/BURYW BL8 38 E3
Haigh Av HTNM SK4 100 B7
Haigh Hall Cl RAMS BL0 17 B8
Haigh La OLD OL1 58 B3
Haigh Pk HTNM SK4 100 B7
Haigh Rd WGNE/HIN WN2 32 E6
Haigh St BOL BL1 2 E2
ROCH OL11 11 G7
Haigh Vw WGN WN1 48 A2
WGNS/IIMK WN3 15 L7
Haig Rd STRET M32 97 G1
TOT/BURYW BL8 38 E2
Haig St WGNS/IIMK WN3 14 D5
Haile Dr WALK M28 68 C6
Hailsham Cl TOT/BURYW BL8 24 F5
Hail St RAMS * BL0 17 A8
Hailwood St ROCH OL11 28 B8
Halbury Wk BOL * BL1 36 C2
Haldon Rd DID/WITH M20 99 G7
Hale Av POY/DIS SK12 129 H2
Hale Cl LEIGH WN7 81 L2
Hale Gv AIMK WN4 63 J7
Hale La FAIL M35 74 B4
Hale Low Rd HALE/TIMP WA15 117 H1
Hale Rd HALE/TIMP WA15 117 G1
HTNM SK4 12 C1
Hales Cl DROY M43 89 J1
Halesden Rd HTNM SK4 100 A7
Halesfield WGNE/HIN WN2 65 L2
Halesworth Wk
NEWH/MOS * M40 72 F8
Hale Vw ALT * WA14 116 F2
Halewood Av GOL/RIS/CU WA3 79 J3
Haley Cl RDSH SK5 100 C4
Haley St CHH M8 72 D5
Half Acre RAD M26 38 C6
Half Acre Dr ROCH OL11 27 M6
Half Acre La HOR/BR BL6 32 F3
ROCH OL11 27 L6
Half Acre Ms ROCH OL11 27 L6
Half Acre Rd ROCH OL11 27 L6
Halfacre Rd WYTH/NTH M22 109 M8
Half Edge La ECC M30 85 J1
Half Moon La OFTN SK2 113 H6
Halford Dr NEWH/MOS M40 73 L4
Half St CSLFD * M3 6 D1
MDTN M24 57 J3
Halifax Rd MILN OL16 29 G1
Halifax St AUL OL6 75 L8
Haliwell St LIT OL15 20 D7
Hallam Rd NEWH/MOS M40 73 L7
Hallam St OFTN SK2 112 D6
RAD M26 39 G8
Hallas Gv NTHM/RTH M23 109 L3
Hall Av HALE/TIMP WA15 108 C5
RUSH/FAL M14 99 G1
SALE M33 96 B6
STLY SK15 76 F7
Hall Bank ECC M30 84 F2
Hallbottom St HYDE SK14 91 J7
Hall Cl HYDE SK14 92 D7
WGNNW/ST WN6 30 E6
The Hall Coppice EDGW/EG BL7 22 A3
Hallcroft PART M31 94 C8
Hallcroft Gdns MILN OL16 29 H6
Hall Dr HYDE SK14 92 D7
MDTN M24 57 J5
Hall Farm Av URM M41 95 L1
Hall Farm Cl BRAM/HZG SK7 122 C1
Hall Fold WHIT OL12 18 D4
Hall Gdns WHIT OL12 27 M2
Hallgate WGN WN1 14 F4
WHTN BL5 50 B7
Hallgate Dr CHD/CHDH SK8 119 J2
Hallgate Rd STKP SK1 112 E4
Hall Green Cl DUK * SK16 90 F3
Hall Green Rd DUK SK16 90 F3
Hall Gv RUSH/FAL M14 99 G1
Hall House La LEIGH WN7 66 F8
Halliday Rd NEWH/MOS M40 73 L8
Halliford Rd NEWH/MOS M40 73 K6
Hallington Cl BOLS/LL BL3 36 C8
Hall I' Th' Wood La BOL BL1 22 D8
Halliwell Av OLDS OL8 75 H1
Halliwell La CHH M8 72 C5
Halliwell Rd BOL BL1 36 A2
PWCH M25 71 J3
Halliwell St BOL * BL1 36 A2
CHAD * OL9 74 D3
MILN OL16 29 H5
WHIT OL12 10 C3
Halliwell St West CHH * M8 72 C5
Hall La FWTH BL4 53 G2
HOR/BR BL6 21 A2
HOR/BR BL6 34 B5
MPL/ROM SK6 101 L6
NTHM/RTH M23 109 L6
PART M31 94 C8
WGN WN1 32 A8
WGNE/HIN WN2 49 G2
WGNW/BIL/O WN5 46 C8
Hall Lane Gv WGNE/HIN WN2 49 G4
Hall Lee Dr WHTN BL5 50 D3
Hall Meadow CHD/CHDH SK8 120 A3
Hall Meadow Rd GLSP SK13 105 G2
Hall Moss La BRAM/HZG SK7 120 D8
Hall Moss Rd BKLY M9 73 K1
Hallows Av CCHDY M21 97 M7
Hallows Farm Av WHIT OL12 28 A2
Hall Pool Dr OFTN SK2 113 H5
Hall Rd ALT WA14 116 E3
AUL OL6 75 M7
BRAM/HZG SK7 120 F3
RNFD/HAY WA11 78 B5
RUSH/FAL M14 99 G1
WILM/AE SK9 126 E5
WILM/AE SK9 127 J1
Hallroyd Brow OLD OL1 9 H2
Hallstead Av LHULT M38 52 B8
Hallstead Gv LHULT M38 52 B8
Hall St AUL OL6 91 H2
BURY BL9 24 F2
CHD/CHDH SK8 111 G6
CMANW M2 6 F6
FAIL M35 74 A6
FWTH BL4 53 G2
HEY OL10 41 G3
HYDE SK14 101 L1
MDTN * M24 57 K4
NM/HAY SK22 124 D4
OLDE OL4 59 L5
RAD M26 38 C6
ROY/SHW OL2 43 G8
STKP SK1 112 E3
SWIN M27 70 C2
TOT/BURYW BL8 4 A1
TOT/BURYW BL8 24 B7
WGN WN1 15 H5
WGNE/HIN WN2 48 C5
WGNE/HIN WN2 64 B5
WHIT OL12 18 D4
Hallsville Rd BNG/LEV M19 99 M3
Halls Wy UPML OL3 61 K6
Hallsworth Rd ECC M30 84 D3
Hall Wood Av RNFD/HAY WA11 78 C4
Hallwood Av SLFD M6 70 F8
Hallwood Rd NTHM/RTH M23 109 K6
Hall Wood Rd WILM/AE SK9 127 H2
Hallwood Rd WILM/AE SK9 127 J1
Hallworth Av DTN/ASHW M34 89 L3
Hallworth Rd CHH M8 72 E4
Hallworthy Cl LEIGH WN7 80 E3
Hallmore Rd NEWH/MOS M40 88 A2
Halsall Cl BURY BL9 25 J6
Halsall Dr BOLS/LL BL3 52 B1
Halsbury Cl WGTN/LGST M12 88 B6
Halsey Cl CHAD OL9 74 B1
Halshaw La FWTH BL4 53 J5
Halsmere Dr BKLY M9 73 H1
Halstead Av CCHDY M21 97 K5
SLFD M6 71 H7
Halstead Dr IRL M44 94 E2
Halstead Gv CHD/CHDH SK8 110 C7
LEIGH WN7 66 E7
Halstead St BOLE BL2 3 H5
BURY BL9 25 K7
Halstead Wk BURY * BL9 25 K7
Halstock Wk NEWH/MOS M40 73 G7
Halston Cl RDSH SK5 100 C8
Halstone Av WILM/AE SK9 126 C8
Halston St HULME M15 87 H6
Halter Cl RAD M26 38 D7
Halton Bank SLFD M6 71 J8
Halton Dr HALE/TIMP WA15 108 E3
Halton Rd OP/CLY M11 88 F2
Halton St BOLE BL2 3 K5
HYDE SK14 102 C1
RNFD/HAY * WA11 78 B6
Halvard Av BURY BL9 25 J6
Halvard Ct BURY BL9 25 J6
Halvis Gv OLDTF/WHR M16 97 L1
Hambleden Cl BOLS/LL BL3 35 J7
Hambledon Cl ATH M46 51 H7
Hambleton Cl TOT/BURYW BL8 38 C3
Hambleton Dr SALE M33 96 A7
Hambleton Rd CHD/CHDH SK8 119 L4
Hamblett St LEIGH WN7 65 L7
Hambridge Cl CHH M8 72 D5
Hamel St BOLS/LL BL3 52 A1
HYDE SK14 91 J7
Hamer Dr OLDTF/WHR M16 87 G7
Hamer Hall Crs WHIT OL12 28 E2
Hamer Hl BKLY M9 72 F1
Hamer La MILN OL16 11 J1
Hamer St BOLE BL2 36 E3
HEY OL10 40 E2
RAD M26 38 F8
RAMS BL0 24 E2
Hamerton Rd NEWH/MOS M40 72 F8
Hamilcar Av ECC M30 85 H2
Hamilton Av IRL M44 94 A8
ROY/SHW OL2 58 E1
Hamilton Cl PWCH M25 71 K1
TOT/BURYW BL8 38 E1
Hamilton Crs HTNM SK4 12 B4
Hamilton Gv OLDTF/WHR M16 87 G7
Hamilton Ms ECC * M30 84 E1
PWCH * M25 71 K1
Hamilton Rd AIMK WN4 62 F8
BRUN/LGST M13 99 J1
PWCH M25 71 K1
TYLD M29 68 A6
WGNE/HIN WN2 49 J8
WHTF M45 55 H4

Hamilton Sq HTNM SK4..............13 G1
WGNW/BIL/O WN5..............47 H4
Hamilton St ATH M46..............66 F2
AULW OL7..............90 C3
BOL BL1..............22 B8
BRO * M7..............72 A5
BURY BL9..............25 J8
CHAD OL9..............58 D5
ECC M30..............84 E1
LEIGH WN7..............66 A6
OLDE OL4..............9M6
OLDTF/WHR M16..............87 C7
STLY SK15..............91 J2
SWIN M27..............70 A3
Hamilton Wy ROY/SHW OL2..............40 B3
Hamlet Dr SALE M33..............96 B6
Hammersmith Rd GTN M18..............88 F6
Hammett Rd CCHDY M21..............97 K4
Hammond Av HTNM SK4..............100 B7
Hamnet Cl BOL BL1..............22 D7
Hamnett St HYDE * SK14..............102 A2
OP/CLY M11..............89 G3
Hamon Rd HALE/TIMP WA15..............108 B8
Hampden Crs GTN M18..............88 F7
Hampden Gv ECC M30..............85 G2
Hampden Pl WGNW/BIL/O WN5..............47 G3
Hampden Rd PWCH M25..............55 L8
ROY/SHW OL2..............44 A6
SALE M33..............108 D1
Hampden St HEY OL10..............41 G3
Hampshire Cl BURY BL9..............5 J9
GLSP SK13..............105 J4
Hampshire Rd CHAD OL9..............8 B8
DROY M43..............89 K1
PART M31..............106 A2
RDSH SK5..............100 F7
Hampshire St BRO M7..............72 A6
ECC M30..............84 E3
Hampson Cl AIMK WN4..............78 E2
Hampson Crs WILM/AE SK9..............119 L8
Hampson Fold RAD M26..............38 C8
Hampson Mill La BURY BL9..............39 J7
Hampson Rd AUL OL6..............76 B6
STRET M32..............96 F2
Hampson St ATH * M46..............66 F1
DROY M43..............89 K2
ECC M30..............84 E3
HOR/BR BL6..............
NEWH/MOS * M40..............73 C8
ORD M5..............6 A5
RAD M26..............54 D1
SALE M33..............97 G8
STKP * SK1..............112 E4
SWIN M27..............70 D3
Hampstead Av URM M41..............95 H3
Hampstead Dr OFTN SK2..............112 F7
Hampstead La OFTN SK2..............112 F7
Hampstead Rd
WGNNW/ST WN6..............31 G3
Hampton Gv ALT WA14..............108 B3
BURY BL9..............25 J6
CHD/CHDH SK8..............120 A2
LEIGH WN7..............67 H5
Hampton Rd BOLS/LL BL3..............52 D1
CCHDY M21..............97 J3
FAIL M35..............74 D4
IRL M44..............94 A8
URM M41..............96 A3
Hampton St OLDS OL8..............59 C8
Hamsell Rd BRUN/LGST M13..............7 L9
Hanborough Ct TYLD M29..............67 H4
Hancock Cl RUSH/FAL M14..............98 E1
Hancock St STRET M32..............97 G4
Handel Av URM M41..............95 K2
Handel Ms SALE M33..............96 F8
Handel St BOL BL1..............2 C5
Handforth Gv BRUN/LGST M13..............99 H2
Handforth Rd RDSH SK5..............100 C7
WILM/AE SK9..............127 J3
Hand La LEIGH WN7..............81 H3
Handley Av RUSH/FAL M14..............98 E3
Handley Cl EDGY/DAV SK3..............111 M7
Handley Rd BRAM/HZG SK7..............121 C1
Handley St BURY BL9..............4 F9
WHIT * OL12..............10 B2
Hands La ROCH OL11..............27 K5
Handsworth St
WGTN/LGST M12..............88 A5
Hanging Chadder La
ROY/SHW OL2..............42 F5
Hankinson Cl PART M31..............106 B2
Hankinson Wy SLFD M6..............86 D1
Hanley Cl MDTN M24..............57 K7
POY/DIS SK12..............123M7
Hanlith Ms BNG/LEV M19..............99 J4
Hanlon St CHH M8..............72 C4
Hanmer St WGNE/HIN WN2..............49 G7
Hannah Baldwin Cl OP/CLY M11..............88 C4
Hannah St WGTN/LGST M12..............99 K2
Hannerton Rd ROY/SHW OL2..............44 A4
Hannesburg Gdns
NTHM/RTH * M23..............109 J8
Hannet Rd WYTH/NTH M22..............118 F3
Hanover Cl BRO M7..............72 A5
WALK * M28..............69 L6
Hanover Crs RUSH/FAL M14..............88 A8
Hanover Gdns BRO M7..............72 B4
Hanover Rd ALT WA14..............107 L5
WGNE/HIN WN2..............48 F6
Hanover St ANC M4..............7 G2
BOL BL1..............2 C5
LEIGH WN7..............66 D6
LIT OL15..............20 B7
MOSL OL5..............76 D7
ROCH OL11..............41 M2
STLY SK15..............91 J2
Hanover St North
DTN/ASHW M34..............90 B4
Hanover St South
DTN/ASHW M34..............90 B4
Hansdon Cl CHH M8..............72 D6
Hanson Cl MDTN M24..............57 K3
Hanson Ms STKP SK1..............112 E2
Hanson Pk MDTN * M24..............57M4
Hanson Rd NEWH/MOS M40..............73 K5
Hanson St BURY BL9..............25 J8
MDTN M24..............57 K3
OLDE OL4..............59M5
Hanstock WGNW/BIL/O WN5..............46 B7
Hanwell Cl LEIGH WN7..............81 G3
Hanworth Cl BRUN/LGST M13..............7 K9
Hapton Av STRET M32..............97 H1
Hapton Pl HTNM SK4..............13 G1
Hapton St BNG/LEV M19..............99 J1
Harbern Cl ECC M30..............70 A4
Harbern Dr LEIGH WN7..............66 G1
Harbord St MDTN M24..............57 K4
Harboro Gv SALE M33..............96 C8
Harboro Rd SALE M33..............96 B8
Harboro Wy SALE M33..............96 C8

Harbour Farm Rd HYDE SK14..............91 H7
Harbour La EDGW/EG BL7..............16 D7
MILN OL16..............29 J7
Harbour La North MILN OL16..............29 J6
Harbourne Av WALK M28..............68 F4
Harbourne Cl WALK M28..............68 F4
Harbury Cl BOLS/LL BL3..............51 K1
WGNNW/ST WN6..............
Harbury Crs WYTH/NTH M22..............109M7
Harcles Dr RAMS BL0..............24 E2
Harcombe Rd DID/WITH M20..............98 F6
Harcourt Av URM M41..............96 C3
Harcourt Cl URM M41..............96 C3
Harcourt Rd ALT WA14..............108 A6
SALE M33..............96 D6
Harcourt St OLD OL1..............59 L4
RDSH SK5..............100 C4
STRET M32..............97 H1
WALK M28..............53 G7
Hardacre St WGNS/IIMK WN3..............15 J8
Hardberry Pl OFTN SK2..............113 H6
Hardcastle Av CCHDY M21..............97M6
Hardcastle Cl BOLE BL2..............22 F6
Hardcastle Gdns BOLE BL2..............22 F6
Hardcastle Rd EDGY/DAV SK3..............12 F8
Hardcastle St BOL BL1..............36 C2
Harden Dr BOLE BL2..............37 G2
Harden Hills ROY/SHW OL2..............44 A4
Harden Pk WILM/AE SK9..............130 D1
Hardfield Rd MDTN M24..............57 K7
Hardfield St HEY OL10..............41 G3
Hardicker St BNG/LEV M19..............99 L5
Hardie Av FWTH BL4..............52 E5
Harding St ANC M4..............88 A3
CSLFD M3..............6 E2
HYDE SK14..............91 G7
SLFD M6..............71 K8
STKP SK1..............112 E3
Hard La WHIT OL12..............19 H4
Hardman Av MPL/ROM SK6..............113 K1
PWCH M25..............72 A2
Hardman Cl RAD M26..............38 C6
Hardman La FAIL M35..............74 B4
Hardman Rd RDSH SK5..............100 C4
Hardmans EDGW/EG BL7..............22 C5
Hardman's La EDGW/EG BL7..............22 C4
Hardman's Rd WHTF M45..............55 J6
Hardman St BURY BL9..............4 F1
CHAD OL9..............74 E1
CSLFD M3..............6 D5
EDGY/DAV SK3..............12 F6
FAIL M35..............74 A5
FWTH BL4..............53 H5
HEY OL10..............41 G2
RAD M26..............38 C6
WGNS/IIMK WN3..............14 E8
Hardon Gv BRUN/LGST M13..............99 J2
Hardrow Cl WGNS/IIMK WN3..............63 L2
Hardrush Fold FAIL M35..............74 D6
Hardshaw Cl BRUN/LGST * M13..............87 L6
Hardwick Cl BOLS/LL BL3..............37 L7
MPL/ROM SK6..............114 F3
Hardwicke St ROCH OL11..............28 B8
Hardwick Rd AIMK WN4..............63 K7
PART M31..............106 D1
Hardwick St AULW OL7..............90 C3
Hardwood Cl CHH M8..............72 D5
Hardy Av CCHDY M21..............97 K4
Hardybutts WGN WN1..............15 K6
Hardy Cl ROCH OL11..............42 C1
WHTN BL5..............
Hardy Dr BRAM/HZG SK7..............120 F5
HALE/TIMP WA15..............108 C5
Hardy Gv SWIN M27..............70 A7
WALK M28..............69 J4
Hardy La CCHDY M21..............97M6
Hardy Mill Rd BOLE BL2..............23 J8
Hardy St ECC M30..............84 E3
OLDE OL4..............9M8
WGNNW/ST WN6..............14 C1
Hardywood Rd
DTN/ASHW M34..............101 K5
Harebell Av WALK * M28..............68 C1
Harebell Cl WHIT OL12..............28 A1
Haredale Dr CHH M8..............72 E6
Hare Dr BURY BL9..............39 L8
Harefield Av ROCH OL11..............10 F8
Harefield Dr DID/WITH M20..............110 D2
HEY OL10..............
WILM/AE SK9..............126 F7
Harefield Rd WILM/AE SK9..............120 A8
Harehill Cl BRUN/LGST M13..............7 K8
Hare Hill Rd HYDE SK14..............102 F1
LIT OL15..............20 B6
Hareshill Rd HEY OL10..............40 F5
Hare St ANC * M4..............7 H3
ROCH OL11..............10 F8
Harewood Av ROCH OL11..............26 F3
SALE M33..............96 A8
Harewood Cl ROCH OL11..............26 F3
Harewood Dr ROCH OL11..............26 F2
ROY/SHW OL2..............42 F7
Harewood Gv RDSH SK5..............100 B4
Harewood Rd IRL M44..............94 C2
ROCH OL11..............26 F2
ROY/SHW OL2..............42 F6
WGNE/HIN WN2..............48 F6
Harewood Wy ROCH OL11..............26 F3
SWIN M27..............70 C2
Harford Cl BRAM/HZG SK7..............121 J3
Hargate Av WHIT OL12..............27 K2
Hargate Cl BURY BL9..............24 E2
Hargate Dr HALE/TIMP WA15..............117 J3
IRL M44..............94 D1
Hargate Hill La GLSP SK13..............104 A5
Hargreaves Rd
HALE/TIMP WA15..............108 F6
Hargreave's St ANC M4..............87 K1
BOL * BL1..............36 B2
CHAD OL9..............8 D6
OLD OL1..............9 H4
ROCH OL11..............27M8
Harland Dr AIMK WN4..............78 F1
CHH M8..............72 E5
Harland Wy WHIT OL12..............28 A2
Harlea Av WGNE/HIN WN2..............65 K1
Harlech Av WGNE/HIN WN2..............49 K8
WHTF M45..............55 L6
Harlech Dr BRAM/HZG SK7..............121 J3
Harlech St AIMK WN4..............63 J7
Harleen Gv OFTN SK2..............113 G5
Harlesden Crs BOLS/LL * BL3..............35 L7
Harley Av BOLE BL2..............38 A3
RUSH/FAL M14..............99 H1
Harley Ct MDTN M24..............57 J3
Harley Rd MDTN M24..............57 J3

SALE M33..............96 F7
Harley St AUL * OL6..............90 E1
OP/CLY M11..............89 G4
Harling Rd WYTH/NTH M22..............110 A5
Harlow Dr GTN M18..............100 A1
Harlyn Av BRAM/HZG SK7..............121 H5
Harmer Cl NEWH/MOS M40..............73 K7
Harmol Gv AULW OL7..............75 J6
Harmony St OLDE OL4..............9 L7
Harmsworth Dr HTNM SK4..............99 L7
Harmsworth St SLFD M6..............86 B2
Harmuir Cl WGNNW/ST WN6..............31 H8
Harold Av AIMK WN4..............63 K7
DUK SK16..............91 G3
GTN M18..............89 J8
Haroldene St BOLE BL2..............36 E2
Harold Lees Rd HEY OL10..............41 J1
Harold Priestnall Cl
NEWH/MOS M40..............73 L7
Harold St BOL BL1..............36 A2
CHAD OL9..............8 E5
FAIL * M35..............74 B5
MDTN M24..............57 H3
MILN OL16..............28 F2
OLDTF/WHR M16..............86 F6
PWCH M25..............55 J8
STKP SK1..............112 E4
WGNE/HIN WN2..............33 G7
Harper Ct EDGY/DAV SK3..............13 H8
Harper Fold Rd RAD M26..............54 A1
Harper Green Rd FWTH BL4..............52 E3
Harper Pl AUL OL6..............90 F1
Harper Rd WYTH/NTH M22..............110 B5
Harper's La BOL BL1..............35 L2
Harper Sq ROY/SHW OL2..............43M5
Harper St EDGY/DAV SK3..............13 G8
FWTH BL4..............52 E2
OLDS OL8..............59 H8
ROCH * OL11..............10 C9
WGN WN1..............15 K5
WGNE/HIN WN2..............48 F8
Harpford Cl BOLE BL2..............37 K7
Harpford Dr BOLE BL2..............37 K7
Harp Rd TRPK M17..............85 K4
Harp St OP/CLY M11..............89 G5
Harptree Gv LEIGH WN7..............66 A5
Harpurhey Rd CHH M8..............72 F4
The Harridge WHIT OL12..............27M1
WHIT OL12..............27M1
Harridge St WHIT OL12..............27M1
Harrier Cl LEIGH WN7..............66 F7
WALK M28..............53 G8
WYTH/NTH M22..............110 B7
Harriet St IRL M44..............94 B7
WALK M28..............53 G8
Harriett St ANC M4..............7M2
MILN OL16..............11 C5
Harringay Rd NEWH/MOS M40..............73 L7
Harrington Cl BURY BL9..............39 K5
Harrington Rd ALT WA14..............107 L7
Harrington St GTN M18..............89 H7
Harris Av DTN/ASHW M34..............100 E1
URM M41..............85 G7
Harris Cl DTN/ASHW M34..............100 E1
HEY OL10..............40 B3
Harris Dr BURY BL9..............55 L2
HYDE SK14..............91 K8
Harrison Av BNG/LEV M19..............99 L2
Harrison Cl WHIT OL12..............27 J3
Harrison Crs HOR/BR BL6..............32 F1
Harrison's Dr MPL/ROM SK6..............101M7
Harrison St ANC M4..............88 A3
BRO M7..............72 A4
ECC M30..............84 D4
HOR/BR BL6..............21 B8
HYDE * SK14..............102 C4
LHULT M38..............52 D8
OFTN SK2..............13 K9
OLD SK1..............9 J6
RAMS BL0..............17 C5
STLY SK15..............91 K2
WGNE/HIN WN2..............65 L1
WGNW/BIL/O WN5..............46 C4
Harrison Wy NEWLW WA12..............78 F8
Harris Rd WGNNW/ST WN6..............30 E2
Harris St BOLS/LL BL3..............2 B7
CHH M8..............72 B8
Harrogate Av PWCH M25..............72 A2
Harrogate Cl OP/CLY M11..............89 H5
Harrogate Rd RDSH SK5..............100 B4
Harrogate St WGN WN1..............15 C5
Harrop Edge La UPML OL3..............45 K8
Harrop Edge Rd HYDE SK14..............92 B8
Harrop Fold OLDS OL8..............75 K3
Harrop Green La UPML OL3..............45M7
Harrop La MCFLDN SK10..............129 J7
Harrop St BOLS/LL BL3..............35 K8
GTN M18..............89 J8
STKP SK1..............13 L8
STLY SK15..............91 J2
WALK M28..............68 E1
Harrow Av BNG/LEV M19..............99 K6
OLDS OL8..............75 C1
ROCH OL11..............27 K6
Harrow Dr NEWH/MOS M40..............73 C7
Harrowby Fold FWTH BL4..............52 E4
Harrowby La FWTH BL4..............52 E4
Harrowby Rd BOL BL1..............35 J2
BOLS/LL * BL3..............51 K1
SWIN M27..............70 B5
Harrowby St FWTH BL4..............52 E4
WGNW/BIL/O WN5..............47 H6
Harrow Cl BURY BL9..............39 J7
WGNW/BIL/O WN5..............46 C4
Harrow Dr SALE M33..............108 D2
Harrow Ms ROY/SHW OL2..............43 L8
Harrow Rd BOL BL1..............35 L5
SALE M33..............108 D2
WGNW/BIL/O WN5..............47 G3
Harrow St CHH M8..............72 E3
ROCH * OL11..............42 C2
Harrycroft Rd MPL/ROM SK6..............101 L7
Harry Hall Gdns BRO * M7..............71M8
Harry Rd RDSH SK5..............100 C4
Harry Rowley Cl
WYTH/NTH * M22..............118 E2
Harry St CHAD OL9..............8 D7
ROCH OL11..............41 L1
ROY/SHW OL2..............59 H2
Harry Thorneycroft Wk
OP/CLY M11..............88 B4
Harrytown MPL/ROM SK6..............113 K2
Hart Av DROY M43..............89 C3
SALE M33..............109 J1

Hart Ct MOSL OL5..............76 E2
Harter St CMANE M1..............7 G6
Hartfield Cl BRUN/LGST M13..............87M6
Hartford Av HEY OL10..............40 E2
HTNM SK4..............100 A6
WILM/AE SK9..............126 D7
Hartford Cl HEY OL10..............40 E2
Hartford Gdns
HALE/TIMP WA15..............109 L8
Hartford Rd SALE M33..............108 A3
URM M41..............85 H8
WHTN BL5..............50 C6
Hartford Sq CHAD * OL9..............8 D7
Hart Hill Dr ORD M5..............86 A1
Harthill St CHH M8..............72 C7
Hartington Cl URM M41..............96 B3
Hartington Dr BRAM/HZG SK7..............122 A4
OP/CLY M11..............88 E1
WGNNW/ST WN6..............31 J5
Hartington Rd ALT WA14..............108 A5
BOL BL1..............35M4
BRAM/HZG SK7..............121 C6
CCHDY M21..............97 L4
CHD/CHDH SK8..............119M4
ECC M30..............84 D1
MPL/ROM SK6..............123 C6
OFTN SK2..............113 C8
Hartis Av BRO M7..............72 B6
Hartland Cl OFTN SK2..............112 F4
POY/DIS SK12..............121M7
TYLD M29..............67 L4
Hartland St HEY OL10..............41 G2
Hartlebury ROCH OL11..............10 D7
Hartlepool Cl RUSH/FAL M14..............98 E1
Hartley Av PWCH M25..............71M1
WGN WN1..............15 K5
Hartley Gv IRL M44..............83 L8
WGNW/BIL/O WN5..............46 E5
Hartley Rd ALT WA14..............107M7
CCHDY M21..............97 K3
Hartley St EDGY/DAV SK3..............12 E7
HEY OL10..............41 C2
HOR/BR BL6..............33 L2
LIT OL15..............20 B7
MILN * OL16..............29 C5
NEWH/MOS M40..............73 J4
STLY * SK15..............92 A1
WGNW/BIL/O WN5..............19 K6
WHIT OL12..............19 K6
WHIT OL12..............27 L1
Hartley Ter WGNS/IIMK WN3..............14 F6
Hart Mill Cl MOSL OL5..............76 E2
Harton Av GTN M18..............99M1
Harton Cl ROY/SHW OL2..............43 K6
Hart Rd RUSH/FAL M14..............98 E3
Hartshead Av AUL OL6..............75M6
STLY SK15..............91 K1
Hartshead Crs FAIL M35..............74 F6
Hartshead Rd AUL * OL6..............75M6
Hartshead St OLDE OL4..............60 C7
Hartshead Vw HYDE SK14..............102 C3
Hartsop Dr MDTN M24..............56 F2
Hart St ALT WA14..............108 A7
CMANE M1..............7 H6
DROY M43..............89 K2
TYLD M29..............67M4
WHTN BL5..............49 L5
Hartswell Cl GOL/RIS/CU WA3..............79 K3
Hartswood Cl DTN/ASHW M34..............90 D8
Hartswood Rd DID/WITH M20..............99 G6
Hartwell Cl BOLE BL2..............36 F2
OP/CLY M11..............88 C4
Harvard Cl MPL/ROM SK6..............101M7
Harvard Gv SLFD M6..............85M1
Harvard St ROCH OL11..............28 D8
Harvest Cl SALE M33..............109 K1
SLFD M6..............71 H7
Harvest Pk BOL BL1..............35M4
Harvey Cl GOL/RIS/CU WA3..............80 E3
Harvey La GOL/RIS/CU WA3..............79 J3
Harvey St BOL BL1..............36 A1
STKP SK1..............13 J4
TOT/BURYW BL8..............38 F1
WGNS/IIMK WN3..............15 J7
WHIT OL12..............28 E3
Harvin Gv DTN/ASHW M34..............101 K2
Harwich Cl BNG/LEV * M19..............99 K3
RDSH SK5..............100 F6
Harwin Cl WHIT OL12..............28 A1
Harwood Cl TOT/BURYW BL8..............24 B5
Harwood Crs TOT/BURYW BL8..............24 B5
Harwood Dr TOT/BURYW BL8..............38 D3
Harwood Gv BOLE * BL2..............36 E3
Harwood Meadow BOLE BL2..............37 J1
Harwood Rd BNG/LEV M19..............99 H6
BOLE BL2..............23 L8
HTNM SK4..............111 H2
Harwood St HTNM SK4..............13 G1
LIT OL15..............20 A7
Harwood V BOLE BL2..............37 H1
Haseldine Cl AIMK WN4..............63 L7
Haseley Cl BOLS/LL BL3..............37 L7
POY/DIS SK12..............122 F7
Haselhurst Wk
NTHM/RTH M23..............109 J2
Hasguard Cl BOL BL1..............35 J5
Haskoll St HOR/BR BL6..............34 A3
Haslam Brow WGN WN1..............4 D8
Haslam Hall Ms BOL BL1..............35 H5
Haslam Hey Cl BOLE * BL2..............37M3
Haslam Rd EDGY/DAV SK3..............112 B6
Haslam St BOLS/LL BL3..............2 B9
BURY BL9..............25 K8
MDTN * M24..............57M5
WHIT OL12..............10 B2
Haslemere Av
HALE/TIMP WA15..............117 L6
Haslemere Dr CHD/CHDH SK8..............120 C5
Haslemere Rd DID/WITH M20..............99 G5
URM M41..............85 C6
Haslington Rd WYTH/NTH M22..............119 G2
Hasper Av DID/WITH M20..............98 C4
Hassall Av DID/WITH M20..............98 C4
Hassall St RAD M26..............57 M1
Hassnes Cl WGNS/IIMK WN3..............63 L1
Hassop Av BRO M7..............71 K5
Hassop Cl OP/CLY M11..............88 B7
Hassop Rd RDSH SK5..............100 D3
Hastings Av CCHDY M21..............97 K4
WHTF M45..............55 L5

Hastings Cl CHD/CHDH SK8..............120 E2
STKP SK1..............112 E5
WHTF M45..............55 L5
Hastings Dr URM M41..............95 H1
Hastings Rd BOL BL1..............35 L4
ECC M30..............69 K8
PWCH M25..............55M7
Hastings St ROCH OL11..............10 F8
Hasty La HALE/TIMP WA15..............118 B5
Hatchett Rd WYTH/NTH M22..............119 G3
Hatchmere Cl
HALE/TIMP WA15..............109 G6
Hatchmere Rd CHD/CHDH SK8..............111 J8
Hatfield Av BNG/LEV M19..............99 K6
Hatfield Rd BOL BL1..............35M3
Hatford Cl TYLD M29..............67M3
Hathaway Cl LEIGH WN7..............66 E6
Hathaway Dr BOL BL1..............22 D7
Hathaway Gdns MPL/ROM SK6..............113 H1
Hathaway Rd BURY BL9..............55 K1
Hathaway Wk WGNS/IIMK WN3..............39 G6
Hatherley Rd DID/WITH M20..............99 G6
Hatherlow MPL/ROM SK6..............113 K2
Hatherlow La BRAM/HZG SK7..............121M2
Hatherop Cl ECC M30..............8 C7
Hathersage Crs GLSP SK13..............104 B2
Hathersage Dr GLSP SK13..............105 J3
Hathersage Rd BRUN/LGST M13..............87M8
Hathersage St CHAD OL9..............8 C7
Hathershaw La OLDS OL8..............75 J1
Hatro Ct URM M41..............96 C3
Hattersley Rd East HYDE SK14..............103 G3
Hattersley Rd West HYDE SK14..............102 F2
Hatter St ANC M4..............7 J2
Hatton Av ATH M46..............87 G1
BRO M7..............72 B6
Hatton Gv BOL BL1..............22 D7
Hattons Ct STRET M32..............96 F1
Hattons Rd TRPK M17..............85 L5
Hatton St STKP SK1..............13 H3
Haugh Hill Rd OLDE OL4..............60 C1
Haugh La MILN OL16..............29M8
Haughton Dr WYTH/NTH M22..............110 A3
Haughton Green Rd
DTN/ASHW M34..............101 K4
Haughton Hall Rd
DTN/ASHW M34..............101 K1
Haughton St DTN/ASHW M34..............90 B7
HYDE SK14..............102 B3
Havana Cl OP/CLY M11..............88 C3
Haveley Rd WYTH/NTH M22..............109M7
Havelock Dr BRO * M7..............72 A8
Havelock St OLDS OL8..............8 J9
The Haven HALE/TIMP WA15..............117 H1
Havenbrook Gv RAMS * BL0..............24 E1
Haven Cl BRAM/HZG SK7..............121 L3
OLDE OL4..............61 G6
RAD M26..............38 A7
Haven Dr DROY M43..............89 H2
Havenscroft Av ECC M30..............60 B1
Haven St SLFD M6..............86 B3
Havenwood Rd WGN WN1..............31 L8
Haverfield Rd BKLY M9..............73 H1
Haverford St WGTN/LGST M12..............88 C6
Haverhill Gv BOLE BL2..............36 E2
Haversham Rd CHH M8..............72 B2
Havers Rd GTN M18..............89 H6
Havisham Cl HOR/BR BL6..............34 E8
Hawarde Cl NEWH/MOS M40..............78 D8
Hawarden Av OLDTF/WHR M16..............97M2
Hawarden Rd ALT WA14..............108 A6
Hawarden St BOL BL1..............22 B8
Haw Clough La UPML OL3..............61M6
Hawes Av FWTH BL4..............52 B4
RUSH/FAL M14..............99 H5
SWIN M27..............70 C6
Hawes Cl OFTN SK2..............112 D6
TOT/BURYW BL8..............24 E7
Hawes Crs AIMK WN4..............63 L7
Haweswater Av TYLD M29..............67 L1
WGNE/HIN WN2..............48 E5
Haweswater Cl
DTN/ASHW M34..............100 D2
Haweswater Ms BURY BL9..............39 L7
MDTN * M24..............57 H2
Hawfinch Gv WALK M28..............68 G4
Hawick Gv BOL BL1..............36 A1
Hawke St STLY SK15..............91M3
Hawk Green Rd MPL/ROM SK6..............123 H1
Hawkhurst Rd BRUN/LGST M13..............99 J1
Hawkhurst St LEIGH WN7..............66 E7
Hawkins St RDSH SK5..............100 B8
Hawkins Wy LIT OL15..............20 D3
Hawkley Av WGNS/IIMK WN3..............63 J2
Hawkshaw Ct ORD M5..............86 D3
Hawkshaw La TOT/BURYW BL8..............23M1
Hawkshaw St HOR/BR BL6..............33 L2
Hawkshead Dr BOLS/LL BL3..............51 K1
MDTN M24..............56 F2
ROY/SHW OL2..............43 G6
Hawkshead Rd GLSP SK13..............105 K4
ROY/SHW OL2..............43 C6
Hawksheath Cl EDGW/EG BL7..............22 B3
Hawksley St HOR/BR BL6..............34 A2
OLDS OL8..............74 F1
Hawksmoor Dr ROY/SHW OL2..............43 L4
Hawkstone Av DROY M43..............89 H1
WHTF M45..............55 G5
Hawkstone Cl BOLE BL2..............37 H1
Hawkswick Dr NTHM/RTH M23..............109 L1
Hawkworth TYLD M29..............67 L7
Hawley Dr HALE/TIMP WA15..............117 K4
Hawley Gn WHIT OL12..............28 A2
Hawley La HALE/TIMP WA15..............117 K4
Hawley St BNG/LEV M19..............99 L4
Haworth Av RAMS BL0..............39 J6
Haworth Cl BURY BL9..............39 J6
Haworth Rd GTN M18..............88 F1
Haworth St EDGW/EG BL7..............16 D7
OLD OL1..............9 H2
RAD M26..............54 E1
TOT/BURYW BL8..............24 B8
Haworth Wy DROY M43..............89 H1
Hawthorn Av AIMK WN4..............62 F7
ECC M30..............84 C5
HALE/TIMP WA15..............108 C3
MPL/ROM SK6..............114 A6

RAD M26 54 E3
RAMS BL0 24 D2
TOT/BURYW BL8 24 F8
URM M41 96 C3
WALK M28 69 H3
WGN WN1 31 L6
WGNE/HIN WN2 65 K1
WGNW/BIL/O WN5 46 C6
WGNW/BIL/O WN5 47 G6
WILM/AE SK9 126 E5
Hawthorn Bank GLSP SK13 93 J8
Hawthorn Cl HALE/TIMP WA15 108 C5
TYLD M29 68 A3
WGNW/BIL/O WN5 62 A7
Hawthorn Crs ROY/SHW * OL2 43 L6
TOT/BURYW BL8 24 C5
Hawthorn Dr BNG/LEV M19 99 J5
IRL M44 94 A7
SLFD M6 70 D8
STLY SK15 91 J4
SWIN M27 70 F5
Hawthorne Av FWTH BL4 52 E4
GOL/RIS/CU WA3 81 M7
HOR/BR BL6 34 B3
Hawthorne Crs OLDS OL8 75 J2
Hawthorne Dr WALK M28 69 K5
Hawthorne Gv AULW OL7 90 C3
CHAD OL9 8 B3
LEIGH * WN7 66 B5
MPL/ROM SK6 101 H8
POY/DIS SK12 122 E8
Hawthorne La MILN OL16 29 K8
Hawthorne Rd BOLS/LL BL3 35 L8
Hawthorne St BOLS/LL BL3 35 L8
Hawthorn Gv BRAM/HZG SK7 120 E6
HTNM SK4 111 L1
HYDE SK14 93 G6
HYDE SK14 102 A3
WILM/AE SK9 126 F5
Hawthorn La CCHDY * M21 97 J4
SALE M33 96 A6
WILM/AE SK9 126 E5
Hawthorn Pk WILM/AE SK9 126 E5
Hawthorn Rd CHD/CHDH SK8 110 D7
DROY M43 89 M2
DTN/ASHW M34 89 L8
FWTH BL4 53 L7
HALE/TIMP WA15 117 G1
HTNM SK4 111 H2
NEWH/MOS M40 74 B3
OLDS OL8 74 E2
ROCH OL11 27 H6
STRET M32 97 H4
WHTN BL5 50 C5
Hawthorn Rd South DROY M43 89 M2
The Hawthorns DTN/ASHW M34 90 A6
Hawthorn St DTN/ASHW M34 90 B6
GTN M18 89 G6
WILM/AE SK9 126 E6
Hawthorn Ter HTNM SK4 12 A1
Hawthorn Vw WILM/AE SK9 126 E5
Hawthorn Wk LIT OL15 20 A7
WILM/AE * SK9 126 E5
Hawthorpe Gv UPML OL3 61 L4
Haxby Rd GTN M18 100 A1
Haybarn Rd NTHM/RTH M23 109 L5
Hayburn Rd OFTN SK2 112 F4
Haycock Cl STLY SK15 92 B5
Hay Cft CHD/CHDH SK8 120 A4
Hayden Fold GLSP SK13 104 A6
Haydn Av RUSH/FAL M14 87 L8
Haydock Av SALE M33 107 L2
Haydock Dr BRAM/HZG SK7 122 B2
HALE/TIMP WA15 108 E7
WALK M28 68 E6
Haydock La EDGW/EG BL7 22 E4
RNFD/HAY WA11 78 A4
Haydock Park Gdns
NEWLW WA12 78 E3
Haydock St AIMK WN4 78 E2
BOL BL1 2 E2
NEWLW WA12 78 D8
Haye's Rd IRL M44 94 B7
Hayes St LEIGH WN7 66 B5
Hayeswater Rd URM M41 95 M1
Hayfell Rd WGNS/IIMK WN3 63 K3
Hayfield Av MPL/ROM SK6 101 K8
TYLD M29 67 M6
Hayfield Cl MDTN M24 57 M1
OLDE OL4 44 C8
TOT/BURYW BL8 24 C3
WGTN/LGST M12 88 B6
Hayfield Rd MPL/ROM SK6 101 K8
NM/HAY SK22 125 G3
SLFD M6 70 E8
Hayfield St SALE M33 96 D8
Hayfield Wk HALE/TIMP WA15 108 F6
Hayle Rd OLD OL1 44 A8
Hayley St BRUN/LGST * M13 88 B8
Hayling Rd SALE M33 96 B7
Haymaker Ri WHIT OL12 19 K6
Hayman Av LEIGH WN7 81 G2
Haymans Wk BRUN/LGST M13 87 L6
The Haymarket BURY BL9 4 F4
Haymarket Cl BRUN/LGST M13 87 M7
Haymarket St BURY BL9 4 E6
Haymill Av LHULT M38 52 D6
Haymond Cl SLFD M6 71 K6
Haynes St BOLS/LL BL3 51 L1
WHIT OL12 10 F2
Haysbrook Av LHULT M38 52 C8
Haysbrook Cl AULW OL7 75 K5
Haythorp Av WYTH/NTH M22 119 G1
Hayward Av BOLS/LL BL3 53 M1
Haywards Cl GLSP SK13 104 F1
Hayward St TOT/BURYW BL8 4 A2
Haywood Cl GOL/RIS/CU WA3 80 B3
Hazel Av AUL OL6 76 B6
BURY BL9 5 L4
CHD/CHDH SK8 111 H7
LHULT M38 52 B7
MILN OL16 43 K1
MPL/ROM SK6 114 A2
OLDTF/WHR M16 98 A2
RAD M26 53 K4
RAMS BL0 24 E3
SALE M33 108 E1
SWIN M27 70 D5
TOT/BURYW BL8 24 C7
WGNNW/ST WN6 31 K8
WHTN BL5 50 C5
Hazelbadge Cl POY/DIS SK12 121 L8
Hazelbadge Rd POY/DIS SK12 121 L8
Hazelbank Av DID/WITH M20 98 E5
Hazelbottom Rd CHH M8 72 E5
Hazel Cl DROY M43 89 M2
MPL/ROM SK6 114 B8
Hazelcroft WILM/AE SK9 130 D4
Hazeldene WHTN BL5 50 A7
Hazel-dene Cl BURY BL9 39 J5
Hazeldene Rd NEWH/MOS M40 74 B3
Hazel Dr OFTN SK2 113 G6
POY/DIS SK12 129 K1
WYTH/NTH M22 119 J4
Hazelfields WALK M28 69 L5
Hazel Gv CHAD OL9 8 B2
FWTH BL4 52 E4
GOL/RIS/CU WA3 79 L4
LEIGH WN7 66 B5
ORD M5 85 M2
RAD M26 54 C4
URM M41 96 B2
Hazel Hall La RAMS BL0 24 E3
Hazelhurst Cl BOL BL1 36 B2
RAMS BL0 17 B8
Hazelhurst Dr MDTN M24 41 J8
Hazelhurst Fold WALK M28 69 M5
Hazelhurst Rd AUL OL6 76 C6
STLY SK15 76 D8
WALK M28 69 L5
Hazel La OLDS OL8 75 G2
Hazelmere Av ECC M30 69 L8
Hazelmere Cl ECC M30 85 H4
Hazelmere Gdns
WGNE/HIN WN2 49 H8
Hazel Mt EDGW/EG BL7 22 B2
Hazel Rd ALT WA14 108 A7
ATH M46 50 F8
CHD/CHDH SK8 120 D3
MDTN M24 57 L2
STLY SK15 91 M1
WHTF M45 55 L4
Hazel St BRAM/HZG * SK7 122 A1
DTN/ASHW M34 90 B6
RAMS BL0 17 A8
Hazel Ter BKLY * M9 57 G8
Hazelton Cl LEIGH WN7 81 H3
Hazelwell SALE M33 108 E1
Hazelwood CHAD OL9 58 B5
Hazelwood Av BOLE BL2 37 H1
Hazelwood Cl HYDE SK14 102 D2
Hazelwood Dr BURY BL9 25 J5
DTN/ASHW M34 90 B6
Hazelwood Rd BOL BL1 35 L2
BRAM/HZG SK7 122 A2
HALE/TIMP WA15 117 G2
OFTN SK2 112 D8
WGN WN1 31 L8
WILM/AE SK9 127 H4
Hazlehurst Gv AIMK WN4 78 F1
Hazlemere FWTH BL4 53 K5
Headen Av WGNW/BIL/O WN5 46 E7
Headingley Dr OLDTF/WHR M16 97 K1
Headingley Rd RUSH/FAL M14 99 G5
Headingley Wy BOLS/LL BL3 52 A1
Headland Cl GOL/RIS/CU WA3 80 B6
Headlands Dr PWCH M25 71 K3
Headlands Rd BRAM/HZG SK7 121 H3
Headlands St WHIT OL12 28 B3
Heady Hill Rd HEY OL10 40 D2
Heald Av RUSH/FAL M14 98 E1
Heald Cl ALT WA14 116 E2
LIT OL15 29 K1
WHIT OL12 27 M1
Heald Dr ALT WA14 116 E2
WHIT OL12 27 M1
Heald Gv CHD/CHDH SK8 119 J3
RUSH/FAL M14 87 L8
Heald Pl RUSH/FAL M14 98 E1
Heald Rd ALT WA14 116 E2
Healds Gn OLD OL1 58 C1
Heald St STKP SK1 13 L2
Healdwood Rd MPL/ROM SK6 101 M8
Healey Av HEY OL10 41 H1
WHIT OL12 18 E8
Healey Cl BRO M7 71 M6
NTHM/RTH M23 109 J2
Healey Gv WHIT OL12 18 D7
Healey La WHIT OL12 28 B1
Healey St MILN OL16 10 D6
Healing St ROCH OL11 11 H9
Heanor Av DTN/ASHW M34 101 K4
Heap Br BURY BL9 39 M2
Heap Brow BURY BL9 40 A3
Heape St ROCH OL11 41 M3
Heapfold WHIT OL12 27 L2
Heaplands TOT/BURYW BL8 24 C3
Heaps Farm Ct STLY SK15 92 A4
Heap St BOLS/LL BL3 36 B8
HEY OL10 40 A3
OLDE OL4 59 M5
WHTF * M45 55 J5
Heapworth Av RAMS BL0 17 B6
Heapy Cl TOT/BURYW BL8 38 C2
Heardman Av WGNNW/ST WN6 14 B1
The Heath AULW OL7 75 K5
MDTN M24 57 L6
Heath Av BRO M7 71 M8
RAMS BL0 24 E3
Heathbank Rd BKLY M9 56 F7
CHD/CHDH SK8 120 B4
EDGY/DAV SK3 12 B9
Heathcliffe Wk BRUN/LGST M13 87 M7
Heath Cl BOLS/LL BL3 51 L2
Heathcote Av HTNM SK4 111 M1
Heathcote Rd GTN M18 88 F8
Heath Crs EDGY/DAV SK3 112 C7
Heather Av DROY M43 89 M2
IRL M44 94 A6
ROY/SHW OL2 44 A4
Heather Bank LIT * OL15 20 E6
TOT/BURYW * BL8 24 B5
Heather Bank Cl GLSP SK13 104 D5
Heather Brae NEWLW WA12 78 D8
Heather Brow STLY SK15 92 B5
Heather Cl HOR/BR BL6 21 B8
OLDE OL4 60 B3
Heatherdale Dr CHH M8 72 D6
Heatherfield BOL BL1 22 A7
EDGW/EG BL7 16 E6
Heatherfield Ct WILM/AE SK9 127 J4
Heather Gv AIMK WN4 64 B8
DROY M43 89 L4
HYDE SK14 93 G6
LEIGH WN7 66 B5
WGNW/BIL/O WN5 47 H5
Heather Lea DTN/ASHW M34 101 J1
Heather Rd ALT WA14 117 G3
The Heathers OFTN SK2 112 E8
Heatherside RDSH SK5 100 D3
STLY SK15 92 A2
Heatherside Av MOSL OL5 77 H3
Heatherside Rd RAMS BL0 17 B5
Heather St OP/CLY M11 88 E4
Heather Wy MPL/ROM SK6 114 B7
Heatherway SALE M33 96 A7
Heath Farm La PART M31 106 D1
Heathfield BOLE BL2 23 J8
FWTH BL4 53 H3
WALK M28 69 J7
WILM/AE SK9 126 E7
Heathfield Av CHD/CHDH SK8 110 E7
DTN/ASHW M34 101 G2
HTNM SK4 99 M7
Heathfield Cl SALE M33 109 J1
Heathfield Dr BOLS/LL BL3 51 L2
SWIN M27 70 D5
TYLD M29 68 A3
Heathfield Rd BURY BL9 55 J1
OFTN SK2 112 C6
Heathfields UPML OL3 61 M4
Heathfield St NEWH/MOS M40 73 M7
Heath Gdns WGNE/HIN WN2 65 M1
Heathland Rd BRO M7 71 L4
Heathlands Dr PWCH M25 71 K3
Heathland Ter EDGY/DAV SK3 13 H9
Heath La GOL/RIS/CU WA3 80 A6
LEIGH WN7 65 L7
Heathlea WGNE/HIN WN2 65 M2
Heathmoor Av GOL/RIS/CU WA3 80 A6
Heath Rd AIMK WN4 78 E2
ALT WA14 116 F2
EDGY/DAV SK3 112 C6
GLSP SK13 104 F1
HALE/TIMP WA15 108 C4
WHIT OL12 19 K6
Heathside Gv WALK M28 69 G1
Heathside Park Rd
EDGY/DAV SK3 111 J5
Heathside Rd DID/WITH M20 98 F7
EDGY/DAV SK3 111 K5
Heath St AIMK WN4 78 F2
CHH M8 72 C5
GOL/RIS/CU WA3 79 K4
ROCH OL11 10 B6
Heathwood UPML OL3 61 M4
Heathwood Rd BNG/LEV M19 99 H8
Heatley Cl DTN/ASHW M34 100 E2
Heatley Rd MILN OL16 29 G6
Heaton Av BOL BL1 35 J3
BOLE BL2 23 H7
BOLS/LL BL3 37 K8
BRAM/HZG SK7 120 F1
FWTH BL4 52 F4
Heaton Cl BURY BL9 39 K7
HTNM SK4 111 K1
Heaton Ct BURY BL9 39 H5
Heaton Dr BURY BL9 39 K7
Heaton Fold BURY BL9 4 E9
Heaton Grange Dr BOL * BL1 35 K5
Heaton Gv BURY BL9 39 H5
Heaton La HTNM SK4 12 F4
Heaton Moor Rd HTNM SK4 111 L1
Heaton Mt BOL BL1 35 J3
Heaton Park Rd BKLY M9 56 D7
Heaton Park Rd West BKLY M9 56 D7
Heaton Rd BOLE BL2 37 L7
DID/WITH M20 98 F5
HOR/BR BL6 34 F7
HTNM SK4 112 A1
Heatons Gv WHTN BL5 50 D2
Heaton St BRO M7 72 B5
DTN/ASHW M34 101 G1
MILN OL16 29 K7
PWCH M25 55 M8
WGN WN1 47 M2
WGNE/HIN WN2 33 G6
WGNNW/ST WN6 31 H3
WGNS/IIMK WN3 15 K7
Heaviley Gv HOR/BR BL6 21 A7
OFTN SK2 112 D6
Hebble Butt Cl MILN * OL16 29 H6
Hebble Cl BOLE BL2 22 E7
Hebburn Dr TOT/BURYW BL8 24 F7
Hebburn Wk RUSH/FAL M14 87 L8
Hebden Av GOL/RIS/CU WA3 81 L8
MPL/ROM SK6 101 K8
SLFD M6 85 M1
Hebden Dr GLSP SK13 105 J4
Hebden Wk HULME M15 87 J7
Hebdon Cl AIMK WN4 63 K7
Heber Pl LIT OL15 20 C7
Heber St RAD M26 54 D1
WGNE/HIN WN2 48 C5
Hebron St ROY/SHW OL2 59 K1
Hector Av MILN OL16 11 J2
Hector Rd BRUN/LGST M13 99 J1
WGNW/BIL/O WN5 47 G3
Heddles Ct LEIGH * WN7 66 B8
Heddon Cl HTNM SK4 111 H1
Hedgemead WGNNW/ST WN6 14 B2
The Hedgerows HYDE SK14 102 D1
RNFD/HAY WA11 78 C5
Hedge Rows WHIT OL12 18 D2
Hedges St FAIL M35 74 D4
Hedley St BOL BL1 35 M2
Heeley St WGN WN1 47 L2
Heginbottom Crs AUL OL6 75 M7
The Heights HOR/BR BL6 34 A3
Heights Av WHIT OL12 28 B3
Heights Cl WHIT OL12 28 B2
Heights La OLD OL1 58 C2
UPML OL3 45 G5
WHIT OL12 28 B3
Helena St SLFD M6 70 F7
Helen St AIMK WN4 63 K8
BRO M7 71 M7
ECC M30 84 E4
FWTH BL4 53 G4
GOL/RIS/CU WA3 79 J2
Helensville Av SLFD M6 71 J7
Helga St NEWH/MOS M40 73 G8
Helias Cl LHULT M38 68 C1
Hell Nook GOL/RIS/CU WA3 79 H3
Helmclough Wy WALK M28 68 F4
Helmet St CMANE M1 7 M7
Helmsdale WALK M28 68 F2
Helmsdale Av BOLS/LL BL3 35 J6
Helmsdale Cl RAMS BL0 24 D1
Helmshore Av OLDE OL4 60 A1
Helmshore Rd RAMS BL0 17 A1
Helmshore Wk BRUN/LGST M13 7 K9
Helmshore Wy ROY/SHW OL2 43 L4
Helmsman Wy WGNS/IIMK WN3 14 D9
Helsby Cl OLDE OL4 60 D6
Helsby Gdns BOL BL1 22 C8
Helsby Rd SALE M33 109 H2
Helsby Wk WGTN/LGST M12 88 B4
Helsby Wy WGNS/IIMK WN3 62 F2
Helston Cl BRAM/HZG SK7 121 H5
IRL M44 94 E2
Helston Dr ROY/SHW OL2 43 J8
Helston Gv CHD/CHDH SK8 119 L4
Helston St NEWH/MOS M40 73 J8
Helston Wy TYLD M29 67 M4
Helvellyn Dr MDTN M24 57 J2
Helvellyn Rd WGNW/BIL/O WN5 46 E5
Helvellyn Wk OLD OL1 9 L1
Hembury Av BNG/LEV M19 99 J6
Hembury Cl MDTN M24 57 L2
Hemfield Ct WGNE/HIN WN2 48 F4
Hemfield Rd WGNE/HIN WN2 48 F4
Hemley Cl WHTN BL5 50 A6
Hemlock Av OLDS OL8 75 H1
Hemming Dr ECC M30 85 H3
Hemmington Dr BKLY M9 73 G5
Hemmons Rd WGTN/LGST M12 99 L2
Hempcroft Rd
HALE/TIMP WA15 108 F7
Hempshaw La STKP SK1 13 K8
Hemsley St BKLY M9 73 H3
Hemsley St South BKLY M9 73 H4
Hemswell Cl SLFD M6 71 H8
Hemsworth Rd BOL BL1 2 B2
GTN M18 100 A1
Henbury Dr MPL/ROM SK6 101 L6
Henbury La CHD/CHDH SK8 120 B6
Henbury Rd WILM/AE * SK9 119 M8
Henbury St OFTN SK2 112 F8
RUSH/FAL M14 98 D1
Henderson Av SWIN M27 70 C3
Henderson St BNG/LEV M19 99 L4
LIT OL15 20 B7
WHIT OL12 28 E2
Henderville St LIT OL15 20 B6
Hendham Cl BRAM/HZG SK7 121 J2
Hendham Dr ALT WA14 107 L6
Hendham V BKLY M9 72 F5
Hendon Dr BURY BL9 39 J7
EDGY/DAV SK3 111 K5
Hendon Gv LEIGH WN7 66 C4
Hendon Rd BKLY M9 56 F8
WGNW/BIL/O WN5 47 G4
Hendon St LEIGH WN7 66 C4
Hendriff Pl WHIT * OL12 28 C3
Hen Fold Rd TYLD M29 67 M5
Hengist St BOLE BL2 3 M4
GTN M18 89 G8
Henley Av CHD/CHDH SK8 120 B2
IRL M44 94 B6
OLDTF/WHR M16 97 L1
Henley Cl TOT/BURYW BL8 38 E4
Henley Dr AULW OL7 75 J8
HALE/TIMP WA15 108 C5
Henley Gv BOLS/LL BL3 51 M1
Henley Pl BNG/LEV M19 99 K6
Henley St CHAD OL9 74 D1
OLD OL1 8 F2
WGNE/HIN WN2 32 E6
WHIT OL12 10 D1
Henley Ter ROCH OL11 10 C9
Henniker Rd BOLS/LL BL3 51 K2
Henniker St SWIN M27 70 B6
WALK M28 69 G3
Hennon St BOL BL1 36 A3
Henrietta St AUL OL6 75 L7
BOLS/LL BL3 35 L8
LEIGH WN7 66 C7
OLDTF/WHR M16 86 F7
Henry Herman St BOLS/LL BL3 51 K1
Henry Lee St BOLS/LL * BL3 51 M1
Henry Park St WGN WN1 15 L5
Henry St ANC M4 7 K3
BOLS/LL BL3 3 G7
DROY M43 89 K3
DTN/ASHW * M34 101 L4
ECC M30 84 F3
FAIL M35 74 C5
GLSP SK13 104 F3
HYDE SK14 102 A2
LEIGH WN7 66 D8
LEIGH WN7 81 K1
LIT OL15 29 J1
MDTN M24 57 J4
OLDTF/WHR M16 86 F7
PWCH M25 55 M7
RAMS BL0 17 D5
ROCH OL11 10 F6
STKP SK1 112 E4
TYLD M29 67 K3
WGNS/IIMK WN3 48 B8
Henshall La ALT WA14 106 F5
Henshaw Ct OLDTF/WHR M16 86 E8
Henshaw La CHAD OL9 74 C2
Henshaw St OLD OL1 9 H5
STRET M32 97 G2
Henshaw Wk BOL BL1 36 B2
Henson Gv HALE/TIMP WA15 108 D8
Henthorn St ROY/SHW OL2 43 L6
Henton Wk NEWH/MOS M40 72 F8
Henwick Hall Av RAMS BL0 17 B8
Henwood Rd DID/WITH M20 98 F7
Hepley Rd POY/DIS SK12 129 L1
Hepple Cl HTNM SK4 111 J1
Heppleton Rd NEWH/MOS M40 74 A2
Hepple Wk AULW * OL7 75 H7
Hepton St OLD OL1 9 G3
Hepworth Cl GOL/RIS/CU WA3 79 J2
Hepworth St HYDE SK14 102 B5
Herbert St BOLS/LL BL3 53 L1
CHAD OL9 8 B5
CHH * M8 72 C7
DROY M43 89 J3
DTN/ASHW M34 90 D8
EDGY/DAV SK3 12 F8
HOR/BR BL6 21 A8
OLDE OL4 59 M3
PWCH M25 55 J8
RAD M26 38 C7
STRET M32 97 G2
WGNS/IIMK WN3 14 D5
WHTN BL5 50 B2
Hereford Av GOL/RIS/CU * WA3 79 L4
Hereford Cl AIMK WN4 78 F2
AUL OL6 76 A5
ROY/SHW OL2 43 J5
Hereford Dr BURY BL9 5 G8
PWCH M25 71 M2
SWIN M27 70 C6
WILM/AE SK9 127 J1
Hereford Gv URM M41 95 M2
Hereford Rd BOL BL1 35 L4
CHD/CHDH SK8 111 K8
ECC M30 70 D7
RDSH SK5 100 F7
WGNE/HIN WN2 49 J6
Hereford St BOL BL1 36 C2
CHAD OL9 8 C8
ROCH OL11 11 G8
SALE M33 96 E8
Hereford Wy MDTN M24 57 M3
STLY SK15 92 A5
Herevale Gra WALK M28 68 E5
Herevale Hall Dr RAMS * BL0 17 B8
Heriston Av DTN/ASHW M34 101 H1
Heritage Gdns DID/WITH M20 110 E2
Herle Dr WYTH/NTH M22 118 E3
Hermitage Av MPL/ROM SK6 114 C2
Hermitage Cl WGNNW/ST WN6 30 B5
Hermitage Gdns
MPL/ROM SK6 114 C2
Hermitage Rd CHH M8 72 D3
HALE/TIMP WA15 117 J1
Hermon Av OLDS OL8 75 H1
Herne St OP/CLY M11 88 D4
Heron Av DUK SK16 91 H5
FWTH BL4 52 C5
Heron Ct SLFD M6 85 L1
Herondale Cl NEWH/MOS M40 73 L7
Heron Dr DTN/ASHW M34 89 M3
IRL M44 94 D1
POY/DIS SK12 128 E1
WGNS/IIMK WN3 63 H2
Heron Ml OLDS * OL8 75 G1
Heron Pl WGNW/BIL/O WN5 46 F4
Heron St EDGY/DAV SK3 12 F7
HULME M15 87 H7
OLDS OL8 74 F1
SWIN M27 70 D3
Heron's Wy BOLE BL2 3 G8
Herries St AUL OL6 76 A8
Herristone Rd CHH M8 72 D2
Herrod Av HTNM SK4 100 B7
Herschel St NEWH/MOS M40 73 K4
Hersey St SLFD * M6 86 B2
Hertford Dr TYLD M29 67 K1
Hertford Rd BKLY M9 73 G3
Hertfordshire Park Cl
ROY/SHW * OL2 43 L4
Hertford St AULW OL7 90 D3
Hesford Av BKLY M9 73 J5
Hesketh Av BOL BL1 22 C7
DID/WITH M20 110 D1
ROY/SHW OL2 43 K7
Hesketh Ct ATH M46 66 F1
Hesketh Dr WGNNW/ST WN6 30 D2
Hesketh Meadow La
GOL/RIS/CU WA3 80 D5
Hesketh Rd MILN OL16 11 L4
SALE M33 108 C1
Hesketh St ATH M46 51 G8
HTNM * SK4 13 G1
HTNM SK4 100 B8
LEIGH WN7 66 A7
WGNW/BIL/O WN5 47 H5
Hesnall Cl GOL/RIS/CU WA3 81 M4
Hessel St SALQ M50 86 A3
Hester Wk HULME * M15 87 J6
Heston Av BRUN/LGST M13 99 H2
Heston Dr URM M41 95 M1
Heswall Av DID/WITH M20 98 E5
Heswall Dr TOT/BURYW BL8 24 B7
Heswall Rd RDSH SK5 100 C3
Hetherington Wk
WGTN/LGST M12 88 C8
Hethorn St NEWH/MOS M40 73 M7
Hetton Av BRUN/LGST M13 99 H2
Heversham Av ROY/SHW OL2 44 A5
Hewart Cl NEWH/MOS M40 72 F8
Hewart Dr BURY BL9 39 M2
Hewitt Av DTN/ASHW M34 100 C1
Hewitt St CSLFD M3 6 D8
Hewlett Rd CCHDY M21 97 K3
Hewlett St BOLE BL2 3 G5
WGN WN1 15 G4
WHTN BL5 49 L5
Hexham Av BOL BL1 35 J3
WGNS/IIMK WN3 63 J1
Hexham Cl ATH M46 51 H8
CHAD OL9 8 C4
OFTN SK2 113 H7
Hexham Rd GTN M18 88 E8
Hexon Cl SLFD M6 86 B1
The Hey ROY/SHW * OL2 44 B3
Hey Bottom La WHIT OL12 19 H6
Heybrook Cl WHTF M45 55 M4
Heybrook Rd NTHM/RTH M23 109 L7
Heybrook St MILN * OL16 11 J1
Heybury Cl OP/CLY M11 88 C4
Hey Crs OLDE OL4 60 C5
Hey Cft WHTF M45 54 F5
Heycrofts Vw RAMS BL0 17 E1
Heyes Av HALE/TIMP WA15 108 E5
RNFD/HAY WA11 78 A7
Heyes Dr HALE/TIMP WA15 108 E5
Heyes La HALE/TIMP WA15 108 E4
WILM/AE SK9 130 E2
Heyes Leigh
HALE/TIMP * WA15 108 E5
Heyes Rd WGNW/BIL/O WN5 46 B6
Heyes Ter HALE/TIMP * WA15 108 E4
Heyford Av NEWH/MOS M40 74 A2
Heyford Rd WGNW/BIL/O WN5 47 G4
Hey Head La LIT OL15 20 C3
Heyheads New Rd MOSL OL5 77 H5
Hey Hill Cl ROY/SHW OL2 43 K7
Heyland Rd NTHM/RTH M23 109 K6
Heyridge Dr WYTH/NTH M22 110 A3
Heyrod St CMANE M1 7 L6
STLY SK15 77 G7
Heyrose Wk HULME M15 87 G6
The Heys PWCH M25 55 L7
RDSH SK5 100 D3
Heys Av MPL/ROM SK6 114 B1
NTHM/RTH M23 109 K3
SWIN M27 69 M2
Heysbank Rd POY/DIS SK12 123 M7
Heys Cl North SWIN M27 69 M2
Heyscroft Rd DID/WITH M20 98 F6
HTNM SK4 111 K2
Heysham Av DID/WITH M20 98 C5
Heysham Rd WGNW/BIL/O WN5 46 E5
Hey Shoot La GOL/RIS/CU WA3 81 M7
Heyside ROY/SHW OL2 43 K8
Heyside Av ROY/SHW OL2 59 K1
Heyside Cl STLY SK15 77 H6
Heyside Wy BURY BL9 5 G6
Heys La HEY OL10 40 D2
MPL/ROM SK6 114 B1
Heys Rd AUL OL6 91 G1
PWCH M25 55 L7
Heys St TOT/BURYW BL8 4 B4
Hey St MILN OL16 11 J3
WGNNW/ST WN6 14 D3
WGNS/IIMK WN3 64 C1
Heys Vw PWCH M25 55 L8
Hey Willow BOLE BL2 22 F5
Heywood Av GOL/RIS/CU WA3 79 L3
OLDE OL4 60 D4
SWIN M27 70 E2
Heywood Cl WILM/AE SK9 130 E2
Heywood Fold Rd OLDE OL4 60 C5
Heywood Gdns BOLS/LL BL3 36 B8
PWCH M25 55 L8
Heywood Gv SALE M33 96 D6
Heywood Hall Rd HEY OL10 41 G1
Heywood La OLDE OL4 60 D5
Heywood Old Rd MDTN M24 56 D4
Heywood Park Vw BOLS/LL BL3 2 D9

Heywood Rd PWCH M25 ....55 L6
ROCH OL11 ....41 L2
SALE M33 ....108 L1
WILM/AE SK9 ....130 E2
Heywood's Hollow BOL BL1 ....36 C1
Heywood St BOL BL1 ....2 E2
BOLS/LL BL3 ....53 L1
BURY BL9 ....5 K2
CHH M8 ....72 D6
FAIL M35 ....74 A5
OLDE OL4 ....60 B4
SWIN M27 ....70 B4
Heyworth Av DTN/ASHW M34 ....102 B3
Heyworth Av MPL/ROM SK6 ....114 A1
Heyworth St ORD * M5 ....86 B3
Hibbert Av DTN/ASHW M34 ....90 A7
HYDE SK14 ....102 B3
Hibbert Crs FAIL M35 ....74 D5
Hibbert La MPL/ROM SK6 ....114 C7
Hibbert St BOL BL1 ....36 C2
HTNM SK4 ....100 B7
NM/HAY SK22 ....124 D6
OLDE OL4 ....60 C5
RUSH/FAL M14 ....98 F1
Hibernia St BOLS/LL BL3 ....35 M7
Hibernia Wy STRET M32 ....85 K7
Hibson Av WHIT OL12 ....27 H2
Hibson Cl WHIT OL12 ....19 K6
Hickenfield Rd HYDE SK14 ....91 J7
Hicken Pl HYDE SK14 ....91 J7
Hickton Dr ALT WA14 ....107 L6
Hieland Rd WGN WN1 ....48 B2
Higginshaw La OLD OL1 ....59 K2
Higginshaw Rd OLD OL1 ....9 K2
Higginson Rd RDSH SK5 ....100 B5
Higgs Cl OLDE OL4 ....60 A5
Higham Cl ROY/SHW OL2 ....43 K7
Higham La HYDE SK14 ....102 C4
Higham Vw SLFD M6 ....86 D1
High Ash Gv DTN/ASHW M34 ....90 A5
High Av BOLE * BL2 ....37 H5
High Bank ALT WA14 ....108 A7
ATH M46 ....51 K6
EDGW/EG BL7 ....22 C5
GTN M18 ....89 H7
Highbank GLSP SK13 ....93 J5
High Bank Av STLY SK15 ....92 A5
High Bank Cl IRL M44 ....94 A6
Highbank Crs OLDE OL4 ....61 H7
High Bank Crs PWCH M25 ....71 M1
Highbank Dr DID/WITH M20 ....110 E4
High Bank Gv PWCH M25 ....71 M1
High Bank La HOR/BR BL6 ....34 E5
High Bank Rd DROY M43 ....89 J4
HYDE SK14 ....102 C1
SWIN M27 ....70 E4
Highbank Rd BURY BL9 ....55 J1
GLSP SK13 ....105 J5
MILN OL16 ....43 M1
High Bank Side STKP SK1 ....13 J4
High Bank St BOLE BL2 ....3 M5
High Barn Cl ROCH OL11 ....10 C9
High Barn La WHIT OL12 ....18 D1
High Barn Rd MDTN M24 ....57 K5
ROY/SHW OL2 ....43 J8
High Barn Rd ROY/SHW OL2 ....43 H8
High Beeches BOLE * BL2 ....37 L7
High Bent Av CHD/CHDH SK8 ....120 C6
Highbridge Cl BOLE BL2 ....37 K6
Highbury Av IRL M44 ....94 D3
URM M41 ....95 H2
Highbury Cl WHTN BL5 ....50 A6
Highbury Rd HTNM SK4 ....99 M6
OLDTF/WHR M16 ....98 B3
Highbury Wy ROY/SHW OL2 ....43 G6
Highclere Av CHH M8 ....72 C6
Highclere Rd CHH M8 ....72 C6
Highcliffe Ct WGNNW/ST WN6 ....31 J5
Highcliffe Rd BKLY M9 ....72 E1
Highclove La WALK M28 ....68 C7
High Crest Av CHD/CHDH SK8 ....120 C6
Highcrest Gv TYLD M29 ....68 A3
Highcroft HYDE SK14 ....102 B5
High Croft Cl DUK SK16 ....91 K4
Highcroft Rd MPL/ROM SK6 ....113 M1
Highcroft Wy WHIT OL12 ....19 G8
Highdales Rd NTHM/RTH M23 ....109 L7
High Elm Dr HALE/TIMP WA15 ....117 L4
High Elm Rd HALE/TIMP WA15 ....117 L4
High Elms MOSL * OL5 ....76 E3
Higher Ainsworth Rd RAD M26 ....38 B5
Higher Ardwick WGTN/LGST M12 ....7 M9
Higher Bank Rd LIT OL15 ....29 K1
Higher Barlow Rw STKP SK1 ....13 K6
Higher Barn HOR/BR BL6 ....34 C1
Higher Barn Rd GLSP SK13 ....93 H8
Higher Bents La MPL/ROM SK6 ....113 J1
Higher Bridge St BOL BL1 ....2 E2
Higher Bury St HTNM SK4 ....12 E3
Higher Cambridge St
HULME M15 ....87 K6
Higher Carr La UPML OL3 ....61 L5
Higher Chatham St
HULME * M15 ....87 K6
Higher Cleggswood Av LIT OL15 ....29 K1
Higher Crft ECC M30 ....84 F4
WHTF M45 ....54 F6
Higher Crossbank OLDE OL4 ....60 C4
Higher Cross La UPML OL3 ....61 M5
Higher Damshead WHTN BL5 ....50 C4
Higher Darcy St BOLE BL2 ....3 L8
Higher Dean St RAD M26 ....54 B1
Higher Downs ALT WA14 ....116 E1
Higher Drake Meadow
WHTN BL5 ....50 A7
Higher Dunscar EDGW/EG BL7 ....22 B3
Higher Fold Farm
MPL/ROM * SK6 ....123 G3
Higher Fold La RAMS BL0 ....17 L5
Higher Fullwood OLD OL1 ....44 A8
Higher Green La TYLD M29 ....67 M8
Higher Henry St HYDE SK14 ....102 A3
Higher Highfield Ct
WGNE/HIN * WN2 ....32 E6
Higher Hillgate STKP SK1 ....13 K6
Higher House Cl CHAD OL9 ....58 D2
Higher Knowles HOR/BR BL6 ....34 B2
Higher La WGNE/HIN WN2 ....32 D3
WHTF M45 ....55 H4
Higher Lime Rd OLDS OL8 ....74 F4
Higher Lomax La HEY OL10 ....40 D1
Higher Lydgate Pk OLDE OL4 ....60 F6
Higher Market St FWTH BL4 ....53 H4
Higher Ormond St
HULME * M15 ....87 K6
Higher Ridings EDGW/EG BL7 ....22 B4

EDGW/EG BL7 ....22 C5
Higher Ri ROY/SHW OL2 ....43 K3
Higher Rd URM M41 ....96 B1
Higher Rw BURY BL9 ....5 K2
Higher Shady La EDGW/EG BL7 ....22 F5
Higher Shore Rd WHIT OL12 ....19 M5
Higher Southfield WHTN BL5 ....50 B5
Higher Summerseat RAMS BL0 ....24 E3
Higher Swan La BOLS/LL BL3 ....36 A8
Higher Tame St STLY SK15 ....91 L2
Higher Turf La OLDE OL4 ....60 E4
Higher Turf Pk ROY/SHW OL2 ....59 H1
Higher Wharf St AULW OL7 ....90 E2
Higher Wheat La MILN OL16 ....11 L3
Higher Wood St MDTN M24 ....57 J2
Higher York St
BRUN/LGST * M13 ....87 K6
Highfield SALE M33 ....108 F1
Highfield Av ATH M46 ....51 H7
BOLE BL2 ....37 K1
GOL/RIS/CU WA3 ....79 J4
HEY OL10 ....40 D2
LEIGH WN7 ....81 M1
MPL/ROM SK6 ....113 J2
RAD M26 ....54 F3
WALK M28 ....68 B4
WGN WN1 ....15 L1
WGNNW/ST WN6 ....30 D6
Highfield Cl EDGY/DAV SK3 ....112 C8
HYDE SK14 ....91 J6
STRET M32 ....96 F4
Highfield Crs WILM/AE SK9 ....127 G3
Highfield Dr ECC M30 ....85 G1
FWTH BL4 ....52 D5
MDTN M24 ....57 J5
MOSL OL5 ....76 F4
ROY/SHW OL2 ....59 H2
SWIN M27 ....70 F5
URM M41 ....95 M1
WGNNW/ST WN6 ....31 J5
Highfield Est WILM/AE SK9 ....127 G3
Highfield Gdns HYDE SK14 ....93 C7
Highfield Gln AUL OL6 ....76 C7
Highfield Grange Av
WGNS/IIMK WN3 ....63 G2
Highfield Gv WGNE/HIN WN2 ....32 F7
Highfield Gv GOL/RIS/CU WA3 ....79 M7
WHTF M45 ....55 J2
Highfield Pk HTNM SK4 ....111 J2
Highfield Park Rd
MPL/ROM SK6 ....101 H8
Highfield Pkwy
BRAM/HZG SK7 ....120 F8
Highfield Pl WTN * M18 ....89 J8
Highfield Range GTN * M18 ....89 J8
WGNNW/ST WN6 ....99 M3
Highfield Rd BNG/LEV M19 ....99 M3
BOL BL1 ....35 L2
BRAM/HZG SK7 ....121 H1
BRAM/HZG SK7 ....122 C2
CHD/CHDH SK8 ....120 B3
ECC M30 ....70 A8
FWTH BL4 ....52 B4
GLSP SK13 ....105 G4
HALE/TIMP WA15 ....108 E7
HALE/TIMP WA15 ....117 J2
HOR/BR BL6 ....33 H3
HTNM SK4 ....99 M4
LHULT M38 ....52 C7
MILN OL16 ....29 K6
MPL/ROM SK6 ....114 C7
NM/HAY SK22 ....125 M1
POY/DIS * SK12 ....121 J8
PWCH M25 ....55 K6
RAMS BL0 ....17 D1
ROCH OL11 ....27 H5
SALE M33 ....96 C6
STRET M32 ....96 F5
Highfield St BRO M7 ....72 C5
CHAD OL9 ....8 F5
DTN/ASHW M34 ....90 B7
DUK SK16 ....90 E3
EDGY/DAV SK3 ....12 C6
FWTH BL4 ....53 K6
MDTN M24 ....57 L4
Highfield Ter BKLY M9 ....73 C4
NM/HAY SK22 ....124 F4
OLDE OL4 ....60 D7
Highgate BOLS/LL BL3 ....50 F2
Highgate Av URM M41 ....84 D8
Highgate Crs GTN M18 ....89 G8
Highgate Dr LHULT M38 ....52 B7
ROY/SHW OL2 ....42 F5
Highgate La LHULT M38 ....52 B7
WHIT OL12 ....18 D1
Highgate Rd ALT WA14 ....107 L8
NM/HAY SK22 ....125 M2
High Gates SALE M33 ....97 H7
The Highgrove BOL BL1 ....35 G3
Highgrove Cl BOLE BL2 ....36 C1
High Grove La OLDE OL4 ....61 H7
High Grove Rd CHD/CHDH SK8 ....110 F7
High Hill Rd NM/HAY SK22 ....124 F3
High Houses BOL * BL1 ....22 A6
High Hurst Cl MDTN M24 ....56 F5
Highland Rd EDGW/EG BL7 ....22 E4
HOR/BR BL6 ....34 B3
Highlands Av OFTN SK2 ....113 J6
ROY/SHW OL2 ....58 F1
Highlands Dr OFTN SK2 ....113 J6
Highlands Rd HEY OL10 ....127 G7
OFTN SK2 ....113 J6
ROY/SHW OL2 ....43 J4
ROY/SHW OL2 ....58 F1
High La CCHDY M21 ....97 L4
GLSP SK13 ....104 B5
MPL/ROM SK6 ....101 L8
High Lea CHD/CHDH SK8 ....110 F7
High Lee La OLDE OL4 ....60 L1
High Lee Rd NM/HAY SK22 ....124 C4
High Legh Rd OP/CLY M11 ....89 G4
High Level Rd ROCH OL11 ....10 F7
Highmarsh Crs NEWLW WA12 ....78 D8
High Meadow
CHD/CHDH * SK8 ....120 A4
Highmeadow RAD M26 ....54 C3
High Mdw EDGW/EG BL7 ....22 F4
GLSP SK13 ....104 E5
High Mead St GTN M18 ....89 G7
Highmead Wk OLDTF/WHR M16 ....87 G7
High Moor Crs OLDE OL4 ....60 B3
Highmore Dr BKLY M9 ....73 H1
High Mt BOLE BL2 ....37 H1
High Pk WGNNW/ST WN6 ....30 F6
High Peak Rd AUL OL6 ....76 C6
WHIT OL12 ....18 D6
High Peak St NEWH/MOS M40 ....73 L6

High Rid La HOR/BR BL6 ....34 E3
Highshore Dr CHH M8 ....72 C5
High Stile St FWTH BL4 ....53 H5
Highstone Dr CHH M8 ....72 F6
Hightones Gdns GLSP * SK13 ....105 J2
High St ALT WA14 ....108 A8
ANC M4 ....7 H3
BOLS/LL BL3 ....36 B8
BOLS/LL BL3 ....53 L1
BRAM/HZG SK7 ....122 B2
CHD/CHDH SK8 ....111 G6
DROY M43 ....89 K3
EDGW/EG BL7 ....22 C5
GOL/RIS/CU WA3 ....79 K4
HEY OL10 ....40 E2
HYDE SK14 ....102 C1
LEIGH WN7 ....66 D7
LIT OL15 ....20 A7
MDTN M24 ....57 K3
MOSL * OL5 ....77 G2
NEWLW WA12 ....79 G8
NM/HAY SK22 ....124 E4
OLD OL1 ....9 H5
OLDE OL4 ....60 B6
ROY/SHW * OL2 ....43 G8
ROY/SHW OL2 ....43 L6
STKP SK1 ....13 J4
STLY SK15 ....91 K3
TOT/BURYW BL8 ....38 C1
TYLD M29 ....67 J3
TYLD M29 ....67 L7
UPML OL3 ....45 H8
UPML OL3 ....61 L4
WALK M28 ....68 F1
WGN WN1 ....48 A2
WGNE/HIN WN2 ....48 E1
WGNNW/ST WN6 ....31 H3
WGNS/IIMK WN3 ....15 L7
WHIT OL13 ....10 E3
High St East GLSP SK13 ....105 H3
High St West GLSP SK13 ....104 E3
Highthorne Gn ROY/SHW OL2 ....42 F4
Highview GLSP SK13 ....105 D5
High View St BOL BL1 ....22 B7
BOLS/LL * BL3 ....35 M8
Highwood ROCH OL11 ....27 H3
Highwood Cl BOLE * BL2 ....37 J3
GLSP SK13 ....104 D4
High Wood Fold
MPL/ROM SK6 ....114 F4
Highwoods Cl BOLS/LL * BL3 ....2 C9
Highworth Dr NEWH/MOS M40 ....74 A2
Higifield Av SALE M33 ....108 F1
Higson Av CCHDY M21 ....97 L5
ECC M30 ....84 F4
Higson St BNG/LEV M19 ....99 M3
Hilary Av ATH M46 ....50 F7
CHD/CHDH SK8 ....119 M4
GOL/RIS/CU WA3 ....80 A3
OLDS OL8 ....75 J3
Hilary Cl HTNM SK4 ....12 E2
Hilary Gv FWTH BL4 ....52 F5
Hilary Rd WYTH/NTH M22 ....118 D3
Hilary St ROCH * OL11 ....42 A3
Hilbre Av ROY/SHW OL2 ....59 G2
Hilbury Av BKLY M9 ....73 C3
Hilda Av CHD/CHDH SK8 ....111 H7
TOT/BURYW BL8 ....38 A5
Hilda Gv RDSH SK5 ....100 C8
Hilda Rd HYDE SK14 ....102 A5
Hilda St BOLS/LL BL3 ....36 D8
CHAD OL9 ....8 F4
HEY OL10 ....41 G2
LEIGH WN7 ....65 M6
Hilden Ct HTNM SK4 ....87 C8
Hilden St BOLE BL2 ....3 H6
LEIGH WN7 ....66 C7
Hilditch Cl NTHM/RTH M23 ....109 L6
Hildyard St WGNW/BIL/O WN5 ....47 C7
Hiley Rd ECC M30 ....84 C4
Hilgay Cl WCNS/IIMK WN3 ....63 C1
Hillam Cl URM M41 ....96 C3
Hillary Av AULW OL7 ....75 L7
WGNW/BIL/O WN5 ....47 G7
Hillary Rd HYDE SK14 ....91 K7
Hillbank WGNNW/ST WN6 ....31 K5
Hillbank Cl BOL BL1 ....35 M1
Hillbank St MDTN M24 ....42 A6
Hillbeck Crs AIMK WN4 ....63 C8
Hillbre Wy WILM/AE SK9 ....119 M8
Hillbrook Av NEWH/MOS * M40 ....73 L2
Hillbrook Rd BRAM/HZG SK7 ....120 F6
STKP SK1 ....112 F4
Hill Cl TOT/BURYW BL8 ....38 D1
Hillcot Av WCNW/ST WN6 ....30 B5
Hillcote Wk GTN * M18 ....88 E6
Hill Cot Rd BOL BL1 ....22 C7
Hill Court Ms MPL/ROM SK6 ....113 L2
Hillcourt Rd MPL/ROM SK6 ....101 M8
MPL/ROM SK6 ....123 C5
Hillcourt St CMANE M1 ....7 H9
Hill Crs BKLY M9 ....72 D1
LEIGH WN7 ....65 M4
Hill Crest ATH M46 ....51 J7
Hillcrest HYDE SK14 ....102 C5
MDTN M24 ....57 J1
SLFD * M6 ....85 K1
WGNE/HIN WN2 ....64 E2
Hillcrest Av HEY OL10 ....40 D1
Hill Crest Av HTNM SK4 ....111 K2
LEIGH WN7 ....65 M4
Hillcrest Dr BNG/LEV M19 ....99 M5
DTN/ASHW M34 ....101 L3
Hillcrest Rd BRAM/HZG SK7 ....121 H3
OFTN SK2 ....112 F6
PWCH M25 ....71 J2
ROCH OL11 ....42 A2
TYLD M29 ....67 J7
Hillcroft OFTN SK2 ....113 H6
OLDS OL8 ....75 K4
Hillcroft Cl CHH M8 ....72 D4
Hillcroft Rd ALT WA14 ....107 K7
Hilldale Av BKLY M9 ....57 C8
Hill End MPL/ROM * SK6 ....102 A8
Hillend La HYDE SK14 ....103 J3
Hill End Rd UPML OL3 ....45 J8
Hill Farm Cl OLDS OL8 ....75 L1
Hillfield SLFD M6 ....86 A2
Hillfield Cl BRUN/LGST M13 ....88 A7
Hillfield Dr BOLE BL2 ....36 E3
WALK M28 ....68 D5
Hillfield Wk BOLE BL2 ....36 E3
Hillfoot Wk HULME * M15 ....87 G6
Hillgate Av ORD M5 ....86 E5

EDGY/DAV SK3 ....12 F6
HYDE * SK14 ....91 J7
LHULT M38 ....52 D8
WGN WN1 ....15 H2
WGNS/IIMK WN3 ....15 K8
Himley Rd OP/CLY M11 ....88 F1
Hinchcombe Cl LHULT * M38 ....52 B8
Hinchley Rd BKLY M9 ....73 L1
Hinchley Wy SWIN M27 ....70 C2
Hinckley St OP/CLY M11 ....88 C4
Hindburn Cl WHTF M45 ....55 L4
Hindburn Dr WALK M28 ....68 D4
Hindle St NEWH/MOS M40 ....73 K4
Hindle Dr ROY/SHW OL2 ....58 F1
Hindles Cl ATH M46 ....66 D2
Hindle St RAD M26 ....54 D1
Hindley Av WYTH/NTH M22 ....118 D2
Hindley Mill La WGNE/HIN WN2 ....49 H5
Hindley Rd WHTN BL5 ....50 A7
STKP SK1 ....90 C3
Hindley Wk NTHM/RTH M23 ....14 F3
Hindley Wk WGN * WN1 ....14 F3
Hindsford Rd WGNW/BIL/O WN5 ....47 G4
Hindsford La NTHM/RTH M23 ....109 C3
Hindsford St ATH M46 ....66 D2
Hinds La RAD M26 ....38 F5
TOT/BURYW BL8 ....4 A8
Hind St BOLE BL2 ....3 M4
Hinkler Av BOLS/LL BL3 ....52 B1
Hinton WHIT OL12 ....10 D2
Hinton Cl ROCH OL11 ....27 H6
Hinton Gv HYDE SK14 ....102 D4
Hinton St ANC * M4 ....7 K4
OLDS OL8 ....9 K8
Hipley Cl MPL/ROM SK6 ....101 K7
Hirons La OLDE OL4 ....60 D7
Hirst Av WALK M28 ....67 M3
Hitchen Cl DTN/ASHW M34 ....90 B6
Hitchen Dr DUK SK16 ....91 J5
Hitchen Wk BRUN/LGST M13 ....87 M7
Hive St OLDS OL8 ....74 E2
Hoade St WGNE/HIN WN2 ....49 H5
Hobart Cl BRAM/HZG SK7 ....121 H7
Hobart St BOL BL1 ....36 A2
GTN M18 ....89 G7
Hobby Gv LEIGH WN7 ....66 E7
Hob Hey La GOL/RIS/CU WA3 ....81 G8
Hobhill Mdw GLSP SK13 ....105 C5
Hob La EDGW/EG BL7 ....16 C5
Hobson Ct DTN/ASHW M34 ....90 B6
Hobson Crs DTN/ASHW M34 ....90 B6
Hobson Moor Rd STLY SK14 ....92 C4
Hobson St FAIL M35 ....74 A6
OLD OL1 ....9 K5
OP/CLY M11 ....89 K5
RDSH SK5 ....99 M8
Hockenhull Cl WYTH/NTH M22 ....119 C2
Hocker La MCFLDN SK10 ....130 E7
Hockery Vw WGNE/HIN WN2 ....48 F8
Hockley Cl POY/DIS SK12 ....129 K1
Hockley Paddock
POY/DIS SK12 ....129 K1
Hockley Rd NTHM/RTH M23 ....109 J6
POY/DIS SK12 ....129 K1
Hodder Av LIT OL15 ....20 A6
WGNE/HIN WN2 ....64 C2
Hodder Bank OFTN SK2 ....113 H7
Hodder Cl WGNW/BIL/O WN5 ....47 H5
Hodder Wy WHTF M45 ....55 M4
Hoddesdon St CHH M8 ....72 E5
Hodge Clough Rd OLD OL1 ....43 M8
SLFD M6 ....86 C3
Hodge Rd OLD OL1 ....60 A1
WALK M28 ....69 G2
Hodges St WGNNW/ST WN6 ....73 J3
Hodgson Dr HALE/TIMP WA15 ....108 D4
Hodgson St AUL OL6 ....90 D2
CHH M8 ....72 C7
Hodnet Dr AIMK WN4 ....78 F1
Hodnett Av URM M41 ....95 H3
Hodson Fold OLDS OL8 ....75 K3
Hodson Rd SWIN M27 ....70 B2
Hodson St WGNS/IIMK WN3 ....14 D1
Hogarth Ri OLD OL1 ....44 A8
Hogarth Rd MPL/ROM SK6 ....114 C4
ROCH OL11 ....42 C2
Holbeach Cl TOT/BURYW BL8 ....25 J7
WGNE/HIN WN2 ....49 H8
Holbeck TYLD M29 ....67 L7
Holbeck Av WHIT OL12 ....18 E8
Holbeck Cl ALT WA14 ....107 L6
FWTH BL4 ....53 K6
OLDE OL4 ....60 D5
SLFD M6 ....86 D7
Holborn Av FAIL M35 ....74 E5
LEIGH WN7 ....66 D6
RAD M26 ....38 A8
WGNS/IIMK WN3 ....72 E7
Holborn Dr CHH M8 ....72 E7
Holborn Gdns ROCH OL11 ....10 A8
Holborn Sq ROCH OL11 ....10 A8
Holborn St ROCH OL11 ....10 A8
STKP SK1 ....13 J5
Holbrook Av LHULT M38 ....52 D6
Holbrook St CMANE * M1 ....7 H7
Holcombe Av GOL/RIS/CU WA3 ....79 M4
TOT/BURYW BL8 ....24 C1
Holcombe Cl ALT WA14 ....107 L6
FWTH BL4 ....53 K6
OLDE OL4 ....60 D5
SLFD M6 ....86 D5
Holcombe Ct RAMS * BL0 ....24 C2
Holcombe Crs FWTH BL4 ....53 K6
Holcombe Lee RAMS BL0 ....24 C1
Holcombe Old Rd
TOT/BURYW BL8 ....24 C1
Holcombe Rd BOLS/LL BL3 ....51 J3
RUSH/FAL M14 ....99 H5
TOT/BURYW BL8 ....24 C1
Holcombe View Cl OLDE OL4 ....60 A2
Holden Av BOL BL1 ....36 B8
BURY BL9 ....26 B8
RAMS BL0 ....17 A7
Holden Brook Cl LEIGH WN7 ....66 A1
Holden Clough Dr AULW OL7 ....75 K5
Holden Fold La ROY/SHW OL2 ....58 F2
Holden Lea WHTN BL5 ....50 A3
Holden Rd BRO M7 ....72 A5
LEIGH WN7 ....66 D6
Holden St AUL OL6 ....75 M8
OLDS OL8 ....9 J8
WHIT * OL12 ....28 D7
Holden Wd WGNW/BIL/O WN5 ....47 H7
Holder Av BOLS/LL BL3 ....37 L7
Holderness Dr ROY/SHW OL2 ....58 F7
Holdgate Cl HULME M15 ....87 J7

Holding St *WGNE/HIN* WN2 ......49 G6
Holdsworth St *SWIN* M27 ......70 A5
Holebottom *AUL* OL6 ......75 M6
Hole House Fold
  MPL/ROM SK6 ......113 L2
Holford Av *RUSH/FAL* M14 ......98 E2
Holford St *SLFD* M6 ......71 M8
Holford Wk *MILN* OL16 ......29 G5
Holgate Dr *WGNW/BIL/O* WN5 ......46 B7
Holgate St *OLDE* OL4 ......60 B3
Holhouse La *TOT/BURYW* BL8 ......24 B2
Holiday La *OFTN* SK2 ......113 J6
Holker Cl *BRUN/LGST* M13 ......88 A7
  POY/DIS SK12 ......122 B8
Holkham Cl *ANC* M4 ......7 M3
Holland Av *STLY* SK15 ......91 K2
Holland Cl *UPML* OL3 ......45 H8
Holland Ct *RAD* M26 ......38 F8
Holland Gv *AUL* OL6 ......75 L6
Holland Ri *WHIT* OL12 ......10 D3
Holland Rd *BRAM/HZG* SK7 ......121 G5
  CHH M8 ......72 A4
  HYDE SK14 ......91 J7
Holland St *BOL* BL1 ......22 C8
  DTN/ASHW M34 ......90 A8
  HEY OL10 ......41 G2
  MILN OL16 ......19 L8
  NEWH/MOS M40 ......88 A2
  RAD M26 ......38 F8
  SLFD M6 ......71 K7
  WHIT OL12 ......10 C4
Holland St East *DTN/ASHW* M34 ......90 A8
Holland St West
  DTN/ASHW M34 ......89 M8
The Hollies *ATH* M46 ......67 G1
  CHD/CHDH SK8 ......110 E7
  DID/WITH M20 ......110 C1
  WGN WN1 ......48 A1
  WGNE/HIN WN2 ......32 E7
Hollies Dr *MPL/ROM* SK6 ......114 D7
Hollies La *WILM/AE* SK9 ......127 K5
Hollin Acre *WHTN* BL5 ......50 C4
Hollin Bank *HTNM* SK4 ......100 A5
Hollinbrook *WGNNW/ST* WN6 ......47 J2
Hollin Crs *OLDE* OL4 ......61 H8
Hollin Cross La *GLSP* SK13 ......104 F4
Hollin Dr *MDTN* M24 ......41 H8
Holliney Av *WYTH/NTH* M22 ......119 H3
Holliney Rd *WYTH/NTH* M22 ......119 H3
Hollingwood Av *AIMK* WN4 ......78 D1
Hollingworth Av
  NEWH/MOS M40 ......74 C2
Hollingworth Cl *STKP* ＊ SK1 ......13 J6
Hollingworth Dr
  MPL/ROM SK6 ......123 H1
Hollingworth Fold *LIT* ＊ OL15 ......29 M2
Hollingworth Rd *LIT* OL15 ......20 C8
  MPL/ROM SK6 ......101 H8
Hollingworth St *CHAD* OL9 ......74 E1
Hollinhall St *OLDE* OL4 ......59 M5
Hollin Hey Rd *BOL* BL1 ......35 H1
Hollinhey Ter *HYDE* SK14 ......92 F8
Hollinhurst Dr *HOR/BR* BL6 ......34 F5
Hollinhurst Rd *RAD* M26 ......54 F2
Hollin La *MDTN* M24 ......41 J8
  ROCH OL11 ......27 H6
  WILM/AE SK9 ......119 H7
Hollinsclough Cl
  WYTH/NTH M22 ......110 B7
Hollinscroft Av
  HALE/TIMP WA15 ......109 G7
Hollins Gn *MDTN* M24 ......57 K1
Hollins Green Rd
  MPL/ROM SK6 ......114 C6
Hollins Gv *SALE* M33 ......96 D8
  WGTN/LGST M12 ......99 K1
Hollins La *BURY* BL9 ......39 K7
  MOSL OL5 ......77 G3
  MPL/ROM SK6 ......114 C6
  MPL/ROM SK6 ......114 F4
  RAMS BL0 ......17 E3
Hollins Ms *BURY* BL9 ......39 M8
  GLSP SK13 ......104 A2
Hollinsmoor Rd *NM/HAY* SK22 ......115 M5
Hollins Mt *MPL/ROM* SK6 ......114 E4
Hollins Rd *OLDE* OL4 ......60 C4
  OLDS OL8 ......74 F2
  WGNE/HIN WN2 ......49 K7
Hollins St *BOLE* BL2 ......3 J7
  OLDE OL4 ......60 C6
  STLY SK15 ......91 J4
Hollinswood Rd *BOLE* BL2 ......3 K6
  WALK M28 ......68 E6
Hollinwood Av *CHAD* OL9 ......74 D2
  NEWH/MOS M40 ......74 A2
Hollinwood La *MPL/ROM* SK6 ......123 K2
Holloway Dr *WALK* M28 ......69 M3
Hollowbrook Wy *WHIT* OL12 ......28 A2
Hollowell La *HOR/BR* BL6 ......34 A3
Hollow End *RDSH* SK5 ......100 E5
Hollowfield *ROCH* OL11 ......27 G3
Hollow Mdw *RAD* M26 ......53 M6
The Hollows *CHD/CHDH* ＊ SK8 ......119 L3
Hollowspell *WHIT* OL12 ......28 F1
Hollow Vale Dr *RDSH* SK5 ......100 D3
Holly Av *CHD/CHDH* SK8 ......111 G7
  URM M41 ......95 L2
  WALK M28 ......69 H2
Holly Bank *GLSP* SK13 ......105 H4
  HYDE SK14 ......93 G7
  NEWH/MOS ＊ M40 ......73 M5
  ROY/SHW OL2 ......43 G7
  SALE M33 ......108 F1
Holly Bank Cl *HULME* ＊ M15 ......86 F5
Holly Bank Ri *DUK* SK16 ......91 J4
Holly Bank Rd *WILM/AE* SK9 ......126 F3
Hollybank St *RAD* M26 ......54 C1
Hollybrook Dene
  MPL/ROM SK6 ......114 B2
Hollybush Sq *GOL/RIS/CU* WA3 ......79 H4
Hollybush St *GTN* M18 ......89 H7
Holly Ct *HALE/TIMP* WA15 ......108 D6
Holly Ct *HYDE* SK14 ......102 D2
Hollycroft Av *BOLE* BL2 ......37 H7
  WYTH/NTH M22 ......110 A6
Hollydene *BRUN/LGST* ＊ WN2 ......32 E7
Holly Dene Dr *HOR/BR* BL6 ......34 F6
Holly Dr *SALE* M33 ......96 D8
Hollyedge Dr *PWCH* M25 ......71 K2
Holly Fold *WHTF* M45 ......55 J3
Holly Gra *ALT* WA14 ......116 F2

  BRAM/HZG SK7 ......121 H1
Holly Gv *BOL* BL1 ......35 M3
  CHAD OL9 ......8 B2
  DTN/ASHW M34 ......101 K1
  DUK SK16 ......91 H4
  FWTH BL4 ......52 D4
  LEIGH WN7 ......66 B5
  OLDE OL4 ......60 B4
  SALE M33 ......97 G8
Holly Heath Dr *WGN* WN1 ......31 L8
Hollyhedge Court Rd
  WYTH/NTH M22 ......110 B7
Hollyhedge Rd
  NTHM/RTH M23 ......109 L7
Hollyhey Dr *NTHM/RTH* M23 ......109 L3
Hollyhouse Dr *MPL/ROM* SK6 ......101 K7
Holly House Dr *URM* M41 ......95 J2
Hollyhurst *WALK* M28 ......69 L6
Holly La *OLDS* OL8 ......74 F2
  WILM/AE SK9 ......119 G7
Holly Mill Crs *BOL* BL1 ......22 C8
Hollymount Av *OFTN* SK2 ......112 F7
Hollymount Dr *OFTN* SK2 ......112 F7
  OLDE OL4 ......60 B1
Hollymount Gdns *OFTN* SK2 ......113 G7
Hollymount Rd *OFTN* SK2 ......112 F7
Holly Oak Gdns *HEY* OL10 ......40 F3
Holly Rd *BRAM/HZG* SK7 ......121 G7
  GOL/RIS/CU WA3 ......79 M4
  HTNM SK4 ......99 M7
  MPL/ROM SK6 ......123 G5
  POY/DIS SK12 ......129 J1
  SWIN M27 ......70 A6
  WGNE/HIN WN2 ......32 E7
  WGNW/BIL/O WN5 ......47 H5
Holly Rd North *WILM/AE* SK9 ......126 E6
Holly Rd South *WILM/AE* SK9 ......126 E6
Holly Royde Cl *DID/WITH* M20 ......98 D6
Holly St *BOL* BL1 ......22 C8
  BURY BL9 ......5 J4
  DROY M43 ......89 G2
  OP/CLY M11 ......88 B4
  RAMS BL0 ......24 F1
  STKP SK1 ......13 M5
  TOT/BURYW BL8 ......24 C6
  WGNE/HIN WN2 ......48 C2
  WHIT OL12 ......19 K6
Hollythorn Av *CHD/CHDH* SK8 ......120 E5
Hollyway *WYTH/NTH* M22 ......110 B4
Hollywood Rd *BOL* BL1 ......35 L2
  MPL/ROM SK6 ......115 H4
Holly Wood Wy *HTNM* SK4 ......12 E5
Holmbrook *TYLD* M29 ......67 M5
Holmbrook Wk *CHH* M8 ......72 D6
Holm Ct *SLFD* ＊ M6 ......86 D1
Holmcroft Rd *GTN* M18 ......100 A2
Holmdale Av *BNG/LEV* M19 ......99 H7
Holme Av *TOT/BURYW* BL8 ......24 F7
  WGN WN1 ......47 M2
Holme Beech Gv *OFTN* SK2 ......112 F4
Holmebrook Dr *HOR/BR* BL6 ......34 A4
Holme Ct *WGN* ＊ WN1 ......47 M2
Holme Crs *ROY/SHW* OL2 ......58 F2
Holmefield *SALE* M33 ......96 E8
Holme House St *LIT* OL15 ......20 E3
Holme Park Gdns *WALK* M28 ......68 D7
Holme Park Wy *FAIL* M35 ......74 E5
Holme Rd *DID/WITH* M20 ......98 E6
Holmes Cottages *BOL* ＊ BL1 ......35 M1
Holmes House Av
  WGNS/IIMK WN3 ......62 F1
Holmes Rd *WHIT* OL12 ......10 B4
Holmes St *BOLS/LL* BL3 ......36 C8
  CHD/CHDH SK8 ......111 H6
  EDGY/DAV SK3 ......13 H8
  WHIT OL12 ......10 B3
  WHIT OL12 ......28 F1
Holme St *HYDE* SK14 ......102 G4
Holmeswood Cl *WILM/AE* SK9 ......127 G4
Holmeswood Rd *BOLS/LL* BL3 ......52 A2
Holme Ter *LIT* OL15 ......20 E3
  WHIT OL12 ......47 L1
Holmfield Av *BKLY* M9 ......73 J5
  PWCH M25 ......71 M1
Holmfield Av West
  NEWH/MOS M40 ......73 J6
Holmfield Cl *HTNM* SK4 ......112 A1
Holmfield Dr *CHD/CHDH* SK8 ......120 D4
Holmfield Gn *BOLS/LL* BL3 ......51 J1
Holmfirth St *BRUN/LGST* M13 ......88 C8
Holmlea Rd *DROY* M43 ......89 H2
Holmleigh Av *BKLY* M9 ......73 H3
Holmpark Rd *OP/CLY* M11 ......89 H5
Holmsfield Cl *WGNE/HIN* WN2 ......48 D2
Holmside Gdns *BNG/LEV* M19 ......99 G8
Holmwood *ALT* WA14 ......116 C1
Holmwood Cl *AIMK* WN4 ......63 K7
Holmwood Rd *DID/WITH* M20 ......98 E7
Holroyd St *MILN* OL16 ......11 G5
  OP/CLY ＊ M11 ......88 D4
Holset Dr *ALT* WA14 ......107 L7
Holst Av *CHH* M8 ......72 D6
Holstein Av *WHIT* OL12 ......18 E8
Holt Av *WGNW/BIL/O* WN5 ......62 A8
Holtby St *BKLY* M9 ......73 H3
Holt Crs *WGNW/BIL/O* WN5 ......62 A8
Holt La *FAIL* M35 ......74 E5
Holt Lane Ms *FAIL* M35 ......74 D5
Holton Av *WGNS/IIMK* WN3 ......63 H3
Holts La *OLDE* OL4 ......60 A8
  WILM/AE SK9 ......126 D1
Holts Ter *WHIT* OL12 ......28 B2
Holt St *ALT* WA14 ......107 M5
  BOLS/LL BL3 ......2 A8
  DTN/ASHW M34 ......90 B4
  ECC M30 ......84 F4
  LEIGH WN7 ......66 B5
  LIT OL15 ......20 C6
  MILN ＊ OL16 ......29 K7
  NEWH/MOS M40 ......73 J7
  OLDE OL4 ......59 M4
  RAMS BL0 ......17 D6
  STKP SK1 ......13 K7
  SWIN M27 ......70 C2
  TYLD M29 ......67 K3
  WGN WN1 ......15 M4
  WGNE/HIN WN2 ......49 J1
  WGNE/HIN WN2 ......49 J6
  WGNS/IIMK WN3 ......48 B8
  WHIT OL12 ......10 E2
Holt St West *RAMS* BL0 ......17 B7
Holtswell Cl *GOL/RIS/CU* WA3 ......80 B3
Holt Town *NEWH/MOS* M40 ......88 B2
Holwick Rd *NTHM/RTH* M23 ......108 F3
Holwood Dr *OLDTF/WHR* M16 ......98 B4
Holy Harbour St *BOL* ＊ BL1 ......35 M2
Holyhurst Wk *BOL* ＊ BL1 ......36 B2

Holyoake Rd *WALK* M28 ......69 G2
Holyoake St *DROY* M43 ......89 M2
Holyoak St *NEWH/MOS* M40 ......73 M6
Holyrood Cl *PWCH* M25 ......55 M6
Holyrood Dr *PWCH* M25 ......55 M6
  SWIN M27 ......69 M5
Holyrood Gv *PWCH* M25 ......55 L6
Holyrood Rd *PWCH* M25 ......55 M7
Holyrood St *NEWH/MOS* M40 ......74 A8
  OLD OL1 ......59 K3
Holy St *ROCH* OL11 ......42 E2
Holywood St *RUSH/FAL* M14 ......98 E1
Homebury Dr *OP/CLY* ＊ M11 ......88 C2
Home Dr *MDTN* M24 ......57 J5
Home Farm Av *HYDE* SK14 ......103 J3
Homelands Cl *SALE* M33 ......108 C2
Homelands Rd *SALE* M33 ......108 C2
Homer Dr *MPL/ROM* SK6 ......114 E4
Homerton Rd *NEWH/MOS* M40 ......73 L8
Homestead Av
  RNFD/HAY ＊ WA11 ......78 B5
Homestead Cl *PART* M31 ......94 D8
Homestead Crs *BNG/LEV* M19 ......111 C1
Homestead Gdns *WHIT* OL12 ......19 L7
Homestead Rd *POY/DIS* SK12 ......123 L6
Hometel *RUSH/FAL* M14 ......98 F3
Homewood Av
  WYTH/NTH M22 ......110 A3
Homewood Rd
  WYTH/NTH M22 ......109 M3
Honduras St *OLDE* OL4 ......9 M5
Hondwith Cl *BOLE* BL2 ......22 E7
Honeybourne Cl *TYLD* M29 ......67 M3
Honeycombe Cottages
  CHD/CHDH ＊ SK8 ......111 H7
Honey St *CHH* M8 ......72 D8
Honeysuckle Av
  WGNNW/ST WN6 ......47 J1
Honeysuckle Cl *MPL/ROM* SK6 ......101 L7
  NTHM/RTH M23 ......109 G3
Honeysuckle Dr *STLY* SK15 ......91 K2
Honeysuckle Wy *WHIT* OL12 ......28 A1
Honey Wk *NTHM/RTH* M23 ......109 G3
Honeywell La *OLDS* OL8 ......75 J1
Honeywood Cl *RAMS* BL0 ......24 D1
Honford Rd *WYTH/NTH* M22 ......109 L8
Hong Kong Av *MANAIR* M90 ......118 C4
Honister Dr *MDTN* M24 ......57 J2
Honister Rd *BKLY* M9 ......73 J5
  WGNW/BIL/O WN5 ......46 B5
Honister Wy *ROCH* OL11 ......27 L8
Honiton Av *HYDE* SK14 ......102 F2
Honiton Cl *CHAD* OL9 ......58 B3
  HEY OL10 ......40 F4
  LEIGH WN7 ......66 B7
Honiton Dr *BOLE* BL2 ......37 K6
Honiton Gv *RAD* M26 ......38 A7
Honiton Wy *ALT* WA14 ......107 K6
Honor St *BRUN/LGST* M13 ......99 H1
Hood Cl *TYLD* M29 ......68 A3
Hood Gv *LEIGH* WN7 ......81 L1
Hood Sq *OLDE* OL4 ......60 D7
Hood St *ANC* M4 ......7 K3
Hook St *WGNE/HIN* WN2 ......48 C5
Hoole Cl *CHD/CHDH* SK8 ......111 K7
Hooley Range *HTNM* SK4 ......111 L1
Hooper St *OLDE* OL4 ......9 M7
  STKP SK1 ......13 H5
  WGTN/LGST M12 ......88 A4
Hooten La *LEIGH* WN7 ......81 M1
Hooton St *BOLS/LL* BL3 ......51 M1
  NEWH/MOS M40 ......88 B1
Hopcroft Cl *BKLY* M9 ......56 F6
Hope Av *BOLE* BL2 ......3 K7
  BOLE BL2 ......23 H7
  LHULT M38 ......52 E8
  STRET M32 ......96 F1
  WILM/AE SK9 ......127 G1
Hope Carr La *LEIGH* WN7 ......81 L2
Hope Carr Rd *LEIGH* WN7 ......81 L1
Hope Carr Wy *LEIGH* WN7 ......81 K1
Hopecourt Cl *SLFD* M6 ......70 E8
Hope Crs *WGNNW/ST* WN6 ......30 E6
Hopedale Rd *RDSH* SK5 ......100 C6
Hopefield St *BOLS/LL* BL3 ......36 A8
Hope Fold Av *ATH* M46 ......66 E2
Hopefold Dr *WALK* M28 ......69 H2
Hope Green Wy *POY/DIS* SK12 ......129 H2
Hope Hey La *LHULT* M38 ......52 A7
Hope La *GOL/RIS/CU* WA3 ......82 D2
  MCFLDN SK10 ......129 H3
Hopelea St *DID/WITH* M20 ......98 E5
Hope Park Cl *PWCH* M25 ......71 L1
Hope Park Rd *PWCH* M25 ......71 L1
Hope Pl *ROCH* ＊ OL11 ......41 M3
Hope Rd *PWCH* M25 ......71 K2
  RUSH/FAL M14 ......88 A8
  SALE M33 ......108 D1
Hopes Carr *STKP* SK1 ......13 K5
Hope St *AIMK* WN4 ......64 A7
  AUL OL6 ......4 A6
  BRAM/HZG SK7 ......121 M2
  BRO M7 ......72 A5
  CMANE M1 ......7 H5
  DTN/ASHW M34 ......90 B7
  DUK SK16 ......90 F4
  GLSP SK13 ......105 H2
  HEY OL10 ......41 G4
  HOR/BR BL6 ......21 B8
  HOR/BR BL6 ......33 H4
  HTNM SK4 ......12 F4
  LEIGH WN7 ......66 C7
  LHULT M38 ......52 D8
  OLD OL1 ......59 L5
  ORD M5 ......86 F3
  RAMS BL0 ......17 B7
  ROY/SHW OL2 ......43 L5
  SWIN M27 ......70 D4
  TYLD M29 ......67 L7
  WN ＊ WN1 ......14 F3
  WGNE/HIN WN2 ......49 J1
  WGNE/HIN WN2 ......49 J6
  WGNS/IIMK WN3 ......48 B8
  WHIT OL12 ......10 E2
Hope St North *HOR/BR* BL6 ......21 B7
Hope Ter *DUK* ＊ SK16 ......90 E4
  EDGY/DAV ＊ SK3 ......13 H7
Hopkin Av *OLD* OL1 ......59 L4
Hopkins Fld *ALT* WA14 ......116 D3
Hopkinson Av *DTN/ASHW* M34 ......90 B7
Hopkinson Cl *UPML* ＊ OL3 ......61 L4
Hopkins Rd *BKLY* M9 ......57 G7
Hopkins St *HYDE* SK14 ......91 H8
Hopkin St *OLD* OL1 ......9 K5
Hoppet La *DROY* M43 ......89 M2
Hopton Av *WYTH/NTH* M22 ......119 G1
Hopwood Av *ECC* M30 ......85 G1
  HEY OL10 ......41 G4
  HOR/BR BL6 ......21 C8
Hopwood Cl *BURY* BL9 ......55 J1
Hopwood Rd *MPL/ROM* SK6 ......113 K2

Hopwood Rd *MDTN* M24 ......41 K8
Hopwood St *CSLFD* ＊ M3 ......6 D2
  NEWH/MOS M40 ......73 L6
  SWIN M27 ......70 D4
Horace Barnes Cl
  RUSH/FAL M14 ......98 D1
Horace Gv *HTNM* SK4 ......100 B8
Horace St *BOL* BL1 ......36 A2
Horatio St *GTN* ＊ M18 ......89 J6
Horbury Av *GTN* M18 ......100 A1
Horbury Dr *TOT/BURYW* BL8 ......38 F2
Horeb St *BOLS/LL* BL3 ......2 A9
Horest La *UPML* OL3 ......44 E4
Horkers Nook *WHTN* BL5 ......50 A5
Horley Cl *TOT/BURYW* BL8 ......24 F5
Hornbeam Cl *HALE/TIMP* WA15 ......109 H7
  SALE M33 ......95 M7
Hornbeam Ct *SLFD* M6 ......86 D1
Hornbeam Crs *AIMK* WN4 ......78 E1
Hornbeam Rd *BNG/LEV* M19 ......99 L2
Hornby Av *BKLY* M9 ......57 H7
Hornby Dr *BOLS/LL* BL3 ......51 G2
Hornby Gv *LEIGH* WN7 ......67 G5
Hornby Rd *STRET* M32 ......86 C8
Hornby Steet *WGN* WN1 ......47 M2
Hornby St *BURY* BL9 ......25 J7
  CHH M8 ......72 C8
  HEY OL10 ......41 G3
  MDTN M24 ......57 K4
  OLDS OL8 ......9 F8
Horncastle Cl *GOL/RIS/CU* WA3 ......80 C4
  TOT/BURYW BL8 ......24 F5
Horncastle Rd *NEWH/MOS* M40 ......73 L3
Hornchurch St *HULME* M15 ......87 H6
Horne Dr *ANC* M4 ......7 L3
Horne Gv *WGNS/IIMK* WN3 ......14 A9
Horne St *BURY* BL9 ......4 F1
Hornsea Cl *CHAD* OL9 ......58 C3
  TOT/BURYW BL8 ......38 C2
Hornsea Rd *OFTN* SK2 ......113 K7
Hornsea Wk *OP/CLY* ＊ M11 ......88 D3
Hornsey Gv *WGNS/IIMK* WN3 ......63 G1
Horridge Av *NEWLW* WA12 ......78 F7
Horridge Fold *EDGW/EG* BL7 ......22 B1
Horridge Fold Av *WHTN* BL5 ......51 J3
Horsa St *TOT/BURYW* BL8 ......38 F2
Horridge St *TOT/BURYW* BL8 ......24 F5
Horrobin Fold *EDGW/EG* ＊ BL7 ......22 F2
Horrobin La *EDGW/EG* BL7 ......22 F2
Horrocks Fold Av *BOL* BL1 ......22 A6
Horrocks Rd *EDGW/EG* BL7 ......16 D5
Horrocks St *ATH* M46 ......67 H3
  LEIGH WN7 ......65 K8
  LEIGH WN7 ......66 B7
  RAD M26 ......38 F8
Horsa St *BOLE* BL2 ......3 J1
Horsedge St *OLD* OL1 ......9 K3
Horsefield Av *WHIT* OL12 ......18 D6
Horsefield Cl *CCHDY* M21 ......98 B5
Horseforth La *UPML* OL3 ......61 K8
Horseshoe La *CHAD* OL9 ......58 C6
  EDGW/EG BL7 ......22 D4
  WILM/AE SK9 ......130 D2
Horsfield St *BOLS/LL* BL3 ......35 K8
Horsfield Wy *MPL/ROM* SK6 ......101 J6
Horsham Av *BRAM/HZG* SK7 ......121 L3
Horsham Cl *TOT/BURYW* BL8 ......24 F5
  WHTN BL5 ......50 C6
Horsham Gv *WGNE/HIN* WN2 ......48 C2
Horsham St *SLFD* M6 ......86 B2
Horstead Wk *BNG/LEV* M19 ......99 K2
Horton Av *BOL* BL1 ......22 B6
Horton Rd *RUSH/FAL* M14 ......98 D3
Horton St *STKP* SK1 ......13 L9
  WGNNW/ST WN6 ......47 H1
Hortree Rd *STRET* M32 ......97 H2
Horwood Crs *DID/WITH* M20 ......99 G7
Hoscar Dr *BNG/LEV* M19 ......99 H5
The Hoskers *WHTN* BL5 ......50 A5
Hoskins Cl *WGTN/LGST* M12 ......88 D7
Hospital Rd *EDGW/EG* BL7 ......22 D4
  SWIN M27 ......70 E5
Hotel Rd *MANAIR* M90 ......118 E5
Hotel St *BOL* BL1 ......2 D4
Hothersall Rd *RDSH* SK5 ......100 C5
Hothersall St *BRO* M7 ......87 H1
Hotspur Cl *DID/WITH* M20 ......98 E8
Hough Dr *OLDS* OL8 ......75 K2
Hough End Av *NTHM/RTH* M23 ......97 M6
Houghend Crs *CCHDY* M21 ......98 B5
Hough Fold Wy *BOLE* BL2 ......23 G8
Hough Hall Rd *NEWH/MOS* M40 ......73 J4
Hough Hill Rd *STLY* SK15 ......91 K3
Hough La *EDGW/EG* BL7 ......22 C5
  HYDE SK14 ......91 J7
  MDTN M24 ......42 C7
  TYLD M29 ......67 M4
  WILM/AE SK9 ......127 H7
  WILM/AE SK9 ......131 C2
Hough St *BOLS/LL* BL3 ......35 K8
  TYLD M29 ......68 A4
Houghton Av *OLDS* OL8 ......75 G2
  WGNW/BIL/O WN5 ......47 H2
Houghton Cl *MILN* OL16 ......11 L6
  NM/HAY SK22 ......125 J2
Houghton La *SWIN* M27 ......70 A7
  WGNNW/ST WN6 ......30 C6
Houghton Rd *CHH* M8 ......72 D3
Houghton St *BOLS/LL* BL3 ......2 C8
  BURY BL9 ......4 D7
  LEIGH WN7 ......66 C7
  ROY/SHW OL2 ......59 H2
  SWIN M27 ......71 G6
Hough Wk *BRO* M7 ......86 F1
Houghwood Gra *AIMK* WN4 ......78 C4
Houldsworth Av *ALT* WA14 ......108 B5
Houldsworth Ml *RDSH* ＊ SK5 ......100 B3
Houldsworth St *CMANE* M1 ......7 J3
  RAD M26 ......38 C7
  RDSH SK5 ......100 B5
Houseley Av *CHAD* OL9 ......74 E1
Houseman Gv *WGNNW/ST* WN6 ......47 K2
Housley Cl *WGNS/IIMK* WN3 ......47 K6
Houson St *OLDS* OL8 ......9 J7
Houston Pk *SALQ* M50 ......86 C3
Hove Cl *TOT/BURYW* BL8 ......24 C3
Hoveden St *CHH* M8 ......72 C8
Hove Dr *RUSH/FAL* M14 ......99 H5
Hove St *BOLS/LL* BL3 ......35 M7
Hove St North *BOLS/LL* ＊ BL3 ......35 M7
Hovey Cl *CHH* ＊ M8 ......72 A5
Hovingham St *MILN* OL16 ......11 J3
Hovis St *OP/CLY* M11 ......88 F4
Howard Av *BOLS/LL* BL3 ......35 K8
  CHD/CHDH SK8 ......120 C3
  ECC M30 ......85 G1
  FWTH BL4 ......53 J5
  HOR/BR BL6 ......21 C8
  HTNM SK4 ......99 M6

  AUL OL6 ......90 E1
  HALE/TIMP ＊ WA15 ......108 E6
Howard Dr *HALE/TIMP* WA15 ......117 J3
Howard Hl *BURY* BL9 ......39 K8
Howard La *DTN/ASHW* M34 ......90 C8
Howard Pl *MILN* OL16 ......10 E3
Howard Rd *WYTH/NTH* M22 ......110 A3
Howard's La *MOSL* OL5 ......77 J3
Howards Meadow *GLSP* SK13 ......104 E5
Howard St *AULW* OL7 ......75 K8
  BOL BL1 ......36 C3
  CHH M8 ......72 C8
  DTN/ASHW M34 ......90 B7
  GLSP SK13 ......104 F3
  OLDE OL4 ......60 B4
  ORD M5 ......54 E1
  RAD M26 ......54 E1
  ROY/SHW OL2 ......43 K5
  STKP SK1 ......13 J5
  STRET M32 ......97 G2
  WGNW/BIL/O WN5 ......46 F7
  WHIT OL12 ......10 D2
Howard Wy *LIT* OL15 ......20 D3
Howarth Av *WALK* M28 ......69 M5
Howarth Cross St *MILN* OL16 ......11 G4
Howarth Dr *IRL* M44 ......94 C3
Howarth Farm Wy *WHIT* OL12 ......28 F1
Howarth Sq *MILN* OL16 ......11 H4
Howarth St *FWTH* BL4 ......53 G5
  LEIGH WN7 ......66 E8
  LIT OL15 ......20 C6
  OLDTF/WHR M16 ......86 F8
  WHTN BL5 ......50 C4
Howbridge Cl *WALK* M28 ......68 F4
Howbro Dr *AULW* OL7 ......75 H7
How Clough Cl *WALK* M28 ......69 J2
How Clough Dr *WALK* M28 ......69 J2
Howcroft Cl *BOL* BL1 ......2 A1
Howcroft Cl *RDSH* SK5 ......100 B2
Howden Dr *WGNS/IIMK* WN3 ......47 K8
Howden Rd *BKLY* M9 ......56 F7
  NM/HAY SK22 ......124 E3
Howe Bridge Cl *ATH* M46 ......66 D3
Howe Dr *RAMS* BL0 ......24 E2
Howell Cft North *BOL* ＊ BL1 ......2 E4
Howell Cft South *BOL* ＊ BL1 ......2 E5
Howells Av *SALE* M33 ......96 D7
Howe St *AULW* OL7 ......90 B4
  BRO M7 ......71 M5
Howgill Crs *OLDS* OL8 ......75 H1
Howgill St *OP/CLY* M11 ......89 G3
How Lea Dr *BURY* BL9 ......39 K6
Howsin Av *BOLE* BL2 ......22 E8
Howton Cl *WGTN/LGST* M12 ......88 D8
Howty Cl *WILM/AE* SK9 ......127 H3
Hoxton Cl *MPL/ROM* SK6 ......101 K8
Hoy Dr *URM* M41 ......85 G7
Hoylake Cl *LEIGH* WN7 ......81 G2
  NEWH/MOS M40 ......74 A4
Hoylake Rd *EDGY/DAV* SK3 ......111 K4
  SALE M33 ......109 J2
Hoyle Av *OLDS* OL8 ......9 G8
Hoyles Ct *RAD* ＊ M26 ......38 F8
Hoyle's Ter *MILN* ＊ OL16 ......29 H6
Hoyle St *RAD* M26 ......54 B1
  WGTN/LGST M12 ......7 M7
  WHIT OL12 ......18 E1
Hoyle Wk *BRUN/LGST* ＊ M13 ......87 L6
Hucclecote Av *WYTH/NTH* M22 ......118 C2
Hucklow Av *NTHM/RTH* M23 ......118 C2
Hudcar La *BURY* BL9 ......5 H1
Huddart Cl *ORD* M5 ......86 E4
Huddersfield Rd *MILN* OL16 ......29 M8
  OLDE OL4 ......60 A8
  STLY SK15 ......77 H6
  STLY SK15 ......91 M2
  UPML OL3 ......45 K8
  UPML OL3 ......61 L2
Hudson Rd *BOLS/LL* BL3 ......51 L1
  HYDE SK14 ......102 B5
Hudson St *CHAD* OL9 ......74 D2
Hudsons Wk *ROCH* OL11 ......27 L5
Hudswell Cl *WHTF* M45 ......55 H4
Hughenden Ct
  TOT/BURYW ＊ BL8 ......24 C5
Hughes Av *HOR/BR* BL6 ......21 A8
Hughes Cl *FAIL* M35 ......74 B4
Hughes St *BOL* BL1 ......35 M2
  OP/CLY M11 ......88 B4
Hughley Cl *ROY/SHW* OL2 ......43 J8
Hugh Lupus St *BOL* BL1 ......22 D7
Hugh Oldham Dr *BRO* M7 ......71 M6
Hugh St *MILN* OL16 ......11 G3
Hughtrede St *MILN* ＊ OL16 ......42 E1
Hugo St *FWTH* BL4 ......52 E2
  NEWH/MOS M40 ......73 K5
  ROCH OL11 ......42 A2
Hulbert St *MDTN* M24 ......57 J3
  TOT/BURYW BL8 ......38 F3
Hullet Cl *WGNNW/ST* WN6 ......30 B4
Hull Mill La *UPML* OL3 ......45 J7
Hull Sq *CSLFD* M3 ......6 A2
Hully St *STLY* SK15 ......91 J2
Hulme Gv *LEIGH* WN7 ......65 M6
Hulme Hall Av *CHD/CHDH* SK8 ......120 C4
Hulme Hall Cl *CHD/CHDH* SK8 ......120 C4
Hulme Hall Crs *CHD/CHDH* SK8 ......120 C4
Hulme Hall La *NEWH/MOS* M40 ......73 H8
Hulme Hall Rd *CHD/CHDH* SK8 ......120 C2
  HULME M15 ......6 A8
Hulme Pl *ORD* ＊ M5 ......86 F3
Hulme Rd *BOLE* BL2 ......23 H6
  DTN/ASHW M34 ......100 E1
  HTNM SK4 ......100 A7
  LEIGH WN7 ......65 M6
  RAD M26 ......53 M5
  SALE M33 ......108 F1
Hulmes Rd *NEWH/MOS* M40 ......74 B7
Hulme St *AUL* OL6 ......76 A8
  BOL BL1 ......36 C3
  HULME M15 ......6 D9
  OLDS OL8 ......59 H8
  ORD M5 ......86 F3
  STKP SK1 ......112 C5
  TOT/BURYW BL8 ......4 B2
Humber Dr *BURY* BL9 ......25 J4
Humber Pl *WGNW/BIL/O* WN5 ......46 F5
Humber Rd *MILN* OL16 ......29 K6
  TYLD M29 ......67 M3

Humberstone Av HULME M15......6 D9
Humber St CHH M8......72 D5
SALQ M50......86 A3
Hume St BNG/LEV * M19......99 L4
MILN OL16......11 H7
Humphrey Crs URM M41......96 D2
Humphrey La URM M41......96 D2
Humphrey Pk URM M41......96 D3
Humphrey Rd OLDTF/WHR M16......86 F2
Humphrey St CHH M8......72 C4
Huncoat Av HTNM SK4......100 A6
Huncote Dr BKLY M9......73 H3
Hunger Hill Av BOLS/LL BL3......51 H2
Hunmanby Av HULME M15......6 E9
Hunstanton Dr TOT/BURYW BL8......25 G7
Hunston Rd SALE M33......108 C1
Hunt Av AULW OL7......75 L7
Hunter Dr RAD M26......38 D7
Hunter Rd WGNW/BIL/O WN5......47 H3
Hunters Cha WGNW/BIL/O WN5......62 B3
Hunters Cl MPL/ROM SK6......113 J1
WILM/AE * SK9......127 K3
Hunters Ct STLY SK15......92 A4
Hunters Gn RAMS BL0......24 C1
Hunters Hl BURY BL9......39 L8
Hunters Hill La UPML OL3......45 M6
Hunters La GLSP SK13......104 C4
MILN OL16......10 E3
OLD OL1......9 K5
Hunters Ms SALE M33......96 D8
WILM/AE SK9......127 G5
Hunters Pool La MCFLDN SK10......131 L5
Hunterston Av ECC M30......85 K2
Hunt Fold Dr TOT/BURYW BL8......24 C3
Huntingdon Av CHAD OL9......8 B8
Huntingdon Crs RDSH * SK5......100 F7
Huntingdon Wk BOL * BL1......36 B2
Huntington Av DID/WITH M20......98 D5
Hunt La CHAD OL9......58 C4
Huntley Mount Rd BURY BL9......5 K1
Huntley Rd CHH M8......72 B2
EDGY/DAV SK3......12 A9
Huntley St BURY BL9......5 L2
Huntly Cha WILM/AE SK9......127 G6
Hunt Rd HYDE SK14......91 K7
RNFD/HAY WA11......78 B6
Huntroyde Av BOLE BL2......3 L1
Hunts Bank CSLFD M3......6 F1
Huntsham Cl ALT WA14......107 L6
Huntsman Dr IRL M44......94 C5
Hunts Rd SLFD M6......71 G7
Hunt St ATH M46......67 G1
BKLY M9......73 G3
WGN WN1......15 K5
Hurdlow Av BRO M7......71 K5
Hurdlow Ms GLSP SK13......104 A3
Hurdsfield Rd OFTN SK2......112 F8
Hurford Av GTN M18......89 G6
Hurlbote Cl WILM/AE SK9......119 M7
Hurley Dr CHD/CHDH SK8......120 A2
Hurlston Rd BOLS/LL BL3......52 A2
Hurst Av CHD/CHDH SK8......120 E6
SALE M33......107 M1
Hurstbank Av BNG/LEV * M19......99 G8
Hurst Bank Rd AUL OL6......76 B8
Hurstbourne Av OP/CLY M11......88 E1
Hurst Brook Cl AUL OL6......75 M8
Hurstbrook Cl GLSP SK13......105 J3
Hurstbrook Dr STRET M32......96 C2
Hurst Cl WHTN BL5......51 J5
Hurstead Gn WHIT * OL12......19 L8
Hurstead Rd MILN OL16......29 J6
Hurstfield Rd WALK M28......68 E4
Hurstfold Av BNG/LEV M19......111 G1
Hurst Green Cl RAD M26......38 C4
Hurst Gv AUL OL6......76 B7
Hurst Hall Dr AUL OL6......76 A7
Hursthead Rd CHD/CHDH SK8......120 D5
Hursthead Wk BRUN/LGST M13......7 K9
Hurst Hill Crs AUL OL6......76 A8
Hurst La GOL/RIS/CU WA3......81 L5
Hurst Lea Rd NM/HAY SK22......124 E5
Hurst Meadow MILN OL16......42 E2
Hurst Mill La GOL/RIS/CU WA3......81 M4
Hurst Rd GLSP SK13......105 J3
Hurst St BOLS/LL BL3......51 M1
BURY BL9......5 H5
CHAD OL9......8 E5
DUK SK16......90 D6
LEIGH WN7......81 L1
RDSH SK5......100 B5
ROCH OL11......11 H9
WALK M28......52 F6
WGNE/HIN WN2......48 F6
Hurstvale Av CHD/CHDH SK8......119 K3
Hurstville Rd CCHDY M21......97 L6
Hurstway Dr BKLY M9......73 H1
Hurstwood BOL BL1......22 A7
Hurstwood Cl OLDS OL8......59 M8
Hurstwood Ct BOLS/LL BL3......36 E8
Hurstwood Rd OFTN SK2......113 J6
Huskisson Wy NEWLW WA12......78 E8
Hus St DROY M43......89 J4
Husteads La UPML OL3......61 H3
Hutchins La OLDE OL4......60 A3
Hutchinson Rd ROCH OL11......27 G3
Hutchinson St ROCH OL11......27 L6
Hutchinson Wy RAD M26......54 D2
Hutton Av AUL OL6......91 H2
WALK M28......68 C6
Hutton Cl GOL/RIS/CU WA3......81 H7
Hutton St WGN WN1......31 K1
Huxley Av CHH M8......72 D6
Huxley Cl BRAM/HZG SK7......121 G5
Huxley Dr BRAM/HZG SK7......121 G5
Huxley Pl WGNS/IIMK WN3......47 K7
Huxley St ALT WA14......108 A5
BOL BL1......35 M2
OLDE OL4......59 M7
Huxley Ter ALT * WA14......116 E3
Huxton Gn BRAM/HZG SK7......121 J2
Hyacinth Cl EDGY/DAV SK3......112 A7
RNFD/HAY WA11......78 C6
Hyatt Crs WGNNW/ST WN6......30 F1
Hyde Bank Rd NM/HAY SK22......124 E4
Hyde Cl WGNS/IIMK WN3......47 K7
Hyde Dr WALK M28......68 F2
Hyde Fold Cl BNG/LEV M19......99 J6
Hyde Gv BRUN/LGST M13......87 M7
SALE M33......96 E8
WALK M28......68 F2
Hyde Pl BRUN/LGST M13......87 M7
Hyde Rd DTN/ASHW M34......101 J1
GTN M18......89 J8
HYDE SK14......103 J1
MDTN M24......58 B6
MPL/ROM SK6......101 L7
WALK M28......68 F2
WGTN/LGST M12......88 E7
Hyde Sq MDTN M24......57 H4
Hyde St BOLS/LL * BL3......51 M1
DROY M43......74 F8
DUK SK16......91 G4
HULME M15......87 G7
Hydon Brook Wk ROCH OL11......27 M8
Hydrangea Cl SALE M33......95 M7
Hyldavale Av CHD/CHDH SK8......110 E6
Hylton Dr CHD/CHDH SK8......120 E4
Hypatia St BOLE BL2......3 K4
Hythe Cl RUSH/FAL M14......98 F1
Hythe Rd EDGY/DAV SK3......12 A7
Hythe St BOLS/LL * BL3......35 K8
Hythe Wk CHAD OL9......8 A7

I

Ian Frazer Ct ROCH OL11......28 C8
Ibsley WHIT OL12......10 D2
Ice House Cl WALK M28......68 C1
Iceland St SLFD M6......86 B2
Idonia St BOL BL1......36 A1
Ilex Gv BRO M7......72 A6
Ilford St OP/CLY M11......88 E2
Ilfracombe Rd OFTN SK2......113 G4
Ilfracombe St NEWH/MOS M40......74 A6
Ilkeston Dr WGNE/HIN WN2......49 J1
Ilkley Cl BOLE BL2......3 L4
CHAD OL9......8 B7
Ilkley Crs RDSH SK5......100 B4
Ilkley Dr URM M41......84 D8
Ilkley St NEWH/MOS M40......73 K3
Ilk St OP/CLY M11......88 E2
Illingworth Av STLY SK15......91 M3
Illona Dr BRO M7......71 K4
Ilminster ROCH OL11......10 C7
Imperial Dr LEIGH WN7......67 G6
Imperial Ter SALE * M33......96 D6
Ina Av BOL BL1......35 J3
Ince Cl DID/WITH M20......98 E5
HTNM SK4......13 G1
Ince Green La WGNS/IIMK WN3......15 L8
Ince Hall Av WGNE/HIN WN2......48 C4
Ince St HTNM SK4......112 B1
Inchcape Dr BKLY M9......56 E8
Inchfield Cl ROCH OL11......27 H3
Inchfield Rd NEWH/MOS M40......73 K3
Inchley Rd BRUN/LGST M13......7 J9
Inchwood Ms OLDE OL4......44 B8
Incline Rd OLDS OL8......74 E2
Independent St BOLS/LL BL3......53 K1
Indigo St SLFD M6......71 J7
Industrial St RAMS BL0......17 C3
WHTN BL5......50 C5
Industry Rd WHIT OL12......10 E1
Industry St CHAD OL9......58 D8
LIT OL15......20 C7
ROCH OL11......27 H3
WHIT OL12......18 E2
Infant St PWCH * M25......55 M8
Infirmary St BOL BL1......2 F5
Ingersol Rd HOR/BR BL6......34 B4
Ingham Rd ALT WA14......108 A3
Inghams La LIT OL15......20 C7
Ingham St BURY BL9......5 H6
LEIGH WN7......66 B4
NEWH/MOS * M40......74 B8
OLD OL1......9 L5
Inghamwood Cl BRO M7......72 C5
Ingleby Av BKLY M9......57 J8
Ingleby Cl ROY/SHW OL2......43 K4
WGNNW/ST WN6......31 G2
WHTN BL5......50 C2
Ingleby Ct STRET M32......97 H3
Ingleby Wy ROY/SHW OL2......43 K4
Ingledene Av BRO M7......72 B3
Ingledene Gv BOL * BL1......35 K2
Ingle Dr OFTN SK2......112 F5
Inglefield ROCH OL11......27 H3
Inglehead Cl DTN/ASHW M34......101 K2
Ingle Rd CHD/CHDH SK8......111 K6
Ingles Fold WALK M28......68 E5
Inglesham Cl LEIGH WN7......81 H3
NTHM/RTH M23......109 L6
Ingleton Av CHH M8......72 E2
Ingleton Cl BOLE BL2......23 G8
CHD/CHDH SK8......110 F6
NEWLW * WA12......78 E8
ROY/SHW OL2......43 G7
Ingleton Ms TOT/BURYW BL8......24 E8
Ingleton Rd EDGY/DAV SK3......12 C7
Inglewhite Av WGN WN1......47 M2
Inglewhite Cl BURY BL9......39 G5
Inglewhite Crs WGN * WN1......47 M2
Inglewood Av WGN WN1......15 K5
Inglewood Cl AULW OL7......75 J7
BURY BL9......5 M1
PART M31......94 B8
Inglewood Hollow STLY SK15......91 M4
Inglewood Rd CHAD OL9......58 B3
Inglewood Wk
BRUN/LGST * M13......87 M6
Inglis St LIT OL15......20 C6
Ingoe Cl HEY OL10......41 J1
Ingoldsby Av BRUN/LGST M13......88 A8
Ingram Dr HTNM SK4......111 H1
Ingram St WGNE/HIN WN2......64 D1
WGNNW/ST WN6......14 A1
Ings Av WHIT OL12......27 L2
Ings La WHIT OL12......27 L2
Inkerman St HYDE SK14......90 F8
NEWH/MOS M40......73 G7
WHIT * OL12......10 E1
Ink St MILN OL16......10 F4
Inman St BURY BL9......4 D8
DTN/ASHW M34......101 J1
Innes St WGTN/LGST M12......99 L1
Innis Av NEWH/MOS M40......73 M7
Institute St BOL BL1......2 F5
Instow Cl BRUN/LGST M13......88 A7
CHAD OL9......58 C3
Intake Rd UPML OL3......77 K1
International Ap
MANAIR * M90......118 D5
Invar Rd WALK M28......70 A3
Inverbeg Dr BOLE BL2......37 K5
Inverlael Av BOL BL1......35 L4
Inverness Av BKLY M9......57 K8
Inverness Rd DUK SK16......90 F5
Inward Dr WGNNW/ST WN6......30 D7
Inwood Wk CHH M8......72 F6
Inworth Cl WHTN BL5......50 C6
Iona Pl BOLE BL2......36 F2
Iona Wy URM M41......95 G1
Ionian Gdns BRO M7......71 M7
Ipswich St ROCH OL11......10 F8
Iqbal Cl WGTN/LGST M12......88 D7
Ireby Cl MDTN M24......56 F2
Iredale Crs WGNNW/ST WN6......31 J5
Iredine St OP/CLY M11......88 F3
Irene Av HYDE SK14......91 H8
Iris Av FWTH BL4......52 D3
FWTH BL4......53 J7
Iris St OLDS OL8......75 J2
RAMS BL0......17 B6
Irkdale St CHH M8......72 F6
Irk St ANC M4......87 K1
Irk Vale Dr OLD OL1......58 B3
Irlam Av ECC M30......85 G3
Irlam Rd SALE M33......96 F7
URM M41......94 E3
URM M41......95 H2
Irlam Sq SLFD M6......71 G7
Irlam St BOL BL1......36 B1
NEWH/MOS M40......73 H7
Irlam Wharf Rd IRL M44......94 D6
Irma St BOL BL1......36 C1
Ironmonger La WGNS/IIMK WN3......14 F6
Iron St DTN/ASHW * M34......101 J1
HOR/BR BL6......33 M2
NEWH/MOS M40......88 B1
Irvin Dr WYTH/NTH M22......119 J4
Irvine Av WALK M28......68 D6
Irvine St LEIGH WN7......66 C6
Irving Cl OFTN SK2......121 J1
Irving St BOL BL1......36 B2
OLDS OL8......74 E2
Irvin St NEWH/MOS M40......73 M6
Irwell Av ECC M30......85 J3
LHULT M38......52 E8
Irwell Gv ECC M30......85 J3
Irwell Pl ECC M30......85 J2
ORD M5......86 F3
WGNW/BIL/O WN5......46 F6
Irwell Rd WGNW/BIL/O WN5......46 C5
Irwell St BURY BL9......4 D5
CHH M8......72 B8
CSLFD M3......6 C4
RAD M26......53 K5
RAD M26......54 E2
RAMS BL0......17 C6
SLFD M6......71 K6
Irwell Valley Wy RAMS BL0......17 C8
Irwin Dr WILM/AE SK9......119 L7
Irwin Rd ALT WA14......107 M4
Irwin St DTN/ASHW M34......101 H1
Isaac Cl ORD M5......86 D4
Isaac St BOL BL1......35 M4
Isabella Cl OLDTF/WHR M16......86 F8
Isabella Sq WGN WN1......15 K3
Isabella St WHIT OL12......28 C2
Isabel Wk BOLS/LL BL3......2 A9
Isaiah St OLDS * OL8......59 J8
Isa St RAMS BL0......17 A8
Isca St OP/CLY M11......88 C3
Isherwood Dr MPL/ROM SK6......114 A6
Isherwood Fold EDGW/EG BL7......16 D5
Isherwood Rd PART M31......95 J6
Isherwood St HEY OL10......41 H3
LEIGH WN7......66 B4
ROCH OL11......11 G8
Isis Cl BRO M7......71 K4
Islington Rd OFTN SK2......112 F8
Islington St CSLFD M3......6 B3
Islington Wy CSLFD M3......6 A4
Isobel Cl ECC M30......84 E3
OLDTF/WHR M16......87 J8
Ivanhoe Av GOL/RIS/CU WA3......80 A3
Ivanhoe Ct FWTH BL4......52 F2
Ivanhoe St BOLS/LL BL3......52 F2
OLD OL1......59 M3
Iveagh Ct MILN OL16......11 J7
Ivor St ROCH OL11......41 L1
Ivy Bank Rd BOL BL1......22 B7
Ivybridge Cl BRUN/LGST M13......88 A7
Ivy Cl DROY M43......89 J1
ROY/SHW OL2......43 L5
Ivy Cottages WHIT OL12......10 A1
Ivycroft GLSP SK13......93 H8
Ivydale Dr LEIGH WN7......66 F7
Ivy Dr MDTN M24......57 J6
Ivy Farm Gdns GOL/RIS/CU WA3......81 G8
Ivygreen Dr OLDE OL4......60 C6
Ivygreen Rd CCHDY M21......97 J4
Ivy Gv FWTH BL4......52 E4
FWTH * BL4......53 J5
LHULT M38......52 C8
Ivy House Rd GOL/RIS/CU WA3......80 A3
Ivyleaf Sq BRO M7......72 B6
Ivylea Rd BNG/LEV M19......99 H8
Ivy Rd BOL BL1......35 M3
GOL/RIS/CU WA3......79 L4
POY/DIS SK12......129 J1
TOT/BURYW BL8......38 E2
WHTN BL5......50 C5
Ivy St BOLS/LL BL3......35 M8
ECC M30......85 G3
NEWH/MOS M40......73 K4
WGNNW/ST WN6......14 E4

J

Jack Brady Cl NTHM/RTH M23......109 H8
Jackdaw Rd RAMS BL0......24 C2
Jack La DROY M43......89 M2
URM M41......96 B2
Jackman Av HEY OL10......41 G5
Jackroom Dr ANC * M4......7 L4
Jack's La WHTN BL5......49 K5
Jackson Av DUK SK16......91 G4
Jackson Cl HALE/TIMP WA15......108 F5
OLDS OL8......9 G8
Jackson Ct URM M41......95 K1
Jackson Crs HULME M15......6 D9
Jackson Gdns DTN/ASHW M34......101 G2
Jackson Ms OLDE OL4......60 A3
Jacksons Edge Rd
POY/DIS SK12......123 J5
Jackson's La BRAM/HZG SK7......121 L4
Jackson's Rw CSLFD M3......6 E5
Jackson St AUL OL6......75 L8
CHD/CHDH SK8......111 H6
FAIL M35......74 A6
FWTH BL4......53 G4
FWTH BL4......53 J5
GLSP SK13......93 M7
GLSP SK13......104 F5
HYDE SK14......102 A2
HYDE * SK14......103 K1
MDTN M24......57 L3
MILN OL16......11 K7
OLDE OL4......59 L5
OLDE * OL4......60 C6
RAD M26......54 E2
SALE M33......97 G7
STRET M32......96 F3
WALK M28......52 F8
WGNE/HIN WN2......48 D5
WHIT OL12......19 K6
WHTF M45......55 J5
Jack St BOLE BL2......3 L1
Jack Taylor Ct WHIT * OL12......11 J1
Jacobite Cl BRO M7......71 M3
Jacobsen Av HYDE SK14......91 J8
Jacob St WGNE/HIN WN2......49 G6
Jaffrey St LEIGH WN7......66 B7
James Andrew St
MDTN * M24......57 L3
James Brindley Basin
CMANE M1......7 L5
James Butterworth Ct
MILN OL16......11 J6
James Butterworth St
MILN OL16......11 K6
James Cl DUK SK16......91 H4
WGNS/IIMK WN3......14 F6
James Corbett Rd SALQ M50......85 M3
James Dr HYDE SK14......102 B2
James Henry Av ORD M5......86 E4
James Hill St LIT * OL15......20 C7
James Leigh St CMANE M1......7 G7
Jameson St ROCH OL11......41 L2
James Pl WGNNW/ST WN6......31 G2
James Rd RNFD/HAY WA11......78 C5
ROY/SHW OL2......43 L4
James Sq WGNNW/ST WN6......31 G2
James's St OLDE OL4......60 A3
James St ATH M46......67 H3
BOLS/LL BL3......53 L1
BURY BL9......5 J6
DROY M43......89 L2
DTN/ASHW * M34......101 K1
EDGW/EG BL7......22 A1
EDGY/DAV SK3......13 G8
FAIL M35......74 D4
FWTH BL4......53 J4
GLSP SK13......104 F4
HEY * OL10......41 G2
HOR/BR BL6......33 J1
LIT OL15......20 A7
MPL/ROM SK6......101 K7
NEWH/MOS M40......88 A1
ORD M5......6 A4
PWCH M25......55 K7
RAD M26......54 E2
ROY/SHW OL2......43 K7
SALE M33......97 G8
STLY * SK15......91 H4
TYLD M29......67 J4
WGNE/HIN WN2......64 B5
WGNS/IIMK WN3......15 J7
WHIT * OL12......11 G1
WHIT OL12......18 E2
WHTN BL5......50 B2
James St South CHAD * OL9......58 D5
Jane St CHAD OL9......8 B7
WHIT OL12......10 C2
Japan St BRO M7......72 C5
Jardine Wy CHAD OL9......58 C8
Jarvis St OLDE OL4......9 M7
WHIT OL12......28 C3
Jasmine Av DROY M43......89 M2
Jasmine Cl NTHM/RTH M23......109 H3
Jasmine Rd WGNW/BIL/O * WN5......47 G5
Jason St ANC M4......87 L1
Jauncey St BOLS/LL BL3......35 M7
Jayton Av DID/WITH M20......110 E4
Jean Av LEIGH WN7......81 H2
Jean Cl BNG/LEV M19......99 K2
Jedburgh Av BOL BL1......35 L4
Jefferson Wy WHIT OL12......28 C1
Jeffreys Dr DUK SK16......91 G4
Jeffrey St WGNE/HIN WN2......48 D4
Jehlum Cl CHH M8......72 E5
Jellicoe Av IRL M44......94 B6
Jenkinson St HULME M15......7 H9
WGNE/HIN WN2......49 G6
Jenner Cl HULME M15......87 H6
Jennet Hey AIMK WN4......63 J6
Jennet's La GOL/RIS/CU WA3......81 M3
Jennings Av ORD M5......86 D4
Jennings Cl HYDE SK14......91 L7
ORD M5......86 D4
Jennings St EDGY/DAV SK3......12 F9
Jennison Cl WGTN/LGST M12......88 E6
Jenny La BRAM/HZG SK7......128 C1
Jenny St OLDS OL8......74 F2
Jepheys Pl WHIT OL12......28 C3
Jepheys St WHIT OL12......28 C3
Jepson St OFTN SK2......112 D6
Jericho Rd BURY BL9......26 B8
Jermyn St WHIT OL12......11 G2
Jerrold St LIT OL15......20 C7
Jersey Rd RDSH SK5......100 C8
Jersey St ANC M4......7 K3
AUL OL6......75 L8
Jerusalem Pl CMANW * M2......6 E6
Jesmond Av PWCH M25......71 L2
Jesmond Dr TOT/BURYW BL8......24 F7
Jesmond Gv CHD/CHDH SK8......120 D4
Jespersen St OLD OL1......9 J4
Jessamine Av BRO M7......72 A8
Jessel Cl BRUN/LGST M13......87 M6
Jessica Wy LEIGH WN7......65 L8
Jessie St BOLS/LL BL3......35 M7
NEWH/MOS M40......73 K6
Jessop Dr MPL/ROM SK6......114 C4
Jessop St GTN M18......89 G7
Jethro St BOLE BL2......3 L3
BOLE BL2......22 F8
Jetson St GTN M18......89 J6
Jimmy McMullen Wk
RUSH/FAL * M14......98 D1
Jinnah Cl OLDE OL4......59 M7
OP/CLY M11......88 F4
J J Thomson Ms
RUSH/FAL * M14......98 F3
Joan St NEWH/MOS M40......73 K5
Jobling St OP/CLY M11......88 C4
Jocelyn St NEWH/MOS M40......73 H6
Joddrell St CSLFD M3......6 D5
Jodrell St NM/HAY SK22......124 D5
Joel La HYDE SK14......102 C5
Johannesburg Gdns
NTHM/RTH M23......109 J8
John Ashworth St WHIT OL12......28 E3
John Atkinson Ct ORD * M5......86 A2
John Av CHD/CHDH SK8......111 H7
John Beeley Av OP/CLY M11......89 G4
John Booth St OLDE OL4......60 C7
John Brown St BOL * BL1......2 C3
John Clynes Av
NEWH/MOS * M40......87 M1
John Cross St BOLS/LL BL3......36 B8
John Dalton St CMANW M2......6 E5
GLSP SK13......93 H7
John Foran Cl NEWH/MOS M40......73 L6
John Gilbert Wy TRPK M17......86 B7
John Heywood St OP/CLY M11......88 E2
John Kennedy Gdn HYDE SK14......103 K1
John Kennedy Rd HYDE SK14......103 J1
John Knott St OLDE OL4......60 C6
John Lee Fold MDTN M24......57 K3
John Nash Crs HULME M15......87 H6
Johnny King Cl NEWH/MOS M40......73 G7
John Roberts Cl ROCH OL11......10 D8
Johns Cl CCHDY M21......97 L4
John Shepley St HYDE SK14......102 B2
John Smeaton Ct CMANE M1......7 L5
Johnson Av NEWLW WA12......78 E7
WGNE/HIN WN2......65 H3
Johnsonbrook Rd DUK SK16......91 G7
Johnson Cl LEIGH WN7......65 L8
Johnson Fold Av BOL BL1......35 H2
Johnson Gv MDTN M24......57 H3
Johnson's Sq NEWH/MOS M40......73 G8
Johnson St ATH M46......66 D3
BOL BL1......2 F6
CSLFD M3......6 D3
RAD M26......54 E2
SWIN M27......71 G6
TYLD M29......67 K3
WGNW/BIL/O WN5......46 E6
John's Pl MPL/ROM SK6......113 M2
John Steet MPL/ROM SK6......113 M2
Johnston WHIT OL12......10 D2
Johnston Av LIT * OL15......29 J1
John St AIMK WN4......64 A7
ALT WA14......108 A8
ANC M4......7 H3
BOLS/LL * BL3......53 L1
BRAM/HZG SK7......121 M1
BRO M7......72 A8
BURY BL9......4 F3
CHAD OL9......9 G6
CSLFD M3......6 D2
DROY M43......89 J4
DTN/ASHW * M34......90 C8
ECC M30......84 E3
EDGW/EG BL7......22 D5
FAIL M35......74 C3
FWTH BL4......53 H4
GLSP SK13......104 F4
GOL/RIS/CU WA3......79 K4
HEY OL10......41 G2
HYDE SK14......102 A1
HYDE * SK14......102 A2
IRL M44......94 B7
LEIGH WN7......66 C7
LIT OL15......20 B7
MILN OL16......11 G4
MILN OL16......28 F1
MPL/ROM SK6......101 K7
MPL/ROM SK6......114 D7
MPL/ROM SK6......114 E2
PWCH M25......56 B4
ROY/SHW OL2......43 G8
ROY/SHW OL2......43 K7
SALE M33......96 E7
STKP SK1......13 J6
STLY SK15......76 F7
SWIN M27......70 D4
TYLD M29......67 K3
WALK M28......53 G8
WGN WN1......15 J4
WGNE/HIN WN2......65 L1
WGNW/BIL/O WN5......47 G7
WHIT OL12......18 E2
John St East AULW OL7......90 D3
John St West AULW OL7......90 C4
John William St ECC M30......85 J2
OP/CLY * M11......88 F3
Joiner St ANC M4......7 H4
ORD M5......86 F3
Join Rd SALE M33......97 G8
Jolly Brows BOLE BL2......37 G1
Jonas St BKLY M9......73 H4
BRO M7......87 H1
Jonathan Fold LEIGH * WN7......67 G7
Jones Sq STKP SK1......13 K8
Jones St GLSP SK13......93 K7
HOR/BR BL6......21 B8
MILN OL16......11 H7
OLD OL1......9 M3
RAD M26......38 E8
ROY/SHW OL2......59 G2
SLFD M6......86 C1
Jonquil Dr LHULT M38......68 C2
Jopson St MDTN M24......57 L3
Jordan Av ROY/SHW * OL2......43 M3
Jordan St GLSP SK13......105 H3
HULME M15......6 D8
Josephine Dr SWIN M27......70 D5
Joseph Johnson Ms
WYTH/NTH * M22......110 B3
Joseph St ECC M30......84 E3
FAIL M35......74 D4
FWTH BL4......53 G3
LIT OL15......20 C6
MDTN M24......57 J3
MPL/ROM * SK6......114 D6
RAD M26......54 E2
WHIT OL12......28 A2
Joshua La MDTN M24......58 A5
Josslyn Rd ORD M5......86 A1
Jo St ORD M5......86 D3
Joule Cl ORD M5......86 D4
Joules Ct STKP SK1......13 K5
Joule St BKLY M9......73 H3
Jowett St OLD OL1......59 M3
RDSH SK5......100 C8
Jowett's Wk AULW OL7......90 C2
Jowkin La ROCH OL11......27 G5
Joyce St NEWH/MOS M40......73 L5
Joynson Av BRO M7......72 A8
Joynson St SALE M33......96 E7
Joy St RAMS BL0......17 B6
WHIT OL12......28 C2
Jubilee Av DUK SK16......91 H3
RAD M26......54 F3
WGNW/BIL/O WN5......46 A8
Jubilee Crs RNFD/HAY WA11......78 C5
Jubilee Gdns NM/HAY SK22......124 E5
Jubilee Houses WALK * M28......68 F1
Jubilee Rd MDTN M24......57 L3
Jubilee St NM/HAY SK22......124 E5
ROY/SHW OL2......43 M5
SLFD M6......86 C2
Jubilee Ter MDTN M24......57 L2
Jubilee Wy BURY BL9......4 C4
Judith St WHIT OL12......27 M1
Judson Av CCHDY M21......97 M7
Judy St BKLY M9......73 J4
Julia St CSLFD M3......87 J1
HOR/BR BL6......21 B8
WHIT OL12......10 D3
Julius St BNG/LEV M19......99 L4

Junction Aly MILN OL16 10 F5
Junction Rd BOLS/LL BL3 35 J7
HYDE SK14 90 F7
OFTN SK2 13 J8
Junction Rd West HOR/BR BL6 34 F7
Junction St MDTN M24 58 A6
OLDS * OL8 59 H8
Junction Ter WGNS/IIMK WN3 15 L8
June Av HTNM SK4 12 B3
LEIGH WN7 65 M6
Juniper Bank RDSH SK5 100 D4
Juniper Cl BOL BL1 36 B3
OLDE OL4 44 C8
SALE M33 96 C6
Juniper Dr MILN OL16 29 G6
WGNE/HIN WN2 65 J1
Juno St OLD OL1 9 L1
Jupiter Gv WGNS/IIMK WN3 63 H2
Jura Cl DUK SK16 91 G4
Jura Dr URM M41 85 H7
Jura Gv HEY OL10 40 E3
Jurby Av BKLY M9 56 F8
Jury St CHH M8 72 C8
LEIGH WN7 66 B5
Justene Cl GOL/RIS/CU WA3 79 K2
Justin Cl BRUN/LGST M13 7 J9
Jutland Av ROCH OL11 27 M4
Jutland Gv WHTN BL5 50 B3
Jutland St CMANE M1 7 K5

K

Kale St BRUN/LGST M13 7 K9
Kalima Gv BRO M7 72 A6
Kane Ct GOL/RIS/CU WA3 80 D3
Kansas Av SALQ M50 86 B4
Kara St SLFD M6 86 B2
Karen Rd WGN WN1 15 L4
Kate St RAMS * BL0 17 B6
Kathan Cl MILN OL16 11 K5
Katherine Rd OFTN SK2 112 F7
Katherine St AUL OL6 90 E1
AULW OL7 90 C2
Kathleen Gv RUSH/FAL M14 98 F2
Kathleen St WHIT OL12 10 B3
Kay Av MPL/ROM SK6 113 G1
Kay Brow HEY OL10 40 F2
RAMS BL0 17 C6
Kay Cl WGN WN1 15 J4
Kayfields BOLE BL2 23 H8
Kay's Av STKP SK1 112 E3
Kays Gdns CSLFD M3 6 B2
Kay St ATH M46 67 G2
BOL BL1 2 E1
BOLS/LL BL3 53 K1
BURY BL9 5 J2
BURY BL9 24 F1
EDGW/EG BL7 16 C8
HEY OL10 40 F2
OP/CLY M11 88 C5
ROCH OL11 10 D8
SLFD M6 71 J6
STLY SK15 91 K3
Kays Wood Rd MPL/ROM SK6 114 A6
Keadby Cl ECC M30 85 G4
Keal Dr IRL M44 83 K8
Kearsley Dr BOLS/LL BL3 52 E1
Kearsley Hall Rd RAD M26 53 M5
Kearsley Rd CHH M8 72 D2
RAD M26 53 M4
Kearsley St ECC M30 84 E2
LEIGH WN7 66 A7
WGNNW/ST WN6 14 D2
Kearsley V RAD M26 53 L4
Kearton Dr ECC M30 85 K3
Keary Cl GTN M18 89 G6
Keaton Cl SLFD M6 71 H8
Keats Av DROY M43 89 K2
DTN/ASHW M34 101 K4
WGNNW/ST WN6 47 H1
WGNS/IIMK WN3 14 C9
WGNW/BIL/O WN5 62 A3
WHIT OL12 27 K3
Keats Crs RAD M26 38 B8
Keats Fold DUK SK16 91 L5
Keats Ms NTHM/RTH M23 108 F4
Keats Rd ECC M30 85 G3
OLD * OL1 59 L3
RAMS BL0 24 C2
Keats St LEIGH WN7 66 A5
Keats Wy WGNE/HIN WN2 64 E3
Keb La OLDS OL8 75 K4
Keble Av OLDS OL8 75 H1
Keble Gv LEIGH WN7 65 M4
Keble St WGNE/HIN WN2 48 C5
Kedleston Av RUSH/FAL M14 88 B8
Kedleston Gn OFTN SK2 113 G5
Keele Cl NEWH/MOS M40 87 M1
Keele Wk NEWH/MOS M40 87 M1
Keepers Dr WHIT OL12 27 H2
Keighley Av DROY M43 89 K1
Keighley Cl TOT/BURYW BL8 38 C2
Keighley St BOL BL1 35 M2
Keilder Ms BOL BL1 35 K4
Keith Dr EDGY/DAV SK3 12 A9
Keith Wk NEWH/MOS M40 88 A1
Kelboro Av DTN/ASHW M34 90 A5
Kelbrook Ct OFTN SK2 113 H7
Kelbrook Rd OP/CLY M11 88 E4
Kelby Av NTHM/RTH M23 109 L5
Keld Cl TOT/BURYW BL8 24 E7
Kelfield Av NTHM/RTH M23 109 K2
Kellaton Cl WGNS/IIMK WN3 15 K7
Kellbank Rd WGNS/IIMK WN3 63 H1
Kellbrook Crs BRO * M7 71 K4
Kellet Cl WGNW/BIL/O WN5 47 G3
Kellets Rw WALK * M28 53 G7
Kellett St BOL BL1 22 C6
MILN OL16 11 J3
Kelling Wk HULME M15 6 B9
Kells Gv WGNNW/ST WN6 47 J2
Kelmarsh Cl OP/CLY * M11 89 G5
Kelsall Crs EDGY/DAV SK3 112 A6
Kelsall Dr DROY M43 89 J1
HALE/TIMP WA15 108 F6
Kelsall Rd CHD/CHDH SK8 111 K7
Kelsall St CHAD OL9 8 E6
MILN OL16 10 F3
SALE M33 96 D8
WGTN/LGST M12 88 C6
Kelso Cl OLDS OL8 75 J3
Kelson Av AULW OL7 75 K7
Kelstern Av BRUN/LGST M13 99 H1
Kelstern Sq BRUN/LGST M13 99 H1
Kelton Cl RDSH SK5 100 C7
Kelverlow St OLDE OL4 59 M6
Kelvin Av MDTN M24 56 E5
SALE M33 96 E8
Kelvin Cl AIMK * WN4 63 G8
Kelvindale Dr
HALE/TIMP WA15 108 F5
Kelvin Gv CHH M8 72 D6
WGNS/IIMK WN3 63 H2
Kelvington Dr BKLY M9 73 G6
Kelvin St ANC M4 7 H3
AULW OL7 90 C4
Kelway Ter WGN WN1 15 J1
Kemble Av NTHM/RTH M23 109 M3
Kemmel Av WYTH/NTH M22 110 B7
Kemp Av ROCH OL11 10 B9
Kempnough Hall Rd WALK M28 69 H5
Kemp Rd MPL/ROM SK6 114 F4
Kempsey Ct CHAD OL9 8 A5
Kempsey St CHAD OL9 8 A5
Kempsford Cl NTHM/RTH M23 109 L6
Kempster St BRO M7 72 A8
Kempston Gdns BOL BL1 36 B2
Kemp St HYDE SK14 91 H8
MDTN M24 57 J4
Kempton Av BOLS/LL BL3 53 K2
SALE M33 108 A1
Kempton Cl BRAM/HZG SK7 122 C2
DROY M43 89 M2
NEWLW WA12 79 G7
Kempton Wy CHAD OL9 8 C5
Kemsing Wk ORD * M5 86 D2
Kenchester Av OP/CLY M11 89 G4
Kendal Av AULW OL7 75 J8
DTN/ASHW M34 101 K3
HYDE SK14 90 F7
SALE M33 108 F1
URM M41 84 B8
WHIT OL12 27 H2
Kendal Cl HALE/TIMP WA15 109 G7
HEY OL10 41 H4
Kendal Dr BRAM/HZG SK7 120 E7
BURY BL9 39 G5
CHD/CHDH SK8 110 F8
ROY/SHW OL2 44 A5
Kendal Gdns MPL/ROM SK6 101 L8
Kendal Gv AIMK WN4 63 L8
LEIGH WN7 66 A7
WALK M28 69 J2
WHTF M45 55 J4
Kendall Rd CHH M8 72 C1
Kendal Rd BOL BL1 35 M4
RAMS BL0 24 C2
SLFD M6 70 F7
STRET M32 97 G1
WALK M28 68 B5
WGNE/HIN WN2 48 D4
Kendal Rd West RAMS BL0 24 C2
Kendal St WGNNW/ST WN6 14 D2
Kendon Gv DTN/ASHW M34 101 H1
Kendrew Rd BOLS/LL BL3 35 K8
Kendrick Pl WGN WN1 15 K3
Kenford Dr WGNS/IIMK WN3 63 H2
Kenhall Rd LEIGH WN7 66 F8
Kenilworth ROCH OL11 10 D7
Kenilworth Av CHAD OL9 58 B3
CHD/CHDH SK8 120 C1
DID/WITH M20 98 C7
SWIN M27 70 E1
WHTF M45 55 K6
WILM/AE SK9 127 H1
Kenilworth Cl MPL/ROM SK6 114 C4
OLDE OL4 60 C7
RAD M26 38 C6
Kenilworth Dr BRAM/HZG SK7 121 M4
LEIGH WN7 67 H5
WGNE/HIN WN2 49 J8
Kenilworth Gv DTN/ASHW M34 89 M4
Kenilworth Rd EDGY/DAV SK3 111 J5
GOL/RIS/CU WA3 80 B5
MILN OL16 42 F4
SALE M33 96 B8
URM M41 94 F3
Kenilworth Sq BOL BL1 35 L3
Kenion Rd ROCH OL11 27 K6
Kenion St MILN OL16 10 F5
Kenley Ldg BRAM/HZG * SK7 120 F5
Kenmay Av BOLS/LL BL3 35 J6
Kenmere Gv NEWH/MOS M40 73 L3
Kenmor Av TOT/BURYW BL8 38 D4
Kenmore Cl WHTF M45 55 L4
Kenmore Dr HALE/TIMP WA15 117 J1
Kenmore Gv AIMK WN4 63 G8
AIMK WN4 78 A1
IRL M44 94 A6
Kenmore Rd SALE M33 107 M3
WHTF M45 55 L4
WYTH/NTH M22 109 M5
Kenmore Wy WHTF M45 55 L4
Kennard Cl BKLY M9 73 J3
Kennedy Dr BOLS/LL BL3 53 M1
BURY BL9 55 L2
Kennedy Rd ORD M5 85 M2
TYLD M29 68 A5
Kennedy St BOLE * BL2 3 M4
CMANW M2 6 F5
OLDS OL8 9 H9
Kennedy Wy DTN/ASHW M34 101 G2
HTNM SK4 12 D3
Kennerley Rd OFTN SK2 112 D7
Kennerley's La WILM/AE SK9 126 E5
Kennet Cl WHTN BL5 50 C3
WILM/AE SK9 127 H2
Kenneth Av LEIGH WN7 66 A6
Kenneth Gv LEIGH WN7 66 A6
Kenneth Sq BRO M7 72 B6
Kennett Rd NTHM/RTH M23 118 C1
Kennet Wy LEIGH WN7 66 C5
Kenninghall Rd
WYTH/NTH M22 118 F1
Kennington Av
NEWH/MOS M40 73 L8
Kennington Fold BOLS/LL BL3 52 A1
Kenny Cl OLDE OL4 60 A7
Kensington Av AUL OL6 76 B8
CHAD OL9 58 B4
HYDE * SK14 102 B3
RAD M26 38 A8
ROY/SHW OL2 42 F6
RUSH/FAL M14 88 A8
Kensington Cl MILN OL16 29 K6
TOT/BURYW BL8 24 D3
Kensington Ct BOL * BL1 2 B3
HYDE SK14 102 B3
WILM/AE SK9 126 E6
Kensington Dr HOR/BR BL6 33 M1
LEIGH WN7 67 H5
ORD M5 86 A1
TOT/BURYW BL8 38 D4
Kensington Gdns
HALE/TIMP WA15 117 H3
Kensington Gv ALT WA14 108 B4
DTN/ASHW M34 89 L8
STLY SK15 91 K3
Kensington Rd CCHDY M21 97 K2
EDGY/DAV SK3 12 A8
FAIL M35 74 E4
OLDS OL8 59 G8
WGNW/BIL/O * WN5 47 G7
Kensington St BOL BL1 2 C4
HYDE SK14 102 B3
ROCH OL11 28 B8
RUSH/FAL M14 98 D1
Kenslow Av CHH M8 72 C2
Kensworth Cl BOL BL1 2 A1
Kensworth Dr BOL BL1 36 A3
Kent Av CHAD OL9 58 D6
CHD/CHDH SK8 111 M8
DROY M43 89 H3
WGNE/HIN WN2 64 D2
Kent Cl UPML OL3 45 M8
WALK M28 68 D2
Kent Ct BOL BL1 2 D3
Kent Dr BURY BL9 5 G8
FWTH BL4 53 L6
Kentford Dr NEWH/MOS M40 72 F8
Kentford Rd BOL BL1 2 D1
Kentmere Av WHIT OL12 28 E1
Kentmere Cl CHD/CHDH SK8 119 K1
Kentmere Dr MDTN M24 57 H1
TYLD M29 67 L5
Kentmere Gv FWTH BL4 52 C5
Kentmere Rd BOLE BL2 37 J3
HALE/TIMP WA15 109 G6
Kentmore Cl HTNM SK4 111 H2
Kenton Av GTN M18 99 M1
Kenton Cl BOL BL1 36 A3
DTN/ASHW M34 90 A5
Kenton Rd ROY/SHW OL2 43 K5
Kenton St OLDS OL8 59 L7
Kent Rd ATH M46 50 F8
DTN/ASHW M34 100 D2
EDGY/DAV SK3 12 A7
FAIL M35 74 B6
GLSP SK13 105 G3
PART M31 106 B2
TYLD M29 67 J2
Kent Rd East RUSH/FAL M14 99 G1
Kent Rd West RUSH/FAL M14 98 F1
Kentsford Dr BOLS/LL BL3 37 L7
Kentstone Av HTNM SK4 111 G1
Kent St BOL BL1 2 D2
BRO M7 72 A8
CMANW * M2 6 F4
LEIGH WN7 67 G8
OLDS OL8 59 J8
ROCH OL11 10 E7
SWIN M27 70 C2
WGN WN1 15 J5
Kentucky St OLDE OL4 59 M6
Kentwell Cl DUK SK16 90 E5
Kenwick Dr NEWH/MOS M40 74 B2
Kenwood Av BNG/LEV M19 99 J6
BRAM/HZG SK7 120 F7
CHD/CHDH SK8 110 D6
HALE/TIMP WA15 117 J2
LEIGH WN7 66 F7
Kenwood Cl LEIGH WN7 66 F8
STRET M32 97 H2
Kenwood La WALK M28 69 J7
Kenwood Rd BOL BL1 35 L1
OLD OL1 58 F3
RDSH SK5 100 B2
STRET M32 97 H3
Kenworthy Av AUL OL6 76 A7
Kenworthy Cl HYDE SK14 103 H2
Kenworthy Gdns UPML OL3 61 L4
Kenworthy La WYTH/NTH M22 110 A2
Kenworthy St MILN OL16 11 L4
STLY SK15 91 K3
Kenwright St ANC M4 7 H2
Kenwyn St NEWH/MOS M40 88 B1
Kenyon Av DUK SK16 91 H5
OLDS OL8 75 J1
SALE M33 109 H2
Kenyon Cl HYDE SK14 91 J7
Kenyon Fold ROCH OL11 27 H7
Kenyon Gv LHULT M38 52 B8
Kenyon La GOL/RIS/CU WA3 80 C6
MDTN M24 57 M4
NEWH/MOS M40 73 K4
PWCH M25 55 M8
Kenyon Rd BOLE BL2 37 L7
WGN WN1 47 M2
WGNNW/ST WN6 31 G2
Kenyon's La North
RNFD/HAY WA11 78 C4
Kenyon's La South
RNFD/HAY WA11 78 C4
Kenyon St AUL OL6 90 C1
BURY BL9 5 H2
DUK SK16 90 E4
GTN M18 89 H6
HEY OL10 40 F2
LEIGH WN7 66 A4
RAMS BL0 17 C5
Kenyon Ter TYLD M29 68 B1
Kenyon Wy LHULT M38 52 B8
TOT/BURYW BL8 24 C7
Keppel Rd CCHDY M21 97 L3
Keppel St AUL OL6 90 F1
Kepwick Dr WYTH/NTH M22 119 G3
Kerans Dr WHTN BL5 50 B3
Kerenhappuch St RAMS BL0 17 B7
Kerfoot Cl WYTH/NTH M22 110 B4
Kerfoot St LEIGH WN7 66 F8
Kermishaw Nook TYLD M29 67 K6
Kermoor Av BOL BL1 22 B6
Kerne Gv NTHM/RTH M23 109 K3
Kerrera Dr ORD * M5 86 A3
Kerridge Dr MPL/ROM SK6 101 J8
Kerris Cl WYTH/NTH M22 119 G3
Kerr St BKLY M9 73 G1
Kerry Gv BOLE BL2 3 K2
Kersal Av LHULT M38 52 E8
SWIN M27 70 F4
Kersal Bank BRO M7 71 M4
Kersal Cl PWCH M25 71 K3
Kersal Crag BRO M7 71 M3
Kersal Dr HALE/TIMP WA15 108 F5
Kersal Hall Av BRO M7 71 K4
Kersal Rd PWCH M25 71 K3
Kersal Vale Rd SWIN M27 71 J3
Kersal Wy BRO M7 71 L5
Kerscott Rd NTHM/RTH M23 109 H3
Kersh Av BNG/LEV M19 99 L4
Kershaw Av BOLS/LL BL3 37 K8
PWCH M25 71 J2
SALE M33 109 G2
Kershaw Dr MDTN M24 58 A8
Kershaw Gv DTN/ASHW M34 89 L4
Kershaw La DTN/ASHW M34 89 L5
Kershaw Rd FAIL M35 74 C4
Kershaw St AULW OL7 90 C4
BOLE BL2 22 F7
BOLS/LL BL3 2 B8
BURY BL9 5 H5
DROY M43 89 J3
GLSP SK13 104 F4
HEY OL10 40 E2
ROY/SHW OL2 43 G7
ROY/SHW OL2 43 L5
TYLD M29 67 K3
WGNW/BIL/O WN5 46 E6
WHIT * OL12 10 E2
Kershaw St East ROY/SHW OL2 43 L5
Kershaw Wk WGTN/LGST M12 88 A6
Kershaw Wy NEWLW WA12 78 F7
Kershope Gv ORD M5 86 D4
Kersley St OLDE OL4 59 L6
Kerwin Wk OP/CLY * M11 88 D4
Kerwood Dr ROY/SHW OL2 59 H1
Kesteven Rd BKLY M9 73 G5
Keston Av BKLY M9 73 K1
DROY M43 89 H3
Keston Crs RDSH SK5 100 E6
Keston Rd OLD OL1 59 M3
Kestor St BOLE BL2 3 H3
Kestrel Av DTN/ASHW M34 89 M3
FWTH * BL4 52 C5
LHULT M38 52 D7
OLDE OL4 59 M7
SWIN M27 70 E2
Kestrel Cl MPL/ROM SK6 123 J1
PWCH M25 55 K6
Kestrel Dr AIMK WN4 63 M6
BURY BL9 5 K1
IRL M44 94 D1
Kestrel Rd TRPK M17 85 J4
Kestrel St BOL * BL1 3 G3
Kestrel Wk WGTN/LGST M12 88 D6
Keswick Av AULW OL7 75 J7
CHAD OL9 58 D5
CHD/CHDH SK8 119 K1
DTN/ASHW M34 90 A8
HYDE SK14 90 F8
OLDS OL8 59 K8
URM M41 95 H3
Keswick Cl BRUN/LGST M13 88 A8
IRL M44 94 A8
MDTN M24 57 G2
STLY SK15 76 D8
Keswick Dr BRAM/HZG SK7 120 E7
BURY BL9 39 G5
Keswick Gv SLFD M6 86 C1
Keswick Pl WGNE/HIN WN2 48 D5
Keswick Rd HALE/TIMP WA15 109 G6
HTNM SK4 100 A5
MPL/ROM SK6 123 G4
STRET M32 96 F1
WALK M28 69 J2
Keswick St BOL BL1 36 C2
ROCH OL11 41 L2
Kettering Rd BNG/LEV M19 99 L2
Kettleshulme Wy
POY/DIS SK12 129 L2
Ketton Cl OP/CLY M11 89 H5
Kevin Av ROY/SHW OL2 59 H2
Kevin St BNG/LEV M19 99 L4
Kew Av HYDE SK14 102 B3
Kew Dr CHD/CHDH SK8 120 A2
URM M41 84 D8
Kew Gdns NEWH/MOS M40 73 K3
Kew Rd FAIL M35 74 D4
OLDE OL4 59 L6
ROCH OL11 42 D1
Key Ct DTN/ASHW M34 101 K4
Keymer St OP/CLY M11 88 B2
Keynsham Rd OP/CLY M11 88 E1
Keystone Cl SLFD M6 71 H8
Key West Cl OP/CLY M11 88 C3
Keyworth Wk NEWH/MOS M40 73 H8
Khartoum St OLDTF/WHR M16 87 G8
OP/CLY M11 89 G2
Kibbles Brow EDGW/EG BL7 22 E4
Kibboth Crew RAMS BL0 17 B5
Kibworth Cl WHTF M45 55 G4
Kidderminster Wy CHAD OL9 58 C3
Kidd Rd GLSP SK13 105 H6
Kid St MDTN * M24 57 J3
Kiel Cl ECC M30 85 H4
Kielder Cl AIMK WN4 63 J5
Kielder Hl MDTN M24 41 J8
Kilbride Av BOLE BL2 37 J6
Kilbuck La RNFD/HAY WA11 78 D4
Kilburn Av AIMK WN4 64 A8
BKLY M9 57 G7
Kilburn Cl CHD/CHDH SK8 119 K5
Kilburn Clqse LEIGH WN7 66 A3
Kilburn Dr WGNNW/ST WN6 30 D5
Kilburn Gv WGNS/IIMK WN3 63 G1
Kilburn Rd EDGY/DAV SK3 12 D8
RAD M26 38 A8
Kilburn St OLD OL1 59 M3
Kildale Cl BOLS/LL BL3 35 H8
Kildare Crs ROCH OL11 42 D2
Kildare Rd CCHDY M21 98 A4
SWIN M27 70 B5
Kildare St FWTH BL4 52 F5
WGNE/HIN WN2 48 F7
WGNW/BIL/O WN5 47 J6
Kildonan Dr BOLS/LL BL3 35 J6
Killer St RAMS * BL0 17 C6
Killington Cl WGNS/IIMK WN3 63 L2
Killingworth Ms HOR/BR * BL6 34 A3
Killon St BURY BL9 5 H7
Kilmaine Dr BOLS/LL BL3 35 H7
Kilmington Dr CHH M8 72 C6
Kilmory Dr BOLE BL2 37 J6
Kilmory Fold GLSP SK13 105 H1
Kiln Bank La WHIT OL12 18 D2
Kilnbrook Cl OLDE OL4 60 E8
Kiln Brow EDGW/EG BL7 22 F4
Kiln Cft MPL/ROM SK6 113 J3
Kiln Croft La WILM/AE SK9 120 A8
Kilner Cl BURY BL9 39 L8
Kilnerdeyne Ter MILN OL16 10 D6
Kilner Wk NEWH/MOS M40 72 F8
Kiln Fld EDGW/EG BL7 22 C4
Kiln Hill Cl OLD OL1 58 C2
Kiln Hill La OLD OL1 58 C2
Kilnhurst Wk BOL * BL1 2 B3
Kiln La GLSP SK13 93 K7
MILN OL16 29 J6
Kilnside Dr BKLY M9 73 G5
Kiln St RAMS BL0 17 B7
Kiln Wk WHIT OL12 28 B2
Kilnwick Cl GTN M18 99 L1
The Kilphin HOR/BR BL6 34 E4
Kilrush Av ECC M30 85 G4
Kilsby Cl FWTH BL4 52 E2
HOR/BR BL6 34 F6
Kilsby Wk NEWH/MOS M40 73 G8
Kilshaw St WGNW/BIL/O WN5 46 F7
Kilton Wk NEWH/MOS * M40 72 F8
Kilvert Dr SALE M33 96 C7
Kilvert St TRPK M17 86 D7
Kilworth Av SALE M33 108 C1
Kilworth Dr HOR/BR BL6 35 G6
Kilworth St ROCH OL11 10 B9
Kimberley Av MPL/ROM SK6 113 L2
Kimberley Pl AIMK WN4 78 F1
Kimberley Rd BOL BL1 22 B7
Kimberley St BRO * M7 72 B5
EDGY/DAV SK3 13 H9
OLDS OL8 74 F1
Kimberley Wk HULME M15 6 B9
Kimberly St WGNNW/ST WN6 14 B1
Kimble Cl TOT/BURYW BL8 24 C2
Kimbolton Cl WGTN/LGST M12 88 D5
Kinburn Rd BNG/LEV M19 111 G2
Kincardine Rd BRUN/LGST M13 7 J9
Kincraig Cl BOLS/LL BL3 35 H8
OP/CLY M11 88 F3
Kinder Av AUL OL6 76 D6
OLDE OL4 60 A7
Kinder Cl GLSP SK13 104 D4
Kinder Dr MPL/ROM SK6 114 D6
Kinder Fold STLY SK15 92 A6
Kinder Gv AIMK WN4 63 J6
MPL/ROM SK6 114 B2
Kinders Crs UPML OL3 61 L7
Kinders Fold LIT OL15 20 A5
Kinders La UPML OL3 61 M6
Kinders Ms UPML * OL3 61 L7
Kinder St EDGY/DAV SK3 13 G8
STLY SK15 91 K2
Kinderton Av DID/WITH M20 98 E5
Kinder Wy MDTN M24 57 J2
Kineton Wk BRUN/LGST M13 87 M6
King Albert St ROY/SHW OL2 43 L5
King Charles Ct GLSP SK13 105 G5
King Edward Av GLSP SK13 105 G3
King Edward Rd HYDE SK14 102 B5
King Edward St BNG/LEV M19 99 L3
ECC M30 84 F2
ORD M5 86 E4
Kingfisher Av DTN/ASHW M34 89 M3
Kingfisher Cl WGTN/LGST M12 88 B7
Kingfisher Ct AIMK WN4 63 L6
Kingfisher Dr BURY BL9 25 L8
FWTH BL4 52 C5
Kingfisher Rd OFTN SK2 113 J8
Kingfisher Wy GLSP SK13 104 C4
King George Cl AIMK WN4 78 E1
King George Rd HYDE SK14 102 B3
RNFD/HAY WA11 78 D5
Kingham Dr ANC M4 7 M2
Kingholm Gdns BOL * BL1 36 A3
King La OLD OL1 44 B8
Kingmoor Av RAD M26 38 E8
King's Acre ALT WA14 116 C3
Kings Av CHD/CHDH SK8 110 D8
CHH M8 72 D4
GOL/RIS/CU WA3 80 C5
WHTF M45 55 H2
Kingsbridge Av BOLE BL2 38 A3
HYDE SK14 102 F2
Kingsbridge Cl MPL/ROM SK6 114 B5
Kingsbridge Dr DUK SK16 90 E5
Kingsbridge Rd BKLY M9 72 F5
OLDS * OL8 59 L7
Kingsbrook Rd
OLDTF/WHR M16 98 B4
Kingsbury Av BOL BL1 35 J3
Kingsbury Dr WILM/AE SK9 127 H4
Kingsbury Rd OP/CLY M11 88 F2
Kingscliffe St BKLY M9 73 H5
King's Cl BRAM/HZG SK7 121 H2
GTN M18 89 J6
PWCH M25 55 M7
WILM/AE SK9 126 E6
Kings Ct RDSH SK5 13 J1
Kingscourt Av BOL BL1 35 M2
Kings Crs OLDTF/WHR M16 97 L1
TYLD M29 67 H4
Kingscroft Ct WGN WN1 15 J5
Kingsdale Rd DTN/ASHW M34 89 K8
Kingsdown Crs WGN WN1 31 M8
Kingsdown Dr BOL BL1 2 E1
Kingsdown Gdns BOL * BL1 2 E1
Kingsdown Rd WGNE/HIN WN2 64 E5
WYTH/NTH M22 118 E3
Kings Dr CHD/CHDH SK8 120 C1
HTNM SK4 111 K1
MDTN M24 57 G4
MPL/ROM SK6 114 B5
Kingsfield Dr DID/WITH M20 110 F2
Kingsfield Wy TYLD M29 67 L4
Kingsfold Av NEWH/MOS * M40 72 F8
Kingsford St ORD M5 86 A2
King's Gdns LEIGH WN7 66 F7
Kingsgate BOL BL1 2 D4
Kingsgate Rd WYTH/NTH M22 118 E3
Kings Gv STRET M32 97 J1
WHIT OL12 19 K8
Kingsheath Av OP/CLY M11 88 E1
Kingshill Ct WGNNW/ST WN6 31 J5
Kingshill Rd CCHDY M21 97 K4
Kingsholme Rd
WYTH/NTH M22 118 E2
Kingsland Cl NEWH/MOS M40 88 A1
Kingsland Rd EDGY/DAV SK3 111 K5
FWTH BL4 52 C3
ROCH OL11 41 L1
Kings La STRET M32 97 J1
Kingslea Rd DID/WITH M20 98 F7
Kingsleigh Rd HTNM SK4 99 J8
Kingsley Av BKLY M9 73 J5
BRO M7 71 K5
HTNM SK4 100 B8
STRET M32 97 J1
URM * M41 95 L2
WGNS/IIMK WN3 63 J1
WHTF M45 55 K5
WILM/AE SK9 127 G2
Kingsley Cl AUL OL6 76 D7
DTN/ASHW M34 101 G3
Kingsley Dr CHD/CHDH SK8 120 C1
OLDE OL4 60 B5
Kingsley Gv DTN/ASHW M34 89 M4
Kingsley Rd HALE/TIMP WA15 108 E5
MDTN M24 57 L2
OLDE OL4 59 M6
SWIN M27 70 A3
WALK M28 52 F8
WGNE/HIN * WN2 49 J7
WYTH/NTH M22 110 A4
Kingsley St BOL BL1 36 A2
LEIGH WN7 65 M5
TOT/BURYW BL8 38 E2
King's Lynn Cl DID/WITH M20 110 E1
Kingsmead Ms BKLY M9 56 F7
Kingsmede WGN WN1 48 A1

166 Kin - Lan

Kingsmere Av BNG/LEV M19 99 J3
Kingsmill Av BNG/LEV M19 99 L4
Kingsmoor Flds GLSP SK13 105 G1
Kingsmoor Rd GLSP SK13 105 G2
Kingsnorth Rd URM M41 95 G1
Kingsoak Cl WGN WN1 15 H3
King's Rd AIMK WN4 63 K7
AUL OL6 76 A7
BRAM/HZG SK7 122 A1
CCHDY M21 98 A4
CHAD OL9 74 B1
CHD/CHDH SK8 120 C1
DTN/ASHW M34 89 K7
GOL/RIS/CU WA3 79 K5
IRL M44 94 B6
MILN OL16 11 J9
MPL/ROM SK6 113 K1
OLDS OL8 9 K9
PWCH M25 71 M2
ROY/SHW OL2 43 K6
SALE M33 96 C8
STRET M32 97 H2
WILM/AE SK9 126 C4
Kings Ter STRET M32 97 J1
Kingston Av BOLE BL2 3 L1
CHAD OL9 58 D8
DID/WITH M20 110 E3
OLD * OL1 59 L3
Kingston Cl BRO M7 72 A4
HYDE SK14 103 H2
ROY/SHW OL2 43 L5
SALE M33 108 A2
TOT/BURYW BL8 38 E4
WGNS/IIMK WN3 63 L1
Kingston Dr ROY/SHW OL2 42 F6
SALE M33 97 G7
URM M41 95 L4
Kingston Gdns HYDE SK14 101 L1
Kingston Gv BKLY M9 57 J8
Kingston Hl CHD/CHDH SK8 111 G8
Kingston Ml EDGY/DAV * SK3 12 F5
Kingston Pl CHD/CHDH SK8 120 A2
Kingston Rd DID/WITH M20 110 E3
FAIL M35 74 E5
RAD M26 38 F6
WILM/AE SK9 119 L8
Kingston St EDGY/DAV SK3 12 F5
King St BOL BL1 2 D4
BOLE BL2 23 G7
BRO M7 72 B5
CHAD OL9 9 H6
CMANW M2 6 F4
CSLFD M3 6 D2
DROY M43 89 K4
DTN/ASHW M34 90 C6
DTN/ASHW M34 101 J1
DUK SK16 90 E4
ECC M30 85 J3
EDGW/EG BL7 22 C4
FAIL M35 74 A6
FWTH BL4 53 G4
GLSP SK13 104 F4
HEY OL10 41 G3
HOR/BR BL6 21 A8
HYDE SK14 93 G7
HYDE SK14 102 A1
HYDE SK14 103 K4
LEIGH WN7 66 C8
MDTN M24 57 K3
MILN OL16 10 E4
MOSL OL5 77 G3
RAD M26 54 E2
RAMS BL0 17 C6
SLFD M6 71 G7
STLY SK15 91 K2
UPML OL3 45 J8
WGN WN1 14 F4
WGNE/HIN WN2 48 D5
WGNE/HIN WN2 49 G6
WHIT OL12 18 E1
WHTN BL5 50 C4
King St East ROCH OL11 10 E8
STKP SK1 13 J2
King Street Rbt OLDS OL8 9 H8
King St South ROCH OL11 10 D8
King St West CSLFD M3 6 E4
HTNM SK4 12 F4
WGN WN1 14 F4
Kings Vw HTNM * SK4 12 D4
Kingsway ALT WA14 108 A7
BNG/LEV M19 99 J3
BRAM/HZG SK7 121 H2
CHD/CHDH SK8 110 F5
CHD/CHDH SK8 110 F8
DID/WITH M20 110 F4
DID/WITH M20 111 G2
DUK SK16 91 H5
FWTH BL4 53 J6
MDTN M24 57 J6
MILN OL16 11 K9
MILN OL16 11 M6
MPL/ROM SK6 113 H1
STKP SK1 13 J3
STRET M32 96 F3
SWIN M27 70 F6
WALK M28 69 G4
WGN WN1 48 A2
WGNE/HIN WN2 15 M6
Kingsway Av BNG/LEV M19 99 J3
Kingsway Cl OLDS OL8 9 G9
Kingsway Crs BNG/LEV M19 99 H7
Kingsway Pk URM M41 85 G8
Kingswear Dr BOL BL1 35 M3
Kingswood Gv RDSH SK5 100 C3
Kingswood Rd ECC M30 69 L8
MDTN M24 57 J1
PWCH M25 55 J7
RUSH/FAL M14 99 H5
Kingthorpe Gdns BOLS/LL * BL3 36 B8
King William St ECC M30 84 D1
ORD M5 86 D4
TYLD M29 67 J3
Kingwood Av BOL BL1 35 J4
Kingwood Crs
WGNW/BIL/O WN5 47 G6
Kinlet Rd WGNS/IIMK WN3 46 F8
Kinley Cl WGTN/LGST M12 88 C6
Kinloch Dr BOL BL1 35 L5
Kinloch St OLDS OL8 59 K8
OP/CLY M11 88 D2
Kinmel Av RDSH SK5 100 F8
Kinnaird Crs STKP SK1 112 E4
Kinnaird Rd DID/WITH M20 98 E7
Kinnerly Gv WALK M28 68 D3
Kinniside Cl WGNS/IIMK WN3 63 K2
Kinross Av AIMK WN4 62 F8
OFTN SK2 121 J1
Kinross Cl RAMS BL0 24 D2
Kinross Dr BOLS/LL BL3 35 J7
Kinross Rd RUSH/FAL M14 99 H1
Kinsey Av NTHM/RTH M23 109 J5
Kinsley Dr WALK M28 68 F2
Kintbury St WGNE/HIN WN2 64 C5
Kintore Av BRAM/HZG SK7 122 B2
Kintyre Av ORD M5 86 A3
Kintyre Cl OP/CLY * M11 88 F3
Kintyre Dr BOLS/LL BL3 35 H7
Kinver Rd NEWH/MOS M40 73 M2
Kipling Av DROY M43 89 K1
DTN/ASHW M34 101 K5
WGNS/IIMK WN3 47 K8
Kipling Cl OFTN SK2 113 H5
Kipling Gv LEIGH WN7 66 C5
Kipling Rd OLD OL1 59 L2
Kipling St BRO M7 72 A6
Kippax St RUSH/FAL M14 98 E1
Kirby Av ATH M46 50 F7
CHAD OL9 74 A1
SWIN M27 70 A7
Kirby Rd LEIGH WN7 66 B7
Kiribati Wy LEIGH WN7 66 B6
Kirkbank St CHAD OL9 8 E4
Kirkbeck LEIGH WN7 81 M1
Kirkburn Vw TOT/BURYW BL8 24 F7
Kirkby Av NEWH/MOS M40 73 L5
SALE M33 108 F2
Kirkby Cl BURY BL9 39 H5
Kirkby Dr SALE M33 109 G2
Kirkby Rd BOL BL1 35 L4
Kirkdale Av NEWH/MOS M40 74 A2
Kirkdale Dr ROY/SHW OL2 42 F7
Kirkebrok Rd BOLS/LL BL3 35 K8
Kirkfell Dr MPL/ROM SK6 123 G4
TYLD M29 67 L5
Kirkfell Wk OLD OL1 9 K1
Kirkgate Cl NEWH/MOS * M40 7 M1
Kirkhall La BOL BL1 35 M4
LEIGH WN7 66 B6
Kirkham Av GOL/RIS/CU * WA3 80 B6
GTN M18 89 G6
Kirkham Cl DTN/ASHW M34 101 J1
Kirkham Rd CHD/CHDH SK8 119 L4
LEIGH WN7 81 G2
Kirkham St BOLE * BL2 3 L1
CHAD OL9 8 F4
LHULT M38 52 D7
ORD M5 86 B3
WGNE/HIN WN2 64 E4
Kirkhaven Sq NEWH/MOS M40 73 H8
Kirkhope Dr BOL BL1 36 A3
Kirkhope Wk BOL BL1 2 B1
Kirklands BOLE BL2 37 G2
SALE M33 108 D2
Kirklee Av CHAD OL9 58 D3
Kirklee Rd ROCH OL11 42 A2
Kirklees St TOT/BURYW BL8 24 D5
WGN WN1 15 L4
Kirkless St WGNE/HIN WN2 48 D1
Kirkless Vls WGNE/HIN * WN2 48 D2
Kirkley St HYDE SK14 102 A3
Kirklinton Dr BKLY M9 73 G6
Kirkman Av ECC M30 84 F4
Kirkman Cl GTN M18 89 G8
Kirkmanshulme La
WGTN/LGST M12 88 D8
Kirkman St BURY BL9 55 J1
Kirkpatrick St WGNE/HIN WN2 65 L1
Kirk Rd BNG/LEV M19 99 L5
Kirkstall WHIT OL12 10 D2
Kirkstall Av HEY OL10 40 F1
LIT OL15 20 B6
Kirkstall Cl POY/DIS SK12 121 M8
Kirkstall Rd MDTN M24 57 J1
URM M41 96 B1
Kirkstall Sq BRUN/LGST M13 87 M6
Kirkstead Cl OP/CLY M11 88 D4
Kirkstead Rd CHD/CHDH SK8 120 E5
Kirkstead Wy GOL/RIS/CU WA3 79 K4
Kirkstile Crs WGNS/IIMK WN3 63 H2
Kirkstile Pl SWIN M27 54 B8
Kirkstone WGNW/BIL/O WN5 46 F5
Kirkstone Av WALK M28 69 J3
Kirkstone Cl OLD OL1 9 K1
Kirkstone Dr MDTN M24 57 H2
ROY/SHW OL2 42 F6
Kirkstone Rd HYDE SK14 90 F7
NEWH/MOS M40 73 M2
Kirk St GTN M18 89 G7
Kirkwall Dr BOLE BL2 3 K8
Kirkway MDTN M24 57 K6
ROCH OL11 42 C2
Kirkwood Dr NEWH/MOS M40 72 F8
Kirtley Av ECC M30 85 G1
Kirtlington Cl ROY/SHW OL2 43 K7
Kitchener St BOLS/LL BL3 52 E1
TOT/BURYW BL8 38 E3
Kitchen St MILN OL16 11 G3
Kite Gv LEIGH WN7 66 E7
Kitepool St ECC * M30 84 D1
Kitter St WHIT OL12 28 E1
Kitt Green Rd
WGNW/BIL/O WN5 46 F4
Kittiwake Cl TYLD M29 67 K5
Kitt's Moss La BRAM/HZG SK7 120 F6
Kitty Wheeldon Gdns
SALE * M33 96 D7
Kiveton Cl WALK M28 68 F2
Kiveton Dr AIMK WN4 78 F2
Kiwi St SLFD M6 86 D2
Knacks La WHIT OL12 18 B7
Knaresborough Cl RDSH SK5 100 B3
Knaresborough Rd
WGNE/HIN WN2 49 H8
Knarr Barn La UPML OL3 61 G1
Knarr La UPML OL3 61 H2
Knight Crs MDTN M24 57 G1
Knightley Wk NEWH/MOS M40 73 G7
Knightsbridge STKP SK1 13 J2
Knightsbridge Cl BRO M7 72 A4
WILM/AE SK9 127 H3
Knightscliffe Crs
WGNNW/ST WN6 30 A6
Knight's Cl PWCH M25 55 L7
Knightshill Crs WGNNW/ST WN6 14 A1
Knight St AULW OL7 90 C2
BOL BL1 2 E2
DID/WITH M20 110 E2
HYDE SK14 102 B3
TOT/BURYW * BL8 38 F2
Knightswood BOLS/LL BL3 51 J1
Knightwake Rd NM/HAY SK22 124 C4
Kniveton Cl WGTN/LGST M12 88 C6
Kniveton Rd WGTN/LGST M12 88 C6
Knivton St HYDE * SK14 102 C1
Knole Av POY/DIS SK12 122 B8
The Knoll MOSL OL5 76 E3
ROY/SHW * OL2 43 M6
Knoll St BRO M7 72 B2
NM/HAY SK22 124 D4
ROCH OL11 41 L1
Knott Fold HYDE SK14 102 A4
Knott Hill La UPML OL3 61 H1
Knott La BOL BL1 35 J2
HYDE SK14 102 A4
Knott Lanes OLDS OL8 75 H4
Knott St ORD M5 86 A3
Knowe Av WYTH/NTH M22 118 F3
Knowl Cl DTN/ASHW M34 100 D2
RAMS BL0 17 C8
Knowldale Wy WGTN/LGST M12 88 B7
Knowle Av AULW OL7 75 K8
Knowle Dr PWCH M25 71 K2
Knowle Pk WILM/AE SK9 127 G1
Knowle Rd MPL/ROM SK6 114 F6
The Knowles OLDS OL8 74 E3
Knowles Av WGNS/IIMK WN3 47 J8
Knowles Edge St BOL BL1 35 M2
Knowles Pl HULME M15 6 F9
WGN WN1 15 L3
Knowles St BOL BL1 3 G1
RAD M26 38 D8
WGNS/IIMK WN3 15 J8
Knowl Hill Dr WHIT OL12 27 H2
Knowl Rd MILN OL16 29 G6
ROY/SHW OL2 43 M6
Knowls La OLDE OL4 60 C7
Knowl St OLDS OL8 74 F2
STLY SK15 91 L2
Knowl Syke St WHIT OL12 19 K5
Knowl Vw LIT OL15 29 J2
TOT/BURYW BL8 24 D6
Knowsley Av ATH M46 50 F8
GOL/RIS/CU WA3 79 L3
OLDE OL4 60 D5
ORD M5 86 E4
URM M41 84 F8
Knowsley Crs STKP SK1 112 E4
Knowsley Dr LEIGH WN7 81 G2
OLDE OL4 60 D5
SWIN M27 70 A6
Knowsley Gra BOL BL1 35 G5
Knowsley Gn OLDE OL4 60 D5
ORD * M5 86 E4
Knowsley Gv HOR/BR BL6 34 A3
Knowsley Rd BOL BL1 35 L2
BOLE BL2 37 M3
BRAM/HZG SK7 122 B4
STKP SK1 112 E4
WGNNW/ST WN6 47 K1
WHTF M45 55 J4
Knowsley St BOL BL1 2 E3
BURY BL9 4 D7
CHH M8 72 D8
LEIGH WN7 66 A7
WHIT OL12 10 D2
Knowsley Ter OLDE * OL4 60 D5
STKP * SK1 112 E4
Knutsford Av HTNM SK4 100 A5
SALE M33 97 H8
Knutsford Rd GTN M18 88 F8
WILM/AE SK9 130 B1
Knutsford St SLFD M6 86 B2
Knutshaw Crs BOLS/LL BL3 51 G2
Knypersley Av OFTN SK2 112 F5
Kranj Wy OLD OL1 9 J4
Krokus Sq CHAD * OL9 58 D5
Kylemore Av BOLS/LL BL3 35 L7
Kyle Rd BRAM/HZG * SK7 122 B3
Kynder St DTN/ASHW M34 101 J1

L

Labrador Quay SALQ M50 86 C5
Labtec St SWIN M27 70 E3
Laburnum Av ATH M46 67 H1
AUL OL6 75 M6
CHAD OL9 8 B1
DTN/ASHW M34 89 M3
ECC M30 84 D4
FAIL M35 74 C6
HYDE SK14 102 A4
LEIGH WN7 66 B4
ROY/SHW OL2 43 L6
STLY SK15 91 J4
SWIN M27 70 B6
TOT/BURYW BL8 24 C5
WGNS/IIMK WN3 15 M7
WHTF * M45 55 J6
Laburnum Cl HALE/TIMP WA15 108 E7
Laburnum Dr WGNNW/ST WN6 31 K8
WHTF M45 55 K3
Laburnum Gv HOR/BR BL6 34 B3
PWCH M25 55 K7
TYLD M29 68 A3
Laburnum La HALE/TIMP WA15 117 G4
MILN OL16 43 K1
Laburnum Pk BOLE BL2 22 E7
Laburnum Rd DTN/ASHW M34 100 C1
FWTH BL4 52 E4
GOL/RIS/CU WA3 80 C4
GTN M18 89 G8
IRL M44 94 A7
MDTN M24 57 M4
OLDS OL8 74 F4
URM M41 84 E8
WALK M28 69 H2
Laburnum St AIMK WN4 78 E2
ATH M46 67 H1
BOL BL1 2 A3
SLFD M6 86 C2
Laburnum Ter ROCH OL11 28 B8
Laburnum Wy EDGY/DAV SK3 12 B6
LIT OL15 20 A7
Lacey Av WILM/AE SK9 126 F4
Lacey Gn WILM/AE SK9 126 F3
Lacey Gv WILM/AE SK9 127 G3
Lackford Dr NEWH/MOS M40 72 F8
Lacrosse Av OLDS OL8 58 F8
Lacy Gv STRET M32 97 G3
Lacy St STKP SK1 13 J6
STRET M32 97 G3
Lacy Wk WGTN/LGST M12 88 A4
Ladbrooke Cl AUL OL6 75 M8
Ladbrooke Rd AUL OL6 75 M7
Ladcastle Rd UPML OL3 61 K3
UPML OL3 61 K6
Ladhill La UPML OL3 61 L7
Ladies La WGNE/HIN WN2 49 G6
Ladybarn Av GOL/RIS/CU WA3 79 J5
Ladybarn Crs BRAM/HZG SK7 121 H6
RUSH/FAL M14 99 G5
Ladybarn La RUSH/FAL M14 99 G4
Ladybarn Rd RUSH/FAL M14 99 G4
Ladybower CHD/CHDH SK8 120 E1
Ladybridge Av WALK M28 68 F4
Lady Bridge La BOL BL1 35 J5
Ladybridge Ri CHD/CHDH SK8 120 E1
Ladybridge Rd CHD/CHDH SK8 120 E1
Ladybrook Av
HALE/TIMP WA15 108 E5
Ladybrook Rd BRAM/HZG SK7 120 E3
Ladyfield St WILM/AE SK9 126 F5
Ladyfield Ter WILM/AE SK9 126 F5
Ladyhill Vw WALK M28 68 F4
Ladyhouse Cl MILN OL16 29 K8
Ladyhouse La MILN OL16 29 J7
Lady La WGNS/IIMK WN3 47 H8
Ladymere Dr WALK M28 68 E4
Ladypit Rd CHF/WBR SK23 125 H8
Lady Rd OLDE OL4 60 B6
Ladys Cl POY/DIS SK12 122 A8
Ladyshore Cl ORD M5 86 C3
Ladyshore Rd BOLS/LL BL3 53 M2
The Ladysmith AUL OL6 76 C7
Ladysmith Av AIMK WN4 78 F1
BURY BL9 25 K7
Ladysmith Dr AUL OL6 76 C7
Ladysmith Rd AUL OL6 76 C7
DID/WITH M20 110 F2
Ladysmith St EDGY/DAV SK3 13 H9
OLDS OL8 74 F1
Ladythorn Av MPL/ROM SK6 114 D7
Ladythorn Ct PWCH M25 71 K2
Ladythorn Crs BRAM/HZG SK7 121 H6
Ladythorne Av PWCH M25 71 K2
Ladythorne Dr PWCH M25 71 K2
Ladythorn Gv BRAM/HZG SK7 121 H6
Ladythorn Rd BRAM/HZG SK7 121 G6
Ladywell Av LHULT M38 52 D8
Ladywell Cl BRAM/HZG SK7 121 J2
Ladywell Gv LHULT M38 52 D7
Lagos Cl RUSH/FAL M14 87 K8
Laindon Rd RUSH/FAL M14 99 H1
Laithwaite Rd
WGNW/BIL/O WN5 47 G5
Lake Bank LIT OL15 29 K1
Lake Dr MDTN M24 57 J5
Lakeland Av AIMK WN4 63 M8
Lakeland Crs BURY BL9 39 H6
Lakeland Dr ROY/SHW * OL2 42 F4
Lakelands Dr BOLS/LL BL3 35 J7
Lakenheath Cl BOL BL1 22 C6
Lakenheath Dr BOL BL1 22 C6
Lake Rd DTN/ASHW M34 90 C8
STLY SK15 76 C8
TRPK M17 85 M5
Lakes Dr WGNW/BIL/O WN5 46 B6
Lakeside BURY BL9 39 J6
CHD/CHDH SK8 119 L1
GLSP SK13 93 K6
Lake Side LEIGH WN7 66 A6
LIT OL15 29 K2
Lakeside Av AULW OL7 75 J8
BOLS/LL BL3 52 D2
WALK M28 53 G7
WGNW/BIL/O WN5 62 B1
Lakeside Cl GTN M18 89 J6
Lakeside Dr POY/DIS SK12 122 A7
Lakeside Gn OFTN SK2 112 F6
Lakeside Wy BURY BL9 4 F6
Lakes Rd DUK SK16 90 F4
MPL/ROM SK6 114 D6
Lakes Ter WGNE/HIN WN2 48 D5
Lake St BOLS/LL * BL3 2 E9
LEIGH WN7 66 D6
OFTN SK2 112 E7
Lakeswood DUK * SK16 90 E4
Lake Vw BKLY M9 73 K2
Lakin St NEWH/MOS M40 73 K5
Laleham Gn BRAM/HZG SK7 120 F1
Lamb Cl WGTN/LGST * M12 88 C7
Lamb Ct CSLFD * M3 6 C3
Lamberhead Rd
WGNW/BIL/O WN5 46 E6
Lambert Dr SALE M33 96 A6
Lamberton Dr NTHM/RTH M23 109 H6
Lambert St AULW OL7 90 C3
Lambeth Av FAIL M35 74 D4
Lambeth Cl HOR/BR BL6 34 A1
Lambeth Gv MPL/ROM SK6 101 K7
Lambeth Rd NEWH/MOS M40 73 M8
RDSH SK5 100 C5
Lambeth St ATH M46 66 E1
Lambeth Ter ROCH OL11 10 A9
Lambgates GLSP SK13 93 K7
Lamb La ALT WA14 116 F7
CSLFD M3 6 C3
Lambley Cl LEIGH WN7 66 A4
Lambourn Cl BOLS/LL * BL3 2 C8
POY/DIS SK12 121 M8
Lambourne Cl WYTH/NTH M22 118 F4
Lambourne Gv MILN OL16 29 J7
Lambourn Rd URM M41 84 A8
Lambs Fold HTNM SK4 100 A7
Lamb St WGN WN1 15 K1
Lambton Rd WALK M28 69 M6
Lambton St BOLS/LL BL3 51 M2
ECC M30 69 L8
WGNW/BIL/O WN5 46 E7
Lamburn Av NEWH/MOS * M40 74 A2
Lamerton Wy WILM/AE SK9 127 J2
Lamorna Cl BRO M7 71 L4
Lamphey Cl BOL BL1 35 G4
Lamplight Wy SWIN M27 71 H5
Lamport Cl CMANE M1 7 J8
Lamport Ct CMANE * M1 7 J8
Lampson St CHH M8 72 B8
Lampton Cl ALT WA14 108 A5
Lamsholme Cl BNG/LEV M19 99 K2
Lanark Av WYTH/NTH M22 110 A4
Lanark Cl BRAM/HZG SK7 122 C2
HEY OL10 40 C3
Lanbury Dr CHH M8 72 C5
Lancashire Ct CHAD OL9 8 C8
Lancashire Hl RDSH SK5 13 H1
Lancashire Rd PART M31 106 B2
Lancashire St NEWH/MOS M40 73 J7
Lancaster Av ATH M46 67 G1
FAIL M35 74 B5
FWTH BL4 52 C4
GOL/RIS/CU WA3 79 M4
HOR/BR BL6 34 A2
MDTN M24 57 M5
RAMS BL0 17 A8
STLY SK15 91 K1
TYLD M29 67 K1
URM M41 96 B1
WHTF M45 55 K5
Lancaster Cl BOL BL1 3 G5
BRAM/HZG SK7 121 M4
MPL/ROM SK6 113 K3
NEWLW WA12 78 C7
Lancaster Dr BOLS/LL BL3 37 L8
BURY BL9 25 J4
PWCH M25 71 M2
Lancaster Rd DID/WITH M20 110 D1
DROY M43 89 J1
DTN/ASHW M34 101 J3
SLFD M6 70 E7
WGNE/HIN WN2 49 H6
WGNW/BIL/O WN5 46 F3
WILM/AE SK9 127 J3
Lancaster St CHAD OL9 58 D8
MOSL * OL5 76 E3
RAD * M26 54 B1
STKP SK1 13 L2
WGNS/IIMK WN3 15 J7
Lancaster Wk BOL * BL1 36 B2
Lancelot Rd WYTH/NTH M22 119 H2
Lancelyn Dr WILM/AE SK9 127 H4
Lance Wood Pl
WGNW/BIL/O WN5 47 G6
Lanchester Dr BOLS/LL BL3 2 A7
Lanchester St NEWH/MOS M40 88 B1
Lancing Av DID/WITH M20 111 G1
Lancing Wk CHAD * OL9 58 D6
Landcross Rd RUSH/FAL M14 98 F3
Landedmans WHTN BL5 50 C5
Lander Gv BKLY M9 73 J1
Land Gate La AIMK WN4 63 K5
Landkey Cl NTHM/RTH M23 109 J2
Land La WILM/AE SK9 127 G6
Landor Cl GOL/RIS/CU WA3 80 B4
Landos Rd NEWH/MOS M40 7 M1
Landrace Dr WALK M28 68 E6
Landsberg Rd FAIL M35 74 E4
Landseer Dr MPL/ROM SK6 114 E5
Landseer St OLDE OL4 9 L8
Lands End Rd MDTN M24 56 E5
Landside LEIGH WN7 81 J2
Land St WGNNW/ST WN6 14 D3
The Lane BOL BL1 35 G5
Lane Brow OLDE OL4 60 E7
Lane Dr OLDE OL4 60 E7
Lane End ECC M30 85 J3
HEY OL10 41 J4
Lane End Rd BNG/LEV M19 99 G8
Lane Ends MPL/ROM SK6 114 A1
Lanegate HYDE SK14 102 A4
Lane Head Av GOL/RIS/CU WA3 80 B4
Lanehead Rd OLDE OL4 76 D1
Lane North BOLS/LL * BL3 35 L8
Laneside Av ROY/SHW OL2 44 A5
Laneside Cl LIT OL15 20 B6
Laneside Dr BRAM/HZG SK7 121 J3
Laneside Rd DID/WITH M20 110 F4
NM/HAY SK22 125 H6
Lanfield Dr CHH M8 72 C5
Langcroft Dr NEWH/MOS M40 73 M7
Langdale Av BNG/LEV M19 99 L4
GOL/RIS/CU WA3 79 M3
MILN OL16 42 F4
OLDS OL8 59 G8
WGN WN1 47 L1
WGNE/HIN WN2 48 E4
Langdale Cl CHD/CHDH SK8 119 L1
DTN/ASHW M34 101 H3
HALE/TIMP WA15 108 B7
MPL/ROM SK6 123 G4
Langdale Crs WGNE/HIN WN2 64 E4
WGNW/BIL/O WN5 46 E4
Langdale Dr BURY BL9 55 K1
MDTN M24 57 H1
WALK M28 69 J3
Langdale Gv WGNE/HIN WN2 64 E1
Langdale Rd BRAM/HZG SK7 120 E7
HTNM SK4 99 M6
MPL/ROM SK6 101 L7
PART M31 106 B1
RUSH/FAL M14 88 A8
SALE M33 108 B3
STRET * M32 96 F1
WGNE/HIN WN2 49 H7
WGNW/BIL/O WN5 46 E5
Langdale St BOLS/LL BL3 52 B1
FWTH BL4 52 F5
LEIGH WN7 66 B7
Langden Cl GOL/RIS/CU WA3 81 G8
ROY/SHW OL2 43 K4
Langdon Cl BOL BL1 2 B2
Langfield GOL/RIS/CU WA3 80 B5
Langfield Av OLDTF/WHR M16 98 A1
Langfield Crs DROY * M43 89 M2
Langford Dr IRL M44 94 D3
LEIGH WN7 81 H2
Langford Gdns BOLS/LL BL3 36 B8
Langford Rd DID/WITH M20 98 D6
HTNM SK4 99 M8
Langford St DTN/ASHW * M34 101 J1
Langham Cl BOL BL1 22 D6
Langham Ct STRET M32 85 K8
Langham Gv HALE/TIMP WA15 108 E4
Langham Rd ALT WA14 116 E2
HTNM SK4 12 B4
OLDS OL8 59 H8
SLFD M6 86 C2
WGNNW/ST WN6 31 G3
Langham St AULW OL7 75 K7
Langholm Cl WGNS/IIMK WN3 63 G2
Langholm Dr BOLE BL2 37 J6
Langholme Cl HULME * M15 6 B9
Langholme Pl ECC M30 84 E2
Langholme Wy HEY OL10 40 C3
Langholm Rd AIMK WN4 62 F8
Langland Cl RDSH SK5 100 A2
Langland Dr ECC M30 84 F5
Langley Av BRAM/HZG SK7 121 K3
MDTN M24 41 H8
OLDE OL4 60 E7
PWCH M25 55 L7
Langley Cl GOL/RIS/CU WA3 79 M3
URM M41 96 B2
WGNNW/ST WN6 31 H2
Langley Ct GLSP SK13 93 K7
Langley Dr GLSP SK13 105 J4
WALK M28 68 B6
WILM/AE SK9 127 J1
Langley Hall Rd PWCH M25 55 L6
Langley La MDTN M24 40 F8
Langley Rd PWCH M25 55 K7
RUSH/FAL M14 98 F3
SALE M33 96 B8
SWIN M27 71 J4
Langley Rd South SLFD M6 71 J7
Langley St WGNW/BIL/O WN5 47 G6
Langness St OP/CLY M11 88 F3
Lango St OLDTF/WHR * M16 86 F7
Langport Av WGTN/LGST M12 88 B7
Langset Av WGNE/HIN WN2 49 G6
Langsett Av SLFD M6 85 M1
Langshaw Rd BOLS/LL BL3 35 M7
Langshaw St ORD M5 86 C3
Langshaw Wk BOLS/LL * BL3 35 M7
Langside Av BKLY M9 57 H8
Langside Dr BOLS/LL BL3 35 H8
Langstone Cl HOR/BR BL6 33 L1
Langston Gn BRAM/HZG SK7 121 J3
Langston St CSLFD * M3 87 J1

Langthorne St BNG/LEV M19 ....99 L4
Langthorne Wk BOLS/LL BL3 ....2 A7
Langton Av WGNW/ST WN6 ....31 H3
Langton CI FAIL M35 ....74 E4
  NEWLW WA12 ....78 D8
Langton PI WGNNW/ST WN6 ....31 H3
Langton St HEY OL10 ....40 F1
  MDTN M24 ....57 K4
  SLFD M6 ....86 B2
Langton Ter ROCH OL11 ....28 B8
Langtree CI WALK M28 ....68 E4
Langtree La WGNNW/ST WN6 ....31 G1
Langworthy Av LHULT M38 ....52 E8
Langworthy Rd
  NEWH/MOS M40 ....73 K5
  SLFD M6 ....86 C1
Lanhill Dr CHH M8 ....72 F6
Lankro Wy ECC M30 ....85 J3
Lansbury St WGNW/BIL/O WN5 ....46 D6
Lansdale Gdns BNG/LEV M19 ....99 H7
Lansdale St ECC M30 ....84 D4
Lansdown CI BRAM/HZG SK7 ....120 C5
  MPL/ROM SK6 ....114 A2
Lansdowne CI BOLE * BL2 ....36 E3
  RAMS BL0 ....17 B7
Lansdowne Ct CHAD OL9 ....8 A6
Lansdowne Dr WALK M28 ....68 F4
Lansdowne Rd ALT WA14 ....108 A6
  ATH M46 ....51 J7
  BOLE BL2 ....36 E2
  CHAD OL9 ....8 C6
  CHH M8 ....72 D4
  ECC M30 ....85 G1
  SALE M33 ....96 D6
  URM M41 ....95 H3
Lansdowne Rd North URM M41 .....95 H3
Lansdowne St ROCH OL11 ....27M5
Lanstead Dr NEWH/MOS M40 ....88 B2
Lantern Pike Vw NM/HAY SK22 ...125 J2
Lantern Vw NM/HAY SK22 ....124 D3
Lapwing CI GOL/RIS/CU WA3 ....80 A4
  ROCH OL11 ....27 H5
  STLY SK15 ....76 D8
Lapwing La DID/WITH M20 ....98 D7
  ROCH OL11 ....100 F6
Larch Av WD CHD/CHDH SK8 .....120 C3
  RAD M26 ....54 C3
  STRET M32 ....97 G3
  SWIN M27 ....69M6
  WGNW/BIL/O WN5 ....47 G6
Larch CI FAIL M35 ....74 C6
  GOL/RIS/CU WA3 ....80 C6
  MPL/ROM SK6 ....114 B7
  NTHM/RTH M23 ....108 F4
  POY/DIS SK12 ....129 K1
  WGNW/BIL/O WN5 ....46 C3
The Larches MOSL OL5 ....77 G3
Larch Gv ATH M46 ....50 F8
  CHAD OL9 ....8 B2
  SWIN M27 ....69 L2
Larch Rd DTN/ASHW M34 ....101 K1
  ECC M30 ....69 K8
  LEIGH WN7 ....66 B4
  PART M31 ....106 B1
  RNFD/HAY * WA11 ....78 B5
Larch St BURY BL9 ....5 L4
  OLDS OL8 ....8 E7
Larchview Rd MDTN M24 ....57M4
Larch Wy GLSP SK13 ....105 J4
Larchway BRAM/HZG SK7 ....120 E5
  MILN OL16 ....29 G5
  MPL/ROM SK6 ....123 H5
Larchwood CHAD OL9 ....58 B5
Larchwood Av BKLY M9 ....73 J5
Larchwood CI SALE M33 ....95MB
Larchwood Dr WGN WN1 ....31 L8
  WILM/AE SK9 ....127 J4
Larchwood St BOL BL1 ....36 C2
Larkfield Av LHULT M38 ....52 E8
  WGN WN1 ....31 L8
Larkfield CI ALUW OL7 ....75 L5
  TOT/BURYW BL8 ....24 B2
Larkfield Gv BOLE * BL2 ....3 K2
Lark Hi FWTH BL4 ....53 C5
  STLY SK15 ....76 D8
Larkhill Av WGNW/ST WN6 ....31 J4
Larkhill CI HALE/TIMP WA15 ....108 E6
Lark Hill La UPML OL3 ....45 K8
Larkhill Pl WHIT OL12 ....28 B3
Larkhill Rd CHD/CHDH SK8 ....111M7
  UPML OL3 ....61 J2
Larkhill Vw EDGY/DAV SK3 ....111M7
Larkhill Wk CHH M8 ....72 E6
Larkside Av WALK M28 ....69 H1
Larkspur CI LEIGH WN7 ....81 J1
Larks Ri DROY M43 ....90 A1
Lark St BOL BL1 ....2 E3
  FWTH * BL4 ....53 C5
  OLD * OL1 ....60 A1
Larkswood Dr OFTN SK2 ....113 J7
Larkwood CI MOSL OL5 ....77 H5
Larmuth Av CCHDY M21 ....97M6
Larne Av EDGY/DAV SK3 ....12 A8
  STRET M32 ....96 F2
Larne St OP/CLY M11 ....88 D4
Larwood Av HTNM SK4 ....12 A4
Lascar Av ORD M5 ....86 D4
Lashbrook CI NEWH/MOS M40 ......88 D4
Lassell Fold HYDE SK14 ....91 L6
Lassell St OP/CLY * M11 ....89 J5
Lastingham St NEWH/MOS M40 ...73M6
Latchford St AULW OL7 ....75 K8
Latchmere Rd RUSH/FAL M14 ....98 F4
Latham Av NEWLW WA12 ....78 C8
Latham CI MPL/ROM SK6 ....101 J7
Latham La WGNW/BIL/O WN5 ......46 F4
Latham St BOL BL1 ....37 H6
  HOR/BR BL6 ....32 F1
  OP/CLY M11 ....89 J5
Lathbury Rd BKLY M9 ....73 G6
Lathom Gv SALE M33 ....109 H1
Lathom Hall Av OLD * OL4 ....60 D5
Lathom Rd DID/WITH M20 ....99 G5
  IRL M44 ....94 C4
Lathom St BURY BL9 ....5 G1
Latimer CI WGNW/BIL/O * WN5 ....46 C5
Latimer St OLDE OL4 ....9M7
Latin St MILN OL16 ....10 C6
Latrigg Crs MDTN M24 ....56 F2
Latrobe St DROY M43 ....89 K4
Lauderdale Crs BRUN/LGST M13 ..87M6
Launceston CI BRAM/HZG SK7 ....121 L5
  OLDS OL8 ....59MB
Launceston Rd RAD M26 ....38 A7
  WGNE/HIN WN2 ....65 M1
Laundry St SLFD M6 ....71 J8
Laureate Wy DTN/ASHW M34 .....101 K5

Laurel Av CHAD OL9 ....58 A4
  CHD/CHDH SK8 ....111 G7
  RUSH/FAL M14 ....98 D2
  STLY SK15 ....91 L4
Laurel Bank HYDE SK14 ....101M4
Laurel Bank Gdns BKLY M9 ....57 G8
Laurel Ct BOL BL1 ....2 E2
  MILN OL16 ....11 J6
Laurel Crs WGNE/HIN WN2 ....65 K1
Laurel Dr HALE/TIMP WA15 ....108 E8
  LHULT M38 ....52 D8
Laurel End La HTNM SK4 ....11 K1
Laurel La DTN/ASHW M34 ....101 K2
Laurel Gv AIMK WN4 ....63 L8
  GOL/RIS/CU WA3 ....80 A4
  LEIGH WN7 ....66 B4
  ORD * M5 ....85M2
Laurel Rd HTNM SK4 ....99 L8
The Laurels MOSL OL5 ....77 G3
Laurel St BOL BL1 ....35M5
  BURY BL9 ....5 K4
  HTNM SK4 ....13 C3
  MDTN M24 ....58 A4
  TOT/BURYW BL8 ....24 C6
Laurel Wk PART M31 ....106 B2
Laurence CI WGTN/LGST M12 ......88 D6
Lauria Ter BOLE BL2 ....38 A3
Laurie PI WHIT * OL12 ....28 C3
Lausanne Rd BRAM/HZG SK7 .....121 G1
  DID/WITH M20 ....98 E5
Lavender CI NTHM/RTH M23 ....109 H3
  SALE M33 ....95M7
Lavender Rd FWTH BL4 ....52 D3
  OLDE OL4 ....60 B8
  WCNNW/ST WN6 ....47 J1
Lavenders Brow STKP SK1 ....13 K4
Lavender St RAD M26 ....54 A1
Lavenham Av OP/CLY M11 ....89 G3
Lavenham CI BRAM/HZG SK7 ......122 A4
  BURY BL9 ....55 J1
Laverton CI HEY OL10 ....40 A3
Lavington Av CHD/CHDH SK8 .....111 H6
Lavington Gv GTN M18 ....89 G8
Lavinia St ECC M30 ....84 E2
Lavister Av BNG/LEV M19 ....111 G1
Lawefield Crs SWIN M27 ....54 A7
Lawers Av CHAD OL9 ....58 D4
Lawflat WHIT OL12 ....19 K7
Lawler Av ORD M5 ....86 E6
Lawnbank CI MDTN M24 ....57 H3
Lawn CI OLDS OL8 ....75M1
Lawn Dr HALE/TIMP WA15 ....108 B6
  SWIN M27 ....70 B5
Lawnfold GLSP SK13 ....93 H8
Lawngreen Av CCHDY M21 ....97 K5
The Lawns ALT WA14 ....116 E1
Lawnside Ms DID/WITH M20 ....98 D7
Lawn St BOL BL1 ....2 A1
Lawnswood ROCH OL11 ....27M8
Lawnswood Dr SWIN M27 ....70 D6
  TYLD M29 ....68 A3
Lawnswood Park Rd SWIN M27 .....70 D6
Lawrence CI WHIT OL12 ....27 K3
Lawrence Ct WGNE/HIN WN2 ....64 E3
Lawrence PI POY/DIS SK12 ....129 H2
Lawrence Rd ALT WA14 ....107M6
  BRAM/HZG SK7 ....122 A1
  URM M41 ....95 H1
Lawrence St BURY BL9 ....39 J8
  STKP SK1 ....13 H5
Lawrie Av RAMS BL0 ....17 B7
Lawson Av CHD/CHDH SK8 ....110 E7
  LEIGH WN7 ....66 B3
Lawson CI MDTN M24 ....41 K8
  WALK M28 ....68 A5
Lawson Gv SALE M33 ....96 D6
Lawson Rd BOL BL1 ....35M2
Lawson St BKLY M9 ....72 F2
  BOL BL1 ....22 B8
Law St ROCH OL11 ....27M7
Lawton Av BRAM/HZG SK7 ....121 G4
Lawton CI MPL/ROM SK6 ....113 J3
Lawton Moor Rd
  NTHM/RTH M23 ....109 K3
Lawton Rd HTNM SK4 ....99M8
Lawton Sq UPML * OL3 ....45 J8
Lawton St DROY M43 ....89 L2
  OP/CLY M11 ....89 G5
  STLY SK15 ....91 L3
  UPML * OL3 ....45 H8
  WHIT OL12 ....11 G1
Laxey Av ATH M46 ....67 H2
Laxey Crs LEIGH WN7 ....65M5
Laxey St NEWH/MOS * M40 ....73 L5
Laxfield Dr URM M41 ....84 A8
Laxford Gv BOLS/LL BL3 ....35 H6
Layard St AUL OL6 ....90 D1
Laycock Av BOLE BL2 ....36 E1
  STLY SK15 ....77 H8
Laycock Crs FAIL M35 ....74 C6
Laycock Dr DUK SK16 ....91 K5
Laycock Gv FAIL M35 ....74 C5
Layfield CI TOT/BURYW BL8 ....24 A4
Laystall St CMANE M1 ....7 J5
Laythe Barn CI MILN OL16 ....29 H6
Layton Av HYDE SK14 ....101 L1
Layton CI STKP SK1 ....13 L6
  WGNW/BIL/O WN5 ....47 G7
Layton Dr FWTH BL4 ....53 J6
  MPL/ROM SK6 ....113M1
Layton St NEWH/MOS M40 ....88 A2
Lazenby Crs AIMK WN4 ....78 C1
Lazonby Av WGNE/HIN WN2 ....49 J1
Leabank St BNG/LEV M19 ....99 K3
Leabrook Dr NEWH/MOS M40 ......74 B4
Leaburn Dr BNG/LEV M19 ....99 H8
Leach CI MILN OL16 ....28 F2
Leaches Rd RAMS BL0 ....17 D4
Leach St BOLS/LL BL3 ....2 C7
  FWTH BL4 ....53 H3
  GTN M18 ....88 E7
  MILN OL16 ....11 J6
  MILN OL16 ....29 J7
  PWCH M25 ....55 J8
  ROY/SHW OL2 ....43M6
Leach Wk OLDE OL4 ....60 B4
Lea Ct FAIL M35 ....74 B5
Leacroft AIMK WN4 ....63 H6
Leacroft CI BOLE BL2 ....37 C7
Leacroft Rd CCHDY M21 ....98 A7
Leadale CI WCNNW/ST WN6 ....31 G3
Leadale Ri OLDE * OL4 ....60 D6
Leader St WGN WN1 ....15 L4
  WGNW/BIL/O WN5 ....46 F6
Leader Williams Rd IRL M44 ....94 C3

Lea Dr BKLY M9 ....73 J1
Leafield CI RAD M26 ....54 B1
Leafield Av DID/WITH M20 ....99 G8
Leafield CI RAD M26 ....54 B1
Leafield Dr CHD/CHDH SK8 ....120 B6
  WALK M28 ....68 D6
Leaford Av DTN/ASHW M34 ....90 A8
Leaford CI DTN/ASHW M34 ....90 A8
Leaf St BOLS/LL BL3 ....3 L8
  HULME M15 ....87 J6
  RDSH SK5 ....100 B5
Leagate URM M41 ....96 B3
Lea Gate CI BOLE BL2 ....23 C7
  WGNS/IIMK * WN3 ....63 H1
League St MILN OL16 ....11 H8
Leaholme CI NEWH/MOS M40 ....74 A7
Leah St LIT * OL15 ....20 C7
Leak St OLDTF/WHR M16 ....86 F6
Leal Holme Av WGNE/HIN WN2 ....48 D2
Leamington Av ECC M30 ....84 E1
  DID/WITH M20 ....98 C8
Leamington Rd ECC M30 ....84 E1
  RDSH SK5 ....100 B5
  URM M41 ....95 L1
Leamington St OLDE OL4 ....59M4
  OP/CLY M11 ....89 G5
  WHIT OL12 ....10 D2
Lea Mount Dr BURY BL9 ....26 A8
Leam St AUL OL6 ....76 A8
Leander CI BKLY M9 ....73 H2
Leander Dr ROCH OL11 ....42 A3
Lea Rd CHD/CHDH SK8 ....119 K3
  HTNM SK4 ....99 L8
  NM/HAY SK22 ....125 L1
The Leas HALE/TIMP WA15 ....117 K1
Leaside Av OLD OL1 ....58 D2
Leaside CI WHIT OL12 ....28 A2
Leaside Dr DID/WITH M20 ....99 G7
Leaside Gv WALK M28 ....69 H1
Leaside Wy WILM/AE SK9 ....127 C6
Lea St NM/HAY SK22 ....124 C4
  WGNS/IIMK WN3 ....14 C5
Lea Thorn BOLE BL2 ....23 C8
Leaton Av NTHM/RTH M23 ....109 K6
Leavale CI LHULT M38 ....52 E8
Lea Vw ROY/SHW OL2 ....58 F1
  WGN WN1 ....15M2
Leaway WGNE/HIN WN2 ....15M5
  WHIT OL12 ....19 K6
Lecester Rd CHH M8 ....72 E6
Leckenby Dr WALK M28 ....68 D6
Leconfield Dr BKLY M9 ....73 H1
Leconfield Rd ECC M30 ....69 J8
Lecturers CI BOLS/LL BL3 ....2 E8
Ledbrooke CI ORD M5 ....86 E5
Ledburn CI HULME M15 ....87 G6
Ledbury Av URM M41 ....95M1
Ledbury CI MDTN M24 ....57 K6
Ledbury St LEIGH WN7 ....66 C6
Ledge Ley CHD/CHDH SK8 ....120 A4
Ledmore Gv AIMK WN4 ....78 A1
Ledsham Av BKLY M9 ....56 D7
Ledson Rd NTHM/RTH M23 ....109 J7
Ledward La ALT WA14 ....116 D2
Lee Av ALT WA14 ....107M5
  BOLS/LL BL3 ....52 A1
Lee Bank WHTN BL5 ....50 D4
Leech Av AUL OL6 ....76 A7
Leech Brook CI DTN/ASHW M34 ...90 B7
Leech St HYDE SK14 ....102 C2
  STLY SK15 ....91 K3
Lee CI IRL M44 ....94 C3
Lee Ct WYTH/NTH * M22 ....110 B4
Lee Crs STRET M32 ....97 H2
Lee Dale CI DTN/ASHW M34 ....101 K2
Leeds CI BURY BL9 ....5 L1
Leeds St WGNS/IIMK WN3 ....14 D5
Leefields CI UPML OL3 ....61 L4
Lee Fold TYLD M29 ....67M4
Leegate CI HTNM SK4 ....99 J8
Leegate Dr BKLY M9 ....57 J8
Leegate Gdns HTNM SK4 ....99 J8
Leegate Rd HTNM SK4 ....99 K8
Leegrange Rd BKLY M9 ....73 H5
Lee Gv FWTH BL4 ....52 C4
Lee Head GLSP SK13 ....103M7
Leek St RAD M26 ....54 B1
Lee La EDGW/EG BL7 ....16 B6
  HOR/BR BL6 ....21 A8
  WGNE/HIN WN2 ....64 E4
Leemans Hill St
  TOT/BURYW BL8 ....24 D7
Lee Mt GLSP SK13 ....104 F5
Lees Av DTN/ASHW M34 ....101 F5
Lees Brook Pk OLDE OL4 ....60 A6
Lees Gv OLDE OL4 ....60 A7
Lees Hall Crs RUSH/FAL M14 ....99 G4
Leeside HTNM SK4 ....111 K8
Lees La MCFLDN SK10 ....127M5
  OLDE OL4 ....60 C8
Lees New Rd AUL OL6 ....76 A5
Lees Park Av DROY M43 ....89M2
Lees Rd AUL OL6 ....76 A5
  BRAM/HZG SK7 ....120 F7
  OLDE OL4 ....60 A6
Lees St AUL OL6 ....75 L8
  DROY M43 ....89 L2
  GTN M18 ....89 G8
  MDTN M24 ....58 A5
  MOSL * OL5 ....76 F2
  OLDS OL8 ....9 M5
  STLY SK15 ....91 K2
  SWIN M27 ....70 C3
Lees St East ROY/SHW OL2 ....43 L7
Leestone Rd WYTH/NTH M22 ......110 B6
Lee St ATH M46 ....67 C2
  BURY BL9 ....25 J4
  LIT OL15 ....20 C6
  MDTN M24 ....57 J1
  OLDS OL8 ....8 F7
  STKP SK1 ....13 J5
  UPML OL3 ....61 L4
Leesway OLDE OL4 ....60 B7
Leesway Dr DTN/ASHW M34 ....101 K2
Leeswood Av CCHDY M21 ....97M6
Lee Vale Dr GLSP SK13 ....104 A5
Leewood SWIN M27 ....54 A8
Left Bank CSLFD M3 ....6 D4
Le Gendre St BOLE BL2 ....36 E2
Legh CI POY/DIS SK12 ....129 J1
Legh Dr MPL/ROM SK6 ....89 J3
  MPL/ROM SK6 ....101 J3
Legh Rd BRO M7 ....72 A4
  MCFLDN SK10 ....129 G7
  POY/DIS SK12 ....123 J6
  SALE M33 ....109 H1

Legh St AIMK WN4 ....78 E2
  BRO M7 ....72 A4
  ECC M30 ....84 F3
  GOL/RIS/CU WA3 ....79 K4
Legion Gv BRO M7 ....72 B6
Legwood Ct URM M41 ....95M2
Leicester Av BRO * M7 ....72 C4
  DROY M43 ....89 J1
  DTN/ASHW M34 ....101 J3
  HALE/TIMP WA15 ....108 D4
  HOR/BR BL6 ....33 K1
  WGNE/HIN WN2 ....65 L3
Leicester Dr GLSP SK13 ....105 J5
Leicester Rd BRO M7 ....74 D7
  FAIL M35 ....74 D7
  HALE/TIMP WA15 ....117 G2
  SALE M33 ....96 E7
  TYLD M29 ....67 K2
  WHTF M45 ....55 C3
Leicester St AULW OL7 ....75 L8
  OLDE OL4 ....59 L6
  RDSH SK5 ....100 B2
  ROCH OL11 ....11 C8
Leigh Ar WGN * WN1 ....14 F3
Leigh Av MPL/ROM SK6 ....114 B6
  SWIN M27 ....70 A7
Leighbrook Rd RUSH/FAL M14 ......98 E4
Leigh CI TOT/BURYW BL8 ....24 B5
Leigh Fold HYDE SK14 ....91 H7
Leigh La TOT/BURYW BL8 ....38 D1
Leigh Rd ATH M46 ....66 D4
  HALE/TIMP WA15 ....117 G2
  WALK M28 ....68 D6
  WGNE/HIN WN2 ....49 J1
  WGNE/HIN WN2 ....65 L3
  WHTN BL5 ....50 B5
  WILM/AE SK9 ....126 B7
Leigh St BRO M7 ....72 A5
  FWTH BL4 ....53 C4
  HEY OL10 ....40 F2
  HYDE SK14 ....102 B2
  LEIGH WN7 ....65M7
  MILN OL16 ....29 C5
  TOT/BURYW BL8 ....24 C8
  WGN WN1 ....15 J5
  WGNE/HIN WN2 ....49 J1
  WGNE/HIN WN2 ....65 L3
  WHTN BL5 ....50 B3
Leighton Av ATH M46 ....66 E1
  BOL BL1 ....35 L4
  LIT OL15 ....29 J2
Leighton Dr LEIGH WN7 ....80 E3
  MPL/ROM SK6 ....114 F4
Leighton Rd OLDTF/WHR M16 ....86 F6
  NEWH/MOS M40 ....73 K4
Leighton St ATH M46 ....66 E1
  NEWH/MOS M40 ....73 K4
Leinster Rd SWIN M27 ....70 B5
Leinster St FWTH BL4 ....52 F4
Leith Av SALE M33 ....97 H8
Leith Rd SALE M33 ....97 H8
Le Mans Crs BOL BL1 ....2 E5
Lemnos St OLD OL1 ....9 L4
Lemon St TYLD M29 ....67 J4
  NEWH/MOS M40 ....73 K3
Lena St BOL BL1 ....36 C2
  CMANE M1 ....7 J5
Len Cox Wk ANC * M1 ....7 J3
Leng Rd NEWH/MOS M40 ....74 A7
Lenham Cl RDSH SK5 ....100 E6
Lenham Gdns BOLE BL2 ....37 H6
Lennox Gdns BOLS/LL BL3 ....35 J7
Lennox St AUL OL6 ....90 F1
Lenora St BOLS/LL BL3 ....35 L7
Lenten Gv HEY OL10 ....41 H5
Lentmead Dr NEWH/MOS M40 .....73 K3
Lenton Gdns WYTH/NTH M22 .....110 B7
Leominster Dr WYTH/NTH M22 ...119 C1
Leominster Rd MDTN * M24 ....57 L6
Leonardin CI ROY/SHW OL2 ....43 J4
Leonard St BOLS/LL BL3 ....52 B1
  ROCH OL11 ....41M3
Leopold Av DID/WITH M20 ....98 D7
Leopold St ROCH OL11 ....10 A5
  WGNW/BIL/O WN5 ....46 E7
Lepp Crs TOT/BURYW BL8 ....24 F6
Leroy Dr BKLY M9 ....73 C2
Lerryn Dr BRAM/HZG SK7 ....120 F3
Lesley Rd STRET M32 ....96 D3
Leslie Av BURY BL9 ....55 J1
  CHAD OL9 ....74 E1
Leslie Gv HALE/TIMP WA15 ....108 D6
Leslie Hough Wy SLFD M6 ....71 L8
Leslie St BOLE BL2 ....3 J1
  RUSH/FAL M14 ....98 E1
Lessingham Av WGN WN1 ....47 L1
Lester Rd LHULT M38 ....52 B7
Lester St STRET M32 ....97 G2
Letchford St ROCH OL11 ....11 C9
Letchworth St RUSH/FAL M14 ....98 E3
Letham St OLDS OL8 ....75 J2
Letitia St HOR/BR BL6 ....33 K1
Levedale Rd BKLY M9 ....57 H8
Leven CI FWTH BL4 ....53 L7
Levenhurst Rd CHH M8 ....72 C5
Levens CI CHD/CHDH SK8 ....110 E8
Levens Dr BOLE BL2 ....37 H3
Levens Rd GTN M18 ....89 C8
Levenshulme Ter
  BNG/LEV * M19 ....99 K3
Levens Pl WGNE/HIN WN2 ....48 D3
  WGNW/BIL/O WN5 ....46 F5
Levens Rd BRAM/HZG SK7 ....121 L2
Levens St NEWH/MOS M40 ....73 K5
  SLFD M6 ....71 L7
Levens Wk CHAD OL9 ....58 D7
Lever Av SWIN M27 ....70 E2
Lever Bridge Pl BOLS/LL BL3 ....3M9
Lever Dr BOLS/LL BL3 ....2 D9
Lever Edge La BOLS/LL BL3 ....51M2
Leverett CI ALT WA14 ....107 K1
Lever Gv BOLS/LL BL3 ....3 J3
Lever Hall Rd BOLE BL2 ....37 C5
Leverhulme Av BOLS/LL BL3 ....52 D1
Lever Park Av HOR/BR BL6 ....21 A7
Lever St BOLS/LL BL3 ....36 B8
  BOLS/LL BL3 ....51 M1
  BRAM/HZG SK7 ....121M2
  CMANE M1 ....7 H4
  HEY OL10 ....41 G1
  MDTN M24 ....57 J1
  RAMS BL0 ....17 C6
  TYLD M29 ....68 A1
  WHTN BL5 ....50 B1
Lever Wk MDTN M24 ....57 K4
Levington Dr OLDS OL8 ....75 K4
Levi St BOL BL1 ....35 J3
Lewes Av DTN/ASHW M34 ....101 J3
Lewis Av BKLY M9 ....73 H3
  URM M41 ....85 C7
Lewis CI WGNS/IIMK WN3 ....14 B9
Lewis Dr HEY OL10 ....40 C3

Lewisham Av NEWH/MOS M40 .....73 L8
Lewisham CI ROY/SHW * OL2 ....42 F6
Lewis Rd DROY M43 ....89 H2
  RDSH SK5 ....100 C3
Lewis St ECC M30 ....85 C5
  HEY * OL10 ....41 H1
  NEWH/MOS M40 ....88 A1
  ROY/SHW OL2 ....43 L7
Lewtas St ECC M30 ....85 H3
Lexton Av CHH M8 ....72 E2
Leybourne Av BNG/LEV M19 ....99 L2
Leybourne St BOL BL1 ....36 B2
Leybrook Rd WYTH/NTH M22 ......118 E1
Leyburn Av ROY/SHW OL2 ....43 C8
  STRET M32 ....96 E2
  URM M41 ....95 K3
Leyburn CI WGN WN1 ....15M2
  WHTF M45 ....55 H4
Leyburne Rd OFTN SK2 ....112 F6
Leyburn Gv MPL/ROM SK6 ....113M2
Leyburn Rd NEWH/MOS M40 ....73M2
Leycett Dr NTHM/RTH M23 ....109 K3
Ley Crs TYLD M29 ....67 L6
Leycroft St CMANE * M1 ....7 K6
Ley Dr HEY OL10 ....41 H5
Leyfield Av MPL/ROM SK6 ....113M2
Leyfield Rd MILN OL16 ....29 C6
Leygate Vw NM/HAY SK22 ....124 D4
Ley Hey Av MPL/ROM SK6 ....114 C5
Ley Hey Rd MPL/ROM SK6 ....114 C5
Leyland Av CHD/CHDH SK8 ....110 E6
  DID/WITH M20 ....111 J1
  IRL M44 ....83 L8
  WGNE/HIN WN2 ....65 G1
Leyland Green Rd AIMK WN4 ....62 F7
Leyland Mill La WGN WN1 ....47M1
Leylands La HYDE SK14 ....103 H6
Leyland St BURY BL9 ....39 J8
  HTNM SK4 ....99 L8
  LEIGH WN7 ....48 F8
  WGNE/HIN WN2 ....64 E3
Leyton Av NEWH/MOS M40 ....73 L5
Leyton CI FWTH BL4 ....52 C3
Leyton Dr BURY BL9 ....39 J7
Leyton St WHIT OL12 ....28 C2
Leywell Dr OLD OL1 ....60 A1
Leywell Rd BKLY M9 ....73 J4
Library La CHAD OL9 ....8 F3
Library St WGN WN1 ....15 C4
  WHTN BL5 ....50 C4
Libra St BOL BL1 ....36 A2
Lichens Crs OLDS OL8 ....75 K1
Lichfield Av AUL OL6 ....76 A5
  BOLE BL2 ....36 E2
  GOL/RIS/CU WA3 ....80 A4
  HALE/TIMP WA15 ....117 L1
  RDSH SK5 ....100 B5
  TYLD M29 ....67M5
Lichfield CI FWTH BL4 ....52 D3
  UPML OL3 ....44 F2
Lichfield Dr CHAD OL9 ....58 D3
  CHH M8 ....72 E5
  PWCH M25 ....71M2
  SWIN M27 ....70 C6
  TOT/BURYW BL8 ....4 C1
Lichfield Rd ECC M30 ....70 C8
  RAD M26 ....38 A7
  URM M41 ....85 C8
Lichfield Ter MILN OL16 ....28 F8
Lichfield Wk MPL/ROM SK6 ....113 K3
Lidbrook Wk WGTN/LGST M12 .....88 B6
Liddington Hall Dr RAMS BL0 ....17 B8
Lidgate CI WGNS/IIMK WN3 ....63 C1
Lidgett CI WALK M28 ....52 F7
Lidiard St CHH M8 ....72 D3
Liffey Av WYTH/NTH M22 ....119 C1
Lifton Av NEWH/MOS M40 ....73 M8
Light Alders La POY/DIS SK12 ......123 J5
Lightborne Rd SALE M33 ....96 B8
Lightbounds Rd BOL BL1 ....35 J1
Lightbourne Av SWIN M27 ....70 C5
Lightbowne Rd
  NEWH/MOS M40 ....73 K6
Lightburn Av LIT OL15 ....19M8
Lightburne Av BOL BL1 ....35 L5
  LEIGH WN7 ....81 H1
Lightcliffe Av WGNE/HIN WN2 ......48 D2
Lighthorne Gv EDGY/DAV SK3 .....111 J5
Lighthorne Rd EDGY/DAV SK3 .....111 J5
Light Oaks Rd GOL/RIS/CU WA3 ...81M6
  SLFD M6 ....70 B8
Lightowlers La LIT OL15 ....20 E5
Lightshaw La GOL/RIS/CU WA3 .....64 E3
Lightwood WALK M28 ....68 D3
Lightwood CI FWTH BL4 ....53 H3
Lignum Av CHAD OL9 ....58 D7
Lilac Av AIMK WN4 ....65 C7
  BURY BL9 ....39 C5
  HYDE SK14 ....102 A4
  LEIGH WN7 ....66 B5
  MILN OL16 ....43 K1
  SWIN M27 ....70 D4
  WGNNW/ST WN6 ....47 K1
Lilac Ct SLFD M6 ....86 D2
Lilac Gdns WGNS/IIMK WN3 ....48 C8
Lilac Gv CHAD OL9 ....8 B2
  NEWH/MOS M40 ....73 K3
  PWCH M25 ....55 K6
  WGNW/BIL/O WN5 ....62 A8
Lilac La OLDS OL8 ....75 C2
Lilac Rd GOL/RIS/CU WA3 ....79 K3
  HALE/TIMP WA15 ....117 J1
  ROCH OL11 ....100 C3
Lilac St OFTN SK2 ....112 C6
Lilac View CI ROY/SHW OL2 ....44 A6
Lila St BKLY M9 ....73 J5
Lilburn CI RAMS BL0 ....17 C8
Liley St MILN OL16 ....11 H5
Liliford CI WGTN/LGST M12 ....88 D6
Liliford St ATH M46 ....67 H6
  LEIGH WN7 ....66 B5
Lilian St WGNNW/ST WN6 ....47 K1
Lillian St OLDTF/WHR M16 ....86 F8
Lilly St BOL BL1 ....2 A2
  HYDE SK14 ....102 C4
Lily Av NEWH/MOS M40 ....73 J8
Lily Av FWTH BL4 ....52 E3
Lily CI EDGY/DAV SK3 ....112 A7
Lily Hill St WHTF M45 ....55 H2
Lily La BKLY M9 ....73 H4
Lily Lanes AUL OL6 ....76 B4
Lily Pl AIMK WN4 ....78 F2

Lily St *AIMK* WN4 ....64 B7
ECC M30 ....84 E3
MDTN M24 ....57 M4
MILN OL16 ....29 J6
OLD OL1 ....9 G1
ROY/SHW OL2 ....43 J8
Lima St *BURY* BL9 ....5 L2
Limbert Cir *CHH* M8 ....72 F3
Lime Av *LEIGH* WN7 ....66 B4
NM/HAY SK22 ....124 F3
SWIN M27 ....69 M6
URM M41 ....95 L2
WHTF M45 ....55 J5
Lime Bank St *WGTN/LGST* M12 ......98 E4
Limebrook Cl *OP/CLY* M11 ....89 H5
Lime Cl *DUK* SK16 ....91 C6
SLFD M6 ....86 D1
WGNE/HIN WN2 ....64 C5
Lime Crs *OLDTF/WHR* M16 ....86 E8
Lime Fld *MILN* OL16 ....29 H5
Limefield *MDTN* M24 ....57 H5
MOSL OL5 ....76 E2
WGN WN1 ....15 H4
Limefield Av *FWTH* BL4 ....53 C8
Limefield Brow *BURY* BL9 ....25 J5
Limefield Rd *BRO* M7 ....72 A3
BURY BL9 ....25 J5
RAD M26 ....54 A1
Limefield Ter *BNG/LEV* M19 ....99 K3
Lime Gdns *DUK* SK16 ....90 E4
MDTN M24 ....57 H4
Lime Ga *OLDS* OL8 ....74 F2
Lime Gn *OLDS* OL8 ....75 G3
Lime Green Rd *OLDS* OL8 ....74 F4
Lime Gv *AUL* OL6 ....75 M7
BURY BL9 ....25 J5
CHD/CHDH SK8 ....111 G6
DTN/ASHW M34 ....90 C8
GOL/RIS/CU WA3 ....80 A6
HALE/TIMP WA15 ....108 E6
HEY OL10 ....40 F1
LIT OL15 ....20 A7
OLDTF/WHR M16 ....86 E8
PWCH M25 ....55 K6
RAMS BL0 ....17 D5
ROY/SHW OL2 ....43 G6
STLY SK15 ....91 H4
WALK M28 ....69 J3
WGNE/HIN WN2 ....65 J1
Limehurst Av *AULW* OL7 ....75 K6
DID/WITH M20 ....98 C4
Limehurst Rd *AULW* OL7 ....75 K6
Lime Kiln La *MPL/ROM* SK6 ....114 D7
Limekiln La *WGTN/LGST* M12 ....88 A4
Lime La *OLDS* OL8 ....74 F3
Lime Rd *STRET* M32 ....97 C3
Limers Ga *WHIT* OL12 ....19 G7
Limerston Dr *NEWH/MOS* M40 ....73 J7
The Limes *GOL/RIS/CU* WA3 ....80 A6
GOL/RIS/CU WA3 ....81 C8
MOSL OL5 ....76 E3
MOSL OL5 ....77 H3
WGNNW/ST WN6 ....31 K6
Limes Av *WGNNW/ST* WN6 ....31 L6
Limesdale Cl *BOLE* BL2 ....37 L7
Limeside Rd *OLDS* OL8 ....74 F2
Limestead Av *CHH* M8 ....72 D4
Lime St *ATH* M46 ....66 C1
BURY BL9 ....25 J6
DUK SK16 ....90 E4
ECC M30 ....85 G3
FWTH BL4 ....53 H4
MPL/ROM SK6 ....101 H8
NEWH/MOS M40 ....88 A1
OLD OL1 ....8 D1
ROCH OL11 ....27 M7
TYLD M29 ....67 J3
WGN WN1 ....15 H3
Lime Tree Cl *URM* M41 ....96 B3
Lime Tree Gv *FAIL* M35 ....74 E5
Limetrees Rd *MDTN* M24 ....57 J4
Lime V *WGNS/IIMK* WN3 ....48 C8
Limley Gv *CCHDY* M21 ....97 M5
Linacre Av *BOLS/LL* BL3 ....52 B2
Linacre Wy *GLSP* SK13 ....105 J5
Linbeck Gv *GOL/RIS/CU* WA3 ....80 B3
Linby St *HULME* M15 ....6 C9
Lincoln Av *BNG/LEV* M19 ....99 L3
BOLS/LL BL3 ....37 K7
CHD/CHDH SK8 ....119 K5
DROY M43 ....89 K1
DTN/ASHW M34 ....101 K3
GOL/RIS/CU WA3 ....80 A3
STRET M32 ....96 C1
Lincoln Cl *AUL* OL6 ....76 A4
GOL/RIS/CU WA3 ....80 F4
ROCH OL11 ....11 G7
TYLD M29 ....67 K2
Lincoln Dr *AIMK* WN4 ....63 J7
BURY BL9 ....5 C8
HALE/TIMP WA15 ....108 E7
LIT OL15 ....29 K1
WGNE/HIN WN2 ....33 G7
Lincoln Gv *BOLE* BL2 ....23 J8
BRUN/LGST M13 ....87 M7
SALE M33 ....97 H8
Lincoln Leach Ct *ROCH* OL11 ......10 E8
Lincoln Mnr *WGNW/BIL/O* WN5 .....46 F4
Lincoln Pl *MPL/ROM* SK6 ....113 K3
Lincoln Rd *BOL* BL1 ....35 L4
FAIL M35 ....74 D6
MDTN M24 ....57 M7
WGNE/HIN WN2 ....49 H7
WILM/AE SK9 ....127 J3
Lincoln St *BRUN/LGST* M13 ....88 C8
CHAD OL9 ....8 B8
ECC M30 ....84 F3
ROCH OL11 ....11 G7
Lincoln Wy *GLSP* SK13 ....105 J4
Lincombe Rd *WYTH/NTH* M22 .....118 E4
Lincroft Rd *WGNE/HIN* WN2 ....65 K1
Linda Dr *BRAM/HZG* SK7 ....121 M3
Lindale Av *HYDE* SK14 ....90 F7
Lindale Av *BOL* BL1 ....35 J4
BURY BL9 ....55 K1
CHAD OL9 ....58 D6
NEWH/MOS M40 ....74 A2
ROY/SHW OL2 ....42 F5
URM M41 ....95 J2
Lindale Cl *MDTN* M24 ....57 H1
Lindale Dr *MDTN* M24 ....57 H1
Lindale Ri *ROY/SHW* OL2 ....44 A5
Lindale Rd *WALK* M28 ....68 B5
Lindbury Av *OFTN* SK2 ....112 F5
Linden Av *AIMK* WN4 ....63 J7
ATH M46 ....66 E2
BOLS/LL BL3 ....37 K7
DTN/ASHW M34 ....90 A5

HALE/TIMP WA15 ....108 B7
OLDE OL4 ....60 A4
RAMS BL0 ....17 D6
SALE M33 ....96 C8
SLFD M6 ....71 H6
SWIN M27 ....70 A5
WGNW/BIL/O WN5 ....46 B6
Linden Dr *ORD* M5 ....86 D4
Linden Gv *BRAM/HZG* SK7 ....120 F8
LEIGH WN7 ....66 B5
OFTN SK2 ....112 E8
RUSH/FAL M14 ....99 G4
WGNW/BIL/O WN5 ....46 B6
Linden Ms *WALK* M28 ....68 C6
Linden Pk *BNG/LEV* M19 ....99 J4
Linden Rd *CHD/CHDH* SK8 ....120 C1
DID/WITH M20 ....98 D8
DTN/ASHW M34 ....101 K1
STLY SK15 ....92 A5
WALK M28 ....68 C6
WGNE/HIN WN2 ....49 H5
Linden St *WGNW/BIL/O* WN5 ....46 F7
Linden Wk *BOLE* BL2 ....22 E7
Lindenwood *CHAD* OL9 ....58 B4
Lindeth Av *GTN* M18 ....89 G8
Lindfield Dr *BOL* BL1 ....36 B3
Lindfield Est North
WILM/AE SK9 ....126 E6
Lindfield Est South
WILM/AE SK9 ....126 D6
Lindfield Rd *RDSH* SK5 ....100 C3
Lindinis Av *SLFD* M6 ....86 D2
Lindisfarne *WHIT* OL12 ....10 D3
Lindisfarne Av *GOL/RIS/CU* WA3 ....80 F4
Lindisfarne Cl *SALE* M33 ....108 E3
Lindisfarne Dr *POY/DIS* SK12 .....121 M8
Lindisfarne Pl *BOLE* BL2 ....36 F2
Lindisfarne Rd *AULW* OL7 ....75 H7
Lindley St *BOLS/LL* * BL3 ....53 L1
FWTH BL4 ....53 L6
LEIGH * WN7 ....66 D7
Lindleywood Rd *RUSH/FAL* M14 .....99 H4
Lindon Wy *DROY* M43 ....89 H4
Lindop Rd *HALE/TIMP* WA15 ....117 H3
Lindow Cl *TOT/BURYW* BL8 ....24 E6
Lindow Ct *BRAM/HZG* SK7 ....121 J6
Lindow Fold Dr *WILM/AE* SK9 .....126 B8
Lindow La *WILM/AE* SK9 ....126 C6
Lindow Rd *OLDTF/WHR* M16 ....97 L2
Lindow St *SALE* M33 ....109 J1
LEIGH WN7 ....66 A7
Lindrick Av *WHTF* M45 ....55 G6
Lindrick Cl *NEWH/MOS* M40 ....73 M5
Lindrick Ter *BOLS/LL* * BL3 ....2 A9
Lindsay Av *BNG/LEV* M19 ....99 J3
CHD/CHDH SK8 ....120 D3
SWIN M27 ....70 B5
Lindsay Cl *OLDE* * OL4 ....60 A2
Lindsay Rd *BNG/LEV* M19 ....99 J4
Lindsay St *HOR/BR* BL6 ....34 A3
STLY SK15 ....91 L2
Lindsay Ter *WGNE/HIN* WN2 ....32 E7
Lindsell Rd *ALT* WA14 ....107 M4
Lindsgate Dr *HALE/TIMP* WA15 ....108 E5
Lind St *NEWH/MOS* M40 ....88 B2
Lindum Av *OLDTF/WHR* M16 ....86 F8
Lindum St *RUSH/FAL* M14 ....98 E1
Lindwall Cl *NTHM/RTH* M23 ....109 L2
Linehan Cl *HTNM* SK4 ....111 G2
Lineholme *ROY/SHW* OL2 ....58 F2
Linen Ct *CSLFD* M3 ....6 A1
Lines Rd *DROY* M43 ....89 L3
IRL M44 ....94 C4
Linfield *BOLE* BL2 ....23 C8
Linfield St *OP/CLY* M11 ....88 E3
Linford Av *NEWH/MOS* M40 ....73 M2
Lingard La *MPL/ROM* SK6 ....101 G7
Lingard St *LEIGH* WN7 ....66 E8
RDSH SK5 ....100 C4
Lingcrest Rd *BNG/LEV* M19 ....99 M5
Lingdale Rd *CHD/CHDH* SK8 ....120 B2
Lingdale Dr *ATH* M46 ....66 C2
Lingfield Av *BRAM/HZG* SK7 ....122 B2
SALE M33 ....107 L2
Lingfield Cl *FWTH* BL4 ....52 F5
TOT/BURYW BL8 ....24 F5
Lingfield Crs *WGNNW/ST* WN6 .....47 H1
Lingholme Dr *MDTN* M24 ....56 C2
Lingmell Cl *BOL* BL1 ....35 J4
MDTN M24 ....57 C2
URM M41 ....84 C8
Lingmoor Dr *MDTN* M24 ....56 F2
WGNS/IIMK WN3 ....63 K3
Lingmoor Dr *TYLD* M29 ....67 L5
Lingmoor Rd *BOL* BL1 ....35 J3
Lingmoor Wk *HULME* * M15 ....87 J7
Lings Wk *WYTH/NTH* M22 ....119 C3
Linhope Cl *HTNM* SK4 ....111 H1
The Link *RDSH* SK5 ....100 F6
ROY/SHW OL2 ....43 J3
WILM/AE SK9 ....127 H1
Link Av *URM* M41 ....96 D3
Linkfield Dr *WALK* M28 ....68 C6
Link La *OLDS* OL8 ....75 H2
Link Rd *OLDE* OL4 ....60 C5
SALE M33 ....108 A2
Links Av *FAIL* M35 ....74 C7
Links Crs *PWCH* M25 ....72 B2
Links Dr *HOR/BR* BL6 ....34 E5
Linksfield *DTN/ASHW* M34 ....90 C7
Linkside Av *ROY/SHW* OL2 ....43 G7
Links Pl *AUL* OL6 ....76 B6
Links Ri *URM* M41 ....84 D8
Links Rd *BOLE* BL2 ....23 K8
HEY OL10 ....41 C4
HOR/BR BL6 ....34 E5
MPL/ROM SK6 ....114 A1
MPL/ROM SK6 ....114 C8
WILM/AE SK9 ....130 B1
Links Vw *PWCH* M25 ....71 K3
ROCH OL11 ....27 L6
Linksway *CHD/CHDH* SK8 ....110 D8
PWCH M25 ....72 A2
SWIN M27 ....70 D6
Linksway Dr *BURY* BL9 ....55 K1
Linkway Av *AIMK* WN4 ....64 B7
Linley Av *RAD* M26 ....39 H7
Linley Cl *WGNNW/ST* WN6 ....30 F8
Linley Dr *OLDE* OL4 ....60 A8

Linley Gv *RAMS* BL0 ....24 D2
Linley Rd *CHD/CHDH* SK8 ....120 D4
SALE M33 ....96 E7
WGNW/BIL/O WN5 ....47 G7
Linnell Dr *ROCH* OL11 ....27 H4
Linnet Cl *DTN/ASHW* M34 ....89 M2
OFTN SK2 ....113 J7
WGTN/LGST M12 ....88 C8
Linnet Dr *BURY* BL9 ....5 L1
IRL M44 ....94 D1
LEIGH WN7 ....66 E7
Linnet Hl *ROCH* OL11 ....27 M6
Linney La *ROY/SHW* OL2 ....43 M5
Linney Rd *BRAM/HZG* SK7 ....120 F2
Linney Sq *WGN* WN1 ....15 K3
Linn St *CHH* M8 ....72 D3
Linslade Gdns *BOLS/LL* * BL3 ....2 C8
Linstead Dr *CHH* * M8 ....72 C6
Linstock Wy *ATH* M46 ....66 D1
Linthorpe Wk *BOLS/LL* BL3 ....35 L8
Linton Av *BURY* BL9 ....25 J7
DTN/ASHW M34 ....100 D1
GOL/RIS/CU WA3 ....79 J2
Linton Cl *ANC* M4 ....88 A4
Linton Rd *SALE* M33 ....96 F6
Linwood Cl *WGNE/HIN* WN2 ....49 G8
Linwood Gv *WGTN/LGST* M12 ....99 K2
Linwood St *FAIL* M35 ....73 M6
Lion Brow *BKLY* M9 ....73 C2
Lion Fold La *BKLY* M9 ....73 C1
Lion La *HOR/BR* BL6 ....32 F2
Lions Dr *SWIN* M27 ....70 D5
Lion St *BKLY* M9 ....73 C2
Liptrot St *WGNW/BIL/O* WN5 ....14 A6
Lisbon St *ROCH* OL11 ....27 L4
Lisburn Av *CCHDY* M21 ....97 M3
SALE M33 ....108 D1
Lisburne Av *OFTN* SK2 ....113 G6
Lisburne Cl *OFTN* * SK2 ....113 G6
Lisburne La *OFTN* SK2 ....112 F7
Lisburn Rd *NEWH/MOS* M40 ....73 K4
Liscard Av *RUSH/FAL* M14 ....98 E3
Liscard St *ATH* M46 ....66 E1
Lisetta Av *OLDE* * OL4 ....59 L7
Liskeard Av *ROY/SHW* OL2 ....59 J1
Liskeard Cl *MILN* OL16 ....11 L1
Liskeard Ct *BRAM/HZG* SK7 ....121 H5
RDSH SK5 ....100 B6
Lismore Av *BOLS/LL* BL3 ....35 J7
EDGY/DAV SK3 ....12 A8
Lismore Dr *BURY* SK16 ....91 C5
Lismore Wy *URM* M41 ....85 G7
Lissadel St *SLFD* M6 ....71 K8
Lisson Gv *HALE/TIMP* WA15 ....117 G2
Lister Rd *MDTN* M24 ....56 E6
Lister St *BOLS/LL* BL3 ....51 L1
Liston St *DUK* SK16 ....91 J4
Litcham Cl *CMANE* M1 ....7 J8
Litchfield Gv *WALK* M28 ....69 L5
Litherland Av *WYTH/NTH* M22 ......119 C3
Litherland Rd *BOLS/LL* BL3 ....52 B2
SALE M33 ....109 H1
Little 66 *BURY* BL9 ....39 L5
Little Ancoats St *CMANE* M1 ....7 J3
Little Bank St *OLDE* OL4 ....59 L6
Littlebourne Wk *BOL* BL1 ....22 D6
Littlebrook Cl *CHD/CHDH* SK8 .....111 M8
GLSP SK13 ....93 K8
Little Brook Rd *SALE* M33 ....107 M3
Little Brow *EDGW/EG* BL7 ....22 D5
Little Clegg Rd *LIT* OL15 ....29 J2
Littledale St *WHIT* OL12 ....10 C3
Little David St *CMANE* M1 ....7 H6
Little Ees La *SALE* M33 ....96 C5
Little Egerton St *STKP* SK1 ....13 H3
Little Factory St *TYLD* M29 ....67 J3
Littlefields *HYDE* SK14 ....92 D8
Little Flatt *WHIT* OL12 ....27 L3
Littlegate *WHTN* BL5 ....50 B7
Little Gn *MDTN* * M24 ....57 L3
Littlegreen Gdns *SLFD* M6 ....86 C1
Little Harwood Lee *BOLE* BL2 ....37 G1
Littlehaven Cl *WGTN/LGST* M12 .....88 B7
Little Heath La *ALT* WA14 ....107 G7
Little Hey St *ROY/SHW* OL2 ....43 L8
Littlehills Cl *MDTN* M24 ....56 E4
Little Holme St *ANC* M4 ....88 A3
Little Holme Wk *BOLS/LL* * BL3 ....36 C8
Little Howarth Wy *WHIT* * OL12 ....19 K8
Little John St *CSLFD* M3 ....6 C6
Little La *WGNS/IIMK* WN3 ....47 H8
Little Lever St *CMANE* M1 ....7 H4
Little London *WGN* WN1 ....15 C2
Little Meadow Rd *ALT* WA14 ....116 D3
Little Mdw *EDGW/EG* * BL7 ....22 C5
Little Moor Clough
EDGW/EG BL7 ....22 B2
Little Moor Cottages *STKP* SK1 ....112 E4
Little Moor La *OLDE* OL4 ....59 M4
Littlemoor La *UPML* OL3 ....45 L8
Littlemoor Rd *HYDE* SK14 ....103 K2
Little Moss La *SWIN* M27 ....70 C2
Littlemoss Rd *DROY* M43 ....89 M1
Little Nelson St *ANC* * M4 ....7 H1
Little Oak Cl *OLDE* OL4 ....60 B6
Little Pasture *LEIGH* WN7 ....66 A5
Little Peter St *HULME* M15 ....6 D8
Little Pitt St *CMANE* * M1 ....7 K4
Little Quay St *CSLFD* M3 ....6 E5
Little Scotland *HOR/BR* BL6 ....32 E2
Little Stones Rd *EDGW/EG* BL7 ......22 B2
Littleton Gv *WGNNW/ST* WN6 ....31 H2
Littleton Rd *BRO* M7 ....71 K4
Little Underbank *STKP* SK1 ....13 J4
Littlewood *ROY/SHW* OL2 ....43 G5
Littlewood Av *BURY* BL9 ....25 J7
Littlewood Rd *WYTH/NTH* M22 ....109 M8
Littlewood St *SLFD* M6 ....86 B2
Littondale Cl *ROY/SHW* OL2 ....43 H7
Litton Ms *GLSP* SK13 ....105 J4
Liverpool Cl *RDSH* SK5 ....100 B5
Liverpool Rd *AIMK* WN4 ....78 C1
CSLFD M3 ....6 C6
ECC M30 ....84 B6
ECC M30 ....84 E3
IRL M44 ....94 C4
IRL M44 ....106 A1
WGNE/HIN WN2 ....48 F7
Liverpool St *RDSH* SK5 ....100 B5
SLFD M6 ....86 B2
Liverstudd Av *RDSH* SK5 ....100 C4
Livesey St *ANC* M4 ....87 M1
BNG/LEV M19 ....99 L4
OLD OL1 ....59 M4
Livingstone Av *MOSL* OL5 ....76 E3
Livingstone St *OLDE* OL4 ....60 B7
Livsey Ct *BOL* BL1 ....2 E1
Livsey La *HEY* OL10 ....40 D2
Livsey St *MILN* OL16 ....11 G5

WHTF M45 ....55 J4
Lizard St *CMANE* M1 ....7 J4
Liza St *LEIGH* WN7 ....66 B4
Lizmar Ter *BKLY* M9 ....73 J4
Llanberis Rd *CHD/CHDH* SK8 ....120 A3
Llanfair Rd *EDGY/DAV* SK3 ....12 D7
Lloyd Av *CHD/CHDH* SK8 ....110 D6
Lloyd Ct *LEIGH* * WN7 ....66 B5
Lloyd Gdns *HALE/TIMP* WA15 .....116 F1
Lloyd Rd *BNG/LEV* M19 ....99 L5
Lloyd Sq *ALT* WA14 ....108 A8
Lloyd St *ALT* WA14 ....108 A8
CMANW M2 ....6 F5
HEY OL10 ....41 G3
HTNM SK4 ....12 F2
HTNM SK4 ....100 A8
ROCH OL11 ....10 B9
WHIT OL12 ....18 D3
Lloyd St South *RUSH/FAL* M14 ......98 D3
Lobden Crs *WHIT* OL12 ....18 E5
Lobelia Av *FWTH* BL4 ....52 D3
Lobley Cl *WHIT* OL12 ....18 F4
Local Board St *WGNE/HIN* * WN2 ...48 C5
Lochawe Cl *HEY* OL10 ....40 D3
Lochinver Gv *HEY* OL10 ....40 D3
Lochmaddy Cl *BRAM/HZG* SK7 ....122 B3
Loch St *WGNW/BIL/O* WN5 ....46 F4
Lock Cl *HEY* OL10 ....41 H4
Lockerbie Pl *WGNS/IIMK* WN3 ....63 H2
Locker La *AIMK* WN4 ....64 C8
Lockett Gdns *CSLFD* M3 ....6 B2
Lockett Rd *AIMK* WN4 ....63 L6
Lockett St *CHH* M8 ....72 B8
SLFD M6 ....71 K7
Lockhart Cl *WGTN/LGST* M12 ....88 D7
Lockhart St *MILN* OL16 ....11 K8
Lockingate St *AUL* OL6 ....75 L6
Locking Gate Ri *OLDE* OL4 ....60 B3
Lockland Cl *IRL* M44 ....94 D2
Lock La *HOR/BR* BL6 ....34 F8
PART M31 ....106 A1
Lock Rd *ALT* WA14 ....107 M6
Lockside *MPL/ROM* SK6 ....114 D6
Lockside Vw *MOSL* OL5 ....61 H8
Locksley Cl *HTNM* SK4 ....12 D2
Locks Vw *WGN* WN1 ....15 M4
Lockton Cl *CMANE* M1 ....7 K8
RDSH SK5 ....100 B6
Lockton Ct *CMANE* M1 ....7 J8
Lockwood St *WGTN/LGST* M12 ......99 L1
The Lodge *GLSP* SK13 ....93 K6
Lodge Av *URM* M41 ....96 B2
Lodge Bank *GLSP* SK13 ....93 K6
Lodge Bank Rd *LIT* OL15 ....29 J1
Lodge Brow *RAD* M26 ....54 E2
Lodge Ct *URM* M41 ....91 H5
HYDE SK14 ....92 D8
Lodge Dr *TYLD* M29 ....67 L6
Lodge Farm Cl *BRAM/HZG* SK7 ....121 G2
Lodge Fold *DROY* M43 ....89 L2
Lodge Gn *DUK* SK16 ....91 H5
Lodge Gn *ATH* M46 ....67 H3
Lodge La *ATH* M46 ....67 G3
DUK SK16 ....91 H5
HYDE SK14 ....91 H8
LEIGH WN7 ....67 H8
NEWLW WA12 ....78 E3
UPML OL3 ....45 H7
Lodgepole Cl *ECC* M30 ....84 C4
Lodge Rd *ATH* M46 ....67 H3
RAD M26 ....54 E2
WGNW/BIL/O WN5 ....46 B8
Lodgeside Cl *DROY* M43 ....89 L2
Lodge St *AULW* OL7 ....90 C3
HYDE SK14 ....57 K3
LIT OL15 ....20 C6
MDTN M24 ....57 K3
NEWH/MOS M40 ....73 H7
RAMS BL0 ....17 C6
RAMS BL0 ....17 L6
WHIT OL12 ....19 K6
Lodge Vw *DROY* M43 ....89 L2
Loeminster Pl *WGNE/HIN* WN2 .....15 M6
Loen Crs *BOL* BL1 ....35 M1
Loganberry Av *SLFD* M6 ....86 D1
Logan St *BOL* BL1 ....22 B7
Logwood Av *TOT/BURYW* BL8 ....4 C2
WGNW/BIL/O WN5 ....14 A5
Logwood Pl *WGNW/BIL/O* WN5 .....47 H4
Loire Dr *WGNW/BIL/O* WN5 ....14 A5
Loisine Cl *ROCH* OL11 ....41 K1
Lois St *CHAD* OL9 ....74 D2
Lomas Cl *BNG/LEV* M19 ....111 G1
Lomas La *EDGY/DAV* SK3 ....74 D3
FAIL M35 ....74 D3
MDTN M24 ....57 L3
Lomax's Buildings *BOL* BL1 ....2 F6
Lomax St *BOL* BL1 ....36 B2
BURY BL9 ....5 H3
CMANE M1 ....7 J3
RAD M26 ....54 D2
WGNE/HIN WN2 ....64 D2
WHIT OL12 ....10 F2
WHTF * M45 ....55 H2
Lombard Cl *MPL/ROM* SK6 ....101 J8
Lombard Gv *RUSH/FAL* M14 ....98 F4
Lombard St *ATH* M46 ....66 E1
OLD OL1 ....9 G3
WHIT * OL12 ....10 B3
Lombardy Ct *SLFD* * M6 ....86 D1
Lomond Av *HALE/TIMP* WA15 ......117 J1
Lomond Cl *OFTN* SK2 ....121 J1
Lomond Dr *TOT/BURYW* BL8 ....24 E8
Lomond Pl *BOLS/LL* BL3 ....35 H6
Lomond Rd *WYTH/NTH* M22 ....119 H2
Lomond Ter *MILN* OL16 ....28 F8
London Cl *WGNW/BIL/O* WN5 ....47 H4
London Flds *WGNW/BIL/O* WN5 .....62 B7
London Pl *STKP* SK1 ....13 J5
London Rd *CMANE* M1 ....7 H6
MCFLDN SK10 ....129 C7
OFTN SK2 ....113 G8
OLD OL1 ....59 L3
WILM/AE SK9 ....130 D3
London Rd North
POY/DIS SK12 ....122 D4
London Rd South
POY/DIS SK12 ....129 H2
London Sq *STKP* SK1 ....13 J5
London St *BOLS/LL* BL3 ....36 B8
SLFD M6 ....71 J8
WHTF M45 ....55 J5
Long Acres Dr *WHIT* OL12 ....18 E3
Longacres La *WHIT* OL12 ....18 E2
Longacre St *CMANE* M1 ....7 J4
Longbow Ct *BRO* * M7 ....72 A4

Longbridge Rd *TRPK* M17 ....85 K6
Longbrook *WGNNW/ST* WN6 ....30 A3
Long Cswy *ATH* WA46 ....66 E5
FWTH BL4 ....53 H5
Longcliffe Wk *BOL* * BL1 ....36 C2
Longclough Dr *GLSP* SK13 ....104 D4
Longcrag Wk *HULME* * M15 ....87 J7
Longcroft *URM* M41 ....67 H8
Longcroft Dr *ALT* WA14 ....107 L4
Longcroft Gv *DTN/ASHW* M34 ....89 L4
NTHM/RTH M23 ....109 K5
Long Croft La *CHD/CHDH* SK8 .....120 A4
Longdale Cl *ROY/SHW* OL2 ....42 F8
Longdale Dr *HYDE* SK14 ....103 K1
Longden Av *OLDE* OL4 ....60 B1
Longden Rd *WGTN/LGST* M12 ....99 K2
Longden St *BOL* BL1 ....35 M4
Longden Ct *BRAM/HZG* * SK7 ....97 H1
Longdendale Rd
WGNNW/ST WN6 ....31 G4
Longfellow Av *BOLS/LL* BL3 ....51 L1
Longfellow Cl *WGNS/IIMK* WN3 .....47 K7
Longfellow Crs *OLD* OL1 ....44 A8
Longfield Av *SLFD* M6 ....71 M8
Longfield *BURY* * BL9 ....25 K8
Longfield Cl *CHD/CHDH* SK8 ....119 L5
HALE/TIMP WA15 ....108 F6
URM M41 ....95 L2
Longfield Crs *OLDE* OL4 ....59 M3
Longfield Dr *URM* M41 ....95 L2
Longfield La *OLDE* OL4 ....60 A3
Longfield Pk *ROY/SHW* OL2 ....43 K7
Longfield Rd *BOLS/LL* BL3 ....51 L1
NTHM/RTH M23 ....109 J4
ROCH OL11 ....27 M4
ROY/SHW OL2 ....43 K6
Longfield Rd West *RDSH* SK5 ......100 A3
Longford Av *BOL* BL1 ....35 M2
STRET M32 ....97 H2
Longford Cl *STRET* M32 ....97 H1
Longford Pk *STRET* M32 ....88 B8
Longford Pl *RUSH/FAL* M14 ....88 B8
RDSH SK5 ....100 A3
Longford Rd *GTN* M18 ....89 G6
HEY OL10 ....40 F7
Longford Rd West *RDSH* SK5 ......100 A3
HEY OL10 ....40 F7
Long Grain *OFTN* SK2 ....113 G7
Longham Cl *BRAM/HZG* SK7 ....120 E3
OP/CLY M11 ....88 B3
Long Hey *HALE/TIMP* WA15 ....117 J1
Longhey Rd *WYTH/NTH* M22 ....110 A7
Long Hi *ROCH* OL11 ....28 A8
Longhirst Cl *BOL* BL1 ....35 L1
Longhope Rd *WYTH/NTH* M22 .....118 D1
Longhurst La *MPL/ROM* SK6 ....114 E5
Longhurst Rd *BKLY* M9 ....73 H8
WGNE/HIN WN2 ....49 J8
Longlands Dr *HYDE* SK14 ....102 E1
Longlands Dr *HYDE* SK14 ....102 E1
NM/HAY SK22 ....124 D4
Longlands Rd *NM/HAY* SK22 ....124 D4
Long La *BOLE* BL2 ....37 G2
BURY BL9 ....25 H5
CHAD OL9 ....74 C1
GLSP SK13 ....103 M5
UPML OL3 ....45 J8
WGNE/HIN WN2 ....49 K8
WHTN BL5 ....49 M2
Longlevens Rd
WYTH/NTH M22 ....118 C2
Longley Dr *WALK* M28 ....69 L6
Longley La *WYTH/NTH* M22 ....110 A4
Longley St *OLD* OL1 ....9 J7
ROY/SHW OL2 ....43 L7
WALK M28 ....69 G2
Long Marl Dr *WILM/AE* SK9 ....126 C8
Longmead Av *AIMK* WN4 ....63 M8
BRAM/HZG SK7 ....121 M3
Longmeade Gdns
WILM/AE SK9 ....127 G6
Long Meadow *BOLE* BL2 ....22 F5
HYDE SK14 ....91 J6
Longmeadow
CHD/CHDH SK8 ....120 C7
Longmeadow Gv
CHD/CHDH SK8 ....101 H2
Long Meadow Pas
HYDE * SK14 ....102 A1
Longmead Rd *SLFD* M6 ....71 G7
Longmere Av *WYTH/NTH* M22 .....118 F1
Long Millgate *ANC* M4 ....6 F2
Longmoor Rd *GLSP* SK13 ....104 D5
Longnor Rd *BRAM/HZG* SK7 ....122 A6
CHD/CHDH SK8 ....119 M5
Longport Av *DID/WITH* M20 ....98 D5
Longridge *EDGW/EG* BL7 ....22 F4
Longridge Av *STLY* SK15 ....76 D8
WGNNW/ST WN6 ....31 J4
Longridge Dr *HEY* OL10 ....40 C2
TOT/BURYW BL8 ....38 C4
Long Rw *STLY* SK15 ....77 J5
Long Rushes *ROY/SHW* OL2 ....43 J4
Longshaw Av *SWIN* M27 ....70 C3
WGNW/BIL/O WN5 ....62 B3
Longshaw Common
WGNW/BIL/O WN5 ....62 B4
Longshaw Dr *WALK* M28 ....68 D8
Longshaw Old Rd
WGNW/BIL/O WN5 ....62 B3
Longshoot Cl *WGN* WN1 ....15 J2
Longshut La *STKP* SK1 ....13 J8
Longshut La West *OFTN* SK2 ....13 J8
Longsides Rd
HALE/TIMP WA15 ....117 L5
Longsight *BOLE* BL2 ....23 C8
Longsight La *BOLE* BL2 ....23 C8
CHD/CHDH SK8 ....120 E7
GTN M18 ....99 L1
RAMS BL0 ....13 E3
Longsight St *HTNM* SK4 ....12 E3
Longson St *BOL* BL1 ....89 H6
Long St *GTN* M18 ....89 H6
MDTN M24 ....70 C5
SWIN M27 ....70 C5
Longton Av *DID/WITH* M20 ....98 E3
GOL/RIS/CU WA3 ....79 M4
SLFD M6 ....70 F7
Longton Rd *BKLY* M9 ....70 F7
WGNE/HIN WN2 ....48 F9
Longton St *BURY* BL9 ....39 J8
WGNE/HIN WN2 ....48 F9
Longtown Gdns *BOL* * BL1 ....36 B2
Longview Dr *SWIN* M27 ....69 M3
Longwall Av *WALK* M28 ....68 C4

Longwood Av OFTN SK2 112 E6
Longwood Cl MPL/ROM SK6 114 B1
Longwood Rd TRPK M17 85 L6
WYTH/NTH M22 119 G1
Longworth Av HOR/BR BL6 32 F1
Longworth Cl URM M41 95 G3
Longworth Clough
EDGW/EG BL7 22 A2
Longworth La BOL BL1 22 A4
Longworth Rd HOR/BR BL6 21 C8
Longworth St BOLE BL2 3 L4
CSLFD M3 6 D6
Lonsdale Av LEIGH WN7 81 G2
MILN OL16 11 K9
RDSH SK5 100 C1
SWIN M27 70 A7
URM M41 84 E8
Lonsdale Rd BNG/LEV M19 99 L2
BOL BL1 35 L4
OLDS OL8 74 E2
Lonsdale St NEWH/MOS M40 73 M6
TOT/BURYW BL8 38 F2
Loom St ANC M4 7 K3
Loonies Ct STKP * SK1 13 J6
Lord Av ATH * M46 67 H3
Lord Byron Sq SALQ M50 86 C4
Lord Derby Rd HYDE SK14 102 B6
Lord Gv ATH M46 67 J3
Lord La FAIL M35 74 B8
Lord Napier Dr ORD M5 86 D5
Lord North St NEWH/MOS M40 73 H8
Lord's Av ORD * M5 86 A2
Lordsfields Av AULW OL7 75 L8
Lords Fold BOL * BL1 35 J2
Lordship Cl BKLY M9 73 J3
Lordsmead St HULME M15 6 B9
Lord Sq MILN OL16 10 E4
Lord's Stile La EDGW/EG BL7 22 E5
Lord St AIMK * WN4 64 A8
ATH M46 67 H3
AUL OL6 75 L8
BOLS/LL BL3 53 L1
BURY BL9 5 G5
CSLFD M3 72 C8
DTN/ASHW M34 89 K8
DUK SK16 91 J4
FWTH BL4 53 H4
GLSP SK13 104 F3
HOR/BR BL6 21 B8
HYDE SK14 93 G8
LEIGH WN7 66 C7
MDTN M24 57 K3
OLD OL1 9 J4
RAD M26 54 D1
STKP SK1 13 H5
TYLD M29 67 J6
WGN WN1 15 G1
WGNE/HIN WN2 48 D5
WGNE/HIN WN2 49 G7
WHTN BL5 50 B3
Lord St South LEIGH WN7 66 D7
Lordy Cl WGNNW/ST WN6 31 L5
Loretto Rd URM M41 96 C3
Lorgill Cl EDGY/DAV SK3 112 C8
Loring St NEWH/MOS M40 73 M7
Lorland Rd EDGY/DAV SK3 12 A8
Lorna Gv CHD/CHDH SK8 110 C6
Lorna Rd CHD/CHDH SK8 120 D2
Lorne Av ROY/SHW OL2 58 E1
Lorne Gv EDGY/DAV SK3 112 B6
URM M41 96 B2
Lorne Rd RUSH/FAL M14 98 F4
Lorne St BOL BL1 2 E4
BRUN/LGST M13 87 M7
ECC M30 84 E4
FWTH BL4 52 F2
HEY OL10 41 G3
MOSL OL5 76 F3
OLDS OL8 59 H8
WGN WN1 15 K4
WHIT OL12 28 E1
Lorne Wy HEY OL10 40 C3
Lorraine Cl HEY OL10 41 H4
Lorraine Rd HALE/TIMP WA15 108 D7
Lorton Cl MDTN M24 56 F2
WALK M28 68 C6
Lorton Gv BOLE BL2 37 J4
Lostock Av BNG/LEV M19 99 L3
BRAM/HZG SK7 121 K3
POY/DIS SK12 121 K8
SALE M33 97 H8
URM M41 95 L1
Lostock Cl HEY OL10 40 E1
WGNW/BIL/O WN5 62 B7
Lostock Dr BURY BL9 25 J6
Lostock Gv STRET M32 96 E1
Lostock Hall Rd POY/DIS SK12 128 F1
Lostock Junction La
HOR/BR BL6 34 F6
Lostock La HOR/BR BL6 34 B6
Lostock Park Dr HOR/BR BL6 34 D5
Lostock Rd ORD M5 86 B2
POY/DIS SK12 129 G2
URM M41 84 F8
WHTN BL5 33 M8
Lostock St NEWH/MOS M40 88 A1
Lostock Wy WILM/AE SK9 119 M8
Lothian Av ECC M30 84 E1
Lottery Rw BOL BL1 2 F5
Lottery St EDGY/DAV SK3 12 F5
Lottie St SWIN M27 70 D4
Loughborough Cl SALE M33 108 A1
Loughfield URM M41 95 K2
Loughrigg Av ROY/SHW OL2 42 F4
Loughrigg Cl TYLD M29 67 L5
Louisa St BOL BL1 36 A2
OP/CLY M11 89 G4
WALK M28 53 G8
Louis Av BURY BL9 25 J8
Louise Cl WHIT OL12 28 F1
Louise Gdns WHIT OL12 28 E1
WHTN BL5 50 B6
Louise St WHIT OL12 28 E1
Louvain St FAIL M35 74 B5
Lovalle St BOL BL1 35 M3
Lovat Rd BOLE BL2 37 J5
Love La HTNM SK4 13 G2
RAMS BL0 17 E3
Lovell Dr HYDE SK14 91 J8
Lovers' La ATH M46 66 C2
OLDE OL4 60 F6
Low Bank Rd AIMK WN4 63 H8
Lowcock St BRO M7 72 B8
Lowcroft Crs CHAD OL9 58 C4
Low Crompton Rd
ROY/SHW OL2 43 G6
Lowcross Rd NEWH/MOS M40 73 K6
Lowe Av ATH M46 50 F7
Lowe Gn ROY/SHW OL2 43 H7
Lowe Mill La WGNE/HIN WN2 49 G7
Lower Albion St CMANE M1 7 J7
Lower Alma St AULW OL7 90 E3
Lowerbank DTN/ASHW M34 90 C7
Lower Bank GLSP SK13 105 G4
Lower Bank Cl GLSP SK13 104 C1
Lower Bank St BURY BL9 4 D4
Lower Barn Rd GLSP SK13 93 H8
Lower Beechwood ROCH OL11 10 A8
Lower Bennett St HYDE SK14 102 A4
Lower Bents La MPL/ROM SK6 101 J8
Lower Birches OLDE OL4 60 C8
Lower Bridgeman St
BOLS/LL BL3 3 G7
Lower Broadacre STLY SK15 92 B6
Lower Brook La WALK * M28 69 K7
Lower Brook St CMANE * M1 7 J6
Lower Broughton Rd BRO M7 71 M8
Lower Bury St HTNM SK4 12 E3
Lower Byrom St CSLFD M3 6 C6
Lower Carr La UPML OL3 61 L6
Lower Carrs STKP SK1 13 K5
Lower Chatham St CMANE M1 7 G8
Lower Cliffe NM/HAY * SK22 124 A2
Lower Cft WHTF M45 54 F6
Lowercroft Rd TOT/BURYW BL8 38 C2
Lower Crossbank OLDE OL4 60 C4
Lower Darcy St BOLS/LL BL3 3 L9
Lower Dingle OLD OL1 43 M8
Lower Drake Fold WHTN BL5 50 A7
Lower Edge Av OLD OL1 9 H2
Lowerfield Dr OFTN SK2 113 J7
Lowerfields OLDS OL8 59 L8
Lower Flds UPML OL3 61 K3
Lowerfields Ri ROY/SHW OL2 43 L4
Lower Fold DTN/ASHW M34 101 K2
MPL/ROM SK6 114 E4
Lower Fold Av ROY/SHW OL2 43 K8
Lowerfold Cl WHIT OL12 18 D8
Lowerfold Crs WHIT OL12 18 D8
Lowerfold Dr WHIT OL12 18 D8
Lowerfold Wy WHIT OL12 18 D8
Lower Frenches Dr UPML OL3 61 K6
Lower Goodwin Cl BOLE BL2 37 H2
Lower Gn AUL OL6 75 M8
MDTN M24 57 J7
WHIT OL12 27 M3
Lower Green La TYLD M29 82 F2
Lower Greenshall La
POY/DIS SK12 124 A5
Lower Hague NM/HAY SK22 124 A4
Lower Hardman St CSLFD M3 6 C5
Lower Hey La MOSL OL5 77 H1
Lower Hillgate STKP SK1 13 J4
Lower House Dr HOR/BR BL6 34 F5
Lower House La WHIT OL12 19 J5
Lower House St OLD OL1 59 L4
Lower House Wk EDGW/EG BL7 22 D4
Lower Jowkin La ROCH OL11 27 G5
Lower Knoll Rd UPML OL3 45 M7
Lower Landedmans WHTN BL5 50 C5
Lower La MILN OL16 29 G8
Lowerlea POY/DIS SK12 123 L6
Lower Leigh Rd WHTN BL5 50 C7
Lower Lime Rd OLDS OL8 74 F4
Lower Longshoot WGN WN1 15 J3
Lower Lyndon Av
WGNNW/ST WN6 30 D6
Lower Makinson Fold
HOR/BR * BL6 34 A3
Lower Marlands EDGW/EG BL7 22 C4
Lower Md EDGW/EG BL7 22 C3
Lower Meadow EDGW/EG BL7 16 D6
Lower Meadow Rd
WILM/AE SK9 120 A8
Lower Moat Cl HTNM SK4 112 B1
Lower Monton Rd ECC M30 85 H2
Lower Mosley St CMANW M2 6 E7
Lower Moss La HULME M15 6 B9
WHTF M45 55 J4
Lower New Rw WALK M28 68 D3
Lower Ormond St CMANE M1 7 G8
Lower Park Crs POY/DIS SK12 121 K6
Lower Park Rd POY/DIS SK12 121 K7
RUSH/FAL M14 87 M8
Lower Rawson St FWTH BL4 53 H3
Lower Rd RAMS BL0 17 D4
Lower St Stephen St
WGNNW/ST WN6 14 C3
Lower Seedley Rd SLFD M6 86 B1
Lower Sheriff St WHIT OL12 10 C3
Lower Southfield WHTN BL5 50 B5
Lower St FWTH BL4 52 F5
ROCH OL11 28 D8
Lower Strines Rd
MPL/ROM SK6 114 D7
Lower Sutherland St SWIN M27 70 B4
Lower Tenterfield ROCH OL11 27 G2
Lower Tong EDGW/EG BL7 22 C5
Lower Turf La OLDE OL4 60 D5
Lower Tweedale St ROCH OL11 10 F7
Lower Vickers St
NEWH/MOS M40 88 A1
Lower Victoria St CHAD OL9 8 B5
Lower Wharf St AUL OL6 90 E2
Lower Wheat End MILN OL16 11 K3
Lower Woodhill Rd
TOT/BURYW BL8 4 B4
Lowerwood La BOLE BL2 36 E3
The Lowes ALT WA14 116 D3
Lowes Rd BURY BL9 25 J6
Lowestead Rd OP/CLY M11 88 F2
Lowestoft St RUSH/FAL M14 98 E2
Lowe St DTN/ASHW M34 101 L1
GOL/RIS/CU WA3 79 K4
RAD M26 38 C8
STKP SK1 13 J5
Loweswater Av TYLD M29 67 K5
Loweswater Rd
CHD/CHDH SK8 119 K1
FWTH BL4 52 B5
Lowfield Av AUL OL6 76 C7
DROY M43 89 J1
Lowfield Gdns GOL/RIS/CU WA3 81 M5
Lowfield Gv OFTN SK2 13 J9
Lowfield Rd EDGY/DAV SK3 13 H9
Low Gate La UPML OL3 45 J3
Low Gn ATH M46 51 J7
Low Grove La OLDE * OL4 61 H7
Low Hl WHIT OL12 28 F1
Lowhouse Cl MILN OL16 29 K5
Lowick Av BOLS/LL BL3 52 D1
Lowick Cl BRAM/HZG SK7 121 M2
Lowick Gn MPL/ROM SK6 101 J7
Lowland Gv AULW OL7 75 K6
Lowland Rd OFTN SK2 112 E8
Lowlands Cl MDTN M24 57 M8
Low Lea Rd MPL/ROM SK6 114 E5
Low Leighton Rd
NM/HAY SK22 124 F5
Low Mdw ROY/SHW OL2 43 G6
Lowndes Cl OFTN SK2 112 E5
Lowndes La OFTN SK2 112 E5
Lowndes St BOL BL1 35 L4
Lowndes Wk
BRUN/LGST * M13 87 M6
Lownorth Rd WYTH/NTH M22 119 G4
Lowood Av URM M41 84 C8
Lowood St LEIGH WN7 66 A7
Lowry Ct WHTF * M45 55 G2
Lowry Dr MPL/ROM SK6 114 E4
SWIN M27 70 C3
Lowry Gv HYDE SK14 103 J1
Lowry Houses ECC * M30 85 H2
Lowry Wk BOL BL1 36 A3
The Lows OLDE OL4 59 L7
Lowside Av HOR/BR BL6 34 F6
MPL/ROM SK6 101 M6
Lowside Dr OLDE OL4 59 L7
Low's Pl WHIT OL12 28 D2
Lowstern Cl EDGW/EG BL7 22 A5
Lowther Av GOL/RIS/CU WA3 81 J8
GTN M18 99 L1
HALE/TIMP WA15 108 D6
ROY/SHW OL2 42 F4
Lowther Cl PWCH M25 71 K1
Lowther Crs MDTN M24 57 H3
Lowther Dr LEIGH WN7 67 H5
Lowther Gdns URM M41 95 G1
Lowther Rd CHH M8 72 D3
PWCH M25 71 J1
ROCH OL11 28 B8
Lowther St BOLS/LL BL3 52 D2
Lowthorpe St RUSH/FAL M14 98 D2
Lowton Av BKLY M9 73 J5
Lowton Gdns GOL/RIS/CU WA3 79 L7
Lowton Rd GOL/RIS/CU WA3 79 L3
SALE M33 108 A2
Lowton St RAD M26 38 D8
Low Wood Cl BRAM/HZG SK7 120 E3
Low Wood Rd DTN/ASHW M34 89 K8
Loxford Ct HULME M15 6 F9
Loxford St HULME M15 87 J6
Loxham St FWTH BL4 53 G2
Loxton Crs WGNS/IIMK WN3 63 L1
Lubeck St BKLY M9 73 H4
Lucas Rd FWTH BL4 52 D4
Lucas St BURY BL9 5 J2
OLDE OL4 59 L5
Lucas Wk OP/CLY M11 88 C4
Lucerne Cl CHAD OL9 8 C7
Lucerne Rd BRAM/HZG SK7 121 G1
Lucien Cl WGTN/LGST M12 88 B7
Luciol Cl TYLD M29 67 M3
Lucknow St ROCH OL11 10 E9
Lucy St BOL BL1 35 K3
BRO M7 72 A7
EDGY/DAV SK3 13 G7
HULME M15 87 G6
Ludford Gv SALE M33 108 C2
Ludgate Hl ANC M4 7 J1
Ludgate Rd NEWH/MOS M40 73 M8
ROCH OL11 42 D2
Ludgate St ANC M4 7 H1
Ludlow Av SWIN M27 70 D2
WGNE/HIN WN2 49 K8
WHTF M45 55 L6
Ludlow Dr LEIGH WN7 67 G5
Ludlow Pk OLDE OL4 60 A6
Ludlow Rd STKP SK1 112 F4
Ludlow St WGNNW/ST WN6 31 J8
Ludovic Ter WGN WN1 31 M8
Lugano Rd BRAM/HZG SK7 121 G1
Luke Rd DROY M43 89 L3
Luke St AIMK WN4 64 A7
Lullington Cl WYTH/NTH M22 118 E3
Lullington Rd SLFD M6 71 G8
Lulworth Av URM M41 95 J2
Lulworth Cl TOT/BURYW BL8 24 F6
Lulworth Crs FAIL M35 74 E4
Lulworth Dr WGNE/HIN WN2 49 K8
Lulworth Gdns
NTHM/RTH M23 109 J4
Lulworth Rd BOLS/LL BL3 51 K1
ECC M30 84 F2
MDTN M24 57 L2
Lumb Carr Av RAMS BL0 17 A8
Lumb Carr Rd RAMS BL0 24 D1
Lumb Cl BRAM/HZG SK7 121 G6
Lumber La WALK M28 69 H4
Lumb La BRAM/HZG SK7 121 G6
DROY M43 74 F8
DROY M43 75 G7
DTN/ASHW M34 89 M4
Lumley Cl RUSH/FAL M14 87 L8
Lumn Hollow HYDE SK14 102 B2
Lumn Rd HYDE SK14 102 B2
Lumn's La SWIN M27 70 F2
Lum St BURY BL9 25 J4
Lumsden St BOLS/LL BL3 2 C9
Lum St BOL BL1 3 G3
Lumwood BOL BL1 35 L1
Luna St ANC M4 7 J3
Lund Av RAD M26 54 E4
Lund St OLDTF/WHR M16 86 F6
Lune Cl WHTF M45 55 K4
Lunedale Gn OFTN SK2 113 H6
Lune Dr WHTF M45 55 K4
Lune Gv HEY OL10 40 D1
LEIGH WN7 65 M7
Lunehurst GOL/RIS/CU WA3 80 B4
Lune Rd WGNE/HIN WN2 64 D2
Lune St OLDS OL8 59 H8
Lune Wy RDSH SK5 100 C7
Lunn Av GTN M18 89 J8
Lupin Av FWTH BL4 52 D3
Lupin Dr RNFD/HAY WA11 78 C6
Lupton St CSLFD * M3 6 B3
DTN/ASHW M34 90 C8
Lurden Wk CHAD * OL9 58 D8
Lurdin La WGN WN1 31 L5
Lurgan Av SALE M33 108 F1
Lutener Av ALT WA14 107 M4
Luton Dr NTHM/RTH M23 109 K8
Luton Gv ATH M46 66 E1
Luton Rd RDSH SK5 100 C4
Luton St BOLS/LL * BL3 36 D8
TOT/BURYW BL8 38 E3
Luxhall Wk NEWH/MOS M40 73 L7
Luxor Gv DTN/ASHW M34 100 C1
Luzley Brook Rd ROY/SHW OL2 43 K7
Luzley Rd AUL OL6 76 D6
Lyceum Pas MILN OL16 10 E4
Lyceum Pl HULME * M15 7 G9
Lychgate WGNW/BIL/O WN5 47 H7
Lychgate Ct OLDE OL4 76 B1
Lychgate Ms HTNM * SK4 111 H2
Lydbrook Cl BOL BL1 2 C6
Lydden Av OP/CLY * M11 89 G1
Lydford ROCH OL11 10 D7
Lydford Gdns BOLE BL2 37 J7
Lydford Gn WGNNW/ST WN6 31 J4
Lydford St SLFD M6 71 L8
Lydford Wk BRUN/LGST * M13 87 M6
Lydgate Av BOLE BL2 37 H4
Lydgate Cl DTN/ASHW M34 101 L3
STLY SK15 77 H6
WHTF M45 55 K4
Lydgate Dr OLDE OL4 59 M7
Lydgate Rd DROY M43 89 H1
SALE M33 108 F2
Lydiate Cl BOLS/LL BL3 52 C1
Lydiat La WILM/AE SK9 130 D4
Lydney Av CHD/CHDH SK8 119 L5
Lydney Rd URM M41 95 G1
Lyefield Av WGN WN1 15 M2
Lyefield Wk MILN OL16 11 J6
Lymbridge Dr HOR/BR BL6 33 G2
Lyme Av WILM/AE SK9 126 F3
Lyme Clough Wy MDTN M24 41 J8
Lymefield Dr WALK M28 68 D5
Lymefield Gv OFTN SK2 112 E6
Lyme Gv ALT WA14 107 M8
DROY M43 89 J4
MPL/ROM SK6 114 A2
MPL/ROM SK6 114 C7
OFTN SK2 13 J8
Lyme Rd BRAM/HZG SK7 122 A3
POY/DIS SK12 123 J5
Lymes ALT WA14 116 E3
Lyme St BRAM/HZG * SK7 121 M1
HTNM SK4 111 H2
NEWLW WA12 78 B8
RNFD/HAY WA11 78 B6
Lymewood Dr POY/DIS SK12 123 K6
WILM/AE * SK9 127 J4
Lymington Cl MDTN M24 57 L7
Lymington Dr NTHM/RTH M23 109 G4
Lymm Cl EDGY/DAV SK3 112 A6
WALK M28 68 D1
Lymn St WGNE/HIN WN2 64 E1
Lynbridge Cl WGNW/BIL/O WN5 46 B7
Lyncombe Cl CHD/CHDH SK8 120 D6
Lyndale Av RDSH SK5 100 C1
SWIN M27 70 A6
Lyndale Dr LIT OL15 20 B6
Lyndene Av WALK M28 69 K4
Lyndene Gdns CHD/CHDH SK8 110 F6
Lyndene Rd WYTH/NTH M22 110 A7
Lyndhurst Av AUL OL6 75 L7
BRAM/HZG SK7 121 L3
CHAD OL9 58 C7
DTN/ASHW * M34 101 H1
IRL M44 94 E1
MPL/ROM SK6 101 J8
PWCH M25 72 B1
ROCH OL11 42 A4
SALE M33 108 C1
URM M41 84 F8
Lyndhurst Cl WILM/AE SK9 126 B7
Lyndhurst Dr HALE/TIMP WA15 117 J2
Lyndhurst Rd DID/WITH M20 98 D8
OLDS OL8 75 G1
RDSH * SK5 100 B2
STRET M32 96 E2
Lyndhurst St SLFD M6 86 B2
Lyndhurst Vw DUK * SK16 90 F3
Lyndon Av WGNNW/ST WN6 30 E5
Lyndon Cl OLDE OL4 60 E4
TOT/BURYW BL8 24 C6
Lyndon Rd IRL M44 94 C3
Lyne Av GLSP SK13 104 D4
Lyne Edge Crs DUK SK16 91 J5
Lyne Edge Rd DUK SK16 91 K5
Lyne Vw HYDE SK14 91 J6
Lyngard Cl WILM/AE SK9 127 H3
Lyngate Cl STKP SK1 13 L6
Lyn Gv HEY OL10 40 D1
Lynham Dr HEY OL10 41 G4
Lynmouth Av DID/WITH M20 98 D6
OLDS OL8 75 J1
RDSH SK5 100 B5
ROY/SHW OL2 58 F1
URM M41 95 L4
Lynmouth Cl CHAD OL9 58 B3
RAD M26 38 F8
WGNNW/ST WN6 47 K2
Lynmouth Gv PWCH M25 71 J1
Lynn Av SALE M33 97 G6
Lynndene Ct HEY * OL10 40 F1
Lynn Dr DROY M43 89 H2
Lynne Cl GLSP SK13 105 J4
Lynn St CHAD OL9 58 F8
Lynnwood Dr ROCH OL11 27 L4
Lynnwood Rd BNG/LEV M19 111 G2
Lynroyle Wy ROCH OL11 42 A1
Lynsted Av BOLS/LL BL3 52 D1
Lynstock Wy HOR/BR BL6 34 B6
Lynthorpe Av IRL M44 94 A6
Lynthorpe Rd NEWH/MOS M40 74 A2
Lynton Av HYDE SK14 102 F2
IRL M44 94 B6
OLDS OL8 74 F2
ROCH OL11 41 L1
SWIN M27 70 A6
URM M41 94 F2
WGNNW/ST WN6 47 K1
Lynton Cl CHAD OL9 58 C3
Lynton Crs WALK M28 69 G4
Lynton Dr BNG/LEV M19 99 J5
MPL/ROM SK6 123 G4
PWCH M25 55 M6
Lynton Gv HALE/TIMP WA15 108 D7
Lynton La WILM/AE SK9 130 D2
Lynton Lea RAD M26 38 F8
Lynton Ms WILM/AE SK9 130 D2
Lynton Park Rd
CHD/CHDH SK8 120 B4
Lynton Rd BOLS/LL BL3 51 M2
CCHDY M21 97 K3
CHD/CHDH SK8 110 F7
HTNM SK4 99 L7
SWIN M27 70 C5
TYLD M29 68 A4
WGNE/HIN WN2 49 J6
Lynton St LEIGH WN7 66 A7
RUSH/FAL * M14 98 E2
Lyntonvale Av CHD/CHDH SK8 110 D6
Lynway Dr DID/WITH M20 98 E7
Lynway Gv MDTN M24 57 L2
Lynwell Rd ECC M30 85 G2
Lynwood HALE/TIMP WA15 117 J4
Lynwood Av BOLS/LL BL3 52 E1
ECC M30 85 G2
GOL/RIS/CU WA3 80 B6
OLDTF/WHR M16 97 M2
Lynwood Cl AULW OL7 75 K5
Lynwood Dr OLDE OL4 60 B4
Lynwood Gv ATH M46 66 E1
BOLE BL2 23 G8
DTN/ASHW M34 89 M3
HTNM SK4 99 M6
SALE M33 96 F7
Lyon Gv WALK M28 69 K4
Lyon Rd ALT WA14 107 M5
FWTH BL4 53 H7
WGNNW/ST WN6 47 K2
Lyons Dr TOT/BURYW BL8 38 D3
Lyons Fold SALE M33 96 E6
Lyons Rd TRPK M17 85 K5
Lyon St AIMK WN4 63 J5
ROY/SHW OL2 43 L5
SWIN M27 70 B5
WGNS/IIMK WN3 14 E5
Lysander Cl RUSH/FAL M14 98 D4
Lytham Av CCHDY M21 97 M5
Lytham Cl AUL OL6 76 B6
Lytham Dr BRAM/HZG SK7 121 J5
HEY OL10 40 F3
Lytham Rd AIMK WN4 63 J7
CHD/CHDH SK8 119 K3
RUSH/FAL M14 99 J3
URM M41 94 F2
Lytham St EDGY/DAV SK3 112 C6
WHIT OL12 28 B1
Lytherton Av IRL M44 94 A8
Lyth St RUSH/FAL M14 99 G5
Lytton Av CHH M8 72 D6
Lytton Rd DROY M43 89 K2
Lytton St BOL BL1 36 A2

M

Mabel Av BOLS/LL BL3 52 D1
WALK M28 69 K5
Mabel Rd FAIL M35 74 D3
Mabel's Brow FWTH BL4 53 H5
Mabel St BOL BL1 35 M4
NEWH/MOS M40 74 A7
WGNW/BIL/O WN5 47 H6
WHIT OL12 28 A2
WHTN BL5 50 C6
Maberry Cl WGNNW/ST WN6 30 A5
Mabfield Rd RUSH/FAL M14 98 F3
Mableden Cl CHD/CHDH SK8 119 M4
Mabs Ct AUL OL6 91 G2
Macaulay St ROCH OL11 41 M3
ROY/SHW OL2 43 H8
Macauley Cl DUK SK16 91 K5
Macauley Pl WGNS/IIMK WN3 47 J8
Macauley Rd OLDTF/WHR M16 97 L2
RDSH SK5 100 A3
Macclesfield Cl WGNE/HIN WN2 48 F7
Macclesfield Rd
BRAM/HZG SK7 122 B4
MCFLDN SK10 129 G5
WILM/AE SK9 127 G6
WILM/AE SK9 130 F4
Macdonald Av FWTH BL4 52 D5
WGNS/IIMK WN3 63 K1
Macdonald Rd IRL M44 94 B5
Macdonald St OLDS OL8 59 J8
WGNW/BIL/O WN5 46 E6
Macefin Av CCHDY M21 98 A8
Mackenzie Av WGNS/IIMK WN3 63 K1
Mackenzie Gv BOL BL1 22 A8
Mackenzie Rd BRO M7 71 L6
Mackenzie St BOL BL1 22 A8
WGTN/LGST M12 99 K1
Mackenzie Wk OLD OL1 44 B7
Mackeson Dr AUL OL6 76 B8
Mackeson Rd AUL OL6 76 B8
Mackintosh Wy OLD OL1 9 J4
Maclaren Dr CHH M8 72 B2
Maclure Rd ROCH OL11 10 F6
Macnair Ms MPL/ROM * SK6 114 C6
Madams Wood Rd WALK M28 68 C1
Maddison Rd DROY M43 89 J3
Madeley Cl ALT WA14 117 G4
WGNS/IIMK WN3 63 H1
Madeley Dr CHAD OL9 8 B7
Madeley Gdns BOL BL1 36 B2
WHIT OL12 10 A1
Maden's Sq LIT OL15 20 C7
Maden St TYLD M29 67 J6
Maden Wk CHAD * OL9 8 B3
Madison Av CHD/CHDH SK8 120 C2
DTN/ASHW M34 89 M4
Madison St GTN M18 89 H6
Madras Rd EDGY/DAV SK3 12 D9
Maesbrook Dr TYLD M29 67 K4
Mafeking Av BURY BL9 25 K7
Mafeking Pl AIMK WN4 78 F1
Mafeking Rd BOLE * BL2 37 H5
Mafeking St OLDS OL8 74 F1
Magdala St HEY * OL10 41 H4
OLD OL1 9 G2
Magdalen Dr AIMK WN4 63 J8
Magda Rd OFTN SK2 112 F7
Magenta Av IRL M44 94 B6
Magnolia Cl SALE M33 95 M7
Magnolia Dr CHH * M8 72 D6
Magpie Cl DROY M43 89 M1
Magpie La OLDE OL4 60 A8
Magpie Wk OP/CLY * M11 88 C3
Maguire Av GLSP SK13 93 K6
Maher Gdns HULME M15 87 H8
Mahood St EDGY/DAV SK3 12 F8
Maida St BNG/LEV M19 99 L2
Maidford Cl ANC * M4 88 A3
STRET M32 97 H2
Maidstone Av CCHDY M21 97 K3
Maidstone Cl WGNE/HIN WN2 65 M2
Maidstone Ms CCHDY M21 97 K3
Maidstone Rd HTNM SK4 111 G1
Main Av BNG/LEV M19 99 J5
TRPK M17 85 M8
Maine Rd RUSH/FAL M14 98 D1
Mainprice Cl SLFD M6 71 J8
Main Rd CHAD OL9 8 D4
SWIN M27 71 G1
Mains Av WGNE/HIN WN2 64 C5
Main St FAIL M35 74 C4
HYDE SK14 91 G8
WGNW/BIL/O WN5 62 B7
Mainwaring Dr WILM/AE SK9 127 H4
Mainwaring Ter
NTHM/RTH M23 109 K2
Mainway MDTN M24 57 J6
Mainway East MDTN M24 57 M6
Mainwood Rd
HALE/TIMP WA15 108 F7
Maismore Rd WYTH/NTH M22 118 C3
Maitland Av CCHDY M21 97 M8
Maitland Cl WHIT OL12 28 F1
Maitland St STKP SK1 112 E5
Maitland Wk CHAD * OL9 8 B3
Major St CMANE M1 7 H6
MILN OL16 29 J6

RAMS BL0 17 B6
WGNW/BIL/O WN5 46 F6
Makants Cl ATH M46 51 J6
TYLD M29 68 B4
Makerfield Dr NEWLW WA12 78 D8
Makerfield Wy WGNE/HIN WN2 48 E5
Makin Ct HEY OL10 41 G3
Makinson Ar WGN WN1 14 F3
Makinson Av HOR/BR BL6 34 B2
WGNE/HIN WN2 49 G5
Makin St CMANE * M1 7 H7
Makkah Cl NEWH/MOS M40 73 K7
Malaga Av MANAIR M90 118 D5
Malakoff St STLY SK15 91 H4
Malbrook Wk BRUN/LGST * M13 87 M6
Malby St OLD OL1 9 J3
Malcolm Av SWIN M27 70 D2
Malcolm Dr SWIN M27 70 D2
Malcolm St ROCH OL11 42 A1
Malden Gv NTHM/RTH M23 109 K5
Maldon Cl BOLS/LL BL3 53 K1
OFTN SK2 113 K7
WGNE/HIN WN2 48 C2
Maldon Crs SWIN M27 70 C6
Maldon Dr ECC M30 70 B8
Maldon Rd WGNNW/ST WN6 31 J4
Maldon St ROCH OL11 10 F8
Maldwyn Av BOLS/LL BL3 51 L2
CHH M8 72 D2
Maleham St BRO * M7 72 B6
Malgam Dr DID/WITH M20 110 E4
Malham Av WGNS/IIMK WN3 63 K2
Malham Cl LEIGH WN7 65 M7
ROY/SHW OL2 43 G8
Malham Ct OFTN SK2 113 G6
Malham Dr WHTF M45 55 K4
Malika Pl AIMK * WN4 63 H6
The Mall BURY BL9 4 F5
STLY SK15 92 B6
Mallard Cl DUK SK16 91 H5
OFTN SK2 113 K7
OLDS OL8 75 G2
Mallard Crs POY/DIS SK12 121 J8
Mallard Dr HOR/BR BL6 33 K1
Mallard Gn ALT WA14 107 L4
Mallards Reach MPL/ROM SK6 113 L2
Mallard St CMANE * M1 7 G8
Mallet Crs BOL BL1 35 J2
Malling Rd NTHM/RTH M23 109 K8
Mallison St BOL BL1 36 C1
Mallory Av AULW OL7 75 L7
Mallory Dr LEIGH WN7 66 E7
Mallory Rd HYDE SK14 91 K8
Mallow Cft MILN OL16 28 F8
Mallowdale WALK M28 68 E4
Mallowdale Cl BOL BL1 35 G6
Mallowdale Rd OFTN SK2 113 K7
Mallow St HULME M15 87 H6
Malls Gdns MOSL OL5 77 G4
Malmesbury Cl POY/DIS SK12 121 M8
Malmesbury Rd
CHD/CHDH SK8 120 D6
Malpas Av WGN WN1 15 J1
Malpas Cl CHD/CHDH SK8 111 K7
WILM/AE SK9 127 H3
Malpas Dr ALT WA14 108 B3
Malpas St OLD OL1 9 K4
WGTN/LGST M12 88 D6
Malpas Wk OLDTF/WHR * M16 87 G7
Malrae HALE/TIMP * WA15 117 G3
Malsham Rd NTHM/RTH M23 109 J2
Malta Cl MDTN M24 58 A4
Malta St ANC M4 88 A3
OLDE OL4 60 A6
Maltby Ct OLDE OL4 60 C7
Maltby Dr BOLS/LL BL3 51 M2
Maltby Rd NTHM/RTH M23 109 J6
Malton Av BOLS/LL BL3 35 K8
CCHDY M21 97 L4
GOL/RIS/CU WA3 80 B5
WHTF M45 55 J2
Malton Cl CHAD OL9 58 C3
LEIGH WN7 65 M6
Malton Dr ALT WA14 107 K6
BRAM/HZG SK7 121 M5
Malton Rd HTNM SK4 99 K8
WALK M28 68 B5
Malton St OLDS OL8 8 F8
Malt St HULME M15 6 A9
Malus Ct SLFD M6 86 D1
Malverley Dr LEIGH WN7 66 F7
Malvern Av ATH M46 51 J7
AUL OL6 75 M5
BOL BL1 35 K3
BURY BL9 25 J7
CHD/CHDH SK8 110 C7
DROY M43 89 M2
URM M41 95 L2
WGNE/HIN WN2 49 K8
Malvern Cl AIMK WN4 63 L8
FWTH BL4 52 C3
HOR/BR BL6 21 C7
HTNM SK4 12 F1
MILN OL16 29 K5
PWCH M25 55 M7
ROY/SHW OL2 43 J4
ROY/SHW OL2 58 F1
SWIN M27 71 G6
WGNS/IIMK WN3 62 F1
Malvern Crs WGNS/IIMK WN3 48 C8
Malvern Dr ALT WA14 107 L7
SWIN M27 71 G6
Malvern Gv DID/WITH M20 98 D6
SLFD M6 85 M1
WALK M28 69 G1
Malvern Ri GLSP SK13 93 K7
Malvern Rd MDTN M24 57 K7
RDSH SK5 100 E7
Malvern Rw HULME * M15 86 F6
Malvern St OLDS OL8 8 F8
WGNNW/ST WN6 30 F1
Malvern St East ROCH OL11 27 M5
Malvern St West ROCH OL11 27 M5
Malvern Ter LEIGH WN7 81 J1
Manby Rd GTN M18 88 E8
Manby Sq GTN M18 88 E8
Manchester Chambers OLD OL1 9 H6
Manchester New Rd MDTN M24 57 J4
PART M31 106 C1
Manchester Old Rd BURY BL9 4 D7
MDTN M24 56 F5
Manchester Rd ALT WA14 108 A6
BOLS/LL BL3 3 G6
BOLS/LL BL3 52 F1
BURY BL9 4 D6
BURY BL9 4 D8
CCHDY M21 97 K4
CHD/CHDH SK8 111 G4
DROY M43 89 H3
DTN/ASHW M34 89 K8
FWTH BL4 53 L6
GLSP SK13 93 H6
HEY OL10 41 G6
HOR/BR BL6 33 G2
HTNM SK4 100 A7
HYDE SK14 101 L1
LEIGH WN7 66 F8
MDTN M24 42 A5
MOSL OL5 76 F5
OLDS OL8 58 F8
PART M31 94 D8
RAMS BL0 17 E7
ROCH OL11 10 C7
ROCH OL11 27 M8
ROCH OL11 41 M1
ROY/SHW OL2 43 K7
SWIN M27 70 C1
TYLD M29 67 L3
WALK M28 69 J2
WGN WN1 15 M4
WGNE/HIN WN2 48 D5
WHTN BL5 50 C2
WILM/AE SK9 126 F4
WILM/AE SK9 127 G4
Manchester Rd East WALK M28 52 D8
Manchester Rd North
DTN/ASHW M34 89 M8
Manchester Rd South
DTN/ASHW M34 100 F1
Manchester Rd West
LHULT M38 52 B7
Manchester St HEY OL10 41 G2
OLDS OL8 8 E8
OLDTF/WHR M16 86 F7
Manchet St ROCH OL11 41 L3
Mancroft Av BOLS/LL * BL3 36 A8
Mancroft Ter BOLS/LL * BL3 36 A8
Mancroft Wk CMANE M1 7 J8
Mancunian Rd DTN/ASHW M34 101 K4
Mancunian Wy WGTN/LGST M12 7 M8
Mandalay Gdns MPL/ROM SK6 114 A5
Mandarin Gn ALT WA14 107 L4
Mandarin Wk SLFD * M6 86 D1
Manderville Cl WGNS/IIMK WN3 63 G2
Mandeville St BNG/LEV M19 99 L4
Mandley Av NEWH/MOS * M40 74 A2
Mandley Cl BOLS/LL BL3 37 K7
Mandley Park Av BRO M7 72 B5
Mandon Cl RAD M26 38 B7
Manesty Cl MDTN M24 56 F2
Manet Cl BRO M7 71 L4
Mangle St CMANE M1 7 J4
Mango Pl SLFD M6 86 D2
Manifold Dr MPL/ROM SK6 123 H6
Manifold St SLFD M6 71 L7
Manilla Wk OP/CLY M11 88 C3
Manipur St OP/CLY M11 88 C4
Manley Av GOL/RIS/CU WA3 79 J2
SWIN M27 54 C8
Manley Cl BURY BL9 24 F2
LEIGH WN7 66 A4
Manley Crs WHTN BL5 50 E3
Manley Gv BRAM/HZG SK7 121 G6
HYDE SK14 103 J1
Manley Rd CCHDY M21 97 M3
OLDS OL8 59 H8
ROCH OL11 27 M8
SALE M33 108 B3
Manley St BRO M7 72 A6
WGNS/IIMK WN3 15 K8
Manley Ter BOL * BL1 22 B8
Manning Av WGNNW/ST WN6 47 K2
Manningham Rd BOLS/LL BL3 35 L7
Mannington Dr BKLY M9 72 F6
Mannock St OLDS OL8 8 F8
Manor Av BOLS/LL BL3 53 M1
GOL/RIS/CU WA3 79 M4
NEWLW WA12 78 C8
OLDTF/WHR M16 98 A2
SALE M33 96 A8
URM M41 96 A3
Manor Cl CHAD OL9 8 C3
CHD/CHDH SK8 120 E4
DTN/ASHW M34 101 L2
OLDE OL4 61 H6
WILM/AE SK9 126 C4
Manor Ct GOL/RIS/CU WA3 79 M4
STRET M32 96 E3
Manor Dr CCHDY M21 98 A8
ROY/SHW OL2 59 H1
Manor Farm Cl AULW OL7 75 J6
Manor Farm Ri OLDE OL4 60 A5
Manorfield Cl BOL BL1 35 K3
Manor Gdns WILM/AE SK9 127 H5
Manor Gate Rd BOLE BL2 37 K4
Manor Gv LEIGH WN7 81 M1
WGNE/HIN WN2 32 E7
WGNW/BIL/O WN5 46 E4
Manor Hill Rd MPL/ROM SK6 114 C5
Manorial Dr LHULT M38 52 B7
Manor Ml CHAD * OL9 8 C2
Manor Pk URM * M41 96 A3
Manor Park Rd GLSP SK13 105 H3
Manor Pl WGNS/IIMK WN3 15 M8
Manor Rd BNG/LEV M19 99 L2
BRAM/HZG SK7 113 G8
CHD/CHDH SK8 120 E3
DROY M43 89 H3
DTN/ASHW M34 89 L5
DTN/ASHW M34 101 L3
HALE/TIMP WA15 108 B8
HOR/BR BL6 21 D8
HYDE SK14 91 J7
MDTN M24 57 J6
MPL/ROM SK6 101 L7
MPL/ROM SK6 114 C5
OLDE OL4 59 M8
RDSH SK5 100 E7
RNFD/HAY WA11 78 D5
ROY/SHW OL2 43 K5
SALE M33 96 E7
SLFD M6 71 G8
STRET M32 96 E3
SWIN M27 70 C6
TYLD M29 67 M6
WGNE/HIN WN2 49 J7
WGNNW/ST WN6 30 C6
WILM/AE SK9 126 C4
Manor St BOL BL1 2 F4
BURY BL9 5 H4
DTN/ASHW M34 90 C5
FWTH BL4 52 F5
FWTH BL4 53 L7
GLSP SK13 105 G3
GOL/RIS/CU WA3 79 L3
MDTN M24 57 K2
MOSL OL5 76 F2
OLD OL1 59 K2
RAMS BL0 17 B5
WGN WN1 14 F4
WGNW/BIL/O WN5 47 J6
WGTN/LGST M12 7 L8
Manor Vw MPL/ROM SK6 101 L6
Mansart Cl AIMK WN4 79 G1
The Manse MOSL OL5 76 F4
Manse Gdns NEWLW WA12 79 G8
Mansell Wy HOR/BR BL6 34 A4
Mansfield Av BKLY M9 57 G8
DTN/ASHW M34 90 A7
RAMS BL0 24 E2
Mansfield Cl AULW OL7 90 C3
DTN/ASHW M34 90 A7
Mansfield Crs DTN/ASHW M34 90 A8
Mansfield Dr BKLY M9 57 H8
Mansfield Gra ROCH OL11 27 M6
Mansfield Gv BOL BL1 35 L3
Mansfield Rd BKLY M9 57 G8
HYDE SK14 102 B3
MOSL OL5 77 H3
OLDS OL8 59 L7
ROCH OL11 27 H5
URM M41 95 K3
Mansfield St AULW OL7 90 B4
GOL/RIS/CU WA3 79 H3
Mansford Dr NEWH/MOS M40 73 J7
Manshaw Crs OP/CLY M11 89 K5
Manshaw Rd OP/CLY M11 89 K5
Mansion Av WHTF M45 55 H1
Manson Av HULME M15 6 A9
Manstead Wk
NEWH/MOS * M40 88 B2
Manston Dr CHD/CHDH SK8 120 C2
Manswood Dr CHH M8 72 D5
Mantley La ROY/SHW OL2 44 D5
Manton Av BKLY M9 73 L1
DTN/ASHW M34 100 D1
Manton Cl CHH M8 72 C6
Manvers St RDSH SK5 112 B1
Manwaring St FAIL M35 74 B4
Maple Av ATH M46 50 E8
BOL * BL1 35 L3
BURY BL9 5 L4
CCHDY M21 97 L4
CHD/CHDH SK8 120 B2
DTN/ASHW M34 89 L3
DTN/ASHW M34 101 H1
ECC M30 69 K8
GOL/RIS/CU WA3 80 C5
HALE/TIMP WA15 109 H7
HOR/BR BL6 34 B3
MPL/ROM SK6 114 C8
POY/DIS SK12 124 C6
POY/DIS SK12 129 K1
STLY SK15 91 J4
STRET M32 97 G3
WGNE/HIN WN2 65 J1
WHTF M45 55 J5
Maple Cl FWTH BL4 53 J7
MDTN M24 58 A4
OFTN SK2 112 E6
ROY/SHW * OL2 43 J4
SLFD M6 86 C1
WGNW/BIL/O WN5 62 A7
Maple Crs LEIGH WN7 66 B5
Maplecroft STKP SK1 112 E4
Mapledon Rd BKLY M9 73 J4
Maple Dr WGNE/HIN WN2 64 E5
Maplefield Dr WALK M28 68 E5
Maple Gv FAIL M35 74 B7
NEWH/MOS M40 74 B2
PWCH M25 55 K6
RAMS BL0 17 D7
TOT/BURYW BL8 24 D7
WALK M28 69 G4
WGNNW/ST WN6 47 K1
Maple Rd BRAM/HZG SK7 121 G7
CHAD OL9 8 B1
FWTH BL4 52 D4
NTHM/RTH M23 108 F4
PART M31 106 B1
SWIN M27 70 B6
WILM/AE SK9 130 E2
Maple Rd West
NTHM/RTH M23 108 F4
Maple St AIMK WN4 63 K6
BOLE BL2 22 F7
BOLS/LL BL3 2 B8
OLDS OL8 74 F1
ROCH OL11 10 B6
Maple Wk NTHM/RTH M23 108 F4
Maplewood Cl ROY/SHW OL2 58 F2
Maplewood Gdns BOL * BL1 36 B2
Maplewood House BOL BL1 36 B3
Maplewood Rd WILM/AE SK9 127 J4
Mapley Av WYTH/NTH M22 110 A4
Maplin Cl BRUN/LGST M13 7 L9
Maplin Dr OFTN SK2 113 K7
Marble St CMANW M2 7 G4
OLD * OL1 59 L4
Marbury Av RUSH/FAL M14 98 E3
Marbury Cl EDGY/DAV SK3 111 K5
URM M41 95 G1
Marbury Gv WGNNW/ST WN6 31 H4
Marbury Rd HTNM SK4 100 A5
WILM/AE * SK9 126 E3
Marcer Rd NEWH/MOS M40 88 A2
March Av HTNM SK4 12 B3
Marchbank WGNE/HIN WN2 48 D2
Marchbank Dr CHD/CHDH SK8 110 F6
March Dr TOT/BURYW BL8 25 G7
Marchioness St GTN * M18 89 J6
Marchmont Cl
BRUN/LGST * M13 88 A6
March St MILN OL16 11 H4
Marchwood Av CCHDY M21 98 A3
Marcliffe Dr BNG/LEV M19 99 M3
ROCH OL11 27 L6
Marcliff Gv HTNM SK4 12 A3
Marcroft Pl ROCH OL11 28 D8
Marcus Gv RUSH/FAL M14 98 F2
Marcus St BOL BL1 35 L3
Mardale Av DID/WITH M20 98 F7
ROY/SHW OL2 42 F4
SWIN M27 69 M2
URM M41 95 J1
Mardale Cl ATH M46 50 F7
BOLE BL2 37 J3
PWCH M25 55 M5
STLY SK15 91 K1
Mardale Dr BOLE BL2 37 J3
CHD/CHDH SK8 110 E6
MDTN M24 57 H3
Mardale Rd SWIN M27 70 A6
Marden Rd NTHM/RTH M23 109 K7
Mardyke WHIT OL12 10 D3
Marfield BKLY * M9 73 H3
Marfield Av CHAD OL9 58 D7
Marford Cl WYTH/NTH M22 110 A6
Marford Crs SALE M33 108 C2
Margaret Ashton Cl BKLY M9 73 J5
Margaret Av MILN OL16 11 L5
WGNNW/ST WN6 30 F8
Margaret Rd DROY * M43 89 H2
DTN/ASHW M34 90 D8
Margaret St AUL OL6 90 D2
BURY BL9 5 G6
HEY OL10 40 E2
OLDS OL8 74 E2
RDSH SK5 100 B5
ROY/SHW * OL2 43 L6
WGNE/HIN WN2 49 G6
WGNNW/ST WN6 14 C2
Margate Av NEWH/MOS M40 73 L7
Margate Rd RDSH SK5 100 C5
Margrove Cha HOR/BR BL6 34 F7
Margrove Cl FAIL M35 74 F5
Margrove Rd SLFD M6 70 F8
Margroy Cl WHIT OL12 28 D2
Marguerita Rd NEWH/MOS M40 74 A8
Marham Cl CCHDY * M21 98 B6
HYDE SK14 91 G6
Marian Rd RNFD/HAY WA11 78 B5
Maria St BOL BL1 36 B2
Marie Cl DTN/ASHW M34 101 J2
Marie St BRO * M7 72 B5
Marigold St ROCH OL11 10 E9
WGNW/BIL/O WN5 47 G5
Mariman Dr CHH M8 72 D2
Marina Av DTN/ASHW M34 101 K3
Marina Cl WILM/AE SK9 119 M7
Marina Crs OP/CLY M11 88 E1
Marina Dr MPL/ROM SK6 113 M5
WGNW/BIL/O WN5 47 G7
Marina Rd DROY M43 89 L2
MPL/ROM SK6 101 H8
Marine Av PART M31 106 A1
Marion Pl WGNE/HIN WN2 64 C4
Marion St BOLS/LL BL3 52 F2
OLDS OL8 75 J1
Maritime Cl NEWLW WA12 78 F7
Marjorie Cl GTN M18 88 E6
Mark Av SLFD M6 71 L8
Markenfield Dr ROY/SHW OL2 43 J5
Market Ap AIMK * WN4 78 E1
Market Hall BOL * BL1 2 E4
Market Pde BURY BL9 4 F5
Market Pl AUL OL6 90 E1
BURY BL9 4 E4
HYDE * SK14 103 K1
LEIGH WN7 66 C7
MDTN M24 57 K3
OLD * OL1 9 H5
RAMS BL0 17 C6
STKP SK1 13 J3
WGN WN1 14 F4
WGNNW/ST WN6 31 H3
Market Sq ROY/SHW OL2 43 G8
Market St ALT WA14 108 A8
ATH M46 66 F1
BOL BL1 2 E4
BOLS/LL BL3 53 K1
BURY BL9 4 E5
BURY BL9 4 F8
CMANE M1 7 G4
DROY M43 89 L2
DTN/ASHW M34 101 J1
FWTH BL4 53 G3
GLSP SK13 104 F4
HEY OL10 40 F2
HYDE SK14 92 D8
HYDE SK14 93 G7
HYDE SK14 102 A1
MDTN M24 57 J3
MOSL OL5 76 F3
NEWLW WA12 78 D8
NM/HAY SK22 124 D5
NM/HAY SK22 125 M1
POY/DIS SK12 123 M6
RAD M26 53 K5
ROY/SHW OL2 43 L6
STLY SK15 91 K2
SWIN M27 70 D3
TOT/BURYW BL8 24 C6
TYLD M29 67 J3
WGN WN1 14 F3
WGNE/HIN WN2 49 G7
WGNNW/ST WN6 31 H3
WHIT OL12 18 D4
WHTN BL5 50 B4
Market Wk SALE * M33 96 E8
Market Wy SLFD M6 86 C1
Markfield Av BRUN/LGST M13 88 A7
Markham Cl WGTN/LGST M12 88 A4
Markham St HYDE SK14 91 G6
Markington St RUSH/FAL M14 98 D1
Markland Hl BOL BL1 35 H4
Markland Hill Cl BOL BL1 35 J3
Markland Hill La BOL BL1 35 H3
Marklands Rd HOR/BR BL6 21 E7
TYLD M29 67 K8
Markland St BOL BL1 2 E6
HYDE SK14 102 B3
RAMS * BL0 17 C6
WGN WN1 15 L5
Mark La ROY/SHW OL2 44 A6
Marks St RAD M26 54 D1
Mark St CHAD OL9 8 F4
WALK M28 68 C5
WHIT * OL12 28 D3
Markwood UPML OL3 45 J8
Marland Av CHD/CHDH SK8 120 B2
OLDS OL8 75 K3
ROCH OL11 27 L8
Marland Cl ROCH OL11 27 L7
Marland Crs RDSH SK5 100 C4
Marland Fold ROCH OL11 27 L8
Marland Fold La OLDS OL8 75 J3
Marland Gn ROCH OL11 27 L8
Marland Hill Rd ROCH OL11 27 M7
Marland Old Rd ROCH OL11 27 L8
Marland St CHAD OL9 74 D1
Marlborough Av CCHDY M21 97 M3
CHD/CHDH SK8 120 D3
WGNS/IIMK WN3 48 C8
WILM/AE SK9 130 E2
Marlborough Cl AULW OL7 90 B4
DTN/ASHW M34 101 J1
MPL/ROM SK6 114 A5
RAMS BL0 24 F1
Marlborough Dr FAIL M35 74 B6
HTNM * SK4 100 A8
Marlborough Gdns FWTH BL4 52 C4
Marlborough Rd ALT WA14 116 F2
ATH M46 51 H8
BRO M7 72 C6
ECC M30 70 D8
HYDE SK14 102 B4
IRL M44 94 E1
ROY/SHW OL2 59 H2
SALE M33 96 E8
STRET M32 96 F1
URM M41 95 J1
Marlborough St AULW OL7 90 C3
BOL BL1 2 A3
HEY OL10 41 H4
OLDE OL4 9 L7
WHIT OL12 27 M3
Marlbrook Dr WHTN BL5 50 B7
Marlbrook Ms WHTN * BL5 50 C7
Marlbrook Wk BOLS/LL BL3 36 C8
Marlcroft Av HTNM SK4 12 B3
Marld Crs BOL BL1 35 J2
Marle Av MOSL OL5 77 H3
Marle Cft WHTF M45 54 F6
Marled Hey EDGW/EG BL7 16 D7
Marle Ri MOSL OL5 77 H3
Marler Rd HYDE SK14 91 H8
Marley Cl HALE/TIMP WA15 108 C5
Marley Dr SALE M33 96 D6
Marleyer Cl NEWH/MOS M40 73 M5
Marleyer Ri MPL/ROM SK6 113 K4
Marley Rd BNG/LEV M19 99 L4
POY/DIS SK12 129 J2
Marlfield Rd HALE/TIMP WA15 117 M5
ROY/SHW OL2 43 H4
Marlfield St BKLY M9 73 H3
Marl Gv WGNW/BIL/O WN5 46 A8
Marlhill Cl OFTN SK2 113 H7
Marlinford Dr NEWH/MOS M40 73 M7
Marlor St DTN/ASHW M34 90 B8
Marlow Brow GLSP SK13 93 K8
Marlow Cl BOLE BL2 37 J3
CHD/CHDH SK8 120 B2
URM M41 84 E8
Marlow Dr ALT WA14 116 B2
IRL M44 94 D1
SWIN M27 70 B6
WILM/AE SK9 119 L7
Marlowe Cl WGNS/IIMK WN3 47 K7
Marlowe Dr DID/WITH M20 98 E8
Marlowe Wks MPL/ROM SK6 113 H2
Marlow Rd BKLY M9 73 J3
Marlow St GLSP SK13 93 K8
Marlwood Rd BOL BL1 35 J2
Marmion Cl GOL/RIS/CU WA3 80 B3
Marmion Dr CCHDY M21 97 K4
Marne Av AUL OL6 76 C7
WYTH/NTH M22 110 B7
Marne Crs ROCH OL11 27 M5
Marnland Gv BOLS/LL BL3 35 H8
Maroon Rd WYTH/NTH M22 119 H5
Marple Av BOL BL1 22 D8
Marple Cl OLDS OL8 75 G2
WGNNW/ST WN6 30 D2
Marple Gv STRET M32 96 F1
Marple Hall Dr MPL/ROM SK6 114 A5
Marple Old Rd OFTN SK2 113 K6
Marple Rd GLSP SK13 103 K7
OFTN SK2 113 G5
Marple St HULME M15 87 G7
Marquis Av BURY BL9 25 H8
Marquis Dr CHD/CHDH SK8 119 M5
Marquis St BNG/LEV M19 100 A3
Marrick Av CHD/CHDH SK8 110 F7
Marrick Cl WGNS/IIMK WN3 63 K2
Marriotts Ct CMANW M2 7 G4
Marriott St DID/WITH M20 98 E6
STKP SK1 13 K7
Marron Pl CMANW * M2 6 E6
Mars Av BOLS/LL BL3 51 M1
Marsden Cl AULW OL7 75 H7
MILN OL16 42 F4
Marsden Dr HALE/TIMP WA15 108 F6
Marsden Rd BOL BL1 2 D4
MPL/ROM SK6 113 M1
Marsden St BURY BL9 4 F2
CMANW M2 6 F4
ECC M30 84 F1
GLSP SK13 93 K8
WALK M28 68 C6
WGN WN1 15 G3
WGNS/IIMK WN3 48 B8
WGNW/BIL/O WN5 47 J5
WHTN BL5 50 B4
Marsett Cl WHIT OL12 27 J3
Marshall Ct AUL OL6 91 G2
OLD * OL1 9 G2
Marshall Rd BNG/LEV M19 99 K3
Marshall Stevens Wy TRPK M17 85 L7
Marshall St ANC M4 7 J2
DTN/ASHW M34 90 B8
LEIGH WN7 66 B8
MILN OL16 11 L5
WGTN/LGST M12 87 M6
Marsham Cl BRUN/LGST M13 88 B8
OLDE OL4 60 E7
Marsham Dr MPL/ROM SK6 114 D7
Marsham Rd BRAM/HZG SK7 121 K3
WHTN BL5 50 C6
Marshbank WHTN BL5 50 B3
Marshbrook Cl WGNE/HIN WN2 49 K6
Marshbrook Dr CHH M8 72 F3
Marsh Brook Fold WHTN BL5 49 K5
Marshbrook Rd URM M41 95 M1
Marsh Cl EDGY/DAV SK3 112 A6
Marshdale Rd BOL BL1 35 J4
Marshfield Rd
HALE/TIMP WA15 108 F7
Marshfield Wk BRUN/LGST M13 87 M6
Marsh Fold La BOL BL1 35 M4
Marsh Gn WGNW/BIL/O WN5 47 G3
Marsh La FWTH BL4 52 D4
NM/HAY SK22 124 F6
WGN WN1 15 G3
Marsh Rd BOLS/LL BL3 37 K8
LHULT M38 52 C8
Marsh Rw WGNE/HIN WN2 49 K8
Marsh St HOR/BR BL6 21 A8
WALK M28 69 J1
WHTN BL5 50 B3
Marshway Dr NEWLW WA12 78 E8
Marsland Av HALE/TIMP WA15 108 E4
Marsland Cl DTN/ASHW M34 100 E1
Marsland Green La TYLD M29 67 H8
Marsland Rd HALE/TIMP WA15 108 E6
MPL/ROM SK6 114 A5
SALE M33 108 D1
Marslands UPML OL3 61 L1
Marsland St BRAM/HZG * SK7 121 M2
STKP SK1 13 K1
Marsland St North BRO M7 72 B5
Marsland St South BRO M7 72 C5
Marsland Ter STKP SK1 112 E4
Mars St CHAD OL9 8 D4
EDGW/EG * BL7 16 E6
Marston Cl FAIL M35 74 E6
HOR/BR BL6 34 C4
WHTF M45 55 M4
Marston Dr IRL M44 94 E2
Marston Rd BRO M7 72 B4
STRET M32 97 H2

Marsworth Dr *ANC* * M4.....7 M3
Martens Rd *IRL* M44.....94 B7
Marthall Dr *SALE* M33.....109 G3
Martham Dr *OFTN* SK2.....113 K6
Martha's Ter *MILN* OL16.....28 F1
Martha St *BOLS/LL* * BL3.....36 A8
CHAD OL9.....8 F3
Martin Av *BOLS/LL* BL3.....53 M1
FWTH BL4.....52 C5
NEWLW WA12.....78 E7
OLDE OL4.....59 M6
Martin Cl *DTN/ASHW* M34.....90 C7
OFTN SK2.....113 J7
Martindale Cl *ROY/SHW* OL2.....43 H7
Martindale Crs *MDTN* M24.....57 G1
WGNW/BIL/O WN5.....47 H6
WGTN/LGST M12.....88 B6
Martindale Gdns *BOL* BL1.....36 B2
Martindale Rd
WGNW/BIL/O WN5.....62 A8
Martin Dr *IRL* M44.....83 K8
Martingale Cl *RAD* M26.....38 D7
Martingale Wy *DROY* M43.....90 A1
Martin Gv *FWTH* BL4.....53 J5
Martin La *WHIT* OL12.....27 L3
Martin Rd *SWIN* M27.....70 E2
Martinscough *HOR/BR* BL6.....34 F6
Martins Ct *WGNE/HIN* WN2.....49 K6
Martinscroft Rd
NTHM/RTH M23.....109 K7
Martins Fld *WHIT* OL12.....27 J3
Martin St *ATH* * M46.....67 G1
BURY BL9.....40 A1
DTN/ASHW M34.....90 C5
EDGW/EG BL7.....16 D8
HYDE SK14.....102 B2
ORD M5.....86 A2
Martland Av *GOL/RIS/CU* WA3.....80 A5
WGNNW/ST WN6.....30 C7
Martland Crs *WGNNW/ST* WN6.....47 H1
Martland Mill La
WGNW/BIL/O WN5.....47 G2
Martlesham Wk *ANC* * M4.....7 H3
Martlet Av *POY/DIS* SK12.....123 L6
ROCH OL11.....27 H5
Martlet Cl *RUSH/FAL* M14.....98 D3
Martlew Dr *ATH* M46.....66 D1
Martock Av *WYTH/NTH* M22.....119 G1
Marton Av *BOLE* BL2.....3 L2
DID/WITH M20.....110 F2
Marton Cl *GOL/RIS/CU* WA3.....81 H8
Marton Dr *ATH* M46.....51 H8
Marton Gra *PWCH* M25.....72 A2
Marton Gn *EDGY/DAV* SK3.....112 A7
Marton Gv *HTNM* SK4.....100 B6
Marton Pl *SALE* M33.....96 D8
Marton St *WGN* WN1.....14 F2
Marus Av *WGNS/IIMK* WN3.....63 J1
Marwick Cl *WGNNW/ST* WN6.....31 G2
Marwood Cl *ALT* WA14.....107 L6
RAD M26.....53 K4
Marwood Dr *NTHM/RTH* M23.....118 B1
Maryfield Cl *GOL/RIS/CU* WA3.....79 K5
Mayfield Ct *OLDTF/WHR* * M16.....98 B4
Mary France St *HULME* M15.....87 H6
Mary Hulton Ct *WHTN* BL5.....50 D4
Maryland Av *BOLE* BL2.....37 G5
Marylebone Pl *WGN* WN1.....47 M1
Marylon Dr *WYTH/NTH* M22.....110 B4
Mary St *CHD/CHDH* SK8.....111 G6
CSLFD M3.....87 J1
DROY M43.....89 L3
DTN/ASHW * M34.....90 C8
DUK SK16.....90 E4
FWTH BL4.....53 G5
HEY OL10.....40 F2
HYDE SK14.....101 M1
MILN OL16.....19 L8
RAMS BL0.....17 B7
STKP SK1.....13 L3
TYLD * M29.....67 K3
Mary St East *HOR/BR* BL6.....21 B8
Mary St West *HOR/BR* BL6.....21 A8
Masboro St *CHH* M8.....72 C5
Masbury Cl *BOL* BL1.....22 B5
Masefield Av *LEIGH* WN7.....66 A5
PWCH M25.....71 J1
RAD M26.....38 B8
WGNW/BIL/O WN5.....46 D6
Masefield Cl *DUK* SK16.....91 L5
Masefield Crs *DROY* M43.....89 K3
Masefield Dr *FWTH* BL4.....52 E5
HTNM SK4.....111 K2
WGNS/IIMK WN3.....47 J8
Masefield Gv *RDSH* SK5.....100 B3
Masefield Rd *BOLS/LL* BL3.....37 L8
DROY M43.....89 K3
OLD OL1.....59 L2
Mason Cl *AIMK* WN4.....64 A8
Mason Gdns *BOLS/LL* BL3.....2 C7
Mason La *ATH* M46.....67 H2
Masons Gv *GLSP* SK13.....93 K6
Mason St *ANC* M4.....7 J2
AULW OL7.....90 C3
BURY BL9.....5 H5
EDGW/EG * BL7.....22 B3
HEY OL10.....40 E2
HOR/BR BL6.....33 K1
MILN OL16.....10 F5
WGNE/HIN WN2.....64 E4
WGNS/IIMK WN3.....14 D5
Massey Av *AUL* OL6.....75 M6
FAIL M35.....74 E4
Massey Cft *WHIT* OL12.....18 D5
Massey Rd *HALE/TIMP* WA15.....108 B8
SALE M33.....97 H8
Massey St *BURY* BL9.....5 G2
ORD M5.....86 F3
STKP SK1.....13 J5
WILM/AE SK9.....130 D3
Massey Wk *WYTH/NTH* M22.....119 H3
Massie St *CHD/CHDH* SK8.....111 G6
Matham Wk *HULME* M15.....7 G9
Mather Av *ECC* M30.....85 H2
GOL/RIS/CU WA3.....80 B6
PWCH M25.....71 M3
WHTF M45.....55 J2
Mather Cl *WHTF* M45.....55 J3
Mather Fold Rd *WALK* M28.....68 E3
Mather La *LEIGH* WN7.....66 D8
Mather Rd *BURY* BL9.....25 J5
ECC M30.....85 H2
Mather St *ATH* M46.....67 G1
BOLS/LL * BL3.....2 D7
FAIL M35.....74 A5
FWTH BL4.....53 H4
RAD M26.....54 D1
Mather Wy *SLFD* * M6.....86 D1
Matheson Dr *WGNW/BIL/O* WN5.....47 G4
Matisse Wy *BRO* M7.....71 L4
Matley Cl *HYDE* SK14.....91 L7
Matley Gn *RDSH* SK5.....100 F6
Matley La *STLY* SK15.....91 M6
Matlock Av *AUL* OL6.....76 C6
BRO M7.....71 K5
DID/WITH M20.....98 C6
DTN/ASHW M34.....101 K4
OFTN SK2.....113 H7
Matlock Cl *ATH* M46.....67 G2
FWTH BL4.....53 H3
SALE M33.....96 F8
Matlock Dr *BRAM/HZG* SK7.....122 A4
Matlock Rd *CHD/CHDH* SK8.....119 L5
RDSH SK5.....100 D3
STRET M32.....96 D1
Matlock St *ECC* M30.....84 F4
Matt Busby Cl *SWIN* M27.....70 E5
Matthew Cl *GLSP* SK13.....93 J5
OLDS OL8.....59 M8
Matthew Moss La *ROCH* OL11.....27 L8
Matthews Av *FWTH* BL4.....53 J5
Matthews La *BNG/LEV* M19.....99 L2
Matthew's St *WGTN/LGST* M12.....88 C5
Matthew St *MPL/ROM* SK6.....114 D6
Mattison St *OP/CLY* M11.....89 H5
Maudsley St *BURY* BL9.....4 D6
Maud St *BOLE* BL2.....22 F7
WHIT OL12.....28 D2
Mauldeth Cl *HTNM* SK4.....111 K1
Mauldeth Rd *DID/WITH* M20.....98 F5
HTNM SK4.....99 H8
Mauldeth Rd West *CCHDY* M21.....98 B4
Maunby Gdns *LHULT* M38.....68 F1
Maureen Av *CHH* M8.....72 D4
Maureen St *WHIT* OL12.....28 D2
Maurice Cl *DUK* SK16.....91 H5
Maurice Dr *SLFD* M6.....71 J8
Maurice St *SLFD* M6.....71 J8
Maveen Gv *OFTN* SK2.....112 D8
Mavis Gv *MILN* OL16.....29 K6
Mavis St *ROCH* OL11.....41 M3
Mawdsley Dr *CHH* M8.....72 F4
Mawdsley St *BOL* BL1.....2 E5
Maxwell Av *OFTN* SK2.....112 F7
Maxwell St *BOL* BL1.....22 B8
BURY BL9.....5 K3
Max Woosnam Wk
RUSH/FAL M14.....98 D1
Mayall St *MOSL* OL5.....76 F3
Mayall St East *OLDE* * OL4.....59 M5
Mayan Av *CSLFD* M3.....6 A2
May Av *CHD/CHDH* SK8.....120 D6
HTNM * SK4.....12 C3
LEIGH WN7.....66 A6
WGNE/HIN WN2.....64 F5
Maybank St *BOLS/LL* BL3.....36 A8
Mayberth Av *CHH* M8.....72 D2
Maybreck Cl *BOLS/LL* BL3.....35 M7
Mayburn Cl *MDTN* M24.....57 M7
Maybury St *GTN* M18.....89 H6
Maycroft Av *DID/WITH* M20.....98 F7
May Dr *BNG/LEV* M19.....99 J6
Mayer St *OFTN* * SK2.....112 F5
Mayes Gdns *ANC* M4.....88 A3
Mayes St *ANC* M4.....7 H2
Mayfair *HOR/BR* BL6.....34 A1
Mayfair Av *RAD* M26.....38 A8
SLFD M6.....85 L1
URM M41.....95 L2
WHTF * M45.....55 J5
Mayfair Cl *DUK* SK16.....91 J4
POY/DIS SK12.....122 A7
Mayfair Ct *HALE/TIMP* * WA15.....108 E5
Mayfair Crs *FAIL* M35.....74 E4
Mayfair Dr *ATH* M46.....51 J8
IRL M44.....94 D2
ROY/SHW OL2.....59 G2
SALE M33.....108 B2
WGNE/HIN WN2.....49 G2
WGNS/IIMK WN3.....63 J2
Mayfair Gdns *ROCH* OL11.....10 A9
Mayfair Ms *DID/WITH* * M20.....98 C8
Mayfair Pk *DID/WITH* * M20.....98 C8
Mayfair Rd *WYTH/NTH* M22.....110 B8
Mayfield *BOLE* BL2.....23 G7
Mayfield Av *BOLS/LL* BL3.....52 E1
DTN/ASHW M34.....101 K5
FWTH BL4.....52 F5
OLDE OL4.....60 D5
RDSH SK5.....100 C7
SALE M33.....97 H8
STRET M32.....96 E3
SWIN M27.....69 M6
WALK M28.....69 G1
Mayfield Cl *HALE/TIMP* WA15.....108 E6
RAMS BL0.....24 D2
Mayfield Dr *GOL/RIS/CU* WA3.....80 F4
Mayfield Gv *GTN* M18.....100 C1
RDSH SK5.....100 C7
WILM/AE SK9.....126 C7
Mayfield Houses *RAD* * M26.....54 B2
Mayfield Rd *BRAM/HZG* SK7.....121 G8
BRO M7.....71 L3
HALE/TIMP WA15.....108 E6
MPL/ROM SK6.....114 E3
OLD OL1.....59 L3
OLDTF/WHR M16.....98 B1
RAMS BL0.....24 D2
WGNW/BIL/O WN5.....46 E4
Mayfield St *AIMK* * WN4.....78 D1
ATH M46.....66 F1
DTN/ASHW M34.....90 B7
MILN OL16.....11 K1
WHTF * M45.....55 H5
Mayfield Ter *MILN* OL16.....28 E3
Mayflower Av *ORD* M5.....86 D4
Mayford Rd *BNG/LEV* M19.....99 K2
Maygate *OLD* OL1.....8 E2
May Gv *BNG/LEV* M19.....99 L4
Mayhill Dr *SLFD* M6.....70 D8
WALK M28.....69 K4
Mayhurst Av *CCHDY* M21.....110 A1
Mayorlowe Av *RDSH* SK5.....100 F8
Mayor's Rd *HALE/TIMP* WA15.....108 B8
Mayor St *BOLS/LL* BL3.....2 B6
TOT/BURYW BL8.....4 A2
Mayo St *WGTN/LGST* M12.....88 A4
Maypool Dr *RDSH* SK5.....100 C6
May Rd *CHD/CHDH* SK8.....120 C6
OLDTF/WHR M16.....98 A1
SWIN M27.....70 E6
Mays St *BOLE* BL2.....3 H5
ECC M30.....69 M8
EDGW/EG BL7.....16 E6
GOL/RIS/CU WA3.....79 L2
HEY * OL10.....41 H4
LEIGH WN7.....65 M7
NEWH/MOS M40.....73 M7
OLDS OL8.....58 F8
RAD M26.....54 D1
Mayton St *OP/CLY* M11.....88 D4
May Tree Dr *WGN* WN1.....47 L1
Mayville Dr *DID/WITH* M20.....98 E7
Maywood Av *DID/WITH* M20.....110 E4
Maze St *BOLS/LL* BL3.....37 G7
McConnell Rd *NEWH/MOS* M40.....73 K5
McCormack Dr *WGN* WN1.....15 J4
McCready Dr *ORD* * M5.....86 E4
McDonna St *BOL* BL1.....35 M1
McDonough Cl *OLDS* OL8.....75 K1
McEvoy St *BOL* BL1.....36 C2
McKean St *BOLS/LL* BL3.....36 D8
McKie Cl *OLDS* OL8.....75 K1
McLaren Ct *CCHDY* M21.....97 K3
McLean Dr *IRL* M44.....83 K8
Mc Naught St *MILN* OL16.....11 J7
Meachin Av *CCHDY* M21.....97 M6
The Mead *CCHDY* * M21.....97 L5
ORD M5.....86 B2
The Meade *BOLS/LL* BL3.....52 B2
WILM/AE SK9.....126 F4
Meade Cl *URM* M41.....95 M2
Meade Gv *BRUN/LGST* M13.....99 J1
Meade Hill Rd *PWCH* M25.....72 B1
Meadfoot Av *PWCH* M25.....71 M1
Meadfoot Rd *GTN* M18.....89 G6
Meadland Gv *BOL* BL1.....22 C8
The Meadow *BOL* BL1.....35 G5
Meadow Av *HALE/TIMP* WA15.....117 K1
SWIN M27.....70 E3
Meadowbank *AULW* OL7.....75 K6
Meadow Bank *CCHDY* M21.....97 K5
GLSP SK13.....104 C5
HALE/TIMP WA15.....108 D5
HTNM SK4.....12 B3
HYDE SK14.....93 G6
MPL/ROM SK6.....113 J1
Meadowbank Av *ATH* M46.....51 H8
Meadowbank Cl *FAIL* M35.....74 D6
Meadow Bank Cl *OLDE* * OL4.....60 B8
Meadow Bank Ct *STRET* M32.....96 E3
Meadowbank Gdns
GOL/RIS/CU WA3.....81 M5
Meadowbank Rd *BOLS/LL* BL3.....51 L2
Meadowbrook Cl *BURY* BL9.....5 M1
HOR/BR BL6.....50 F1
Meadow Brook Wy
CHD/CHDH SK8.....111 L8
Meadow Brow *WILM/AE* SK9.....130 D2
Meadow Cl *BOLS/LL* BL3.....53 L2
BRAM/HZG SK7.....122 A1
DTN/ASHW M34.....101 K5
HALE/TIMP WA15.....117 K1
HEY OL10.....40 F2
LEIGH WN7.....81 H2
MOSL OL5.....77 H1
MPL/ROM SK6.....101 K7
MPL/ROM SK6.....123 H4
STRET M32.....97 H3
WILM/AE SK9.....126 C8
Meadow Ct *CCHDY* M21.....97 J4
Meadow Cft *BRAM/HZG* SK7.....122 A1
WHTF M45.....54 F6
Meadowcroft *AIMK* WN4.....63 J6
HYDE SK14.....92 C8
RAD M26.....38 C7
WHTN BL5.....50 C5
Meadowcroft La *OLD* OL1.....9 M1
ROCH OL11.....27 J6
Meadowfield *HOR/BR* BL6.....34 E5
MILN OL16.....42 E1
Meadowfield Cl *GLSP* SK13.....104 C1
Meadowfield Ct *HYDE* SK14.....91 G8
Meadowfield Dr *WALK* M28.....68 E6
Meadow Fold *UPML* OL3.....61 M4
Meadowgate *URM* M41.....96 A3
WALK M28.....69 J4
Meadowgate Rd *SLFD* M6.....85 M1
Meadow Head Av *WHIT* OL12.....18 E6
Meadow La *ALT* WA14.....106 D8
BOLE BL2.....37 K5
DTN/ASHW M34.....101 K5
DUK SK16.....91 G4
OLDS OL8.....75 H2
POY/DIS SK12.....123 M6
ROY/SHW OL2.....43 K6
WALK M28.....69 J7
Meadow Pit La *WGNE/HIN* WN2.....32 D5
Meadow Ri *GLSP* SK13.....104 C5
ROY/SHW OL2.....43 K3
Meadow Rd *BRO* M7.....86 F1
MDTN M24.....57 H6
URM M41.....96 A3
The Meadows *GLSP* SK13.....105 H4
IRL M44.....94 A6
MDTN M24.....57 L6
MPL/ROM SK6.....101 L8
OLDE OL4.....60 D6
PWCH M25.....55 L8
RAD M26.....38 B7
WHIT OL12.....18 D3
Meadows *UPML* OL3.....61 L5
Meadows Cl *WGNE/HIN* WN2.....49 G7
Meadows Gn *GOL/RIS/CU* WA3.....80 B7
Meadowside *BRAM/HZG* SK7.....120 E2
MCFLDN SK10.....129 M4
MILN OL16.....29 M8
NM/HAY SK22.....124 C6
Meadowside Av *AIMK* WN4.....63 K4
BOLE BL2.....3 M4
IRL M44.....94 D2
WALK M28.....53 H8
WYTH/NTH M22.....110 B8
Meadowside Cl *RAD* M26.....38 D7
Meadowside Gv *WALK* M28.....69 H1
Meadowside Rd
WGNE/HIN WN2.....49 K8
Meadows La *BOLE* BL2.....37 J1
Meadows Rd *CHD/CHDH* SK8.....119 K3
CHD/CHDH SK8.....120 B4
HTNM SK4.....99 M6
NM/HAY SK22.....125 M2
SALE M33.....96 F6
Meadows St *WGNNW/ST* WN6.....14 B2
Meadow St *HYDE* SK14.....102 B3
NM/HAY SK22.....124 E4
OFTN SK2.....112 F7
Meadowvale Dr
WGNW/BIL/O WN5.....46 F6
Meadow Vw *WHIT* OL12.....27 K3
Meadow Wk *FWTH* BL4.....52 D5
LIT * OL15.....20 A7
Meadow Wy *EDGW/EG* BL7.....16 D6
HALE/TIMP WA15.....117 K1
HOR/BR BL6.....33 H3
NEWH/MOS M40.....73 K3
TOT/BURYW BL8.....24 B6
WILM/AE SK9.....126 C8
The Meads *CHAD* OL9.....58 D6
Meadscroft Dr *WILM/AE* SK9.....130 C3
Meads Gv *FWTH* BL4.....52 A4
TYLD M29.....67 M6
Meadway *BRAM/HZG* SK7.....121 G7
BURY BL9.....39 J6
CHAD OL9.....74 B2
DUK SK16.....91 H5
GOL/RIS/CU WA3.....80 A4
MPL/ROM SK6.....123 H4
POY/DIS SK12.....121 K7
RAMS BL0.....17 C3
ROCH OL11.....27 L8
SALE M33.....108 B2
STLY SK15.....92 B6
TYLD M29.....68 A3
WGNE/HIN WN2.....15 M6
Meadway Cl *HOR/BR* BL6.....34 A1
SALE M33.....108 B1
Meadway Rd *CHD/CHDH* SK8.....120 D1
Mealhouse Brow *STKP* SK1.....13 J4
Mealhouse Ct *ATH* M46.....66 F1
Mealhouse La *ATH* M46.....66 F1
BOL BL1.....2 E4
Meal St *HTNM* SK4.....112 B1
NM/HAY SK22.....124 E4
Meanley Rd *TYLD* M29.....67 J5
Meanley St *TYLD* M29.....67 J3
Meanwood Brow *WHIT* OL12.....10 A2
Meanwood Fold *ROCH* OL11.....27 M4
WHIT OL12.....10 A2
Measham Ms *CMANE* * M1.....7 G8
Meddings Cl *WILM/AE* SK9.....130 D4
Medina Cl *CHD/CHDH* SK8.....111 L8
Medlar Wy *AIMK* WN4.....63 J7
Medley St *WHIT* OL12.....28 C3
Medlock Cl *FWTH* BL4.....52 E4
Medlock Dr *OLDS* OL8.....75 K3
Medlock Rd *FAIL* M35.....74 D7
Medlock St *DROY* M43.....89 K2
HULME M15.....6 E8
OLD OL1.....9 M4
Medlock Valley Wy *OLDE* OL4.....44 D7
Medlock Wy *OLDE* OL4.....60 B6
WGNE/HIN WN2.....64 D2
WHTF M45.....55 M4
The Medway *HEY* OL10.....40 E1
Medway Cl *AIMK* * WN4.....63 J6
LEIGH WN7.....80 F4
OLDS OL8.....74 F1
ORD M5.....86 A1
WILM/AE SK9.....127 H2
Medway Crs *ALT* WA14.....107 M6
Medway Dr *FWTH* BL4.....53 L7
HOR/BR BL6.....34 A1
Medway Pl *WGNW/BIL/O* WN5.....47 G5
Medway Rd *OLDS* OL8.....74 F1
ROY/SHW OL2.....43 K4
WALK M28.....68 E4
Medway Wk *NEWH/MOS* M40.....88 A1
Meech St *OP/CLY* M11.....88 F4
Meek St *OLD* OL1.....59 K2
Meerbrook Rd *EDGY/DAV* SK3.....111 K4
Mee's Sq *ECC* M30.....85 G4
Megfield *WHTN* BL5.....50 B6
Megna Cl *CHAD* OL9.....8 D4
Melandra Castle Rd *GLSP* SK13.....104 A3
Melandra Crs *HYDE* SK14.....103 H2
Melandra Rd *GLSP* SK13.....104 A1
Melanie Cl *GLSP* SK13.....104 D4
Melanie Dr *RDSH* SK5.....100 C4
Melba St *OP/CLY* M11.....89 H4
Melbecks Wk *NTHM/RTH* M23.....109 J2
Melbourne Av *CHAD* OL9.....58 D5
MANAIR M90.....118 C4
STRET M32.....97 G2
Melbourne Cl *HOR/BR* BL6.....33 M1
ROCH OL11.....42 D2
Melbourne Gv *HOR/BR* BL6.....33 M1
Melbourne Rd *BOLS/LL* BL3.....35 L7
BRAM/HZG SK7.....121 G6
ROCH OL11.....42 D2
Melbourne St *BKLY* M9.....73 H4
BRO M7.....72 A7
CHAD OL9.....8 A5
DTN/ASHW M34.....101 H2
HULME M15.....6 D9
RDSH SK5.....100 C4
STLY SK15.....91 K3
SWIN M27.....70 E4
Melbourne St North *AUL* OL6.....75 M8
Melbourne St South *AUL* OL6.....90 F1
Melbury Av *DID/WITH* M20.....99 G8
Melbury Dr *HOR/BR* BL6.....34 C3
Melbury Rd *CHD/CHDH* SK8.....120 D6
Meldon Rd *BRUN/LGST* M13.....99 H2
Meldrum St *OLDS* OL8.....59 J8
Melford Av *NEWH/MOS* M40.....74 B3
Melford Dr *AIMK* WN4.....63 K8
WGNW/BIL/O WN5.....62 A1
Melford Gv *OLDE* OL4.....60 A6
Melford Rd *BRAM/HZG* SK7.....122 B3
Melfort Av *STRET* M32.....97 H3
Meliden Crs *BOL* * BL1.....35 L3
WYTH/NTH M22.....119 G2
Melksham Cl *ORD* M5.....86 E2
Mellalieu St *MDTN* M24.....57 H3
ROY/SHW OL2.....59 H2
Melland Av *CCHDY* M21.....97 M7
Melland Rd *GTN* M18.....99 M1
Meller Rd *BRUN/LGST* M13.....99 J2
Melling Av *CHAD* OL9.....58 B3
HTNM SK4.....100 B6
Melling Cl *LEIGH* WN7.....81 J3
Melling Rd *OLDE* OL4.....59 M6
Mellings Av *WGNW/BIL/O* * WN5.....62 B3
Melling St *WGNW/BIL/O* WN5.....47 H7
WGTN/LGST M12.....88 D8
Mellington Av *DID/WITH* M20.....110 F4
Melling Wy *WGNS/IIMK* WN3.....63 G3
Mellodew Dr *OLD* OL1.....60 A1
Mellor Brook Dr
WGNE/HIN * WN2.....64 D2
Mellor Brow *HEY* OL10.....40 E2
Mellor Cl *AUL* OL6.....91 H2
WGNNW/ST WN6.....31 H2
Mellor Ct *OFTN* SK2.....113 H5
Mellor Dr *BURY* BL9.....39 G5
WALK M28.....68 F3
Mellor Gv *BOL* BL1.....35 L3
Mellor Rd *AUL* OL6.....91 H1
CHD/CHDH SK8.....120 D3
NM/HAY SK22.....124 E1
Mellors Rd *TRPK* M17.....85 L5
Mellor St *DROY* M43.....89 J3
ECC M30.....85 G3
FAIL M35.....74 A5
NEWH/MOS M40.....88 A1
OLDE OL4.....60 B6
PWCH M25.....55 J8
RAD M26.....54 E2
ROCH OL11.....10 A3
ROY/SHW OL2.....43 G7
STRET M32.....86 A8
Mellor Wy *CHAD* OL9.....58 E8
Mellowstone Dr
OLDTF/WHR M16.....98 C4
Melloy Pl *CHH* M8.....72 D8
Melmerby Cl *AIMK* WN4.....78 C1
Melon Pl *SLFD* M6.....86 E2
Melrose *WHIT* OL12.....10 D3
Melrose Av *BOL* BL1.....35 K3
DID/WITH M20.....110 F1
ECC M30.....69 K8
EDGY/DAV * SK3.....111 J5
HEY OL10.....40 F1
LEIGH WN7.....66 A3
LIT OL15.....20 B5
SALE M33.....108 E1
TOT/BURYW BL8.....38 F1
Melrose Cl *WHTF* M45.....55 J2
Melrose Ct *CHAD* * OL9.....58 D8
Melrose Crs *EDGY/DAV* SK3.....112 A8
HALE/TIMP WA15.....117 K3
POY/DIS SK12.....122 F7
Melrose Dr *WGNS/IIMK* WN3.....63 G1
Melrose Gdns *RAD* M26.....38 B7
Melrose Rd *BOLS/LL* BL3.....53 J1
RAD M26.....38 B7
Melrose St *BURY* BL9.....24 E2
NEWH/MOS M40.....73 M7
OLD OL1.....59 L3
ROCH OL11.....10 A5
Melsomby Rd *NTHM/RTH* M23.....109 K2
Meltham Av *DID/WITH* M20.....98 D6
Meltham Cl *HTNM* SK4.....111 H3
Meltham Pl *BOLS/LL* * BL3.....35 M8
Meltham Rd *HTNM* SK4.....111 H3
Melton Av *DTN/ASHW* M34.....100 D1
URM M41.....94 F1
Melton Cl *HEY* OL10.....40 E3
TYLD M29.....67 L4
WALK M28.....68 F2
Melton Dr *BURY* BL9.....39 K7
Melton Rd *CHH* M8.....72 B3
Melton St *BKLY* M9.....73 J3
HEY OL10.....40 E3
RAD M26.....38 C8
RDSH SK5.....100 C8
Melverley Rd *BKLY* M9.....56 D7
Melverley St *WGNS/IIMK* WN3.....14 C6
Melville Cl *OP/CLY* M11.....89 H5
Melville Rd *FWTH* BL4.....53 J6
STRET M32.....96 E1
Melville St *AUL* OL6.....75 L8
BOLS/LL BL3.....36 D8
CSLFD M3.....6 B3
OLDE OL4.....60 B7
ROCH OL11.....42 A3
Melvin Av *WYTH/NTH* M22.....110 B8
Melyncourt Rd *HYDE* * SK14.....103 H1
Memorial Cottages *SWIN* * M27.....70 C1
Memorial Rd *WALK* M28.....69 G1
Menai Gv *CHD/CHDH* SK8.....111 K6
Menai Rd *EDGY/DAV* SK3.....112 B6
Menai St *BOLS/LL* * BL3.....35 L8
Mendip Av *WGNS/IIMK* WN3.....62 F1
WYTH/NTH M22.....110 C8
Mendip Cl *BOLE* BL2.....37 K5
CHAD * OL9.....58 D7
CHD/CHDH SK8.....119 K5
HOR/BR BL6.....21 C7
HTNM SK4.....13 G1
ROY/SHW OL2.....58 F1
Mendip Crs *TOT/BURYW* BL8.....38 D1
Mendip Dr *BOLE* BL2.....37 K6
MILN OL16.....29 K6
Mendip Rd *OLDS* OL8.....75 G1
Mendips Cl *ROY/SHW* OL2.....43 J4
Menston Av *NEWH/MOS* M40.....74 B3
Mentmore Rd *MILN* OL16.....29 G5
Mentone Crs *WYTH/NTH* M22.....110 B8
Mentone Rd *HTNM* SK4.....111 L1
Mentor St *BRUN/LGST* M13.....99 J2
Mercer La *ROCH* OL11.....27 H4
Mercer Rd *GTN* M18.....89 G7
HEY OL10.....41 G5
Mercer St *BNG/LEV* M19.....99 L3
DROY M43.....89 L2
NEWLW WA12.....79 G8
Merchants Crs *GOL/RIS/CU* WA3.....80 B3
Merchants Quay *SALQ* M50.....86 D6
Mercian Wy *EDGY/DAV* SK3.....12 F8
Mercia St *BOLS/LL* BL3.....35 M7
Mercury Pk *URM* * M41.....85 J6
Mercury Wy *URM* M41.....85 J7
The Mere *AUL* OL6.....76 B6
Mere Av *DROY* M43.....89 M4
LEIGH WN7.....66 A7
MDTN M24.....57 K6
SLFD M6.....86 B2
Merebank Cl *ROCH* OL11.....27 H4
Mere Cl *BURY* BL9.....39 L7
DTN/ASHW M34.....100 E2
SALE M33.....109 J1
Mereclough Av *WALK* M28.....69 J3
Meredew Av *SWIN* M27.....70 B6
Meredith St *BOLS/LL* BL3.....52 C1
RUSH/FAL M14.....99 G5
Mere Dr *DID/WITH* M20.....98 E8
SWIN M27.....70 D2
Merefield Av *ROCH* OL11.....10 C9
Merefield Rd *HALE/TIMP* WA15.....108 F7
Merefield St *ROCH* OL11.....10 C9
Merefield Ter *ROCH* * OL11.....10 C9
Merefold *HOR/BR* BL6.....33 J1
Mere Fold *WALK* M28.....68 E1
Mere Gdns *BOL* BL1.....2 C2
Merehall Cl *BOL* BL1.....2 C2
Merehall Dr *BOL* BL1.....2 C2
Merehall St *BOL* BL1.....2 B1
Mereland Av *DID/WITH* M20.....98 F8
Mereland Cl *WGNW/BIL/O* WN5.....46 B6
Mere La *ROCH* OL11.....10 E8
Meremanor *WALK* M28.....69 J3
Merepool Cl *MPL/ROM* SK6.....113 M5
Mere Rd *AIMK* WN4.....63 M8
NEWLW WA12.....79 J8
Mere Side *STLY* SK15.....76 C8
Mereside Cl *CHD/CHDH* SK8.....111 J8
Mereside Gv *WALK* M28.....69 H1
Mere St *LEIGH* WN7.....66 A7
ROCH OL11.....10 E7
WGNW/BIL/O WN5.....14 A8
CHD/CHDH SK8.....111 J8
Mere Wk *BOL* BL1.....2 C2
Merewood Av *WYTH/NTH* M22.....110 A6
Meriden Cl *RAD* M26.....38 C6
Meriden Gv *HOR/BR* BL6.....35 G6
Meridian Pl *DID/WITH* M20.....98 D8
Merinall Cl *MILN* OL16.....11 M5
Meriton Rd *WILM/AE* SK9.....119 L8
Merlewood *RAMS* BL0.....17 E1

Merlewood Av *BNG/LEV* M19 ....99 M5
*DTN/ASHW * M34 ....89 L3
UPML OL3 ....61 L4
Merlewood Dr *SWIN* M27 ....69 M6
TYLD M29 ....67 L4
Merlin Cl *LIT* OL15 ....29 K2
OLDS SK2 ....113 K6
OLDS OL8 ....35 L3
Merlin Gv *BOL* BL1 ....35 J3
Merlin Rd *IRL* M44 ....83 K8
MILN OL16 ....29 J6
Merlyn Av *DID/WITH* M20 ....98 F8
DTN/ASHW M34 ....101 K2
SALE M33 ....96 F6
Merrick Av *WYTH/NTH* M22 ....110 B8
Merrick St *HEY* OL10 ....41 H3
The Merridale
HALE/TIMP WA15 ....117 H4
Merrill St *ANC* M4 ....88 A3
Merriman St *OLDTF/WHR* M16 ....87 H8
Merrion St *FWTH* BL4 ....52 F2
Merrow Wk *CMANE* M1 ....7 J8
Merrybent Ct *WGN* 113 G8
Merrybower Rd *BRO* M7 ....72 B4
Merrydale Av *ECC* M30 ....70 B8
Merryman Hall *MILN * OL16 ....28 E2
Merseybank Av *CCHDY* M21 ....98 A8
Mersey Bank Rd *GLSP* SK13 ....93 J8
Mersey Cl *WGNE/HIN* WN2 ....65 M1
WHTF M45 ....55 L3
Mersey Crs *DID/WITH* M20 ....110 A1
WHTF M45 ....55 L3
Mersey Dr *PART* M31 ....94 D8
WHTF M45 ....55 L3
Mersey Mdw *DID/WITH* M20 ....110 C1
Mersey Rd *DID/WITH* M20 ....110 C1
HTNM SK4 ....111 J2
SALE M33 ....96 E6
WGNE/HIN WN2 ....64 C2
WGNW/BIL/O WN5 ....46 C5
Mersey Rd North *FAIL* M35 ....74 D3
Mersey Sq *STKP* SK1 ....13 G4
Mersey St *LEIGH* WN7 ....65 M8
OP/CLY M11 ....13 L3
STKP SK1 ....13 G4
Mersey Vw *URM * M41 ....95 H4
Merseyway *STKP* SK1 ....13 H3
Merston Dr *DID/WITH* M20 ....110 F5
Merton Av *BRAM/HZG* SK7 ....122 B4
MPL/ROM SK6 ....101 K8
OLDS OL8 ....75 G1
Merton Cl *BOLS/LL * BL3 ....35 M7
Merton Dr *DROY* M43 ....89 H3
Merton Gv *CHAD* OL9 ....74 A1
HALE/TIMP WA15 ....108 E6
TYLD M29 ....67 M6
Merton Rd *EDGY/DAV* SK3 ....12 A3
POY/DIS SK12 ....121 K8
PWCH M25 ....55 M7
SALE M33 ....96 D7
WGNS/IIMK WN3 ....46 E8
Merton St *TOT/BURYW* BL8 ....4 B2
Merville Av *NEWH/MOS* M40 ....73 J3
Mervyn Pl *WGNS/IIMK* WN3 ....47 K8
Mervyn Rd *BRO* M7 ....71 K6
Merwell Rd *URM* M41 ....95 H3
Merwood Av *CHD/CHDH* SK8 ....119 M4
Merwood Gv *RUSH/FAL* M14 ....88 B8
Meshaw Ct *NTHM/RTH* M23 ....109 H2
Mesnefield Rd *BRO* M7 ....71 K4
Mesne Lea Gv *WALK * M28 ....69 H4
Mesne Lea Rd *WALK* M28 ....69 H4
Mesnes Av *WGNS/IIMK* WN3 ....14 B9
Mesnes Park Ter *WGN* WN1 ....14 F2
Mesnes Rd *WGN* WN1 ....47 M2
Mesnes St *WGN* WN1 ....14 F3
Mesnes Ter *WGN* WN1 ....14 F3
Metal Box Wy *WHTN* BL5 ....50 C2
Metcalfe Ct *LHULT * M38 ....52 C8
Metfield Pl *BOL* BL1 ....35 M4
Methuen St *WGTN/LGST* M12 ....99 L1
Methwold St *BOLS/LL * BL3 ....35 M8
The Mews *BOL* BL1 ....35 L4
CHD/CHDH SK8 ....110 E7
NEWH/MOS M40 ....88 B1
PWCH M25 ....71 L1
*SALE * M33 ....108 F1
WGNE/HIN WN2 ....49 G7
*WHTF * M45 ....55 G4
Meyer St *EDGY/DAV * SK3 ....112 C6
Meynell Dr *LEIGH* WN7 ....81 J2
Meyrick Rd *SLFD* M6 ....86 F3
Meyrick St *WGNW/BIL/O* WN5 ....14 A7
Miall St *ROCH* OL11 ....10 F8
Micawber Rd *POY/DIS* SK12 ....129 L2
Michael St *MDTN* M24 ....57 J4
Michael Wife La *RAMS* BL0 ....17 E2
Michigan Av *SALQ* M50 ....86 C4
Mickleby Wk *NEWH/MOS * M40 ....7 M1
Micklehurst Av *DID/WITH* M20 ....98 B8
Micklehurst Gn *OFTN* SK2 ....113 H7
Micklehurst Rd *MOSL* OL5 ....77 C4
Mickleton *ATH* M46 ....51 H8
Middlebourne St *SLFD* M6 ....86 B2
Middlebrook Dr *HOR/BR* BL6 ....34 F6
Middlecot Cl *WGNW/BIL/O* WN5 ....46 B7
Middlefield *OLDS* OL8 ....75 K4
Middle Fld *ROCH* OL11 ....27 H3
Middlefields *CHD/CHDH* SK8 ....111 L8
Middlegate *NEWH/MOS* M40 ....74 A1
Middle Ga *OLDS* OL8 ....75 H2
Middle Gn *AUL* OL6 ....75 M8
Middleham St *RUSH/FAL* M14 ....98 D2
Middle Hl *WHIT* OL12 ....19 G8
Middle Hillgate *STKP* SK1 ....13 K5
Middlesex Dr *BURY* BL9 ....73 C2
Middlesex Rd *BKLY* M9 ....73 C2
RDSH SK5 ....100 F6
Middlesex Wk *CHAD* OL9 ....8 A5
Middlestone Dr *BKLY* M9 ....73 G5
Middle St *WHIT* OL12 ....18 D3
Middleton Av *FAIL* M35 ....74 C5
Middleton Dr *BURY* BL9 ....55 J1
Middleton Old Rd *BKLY* M9 ....73 G2
Middleton Rd *BKLY* M9 ....56 C7
CHAD OL9 ....8 B4
CHAD OL9 ....8 F5
CHAD OL9 ....58 A3
CHH M8 ....72 C2
HEY OL10 ....41 H5
RDSH SK5 ....100 C2
ROY/SHW OL2 ....58 E1
Middleton Rd West *CHAD* OL9 ....58 E1
Middleton Wy *MDTN* M24 ....57 J4
Middle Turn *EDGW/EG* BL7 ....16 D5
Middleway *OLDE* OL4 ....60 E7
Middlewood *GOL/RIS/CU* WA3 ....80 A4
Middlewood Gn *CHAD* OL9 ....58 D5
Middle Wood La *WHIT* OL12 ....19 M6
Middlewood Rd *POY/DIS* SK12 ....122 C8

POY/DIS SK12 ....122 E5
Middlewood Wy *MCFLDN* SK10 ....129 L6
Midford Av *BNG/LEV* M19 ....99 M5
Midford Dr *BOL* BL1 ....22 B5
Midge Hall Dr *ROCH* OL11 ....27 K6
Midgley Av *GTN* M18 ....89 H6
Midgley Crs *AUL* OL6 ....76 B8
Midgley St *SWIN* M27 ....70 A6
Midgrove La *UPML* OL3 ....61 J1
Midhurst Av *NTHM/MOS * M40 ....73 L8
Midhurst Cl *CHD/CHDH* SK8 ....120 B4
Midhurst St *ROCH* OL11 ....10 F9
Midland Cl *WGTN/LGST* M12 ....88 A5
Midland Rd *BRAM/HZG* SK7 ....121 G1
RDSH SK5 ....100 C2
Midland St *WGTN/LGST* M12 ....88 A5
Midland Ter *ALT * WA14 ....116 F2
NM/HAY SK22 ....124 E5
Midland Wk *BRAM/HZG* SK7 ....121 G1
Midlothian St *OP/CLY* M11 ....88 E2
Midville Rd *OP/CLY* M11 ....88 F1
Midway *CHD/CHDH* SK8 ....120 D7
Midway St *BNG/LEV* M19 ....99 K2
Milan St *BRO* M7 ....72 B6
Milbourne Rd *BURY* BL9 ....25 J6
Milburn Av *NTHM/RTH* M23 ....109 L2
Milbury Dr *LIT* OL15 ....29 K2
Milden Cl *DID/WITH * M20 ....98 F8
Mildred Av *OLDE* OL4 ....60 E7
PWCH M25 ....71 M2
ROY/SHW OL2 ....59 H2
Mildred St *BRO* M7 ....71 M7
Mile End La *OFTN* SK2 ....112 F7
Mile La *TOT/BURYW* BL8 ....38 C3
Miles La *WGNNW/ST* WN6 ....30 A4
Miles St *BOL* BL1 ....36 A2
HYDE SK14 ....102 C2
OLD OL1 ....59 L4
WGTN/LGST M12 ....88 D5
Milford Av *OLDS* OL8 ....74 F2
Milford Brow *OLDE* OL4 ....60 B5
Milford Cr *LIT* OL15 ....20 C6
Milford Dr *BNG/LEV* M19 ....99 M5
Milford Gv *OFTN* SK2 ....112 F5
Milford Rd *BKLY* M9 ....72 E1
BOLS/LL BL3 ....52 B1
WGNE/HIN WN2 ....48 C2
Milford St *BKLY* M9 ....72 E1
SLFD M6 ....86 B3
WGNS/IIMK WN3 ....15 K7
WHIT/CU OL12 ....18 E3
Milkstone Pl *ROCH* OL11 ....10 E7
Milkstone Rd *ROCH* OL11 ....10 E6
Milk St *CMANW* M2 ....7 G4
HYDE SK14 ....102 A2
*RAMS * BL0 ....17 B7
ROCH OL11 ....10 F6
TYLD M29 ....67 K3
WHIT OL12 ....14 F5
Milkwood Gv *GTN* M18 ....89 G8
Millais St *NEWH/MOS* M40 ....73 J3
Millard St *CHAD* OL9 ....58 D5
Mill Bank *RAD* M26 ....54 E2
WGNNW/ST WN6 ....30 A5
Millbank Gdns *BOL * BL1 ....35 M3
Millbank St *CMANE* M1 ....7 L5
HEY OL10 ....40 E2
Millbeck Farm
WGNW/BIL/O WN5 ....47 G7
Millbeck Cl *BOLS/LL * BL3 ....36 B8
Millbeck Rd *MDTN* M24 ....57 G2
Millbeck St *HULME* M15 ....87 K6
Millbrae Gdns *ROY/SHW* OL2 ....43 J5
Millbrook Av *ATH* M46 ....51 H7
DTN/ASHW M34 ....101 G3
ROY/SHW OL2 ....44 A6
Millbrook Bank *ROCH * OL11 ....27 G3
Millbrook Cl *GOL/RIS/CU* WA3 ....81 M7
ROY/SHW OL2 ....44 A6
Millbrook Fold *BRAM/HZG* SK7 ....122 C5
Millbrook Rd *NTHM/RTH* M23 ....118 C1
Millbrook St *STKP* SK1 ....13 J6
Mill Brow *AUL* OL6 ....75 M3
BKLY M9 ....72 F2
*HYDE * SK14 ....103 K4
MPL/ROM SK6 ....115 G4
OLD OL1 ....58 D2
WALK M28 ....69 J6
Mill Brow Rd *MPL/ROM* SK6 ....115 H4
Millcrest Cl *WALK* M28 ....68 C7
Mill Cft *BOL* BL1 ....2 B8
Millcroft Av *WGNW/BIL/O* WN5 ....46 A7
Mill Croft Cl *ROCH* OL11 ....27 G3
Millcroft La *UPML* OL3 ....45 J6
Milldale Cl *ATH* M46 ....66 F1
HOR/BR BL6 ....34 C5
Milldale Rd *LEIGH* WN7 ....80 E3
Miller Meadow Cl *ROY/SHW* OL2 ....43 M4
Miller St *OLDS* OL8 ....75 H1
Millers Brook Cl *HEY * OL10 ....41 G1
Millers Cl *SALE* M33 ....109 K1
Millers Ct *ORD* M5 ....85 K2
Millersdale Ct *GLSP* SK13 ....105 J3
Miller's La *ATH* M46 ....67 G3
WGNE/HIN WN2 ....64 D2
Millers St *ANC* M4 ....84 F3
Miller St *AUL* OL6 ....7 H2
AUL OL6 ....75 M8
BOL BL1 ....22 B8
BURY BL9 ....24 F2
HEY OL10 ....41 G2
RAD M26 ....38 C6
Millett St *BURY* BL9 ....4 C5
RAMS BL0 ....17 D5
Millfield *HALE/TIMP* WA15 ....117 H2
Millfield Dr *WALK* M28 ....68 E6
Millfield La *AIMK* WN4 ....78 E8
Millfield Rd *BOLE* BL2 ....37 K5
Millfold *WHIT* OL12 ....18 E2
Mill Fold Rd *MDTN* M24 ....57 H5
Mill Ga *URM* M41 ....95 H3
Mill Ga *MILN* OL16 ....28 D8
OLDS OL8 ....75 G1
Millgate *ANC * M4 ....7 H2
EDGW/EG BL7 ....22 A2
STKP SK1 ....13 J4
UPML OL3 ....45 J8
Millgate La *DID/WITH* M20 ....110 A3
Mill Green St *WGTN/LGST * M12 ....88 A4
Millhall Cl *HULME* M15 ....87 H7
Millhead Av *NEWH/MOS* M40 ....88 B2
Mill HI *BOL * BL1 ....3 H3
LHULT M38 ....52 B6
Mill Hill Av *POY/DIS* SK12 ....121 M5
Mill Hill Caravan Pk *BOLE* BL2 ....3 H3
Mill Hill Gv *HYDE* SK14 ....103 J2
Mill Hill Hollow *POY/DIS* SK12 ....121 M5

Mill Hill St *BOLE* BL2 ....3 H3
Millhouse Av *NTHM/RTH* M23 ....109 K8
Mill House Cl *WHIT* OL12 ....19 L8
Millhouse St *RAMS* BL0 ....17 E4
Milliner Ct *OFTN * SK2 ....113 G5
Millingford Av *GOL/RIS/CU* WA3 ....79 J2
Millingford Gv *AIMK* WN4 ....78 E1
Millington Wk *HULME* M15 ....87 G6
Mill La *AUL* OL6 ....90 E2
BRAM/HZG SK7 ....122 B4
CHAD OL9 ....8 D8
CHD/CHDH SK8 ....111 C6
CHD/CHDH SK8 ....120 D1
DTN/ASHW M34 ....101 L3
FAIL M35 ....74 A6
HALE/TIMP WA15 ....118 A8
HOR/BR BL6 ....21 D8
LEIGH WN7 ....66 E8
MCFLDN SK10 ....128 A7
MOSL OL5 ....76 F2
MPL/ROM SK6 ....101 K7
OLDE OL4 ....61 G3
RDSH SK5 ....100 D3
ROY/SHW OL2 ....42 F8
WGNE/HIN WN2 ....49 J1
WHTN BL5 ....50 B8
WYTH/NTH M22 ....110 B3
Mill Meadow *WGN* WN1 ....15 H5
Millom Av *NTHM/RTH* M23 ....109 L3
Millom Cl *MILN* OL16 ....11 L1
Millom Ct *HALE/TIMP * WA15 ....109 C6
Millom Dr *BURY* BL9 ....55 K2
Millow Pl *CHD/CHDH* SK8 ....119 K1
Millow St *ANC* M4 ....7 G1
Mill Pond Av *NM/HAY* SK22 ....124 F3
Mill Rd *BURY* BL9 ....25 J4
WGNW/BIL/O WN5 ....46 A7
WILM/AE SK9 ....126 F5
Mills Farm Cl *OLDS* OL8 ....75 K3
Millstead Cl *HYDE* SK14 ....102 D3
Millstone Cl *POY/DIS* SK12 ....122 B7
Millstone Rd *BOL* BL1 ....35 J3
Millstream La *NEWH/MOS* M40 ....73 L7
Mill St *AIMK* WN4 ....78 F2
ALT WA14 ....108 B7
ATH M46 ....67 H3
BOL BL1 ....3 G4
BRAM/HZG SK7 ....121 M1
EDGW/EG BL7 ....22 C4
FAIL M35 ....73 M5
FWTH BL4 ....52 F4
GLSP SK13 ....105 C3
GOL/RIS/CU WA3 ....79 K4
HYDE SK14 ....91 H7
LEIGH WN7 ....66 D8
MOSL OL5 ....76 F4
OP/CLY M11 ....88 D4
RAD M26 ....54 E2
*RAMS * BL0 ....17 A8
ROY/SHW OL2 ....43 G8
SLFD M6 ....71 K8
STLY SK15 ....91 M3
TOT/BURYW BL8 ....24 C4
UPML OL3 ....61 L4
WALK M28 ....68 D5
WGNE/HIN WN2 ....49 G7
WGNS/IIMK WN3 ....14 E5
WHTN BL5 ....50 C4
Milltown *GLSP* SK13 ....105 G3
Milltown St *RAD* M26 ....54 E2
Millwall Cl *GTN* M18 ....89 G7
Millway *HALE/TIMP* WA15 ....117 L5
Millwell La *BOL * BL1 ....2 E4
Millwood Av *AIMK* WN4 ....63 K7
CHD/CHDH SK8 ....120 A4
Millwood Ct *BURY* BL9 ....39 K6
Millwood Ter *HYDE* SK14 ....101 M2
Millwright St *NEWH/MOS* M40 ....73 L7
Mill Yd *BURY* BL9 ....5 H3
Milne Cl *WGTN/LGST* M12 ....88 D6
Milner Av *ALT* WA14 ....107 L5
BURY BL9 ....25 J7
Milner St *OLDTF/WHR* M16 ....87 G8
RAD M26 ....54 B1
SWIN M27 ....70 D4
WHIT OL12 ....18 D4
Milnes Av *LEIGH* WN7 ....81 J2
Milne St *CHAD* OL9 ....8 B4
CHAD OL9 ....8 C8
OLD OL1 ....59 K2
ROCH OL11 ....41 M2
ROY/SHW OL2 ....43 L6
Milngate Cl *MILN* OL16 ....42 F1
Milnholme Rd *BOL* BL1 ....35 L1
Milnrow Cl *CMANE* M1 ....7 K8
Milnrow Rd *LIT* OL15 ....29 J2
MILN OL16 ....11 H6
ROY/SHW OL2 ....43 M3
Milnthorpe Rd *BOLE* BL2 ....37 H4
Milnthorpe St *SLFD* M6 ....71 K7
Milnthorpe Wy *WGTN/LGST* M12 ....88 B6
Milo St *BKLY * M9 ....73 G1
Milsom Av *BOLS/LL* BL3 ....51 M1
Milton Av *BOLS/LL* BL3 ....37 L8
*BOLS/LL * BL3 ....51 L1
DROY M43 ....89 K3
IRL M44 ....94 B6
*ORD * M5 ....86 A2
STLY SK15 ....77 H8
Milton Cl *DUK* SK16 ....91 L5
MPL/ROM SK6 ....114 C8
STRET M32 ....97 H1
Milton Crs *CHD/CHDH* SK8 ....110 F7
FWTH BL4 ....52 E6
Milton Dr *CHAD* OL9 ....58 D6
HALE/TIMP WA15 ....108 D3
POY/DIS SK12 ....121 M8
SALE M33 ....96 D6
Milton Gv *OLDTF/WHR* M16 ....97 M2
SALE M33 ....96 D6
WGN WN1 ....47 M1
WGNW/BIL/O WN5 ....46 D6
WGNW/BIL/O WN5 ....62 A3
Milton La *SLFD* M6 ....86 D1
Milton Mt *DTN/ASHW* M34 ....90 A3
GOL/RIS/CU WA3 ....80 A5
PWCH M25 ....55 M7
RAD M26 ....38 A8
STRET M32 ....97 H1
SWIN M27 ....70 A3
Milton St *BRO* M7 ....72 B8
DTN/ASHW M34 ....90 B8
ECC M30 ....85 G2
HYDE SK14 ....91 G8

LEIGH WN7 ....66 B7
MDTN M24 ....57 J3
MILN OL16 ....10 F7
MOSL OL5 ....76 F2
RAMS BL0 ....17 B6
ROY/SHW OL2 ....43 H7
Milton Vw *MOSL* OL5 ....77 G2
Milverton Av *HYDE* SK14 ....102 F2
Milverton Cl *HOR/BR* BL6 ....35 G7
Milverton Dr *CHD/CHDH* SK8 ....120 D7
Milverton Rd *RUSH/FAL* M14 ....99 G1
Milverton Wk *HYDE* SK14 ....102 F2
Milwain Dr *HTNM* SK4 ....99 M6
Milwain Rd *BNG/LEV* M19 ....99 J4
STRET M32 ....96 F3
Mimosa Dr *SWIN* M27 ....70 C2
Mincing St *ANC * M4 ....7 H1
Minden Cl *DID/WITH* M20 ....98 F8
TOT/BURYW BL8 ....38 E2
Minden Pde *BURY* BL9 ....4 F5
Minden St *SLFD* M6 ....71 H6
Minehead Av *DID/WITH* M20 ....98 C5
LEIGH WN7 ....66 A2
URM M41 ....95 L4
Minerva Rd *DUK* SK16 ....90 F2
FWTH BL4 ....52 C3
Mine St *HEY* OL10 ....27 G8
Mine Wy *RNFD/HAY * WA11 ....78 C5
Minnie St *BOLS/LL * BL3 ....35 L8
*WHIT * OL12 ....18 E2
Minoan Gdns *BRO* M7 ....71 M7
Minorca Cl *ROCH* OL11 ....27 H4
Minorca St *BOLS/LL* BL3 ....36 B8
Minor St *FAIL* M35 ....74 D3
OLDS OL8 ....9 H8
ROCH OL11 ....41 M3
Minshull St *CMANE* M1 ....7 H5
Minshull St South *CMANE* M1 ....7 J6
Minstead Cl *HYDE* SK14 ....102 D3
Minster Cl *BOLE* BL2 ....36 F2
DUK SK16 ....91 G6
Minster Dr *ALT* WA14 ....116 C3
CHD/CHDH SK8 ....111 K7
URM M41 ....84 F8
Minster Gv *TYLD* M29 ....67 L5
Minster Rd *BKLY* M9 ....73 J4
BOLE BL2 ....36 F2
Minster Wy *CHAD* OL9 ....58 D3
Minstrel Cl *SWIN* M27 ....70 A5
WGNE/HIN WN2 ....64 E5
Minton St *NEWH/MOS* M40 ....73 M4
OLDE OL4 ....9 L8
Minto St *AULW* OL7 ....75 K8
Mint St *RAMS* BL0 ....17 C2
Mirabel St *CSLFD* M3 ....6 E1
Mirfield Av *BKLY* M9 ....57 G8
HTNM SK4 ....12 A3
OLDS OL8 ....59 H8
Mirfield Cl *GOL/RIS/CU* WA3 ....80 A5
Mirfield Dr *ECC* M30 ....70 A8
MDTN M24 ....57 J3
URM M41 ....84 F8
Mirfield Rd *BKLY* M9 ....57 G8
Miriam Gv *LEIGH* WN7 ....66 D8
Miriam St *BOLS/LL * BL3 ....35 L8
NEWH/MOS M40 ....74 A6
Miry La *WGNNW/ST* WN6 ....14 B3
WHTN BL5 ....50 B7
Mission St *HEY* OL10 ....40 F2
Missouri Av *ORD* M5 ....86 B3
Mistletoe Gv *CSLFD * M3 ....6 B1
Mitcham Av *BKLY* M9 ....73 K1
Mitchell Cl *CHD/CHDH * SK8 ....110 C6
Mitchell Hey *WHIT* OL12 ....10 C4
Mitchell Rd *WGNW/BIL/O* WN5 ....62 B7
Mitchells Quay *FAIL* M35 ....74 B5
Mitchell St *AIMK* WN4 ....78 F5
ECC M30 ....84 F1
GOL/RIS/CU WA3 ....79 K5
LEIGH WN7 ....65 L7
MDTN M40 ....57 J3
MILN OL16 ....28 F1
NEWH/MOS M40 ....73 L7
OLD OL1 ....8 F7
*OP/CLY * M11 ....88 C5
TOT/BURYW BL8 ....24 F8
WGNE/HIN WN2 ....48 D5
WGNW/BIL/O WN5 ....47 H6
WHIT OL12 ....10 B3
Mitcheson Gdns *SLFD* M6 ....86 C1
Mitford Rd *RUSH/FAL* M14 ....98 F5
Mitford St *STRET* M32 ....96 F3
Mitre Rd *BRUN/LGST* M13 ....88 C8
Mitre St *BOL* BL1 ....22 B8
FAIL M35 ....74 C4
Mitton Cl *GOL/RIS/CU* WA3 ....81 G7
HEY OL10 ....40 C2
TOT/BURYW BL8 ....38 E2
Mizpah Gv *TOT/BURYW* BL8 ....38 E2
Mizzy Rd *WHIT* OL12 ....28 B3
Moadlock *MPL/ROM* SK6 ....101 M8
Moat Av *WYTH/NTH* M22 ....109 M8
Moatfield Gdns *BOL* BL1 ....2 A2
Moat Gdns *WYTH/NTH* M22 ....109 M8
Moat Hall Av *ECC* M30 ....84 D4
Moat House St *WGNE/HIN* WN2 ....48 D5
Moat Rd *WYTH/NTH* M22 ....109 M8
Mobberley Cl *BNG/LEV* M19 ....99 H8
Mobberley Rd *BOLE* BL2 ....37 H4
WILM/AE SK9 ....126 A3
Mocha Pde *BRO* M7 ....87 C1
Modbury Cl *BRAM/HZG* SK7 ....121 J3
Mode Hill La *WHTF* M45 ....55 M4
Model Cottages *HALE/TIMP * WA15 ....109 C8
Mode Wheel Rd South *ORD* M5 ....86 A4
Modwen Rd *ORD * M5 ....86 B6
Moelfre Dr *CHD/CHDH* SK8 ....120 E5
Moffat Cl *BOLE* BL2 ....37 J8
Moggle La *MCFLDN* SK10 ....129 K3
Moisant St *BOLS/LL* BL3 ....52 A1
Mold St *BOL* BL1 ....36 B1
OLD OL1 ....9 H2
Molesworth St *MILN* OL16 ....11 L5
Mollets Wd *DTN/ASHW* M34 ....90 D7
Mollington Rd *WYTH/NTH* M22 ....119 L4
Molyneux Rd *BNG/LEV* M19 ....99 M3
WHTN BL5 ....50 B1
Molyneux St *WGN* WN1 ....15 J3
WHIT OL12 ....10 A2
Mona Av *CHD/CHDH* SK8 ....119 M4
STRET M32 ....96 F1
Monaco Dr *WYTH/NTH* M22 ....110 A2
Monarch Cl *IRL* M44 ....94 B6
ROY/SHW OL2 ....59 H2
Monart Rd *BKLY* M9 ....73 H3
Mona St *HYDE* SK14 ....102 B2
SLFD M6 ....71 K8
WGN WN1 ....14 E5

Mond Rd *IRL* M44 ....83 L8
Money Ash Rd
HALE/TIMP WA15 ....116 F1
Monica Av *CHH* M8 ....72 C2
Monica Gv *BNG/LEV* M19 ....99 J4
Monica Ter *AIMK* WN4 ....78 E2
Monks Cl *MILN* OL16 ....29 H6
Monksdale Av *URM* M41 ....95 L2
Monks Hall Gv *ECC* M30 ....85 G2
Monks La *BOLE* BL2 ....37 G2
Monks' Rd *GLSP* SK13 ....104 B6
Monkton Av *GTN* M18 ....99 M1
Monkwood Dr *BKLY * M9 ....73 H4
SALE M33 ....96 C7
Monmouth Av *BURY* BL9 ....25 J7
SALE M33 ....96 C7
Monmouth Crs *AIMK* WN4 ....78 F2
Monmouth Rd *CHD/CHDH* SK8 ....120 D3
Monmouth St *CHAD* OL9 ....89 H6
GTN M18 ....89 H6
MDTN M24 ....57 J3
ROCH OL11 ....10 E8
Monroe Cl *SLFD* M6 ....71 H8
WCNS/IIMK WN3 ....63 K1
Monsal Av *BRO* M7 ....71 K5
OFTN SK2 ....113 G5
Monsall Rd *NEWH/MOS* M40 ....73 H6
Monsall St *NEWH/MOS* M40 ....73 H6
OLDS OL8 ....75 H1
Mons Av *ROCH* OL11 ....27 M4
Montague Rd *AUL* OL6 ....91 C1
OLDTF/WHR M16 ....98 C3
SALE M33 ....96 E8
Montague St *BOLS/LL * BL3 ....35 L2
Montague Wy *STLY* SK15 ....91 K2
Montagu Rd *OFTN* SK2 ....113 G5
Montagu St *MPL/ROM* SK6 ....114 E2
Montana Sq *OP/CLY* M11 ....89 H5
Montcliffe Crs *OLDTF/WHR* M16 ....98 C3
Monteagle St *BKLY* M9 ....56 E8
Montford Ri *WGNE/HIN* WN2 ....48 D2
Montford St *SALQ* M50 ....86 C6
Montfort Cl *WHTN* BL5 ....50 A6
Montgomery *ROCH* OL11 ....10 D7
Montgomery Dr *BURY* BL9 ....55 L2
Montgomery Rd
BRUN/LGST M13 ....99 J2
Montgomery St *OLDS* OL8 ....74 E2
ROCH OL11 ....10 D7
Montgomery Wy *RAD* M26 ....37 M7
Monton Av *ECC* M30 ....85 H1
Montondale *ECC* M30 ....84 F1
Montonfields Rd *ECC* M30 ....84 E1
Monton Gn *ECC* M30 ....70 A8
Monton La *ECC* M30 ....84 F2
Monton Mill Gdns *ECC* M30 ....84 F1
Monton Rd *ECC* M30 ....85 H1
RDSH SK5 ....100 F8
Monton St *BOLS/LL* BL3 ....52 C1
RAD M26 ....54 C1
RUSH/FAL M14 ....87 K8
Montpelier Rd
WYTH/NTH M22 ....118 C2
Montreal St *BNG/LEV* M19 ....99 L3
OLDS OL8 ....59 J8
Montrose Av *BOLE* BL2 ....3 L1
DID/WITH M20 ....98 F5
DUK SK16 ....90 F5
EDGY/DAV SK3 ....121 J1
RAMS BL0 ....24 D2
STRET M32 ....97 H1
WGNW/BIL/O WN5 ....46 F5
Montrose Crs *BNG/LEV* M19 ....99 K3
Montrose Dr *EDGW/EG* BL7 ....22 E5
Montrose St *ROCH* OL11 ....41 M4
Montserrat Brow *HOR/BR* BL6 ....34 F1
Montserrat Rd *BOL* BL1 ....35 H2
Monument Man *WGN* WN1 ....47 M2
Monument Rd *WGN* WN1 ....48 A1
Monyash Ms *GLSP* SK13 ....104 A3
Monyash Vw *WGNE/HIN* WN2 ....65 J1
Moody St *CHAD* OL9 ....8 D2
Moon Gv *RUSH/FAL* M14 ....98 E1
Moon St *CHAD* OL9 ....8 D2
Moor Av *WGNNW/ST* WN6 ....30 B4
Moor Bank La *MILN* OL16 ....29 G8
Moorby Av *BNG/LEV* M19 ....99 H8
Moorby Wk *BOLS/LL * BL3 ....2 D6
Moor Cl *RAD* M26 ....38 B7
Moorclose St *MDTN* M24 ....57 H3
Moorcock Av *SWIN* M27 ....70 E4
Moor Crs *UPML* OL3 ....61 J3
Moorcroft *RAMS* BL0 ....17 D2
ROCH OL11 ....10 B5
Moorcroft Dr *BNG/LEV* M19 ....99 J8
Moorcroft Rd *NTHM/RTH* M23 ....109 J3
Moorcroft St *DROY * M43 ....89 K3
OLDS OL8 ....74 F2
Moordale Av *OLDE* OL4 ....60 B3
Moordale St *DID/WITH* M20 ....98 D7
Moordown Cl *CHH* M8 ....72 E6
Moor Edge Rd *STLY* SK15 ....77 J4
Mooredge Ter *ROY/SHW* OL2 ....59 H2
Moore Dr *RNFD/HAY* WA11 ....78 C6
Moor End *ECC* M30 ....84 F1
Moor End Av *BRO* M7 ....71 M4
Moor End Rd *MPL/ROM* SK6 ....115 K7
Moore's Ct *BOL* BL1 ....35 M4
Moores La *WGNNW/ST* WN6 ....31 G2
Moore St *MILN* OL16 ....10 F5
WGN WN1 ....15 K1
Moore St East *WGN* WN1 ....15 K1
Moorfield *EDGW/EG* BL7 ....16 D6
WALK M28 ....68 C5
WALK M28 ....68 C5
Moorfield Av *DTN/ASHW* M34 ....101 K3
LIT OL15 ....20 B5
RUSH/FAL M14 ....98 D2
STLY SK15 ....77 J4
Moorfield Cha *FWTH* BL4 ....53 G5
Moorfield Cl *IRL * M44 ....94 E1
SWIN M27 ....70 A6
Moorfield Crs *GOL/RIS/CU* WA3 ....80 D7
Moorfield Dr *HYDE * SK14 ....91 H7
WILM/AE SK9 ....126 C7
Moorfield Gv *BOLE* BL2 ....36 E3
HTNM SK4 ....12 C2
SALE M33 ....109 G1
Moorfield Hamlet
ROY/SHW OL2 ....43 J5
Moorfield Hts *MOSL* OL5 ....77 L5
Moorfield Ms *ROY/SHW * OL2 ....43 L5
Moorfield Pl *WHIT * OL12 ....10 D4
Moorfield Rd *DID/WITH* M20 ....98 C8
IRL M44 ....94 D1
OLDS OL8 ....74 E2
SLFD M6 ....71 H8
SWIN M27 ....69 M6
Moorfield St *DID/WITH * M20 ....98 E5

HYDE SK14 93 G6
WGNE/HIN WN2 64 E1
Moorfield Ter HYDE SK14 93 G7
Moor Ga BOLE BL2 23 G7
Moorgate BURY BL9 5 G3
Moorgate Av DID/WITH M20 98 G6
ROCH OL11 27 K5
Moorgate Ct BOLE BL2 3 K1
Moorgate Dr STLY SK15 77 H6
TYLD M29 67 M6
Moor Gate La WHIT OL12 19 M5
Moorgate Ms MOSL * OL5 77 H5
Moorgate Rd RAD M26 38 B4
STLY SK15 77 H5
Moorgate St UPML OL3 61 L4
Moorhead St ANC M4 7 K1
Moorhey Rd LHULT M38 52 C6
Moorhey St OLDE OL4 59 L6
Moor Hl ROCH OL11 27 H3
Moorhouse Farm MILN OL16 29 H6
Moor House Fold MILN OL16 29 H6
The Moorings MOSL OL5 77 H1
POY/DIS SK12 124 A6
WALK M28 69 K7
Moorings Cl WGN WN1 15 M4
Moorings Rd TRPK M17 85 L4
Moorland Av CHH M8 72 C2
DROY M43 89 H3
MILN OL16 29 J7
ROCH OL11 27 J3
SALE M33 108 F1
UPML OL3 61 J1
WHIT OL12 18 D6
Moorland Crs WHIT OL12 18 D5
Moorland Dr CHD/CHDH SK8 120 B4
HOR/BR BL6 34 C1
LHULT M38 52 D6
Moorland Gv BOL BL1 35 K2
Moorland Rd AIMK WN4 64 B7
DID/WITH M20 110 E1
OFTN SK2 112 D8
STLY SK15 77 H7
WGNE/HIN WN2 48 F7
Moorlands Av LEIGH WN7 81 J1
URM * M41 95 L1
Moorlands Crs MOSL OL5 77 G3
Moorlands Dr MOSL OL5 77 H1
Moorlands St ROY/SHW OL2 43 M5
Moorland St WHIT OL12 28 B3
Moorlands Vw BOLS/LL BL3 51 K2
Moorland Ter WHIT OL12 27 K3
Moor La BOL BL1 2 D5
BRAM/HZG SK7 128 B1
BRO M7 71 K4
LEIGH WN7 66 B4
NTHM/RTH M23 109 K2
UPML OL3 61 M2
URM M41 95 K1
WILM/AE SK9 126 A7
Moor Nook SALE M33 109 G1
Moor Park Av ROCH OL11 41 L2
Moor Park Rd DID/WITH M20 110 F4
Moor Platt Cl HOR/BR BL6 34 C1
Moor Rd LIT OL15 20 D3
NTHM/RTH M23 109 H4
TOT/BURYW BL8 17 A6
WGNW/BIL/O WN5 46 B6
Moorsholme Av
NEWH/MOS M40 73 K5
Moorside HALE/TIMP * WA15 108 F5
ROCH OL11 42 C1
Moorside Av BOL BL1 35 K2
BOLE BL2 38 A3
DROY M43 89 M1
FWTH BL4 52 E5
HOR/BR BL6 21 C8
OLDE OL4 44 C8
Moorside Cl GLSP SK13 104 E4
Moorside Ct DTN/ASHW M34 90 C8
Moorside Crs DROY M43 89 M2
Moorside La DTN/ASHW M34 90 D8
Moorside Rd BRO M7 71 M3
CHH * M8 72 D3
EDGW/EG BL7 16 D3
HTNM SK4 111 K2
MOSL OL5 77 H3
SWIN M27 70 A4
TOT/BURYW BL8 24 B7
URM M41 95 H1
URM M41 95 L1
Moorside St DROY M43 89 L2
Moorside Vw TOT/BURYW BL8 24 C6
Moorsley Dr BKLY M9 57 J8
Moor St BURY BL9 5 G2
ECC M30 84 E3
HEY OL10 40 E2
OLD * OL1 59 L5
ROY/SHW OL2 43 K6
SWIN M27 70 C5
Moorsview RAMS BL0 17 B6
Moorton Av BNG/LEV M19 99 J5
Moorton Pk BNG/LEV M19 99 J5
Moortop Cl BKLY M9 56 F7
Moor Top Pl HTNM SK4 12 A1
Moor View Cl WHIT OL12 27 J3
Moorville Rd SLFD M6 70 F7
Moor Wy TOT/BURYW BL8 23 L1
Moorway Dr BKLY M9 57 K8
Moorwood Dr OLDS OL8 59 M8
SALE M33 108 B1
Mora Av CHAD OL9 8 B1
Moran Cl WILM/AE SK9 127 H2
Moran Wk HULME M15 87 J6
Morar Dr BOLE BL2 37 K5
Morar Rd DUK SK16 91 G5
Mora St BKLY M9 73 J4
Moravian Cl DUK SK16 90 F3
Moravian Fld DROY * M43 89 K4
Moray Cl RAMS BL0 17 A8
Moray Rd CHAD OL9 58 D8
Morbourne Cl WGTN/LGST M12 88 B6
Morden Av AIMK WN4 78 E1
Morecambe Cl NEWH/MOS M40 73 L6
Morely St OLDE OL4 60 A3
Moresby Cl LEIGH WN7 66 A7
Moresby Dr DID/WITH M20 110 E4
Moreton Av BRAM/HZG SK7 121 G7
SALE M33 108 B1
STRET M32 97 G2
WHTF M45 55 J3
Moreton Cl DUK SK16 91 G6
GOL/RIS/CU WA3 79 J3
Moreton Dr LEIGH WN7 81 H3
POY/DIS SK12 122 B8
TOT/BURYW BL8 38 E1
WILM/AE SK9 127 J1
Moreton La OFTN SK2 112 F5
Moreton St CHAD OL9 58 C4
Morgan Pl RDSH SK5 100 C8
Morgan St LIT OL15 20 C7
Morillon Rd IRL M44 83 K8
Morland Rd NM/HAY SK22 125 J2
OLDTF/WHR M16 86 F8
Morley Av RUSH/FAL M14 98 D3
SWIN M27 70 B6
Morley Gn WILM/AE SK9 126 A3
Morley Rd RAD M26 38 A8
Morley's La TYLD M29 82 D1
Morley St ATH M46 66 F1
BOLS/LL BL3 2 B6
BURY BL9 4 F8
GLSP SK13 105 G4
MILN OL16 11 J1
WHTF M45 55 J4
Morley Wy UPML OL3 61 L7
Morna Wk WGTN/LGST M12 88 A4
Morningside Cl DROY M43 89 J5
MILN * OL16 11 J6
Morningside Dr DID/WITH M20 110 F4
Mornington Av CHD/CHDH SK8 111 G8
Mornington Crs RUSH/FAL M14 98 D4
Mornington Rd ATH M46 51 J6
BOL BL1 35 M3
CHD/CHDH SK8 111 G8
ROCH OL11 42 C2
SALE M33 97 G7
WGNE/HIN WN2 49 J7
Morpeth Cl AULW OL7 75 H8
WGTN/LGST M12 88 B7
Morpeth St SWIN M27 70 B6
Morrell Rd WYTH/NTH M22 110 B4
Morris Fold Dr HOR/BR BL6 34 F6
Morris Gn BOLS/LL BL3 51 M2
Morris Green La BOLS/LL BL3 51 M1
Morris Green St BOLS/LL * BL3 51 M2
Morris Gv URM M41 95 H4
Morrison St BOLS/LL BL3 52 B1
Morris St BOL BL1 3 G4
DID/WITH M20 98 E5
OLDE OL4 9 M8
RAD M26 39 H7
TYLD M29 67 J3
WGN WN1 15 H3
WGNE/HIN WN2 49 G7
WGNS/IIMK WN3 48 B8
Morrowfield Av CHH M8 72 C5
Morse Rd NEWH/MOS M40 73 L7
Mortar St OLDE OL4 59 M5
Mortfield Gdns BOL BL1 2 A2
Mortfield La BOL BL1 2 A2
Mortimer Av BKLY M9 57 H8
Mortimer St OLD OL1 9 L1
Mortlake Cl LHULT M38 68 C1
Mortlake Dr NEWH/MOS M40 73 L7
Mort La TYLD M29 68 B2
Morton Av WGNS/IIMK WN3 14 D9
Morton Cl WGNS/IIMK WN3 62 F2
Morton St FAIL M35 73 M5
HTNM SK4 100 B8
MDTN M24 57 K3
RAD M26 54 E2
Mort St FWTH BL4 52 E4
HOR/BR BL6 21 B8
TYLD M29 67 J3
WGNE/HIN WN2 49 K7
WGNNW/ST WN6 14 B1
Morven Av BRAM/HZG SK7 122 B1
Morven Dr NTHM/RTH M23 109 K7
Morven Gv BOLE BL2 37 J5
Morville Dr WGNS/IIMK WN3 47 L8
Morville Rd CCHDY M21 98 A3
Morville St CMANE * M1 7 L6
Moscow Rd EDGY/DAV SK3 12 F9
Moscow Rd East EDGY/DAV SK3 12 F9
Mosedale Cl NTHM/RTH M23 109 H6
TYLD M29 67 M6
Mosedale Rd MDTN M24 57 G2
Moseldene Rd OFTN SK2 113 G7
Moseley Rd CHD/CHDH SK8 120 B1
RUSH/FAL M14 99 H4
Moseley St EDGY/DAV SK3 13 G7
Mosley Av BURY BL9 25 J7
RAMS BL0 24 E2
Mosley Cl HALE/TIMP WA15 108 C5
Mosley Common Rd TYLD M29 68 B4
Mosley Rd HALE/TIMP WA15 108 E6
TRPK M17 85 M6
Mosley Rd North TRPK M17 85 M4
Mosley St CMANW M2 7 G5
RAD M26 38 C8
The Moss MDTN M24 57 L6
Mossack Av WYTH/NTH M22 118 F3
Moss Av LEIGH WN7 66 E7
MILN OL16 11 M6
WGNW/BIL/O WN5 62 A1
Moss Bank CHD/CHDH SK8 120 E7
CHH M8 72 D4
Moss Bank Av DROY M43 89 M2
Moss Bank Cl BOL BL1 22 A8
Mossbank Cl GLSP SK13 93 H8
Moss Bank Ct DROY * M43 89 M2
Mossbank Gv HEY OL10 40 F1
Moss Bank Gv SWIN M27 69 M2
Moss Bank Pk BOL * BL1 35 J1
Moss Bank Rd SWIN M27 70 A2
Moss Bank Wy BOL BL1 35 K2
Mossbray Av BNG/LEV M19 99 G8
Moss Bridge Rd MILN OL16 11 K8
Mossbrook Dr LHULT M38 52 B6
Moss Brook Rd BKLY M9 73 H5
Moss Cl RAD M26 38 A7
Mossclough Ct BKLY M9 73 H5
Moss Colliery Rd SWIN M27 70 A1
Mosscot Wk BRUN/LGST M13 7 K8
Moss Croft Cl URM M41 95 H1
Mossdale Av BOL BL1 35 G5
Mossdale Rd AIMK WN4 63 K4
NTHM/RTH M23 109 J3
SALE M33 108 B3
Mossdown Rd ROY/SHW OL2 59 K1
Moss Dr HOR/BR BL6 34 C1
Mossfield Cl BURY BL9 5 L1
HTNM SK4 12 A2
Mossfield Ct BOL BL1 2 C2
Mossfield Dr BKLY M9 57 K8
Mossfield Rd FWTH BL4 52 E4
FWTH BL4 53 J7
HALE/TIMP WA15 109 G6
SWIN M27 70 B2
Moss Fold TYLD M29 67 M5
Moss Gate Rd ROY/SHW OL2 43 K3
Moss Grange Av
OLDTF/WHR * M16 98 A1
Moss Gn PART M31 95 J6
Moss Gv ROY/SHW OL2 43 H3
WGNNW/ST WN6 31 H4
Mossgrove Rd
HALE/TIMP WA15 108 C6
Mosshall Cl HULME M15 87 G6
Moss Hall Rd BURY BL9 40 A3
Moss Hey Dr NTHM/RTH M23 109 L3
Moss Hey St ROY/SHW OL2 43 L6
Moss House La WALK M28 68 C7
Moss House Ter BKLY * M9 72 F3
Mossland Cl HEY OL10 41 G4
Mossland Gv BOLS/LL BL3 51 G2
Moss La AULW OL7 90 C2
BOL BL1 35 K1
BRAM/HZG SK7 120 F7
FWTH BL4 53 L7
GOL/RIS/CU WA3 79 L7
GOL/RIS/CU WA3 82 A7
HALE/TIMP WA15 108 B8
HALE/TIMP WA15 108 C5
HOR/BR BL6 33 J2
HYDE SK14 103 J4
IRL M44 94 A7
LYMM WA13 106 B3
LYMM WA13 106 E4
MCFLDN SK10 131 K2
MDTN M24 57 J7
MILN OL16 11 G6
PART M31 106 D1
ROY/SHW OL2 59 K1
SALE M33 107 L1
SWIN M27 70 A3
TYLD M29 82 D3
URM M41 85 G7
WALK M28 53 H8
WALK M28 69 H1
WGNE/HIN WN2 64 D1
WHTF M45 55 J4
WILM/AE SK9 118 F7
WILM/AE SK9 130 E3
Moss La East OLDTF/WHR M16 87 H8
Moss La West HULME M15 87 H8
Moss Lea BOL BL1 22 A8
Mosslee Av CHH M8 72 C1
Mossley Rd AUL OL6 76 C7
AUL OL6 90 F1
OLDE OL4 61 G8
Moss Meadow WHTN BL5 50 B2
Moss Meadow Rd SLFD * M6 70 F8
Mossmere Rd CHD/CHDH SK8 111 K8
Moss Mill St MILN OL16 11 J8
Moss Park Rd STRET M32 96 D2
Moss Pl BURY BL9 4 E9
Moss Rd FWTH BL4 53 H5
PART M31 95 L8
STRET M32 96 F1
WGNW/BIL/O WN5 62 A1
WILM/AE SK9 130 F2
Moss Rose WILM/AE SK9 130 E2
Moss Rw BURY BL9 4 F6
Moss Shaw Wy RAD M26 38 B7
Moss Side La MILN OL16 11 M9
Moss Side Rd IRL M44 94 A6
Moss St BRO M7 72 A7
BURY BL9 4 E5
BURY BL9 25 G2
DTN/ASHW M34 89 L3
FWTH BL4 53 H3
HEY OL10 40 F2
HYDE SK14 93 G7
MILN OL16 11 J6
OLDE OL4 60 B4
WGNNW/ST WN6 14 B1
WGNS/IIMK WN3 64 C1
WGNW/BIL/O * WN5 46 E6
Moss St West AULW OL7 90 C2
Moss Ter MILN OL16 11 H6
WGNW/BIL/O WN5 46 E7
Moss Vale Crs STRET M32 85 J8
Moss Vale Rd URM M41 96 B2
Moss View Rd BOLE * BL2 37 H4
PART M31 106 D1
Mossway MDTN M24 57 J7
Moss Wy SALE M33 96 B8
Mosswood Pk DID/WITH M20 110 E4
Mosswood Rd WILM/AE SK9 127 J3
Mossylea Cl MDTN M24 57 L7
Mossy Lea Fold
WGNNW/ST WN6 30 C1
Moston Bank Av BKLY M9 73 H5
Moston La BKLY M9 73 H4
NEWH/MOS M40 73 K3
Moston La East
NEWH/MOS M40 74 A2
Moston Rd MDTN M24 58 A6
Moston St BRO M7 72 C5
Mostyn Av BURY BL9 25 J7
CHD/CHDH SK8 120 A3
RUSH/FAL M14 98 E4
Mostyn Rd BRAM/HZG SK7 121 L3
Mostyn St DUK SK16 91 J4
Motcombe Farm Rd
CHD/CHDH SK8 119 K3
Motcombe Gv CHD/CHDH SK8 119 J1
Motcombe Rd CHD/CHDH SK8 119 J2
Motherwell Av BNG/LEV M19 99 K3
Mottershead Av BOLS/LL BL3 37 K8
Mottershead Rd
WYTH/NTH M22 109 L8
Mottram Av CCHDY M21 97 M7
Mottram Cl CHD/CHDH SK8 111 K7
Mottram Dr HALE/TIMP WA15 108 D7
WGNS/IIMK WN3 47 L7
Mottram Fold STKP SK1 13 J6
Mottram Moor HYDE SK14 92 F8
Mottram Old Rd HYDE SK14 102 D4
STLY SK15 91 M3
Mottram Rd HYDE SK14 102 E1
HYDE SK14 103 K4
SALE M33 109 H1
STLY SK15 91 M3
WILM/AE SK9 130 E3
Mottram St HOR/BR BL6 21 B8
STKP SK1 13 J6
Mough La CHAD OL9 74 A1
Mouldsworth Av DID/WITH M20 98 D5
HTNM SK4 100 A6
Moulton St CHH M8 72 B8
Mouncey St CMANE * M1 7 G8
The Mount ALT WA14 108 A7
HALE/TIMP WA15 117 L4
Mountain Ash WHIT OL12 27 L1
Mountain Ash Cl SALE M33 95 M7
WHIT OL12 27 L1
Mountain Gv WALK M28 52 F8
Mountain St MOSL OL5 76 F3
NEWH/MOS M40 74 A8
STKP SK1 13 M3
WALK M28 52 F8
Mount Av LIT OL15 20 B5
WHIT OL12 19 M8
Mountbatten Av DUK SK16 91 J5
Mountbatten Cl BURY BL9 55 L2
Mountbatten St GTN M18 88 F7
Mount Carmel Crs ORD * M5 86 F5
Mount Crs WGNW/BIL/O WN5 46 C6
Mount Dr MPL/ROM SK6 114 C7
URM M41 96 C2
Mountfield PWCH M25 55 L8
Mountfield Rd BRAM/HZG SK7 121 G7
EDGY/DAV SK3 12 D9
Mountfield Wk OP/CLY M11 88 C3
Mount Fold MDTN M24 57 K5
Mountford Av CHH * M8 72 C2
Mount Gv WYTH/NTH M22 110 C7
Mount La UPML OL3 61 H3
Mountmorres Cl WHTN BL5 51 J5
Mount Pleasant BOLS/LL * BL3 3 M9
BRAM/HZG SK7 121 M1
LIT * OL15 20 D4
MDTN M24 56 F4
PWCH M25 56 B4
WILM/AE SK9 126 F3
Mount Pleasant Rd
DTN/ASHW M34 101 J2
FWTH BL4 52 C4
Mount Pleasant St AUL OL6 75 M8
DTN/ASHW M34 90 C5
HOR/BR BL6 34 A3
OLDE * OL4 59 L5
Mount Pleasant Wk RAD M26 38 D8
Mount Rd GTN M18 88 F7
HTNM SK4 12 D2
HYDE SK14 102 D6
MDTN M24 57 K5
PWCH M25 55 M5
Mountroyal Cl HYDE SK14 91 J7
Mount St Joseph's Rd
BOLS/LL BL3 35 L7
Mountside Crs PWCH M25 55 J8
Mount Sion Houses RAD * M26 54 A2
Mount Sion Rd RAD M26 54 B2
Mount Skip La LHULT M38 52 D8
Mount St BOL BL1 36 B3
CMANW M2 6 F6
CSLFD M3 6 B2
ECC M30 84 F4
GLSP SK13 104 F4
HEY OL10 41 G3
HOR/BR BL6 34 A3
HYDE SK14 102 B2
LEIGH WN7 65 M8
RAMS BL0 17 B5
ROCH OL11 41 M3
ROY/SHW OL2 59 H1
SWIN M27 70 C5
WHIT OL12 10 C3
Mount Vw WGNS/IIMK WN3 15 J9
Mount View Rd ROY/SHW OL2 43 M6
Mount Zion Rd BURY BL9 39 J7
Mousell St CHH M8 72 D8
Mouselow Cl GLSP SK13 104 C1
Mowbray Av PWCH M25 71 M2
SALE M33 108 F1
Mowbray St AULW OL7 90 C2
BOL * BL1 35 L3
OLD OL1 9 K6
ROCH OL11 41 L1
STKP SK1 13 K6
Mow Halls La UPML OL3 61 K3
Moxley Rd CHH M8 72 B3
Moxon Wy AIMK WN4 64 A8
Moyse Av TOT/BURYW BL8 24 C7
Mozart Cl ANC M4 7 M2
Muirfield Av MPL/ROM SK6 101 K8
Muirfield Cl BOLS/LL BL3 51 J1
HEY OL10 41 G3
NEWH/MOS M40 73 M5
WILM/AE SK9 127 H4
Muirfield Dr TYLD M29 67 M5
Mulberry Av GOL/RIS/CU WA3 80 C5
Mulberry Cl CHD/CHDH SK8 119 L5
ROCH OL11 10 C8
WGNW/BIL/O WN5 47 G6
Mulberry Ct SLFD * M6 86 D1
Mulberry Ms HTNM SK4 13 G2
Mulberry Mount St
EDGY/DAV SK3 13 H7
Mulberry Rd SLFD M6 86 D2
Mulberry St AUL * OL6 90 F1
CMANW M2 6 E5
Mulberry Wk DROY M43 89 H4
SALE M33 96 A6
Mule St BOLE BL2 3 H3
Mulgrave Rd WALK M28 69 K4
Mulgrave St BOLS/LL BL3 51 M2
SWIN M27 70 A3
Mullacre Rd WYTH/NTH M22 110 A6
Mull Av WGTN/LGST M12 88 B7
Mullein Cl GOL/RIS/CU WA3 80 A4
Mulliner St BOL * BL1 35 M4
Mullins Av NEWLW WA12 78 F7
Mullion Cl RDSH SK5 100 A2
Mullion Dr HALE/TIMP WA15 108 B5
Mullion Wk CHH M8 72 D6
Mulmount Cl OLDS OL8 74 F1
Munday St ANC M4 88 A3
Municipal Cl HEY * OL10 40 E2
Munn Rd BKLY M9 56 E7
Munro Av WGNW/BIL/O WN5 46 B6
WYTH/NTH M22 119 H2
Munster St ANC * M4 7 G1
Muriel St BRO M7 72 A7
HEY OL10 41 H2
MILN OL16 11 K8
Murieston Rd
HALE/TIMP WA15 117 G2
Murphy Cl WGNS/IIMK WN3 14 B9
Murrayfield ROCH OL11 27 H6
Murray Rd BURY BL9 4 F5
Murray St ANC M4 7 L3
ATH M46 66 E2
BRO M7 72 A6
Musabbir Sq WHIT * OL12 11 G3
Musbury Av CHD/CHDH SK8 120 D2
Museum St CMANW M2 6 F6
Musgrave Gdns BOL BL1 35 M4
Musgrave Rd BOL BL1 35 M4
WYTH/NTH M22 118 F1
Muslin St ORD M5 86 F3
Muter Av WYTH/NTH M22 119 H2
Mutual St HEY OL10 41 H1
Mycroft Cl LEIGH WN7 66 B4
Myerscroft Cl NEWH/MOS M40 74 A4
Myrrh St BOL BL1 36 B1
Myrtle Av AIMK WN4 63 J6
LEIGH WN7 66 B5
Myrtle Bank PWCH M25 71 K3
Myrtle Cl OLDS OL8 9 H9
Myrtle Gdns BURY BL9 5 K4
Myrtle Gv DROY M43 89 M2
DTN/ASHW M34 100 C1
PWCH M25 71 L2
WGNW/BIL/O * WN5 62 A8
WHTF M45 55 G2
Myrtleleaf Gv ORD * M5 86 A2
Myrtle Pl BRO M7 71 M8
Myrtle Rd MDTN M24 57 M3
PART M31 106 A2
Myrtle St BOL * BL1 2 B3
EDGY/DAV SK3 12 B6
OLDTF/WHR * M16 86 F8
OP/CLY M11 88 B4
WGN WN1 14 E3
Myrtle St North BURY BL9 5 K4
Myrtle St South BURY BL9 5 K5
My St ORD M5 86 B3
Mytham Gdns BOLS/LL BL3 53 L2
Mytham Rd BOLS/LL BL3 53 L1
Mytton Rd BOL BL1 35 L1
Mytton St HULME M15 87 H7

N

Nabbs Fold RAMS BL0 24 C1
Nabbs Wy TOT/BURYW BL8 24 D3
Naburn Cl RDSH SK5 100 F6
Naburn St BRUN/LGST M13 88 A8
Nada Rd CHH M8 72 C3
Nadine St SLFD M6 86 B1
Nadin St OLDS OL8 75 H1
Nairn Cl NEWH/MOS * M40 88 B1
WGNNW/ST WN6 31 G3
Nall St BNG/LEV M19 99 L5
MILN OL16 29 H6
Nameplate Cl ECC M30 84 E2
Nancy St HULME M15 87 G6
Nandywell BOLS/LL BL3 53 L1
Nangreave Rd OFTN SK2 112 D6
Nangreaves St LEIGH WN7 65 M7
Nan Nook Rd NTHM/RTH M23 109 J3
Nansen Av ECC M30 84 F1
Nansen Cl STRET M32 86 B8
Nansen Rd CHD/CHDH SK8 110 D8
Nansen St OP/CLY M11 88 B4
SLFD M6 86 B2
STRET M32 97 G1
Nansmoss La WILM/AE SK9 126 B3
Nantwich Av WHIT OL12 28 C1
Nantwich Rd RUSH/FAL M14 98 D3
Nantwich Wk BOLS/LL * BL3 36 B8
Napier Ct HULME * M15 86 F6
Napier Gn ORD M5 86 E5
Napier Rd CCHDY M21 97 L4
ECC M30 84 F1
HTNM SK4 111 L1
Napier St BRAM/HZG SK7 121 M1
HYDE SK14 102 B3
ROY/SHW OL2 43 L4
SWIN M27 70 A5
Napier St East OLDS OL8 8 F8
Napier St West OLDS OL8 8 D9
Naples Rd EDGY/DAV SK3 111 L6
Naples St ANC M4 7 J1
Narbonne Av ECC M30 70 D8
Narborough Cl WGNE/HIN WN2 49 H8
Narbuth Dr CHH M8 72 C5
Narrow La MCFLDN SK10 129 L3
The Narrows ALT WA14 107 M8
Naseby Av BKLY M9 57 J8
Naseby Pl PWCH M25 55 M7
Naseby Rd RDSH SK5 100 B4
Naseby Wk WHTF M45 55 M4
Nash Rd TRPK M17 85 H4
Nash St HULME M15 87 H6
Nasmyth Av DTN/ASHW M34 90 D8
Nasmyth Rd ECC M30 84 F4
Nasmyth St CHH M8 72 F7
HOR/BR BL6 33 M1
Nately Rd OLDTF/WHR * M16 97 K2
Nathan Dr CSLFD M3 6 C2
RNFD/HAY WA11 78 B6
Nathans Rd WYTH/NTH M22 109 M8
National Dr ORD M5 86 D4
Naunton Av LEIGH WN7 65 M7
Naunton Rd MDTN M24 57 L5
Naval St ANC M4 7 L3
Nave Ct SLFD M6 71 J8
Navenby Av OLDTF/WHR M16 86 F8
Navenby Rd WGNS/IIMK WN3 63 K2
Navigation Cl LEIGH WN7 66 B8
Navigation Rd ALT WA14 108 A5
Naylor Av GOL/RIS/CU WA3 79 L4
Naylorfarm Av WGNNW/ST WN6 30 C7
Naylor St ATH M46 66 F1
NEWH/MOS M40 88 A1
OLD OL1 9 H4
Nazeby Wk CHAD OL9 8 D9
Naze Ct OLD * OL1 9 G2
Neal Av AUL OL6 91 G1
CHD/CHDH SK8 119 J4
Neale Av UPML OL3 61 M7
Neale Rd CCHDY M21 97 K5
Near Birches Pde OLDE OL4 60 B8
Nearbrook Rd WYTH/NTH M22 109 M8
Nearcroft Rd NTHM/RTH M23 109 K5
Near Hey Cl RAD M26 54 B1
Nearmaker Av WYTH/NTH M22 109 M8
Nearmaker Rd WYTH/NTH M22 109 M8
Neary Wy URM M41 84 F7
Neasden Gv BOLS/LL * BL3 35 M7
Neath Av WYTH/NTH M22 110 A5
Neath Cl POY/DIS SK12 121 M7
WHTF M45 55 M5
Neath Fold BOLS/LL BL3 52 A1
Neath St CHAD OL9 8 F5
Nebo St BOLS/LL BL3 36 A8
Nebraska St BOL * BL1 36 B3
Neden Cl OP/CLY M11 88 E4
Needham Av CCHDY M21 97 L4
Needwood Cl NEWH/MOS M40 73 G7
Needwood Rd MPL/ROM SK6 101 M7
Neenton Sq WGTN/LGST M12 88 D5
Neild Gdns LEIGH WN7 66 B8
Neild St CMANE M1 7 K7
OLDS OL8 59 H8
Neill St BRO M7 72 B8
Neilson Cl MDTN M24 57 M5
Nell Carrs RAMS BL0 17 E5
Nellie St HEY OL10 40 E2
Nell La CCHDY M21 98 A5
Nell St BOL BL1 22 C8
Nel Pan La LEIGH WN7 65 M4
Nelson Av ECC M30 85 G1
POY/DIS SK12 129 L1
Nelson Cl POY/DIS SK12 129 L1
Nelson Dr DROY M43 89 G2
IRL M44 94 B6
WGNE/HIN WN2 48 D4
Nelson Fold SWIN M27 70 D3
Nelson Rd BKLY M9 57 G7
Nelson Sq BOL BL1 2 F5
Nelson St ATH M46 50 E8
ATH M46 66 E1

BOLS/LL BL3 .... 3 G9
BOLS/LL * BL3 .... 53 L1
BRAM/HZG SK7 .... 113 M8
BRO M7 .... 72 A7
BRUN/LGST M13 .... 87 L1
BURY BL9 .... 4 F8
DTN/ASHW M34 .... 90 C6
ECC M30 .... 85 G2
FWTH BL4 .... 53 H4
HEY OL10 .... 41 G3
HOR/BR BL6 .... 34 A1
HYDE SK14 .... 102 B2
LIT OL15 .... 20 C7
MDTN M24 .... 57 M5
MILN OL16 .... 10 E5
NEWH/MOS M40 .... 73 G8
OLDE * OL4 .... 60 B7
ORD M5 .... 86 B3
STRET M32 .... 97 G3
TYLD M29 .... 67 L4
WGNE/HIN WN2 .... 49 G6
Nelson Wy CHAD * OL9 .... 58 D8
Nelstrop Crs HTNM SK4 .... 100 A6
Nelstrop Rd HTNM SK4 .... 99 M6
Nelstrop Rd North RDSH SK5 .... 100 A4
Nene Gv WGNE/HIN WN2 .... 49 H8
Nepaul Rd BKLY M9 .... 73 H3
Neptune Gdns BRO M7 .... 71 M8
Nesbit St BOLE * BL2 .... 36 E1
Nesfield Rd NTHM/RTH M23 .... 109 J2
Neston Av BOL BL1 .... 22 C7
DID/WITH M20 .... 98 D6
SALE M33 .... 109 H2
Neston Cl ROY/SHW OL2 .... 44 A5
Neston Gv EDGY/DAV SK3 .... 112 A4
Neston Rd MILN OL16 .... 28 F8
TOT/BURYW BL8 .... 24 C8
Neston Wy WILM/AE SK9 .... 127 H1
Netherby Rd WGNNW/ST WN6 .... 47 K1
Nethercote Av
  NTHM/RTH M23 .... 109 L6
Nethercroft ROCH OL11 .... 27 H4
Nethercroft Rd
  HALE/TIMP WA15 .... 108 F7
Netherfield Cl OLDS OL8 .... 58 F8
Netherfield Rd BOLS/LL BL3 .... 52 B2
Netherfields LEIGH WN7 .... 66 A5
  WILM/AE SK9 .... 130 D4
Netherhey La ROY/SHW OL2 .... 58 F2
Nether Hey St OLDS OL8 .... 59 L8
Netherhouse Rd ROY/SHW OL2 .... 43 K5
Netherland St SALQ M50 .... 86 C3
Netherlees OLDE OL4 .... 60 A7
Nether St HYDE SK14 .... 102 C4
  WGTN/LGST * M12 .... 7 L7
Netherton Rd RUSH/FAL M14 .... 98 D3
Nethervale Dr BKLY M9 .... 73 H5
Netherwood OLDS OL8 .... 74 E4
Netherwood Rd
  WYTH/NTH M22 .... 109 M5
Netley Av WHIT OL12 .... 28 C1
Netley Gv OLDS * OL8 .... 59 M8
Netley Rd NTHM/RTH M23 .... 109 K8
Nettlebarn Rd WYTH/NTH M22 .... 109 M7
Nettleford Rd CCHDY M21 .... 98 B4
Nettleton Gv BKLY M9 .... 73 J3
Nevada St BOL * BL1 .... 36 B3
Nevendon Dr NTHM/RTH M23 .... 109 J8
Nevern Cl BOL BL1 .... 35 J4
Nevile St ROCH OL11 .... 42 D2
Neville Cardus Wk
  RUSH/FAL M14 .... 98 F2
Neville Cl BOL BL1 .... 2 D3
Neville Dr IRL M44 .... 83 K8
Neville St BRAM/HZG SK7 .... 121 M1
  CHAD OL9 .... 8 D4
  WGNE/HIN WN2 .... 64 D1
Nevill Rd BRAM/HZG SK7 .... 121 G2
Nevin Av OP/CLY M11 .... 120 A3
Nevin Cl BRAM/HZG SK7 .... 120 A3
Nevin Rd NEWH/MOS M40 .... 74 A3
Nevis Gv BOL BL1 .... 22 A7
Nevis St ROCH OL11 .... 42 D2
Nevy Fold Av HOR/BR BL6 .... 34 C1
New Allen St NEWH/MOS M40 .... 87 M1
Newall Gv LEIGH WN7 .... 66 C5
Newall Rd NTHM/RTH M23 .... 118 B1
Newall St CHAD OL9 .... 74 E2
  LIT OL15 .... 20 C6
Newark Av RAD M26 .... 37 M7
  RUSH/FAL M14 .... 98 E1
Newark Park Wy ROY/SHW OL2 .... 42 F6
Newark Rd RDSH SK5 .... 100 C7
  SWIN M27 .... 70 C2
  WGNE/HIN WN2 .... 48 F8
  WHIT OL12 .... 28 C1
Newark Sq WHIT OL12 .... 28 C1
Newark St WGNNW/ST WN6 .... 14 A1
New Bailey St CSLFD M3 .... 6 C4
Newbank Cha CHAD OL9 .... 58 D4
New Bank St GLSP SK13 .... 93 K7
  TYLD * M29 .... 67 K4
  WGTN/LGST * M12 .... 88 B7
New Barn Av AIMK WN4 .... 78 F1
Newbarn Cl ROY/SHW OL2 .... 43 K5
New Barn La LEIGH WN7 .... 81 H2
  ROCH OL11 .... 10 C9
New Barn Rd OLDS OL8 .... 75 K2
New Barns Av CCHDY M21 .... 97 M6
New Barn St BOL BL1 .... 35 L3
  ROCH OL11 .... 11 H9
  ROY/SHW OL2 .... 43 K5
New Barton St SLFD M6 .... 70 F7
Newbeck St ANC * M4 .... 7 H1
New Beech Rd HTNM SK4 .... 111 H2
Newberry Gv EDGY/DAV SK3 .... 112 A7
Newbold Cl HULME * M15 .... 87 J6
Newbold Moss MILN OL16 .... 11 K4
Newbold St MILN OL16 .... 11 M4
  TOT/BURYW BL8 .... 38 F2
Newboult Rd CHD/CHDH SK8 .... 111 H6
Newbourne Cl BRAM/HZG SK7 .... 121 M1
Newbreak Cl OLDE OL4 .... 60 A4
Newbridge Gdns BOLE BL2 .... 23 H8
Newbridge La STKP SK1 .... 13 L4
New Bridge La CSLFD M3 .... 6 E1
Newbridge Vw MOSL * OL5 .... 77 J2
New Briggs Fold EDGW/EG BL7 .... 22 B2
New Broad La MILN OL16 .... 11 K7
Newbrook Av CCHDY M21 .... 110 A1
Newbrook Rd ATH M46 .... 51 J6
New Brunswick St HOR/BR BL6 .... 33 L1
New Buildings PI MILN OL16 .... 10 E3
Newburn Av BKLY M9 .... 57 J8
Newbury Av SALE M33 .... 95 M3
Newbury Cl CHD/CHDH SK8 .... 120 C6

Newbury Ct
  HALE/TIMP * WA15 .... 108 C5
Newbury Dr ECC M30 .... 84 E1
  URM M41 .... 84 F7
Newbury Gv HEY OL10 .... 40 F4
Newbury Rd BOLS/LL BL3 .... 53 J1
  CHD/CHDH SK8 .... 119 L5
Newbury Wk BOL * BL1 .... 2 C2
  CHAD OL9 .... 8 C4
New Bury Dr ALT * WA14 .... 108 A6
  CHD/CHDH SK8 .... 110 D7
  MDTN M24 .... 57 J1
  SALE M33 .... 109 G1
Newby Rd BOLE BL2 .... 37 H3
  BRAM/HZG SK7 .... 121 G2
  HTNM SK4 .... 12 C3
Newby Sq WGNW/BIL/O * WN5 .... 46 E7
Newcastle St HULME M15 .... 6 F9
New Chapel La EDGW/EG BL6 .... 34 B2
Newchurch OLDS OL8 .... 75 K4
New Church St BOL BL1 .... 35 J2
Newchurch St OP/CLY M11 .... 88 C4
New Church St M26 .... 54 D1
Newchurch St ROCH OL11 .... 41 M3
New City Rd WALK M28 .... 68 D4
Newcliffe Rd BKLY M9 .... 57 J8
New Coin St ROY/SHW OL2 .... 59 G1
Newcombe Cl OP/CLY M11 .... 88 C3
Newcombe Dr LHULT M38 .... 52 C6
Newcombe Rd RAMS BL0 .... 24 D3
Newcombe St CSLFD * M3 .... 87 J1
New Court Dr EDGW/EG BL7 .... 22 A1
Newcroft FAIL M35 .... 74 E6
Newcroft Crs URM M41 .... 96 C3
Newcroft Dr EDGY/DAV SK3 .... 112 A6
  URM M41 .... 96 C3
Newcroft Rd URM M41 .... 96 C3
New Cross St SLFD M6 .... 85 M2
  SWIN M27 .... 70 D5
Newdale Rd BNG/LEV M19 .... 99 L2
New Drake Gn WHTN BL5 .... 50 B7
Newearth Rd WALK M28 .... 68 E4
New Earth St MOSL OL5 .... 77 G2
  OLDE OL4 .... 59 M7
New Elizabeth St CHH M8 .... 72 D7
New Ellesmere Ap WALK M28 .... 52 F8
New Elm Rd CSLFD M3 .... 6 B7
Newenden Rd WGN WN1 .... 31 L8
New Field Cl MILN OL16 .... 11 K3
  RAD M26 .... 54 B1
Newfield Head La MILN OL16 .... 11 K3
Newfield Vw MILN OL16 .... 29 K7
New Forest Rd
  NTHM/RTH M23 .... 108 F4
Newgate MILN OL16 .... 11 G4
Newgate Cottages WHTN * BL5 .... 51 K3
Newgate Dr LHULT M38 .... 52 C6
Newgate Rd SALE M33 .... 107 L3
  WILM/AE SK9 .... 126 B5
Newgate St ANC M4 .... 7 H1
New George St TOT/BURYW BL8 .... 38 F1
Newhall Av BOLE BL2 .... 37 L6
  ECC M30 .... 84 D5
  WYTH/NTH M22 .... 119 K5
New Hall Cl SALE M33 .... 97 J8
Newhall Dr NTHM/RTH M23 .... 109 K2
New Hall La BOL BL1 .... 35 K4
New Hall Ms HOR/BR BL6 .... 34 F3
New Hall PI BOL BL1 .... 35 K4
New Hall Rd BRO M7 .... 72 A5
  BURY BL9 .... 26 B8
New Hall Rd SALE * M33 .... 109 J1
Newham Dr TOT/BURYW BL8 .... 38 E3
Newhart Gv WALK M28 .... 68 F2
Newhaven Av LEIGH WN7 .... 66 C4
  OP/CLY M11 .... 89 J5
Newhaven Cl CHD/CHDH SK8 .... 120 E2
  TOT/BURYW BL8 .... 24 F5
New Herbert St SLFD M6 .... 70 F7
New Hey Av WYTH/NTH M22 .... 110 A3
New Hey Rd CHD/CHDH SK8 .... 111 H7
Newhey Rd MILN OL16 .... 29 K8
  WYTH/NTH M22 .... 110 A3
New Heys Wy BOLE BL2 .... 23 G6
New Holder St BOL BL1 .... 2 D5
Newholme Gdns LHULT M38 .... 68 F1
Newholme Rd DID/WITH M20 .... 98 B7
New Houses OLDE OL4 .... 60 F4
Newington Av CHH M8 .... 72 C1
Newington Ct ALT * WA14 .... 116 D1
Newington Dr BOL * BL1 .... 2 D1
  TOT/BURYW BL8 .... 38 D4
Newington Wk BOL * BL1 .... 2 D1
New Islington ANC M4 .... 7 M3
New Kings Head Yd CSLFD * M3 .... 6 E2
Newland Av WGNW/BIL/O WN5 .... 47 G7
Newland Dr WHTN BL5 .... 50 C6
Newland Ms GOL/RIS/CU WA3 .... 81 H7
Newlands Av BOLE BL2 .... 37 J3
  BRAM/HZG SK7 .... 121 G4
  CHD/CHDH SK8 .... 120 C5
  ECC M30 .... 84 C4
  IRL M44 .... 94 C1
  TYLD M29 .... 67 K6
  WHTF * M45 .... 55 H3
Newlands Cl CHD/CHDH SK8 .... 120 C5
  WHIT OL12 .... 28 C1
Newlands Dr DID/WITH M20 .... 110 F4
  GLSP SK13 .... 93 J8
  GOL/RIS/CU WA3 .... 79 M4
  STLY SK15 .... 91 G3
  SWIN M27 .... 70 F6
Newlands Rd CHD/CHDH SK8 .... 120 C5
  LEIGH WN7 .... 81 H1
  NTHM/RTH M23 .... 109 H4
Newland St CHH M8 .... 72 C5
New La BOLE BL2 .... 37 J3
  ECC M30 .... 84 E2
  OLDE OL4 .... 60 F4
  ROY/SHW OL2 .... 43 G8
New Lane Ct BOLE * BL2 .... 37 H2
New Lawns RDSH SK5 .... 100 D3
Newlea Cl BOL BL1 .... 35 M2
New Lees St AUL OL6 .... 76 A7
New Lester Cl TYLD M29 .... 67 L3
New Lester Wy LHULT M38 .... 52 B8
New Ldg WGN WN1 .... 47 M2
Newlyn Av STLY SK15 .... 92 A1
Newlyn Cl BRAM/HZG SK7 .... 121 M3

Newlyn Dr AIMK WN4 .... 78 E2
  MPL/ROM SK6 .... 113 K1
  SALE M33 .... 108 F3
Newlyn St RUSH/FAL M14 .... 98 E2
Newman Av WGNNW/ST WN6 .... 47 K2
Newman Cl AUL OL6 .... 90 D1
  HYDE SK14 .... 102 B1
  MILN OL16 .... 28 F1
  WGN WN1 .... 48 B2
New Market CMANW M2 .... 6 F4
Newmarket Cl SALE M33 .... 107 L2
Newmarket Gv AULW OL7 .... 75 H7
New Market La CMANW M2 .... 6 F4
Newmarket Rd AULW OL7 .... 75 H7
  BOLS/LL BL3 .... 53 K2
New Market St WGN WN1 .... 14 F3
New Meadow HOR/BR BL6 .... 34 F5
New Miles La WGNNW/ST WN6 .... 30 C6
New Mills Rd GLSP SK13 .... 115 L1
  NM/HAY SK22 .... 125 K2
New Mill St LIT OL15 .... 20 B7
New Moor La BRAM/HZG SK7 .... 121 M1
New Moss Rd IRL M44 .... 94 A6
New Mount St * M4 .... 7 H1
Newnham St BOL BL1 .... 36 B1
New Park Rd ORD M5 .... 86 E5
Newport Ar BOL BL1 .... 2 E5
Newport Rd BOLS/LL BL3 .... 52 D1
  CCHDY M21 .... 97 K3
  DTN/ASHW M34 .... 101 L4
  OLDS OL8 .... 8 E8
Newport St BOL BL1 .... 2 E6
  FWTH BL4 .... 53 G5
  MDTN M24 .... 57 M3
  OLDS OL8 .... 8 E8
  RUSH/FAL M14 .... 98 E1
  SLFD M6 .... 86 B2
  TOT/BURYW BL8 .... 24 D7
Newquay Av BOLE BL2 .... 38 A3
  RDSH SK5 .... 100 B5
Newquay Dr BRAM/HZG SK7 .... 121 H5
New Quay St CSLFD M3 .... 6 C5
New Raven Cl BOLS/LL * BL3 .... 53 K1
New Ridd Ri HYDE SK14 .... 102 A4
New Rd GLSP SK13 .... 93 J5
  LIT OL15 .... 19 M8
  OLDS OL8 .... 59 H8
  RAD M26 .... 54 C2
  WGNE/HIN WN2 .... 48 F8
  WHIT OL12 .... 18 C4
New Royd Av OLDE OL4 .... 60 C3
Newry Rd ECC M30 .... 85 H4
Newry St BOL BL1 .... 36 A1
Newsham Cl BOLS/LL BL3 .... 2 A7
Newsham Rd EDGY/DAV SK3 .... 112 B6
Newsham Wk
  WGNNW/ST * WN6 .... 14 A1
  WGTN/LGST * M12 .... 99 L1
Newshaw La GLSP SK13 .... 104 C1
Newsholme St CHH M8 .... 72 C5
New Springs BOL * BL1 .... 35 L1
Newstead WHIT OL12 .... 10 D3
Newstead Av AUL OL6 .... 75 M5
  DID/WITH M20 .... 99 G7
Newstead Cl POY/DIS SK12 .... 121 M7
Newstead Dr BOLS/LL BL3 .... 53 K2
Newstead Gv MPL/ROM SK6 .... 113 J1
Newstead Rd URM M41 .... 96 B1
  WGNS/IIMK WN3 .... 63 H1
Newstead Ter
  HALE/TIMP WA15 .... 108 C5
New St ALT WA14 .... 107 M8
  BOL BL1 .... 2 D6
  DROY M43 .... 89 K4
  ECC M30 .... 84 F3
  HYDE SK14 .... 103 K4
  LIT OL15 .... 20 A8
  MILN OL16 .... 29 K7
  NEWH/MOS M40 .... 73 H8
  NM/HAY SK22 .... 124 E5
  OLDE OL4 .... 60 B6
  RAD M26 .... 54 E2
  STLY SK15 .... 91 K4
  SWIN M27 .... 70 D3
  TOT/BURYW BL8 .... 24 C6
  UPML OL3 .... 61 L4
  WGNE/HIN WN2 .... 64 D3
  WGNW/BIL/O WN5 .... 46 E7
  WHIT OL12 .... 28 B2
New Tempest Rd HOR/BR BL6 .... 34 F8
New Ter HYDE * SK14 .... 102 B3
New Thomas St SLFD * M6 .... 71 K8
Newton Av DID/WITH M20 .... 99 G7
  WGTN/LGST M12 .... 88 C7
Newton Cl WGN WN1 .... 48 A2
Newton Crs MDTN M24 .... 57 G1
Newton Dr ROY/SHW OL2 .... 43 J5
Newton Hall Rd HYDE SK14 .... 90 F7
Newton La HYDE SK14 .... 79 H6
Newton Rd ALT WA14 .... 108 B5
  FAIL M35 .... 74 B4
  GOL/RIS/CU WA3 .... 80 B6
  MDTN M24 .... 56 E5
  URM M41 .... 95 M2
  WGNW/BIL/O WN5 .... 62 C6
Newton St AUL * OL6 .... 90 F1
  BOL BL1 .... 36 B2
  BURY BL9 .... 25 J6
  CMANE M1 .... 7 J4
  DROY M43 .... 89 M1
  OP/CLY M11 .... 89 G7
  STLY SK15 .... 91 G3
  WGTN/LGST * M12 .... 88 B7
Newton Wk BOL * BL1 .... 36 B2
Newton Wood Rd DUK SK16 .... 90 E6
Newtown Av DTN/ASHW M34 .... 101 J3
Newtown Cl OP/CLY M11 .... 88 E4
  SWIN M27 .... 70 C2
Newtown St PWCH M25 .... 71 M3
  ROY/SHW OL2 .... 43 L6
New Union St ANC M4 .... 7 L3
New Vernon St BURY BL9 .... 5 G1
New Viaduct St OP/CLY M11 .... 88 B2
Newville Dr DID/WITH M20 .... 99 G7
New Vine St HULME * M15 .... 87 J6
New Wakefield St CMANE M1 .... 7 G8
New Welcome St HULME * M15 .... 87 J6
New York OLDS OL8 .... 59 M8
New York St HEY OL10 .... 40 E2
New Zealand Rd STKP SK1 .... 13 M3

Neyland Cl BOL BL1 .... 35 J5
Ney St AULW OL7 .... 75 J6
Niagara St OFTN SK2 .... 112 D6
Nicholas Cft ANC M4 .... 7 G3
Nicholas Owen Cl OP/CLY M11 .... 88 F4
Nicholas St BOLE BL2 .... 3 H3
  CMANW M2 .... 7 G5
Nicholls St SLFD * M6 .... 86 D1
Nicholson Rd HYDE SK14 .... 90 F7
Nicholson Sq DUK * SK16 .... 90 E4
Nicholson St HTNM SK4 .... 13 H2
  OLDE OL6 .... 60 B6
  ROCH OL11 .... 11 H9
Nickerty Rd POY/DIS SK12 .... 129 J1
Nicolas Rd CCHDY M21 .... 97 K3
Nicol Mere Dr AIMK WN4 .... 63 K6
Nicol St AIMK WN4 .... 63 K7
Nield Rd DTN/ASHW M34 .... 101 J1
Nield's Brow ALT * WA14 .... 116 E2
Nield St MOSL OL5 .... 76 C2
Nields Wy MPL/ROM SK6 .... 115 G8
Nigel Rd BKLY M9 .... 73 J5
Nigher Moss Av MILN OL16 .... 11 M5
Nightingale Dr DTN/ASHW M34 .... 89 M2
Nightingale Gdns
  NTHM/RTH M23 .... 109 K3
Nightingale Rd HOR/BR BL6 .... 32 F1
Nile St AULW OL7 .... 90 C4
  BOLS/LL BL3 .... 2 E8
  MILN OL16 .... 11 H3
  OLDE * OL1 .... 9 H3
Nile Ter BRO M7 .... 72 A7
Nimble Nook CHAD OL9 .... 58 D7
Nina Dr NEWH/MOS M40 .... 73 M1
Nine Acre Dr ORD M5 .... 86 C5
Ninfield Rd NTHM/RTH M23 .... 109 L8
Ninth Av OLDS OL8 .... 75 G3
Nipper La WHTF M45 .... 55 H3
Nisbet Av WYTH/NTH M22 .... 119 G1
Niven St WGTN/LGST M12 .... 7 L8
Nixon St EDGY/DAV SK3 .... 51 M1
Nixon Rd BOLS/LL BL3 .... 51 M1
Nixon Rd South BOLS/LL BL3 .... 51 M1
Nixon St EDGY/DAV SK3 .... 13 H7
  FAIL M35 .... 74 B5
  ROCH OL11 .... 11 H9
No 11 Pas DID/WITH * M20 .... 98 C7
Noble Meadow WHIT OL12 .... 19 L8
Noble St BOLS/LL BL3 .... 2 C8
  LEIGH * WN7 .... 66 D7
  OLDS OL8 .... 59 J8
Noel Dr SALE M33 .... 97 G8
Noel St BOL BL1 .... 2 D4
Nolan St BKLY M9 .... 73 H5
Nona St SLFD M6 .... 86 B2
The Nook ECC M30 .... 84 D1
  URM M41 .... 96 A3
  WGNNW/ST WN6 .... 30 B5
Nook Fld BOLE BL2 .... 37 H2
Nook La AUL OL6 .... 76 B6
  GOL/RIS/CU WA3 .... 79 L4
  TYLD M29 .... 83 G2
Noon Sun Cl UPML OL3 .... 61 K8
Noon Sun St WHIT OL12 .... 28 C3
Norbet Wk BKLY M9 .... 73 H5
Norbreck Av CCHDY M21 .... 97 L5
  CHD/CHDH SK8 .... 111 K6
Norbreck Crs WGNNW/ST WN6 .... 47 K2
Norbreck Gdns BOLE BL2 .... 3 L3
Norbreck St BOLE BL2 .... 3 L3
Norbrook Gv LEIGH WN7 .... 66 B7
Norburn Rd BRUN/LGST M13 .... 99 J2
Norbury Av MPL/ROM SK6 .... 114 B6
  OLDE OL4 .... 60 F6
  SALE M33 .... 96 C8
  SLFD M6 .... 71 G7
  WGNW/BIL/O WN5 .... 62 A6
Norbury Cl NEWH/MOS * M40 .... 73 G8
Norbury Crs BRAM/HZG SK7 .... 121 M2
Norbury Dr MPL/ROM SK6 .... 114 C6
Norbury Gv BOL BL1 .... 22 C8
  BRAM/HZG SK7 .... 121 M2
  SWIN M27 .... 70 C3
Norbury Hollow Rd
  BRAM/HZG SK7 .... 122 D4
Norbury La OLDS OL8 .... 76 A1
Norbury Ms MPL/ROM * SK6 .... 114 C6
Norbury St BRO M7 .... 72 B6
  LEIGH WN7 .... 66 A4
  MILN * OL16 .... 28 E8
  STKP SK1 .... 13 L1
Norcot Wk HULME * M15 .... 87 G6
Norcross Cl OFTN SK2 .... 113 G7
Nordale Pk WHIT OL12 .... 27 G2
Nordek Cl ROY/SHW OL2 .... 43 G7
Nordek Dr ROY/SHW OL2 .... 43 G7
Norden Av DID/WITH M20 .... 98 D6
Norden Cl ROCH OL11 .... 26 F2
Norden Ct BOLS/LL BL3 .... 36 B8
Norden Rd HEY OL10 .... 27 G7
Nordens Dr CHAD OL9 .... 58 C3
Nordens Rd CHAD OL9 .... 58 C4
Nordens St CHAD OL9 .... 58 C4
Norden Wy ROCH OL11 .... 26 F2
Noreen Av PWCH M25 .... 55 M7
Norfield Cl DUK SK16 .... 90 F4
Norfolk Av DROY M43 .... 89 J1
  DTN/ASHW M34 .... 100 D1
  HEY OL10 .... 40 C2
  HTNM SK4 .... 99 M6
  WHTF M45 .... 55 K4
Norfolk Cl BOLS/LL BL3 .... 37 L8
  ROY/SHW OL2 .... 43 J5
  WGNE/HIN WN2 .... 49 K6
Norfolk Crs FAIL M35 .... 74 B6
Norfolk Dr FWTH BL4 .... 53 C3
Norfolk Gdns URM M41 .... 95 G1
Norfolk Rd ATH M46 .... 50 F7
  GTN M18 .... 88 B3
  WGNW/BIL/O WN5 .... 62 B3
Norfolk St CHAD OL9 .... 58 E8
  CMANW M2 .... 6 F4
  GLSP SK13 .... 105 G3
  HYDE SK14 .... 102 A2
  ROCH OL11 .... 10 D6
  SLFD M6 .... 71 K7
  WALK M28 .... 53 G6
  WGNNW/ST WN6 .... 47 K2
  WGNW/BIL/O WN5 .... 14 A7
Norfolk Wy ROY/SHW OL2 .... 59 G2
Norford Wy ROCH OL11 .... 26 F2
Norgate St DID/WITH M20 .... 110 B1
Norlan Av DTN/ASHW M34 .... 90 B5
Norleigh Rd WYTH/NTH M22 .... 110 A4
Norley Av STRET M32 .... 97 J1
Norley Cl OLD OL1 .... 58 E2
Norley Dr BNG/LEV M19 .... 99 M2

SALE M33 .... 109 H1
Norley Hall Av
  WGNW/BIL/O WN5 .... 46 F6
Norley Rd LEIGH WN7 .... 65 L8
  WGNW/BIL/O WN5 .... 46 F5
Norman Av RNFD/HAY WA11 .... 78 D5
Normanby Cha SALE M33 .... 107 L8
Normanby Gv SWIN M27 .... 70 B3
Normanby Rd WALK M28 .... 68 F3
Normanby St BOLS/LL BL3 .... 51 L2
  RUSH/FAL M14 .... 87 K8
  SWIN M27 .... 70 B3
  WGNW/BIL/O WN5 .... 46 E6
Normandale Av BOL BL1 .... 35 K3
Normandy Crs RAD M26 .... 54 C1
Norman Gv RDSH SK5 .... 100 B5
  WGTN/LGST * M12 .... 88 D8
Norman Rd ALT WA14 .... 107 M6
  AUL OL6 .... 75 M6
  BRO * M7 .... 72 B5
  HTNM SK4 .... 111 L1
  ROCH OL11 .... 10 B6
  RUSH/FAL M14 .... 99 G2
  SALE M33 .... 96 E8
  STLY SK15 .... 91 J3
Norman Rd West BKLY * M9 .... 73 J5
Norman's PI ALT WA14 .... 108 A8
Norman St BURY BL9 .... 5 K1
  CHAD OL9 .... 8 F3
  FAIL M35 .... 74 D3
  HYDE SK14 .... 102 B2
  MDTN M24 .... 57 L3
  WGTN/LGST M12 .... 88 E7
Normanton Av SLFD M6 .... 85 M1
Normanton Cl WGNNW/ST WN6 .... 31 H8
Normanton Dr BKLY M9 .... 57 H8
Normanton Rd EDGY/DAV SK3 .... 112 B6
Norman Weall Ct MDTN * M24 .... 57 K2
Normington St OLDE * OL4 .... 59 L5
Norreys Av URM M41 .... 95 H1
Norreys St MILN OL16 .... 11 G3
Norris Av HTNM SK4 .... 12 C3
Norris Bank Ter HTNM SK4 .... 12 C4
Norris Hill Dr HTNM SK4 .... 12 C2
Norris Rd SALE M33 .... 108 F2
Norris St BOLS/LL BL3 .... 53 K1
  BOLS/LL BL3 .... 53 K1
  FWTH BL4 .... 52 F5
  TYLD * M29 .... 67 K4
Northallerton Rd BRO M7 .... 71 L6
Northampton Rd
  NEWH/MOS M40 .... 73 H6
North Av BNG/LEV M19 .... 99 J3
  BURY BL9 .... 39 L8
  FWTH BL4 .... 52 D4
  STLY SK15 .... 91 H5
  TOT/BURYW BL8 .... 24 C2
  UPML OL3 .... 61 L7
  URM M41 .... 85 H5
North Back Rock BURY BL9 .... 4 F5
Northbank Gdns BNG/LEV M19 .... 99 H6
North Blackfield La BRO * M7 .... 71 M4
Northbourne St SLFD M6 .... 86 B2
Northbrook Av CHH M8 .... 56 C8
North Brook Rd GLSP SK13 .... 93 H8
North Broughton St CSLFD M3 .... 6 C3
North Cir WHTF M45 .... 55 K6
North Clifden La BRO M7 .... 72 B6
Northcliffe Rd OFTN SK2 .... 112 F4
North Cft OLDS OL8 .... 75 K1
North Crs NEWH/MOS M40 .... 74 A1
  OP/CLY M11 .... 89 G1
North Cft OLDS OL8 .... 75 K1
Northcroft WGN WN1 .... 48 C5
Northdale Rd BKLY M9 .... 56 E7
North Dean St SWIN M27 .... 70 D3
Northdene Dr ROCH OL11 .... 27 J6
Northdown Av HULME M15 .... 87 G6
  MPL/ROM SK6 .... 101 M7
North Downs Rd
  CHD/CHDH SK8 .... 120 B1
Northdowns Rd ROY/SHW OL2 .... 43 K6
North Dr DTN/ASHW M34 .... 89 M3
  SWIN M27 .... 70 E5
North Edge LEIGH WN7 .... 66 E6
Northenden Rd
  CHD/CHDH SK8 .... 110 D6
  SALE M33 .... 96 F8
  SALE M33 .... 109 H1
Northend Rd STLY SK15 .... 91 L2
Northen Gv DID/WITH M20 .... 98 C8
Northern Av BOL BL1 .... 70 F1
Northern Gv BOL BL1 .... 35 M3
Northern Service Rd
  NTHM/RTH * M23 .... 109 J7
Northfield Av NEWH/MOS M40 .... 73 J8
Northfield Dr WILM/AE SK9 .... 127 H4
Northfield Rd BURY BL9 .... 25 J6
  NEWH/MOS M40 .... 74 C2
Northfleet Rd ECC M30 .... 84 C4
North Florida Rd
  RNFD/HAY WA11 .... 78 A4
North Ga OLDS OL8 .... 75 H1
Northgate WHIT OL12 .... 18 D5
Northgate La OLD OL1 .... 60 B1
Northgate Rd EDGY/DAV SK3 .... 12 C6
North George St CSLFD M3 .... 6 A2
North Gv BRUN/LGST M13 .... 88 A7
  URM M41 .... 95 M3
  WALK M28 .... 68 F1
North Harvey St STKP SK1 .... 13 K4
North Hill St CSLFD M3 .... 6 B2
Northland Rd BKLY M9 .... 73 K1
  BOL BL1 .... 38 B7
Northlands RAD M26 .... 38 B7
North La TYLD M29 .... 67 K6
  WHIT OL12 .... 10 F7
Northleach Cl TOT/BURYW BL8 .... 24 F1
Northleigh Dr PWCH * M25 .... 72 A1
Northleigh Rd OLDTF/WHR M16 .... 97 L1
North Lonsdale St STRET * M32 .... 97 H1
Northmoor Rd WGTN/LGST M12 .... 88 D3
North Nook OLDE OL4 .... 60 F4
Northolme Gdns BNG/LEV M19 .... 99 H8
Northolt Ct OP/CLY * M11 .... 89 G2
Northolt Dr BOLS/LL BL3 .... 36 B8
Northolt Rd NTHM/RTH M23 .... 109 J3
North Pde CSLFD M3 .... 6 E4
  MILN OL16 .... 29 M8
  SALE M33 .... 109 G2
North Park Rd BRAM/HZG SK7 .... 121 G2
North Phoebe St ORD M5 .... 86 B3

North Pl STKP SK1 13 J4
Northridge Rd BKLY M9 57 G6
North Ri UPML OL3 61 L7
North Rd ATH M46 50 E7
DTN/ASHW M34 90 A3
GLSP SK13 104 F1
HALE/TIMP WA15 117 J4
MANAIR M90 118 E6
NM/HAY SK22 125 M1
OP/CLY M11 88 F2
PART M31 95 G8
PWCH M25 55 J7
STRET M32 85 L8
Northside Av URM M41 95 J3
North Star Dr CSLFD M3 6 B4
Northstead Av DTN/ASHW M34 101 L2
North St AIMK WN4 64 A7
ATH M46 67 H1
AUL OL6 90 D2
CHH M8 72 D7
HEY OL10 40 E2
LEIGH WN7 66 E8
MDTN M24 57 K2
MILN OL16 11 G2
NEWLW WA12 78 C8
RAD M26 38 F8
RAMS BL0 17 C2
RNFD/HAY WA11 78 B6
ROY/SHW OL2 59 G1
WHIT OL12 18 D3
Northumberland Av AULW OL7 75 L8
Northumberland Cl
OLDTF/WHR M16 86 F7
Northumberland Crs
OLDTF/WHR * M16 86 F7
Northumberland Rd
OLDTF/WHR M16 86 F8
PART M31 106 B2
RDSH SK5 100 E6
Northumberland St BRO M7 72 A5
WGN WN1 15 K2
Northumbria St BOLS/LL BL3 35 M7
Northurst Dr CHH M8 72 C1
North Vale Rd
HALE/TIMP WA15 108 C6
North Veiw WHTF M45 55 H2
North View Cl OLDE OL4 60 F7
Northward Rd WILM/AE SK9 126 D6
North Wy BOL BL1 22 E8
HYDE SK14 102 B2
RDSH SK5 100 F6
Northway DROY M43 89 K4
WGN WN1 14 F2
Northways WGNNW/ST WN6 31 G2
Northwell St LEIGH WN7 66 B4
North Western St BNG/LEV M19 99 K4
CMANE M1 7 L6
Northwold Cl WGNS/IIMK WN3 62 F1
Northwold Dr BKLY M9 73 L1
BOL BL1 35 H4
Northwood BOLE BL2 23 G8
Northwood Av CHD/CHDH SK8 120 C1
NEWLW WA12 79 J8
Northwood Crs BOLS/LL * BL3 35 M7
Northwood Gv SALE M33 96 E8
North Zetland Av BOLS/LL BL3 51 L2
Norton Av DTN/ASHW M34 100 D1
SALE M33 96 A7
URM M41 85 G8
WGTN/LGST M12 99 L1
Norton Gra PWCH M25 72 A1
Norton Gv HTNM SK4 12 B4
Norton Rd WALK M28 68 B5
WHIT OL12 28 C1
Norton St BOL BL1 36 C1
BRO M7 72 B5
CMANE * M1 7 M5
CSLFD M3 6 E2
NEWH/MOS M40 73 H8
Norview Dr DID/WITH M20 110 E5
Norville Av NEWH/MOS M40 74 A1
Norway Gv RDSH * SK5 100 C8
Norway St BOL * BL1 36 A2
OP/CLY M11 88 B4
SLFD M6 86 B2
STRET M32 97 H1
Norweb Wy LEIGH WN7 81 L1
Norwell Rd WYTH/NTH M22 110 B7
Norwich Av AIMK WN4 79 G2
CHAD OL9 58 D3
DTN/ASHW M34 101 J3
GOL/RIS/CU WA3 80 A4
ROCH OL11 27 K5
Norwich Cl AUL OL6 76 A4
DUK SK16 91 K5
Norwich Dr TOT/BURYW BL8 4 B2
Norwich Rd STRET M32 96 C1
Norwich St ROCH OL11 11 G8
Norwick Cl BOLS/LL BL3 35 H8
Norwood PWCH M25 71 L2
Norwood Av AIMK WN4 63 J6
BRAM/HZG SK7 120 E7
BRO M7 71 L4
DID/WITH M20 99 G8
GOL/RIS/CU WA3 80 B5
MPL/ROM SK6 122 F5
TYLD M29 67 K6
WGNNW/ST WN6 47 K1
Norwood Cl ROY/SHW OL2 43 K4
WALK M28 69 H4
Norwood Crs ROY/SHW OL2 59 H2
Norwood Dr HALE/TIMP WA15 109 G7
SWIN M27 69 M5
Norwood Gv BOL * BL1 35 M4
Norwood Rd CHD/CHDH SK8 110 E6
OFTN SK2 112 E8
STRET M32 97 H3
Nostell Rd AIMK WN4 63 K7
Nottingham Av RDSH SK5 100 F6
Nottingham Cl RDSH SK5 100 F6
Nottingham Dr AUL OL6 75 L5
BOL BL1 2 C1
FAIL M35 74 D7
RDSH SK5 100 F6
Nottingham Pl WGN WN1 15 L1
Nowell Rd MDTN M24 57 K1
Nudger Cl UPML OL3 61 J2
Nudger Gn UPML OL3 61 K2
Nuffield Rd WYTH/NTH M22 110 B8
Nugent Rd BOLS/LL BL3 52 B1
Nugget St OLDE * OL4 59 L6
Nuneaton Dr NEWH/MOS M40 88 A1
Nuneham Av DID/WITH M20 98 F5
Nunfield Cl NEWH/MOS M40 73 L2
Nunnery Rd BOLS/LL BL3 35 L8
Nunthorpe Dr CHH M8 72 F4
Nursery Av HALE/TIMP WA15 117 G4
Nursery Cl GLSP SK13 104 F4
OFTN SK2 113 G5
SALE M33 97 G8
Nursery Dr POY/DIS SK12 121 M8
Nursery Gdns MILN OL16 11 M3
Nursery Gv PART M31 94 C8
Nursery La EDGY/DAV SK3 111 K5
MCFLDN SK10 130 A7
WILM/AE SK9 126 D6
Nursery Rd CHD/CHDH SK8 120 B3
FAIL M35 74 D6
HTNM SK4 12 C2
PWCH M25 55 K6
URM M41 84 E8
Nursery St OLDTF/WHR M16 98 C1
SLFD M6 71 J8
Nuthatch Av WALK M28 69 G4
Nuthurst Rd NEWH/MOS M40 73 M2
Nutsford V WGTN/LGST M12 88 D8
Nuttall Av BOLS/LL BL3 53 M1
HOR/BR BL6 33 K1
WHTF M45 55 J3
Nuttall Cl RAMS BL0 17 C7
Nuttall Hall Rd RAMS BL0 17 D8
Nuttall La RAMS BL0 17 B7
Nuttall Ms WHTF M45 55 J4
Nuttall Rd RAMS BL0 17 D8
Nuttall Sq BURY BL9 39 J7
Nuttall St ATH M46 67 H1
BURY BL9 5 H6
IRL M44 94 B6
OLDS * OL8 59 L8
OLDTF/WHR M16 86 F7
OP/CLY M11 88 D5
Nutt La PWCH M25 56 B4
Nutt St WGN WN1 15 K1

O

Oadby Cl WGTN/LGST M12 88 D8
Oak Av BOLS/LL BL3 53 L1
CCHDY M21 97 L4
CHD/CHDH SK8 120 B2
GOL/RIS/CU WA3 79 L4
GTN M18 89 J8
HTNM SK4 12 A2
IRL M44 94 A7
MDTN M24 57 K5
MPL/ROM SK6 113 M2
POY/DIS SK12 121 M8
RAMS BL0 24 D2
RNFD/HAY WA11 78 B5
ROY/SHW OL2 43 G6
WGNE/HIN WN2 64 F5
WGNE/HIN WN2 65 K1
WGNNW/ST WN6 31 J4
WHTF M45 55 J5
WILM/AE SK9 126 D7
Oak Bank BKLY M9 73 G4
PWCH M25 71 J3
Oakbank WGNE/HIN WN2 64 E1
Oak Bank Av BKLY M9 73 J3
Oakbank Av CHAD OL9 58 B4
Oak Bank Cl WHTF M45 55 L4
Oakbank Dr BOL BL1 22 A6
Oakbarton HOR/BR BL6 34 F8
Oakcliffe Rd WHIT OL12 19 K8
Oak Cl HYDE SK14 92 D8
WILM/AE SK9 126 D6
Oak Coppice BOL BL1 35 K5
Oakcroft STLY SK15 92 B5
Oakcroft Wy WYTH/NTH M22 110 B6
Oakdale BOLE BL2 23 G8
Oakdale Cl WHTF M45 55 G4
Oakdale Ct UPML OL3 61 H1
Oakdale Dr CHD/CHDH SK8 119 K2
DID/WITH M20 111 G1
TYLD M29 67 M6
Oakdene SWIN M27 69 L6
Oakdene Av CHD/CHDH SK8 119 K5
HTNM SK4 100 A7
Oakdene Crs MPL/ROM SK6 114 C5
Oakdene Gdns MPL/ROM SK6 114 C5
Oakdene Rd HALE/TIMP WA15 108 E4
MDTN M24 57 M4
MPL/ROM SK6 114 C5
Oakdene St BKLY M9 73 J4
Oak Dr BRAM/HZG SK7 120 E5
DTN/ASHW M34 89 K8
MPL/ROM SK6 114 A6
RUSH/FAL M14 99 G3
Oaken Bank Rd MDTN M24 41 J6
Oakenbottom Rd BOLE BL2 37 G6
Oaken Clough AULW OL7 75 J6
Oakenclough Cl WILM/AE SK9 127 H2
Oaken Clough Dr AULW OL7 75 J6
Oakenclough Dr BOL BL1 35 J2
Oakenden Cl AIMK WN4 63 K6
Oakengates WGNNW/ST WN6 31 J3
Oakenrod Hl ROCH OL11 27 M5
Oakenshaw Av WHIT OL12 18 D6
Oakenshaw Vw WHIT OL12 18 D6
Oaker Av DID/WITH M20 98 B8
The Oakes GLSP SK13 104 D5
Oakes St FWTH BL4 53 J5
Oakfield DUK SK16 91 H6
PWCH M25 72 A1
SALE M33 96 D7
Oakfield Av ATH M46 50 F8
CHD/CHDH SK8 111 H6
DROY M43 89 L2
GOL/RIS/CU WA3 79 J3
OLDTF/WHR M16 97 K1
OLDTF/WHR M16 98 A1
STLY SK15 77 H6
Oakfield Cl BRAM/HZG SK7 121 G8
HOR/BR BL6 34 C2
WILM/AE SK9 130 E1
Oakfield Crs WGNE/HIN WN2 32 F7
Oakfield Dr LHULT M38 52 B7
Oakfield Gv FWTH BL4 52 F6
GTN M18 89 G8
Oakfield Rd DID/WITH M20 110 D1
EDGY/DAV SK3 112 C7
GLSP SK13 104 B1
HALE/TIMP WA15 108 B7
HYDE SK14 91 H7
POY/DIS SK12 122 B8
WILM/AE SK9 130 E2
Oakfield St CHH M8 72 D6
HALE/TIMP WA15 108 B7
Oakfield Ter ROCH OL11 27 M4
Oakfold Av AUL OL6 76 A6
Oakford Av NEWH/MOS M40 7 M1
Oakford Wk BOLS/LL BL3 35 M8
Oak Gates EDGW/EG BL7 22 B3
Oak Gv AUL OL6 76 A6
CHD/CHDH SK8 111 H7
ECC M30 84 E3
POY/DIS SK12 121 M8
URM M41 96 B2
Oakham Cl TOT/BURYW BL8 25 H7
Oakham Ms BRO M7 71 M3
Oakham Rd DTN/ASHW * M34 101 K3
Oakhead LEIGH WN7 81 M1
Oak Hl LIT OL15 20 A7
Oakhill Cl BOLE BL2 37 K5
Oak Hill Cl WGN * WN1 47 L1
Oakhill Wy CHH M8 72 C5
Oakhouse Dr CCHDY M21 97 L5
Oakhurst Cha WILM/AE SK9 130 D2
Oakhurst Dr CHD/CHDH SK8 111 L7
Oakhurst Gv WHTN BL5 49 M5
Oakington Av RUSH/FAL * M14 98 E1
Oakland Av BNG/LEV M19 99 H8
OFTN SK2 112 F6
SLFD M6 70 D8
Oakland Gv BOL * BL1 35 K2
Oaklands BOL BL1 35 J5
Oaklands Av CHD/CHDH SK8 120 C2
MPL/ROM SK6 114 F4
Oaklands Cl WILM/AE SK9 127 J3
Oaklands Dene HYDE SK14 102 D2
Oaklands Dr BRAM/HZG SK7 122 A3
HYDE SK14 102 D2
PWCH M25 55 L7
SALE M33 96 D7
Oaklands Pk OLDE OL4 61 H7
Oaklands Rd BRO M7 71 K5
GOL/RIS/CU WA3 80 C5
OLDE OL4 61 J7
RAMS BL0 17 D2
ROY/SHW OL2 59 H2
SWIN M27 69 M6
Oak La WHTF M45 55 L4
WILM/AE SK9 126 D6
Oaklea WGNNW/ST WN6 30 D2
Oak Lea Av WILM/AE SK9 126 E7
Oaklea Rd SALE M33 96 B6
Oakleigh Av BNG/LEV M19 99 J5
BOLS/LL BL3 52 D2
HALE/TIMP WA15 108 D5
Oakleigh Cl HEY OL10 41 H5
Oakleigh Rd CHD/CHDH SK8 120 A4
Oakley Av WGNW/BIL/O WN5 62 A6
Oakley Cl NEWH/MOS M40 73 M7
RAD M26 54 D4
Oakley Dr WGNW/BIL/O WN5 47 H6
Oakley Pk BOL BL1 35 J5
Oakley St ORD M5 86 A3
Oakley Vls HTNM SK4 12 B1
The Oaklings WGNE/HIN WN2 65 K1
Oak Ldg BRAM/HZG * SK7 121 H5
Oakmere Av ECC M30 69 M8
Oakmere Cl WYTH/NTH M22 110 A8
Oakmere Rd CHD/CHDH SK8 111 J8
WILM/AE SK9 119 M7
Oak Ms WILM/AE SK9 127 G3
Oakmoor Dr BRO M7 71 K4
Oakmoor Rd NTHM/RTH M23 109 K6
Oak Mt DID/WITH * M20 110 E1
Oak Rd BRO M7 71 M6
CHD/CHDH SK8 111 H6
DID/WITH M20 98 E7
FAIL M35 74 C6
HALE/TIMP WA15 117 G1
MCFLDN SK10 131 L3
MCFLDN SK10 131 L7
OLDS OL8 74 F2
PART M31 106 A2
SALE M33 97 G8
The Oaks CHD/CHDH SK8 119 J2
HYDE SK14 102 D1
Oaks Av BOLE BL2 22 F8
NM/HAY SK22 125 M2
Oak Shaw Cl BKLY M9 72 F2
Oakshaw Dr WHIT OL12 27 K3
Oaks La BOL BL1 22 E7
Oak St ANC M4 7 H3
ATH M46 66 D3
BRAM/HZG SK7 121 M1
DTN/ASHW M34 90 C6
ECC M30 85 G3
EDGY/DAV SK3 12 B7
GLSP SK13 104 F3
HEY OL10 40 E1
HYDE SK14 91 H8
LEIGH WN7 81 J1
LIT OL15 20 D7
MDTN * M24 58 A5
MILN OL16 10 E5
MILN OL16 43 K1
RAMS * BL0 17 B7
ROY/SHW OL2 43 M6
SWIN M27 70 D3
TYLD M29 67 K3
WGN WN1 15 K4
Oak Ter LIT OL15 20 E2
Oak Tree Cl ATH M46 66 D3
HYDE SK14 102 D2
OFTN SK2 113 G4
Oak Tree Ct CHD/CHDH SK8 111 G6
Oak Tree Crs STLY SK15 77 K6
Oak Tree Dr DUK SK16 91 J5
Oak View Rd UPML OL3 61 L7
Oakville Dr SLFD M6 70 D8
Oakville Ter NEWH/MOS M40 73 J3
Oakway DID/WITH M20 110 F4
MDTN M24 41 J8
Oakwell Dr BURY BL9 55 L1
CHH M8 72 B3
Oakwell Man BRO M7 72 B3
Oakwood CHAD OL9 58 B5
GLSP SK13 104 C4
SALE M33 95 M8
Oakwood Av AIMK WN4 78 D2
CHD/CHDH SK8 110 E7
DTN/ASHW M34 90 A5
NEWH/MOS M40 74 A3
SWIN M27 54 B8
WALK M28 69 J2
WGNNW/ST WN6 30 C7
WILM/AE SK9 126 C6
Oakwood Cl TOT/BURYW BL8 38 E1
Oakwood Ct ALT WA14 116 D4
Oakwood Dr BOL BL1 35 J4
LEIGH WN7 81 H3
SLFD M6 70 E7
WALK M28 69 J2
Oakwood La ALT WA14 116 C3
Oakwood Rd MPL/ROM SK6 113 M2
POY/DIS * SK12 123 M6
Oakworth Cft OLDE OL4 44 C8
Oakworth Dr BOL BL1 22 A7
Oakworth St BKLY M9 72 F1
Oatlands WILM/AE SK9 119 M8
Oatlands Rd WYTH/NTH M22 118 E2
Oat St STKP SK1 13 L8
Oban Av NEWH/MOS M40 73 L8
OLD OL1 59 L3
Oban Crs EDGY/DAV SK3 112 A8
Oban Dr AIMK WN4 62 F8
SALE M33 109 H1
Oban Gv BOL BL1 22 B7
Oban St BOL * BL1 36 A1
Oban Wy WGNE/HIN * WN2 33 G7
Oberlin St OLDE OL4 60 A5
ROCH OL11 10 B9
Occlestone Cl SALE M33 109 H3
Occupiers La BRAM/HZG * SK7 122 D3
Ocean St ALT WA14 107 L6
Ockendon Dr BKLY M9 73 H5
Octagon Ct BOL * BL1 2 E5
Octavia Dr NEWH/MOS M40 73 M8
Odell St OP/CLY * M11 88 E5
Odessa Av SLFD M6 70 E7
Odette St GTN M18 88 F8
Offerton Dr OFTN SK2 113 G5
Offerton Fold OFTN SK2 112 F5
Offerton Gn OFTN SK2 113 K6
Offerton La OFTN SK2 112 F4
Offerton Rd BRAM/HZG SK7 122 C1
OFTN SK2 113 K8
Offerton St HOR/BR BL6 33 K1
STKP SK1 112 E2
Off Grove Rd STLY SK15 77 G8
Off Ridge Hill La STLY * SK15 91 J2
Off Stamford St STLY * SK15 77 G8
Ogbourne Wk BRUN/LGST M13 87 M6
Ogden Cl HEY OL10 40 D2
WHTF M45 55 K3
Ogden Gv CHD/CHDH * SK8 110 C8
Ogden La OP/CLY M11 89 G5
Ogden Rd BRAM/HZG SK7 120 F7
FAIL M35 74 C6
Ogden Sq DUK SK16 90 E4
Ogden St CHAD OL9 8 B3
DID/WITH M20 110 E1
HYDE SK14 103 L4
MDTN M24 57 K4
OLDE * OL4 60 A6
PWCH M25 55 M8
ROCH OL11 41 M2
SWIN M27 70 C5
Ogwen Dr PWCH M25 55 L7
Ohio Av SALQ M50 86 C4
Okehampton Cl RAD M26 37 M7
Okehampton Crs SALE M33 96 A7
Okell Gv LEIGH WN7 66 A7
Okeover Rd BRO M7 72 A4
Olaf St BOLE BL2 3 J1
Old Bank Cl MPL/ROM SK6 113 K1
Old Bank St CMANW M2 6 F4
Old Bank Vw OLD OL1 43 M8
Old Barn Pl EDGW/EG BL7 22 D4
Old Barton Rd TRPK M17 84 F5
Old Bent La WHIT OL12 19 H5
Old Birley St HULME M15 87 J7
Old Boston RNFD/HAY WA11 78 D5
Oldbridge Dr WGNE/HIN WN2 49 G6
Old Broadway DID/WITH M20 98 E7
Old Brook Cl ROY/SHW OL2 44 A4
Oldbrook Fold
HALE/TIMP WA15 108 E8
Old Brow MOSL OL5 76 F4
Old Brow La MILN OL16 28 F1
Old Brown Ct MOSL OL5 76 F4
Oldbury Cl HEY OL10 41 G5
NEWH/MOS M40 88 A1
Oldcastle Av DID/WITH M20 98 D5
Old Chapel St EDGY/DAV SK3 12 D8
Old Church Ms DUK SK16 91 H4
Old Church St NEWH/MOS M40 73 L6
OLD OL1 9 K5
Old Clay Dr WHIT OL12 19 L8
Old Clough La WALK M28 69 J4
Oldcott Cl WALK M28 68 C7
The Old Ctyd WYTH/NTH * M22 110 C7
Old Cft OLDE OL4 60 D6
Old Croft Ms STKP SK1 112 E5
Old Crofts Bank URM M41 84 F8
Old Cross St AUL * OL6 90 F1
Old Dairy Ms HYDE SK14 90 F7
Old Delph Rd ROCH OL11 27 H3
Old Doctors St TOT/BURYW BL8 24 C5
Old Eagley Ms BOL BL1 22 C6
Old Edge La ROY/SHW OL2 59 H2
Old Elm St BRUN/LGST * M13 87 M6
Oldershaw Dr BKLY M9 73 G6
Old Farm Crs DROY M43 89 J4
Old Farm Dr OFTN SK2 113 J6
Oldfield Cl WHTN BL5 50 C4
Oldfield Dr HALE/TIMP WA15 108 C6
Oldfield Gv SALE M33 96 F7
Oldfield Rd ALT WA14 107 K7
ORD M5 86 F5
PWCH M25 55 M5
SALE M33 96 F7
Oldfield St OP/CLY M11 88 E3
Old Fold WGNW/BIL/O WN5 46 E6
Old Fold Rd WGNE/HIN WN2 33 G7
The Old Gdn HALE/TIMP WA15 108 E5
Old Gardens St STKP SK1 13 K6
Oldgate Wk HULME * M15 87 G6
Old Gn BOLE BL2 23 H6
Old Greenwood La HOR/BR BL6 34 A3
Old Ground St RAMS * BL0 17 C6
Old Hall Cl GLSP SK13 105 G2
TOT/BURYW BL8 24 E5
Old Hall Clough HOR/BR BL6 34 F5
Old Hall Crs WILM/AE SK9 127 J1
Old Hall Dr AIMK WN4 78 D2
GTN M18 89 G8
OFTN SK2 113 H6
Old Hall La BRAM/HZG SK7 128 B3
BRUN/LGST M13 99 H2
HOR/BR BL6 34 F3
HYDE SK14 92 D7
MPL/ROM SK6 114 F7
PWCH M25 56 C5
WALK M28 69 H5
WHTF M45 54 F6
WHTN BL5 50 B7
Old Hall Mill La LEIGH WN7 66 D4
Old Hall Rd BRO M7 72 A4
CHD/CHDH SK8 110 D6
NEWH/MOS M40 73 L5
SALE M33 97 H8
STRET M32 85 K8
WHTF M45 54 F5
Old Hall Sq GLSP SK13 93 K7
Old Hall St DUK SK16 90 D5
FWTH BL4 53 H5
MDTN M24 57 K4
OP/CLY * M11 89 H5
WGNS/IIMK WN3 15 L8
Old Hall St North BOL * BL1 2 E5
Oldham Av STKP SK1 112 E3
Oldham Dr MPL/ROM SK6 101 K8
Oldham Rd ANC M4 7 K2
AULW OL7 75 K6
AULW OL7 75 K8
AULW OL7 90 D1
FAIL M35 74 B5
MDTN M24 57 J4
MILN OL16 10 F5
NEWH/MOS M40 73 J7
OLDE OL4 60 D6
OLDE OL4 61 G3
OLDE OL4 61 J6
ROCH OL11 42 E4
ROY/SHW OL2 43 L8
UPML OL3 44 D6
UPML OL3 44 F3
Oldhams La BOL BL1 22 A7
Oldham Sq NM/HAY * SK22 124 E5
Oldham St CMANE M1 7 H4
DROY M43 89 L2
DTN/ASHW M34 100 F2
HYDE SK14 102 A2
ORD M5 6 A5
RDSH * SK5 100 B5
Oldham Wy CHAD OL9 8 F4
MILN OL16 43 J3
OLDE OL4 61 G7
OLDS OL8 9 G7
ROY/SHW OL2 44 D2
UPML OL3 45 M1
UPML OL3 77 M1
Old Kiln La BOL BL1 35 G2
OLDE OL4 60 E8
Oldknow Rd MPL/ROM SK6 114 D6
Old La BURY BL9 25 J4
CHAD OL9 58 E8
GLSP SK13 104 D5
HOR/BR BL6 34 C2
LHULT M38 52 C6
OLDE OL4 60 C4
OLDE OL4 61 H6
OP/CLY M11 89 G5
UPML OL3 61 L2
WGNNW/ST WN6 30 E6
WHTN BL5 50 A4
Old Lansdowne Rd
DID/WITH M20 98 C8
Old Lees St AUL OL6 76 A7
Old Lord's Crs HOR/BR BL6 21 B7
Old Malt La DID/WITH M20 98 D5
Old Manor Pk ATH M46 66 D2
Old Market Pl ALT WA14 108 A7
Old Market St BKLY M9 72 F2
Old Meadow Dr DTN/ASHW M34 90 C7
Old Meadow La
HALE/TIMP WA15 117 K1
Old Medlock St CSLFD * M3 6 B6
Old Mill Cl SWIN M27 70 E4
Old Mill La BRAM/HZG SK7 122 C4
OLDE OL4 60 D7
Old Mills Hl MDTN M24 58 A3
Old Mill St ANC M4 7 M4
Oldmill St WHIT OL12 10 E2
Old Moat La DID/WITH M20 98 E6
Oldmoor Rd MPL/ROM SK6 101 H7
Old Moss La GOL/RIS/CU WA3 82 A6
Old Mount St ANC M4 7 H1
Old Nans La BOLE BL2 37 J2
Old Nursery Fold BOLE BL2 23 H8
Old Oak Cl BOLE BL2 37 L7
Old Oak Dr DTN/ASHW M34 101 K1
Old Oake Cl WALK * M28 69 H2
Old Oak St DID/WITH M20 110 E1
The Old Orch HALE/TIMP WA15 108 E4
Old Orch WILM/AE SK9 126 E5
Old Pack Horse Rd UPML OL3 45 L6
Old Park La TRPK M17 84 F6
Old Parrin La ECC M30 84 E1
Old Pasture Cl OFTN SK2 113 H5
Old Pepper La WGNNW/ST WN6 30 E2
Old Quarry La EDGW/EG BL7 22 C3
Old Rake HOR/BR BL6 21 D6
Old Rectory Gdns
CHD/CHDH SK8 111 G7
Old River Cl IRL M44 94 D2
Old Rd AIMK WN4 63 K7
AUL OL6 76 C7
BKLY M9 73 G2
BOL BL1 36 B1
CHD/CHDH SK8 111 J6
DUK SK16 90 F4
FAIL M35 74 B5
GLSP SK13 93 K5
HTNM SK4 112 B1
HYDE SK14 91 G8
HYDE SK14 92 C7
MILN OL16 19 M8
STLY SK15 91 M4
WILM/AE SK9 126 F4
WILM/AE SK9 127 H1
Old School Dr BKLY * M9 72 F2
Old School Ms DUK * SK16 91 H4
Old School Pl AIMK WN4 78 D1
Old Shaw St ORD * M5 86 D4
Old Station St ECC M30 84 F3
Oldstead Gv BOLS/LL BL3 35 J8
Old St AUL OL6 90 D2
HYDE SK14 103 K4
OLDE OL4 60 A7
STLY SK15 91 K2
Old Swan Cl EDGW/EG * BL7 22 B2
Old Towns Cl TOT/BURYW BL8 24 C5
Old Vicarage WHTN BL5 50 B7
Old Vicarage Gdns WALK M28 69 G1
Old Vicarage Rd HOR/BR BL6 34 C1
Old Wellington Rd ECC M30 85 H2
Old Wells Cl LHULT M38 52 D6
Old Will's La HOR/BR BL6 21 B6
Oldwood Rd NTHM/RTH M23 118 C1
Old Wool La CHD/CHDH SK8 111 J8
Old York St HULME M15 87 H6
Olebrook Cl WGTN/LGST M12 88 A6
Oleo Ter IRL M44 94 F1
Olga St BOL BL1 36 A2
Olga Ter BKLY * M9 73 G2
Olivant St BURY BL9 4 D8
Olive Bank TOT/BURYW BL8 24 E8
Olive Gv WGNNW/ST WN6 47 J1
Oliver Cl LIT OL15 20 A7
Oliver Rd HALE/TIMP WA15 108 D4
Oliver St ATH M46 67 G1
EDGY/DAV SK3 13 J7
OP/CLY * M11 88 C4
Olive Shapley Av
DID/WITH M20 110 E1
Olive St BOLS/LL BL3 36 A8
FAIL M35 74 B4
HEY OL10 41 H2
RAD M26 54 F1
ROCH * OL11 41 M3
TOT/BURYW BL8 4 B4
Olivia Gv RUSH/FAL M14 99 G1

Ollerbarrow Rd
HALE/TIMP WA15.........117 G2
Ollerbrook Ct BOL BL1..........36 C2
Ollersett Av NM/HAY SK22....124 E4
Ollersett La NM/HAY SK22....124 F4
Ollerton WHIT OL12...........10 D3
Ollerton Av SALE M33..........96 A7
Ollerton Cl WGNE/HIN WN2....48 D2
Ollerton Rd WILM/AE SK9....119M7
Ollerton St BOL BL1...........22 C6
Ollier Av WGTN/LGST M12....99 G3
Olney ROCH OL11...........10 D7
Olney Av WYTH/NTH M22....110 A6
Olney St BRUN/LGST M13....88 A8
Olsego Cl RAD M26...........38 F8
Olwen Crs RDSH SK5.........100 C4
Olympic Ct SALQ M50.........86 C4
Omer Av WGNE/HIN WN2....99 J2
Omer Dr BNG/LEV M19.........99 H5
Onchan Av OL4...........59 L6
One Ash Cl WHIT OL12.........28 C2
One Oak La WILM/AE SK9....127 K5
Onslow Av NEWH/MOS M40....74 B3
Onslow Cl OLD OL1...........9 C3
Onslow Rd CHD/CHDH SK3....12 C7
Onslow St ROCH OL11.........27M8
Onward St HYDE SK14.........102 A2
Oozewood Rd ROY/SHW OL2....42 D7
Opal Ct RUSH/FAL * M14....99 L4
Opal Gv LEIGH WN7...........66 B8
Opal St BNG/LEV M19.........99 L4
Openshaw Fold Rd BURY BL9....39 G5
Openshaw La IRL M44.........94 B6
Openshaw Pl FWTH BL4.........52 E4
Openshaw St BURY BL9.........5 H6
Orama Av SLFD M6...........70 D8
Orama Ml WHIT * OL12.........18 D4
Oram St BURY BL9...........25 K8
Orange Hill Rd PWCH M25....55M7
Orange St SLFD M6...........86 D1
Orbital Wy DTN/ASHW M34....101 G1
The Orchard URM M41.........95M3
WHTN BL5...........50 B3
Orchard Av BOL BL1.........36 C1
GTN M18...........89 H8
PART M31...........94 C8
WALK M28...........68 E5
Orchard Cl CHD/CHDH SK8....120 E5
LEIGH WN7...........66 C5
POY/DIS SK12...........129 J1
WGNNW/ST WN6...........30 D5
WILM/AE SK9...........126 D7
Orchard Ct OFTN * SK2....113 G6
Orchard Crs MCFLDN SK10....130 C6
Orchard Dr GLSP SK13.........104 B3
HALE/TIMP WA15...........117 J1
WILM/AE SK9...........127 J1
Orchard Gdns BOLE BL2....37 J1
Orchard Gn WILM/AE SK9....130 E3
Orchard Gv DID/WITH M20....98 C7
ROY/SHW OL2...........43 K5
Orchard La LEIGH WN7....66 C5
Orchard Pl HALE/TIMP WA15....108 E5
POY/DIS * SK12...........121 M8
SALE M33...........96 E7
Orchard Ri HYDE SK14.........102 C4
Orchard Rd FAIL M35.........74 C5
HALE/TIMP WA15...........108 B7
MPL/ROM SK6...........114 E2
Orchard Rd East
WYTH/NTH M22...........110 A2
Orchard Rd West
WYTH/NTH M22...........110 A2
The Orchards
WGNNW/BIL/O WN5...........46 B7
Orchard St AIMK WN4.........78 F1
DID/WITH M20...........98 C7
HEY OL10...........41 H1
HYDE SK14...........102 B2
SLFD M6...........71 K7
STKP SK1...........13 K4
WGN WN1...........15 H3
Orchard V EDGY/DAV SK3....111M6
Orchid Av FWTH BL4.........52 E3
Orchid Cl IRL M44.........94 B4
OLD OL1...........8 E1
Orchid Dr BKLY M9.........73 G5
Orchid St BKLY M9.........73 G5
Ordsall Av LHULT M38.........52 E8
Ordsall Dr ORD M5.........86 E5
Ordsall La ORD M5.........6 A6
ORD M5...........86 D6
Oregon Av OLD OL1.........9 G1
Oregon Cl BRUN/LGST M13....87M6
Orford Av POY/DIS SK12....123M6
Orford Cl MPL/ROM SK6....123 C5
Orford Rd NEWH/MOS M40....55 K7
PWCH M25...........55 K7
Organ St LEIGH WN7.........66 B7
WGNE/HIN WN2...........65 L1
Oriel Av OLDS OL8.........75 H1
Oriel Cl CHAD OL9.........58 D8
OFTN SK2...........112 E6
Oriel Rd AIMK WN4.........63 J8
DID/WITH M20...........98 C7
Oriel St BOLS/LL BL3.........35M7
ROCH OL11...........10 F9
Orient Rd SLFD M6.........70 D8
Orient St BRO M7.........72 C5
Oriole Cl WALK M28.........68 E5
Oriole Dr WALK M28.........68 E4
Orion Pl BRO * M7.........71M8
Orkney Cl NTHM/RTH M23....109 K8
RAD M26...........38 E8
Orkney Dr URM M41.........85 G7
Orlanda Av SLFD M6.........70 D8
Orlanda Dr BRO M7.........72 C6
Orlando St BOLS/LL BL3....3 G8
Orleans Wy OLD OL1.........9 H4
Orley Wk OLD OL1.........44 A8
Orme Av MDTN M24.........57 K5
SLFD M6...........70 E7
Orme Cl OP/CLY M11.........88 B3
URM M41...........96 C2
Ormerod Av ROY/SHW OL2....59 H1
Ormerod Cl MPL/ROM SK6....113 J3
Ormerod St HEY OL10.........41 H3
Orme St OLDE OL4.........9 L8
STKP * SK1...........112 E2
WILM/AE SK9...........112 B8
Ormonde Av SLFD M6.........70 E8
Ormonde Ct AUL OL6.........75M8
Ormond St BOLS/LL BL3....37 G7
BURY BL9...........5 J5
Ormrod St BOL BL1.........2 D6
BOLE BL2...........22 F7
BURY BL9...........5 J5
FWTH BL4...........52 F4
Ormsby Av GTN M18.........88 E8
Ormsby Cl EDGY/DAV SK3....112 B8

WGNNW/ST WN6...........31 H3
Ormsgill Cl HULME M15.........87 J6
Orms Gill Pl OFTN * SK2....113 H6
Ormsgill St NEWH/MOS M40....87 J6
Ormside Cl WGNE/HIN WN2....65 L1
Ormskirk Av DID/WITH M20....98 C6
Ormskirk Cl TOT/BURYW BL8....38 C4
Ormskirk Rd RDSH SK5....100 C6
WGNNW/BIL/O WN5...........14 B6
Ormston Av HOR/BR BL6....21 B7
Ormston Gv LEIGH WN7....66 C5
Ornatus St BOL * BL1.........22 C7
Orphanage St HTNM SK4.........13 H1
Orpington St TOT/BURYW BL8....38 E3
Orpington Rd BKLY M9.........73 H5
Orpington St WGNNW/BIL/O WN5....46 C6
Orrell Ar WGN WN1...........14 F3
Orrell Gdns WGNNW/BIL/O WN5....46 C6
Orrell Hall Cl WGNNW/BIL/O WN5....46 C6
Orrell Rd WGNNW/BIL/O WN5....46 C6
Orrell St OP/CLY * M11.........89 G4
TOT/BURYW BL8...........4 A3
WGN WN1...........15 H6
Orrishmere Rd CHD/CHDH SK8....120 B1
Orron St LIT OL15...........20 B7
Orsett Cl NEWH/MOS M40....87M1
Orthes Gv HTNM SK4.........100 A7
Orton Av NTHM/RTH M23....109 K3
Orton Rd NTHM/RTH M23....109 K3
Orton Wy AIMK WN4.........78 C1
Orvietto Av SLFD M6.........70 D8
Orville Dr BNG/LEV M19....99 J5
Orwell Av DTN/ASHW M34....100 D1
WYTH/NTH M22...........110 A6
Orwell Cl TOT/BURYW BL8....4 C2
WILM/AE SK9...........127 H2
Orwell Rd BOL BL1.........35 L2
Osborne Av BOLE BL2.........37 H1
Osborne Ct ATH M46.........66 F1
Osborne Gv BOL BL1.........35M3
CHD/CHDH SK8...........119 J1
LEIGH WN7...........67 G6
Osborne Rd AIMK WN4.........63 K8
BKLY * M9...........73 H5
BNG/LEV M19...........99 J3
DTN/ASHW M34...........90 C8
GOL/RIS/CU WA3...........80 B5
HALE/TIMP WA15...........108 B7
HYDE SK14...........102 B3
OFTN SK2...........112 E6
OLDS OL8...........8 E9
SLFD * M6...........85 K1
Osborne St CHAD OL9.........8 D3
HEY OL10...........41 G3
MPL/ROM SK6...........112 F1
NEWH/MOS M40...........72 F8
ROCH OL11...........10 D9
ROY/SHW OL2...........43 L6
SLFD M6...........86 C1
Osborne Ter SALE M33.........96 E8
Osbourne Cl FWTH BL4.........53 G3
WILM/AE SK9...........127 H6
Osbourne Pl WH WA14.........108 A8
Osbourne St DID/WITH M20....110 D1
Oscar St BOL * BL1...........35M2
NEWH/MOS M40...........73 K5
Oscott Av LHULT M38.........52 D7
Oscroft Cl CHH M8.........72 C6
Osmond St OLDE OL4.........59M5
Osmund Av BOLE BL2.........37 G5
Osprey Av WHTN BL5.........49M6
Osprey Cl DUK SK16.........91 H5
HULME M15...........87 H7
Osprey Dr DROY M43.........89M1
IRL M44...........94 D1
WILM/AE SK9...........127 G4
The Ospreys WGNS/IIMK WN3....62 F1
Osprey Wk BRUN/LGST * M13....87M6
Ossory St RUSH/FAL M14....98 E1
Osterley Rd BKLY M9.........73 K1
Ostlers Gdns DROY M43....90 A2
Ostrich La PWCH M25.........71M1
Oswald Cl SLFD M6.........71 K7
Oswald La CCHDY M21.........97 L3
Oswald St ANC M4.........7 L1
BOLS/LL BL3...........35M8
MILN OL16...........11 H2
RDSH SK5...........100 C1
ROY/SHW OL2...........43M4
Oswestry Cl TOT/BURYW BL8....24 B4
Otago St OLDE * OL4.........59M3
Otago St OLDE * OL4.........59M3
Othello Dr ECC M30.........85 C2
Otley Av SLFD M6...........85M1
Otley Cl CHAD OL9.........8 B7
Otley Gv EDGY/DAV SK3....112 A8
Otmoor Wy ROY/SHW OL2....43 K8
Otranto Av SLFD M6.........70 E6
Ottawa Cl NTHM/RTH M23....109 J3
Otterburn Pl OFTN SK2....113 G6
Otterbury Cl TOT/BURYW BL8....38 C2
Otter Dr BURY BL9.........39 L8
CHH M8...........72 B7
Otterspool Rd MPL/ROM SK6....113 L3
Otterspool Sq
WGNNW/ST WN6...........46 F2
Oulder Hl ROCH OL11.........27 K5
Oulder Hill Dr ROCH OL11....27 L5
Oulder Mt ROCH OL11.........27 L5
Ouldfield Cl MILN OL16....11 J6
Oulton Av SALE M33.........97 H7
Oulton Cl LEIGH WN7.........66 D8
Oulton St BOL BL1...........22 D7
Oulton Wk NEWH/MOS M40....88 A2
Oundle Cl RUSH/FAL M14....98 F1
Ouse St SLFD M50...........85M3
Outram Cl MPL/ROM * SK6....114 C8
Outram Rd DUK SK16.........90 E6
Outram Sq DROY * M43....89 M8
Outrington Dr OP/CLY M11....88 D4
Outwood Av SWIN M27.........54 A8
Outwood Dr CHD/CHDH SK8....119 J4
Outwood Gv BOL BL1.........22 B7
Outwood La MANAIR M90....118 E4
Outwood La West
MANAIR M90...........118 D4
Outwood Rd CHD/CHDH SK8....119 K4
RAD M26...........54 D3
The Oval WGNNW/ST WN6....30 C7
WYTH/NTH M22...........119 J4
Oval Dr DUK SK16.........90 E5
Oven Hill Rd NM/HAY SK22....125 J4
Overbeck Cl WGNNW/ST WN6....31 K8
Overbridge Rd BRO M7.........72 B8
Overbrook Av NEWH/MOS M40....73 G7

Overbrook Dr PWCH M25.........71 L1
Overdale SWIN M27...........70 D6
Overdale Cl OLD OL1.........9 H1
Overdale Crs URM M41.........95 J2
Overdale Dr BOL BL1.........35 K5
GLSP SK13...........104 E4
Overdale Rd MPL/ROM SK6....113 K5
POY/DIS SK12...........124 B6
WYTH/NTH M22...........110 A7
Overdell Dr WHIT OL12.........27M1
Overdene Cl HOR/BR BL6....34 E6
Overens St OLDE OL4.........59 L5
Overfield Wy WHIT OL12....28 C2
Overgreen BOLE BL2.........37 H1
Overhill Dr WILM/AE SK9....127 J5
Overhill La WILM/AE SK9....127 J5
Overhill Rd CHAD OL9.........58 C4
Over Hill Rd NM/HAY SK22....125 J7
Overhill Wy WGNS/IIMK WN3....63 C1
Overlea Dr BNG/LEV M19....99 H7
Overlinks Dr SLFD M6.........70 E7
Overshores Rd EDGW/EG BL7....16 A5
Overstone Dr CHH M8.........72 C5
Overton Av WYTH/NTH M22....110 A4
Overton Crs BRAM/HZG SK7....113 H8
SALE M33...........108 A2
Overton Rd WYTH/NTH M22....110 A7
Overton St LEIGH WN7.........66 B8
Overton Wy WILM/AE SK9....127 J1
Over Town La WHIT OL12....26 D1
Overt St ROCH OL11.........10 F8
Overwood Rd WYTH/NTH M22....110 A4
Owen Fold Cl OLDE OL4....60 C5
Owenington Gv LHULT M38....52 D7
Owens Cl CHAD OL9.........58 B4
Owens Farm Dr OFTN SK2....113 H5
Owens Pk RUSH/FAL * M14....99 G3
Owen St ECC M30...........84 E3
EDGY/DAV SK3...........12 F5
LEIGH * WN7...........66 A7
OLD OL1...........60 B1
SLFD M6...........71 K7
Owlerbarrow Rd
TOT/BURYW BL8...........38 D1
Owler La AIMK WN4.........74 A1
Owlwood Cl LHULT M38.........68 B1
Owlwood Dr LHULT M38....68 B1
Oxbridge Cl SALE M33....108 A1
Oxbrow Wy WHTF M45.........55 K4
Oxburgh Rd WGNS/IIMK WN3....48 C3
Oxendale Dr MDTN M24....56 F3
Oxenhurst Gn OFTN SK2....113 H7
Oxford Av DROY M43.........89 J1
ROCH OL11...........27 K6
SALE M33...........96 A8
WHTF M45...........55 K4
Oxford Dr MDTN M24.........57M2
MPL/ROM SK6...........101 M8
Oxford Gv BOL BL1.........2 A2
Oxford Ml AULW * OL7.........90 C4
Oxford Pl ROCH * OL11....11 H9
RUSH/FAL M14...........87M8
Oxford Rd ALT WA14.........116 F1
ATH M46...........50 E7
BOLS/LL BL3...........53 J1
BRUN/LGST M13...........87 L7
CMANE M1...........7 G8
DUK SK16...........91 G4
HOR/BR BL6...........34 C4
SLFD M6...........70 D8
WGNW/BIL/O WN5...........46 C5
Oxford St BOL BL1.........2 E4
BURY BL9...........5 H4
CHAD OL9...........8 C9
CMANW M2...........6 F6
ECC M30...........85 H3
LEIGH WN7...........66 C5
ROY/SHW OL2...........43 L5
STLY SK15...........91M3
WGNE/HIN WN2...........49 J5
Oxford St East AULW OL7....90 C4
Oxford St West AULW OL7....90 C4
Oxford Wy HTNM SK4.........12 F1
Ox Ga BOLE BL2...........23 C7
Ox Hey Cl HOR/BR BL6....34 B4
Ox Hey La HOR/BR BL6....34 B5
UPML OL3...........
Oxlea Gv WHTN BL5.........50 B5
Oxley St OP/CLY M11.........88 D2
Oxney Rd RUSH/FAL M14....87M8
Ox St RAMS BL0...........17 B7
Oxton Av WYTH/NTH M22....109M8
Oxton St OP/CLY M11.........89 J5

P

Pacific Rd ALT WA14.........107 K6
Pacific Wy SALO M50.........85M4
Packer St BOL BL1...........35M2
MILN OL16...........10 E4
Packwood Cha CHAD OL9....58 C4
Padbury Cl URM M41.........95 G1
Padbury Wy BOLE BL2.........37 H2
Padden Brook MPL/ROM SK6....113 L2
Paddington Av
NEWH/MOS * M40...........73 L7
Paddington Cl SLFD M6....86 D2
Paddison St SWIN M27.........70 B5
The Paddock AIMK WN4....63 J6
BRAM/HZG SK7...........120 F3
CHD/CHDH SK8...........111 H4
HALE/TIMP WA15...........108 E8
HYDE SK14...........93 H7
RAMS BL0...........17 B5
UPML OL3...........61 J8
WALK M28...........69 H5
Paddock Cha POY/DIS SK12....122 B6
Paddock Cl ATH M46.........51 H7
Paddock La FAIL M35.........74 C7
LYMM WA13...........106 A5
LYMM WA13...........106 D7
Paddock Rd WGNNW/ST WN6....47 H1
Paddock Ri HYDE * SK14....102 A4
The Paddocks EDGY/DAV SK3....112 D7
Paddock St WGTN/LGST M12....7 L8
WILM/AE SK9...........126 F3
Paderborn Ct BOL BL1.........2 C6
Padfield Ga GLSP SK13....105 G5
Padfield Main Rd GLSP SK13....93 L6
Padiham Cl BURY BL9.........39 L5
LEIGH WN7...........66 D7
Padstow Cl HYDE SK14....103 G1
Padstow Dr BRAM/HZG SK7....121 H5
Padstow St NEWH/MOS * M40....88 B1

Padstow Wk HYDE SK14....103 G1
Pagan St MILN OL16.........10 F3
Pagefield Cl WGNNW/ST WN6....14 C1
Pagefield St WGNNW/ST WN6....14 C1
Paget St NEWH/MOS M40....73 G7
Pagnall Ct CHAD * OL9....8 A8
Paignton Av BNG/LEV M19....99 J3
HYDE SK14...........103 G1
Paignton Dr SALE M33....96 A7
Paignton Gv HTNM SK4....100 B5
Pailin Dr DROY M43.........89M2
Pailton Cl HOR/BR BL6....35 G5
Painswick Rd WYTH/NTH M22....118 D3
Paisley Pk FWTH BL4.........52 F3
Paiton St BOL BL1.........35M5
Palace Ar AIMK WN4.........78 E1
Palace Gdns ROY/SHW OL2....59 C2
Palace Rd AUL OL6.........76 B7
SALE M33...........96 D7
Palace St BOL BL1.........2 E3
BURY BL9...........5 J5
CHAD OL9...........8 D5
Palatine Av DID/WITH M20....98 E6
DTN/ASHW M34...........100 E1
WGNS/IIMK WN3...........47 H8
Palatine Crs DID/WITH M20....98 E7
Palatine Dr BURY BL9.........25 J4
Palatine Rd DID/WITH M20....110 C1
ROCH OL11...........27 K4
WYTH/NTH M22...........110 A3
Palatine Sq LEIGH WN7....66 A7
Palatine St BOL BL1.........2 E4
DTN/ASHW M34...........90 B7
MILN OL16...........11 L5
RAMS BL0...........17 C6
Palewood Cl WGN WN1....15 K1
Paley St BOL BL1.........2 E4
Palfrey Pl WGTN/LGST M12....7M9
Palin Dr WGNE/HIN WN2....65 L1
Palin Wood Rd UPML OL3....45 J7
Pall Ml CMANW M2...........6 F5
HOR/BR * BL6...........21 A5
Palma Av MANAIR M90....118 C4
Palm Av AIMK WN4.........63 G7
Palm Cl SALE M33.........95M7
Palmer Av CHD/CHDH SK8....111 J6
OLDS OL8...........59 J8
Palmer Gv LEIGH WN7....66 B3
Palmerston Av
OLDTF/WHR M16...........98 A2
RAMS BL0...........24 C1
Palmerston Cl DTN/ASHW M34....100 E1
RAMS BL0...........17 C6
Palmerston Rd
DTN/ASHW M34...........100 E1
OFTN SK2...........121 J1
Palmerston St WGTN/LGST M12....88 A4
Palmer St BRO M7.........71M7
DUK SK16...........91 C8
SALE M33...........96 D8
Palm Gv CHAD OL9.........8 B2
Palm St BRUN/LGST M13....99 J1
DROY M43...........89 G2
OLDE OL4...........59M4
Pandora St DID/WITH M20....98 D5
Panfield Rd WYTH/NTH M22....109M8
Pangbourne Av URM M41....96 B1
Pangbourne Cl EDGY/DAV SK3....111M6
Pankhurst Wk RUSH/FAL M14....98 E1
Panmure St OLDS OL8....59 J8
Pansy Rd FWTH BL4.........52 D4
Panton St HOR/BR BL6....34 A3
Paper Mill Rd EDGW/EG BL7....22 C5
Parade Rd MANAIR M90....118 E5
Paradise St DTN/ASHW M34....90 C5
GLSP SK13...........93 J7
RAMS BL0...........17 C6
Parbold Av DID/WITH M20....98 D5
Parbrook La WGNNW/ST WN6....30 E5
The Parchments NEWLW WA12....79 G8
Pargate Cha ROCH OL11....27 K4
Paris Av ORD M5...........86 E5
WGNS/IIMK WN3...........62 F1
Parish Vw ORD M5.........86 E4
Paris St BOLS/LL BL3.........35 L8
The Park OLDE OL4.........61 G7
UPML OL3...........61M7
Park 66 BURY * BL9.........39 L6
Park Av ALT WA14.........108 A6
BNG/LEV M19...........99 J3
BOL * BL1...........22 E8
BRAM/HZG SK7...........120 E7
BRO M7...........72 C4
CHAD OL9...........58 E3
CHD/CHDH SK8...........120 B3
EDGY/DAV SK3...........111 J5
FAIL M35...........74 A4
GOL/RIS/CU WA3...........79 J2
HALE/TIMP WA15...........117 H3
HYDE SK14...........91 C8
NEWH/MOS M40...........86 F7
POY/DIS SK12...........122 A8
PWCH M25...........55 L8
RAMS BLO...........17 D6
SALE M33...........96 D6
URM M41...........95M2
WGNNW/ST WN6...........30 E5
WGNW/BIL/O WN5...........62 B3
WHTF M45...........55 G6
WILM/AE SK9...........127 G4
Park Bank ATH M46.........51 A8
Park Bridge Rd AULW OL7....75 L4
Parkbrook Rd NTHM/RTH M23....109 L5
Park Brow Cl CCHDY M21....97M5
Park Cl ALT WA14.........108 C4
CHAD OL9...........8 A1
GLSP SK13...........105 G2
STLY SK15...........91 J1
WHTF M45...........55 G5
Park Cottages BOL * BL1....35M1
ROY/SHW OL2...........43 J4
Park Court Ms
CHD/CHDH * SK8...........111 H8
Park Crs AUL OL6.........91 H2
CHAD OL9...........58 C3
GLSP SK13...........104 E1
RUSH/FAL M14...........98 F1
WGN WN1...........15 J3
WILM/AE SK9...........126 F3
Park Crs West WGN WN1....15 J3
Parkdale CHAD OL9.........58 E3
TYLD M29...........68 D7
Parkdale Av DTN/ASHW M34....90 A5
GTN M18...........89 H7
Parkdale Rd BOLE BL2.........3 L1
BOLE BL2...........37 J1

Park Dene Dr GLSP SK13....104 F2
Park Dr ECC M30...........70 A8
HALE/TIMP WA15...........108 D5
HALE/TIMP WA15...........117 H3
HTNM SK4...........12 B3
HYDE SK14...........91 C8
OLDTF/WHR M16...........97M2
Park Edge WHTN BL5.........50 B5
Parkend Dr LEIGH WN7....81 G2
Parkend Rd NTHM/RTH M23....109 K7
Parker St BURY BL9.........5 H5
CMANE M1...........7 H5
Parkfield CHAD OL9.........58 D3
ECC * M30...........86 A2
ORD M5...........86 A2
Parkfield Av FWTH BL4....52 F5
MPL/ROM SK6...........114 C6
OLDS OL8...........74 E2
PWCH M25...........72 A1
RUSH/FAL M14...........98 E1
TYLD M29...........67 L6
URM M41...........95 L3
Parkfield Cl LEIGH WN7....66 D5
TYLD M29...........68 A3
Parkfield Dr MDTN M24....57 H4
TYLD M29...........68 A3
Parkfield Rd ALT WA14....107M8
BOLS/LL BL3...........52 C1
CHD/CHDH SK8...........120 B3
OLDE OL4...........61 H6
Parkfield Rd North
NEWH/MOS M40...........74 B2
Parkfield Rd South
DID/WITH M20...........98 D8
Parkfields STLY SK15.........92 A1
WGNE/HIN WN2...........65 L1
Parkfield St ROCH OL11....42 E2
RUSH/FAL M14...........98 E1
Parkgate CHAD OL9.........58 E3
TOT/BURYW BL8...........4 E1
Park Gate Av DID/WITH M20....98 E6
Park Gate Cl MPL/ROM SK6....101 H7
Parkgate Dr BOL BL1.........22 C7
OFTN SK2...........70 E5
SWIN M27...........70 E5
Park Gates Av CHD/CHDH SK8....120 E3
Park Gates Dr CHD/CHDH SK8....120 E3
Park Gv BNG/LEV M19.........99 K2
HTNM SK4...........99 L8
RAD M26...........38 A2
WALK M28...........69 G4
Parkham Cl WHTN BL5....50 C6
Park Hey Dr WGNNW/ST WN6....30 E5
Park Hill PWCH * M25.........72 A2
Parkhill Av CHH M8.........72 E2
Park Hill Cl NM/HAY SK22....124 E3
Park Hill Dr WHTF M45....55 H5
Park Hill Rd HALE/TIMP WA15....117 J3
Parkhills Rd BURY BL9....5 G7
Park Hill St BOL BL1.........2 A3
Park House Bridge Est
SLFD * M6...........71 J5
Park House Bridge Rd SLFD M6....71 J5
Parkhouse St OP/CLY M11....88 E4
Parkhurst Av NEWH/MOS M40....74 B3
Parkin Cl DUK * SK16....90 F4
Parkinson St BOLS/LL BL3....35 K7
BURY BL9...........25 J7
Parkin St WGTN/LGST M12....99 K1
Parklake Av BRO M7.........72 K4
Parkland Av NM/HAY SK22....124 E3
The Parklands HTNM SK4....100 B8
Parklands ROY/SHW OL2....44 A4
WHTF M45...........55 H5
Parklands Dr SALE M33....108 A2
WGNE/HIN WN2...........32 F6
Parklands Rd NTHM/RTH M23....109 J3
Parklands Wy POY/DIS SK12....122 A8
Park La BRO M7...........72 A4
DUK SK16...........90 F4
HALE/TIMP WA15...........117 J3
HOR/BR BL6...........66 F8
LEIGH WN7...........66 F8
MILN OL16...........10 E7
OLDS OL8...........75 J2
POY/DIS SK12...........122 A8
ROY/SHW OL2...........43 G8
SLFD M6...........70 F7
STRAP SK1...........112 E4
UPML OL3...........61M7
WGNE/HIN WN2...........64 E5
WGNE/HIN WN2...........65 H6
WHTF M45...........55 H5
Park Lane Ct WHTF * M45....55 G5
Park La West SWIN M27....71 G5
Parkleigh Dr NEWH/MOS M40....74 B2
Park Ldg BNG/LEV M19....99 K3
Park Lodge Cl CHD/CHDH SK8....111 H8
Park Meadow WHTN BL5....50 D4
Park Ms OLDTF/WHR M16....97M2
Parkmount Rd BKLY M9....73 H3
Park Pde AULW OL7.........90 C4
ROY/SHW OL2...........43M3
Park Pl ANC M4...........87 K1
HTNM SK4...........111 J2
PWCH M25...........55M7
SLFD M6...........86 A2
Park Range RUSH/FAL M14....99 G1
Park Ri MPL/ROM SK6....101 H7
Park Rd ALT WA14.........116 C2
BOL * BL1...........35M5
BOLS/LL BL3...........37 J8
BURY BL9...........4 E1
CHD/CHDH SK8...........111 H6
CHD/CHDH SK8...........120 E3
DTN/ASHW M34...........90 A4
DTN/ASHW M34...........101 G1
ECC M30...........70 A8
GLSP SK13...........93 L8
HALE/TIMP WA15...........108 C4
HALE/TIMP WA15...........117 H5
HTNM SK4...........99 L7
HYDE SK14...........91 G8
MDTN M24...........57 J4
MPL/ROM SK6...........113M1
NEWLW WA12...........79 J3
NM/HAY SK22...........124 E3
OLDS OL8...........9 J8
PART M31...........106 D7
POY/DIS SK12...........123 H6
PWCH M25...........72 A1
RAMS BLO...........24 C1
SALE M33...........96 D6
SLFD M6...........70 D8
STRET M32...........96 F1

WALK M28 .....68 F3
WCGNE/HIN WN2 .....65 H1
WCGNNW/ST WN6 .....14 C1
WCGNNW/ST WN6 .....31 H4
WCGNW/BIL/O WN5 .....46 D6
WCGNW/BIL/O WN5 .....62 B3
WHIT OL12 .....28 E3
WILM/AE SK9 .....126 D5
Park Rd North *URM* M41 .....95 M1
Park Rd South *URM* M41 .....95 M2
HTNM SK4 .....111 J3
Park Rw *BOL* BL1 .....22 C6
Park Seventeen *WHTF* M45 .....55 J4
The Parks *RNFD/HAY* WA11 .....78 E3
WCGNE/HIN WN4 .....49 H6
Parkside *MDTN* M24 .....57 H6
Park Side Av *AIMK* WN4 .....63 J4
BRO M7 .....72 B4
ECC M30 .....84 F3
FAIL M35 .....74 B7
WALK M28 .....69 G3
Parkside CI *MPL/ROM* SK6 .....122 F4
RAD M26 .....39 H8
Parkside Crs *WCGNW/BIL/O* WN5 .....46 C6
Parkside La *WCGNW/ST* WN6 .....114 F6
Parkside Rd *RUSH/FAL* M14 .....98 C2
SALE M33 .....109 C1
Parkside St *BOLE* * BL2 .....36 F5
WCGTN/LGST * M12 .....7 M8
BURY BL9 .....4 F7
Parks Nook *FWTH* BL4 .....52 F5
Park Sq *OLDTF/WHR* M16 .....97 K2
Parkstead Dr *BKLY* M9 .....73 G6
Parkstone Av *GTN* M18 .....89 J6
WHTF M45 .....55 G6
Parkstone CI *TOT/BURYW* BL8 .....38 C2
Parkstone Dr *BOLE* * BL2 .....70 E6
Parkstone La *WALK* M28 .....69 J8
Parkstone Rd *IRL* M44 .....94 D1
Park St *ATH* M46 .....51 H8
AULW OL7 .....90 D3
BOL BL1 .....2 A3
BRO M7 .....71 M4
CSLFD M3 .....6 A4
DROY M43 .....89 M2
DTN/ASHW M34 .....101 G1
FWTH BL4 .....53 C3
HEY OL10 .....41 H4
MILN OL16 .....10 E6
MOSL OL5 .....76 F4
MPL/ROM SK6 .....113 J1
OLDS OL8 .....9 G8
PWCH M25 .....55 M8
RAD M26 .....38 F8
ROY/SHW OL2 .....43 H8
ROY/SHW OL2 .....43 L6
STKP SK1 .....13 J3
STLY SK15 .....91 L3
SWIN M27 .....70 D5
TYLD M29 .....67 K3
WCGNS/IIMK WN3 .....14 E7
Parksway *BKLY* M9 .....56 E6
PWCH M25 .....71 M2
SWIN M27 .....70 F6
Parks Yd *BURY* BL9 .....4 E4
Park Ter *OL10 .....41 C1
MOSL * OL5 .....76 F4
Park Vw *AIMK* WN4 .....78 E2
BKLY M9 .....72 F6
CHAD OL9 .....58 D3
DTN/ASHW * M34 .....90 A4
EDGY/DAV SK3 .....111 J5
FWTH BL4 .....53 C3
FWTH BL4 .....53 J5
LIT OL15 .....20 C6
RUSH/FAL * M14 .....99 H5
STKP SK1 .....112 E5
WCGNE/HIN WN2 .....64 E3
WCGNW/BIL/O * WN5 .....46 E7
WILM/AE SK9 .....127 G4
Park View Ct *PWCH* * M25 .....71 J1
Park View Ri *NM/HAY* SK22 .....124 E3
Park View Rd *BOLS/LL* * BL3 .....35 M8
PWCH M25 .....71 L1
Parkville Rd *DID/WITH* M20 .....98 F7
PWCH M25 .....55 M8
Park Wy *STRET* M32 .....85 J8
Parkway *BRAM/HZG* SK7 .....121 G2
CHAD OL9 .....58 D3
DTN/ASHW M34 .....100 F1
EDGY/DAV SK3 .....111 J5
LHULT M38 .....52 E8
NM/HAY SK22 .....124 E3
ROCH OL11 .....27 L4
WCGNNW/ST WN6 .....30 D2
WHTN BL5 .....50 A7
WILM/AE SK9 .....126 F6
Parkway Gv *LHULT* M38 .....52 E8
Parkwood CI *WCGNS/IIMK* WN3 .....15 L3
Parkwood Dr *WHTN* BL5 .....51 J5
Parkwood Rd *NTHM/RTH* M23 .....109 M5
Parlane St *ANC* M4 .....87 K1
Parliament PI *BURY* BL9 .....4 D7
Parliament St *BURY* BL9 .....4 E7
WCGNS/IIMK WN3 .....15 J7
Parndon Dr *OFTN* SK2 .....112 F5
Parnell Av *WYTH/NTH* M22 .....110 A4
Parnell CI *TYLD* M29 .....67 L7
Parnham CI *BOLS/LL* BL3 .....37 L7
Parrbrook CI *WHTF* M45 .....55 L5
Parr CI *FWTH* BL4 .....52 E4
Parrenthorn Rd *PWCH* M25 .....55 M4
Parrfield Rd *WALK* M28 .....69 G5
Parr Fold *BURY* BL9 .....55 L2
Parr Fold Av *WALK* M28 .....68 F3
Parrin La *ECC* M30 .....84 F1
Parr La *BURY* BL9 .....55 K3
Parrot St *BOLS/LL* BL3 .....2 C9
OP/CLY M11 .....88 F3
Parrs Mount Ms *HTNM* * SK4 .....111 J2
Parr St *ECC* M30 .....85 G3
OP/CLY * M11 .....89 H5
TYLD M29 .....67 J4
Parrs Wood Av *DID/WITH* M20 .....110 F3
Parrs Wood La *DID/WITH* M20 .....111 C3
Parrs Wood Rd *DID/WITH* M20 .....110 E4
Parry Md *MPL/ROM* SK6 .....101 M8
Parslow Av *CHH* M8 .....72 D4
Parsonage Dr *WALK* M28 .....68 F2
Parsonage Gdns *CSLFD* * M3 .....6 C3
MPL/ROM SK6 .....114 D8
Parsonage La *CSLFD* M3 .....6 C3
DID/WITH M20 .....98 E7
HTNM SK4 .....99 L3
RAD * M26 .....53 M5

URM M41 .....95 H3
WALK M28 .....68 F2
Parsonage St *BURY* BL9 .....5 J4
CHH M8 .....72 C3
HTNM SK4 .....13 G3
HULME M15 .....87 H7
HYDE * SK14 .....102 A2
Parsonage Wk *MILN* * OL16 .....29 J5
Parsonage Wy *CHD/CHDH* SK8 .....111 K7
LEIGH WN7 .....66 B6
Parsons Dr *MDTN* M24 .....57 J2
Parsons Fld *SLFD* * M6 .....71 K7
Parson's La *BURY* BL9 .....4 F3
Parsons St *CHAD* OL9 .....8 D7
Parson's Wk *WCGN* WN1 .....14 E2
Parth St *HEY* OL10 .....40 A3
Partington CI *FWTH* BL4 .....52 F3
GLSP SK13 .....105 J4
Partington La *SWIN* M27 .....70 B5
Partington Pk *GLSP* SK13 .....104 F2
ROCH OL11 .....41 M4
Partington PI *SALE* M33 .....96 E7
Partington St *BOLS/LL* BL3 .....51 M2
ECC M30 .....85 G1
FAIL M35 .....74 C5
HEY OL10 .....40 D2
NEWH/MOS M40 .....73 J7
OLD * OL1 .....9 L5
ROCH OL11 .....41 L2
WALK M28 .....69 M4
WCGNW/BIL/O WN5 .....47 H4
Partridge Av *NTHM/RTH* M23 .....109 L6
Partridge CI *ROCH* OL11 .....27 J5
Partridge Ct *OFTN* * SK2 .....112 E8
Partridge Ri *DROY* M43 .....90 A1
Partridge Rd *FAIL* M35 .....74 F6
Partridge St *STRET* M32 .....86 C7
Partridge Wy *CHAD* OL9 .....58 A4
Parvet Av *DROY* M43 .....89 J1
Pascal St *BNG/LEV* M19 .....99 K4
The Pass *MILN* OL16 .....11 H3
Passmonds Crs *ROCH* OL11 .....27 L4
Passmonds Wy *ROCH* OL11 .....27 L4
Pass St *CHAD* OL9 .....8 E7
Paston Rd *WYTH/NTH* M22 .....110 A5
HEY OL10 .....40 E3
Pasturefield CI *SALE* M33 .....109 J1
Pasture Field Rd
WYTH/NTH M22 .....119 H3
Pasturegreen Wy *IRL* M44 .....94 E1
Pastures La *OLDE* OL4 .....60 E4
Patch Croft Rd
WYTH/NTH M22 .....119 H3
Patchett St *WCGTN/LGST* M12 .....88 C6
Patch La *BRAM/HZG* SK7 .....120 F7
Pateley Sq *WCGNNW/ST* WN6 .....47 L2
Patey St *WHIT* OL12 .....27 M3
Patience St *WHIT* OL12 .....27 M3
Patmos St *RAMS* BL0 .....17 D6
Paton Av *BOLS/LL* BL3 .....51 J1
Paton Ct *BRO* M7 .....71 M8
Paton St *CMANE* M1 .....7 J5
WHIT OL12 .....28 A1
Patricia Dr *WALK* M28 .....69 H2
Patricroft Rd *WCGNE/HIN* WN2 .....15 M7
Patten St *DID/WITH* M20 .....98 E6
URM M41 .....84 E3
Patterdale Av *AULW* OL7 .....75 J7
URM M41 .....84 E3
Patterdale CI *OLD* OL1 .....9 L1
ROCH OL11 .....41 L1
MDTN M24 .....57 H2
Patterdale Dr *BURY* BL9 .....39 H5
Patterdale CI *NTHM/RTH* M23 .....48 D5
Patterdale Rd *AIMK* WN4 .....63 K4
AULW OL7 .....75 J7
BOLE BL2 .....23 H8
LEIGH WN7 .....66 F8
MPL/ROM SK6 .....101 L8
OFTN SK2 .....112 E6
PART M31 .....106 B1
WYTH/NTH M22 .....110 B4
Patterson Av *CCHDY* M21 .....97 K3
Patterson St *BOLS/LL* BL3 .....35 K8
DTN/ASHW M34 .....90 C8
NEWLW WA12 .....78 E8
WHTN BL5 .....49 L5
Patting CI *IRL* M44 .....94 F1
Pattishall CI *ANC* M4 .....88 A3
Pattison CI *WHIT* OL12 .....27 M1
Patton CI *BURY* BL9 .....55 L2
Paulden Av *NTHM/RTH* M23 .....109 L6
OLDE OL4 .....60 B3
Paulden Dr *FAIL* M35 .....74 D5
Paulette St *BOL* BL1 .....36 B2
Paulhan Rd *DID/WITH* M20 .....99 G8
Paulhan St *BOLS/LL* BL3 .....52 B1
Pauline St *WCGNE/HIN* WN2 .....65 L3
Pavilion CI *WHIT* OL12 .....28 C2
Pavilion Dr *AUL* OL6 .....76 A7
The Pavilions *CHD/CHDH* SK8 .....111 G8
Pavilion Wk *RAD* M26 .....38 C8
Paxford PI *WILM/AE* SK9 .....126 E7
Paythorne Av *OFTN* SK2 .....113 H7
Peabody St *BOLS/LL* BL3 .....36 B8
Peacefield *MPL/ROM* SK6 .....114 B7
Peace St *ATH* M46 .....67 H1
BOLS/LL BL3 .....2 A9
FAIL * M35 .....74 D3
TYLD M29 .....67 J6
Peaceville Rd *BNG/LEV* M19 .....99 J3
Peach Bank *MDTN* M24 .....57 K4
Peach Gv *RNFD/HAY* * WA11 .....78 B5
Peach Rd *OLDE* OL4 .....60 A3
Peach St *PWCH* M25 .....55 M7
Peach Tree CI *BRO* * M7 .....72 C6
Peach Tree Ct *SLFD* M6 .....86 D2
Peacock Av *GLSP* SK13 .....93 H8
GTN M18 .....88 F6
Peacock Dr *CHD/CHDH* SK8 .....119 K6
Peacock Fold *LEIGH* WN7 .....66 A6
Peacock Gv *GTN* M18 .....89 G8
Peak Av *ATH* M46 .....50 F7
Peak Bank *MPL/ROM* SK6 .....113 K2
Peak CI *OLDE* OL4 .....44 C8
Peakdale Av *CHH* M8 .....72 C3
CHH M8 .....72 C3
Peakdale Rd *DROY* M43 .....89 H1
GLSP SK13 .....104 B1
MPL/ROM SK6 .....114 D8
SWIN M27 .....70 E4
Peaknaze CI *GLSP* SK13 .....104 D4
SWIN M27 .....70 E4
Peak St *BOL* BL1 .....36 A2
CHAD OL9 .....8 B7
CMANE M1 .....7 K5
STKP SK1 .....13 L4
Pear Av *BURY* BL9 .....5 M3

Pear CI *MDTN* M24 .....57 L6
Pearl Av *BRO* M7 .....72 B3
Pearl Mill CI *OLDS* OL8 .....59 L8
Pearl St *BRAM/HZG* SK7 .....113 H8
DTN/ASHW M34 .....101 H1
ROCH OL11 .....27 M4
WCGNNW/ST WN6 .....47 L1
Pearly Bank *OLD* OL1 .....44 A8
Pearn Rd *BNG/LEV* M19 .....99 J7
Pearson CI *MILN* OL16 .....29 J5
PART M31 .....106 D1
Pearson Gv *OLDE* OL4 .....60 B6
Pearson St *BURY* BL9 .....5 K2
DUK SK16 .....90 F6
MILN OL16 .....11 M2
RDSH SK5 .....112 C1
Pear Tree CI *GLSP* SK13 .....93 H8
MPL/ROM SK6 .....114 E4
SLFD M6 .....86 D2
Pear Tree Ct *SLFD* M6 .....86 D2
Pear Tree Dr *STLY* SK15 .....91 L2
Pear Tree Gv *TYLD* M29 .....68 B3
Peart St *DTN/ASHW* M34 .....101 H1
Peary St *ANC* M4 .....87 L1
Peaslake CI *MPL/ROM* SK6 .....114 A2
Peatfield Av *SWIN* M27 .....70 A2
Peatfield Wk *HULME* * M15 .....87 J7
Pebble CI *STLY* SK15 .....76 D8
Pebworth CI *MDTN* M24 .....57 J7
Peckford Dr *NEWH/MOS* M40 .....73 K7
Peckforton CI *CHD/CHDH* SK8 .....110 D7
Peckmill CI *WILM/AE* SK9 .....127 C2
Pedder St *BOL* BL1 .....35 M3
Pedler Brow La *WHIT* OL12 .....19 M6
Pedley HI *MCFLDN* SK10 .....129 K5
Pedley Wk *BRUN/LGST* M13 .....7 K8
Peebles CI *CMANE* M4 .....62 F8
Peebles Dr *NEWH/MOS* M40 .....74 A7
Peel Av *ALT* WA14 .....116 F2
Peel Brow *RAMS* BL0 .....17 D6
Peel Cir *URM* M41 .....85 H6
Peel CI *ATH* M46 .....67 H1
Peel Cross Rd *ORD* M5 .....86 D3
Peel Dr *LHULT* M38 .....52 C8
SALE M33 .....97 H8
Peel Gv *WALK* M28 .....69 H4
WCGTN/LGST M12 .....88 D8
Peelgate Dr *CHD/CHDH* SK8 .....119 J2
Peel Green Rd *ECC* M30 .....84 E4
Peel Hall Av *TYLD* M29 .....67 L3
Peel Hall Rd *BURY* BL9 .....24 E2
WYTH/NTH M22 .....119 H1
Peel La *CHH* M8 .....72 D8
HEY OL10 .....40 E1
LHULT M38 .....52 C8
TYLD M29 .....67 L8
Peel Moat Rd *HTNM* SK4 .....99 L7
Peel Mt *RAMS* BL0 .....17 A8
Peel Park Crs *LHULT* M38 .....52 C8
Peel Rd *HALE/TIMP* WA15 .....117 C1
Peels Av *OLDE* OL4 .....60 D5
Peel St *AUL* OL6 .....90 E1
CHAD OL9 .....8 B6
DROY M43 .....89 J4
DTN/ASHW M34 .....90 B7
DUK SK16 .....90 F3
ECC M30 .....85 J2
FAIL M35 .....74 A6
FWTH BL4 .....53 H4
GLSP SK13 .....93 M7
HEY OL10 .....40 E2
HYDE SK14 .....102 C3
LIT OL15 .....20 C7
OFTN SK2 .....112 C6
RAD M26 .....54 E2
STLY SK15 .....91 J3
WCGNE/HIN WN2 .....64 D2
WHIT OL12 .....10 C2
WHTN BL5 .....50 B3
Peel Vw *TOT/BURYW* BL8 .....24 D6
Peel Wk *BURY* BL9 .....25 H6
TOT/BURYW BL8 .....4 D1
Peel Wy *BURY* BL9 .....4 E4
Peelwood Av *LHULT* M38 .....52 D7
Peelwood Gv *ATH* M46 .....67 H2
Peers CI *URM* M41 .....84 A8
Peers St *TOT/BURYW* BL8 .....4 A5
Pegamoid St *BOLE* M2 .....36 E5
Pegasus Sq *BRO* M7 .....86 E1
Pegwell Dr *BRO* M7 .....72 B7
Pekin St *AUL* OL6 .....75 M8
Pelham PI *CHH* M8 .....72 E2
Pelham St *AULW* OL7 .....90 B4
BOLS/LL BL3 .....51 M1
OLDS OL8 .....75 J2
Pellowe Rd *OLDS* OL8 .....75 H1
Pelton Av *SWIN* M27 .....70 A2
Pemberlei Rd *WCGNE/HIN* WN2 .....49 G2
Pemberton La *WCGN* WN1 .....31 M6
Pemberton St *BOL* * BL1 .....52 E8
LHULT M38 .....52 E8
ROCH OL11 .....41 M8
Pemberton Wy *ROY/SHW* OL2 .....43 L4
Pembridge Fold *MDTN* M24 .....57 M4
Pembridge Rd *BKLY* M9 .....57 J8
Pembroke Av *ECC* M30 .....85 G2
SALE M33 .....96 C7
Pembroke CI *BRUN/LGST* M13 .....88 A6
HOR/BR BL6 .....21 A8
Pembroke Ct *BRAM/HZG* * SK7 .....122 A2
WHIT OL12 .....10 E1
Pembroke Dr *BURY* BL9 .....39 H5
OLDE OL4 .....44 B8
Pembroke Rd *WCGNE/HIN* WN2 .....49 G3
WCGNW/BIL/O WN5 .....47 G3
Pembroke St *BOL* BL1 .....2 B3
BRO M7 .....72 B6
LIT OL15 .....20 C6
OLDS * OL8 .....8 F7
SLFD M6 .....86 B3
Pembry CI *RDSH* SK5 .....100 E6
Pembury CI *WYTH/NTH* M22 .....118 E1
Penarth Rd *BOLS/LL* BL3 .....35 L8
WYTH/NTH M22 .....110 A4
Penbury Rd *WGN* WN1 .....14 F1
Pencarrow CI *DID/WITH* M20 .....110 C1
Pencombe CI *WCGTN/LGST* M12 .....88 D8
Pencroft Wy *HULME* M15 .....87 K7
Pendeen CI *TYLD* M29 .....67 K5
WYTH/NTH M22 .....119 G3
Pendennis *ROCH* OL11 .....10 F5
Pendennis Av *HOR/BR* BL6 .....35 G7
Pendennis CI *RAD* M26 .....39 H7
Pendennis Crs *WCGNE/HIN* WN2 .....65 K1
Pendennis Rd *HTNM* SK4 .....12 B6
Pendle Av *BOL* BL1 .....22 B6

Pendlebury CI *PWCH* M25 .....71 J2
Pendlebury Fold *BOLS/LL* BL3 .....51 C2
Pendlebury La *WCGNE/HIN* WN1 .....31 M6
Pendlebury Rd *CHD/CHDH* SK8 .....110 D6
SWIN M27 .....70 D4
Pendlebury St *BOL* BL1 .....36 C1
Pendle CI *OLDE* OL4 .....60 A7
TOT/BURYW BL8 .....38 E1
WCGNW/BIL/O WN5 .....47 G7
Pendle Ct *BOL* BL1 .....36 A1
Pendlecroft Av *SWIN* M27 .....70 F5
Pendlegreen CI *OP/CLY* M11 .....88 C4
Pendle Gv *ROY/SHW* OL2 .....58 F1
Pendle Rd *DTN/ASHW* M34 .....101 J3
GOL/RIS/CU WA3 .....79 M3
Pendleton Gn *SLFD* * M6 .....86 C1
Pendleton Wy *SLFD* M6 .....86 D1
Pendleway *SWIN* M27 .....70 D3
Pendragon PI *FAIL* M35 .....74 D5
Penelope Rd *SLFD* M6 .....71 G7
Penerly Dr *BKLY* M9 .....73 G6
Penfield CI *CMANE* M1 .....7 J8
Penfold Wk *WCGTN/LGST* * M12 .....88 C6
Pengarth Rd *HOR/BR* BL6 .....21 C8
Pengwern Av *BOLS/LL* BL3 .....51 L1
Penhale Ms *BRAM/HZG* SK7 .....121 H5
Penistone Av *BKLY* M9 .....73 K1
MILN OL16 .....11 M7
SLFD M6 .....85 M1
Penketh Av *GTN* M18 .....88 E8
TYLD M29 .....67 L6
Penketh Av *WCGNNW/ST* WN6 .....47 L2
Penleach Av *LEIGH* WN7 .....66 E7
Penmere Gv *SALE* M33 .....108 B3
Penmoor Cha *BRAM/HZG* SK7 .....121 K3
Penmore CI *ROY/SHW* OL2 .....43 M5
Pennant Dr *PWCH* M25 .....55 K7
Pennant St *OLD* OL1 .....59 L4
Pennell St *OP/CLY* M11 .....89 G3
Penn House CI *BRAM/HZG* SK7 .....121 C5
Penn Gn *CHD/CHDH* SK8 .....120 D3
Pennine Av *CHAD* OL9 .....58 D7
WCGNS/IIMK WN3 .....62 F1
Pennine CI *BKLY* M9 .....57 J8
HOR/BR BL6 .....21 C7
TOT/BURYW BL8 .....38 D1
Pennine Dr *STLY* SK15 .....92 A1
WCGNS/IIMK WN3 .....62 F1
Pennine Gv *ALT* WA14 .....107 L2
AUL OL6 .....76 B8
MILN OL16 .....29 K6
WHIT OL12 .....19 K6
LEIGH WN7 .....65 M4
Pennine La *GOL/RIS/CU* WA3 .....79 M3
Pennine Rd *BRAM/HZG* SK7 .....121 K3
GLSP SK13 .....104 D4
HOR/BR BL6 .....21 C7
MPL/ROM SK6 .....101 M6
Pennine Vw *ROY/SHW* OL2 .....43 M4
Pennine Vw *LIT* OL15 .....20 E2
MOSL OL5 .....77 G3
ROY/SHW OL2 .....43 H8
STLY SK15 .....76 F7
Pennington Av *LEIGH* WN7 .....81 H1
Pennington CI *LHULT* M38 .....52 B8
WCGNE/HIN WN2 .....49 H3
Pennington Gdns *LEIGH* WN7 .....81 H1
Pennington Green La
WCGNE/HIN WN2 .....49 G2
Pennington La *WCGNE/HIN* WN2 .....32 B3
WCGNE/HIN WN2 .....48 D4
Pennington Rd *BOLS/LL* BL3 .....52 C1
LEIGH WN7 .....81 J1
Pennington St *CHAD* OL9 .....74 E1
TOT/BURYW BL8 .....24 B8
WALK M28 .....69 H2
WCGNE/HIN WN2 .....49 G6
WCGTN/LGST M12 .....99 K2
Pennon CI *BRO* M7 .....72 B6
Penn St *FWTH* BL4 .....52 F4
HEY OL10 .....41 G3
HOR/BR BL6 .....33 M1
MILN OL16 .....10 F3
NEWH/MOS M40 .....73 J4
OLDS OL8 .....8 E8
Penny Bridge La *URM* M41 .....95 K2
Pennygate CI *WCGNE/HIN* WN2 .....49 G6
Pennyhurst St *WCGNS/IIMK* WN3 .....14 C5
Penny La *RDSH* SK5 .....100 E5
RNFD/HAY WA11 .....78 D5
Penny Meadow *AUL* OL6 .....90 E1
Pennymoor Dr *ALT* WA14 .....107 L6
Penrhos Av *CHD/CHDH* SK8 .....110 C8
Penrhyn Av *CHD/CHDH* SK8 .....120 A3
MDTN M24 .....57 K5
Penrhyn Crs *BRAM/HZG* SK7 .....121 L4
Penrhyn Dr *BRAM/HZG* SK7 .....121 L3
PWCH M25 .....55 L8
Penrhyn Gv *ATH* M46 .....50 F7
Penrhyn Rd *EDGY/DAV* SK3 .....12 C7
Penrice CI *RAD* M26 .....38 A7
Penrice Fold *WALK* M28 .....68 E5
Penrith Av *AULW* OL7 .....75 J7
BOL BL1 .....35 K3
OLDS OL8 .....74 F1
RDSH SK5 .....100 C3
SALE M33 .....108 F2
WALK M28 .....69 J2
WHTF M45 .....55 L5
Penrith CI *PART* M31 .....94 B8
Penrith Crs *AIMK* WN4 .....63 L8
Penrith St *ROCH* OL11 .....10 F9
Penrod PI *SLFD* M6 .....71 L8
Penrose Gdns *MDTN* M24 .....57 L3
Penrose St *BOLE* * BL2 .....3 L4
Penrose Wk *MDTN* M24 .....41 J8
Penroy Av *DID/WITH* M20 .....110 A1
Penruddock Wk
BRUN/LGST * M13 .....88 C8
Penry Av *IRL* M44 .....94 D1
Penryn Av *ROY/SHW* OL2 .....59 J1
SALE M33 .....108 F1
Pensarn Av *RUSH/FAL* M14 .....99 H4
Pensarn Gv *RDSH* SK5 .....100 C8
Pensby CI *SWIN* M27 .....70 F5
Pensford Ct *BOLE* BL2 .....23 H6
Pensford Rd *NTHM/RTH* M23 .....118 B1
Penshaw Av *WCGNS/IIMK* WN3 .....63 J1
Penshurst Rd *RDSH* SK5 .....100 E6
Penson St *WCN* WN1 .....48 A2
Penthorpe Dr *ROY/SHW* OL2 .....59 J1
Pentland Av *NEWH/MOS* M40 .....73 M2
Pentland CI *BRAM/HZG* SK7 .....121 K3
The Pentlands *ROY/SHW* OL2 .....43 J4
Pentlands Av *BRO* M7 .....72 A6
Pentland Ter *BOL* * BL1 .....36 B3
Pentland Wy *HYDE* SK14 .....91 L6
Pentwyn Gv *NTHM/RTH* M23 .....109 L5

Penwortham St
NEWH/MOS M40 .....73 J8
Penzance St *NEWH/MOS* M40 .....88 C1
Penznance St
NEWH/MOS * M40 .....88 B1
Peover Av *SALE* M33 .....97 H8
Peover Rd *WILM/AE* SK9 .....120 A7
Pepler Av *NTHM/RTH* M23 .....109 L2
Pepperhill Rd *OLDTF/WHR* M16 .....87 J2
Pepper La *WCGNNW/ST* WN6 .....30 E2
Pepper Mill La *WGN* WN1 .....15 H6
Peppermint CI *MILN* OL16 .....29 M8
Pepper Rd *BRAM/HZG* SK7 .....121 K2
Pepperwood Dr
WCGNS/IIMK WN3 .....63 H2
Pepys PI *WCGNS/IIMK* WN3 .....47 K8
Perch St *WGN* WN1 .....15 K2
Percival CI *BRO* * M7 .....72 C6
Percival Rd *DROY* M43 .....89 L3
Percival Wy *WCGNE/HIN* WN2 .....49 G8
Percy Dr *ORD* M5 .....86 E5
Percy St *BOL* * BL1 .....36 C2
BURY BL9 .....5 J2
FWTH * BL4 .....53 H5
HULME M15 .....87 G6
MILN OL16 .....11 J9
OLDE OL4 .....59 M5
RAMS * BL0 .....17 B7
STKP SK1 .....13 J3
STLY * SK15 .....91 L3
Peregrine Crs *DROY* M43 .....89 M1
Peregrine Dr *IRL* M44 .....94 D1
LEIGH WN7 .....66 E7
Peregrine Rd *OFTN* SK2 .....113 K8
Peregrine St *HULME* M15 .....87 J7
Perendale Ri *BOL* BL1 .....22 B3
Perivale Dr *OLDS* OL8 .....59 L8
Pernham St *OLDE* OL4 .....59 M5
Perrin St *HYDE* SK14 .....102 A2
Perry Av *HYDE* SK14 .....91 K8
Perry CI *ROCH* OL11 .....10 B9
Perrygate Av *DID/WITH* M20 .....98 D6
Perrymead *PWCH* M25 .....55 L6
Perryn PI *WCGNNW/ST* WN6 .....31 J5
Perry Rd *HALE/TIMP* WA15 .....108 E6
Pershore *WHIT* OL12 .....10 D3
Pershore Rd *MDTN* M24 .....57 K1
Perth Av *CHAD* OL9 .....58 D8
WCGNE/HIN WN2 .....48 D4
Perth CI *BRAM/HZG* SK7 .....121 G2
Perth Rd *ROCH* OL11 .....42 E2
Perth St *BOLS/LL* BL3 .....51 M1
ROY/SHW OL2 .....59 K1
SWIN M27 .....70 A3
Peru St *CSLFD* M3 .....6 A2
Peterborough CI *AUL* OL6 .....75 L6
Peterborough Dr *BOL* BL1 .....22 C1
Peterborough St *GTN* M18 .....89 J6
Peterborough Wk *BOL* BL1 .....2 B1
Peterhead CI *BOL* BL1 .....2 B1
Peterhead Wk *ORD* * M5 .....86 D3
Peterhouse Gdns
MPL/ROM SK6 .....101 M8
Peterloo Ct *SLFD* * M6 .....86 D2
Peter Martin St *HOR/BR* BL6 .....21 B8
Peter Moss Wy *BNG/LEV* M19 .....99 M3
Petersburg Rd *EDGY/DAV* SK3 .....111 M4
Petersfield Dr *NTHM/RTH* M23 .....109 G5
Petersfield Gdns
GOL/RIS/CU WA3 .....81 M3
Petersfield Wk *BOL* BL1 .....2 C1
Peter St *AIMK* WN4 .....78 F1
ALT WA14 .....116 F1
BRAM/HZG SK7 .....121 M1
BURY BL9 .....5 J2
CMANW M2 .....6 E4
DTN/ASHW M34 .....101 K1
ECC M30 .....85 G3
GLSP SK13 .....93 K6
GOL/RIS/CU WA3 .....79 K4
LEIGH WN7 .....66 E8
OLD OL1 .....9 G3
STKP SK1 .....13 C1
TYLD M29 .....67 J3
WCGNE/HIN WN2 .....49 G7
WCGNW/BIL/O WN5 .....46 E4
WHTN BL5 .....49 K5
Peterswood CI
WYTH/NTH M22 .....118 D1
Petheridge Dr *WYTH/NTH* M22 .....118 D3
Petrel Av *POY/DIS* SK12 .....121 J8
Petrel CI *DROY* M43 .....89 M1
EDGY/DAV SK3 .....112 A6
ROCH OL11 .....27 J5
TYLD M29 .....67 K4
Petrie St *WHIT* OL12 .....10 E1
Petrock Wk *NEWH/MOS* M40 .....73 M7
Petticoat La *WCGNE/HIN* WN2 .....48 E5
Petts Crs *LIT* OL15 .....20 E6
Petworth Av *WCGNS/IIMK* WN3 .....63 G2
Petworth CI *WYTH/NTH* M22 .....110 B7
Petworth Rd *CHAD* OL9 .....8 A6
Pevensey Rd *SLFD* M6 .....71 H7
Pevensey Wk *CHAD* OL9 .....8 A7
Peveril Av *NM/HAY* SK22 .....124 E3
Peveril CI *WHTF* M45 .....55 M5
Peveril Crs *CCLSP* SK13 .....105 J4
Peveril Dr *BRAM/HZG* SK7 .....122 A6
Peveril Gdns *POY/DIS* SK12 .....124 C6
Peveril Ms *POY/DIS* SK12 .....124 C6
Peveril Rd *ALT* WA14 .....107 M5
OLD OL1 .....59 M5
ORD M5 .....86 A2
Peveril St *BOLS/LL* BL3 .....51 L1
HYDE SK14 .....102 C4
The Pewfist *WHTN* BL5 .....50 B5
Pewfist Gn *WHTN* BL5 .....50 B5
The Pewfist Spinney *WHTN* BL5 .....50 A5
Pewsey Rd *WYTH/NTH* M22 .....119 H1
Pexwood *OLD* OL1 .....58 B3
Pheasant CI *WALK* M28 .....68 E6
Pheasant Dr *CCHDY* M21 .....98 A5
Pheasant Ri *ALT* WA14 .....116 F3
Phelan CI *NEWH/MOS* M40 .....73 L7
Phethean St *BOLE* BL2 .....3 H4
FWTH BL4 .....52 F3
Philip Av *DTN/ASHW* M34 .....90 A7
Philip CI *WCGNW/BIL/O* WN5 .....47 G7
Philip Dr *SALE* M33 .....108 D3
Philip Howard Rd *GLSP* SK13 .....104 F4
Philips Av *FWTH* BL4 .....53 C5
Philips Dr *WHTF* M45 .....55 G6
Philips Park Rd *OP/CLY* M11 .....88 B2
Philip St *BOLS/LL* BL3 .....2 B9
ECC M30 .....85 G3
OLDE OL4 .....59 M4
ROCH OL11 .....10 F8
Phillimore St *OLDE* OL4 .....60 B7

Phillips Park Rd WHTF M45 55 J6
Phillips St LEIGH WN7 66 B4
Phipps St WALK M28 52 F8
Phoebe St BOLS/LL * BL3 35 M8
ORD M5 86 D4
Phoenix Cl HEY OL10 41 J3
Phoenix St BOL BL1 3 G2
BURY BL9 4 C4
CMANW * M2 7 G4
FWTH BL4 53 G5
LIT OL15 20 C6
OLD OL1 9 J7
WHIT OL12 27 M3
Phoenix Wy RAD M26 54 D2
URM M41 85 H6
Phyllis St MDTN M24 57 M5
WHIT OL12 27 L3
Picadilly WGNW/BIL/O WN5 62 B7
Piccadilly CMANE M1 7 H4
CMANE M1 7 J5
STKP SK1 13 J5
Piccadilly Plaza CMANE M1 7 H5
Piccadilly South CMANE M1 7 J6
Piccard Cl ANC M4 7 L1
Pickering Cl HALE/TIMP WA15 108 D5
RAD * M26 53 K4
TOT/BURYW BL8 24 E7
URM M41 95 L2
Pickford Av BOLS/LL BL3 53 M1
Pickford Ct DUK * SK16 90 F4
Pickford La DUK SK16 90 F4
Pickford Ms DUK * SK16 90 F4
Pickford's Brow STKP SK1 13 J4
Pickford St ANC M4 7 K3
Pickhill La UPML OL3 61 L4
Pickhill Ms UPML OL3 61 L4
Pickley Gdns LEIGH WN7 66 B3
Pickmere Av DID/WITH M20 98 E4
Pickmere Cl DROY M43 89 L3
EDGY/DAV SK3 111 M6
SALE M33 109 J2
Pickmere Gdns CHD/CHDH SK8 111 J7
Pickmere Ms UPML OL3 61 L4
Pickmere Rd WILM/AE SK9 119 M7
Picksley St LEIGH WN7 66 E8
Pickthorn Cl WGNE/HIN WN2 64 E1
Pickup St MILN OL16 11 G5
WGNE/HIN WN2 48 C5
Pickwick Rd POY/DIS SK12 129 H1
Picton Cl CSLFD M3 6 C2
Picton Dr WILM/AE SK9 127 J3
Picton Sq OLDE OL4 9 L7
Picton St AULW OL7 75 K6
CSLFD M3 87 G1
Picton Wk OLDTF/WHR M16 98 C1
Piele Rd RNFD/HAY WA11 78 B5
Pierce St OLD OL1 59 M3
Piercy Av BRO M7 72 A8
Piercy St ANC M4 88 A3
FAIL * M35 74 B5
Pierpoint St NEWLW WA12 79 K5
Piethorne Cl MILN OL16 29 M8
Pigeon St CMANE M1 7 K4
Piggott St FWTH BL4 52 F5
Pigot St WGNW/BIL/O WN5 46 E6
Pike Av ATH M46 66 D2
FAIL M35 74 F6
Pike Fold La BKLY M9 72 F1
Pike Rd BOLS/LL BL3 36 A8
Pike's La GLSP SK13 104 E4
Pike St ROCH OL11 10 F9
Pike View Cl OLDE OL4 59 L7
Pilgrim Dr OP/CLY M11 88 C3
Pilgrims Wy WGNNW/ST WN6 31 K5
Pilkington Dr WHTF M45 55 L2
Pilkington Rd BKLY M9 73 K2
FWTH BL4 53 J6
RAD M26 38 C7
Pilkington St BOLS/LL BL3 2 D8
MDTN M24 57 L3
RAMS BL0 17 B7
WGNE/HIN WN2 49 G6
Pilkington Wy RAD M26 54 D2
Pilling Fld EDGW/EG BL7 22 B3
Pilling St DTN/ASHW M34 101 J1
LEIGH WN7 66 A7
NEWH/MOS M40 73 J7
TOT/BURYW BL8 38 F1
WHIT OL12 10 B2
Pilning St BOLS/LL BL3 36 D8
Pilot St BURY BL9 5 G7
Pilsley Cl WGNW/BIL/O WN5 46 D3
Pilsworth Rd BURY BL9 39 K6
BURY BL9 40 A5
HEY OL10 40 E3
Pilsworth Wy BURY BL9 39 K6
Pimblett Rd RNFD/HAY WA11 78 B5
Pimblett St CSLFD M3 87 J1
GOL/RIS/CU * WA3 79 K5
Pimhole Fold BURY BL9 5 J6
Pimhole Rd BURY BL9 5 J5
Pimlico Cl BRO * M7 72 A6
Pimlott Gv HYDE SK14 91 G7
PWCH M25 71 H2
Pimlott Rd BOL BL1 36 E1
Pimmcroft Wy SALE M33 109 J1
Pine Av WHTF M45 55 J5
Pine Cl DTN/ASHW M34 90 B6
MPL/ROM SK6 114 B8
Pine Gv DTN/ASHW M34 101 K1
DUK SK16 91 J4
ECC M30 70 B8
FWTH BL4 52 E4
GOL/RIS/CU WA3 79 M4
PWCH M25 55 K6
ROY/SHW OL2 43 G6
RUSH/FAL M14 88 B8
SALE M33 96 A6
SWIN M27 70 A5
WALK M28 69 H4
WHTN BL5 50 B5
Pinehurst Rd NEWH/MOS M40 73 H7
Pine Ldg BRAM/HZG * SK7 121 H5
Pine Meadow RAD M26 53 M6
Pine Rd BRAM/HZG SK7 121 H4
DID/WITH M20 98 D8
DUK SK16 91 H4
POY/DIS SK12 129 K1
WGNW/BIL/O WN5 47 H6
The Pines LEIGH WN7 81 J1
Pine St AUL OL6 75 L8
BOL BL1 36 C2
BURY BL9 5 K4
CHAD OL9 58 D4
CMANE M1 7 G5
EDGY/DAV SK3 12 E6
HEY OL10 41 G2
HYDE SK14 91 G7
LIT OL15 20 C6
MDTN M24 57 M5
MILN * OL16 11 J5
MILN OL16 43 L1
MPL/ROM SK6 101 L7
TYLD M29 67 K3
Pine St North BURY BL9 5 K3
Pinetop Cl CCHDY M21 98 A5
Pine Tree Rd OLDS OL8 75 G3
Pinetree St GTN M18 88 F7
Pinevale WGNNW/ST WN6 31 K5
Pine Vw WGNS/IIMK WN3 62 E3
Pineway OLDE OL4 60 C6
Pinewood AIMK WN4 78 D2
ALT WA14 116 C2
CHAD OL9 58 B5
SALE M33 96 A8
Pinewood Cl BOL BL1 36 B2
DUK SK16 90 F3
WGNE/HIN WN2 64 E5
Pinewood Ct ALT WA14 117 G3
SALE M33 97 G7
Pinewood Crs WGNE/HIN WN2 15 M7
WGNW/BIL/O WN5 46 B6
Pinewood Rd CCHDY * M21 97 K5
WILM/AE SK9 127 J4
The Pinewoods MPL/ROM SK6 101 L7
Pinfold GLSP SK13 93 H8
Pinfold Av BKLY M9 73 K2
Pinfold Cl HALE/TIMP WA15 117 M5
WHTN BL5 50 A6
Pinfold Dr CHD/CHDH SK8 120 C3
Pinfold La MANAIR M90 118 B6
MPL/ROM SK6 102 A8
WHTF M45 55 H4
Pinfold Rd WALK M28 68 F3
Pinfold St WGNE/HIN WN2 48 D5
Pingate Dr CHD/CHDH SK8 120 C6
Pingate La CHD/CHDH SK8 120 C6
Pingate La South
CHD/CHDH SK8 120 C6
Pingle La UPML OL3 45 G7
The Pingot IRL M44 94 E1
LEIGH WN7 66 A7
Pingot Av NTHM/RTH M23 109 L2
Pingot La HYDE SK14 103 L3
Pingot Rd NM/HAY SK22 124 F4
WGNW/BIL/O WN5 62 B7
Pingott La GLSP SK13 93 K7
Pink Bank La WGTN/LGST M12 88 D8
Pin Mill Brow WGTN/LGST M12 88 A4
Pinnacle Dr EDGW/EG BL7 22 A2
Pinner Pl BNG/LEV M19 99 K6
Pinners Cl RAMS BL0 17 C5
Pinnington La STRET * M32 97 G3
Pinnington Rd GTN M18 89 G6
Pintail Av EDGY/DAV SK3 112 A6
Pioneer Cl HOR/BR BL6 21 G8
Pioneer Rd SWIN M27 71 G2
Pioneer St HOR/BR BL6 21 C8
LIT OL15 20 C7
OP/CLY M11 88 E1
ROCH OL11 11 G7
Piperhill Av WYTH/NTH M22 110 A3
The Pipers GOL/RIS/CU WA3 80 C4
Pipers Cl ROCH OL11 27 G4
Pipewell Av GTN M18 88 F7
Pipit Cl DTN/ASHW M34 89 M2
Pitchcombe Rd
WYTH/NTH M22 118 D2
Pitcombe Cl BOL BL1 22 A5
Pitfield Gdns NTHM/RTH M23 109 J5
Pitfield La BOLE BL2 37 J1
Pitfield St BOLE BL2 3 J5
Pit La ROY/SHW OL2 43 G3
Pitman Cl OP/CLY M11 88 D4
Pits Farm Av ROCH OL11 27 M5
Pitsford Rd NEWH/MOS M40 73 H7
Pitshouse La WHIT * OL12 27 H2
Pit St CHAD OL9 58 E8
DTN/ASHW M34 101 J1
Pittbrook St WGTN/LGST M12 88 A5
Pitt St EDGY/DAV SK3 12 F7
HEY OL10 40 F2
HYDE SK14 102 A1
OLDE OL4 9 M7
RAD M26 54 B1
WGNS/IIMK WN3 14 E5
WGNS/IIMK * WN3 15 J7
WHIT OL12 10 F2
Pitt St East OLDE OL4 59 L7
Pixmore Av BOL BL1 22 E8
Place Rd ALT WA14 107 M6
Plain Pit St HYDE SK14 90 F7
Plainsfield Cl OLDTF/WHR M16 87 J8
Plane Av WGNW/BIL/O WN5 47 H5
Plane Ct SLFD * M6 86 D2
Plane Rd FAIL M35 74 C7
Plane St OLDE OL4 59 L5
Plane Tree Cl MPL/ROM SK6 114 A7
Plane Tree Gv
RNFD/HAY * WA11 78 D5
Planetree Rd HALE/TIMP WA15 117 J2
Plane Tree Rd PART M31 106 A1
Planet Wy DTN/ASHW M34 90 B7
Plank La LEIGH WN7 65 K8
Plantation Av WALK M28 52 F8
Plantation Gates WGN WN1 48 B2
Plantation St DUK SK16 91 G3
GTN M18 89 H7
Plant Cl SALE M33 96 D7
Plant Hill Rd BKLY M9 56 F7
Plant St CMANE * M1 7 J5
Plant Ter BKLY * M9 57 G7
Plate St OLD OL1 9 K5
Plato St CHAD OL9 8 E5
Platt Av AUL OL6 75 M6
Plattbrook Cl RUSH/FAL M14 98 E3
Platt Cl MILN OL16 29 K7
Platt Cft LEIGH WN7 66 F8
Platt Fold Rd LEIGH WN7 66 D6
Platt Fold St LEIGH WN7 66 D7
Platt Hill Av BOLS/LL BL3 35 K8
Platting La ROCH OL11 28 D8
Platting Rd OLDE OL4 60 F6
Platt La RUSH/FAL M14 98 C3
UPML OL3 61 J2
WGN WN1 15 K3
WGN WN1 31 L1
WGNE/HIN WN2 49 G7
WHTN BL5 50 E6
Platts Dr IRL M44 94 D2
Platt St CHD/CHDH SK8 111 H6
DUK SK16 90 D5
GLSP SK13 93 L7
LEIGH WN7 66 C6
WGNE/HIN WN2 64 D2
Plattwood Wk HULME * M15 87 G6
Playfair Cl HEY OL10 41 H5
Playfair St BOL BL1 22 C6
RUSH/FAL M14 87 L8
Pleachway HTNM SK4 111 J2
Pleasance Wy NEWLW WA12 78 F8
Pleasant Gdns BOL BL1 2 C2
Pleasant Rd ECC M30 85 H3
Pleasant St BKLY M9 73 G5
HEY OL10 26 F8
ROCH OL11 41 M2
TOT/BURYW BL8 24 C8
Pleasant Wy CHD/CHDH SK8 120 E6
Pleasington Dr NEWH/MOS M40 73 M2
TOT/BURYW BL8 38 B2
Plevna St BOLE BL2 3 G4
Plodder La FWTH BL4 52 A4
WHTN BL5 51 K4
Ploughbank Dr CCHDY M21 98 A5
Plough Cl URM M41 94 F3
Plough Flds WALK M28 68 C7
Ploughfields WHTN BL5 50 B1
Plough St DUK SK16 91 G4
Plover Cl ROCH OL11 27 H5
Plover Dr ALT WA14 107 L4
BURY BL9 25 L8
IRL M44 83 K8
Plover Wy GOL/RIS/CU WA3 80 B4
Plowden Av BOLS/LL BL3 51 M1
Plowden Rd WYTH/NTH M22 118 D2
Plowley Cl DID/WITH M20 110 E2
Plucksbridge Rd
MPL/ROM SK6 123 J1
Plumbley Dr OLDTF/WHR M16 97 M1
Plumbley St OP/CLY * M11 89 H5
Plumley Cl EDGY/DAV SK3 112 C7
Plumley Rd WILM/AE SK9 119 M7
Plummer Av CCHDY M21 97 L6
Plumpton Cl ROY/SHW OL2 59 H3
Plumpton Dr BURY BL9 25 H6
Plumpton Rd ROCH OL11 42 E4
Plumpton Wk
BRUN/LGST * M13 88 C8
Plum St OLDS OL8 8 E8
Plum Tree Ct SLFD M6 86 D2
Plunge Rd RAMS BL0 17 E1
Pluto Cl SLFD * M6 71 M8
Plymouth Av BRUN/LGST M13 88 B7
Plymouth Cl AUL OL6 75 M5
Plymouth Dr BRAM/HZG SK7 121 G5
FWTH BL4 52 C4
Plymouth Gv BRUN/LGST M13 88 A7
EDGY/DAV SK3 12 A8
RAD M26 38 A7
WGNNW/ST WN6 31 K5
Plymouth Gv West
BRUN/LGST M13 88 A7
Plymouth Rd SALE M33 96 A7
Plymouth St OLDS OL8 59 J8
Plymouth Vw BRUN/LGST M13 87 M6
Plymtree Cl CHH M8 72 B2
Pochard Dr ALT WA14 107 L5
POY/DIS SK12 121 J8
Pochin St NEWH/MOS M40 88 B1
Pocket Nook La
GOL/RIS/CU WA3 80 D4
Pocket Nook Rd HOR/BR BL6 50 E1
Pocklington Dr
NTHM/RTH M23 109 J5
Podnor La MPL/ROM SK6 115 K6
Podsmead Rd WYTH/NTH M22 118 D2
Poet's Nook LEIGH WN7 66 B8
Poise Brook Dr OFTN SK2 113 J7
Poise Brook Rd OFTN SK2 113 J7
Poise Cl BRAM/HZG SK7 122 C1
Poke St WGNW/BIL/O WN5 46 E6
Poland St ANC M4 7 L2
DTN/ASHW M34 90 B4
Poleacre La MPL/ROM SK6 101 M6
Polebrook Av WGTN/LGST M12 88 A6
Pole Ct BURY * BL9 55 M1
Polefield Ap PWCH M25 55 L6
Polefield Cir PWCH M25 55 L6
Polefield Gdns PWCH M25 55 L6
Polefield Gra PWCH M25 55 L6
Polefield Gv PWCH M25 55 L6
Polefield Hall Rd PWCH M25 55 L6
Polefield Rd BKLY M9 73 G2
PWCH M25 55 L5
Polegate Dr WGNE/HIN WN2 65 M2
Pole La BURY BL9 55 M2
FAIL M35 74 C4
Pole St BOLE BL2 3 J1
WGNNW/ST WN6 31 H3
Polesworth Cl WGTN/LGST M12 88 D6
Police St ALT WA14 108 A7
CMANW M2 6 E4
ECC M30 84 F2
Pollard Ct OLD * OL1 9 G2
Pollard Gv LIT OL15 20 D4
Pollards La BURY BL9 24 F2
Pollard Sq PART M31 106 D1
Pollard St ANC M4 7 M5
Pollard St East NEWH/MOS M40 88 A2
Pollen Cl SALE M33 108 F2
Pollen Rd ALT WA14 107 M6
Polletts Av RDSH SK5 100 F6
Pollit Cft MPL/ROM SK6 113 J3
Pollitt Av AUL OL6 75 M7
Pollitt Cl WGTN/LGST * M12 88 C6
Pollitts Cl ECC M30 84 E2
Polonia Ct OLDS OL8 74 F1
Polperro Cl ROY/SHW OL2 43 K8
Polruan Rd CCHDY M21 97 K2
Polworth Rd BKLY M9 73 H3
The Polygon BRO M7 71 M6
ECC M30 85 K2
Polygon Av BRUN/LGST M13 87 M6
Polygon Rd CHH M8 72 C3
Polygon St BRUN/LGST M13 7 L9
Pomfret St SLFD * M6 70 F7
WGTN/LGST M12 88 D6
Pomona Crs ORD M5 86 E5
Pomona Strd HULME M15 86 D7
Pomona St ROCH OL11 10 F9
Ponds Cl CCHDY * M21 97 L3
Pond St GOL/RIS/CU WA3 80 D4
Pondwater Cl LHULT M38 68 C1
Ponsford Av BKLY M9 73 K1
Ponsonby Rd STRET M32 97 G1
Pontefract Cl SWIN M27 70 B5
Pool Bank St MDTN M24 56 E5
Poolcroft SALE M33 109 J1
Poole Cl BRAM/HZG SK7 120 F3
Pooley Cl MDTN M24 56 E3
Poolfield Cl RAD M26 54 B1
Pool Fold FAIL M35 74 D6
Pool House Rd POY/DIS SK12 122 E7
Poolstock WGNS/IIMK WN3 14 E8
Poolstock La WGNS/IIMK WN3 47 K8
Pool St BOL BL1 2 D4
OLDS OL8 59 J8
WGNE/HIN WN2 49 G8
WGNS/IIMK WN3 14 E8
Pool Ter BOL BL1 35 K2
Poolton Rd BKLY M9 56 E8
Poorfield St OLDS OL8 9 H8
Poplar Av AIMK WN4 63 G7
ALT WA14 108 A6
BNG/LEV M19 99 L5
BOL BL1 22 C8
BOLE BL2 22 F6
BURY BL9 5 L3
HOR/BR BL6 34 B3
NM/HAY SK22 124 F3
OLDE OL4 60 F8
OLDS OL8 75 G2
WGNW/BIL/O WN5 47 G6
WILM/AE SK9 126 C7
Poplar Cl CHD/CHDH SK8 110 E7
Poplar Ct DTN/ASHW * M34 90 C6
EDGY/DAV * SK3 112 C7
Poplar Dr PWCH M25 71 K2
Poplar Gv AUL OL6 75 M7
GTN M18 89 G8
IRL M44 94 A6
OFTN SK2 112 F8
RAMS BL0 17 D5
SALE M33 108 E1
URM M41 96 B2
WGNE/HIN WN2 65 L2
WHTN BL5 50 B4
Poplar Rd BNG/LEV M19 111 G1
DUK SK16 91 J5
ECC M30 70 B8
STRET M32 96 F4
SWIN M27 70 A5
WALK M28 69 H2
The Poplars LEIGH WN7 80 F4
MOSL OL5 77 H3
Poplars Rd STLY SK15 92 A1
Poplar St DTN/ASHW M34 90 C6
FAIL M35 74 A6
GOL/RIS/CU WA3 79 L3
HTNM SK4 111 H2
LEIGH WN7 81 J1
OP/CLY M11 88 B4
TYLD M29 67 K3
Poplar Wk CHAD OL9 8 A3
Poplar Wy MPL/ROM SK6 123 J5
Poplin Dr CSLFD M3 6 D1
Poppy Cl MDTN M24 58 A5
NTHM/RTH M23 109 H3
Poppyfield Vw ROCH OL11 27 H4
Poppythorn La PWCH M25 55 K7
Porchester Dr RAD M26 37 M7
Porchfield Sq CSLFD M3 6 D6
Porlock Av DTN/ASHW M34 89 M4
HYDE SK14 102 F2
Porlock Cl STKP SK1 112 F4
WGNE/HIN WN2 64 D3
Porlock Rd NTHM/RTH M23 109 L6
URM M41 95 L4
Porritt Cl ROCH OL11 27 H6
Porritt St BURY BL9 5 J1
Porritt Wy RAMS BL0 17 C5
Portal Gv DTN/ASHW M34 101 L3
Porter Av NEWLW WA12 78 F7
Porter Dr NEWH/MOS M40 73 M7
Porter St BURY BL9 25 J8
Porters Wood Cl
WGNW/BIL/O * WN5 46 E5
Porthleven Crs TYLD M29 67 M4
Porthleven Dr NTHM/RTH M23 109 H6
Portinscale Cl TOT/BURYW BL8 38 E1
Portland Cl BRAM/HZG SK7 121 K3
WGNE/HIN WN2 64 D3
Portland Crs BRUN/LGST M13 88 A7
Portland Gv HTNM SK4 99 L8
Portland Houses
MPL/ROM * SK6 114 B7
Portland Pl AULW OL7 90 D3
HOR/BR BL6 33 M1
Portland Rd ALT WA14 116 E1
BRUN/LGST M13 99 J1
ECC M30 85 J1
NM/HAY SK22 124 F3
STRET M32 86 B8
SWIN M27 70 D5
WALK M28 52 F7
Portland St BOL BL1 36 B2
BURY BL9 5 H1
CMANE M1 7 G6
MILN OL16 10 F3
NEWLW WA12 78 C8
WGNW/BIL/O WN5 47 H6
Portland St North AUL OL6 90 D1
Portland St South AULW OL7 90 D2
Portloe Rd CHD/CHDH SK8 119 K5
Portman Rd OLDTF/WHR M16 98 B1
Portman St MOSL OL5 76 F3
Portrea Cl EDGY/DAV SK3 112 B7
Portree Cl ECC M30 84 E2
Portrush Rd WYTH/NTH M22 119 G2
Portside Cl WALK M28 68 E7
Portsmouth Cl BRO M7 72 A7
Portsmouth St BRUN/LGST M13 87 L6
Port Soderick Av ORD M5 86 D3
Portstone Cl OLDTF/WHR M16 87 H8
Portstone St OLDTF/WHR * M16 87 H8
Port St CMANE M1 7 J4
OLDS OL8 59 J8
STKP SK1 13 G3
Portugal Rd PWCH M25 71 L2
Portugal St ANC M4 7 M1
AULW OL7 90 C4
BOLE BL2 3 J5
Portugal St East CMANE M1 7 L6
Portville Rd BNG/LEV M19 99 K3
Portway WYTH/NTH M22 118 D2
Portwood Pl RDSH SK5 13 J2
Posnett St EDGY/DAV SK3 12 C6
Postal St CMANE * M1 7 J4
Postbridge Cl BRUN/LGST M13 87 M6
Post Office St ALT WA14 108 A8
Post St GLSP SK13 93 L7
Potato Whf CSLFD M3 6 B7
Pot Hl AUL OL6 75 M8
Pot Hill Sq AUL * OL6 75 M8
Potter Rd GLSP SK13 104 B1
Potters La BKLY M9 73 H5
Potter St BURY BL9 5 J2
RAD M26 39 G8
Pottery La OP/CLY M11 88 D4
Pottery Rd WGNS/IIMK WN3 14 C6
Pottery Ter WGNS/IIMK WN3 14 D6
Pottinger St AULW OL7 90 C4
Pott St SWIN M27 70 C2
Poulton Av BOLE BL2 37 H5
Poulton Dr AIMK * WN4 63 J8
Poulton St OP/CLY M11 89 H5
Poundswick La
WYTH/NTH M22 118 F1
Powell Av HYDE SK14 102 B1
Powell St OLDTF/WHR M16 86 F8
OP/CLY M11 89 G2
TOT/BURYW BL8 38 E3
WGN WN1 15 G2
WGNE/HIN WN2 64 E3
Powicke Dr MPL/ROM SK6 113 J3
Powicke Wk MPL/ROM SK6 113 J3
Powis Rd URM M41 94 F3
Pownall Av BRAM/HZG SK7 121 H6
DID/WITH M20 98 D4
Pownall Rd ALT WA14 116 F1
CHD/CHDH SK8 120 C3
WILM/AE SK9 126 D4
Pownall St BRAM/HZG SK7 121 M1
LEIGH WN7 66 D7
Powys St ATH M46 67 H3
Poynings Dr WYTH/NTH M22 118 E3
Poynt Cha WALK M28 68 E7
Poynter St NEWH/MOS M40 73 M3
Poynton St BURY BL9 5 H7
HULME M15 87 J6
Praed Rd TRPK M17 85 M7
Preece Cl HYDE SK14 91 K8
Preesall Av CHD/CHDH SK8 119 K4
Preesall Cl TOT/BURYW BL8 38 C4
Prefect Pl WGNW/BIL/O WN5 46 F4
Premier Rd CHH M8 72 C8
Premier St OLDTF/WHR M16 87 G8
Prenton St OP/CLY M11 89 H4
Prenton Wy TOT/BURYW BL8 24 C7
Presall St BOLE * BL2 3 L3
Presbyterian Fold
WGNE/HIN WN2 49 G6
Prescot Av ATH M46 51 H8
TYLD M29 67 M3
Prescot Cl BURY BL9 5 H7
Prescot Rd BKLY M9 73 G5
HALE/TIMP WA15 117 H2
Prescott Av GOL/RIS/CU WA3 79 J2
Prescott La WGNW/BIL/O WN5 46 E4
Prescott Rd WILM/AE SK9 126 F3
Prescott St BOLS/LL * BL3 35 M8
GOL/RIS/CU WA3 79 K3
LEIGH WN7 66 C6
MILN OL16 28 F2
WALK M28 68 E1
WGNE/HIN WN2 49 G7
WGNNW/ST WN6 14 C4
Press St OP/CLY M11 89 G5
Presswood Ct SLFD * M6 70 F6
Prestage St BNG/LEV M19 99 L2
OLDTF/WHR M16 87 G8
Prestbury Av HALE/TIMP WA15 108 B6
RUSH/FAL M14 98 C3
WGNS/IIMK WN3 63 H1
Prestbury Cl BURY BL9 5 H7
OFTN SK2 113 G8
Prestbury Dr MPL/ROM SK6 113 H1
OLD OL1 59 G3
Prestbury Rd BOL BL1 22 D7
MCFLDN SK10 131 K6
WILM/AE SK9 127 J7
Prestfield Rd WHTF M45 55 K5
Presto Gdns BOLS/LL * BL3 35 L8
Prestolee Rd BOLS/LL BL3 53 K3
RAD M26 53 M3
Preston Av ECC M30 85 K1
IRL M44 94 C5
Preston Cl ECC * M30 85 K1
Preston Rd BNG/LEV M19 99 K4
Preston St BOLS/LL * BL3 36 E8
GTN M18 88 F6
MDTN M24 57 K4
OLDE OL4 9 L7
WHIT OL12 27 M4
Presto St BOLS/LL BL3 35 L8
FWTH BL4 53 H3
Prestt Gv WGNS/IIMK WN3 14 B8
Prestwich Av LEIGH WN7 66 E7
Prestwich Cl OFTN SK2 112 E5
Prestwich Hills PWCH M25 71 K2
Prestwich Park Rd South
PWCH M25 71 K1
Prestwich St ATH M46 50 E8
DTN/ASHW M34 90 B8
Prestwood Cl BOL BL1 35 M3
Prestwood Dr BOL BL1 36 A3
Prestwood Rd FWTH BL4 52 D3
SLFD M6 70 F8
Pretoria Rd AIMK WN4 63 K8
BOLE BL2 37 H5
OLDS OL8 74 F1
Pretoria St WHIT * OL12 27 M3
Prettywood BURY BL9 40 A2
Price St ANC * M4 88 A3
BURY BL9 5 H7
DUK * SK16 90 F4
FWTH BL4 53 G3
Prichard St STRET M32 97 G2
Prickshaw La WHIT OL12 18 C6
Pridmouth Rd DID/WITH M20 98 F6
Priest Av CHD/CHDH SK8 110 D8
Priest La MCFLDN SK10 131 L3
Priestley Rd WALK M28 69 M4
Priestley Wy ROY/SHW OL2 44 A5
Priestnall Rd HTNM SK4 111 J1
Priestners Wy LEIGH WN7 66 B6
Priest St STKP SK1 13 K9
Priestwood Av OLDE OL4 44 C8
Primrose Av FWTH BL4 52 D3
HYDE SK14 102 A5
MPL/ROM SK6 114 B6
UPML OL3 61 M3
URM * M41 96 A2
WALK M28 68 E2
Primrose Bank ALT WA14 116 E3
OLDS OL8 9 G9
TOT/BURYW BL8 24 B5
WALK M28 68 E2
Primrose Cl BOLE BL2 23 K8
ORD M5 86 C2
Primrose Cottages
ALT * WA14 116 E3
Primrose Crs HYDE SK14 102 A4
Primrose Dr BURY BL9 26 A8
DROY M43 89 M1
Primrose Gv RNFD/HAY WA11 78 B5
WGNW/BIL/O * WN5 47 H5
Primrose Hl GLSP SK13 104 E4
Primrose La GLSP SK13 104 D3
WGNNW/ST WN6 31 G2
Primrose St ANC M4 7 K2
BOL * BL1 22 C8
FWTH BL4 53 H5
LEIGH * WN7 66 A7
OLDS OL8 9 H8
WHIT OL12 10 B3
Primrose St North TYLD M29 67 K3
Primrose Ter GLSP SK13 104 E4
Primrose Vw AIMK WN4 78 E2
Primrose Wk OLDS OL8 9 H8

Primula Dr GOL/RIS/CU WA3 ....80 A4
Primula Rd BOL BL1 ....22 C7
Prince Albert Av BNG/LEV * M19..99 K2
Prince Charlie St OLD OL1 ....59 L4
Princedom St BKLY M9 ....73 H4
Prince Edward Av
  DTN/ASHW M34 ....101 J2
  OLDE OL4 ....59M5
Prince George St OLD OL1 ....59M3
Prince Rd POY/DIS SK12 ....122 F7
Prince's Av BOLS/LL BL3 ....37 L8
  DID/WITH M20 ....98 F8
  IRL M44 ....94 F1
  MPL/ROM SK6 ....113 K1
  TYLD M29 ....67 K6
Princes Ct ECC * M30 ....85 G1
Prince's Dr MPL/ROM SK6 ....114 A5
  SALE M33 ....109 G1
Princes Gdns LEIGH WN7 ....66 F7
Princes Pk WGNNW/ST WN6 ....30 C8
Princes Rd ALT WA14 ....108 A6
  HTNM SK4 ....99 K8
  MPL/ROM SK6 ....113 K1
  SALE M33 ....108 F1
Princess Av AIMK WN4 ....78 F1
  ATH M46 ....50 F7
  CHD/CHDH SK8 ....120 C1
  DTN/ASHW M34 ....101 H1
  FWTH BL4 ....53 J7
  PWCH M25 ....71M2
  RNFD/HAY WA11 ....78 D5
  WHIT OL12 ....19 K8
Princess Cl DUK SK16 ....91 G4
  HEY OL10 ....41 G3
  MOSL OL5 ....77 H4
Princess Dr MDTN M24 ....57 H4
Princess Gv FWTH BL4 ....53 C4
Princess Pde BURY BL9 ....4 F5
  RUSH/FAL M14 ....98 C3
Princess Pkwy WYTH/NTH M22..109M3
Princess Rd AIMK WN4 ....78 E1
  CHAD OL9 ....74 B1
  DID/WITH M20 ....98 A8
  HOR/BR BL6 ....34 C5
  HULME M15 ....87 G6
  MILN OL16 ....29 G5
  PWCH * M25 ....55M8
  ROY/SHW OL2 ....43 K6
  RUSH/FAL M14 ....98 C4
  URM M41 ....95 L2
  WGNNW/ST WN6 ....30 F1
  WILM/AE SK9 ....126 D7
Princess St ALT WA14 ....107M4
  AUL OL6 ....76 A8
  BOL BL1 ....2 F5
  CMANW M2 ....6 F5
  ECC M30 ....84 F2
  FAIL M35 ....74 B5
  GLSP SK13 ....104 E4
  HULME M15 ....87 G6
  HYDE SK14 ....102 B2
  LEIGH * WN7 ....66 D7
  NEWH/MOS M40 ....73 H8
  OLDE OL4 ....60 B6
  OP/CLY M11 ....88 D2
  RAD M26 ....54 B1
  SLFD M6 ....71 K8
  SWIN M27 ....70 D5
  WGNE/HIN WN2 ....49 H5
  WGNS/IIMK WN3 ....14 F6
  WHIT OL12 ....10 E2
Prince's St STKP SK1 ....13 H4
Prince St AIMK WN4 ....63 K7
  BOL BL1 ....2 D2
  HEY OL10 ....41 G2
  MILN OL16 ....11 H9
  OLD OL1 ....9 L5
  RAMS BL0 ....17 C6
Princes Wk BRAM/HZG SK7 ....121 J5
Princethorpe Cl HOR/BR BL6 ....35 G6
Princeton Cl SLFD M6 ....85M1
Prinknash Rd WYTH/NTH M22..118 F5
Printers Fold HYDE SK14 ....93 C7
Printers La BOLE BL2 ....22 F6
Printers Pk HYDE SK14 ....93 H7
Printer St OLD OL1 ....9 J6
  OP/CLY * M11 ....89 G4
Printon Av BKLY M9 ....72 E1
Printshop La ATH M46 ....67 H3
Printworks La BNG/LEV M19 ....99M3
Printworks Rd STLY SK15 ....91 L1
Prior St OLDS OL8 ....59 L8
The Priory BRO M7 ....71M6
Priory Av BRO M7 ....71M6
  CCHDY M21 ....97 L4
  LEIGH WN7 ....66 A3
Priory Cl DUK SK16 ....91 G6
  OLDS OL8 ....75 C1
  SALE M33 ....97 C6
  WGNE/BIL/O WN5 ....46 F7
Priory Crt RDSH SK5 ....100 B4
Priory Gv BRO M7 ....71M6
  CHAD OL9 ....58 D8
Priory La RDSH SK5 ....100 B4
Priory Pl BOLE BL2 ....36 F2
Priory Rd AIMK WN4 ....63 J7
  ALT WA14 ....116 D4
  CHD/CHDH SK8 ....111 K7
  SALE M33 ....97 C2
  SWIN M27 ....70 B3
  WILM/AE SK9 ....126 C4
Priory St ALT WA14 ....116 E4
Pritchard St CMANE * M1 ....7 H7
Privet St OLD OL4 ....60 A3
Proctor Cl WGNW/BIL/O WN5 ....47 H3
Proctor St TOT/BURYW BL8 ....38 F3
Prodesse Ct WGNE/HIN WN2 ....49 G6
Progress Av DTN/ASHW M34 ....90 C6
Progress St AUL OL6 ....90 D1
  BOL BL1 ....36 C3
  ROCH OL11 ....41M3
  WGNE/HIN WN2 ....49 G7
Promenade St HEY OL10 ....41 H2
Propps Hall Dr FAIL M35 ....74 A6
Prospect Av FWTH BL4 ....53 G5
  IRL M44 ....94 B6
Prospect Ct FAIL M35 ....74 A6
  HALE/TIMP WA15 ....117M5
Prospect Pl AUL OL6 ....76 B7
  FWTH BL4 ....52 F5
  HEY OL10 ....41 G1
Prospect Rd AUL OL6 ....76 B7
  CHAD OL9 ....8 C1
  DUK SK16 ....91 C4
  IRL M44 ....94 B6
  WGNNW/ST WN6 ....31 H5
Prospect St BOL BL1 ....36 C3
  HEY OL10 ....41 H4

LIT * OL15 ....20 C6
ROCH OL11 ....28 D8
TYLD M29 ....67 J5
WGNE/HIN WN2 ....49 G7
Prospect Ter TOT/BURYW BL8...4 A3
Prospect V CHD/CHDH SK8....119 K3
Prospect Vw SWIN M27 ....70 D5
Prosser Av ATH M46 ....66 D2
Prout St WGTN/LGST M12 ....99 K1
Providence St ANC M4 ....88 A3
  AUL * OL6 ....75M8
  BOLS/LL BL3 ....2 F8
  DTN/ASHW M34 ....90 C5
Provident Av BNG/LEV M19 ....99M3
Provident St ROY/SHW * OL2 ....43 L5
Provident Wy
  HALE/TIMP WA15 ....108 D5
Provis Rd CCHDY M21 ....97 L5
Prubella Av DTN/ASHW M34 ....90 B7
Pryce Av WGNE/HIN WN2 ....15M5
Pryce St BOL BL1 ....2 B1
Pryme St HULME M15 ....6 C8
Pudding La HYDE SK14 ....102 F1
Puffin Av POY/DIS SK12 ....128 E1
Puffingate Cl STLY SK15 ....77 H5
Pulborough Cl TOT/BURYW BL8 ..24 C5
Pulford Av CCHDY M21 ....98 A8
Pulford Rd SALE M33 ....108 F2
Pullman Cl BNG/LEV M19 ....99 L4
Pullman Dr STRET M32 ....96 C2
Pullman St ROCH OL11 ....10 F9
Pump St WGNE/HIN WN2 ....49 G7
Punch La BOLS/LL BL3 ....51 G2
Punch St BOLS/LL BL3 ....2 B7
The Pungle WHTN BL5 ....52 A7
Purbeck Cl WYTH/NTH M22 ....118 E3
Purbeck Dr HOR/BR BL6 ....34 C4
  TOT/BURYW BL8 ....4 A5
Purbeck Wy TYLD M29 ....67 K5
Purcell Cl BOL BL1 ....36 A3
Purcell St WGTN/LGST M12 ....99 K1
Purdon St BURY BL9 ....25 J6
Purley Av NTHM/RTH M23 ....109 L3
Purple St BOL BL1 ....2 F4
Purslow Cl WGTN/LGST M12 ....88 B3
Putney Cl OLD OL1 ....59 H3
Pye Cl RNFD/HAY WA11 ....78 E4
Pyegrove GLSP SK13 ....105 J3
Pyegrove Rd GLSP SK13 ....105 H3
Pyke St WGN WN1 ....15 J1
Pymgate Dr CHD/CHDH SK8 ....119 J2
Pymgate La CHD/CHDH SK8....119 J2
Pym St ECC M30 ....85 G2
  HEY OL10 ....41 G3
  NEWH/MOS * M40 ....73 J4
Pyramid Ct BRO M7 ....72 A6
Pyrus Cl ECC M30 ....84 C4
Pytha Fold Rd DID/WITH M20 ....99 G7

Q

The Quadrant BKLY M9 ....73 K1
  DROY M43 ....89 J3
  MPL/ROM SK6 ....113 K2
  STKP SK1 ....112 E3
Quail Dr IRL M44 ....94 D1
Quail St OLDE OL4 ....59M7
Quakerfields WHTN BL5 ....50 A5
Quakers Fld TOT/BURYW BL8 ....24 C4
Quakers' Pl WGNNW/ST WN6....31 H3
Quantock Cl HTNM SK4 ....13 C2
Quantock St OLDTF/WHR * M16 ..87 H8
Quarlton Dr TOT/BURYW BL8....23 L1
Quarmby Rd GTN M18 ....89 J8
Quarry Bank Rd WILM/AE SK9 ..126 D1
Quarry Cl GLSP SK13 ....105 C3
Quarry Clough STLY SK15 ....92 A4
Quarry Hts STLY SK15 ....91 J4
Quarry Pl WGN WN1 ....15 K3
Quarry Pond Rd WALK M28 ....68 D1
Quarry Ri MPL/ROM SK6 ....113 L1
  STLY SK15 ....91 J4
Quarry Rd FWTH BL4 ....53 K5
  MPL/ROM SK6 ....113 L2
  NM/HAY SK22 ....124 F5
  NM/HAY SK22 ....125 H1
Quarry St MPL/ROM * SK6 ....101 L7
  RAD M26 ....54 E1
  RAMS BL0 ....17 C6
  STLY SK15 ....91 J3
  WHIT OL12 ....10 D1
Quarry Wk OP/CLY * M11 ....88 C3
The Quays SALO M50 ....86 C5
Quayside LEIGH WN7 ....66 B8
Quayside Dr WALK M28 ....68 E7
Quay St CSLFD M3 ....6 C5
  HEY * OL10 ....41 H4
Quay Vw ORD M5 ....86 D4
Quebec Pl BOLS/LL * BL3 ....35M7
Quebec St BOLS/LL BL3 ....2 A9
  CHAD OL9 ....8 D3
  DTN/ASHW M34 ....90 C5
Queen Alexandra Cl ORD * M5 ..86 F4
Queen Ann Dr WALK M28 ....68 D5
Queenhill Dr HYDE SK14 ....91 J7
Queenhill Rd WYTH/NTH M22 ..110 B3
Queen's Av AIMK WN4 ....63 L8
  ATH M46 ....50 F7
  EDGW/EG BL7 ....22 D5
  GOL/RIS/CU WA3 ....81M5
  MPL/ROM SK6 ....113 K1
  WHIT OL12 ....19 K8
Queensbrook Bol BL1 ....2 C2
Queensbury Cl BOL BL1 ....22 K7
  WILM/AE SK9 ....127 H4
Queensbury Pde
  NEWH/MOS * M40 ....88 B1
Queens Cl HTNM SK4 ....111 K2
  HYDE * SK14 ....102 B5
  WALK M28 ....68 C5
Queens Ct NEWH/MOS M40 ....73 G7
Queens Dr CHD/CHDH SK8 ....120 C1
  GLSP SK13 ....105 J3
  GOL/RIS/CU WA3 ....79M4
  HTNM SK4 ....111 K2
  HYDE SK14 ....102 C5
  NEWLW M12 ....78 F8
  PWCH M25 ....71M2
  ROCH OL11 ....42 A1
Queensferry St
  NEWH/MOS M40 ....73M6
Queens Gdns LEIGH WN7 ....66 F7
Queensgate BOL BL1 ....35 L4
  BRAM/HZG SK7 ....121 G4
Queensgate Dr ROY/SHW OL2 ..42 F6
Queen's Gv WGTN/LGST M12 ....88 D2
Queens Hall Pas WGN * WN1 ....14 F4

Queensland Rd GTN M18 ....88 E7
Queens Pk BOL * BL1 ....2 A5
Queen's Park Rd HEY OL10 ....41 G1
Queen's Rd AIMK WN4 ....78 E1
  AUL OL6 ....76 A7
  BOLS/LL BL3 ....35 L8
  BRAM/HZG SK7 ....122 A1
  CHAD OL9 ....58 D5
  CHD/CHDH SK8 ....111 J8
  CHH M8 ....72 E7
  HALE/TIMP WA15 ....117 G1
  LIT OL15 ....20 C7
  MPL/ROM SK6 ....113 K1
  NEWH/MOS M40 ....73 G7
  OLDS OL8 ....9 L8
  RNFD/HAY WA11 ....78 D5
  SALE M33 ....96 C8
  URM M41 ....96 A3
  WILM/AE SK9 ....126 E6
Queenston Rd DID/WITH M20 ..98 E5
Queen St AUL OL6 ....91 G1
  BOL BL1 ....2 D5
  BURY BL9 ....5 H4
  CHD/CHDH SK8 ....111 H6
  CMANW M2 ....6 E5
  CSLFD M3 ....6 D2
  DTN/ASHW M34 ....90 B8
  DTN/ASHW M34 ....90 C6
  DUK SK16 ....90 E3
  ECC * M30 ....85 J3
  FAIL M35 ....74 B5
  FWTH BL4 ....53 G4
  GLSP SK13 ....93 K8
  GLSP SK13 ....104 E4
  GOL/RIS/CU * WA3 ....79 L4
  HEY OL10 ....41 G2
  HOR/BR BL6 ....33 K1
  HYDE SK14 ....102 B3
  LHULT M38 ....68 E1
  LIT OL15 ....20 C7
  MDTN M24 ....57M4
  MOSL OL5 ....76 F3
  MPL/ROM SK6 ....9 K5
  OLD OL1 ....60 C6
  OLDE OL4 ....60 C6
  RAD M26 ....54 F2
  RAMS BL0 ....17 C6
  ROY/SHW OL2 ....43 C8
  ROY/SHW OL2 ....43 L6
  SLFD M6 ....71 G7
  STKP SK1 ....13M2
  STLY * SK15 ....91 K2
  TOT/BURYW BL8 ....24 D7
  WGNE/HIN WN2 ....49 G6
  WGNE/HIN WN2 ....64 D2
  WGNS/IIMK WN3 ....14 F5
  WGNW/BIL/O WN5 ....46 E6
  WHIT OL12 ....10 E2
  WHTN BL5 ....49 H5
Queen St West DID/WITH M20...98 E5
Queens Vw LIT OL15 ....29 K1
Queensway BNG/LEV M19 ....111 G2
  CHD/CHDH SK8 ....119 L4
  DUK SK16 ....91 J5
  FWTH BL4 ....53 J6
  IRL M44 ....94 C2
  LEIGH WN7 ....67 G7
  MOSL OL5 ....77 C5
  PART M31 ....94 C8
  POY/DIS SK12 ....129 H1
  ROCH OL11 ....28 D8
  ROCH OL11 ....42 A1
  SWIN M27 ....70 D2
  UPML OL3 ....61 L6
  URM M41 ....85 H8
  WALK M28 ....47 L2
  WGN WN1 ....47 L2
  WGNE/HIN WN2 ....49 H5
  WGNNW/ST WN6 ....30 D4
Queen Victoria St ECC M30 ....84 F2
  ROCH OL11 ....42 D1
Quenby St HULME M15 ....87 G6
Quendon Av BRO M7 ....72 B8
Quick Edge La OLDE OL4 ....60 E8
Quickedge Rd MOSL OL5 ....76 F2
Quick Rd OLDE OL4 ....60 F8
Quick Vw MOSL OL5 ....77 H1
Quill Ct IRL M44 ....94 B6
Quilter Gv BKLY M9 ....72 F2
Quinney Crs OLDTF/WHR M16 ..98 C1
Quinn St OP/CLY M11 ....88 D3
Quinton Wk BRUN/LGST M13...87 L6
Quixall St OP/CLY M11 ....88 D2

R

Radnormere Dr
  CHD/CHDH SK8 ....111 J8
Radnor Cl CHAD OL9 ....8 C8
  GTN M18 ....88 F8
  HULME M15 ....87 J7
  STRET M32 ....97 G2
Radstock Cl BOL BL1 ....22 B5
  RUSH/FAL M14 ....98 E3
Radstock Rd STRET M32 ....96 F2
Radway TYLD M29 ....67M3
Raeburn Dr MPL/ROM SK6 ....114 E4
Rae St EDGY/DAV SK3 ....12 D6
Raglan Av SWIN M27 ....70 E2
  WHTF M45 ....55 L5
Raglan Dr ALT WA14 ....108 B4
Raglan Rd SALE M33 ....108 C1
  STRET M32 ....96 F1
Raglan St BOL BL1 ....36 A2
  HYDE SK14 ....101M2
  ROCH OL11 ....41M3
Raglan Wk HULME * M15 ....87 J6
Ragley Cl POY/DIS SK12 ....122 B8
Raikes La BOLS/LL BL3 ....36 E8
Raikes Rd BOLS/LL BL3 ....37 G7
Railton Av OLDTF/WHR M16 ....98 A1
Railton Ter BKLY * M9 ....73 J5
Railway Ap ROCH OL11 ....41M2
Railway Brow ROCH OL11 ....41M3
Railway Rd CHAD OL9 ....8 E7
  CHAD OL9 ....74 D2
  EDGY/DAV SK3 ....13 H6
  GOL/RIS/CU * WA3 ....79 L4
  LEIGH WN7 ....66 B7
  STRET M32 ....86 C7
  URM M41 ....96 A2
Railway St ALT WA14 ....108 A8
  ATH M46 ....50 E8
  BURY BL9 ....24 E2
  DUK SK16 ....90 E4
  FWTH BL4 ....53 H3
  GLSP SK13 ....93 K8
  GTN M18 ....88 F6
  HEY OL10 ....41 H5
  HTNM SK4 ....12 F4
  LIT OL15 ....20 C7
  MILN OL16 ....11 C6
  MILN OL16 ....29M8
  RAD M26 ....54 D2
  RAMS BL0 ....17 C6
  WGNE/HIN WN2 ....49 H5
  WGNNW/ST WN6 ....14 B2
Railway Ter TOT/BURYW BL8 ....4 A6
Railway Vw OLDE OL4 ....60 C6
  ROY/SHW * OL2 ....43M4
Raimond St BOL BL1 ....35M1
Rainbow Cl CCHDY M21 ....97 L5
Rainbow Dr ATH M46 ....51 C8
Raincliff Av BRUN/LGST M13 ....99 J2
Raines Crest MILN OL16 ....29 K6
Rainford Av DID/WITH M20 ....98 D4
  HALE/TIMP WA15 ....108 D7
Rainford Rd WGNW/BIL/O WN5 ..62 A7
Rainford St BOLE BL2 ....22 F6
Rainforth St BRUN/LGST M13 ..99 J1
Rainham Dr BOL BL1 ....2 D1
  CHH M8 ....72 D5
Rainham Wy CHAD * OL9 ....8 B7
  RDSH SK5 ....100 E6
Rainow Av DROY M43 ....89 H4
Rainow Dr POY/DIS SK12 ....129 L2
Rainow Rd EDGY/DAV * SK3 ....111M6
Rainshaw St BOL BL1 ....22 C8
  OLDE * OL4 ....60 A4
Rainsough Av PWCH M25 ....71 J3
Rainsough Brow PWCH M25 ....71 J3
Rainsough Cl PWCH M25 ....71 K3
Rainwood CHAD OL9 ....58 B4
Raithby Dr WGNS/IIMK WN3 ....63 K1
Raja Cl CHH M8 ....72 E5
Rake ROCH OL11 ....27 C5
Rake La SWIN M27 ....70 C1
Rake St BURY BL9 ....25 J8
Rake Ter LIT OL15 ....20 D6
Rakewood Dr OLDE OL4 ....44 B8
Rakewood Rd LIT OL15 ....29 L1
Raleigh Cl DID/WITH M20 ....98 D7
  OLD OL1 ....9 J2
Raleigh Gdns LIT OL15 ....20 D3
Raleigh St RDSH SK5 ....100 B8
  STRET M32 ....97 G2
Ralli Cts CSLFD M3 ....6 C4
Ralph Av HYDE SK14 ....102 B5
Ralph Green St CHAD OL9 ....74 E1
Ralph St BOL BL1 ....35 H1
  OP/CLY M11 ....89 G3
  WHIT OL11 ....11 G1
Ralston Cl BRO M7 ....72 C4
Ralstone Av OLDS OL8 ....59 J8
Ramage Wk WGTN/LGST M12...88 B3
Ramillies Av CHD/CHDH SK8....120 D3
Rampit Cl RNFD/HAY WA11 ....78 C5
Ramp Rd East MANAIR M90 ..118 E5
Ramp Rd South MANAIR M90...118 D5
Ramp Rd West MANAIR M90 ..118 D5
Ramsay Av FWTH BL4 ....52 E5
Ramsay Pl MILN OL16 ....11 C3
Ramsay St BOL BL1 ....22 B8
  MILN OL16 ....11 C3
Ramsay Ter MILN * OL16 ....11 C3
Ramsbottom La RAMS BL0 ....17 C5
Ramsbottom Rd BOLE BL2 ....23 J2
  HOR/BR BL6 ....33 L1
Ramsbury Dr NEWH/MOS M40 ..74 A2
Ramsdale Rd BRAM/HZG SK7...121 G4
Ramsdale St CHAD OL9 ....58 D5
Ramsden Cl GLSP SK13 ....104 F2
  OLD OL1 ....9 G4
  WGNS/IIMK WN3 ....14 B9
Ramsden Crs OLD OL1 ....9 G4
Ramsden Rd WHIT OL12 ....19 K5
Ramsden St AUL OL6 ....75 L8
  BOLS/LL BL3 ....37 G7
  OLD OL1 ....9 C4
Ramsey Av BNG/LEV M19 ....100 A3
Ramsey Cl AIMK WN4 ....63 J7
  ATH M46 ....67 H2
Ramsey Gv TOT/BURYW BL8 ....38 E2
Ramsey St CHAD OL9 ....8 A9
  LEIGH * WN7 ....66 D8
  NEWH/MOS M40 ....73 L5
Ramsgate Rd NEWH/MOS M40 ..73M8
  RDSH SK5 ....100 C5
Ramsgate St BRO M7 ....72 B7
Ramsgill Cl NTHM/RTH M23 ..109 H3
Ramsgreave Cl BURY BL9 ....39 C5
Ram St LHULT M38 ....52 C8

Ramwell Gdns BOLS/LL BL3 ....2 A8
Ramwells Brow EDCW/EG BL7 ..22 C4
Ramwells Ct EDGW/EG * BL7 ....22 C4
Ramwells Ms EDGW/EG * BL7 ..22 C4
Ranby Av BKLY M9 ....57 J8
Randale Dr BURY BL9 ....55 K2
Randall Av WGNNW/ST WN6 ....30 D7
Randal St BOLS/LL BL3 ....35M8
Randerson St WGTN/LGST * M12..7 L8
Randlesham St PWCH M25 ....55M8
Randolph Pl EDGY/DAV SK3 ....13 H8
Randolph Rd FWTH BL4 ....53 J5
Randolph St BNG/LEV M19 ....99 K2
  BOLS/LL BL3 ....35M6
  OLDS OL8 ....74 F2
Rands Clough Dr WALK M28 ....68 E6
Rand St OLD OL1 ....60 A3
Ranelagh Rd SWIN M27 ....70 E5
Ranelagh St OP/CLY M11 ....88 E2
Raneley Gv ROCH OL11 ....42 D5
Ranford Rd BNG/LEV M19 ....99 K4
Range Dr MPL/ROM SK6 ....101M6
Range La UPML OL3 ....45 G3
Rangemore Av
  WYTH/NTH * M22 ....110 A3
Range Rd DUK SK16 ....91 L6
  EDGY/DAV SK3 ....13 H9
  OLDTF/WHR M16 ....98 B1
  STLY SK15 ....91 L4
Range St BOLS/LL BL3 ....36 A8
  OP/CLY M11 ....88 F4
Ranicar Steet WGNE/HIN WN2...65M1
Rankine Ter BOLS/LL * BL3 ....2 B8
Ranmore Av AIMK WN4 ....63 C8
Rannoch Rd BOLE BL2 ....37 J5
Ransfield Rd CCHDY M21 ....97 K2
Ranulph Ct SLFD * M6 ....71 C7
Ranworth Av HTNM SK4 ....111 J2
  BURY BL9 ....22 D6
Ranworth Dr GOL/RIS/CU WA3 ..80 B5
Raper St OLDE OL4 ....59M4
Raphael St BOL BL1 ....35M2
Rappax Rd HALE/TIMP WA15...117 J4
Rasbottom St BOLS/LL BL3 ....2 B7
Raspberry La IRL M44 ....83 J8
Rassbottom Brow STLY * SK15 ..91 J2
Rassbottom St STLY SK15 ....91 J2
Rassey Cl WGNNW/ST WN6 ....31 K5
Ratcliffe Av IRL M44 ....94 D2
Ratcliffe Rd WGNE/HIN WN2 ....32 F6
Ratcliffe St BNG/LEV M19 ....99 L3
  LEIGH WN7 ....66 C6
  STKP SK1 ....13 J7
  TYLD M29 ....67 L3
  WGNNW/ST WN6 ....14 B2
Rathan Rd URM M41 ....84 F8
Rathbone St MILN OL16 ....11 L5
Rathbourne Av BKLY M9 ....73 G1
Rathen Av WGNE/HIN WN2 ....48 D3
Rathen Rd DID/WITH M20 ....98 E7
Rathmel Rd NTHM/RTH M23 ..109 J2
Rathmore Av NEWH/MOS M40 ..73 H7
Rathvale Dr WYTH/NTH M22 ..118 E4
Rathybank Cl BOL BL1 ....35 L2
Rattenbury Ct SLFD M6 ....70 F7
Raveden Cl BOL BL1 ....35M1
Raveley Av RUSH/FAL M14 ....99 G4
Ravelston Dr BKLY M9 ....73 G6
Raven Av CHAD OL9 ....58 D7
Raven Cl DROY M43 ....89M1
Ravendale Cl WHIT OL12 ....27 K3
Raven Dr IRL M44 ....94 D1
Ravenfield Gv BOL * BL1 ....2 B2
Ravenhead Cl RUSH/FAL M14 ..99 C4
Ravenhead Sq STLY SK15 ....77 H7
Ravenhurst Dr BOL BL1 ....35 G5
Ravenna Av NTHM/RTH M23 ..109 C5
Ravenoak Dr FAIL M35 ....74 D4
Ravenoak Park Rd
  CHD/CHDH SK8 ....120 C8
Ravenoak Rd CHD/CHDH SK8 ..120 C5
  EDGY/DAV SK3 ....112 D8
Raven Rd BOLS/LL * BL3 ....35 K8
  HALE/TIMP WA15 ....108 C3
Ravensbury St OP/CLY M11 ....88 F2
Ravenscar Crs WYTH/NTH M22..118 F4
Ravens Cl PWCH M25 ....72 B2
Ravenscraig Rd LHULT M38 ....52 E6
Ravensdale Gdns ECC M30 ....85 H1
Ravensdale Rd BOL BL1 ....35 C5
Ravensdale St RUSH/FAL M14 ..98 F1
Ravens Holme BOL BL1 ....35 H5
Ravenside Pk CHAD OL9 ....58 D7
Ravenstonedale Dr
  ROY/SHW OL2 ....43 H7
Ravenstone Dr SALE M33 ....97 H7
  UPML OL3 ....61M1
Raven St BURY BL9 ....5 C7
  ROCH OL11 ....27 C3
  WGTN/LGST M12 ....7M7
Ravensway PWCH M25 ....72 A2
Ravenswood BOL BL1 ....35 H5
Ravenswood Av HTNM SK4 ....111 K3
  WGNS/IIMK WN3 ....63 C1
Ravenswood Dr BKLY M9 ....73 H1
  BOL BL1 ....35 H5
  CHD/CHDH SK8 ....120 D4
  WGNE/HIN WN2 ....49 H6
Ravenswood Rd STRET M32 ....86 C7
  WILM/AE SK9 ....126 D8
Raven Wy SLFD M6 ....86 C1
Ravenwood CHAD OL9 ....58 A5
Ravenwood Dr DTN/ASHW M34 ..90 B6
  HALE/TIMP WA15 ....117M5
Ravine Av BKLY M9 ....73 H5
Rawcliffe Av BOLE BL2 ....37 J5
Rawcliffe St RUSH/FAL M14 ....98 E1
Rawdon Cl BNG/LEV M19 ....99 L3
Rawkin Cl HULME M15 ....87 H7
Rawlinson St HOR/BR BL6 ....21 D7
Rawlyn Rd BOL BL1 ....35 J3
Rawpool Gdns NTHM/RTH M23..109 H3
Rawson Av FWTH BL4 ....53 H3
Rawson Rd BOL BL1 ....35M4
Rawsons Rake TOT/BURYW BL8 ..17 A6
Rawson St FWTH BL4 ....53 G3
Rawsthorne Av RAMS BL0 ....17 G6
Rawsthorne St BOL BL1 ....36 B2
  TYLD M29 ....68 A4
Rawstron St WHIT OL12 ....18 C5
Rayburn Wy CHH M8 ....72 C7
Raycroft Av BKLY M9 ....73 K2
Raydale Cl GOL/RIS/CU WA3 ....80 A4
Rayden Crs WHTN BL5 ....50 B5
Raydon Av NEWH/MOS * M40 ..73 G7
Rayleigh Av OP/CLY M11 ....89 J5
Raymond Av BURY BL9 ....25 J7
  CHAD OL9 ....58 C8

Raymond Rd NTHM/RTH M23 .....109 L2
Raymond St SWIN M27 .....70 C3
Rayner Av WGNE/HIN WN2 .....65 H1
Rayner La AULW M28 .....90 B2
Rayners Cl STLY SK15 .....91 J3
Rayner St STKP SK1 .....112 E4
Raynham Av DID/WITH M20 .....110 E1
Raynham St AUL OL6 .....90 F1
Rayson Hill Dr BKLY * M9 .....72 F2
Rayson St BKLY M9 .....72 F2
Reabrook Av WGTN/LGST M12 .....88 C2
The Reach WALK M28 .....69 H2
Read Cl BURY BL9 .....39 C5
Reade Av URM M41 .....95 H3
Reading Cl OP/CLY M11 .....88 F4
Reading Dr SALE M33 .....96 A8
Reading St SLFD M6 .....71 L7
Readitt Wk OP/CLY M11 .....88 E2
Read St HYDE SK14 .....101 M1
Read St West HYDE SK14 .....101 M1
Reaney Wk WGTN/LGST * M12 .....88 C6
Reather Wk NEWH/MOS M40 .....87 M1
Rebecca St CHH M8 .....72 D4
Recreation Av AIMK WN4 .....64 A8
Recreation Dr
  WGNW/BIL/O * WN5 .....62 B7
Recreation Rd FAIL M35 .....74 D3
Recreation St BOLE BL2 .....23 H7
  BOLS/LL BL3 .....36 B8
  PWCH M25 .....55 M8
Rectory Av CHH M8 .....72 D3
  GOL/RIS/CU WA3 .....79 M4
  PWCH M25 .....55 L8
Rectory Cl DTN/ASHW M34 .....101 K2
  RAD M26 .....39 C8
Rectory Flds STKP SK1 .....13 L4
  WHTN BL5 .....50 B8
Rectory Gdns PWCH M25 .....55 L8
  STKP SK1 .....13 L4
Rectory Gn PWCH M25 .....55 K8
Rectory Gv PWCH M25 .....71 L1
Rectory Hl BURY BL9 .....26 A8
Rectory La BURY BL9 .....26 A8
  PWCH M25 .....55 K8
  RAD M26 .....54 F1
  WGNNW/ST WN6 .....31 J3
Rectory Rd AIMK WN4 .....63 G7
  CHH M8 .....72 C5
Rectory St MDTN M24 .....57 J3
Redacre POY/DIS SK12 .....122 B6
Redacre Rd GTN M18 .....89 H7
Red Bank ANC M4 .....87 K1
Red Bank Rd RAD M26 .....38 C7
Redbarn Cl MPL/ROM SK6 .....101 J8
Redbourne Dr URM M41 .....84 C8
Redbrick Ct AULW OL7 .....90 D3
Redbrook Av NEWH/MOS M40 .....73 H7
Redbrook Cl FWTH * BL4 .....53 H3
Redbrook Rd HALE/TIMP WA15 .....106 C3
  PART M31 .....106 B2
  WGNS/IIMK WN3 .....15 K7
Red Brook St ROCH OL11 .....10 B4
Redbrook Wy MCFLDN SK10 .....129 G7
Redburn Cl WGNS/IIMK WN3 .....14 E8
Redburn Rd NTHM/RTH M23 .....109 L5
Redby St OP/CLY * M11 .....88 E5
Redcar Av DID/WITH M20 .....98 E6
  URM M41 .....84 D8
Redcar Cl BRAM/HZG SK7 .....122 C3
  OLD OL1 .....59 J3
Redcar Rd BOLS/LL BL3 .....53 K1
  SWIN M27 .....70 F5
Redcar St WHIT OL12 .....10 D2
Redclyffe Av RUSH/FAL M14 .....98 F1
Redclyffe Rd DID/WITH M20 .....98 D7
  URM M41 .....85 G4
Redcot BOL * BL1 .....35 L5
Redcote St NEWH/MOS M40 .....73 K4
Redcourt Av DID/WITH M20 .....98 E8
Redcroft Gdns BNG/LEV M19 .....99 H8
Redcroft Rd SALE M33 .....96 B6
Redcross St WHIT OL12 .....10 E1
Redcross St North WHIT OL12 .....10 D1
Reddaway Cl SLFD M6 .....71 K7
Reddish Cl BOLE BL2 .....23 H6
Reddish La GTN M18 .....100 B3
Reddish Rd RDSH SK5 .....100 C6
Reddish Vale Rd RDSH SK5 .....100 D5
Reddyshore Brow LIT OL15 .....20 E4
Redesmere Cl DROY M43 .....89 L3
  HALE/TIMP WA15 .....109 G6
  WILM/AE SK9 .....130 C3
Redesmere Pk URM M41 .....95 L4
Redesmere Rd WILM/AE SK9 .....119 M7
Redfearn Wd WHIT OL12 .....27 L2
Redfern Av SALE M33 .....109 H1
Redfern Cl GLSP SK13 .....93 K6
Redfern St ANC M4 .....7 G3
Redfern Wy ROCH OL11 .....27 G3
Redfield Cl OP/CLY M11 .....88 C2
Redford Cl LEIGH WN7 .....66 D7
Redford Dr BRAM/HZG SK7 .....121 J2
Redford St CHH M8 .....56 C8
Redford St TOT/BURYW BL8 .....38 F1
Redgate GLSP SK13 .....93 M8
  HYDE SK14 .....102 A3
Redgate La WGTN/LGST M12 .....88 D7
Redgate Rd AIMK WN4 .....63 G6
Redgates Wk CCHDY * M21 .....97 L3
Redgrave Pas OLDE OL4 .....60 A4
Redgrave Ri OLDE OL4 .....60 A4
Redgrave St OLDE OL4 .....60 A4
Red Hall St OLDE OL4 .....59 M6
Redhill Gv BOL BL1 .....2 C1
Redhill St ANC M4 .....7 K4
Red Hill Wy WGNE/HIN * WN2 .....49 G6
Red House La ALT WA14 .....106 F4
Red House La MPL/ROM SK6 .....101 J8
  POY/DIS SK12 .....124 A6
Redington Cl WALK M28 .....68 D7
Redisher Cft TOT/BURYW BL8 .....24 C1
Redisher La TOT/BURYW BL8 .....24 B1
Redland Av RDSH SK5 .....100 C7
Redland Cl LIT OL15 .....20 C6
Redland Ct WGNE/HIN WN2 .....64 B5
Redland Crs CCHDY M21 .....97 L6
Red La BOLE BL2 .....37 H3
  POY/DIS SK12 .....123 K7
  WHIT OL12 .....28 E2
Red Lion St ANC * M4 .....7 H3
Redmain Gv GOL/RIS/CU WA3 .....80 B4
Redmayne Cl NEWH/MOS M40 .....73 J4
Redmere Dr BURY BL9 .....5 J9
Redmere Gv RUSH/FAL M14 .....98 F4
Redmire Ms DUK SK16 .....91 J3
Redmond Cl DTN/ASHW M34 .....90 B5
Redmoor La NM/HAY SK22 .....124 D8

POY/DIS SK12 .....124 C8
Redmoor Sq CMANE * M1 .....7 K8
Rednal Wk WGNS/IIMK WN3 .....14 D8
Red Pike Wk OLD OL1 .....9 L2
Redpol Av LEIGH WN7 .....66 E6
Redpoll Cl WALK M28 .....68 E5
Red Rock La RAD M26 .....54 A6
  WGNE/HIN WN2 .....32 A4
Red Rose Crs BNG/LEV M19 .....99 M5
Redruth St RUSH/FAL M14 .....98 E2
Redshank Gv LEIGH WN7 .....66 D6
Redshank Cl RUSH/FAL M14 .....99 G3
Redshaw Cl RUSH/FAL M14 .....99 G3
Redstart Cl GOL/RIS/CU WA3 .....80 B4
Redstart Gv WALK M28 .....69 G4
Redstock Cl WHTN BL5 .....50 D3
Redstone Rd BNG/LEV M19 .....111 C1
Red St ATH M46 .....67 H1
Redthorn Av BNG/LEV M19 .....99 J5
Redvale Rd BRO M7 .....72 B6
Redvales Rd BURY BL9 .....39 H5
Redvers St OLD OL1 .....88 F3
  OP/CLY M11 .....88 B4
Redwater Cl WALK M28 .....68 D6
Red Waters LEIGH WN7 .....66 D6
Redwing Rd TOT/BURYW BL8 .....24 C2
Redwood CHAD OL9 .....58 A5
  SALE M33 .....95 M4
  WGNNW/ST WN6 .....30 E6
  WHTN BL5 .....50 A6
Redwood Av WGNNW/ST WN6 .....47 J1
Redwood Cl WHIT OL12 .....27 L1
Redwood Dr CHH M8 .....72 E7
  DTN/ASHW M34 .....90 B6
  MPL/ROM SK6 .....113 J1
Redwood La OLDE OL4 .....60 B5
Redwood Park Gv MILN OL16 .....29 C5
Redwood Rd UPML OL3 .....61 M5
Redwood St SLFD M6 .....71 K8
Reedbank Rd RAD M26 .....54 D4
Reed Ct OLD OL1 .....9 G2
Reed Crs WGNS/IIMK WN3 .....47 K8
Reedham Cl BOL BL1 .....35 M4
Reedham Ct WALK * OL9 .....58 F8
  NEWH/MOS * M40 .....73 G8
Reed Hl MILN OL16 .....10 E3
Reedley Dr WALK M28 .....68 F4
Reedmace Cl WALK M28 .....69 H3
Reedshaw Bank OFTN SK2 .....113 G7
Reedshaw Rd BKLY M9 .....72 F6
Reedsmere Cl
  WGNW/BIL/O WN5 .....47 J6
Reed St GTN M18 .....89 G6
  OLD * OL1 .....9 L5
Reeman Cl MPL/ROM SK6 .....101 K8
Reepham Cl WGNS/IIMK WN5 .....63 G1
Rees St OFTN SK2 .....113 J7
Reeves Rd CCHDY M21 .....97 L5
Reeves St GOL/RIS/CU WA3 .....80 E4
Reeve St GOL/RIS/CU WA3 .....80 E4
Reevey Av BRAM/HZG SK7 .....121 L2
Reform Cl OP/CLY M11 .....10 E2
Reform Wk OP/CLY M11 .....88 E4
Refuge St ROY/SHW OL2 .....43 L6
Regaby Gv WGNE/HIN WN2 .....49 K7
Regal Cl WHTF M45 .....55 L4
Regan Av CCHDY M21 .....98 A5
Regan St BOL BL1 .....36 A1
  RAD M26 .....54 E2
Regatta Cl CHAD OL9 .....74 D1
Regatta St SLFD M6 .....71 J6
Regency Cl GLSP SK13 .....105 G3
  NEWH/MOS M40 .....73 G7
  OLDS OL8 .....59 G8
Regency Ct HALE/TIMP * WA15 .....117 K3
  ROCH OL11 .....27 J3
  WGN WN1 .....14 A5
Regency Gdns CHD/CHDH SK8 .....120 A4
Regency Ldg PWCH * M25 .....71 K1
Regency Pk WILM/AE SK9 .....126 D7
Regent Av AIMK WN4 .....63 J7
  LHULT M38 .....52 F8
  RUSH/FAL M14 .....98 C2
Regent Cl BRAM/HZG SK7 .....120 F8
  CHD/CHDH SK8 .....111 M8
  WILM/AE SK9 .....126 D7
Regent Ct HTNM SK4 .....99 M7
Regent Crs FAIL M35 .....74 B6
  ROY/SHW OL2 .....59 G2
Regent Dr DTN/ASHW M34 .....101 C3
  HOR/BR BL6 .....34 E5
  LEIGH WN7 .....67 G5
Regent Pl RUSH/FAL M14 .....87 M8
Regent Rd ALT WA14 .....108 A8
  HOR/BR BL6 .....34 E6
  OFTN SK2 .....112 D6
  ORD M5 .....86 E4
  RAD M26 .....64 D1
Regent Sq ORD M5 .....86 A4
Regent St ATH M46 .....67 H2
  BURY BL9 .....4 F1
  ECC M30 .....85 K2
  GLSP SK13 .....105 C3
  HEY OL10 .....40 E3
  LIT OL15 .....20 C7
  MDTN M24 .....57 J2
  NEWH/MOS M40 .....74 A7
  OLD OL1 .....9 L5
  RAMS BL0 .....17 A7
  WGNE/HIN WN2 .....49 G7
  WHTN BL5 .....49 G7
  WILM/AE SK9 .....28 C3
Regent Wk FWTH * BL4 .....53 G4
Regina Av STLY SK15 .....91 K2
Regina Crs LEIGH WN7 .....67 H6
Reginald St BOLS/LL * BL3 .....51 K2
  ECC M30 .....84 D4
  OP/CLY M11 .....89 J5
  SWIN M27 .....70 A3
Reid Cl DTN/ASHW M34 .....101 K4
Reigate Cl TOT/BURYW BL8 .....38 E3
Reigate Rd URM M41 .....95 H4
Reilly St HULME M15 .....87 J6
Reins Lee Av OLDS OL8 .....75 K2
Reins Lee Rd AULW OL7 .....75 K2
Reliance St NEWH/MOS M40 .....73 M6
Rembrandt Wk OLD OL1 .....44 A7
Rena Cl HTNM SK4 .....12 E1
Renald St ETRET M32 .....97 G2
Renfrew Cl WGNS/IIMK WN3 .....63 K1
Renfrew Dr BOLS/LL BL3 .....51 J1
Renfrew Rd WGNE/HIN WN2 .....33 G2
Rennie Cl STRET M32 .....96 F2
Renshaw Av ECC M30 .....85 C3
Renshaw Dr BURY BL9 .....5 M2
Renshaw St ECC M30 .....85 C3

Renton Rd BOLS/LL BL3 .....51 L1
  STRET M32 .....97 H2
  WYTH/NTH M22 .....110 A8
Renwick Sq AIMK WN4 .....78 C1
Repton Av DROY M43 .....89 G1
  DTN/ASHW M34 .....100 D1
  HYDE SK14 .....102 B1
  NEWH/MOS M40 .....74 B3
  OLDS OL8 .....75 G1
  URM M41 .....95 G2
Reservoir Rd EDGY/DAV SK3 .....12 F9
Reservoir St CSLFD M3 .....6 D1
  MILN OL16 .....11 L2
  SLFD M6 .....86 C2
  WGNE/HIN WN2 .....48 D4
  WGNNW/ST WN6 .....48 D4
Restormel Av WGNE/HIN WN2 .....33 G7
Retford Av MILN OL16 .....28 E8
Retford Cl TOT/BURYW BL8 .....25 H7
Retford St OLDE * OL8 .....59 L7
Retiro St OLD OL1 .....9 K5
The Retreat MPL/ROM SK6 .....113 L3
Reuben St HTNM SK4 .....100 B8
Revers St TOT/BURYW BL8 .....4 B3
Reveton Gn BRAM/HZG SK7 .....121 J2
Reynard Av CCHDY M21 .....97 L5
Reynard St HYDE * SK14 .....102 A1
Reynell Rd BRUN/LGST M13 .....99 J2
Reyner St AUL OL6 .....91 H2
  CMANE M1 .....7 G6
Reynolds Cl WHTN BL5 .....51 J6
Reynolds Dr GTN M18 .....89 G6
  MPL/ROM SK6 .....114 E4
  WHTN BL5 .....51 J5
Reynolds Ms WILM/AE SK9 .....127 J4
Reynolds Rd OLDTF/WHR M16 .....86 F8
Reynold St HYDE SK14 .....102 A2
Rhine Cl TOT/BURYW BL8 .....24 C5
Rhine Dr CHH M8 .....72 B7
Rhiwlas Dr BURY BL9 .....5 G8
Rhodes Av OLDE OL4 .....60 C7
  UPML OL3 .....61 M3
Rhodes Crs ROCH OL11 .....42 C1
Rhodes Dr BURY BL9 .....55 K2
Rhodes Hl OLDE OL4 .....60 C7
Rhodes St GLSP SK13 .....93 L7
  HYDE SK14 .....101 M1
  NEWH/MOS M40 .....73 H8
  OLD OL1 .....9 L5
  WHIT OL12 .....10 E1
Rhodes St North HYDE SK14 .....101 M1
Rhodeswood Dr GLSP SK13 .....93 K6
Rhos Av CHD/CHDH SK8 .....120 B5
  MDTN M24 .....57 K5
  RUSH/FAL M14 .....99 H4
Rhos Dr BRAM/HZG SK7 .....121 M3
Rhosleigh Av BOL BL1 .....22 B8
Rhyl Fold LEIGH * WN7 .....67 H7
Ribbesford Rd WGNS/IIMK WN3 .....46 F8
Ribble Av BOLE BL2 .....37 H5
  CHAD OL9 .....58 C3
  LIT OL15 .....20 A6
Ribble Dr BURY BL9 .....25 J4
  FWTH BL4 .....53 L7
  WALK M28 .....69 J1
  WGNW/BIL/O WN5 .....46 F5
  WHTF M45 .....55 J5
Ribble Gv LEIGH WN7 .....65 M7
Ribble Rd OLDS OL8 .....74 F1
  NEWH/HIN WN2 .....64 D2
Ribblesdale Cl HEY * OL10 .....41 H5
Ribblesdale Dr NEWH/MOS M40 .....72 F7
Ribblesdale Rd BOLS/LL BL3 .....36 A8
Ribble St ROCH OL11 .....28 A8
Ribbleton Cl TOT/BURYW BL8 .....38 C3
Ribchester Dr BURY BL9 .....39 G5
Ribchester Gv BOLE BL2 .....37 H3
Ribchester Wk HULME * M15 .....87 J4
Ribston St HULME M15 .....87 H4
Rice St CSLFD M3 .....6 C7
Richard Burch St BURY BL9 .....5 C7
Richard Gwyn Cl WHTN BL5 .....50 A6
Richards Cl DTN/ASHW M34 .....90 B5
Richardson Cl WHTF M45 .....55 J3
Richardson Rd ECC M30 .....85 H2
Richardson St OP/CLY M11 .....89 H5
  STKP SK1 .....13 L9
Richards Rd FAIL M35 .....74 C5
  RAD M26 .....54 C1
  RAMS BL0 .....17 E5
  ROCH OL11 .....10 D6
  STKP SK1 .....13 K2
  WGNE/HIN WN2 .....49 H6
Richbell Cl IRL M44 .....94 B5
Richborough Cl BRO M7 .....72 B7
Richelieu St BOLS/LL BL3 .....36 D8
Richmond Av CHAD OL9 .....58 D8
  PWCH M25 .....71 M3
  ROY/SHW OL2 .....43 L7
  URM M41 .....96 B2
  WILM/AE SK9 .....119 M7
Richmond Cl DUK SK16 .....91 G6
  GLSP SK13 .....93 K7
  GOL/RIS/CU WA3 .....81 C8
  MILN OL16 .....42 F1
  MOSL OL5 .....77 H4
  ROY/SHW OL2 .....43 L7
  SALE M33 .....109 J1
  STLY SK15 .....91 K3
  TOT/BURYW BL8 .....24 C6
  WGN WN1 .....31 L5
  WHTF M45 .....55 C5
Richmond Crs MOSL OL5 .....77 H4
Richmond Dr LEIGH WN7 .....67 H5
  WALK M28 .....69 G1
Richmond Gdns BOLS/LL BL3 .....52 E1
Richmond Gn ALT WA14 .....116 D2
  BRAM/HZG * SK7 .....121 H6
Richmond Gv BRUN/LGST M13 .....88 A8
  CHD/CHDH SK8 .....120 A4
  FWTH * BL4 .....52 D3
  LEIGH WN7 .....67 G6
Richmond Gv East
  WGTN/LGST M12 .....88 B7
Richmond Hl WGNW/BIL/O WN5 .....86 F6
Richmond Hill Rd
  CHD/CHDH SK8 .....110 F7
Richmond Rd AIMK WN4 .....63 J7
  ALT WA14 .....108 A7
  DTN/ASHW * M34 .....100 D1
  DUK SK16 .....91 G6
  FAIL M35 .....74 D4

HTNM SK4 .....111 J2
  MPL/ROM SK6 .....113 M1
  RUSH/FAL M14 .....99 G4
  TRPK M17 .....85 K5
  WALK M28 .....68 B5
  WGNE/HIN WN2 .....65 K1
Richmond St AULW OL7 .....75 J8
  BURY BL9 .....4 E9
  CMANE M1 .....7 H6
  CSLFD M3 .....6 C1
  DROY * M43 .....89 M2
  DTN/ASHW M34 .....90 B6
  HOR/BR BL6 .....33 L1
  HYDE SK14 .....102 B2
  STLY SK15 .....91 L2
  WGN WN1 .....14 E3
  WGNS/IIMK WN3 .....47 K7
Richmond Wk CHAD OL9 .....8 E6
Ricroft Rd MPL/ROM SK6 .....114 E1
Ridding Av WYTH/NTH M22 .....119 G1
Ridding Cl OFTN SK2 .....113 G6
Riddings Ct HALE/TIMP WA15 .....108 C4
Riddings Rd HALE/TIMP WA15 .....108 D4
  HALE/TIMP WA15 .....117 H3
Ridge Av HALE/TIMP WA15 .....117 L6
  MPL/ROM SK6 .....114 B2
  WGN WN1 .....31 L5
Ridge Cl GLSP SK13 .....93 H8
  MPL/ROM SK6 .....114 B2
Ridgecroft AULW OL7 .....75 L6
The Ridgedales OLD * OL1 .....44 B8
Ridge End Fold MPL/ROM SK6 .....123 J3
Ridgefield CMANW M2 .....6 E5
Ridgefield St FAIL M35 .....74 A5
Ridgegreen WALK * M28 .....68 D7
Ridge Gv WHTF M45 .....55 L4
Ridge Hill La STLY SK15 .....91 L2
Ridgemont Av HTNM SK4 .....12 B2
Ridgemont Cl HOR/BR BL6 .....34 C1
Ridge Pk BRAM/HZG SK7 .....120 F6
Ridge Rd MPL/ROM SK6 .....114 B2
Ridge Top La NM/HAY SK22 .....125 L2
The Ridgeway BOL * BL1 .....2 E4
  GOL/RIS/CU WA3 .....80 B5
  SWIN M27 .....70 E3
  WILM/AE SK9 .....127 K5
Ridgeway Gates BOL BL1 .....2 E4
Ridgeway Rd
  HALE/TIMP WA15 .....108 F7
The Ridgeways NM/HAY SK22 .....125 M2
Ridgeway St NEWH/MOS M40 .....88 A2
Ridgeway St East
Ridgewell Av GOL/RIS/CU WA3 .....80 A4
Ridgewood CHAD OL9 .....58 B4
Ridgewood Av NEWH/MOS M40 .....73 H7
  WALK M28 .....68 D7
Ridgmont Dr HOR/BR BL6 .....34 C1
Ridgmont Rd BRAM/HZG SK7 .....121 G8
The Ridgway MPL/ROM SK6 .....113 K3
Ridgway HOR/BR BL6 .....32 F2
Riding Cl TYLD M29 .....68 A5
Riding Fold DROY M43 .....90 A1
Riding Fold La WALK M28 .....69 K7
Riding Ga BOLE BL2 .....23 H6
Riding Gate Ms BOLE BL2 .....23 H6
Riding La AIMK WN4 .....64 B7
Ridings Ct UPML OL3 .....61 K2
Ridings Rd GLSP SK13 .....93 J7
Ridings St NEWH/MOS M40 .....73 J7
  OP/CLY M11 .....88 E4
Riding Wy CHAD OL9 .....8 D7
Ridley Dr ALT WA14 .....108 B3
Ridley Gv SALE M33 .....109 J1
Ridley St OLDE OL4 .....9 M7
Ridley Wk HULME * M15 .....87 J7
Ridling La HYDE SK14 .....102 B2
Ridsdale Av DID/WITH M20 .....98 E6
Ridyard St LHULT M38 .....52 F8
  WGNE/HIN WN2 .....64 E1
  WGNW/BIL/O WN5 .....47 H5
Riefield BOL OL1 .....35 L1
Rifle Rd SALE M33 .....97 J7
Rifle St OLD OL1 .....9 J3
Riga Rd RUSH/FAL M14 .....98 F3
Riga St ANC M4 .....7 H2
Rigby Av HOR/BR * BL6 .....32 F2
  RAD M26 .....38 F7
Rigby Cl BOLS/LL BL3 .....36 C8
Rigby Gv LHULT M38 .....52 F7
Rigby La BOLE BL2 .....22 F6
Rigbys La AIMK WN4 .....79 C1
Rigby St AIMK WN4 .....78 D1
  ALT WA14 .....116 F1
  BOLS/LL BL3 .....36 C8
  BRO M7 .....72 A5
  GOL/RIS/CU WA3 .....79 K4
  WGNE/HIN WN2 .....49 H6
Rigel Pl BRO M7 .....86 F1
Rigel St ANC M4 .....7 M1
Rigton Cl WGTN/LGST M12 .....88 D7
Rildene Wk ROCH OL11 .....27 G4
Riley Cl SALE M33 .....107 J3
Riley Ct BOL BL1 .....36 C3
Riley La WGNE/HIN WN2 .....32 E5
Riley Sq WGN WN1 .....15 J3
Riley St ATH M46 .....66 C6
Riley Wood Cl MPL/ROM * SK6 .....113 J3
Rimington Av GOL/RIS/CU WA3 .....79 M3
Rimington Fold MDTN M24 .....41 G8
Rimmer Cl OP/CLY M11 .....88 B4
Rimmington Cl BKLY M9 .....73 K2
Rimsdale Cl CHD/CHDH SK8 .....119 J1
Rimworth Dr NEWH/MOS M40 .....72 F8
Rindle Rd TYLD M29 .....82 A7
Ringcroft Gdns
  NEWH/MOS M40 .....73 L3
Ringley Av GOL/RIS/CU WA3 .....79 J3
Ringley Cha WHTF M45 .....55 H4
Ringley Cl WHTF M45 .....55 H4
Ringley Dr WHTF M45 .....55 C5
Ringley Gv BOL BL1 .....22 E1
Ringley Hey WHTF M45 .....55 G4
Ringley Mdw RAD M26 .....53 M5
Ringley Old Brow RAD M26 .....53 M5
Ringley Pk WHTF M45 .....55 G4
Ringley Rd RAD M26 .....54 B4
Ringley Rd West RAD M26 .....54 B4
Ringley St BKLY * M9 .....73 G4
Ringlow Av SWIN M27 .....69M5
Ringlow Park Rd SWIN M27 .....69 M6
Ring Lows La WHIT OL12 .....19 H8
Ringmer Av WYTH/NTH M22 .....118 D3
Ringmere Ct OLD * OL1 .....9 J2
Ringmore Rd BRAM/HZG SK7 .....121 J4
Ring-o-bells La POY/DIS SK12 .....123 N6
Rings Cl FAIL M35 .....74 C6

Ringstead Cl WILM/AE SK9 .....127 H3
Ringstead Dr NEWH/MOS M40 .....87 M1
  WILM/AE SK9 .....127 H3
Ringstone PWCH M25 .....71 K1
Ringway Av LEIGH WN7 .....66 C4
Ringway Rd MANAIR M90 .....118 E5
Ringway Rd West
  MANAIR 118 E4
Ringwood Av BRAM/HZG SK7 .....121 K3
  DTN/ASHW M34 .....89 M3
  HYDE SK14 .....102 D3
  RAD M26 .....54 E3
  RAMS BL0 .....17 A8
  WGTN/LGST M12 .....99 L2
Rink St RUSH/FAL M14 .....99 C5
Ripley Av CHD/CHDH SK8 .....120 D7
  OFTN SK2 .....112 E8
Ripley Cl ANC * M4 .....88 A4
  BRAM/HZG SK7 .....122 A4
Ripley Crs URM M41 .....84 C7
Ripley Dr LEIGH WN7 .....66 C6
  WGNS/IIMK WN3 .....46 F8
Ripley St BOL BL1 .....22 E8
Ripon Av BOL BL1 .....35 J3
  GOL/RIS/CU WA3 .....80 A4
  WHTF M45 .....55 J2
Ripon Cl BOLS/LL BL3 .....53 J1
  CHAD OL9 .....8 B7
  HALE/TIMP WA15 .....117 L3
  NEWLW WA12 .....78 F8
  RAD M26 .....39 G7
  STKP SK1 .....13 J7
  WHTF M45 .....55 J2
Ripon Crs STRET M32 .....96 C1
Ripon Dr AIMK WN4 .....79 G2
  BOL BL1 .....35 J3
Ripon Gv SALE M33 .....96 C6
Ripon Hall Av RAMS BL0 .....17 B8
Ripon Rd STRET M32 .....96 C1
Ripon St AUL * OL6 .....90 F1
  OLD OL1 .....8 F2
Rippenden Av CCHDY M21 .....97 K2
Rippingham Rd DID/WITH M20 .....98 E5
Rippleton Rd WYTH/NTH M22 .....110 B8
Ripponden Rd OLDE OL4 .....60 A3
  UPML OL3 .....45 G2
Ripponden St OLD OL1 .....59M3
The Rise OLDE OL4 .....60 C5
  WGNNW/ST WN6 .....46 F1
The Rises GLSP SK13 .....93 J7
Rishton Av BOLS/LL BL3 .....52 C2
Rishton La BOLS/LL BL3 .....36 C8
Rishworth Cl OFTN SK2 .....113 G7
Rishworth Dr NEWH/MOS M40 .....74 B4
Rishworth Ri ROY/SHW OL2 .....43 J3
Rising La OLDS OL8 .....75 H2
Risley Av BKLY M9 .....73 G4
Risley St OLD OL1 .....9 J2
Rissington Av NTHM/RTH M23 .....109 L6
Rita Av RUSH/FAL * M14 .....98 E1
Ritson Cl GTN M18 .....88 E6
Riva Rd BNG/LEV M19 .....111 G2
The Riverbank RAD M26 .....53 K4
Riverbank Dr TOT/BURYW BL8 .....4 C1
Riverbanks BOLS/LL BL3 .....3M9
Riverbank Wy GLSP SK13 .....105 J3
Riverdale Cl WGNNW/ST WN6 .....47 G1
Riverdale Rd BKLY M9 .....72 D1
Riverdale Vw MPL/ROM SK6 .....101 K7
The Rivers Edge WHIT OL12 .....18 D4
Rivershill SALE M33 .....96 D6
Rivershill Dr HEY OL10 .....40 F3
Rivershill Gdns
  HALE/TIMP WA15 .....117 L6
Riverside BOL BL1 .....36 C2
  BRO M7 .....86 F1
  DUK SK16 .....90 F2
  HOR/BR BL6 .....32 B5
Riverside Av IRL M44 .....94 D3
  WGN WN1 .....15 J1
Riverside Cl GLSP SK13 .....105 J3
Riverside Ct MPL/ROM * SK6 .....114 D4
Riverside Dr MILN OL16 .....28 E2
  RAD M26 .....53 L4
  RAMS BL0 .....24 E1
Riverside Gdns SALE M33 .....96 D6
Riverside Rd RAD M26 .....39 G8
Rivers La URM M41 .....84 F7
Riversleigh Cl BOL BL1 .....35 J1
Riversmeade BOLE BL2 .....22 F5
  LEIGH WN7 .....66 D6
Rivers St WCNW/BIL/O WN5 .....46 B6
Riverstone Br LIT OL15 .....20 D3
Riverstone Dr NTHM/RTH M23 .....109 G3
River St BOLE BL2 .....3 G5
  HEY OL10 .....27 G8
  HULME M15 .....6 F4
  MILN OL16 .....10 F4
  RAD M26 .....54 E1
  RAMS BL0 .....17 C6
  STKP SK1 .....112 E1
  WGTN/LGST M12 .....7M7
  WILM/AE SK9 .....126 F4
Riverton Rd DID/WITH M20 .....110 E3
River Vw RDSH SK5 .....100 D5
River View Cl PWCH M25 .....71 J2
Riverview Wk BOL * BL1 .....2 A6
River Wy WGN WN1 .....14 E1
Riviera Ct ROCH OL11 .....26 C2
Rivington Av GOL/RIS/CU WA3 .....79M3
  SWIN M27 .....70 D5
  WGN WN1 .....31 H1
  WGNE/HIN WN2 .....64 E1
Rivington Gv DTN/ASHW M34 .....89M4
  IRL M44 .....94 D3
Rivington Rd HALE/TIMP WA15 .....117 H2
  OLDE OL4 .....60 B6
  SLFD M6 .....70 F8
Rivington St ATH M46 .....66 E7
  HOR/BR BL6 .....33 G2
  OLD OL1 .....9 H4
  WHIT OL12 .....10 F1

Rivington Wk
WGTN/LGST * M12 88 B7
Rivington Wy WGNNW/ST WN6 31 J4
Rixon St OLDE OL4 60 A3
Rixson St OLDE * OL4 60 A3
Rix St BOL BL1 36 B2
Rixton Dr TYLD M29 67 L4
Roach Bank Rd BURY BL9 39 M5
Roaches Ms MOSL OL5 77 G1
Roaches Wy MOSL OL5 77 H1
Roach Gn WGN WN1 15 L2
Roachill Cl ALT WA14 107 L7
Roach Pl MILN OL16 11 G3
Roach St BURY BL9 39 J8
Roach V MILN OL16 28 F2
Roachwood Cl CHAD OL9 58 B5
Roading Brook Rd BOLE BL2 37 K1
Road La WHIT OL12 18 E8
Roads Ford Av MILN OL16 29 J5
Roadside Ct GOL/RIS/CU WA3 79 M4
Roan Wy WILM/AE SK9 130 E4
Roaring Gate La
HALE/TIMP WA15 118 A1
Robert Hall St ORD M5 86 E4
Robert Lawrence Ct URM * M41 95 K3
Robert Malcolm Cl
NEWH/MOS M40 73 G7
Robert Owen Gdns
WYTH/NTH * M22 110 A4
Robert Salt Ct ALT * WA14 108 B6
Robertscroft Cl
WYTH/NTH M22 109 M8
Robertshaw Av CCHDY M21 97 L6
Robertshaw St LEIGH WN7 66 B5
Robertson St RAD M26 38 D8
Roberts St ECC M30 85 G3
Robert St ATH * M46 67 H3
BOLE * BL2 23 H7
CSLFD M3 87 J1
DUK SK16 90 E4
FAIL M35 74 D3
HEY OL10 41 H4
HYDE SK14 101 M2
MILN OL16 10 F3
NEWH/MOS M40 73 J7
PWCH M25 55 M8
RAMS BL0 17 C3
SALE M33 97 H8
TOT/BURYW BL8 38 F1
WGNE/HIN WN2 64 D1
Robeson Wy WYTH/NTH M22 110 C6
Robin Cft MPL/ROM SK6 113 G1
Robin Dr IRL M44 94 D1
Robin Hill Dr WGNNW/ST WN6 30 E2
Robin Hill La WGNNW/ST WN6 30 E1
Robin Hood St CHH M8 72 C4
Robinia Cl ECC M30 84 C4
Robin Park Rd
WGNW/BIL/O WN5 14 A5
Robin Rd RAMS BL0 24 E1
Robinsbay Rd WYTH/NTH M22 119 G5
Robins Cl BRAM/HZG SK7 121 G5
DROY M43 89 M1
Robin's La BRAM/HZG SK7 120 F5
Robinson La AULW OL7 90 C1
Robinson St CHAD OL9 8 A7
EDGY/DAV SK3 12 F8
HOR/BR BL6 21 B8
HYDE * SK14 102 C1
MILN OL16 11 G4
OLDS OL8 75 J1
STLY SK15 91 H4
Robin St OLD OL1 9 G2
Robinsway ALT WA14 116 E3
Robinswood Rd
WYTH/NTH M22 118 F3
Rob La NEWLW WA12 79 H8
Robson Av URM M41 85 H5
Robson St OLD OL1 9 K6
Robson Wy GOL/RIS/CU WA3 80 C4
Roby Rd ECC M30 84 F4
Roby St CMANE M1 7 J5
Roby Well Wy
WGNW/BIL/O WN5 62 A7
Roch Av HEY OL10 40 D2
Rochbury Cl ROCH OL11 27 J6
Roch Cl WHTF M45 55 L3
Roch Crs WHTF M45 55 L3
Rochdale La HEY OL10 41 G2
ROY/SHW OL2 43 G7
Rochdale Old Rd BURY BL9 39 M1
Rochdale Rd ANC M4 7 J2
BKLY M9 73 G1
BURY BL9 5 G4
HEY OL10 41 G2
MDTN M24 57 L1
MILN OL16 29 G5
MILN OL16 43 H3
OLD OL1 9 G2
ROY/SHW OL2 42 F6
ROY/SHW OL2 43 H4
UPML OL3 44 E1
Rochdale Rd East HEY OL10 41 H2
Roche Gdns CHD/CHDH SK8 120 D6
Roche Rd UPML OL3 45 H7
Rochester Av BOLE BL2 37 H3
CCHDY M21 98 A6
PWCH M25 71 M2
WALK M28 68 F3
Rochester Cl AUL OL6 75 M5
DUK SK16 91 K5
GOL/RIS/CU WA3 79 K4
Rochester Dr ALT WA14 108 B3
Rochester Gv BRAM/HZG SK7 122 A1
Rochester Rd URM M41 85 G8
Rochester Wy CHAD OL9 8 A7
Rochford Av WHTF M45 55 G5
WYTH/NTH M22 118 F4
Rochford Rd ECC M30 84 C4
Roch Mills Crs ROCH OL11 27 M7
Roch Mills Gdns ROCH OL11 27 M7
Roch Pl WGNE/HIN WN2 64 C2
Roch St MILN OL16 28 E3
Roch Valley Wy ROCH OL11 27 M6
Roch Wy WHTF M45 55 L3
The Rock BURY BL9 4 E4
BURY BL9 5 G3
Rockall Wk OP/CLY * M11 88 C3
Rock Av BOL BL1 35 M2
Rock Bank BRO * M7 71 M6
MOSL * OL5 76 F3
Rockbourne Cl WGNE/HIN WN2 49 G8
Rockdove Av HULME M15 6 E9
Rocket St CSLFD M3 6 B4
Rockfield Dr BKLY * M9 73 H4
Rock Fold EDGW/EG * BL7 22 C3
Rockhampton St GTN M18 89 H7
Rockhaven Av HOR/BR BL6 21 C8
Rockhouse Cl ECC M30 85 H4
Rockingham Cl ROY/SHW OL2 43 H4
WGTN/LGST M12 88 A6
Rockingham Dr WGNE/HIN WN2 48 F8
Rockley Gdns SLFD M6 71 L8
Rocklyn Av NEWH/MOS M40 73 M2
Rocklynes MPL/ROM SK6 113 L2
Rockmead Dr BKLY M9 73 H1
Rock Rd URM M41 96 C2
WALK M28 83 L2
Rock St AULW OL7 75 K7
BRO M7 72 A6
GOL/RIS/CU WA3 79 K2
HEY OL10 41 H3
HOR/BR BL6 33 L1
HYDE SK14 102 B5
NM/HAY SK22 124 D5
OLD OL1 9 L5
OP/CLY M11 89 H5
RAD M26 54 E2
RAMS BL0 17 E5
Rock Ter EDGW/EG BL7 22 C3
MOSL OL5 77 G1
Rocky Bank Ter
WGNS/IIMK * WN3 15 K9
Rocky La ECC M30 70 A8
Roda St BKLY M9 73 J5
Rodborough Rd
NTHM/RTH M23 118 B1
Rodeheath Cl WILM/AE SK9 127 H5
Rodenhurst Dr NEWH/MOS M40 73 K6
Rodepool Cl WILM/AE SK9 127 H2
Rodgers Cl WHTN BL5 50 B6
Rodgers Wy WHTN BL5 50 B6
Rodmell Av NEWH/MOS * M40 73 G7
Rodmell Cl EDGW/EG BL7 22 C5
Rodmill Ct RUSH/FAL M14 98 F3
Rodmill Dr CHD/CHDH SK8 110 D8
Rodney Ct ANC M4 7 L1
Rodney Dr MPL/ROM SK6 101 K7
Rodney St ANC M4 7 M2
ATH * M46 66 F2
AUL OL6 76 A8
CSLFD M3 6 A4
ROCH OL11 41 L2
WGN WN1 15 G5
Roeacre St HEY OL10 41 H2
Roebuck Gdns SALE * M33 96 D8
Roebuck La OLDE OL4 60 D1
SALE M33 96 D8
Roebuck St WGNE/HIN WN2 65 M1
Roecliffe Cl WGNS/IIMK WN3 14 D8
Roe Cross Gn HYDE SK14 92 C7
Roe Cross Rd HYDE SK14 92 C7
Roedean Gdns URM M41 95 G2
Roefield Ter ROCH OL11 27 M4
Roe Gn WALK M28 69 K4
Roe Green Av WALK M28 69 K4
Roe La OLDE OL4 60 A7
Roe St ANC M4 7 L1
WHIT OL12 27 M3
Rogate Dr NTHM/RTH M23 109 K7
Roger Cl MPL/ROM SK6 113 J3
Rogerstead BOLS/LL * BL3 35 M6
Roger St ANC M4 87 K1
Rogerton Cl LEIGH WN7 66 E8
Rokeby Av GOL/RIS/CU WA3 80 A3
STRET M32 97 G3
Rokeden NEWLW WA12 79 G8
Roker Av BRUN/LGST M13 99 J2
Roker Park Av DTN/ASHW M34 90 A5
Roland Rd BOLS/LL BL3 35 M7
RDSH SK5 100 C5
Rolla St CSLFD M3 6 D2
Rollesby Cl TOT/BURYW BL8 25 G7
Rolleston Av NEWH/MOS M40 88 A2
Rollins La MPL/ROM SK6 114 D3
Rolls Crs HULME M15 87 J6
Rollswood Dr NEWH/MOS M40 73 K6
Roman Rd AIMK WN4 63 K7
FAIL M35 74 D4
HTNM SK4 13 H3
PWCH M25 71 J3
ROY/SHW OL2 59 H1
Roman St RAD M26 54 B1
Romer Av NEWH/MOS * M40 74 B3
Rome Rd NEWH/MOS M40 7 L1
Romer St BOLE BL2 3 M5
Romford Av DTN/ASHW M34 90 D8
LEIGH WN7 66 C6
Romford Cl OLDS * OL8 9 H9
Romford Pl WGNE/HIN WN2 49 H7
Romford Rd SALE M33 96 B6
Romford St WGNE/HIN WN2 49 G7
Romiley Crs BOLE BL2 37 G4
Romiley Dr BOLE BL2 37 G4
Romiley Sq WGNNW/ST WN6 31 H4
Romiley St SLFD M6 71 G7
STKP SK1 112 E2
Romley Rd URM M41 85 G8
Romney Av ROCH OL11 42 B2
Romney Rd BOL BL1 35 H2
Romney St AUL OL6 90 F1
NEWH/MOS M40 73 K4
SLFD M6 71 K7
Romney Wk CHAD OL9 8 A7
Romney Wy RDSH SK5 100 E6
Romsey WHIT OL12 10 D3
Romsey Av MDTN M24 57 J1
Romsey Dr CHD/CHDH SK8 120 D6
Romsey Gv WGNS/IIMK WN3 63 G2
Romsley Cl WGTN/LGST M12 88 D6
Romsley Dr BOLS/LL BL3 51 M1
Ronaldsay Gdns ORD M5 86 B3
Ronald St OLDE OL4 59 M5
OP/CLY M11 89 G3
ROCH OL11 41 M3
Rondin Cl WGTN/LGST M12 88 B5
Rondin Rd WGTN/LGST M12 88 B5
Roocroft Ct BOL BL1 2 B1
Roocroft Sq HOR/BR BL6 32 F2
Roods La ROCH OL11 26 F3
The Rookery NEWLW WA12 79 G8
Rookery Av AIMK WN4 78 E2
GTN M18 89 J6
WGNNW/ST WN6 30 B4
Rookery Cl STLY SK15 92 B5
Rookerypool Cl WILM/AE SK9 127 H2
Rooke St ECC M30 84 D4
Rookfield Av SALE M33 96 F7
Rookley Wk RUSH/FAL * M14 98 F1
Rook St HULME M15 87 H7
OLDE OL4 59 M7
RAMS BL0 17 C6
Rookswood Dr ROCH OL11 41 L1
Rookway MDTN M24 57 J5
Rookwood OLD OL1 58 B3
Rookwood Av NTHM/RTH M23 109 J5
Rookwood Hl BRAM/HZG SK7 121 G3
Rooley Moor Rd WHIT OL12 27 L2
Rooley St WHIT OL12 27 M3
Roosevelt Rd FWTH BL4 53 J5
Rooth St HTNM SK4 12 E3
Ropefield Wy WHIT OL12 28 B1
Rope St WHIT OL12 10 E2
Rope Wk CSLFD M3 6 D1
Rosa Gv BRO M7 72 A6
Rosamond Dr CSLFD M3 6 B3
Rosamond St BOLS/LL BL3 35 M8
HULME M15 87 K6
Rosamond St West HULME M15 87 K6
Rosary Cl OLDS OL8 75 J3
Rosary Rd OLDS OL8 75 K3
Roscoe Ct WHTN BL5 50 C5
Roscoe Rd IRL M44 94 B3
Roscoe St EDGY/DAV SK3 12 F6
OLD OL1 9 K6
WGN WN1 15 K6
Roscow Av BOLE BL2 37 H4
Roscow Rd FWTH BL4 53 K6
Rose Acre WALK M28 68 E5
Roseacre Cl BOLE BL2 3 L2
Roseacre Dr CHD/CHDH SK8 119 L3
Rose Av IRL M44 94 C3
LIT OL15 29 J1
RNFD/HAY WA11 78 B6
ROCH OL11 27 G2
WGNE/HIN WN2 64 E5
WGNNW/ST WN6 47 J1
Rosebank HOR/BR BL6 34 F5
Rosebank Cl BOLE BL2 37 M3
Rose Bank Cl HYDE SK14 93 G7
WGN WN1 31 L8
Rosebank Rd NEWH/MOS M40 73 L8
Roseberry Cl RAMS BL0 24 F1
Roseberry Rd AIMK WN4 63 K7
Roseberry St BOLS/LL BL3 35 M8
OFTN SK2 113 G8
OLDS * OL8 8 F7
Rosebery St RUSH/FAL M14 98 C1
WHTN BL5 50 C4
Rosebridge Ct WGN * WN1 15 M5
Rosebridge Wy WGN WN1 15 M5
Rosebury Av LEIGH WN7 66 D7
OLD OL1 59 L3
Rosebury Gv LEIGH WN7 66 E6
Rose Cottage Rd DID/WITH M20 98 E5
Rose Crs IRL M44 94 C3
Rosecroft Cl EDGY/DAV SK3 112 B8
Rosedale Av ATH M46 66 F1
BOL BL1 22 B7
GOL/RIS/CU WA3 79 M5
Rosedale Cl OLD OL1 59 L3
Rosedale Ct DTN/ASHW * M34 101 H1
Rosedale Dr LEIGH WN7 66 F7
Rosedale Rd HTNM SK4 100 A7
RUSH/FAL M14 98 D2
Rosedale Wy DUK SK16 90 F6
Rosefield Cl EDGY/DAV SK3 112 B7
Rosefield Crs MILN OL16 11 K5
Rosegarth Av DID/WITH M20 98 A8
Rose Gv FWTH BL4 53 J5
TOT/BURYW BL8 38 D2
Rosehay Av DTN/ASHW M34 101 J2
Rose Hey La FAIL M35 74 B8
Rose Hl BOLS/LL BL3 3 H8
DTN/ASHW M34 101 G1
DUK SK16 91 J4
UPML OL3 61 J1
Rose Hill Av NEWH/MOS * M40 73 L8
WGNW/BIL/O WN5 46 F6
Rose Hill Cl EDGW/EG BL7 22 D5
Rosehill Cl SLFD M6 86 C2
Rose Hill Dr EDGW/EG BL7 22 D5
Rose Hill Rd AUL OL6 76 C7
Rosehill Rd SWIN M27 70 C2
Rose Hill St HEY OL10 40 E2
Rose Hill Vw AIMK WN4 63 J5
Roseland Av DID/WITH M20 98 E8
Roseland Dr PWCH M25 55 M6
Roselands Av SALE M33 108 C2
Rose La MPL/ROM SK6 114 B7
Rose Lea BOLE BL2 23 H8
Rosemary Crs WGN WN1 48 A2
Rosemary Dr HYDE SK14 102 A5
LIT OL15 20 A6
Rosemary Gv BRO M7 71 M7
Rosemary La STKP SK1 13 L5
WHTN BL5 51 L6
Rosemary Rd CHAD OL9 58 B4
Rosemount HYDE SK14 91 G7
Rose Mt MDTN M24 57 J2
Rosemount Crs HYDE SK14 91 G7
Roseneath BRAM/HZG SK7 120 F3
Roseneath Av BNG/LEV M19 99 M3
Roseneath Gv BOLS/LL BL3 52 A1
Roseneath Rd BOLS/LL BL3 52 A1
URM M41 95 M1
Rosen Sq CHAD OL9 8 A4
Rose St BOLS/LL BL3 3 G8
CHAD OL9 74 D1
MDTN M24 57 M4
RDSH SK5 112 C1
WGN WN1 15 M5
WGNE/HIN WN2 49 G7
Rose Ter STLY SK15 91 K3
Rosethorns Cl MDTN M24 41 J8
Rose V CHD/CHDH SK8 119 K3
Rosevale Av BNG/LEV M19 99 H7
Roseway BRAM/HZG SK7 121 H2
Rosewell Cl NEWH/MOS M40 73 G8
Rose Wd DTN/ASHW M34 101 G1
Rosewood ROCH OL11 27 H3
WHTN BL5 49 M6
Rosewood Av DROY M43 89 L2
HTNM SK4 111 K3
TOT/BURYW BL8 24 D7
Rosewood Cl DUK SK16 91 G6
WGNE/HIN WN2 64 E5
Rosewood Crs CHAD OL9 58 E4
Rosewood Gdns
CHD/CHDH SK8 110 C6
Rosford Av RUSH/FAL M14 98 E2
Rosgill Cl HTNM SK4 111 H2
Rosina Cl AIMK WN4 63 J6
Rosina St OP/CLY M11 89 J5
Rosley Rd WGNS/IIMK WN3 63 L1
Roslin St OP/CLY M11 89 G2
Roslyn Av URM M41 95 M2
Roslyn Rd EDGY/DAV SK3 112 B7
Rossall Av RAD M26 54 F4
STRET M32 96 F1
Rossall Cl BOLE BL2 3 L2
Rossall Crs LEIGH WN7 81 K1
Rossall Dr BRAM/HZG SK7 121 H6
Rossall Rd BOLE BL2 3 L2
WHIT OL12 28 D2
Rossall St BOLE BL2 3 J2
Rossall Wy SLFD M6 86 D1
Ross Av CHAD OL9 74 C1
EDGY/DAV SK3 112 B7
WHTF M45 55 J6
Ross Cl WGNE/HIN WN2 48 C2
WGNW/BIL/O WN5 62 B7
Rossdale Gv WGNNW/ST WN6 31 K5
Ross Dr SWIN M27 54 B8
Rossenclough Rd
WILM/AE SK9 127 H3
Rossendale Av BKLY M9 73 J3
Rossendale Cl ROY/SHW OL2 44 A5
Rossendale Rd CHD/CHDH SK8 119 L4
Rossendale Wy WHIT OL12 18 A4
WHIT OL12 19 H1
Rossett Av HALE/TIMP WA15 108 D4
WYTH/NTH M22 118 F3
Rossett Cl WGNS/IIMK WN3 63 G2
Rossett Dr URM M41 84 C8
Ross Gv URM M41 95 M2
Rosshill Wk HULME * M15 87 G6
Rossington St NEWH/MOS M40 74 A7
Rossini St BOL BL1 36 A1
Rosslare Rd WYTH/NTH M22 119 G2
Ross Lave La DTN/ASHW M34 100 F4
Rosslyn Gv HALE/TIMP WA15 108 D6
Rosslyn Rd CHD/CHDH SK8 119 M3
NEWH/MOS M40 73 K3
OLDTF/WHR M16 97 K2
Rossmere Av ROCH OL11 27 M6
Rossmill La HALE/TIMP WA15 117 L5
Ross St OLDS OL8 8 F8
Rostherne Av GOL/RIS/CU WA3 80 A4
MPL/ROM SK6 123 G4
RUSH/FAL M14 98 D3
Rostherne Gdns BOLS/LL BL3 35 L8
Rostherne Rd EDGY/DAV SK3 112 B7
SALE M33 109 J1
WILM/AE SK9 126 C7
Rostherne St ALT WA14 116 F1
SLFD * M6 86 B3
Rosthernmere Rd
CHD/CHDH SK8 111 J8
Rosthwaite Cl MDTN M24 56 F3
WGNS/IIMK WN3 63 K2
Roston Rd BRO M7 72 B4
Rostrevor Rd EDGY/DAV SK3 112 B7
Rostron Av WGTN/LGST M12 88 B6
Rostron Rd RAMS BL0 17 B6
Rostron St BNG/LEV M19 99 L3
Rothay Cl BOLE BL2 37 J3
Rothay Dr MDTN M24 57 H1
RDSH SK5 100 C4
Rothay St LEIGH WN7 66 E8
Rothbury Av AULW OL7 75 H7
Rothbury Cl TOT/BURYW BL8 38 C2
Rothbury Ct BOLS/LL BL3 51 L1
Rotherby Rd WYTH/NTH M22 110 B8
Rotherdale Av
HALE/TIMP WA15 109 G7
Rotherhead Cl HOR/BR BL6 33 J2
Rotherwood Av STRET M32 97 H1
Rotherwood Rd WILM/AE SK9 126 B7
Rothesay Av DUK SK16 90 F5
Rothesay Crs SALE M33 107 M2
Rothesay Rd BOLS/LL * BL3 51 L1
CHH M8 72 B2
OLD OL1 59 M3
Rothesay Ter MILN OL16 28 F8
Rothiemay Rd URM M41 95 H3
Rothley Av WYTH/NTH M22 110 A7
Rothman Cl FAIL M35 73 M6
Rothwell Crs LHULT M38 52 B6
Rothwell La LHULT M38 52 B7
Rothwell Rd GOL/RIS/CU WA3 79 M3
Rothwell St BOLS/LL BL3 2 C8
NEWH/MOS M40 73 M6
RAMS BL0 17 B6
ROY/SHW OL2 58 F1
WALK M28 69 J1
WHIT OL12 28 D3
Rottingdene Dr
WYTH/NTH M22 118 E3
Roughey Gdns WYTH/NTH M22 109 M8
Rough Hey Wk MILN OL16 11 J7
Rough Hill La BURY BL9 26 B8
Roughlea Av GOL/RIS/CU WA3 81 G8
Roughlee Av SWIN M27 70 A5
Roughtown Ct MOSL OL5 77 G2
Roughtown Rd MOSL OL5 77 G2
Round Barn EDGW/EG * BL7 16 B1
Roundcroft MPL/ROM SK6 114 A1
Roundhey CHD/CHDH SK8 119 K4
Round Hey MOSL OL5 76 F4
Round Hill Cl GLSP SK13 104 C1
Round Hill Wy BOL BL1 2 F2
Roundhill Wy OLDE OL4 60 B3
Round House Av WGN WN1 15 L1
Roundmoor Rd
WGNNW/ST WN6 31 K5
Roundthorn La WHTN BL5 50 B5
Round Thorn Rd MDTN M24 57 L5
Roundthorn Rd
NTHM/RTH M23 109 J6
OLDE OL4 59 M7
Roundway BRAM/HZG SK7 120 F6
Round Wy NM/HAY SK22 124 F4
Roundwood Rd
WYTH/NTH M22 110 A5
Roundy La MCFLDN SK10 129 K7
Rousdon Cl NEWH/MOS * M40 73 G7
Rouse St ROCH OL11 27 M8
Rowan Av GOL/RIS/CU WA3 80 C5
OLDTF/WHR M16 98 A1
SALE M33 108 F2
URM M41 96 A1
WGNNW/ST WN6 47 J1
Rowan Cl FAIL M35 74 C7
WHIT OL12 27 K1
Rowan Crs DUK SK16 91 J5
Rowan Dr CHD/CHDH SK8 120 E4
Rowanhill WGN WN1 15 J1
Rowanlea PWCH * M25 55 M8
Rowan Pl PWCH M25 71 L1
The Rowans BOL BL1 35 H5
MOSL OL5 77 G3
Rowans Cl STLY SK15 91 M1
Rowanside Dr WILM/AE SK9 127 J4
Rowans St TOT/BURYW BL8 4 A1
Rowan St HYDE SK14 102 C3
Rowanswood Dr HYDE SK14 102 D1
Rowan Tree Dr SALE M33 108 E3
Rowan Tree Rd OLDS OL8 75 G3
Rowan Wk GLSP SK13 93 H8
Rowanwood CHAD OL9 58 B5
Rowany Cl PWCH M25 71 K2
Rowarth Av DTN/ASHW M34 101 K4
Rowarth Rd NTHM/RTH M23 118 B2
Rowbottom Sq WGN WN1 14 F4
Rowbottom Wk OLDS OL8 9 H9
Rowcon Cl DTN/ASHW M34 90 B7
Rowden Rd OLDE OL4 60 B8
Rowe Gn DTN/ASHW M34 101 J1
Rowena St BOLS/LL BL3 52 F2
Rowendale St CMANE * M1 6 E7
Rowe St TYLD * M29 67 L4
Rowfield Dr NTHM/RTH M23 118 B1
Rowland Av URM M41 96 B1
Rowland Ct MILN OL16 11 J7
Rowlands Rd BURY BL9 25 H3
Rowland St ATH M46 67 G2
MILN OL16 11 K7
ORD M5 86 D4
Rowlandsway WYTH/NTH M22 118 F2
Rowland Wy OLDE OL4 60 B5
Rowley Rd BRAM/HZG SK7 122 A4
Rowley St AUL OL6 76 A6
Rowood Av CHH M8 72 E6
RDSH SK5 100 C2
Rowrah Crs MDTN M24 56 E3
Rowsley Av BOL BL1 35 K3
DID/WITH M20 98 B8
Rowsley Gv RDSH SK5 100 B5
Rowsley Ms GLSP SK13 104 B2
Rowsley Rd ECC M30 84 F4
STRET M32 96 D1
Rowsley St OP/CLY M11 88 B2
SLFD M6 71 L7
Rowson Ct SALE * M33 97 G8
Rowson Dr IRL M44 94 A6
Rowton Ri WGN WN1 31 L4
Rowton St BOLE BL2 36 E1
Roxalina St BOLS/LL BL3 36 B8
Roxburgh St GTN M18 89 G7
Roxbury Av OLDE OL4 60 A7
Roxby Cl WALK M28 68 E1
Roxholme Wk WYTH/NTH M22 118 E4
Roxton Rd HTNM SK4 99 M6
Royal Ar WGN WN1 15 G3
Royal Av BURY BL9 25 J7
CCHDY M21 97 K5
DROY M43 89 L2
HEY OL10 41 G3
URM M41 96 A2
Royal Court Dr BOL BL1 2 B3
Royal Dr LEIGH WN7 67 G6
Royal Ex CMANW * M2 6 F4
Royal Exchange Ar CMANW * M2 6 F4
Royal Gdns ALT WA14 116 B2
Royal George St EDGY/DAV SK3 13 H7
Royal Oak Rd NTHM/RTH M23 109 J5
Royal Rd POY/DIS SK12 123 M7
Royal St MILN OL16 28 F2
Royalthorn Dr WYTH/NTH M22 109 M6
Royalthorn Rd WYTH/NTH M22 110 A6
Royce Av HALE/TIMP WA15 108 B7
Royce Rd HULME M15 87 H6
Roydale St NEWH/MOS M40 88 B1
Royden Av BKLY M9 57 G7
IRL M44 94 C4
WGNS/IIMK WN3 63 J2
Royden Crs WGNW/BIL/O WN5 62 B7
Royden Rd WGNW/BIL/O WN5 62 B7
Roydes St MDTN M24 57 L2
Royds Cl BRUN/LGST M13 88 A7
TOT/BURYW BL8 24 D7
Royds Pl MILN OL16 11 H8
Royds St BURY BL9 26 A8
LIT OL15 20 D7
MILN OL16 11 J8
MILN OL16 29 K7
TOT/BURYW BL8 24 C5
Royds St West ROCH OL11 11 H9
Royd St OLDS OL8 58 F8
Royland Av BOLS/LL BL3 52 D1
Royle Barn Rd ROCH OL11 41 M2
Royle Cl OFTN SK2 112 D7
OLDS OL8 75 J1
Royle Green Rd
WYTH/NTH M22 110 B4
Royle Rd ROCH OL11 42 A1
Royle St DTN/ASHW M34 90 C7
OFTN SK2 13 K8
ORD * M5 86 C3
RUSH/FAL M14 99 G5
WALK M28 69 G2
Royley ROY/SHW OL2 58 F1
Royley Crs ROY/SHW OL2 58 F1
Royley Rd OLDS OL8 59 H8
Roynton Rd HOR/BR BL6 21 B6
Royon Dr EDGY/DAV SK3 12 A9
Royston Av BOLE BL2 3 K2
DTN/ASHW M34 100 C1
OLDTF/WHR M16 98 A1
Royston Cl GOL/RIS/CU WA3 80 B4
TOT/BURYW BL8 24 C3
Royston Rd OLDTF/WHR M16 97 L1
URM M41 96 B1
Roy St BOLS/LL BL3 35 L8
ROY/SHW OL2 43 G8
Royton Av SALE M33 109 H2
Rozel Sq CSLFD M3 6 D6
Ruabon Crs WGNE/HIN WN2 49 J8
Ruabon Rd DID/WITH M20 110 F2
Rubens Cl MPL/ROM SK6 114 F4
Ruby Gv LEIGH WN7 66 B8
Ruby St BOL BL1 36 C1
DTN/ASHW M34 101 H1
HULME M15 87 K6
RAMS BL0 24 F1
Rudcroft Cl BRUN/LGST M13 87 L6
Rudding St ROY/SHW OL2 59 K2
Ruddpark Rd WYTH/NTH M22 118 F3
Rudd St NEWH/MOS M40 73 K5
Rudford Gdns BOLS/LL * BL3 36 C8
Rudgwick Dr TOT/BURYW BL8 24 F5
Rudheath Av DID/WITH M20 98 D5
Rudman Dr ORD M5 86 F4
Rudman St WHIT OL12 28 B2
Rudolph St BOLS/LL BL3 52 C1
Rudston Av NEWH/MOS M40 73 L2
Rudyard Av MDTN M24 57 M1
WGNNW/ST WN6 31 H2
Rudyard Gv HTNM SK4 100 A6
ROCH OL11 42 C2
SALE M33 108 B2
Rudyard Rd SLFD M6 70 F7
Rudyard St BRO M7 72 A6
Ruecroft Cl WGNNW/ST WN6 30 A4
Rufford Av HYDE SK14 102 C2
ROCH OL11 28 A8
Rufford Cl AUL OL6 75 M5
ROY/SHW OL2 43 J5
WHTF M45 55 K2
Rufford Dr BOLS/LL BL3 52 A2
WHTF M45 55 J2
Rufford Gv BOLS/LL BL3 52 A2
Rufford Pl GTN * M18 89 J8
TYLD M29 67 J8
Rufford Rd OLDTF/WHR M16 98 A1
Rufus St RUSH/FAL M14 99 H5
Rugby Dr SALE M33 108 D2
WGNW/BIL/O WN5 46 C4

Rugby Rd LEIGH WN7 81 J1
SLFD M6 85 K1
WHIT OL12 11 G1
Rugby St BRO M7 72 B8
Rugeley St SLFD M6 71 L7
Ruins La BOLE BL2 23 H8
Ruislip Av NEWH/MOS M40 73 H7
Ruislip Cl OLDS OL8 59 L8
Rumbles La UPML OL3 45 J8
Rumworth Rd HOR/BR BL6 34 F6
Rumworth St BOLS/LL BL3 36 A8
Runcorn St HULME M15 86 F5
Runger La MANAIR M90 118 B4
Runhall Cl WGTN/LGST M12 88 D6
Runnymeade SLFD M6 70 D6
Runnymede Cl EDGY/DAV SK3 12 D9
Runnymede Ct BOLS/LL BL3 2 A8
ROY/SHW OL2 43 H8
Runshaw Av WGNNW/ST WN6 30 B4
Rupert St BOLS/LL BL3 36 C8
NEWH/MOS M40 74 B8
RAD M26 54 E3
RDSH SK5 100 B5
WGN WN1 15 J5
WHIT OL12 27 M3
Ruscombe Fold MDTN M24 57 G1
Rush Acre Cl RAD M26 54 B1
Rush Bank ROY/SHW OL2 43 J4
Rushbrooke Av OP/CLY M11 88 F1
Rushbury Dr ROY/SHW OL2 43 K8
Rushcroft Rd ROY/SHW OL2 43 J4
Rushdene WGNS/IIMK WN3 47 K8
Rushden Rd BNG/LEV M19 99 L2
Rushen St OP/CLY M11 88 F3
The Rushes GLSP SK13 93 J8
Rushey Cl HALE/TIMP WA15 117 M5
Rushey Fld EDGW/EG BL7 22 C4
Rushey Fold La BOL BL1 36 A2
Rusheylea Cl BOL BL1 35 M2
Rushey Rd WYTH/NTH M22 109 M7
Rushfield Dr BRUN/LGST M13 99 H1
Rushfield Rd CHD/CHDH SK8 120 C6
Rushford Av BNG/LEV M19 99 K2
Rushford Gv BOL BL1 22 C8
Rushford St WGTN/LGST M12 88 D8
Rush Gv UPML OL3 61 L5
Rush Hill Rd UPML OL3 61 L5
Rush Hill Ter UPML OL3 61 L5
Rushlake Dr BOL BL1 36 B3
Rushlake Gdns ROCH OL11 27 H4
Rushley Av BRO M7 71 L5
Rushmere AUL OL6 76 B6
GLSP SK13 105 H4
Rushmere Av BNG/LEV M19 99 L3
Rushmere Dr TOT/BURYW BL8 24 F7
Rushmere Wk OLDTF/WHR M16 87 G7
Rushmoor Av AIMK WN4 64 B8
Rushmoor Cl IRL M44 94 D2
Rush Mt ROY/SHW OL2 43 J3
Rusholme Gv RUSH/FAL M14 98 F1
Rusholme Pl RUSH/FAL M14 87 M8
Rushside Rd CHD/CHDH SK8 120 B6
Rush St DUK SK16 91 J4
Rushton Av LEIGH WN7 66 A4
NEWLW WA12 78 E8
Rushton Cl MPL/ROM * SK6 114 D7
Rushton Dr BRAM/HZG SK7 120 F1
MPL/ROM SK6 113 M1
MPL/ROM SK6 114 C8
Rushton Fold MCFLDN SK10 131 K2
Rushton Gv OLDE OL4 60 B1
OP/CLY M11 89 H5
Rushton Rd BOL BL1 35 L3
CHD/CHDH SK8 120 C6
EDGY/DAV SK3 12 B9
Rushton St DID/WITH M20 110 E2
WALK M28 69 G2
Rushwick Av NEWH/MOS M40 73 H6
Rushworth Ct HTNM SK4 99 M7
Rushycroft HYDE SK14 92 D8
Rushyfield Crs MPL/ROM SK6 114 A1
Rushy Hill Vw WHIT * OL12 27 L3
Rushy Vw NEWLW WA12 78 D8
Ruskin Av CHAD OL9 74 C1
DTN/ASHW M34 89 M5
DTN/ASHW M34 101 H3
FWTH BL4 53 J5
NEWLW WA12 78 F8
RUSH/FAL M14 87 L8
WGNS/IIMK WN3 63 J1
Ruskin Crs PWCH M25 71 J1
WGNE/HIN WN2 64 E3
Ruskin Dr SALE M33 95 M8
Ruskin Gdns MPL/ROM SK6 113 K1
Ruskin Gv MPL/ROM SK6 113 K1
Ruskington Dr BKLY M9 73 G5
Ruskin Rd DROY M43 89 K2
OLDTF/WHR M16 97 M1
PWCH M25 71 H1
RDSH SK5 100 B3
ROCH OL11 42 B2
Ruskin St CHAD OL9 8 F3
RAD M26 38 F8
Rusland Ct STKP * SK1 112 E5
Rusland Dr BOLE BL2 37 H2
Russeldene Rd WGNS/IIMK WN3 63 H1
Russell Av MPL/ROM SK6 123 G5
OLDTF/WHR M16 98 A2
SALE M33 97 G7
Russell Cl BOL BL1 35 M4
Russell Ct FWTH * BL4 53 H4
LHULT M38 68 F1
Russell Dr IRL M44 94 D2
Russell Gdns HTNM SK4 12 B4
Russell Rd OLDTF/WHR M16 98 A1
PART M31 106 D1
SLFD M6 70 E7
Russell St ATH M46 66 F1
AUL OL6 76 A8
BOL BL1 35 M4
BURY BL9 5 G1
CHAD OL9 8 B4
CHH M8 72 C8
DTN/ASHW M34 101 J1
DUK SK16 90 F4
ECC M30 85 H2
FWTH BL4 53 G5
HEY OL10 41 H2
LHULT M38 68 F1
MOSL OL5 76 F3
OFTN SK2 112 D6
OLDTF/WHR M16 98 C1
PWCH M25 55 M8
WGNE/HIN WN2 48 D4
WGNE/HIN WN2 65 M2
Russet Rd BKLY M9 73 G3
Ruth Av NEWH/MOS M40 74 B3
Ruthen La OLDTF/WHR M16 86 E8
Rutherford Av RUSH/FAL M14 98 E1
Rutherford Cl HYDE SK14 102 A2
Rutherford Dr WHTN BL5 51 J5
Rutherglade Cl NEWH/MOS M40 72 F6
Rutherglen Dr BOLS/LL BL3 35 H6
Rutherglen Wk
NEWH/MOS M40 73 H7
Ruthin Av BKLY M9 56 F7
CHD/CHDH SK8 120 A2
MDTN M24 57 K6
Ruthin Cl OLDS OL8 74 E2
Ruth St BOL BL1 2 C3
BURY BL9 5 G1
GTN M18 100 A1
OLD OL1 9 K3
WHIT OL12 18 E3
Rutland ROCH OL11 10 D7
Rutland Av ATH M46 51 J7
DID/WITH M20 98 D7
GOL/RIS/CU WA3 80 A5
OLDTF/WHR M16 97 K1
SWIN M27 70 C2
URM M41 96 B2
Rutland Cl AUL OL6 91 G2
BOLS/LL BL3 37 L8
CHD/CHDH SK8 110 E6
Rutland Crs RDSH SK5 101 G7
Rutland Dr AIMK WN4 63 M8
BRO M7 71 M4
BURY BL9 5 H9
Rutland Gv BOL BL1 35 M3
FWTH * BL4 52 F5
Rutland La SALE M33 97 J8
Rutland Rd ALT WA14 108 A6
BRAM/HZG SK7 122 A4
DROY M43 89 H2
ECC M30 85 J1
IRL M44 94 A7
PART M31 106 B2
TYLD M29 67 J2
WALK M28 68 F3
WGNE/HIN WN2 49 J6
Rutland St AUL OL6 91 G2
BOLS/LL BL3 36 A8
CHAD OL9 8 C9
FAIL * M35 74 C4
GTN M18 89 H6
HEY OL10 41 G2
HYDE SK14 91 G7
LEIGH WN7 67 H8
SWIN M27 70 B3
Rutland Wy ROY/SHW OL2 43 M4
Rutter's La BRAM/HZG SK7 121 L2
Ryall Av ORD M5 86 E4
Ryall Av South ORD M5 86 E4
Ryan St OP/CLY M11 89 H5
Rydal Av BRAM/HZG SK7 121 L1
CHAD OL9 58 B3
DROY M43 89 H3
ECC M30 69 L8
HYDE SK14 90 F7
MDTN M24 57 J6
MPL/ROM SK6 123 G4
ROY/SHW OL2 42 F4
SALE M33 96 C7
URM M41 95 K4
WGNE/HIN WN2 49 H7
WGNW/BIL/O WN5 46 C5
Rydal Cl AIMK WN4 63 M8
BURY BL9 39 H5
CHD/CHDH SK8 119 K1
DTN/ASHW M34 100 E2
HOR/BR BL6 32 F1
TYLD M29 67 K5
Rydal Ct BOL * BL1 35 J3
Rydal Crs SWIN M27 70 C6
WALK M28 69 H3
Rydal Dr HALE/TIMP WA15 117 M4
Rydal Gv AULW OL7 75 J8
FWTH BL4 52 C5
HEY OL10 41 G4
WHTF M45 55 J4
Rydal Pl WGNE/HIN WN2 48 E4
WGNE/HIN WN2 64 E4
Rydal Rd BOL BL1 35 K3
BOLS/LL BL3 53 K1
STRET M32 97 G1
Rydal St LEIGH WN7 66 B7
Ryde Av DTN/ASHW M34 101 L4
HTNM SK4 12 A2
Ryder Av ALT WA14 108 B5
Ryder Brow GTN M18 89 G8
Ryderbrow Rd GTN M18 89 G8
Ryder Gv LEIGH WN7 81 M2
Ryder St BOL BL1 35 M2
HEY * OL10 41 G2
NEWH/MOS M40 73 G8
Ryde St BOLS/LL * BL3 35 K8
WGNW/BIL/O WN5 47 H6
Rydings La WHIT OL12 19 H6
Rydings Rd WHIT OL12 19 J8
Rydley St BOLE BL2 3 J6
Ryebank Gv AUL OL6 76 A7
Ryebank Ms CCHDY * M21 97 J3
Ryebank Rd CCHDY M21 97 J3
Rye Bank Rd OLDTF/WHR M16 97 K2
Ryeburn Av WYTH/NTH M22 118 F1
Ryeburn Dr BOLE BL2 22 E7
Ryeburne St OLDE OL4 59 M5
Ryeburn Wk URM M41 84 C8
Rye Cft WHTF M45 54 F5
Rye Croft Av SLFD M6 85 M1
Ryecroft Av GOL/RIS/CU WA3 80 B3
HEY OL10 41 H2
TOT/BURYW BL8 24 C6
Ryecroft Cl CHAD OL9 74 C1
Ryecroft Dr WHTN BL5 50 A1
Ryecroft Gv NTHM/RTH M23 109 K5
Ryecroft La DTN/ASHW M34 90 B5
WALK M28 69 J8
Ryecroft Rd STRET M32 96 F3
Ryecroft St AULW OL7 90 C3
Ryecroft Vw DTN/ASHW M34 89 M4
Ryedale Av NEWH/MOS M40 73 G7
Ryedale Cl HTNM SK4 12 B1
Ryefield Cl HALE/TIMP WA15 108 F7
Ryefield Rd SALE M33 107 M2
Ryefields ROCH OL11 27 K6
Ryefields Dr UPML OL3 61 L3
Ryefield St BOL BL1 3 G1
Ryeford Cl WGNS/IIMK WN3 15 M8
Rye Hl WHTN * BL5 50 C4
Ryeland Cl MILN OL16 28 E8
Ryelands WHTN BL5 50 C4
Ryelands Ct WHTN * BL5 50 C4
Rye St HEY OL10 41 H1
Rylance St OP/CLY M11 88 B3
Rylands St GTN * M18 89 H6
WGNNW/ST WN6 47 K2
Rylane Wk NEWH/MOS M40 73 G7
Ryley Av BOLS/LL BL3 35 L7
Ryleys La WILM/AE SK9 130 C3
Ryley St BOLS/LL * BL3 2 A7
Rylstone Av CCHDY M21 110 A1
Ryther Gv BKLY M9 56 E7
Ryton Av GTN M18 99 M1
Ryton Cl WGNS/IIMK WN3 14 D8

S

Sabden Brook Dr
WGNE/HIN * WN2 64 C2
Sabden Cl BURY BL9 25 J5
HEY OL10 40 D2
NEWH/MOS M40 88 B1
Sabden Rd BOL BL1 35 H2
Sabrina St CHH M8 72 B7
Sackville Cl ROY/SHW OL2 43 K3
Sackville St AUL OL6 90 E1
BOLE * BL2 3 M4
CMANE M1 7 G6
CSLFD M3 6 C3
ROCH OL11 41 M3
Saddleback Cl WALK M28 68 E6
Saddleback Crs
WGNW/BIL/O WN5 46 E5
Saddleback Rd
WGNW/BIL/O WN5 46 E5
Saddlecote WALK * M28 69 K8
Saddle Gv DROY M43 90 A1
Saddle St BOLE BL2 36 E2
Saddlewood Av BNG/LEV M19 111 G2
Sadie Av STRET M32 85 K8
Sadler Ct HULME M15 87 H7
Sadler St BOLS/LL BL3 36 D8
MDTN M24 57 J3
Saffron Cl GOL/RIS/CU WA3 80 B4
Saffron Dr OLDE OL4 60 A2
Sagars Rd WILM/AE SK9 119 L8
Sagar St CHH M8 72 C8
St Agnes Rd BRUN/LGST M13 99 J2
St Agnes St RDSH SK5 100 C1
St Aidan's Cl ROCH OL11 10 A9
WGNW/BIL/O WN5 62 B6
St Aidan's Gv BRO M7 71 L6
St Albans Av AUL OL6 75 L6
HTNM SK4 99 M7
NEWH/MOS M40 73 L7
St Albans Cl OLDS OL8 59 J8
RNFD/HAY WA11 78 C5
St Albans Crs ALT WA14 107 M4
St Albans Pl NM/HAY SK22 124 E5
St Alban's St MILN OL16 10 D6
NM/HAY SK22 124 E4
St Alban's Ter CHH M8 72 C7
ROCH OL11 10 C7
St Aldates MPL/ROM SK6 113 J2
St Aldwyn's Rd DID/WITH M20 98 E7
St Ambrose Gdns SLFD * M6 86 C2
St Ambrose Rd OLD OL1 59 M3
TYLD M29 67 K7
St Andrew's Av DROY M43 89 H3
ECC M30 85 H3
HALE/TIMP WA15 108 B5
St Andrews Cl ALT WA14 107 M3
HTNM SK4 99 L8
MPL/ROM SK6 113 L3
RAMS BL0 17 C7
WHIT OL12 19 M8
St Andrews Ct BOL * BL1 2 E5
St Andrew's Crs
WGNE/HIN WN2 49 G7
St Andrew's Dr HEY OL10 41 G3
LEIGH WN7 66 F7
WGNNW/ST WN6 47 J2
St Andrews Rd CHD/CHDH SK8 119 L3
HOR/BR BL6 34 D5
HTNM SK4 99 L8
RAD M26 38 C6
STRET M32 96 E2
St Andrew's Sq CMANE M1 7 M6
St Andrew's St CMANE M1 7 L6
St Andrew's Vw RAD M26 38 C6
St Anne's Av ATH M46 67 H3
ROY/SHW OL2 59 G1
SLFD M6 86 B1
St Anne's Ct DTN/ASHW * M34 90 C6
SALE M33 96 F8
SLFD * M6 71 J8
WGNNW/ST WN6 30 C7
St Anne's Crs OLDE OL4 60 F7
St Anne's Dr DTN/ASHW M34 90 D8
WGNNW/ST WN6 30 D7
St Annes Gdns HEY OL10 41 J2
St Anne's Meadow
TOT/BURYW BL8 24 C5
St Annes Rd CCHDY M21 97 L5
DTN/ASHW M34 90 C6
DTN/ASHW M34 90 D8
HOR/BR BL6 21 C8
St Annes Sq UPML OL3 45 J8
St Annes St BURY * BL9 25 J8
HYDE SK14 103 K4
NEWH/MOS M40 73 J6
St Anns Cl PWCH M25 71 K1
St Anns Pas CMANW M2 6 F4
St Ann's Rd BRAM/HZG SK7 121 L3
MILN OL16 11 M3
PWCH M25 71 J1
St Ann's Rd North
CHD/CHDH SK8 119 K3
St Ann's Rd South
CHD/CHDH SK8 119 L3
St Ann's Sq CHD/CHDH SK8 119 L4
CMANW M2 6 F4
St Ann's St CMANW M2 6 E4
SALE M33 109 J1
SWIN M27 70 B4
St Ann St BOL * BL1 36 B3
St Asaphs Dr AUL OL6 75 L5
St Aubin's Rd BOLE BL2 3 J7
St Aubyn's Rd WGN * WN1 47 M1
St Augustine's Rd
EDGY/DAV SK3 12 B7
St Augustine St BOL BL1 36 A2
NEWH/MOS M40 73 G7
St Austell Av TYLD M29 67 M4
St Austell Dr CHD/CHDH SK8 119 K4
TOT/BURYW BL8 24 C2
St Austell Rd OLDTF/WHR M16 98 B3
St Austells Dr PWCH M25 55 L7
SWIN M27 70 F6
St Barnabas's Dr LIT OL15 20 B6
St Barnabas Sq OP/CLY M11 88 E4
St Bartholomew's Dr ORD M5 86 F4
St Bartholomew St BOLS/LL BL3 36 D8
St Bede's Av BOLS/LL BL3 51 L2
St Bees Cl CHD/CHDH SK8 119 K1
RUSH/FAL M14 87 K8
St Bees Rd BOLE BL2 36 F2
St Benedicts Av
WGTN/LGST * M12 88 C6
St Benedict's Sq
WGTN/LGST M12 88 C6
St Bernard's Av SLFD M6 71 M7
St Boniface Rd BRO M7 71 M8
St Brannock's Rd CCHDY M21 97 M3
CHD/CHDH SK8 120 D5
St Brelades Dr BRO M7 72 C4
St Brendan's Rd DID/WITH M20 98 E5
St Brendan's Rd North
DID/WITH M20 98 E5
St Brides Cl HOR/BR BL6 21 A8
St Brides Wy OLDTF/WHR M16 87 G7
St Catherines Dr FWTH BL4 52 C4
St Catherine's Rd DID/WITH M20 98 E5
St Chad's Av MPL/ROM SK6 113 M2
St Chad's Cl MILN OL16 10 F6
St Chads Ct MILN OL16 10 F5
St Chads Crs OLDS OL8 75 G3
UPML OL3 61 M4
St Chad's Gv MPL/ROM SK6 113 M2
St Chad's Rd DID/WITH M20 99 G5
St Chad's St CHH * M8 72 D8
St Charles Cl GLSP SK13 93 J7
St Christopher Ct
WGNNW/ST * WN6 30 F8
St Christopher's Av AUL OL6 76 B6
St Christophers Cl
DID/WITH M20 98 C6
St Christopher's Dr
MPL/ROM SK6 113 K2
St Christopher's Rd AUL OL6 76 A6
St Clair Rd RAMS * BL0 24 C1
St Clare Ter HOR/BR * BL6 34 C4
St Clements Ct OLDS OL8 9 J8
St Clement's Dr ORD M5 86 E5
St Clements Fold URM * M41 96 B2
St Clement's Rd CCHDY M21 97 K4
WGN WN1 47 M1
St Clement's St
WGNS/IIMK WN3 48 C8
St Cuthberts Fold OLDS OL8 75 K3
St Davids Av CHD/CHDH SK8 111 K7
MPL/ROM SK6 113 L2
St David's Cl AUL OL6 76 A5
St David's Crs WGNE/HIN WN2 32 E7
St David's Rd BRAM/HZG SK7 121 L3
CHD/CHDH SK8 111 K6
St Domingo Pl OLD * OL1 9 H5
St Dominics Ms BOLS/LL BL3 51 M1
St Dominics Wy MDTN M24 57 K5
St Edmund Hall Cl RAMS BL0 17 C8
St Edmund's Rd
NEWH/MOS M40 73 H6
St Edmund St BOL BL1 2 D4
St Elisabeth's Wy RDSH SK5 100 B5
St Elizabeth's Rd
WGNE/HIN WN2 32 E7
St Elmo Av OFTN SK2 113 G5
St Elmo Pk POY/DIS SK12 122 E8
St Ethelbert's Av BOLS/LL BL3 35 L7
St Gabriel's Cl ROCH OL11 42 A3
St George's Av
HALE/TIMP WA15 108 D4
HULME M15 87 G6
WHTN BL5 50 B6
St George's Ct ALT WA14 107 L5
BOL BL1 2 E3
HYDE * SK14 102 A2
STRET * M32 96 F3
TYLD M29 67 J4
St George's Crs
HALE/TIMP WA15 108 D4
SLFD * M6 85 K1
WALK M28 69 G2
St Georges Dr HYDE SK14 102 A3
NEWH/MOS M40 73 L5
St George's Gdns
DTN/ASHW M34 101 K3
St George's Pl ATH * M46 50 E8
St George's Rd BOL BL1 2 B3
BURY BL9 39 M8
DROY M43 89 J1
NM/HAY SK22 124 E4
PART M31 95 G6
ROCH OL11 27 J4
RUSH/FAL M14 99 H5
STRET M32 96 E2
St Georges Sq BOL BL1 2 F3
CHAD OL9 74 B1
St George's St BOL BL1 2 E3
STLY SK15 91 K1
TYLD M29 67 J4
St George's Wy SLFD * M6 71 K8
SLFD M6 71 K8
St Germain St FWTH BL4 52 F4
St Giles Dr HYDE SK14 102 C2
St Gregorys Cl FWTH BL4 52 F5
St Helena Rd BOL BL1 2 C4
St Helens Rd BOLS/LL BL3 35 M8
LEIGH WN7 80 F3
WHTN BL5 51 J3
St Helier's Dr BRO M7 72 C4
St Heliers St BOLS/LL BL3 36 A8
St Hilda's Dr OLD OL1 8 F2
St Hilda's Rd DTN/ASHW M34 90 B6
OLDTF/WHR M16 86 E7
WYTH/NTH M22 110 A3
St Hilda's Vw DTN/ASHW * M34 90 B7
St Hugh's Cl ALT WA14 108 B4
St Ignatius Wk ORD * M5 86 E4
St Ives Av CHD/CHDH SK8 111 K6
St Ives Crs SALE M33 108 D3
St Ives Rd RUSH/FAL M14 98 E2
St James Av BOLE BL2 37 H4
TOT/BURYW BL8 38 E1
St James Cl GLSP SK13 104 F4
MILN OL16 42 F4
St James Ct HALE/TIMP WA15 108 B8
SLFD * M6 85 L1
St James Crs WGNE/HIN WN2 65 J4
St James Dr SALE M33 108 D1
WILM/AE SK9 126 E6
St James Gv WGNS/IIMK WN3 14 E8
St James Rd HTNM SK4 99 L7
WGNW/BIL/O WN5 46 A8
St James's Gv ALT WA14 108 C3
St James's Rd BRO M7 72 B6
St James's Sq CMANW * M2 6 F5
St James's St OLD OL1 59 L5
St James's Ter HEY OL10 40 F2
St James St AUL OL6 91 G2
CMANE M1 7 G6
ECC * M30 85 H2
FWTH BL4 52 E5
HEY OL10 40 F2
MILN OL16 29 J6
ROY/SHW OL2 43 L5
WHTN BL5 50 C7
St James' Wy CHD/CHDH SK8 120 B6
St John's Av DROY M43 89 L2
WHTN BL5 50 A1
St John's Cl BRO * M7 72 A6
DUK SK16 91 H4
MPL/ROM SK6 113 L2
St Johns Ct BRO * M7 72 A6
HOR/BR BL6 34 E8
HYDE SK14 102 C1
MILN OL16 11 J6
OLDE OL4 60 C5
RAD M26 54 E2
St John's Dr HYDE SK14 102 C1
MILN OL16 11 J6
St John's Gdns MOSL OL5 76 F2
St John's Rd ALT WA14 116 E1
BRAM/HZG SK7 121 K3
BRUN/LGST M13 88 C8
DTN/ASHW M34 90 C7
HOR/BR BL6 50 E1
HTNM SK4 111 H2
OLDTF/WHR M16 86 F8
WALK M28 68 B5
WGNE/HIN WN2 32 E7
WILM/AE SK9 130 B1
St John's St BRO M7 72 A6
CHAD OL9 8 D8
FWTH BL4 53 H4
RAD M26 54 E2
WGNE/HIN WN2 64 E4
St John St ATH M46 67 G1
CSLFD M3 6 D6
DUK * SK16 91 H4
ECC M30 85 G3
HOR/BR BL6 21 B8
IRL M44 94 D2
NM/HAY SK22 125 L2
OLDE OL4 60 B6
SWIN M27 71 G6
WALK M28 52 F8
WGNW/BIL/O WN5 46 E6
St John's Wk CHAD OL9 8 D7
EDGY/DAV * SK3 12 B6
St Johns Wd HOR/BR BL6 34 E8
St Josephs Av WHTF M45 55 L5
St Joseph's Dr MILN OL16 28 E8
ORD M5 86 E4
St Joseph St BOL BL1 36 A2
St Katherines Dr HOR/BR BL6 32 F1
St Kilda Av FWTH BL4 53 J6
St Kildas Av DROY M43 89 J1
St Lawrence Quay SALQ M50 86 C5
St Lawrence Rd
DTN/ASHW M34 101 J1
St Leonard's Av HOR/BR BL6 34 C3
St Leonard's Ct SALE M33 96 C8
St Leonards Dr
HALE/TIMP WA15 108 C6
St Leonard's Rd HTNM SK4 100 A7
St Leonard's St MDTN M24 57 K3
St Lesmo Rd EDGY/DAV SK3 12 C8
St Luke's Av GOL/RIS/CU WA3 80 A4
St Lukes Ct CHAD OL9 58 D5
St Luke's Dr WGNW/BIL/O WN5 46 A8
St Luke's Rd SLFD M6 86 A2
St Luke St ROCH OL11 10 F8
St Malo Rd WGN WN1 31 M8
St Margaret's Av BNG/LEV M19 99 J6
St Margaret's Cl BOL * BL1 35 L4
PWCH M25 55 M6
St Margarets Gdns OLDS * OL8 74 F1
St Margaret's Rd ALT WA14 107 M8
BOL BL1 35 L4
CHD/CHDH SK8 111 K6
NEWH/MOS M40 74 A1
PWCH M25 55 M7
St Mark's Av ALT WA14 107 K7
ROY/SHW OL2 43 K8
WGNW/BIL/O WN5 47 J5
St Mark's Cl ROY/SHW OL2 43 K8
St Mark's Crs WALK M28 69 G3
St Mark's La CHH M8 72 C5
St Mark's Sq BURY BL9 5 G1
St Mark's St BNG/LEV M19 99 M3
BOLS/LL BL3 2 E9
MPL/ROM SK6 101 K8
St Mark St DUK SK16 90 E3
St Mark's Vw BOLS/LL * BL3 2 E9
St Marks Wk BOLS/LL BL3 36 B8
St Martin's Av HTNM SK4 12 C3
St Martins Cl DROY M43 89 J1
DROY * M43 89 J1
HYDE * SK14 102 C2
St Martin's Dr BRO M7 72 C4
St Martin's Rd MPL/ROM SK6 114 D6
OLDS OL8 75 K2
SALE M33 96 A6
St Martin's St ROCH OL11 41 M3
St Mary's Av BOLS/LL BL3 35 K7
DTN/ASHW M34 101 K4
St Mary's Cl ATH M46 67 H1
MILN OL16 28 E8
PWCH M25 55 K8
STKP SK1 13 L4
WGNE/HIN * WN2 32 E7
St Marys Ct NEWH/MOS M40 73 L4
NEWH/MOS * M40 73 L4
OLD * OL1 9 H4
St Mary's Crest UPML OL3 61 M7
St Mary's Dr CHD/CHDH * SK8 111 J6
RDSH SK5 100 C7
UPML OL3 61 M7
St Marys Est OLD OL1 9 J4
St Mary's Ga CMANE M1 6 F3
ROY/SHW * OL2 43 L5
UPML * OL3 61 L4
WHIT OL12 10 D4
St Mary's Hall Rd CHH M8 72 C3
St Mary's Parsonage CSLFD M3 6 E4
CSLFD * M3 6 E4
St Mary's Pl BURY BL9 4 D5
St Mary's Rd ALT WA14 116 D2
ECC M30 85 J2
GLSP SK13 104 F3
HYDE SK14 91 H7
NEWH/MOS M40 73 L5
NM/HAY SK22 124 D4
POY/DIS SK12 123 M7
PWCH M25 55 K8
SALE M33 96 C7
WALK M28 52 F8
WGNE/HIN WN2 32 E6
St Mary's St CSLFD M3 6 E4
HULME M15 87 H7
OLD OL1 9 J3
OLDTF/WHR M16 87 J8
St Mary's Wy LEIGH * WN7 66 C7
OLD OL1 9 H4
STKP SK1 13 L7
STKP SK1 13 M3

St Matthews Rd
EDGY/DAV * SK3 ....12 F7
St Matthew's Cl
WGNS/IIMK WN3 ....46 F8
St Matthew's Dr *STRET* * M32 ...58 D2
St Matthews Gra *BOL* * BL1 ...36 B3
St Matthew's Rd *EDGY/DAV* SK3 ...12 F7
St Matthews Ter
EDGY/DAV * SK3 ....12 F7
St Matthews Wk *BOL* * BL1 ...36 B6
St Mawes Ct *RAD* * M26 ...37M7
St Michael's Av *ATH* M46 ...66 D3
BOLS/LL BL3 ....52 E2
BRAM/HZG SK7 ....121 G5
St Michaels Cl *TOT/BURYW* BL8 ...38 C4
St Michaels Cl *SALE* M33 ...96 B6
WGN WN1 ....14 F1
St Michaels Gdns *WHTF* M45 ...55 L3
St Michael's Rd *HYDE* SK14 ...102 C1
St Michael's Sq *ANC* * M4 ...7 H1
St Modwen Rd *STRET* M32 ...85 J7
St Nicholas Rd *GOL/RIS/CU* WA3 ...80 D3
St Osmund's Dr *BOLE* BL2 ...37 H5
St Osmund's Gv *BOLE* BL2 ...37 H5
BNG/LEV M19 ....99 L2
St Oswalds Rd *AIMK* WN4 ...78 D2
St Patrick St *WGN* WN1 ...15 J4
St Patricks Wy *WGN* WN1 ...15 J4
St Pauls Cl *STLY* SK15 ...91M2
St Paul's Av *WGNS/IIMK* WN3 ...47 J8
St Paul's Ct *RAD* M26 ...54 D3
St Paul's Hill Rd *HYDE* SK14 ...102 C2
St Paul's Rd *BRO* M7 ...71M3
DID/WITH M20 ....98 F6
HTNM SK4 ....99 L8
WALK * M28 ....69 H2
St Paul's St *BURY* BL9 ...5 J3
HYDE SK14 ....102 B1
RAMS * BL0 ....17 C6
STKP SK1 ....13M1
STLY SK15 ....91M2
St Pauls Vis *BURY* BL9 ...5 J3
St Peter's Av *BOL* BL1 ...35 K2
St Peters Cl *AULW* OL7 ...90 C2
St Peters Ct *STRET* * M32 ...97 H1
St Petersgate *STKP* SK1 ...13 H5
St Peter's Dr *HYDE* * SK14 ...102 C2
St Peter's Rd *BURY* BL9 ...39 J6
SWIN M27 ....70 B5
St Peter's Sq *CMANW* M2 ...6 F6
CMANW * M2 ....6 F6
STKP SK1 ....13 H4
St Peter's St *AUL* OL6 ...90 D2
MILN OL16 ....11 J7
St Peter's Ter *FWTH* BL4 ...53 G5
BOLE BL2 ....2 F3
BOLS/LL BL3 ....36 E8
St Philip's Av *BOLS/LL* BL3 ...36 A8
St Philip's Pl *CSLFD* * M3 ...6 A3
St Philip's Rd *GTN* M18 ...89 J2
St Phillip's Dr *ROY/SHW* OL2 ...59 H3
St Saviour's Rd *OFTN* SK2 ...112 F7
Saintsbridge Rd
WYTH/NTH M22 ....118 E2
St Simons Cl *OFTN* SK2 ...112 F4
St Simon St *CSLFD* M3 ...87 G1
St Stephen's Av *DTN/ASHW* M34 ...90 B4
WGN WN1 ....88 B2
St Stephen's Cl *BOLS/LL* BL3 ...3 L8
BRUN/LGST M13 ....88 A7
TYLD M29 ....67 K7
St Stephens Ct *BKLY* * M9 ...73 G5
St Stephen's Rd
WGNNW/ST WN6 ....30 F3
St Stephen St *OLD* OL1 ...9 L3
CSLFD M3 ....6 C3
OLD OL1 ....9 L3
St Stephens Vw *DROY* M43 ...89 K2
St Teresa's Rd *OLDTF/WHR* M16 ...97 K1
St Thomas's Rd *UPML* * OL3 ...45 H8
St Thomas's Pl *CHH* * M8 ...72 D8
St Thomas's Cir *OLDS* OL8 ...8 A7
St Thomas's Pl *STKP* SK1 ...13 J7
St Thomas St *BOL* * BL1 ...36 A2
WGNS/IIMK WN3 ....14 F6
St Thomas St North *OLDS* OL8 ...8 F8
St Thomas St South *OLDS* OL8 ...8 F9
St Vincent St *ANC* M4 ...7 M4
HALE/TIMP WA15 ....108 B8
St Werburgh's Rd *CCHDY* M21 ...97M4
St Wilfred's Dr *WHIT* * OL12 ...18 E8
St Wilfrid's Rd *WGNNW/ST* WN6 ...31 J4
St Wilfrids St *HULME* M15 ...87 H6
St Williams Av *BOLS/LL* BL3 ...52 B1
Salcombe Av *BOLE* BL2 ...38 A3
Salcombe Cl *SALE* M33 ...96 B7
WGN WN1 ....48 B2
Salcombe Gv *BOLE* BL2 ...37 J6
Salcombe Rd *OFTN* SK2 ...112 F4
OP/CLY M11 ....89 C4
Salcot Wk *NEWH/MOS* * M40 ...87M1
Sale Heys Rd *SALE* M33 ...108 C1
Sale La *TYLD* M29 ...68 A3
Salem Gv *OLDE* OL4 ...60 A6
Sale Rd *NTHM/RTH* M23 ...109 K2
Sales's La *BURY* BL9 ...25 L2
Sale St *LIT* OL15 ...20 C6
Salford Ap *CSLFD* M3 ...6 E2
Salford Rd *WHTN* BL5 ...51 K4
OLDE OL4 ....59M7
Salik Gdns *ROCH* OL11 ...10 E8
Salisbury Av *HEY* OL10 ...40 F4
WGNE/HIN WN2 ....49 J6
Salisbury Crs *AUL* OL6 ...76 A5
Salisbury Dr *DUK* SK16 ...91 K5
PWCH M25 ....71M2
Salisbury Rd *AIMK* * WN4 ...63 K7
ALT WA14 ....108 A5
CCHDY M21 ....97 L3
ECC M30 ....70 C8
HOR/BR BL6 ....34 B3
OLDE OL4 ....59 L6
RAD M26 ....38 A2
RNFD/HAY WA11 ....78 B3
SWIN M27 ....70 B5
URM M41 ....85 G8
WHTF M45 ....55 J4
Salisbury Ter *BOLS/LL* BL3 ...2 B5
GLSP SK13 ....93 K7
GOL/RIS/CU WA3 ....79 K4
MDTN M24 ....57 L3
RDSH SK5 ....100 C4
ROY/SHW OL2 ....43 J4
RUSH/FAL M14 ....87 K8
Salisbury Ter *BOLS/LL* BL3 ...53M1

Salisbury Wy *TYLD* M29 ...67 L4
Salkeld Av *AIMK* WN4 ...78 C1
Salkeld St *ROCH* OL11 ...10 F9
Sallowfields Wk *WGNNW/BIL/O* WN5 ...46 A7
Salmon Flds *ROY/SHW* OL2 ...59 J1
Salmon St *ANC* M4 ...7 H3
WGN * WN1 ....15 K1
Salmsbury Hall Cl *RAMS* BL0 ...17 B8
Salop St *BOLE* BL2 ...3 G6
SLFD M6 ....71 K8
Saltash Cl *WYTH/NTH* M22 ...118 F3
Saltdene Rd *WYTH/NTH* M22 ...118 D3
Saltergate *BOLS/LL* BL3 ...35 J8
Saltergate Ms *SLFD* * M6 ...86 D2
Salters St *ATH* M46 ...67 G1
Salterton Dr *BOLS/LL* BL3 ...51 J7
Salteye Rd *ECC* M30 ...84 D3
Saltford Av *ANC* M4 ...7M3
Saltford Ct *ANC* M4 ...7M3
Salthill Av *HEY* OL10 ...41 H5
Salthill Dr *WYTH/NTH* M22 ...119 C2
Salthouse Cl *TOT/BURYW* BL8 ...24 F6
Saltire Gdns *BRO* M7 ...72 B4
Saltney Av *DID/WITH* M20 ...98 C5
Saltram Cl *BOLS/LL* BL3 ...37M7
Saltram Rd *WGNS/IIMK* WN3 ...46 F8
Saltrush Rd *WYTH/NTH* M22 ...118 F2
Salts Dr *LIT* OL15 ...20 B6
Salts St *ROY/SHW* OL2 ...43 L5
Saltwood Gv *BOL* BL1 ...2 E1
Salutation St *HULME* M15 ...87 J6
Salvin Cl *AIMK* WN4 ...79 C1
Salwick Cl *WGNS/IIMK* WN3 ...47 H8
Sam Cowan Rd *RUSH/FAL* M14 ...98 D1
Samian Gdns *BRO* M7 ...71M7
Samlesbury Cl *DID/WITH* M20 ...110 C1
ROY/SHW OL2 ....43 J5
Samouth Cl *NEWH/MOS* M40 ...88 A1
Sampson Sq *RUSH/FAL* M14 ...87 K8
Sam Rd *UPML* OL3 ...45M8
Samson St *MILN* OL16 ...11M2
Sam Swire St *HULME* M15 ...87 H7
Samuel La *ROY/SHW* OL2 ...43 H4
Samuel Ogden St *CMANE* M1 ...7 H7
Samuel St *ATH* M46 ...67 J3
BNG/LEV M19 ....99 L4
BURY BL9 ....5 H2
FAIL M35 ....74 C4
HEY OL10 ....40 F2
HTNM SK4 ....112 A1
ROCH OL11 ....41M2
Sanby Av *GTN* M18 ...88 F8
Sanby Rd *GTN* M18 ...88 F8
The Sanctuary *HULME* M15 ...87 H6
Sanctuary Cl *BRUN/LGST* M13 ...87 L7
Sandacre Rd *NTHM/RTH* M23 ...109 L5
Sandal St *NEWH/MOS* M40 ...88 B1
Sandalwood *WGNNW/ST* WN6 ...47 J2
Sandalwood Dr
WGNNW/ST WN6 ....47 J2
Sandbach Av *RUSH/FAL* M14 ...98 C4
Sandbach Rd *RDSH* * SK5 ...100 B2
SALE M33 ....109 J1
Sandbank Gdns *WHIT* OL12 ...18 D2
Sand Banks *BOL* BL1 ...22 C6
Sandbed La *MOSL* OL5 ...76 F2
UPML OL3 ....45 K7
Sandbrook Gdns
WGNNW/BIL/O WN5 ....46 A7
Sandbrook Rd *ROCH* * OL11 ...28 B8
Sandbrook Wy *DTN/ASHW* M34 ...90 C7
ROCH OL11 ....28 B8
Sandby Dr *MPL/ROM* SK6 ...114 E4
Sanderling Dr *WHTN* BL5 ...50 A6
Sanderling Dr *LEIGH* WN7 ...66 D7
Sanderling Rd *OFTN* SK2 ...113 K7
Sanderson Cl *WALK* M28 ...69 L4
Sanderson's Cft *LEIGH* WN7 ...66 F4
Sanderson St *BURY* BL9 ...5 J3
LEIGH WN7 ....66 B7
NEWH/MOS M40 ....73 H7
Sanderstead Dr *BKLY* M9 ...73 H1
Sandfield Cl *GOL/RIS/CU* WA3 ...80 A4
Sandfield Crs *GOL/RIS/CU* WA3 ...81M5
Sandfield Dr *HOR/BR* BL6 ...34 F6
Sandfield Rd *MILN* OL16 ...11 J9
Sandford Av *GTN* * M18 ...89 C6
Sandford Cl *BOLE* BL2 ...37 H1
Sandford Rd *SALE* M33 ...109 J1
Sandford Station La *RDSH* SK5 ...100 A2
Sandford St *RAD* M26 ...39 G8
Sandgate Av *OP/CLY* M11 ...89 G2
RAD M26 ....53 L5
Sandgate Cl *LEIGH* WN7 ...66 C6
Sandgate Dr *URM* M41 ...84 F8
Sandgate Rd *CHAD* OL9 ...8 A7
WHTF M45 ....55 L5
Sandham St *BOLS/LL* BL3 ...36 C8
Sandham Wk *BOLS/LL* * BL3 ...36 C8
Sandheys *DTN/ASHW* M34 ...90 C7
Sandheys Gv *GTN* M18 ...89 H8
Sandhill Cl *BOLS/LL* * BL3 ...36 C8
Sandhill La *MPL/ROM* SK6 ...115 H3
Sandhill St *HYDE* SK14 ...102 C1
Sandhill Wk *WYTH/NTH* M22 ...118 D2
Sand Hole La *ROCH* OL11 ...27 H7
ROCH OL11 ....42 C3
Sand Hole Rd *FWTH* BL4 ...53 K6
Sandhurst Av *DID/WITH* M20 ...98 D5
Sandhurst Cl *TOT/BURYW* BL8 ...38 E1
Sandhurst Ct *BOLE* BL2 ...37 H6
Sandhurst Dr *BOLE* BL2 ...37 H6
WILM/AE SK9 ....127 C3
Sandhurst Rd *DID/WITH* M20 ...110 D2
OFTN SK2 ....112 F7
Sandhutton Rd *BKLY* M9 ...73 C3
Sandiacre *WGNNW/ST* WN6 ...31 H4
Sandilands Rd *NTHM/RTH* M23 ...109 C4
Sandileigh Av *CHD/CHDH* SK8 ...111 K6
DID/WITH M20 ....98 E7
HALE/TIMP WA15 ....117 H1
RDSH SK5 ....100 C2
Sandileigh Dr
HALE/TIMP WA15 ....117 H1
Sandiway *BRAM/HZG* SK7 ...121 C2
GLSP SK13 ....105 J3
HEY OL10 ....41 H2
IRL M44 ....94 D2
MPL/ROM SK6 ....113 J4
Sandiway Cl *MPL/ROM* SK6 ...114 C4
WHTN BL5 ....50 A4
Sandiway Dr *DID/WITH* M20 ...110 D1
Sandiway Pl *ALT* WA14 ...108 A7
Sandiway Rd *ALT* WA14 ...108 A6
SALE M33 ....96 E1
WILM/AE SK9 ....119M7
Sand La *MCFLDN* SK10 ...130 C7
Sandling Dr *GOL/RIS/CU* WA3 ...79 K2
Sandon St *BOLS/LL* BL3 ...36 A8
Sandown Av *SLFD* M6 ...86 B2

Sandown Cl *GOL/RIS/CU* * WA3 ...81 J8
OLD OL1 ....59 K3
WILM/AE SK9 ....127 H4
Sandown Crs *BOLS/LL* BL3 ...53 K2
GTN M18 ....100 A1
Sandown Dr *DTN/ASHW* M34 ...101 L4
HALE/TIMP WA15 ....117M6
SALE M33 ....108 B1
Sandown Gdns *URM* M41 ...95 K2
Sandown Rd *BOLE* BL2 ...37 H1
BRAM/HZG SK7 ....122 C3
BURY BL9 ....55 K2
EDGY/DAV SK3 ....12 A7
WGNNW/ST WN6 ....47 H1
Sandown St *GTN* M18 ...89 H6
Sandpiper Cl *DUK* SK16 ...91 H5
FWTH BL4 ....52 C5
NEWLW WA12 ....78 F8
ROCH OL11 ....27 J5
Sandpiper Dr *EDGY/DAV* SK3 ...112 A6
Sandpiper Rd *WGNS/IIMK* WN3 ...46 E8
Sandray Cl *BOLS/LL* BL3 ...35 J7
Sandridge Cl *FWTH* BL4 ...53 H4
Sandringham Wk *WGTN/LGST* M12 ...88 B6
Sandringham Av
DTN/ASHW M34 ....90 A6
DTN/ASHW M34 ....100 D1
STLY SK15 ....91 K1
Sandringham Cl *ALT* WA14 ...116 B3
WGNNW/BIL/O WN5 ....47 H7
Sandringham Dr *DUK* SK16 ...91 J5
HTNM SK4 ....111 K3
LEIGH WN7 ....66 A7
MILN OL16 ....29 K6
POY/DIS SK12 ....129 H1
RAMS BL0 ....24 D3
Sandringham Gra *PWCH* M25 ...72 B1
Sandringham Rd
BRAM/HZG SK7 ....122 B2
CHD/CHDH SK8 ....120 C1
HOR/BR BL6 ....34 A2
HYDE SK14 ....102 B5
MPL/ROM SK6 ....112 F1
WALK M28 ....68 D6
WGNE/HIN WN2 ....49 H8
Sandringham St *GTN* M18 ...88 F8
Sandringham Wy *ROY/SHW* OL2 ...42 F6
WILM/AE SK9 ....126 E6
Sands Av *CHAD* OL9 ...58 A4
Sands Cl *HYDE* SK14 ...103 G3
Sandsend Cl *CHH* M8 ...72 B7
Sandsend Rd *URM* M41 ...95M1
Sandstone Rd *MILN* OL16 ...29 J5
WGNS/IIMK WN3 ....63 C2
Sandstone Wy *CCHDY* M21 ...98 A6
Sand St *NEWH/MOS* M40 ...72 F8
STLY SK15 ....91 J4
Sandway *WGNNW/ST* WN6 ...47 J2
Sandwell Dr *SALE* M33 ...96 E6
Sandwich Rd *ECC* M30 ...85 J1
Sandwich St *WALK* M28 ...68 G2
Sandwick Crs *BOLS/LL* BL3 ...2 B5
Sandwood Av *BOLS/LL* BL3 ...35 H7
Sandy Acre *WHTN* BL5 ...51 K6
Sandyacre Cl *WHTN* BL5 ...51 K6
Sandy Bank *ROY/SHW* OL2 ...43 J4
Sandybank Cl *GLSP* SK13 ...93 H8
Sandy Bank Rd *CHH* M8 ...72 C4
Sandy Bank Wk *HYDE* * SK14 ...103 G3
Sandybrook Cl *TOT/BURYW* BL8 ...24 C6
Sandy Brook *BKLY* M9 ...73 C2
Sandy Cl *SWIN* M27 ...70 B5
Sandycroft Av *SWIN* M27 ...70 B5
Sandy Gv *DUK* SK16 ...91 C4
SLFD M6 ....86 B3
SWIN M27 ....70 C4
Sandy Haven Cl *HYDE* SK14 ...103 G3
Sandyhill Rd *BKLY* M9 ...72 D1
Sandyhills *BOLS/LL* BL3 ...36 B8
Sandylands Dr *PWCH* M25 ...71 J3
Sandy La *CCHDY* M21 ...97 L4
DROY M43 ....89M1
DUK SK16 ....91 C4
GLSP SK13 ....103 K4
GOL/RIS/CU WA3 ....80 D2
IRL M44 ....94 D1
MDTN M24 ....57 L5
MPL/ROM SK6 ....113M1
NEWLW WA12 ....79 J4
NTHM/RTH M23 ....109 C5
OLDS * OL8 ....8 F7
PWCH M25 ....71 K2
RDSH SK5 ....112 B1
ROCH OL11 ....27M5
ROY/SHW OL2 ....43 G8
SLFD M6 ....86 E1
STRET M32 ....96 E3
TYLD M29 ....67 K8
TYLD M29 ....82 E3
UPML OL3 ....61 L2
WGNE/HIN WN2 ....49 J6
WGNNW/BIL/O WN5 ....46 A3
WILM/AE SK9 ....126 B4
Sandy Meade *PWCH* M25 ...71 K1
Sandy Pk *WGNE/HIN* WN2 ...49 K6
Sandyway *PWCH* * M25 ...71 K1
Sandywell Cl *OP/CLY* M11 ...89 C5
Sandywell St *OP/CLY* M11 ...89 C4
Sandy Wd *SLFD* M6 ...86 B1
Sanfold La *BNG/LEV* M19 ...99M2
Sangster St *ORD* M5 ...6 B9
Sankey Gv *BKLY* M9 ...72 E1
Sankey St *BURY* BL9 ...4 E5
GOL/RIS/CU WA3 ....79 K4
Santiago St *RUSH/FAL* M14 ...98 E1
Santley St *WGTN/LGST* M12 ...99 J1
Santon Av *RUSH/FAL* M14 ...99 H4
Santon Dr *GOL/RIS/CU* WA3 ...80 B4
Sapling Gv *SALE* M33 ...108 A2
Sapling Rd *BOLS/LL* BL3 ...51M2
SWIN M27 ....70 A7
Sarah Butterworth Ct
MILN OL16 ....11 K5
Sarah Butterworth St
MILN OL16 ....11 K6
Sarah St *ECC* M30 ...84 E3
MDTN M24 ....57 J4
OP/CLY M11 ....88 C4
RAMS BL0 ....17 E1
ROY/SHW OL2 ....43 L7
Sargent Dr *OLDTF/WHR* M16 ...87 H8
Sargent Rd *MPL/ROM* SK6 ...113 G2
Sark Rd *CCHDY* M21 ...97M4

Sarn Av *WYTH/NTH* M22 ...110 A8
Sarsfield Av *GOL/RIS/CU* WA3 ...80 A4
Satinwood Cl *AIMK* WN4 ...78 C1
Saturn Gv *SLFD* M6 ...71M8
Saunton Av *BOLE* BL2 ...37 J6
Saunton Rd *OP/CLY* M11 ...89 G4
Sautridge Cl *MDTN* M24 ...58 D1
Savernake Rd *MPL/ROM* SK6 ...101M7
Savick Av *BOLE* BL2 ...37 H5
Saville Rd *CHD/CHDH* SK8 ...110 E6
RAD M26 ....38 C5
Saville St *BOLE* BL2 ...3 G5
MDTN M24 ....58 A5
Saviours Ter *BOLS/LL* * BL3 ...35M7
Savio Wy *MDTN* M24 ...58 D1
Savoy Ct *WHTF* * M45 ...55 H3
Savoy Dr *ROY/SHW* OL2 ...59 C2
Savoy St *OLDE* OL4 ...59 L7
ROCH OL11 ....27M4
Sawley Av *GOL/RIS/CU* WA3 ...80 A3
LIT OL15 ....20 B5
OLDE OL4 ....60 A8
WGNNW/ST WN6 ....47 J1
WHTF M45 ....55 J2
Sawley Dr *CHD/CHDH* SK8 ...120 D6
Sawley Rd *NEWH/MOS* M40 ...73 G8
Sawpit St *LYMM* WA13 ...106 D5
Saw St *BOL* BL1 ...36 B2
Sawyer Brow *HYDE* SK14 ...91 J8
Sawyer Dr *AIMK* WN4 ...79 C1
Sawyer St *TOT/BURYW* BL8 ...24 E8
WHIT OL12 ....10 E1
Saxby Av *EDGW/EG* BL7 ...22 C4
Saxby St *SLFD* M6 ...70 F7
Saxby Dr *CHH* M8 ...72 E6
Saxfield Dr *NTHM/RTH* M23 ...109M4
Saxon Av *CHH* M8 ...72 D2
DUK SK16 ....90 F4
Saxon Cl *TOT/BURYW* BL8 ...38 E2
Saxon Dr *CHAD* OL9 ...58 B4
DROY M43 ....89 K2
DTN/ASHW M34 ....90 B5
Saxonholme Rd *ROCH* OL11 ...41M4
Saxon St *DROY* M43 ...89 L2
DTN/ASHW M34 ....101 J1
MDTN M24 ....57 L4
NEWH/MOS M40 ....88 B1
OLDE OL4 ....59M5
RAD M26 ....54 C1
Saxthorpe Cl *SALE* M33 ...96 A7
WGNS/IIMK WN3 ....63 G3
Saxthorpe Wk *WGTN/LGST* M12 ...88 D7
Saxwood Av *BKLY* M9 ...73 G3
Saxwood Cl *WHIT* OL12 ...27 J3
Scafell Av *AULW* OL7 ...75 J8
Scafell Cl *MPL/ROM* SK6 ...123 G4
OLD OL1 ....9 K1
Scafell Dr *WGNNW/BIL/O* WN5 ...46 E6
WGNE/HIN WN2 ....64 E2
Scale St *ORD* M5 ...86 E3
Scaliot Cl *NM/HAY* SK22 ...124 D4
Scant Rw *HOR/BR* * BL6 ...34 F1
Scarborough St
NEWH/MOS M40 ....73 K4
Scarcroft Rd *WGTN/LGST* M12 ...88 D7
Scardale Av *BOL* BL1 ...35 K3
Scarfield Dr *ROCH* OL11 ...27 H3
Scargill Cl *RUSH/FAL* * M14 ...98 F4
Scargill Rd *BOLS/LL* BL3 ...35 K8
Scarisbrick Av *DID/WITH* M20 ...111 G1
Scarisbrick Rd *BNG/LEV* M19 ...99 H3
Scarisbrick St *WGN* WN1 ...15 G1
Scarr Av *RAD* M26 ...54 F2
Scarr Dr *WHIT* OL12 ...28 C2
Scarr La *ROY/SHW* OL2 ...43M5
Scarsdale Rd *RUSH/FAL* M14 ...88 B8
Scarsdale St *SLFD* M6 ...86 E1
Scarthwood Cl *BOLE* BL2 ...23 H7
Scawfell Av *BOLE* BL2 ...37 J6
Schofield Gdns *LEIGH* WN7 ...81 H1
Schofield La *ATH* M46 ...66 E1
Schofield Rd *DROY* M43 ...89 L3
ECC M30 ....84 D3
Schofield St *FAIL* * M35 ...74 C4
HEY OL10 ....41 G3
LEIGH WN7 ....81 H1
LIT OL15 ....20 D6
LIT OL15 ....20 E2
MILN OL16 ....29 K7
OLDS OL8 ....75 H1
OP/CLY M11 ....88 F2
ROCH OL11 ....28 D8
ROY/SHW OL2 ....43 G7
Scholars Dr *DID/WITH* M20 ...98 D5
Scholars Wy *MDTN* M24 ...57 J3
Scholefield La *WGN* WN1 ...15 J3
Scholes Bank *HOR/BR* BL6 ...21 A7
Scholes Dr *NEWH/MOS* M40 ...74 B2
Scholes La *PWCH* M25 ...71M1
Scholes St *CHAD* OL9 ...58 D8
FAIL M35 ....74 B4
OLD OL1 ....9 L5
ROCH OL11 ....41M3
SWIN M27 ....70 D4
TOT/BURYW BL8 ....38 F1
Scholes Wk *PWCH* M25 ...71 L1
Scholey St *BOLS/LL* BL3 ...3 H6
Scholfield Av *URM* M41 ...96 C3
School Av *AUL* OL6 ...76 A1
STRET * M32 ....97 J1
WGN WN1 ....14 F1
School Brow *BURY* BL9 ...4 F4
MPL/ROM SK6 ....113 K2
WALK M28 ....69 J6
WGNNW/BIL/O WN5 ....62 B7
School Cl *POY/DIS* SK12 ...129 K5
School La *ANC* M4 ...7 L3
EDGY/DAV SK3 ....112 C6
RAMS BL0 ....17 D3
School Crs *STLY* SK15 ...91 J3
School Dr *WGNNW/BIL/O* WN5 ...62 B7
Schoolfold La *MCFLDN* SK10 ...129 L5
School Gv *DID/WITH* M20 ...71 K2
PWCH M25 ....71 K2
School Gv West
DID/WITH * M20 ....98 F6
School Hi *BOL* BL1 ...2 D2
School House Flats *OLDS* * OL8 ...74 F2
School La *ALT* WA14 ...107 C8
BKLY M9 ....72 F2
BURY BL9 ....5 H4
CHD/CHDH SK8 ....120 C4
DID/WITH M20 ....110 F1
EDGW/EG BL7 ....16 D4
HTNM SK4 ....99M7
HYDE SK14 ....102 B5
IRL M44 ....94 A1
IRL M44 ....94 C2
MCFLDN SK10 ....131 J6

MILN OL16 ....10 A1
MOSL OL5 ....77 H5
MPL/ROM SK6 ....102 E7
MPL/ROM SK6 ....114 E1
PART M31 ....95 H6
POY/DIS SK12 ....122 D8
POY/DIS SK12 ....129 K1
ROCH OL11 ....26 F4
WGN WN1 ....15 H3
WGNE/HIN WN2 ....32 B4
WGNE/HIN WN2 ....31 G3
School Ms *MILN* * OL16 ...29 L8
School Rd *ECC* M30 ...84 F4
FAIL M35 ....74 C5
HALE/TIMP WA15 ....117 H1
OLDS OL8 ....74 E2
SALE M33 ....96 D7
STRET M32 ....96 F2
WILM/AE SK9 ....119M8
Schools Hi *CHD/CHDH* SK8 ...119M1
Schoolside Cl *CHH* M8 ...72 E6
Schoolside La *MDTN* M24 ...56 E5
Schools Rd *GTN* M18 ...89 H7
School St *AIMK* WN4 ...64 A7
ANC M4 ....7 H1
ATH M46 ....66 E2
BOLS/LL BL3 ....53 L1
BRAM/HZG SK7 ....122 A2
BRO M7 ....72 B8
BURY BL9 ....5 J6
ECC M30 ....84 E1
EDGW/EG BL7 ....16 C4
GOL/RIS/CU WA3 ....79 K4
HEY OL10 ....40 F2
HOR/BR BL6 ....33M1
LEIGH WN7 ....66 B4
LIT OL15 ....19M7
OLDE OL4 ....60 D6
OLDS OL8 ....8 E8
RAD M26 ....54 C1
RAMS BL0 ....17 B7
TYLD M29 ....67 J4
UPML OL3 ....61 L4
WGN WN1 ....15 H3
WGNE/HIN WN2 ....48 C5
WGNE/HIN WN2 ....49 K4
WHIT OL12 ....10 E5
WHIT OL12 ....10 D5
WHIT OL12 ....50 B4
School Ter *GOL/RIS/CU* * WA3 ...79 K4
School Wk *OLDTF/WHR* M16 ...87 G7
School Wy *WGNNW/BIL/O* WN5 ...46 B7
Schuter Rd *RUSH/FAL* M14 ...99 G1
Schwabe St *MDTN* M24 ...56 F4
Scobell St *TOT/BURYW* BL8 ...24 C7
Score St *OP/CLY* M11 ...88 D3
Scorton Av *BOLE* BL2 ...37 J5
Scorton St *BOL* * BL1 ...35M4
Scotforth Cl *HULME* M15 ...6 C9
Scotland *ANC* M4 ...7 G1
Scotland Hall Rd
NEWH/MOS M40 ....73 L7
Scotland La *BURY* BL9 ...25 K6
Scotland St *AUL* OL6 ...90 F2
NEWH/MOS M40 ....73M7
Scot La *WGNE/HIN* WN2 ...33 G6
WGNNW/BIL/O WN5 ....47 H5
Scott Av *BURY* BL9 ...39 J6
CCHDY M21 ....97 L2
ECC M30 ....84 F1
WGNE/HIN WN2 ....49 H6
Scott Dr *HALE/TIMP* WA15 ...108 C8
MPL/ROM SK6 ....114 E4
Scottfield *OLDS* OL8 ...9 H9
Scottfield Rd *OLDS* OL8 ...9 J9
Scott Ga *DTN/ASHW* M34 ...90 B5
Scottia Rd *ECC* M30 ...84 E4
Scottia Rd *ECC* M30 ...84 E4
Scott Rd *DROY* M43 ...89 K3
DTN/ASHW M34 ....101 H3
GOL/RIS/CU WA3 ....80 A3
PWCH M25 ....71 J1
Scott St *LEIGH* WN7 ...66 A7
OLDS OL8 ....8 A8
RAD M26 ....54 A5
SLFD M6 ....71M8
TYLD M29 ....67M8
WGNNW/ST WN6 ....14 D2
WHTN BL5 ....50 B2
Scout Dr *NTHM/RTH* M23 ...109 J8
Scout Gn *MDTN* M24 ...57 K1
Scout Vw *TOT/BURYW* BL8 ...24 D6
Scovell St *BRO* M7 ...72 A6
Scowcroft La *ROY/SHW* OL2 ...43 K6
Scowcroft St *BOLE* BL2 ...3 J1
Scroggins La *PART* M31 ...94 C8
Scropton St *NEWH/MOS* M40 ...73 C7
Seabright Wk *OP/CLY* * M11 ...88 C4
Seabrook Crs *URM* M41 ...84 C8
Seabrook Rd *NEWH/MOS* M40 ...73M7
Seacombe Av *RUSH/FAL* M14 ...98 D3
Seacombe Gv *EDGY/DAV* SK3 ...12 A6
Seaford Rd *BOLE* BL2 ...23 H6
SLFD M6 ....71 L7
Seaford Wk *CHAD* * OL9 ...8 B7
Seaforth Av *ATH* M46 ...50 F8
Seaforth Rd *BOL* BL1 ...22 B7
Seaham Dr *TOT/BURYW* BL8 ...24 F7
Seaham Wk *RUSH/FAL* M14 ...98 E1
Sealand Cl *SALE* M33 ...109 H2
Sealand Dr *ECC* M30 ...84 D4
Sealand Rd *NTHM/RTH* M23 ...109 J2
Seale Av *DTN/ASHW* M34 ...90 A3
Sealey Wk *NEWH/MOS* * M40 ...73 H8
Seal Rd *BRAM/HZG* SK7 ...121 H4
Seaman Wy *WGNE/HIN* WN2 ...48 D6
Seamon's Dr *ALT* WA14 ...107 K6
Seamon's Rd *ALT* WA14 ...107 K6
Searby Rd *GTN* M18 ...88 B8
Searness Rd *MDTN* M24 ...56 F2
Seascale Av *OP/CLY* M11 ...88 C1
Seascale Crs *WGN* WN1 ...47M1
Seathwaite Cl *TYLD* M29 ...67 K5
Seathwaite Rd *FWTH* BL4 ...52 C5
Seatoller Dr *MDTN* M24 ...56 F2
Seatoller Pl *WGNNW/BIL/O* WN5 ...46 E5
Seaton Cl *BRAM/HZG* SK7 ...121M3
Seaton Ms *AULW* OL7 ...75 H8
Seaton Rd *BOL* BL1 ...35M6
Sebastian Cl *MPL/ROM* SK6 ...114 E5
Sebastopol Wk *ANC* M4 ...7 L3
Second Av *ATH* M46 ...51 C8
BOL BL1 ....35 L5
BURY BL9 ....26 A8
MCFLDN SK10 ....129 H3
OLDS OL8 ....74 F2
OP/CLY M11 ....89 G2
STLY SK15 ....77 H7
SWIN M27 ....70 A7
TRPK M17 ....86 A7
TYLD M29 ....67 L8

WGNNW/ST WN6 47 K2
Section St BOL BL1 2 E6
Sedan Cl ORD M5 86 D3
Sedburgh Cl SALE M33 108 A1
Sedbury Cl NTHM/RTH M23 109 J3
Seddon Av GTN M18 89 G6
RAD M26 39 H7
Seddon Cl ATH M46 66 F1
RAD M26 38 D8
Seddon Gdns RAD M26 53 K4
Seddon House Dr
WGNNW/ST WN6 47 H1
Seddon La RAD M26 53 K4
Seddon Rd ALT WA14 116 F2
Seddons Av TOT/BURYW BL8 38 D4
Seddon St BNG/LEV M19 99 L2
BOLS/LL * BL3 53 L1
LHULT M38 52 C7
RAD M26 54 D1
WHTN BL5 50 B1
Sedgeborough Rd
OLDTF/WHR M16 98 B1
Sedge Cl RDSH SK5 100 D4
Sedgefield Cl ORD M5 86 D2
Sedgefield Dr BOL BL1 35 L1
WGNNW/ST WN6 47 H1
Sedgefield Pk OLDE OL4 60 A6
Sedgefield Rd RAD M26 54 C4
Sedgeford Cl WILM/AE SK9 127 G3
Sedgeford Rd NEWH/MOS M40 73 G7
Sedgely WGNNW/ST WN6 31 K5
Sedgemoor Cl CHD/CHDH SK8 120 D2
Sedgemoor V BOLE BL2 37 J2
Sedgemoor Wy OLD OL1 9 H4
Sedgley Av MILN OL16 28 E8
PWCH M25 71 M2
Sedgley Cl MDTN M24 57 M5
Sedgley Dr WHTN BL5 50 B7
Sedgley Park Rd PWCH M25 71 M2
Sedgley Rd CHH M8 72 D4
Sedgley St MDTN M24 57 M5
Sedgwick Cl ATH M46 67 H1
WHTN BL5 50 C6
Sedwyn St WGN WN1 15 K1
Seedfield Rd BURY BL9 25 J7
Seedley Av LHULT M38 52 E8
Seedley Park Rd SLFD M6 86 B2
Seedley Rd SLFD M6 86 C1
Seedley St RUSH/FAL M14 98 E1
Seedley Ter SLFD M6 86 B1
Seedley View Rd ORD M5 86 B1
Seed St BOL BL1 35 M5
Seel St MOSL OL5 76 E3
Sefton Av ATH M46 50 F7
WGNW/BIL/O WN5 46 A7
Sefton Cl BRUN/LGST M13 87 L6
MDTN M24 57 H4
OLD OL1 44 A8
WGNW/BIL/O WN5 46 A7
Sefton Crs SALE M33 96 E6
Sefton Dr BURY BL9 25 K6
SWIN M27 70 A6
WALK M28 69 K6
WILM/AE SK9 127 G2
Sefton Fold Dr
WGNW/BIL/O WN5 62 A7
Sefton Fold Gdns
WGNW/BIL/O WN5 62 A7
Sefton La HOR/BR BL6 34 A3
Sefton Rd AIMK WN4 63 J6
BOL BL1 35 L2
CCHDY M21 97 L4
MDTN M24 57 H4
SALE M33 96 E7
SWIN M27 70 C3
WGNS/IIMK WN3 47 J8
WGNW/BIL/O WN5 46 A7
Sefton St BURY BL9 25 J6
CHAD OL9 74 D2
CHH M8 72 D4
GLSP SK13 104 F4
HEY OL10 41 H3
LEIGH WN7 66 C7
RAD M26 54 F3
ROCH OL11 10 E9
WHTF M45 55 J5
Sefton Vw WGNW/BIL/O WN5 46 A7
Selborne Rd CCHDY M21 97 L3
Selbourne Cl WHTN BL5 50 D3
Selbourne St LEIGH WN7 66 C5
Selby Av CHAD OL9 58 C3
WHTF M45 55 J2
Selby Cl MILN OL16 29 H6
POY/DIS * SK12 121 M7
RAD M26 39 G7
STRET M32 96 C1
Selby Dr SLFD M6 85 L1
URM M41 84 C7
WGNS/IIMK WN3 46 F8
Selby Gdns CHD/CHDH SK8 120 E6
Selby Rd MDTN M24 57 J1
STRET M32 96 D1
Selby St HTNM SK4 100 A8
MILN OL16 11 J2
OP/CLY M11 88 D4
Selham Wk BRUN/LGST * M13 7 L9
Selhurst Av OP/CLY M11 88 F2
Selkirk Av AIMK WN4 63 G8
OLDS OL8 59 G8
Selkirk Dr BKLY M9 73 J1
Selkirk Gv WGNW/BIL/O WN5 46 E4
Selkirk Rd BOL BL1 22 A7
CHAD OL9 58 C8
Sellars Sq DROY M43 89 K4
Sellers Wy CHAD OL9 74 D1
Selsby Av ECC M30 84 E2
Selsey Av EDGY/DAV SK3 111 J5
SALE M33 108 C1
Selsey Dr DID/WITH M20 110 F4
Selside WGNS/IIMK WN3 63 L2
Selside Wk RUSH/FAL M14 98 F4
Selstead Rd WYTH/NTH M22 118 E3
Selston Rd BKLY M9 56 E8
Selworth Av SALE M33 97 H8
Selworth Cl HALE/TIMP WA15 108 B6
Selworthy Rd OLDTF/WHR M16 87 H8
Selwyn Av BKLY M9 73 G4
Selwyn Cl NEWLW WA12 78 E7
OLDS * OL8 9 G8
Selwyn Dr CHD/CHDH SK8 120 E5
Selwyn St BOLE BL2 3 H6
LEIGH WN7 66 C6
Senecar Cl WGNE/HIN WN2 48 E2
Senior Av RUSH/FAL M14 99 H5
Senior Rd ECC M30 84 C4
Senior St CSLFD M3 6 D1
Senior Vw HYDE * SK14 91 H7
Sennicar La WGN WN1 31 M7
WGN WN1 32 B6
Sepal Cl RDSH SK5 100 D3
Sephton St WGNS/IIMK WN3 15 M7
Sepia Gv MDTN M24 57 J3
Sequoia St BKLY M9 73 H4
Sergeants La WHTF M45 54 F5
Serin Cl OFTN SK2 113 J8
Service St EDGY/DAV SK3 12 B6
Set St STLY SK15 91 J3
Settle Cl TOT/BURYW BL8 38 C2
Settle St BOLS/LL BL3 52 B1
BOLS/LL BL3 53 M2
Sett Valley Trail NM/HAY SK22 125 H2
Sevenacres UPML OL3 45 J7
Seven Acres La WHIT OL12 27 H2
Seven Acres Rd WHIT OL12 27 H2
Seven Oaks LEIGH WN7 66 D6
Sevenoaks Av HTNM SK4 99 K7
URM M41 85 G8
Sevenoaks Dr BOLS/LL BL3 52 B1
SWIN M27 70 D6
Sevenoaks Rd CHD/CHDH SK8 110 E6
Sevenoaks Wk
BRUN/LGST * M13 87 M7
Seven Stars Rd
WGNS/IIMK WN3 14 C5
Seven Stiles Dr MPL/ROM SK6 114 B5
Seventh Av OLDS OL8 74 F3
Severn Cl ALT WA14 107 M6
BURY BL9 25 J5
WGNW/BIL/O WN5 62 A8
Severn Dr BRAM/HZG SK7 120 E6
MILN OL16 29 K6
WGNE/HIN WN2 65 M1
WGNW/BIL/O WN5 46 F6
Severn Rd AIMK WN4 64 B7
CHAD OL9 58 C4
HEY OL10 40 D1
OLDS OL8 75 K1
Severn St LEIGH WN7 66 E8
Severn Wy FWTH BL4 53 L6
RDSH SK5 100 C7
Seville St ROY/SHW OL2 43 K7
ROY/SHW OL2 59 H2
Sewell Wy LHULT M38 68 C1
Sewerby Cl OLDTF/WHR M16 87 J8
Sewerby St OLDTF/WHR M16 87 H8
Sexa St OP/CLY M11 89 G4
Sexton St GLSP SK13 93 J5
HEY OL10 40 F2
Seymour Av OP/CLY M11 89 G2
Seymour Cl OLDTF/WHR M16 86 F7
Seymour Dr BOLE BL2 22 F6
Seymour Gv FWTH * BL4 52 D3
HALE/TIMP WA15 108 D7
MILN OL16 42 E1
MPL/ROM SK6 114 B6
OLDTF/WHR M16 86 E8
SALE M33 96 E8
Seymour Pl OLDTF/WHR * M16 86 E7
Seymour Rd BOL BL1 36 C1
CHD/CHDH SK8 120 C4
CHH M8 72 C3
OFTN SK2 112 E6
Seymour Rd South OP/CLY M11 89 G2
Seymour St BOLE BL2 22 F6
DTN/ASHW M34 90 A8
GTN M18 89 G6
HEY OL10 40 E3
RAD M26 54 E1
Shackleton Gv BOL BL1 35 H2
Shackleton St ECC M30 84 F1
Shackliffe Rd NEWH/MOS M40 73 J5
Shaddock Av ROCH OL11 27 J3
Shade Av OLDE OL4 60 C7
Shadowbrook Cl OLD OL1 9 H1
Shadowmoss Rd
WYTH/NTH M22 119 G4
Shadows La MOSL OL5 61 H8
Shadwell Gv LEIGH WN7 65 M4
Shadwell St East HEY OL10 41 G1
Shadwell St West HEY OL10 41 G1
Shady La BOLE BL2 22 E6
NTHM/RTH M23 109 G5
Shady Oak Rd OFTN SK2 113 J6
Shaftesbury Av
CHD/CHDH SK8 120 D3
ECC M30 84 F4
HALE/TIMP WA15 108 E7
HOR/BR BL6 34 C4
LIT OL15 29 K2
Shaftesbury Dr WHIT OL12 19 L6
Shaftesbury Gdns URM M41 94 F2
Shaftesbury Rd CHH M8 72 D5
EDGY/DAV SK3 111 K6
SWIN M27 70 C5
Shaftsbury Dr HEY OL10 40 F4
Shaftsbury Rd
WGNW/BIL/O WN5 46 D4
Shaftsbury St WGNNW/ST WN6 47 J1
Shaftway Cl RNFD/HAY WA11 78 C5
Shakerley La TYLD M29 51 J8
Shakerley Rd TYLD M29 67 J3
Shakespeare Av BURY BL9 39 J6
DTN/ASHW M34 101 J4
RAD M26 38 B8
STLY SK15 92 B1
Shakespeare Cl LIT OL15 20 D3
Shakespeare Crs DROY M43 89 K2
ECC M30 85 G2
Shakespeare Dr
CHD/CHDH SK8 111 J6
Shakespeare Gv
WGNS/IIMK WN3 47 K8
Shakespeare Rd DROY M43 89 K2
MPL/ROM SK6 113 H1
OLD OL1 59 L2
PWCH M25 71 J1
SWIN M27 70 A4
Shakespeare Wk
BRUN/LGST * M13 87 M6
Shakleton Av BKLY M9 73 K1
Shalbourne Rd WALK M28 68 F1
Shaldon Dr NEWH/MOS M40 74 B8
Shalfleet Cl BOLE BL2 23 H7
Shalford Dr WYTH/NTH M22 118 F4
Shambles Sq ANC M4 6 F3
Shandon Av WYTH/NTH M22 110 A3
Shanklin Av URM M41 95 M2
Shanklin Cl CCHDY M21 97 K3
DTN/ASHW * M34 101 L4
Shanklin Wk BOLS/LL BL3 3 M9
Shanley Ct CHAD * OL9 8 B3
Shannon Cl HEY OL10 40 D1
Shannon Rd WYTH/NTH M22 119 G1
Shap Av HALE/TIMP WA15 109 G7
Shap Dr WALK M28 69 G1
Shap Ga WGNW/BIL/O WN5 46 E5
Sharcott Cl OLDTF/WHR M16 87 J8
Shardlow Cl NEWH/MOS M40 73 G8
Shared St WGN WN1 15 J5
Shargate Cl WILM/AE SK9 127 G3
Sharman St BOLS/LL BL3 3 J9
Sharnford Cl BOLE BL2 3 J7
Sharnford Sq WGTN/LGST * M12 88 D6
Sharon Av OLDE OL4 61 G7
Sharon Cl AULW OL7 90 B3
Sharon Sq WGNE/HIN WN2 64 C4
Sharples Av BOL BL1 22 B6
Sharples Dr TOT/BURYW BL8 24 C8
Sharples Gn EDGW/EG BL7 16 D6
Sharples Hall Dr BOL BL1 22 C6
Sharples Hall Fold BOL BL1 22 C7
Sharples Hall Ms BOL BL1 22 C6
Sharples Hall St OLDE OL4 60 A3
Sharples Pk BOL BL1 22 A8
Sharples St HTNM SK4 112 B1
Sharp St ANC M4 7 J1
MDTN M24 57 K4
PWCH * M25 55 K8
WALK M28 69 H1
WGNS/IIMK WN3 15 K8
Sharrington Dr
NTHM/RTH M23 109 H6
Sharston Rd WYTH/NTH M22 110 B5
Shaving La WALK M28 69 G3
Shaw Av HYDE SK14 102 C4
Shawbrook Av WALK M28 68 E4
Shawbrook Rd BNG/LEV M19 99 K7
Shawbury Cl HOR/BR BL6 33 G3
Shawbury Gv SALE M33 108 C2
Shawbury Rd NTHM/RTH M23 109 L8
Shawbury St MDTN M24 57 M5
Shawclough Cl WHIT OL12 28 A1
Shawclough Dr WHIT OL12 27 M1
Shawclough Ri WHIT * OL12 28 A2
Shawclough Rd WHIT OL12 27 M1
Shawclough Wy WHIT OL12 27 M1
Shawcroft Cl ROY/SHW OL2 43 K7
Shawcross Fold STKP * SK1 13 J3
Shawcross La WYTH/NTH M22 110 C4
Shawcross St HYDE SK14 102 C4
SLFD M6 86 C3
STKP SK1 13 K7
Shawdene Rd WYTH/NTH M22 109 M4
Shawe Hall Av URM M41 95 K4
Shawe Hall Crs URM M41 95 K4
Shawe Rd URM M41 95 K2
Shawe Vw URM M41 95 K2
Shawfield Cl RUSH/FAL M14 98 D4
Shawfield La WHIT OL12 27 K2
Shawfield Rd GLSP SK13 104 C1
Shawfields STLY SK15 92 A1
Shawford Rd NEWH/MOS M40 73 M2
Shawgreen Cl HULME M15 87 G6
Shaw Hall Av HYDE SK14 91 L7
Shaw Hall Bank Rd UPML OL3 61 J7
Shaw Hall Cl UPML OL3 61 J7
Shaw Head Dr FAIL M35 74 C6
Shaw Heath EDGY/DAV SK3 13 G7
Shawheath Cl HULME M15 87 G6
Shawhill Wk NEWH/MOS M40 88 B2
Shaw La GLSP SK13 104 B2
MILN OL16 29 J3
Shawlea Av BNG/LEV M19 99 H6
Shaw Moor Av STLY SK15 91 M3
Shaw Rd HOR/BR BL6 21 B7
HTNM SK4 99 L7
MILN OL16 42 E3
MILN OL16 43 L1
OLD OL1 9 L2
ROY/SHW OL2 43 J8
Shaw Rd South EDGY/DAV SK3 13 J9
Shaws Fold OLDE * OL4 60 D5
Shaws La UPML OL3 61 L4
Shaw's Rd ALT WA14 108 A8
Shaw St AIMK WN4 63 L7
AUL OL6 91 G1
BOLS/LL BL3 2 C8
BURY BL9 5 K3
CSLFD M3 6 F1
FWTH * BL4 52 F2
GLSP SK13 104 F4
HYDE SK14 92 D8
OLD OL1 9 K4
OLDE OL4 60 D6
RNFD/HAY WA11 78 B6
ROY/SHW OL2 43 H8
UPML OL3 61 K6
WGN WN1 15 G1
WHIT OL12 28 E2
Shay Av HALE/TIMP WA15 118 A3
Shayfield Av CHAD OL9 58 B4
WYTH/NTH M22 110 A7
Shayfield Dr WYTH/NTH M22 110 A7
Shayfield Rd WYTH/NTH M22 110 A7
Shay La HALE/TIMP WA15 117 M3
Sheader Dr ORD M5 85 M2
Sheard Av AUL OL6 76 A6
Sheardhall Av POY/DIS SK12 124 A7
Shearer Wy SWIN M27 71 G5
Shearing Av WHIT OL12 27 J3
Shearsby Cl HULME M15 87 H6
Shearwater Av TYLD M29 67 K4
Shearwater Dr WALK M28 68 F1
WHTN BL5 50 A6
Shearwater Gdns ECC M30 84 D4
Shearwater Rd OFTN SK2 113 J7
The Sheddings BOLS/LL BL3 36 D8
Shed St WHIT OL12 18 E3
Sheepfoot La OLD OL1 59 G3
PWCH M25 72 A1
Sheep Gap WHIT OL12 27 L3
Sheep Gate Dr TOT/BURYW BL8 24 B7
Sheep Hey RAMS * BL0 17 D3
Sheerness St GTN M18 89 G7
Sheffield Rd GLSP SK13 105 H3
HYDE SK14 91 J8
Sheffield St CMANE M1 7 K6
HTNM SK4 13 H1
Shefford Cl OP/CLY M11 88 C4
Shefford Crs WGNS/IIMK WN3 62 F2
Sheiling Ct ALT WA14 107 M8
The Sheilings GOL/RIS/CU WA3 80 C4
Shelbourne Av BOL BL1 35 L2
Shelburne Dr WGNE/HIN WN2 48 F8
Shelden Ms GLSP SK13 104 A3
Shelderton Cl NEWH/MOS M40 73 K5
Sheldon Av WGNNW/ST WN6 31 H2
Sheldon Cl PART M31 106 B1
Sheldon Ct AULW OL7 75 L7
Sheldon Rd BRAM/HZG SK7 122 A5
Sheldon St OP/CLY M11 88 E2
Sheldrake Cl DUK SK16 91 H5
Sheldrake Rd ALT WA14 107 L4
Sheldwich Cl LEIGH WN7 81 J1
Shelfield Cl ROCH OL11 27 J3
Shelfield La ROCH OL11 27 J3
Shelford Av GTN M18 88 E8
Shelley Av MDTN M24 57 L1
Shelley Dr WGNE/HIN WN2 64 E3
WGNW/BIL/O WN5 46 D6
Shelley Gv DROY M43 89 K3
HYDE SK14 91 G8
STLY SK15 77 H8
Shelley Ri DUK SK16 91 L5
Shelley Rd CHAD OL9 74 C1
LHULT * M38 52 D7
OLD OL1 59 M3
PWCH M25 71 J1
RDSH SK5 100 A3
SWIN M27 70 A4
Shelley St LEIGH WN7 65 M5
NEWH/MOS M40 73 M4
Shelley Wk BOL BL1 36 A3
Shellingford Cl WGNNW/ST WN6 30 A5
Shelton Av SALE M33 96 A8
Shenfield Wk NEWH/MOS M40 88 A1
Shenhurst Cl WILM/AE SK9 126 C8
Shentonfield Rd
WYTH/NTH M22 110 B6
Shenton Park Av SALE M33 107 M3
Shenton St HYDE SK14 90 F8
Shepherd Cross St BOL BL1 35 M3
Shepherds Cl HOR/BR BL6 32 F1
TOT/BURYW BL8 24 C3
Shepherd's Dr HOR/BR BL6 34 D1
Shepherd St BKLY * M9 73 G3
BURY BL9 5 G6
HEY * OL10 40 F2
ROCH OL11 27 G3
ROY/SHW OL2 43 H8
TOT/BURYW BL8 24 C4
WHIT * OL12 10 E2
Shepherds Wy MILN OL16 29 H7
Shepley Av BOLS/LL BL3 35 M7
Shepley Cl BRAM/HZG SK7 121 M4
DUK SK16 91 G4
Shepley Dr BRAM/HZG SK7 121 M3
Shepley La MPL/ROM SK6 114 C8
Shepley Rd DTN/ASHW M34 90 C6
Shepley St CMANE M1 7 J6
DTN/ASHW M34 90 C5
FAIL M35 74 D3
GLSP SK13 105 H2
HYDE SK14 102 B2
OLDE * OL4 60 B6
Shepton Av WGNE/HIN WN2 64 D3
Shepton Cl BOL BL1 22 A5
Shepton Dr NTHM/RTH M23 118 C2
Sheraton Cl WGNW/BIL/O WN5 46 E3
Sheraton Rd OLDS OL8 59 H8
Sherborne Av WGNE/HIN WN2 49 K7
Sherborne Rd EDGY/DAV SK3 111 K5
MDTN M24 57 J1
URM M41 96 B1
WGNW/BIL/O WN5 46 D4
Sherborne St CHH M8 72 C7
Sherborne St West CSLFD M3 87 H1
Sherbourne Cl CHD/CHDH SK8 120 D6
OLDS OL8 59 M8
RAD M26 38 A7
Sherbourne Dr HEY OL10 40 D1
Sherbourne Pl WGNS/IIMK WN3 15 K9
Sherbourne Rd BOL BL1 35 K3
Sherbourne St PWCH * M25 55 K8
Sherbrook Cl SALE M33 108 C1
Sherbrooke Av UPML OL3 61 M3
Sherbrooke Rd POY/DIS SK12 123 M6
Sherbrook Ri WILM/AE SK9 127 G6
Sherdley Ct CHH M8 72 D3
Sherdley Rd CHH M8 72 D3
Sherford Cl BRAM/HZG SK7 121 J2
Sheridan Av GOL/RIS/CU WA3 80 A5
Sheridan Wy CHAD * OL9 58 B4
Sheriffs Dr TYLD M29 68 A3
Sheriff St BOLE BL2 36 E3
MILN OL16 29 K7
WHIT OL12 10 C3
Sheringham Dr HYDE SK14 102 D1
SWIN M27 70 C6
TOT/BURYW BL8 24 F7
Sheringham Pl BOLS/LL BL3 2 A9
Sheringham Rd RUSH/FAL M14 99 G5
Sherlock Av RNFD/HAY WA11 78 B5
Sherlock St RUSH/FAL M14 99 G5
Sherratt St ANC M4 7 K2
Sherrington St WGTN/LGST M12 99 K1
Sherway Dr HALE/TIMP WA15 108 F6
Sherwell Rd BKLY M9 72 E1
Sherwin Wy ROCH OL11 42 A3
Sherwood Av AIMK * WN4 63 M8
BRO M7 71 L5
DROY M43 89 M2
HTNM SK4 111 K3
RAD M26 38 C4
RUSH/FAL M14 98 F4
SALE M33 96 F7
TYLD M29 67 K6
Sherwood Cl AUL OL6 75 M5
MPL/ROM SK6 114 C8
ORD M5 86 A1
TOT/BURYW BL8 24 C5
Sherwood Crs WGNE/HIN WN2 64 D2
WGNW/BIL/O WN5 47 G5
Sherwood Dr SWIN M27 70 E5
WGNW/BIL/O WN5 47 G5
Sherwood Fold GLSP SK13 104 A5
Sherwood Gv LEIGH WN7 81 L2
WGNW/BIL/O WN5 47 G5
Sherwood Rd DTN/ASHW M34 100 E1
MPL/ROM SK6 101 L7
Sherwood St BOL BL1 36 C1
OLD OL1 8 E2
ROCH OL11 42 A2
RUSH/FAL M14 98 F4
Sherwood Wy ROY/SHW OL2 43 H4
Shetland Rd NEWH/MOS M40 88 A1
Shetland Wy RAD M26 38 D7
URM M41 85 G7
Shevington Gdns
NTHM/RTH M23 109 L3
Shevington La WGNNW/ST WN6 30 E3
Shevington Moor
WGNNW/ST WN6 30 D2
Shieldborn Dr BKLY M9 73 G5
Shield Cl OLDS OL8 9 G7
Shield Dr WALK M28 69 M3
Shield St EDGY/DAV SK3 13 G6
Shiel St WALK M28 69 G1
Shiers Dr CHD/CHDH SK8 111 H8
Shiffnall St BOLE BL2 3 G6
Shildon Cl WGNE/HIN WN2 48 C2
Shilford Dr ANC M4 7 K1
Shillingford Rd FWTH BL4 52 F4
Shillingstone Cl BOLE BL2 37 J1
Shillingten Cl LHULT M38 68 C1
Shiloh La OLDE OL4 60 E2
Shiloh Rd NM/HAY SK22 115 M5
Shilton Gdns BOLS/LL BL3 2 C8
Shilton St RAMS BL0 17 B7
Shipgate BOL BL1 2 F4
Shipham Cl LEIGH WN7 66 A4
Shipla Cl CHAD OL9 9 G4
Ship La OLDE OL4 44 D7
Shipley Av SLFD M6 85 M1
Shipley Vw URM M41 84 C7
Shipper Bottom La RAMS BL0 17 D7
Shippey St RUSH/FAL M14 99 G5
Shipston Cl TOT/BURYW BL8 38 E1
Shipton St BOL BL1 35 L3
Ship Yd WGN WN1 15 G4
Shirburn ROCH OL11 10 D7
Shirebrook Dr GLSP SK13 105 H4
RAD M26 38 E8
Shireburn Av BOLE BL2 3 M3
Shiredale Cl CHD/CHDH SK8 111 L8
Shiredale Dr BKLY M9 73 G5
Shiregreen Av NEWH/MOS M40 72 F7
Shirehills PWCH M25 71 K1
Shireoak Rd DID/WITH M20 99 G5
The Shires DROY M43 90 A1
RAD M26 38 D7
Shires Cl WGNE/HIN WN2 49 H8
Shire Wy GLSP SK13 105 H1
Shirewell Rd WGNW/BIL/O WN5 46 B7
Shirley Av BRO M7 71 K5
CHAD OL9 74 B2
CHD/CHDH SK8 119 L6
DTN/ASHW M34 89 M4
ECC M30 84 F4
HYDE SK14 91 G7
MPL/ROM SK6 114 B6
STRET M32 97 J1
SWIN M27 70 F5
Shirley Cl BRAM/HZG SK7 121 L2
Shirley Gv EDGY/DAV SK3 112 B7
Shirley Rd CHH M8 72 D5
Shirley St ROCH OL11 41 M2
Shoecroft Av DTN/ASHW M34 101 H2
Sholver Hill Cl OLD OL1 44 B8
Sholver La OLD OL1 44 A8
Shone Av WYTH/NTH M22 119 H2
Shore Av ROY/SHW OL2 43 M3
Shoreditch Cl HTNM SK4 99 L7
Shorefield Cl MILN OL16 29 J5
Shorefield Mt EDGW/EG BL7 22 B4
Shore Fold LIT OL15 20 A6
Shoreham Wk CHAD * OL9 58 D6
Shore Hl LIT OL15 20 D6
Shore Lea LIT OL15 20 A6
Shore Mt LIT OL15 20 A6
Shore Rd LIT OL15 20 A5
Shore St MILN OL16 29 J6
OLD OL1 9 M4
Shoreswood BOL BL1 22 A6
Shorland St SWIN M27 69 M5
Shorrocks St TOT/BURYW BL8 38 C1
Short Av DROY M43 89 J4
Shortcroft St HULME M15 6 E8
Shortland Crs BNG/LEV M19 111 G1
Shortland Pl WGNE/HIN WN2 65 K4
Shortlands Av BURY BL9 5 G7
Short St ANC M4 7 H4
BRAM/HZG SK7 121 M1
BRO M7 87 H1
GOL/RIS/CU * WA3 79 L3
HEY OL10 40 E3
HTNM SK4 13 G1
RNFD/HAY WA11 78 B6
WGNW/BIL/O WN5 46 E6
Short St East HTNM SK4 13 H1
Shotton Wk RUSH/FAL * M14 98 E1
Shrewsbury Cl WGNE/HIN WN2 49 J6
Shrewsbury Ct
OLDTF/WHR * M16 87 G7
Shrewsbury Gdns
CHD/CHDH SK8 120 E6
Shrewsbury Rd BOL BL1 35 L4
DROY M43 89 K2
PWCH M25 71 K1
SALE M33 108 D2
Shrewsbury St GLSP SK13 104 F3
OLDE OL4 59 M4
OLDTF/WHR M16 87 G7
Shrigley Cl WILM/AE SK9 127 H3
Shrigley Rd MCFLDN SK10 129 M8
Shropshire Av RDSH SK5 100 F6
Shropshire Dr GLSP SK13 105 J4
Shropshire Rd FAIL M35 74 D6
Shropshire Sq
WGTN/LGST * M12 88 B6
Shrowbridge Wk
WGTN/LGST M12 88 D6
Shudehill ANC M4 7 H2
NM/HAY * SK22 125 M1
Shudehill Cl NM/HAY SK22 125 M1
Shurdington Rd ATH M46 51 J7
Shurmer St BOLS/LL BL3 35 M8
Shutt La UPML OL3 61 J2
Shuttle Hillock Rd
WGNE/HIN WN2 65 J5
Shuttle St ECC * M30 85 J2
RAD M26 54 F3
TYLD M29 67 J3
WGNE/HIN WN2 49 H6
Shuttleworth Cl
OLDTF/WHR M16 98 B4
Shutts La STLY SK15 92 A4
Siam St OP/CLY M11 88 C4
Sibley Av AIMK WN4 64 A8
Sibley Rd HTNM SK4 111 L1
Sibley St GTN M18 89 G7
Sibson Rd CCHDY M21 97 K3
SALE M33 96 D8
Sickle St CMANW M2 7 G4
OLDE OL4 9 L8
Sidbrook St WGNE/HIN WN2 48 F7
Sidbury Rd CCHDY M21 97 M4
Sidcup Rd NTHM/RTH M23 109 J7
Siddall St HEY OL10 41 H4
OLD OL1 9 J3
RAD M26 38 D8
ROY/SHW OL2 43 L5
WGTN/LGST M12 99 K2
Siddeley St LEIGH WN7 66 A7
Siddington Av DID/WITH M20 98 D4
EDGY/DAV SK3 111 M6
Siddington Rd POY/DIS SK12 129 K2
WILM/AE * SK9 119 M7
Siddow Common LEIGH WN7 81 K1
Side Av ALT WA14 116 E3
Sidebotham St MPL/ROM SK6 101 J8
Sidebottom St DROY * M43 89 J3
OLDE OL4 60 B4
STLY SK15 91 K2
Side St OLDS OL8 74 F2
OP/CLY M11 88 E3
Sidford Cl BOLS/LL BL3 37 G7
The Sidings WALK M28 69 K7
Sidley Av BKLY M9 57 J8
Sidley St HYDE SK14 102 C1

Sidmouth Av *URM* M41 .....95 H1
Sidmouth Dr *BKLY* M9 .....73 C2
Sidmouth Gv *CHD/CHDH* SK8 ..120 B5
  WGNS/IIMK WN3 .....63 H1
Sidmouth Rd *SALE* M33 .....96 A7
Sidmouth St *CHAD* OL9 .....8 B8
  DTN/ASHW M34 .....90 A5
Sidney Rd *BKLY* M9 .....73 C3
Sidney St *BOLS/LL* BL3 .....2 F8
  CMANE M1 .....7 H9
  CSLFD M3 .....6 B3
  CSLFD * M3 .....6 E5
  LEIGH WN7 .....66 D7
  OLD OL1 .....59 K3
Sidwell Wk *ANC* * M4 .....88 A3
Siebers Bank *WHIT* * OL12 .....28 A2
Siemens Rd *IRL* M44 .....94 B7
Siemens St *HOR/BR* BL6 .....33 M2
Sienna Cl *IRL* M44 .....94 B6
Signal Cl *ECC* M30 .....84 E2
Signal Dr *NEWH/MOS* M40 .....73 C6
Signet Wk *CHH* M8 .....72 E7
Silas St *AUL* * OL6 .....76 A7
Silburn Wy *MDTN* M24 .....56 F5
Silchester Wy *BOLE* BL2 .....37 H3
Silcock St *GOL/RIS/CU* WA3 .....79 K4
Silfield Cl *OP/CLY* M11 .....88 B5
Silkhey Gv *WALK* M28 .....69 C3
Silkin Cl *BRUN/LGST* M13 .....7 J9
Silkstone St *OP/CLY* M11 .....88 F5
Silk St *ANC* M4 .....7 K2
  CSLFD M3 .....6 A1
  GLSP SK13 .....105 H3
  LEIGH WN7 .....66 C7
  MDTN M24 .....57 J4
  NEWH/MOS M40 .....73 M6
  ROCH OL11 .....28 A8
  WHTN * BL5 .....50 B3
Sillavan Wy *CSLFD* M3 .....6 C3
Sillitoe Dr *WHIT* * OL12 .....14 C2
Silsbury Gv *WGNNW/ST* WN6 .....31 K4
Silsden Av *BKLY* M9 .....56 E7
  GOL/RIS/CU WA3 .....80 E4
Silton St *BKLY* M9 .....73 J5
Silverbirch Cl *SALE* M33 .....108 A2
Silver Birches *DTN/ASHW* M34 ..101 L3
Silver Birch Gv *AIMK* WN4 .....63 K7
  SWIN M27 .....70 E6
Silverbirch Wy *FAIL* M35 .....74 C5
Silver Cl *DUK* SK16 .....90 E5
Silvercroft St *HULME* M15 .....6 C8
Silverdale *SWIN* M27 .....70 D2
  WGN WN1 .....47 M2
Silverdale Av *CHAD* OL9 .....58 D6
  DTN/ASHW M34 .....101 K2
  IRL M44 .....83 L8
  PWCH M25 .....72 B2
  WGNE/HIN WN2 .....48 D4
Silverdale Cl *BURY* BL9 .....5 J9
  MPL/ROM SK6 .....123 C4
Silverdale Ct *WGN* WN1 .....5 G4
Silverdale Dr *OLDE* OL4 .....60 C6
  WILM/AE SK9 .....126 E8
Silverdale Rd *BOL* BL1 .....35 M5
  CCHDY M21 .....97 M3
  CHD/CHDH SK8 .....110 E8
  FWTH BL4 .....52 D3
  HTNM SK4 .....99 M8
  NEWLW WA12 .....78 E4
  WGNE/HIN WN2 .....49 J7
  WGNW/BIL/O WN5 .....46 E4
Silverdale St *OP/CLY* M11 .....89 J5
Silver Hl *MILN* OL16 .....29 J6
Silver Hill Rd *HYDE* SK14 .....102 B3
Silver Jubilee Wk *ANC* M4 .....7 J3
Silverlea Dr *BKLY* M9 .....72 F2
Silvermere *AUL* OL6 .....76 B6
Silver Spring *HYDE* SK14 .....102 C4
Silverstone Dr *NEWH/MOS* M40 ..74 A8
Silver St *BURY* BL9 .....4 E5
  CMANE M1 .....7 H5
  IRL M44 .....83 L8
  OLD OL1 .....9 H6
  RAMS BL0 .....17 C6
  WGNE/HIN WN2 .....64 E2
  WHIT OL12 .....10 B2
  WHTF * M45 .....55 H1
Silver Ter *WGN* WN1 .....15 H4
Silverthorne Cl *STLY* SK15 .....91 K3
Silverton Cl *HYDE* SK14 .....103 C2
Silverton Gv *BOL* BL1 .....22 C8
  MDTN M24 .....41 G8
Silverwell La *BOL* BL1 .....2 F5
Silverwell St *BOL* BL1 .....2 F5
  HOR/BR BL6 .....21 D8
  NEWH/MOS M40 .....74 A7
Silverwood *CHAD* OL9 .....58 B5
Silverwood Av *CCHDY* M21 .....97 L4
Silvester St *HOR/BR* * BL6 .....33 C2
Silvington Wy *WGNE/HIN* WN2 ..48 D2
Simeon St *ANC* * M4 .....7 J1
Simfield Cl *WGNNW/ST* WN6 .....31 C3
Simister Dr *BURY* BL9 .....55 K2
Simister Gn *PWCH* M25 .....56 B4
Simister La *PWCH* M25 .....56 A4
Simister Rd *FAIL* M35 .....74 C5
Simister St *BKLY* M9 .....73 H4
Simkin Wy *OLDS* OL8 .....75 K3
Simmondley Gv *GLSP* SK13 .....104 D3
Simmondley La *GLSP* SK13 ......104 D4
Simmondley New Rd
  GLSP SK13 .....104 D5
Simms Cl *CSLFD* M3 .....6 A3
Simonbury Cl *TOT/BURYW* BL8 ..38 C2
Simon Freeman Cl
  BNG/LEV M19 .....99 M6
Simon La *MDTN* M24 .....56 D2
Simons Cl *GLSP* SK13 .....104 D5
  SALE M33 .....108 D1
Simon St *MILN* OL16 .....29 J6
Simonsway *NTHM/RTH* M23 ...118 C1
Simpkin St *WGNE/HIN* WN2 .....64 E3
Simpson Av *SWIN* M27 .....70 F2
Simpson Gv *WALK* M28 .....68 D6
Simpson Hill Cl *HEY* OL10 .....41 J1
Simpson Rd *WALK* M28 .....68 D6
Simpson St *ANC* M4 .....7 H1
  CHAD OL9 .....58 B3
  EDGY/DAV * SK3 .....13 H7
  HYDE SK14 .....101 M1
  OP/CLY M11 .....88 D3
  WILM/AE * SK9 .....126 C6
Sinclair Pl *WGNW/BIL/O* WN5 ...47 H4
Sinclair St *ROCH* OL11 .....42 A1
Sinderland La *LYMM* WA13 .....106 E4
Sinderland Rd *ALT* WA14 .....107 L4
  PART M31 .....106 F1
Sindsley Gv *BOLS/LL* BL3 .....52 B1
Sindsley Rd *SWIN* M27 .....70 A2

Singapore Av *MANAIR* M90 ....118 C4
Singleton Av *BOLE* BL2 .....37 H5
  HOR/BR BL6 .....21 C7
Singleton Cl *WHTN* M7 .....71 M3
Singleton Gv *WHTN* BL5 .....50 E4
Singleton Rd *BRO* M7 .....71 M3
  HTNM SK4 .....99 L8
Singleton St *RAD* M26 .....38 A8
Sion St *RAD* M26 .....54 C2
Sirdar St *OP/CLY* * M11 .....89 J4
Sirius Pl *BRO* M7 .....87 G1
Sir Matt Busby Wy
  OLDTF/WHR M16 .....86 C7
Sir Richard Fairey Rd *HTNM* SK4 ..99 L6
Sir Robert Thomas Ct
  BKLY * M9 .....73 C4
Siskin Cl *LEIGH* WN7 .....66 E7
Siskin Rd *OFTN* SK2 .....113 J7
Sisley Cl *BRO* M7 .....71 L4
Sisson St *FAIL* M35 .....74 B5
Sisters' St *DROY* M43 .....89 K4
Sitch La *MPL/ROM* SK6 ......125 H1
Sittingbourne Rd *WGN* WN1 ....31 M8
Sixpools Gv *WALK* M28 .....68 F4
Sixth Av *BOL* BL1 .....35 L5
  BURY BL9 .....26 A8
  OLDS OL8 .....74 F3
Size House Pl *LEIGH* * WN7 .....66 D8
Size St *WHIT* OL12 .....18 E3
Skagen Ct *BOL* BL1 .....2 D1
Skaife Rd *SALE* M33 .....97 H8
Skarratt Cl *WGTN/LGST* M12 .....88 C6
Skegness Cl *TOT/BURYW* BL8 ....25 C7
Skelton Green La
  MCFLDN SK10 .....129 K4
Skelton Gv *BOLE* BL2 .....37 J4
  BRUN/LGST M13 .....99 J2
Skelton Rd *ALT* WA14 ......108 B5
  STRET M32 .....97 G1
Skelton St *AIMK* WN4 .....63 J6
Skelwith Av *BOLS/LL* BL3 .....52 C2
Skelwith Cl *URM* M41 .....84 D8
Skerry Cl *BRUN/LGST* M13 .....7 K9
Skerton Rd *OLDTF/WHR* M16 .....86 E8
Skiddaw Pl *WGNW/BIL/O* WN5 ...46 F6
Skip Pl *CSLFD* M3 .....87 K1
Skipton Av *CHAD* OL9 .....58 C3
  NEWH/MOS M40 .....74 A3
  WGNE/HIN WN2 .....49 K8
Skipton Cl *BRAM/HZG* SK7 .....121 L4
  RDSH SK5 .....100 B4
  TOT/BURYW BL8 .....38 C2
Skipton Dr *URM* M41 .....84 C7
Skipton St *BOLE* BL2 .....3 L4
  OLDS OL8 .....59 L8
Skipton Wk *BOLE* * BL2 .....3 L4
Skull House La *WGNNW/ST* WN6 ..30 A4
Skye Cl *OLD* OL1 .....40 C3
Skye Cft *MPL/ROM* SK6 .....114 A1
Skye Rd *URM* M41 .....85 C7
Slackcote La *UPML* OL3 .....44 M1
Slackey Brow *FWTH* BL4 .....53 M7
Slackey Fold *WGNE/HIN* WN2 ....65 L3
Slack Fold La *FWTH* BL4 .....52 A3
Slack Ga *WHIT* OL12 .....18 F4
Slack Gate La *UPML* OL3 .....45 C4
Slack La *BOLE* BL2 .....23 H5
  SWIN M27 .....70 D3
  UPML OL3 .....45 C6
  WHTN BL5 .....50 C2
Slack Rd *CHH* M8 .....72 F3
Slack St *HYDE* SK14 .....91 J8
  MILN OL16 .....10 F4
Slade Gv *BRUN/LGST* M13 .....99 J1
Slade Hall Rd *WGTN/LGST* M12 ..99 K2
Slade La *BNG/LEV* M19 .....99 J3
  MCFLDN SK10 .....131 H7
Slade Mt *BNG/LEV* * M19 .....99 J4
Sladen St *WHIT* OL12 .....10 E1
Slade St *BOLS/LL* BL3 .....53 K1
Slag La *GOL/RIS/CU* WA3 .....80 C2
Slaidburn Av *BOLE* BL2 .....37 K2
Slaidburn Cl *MILN* OL16 .....29 J7
  WGNS/IIMK WN3 .....63 K1
Slaidburn Crs *GOL/RIS/CU* WA3 ..79 J7
Slaidburn Dr *TOT/BURYW* BL8 ...38 B1
Slaithwaite Dr *OP/CLY* M11 .....88 F2
Slant Cl *GLSP* SK13 .....105 C4
Slateacre Rd *HYDE* SK14 ......102 C5
Slate Av *ANC* M4 .....7 M4
Slatelands Av *GLSP* SK13 ......104 E4
Slatelands Rd *GLSP* SK13 ......104 E4
Slate La *DTN/ASHW* M34 ......89 M4
Slater Av *HOR/BR* BL6 .....21 C8
Slaterfield *BOLS/LL* BL3 .....2 D9
Slater La *BOL* BL1 .....3 C2
Slater's Nook *WHTN* BL5 .....50 B3
Slater St *BOL* BL1 .....2 D2
  CHAD OL9 .....9 G7
  ECC M30 .....84 E2
  FAIL M35 .....74 C3
Slater St North *LEIGH* WN7 .....66 A7
Slate Whf *HULME* * M15 .....6 B7
Slawson Wy *HEY* OL10 .....41 J1
Sleaford Cl *NEWH/MOS* M40 .....88 A1
  TOT/BURYW BL8 .....25 C7
Sledbrook St
  WGNW/BIL/O * WN5 .....46 F7
Sleddale Cl *OFTN* SK2 .....113 C7
Sledmere Cl *BOL* BL1 .....36 C2
  OP/CLY M11 .....88 D7
Sledmoor Cl *NTHM/RTH* M23 ...109 J3
Slimbridge Cl *BOLE* BL2 .....37 K3
Sloane Av *OLDE* OL4 .....60 B4
Sloane St *AUL* OL6 .....90 F1
  BOLS/LL BL3 .....51 M1
  OP/CLY * M11 .....88 D2
Smallbridge Cl *WALK* M28 .....68 F4
Smallbrook La *LEIGH* WN7 .....66 F3
Smallbrook Rd *ROY/SHW* OL2 ...43 L2
  ROY/SHW OL2 .....43 M4
Smalldale Av *OLDTF/WHR* M16 ..98 C1
Smalley St *ROCH* OL11 .....41 M2
Smallfield Dr *BKLY* M9 .....73 G1
Smallfield Dr *NEWH/MOS* M40 ..88 A1
Smallshaw La *AUL* OL6 .....75 M7
Smallshaw Rd *WHIT* OL12 .....19 C1
Smallwood Rd *NEWH/MOS* M40 ..73 M6
Smart St *WGTN/LGST* M12 .....99 H1
Smeaton Cl *STRET* M32 .....97 H2
Smeaton St *CHH* M8 .....72 F6
  HOR/BR * BL6 .....33 C2
Smedley Av *BOLS/LL* BL3 .....52 D1
Smedley La *CHH* M8 .....72 E6
Smedley Rd *CHH* M8 .....72 E6
Smedley St *CHH* M8 .....72 D6
Smethurst Hall Rd *BURY* BL9 .....26 B8

Smethurst La *BOLS/LL* BL3 .....51 L2
  WGNW/BIL/O WN5 .....46 F7
Smethurst St *BKLY* M9 .....73 C3
  HEY OL10 .....40 E2
  MDTN M24 .....58 A5
  TOT/BURYW BL8 .....24 E8
  WGNW/BIL/O WN5 .....46 F7
Smith Av *WGNW/BIL/O* WN5 .....46 E4
Smith Brow *HOR/BR* BL6 .....32 F7
Smith Farm Cl *OLDE* OL4 .....60 C4
Smith Fold La *WALK* M28 .....68 D1
Smith Hl *MILN* OL16 .....29 J6
Smith La *EDGW/EG* BL7 .....22 C4
Smiths Av *MDTN* M24 .....57 K2
Smiths Dr *BOL* BL1 .....35 J2
Smithies St *HEY* OL10 .....41 H2
Smithills Croft Rd *BOL* BL1 .....35 K1
Smithills Dr *BOL* BL1 .....35 J2
Smithills Hall Cl *RAMS* BL0 .....17 B8
Smith's La *WGNE/HIN* WN2 .....65 K4
Smiths Lawn *WILM/AE* SK9 ....126 E7
Smith's Rd *BOLS/LL* BL3 .....53 G1
Smith St *ATH* * M46 .....66 F1
  AULW OL7 .....90 C3
  BURY BL9 .....5 H2
  CHD/CHDH * SK8 .....111 J6
  DTN/ASHW M34 .....101 J2
  HEY OL10 .....41 G2
  HYDE SK14 .....91 C7
  LIT OL15 .....20 C7
  MILN OL16 .....11 H5
  MOSL OL5 .....76 E4
  OLDE OL4 .....44 E6
  OLDTF/WHR M16 .....86 F6
  RAMS BL0 .....17 B7
  WALK M28 .....69 C1
Smithwood Av *WGNE/HIN* WN2 ..49 J6
  OP/CLY M11 .....89 C2
Smithybridge Rd *LIT* OL15 .....19 M8
Smithy Bridge Rd *LIT* OL15 .....29 K2
Smithy Cl *GLSP* SK13 .....105 C3
Smithy Cft *EDGW/EG* BL7 .....22 C4
Smithy Fold *WHIT* OL12 .....27 L3
Smithy Fold La *HYDE* SK14 ....102 B4
Smithy Gn *CHD/CHDH* * SK8 ...120 C4
  MPL/ROM SK6 .....101 L7
  WGNE/HIN * WN2 .....48 C5
Smithy Gv *AUL* OL6 .....75 M8
Smithy Hl *BOLS/LL* BL3 .....35 K8
Smithy La *CSLFD* * M3 .....6 E4
  HYDE SK14 .....102 B3
  MCFLDN SK10 .....131 M2
  MPL/ROM SK6 .....115 J3
  PART M31 .....106 C1
  UPML OL3 .....61 L4
Smithy St *BRAM/HZG* SK7 .....121 M1
  LEIGH WN7 .....66 C8
  RAMS * BL0 .....17 C6
Smock La *AIMK* WN4 .....62 F8
Smyrna St *HEY* OL10 .....40 F3
  OLDS OL8 .....59 M7
  ORD M5 .....86 C3
  RAD M26 .....38 C8
Snake Pass *GLSP* SK13 ......105 M4
Snake Rd *GLSP* SK13 ......105 M4
Snape St *RAD* M26 .....38 A8
Snell St *ANC* M4 .....88 A3
Snipe Av *ROCH* OL11 .....27 J5
Snipe Cl *POY/DIS* SK12 ......128 E1
Snipe Rd *OLDS* OL8 .....75 L2
Snipe St *BOLS/LL* BL3 .....2 F9
Snipe Wy *DTN/ASHW* M34 .....90 A4
Snowden Av *URM* M41 .....95 L4
  WGNS/IIMK WN3 .....47 K8
Snowden St *BOL* BL1 .....2 C3
  HEY OL10 .....41 H4
  OLDS OL8 .....59 J8
Snowdon Dr *HOR/BR* BL6 .....21 C7
Snowdon Rd *ECC* M30 .....85 K1
Snowdon St *ROCH* OL11 .....42 D2
Snow Hill Rd *BOLS/LL* BL3 .....37 G7
Snowshill Dr *WGNS/IIMK* WN3 ...46 F8
Snydale Cl *WHTN* BL5 .....50 D2
Snydale Wy *BOLS/LL* BL3 .....51 C2
Soane Cl *AIMK* WN4 .....79 G1
Soapstone Wy *IRL* M44 .....94 D4
Soap St *ANC* M4 .....7 H3
Sofa St *BOL* BL1 .....35 L3
Soham Cl *WGNE/HIN* WN2 .....49 H8
Soho St *BOL* BL1 .....35 L5
  OLDE OL4 .....59 L5
Solent Av *CHH* M8 .....72 D2
Solent Dr *BOLS/LL* BL3 .....51 M8
Sole St *WGN* WN1 .....15 L1
Solness St *BURY* BL9 .....25 J6
Solway Cl *AIMK* WN4 .....63 K8
  BOLS/LL BL3 .....52 A1
  OLDS OL8 .....9 H9
  SWIN M27 .....54 B8
Solway Rd *WYTH/NTH* M22 ....110 B8
Somerby Dr *WYTH/NTH* M22 ...118 E3
Somerdale Av *BOL* BL1 .....35 K4
Somerfield Rd *BKLY* M9 .....73 C3
Somerford Av *DID/WITH* M20 ..98 D4
Somerford Rd *RDSH* SK5 .....100 D2
Somersby Dr *EDGW/EG* BL7 .....22 C4
Somersby Wk *BOLS/LL* * BL3 .....36 C8
Somerset Av *ROY/SHW* OL2 .....43 J5
  TYLD M29 .....67 J1
Somerset Cl *IRL* M44 .....94 A6
  RDSH SK5 .....100 F8
Somerset Dr *BURY* BL9 .....5 L8
Somerset Gv *ROCH* OL11 .....27 K4
Somerset Pl *SALE* M33 .....96 E6
Somerset Rd *ALT* WA14 ......108 A6
  ATH M46 .....50 E8
  BOL BL1 .....35 L4
  DROY M43 .....89 K1
  ECC M30 .....70 D8
  FAIL M35 .....74 B6
  WGNW/BIL/O WN5 .....46 F6
Somerset St *OLDE* OL4 .....59 M6
Somers Rd *RDSH* SK5 .....100 C3
Somerton Av *SALE* M33 .....108 F1
  WYTH/NTH * M22 .....118 E1
Somerton Rd *BOLE* BL2 .....37 J7
Somerville Gdns
  HALE/TIMP WA15 .....108 C5
Somerville Rd *WGN* WN1 .....31 M8
Somerville Sq *BOL* BL1 .....35 M1
Somerville St *BOL* BL1 .....35 M1
Somerwood Wk
  WGTN/LGST M12 .....88 C6
Sonning Dr *BOLS/LL* BL3 .....51 L2
Sopwith Dr *RUSH/FAL* M14 .....98 D3
Sorbus Cl *SLFD* M6 .....86 D2
Sorby Rd *IRL* M44 .....94 B5
Sorrel Bank *SLFD* M6 .....71 J8
Sorrel Dr *LIT* OL15 .....20 A6

Sorrel Bank *RDSH* SK5 ......100 D3
Sorrell St *HULME* M15 .....87 H6
Sorrel Wy *OLDE* OL4 .....60 B2
Sorton St *CMANE* M1 .....7 H8
Sossmoss La *MCFLDN* SK10 .....130 A6
Soudan Rd *OFTN* SK2 ......112 D6
Soudan St *MDTN* M24 .....57 M3
Sougher's La *AIMK* WN4 .....63 J6
The Sound *UPML* OL3 .....45 J8
Souracre Fold *STLY* SK15 .....91 L1
South Acre Dr *WILM/AE* SK9 ...127 H1
Southall St *CSLFD* M3 .....87 J1
Southampton Cl *BRO* M7 .....72 A7
Southam St *BRO* M7 .....72 C5
South Av *BNG/LEV* M19 .....99 J5
  FWTH BL4 .....53 J6
  HEY OL10 .....40 E2
  LEIGH WN7 .....81 M1
  SWIN M27 .....70 A7
  UPML OL3 .....61 L6
  WHTF M45 .....55 H3
South Back Rock *BURY* BL9 .....4 F4
South Bank Dr *GLSP* * SK13 .....130 A2
Southbank Rd *BNG/LEV* M19 .....99 C7
South Bank Rd *BURY* BL9 .....26 B4
Southbourne Av *URM* M41 .....96 C2
Southbourne St *SLFD* M6 .....86 B2
South Bourne Av *CHH* M8 .....72 C1
Southbrook Cl *GLSP* SK13 .....93 H8
Southbrook Gv *BOLS/LL* BL3 .....52 B1
Southcliffe Rd *RDSH* SK5 .....100 C6
South Cliffe St *OP/CLY* M11 .....89 J5
South Cl *BURY* BL9 .....55 K1
  GLSP SK13 .....93 J6
  WILM/AE SK9 .....123 C6
Southcourt *LEIGH* WN7 .....66 E6
South Crs *NEWH/MOS* M40 .....74 A1
  OP/CLY M11 .....89 C2
South Croston St
  OLDTF/WHR M16 .....87 G8
Southdene Av *DID/WITH* M20 ...98 B8
Southdown Cl *HTNM* SK4 .....12 F2
  ROCH OL11 .....27 M7
Southdown Crs *BKLY* M9 .....73 K2
  CHD/CHDH SK8 .....120 B4
Southdown Dr *WALK* M28 .....68 C6
Southdowns Rd *CHD/CHDH* SK8 ..43 J4
South Downs Dr *ALT* WA14 ....116 F3
South Downs Rd *ALT* WA14 ....116 E3
South Dr *BOLE* BL2 .....37 H1
  CCHDY M21 .....97 L6
  CHD/CHDH SK8 .....110 D8
  HALE/TIMP WA15 .....108 D5
Southend Av *HULME* M15 .....87 C6
Southend St *BOLS/LL* BL3 .....51 M1
Southern Av *SWIN* M27 .....70 F2
Southernby Cl
  BRUN/LGST * M13 .....88 C3
Southern Cl *BRAM/HZG* SK7 ...121 H2
  DTN/ASHW M34 .....101 H4
Southern Crs *BRAM/HZG* SK7 ..121 H3
Southern Rd *SALE* M33 .....96 D6
Southern's Fold
  WGNE/HIN WN2 .....48 D1
Southern St *CSLFD* M3 .....6 D7
  SLFD M6 .....86 B2
  WALK M28 .....53 G7
  WGNW/BIL/O WN5 .....47 G7
Southey Av *WGNS/IIMK* WN3 .....63 C1
Southey Cl *LIT* OL15 .....29 J2
Southfield *WGNE/HIN* WN2 .....64 E2
Southfield Av *BURY* BL9 .....25 H6
Southfield Cl *DUK* SK16 .....91 C6
Southfield Dr *WHTN* BL5 .....50 C5
Southfield Rd *RAMS* BL0 .....24 D2
Southfields Dr
  HALE/TIMP WA15 .....108 E5
Southfield St *BOLS/LL* BL3 .....36 E8
South Gdns *TYLD* * M29 .....67 K7
Southgarth Rd *SLFD* M6 .....86 B2
Southgate *BOLE* BL2 .....23 H8
  CCHDY M21 .....97 L5
  HTNM SK4 .....99 M7
  UPML OL3 .....61 L4
  URM M41 .....95 L4
  WHIT OL12 .....18 C5
Southgate Av
  NEWH/MOS * M40 .....73 K8
Southgate College Land
  CSLFD M3 .....6 E4
Southgate Rd *BURY* BL9 .....55 J1
  CHAD OL9 .....74 B1
Southgate St *OLD* OL1 .....9 G6
South Gv *BRUN/LGST* M13 .....88 A7
  SALE M33 .....108 E1
  WALK M28 .....68 F2
  WILM/AE SK9 .....130 D3
Southgrove Av *BOL* BL1 .....22 B6
South Hall St *ORD* * M5 .....86 F4
South Hey *LEIGH* WN7 .....65 M7
South Hl *OLDE* OL4 .....60 C7
South Hill St *OLDE* OL4 .....9 M7
South King St *CMANW* M2 .....6 E4
  ECC M30 .....84 E2
Southlands Av *ECC* M30 .....84 C4
  WGNNW/ST WN6 .....31 H4
South La *TYLD* M29 .....67 K7
South Langworthy Rd *ORD* M5 ..86 C3
Southlea Rd *DID/WITH* M20 .....99 C7
Southleigh Dr *BOLE* BL2 .....37 K6
Southlink *OLDE* * OL4 .....9 M6
South Lonsdale St *STRET* M32 ...97 H1
South Marlow St *GLSP* SK13 .....93 K8
South Md *POY/DIS* SK12 .....121 K7
South Meade *CCHDY* M21 .....97 L5
  HALE/TIMP WA15 .....108 D5
  PWCH M25 .....71 J1
  SWIN M27 .....70 B6
South Meadway
  MPL/ROM SK6 .....123 H5
Southmere Cl *BKLY* M9 .....73 M2
South Mesnefield Rd *BRO* M7 ....71 K5
Southmill St *CMANW* M2 .....6 E6
Southmoor Rd
  NTHM/RTH M23 .....109 H7
Southmoor Wk *BOLS/LL* * BL3 .....2 C9
South Oak La *WILM/AE* SK9 ....126 D6
Southover *WHTN* BL5 .....50 B6
South Pde *BRAM/HZG* SK7 .....121 J7
  MILN OL16 .....10 E4
South Park Dr *POY/DIS* SK12 ...122 A8
South Park Rd *CHD/CHDH* SK8 ..110 D6
South Pine St *BURY* BL9 .....5 K5
Southpool Cl *BRAM/HZG* SK7 ..121 J2
South Pump St *CMANE* M1 .....7 H5
South Radford St *BRO* M7 .....71 K5

South Rdg *DTN/ASHW* M34 .....90 C7
South Rd *ALT* WA14 .....116 E2
  DID/WITH M20 .....110 C2
  STRET M32 .....85 K8
  SWIN M27 .....71 C2
South Rw *PWCH* M25 .....71 J3
South Royd St *TOT/BURYW* BL8 ..24 C5
Southsea St *OP/CLY* M11 .....89 C5
Southsea *MPL/ROM* SK6 .....101 M4
  WILM/AE SK9 .....118 D8
South St *ATH* M46 .....67 H4
  AULW OL7 .....90 B4
  BOLS/LL BL3 .....52 B1
  MILN OL16 .....11 C3
  OLDS OL8 .....74 E2
  OP/CLY M11 .....88 E4
  RAMS BL0 .....17 C6
  WGTN/LGST M12 .....88 B7
  WILM/AE SK9 .....130 D3
South Ter *RAD* M26 .....39 C5
South Terrace Ct *ROCH* OL11 .....11 H9
South Vale Crs
  HALE/TIMP WA15 .....108 C7
South Vw *ATH* M46 .....66 F1
  MPL/ROM SK6 .....101 M6
  RDSH SK5 .....100 C1
  ROCH OL11 .....27 H6
  STLY SK15 .....77 J6
South View Gdns
  CHD/CHDH SK8 .....119 L1
Southview Rd *GLSP* SK13 .....105 J5
South View Rd *MILN* OL16 .....29 H1
South View St *BOLE* BL2 .....3 M5
South View Ter *MILN* OL16 .....19 M8
Southview Wk *OLDE* * OL4 .....60 B3
Southward Rd *RNFD/HAY* WA11 ..78 D5
Southwark Dr *DUK* SK16 .....91 C6
Southway *ALT* WA14 .....108 B6
  AULW OL7 .....75 K6
  DROY M43 .....89 K4
  NEWH/MOS M40 .....74 C2
South Wy *OLDS* OL8 .....75 H2
Southwell Cl *BOL* BL1 .....2 C2
  GOL/RIS/CU WA3 .....79 M4
  MPL/ROM SK6 .....113 K3
Southwell Ct *STRET* * M32 .....96 F3
Southwell Gdns *AUL* OL6 .....75 L5
Southwell St *BKLY* M9 .....73 H5
Southwick Rd *NTHM/RTH* M23 ..109 K2
South William St *CSLFD* * M3 .....6 A4
Southwood Cl *BOLS/LL* BL3 .....52 C1
Southwood Dr *BKLY* M9 .....56 D7
Southwood Rd *OFTN* SK2 .....112 E8
Southworth Rd *NEWLW* WA12 ....79 J8
Southyard St *BNG/LEV* M19 .....99 L4
Sovereign Cl *GOL/RIS/CU* WA3 ...80 B5
Sovereign Fold Rd *LEIGH* WN7 ...66 B3
Sovereign Rd *WGN* WN1 .....15 H6
Sovereign St *SLFD* M6 .....71 K8
Sowerby Cl *TOT/BURYW* BL8 .....38 C2
Spa Cl *RDSH* SK5 .....100 B4
Spa Crs *LHULT* M38 .....52 D6
Spa La *LHULT* M38 .....52 D6
  OLDE OL4 .....60 A7
Spalding Dr *NTHM/RTH* M23 ...118 C2
Sparkford Av *NTHM/RTH* M23 ..109 G3
Sparkle St *CMANE* M1 .....7 K5
Spark Rd *NTHM/RTH* M23 .....109 J5
Spa Rd *ATH* M46 .....50 F7
  BOL BL1 .....2 B5
Sparrow Cl *RDSH* SK5 .....100 B2
Sparrowfield Cl *STLY* SK15 .....77 H5
Sparrow Hl *MILN* OL16 .....10 D5
Sparrow St *ROY/SHW* OL2 .....59 H2
Sparta Av *WALK* M28 .....68 F2
Sparth Bottoms Rd *ROCH* OL11 ..10 B9
Sparthfield Av *ROCH* OL11 .....10 C9
Sparthfield Rd *HTNM* SK4 .....12 E1
Sparth La *HTNM* SK4 .....12 E1
Sparth Rd *NEWH/MOS* M40 .....74 A7
Spa St *HULME* M15 .....87 L7
Spath La *WILM/AE* SK9 ......119 M7
Spath La East *CHD/CHDH* SK8 ..120 D7
Spath Rd *DID/WITH* M20 .....110 D1
Spath Wk *CHD/CHDH* SK8 .....120 D7
Spawell Cl *GOL/RIS/CU* WA3 .....80 B3
Spaw St *CSLFD* M3 .....6 C5
Speakman Av *LEIGH* WN7 .....66 E7
  NEWLW WA12 .....78 E7
Spear St *CMANE* M1 .....7 J4
Spectator St *ANC* M4 .....88 A2
Speedwell Cl *GLSP* SK13 .....93 J5
  GOL/RIS/CU WA3 .....80 B5
Spelding Dr *WGNNW/ST* WN6 ...31 C8
Spencer Av *BOLS/LL* BL3 .....53 M1
  HYDE SK14 .....91 C7
  OLDTF/WHR M16 .....97 M2
  WHTF M45 .....55 H2
Spencer La *ROCH* OL11 .....27 H7
Spencer Rd *WGN* WN1 .....47 L1
Spencer Rd West
  WGNNW/ST WN6 .....47 K1
Spencer's La *WGNW/BIL/O* WN5 ..46 A5
Spencer St *CHAD* OL9 .....58 E8
  DUK SK16 .....90 F4
  ECC M30 .....84 F3
  MOSL OL5 .....76 E3
  OLD OL1 .....9 M3
  RAD * M26 .....38 F8
  RAMS BL0 .....17 B7
  RDSH SK5 .....100 C4
  TOT/BURYW BL8 .....4 C3
Spender Av *CHH* M8 .....72 D6
Spenlow Cl *LEIGH* WN7 .....81 M1
Spenlow Cl *MCFLDN* SK10 .....129 J3
Spennithorne Rd *URM* M41 .....95 L2
Spenser Av *DTN/ASHW* M34 ....101 K4
  RAD M26 .....38 B3
Spenwood Rd *LIT* OL15 .....20 A7
Spey Cl *ALT* WA14 .....107 M6
  WGNNW/ST WN6 .....31 C3
Speyside Cl *WHTF* * M45 .....55 K4
Spinnerbottom *NM/HAY* SK22 ...125 H2
Spilsby Sq *WGNS/IIMK* WN3 .....51 M1
Spindle Av *STLY* SK15 .....91 M1
Spindle Cl *OLDS* OL8 .....9 H9
Spindle Hillock *AIMK* WN4 .....63 C3
Spindlepoint Dr *WALK* M28 .....68 F4
The Spindles *MOSL* OL5 .....77 C4
Spindle Wk *WHTN* BL5 .....50 C2
Spindlewood Cl *STLY* SK15 .....92 A2
Spindlewood Rd
  WGNS/IIMK WN3 .....15 L3
Spingdale *LHULT* M38 .....52 A6
Spinks St *OLDE* OL4 .....59 L7
Spinnerbottom *NM/HAY* SK22 ..125 H2
Spinnerette Cl *LEIGH* WN7 .....66 D7
Spinners Gdns *WHIT* OL12 .....19 K8

Spinners Gn WHIT OL12.....28 C2
Spinners La POY/DIS SK12.....121 L2
Spinners Ms BOL BL1.....2 D2
Spinners Wy OLDE OL4.....44 C8
The Spinney CHD/CHDH SK8.....120 A1
EDGW/EG BL7.....22 F2
OLDE OL4.....60 D4
SWIN * M27.....69 M6
URM * M41.....95 K2
WGNW/BIL/O WN5.....47 H1
WHIT OL12.....28 A1
WHTF M45.....54 F5
Spinney Cl GLSP SK13.....104 F2
Spinney Dr BURY BL9.....25 J6
SALE M33.....108 A1
Spinney Gv DTN/ASHW M34.....90 C7
Spinney Nook BOLE BL2.....37 G2
Spinney Rd NTHM/RTH M23.....109 L5
Spinningfields BOL * BL1.....2 A2
Spinningfield Wy HEY OL10.....41 G5
Spinning Jenny Wk ANC M4.....7 M3
Spinning Jenny Wy LEIGH WN7.....66 C8
Spinning Meadow BOL BL1.....2 B2
Spinning Mdw BOL BL1.....2 B2
The Spinnings RAMS * BL0.....24 F1
Spion Kop AIMK WN4.....78 D1
Spiredale Brow
    WGNNW/ST WN6.....31 J3
Spire Hollin GLSP SK13.....104 F2
Spire Wk WGTN/LGST * M12.....88 A4
Spirewood Gdns
    MPL/ROM SK6.....113 K2
Spodden Fold WHIT OL12.....18 D4
Spodden St WHIT OL12.....10 A3
Spod Rd WHIT OL12.....27 M3
Spokeshave Wy MILN OL16.....28 F2
Sportside Av WALK M28.....53 H8
Sportside Cl WALK M28.....53 G8
Sportside Gv WALK M28.....53 G8
Sportsmans Dr OLDS OL8.....75 K1
Sportsman St LEIGH WN7.....66 A7
Spotland Rd WHIT OL12.....10 B2
Spotland Tops WHIT OL12.....27 K1
Spreadbury St NEWH/MOS M40.....73 K5
Spring Av HYDE SK14.....102 C4
    WHTF M45.....55 H2
Springbank CHAD * OL9.....58 D5
    GLSP SK13.....93 J7
Spring Bank GLSP * SK13.....104 E4
    STLY SK15.....91 L4
Spring Bank Av OL6.....75 L7
    DTN/ASHW M34.....90 A5
Springbank Rd MPL/ROM SK6.....101 M6
Spring Bank La ROCH OL11.....27 H4
    STLY SK15.....76 F7
Spring Bank Pl EDGY/DAV * SK3.....13 H6
Springbank Rd MPL/ROM SK6.....101 M6
Spring Bank Rd NM/HAY SK22.....124 E4
Spring Bank St CHAD OL9.....58 F8
Springbourne WGNNW/ST WN6.....47 J2
Spring Bridge Rd
    OLDTF/WHR M16.....98 C2
Springburn Cl WALK M28.....68 D6
Spring Cl OLDE OL4.....60 A7
    RAMS BL0.....17 B6
    TOT/BURYW BL8.....24 B6
Spring Clough SWIN M27.....69 L7
Spring Clough Av WALK M28.....69 J2
Spring Clough Dr OLDS OL8.....59 L8
    WALK M28.....69 J2
Springdale Gdns
    DID/WITH M20.....110 D1
Springfield GLSP SK13.....103 M8
    RAD M26.....53 M6
Springfield Av BRAM/HZG SK7.....121 M1
    GOL/RIS/CU WA3.....79 J4
    HTNM SK4.....100 B5
    LIT OL15.....20 B5
    MPL/ROM * SK6.....114 C6
Springfield Cl FAIL M35.....74 B4
    GLSP SK13.....93 H8
Springfield Dr WILM/AE SK9.....126 B7
Springfield Gdns FWTH BL4.....53 K6
Springfield La CSLFD M3.....6 D1
    IRL M44.....94 C2
    MILN OL16.....29 C1
    ROY/SHW OL2.....42 F5
Springfield Rd ALT WA14.....108 A7
    ATH M46.....51 H8
    BOL BL1.....2 B5
    CHD/CHDH SK8.....110 E7
    DROY M43.....89 J1
    FWTH BL4.....52 D3
    FWTH BL4.....53 J6
    HOR/BR BL6.....34 A4
    MDTN M24.....57 J2
    RAMS BL0.....24 D2
    SALE M33.....96 E8
    WGNE/HIN WN2.....48 E6
    WGNNW/ST WN6.....47 J2
Springfield St AUL * OL6.....76 B7
    BOLS/LL BL3.....36 D8
    DTN/ASHW M34.....90 C6
    HEY OL10.....40 D7
    WGN WN1.....47 M2
Springfield Ter NM/HAY * SK22.....125 M2
Spring Gdns BOLE BL2.....23 J8
    BRAM/HZG SK7.....121 M1
    CMANW M2.....7 G4
    GLSP SK13.....93 J7
    HALE/TIMP WA15.....108 F7
    HOR/BR BL6.....21 B8
    HYDE SK14.....91 G8
    MDTN M24.....57 K2
    SLFD M6.....86 C1
    STKP SK1.....13 L5
    WGN WN1.....14 E4
Spring Gv UPML OL3.....61 L2
    WGN WN1.....15 J5
Spring Hall Ri OLDE OL4.....44 C8
Springhead Av DID/WITH M20.....98 D5
    OLDE OL4.....60 D7
Springhill ROY/SHW OL2.....43 G8
Spring La OLDE OL4.....60 B7
    RAD M26.....54 E1
Springlawns WALK * BL1.....35 J4
Springmeadow GLSP SK13.....104 A5
Spring Meadow La UPML OL3.....61 M4
Spring Mill Wk MILN OL16.....28 F2
Springmount GOL/RIS/CU WA3.....80 B5
Spring Mt NM/HAY SK22.....124 E4
Spring Pl WHIT OL12.....18 E2
Springpool WGNS/IIMK WN3.....62 E2
Spring Ri GLSP SK13.....104 C5
    ROY/SHW OL2.....43 K3
Spring Rd ALT WA14.....116 F2
    POY/DIS SK12.....129 K2
    WGNW/BIL/O WN5.....46 C4
Springside HTNM SK4.....100 A5
Springside Av WALK M28.....69 H1

Springside Cl WALK * M28.....69 H1
Springside Gv WALK M28.....69 H1
Springside Rd BURY BL9.....25 H4
Springside Vw TOT/BURYW BL8.....24 F5
Springside Wk HULME * M15.....87 G6
Springs La STLY SK15.....76 C8
Springs Rd MDTN M24.....58 B6
The Springs ALT WA14.....116 D2
    ROCH OL11.....27 H5
Spring St BOLS/LL BL3.....2 E9
    BURY BL9.....5 G6
    GLSP SK13.....104 E4
    HOR/BR BL6.....21 B8
    HYDE SK14.....92 F7
    MOSL OL5.....76 F2
    OLDE OL4.....59 M4
    RAMS BL0.....17 B6
    RAMS BL0.....17 D5
    STLY SK15.....91 K2
    TOT/BURYW BL8.....24 B5
    TOT/BURYW BL8.....24 C8
    UPML * OL3.....61 L4
    WGN WN1.....15 J5
    WGNS/IIMK WN3.....48 B8
    WGTN/LGST M12.....99 K2
    WILM/AE SK9.....126 E5
Spring Ter CHAD OL9.....58 D5
    MILN * OL16.....43 L1
Spring V BRAM/HZG * SK7.....122 A2
    MDTN M24.....57 K4
    PWCH M25.....71 K2
Springvale Cl AULW OL7.....75 J7
Spring Vale Dr TOT/BURYW BL8.....24 B5
Spring Vale Rd NM/HAY SK22.....125M2
Spring Vale St TOT/BURYW BL8.....24 B6
Spring Vale Ter LIT OL15.....20 C7
Spring Vw BURY * BL9.....26 A7
Springville Av BKLY M9.....73 J5
Springwater Av BOLE BL2.....24 D1
Springwater Cl BOLE BL2.....37 H1
Spring Water Dr GLSP SK13.....104 B1
Springwater La WHTF M45.....55 H2
Springwell Cl SLFD * M6.....86 B2
Springwell Gdns HYDE SK14.....103 H3
Springwood GLSP SK13.....104 C4
    UPML OL3.....45 H7
Springwood Av OLDE OL4.....58 B3
    SWIN M27.....70 E6
Springwood Crs MPL/ROM SK6.....114 B2
Springwood Hall Rd OLDS OL8.....75 K2
Springwood La MPL/ROM SK6.....114 C2
Spring Wood St RAMS BL0.....17 B5
Spruce Av BURY BL9.....5 L4
Spruce Cl COL/RIS/CU WA3.....80 C5
Spruce Ct SLFD M6.....86 E2
Spruce Crs BURY BL9.....5 L4
Spruce St HULME M15.....87 H6
    MILN * OL16.....11 H5
    RAMS BL0.....17 A8
Sprucewood CHAD OL9.....58 A4
The Spur OLDS OL8.....75 K2
Spurn La UPML OL3.....61 L1
The Square DUK * SK16.....91 J5
    HALE/TIMP WA15.....117 L4
    HTNM SK4.....12 C1
    SWIN M27.....70 B7
    UPML OL3.....61 K2
    WHTF * M45.....55 H4
Square St RAMS BL0.....17 C6
Squire Rd CHH M8.....72 C5
Squires La TYLD M29.....67 H4
Squirrel Dr ALT WA14.....107 M4
Squirrel La HOR/BR BL6.....21 A7
Squirrel's Jump WILM/AE SK9.....130 E3
Stablefold MOSL OL5.....76 F4
Stable Fold RAD M26.....38 D8
Stablefold WALK M28.....69 K7
Stableford Av ECC M30.....69 M8
The Stables DROY M43.....90 A1
Stable St CHAD OL9.....74 D2
The Stablings WILM/AE SK9.....126 E7
Stadium Wy WGNNW/ST WN6.....14 B3
    WGNW/BIL/O WN5.....47 H3
Stafford Cl GLSP SK13.....105 J4
Stafford Rd ECC M30.....84 F4
    FAIL M35.....74 D7
    SWIN M27.....70 C4
    WALK M28.....68 F3
Stafford St CHAD OL9.....58 F8
    LEIGH WN7.....67 G8
    NM/HAY SK22.....124 E3
    TOT/BURYW BL8.....25 G8
Stag Pasture Rd OLDS OL8.....75 J4
Stainburn Cl WGNNW/ST WN6.....30 A6
Stainburne Rd OFTN SK2.....112 F6
Staindale OLDE OL4.....60 A6
Stainer Cl NEWLW WA12.....78 E7
Stainer St WGTN/LGST M12.....99 K1
Stainforth St GOL/RIS/CU WA3.....81 G8
    TOT/BURYW BL8.....38 C1
Stainforth St OP/CLY M11.....88 C5
Stainmoor Ct OFTN SK2.....113 G6
Stainsbury St BOLS/LL BL3.....35M8
Stainton Av GTN M18.....89 H8
Stainton Cl RAD M26.....38 B8
Stainton Dr MDTN M24.....57 C1
Stainton Rd RAD M26.....38 B7
Stairgate WGN WN1.....15 G4
Staithes Rd WYTH/NTH M22.....118 F4
Stakeford Dr CHH M8.....72 F4
Stakehill La MDTN M24.....42 B7
Staley Cl STLY * SK15.....91M2
Staley Hall Crs STLY SK15.....91M1
Staley Hall Rd STLY SK15.....91M2
Staley St OLDE * OL4.....59 M6
    OLDE OL4.....60 B7
Stalham Cl NEWH/MOS M40.....88 A1
Stalmine Av CHD/CHDH SK8.....119 K4
Stalybridge Rd HYDE SK14.....92 D8
Stalyhill Dr STLY SK15.....92 B5
    STLY SK15.....91 M8
Stamford Av ALT WA14.....107 K6
    STLY SK15.....91 K2
Stamford Dr FAIL M35.....74 E7
    STLY SK15.....91 K2
Stamford Gv STLY SK15.....91 J3
Stamford New Rd ALT WA14.....108 A8
Stamford Park Rd
    HALE/TIMP WA15.....117 G1
Stamford Pl SALE M33.....96 F8
Stamford Rd ALT WA14.....116 E2
    BRO M7.....71 L6
    BRUN/LGST M13.....99 J3

DTN/ASHW M34.....90 A5
MOSL OL5.....76 F2
OLDE OL4.....60 C4
PART M31.....95 L2
URM M41.....95 L2
WILM/AE SK9.....126 E3
WILM/AE SK9.....130 D3
Stamford Sq AUL OL6.....91 G2
Stamford St ALT WA14.....108 A7
    ATH M46.....51 H8
    HEY OL10.....41 H3
    MILN OL16.....11 J6
    MOSL OL5.....76 E3
    OLDE * OL4.....60 B6
    OLDTF/WHR M16.....87 G8
    SALE M33.....96 D6
    STLY SK15.....77 G8
    STLY SK15.....91 K2
    SWIN M27.....70 D3
Stamford St Central AUL OL6.....90 F2
Stamford St East AUL OL6.....90 F2
Stamford St West AUL OL6.....90 D2
Stamford Wy ALT WA14.....108 A7
Stampstone St OLD OL1.....59 L5
Stanage Av BKLY * M9.....57 J8
Stanbank St HTNM SK4.....100 B8
Stanbourne Dr BOL BL1.....22 C8
Stanbrook St BNG/LEV M19.....99M3
Stanbury Cl HEY * OL10.....40 A3
Stanbury Dr DUK SK16.....91 G4
Stancliffe Gv WGNE/HIN WN2.....32 F6
Stancliffe Rd WYTH/NTH M22.....110 B7
Stancross Rd NTHM/RTH M23.....108 F3
Stand Av WHTF M45.....55 H3
Stand Cl WHTF M45.....54 F4
Standedge St OP/CLY M11.....88 C5
Standfield Dr WALK M28.....68 D5
Standish Av WGNNW/BIL/O WN5.....62 B7
Standish Gallery WGN * WN1.....15 G3
Standishgate WGN WN1.....15 G3
Standish Rd RUSH/FAL M14.....99 G4
Standish Wood La
    WGNNW/ST WN6.....31 H5
Stand La RAD M26.....54 E2
Standmoor Ct WHTF * M45.....55 G5
Standmoor Rd WHTF M45.....55 G5
Standring Av BURY BL9.....53 L2
Stand Ri RAD M26.....54 E4
Stanedge Rd RAMS BL0.....17 L6
Stanedge Gv WGNS/IIMK WN3.....63 L2
Stanford Cl RAD * M26.....53M5
Stanford Hall Crs RAMS OL10.....17 B8
Stanhope Av DTN/ASHW M34.....90 B7
    PWCH M25.....55M8
Stanhope Cl WILM/AE SK9.....127 H4
Stanhope Ct PWCH M25.....55 K6
Stanhope Rd ALT WA14.....116 C2
    SLFD M6.....71 H7
Stanhope St AUL * OL6.....76 A8
    BNG/LEV M19.....99 L3
    DTN/ASHW M34.....90 B7
    LEIGH WN7.....66 A6
    MOSL OL5.....76 F4
    RDSH * SK5.....100 B5
    ROCH OL11.....10 F9
Stanhope Wy FAIL M35.....74 B4
Stanhorne Av CHH M8.....72 D2
Stanier Av ECC M30.....85 G1
Stanier Pl HOR/BR * BL6.....33M2
Stanier St BKLY M9.....73 H4
Stanion Gv DUK SK16.....90 F4
Stan Jolly Wk OP/CLY M11.....88 F4
Stanley Av BRAM/HZG SK7.....121 M1
    HYDE SK14.....91 H8
    MPL/ROM SK6.....114 A5
    RUSH/FAL M14.....98 F1
Stanley Av North PWCH M25.....55 K6
Stanley Av South PWCH M25.....55 K6
Stanley Cl WHTF M45.....55 J3
    WHTN BL5.....50 D5
Stanley Ct BURY BL9.....5 G3
    OLDTF/WHR M16.....86 F7
Stanley Dr CHD/CHDH SK8.....119M6
    HALE/TIMP WA15.....108 D7
    LEIGH WN7.....66 A4
    WHTF M45.....55 J6
Stanley Gv HOR/BR BL6.....34 A3
    HTNM SK4.....91 L8
    URM M41.....96 A2
    WGTN/LGST M12.....88 D8
Stanley Hall La POY/DIS SK12.....123 L5
Stanley La WGNE/HIN WN2.....32 F5
Stanley Ms BOLE BL2.....37 L3
Stanley Mt SALE M33.....108 D1
Stanley Park Wk BOLE * BL2.....35M8
Stanley Pl WGN WN1.....15 K3
    WHIT OL12.....10 D2
Stanley Rd BOL BL1.....35 L3
    BRO M7.....72 B4
    CHAD OL9.....58 E8
    CHD/CHDH SK8.....119M6
    DTN/ASHW M34.....100 E1
    ECC M30.....84 F3
    FWTH BL4.....52 B4
    HTNM SK4.....99 L8
    OLDTF/WHR M16.....86 F7
    OLDTF/WHR M16.....98 B2
    RAD M26.....38 B6
    SWIN M27.....70 D4
    WALK M28.....69 G2
    WGNE/HIN WN2.....32 F6
    WGNE/HIN WN2.....64 D1
    WHIT OL12.....18 C7
    WHIT OL12.....18 E1
    WILM/AE SK9.....126 E1
    WILM/AE SK9.....126 E5
    WILM/AE SK9.....127 H1
Stanley St ATH M46.....66 F2
    BKLY * M9.....73 H4
    CHAD OL9.....8 B4
    CHH M8.....72 D8
    HEY OL10.....41 G3
    NEWH/MOS M40.....73 J7
    OLDE OL4.....60 B7
    OP/CLY M11.....89 H5
    ORD M5.....6 A6
    PWCH M25.....55M8
    RAMS BL0.....17 C8
    STKP SK1.....13 L3
    STLY * SK15.....91 K2
    WGNW/BIL/O WN5.....14 A7
    WHIT OL12.....18 D7
    WHTF * M45.....55 J3
Stanley St South BOLS/LL BL3.....2 C6
Stanmoor Dr WGNE/HIN WN2.....32 F6
Stanmore Av STRET M32.....96 E2
Stanmore Dr BOLS/LL BL3.....35M7
Stanmore Rd ECC M30.....84 C3
Stanneybrook Cl MILN OL16.....11 K3
Stanney Cl MILN OL16.....29 H7
Stanneylands Cl WILM/AE SK9.....127 G2
Stanneylands Dr WILM/AE SK9.....126 F2

Stanneylands Rd WILM/AE SK9.....119 K8
Stanney Rd MILN OL16.....11 K2
Stannybrook Rd FAIL M35.....75 G4
Stanrose Cl EDGW/EG BL7.....22 B3
Stansbury Pl OFTN SK2.....113 H6
Stansby Gdns WGTN/LGST M12.....88 B9
    LEIGH WN7.....81M2
Stansfield Dr ROCH OL11.....27 H3
Stansfield Hall LIT OL15.....20 D3
Stansfield Rd BOLE BL2.....3 J3
    FAIL M35.....74 D3
    HYDE SK14.....91 H8
Stansfield St CHAD OL9.....8 B8
    NEWH/MOS M40.....74 A8
    OLD OL1.....9 G2
    OP/CLY M11.....89 G4
Stanstead Cl WGNE/HIN WN2.....48 C2
Stanthorne Av DID/WITH M20.....98 D5
Stanton Av BRO M7.....71 L6
    DID/WITH * M20.....98 B8
Stanton Cl WGNS/IIMK WN3.....63 L1
Stanton Gdns HTNM SK4.....12 E1
Stanton St CHAD OL9.....74 D2
    STRET M32.....86 B8
Stanway Av BOLS/LL * BL3.....2 B7
Stanway Cl BOLS/LL * BL3.....2 B7
    MDTN M24.....57 L6
Stanway Dr HALE/TIMP WA15.....117 H1
Stanway Rd WHTF M45.....55 L4
Stanway St BKLY M9.....73 H4
    STRET M32.....86 A8
Stanwell Rd NEWH/MOS M40.....73M3
    SWIN M27.....70 B5
Stanwick Av BKLY M9.....56 D8
Stanworth Av BOLE BL2.....37 H5
Stanyard Ct ORD M5.....86 D4
Stanycliffe La MDTN M24.....57 L1
Stanyforth St GLSP SK13.....93 K8
    SALE M33.....97 H7
    WHTN BL5.....51 K6
Stapleford Gv TOT/BURYW BL8.....38 D2
Staplehurst Cl WGNE/HIN WN2.....65M2
Staplehurst Rd NEWH/MOS M40.....73 K4
Stapleton Av BOL BL1.....35 H4
Stapleton St SLFD M6.....70 F7
    WGNE/HIN WN2.....64 D2
Starbeck Cl TOT/BURYW BL8.....38 C2
Starcliffe St BOLS/LL BL3.....53 G2
Starfield Av LIT OL15.....29 J2
Star Gv BRO M7.....72 B6
Starkey St HEY OL10.....41 G1
Starkie Rd BOLE BL2.....3 K1
The Starkies BURY * BL9.....39 H5
Starkie St WALK M28.....69 K4
Star La HOR/BR BL6.....33 J1
Starling Dr DROY M43.....90 A1
Starling Dr FWTH BL4.....52 C5
Starling Rd RAD M26.....38 B4
Starmoor Dr CHH M8.....72 D6
Starmount Cl BOLE BL2.....37 K6
Starring La LIT OL15.....19M7
Starring Rd WHIT OL12.....19M7
Starring Wy LIT OL15.....20 A7
Stash Gv NTHM/RTH M23.....109 L5
Statford Av DTN/ASHW M34.....101 K1
Statham Fold HYDE SK14.....91 K8
Statham St SLFD M6.....86 E2
Station Ap CMANE * M1.....7 G8
    CMANE M1.....7 J5
Station Av WGNE/HIN WN2.....65 G3
    WGNW/BIL/O WN5.....46 A7
Station Cl HYDE SK14.....101M2
Station Cottages TYLD * M29.....82 F5
Stationers Entry MILN OL16.....10 E8
Station La OLDE OL4.....60 E7
Station Ms AIMK WN4.....78 A1
Station Rd ALT WA14.....106 E7
    CHD/CHDH SK8.....120 D3
    CHF/WBR SK23.....124 F8
    CHH M8.....72 D3
    ECC M30.....84 F3
    EDGW/EG BL7.....16 C8
    EDGY/DAV SK3.....13 H6
    FWTH BL4.....53 L6
    GLSP SK13.....93 K7
    HOR/BR BL6.....33 J3
    HTNM SK4.....111 H3
    HYDE SK14.....102 E2
    IRL M44.....94 B5
    LIT OL15.....20 C7
    MILN OL16.....29 J7
    MOSL OL5.....77 G3
    MPL/ROM SK6.....101 L7
    MPL/ROM SK6.....114 C6
    MPL/ROM SK6.....123 M4
    NM/HAY SK22.....124 D6
    NM/HAY SK22.....125 J2
    OLDE OL4.....60 D7
    RDSH SK5.....100 B2
    ROCH OL11.....10 F7
    STRET M32.....97 G1
    SWIN M27.....70 C3
    TOT/BURYW BL8.....24 C3
    UPML OL3.....61 L4
    URM M41.....96 A3
    WGN WN1.....15 G4
    WHIT OL12.....18 C7
    WHIT OL12.....18 E1
    WILM/AE SK9.....126 E1
    WILM/AE SK9.....126 E5
    WILM/AE SK9.....127 H1
Station St AULW OL7.....90 C3
    BOLS/LL BL3.....2 F7
    BRAM/HZG SK7.....121 M2
    OLDE OL4.....60 C6
Station Vw BNG/LEV M19.....99 K3
Staton Av BOLE BL2.....36 F1
Staton St OP/CLY M11.....88 F2
Statter St BURY BL9.....39 K8
Staveley Av BOL BL1.....22 B6
    STLY SK15.....91 K1
Staveley Cl ROY/SHW OL2.....44 A6
    SALE M33.....96 E7
Staveley Rd MOSL OL5.....77 G4
Stead St RAMS BL0.....17 C6
Steadway UPML OL3.....61M7
Stedman Cl OP/CLY M11.....88 B3

Steele Gdns BOLE BL2.....37 G7
Steeles Av HYDE SK14.....102 B1
Steeple Cl CHH M8.....72 C7
Steeple Dr ORD M5.....86 D4
Steeple Vw ROY/SHW OL2.....43 G8
Stelfox Av GOL/RIS/CU WA3.....80 B4
Stelfox La DTN/ASHW * M34.....90 C5
Stelfox St ECC M30.....84 E4
Stella St BKLY M9.....56 E8
Stelling St GTN M18.....89 G7
Stenbury Cl RUSH/FAL M14.....98 F1
Stenner La DID/WITH * M20.....110 D2
Stephen Cl TOT/BURYW BL8.....38 F2
Stephens Av DROY M43.....89 K3
Stephenson Rd STRET M32.....97 G3
    HOR/BR BL6.....33 L2
    OLDE OL4.....60 A4
    WGNE/HIN WN2.....64 E4
Stephens Rd DID/WITH M20.....98 F6
    STLY SK15.....76 C8
Stephen St BOLE BL2.....37 H4
Stephen St CSLFD M3.....72 C8
    STKP SK1.....112 E4
    TOT/BURYW BL8.....38 F2
    URM M41.....96 B2
    WGNE/HIN WN2.....64 D2
Stephen St South
    TOT/BURYW BL8.....38 F3
Stephen Wk STKP * SK1.....112 E4
Steps Meadow WHIT OL12.....19 K8
Stern Av ORD M5.....86 D4
Sterndale Rd WGNNW/ST WN6.....31 H2
Sterndale Rd EDGY/DAV SK3.....112 B7
    MPL/ROM SK6.....113 L3
    WALK M28.....68 C6
Sterratt St BOL BL1.....2 E5
Stetchworth Dr WALK M28.....68 E5
Stevenson Cl WGNS/IIMK WN3.....47 K7
Stevenson Dr OLD OL1.....44 B8
Stevenson Rd SWIN M27.....70 B4
Stevenson Sq CMANE * M1.....7 J4
Stevenson St CSLFD * M3.....6 A4
    WALK M28.....68 E1
Stevens St WILM/AE SK9.....130 D3
Stewart Av FWTH BL4.....52 E5
    STLY SK15.....91 L1
Stewart St AULW OL7.....90 C2
    BOL BL1.....36 B3
    MILN OL16.....43 L1
    TOT/BURYW BL8.....38 F2
Steverton Cl COL/RIS/CU WA3.....79 J2
Steynton Cl BOL BL1.....35 J4
Stile Cl URM M41.....94 F2
Stiles Av MPL/ROM SK6.....114 B5
Stiles Cl GLSP SK13.....93 H7
Stilton Dr OP/CLY * M11.....88 D4
Stirling Av BRAM/HZG SK7.....121M3
    DID/WITH M20.....98 C4
    MPL/ROM SK6.....114 C7
    WGNE/HIN WN2.....48 D4
Stirling Cl EDGY/DAV SK3.....111M6
    LEIGH WN7.....67 G7
Stirling Dr AIMK WN4.....63 G8
    STLY SK15.....91 K1
Stirling Gv WHTF M45.....55 K4
Stirling Rd BOL BL1.....22 B7
    CHAD OL9.....58 C8
    WGNE/HIN WN2.....49 J8
Stirling St CHAD OL9.....8 D4
    WGN WN1.....47 L2
Stirrup Brook Gv WALK M28.....68 C7
Stirrup Ga WALK M28.....69 K7
Stitch La HTNM SK4.....12 F1
Stitch-mi-lane BOLE BL2.....37 H2
Stiups La MILN OL16.....28 F3
Stobart Av PWCH M25.....71M2
Stockburn Dr FAIL M35.....74 E5
Stock Cl WHIT OL12.....28 B2
Stockdale Av EDGY/DAV SK3.....112 C7
Stockdale Gv BOLE BL2.....37 J3
Stockdale Rd BKLY M9.....57 H8
Stockfield Mt CHAD OL9.....8 B6
Stockfield Rd CHAD OL9.....8 B6
Stock Gv MILN OL16.....29 J5
Stockholm Rd EDGY/DAV SK3.....112 A6
Stockholm St OP/CLY M11.....88 E2
Stockland Cl BRUN/LGST M13.....7 J9
Stock La CHAD OL9.....8 A5
Stockley Av BOLE BL2.....37 K2
Stockley Wk HULME * M15.....87 G6
Stockport Rd AULW OL7.....90 C4
    CHD/CHDH SK8.....111 G6
    DTN/ASHW M34.....101 H3
    HALE/TIMP WA15.....108 C7
    HYDE SK14.....102 B3
    HYDE SK14.....103 H3
    MOSL OL5.....76 F2
    MPL/ROM SK6.....113 L2
    MPL/ROM SK6.....113M6
    MPL/ROM SK6.....114 B6
    OLDE OL4.....60 F7
Stockport Rd East
    MPL/ROM SK6.....101 J8
Stockport Rd West
    MPL/ROM SK6.....112 F1
The Stocks GLSP SK13.....93 K5
Stocks Brow GLSP SK13.....93 K5
Stocks Cottages HOR/BR * BL6.....21 B8
Stocksfield Dr BKLY M9.....73 H1
    LHULT M38.....52 C7
Stocks Gdns STLY SK15.....91M8
Stocks La STLY SK15.....91 L3
Stocks Park Dr HOR/BR BL6.....33M1
Stocks St CHH M8.....72 D8
Stocks St East CHH M8.....72 D8
Stock St TOT/BURYW BL8.....25 H7
Stockton Av EDGY/DAV SK3.....12 B7
Stockton Dr TOT/BURYW BL8.....24 F6
Stockton Pk OLDE OL4.....60 A6
Stockton Rd CCHDY M21.....97 K4
    FWTH BL4.....52 E2
    WILM/AE SK9.....126 D3
Stockton St LIT OL15.....20 C7
    SWIN M27.....70 B5
Stoke Abbott Cl
    BRAM/HZG SK7.....121 G5
Stokesay Cl BURY BL9.....39 J7
    ROY/SHW OL2.....43 K4
Stokesay Dr BRAM/HZG SK7.....121 G3
Stokesay Rd SALE M33.....95M2
Stokes St OP/CLY M11.....89 G3
Stoke St MILN OL16.....11 K7
Stokoe Av ALT WA14.....107 K6
Stonall Av HULME M15.....87 G6

Stoneacre HOR/BR BL6....34 C4
Stoneacre Ct SWIN M27....70 C5
Stoneacre Rd WYTH/NTH M22....118 E2
Stonebeck Rd NTHM/RTH M23....109 J7
Stone Breaks Rd OLDE OL4....60 E5
Stonebridge Cl HOR/BR BL6....34 F6
Stonechat Cl DROY *M43....89M1
  GOL/RIS/CU WA3....80 B4
  WALK M28....68 E4
Stonecliffe Av STLY SK15....91 K2
Stone Cl RAMS BL0....17 A8
Stoneclough Rd FWTH BL4....53 J5
Stonecrop WGNNW/ST WN6....30 A3
Stone Cross La North
  GOL/RIS/CU WA3....79M5
Stone Cross La South
  GOL/RIS/CU WA3....79M6
Stonedelph Cl BOLE BL2....38 A3
Stonefield TYLD M29....67M3
Stonefield Dr CHH M8....72 B7
Stonefield St MILN OL16....29 J7
Stoneflat Ct WHIT OL12....10 B3
Stonehaven BOLS/LL BL3....51 J1
Stone Hvn WGNS/IIMK WN3....63 G2
Stonemead St BKLY * M9....73 J5
Stonehewer St RAD M26....54 E2
Stonehill Crs WHIT OL12....27 K1
Stonehill Dr WHIT OL12....27 K1
Stone Hill La WHIT OL12....27 K2
Stone Hill Rd FWTH BL4....53 H6
Stonehill Rd WHIT OL12....27 K1
Stonehouse EDGW/EG BL7....22 E5
Stonehurst Cl WGTN/LGST M12....88 D0
Stonelands Wy OLDE OL4....60 D8
Stoneleigh Av SALE M33....96 A7
Stoneleigh Dr RAD M26....53 L5
Stoneleigh Rd OLDE OL4....60 D5
Stoneleigh St OLD OL1....59 L3
Stonelow Cl HULME M15....87 J2
Stone Md MPL/ROM SK6....114 B1
Stone Mead Av
  HALE/TIMP WA15....117 L5
Stonemead Cl BOLS/LL BL3....34 B8
Stonepail Cl CHD/CHDH SK8....110 C7
Stonepail Cottages
  CHD/CHDH * SK8....110 D7
Stonepail Rd CHD/CHDH SK8....110 D7
Stone Pale WHTF M45....55 J5
Stone Pit Cl GOL/RIS/CU WA3....80 B3
Stone Pits RAMS BL0....17 E1
Stone Pl RUSH/FAL M14....98 F1
Stoneridge GLSP SK13....93 J7
Stone Rw MPL/ROM SK6....114 D6
Stonesby Cl OLDTF/WHR * M16....87 G8
Stonesdale Cl ROY/SHW OL2....43 H7
Stonesteads Dr EDGW/EG BL7....22 D4
Stonesteads Wy EDGW/EG BL7....22 D4
Stone St BOLE BL2....3 J1
  CSLFD M3....6 D7
Stoneswood Dr MOSL OL5....77 G2
Stoneswood Rd UPML OL3....61 H1
Stoney Bank RAD M26....53M5
Stoneycroft Av HOR/BR BL6....21 D8
Stoneycroft Cl HOR/BR BL6....21 D7
Stoneyfield STLY SK15....76 D8
Stoneyfield Cl OLDTF/WHR M16....98 C2
Stoneyhurst Cl HULME M15....87 J6
Stoneyland Dr NM/HAY SK22....124 C4
Stoney La UPML OL3....45 G5
  WILM/AE SK9....126 D7
Stoneyroyd WHIT * OL12....18 E2
Stoneyside Av WALK M28....53 H8
Stoneyside Gv WALK M28....69 H1
Stonie Heyes Av WHIT OL12....28 E2
Stonyford Rd SALE M33....97 G8
Stonyhurst BOL BL1....22 B7
  WGNS/IIMK WN3....15 J8
Stonyhurst Crs
  GOL/RIS/CU WA3....81 G7
Stopes Rd BOLS/LL BL3....37M8
Stopford Av LIT OL15....19M8
Stopford St EDGY/DAV SK3....12 F7
  OP/CLY M11....89 H5
  WGNE/HIN WN2....48 C5
Stopforth St WGNNW/ST WN6....14 B2
Stores Cottages OLDE * OL4....61 H6
Stores St PWCH M25....55M8
Store St AULW OL7....75 K7
  CMANW M1....7 L5
  HOR/BR BL6....21 C8
  OFTN SK2....112 F8
  OP/CLY * M11....88 C5
  RAD M26....39 C8
  ROCH OL11....27 H3
  ROY/SHW OL2....43M4
Storeton Cl WYTH/NTH M22....119 C2
Stortford Dr NTHM/RTH M23....109 L2
Storth Bank GLSP SK13....104 C5
Storth Meadow Rd GLSP SK13....104 C5
Stothard Rd STRET M32....96 E3
Stott Dr URM M41....94 F3
Stottfield ROY/SHW OL2....58 E1
Stott La BOLE BL2....36 E3
  MDTN M24....41 J7
  SLFD M6....85 L1
Stott Milne St CHAD OL9....8 A4
Stott Rd CHAD OL9....74 B1
  SWIN M27....70 A6
Stott's La NEWH/MOS M40....74 A6
Stott St MILN OL16....29 C1
  MILN OL16....29 J8
  NEWH/MOS M40....74 A6
  WHIT OL12....10 F1
Stourbridge Av LHULT M38....52 D6
Stour Cl ALT WA14....107M4
Stourport Cl MPL/ROM SK6....113 X3
Stourport St OLD OL1....9M1
Stout Rd TYLD M29....67 L4
Stout St LEIGH WN7....65M8
Stovell Av WGTN/LGST M12....99 K2
Stovell Rd NEWH/MOS M40....73 K4
Stow Cl TOT/BURYW BL8....25 G7
Stowe Gdns LEIGH WN7....67 G7
Stowell St BKLY M9....56 E8
Stowell St BOL BL1....36 B3
  ORD M5....86 B3
Stow Gdns DID/WITH M20....98 D6
Stracey St NEWH/MOS M40....88 B1
Stradbroke Cl GOL/RIS/CU WA3....80 D5
  GTN M18....88 E7
Strain Av BKLY M9....57 C8
The Straits TYLD M29....67M6
The Strand AIMK WN4....63 L8
  HOR/BR BL6....34 A2
  ROCH OL11....42 C1
Strand Av AIMK WN4....63 L8
Strand Ct STRET M32....96 F4
Strand Wy ROY/SHW OL2....59 C2

Strange Rd AIMK WN4....78 A1
Strange St LEIGH WN7....65 L8
Strangford St RAD M26....38 A3
Strang St RAMS BL0....17 C6
Stranraer Rd WGNW/BIL/O WN5....46 F3
Stranton Dr WALK M28....69M4
Stratfield Av NTHM/RTH M23....109 G3
Stratford Av BOL BL1....35 L3
  BURY BL9....25 H4
  DID/WITH M20....98 C7
  OLDS OL8....75 H1
  ROCH OL11....10 C9
Stratford Cl FWTH BL4....52 C3
Stratford Gdns MPL/ROM SK6....113 J1
Stratford Rd MDTN M24....57 L7
Stratford St WGNNW/ST WN6....14 B1
Strathblane Cl DID/WITH M20....98 E5
Strathfield Dr OP/CLY M11....88 E2
Strathmore Av STRET M32....97 C4
Strathmore Cl AIMK WN4....63 K7
  CCHDY M21....97 L2
  DTN/ASHW M34....101 L2
Strathmore Cl RAMS BL0....24 F1
Strathmore Rd BOLE BL2....37 H3
Stratton Dr WGNE/HIN WN2....34 H4
Stratton Rd OFTN SK2....112 F4
  OLDTF/WHR M16....97 L2
  SWIN M27....70 C3
Strawberry Bank SLFD * M6....86 E1
Strawberry Cl ALT WA14....107 L5
Strawberry Hl SLFD M6....86 E1
Strawberry Hill Rd BOLE BL2....3 J8
Strawberry La WILM/AE SK9....126 C6
Strawberry Rd SLFD M6....86 D1
The Stray BOL BL1....22 E8
Stray St OP/CLY M11....89 H4
Streamside Cl
  HALE/TIMP WA15....108 E8
Stream Ter STKP SK1....112 E3
Streetbridge OLD OL1....58 D2
Street Bridge Rd OLD OL1....58 D2
Streetgate LHULT M38....52 D7
Streethouse La UPML OL3....61 J3
Street Kirklees TOT/BURYW BL8....24 C5
Street La MCFLDN SK10....129 H4
  RAD M26....38 B4
Stretford Rd HULME M15....87 J6
  OLDTF/WHR M16....86 F7
  URM M41....96 A3
Stretton Av DID/WITH M20....110 F1
  GOL/RIS/CU * WA3....80 A5
  SALE M33....96 B5
  STRET M32....96 D1
  WGNW/BIL/O WN5....62 B7
Stretton Cl NEWH/MOS M40....73 C7
  WGNNW/ST WN6....31 H4
Stretton Rd BOLS/LL BL3....35 L8
  RAMS BL0....24 D2
Striding Edge Wk OLD OL1....9 L1
Strines Cl WGNE/HIN WN2....49 C6
Strines Rd MPL/ROM SK6....114 D7
Stringer Av HYDE SK14....103 J2
Stringer Cl HYDE SK14....103 J1
Stringer St LEIGH WN7....66 C7
  STKP SK1....13M3
Stroma Gdns URM M41....84 F7
Strong St BRO M7....72 B8
Strongstry Rd RAMS BL0....17 C2
Stroud Av ECC M30....84 E1
Stroud Cl MDTN M24....57 K7
  WGNE/HIN WN2....48 C2
Stuart Av IRL M44....94 C2
  WGNE/HIN WN2....65 L1
Stuart Dr MPL/ROM SK6....113M5
Stuart Rd ALT WA14....107 L5
  MPL/ROM SK6....101 G6
  STRET M32....97 G1
Stuart St MDTN M24....57M4
  MILN OL16....11 H7
  OLDS OL8....9 G9
  OP/CLY M11....88 D2
Stuart St East OP/CLY M11....88 D2
Stuart Wk MDTN M24....57 J5
Stubbins La NTHM/RTH M23....109 H3
Stubbins La RAMS BL0....17 C4
Stubbins Vale Rd RAMS BL0....17 C3
Stubbs Cl BRO M7....71 L4
Stubley Gdns LIT OL15....20 B7
Stubley La LIT OL15....20 A8
Stubley Mill Rd LIT OL15....19M8
Studforth Wk HULME * M15....87 J7
Studland Rd WYTH/NTH M22....119 H1
Studley Cl ROY/SHW OL2....43 K8
Studley Ct TYLD M29....67 H4
Sturton Av WGNS/IIMK WN3....63 H1
Styal Av RDSH SK5....100 C3
  STRET M32....96 D1
Styal Gv CHD/CHDH SK8....119 J1
Styal Rd WILM/AE SK9....126 E3
  WYTH/NTH M22....110 B5
Styal vw WILM/AE SK9....126 F2
Styhead Dr MDTN M24....57 L7
Style St ANC M4....7 H1
Styperson Wy POY/DIS SK12....129 J7
Sudbrook Cl GOL/RIS/CU WA3....80 B4
Sudbury Cl WGNS/IIMK WN3....63 L2
Sudbury Dr CHD/CHDH SK8....119 L5
  HOR/BR BL6....34 F6
Sudbury Rd BRAM/HZG SK7....122 A4
Sudden St ROCH OL11....27M8
Sudell St ANC M4....7 K1
Sudley Rd ROCH OL11....27M7
Sudlow St MILN OL16....28 E2
Sudren St TOT/BURYW * BL8....38 C1
Suffield St MDTN M24....57 J4
Suffolk Av DROY M43....89 K1
Suffolk Cl BOLS/LL BL3....37 L7
  WGN WN1....31 L4
Suffolk Dr RDSH SK5....100 F6
  WILM/AE SK9....126 B8
Suffolk Gv LEIGH WN7....65M7
Suffolk Rd ALT WA14....107 L8
Suffolk St CHAD OL9....58 E8
  ROCH OL11....10 E6
  SLFD M6....71 K7
Sugar La MCFLDN SK10....129 K8
  UPML OL3....61 K2
Sugden St ALT OL6....91 G1
Sulby Av STRET M32....97M3
Sulby St NEWH/MOS M40....73 K4
  RAD M26....53 L4
Sulgrave Av POY/DIS SK12....122 B8
Sullivan St WGTN/LGST M12....99 K1
Sullivan Wy WGN WN1....15 J2
Sultan St BURY BL9....4 E9
Sulway Cl SWIN * M27....70 D5
Sumac St OP/CLY M11....89 G2
Summer Av URM M41....96 B2

Summer Castle MILN OL16....10 F5
Summercroft CHAD OL9....74 E1
Summerdale Dr RAMS BL0....24 E2
Summerfield Av DROY M43....89 H1
Summerfield Dr MDTN M24....57M2
  TYLD M29....67 L4
Summerfield Pl WILM/AE SK9....126 E6
Summerfield Rd BOLS/LL BL3....36 E8
  WALK M28....69 K5
  WYTH/NTH M22....118 E2
Summer Hl MOSL * OL5....77 G2
Summerhill Vw UPML OL3....45 G3
Summerlea CHD/CHDH * SK8....120 D4
Summer Pl RUSH/FAL M14....98 F2
Summers Av STLY SK15....91M2
Summerseat Cl OLDE OL4....60 D5
  ORD * M5....86 D4
Summerseat La RAMS BL0....24 D2
Summershades La OLDE OL4....61 C6
Summershades Ri OLDE OL4....61 C6
Summer St CHAD OL9....8 C5
Summer St HOR/BR BL6....21 B8
  MILN OL16....11 C5
Summerville Av BKLY M9....73 J5
Summerville Rd SLFD M6....71 H7
Summit St HEY OL10....40 C2
Summit St HEY OL10....40 C2
Sumner Av BOLE BL2....38 A3
Sumner Rd SLFD M6....71 C7
Sumner St ATH M46....66 F1
  GLSP SK13....104 F4
  ROY/SHW OL2....43 L7
  WGNE/HIN WN2....33 G7
Sumner Wy URM M41....95M2
Sunadale Cl BOLS/LL BL3....35 L7
Sunbank Cl WHIT OL12....28 A2
Sunbank La HALE/TIMP WA15....117M6
Sunbury Cl DUK SK16....91 J4
  WILM/AE SK9....127 J2
Sunbury Dr NEWH/MOS M40....74 A8
Sunderland Av ATH M46....75M8
Sunderland Pl
  WGNW/BIL/O WN5....47 G3
Sundial Cl HYDE SK14....103 G1
Sundial Rd OFTN SK2....113 G6
Sundown Cl NM/HAY SK22....124 C4
Sundridge Cl BOLS/LL BL3....51 K1
Sunfield Av OLDE OL4....60 B1
Sunfield Crs ROY/SHW OL2....59 H1
Sunfield Dr ROY/SHW OL2....59 J1
Sunfield Est UPML OL3....45M8
Sunfield La UPML OL3....45M8
Sunfield Rd OLD OL1....9 H2
Sunfield Wy OLDE OL4....60 B5
Sunflower Meadow IRL M44....94 E2
Sunhill Cl MILN OL16....42 E2
Sunk La MDTN M24....57 K5
Sunlaws St GLSP SK13....104 E4
Sunleigh Rd WGNE/HIN WN2....49 H6
Sunlight Rd BOL BL1....35M5
Sunningdale Cl HYDE SK14....91 H7
Sunningdale Ct HYDE SK14....91 H7
  RAD M26....38 A7
  SALE M33....109 H1
  WHTF M45....54 F5
Sunningdale Dr
  BRAM/HZG SK7....121 J5
  GLSP SK13....105 H3
  HEY OL10....41 C4
  IRL M44....94 C1
  PWCH M25....55 K7
  SLFD M6....70 D7
Sunningdale Gv LEIGH WN7....67 C5
Sunningdale Rd
  CHD/CHDH SK8....120 C3
  DTN/ASHW M34....101 K4
  URM M41....95 L3
Sunningdale Wk BOLS/LL * BL3....35M7
Sunning Hill St BOLS/LL BL3....36 A8
Sunny Av BURY BL9....25 J7
Sunny Bank OLDE OL4....60 B7
  RAD M26....53 K4
  WILM/AE SK9....126 B8
Sunny Bank Av DROY M43....89 J5
Sunnybank Av ECC M30....89 J3
  HTNM SK4....99 J8
Sunnybank Cl NEWLW WA12....78 F8
Sunny Bank Rd ALT WA14....116 E4
  BRUN/LGST M13....99 H1
  BURY BL9....55 K1
  DROY M43....89 J3
  TYLD M29....67 H4
Sunny Banks GLSP SK13....104 E4
Sunny Bower St
  TOT/BURYW BL8....24 B6
Sunny Brow Rd GTN M18....88 F7
  MDTN M24....57 H4
Sunny Dr PWCH M25....55 J8
  WGNW/BIL/O WN5....46 C6
Sunnyfield Rd HTNM SK4....111 J1
  PWCH M25....55M5
Sunnyfields WGNS/IIMK WN3....62 F2
Sunny Garth WHTN BL5....50 B4
Sunnylea Av BNG/LEV M19....99 H7
Sunnymead Av BL1 BL1....22 C8
Sunnymede V RAMS BL0....24 D1
Sunnyside AULW OL7....75 H7
Sunnyside Av DROY M43....74 C8
Sunnyside Ct DROY * M43....89 J1
Sunnyside Crs AUL * OL6....91 C2
Sunnyside Gv AUL OL6....91 C2
Sunnyside Rd AIMK WN4....63 J6
  BOL BL1....35M2
  DROY M43....89 J1
Sunnywood Dr TOT/BURYW BL8....24 D6
Sunnywood La TOT/BURYW BL8....24 D6
Sunset Av WYTH/NTH M22....110 A2
Sun St MOSL OL5....76 F3
  RAMS BL0....17 C6
Sunwell Ter MPL/ROM SK6....123 H1
Surbiton Rd NEWH/MOS M40....73 L7
Surma Cl CHAD OL9....8 E4
  MILN OL16....11 J8
Surrey Av DROY M43....89 J1
  LEIGH WN7....67 H8
  ROY/SHW OL2....43 J5
Surrey Dr BURY BL9....5 J1
Surrey Park Cl ROY/SHW * OL2....43 J4
Surrey Rd BKLY M9....73 G2
Surrey St AUL OL6....76 A7
  BKLY * M9....72 F2
  CHAD OL9....8 D3
  GLSP SK13....104 F3
  RAMS BL0....17 C6
Surrey Wy RDSH SK5....100 F7

Surtees Rd NTHM/RTH M23....109 K2
Sussex Av DID/WITH M20....98 E8
  HEY OL10....40 B3
Sussex Cl CHAD OL9....8 A7
  SWIN M27....70 D2
  WGN WN1....31 L3
  WGNE/HIN WN2....49 K7
Sussex Dr BURY BL9....5 G9
  DROY M43....89 K1
Sussex Pl HYDE SK14....91 J7
Sussex Rd EDGY/DAV SK3....12 A7
  PART M31....106 B2
Sussex St BRO M7....87 G1
  CMANW M2....6 F4
  LEIGH WN7....67 H8
  ROCH OL11....10 E6
Sutcliffe Av WGTN/LGST M12....99 K2
Sutcliffe St AULW OL7....90 C3
  BOL BL1....36 B2
  LIT OL15....20 C6
  MDTN M24....57M4
  OLDS OL8....9 H9
  ROY/SHW OL2....59 K1
Sutherland Cl OLDS OL8....75 J3
Sutherland Gv FWTH BL4....52 F4
Sutherland Rd BOL BL1....35 K4
  HEY OL10....40 C3
  OLDTF/WHR M16....97 K1
  WGNS/IIMK WN3....63 K1
Sutherland St ATH M46....66 F1
  ECC M30....84 E1
  FWTH BL4....52 F4
  SWIN M27....70 B3
  WGNE/HIN WN2....48 F7
  WGNW/BIL/O WN5....47 J6
Suthers St CHAD OL9....8 C7
  RAD M26....54 F3
Sutton Av GOL/RIS/CU WA3....81 H8
Sutton Cl TOT/BURYW BL8....38 E4
Sutton Dr DROY M43....89 H1
Sutton Dwellings SLFD M6....85 C1
Sutton Rd BOLS/LL BL3....35 C1
  GTN M18....99M1
  HTNM SK4....111M1
  POY/DIS SK12....129 K2
  WILM/AE SK9....130 C3
Suttons La MPL/ROM SK6....114 D7
Sutton Wy GLSP SK13....93 K7
Swailes St OLDE OL4....59 L6
Swaine St EDGY/DAV SK3....13 G5
Swainsthorpe Dr BKLY M9....73 H4
Swain St WHIT * OL12....28 B3
Swalecliff Av NTHM/RTH M23....108 F5
Swale Cl WILM/AE SK9....127 J2
Swaledale Cl ROY/SHW OL2....43 H7
Swale Dr ALT WA14....107M6
Swallow Bank Dr ROCH * OL11....41 L1
Swallow Cl STLY SK15....77 J5
Swallow Dr BURY BL9....25 L8
  IRL M44....94 D1
  ROCH OL11....27 J5
Swallowfield LEIGH WN7....66 D7
Swallow House Crs
  NM/HAY SK22....125 L1
Swallow House La
  NM/HAY SK22....125 K1
Swallow La STLY SK15....77 J5
Swallow St OLDS OL8....75 C2
  OP/CLY M11....88 C3
  STKP SK1....13 K8
  WGTN/LGST * M12....99 K2
Swanage Av NTHM/RTH M23....109 C4
  OFTN SK2....113 G6
Swanage Cl TOT/BURYW BL8....24 F6
Swanage Rd ECC M30....84 E1
Swanbourne Gdns
  EDGY/DAV SK3....111M6
Swan Cl POY/DIS SK12....121 K8
Swan Ct ROY/SHW * OL2....43 L6
Swanhill Cl GTN M18....89 J6
Swan La BOLS/LL BL3....36 A8
Swanley Av NEWH/MOS M40....73 H7
Swan Meadow Rd
  WGNS/IIMK WN3....14 D6
Swann La CHD/CHDH SK8....120 D4
Swann Ct CHD/CHDH SK8....120 D3
Swann St WGNS/IIMK WN3....14 D5
Swan Rd HALE/TIMP WA15....108 D3
  NEWLW WA12....78 B8
  TOT/BURYW BL8....24 F6
Swansea St OLDS OL8....59 L8
Swan St ANC M4....7 H2
  AUL OL6....90 F1
  RAD M26....54 E2
  WILM/AE SK9....126 F5
Swarbrick Dr PWCH M25....71 J2
Swayfield Av BRUN/LGST M13....99 J1
Swaylands Dr SALE M33....108 L3
Sweetbriar Cl ROY/SHW OL2....43 L5
Sweet Briar St WHIT OL12....28 B2
Sweet Briar La WHIT * OL12....28 B2
Sweetloves Gv BOL BL1....22 B7
Sweetloves La BOL BL1....22 B7
Sweetnam Dr OP/CLY M11....88 E2
Swettenham Rd WILM/AE SK9....119M7
Swift Cl OLDE OL4....60 B1
  ROCH OL11....44 B7
Swift Rd OLD OL1....44 B7
  ROCH OL11....27 L1
Swift St AUL * OL6....76 A7
  WGNW/BIL/O WN5....46 B6
Swinbourne Gv DID/WITH M20....98 E3
Swinburne Av DROY M43....89 K1
Swinburne Gn RDSH SK5....100 A3
Swinburn Gv WGNW/BIL/O WN5....62 A3
Swinburn St BKLY M9....73 J3
Swindells St HYDE SK14....91 H7
  OP/CLY * M11....89 H5
Swinfield Av CCHDY M21....97 J4
Swinford Gv ROY/SHW OL2....43 K7
Swinley Cha WILM/AE SK9....127 K3
Swinley La WGN WN1....47M2
Swinley Rd WGN WN1....47M2
Swinley St WGN WN1....47M2
Swinside WGN WN1....48 A3
Swinside Rd BOLE BL2....37 H4
Swinstead Av
  NEWH/MOS * M40....73 H7
Swinton Crs BURY BL9....55 K3
Swinton Gv BRUN/LGST M13....87M8
Swinton Hall Rd SWIN M27....70 D4
Swinton Park Rd SLFD M6....70 F5
Swinton St BOLE BL2....37 H5
  OLDS OL8....9M7
Swiss Hl WILM/AE SK9....130 E3
Swithemby St HOR/BR BL6....21 A8
Swithin Rd WYTH/NTH M22....119 C4
Swythamley Cl EDGY/DAV SK3....111 K4

Swythamley Rd EDGY/DAV SK3....111 K4
Sybil St LIT OL15....20 B6
Sycamore Av ALT WA14....107 K7
  CHAD OL9....74 C1
  DTN/ASHW M34....101 J3
  GOL/RIS/CU WA3....79 K3
  HEY OL10....41 H4
  MILN OL16....43 K1
  OLDE OL4....60 A4
  RAD M26....54 C4
  TYLD M29....68 A3
  WGNE/HIN WN2....65 J1
  WGNNW/ST WN6....31 J8
Sycamore Cl AUL OL6....91 H2
  DID/WITH * M20....98 F5
  DUK SK16....91 J4
  LIT OL15....20 A7
  NM/HAY SK22....125 C3
  WILM/AE SK9....126 F2
Sycamore Ct SLFD M6....86 D1
Sycamore Crs AUL OL6....75M7
Sycamore Dr BURY BL9....25 J6
  RAD M26....38 D7
  WGNS/IIMK WN3....62 E2
Sycamore Gv FAIL M35....74 E5
Sycamore Ldg
  BRAM/HZG * SK7....121 H5
Sycamore Pl WHTF M45....55 J6
Sycamore Rd ATH M46....67 H1
  ECC M30....69 K8
  MPL/ROM SK6....101 K8
  NM/HAY SK22....125 C3
  PART M31....106 A1
  TOT/BURYW BL8....24 C7
The Sycamores GLSP SK13....104 C1
  MOSL OL5....77 H3
  OLDE OL4....60 C4
  RAD M26....53 L6
  STLY SK15....91 L4
Sycamore St EDGY/DAV SK3....12 B7
  SALE M33....97 H8
Sycamore Wk CHD/CHDH SK8....111 C6
Sydall St DTN/ASHW M34....101 J1
Syddal Cl BRAM/HZG SK7....120 F7
Syddal Crs BRAM/HZG SK7....120 F8
Syddall Av CHD/CHDH SK8....119M4
Syddal Gn BRAM/HZG SK7....120 F7
Syddal Rd BRAM/HZG SK7....120 F7
Syddal St HYDE SK14....102 A2
Syddall St HYDE SK14....102 A2
Sydenham St OLD OL1....59 L3
Syderstone Cl WGNE/HIN WN2....49 H8
Sydney Av ECC M30....85 C2
  LEIGH WN7....
  MANAIR M90....118 C4
Sydney Gdns LIT OL15....20 D3
Sydney Jones Ct
  NEWH/MOS M40....73M3
Sydney Rd BRAM/HZG SK7....121 H7
Sydney St FAIL M35....74 B5
  OFTN SK2....112 F5
  SLFD M6....86 B2
  STRET M32....97 C2
  SWIN M27....70 A4
  WGNE/HIN WN2....64 D1
Syke La WHIT OL12....19 C3
Syke Rd LIT OL15....29M2
  WHIT OL15....19 C8
Sykes Av BURY BL9....39 L8
Sykes Cl UPML OL3....61 L7
Sykes Ct MILN OL16....11 K6
Sykes Crs WGNS/IIMK WN3....62 F3
Sykes Meadow EDGY/DAV SK3....12 E9
Sykes St BURY BL9....5 H2
  MILN * OL16....11 J6
  MILN OL16....29 K8
  RDSH SK5....100 C4
Sylvan Av FAIL M35....74 B7
  HALE/TIMP WA15....108 C4
  SALE M33....108 F1
  URM M41....96 A1
  WILM/AE SK9....126 D7
Sylvan Cl MDTN M24....57 C2
Sylvandale Av BNG/LEV M19....99 K3
Sylvan Gv ALT WA14....108 A7
Sylvan St CHAD OL9....8 D4
Sylvester Av STKP SK1....112 E6
Sylvester Cl HYDE SK14....103 H2
Sylvia Gv RDSH SK5....100 B5
Symms St SLFD M6....71 L8
Symond Rd BKLY M9....57 H7
Symons Rd SALE M33....96 F2
Symons St BRO M7....72 B5
Syndall Av WGTN/LGST M12....88 A2
Syndall St WGTN/LGST M12....88 A6
Syresham St WGNE/HIN WN2....64 E2

T

Taberner Cl WGNNW/ST WN6....31 J3
Taberner St WGNE/HIN WN2....64 E2
Tabley Av RUSH/FAL M14....98 E2
Tabley Gdns MPL/ROM SK6....114 D8
Tabley Gv BRUN/LGST M13....99 J2
  HALE/TIMP WA15....108 D4
  RDSH SK5....100 B5
Tabley Mere Gdns
  CHD/CHDH SK8....120 B1
Tabley Ms ALT WA14....107 K6
Tabley Rd BOLS/LL BL3....35 L8
  SALE * M33....109 H2
  WILM/AE SK9....119M7
Tabley St DUK SK16....91 H4
  MOSL OL5....77 C4
  SLFD M6....71 L7
Tabor St MDTN M24....57 J2
Tackler Cl SWIN M27....70 C5
Tadman Gv ALT WA14....107 K6
Tadmor Cl LHULT M38....52 C8
Tagore Cl BRUN/LGST M13....88 B3
Tahir Cl CHH M8....72 E5
Talavera St BRO M7....72 A7
Talbenny Cl BOL BL1....35 J4
Talbot Cl OLDE OL4....59M4
Talbot Ct BOL BL1....22 C8
Talbot Gv BURY BL9....25 K6
Talbot Pl OLDTF/WHR M16....116 D2
Talbot Rd ALT WA14....116 D2
  GLSP SK13....104 F2
  HYDE SK14....91 H7
  RUSH/FAL M14....99 H5
  SALE * M33....97 H8
  STRET M32....86 C8
  WILM/AE SK9....130 C5
Talbot St AIMK * WN4....64 A8
  OLDE OL4....90 D1
  BRAM/HZG SK7....113 C8
  ECC M30....85 H3
  GLSP SK13....104 F3

GOL/RIS/CU WA3 .....79 K4
MDTN M24 .....57 K2
ROCH OL11 .....10 E7
Talford Gv MDTN M24 .....98 D7
Talgarth Rd NEWH/MOS M40 .....72 F8
Talkin Dr MDTN M24 .....57 H1
Talland Wk BRUN/LGST M13 .....87 A7
Tallarn Cl DID/WITH M20 .....98 F5
Tallis St WGTN/LGST M12 .....99 K1
Tallow Wy IRL M44 .....94 D4
Tall Trees Cl BURY BL9 .....42 F8
Tall Trees Pl OFTN SK2 .....112 F6
Tallyman Wy SWIN M27 .....71 H5
Talman Gv AIMK WN4 .....79 G1
Talmine Av NEWH/MOS M40 .....73 H7
Tamar Cl FWTH BL4 .....53 L7
Tamar Ct HULME M15 .....87 G6
Tamar Dr NTHM/RTH M23 .....109 K8
Tamarin Cl SWIN M27 .....69 M3
Tamebank MOSL OL5 .....77 C1
Tame Barn Cl MILN * OL16 .....29 K6
Tame Cl STLY SK15 .....91 M1
Tame La UPML OL3 .....44 F5
Tamer Gv LEIGH WN7 .....65 M4
Tamerton Dr CHH M8 .....72 D6
Tameside Ct DUK * SK16 .....90 E5
Tame St ANC M4 .....88 A3
DTN/ASHW M34 .....90 C5
DTN/ASHW M34 .....90 C8
MOSL OL5 .....77 H1
STLY SK15 .....91 H3
UPML OL3 .....61 L4
Tamworth Av ORD M5 .....86 E4
WHTF M45 .....55 L5
Tamworth Av West ORD * M5 .....86 D4
HULME M15 .....87 G6
Tamworth Dr TOT/BURYW BL8 .....24 F7
WGNE/HIN WN2 .....48 C2
Tamworth Gn STKP SK1 .....112 E2
Tamworth St CHAD OL9 .....8 C8
STKP SK1 .....112 E2
Tamworth Wk ORD M5 .....86 D4
Tandis Ct SLFD * M6 .....85 K1
Tandle Hill Rd ROY/SHW OL2 .....42 E6
Tandlewood Ms
NEWH/MOS M40 .....73 M7
Tandlewood Pk ROY/SHW OL2 .....42 E6
Tanfield Dr RAD M26 .....53 L5
Tanfield Rd DID/WITH M20 .....110 E5
Tangmere Cl NEWH/MOS * M40 .....73 M1
Tanhill Cl STKP SK2 .....113 H6
Tanhill La OLDS OL8 .....75 L2
Tanhouse Av TYLD M29 .....68 A5
Tan House Dr WGNS/IIMK WN3 .....62 F3
Tan House La WGNS/IIMK WN3 .....62 F3
Tanhouse Rd URM M41 .....95 G1
Tanners Cft RAMS BL0 .....17 B6
Tanners Fold OLDS OL8 .....75 K2
Tanners Gn SLFD M6 .....86 C1
Tanner's La GOL/RIS/CU WA3 .....79 L4
Tanners St RAMS BL0 .....17 B6
Tanner St HYDE * SK14 .....102 A1
Tannery Wy ALT WA14 .....108 B5
Tannock Rd BRAM/HZG SK7 .....122 B3
Tanpits Rd BURY BL9 .....4 D3
Tansey Gv BRO M7 .....72 C2
Tansley Rd CHH M8 .....72 D2
Tansley Sq WGNNW/BIL/O WN5 .....47 G7
Tanworth Wk BOL * BL1 .....36 B2
Tan Yard Brow GTN M18 .....89 H8
Tanyard Dr HALE/TIMP WA15 .....117 L6
Tanyard Gn RDSH SK5 .....100 C7
Tanyard La HALE/TIMP WA15 .....117 H7
Tape St RAMS BL0 .....17 B6
Tapley Av POY/DIS SK12 .....129 J2
Taplin Dr GTN M18 .....88 F7
Taplow Gv CHD/CHDH SK8 .....120 B2
Taplow Wk RUSH/FAL M14 .....99 H1
Tarbet Dr BOLE BL2 .....37 J6
Tarbet Rd DUK SK16 .....90 F5
Tarbolton Crs
HALE/TIMP WA15 .....117 L1
Tariff St CMANE M1 .....7 K4
Tarleton Av ATH M46 .....50 E7
Tarleton Pl BOLS/LL BL3 .....51 K1
Tarleton Wk BRUN/LGST * M13 .....87M6
Tarnbrook Cl WHTF M45 .....55M4
Tarnbrook Dr WGNE/HIN WN2 .....32 E2
Tarnbrook Wk HULME * M15 .....87 J1
Tarn Cl AIMK WN4 .....63 L7
Tarn Dr BURY BL9 .....39 H6
Tarn Gv WALK M28 .....69 J3
Tarnrigg Cl WGNS/IIMK WN3 .....63 H1
The Tarns CHD/CHDH SK8 .....119 K1
Tarnside Cl MILN OL16 .....28 F1
OFTN SK2 .....113 J6
Tarnside Fold GLSP SK13 .....104 D4
Tarnside Rd WGNNW/BIL/O WN5 .....46 B6
Tarnway GOL/RIS/CU WA3 .....80 C5
Tarporley Av RUSH/FAL M14 .....98 D4
Tarporley Cl EDGY/DAV SK3 .....111M7
Tarran Gv DTN/ASHW M34 .....101 L3
Tarrant Cl WGNS/IIMK WN3 .....63 G3
Tarrington Cl WGTN/LGST M12 .....88 D7
Tartan St OP/CLY M11 .....88 C3
Tarvin Av DID/WITH M20 .....98 D5
HTNM SK4 .....100 A5
Tarvin Cl GOL/RIS/CU WA3 .....80 B5
Tarvin Dr MPL/ROM SK6 .....101 H8
Tarvington Cl NEWH/MOS * M40 .....72 F6
Tarvin Rd CHD/CHDH SK8 .....111 K8
Tarvin Wk BOL BL1 .....36 B2
Tasle Aly CMANW M2 .....6 F5
Tatchbury Rd FAIL M35 .....74 C5
Tate St OLDS OL8 .....59 L8
Tatham Cl BRUN/LGST M13 .....99 J1
Tatham Gv WGNS/IIMK WN3 .....63 G3
Tatham St MILN OL16 .....11 G5
Tatland Dr WYTH/NTH M22 .....119 H1
Tatlock Cl WGNNW/BIL/O WN5 .....62 B7
Tattersall Av BOL BL1 .....35 H2
Tattersall St CHAD OL9 .....8 E7
Tatton Cl BRAM/HZG SK7 .....113 J8
CHD/CHDH SK8 .....111 K8
Tatton Dr AIMK WN4 .....63 J8
Tatton Gdns MPL/ROM SK6 .....102 A7
Tatton Cl DID/WITH M20 .....98 E6
Tatton Mere Dr DROY M43 .....89 J3
Tattonmere Gdns
CHD/CHDH SK8 .....111 K8
Tatton Pl SALE M33 .....96 E7
Tatton Rd DTN/ASHW M34 .....101 K3
SALE M33 .....96 E7
WILM/AE SK9 .....120 A7
Tatton Rd North HTNM SK4 .....99M7
Tatton Rd South HTNM SK4 .....99M8
Tatton St HULME M15 .....87 G6
HYDE SK14 .....102 B3

ORD M5 .....86 E4
STKP SK1 .....13 J4
STLY SK15 .....91 L2
Taunton Av AULW OL7 .....75 K8
ECC M30 .....84 E1
LEIGH WN7 .....66 A2
RDSH SK5 .....100 F7
URM M41 .....95 L4
Taunton Cl BOL * BL1 .....35M3
BRAM/HZG BL4 .....122 C2
Taunton Dr FWTH BL4 .....52 C3
Taunton Gn AULW OL7 .....75 J7
Taunton Gv WHTF M45 .....55 K6
Taunton Hall Cl AULW * OL7 .....75 K8
Taunton Lawns AULW * OL7 .....75 K8
Taunton Pl AULW * OL7 .....75 J7
Taunton Platting AULW * OL7 .....75 K7
Taunton Rd AULW OL7 .....75 K7
CHAD OL9 .....58 D3
SALE M33 .....96 A8
Taunton St ANC M4 .....88 A3
Taurus St OLDE OL4 .....59M4
Tavern Court Av FAIL M35 .....74 D5
Tavern Rd GLSP SK13 .....104 B1
Tavery Cl ANC * M4 .....7 M3
Tavistock Cl HYDE SK14 .....103 H2
Tavistock Dr CHAD OL9 .....58 D3
Tavistock Rd BOL BL1 .....2 A6
ROCH OL11 .....42 C1
SALE M33 .....96 A7
WGNE/HIN WN2 .....49 K8
Tavistock St ATH M46 .....66 E1
Tawton Av HYDE SK14 .....103 H2
Taxi Rd MANAIR M90 .....118 D5
Tay Cl OLDS OL8 .....9 G9
Tayfield Rd WYTH/NTH M22 .....118 E2
Taylor Av WGNE/HIN WN2 .....27 J4
Taylor Green Wy OLDE OL4 .....60 C5
Taylor Gv WGNE/HIN WN2 .....65M1
Taylor La DTN/ASHW M34 .....90 E4
Taylor Rd ALT WA14 .....107 K7
RNFD/HAY WA11 .....78 C6
URM M41 .....85 H5
WGNE/HIN WN2 .....65M1
Taylor's La BOLE BL2 .....37 L5
WGNS/IIMK WN3 .....64 C1
Taylorson St ORD M5 .....86 E5
Taylorson St South ORD M5 .....86 D5
Taylors Pl WHIT * OL12 .....10 E1
Taylor's La STRET M32 .....97 H7
Taylor St BOL * BL1 .....2 F6
BURY BL9 .....5 H2
CHAD OL9 .....58 D5
DROY M43 .....89 K3
DTN/ASHW M34 .....90 E4
GTN M18 .....88 F6
HEY OL10 .....40 F2
HOR/BR BL6 .....33 L1
HYDE SK14 .....93 G7
HYDE SK14 .....102 C1
LEIGH WN7 .....66 A4
MDTN M24 .....57 K4
OLD OL1 .....59M4
OLDE OL4 .....60 B6
PWCH M25 .....55M8
RAD M26 .....54 D1
ROY/SHW * OL2 .....43 G7
RUSH/FAL M14 .....98 F1
STLY SK15 .....91 L3
WGNS/IIMK WN3 .....14 D4
WHIT OL12 .....18 E4
Taylton Cl TYLD M29 .....28 C3
Taywood Rd BOLS/LL BL3 .....51 G2
Teak Dr FWTH BL4 .....52 C4
Teak St BURY BL9 .....5 K4
Teal Av POY/DIS SK12 .....121 J8
Tealby Av OLDTF/WHR M16 .....86 F8
Tealby Rd GTN M18 .....88 E8
Teal Cl ALT WA14 .....107 L4
OFTN SK2 .....113 J7
Teal Ct ROCH OL11 .....27 J5
Teal St BOLS/LL BL3 .....36 C8
Teasdale Cl CHAD OL9 .....74 B1
Tebbutt St ANC M4 .....7 K1
Tebworth Dr WGNE/HIN WN2 .....48 A8
Tedder Dr WYTH/NTH M22 .....119 H5
Teddington Rd NEWH/MOS M40 .....73M3
Ted Jackson Wk OP/CLY * M11 .....88 C4
Teer St NEWH/MOS M40 .....88 A3
Teesdale Av AUL OL6 .....84 D8
Teesdale Cl OFTN SK2 .....113 H6
Teesdale Dr LEIGH WN7 .....66 F7
Tees St MILN * OL16 .....11 K7
Teignmouth Av
NEWH/MOS * M40 .....72 F8
Telfer Av BRUN/LGST M13 .....99 H2
Telford Cl DTN/ASHW M34 .....90 B5
Telford Crs LEIGH WN7 .....66 A4
Telford Ms UPML OL3 .....61 L3
Telford Rd MPL/ROM SK6 .....114 D8
Telford St ATH M46 .....66 D2
CHH M8 .....72 F7
HOR/BR BL6 .....33 M2
Telford Wk OLDTF/WHR M16 .....87 G8
Telford Wy ROCH OL11 .....42 D2
Tellers Cl ATH M46 .....67 G1
Telson Cl SLFD M6 .....71 G6
Telson Crs SLFD M6 .....71 G6
Tell St WHIT OL12 .....10 B4
Temperance St BOLS/LL BL3 .....2 C8
HYDE * SK14 .....103 K4
WGTN/LGST M12 .....7 L7
Tempest Cha HOR/BR * BL6 .....34 E8
Tempest Dr HOR/BR * BL6 .....34 F8
Tempest Rd HOR/BR BL6 .....34 E8
WILM/AE SK9 .....130 F3
Tempest St BOLS/LL BL3 .....35 L8
Temple Av GLSP SK13 .....93M7
Temple Cl OLDE OL4 .....60 B4
Templecombe Dr BOL BL1 .....22 A6
Temple Dr BOL * BL1 .....35M1
SWIN M27 .....70 E5
Templegate Cl WGNNW/ST WN6 .....20 D3
Temple La LIT OL15 .....20 D3
Temple Rd BOL * BL1 .....35M1
SALE M33 .....97 G8
Temple St GLSP SK13 .....93M7
HEY OL10 .....41 G2
MDTN M24 .....57 J3
OLD OL1 .....59 L5
Templeton Cl ALT WA14 .....107 L4
WHTN BL5 .....50 B4
Templeton Rd WGNE/HIN WN2 .....46 D3
Ten Acre Ct WHTF * M45 .....55 G5
Ten Acre Dr WHTF M45 .....55 G5

Ten Acres La NEWH/MOS M40 .....73 K7
Tenax Rd TRPK M17 .....85 L5
Tenbury Cl SLFD * M6 .....86 C1
Tenbury Dr AIMK WN4 .....63 J8
MDTN M24 .....57 K7
Tenby Av BOL BL1 .....35 K5
STRET M32 .....86 B8
Tenby Ct HULME * M15 .....86 B6
Tenby Dr CHD/CHDH SK8 .....120 D3
SLFD M6 .....71 G7
Tenby Gv WHIT OL12 .....27M3
Tenby Rd EDGY/DAV SK3 .....12 A8
OLDS OL8 .....74 E2
Tenby St WHIT OL12 .....27M3
Tenement La BRAM/HZG SK7 .....120 C2
Tenement St WGNE/HIN WN2 .....64 E3
Teneriffe St BRO M7 .....72 A7
Ten Foot Cl GLSP SK13 .....104 E2
Tennis St BOL BL1 .....36 A2
OLDTF/WHR M16 .....86 E8
Tennyson Av BURY BL9 .....39 J6
DTN/ASHW * M34 .....101 K5
DUK SK16 .....91 K5
LEIGH WN7 .....65M4
RAD M26 .....38 B8
Tennyson Cl HTNM SK4 .....111 K3
Tennyson Dr WGN WN1 .....47M1
WGNW/BIL/O WN5 .....62 A3
Tennyson Gdns PWCH M25 .....71 J1
Tennyson Rd CHD/CHDH SK8 .....111 J6
DROY M43 .....89 K2
FWTH BL4 .....52 E2
MDTN M24 .....57 L2
RDSH SK5 .....100 A3
SWIN M27 .....70 A4
Tennyson St BOL BL1 .....36 B3
BRUN/LGST M13 .....87M7
OLD OL1 .....59M3
ROCH OL11 .....11 G9
SLFD M6 .....71M8
Tensing Av ATH M46 .....50 F7
AULW OL7 .....75 L7
Tensing St OLDS OL8 .....75 K4
Tentercroft WHIT OL12 .....10 C4
Tenterden St BURY BL9 .....4 C5
Tenter Dr WGNNW/ST WN6 .....31 L5
Tenterhill La WHIT OL12 .....27 G2
Tenters St BURY BL9 .....4 C5
Tenth St TRPK M17 .....86 A6
Terence St NEWH/MOS M40 .....74 A7
Terminal Rd East MANAIR M90 .....118 D5
Terminal Rd North
MANAIR M90 .....118 D5
Terminal Rd South
MANAIR M90 .....118 D5
Tern Av FWTH BL4 .....52 C4
Tern Cl ALT WA14 .....107 L4
DUK SK16 .....91 H5
ROCH OL11 .....27 J5
Tern Dr POY/DIS SK12 .....121 K8
Ternhill Ct FWTH BL4 .....52 F4
The Terrace PWCH M25 .....71 L1
Terrace St OLDE OL4 .....59 L5
Terrington Cl CCHDY M21 .....98 B5
Tetbury Cl WGNNW/BIL/O WN5 .....47 G3
Tetbury Dr BOLE BL2 .....37 J4
Tetlow Gv ECC M30 .....84 F3
Tetlow La BRO M7 .....72 B4
Tetlow St HYDE * SK14 .....91 H7
MDTN M24 .....57 K4
NEWH/MOS M40 .....73M7
OLDS * OL8 .....8 F7
Teviot St BRUN/LGST M13 .....88 B8
Teviot Wy STKP SK1 .....112 C1
Tewkesbury Av AUL OL6 .....75M5
CHD/CHDH SK8 .....120 D6
DROY M43 .....89 K1
HALE/TIMP WA15 .....117 L1
MDTN M24 .....57 J1
URM M41 .....85 G8
Tewkesbury Cl CHD/CHDH SK8 .....120 D6
POY/DIS SK12 .....121M8
Tewkesbury Dr PWCH M25 .....71M2
Tewkesbury Rd EDGY/DAV SK3 .....111 L6
GOL/RIS/CU WA3 .....79 L4
NEWH/MOS M40 .....88 A1
Texas St DUK SK16 .....90 F2
Textile St WGTN/LGST M12 .....88 D5
Textilose Rd TRPK M17 .....85 L7
Thackeray Cl CHH M8 .....72 D6
Thackeray Pl WGNS/IIMK WN3 .....47 K7
Thackeray Rd OLD OL1 .....59M3
Thames Av BURY BL9 .....25 J5
Thames Cl BURY BL9 .....25 J5
OP/CLY M11 .....88 E4
Thames Ct HULME M15 .....87 G6
Thames Dr WGNNW/BIL/O WN5 .....46 C5
Thames Rd MILN OL16 .....29 K6
Thames St MILN OL16 .....11 J7
OLD OL1 .....9 L3
Thanet Cl BRO M7 .....72 B7
Thanet Gv LEIGH WN7 .....66 D7
Thatcham Av DTN/ASHW M34 .....90 A3
Thatcher Cl ALT WA14 .....116 F3
Thatcher St OLDS OL8 .....75 K1
Thatch Leach CHAD OL9 .....58 C7
Thatch Leach La WHTF M45 .....55 K5
Thaxmead Dr NEWH/MOS M40 .....74 A8
Thaxted Dr OFTN SK2 .....113 K7
Thaxted Pl BOL BL1 .....35M4
Thbeechwood La STLY SK15 .....76 F8
Theatre St OLD OL1 .....9 K5
Thekla St CHAD OL9 .....8 F3
Thelma St RAMS BL0 .....17 B6
Thelwall Av BOLE BL2 .....37 G4
RUSH/FAL M14 .....98 C4
Thelwall Cl HALE/TIMP WA15 .....108 B6
LEIGH WN7 .....65 L8
Thelwall Rd SALE M33 .....109 H1
Theobald Rd ALT WA14 .....116 F5
Theta Cl OP/CLY M11 .....88 E2
Thetford WHIT OL12 .....10 C3
Thetford Cl TOT/BURYW BL8 .....25 G7
WGNE/HIN WN2 .....49 H8
Thetford Dr CHH M8 .....72 E5
Thicketford Brow BOLE BL2 .....37 G3
Thicketford Cl BOLE BL2 .....36 F2
Thicketford Rd BOLE BL2 .....36 F3
Thicknesse Av WGNNW/ST WN6 .....47 J1
Thimble Cl WHIT OL12 .....19 L8
The Thimbles WHIT OL12 .....19 L8
Third Av BOL BL1 .....35 L5
BOLS/LL BL3 .....37 J8
BURY BL9 .....26 A8
OLDS OL8 .....74 F2
OP/CLY M11 .....88 F2
POY/DIS SK12 .....129 H3
STLY SK15 .....77 H6

SWIN M27 .....70 B7
TRPK M17 .....86 A7
TYLD M29 .....67 L8
Thirlby Dr WYTH/NTH M22 .....118 F3
Thirlemere Rd STKP SK1 .....112 C5
Thirlmere Av AIMK WN4 .....63M8
AULW OL7 .....75 J8
HOR/BR BL6 .....33M2
STRET M32 .....96 F1
SWIN M27 .....70 D5
TYLD M29 .....67 K5
WGNE/HIN WN2 .....48 E5
WGNE/HIN WN2 .....64 E4
WGNNW/ST WN6 .....31 K5
WHTN BL5 .....51 J5
WYTH/NTH M22 .....118 D2
Thirlmere Dr BURY * BL9 .....39 H5
LHULT M38 .....52 D7
MDTN M24 .....57 H2
Thirlmere Gv FWTH BL4 .....52 B4
ROY/SHW OL2 .....43 G6
Thirlmere Rd GOL/RIS/CU WA3 .....79M3
HOR/BR BL6 .....32 F1
PART M31 .....94 B8
ROCH OL11 .....27 L8
URM M41 .....95 H1
WGNE/HIN WN2 .....49 H7
WGNNW/BIL/O WN5 .....46 C5
WHTN BL5 .....51 J5
WYTH/NTH M22 .....118 D2
Thirlmere St LEIGH WN7 .....66 B7
Thirlspot Cl BOL BL1 .....22 B6
Thirlstone Av OLDE * OL4 .....44 C8
Thirsfield Dr OP/CLY M11 .....88 F2
Thirsk Av CHAD OL9 .....58 C3
SALE M33 .....107M1
Thirsk Cl TOT/BURYW BL8 .....24 F7
Thirsk Rd BOLS/LL BL3 .....53 K1
Thirsk St WGTN/LGST M12 .....7 L8
Thistle Cl STLY SK15 .....92 B5
Thistledown Cl ECC M30 .....84 F4
WGNNW/ST WN6 .....47 K2
Thistle Gn MILN OL16 .....29 H5
Thistle Sq PART M31 .....106 B2
Thistleton Rd BOLS/LL BL3 .....51 J1
Thistle Wy OLDE OL4 .....60 A2
Thistlewood Dr WILM/AE SK9 .....127 H5
Thistleyfields MILN OL16 .....29 H5
Thomas Cl DTN/ASHW M34 .....90 D8
Thomas Dr BOLS/LL BL3 .....2 B9
Thomas Gibbon Cl STRET * M32 .....96 F3
Thomas Henshaw Ct
ROCH OL11 .....27M8
Thomas Holden St BOL BL1 .....2 B3
Thomas Johnson Cl ECC * M30 .....84 F1
Thomas More Cl FWTH BL4 .....53 J6
Thomasson Cl BOL BL1 .....36 B3
Thomas St ANC M4 .....7 H3
ATH M46 .....67 G1
BOLS/LL BL3 .....2 B9
CHH M8 .....72 C4
FWTH BL4 .....53 H4
GLSP SK13 .....105 H3
GOL/RIS/CU WA3 .....79 K4
HALE/TIMP WA15 .....108 B8
MILN OL16 .....11 G2
MPL/ROM SK6 .....113 K1
MPL/ROM SK6 .....114 E2
OLDE OL4 .....60 B7
RAD M26 .....54 E1
ROY/SHW OL2 .....59 J1
STKP SK1 .....13 J8
STRET M32 .....97 G1
WGNE/HIN WN2 .....65 L1
WHTN * BL5 .....50 B1
Thomas St West OFTN SK2 .....13 J8
Thomas Telford Basin
CMANE M1 .....7 K5
Thompson Av BOLE BL2 .....38 A3
WHTF M45 .....55 K5
Thompson Cl DTN/ASHW M34 .....100 E1
Thompson Dr BURY BL9 .....5M3
Thompson Fold STLY SK15 .....91 J2
Thompson La CHAD OL9 .....58 D8
Thompson Rd BOL BL1 .....35 L3
DTN/ASHW M34 .....100 E1
TRPK M17 .....85M4
Thompson St AIMK WN4 .....64 A8
ANC M4 .....7 J2
BOLS/LL BL3 .....2 E9
CSLFD M3 .....87 J1
HOR/BR BL6 .....33 K1
LEIGH WN7 .....65 G1
NEWH/MOS M40 .....73 J7
WGN WN1 .....15 K1
Thomson Rd GTN M18 .....88 F8
Thomson St BRUN/LGST M13 .....87M6
EDGY/DAV SK3 .....13 H7
Thoralby Cl BRUN/LGST M13 .....99 H1
Thorburn Dr WGNNW/BIL/O WN5 .....18 C5
Thorburn Rd WGNNW/BIL/O WN5 .....46 F6
Thoresby Cl BOLS/LL BL3 .....37M7
WGNS/IIMK WN3 .....63 H1
Thoresway Rd BRUN/LGST M13 .....99 H1
WILM/AE SK9 .....126 D7
Thor Gv ORD M5 .....86 E4
Thorley Cl CHAD OL9 .....74 B2
Thorley Dr HALE/TIMP WA15 .....108 E7
URM M41 .....96 A2
Thorley La HALE/TIMP WA15 .....108 E6
HALE/TIMP WA15 .....118 B3
Thorley Ms BRAM/HZG SK7 .....121 H5
Thorley St FAIL M35 .....74 C4
Thornage Dr NEWH/MOS M40 .....72 F5
Thorn Av FAIL M35 .....74 C6
Thornbank BOLS/LL BL3 .....35M6
Thorn Bank DROY * M43 .....89 J1
Thornbank Cl HEY OL10 .....41 H5
Thornbeck Dr BOL BL1 .....35 J3
Thornbeck Rd BOL BL1 .....35 J3
Thornbridge Av CCHDY M21 .....97 L4
Thornbury ROCH OL11 .....10 D7
Thornbury Av GOL/RIS/CU WA3 .....80 B5
HYDE SK14 .....103 H1
Thornbury Cl CHD/CHDH SK8 .....120 E3
Thornbury Rd STRET M32 .....86 B8
Thornbury Wy GTN M18 .....88 F7
Thornbush Wy MILN OL16 .....11 K3
Thorncliff Av OLDS OL8 .....75 H4
Thorncliffe Av DUK SK16 .....90 F5
ROY/SHW OL2 .....42 F6
Thorncliffe Gv BNG/LEV M19 .....99M3
Thorncliffe Pk ROY/SHW OL2 .....42 F6
Thorncliffe Rd BOL BL1 .....22 B7
GLSP SK13 .....104 C1
Thorn Cl HEY OL10 .....40 F1

Thorncombe Rd
OLDTF/WHR M16 .....98 B1
Thorn Ct SLFD M6 .....86 E2
Thorncross Cl HULME M15 .....86 F5
Thorndale Cl ROY/SHW OL2 .....43 H7
Thorndale Gv HALE/TIMP WA15 .....108 D7
Thorn Dr WYTH/NTH M22 .....119 J4
Thorne Av URM M41 .....95 K1
Thorneside DTN/ASHW M34 .....90 C7
Thorne St FWTH BL4 .....52 F3
Thorneycroft LEIGH WN7 .....66 F7
Thorneycroft Av CCHDY M21 .....97 L7
Thorneycroft Rd
HALE/TIMP WA15 .....108 E7
Thorney Dr BRAM/HZG SK7 .....120 E6
Thorney Hill Cl OLDE * OL4 .....60 A4
Thorneyholme Cl HOR/BR BL6 .....34 F6
Thorneylea WHIT OL12 .....18 E3
Thornfield Av AUL OL6 .....91 H1
Thornfield Cl GOL/RIS/CU WA3 .....79M4
Thornfield Crs LHULT M38 .....52 C7
Thornfield Gv CHD/CHDH SK8 .....120 C2
LHULT M38 .....52 C7
Thornfield Hey WILM/AE SK9 .....127 J4
Thornfield Houses
CHD/CHDH * SK8 .....120 C2
Thornfield Rd BNG/LEV M19 .....99 H7
HTNM SK4 .....111 K1
TOT/BURYW BL8 .....24 A5
Thornfield St ORD M5 .....86 A3
Thorngate Rd CHH M8 .....72 D7
Thorn Gv CHD/CHDH SK8 .....120 D5
HALE/TIMP WA15 .....117 G1
RUSH/FAL M14 .....99 G4
SALE M33 .....96 B8
Thorngrove Av NTHM/RTH M23 .....109 G5
Thorngrove Dr WILM/AE SK9 .....127 G6
Thorngrove Hl WILM/AE SK9 .....127 G6
Thorngrove Rd WILM/AE SK9 .....127 G6
Thornham Cl TOT/BURYW BL8 .....24 F6
Thornham Dr BOL BL1 .....22 C6
Thornham La MDTN M24 .....42 A6
ROY/SHW OL2 .....42 F4
Thornham New Rd ROCH OL11 .....42 D3
Thornham Old Rd
ROY/SHW OL2 .....42 C5
Thornham Rd ROY/SHW OL2 .....43 C5
SALE M33 .....108 B2
Thornhill Cl DTN/ASHW M34 .....100 D2
Thornhill Dr WALK M28 .....69 H4
Thornhill Rd AIMK WN4 .....62 E8
DROY M43 .....89 L2
RAMS BL0 .....24 D3
Thornholme Cl GTN M18 .....89 G1
Thornholme Rd MPL/ROM SK6 .....114 C3
Thorniley Brow ANC M4 .....7 G3
Thorn Lea ATH M46 .....67 H2
Thornlea DROY M43 .....89 H3
Thornlea Av OLDS OL8 .....74 E3
SWIN M27 .....69 J6
Thorn Lea Cl BOL BL1 .....35 J3
Thornlea Dr WHIT OL12 .....27 L2
Thornleigh Rd RUSH/FAL M14 .....98 E3
Thornley Av BOL BL1 .....35M2
Thornley Cl OLDE OL4 .....60 D7
Thornley Crs MPL/ROM SK6 .....101 K8
OLDE OL4 .....60 D7
Thornley La North RDSH SK5 .....100 C1
Thornley La South RDSH SK5 .....100 D3
Thornley Ms HYDE SK14 .....102 B3
Thornley Park Rd OLDE OL4 .....60 D7
Thornley Rd WHTF M45 .....55M5
MDTN M24 .....57 L3
RAD M26 .....54 E2
Thornmere Cl SWIN M27 .....69M2
Thorn Rd BRAM/HZG SK7 .....121 J5
OLDS OL8 .....75M1
SWIN M27 .....70 B3
The Thorns CCHDY M21 .....97 L5
Thorns Av BOL BL1 .....36 A1
Thorns Cl BOL BL1 .....36 A1
Thorns Clough UPML OL3 .....45M7
Thornsett Cl BKLY * M9 .....73 H4
Thornsgreen Rd
WYTH/NTH M22 .....118 F4
Thorns Rd BOL BL1 .....36 A1
Thorn St BOL BL1 .....36 C2
RAMS BL0 .....24 F1
WGNE/HIN WN2 .....65 G5
Thorns Villa Gdns WALK M28 .....68 D7
Thornton Av BOL BL1 .....35 J3
DTN/ASHW M34 .....89M4
URM M41 .....95 K2
Thornton Cl AIMK WN4 .....63 J8
BOLS/LL BL3 .....53M1
FWTH BL4 .....52 E5
LEIGH WN7 .....81 J3
WALK M28 .....68 B5
Thornton Crs PWCH M25 .....55 J7
Thornton Dr WILM/AE SK9 .....127 H1
Thornton Ga CHD/CHDH SK8 .....110 D6
Thornton Pl HTNM SK4 .....111 K2
Thornton Rd CHD/CHDH SK8 .....119 L3
RUSH/FAL M14 .....98 D2
WALK M28 .....68 B5
Thornton St BOLE BL2 .....3 H4
NEWH/MOS M40 .....72 F8
OLDE OL4 .....60 B7
ROCH OL11 .....10 E9
Thornton St North
NEWH/MOS M40 .....72 F7
Thorntree Cl BKLY M9 .....73 H5
Thorntree Pl WHIT OL12 .....10 B2
Thornvale WGNE/HIN WN2 .....64 F5
Thorn Vw BURY BL9 .....39M1
Thornway BRAM/HZG SK7 .....120 E4
MPL/ROM SK6 .....123 H5
WALK M28 .....68 B5
Thorn Well WHTN BL5 .....50 B5
Thornwood Av GTN M18 .....89 H8
Thorndyke Av BOL BL1 .....22 D8
Thorold Gv SALE M33 .....97 H8
Thorpe Av RAD M26 .....39 G7
SWIN M27 .....70 B3
Thorpebrook Rd
NEWH/MOS M40 .....73 K6
Thorpe Cl DTN/ASHW M34 .....90 C8
OLDE OL4 .....60 C4
Thorpe Gv HTNM SK4 .....100 A6
Thorpe Hall Gv HYDE SK14 .....91 J6
Thorpe La OLDE OL4 .....60 D4
Thorpeness Sq GTN M18 .....88 F7

Thorpe St *BOL* BL1 ....36 A2
  GLSP SK13 ....105 G1
  MDTN M24 ....56 F5
  OLDTF/WHR M16 ....86 F8
  RAMS * BL0 ....17 B7
  WALK M28 ....53 G8
Thorp Rd *NEWH/MOS* M40 ......73 K6
  ROY/SHW OL2 ....43 G8
Thorp St *ECC* M30 ....84 E4
  WHTF M45 ....55 H2
Thorp Vw *ROY/SHW* OL2 ....55 K6
Thorsby Av *HYDE* SK14 ......102 C2
Thorsby Cl *EDGW/EG* BL7 .....22 C4
Thorsby Rd *HALE/TIMP* WA15 .108 B7
Thrapston Av *DTN/ASHW* M34 ..90 A3
Threadfold Wy *EDGW/EG* BL7 ..22 C5
Threaphurst La *BRAM/HZG* SK7 122 E2
Threapwood Rd
  WYTH/NTH M22 ....119 G3
Three Acre Av *ROY/SHW* OL2 ..43 K8
Three Sisters Rd *AIMK* WN4 ...63 L6
Threlkeld Cl *MDTN* M24 ....56 F3
Threlkeld Rd *BOL* BL1 ....22 A5
  MDTN M24 ....56 F3
Thresher Cl *SALE* M33 ....109 J1
Threshfield Cl *BURY* BL9 .....25 J5
Threshfield Dr
  HALE/TIMP WA15 ....108 F5
Throstle Bank St *HYDE* SK14 ..90 F8
  TOT/BURYW BL8 ....24 F7
Throstle Gv *MPL/ROM* SK6 ...114 B7
Throstle Hall Ct *MDTN * M24 ..57 J3
Throstle Nest Av
  WGNNW/ST WN6 ....14 B1
Throstles Cl *DROY* M43 ....89M1
Thrum Fold *WHIT* OL12 ....18 E8
Thrum Hall La *WHIT* OL12 .....28 B1
Thrush Av *FWTH* BL4 ....52 C4
Thrush Dr *BURY* BL9 ....5 K1
Thrush St *WHIT* OL12 ....27M3
Thruxton Cl *OLDTF/WHR* M16 ..98 B1
Thurland Rd *OLDE* OL4 ....59M6
Thurland St *CHAD* OL9 ....58 B4
Thurlby Av *BKLY* M9 ....57 H7
Thurlby Cl *AIMK* WN4 ....64 A8
Thurlby St *BRUN/LGST* M13 ....88 A8
Thurleigh Rd *DID/WITH* M20 ...98 E8
Thurlestone Av *BOLE* BL2 .....38 A3
  URM M41 ....95M1
Thurlestone Dr *BRAM/HZG* SK7 121 K2
Thurloe St *RUSH/FAL* M14 .....98 F1
Thurlow *GOL/RIS/CU* WA3 ......80 B5
Thurlow St *SALQ* M50 ....86 C3
Thurlston Crs *CHH* M8 ....72 E5
Thurlwood Av *DID/WITH* M20 ...98 D5
Thurnham St *BOLS/LL* BL3 ....51M1
Thursfield St *SLFD* M6 ....71 L7
Thursford Gv *HOR/BR* BL6 .....33 G3
Thurstane St *BOL* BL1 ....35M2
Thurston Av *WGNS/IIMK* WN3 ...63 L1
Thurston Cl *BURY* BL9 ....55 K2
Thurston Clough Rd *OLDE* OL4 .61 G3
Thurston Gn *WILM/AE* SK9 ...130 D3
Thynne St *BOLS/LL* BL3 ....2 F1
  FWTH BL4 ....52 F3
Tiber Av *OLDS* OL8 ....74 F3
Tib La *CMANW* M2 ....6 F5
Tib St *ANC* M4 ....7 H4
  DTN/ASHW M34 ....101 J2
  RAMS * BL0 ....17 B7
Tideswell Av *NEWH/MOS* M40 ..88 A1
  WGNNW/ST WN6 ....46 D3
Tideswell Cl *CHD/CHDH* SK8 ..119M4
Tideswell Rd *BRAM/HZG* SK7 ..122 A4
  DROY M43 ....89 H1
Tideway Cl *SWIN* M27 ....71 J4
Tidworth Av *ANC* M4 ....7M5
Tiflis St *WHIT* OL12 ....10 D2
Tig Fold Rd *FWTH* BL4 ....52 B4
Tilbury Gv *WGNNW/ST* WN6 ....30 A5
Tilbury St *OLD* OL1 ....9 G2
Tilby Cl *URM* M41 ....95 H2
Tildsley St *BOLS/LL* BL3 .....36 B8
Tile St *BURY* BL9 ....4 F2
Tillard Av *EDGY/DAV* SK3 ....12 B7
Tillhey Rd *WYTH/NTH* M22 ...118 F2
Tilney Av *STRET* M32 ....97 H3
Tilshead Wk *BRUN/LGST* M13 .87M6
Tilson Rd *NTHM/RTH* M23 ....109 J7
Tilton St *OLD* OL1 ....59M2
Timberbottom *BOLE* BL2 ....22 F8
Timberhurst *BURY* BL9 ....40 A2
Times St *MDTN* M24 ....57 L4
Timothy Cl *SLFD* M6 ....85 L1
Timperley Cl *OLDS* OL8 ....75 K2
Timperley Fold *OLD* OL6 .....75M6
Timperley La *LEIGH* WN7 ......81 L2
Timperley Rd *AUL* OL6 ....75 L6
Timperley St *OP/CLY * M11 ....88 F4
Timpson Rd *NTHM/RTH* M23 ...109 H5
Timson St *FAIL* M35 ....74 C5
Tindall St *ECC* M30 ....84 E4
  RDSH SK5 ....100 C1
Tindle St *WALK* M28 ....69 J1
Tinkerfield *LEIGH* WN7 ....66 A5
Tinline St *BURY* BL9 ....5 J5
Tinningham Cl *OP/CLY* M11 ....89 H5
Tinshill Gv *WGN/LGST* M12 ....88 D7
Tinsley Cl *NEWH/MOS* M40 ....88 B2
Tinsley Gv *BOLE* BL2 ....3 K2
Tin St *BOLS/LL* BL3 ....2 D8
Tintagel Ct *RAD* M26 ....37M7
  STLY SK15 ....91 J2
Tintagel Rd *WGNE/HIN* WN2 ...49 K8
Tintern Av *AIMK* WN4 ....79 C1
  BOLE * BL2 ....36 E2
  DID/WITH M20 ....98 C2
  HEY OL10 ....26 F8
  LIT OL15 ....20 B5
  TYLD M29 ....67M5
  URM M41 ....95 K4
  WHIT OL12 ....28 B2
  WHTF M45 ....55 J3
Tintern Cl *POY/DIS* SK12 ...121M7
Tintern Dr *HALE/TIMP* WA15 .117 L2
Tintern Gv *STKP* SK1 ....112 E3
Tintern Pl *HEY* OL10 ....26 F8
Tintern Rd *CHD/CHDH* SK8 ...120 D6
  MDTN M24 ....57 J1
Tintern St *RUSH/FAL* M14 .....98 E2
Tinwald Pl *WGN* WN1 ....15M2
Tipperary St *STLY* SK15 .....77 H7
Tipping St *ALT* WA14 ....116 F1
  WGNS/IIMK WN3 ....14 D8
Tipton Cl *CHD/CHDH* SK8 ....111 L8
Tipton Dr *NTHM/RTH* M23 ....109 K2
Tiree Cl *BRAM/HZG* SK7 .....122 B3

Tirza Av *BNG/LEV* M19 ....99 J5
Titanian Ri *OLD* OL1 ....44 A7
Titchfield Rd *OLDS* OL8 .....59M8
Tithe Barn Cl *WHIT * OL12 ....19 L8
Tithe Barn Crs *BOL* BL1 ......22 E8
Titheburn Rd *HALE/TIMP* WA15 117 L4
Tithebarn St *BURY* BL9 ....4 F4
Tithe Barn St *WHTN* BL5 .....50 B3
Titherington Cl *RDSH * SK5 ...100 A3
Titherington Av *CCHDY* M21 ..97 J2
Tiverton Av *LEIGH* WN7 ....66 A2
  SALE M33 ....108 C1
Tiverton Cl *RAD* M26 ....38 A7
  TYLD M29 ....67M5
Tiverton Dr *SALE* M33 ....108 C1
  WILM/AE SK9 ....127 H3
Tiverton Pl *AULW* OL7 ....75 K7
Tiverton Rd *URM* M41 ....85 H8
Tiverton Wk *BOL* * BL1 ......35M3
Tiviot Dl *STKP* SK1 ....13 J3
Tiviot Wy *RDSH* SK5 ....112 C1
Tivoli St *CSLFD* M3 ....6 D5
Toad La *WHIT* OL12 ....10 D3
Tobermory Cl *OP/CLY* M11 ....89 G3
Tobermory Rd *CHD/CHDH* SK8 .119 L2
Toddington La *WGNE/HIN* WN2 .32 E4
Todd St *BRO* M7 ....72 A6
  BURY BL9 ....4 F1
  CSLFD M3 ....7 G2
  HEY OL10 ....40 D2
  MILN OL16 ....11 G5
Todmorden Rd *LIT* OL15 ....20 D6
Toft Rd *GTN* M18 ....88 F8
Toledo St *OP/CLY* M11 ....89 G3
Tolland La *HALE/TIMP* WA15 ..117 H4
Tollard Av *NEWH/MOS* M40 ....73 G7
Tollard Cl *CHD/CHDH* SK8 ...120 D5
Toll Bar St *STKP* SK1 ....13 K6
  WGTN/LGST M12 ....88 B6
Tollemache Cl *HYDE* SK14 .....92 D7
Tollemache Rd *HYDE* SK14 ....92 D7
Tollesbury Cl *NEWH/MOS* M40 .73 F8
Toll Gate Cl *BRUN/LGST* M13 .88 B3
Tollgate Wy *MILN* OL16 ....11 L3
Tollgreen Cl *WGNE/HIN* WN2 ..49 G5
Toll St *WGNE/HIN* WN2 ....64 D3
Tolworth Dr *CHH* M8 ....72 E5
Tomcroft La *DTN/ASHW* M34 ..101 G2
Tom La *ALT* WA14 ....116 A6
Tomlinson Cl *OLDS* OL8 ....9 H9
Tomlinson St *HOR/BR* BL6 .....33 L1
  HULME M15 ....87 H6
  NEWH/MOS M40 ....73M1
  ROCH OL11 ....27M8
Tomlin Sq *BOLE* BL2 ....3M4
Tommy Browell Cl
  RUSH/FAL M14 ....98 D1
Tommy Johnson Wk
  RUSH/FAL M14 ....98 D1
Tommy La *BOLE* BL2 ....37M3
Tommy Taylor Cl
  *NEWH/MOS * M40 ....73M7
Tom Shepley St *HYDE* SK14 ..102 B2
Tomwood Ri *GLSP* SK13 ......103M6
Tonacliffe Rd *WHIT* OL12 ....18 D5
Tonacliffe Wy *WHIT* OL12 ....18 D6
Tonbridge Cl *TOT/BURYW* BL8 .24 F5
Tonbridge Rd *BNG/LEV* M19 ...99 L4
  RDSH SK5 ....100 C4
Tonge Bridge Wy *BOLE* BL2 ....3 J4
Tonge Cl *WHTF* M45 ....55 L3
Tonge Fold Rd *BOLE* BL2 ......3 L5
Tonge Gn *STLY * SK15 ....92 B6
Tonge Hall Cl *MDTN* M24 .....57 L4
Tonge Moor Rd *BOLE* BL2 ......3 K1
Tonge End *WHIT* OL12 ....18 D2
Tonge Old Rd *BOLE* BL2 ....3M4
Tonge Park Av *BOLE* BL2 .....36 F3
Tonge Roughs *MDTN* M24 ......58 A4
Tonge St *HEY* OL10 ....41 G2
  MILN * OL16 ....11 G6
  WGTN/LGST * M12 ....88 A5
Tongfields *EDGW/EG* BL7 .....22 C5
Tong Head Av *BOL* BL1 ....22 E8
Tong La *WHIT* OL12 ....18 D3
Tong Rd *BOLS/LL* BL3 ....37 K8
Tong St *FWTH* BL4 ....53 L7
Tonman St *CSLFD* M3 ....6 D6
Tonnacliffe Rd *WHIT* OL12 ...18 D7
Toon Crs *TOT/BURYW* BL8 .....24 F6
Tootal Dr *SLFD* M6 ....85M2
Tootal Gv *SLFD* M6 ....85M2
Tootal Rd *ORD* M5 ....85M2
Toothill Dr *AIMK* WN4 ....63 L7
Topcroft La *WYTH/NTH* M22 ..110 B4
Topfield Rd *WYTH/NTH* M22 ..118 E1
Topham St *BURY* BL9 ....5 H8
Topley St *BKLY* M9 ....72 F6
Top O' Th' Brow *BOLE * BL2 ..23 H6
Top O' Th' Gorses *BOLE * BL2 .3M8
Top O' Th' Gn *CHAD* OL9 .....58 F3
Top O' Th' La *BOLS/LL * BL3 ..37 G7
Top O' Th' Meadows La
  OLDE OL4 ....60 D3
Topping Fold Rd *BURY* BL9 ...5M2
The Toppings *NEWH/MOS* M40 .113 K1
Toppings Gn *EDGW/EG* BL7 ....22 D5
Topping St *BOL* BL1 ....5 C2
  BURY BL9 ....5 G4
Topp Wy *BOL* BL1 ....2 D3
Topp Schwabe St *MDTN* M24 ...56 F4
Top St *MDTN* M24 ....57 H3
  OLDE OL4 ....60 A4
Torah St *CHH* M8 ....72 D8
Tor Av *TOT/BURYW* BL8 ....24 C3
Torbay Dr *OFTN* SK2 ....112 E5
Torbay Rd *CCHDY* M21 ....97M4
  URM M41 ....96 B3
Torcross Rd *BKLY* M9 ....56 F7
Torkington Av *SWIN* M27 .....70 C3
Torkington La *BRAM/HZG* SK7 122 F1
Torkington Rd *BRAM/HZG* SK7 122 C2
  CHD/CHDH SK8 ....110 E7
  WILM/AE SK9 ....127 G6
Torkington St *EDGY/DAV* SK3 .12 A5
Torness Wk *OP/CLY* M11 ......89 K3
Toronto Av *MANAIR* M90 .....118 D5
Toronto Rd *OFTN* SK2 ....112 D6
Toronto St *BOLE* BL2 ....37 H4
Torquay Cl *BRUN/LGST* M13 ..87M7
Torquay Dr *WGNW/BIL/O* WN5 .62 A6
Torquay Gv *OFTN* SK2 ....112 E8
Torra Barn Cl *EDGW/EG* BL7 ..22 B2
Torrax Cl *SLFD* M6 ....70 E6
Torre Cl *MDTN* M24 ....57 K1
Torrens St *SLFD* M6 ....71 G7
Torridon Rd *WGNNW/ST* WN6 ..31 K5
Torridon Cl *BOLE* BL2 ....37 J5

Torrin Cl *EDGY/DAV* SK3 ....112 C7
Torrington Av *BKLY* M9 ....73 K2
  BOL BL1 ....36 B2
Torrington Dr *HYDE* SK14 ...103 G2
Torrisdale Cl *BOLS/LL* BL3 ...35 L7
Torrs Va *NM/HAY* SK22 ......124 E5
Tor Top St *NM/HAY* SK22 ....124 E4
Torvale Rd *NM/HAY* SK22 ....124 D5
Torside Cl *WGNE/HIN* WN2 ....49 G6
Torside Wy *GLSP* SK13 ....93 K7
Torvin M27 ....70 C2
Torver Cl *WGNS/IIMK* WN3 ....63 K2
Torver Dr *BOLE* BL2 ....37 J4
  MDTN M24 ....57 G2
Torwood Dr *CHAD* OL9 ....58 B3
Totland Cl *WGTN/LGST* M12 ...99 K1
Totley Ms *GLSP* SK13 ....104 A3
Totnes Av *BRAM/HZG* SK7 ....121 J2
  CHAD OL9 ....58 C3
Totnes Rd *CCHDY* M21 ....97M4
  SALE M33 ....96 A7
Totridge Cl *OFTN* SK2 ....113 G7
Tottenham Dr *NTHM/RTH* M23 ..109 G7
Tottington Av *OLDE* OL4 .....60 C5
Tottington Cl *OFTN* SK2 ....112 F7
Tottington La *PWCH* M25 .....55 H7
Tottington Rd *BOLE* BL2 .....23 H7
  BOLE BL2 ....23 J2
  TOT/BURYW BL8 ....4 B3
Totton Rd *FAIL* M35 ....74 C5
Touchet Hall Rd *MDTN* M24 ...42 A8
Towcester Cl *ANC* M4 ....88 A3
Tower Buildings *HOR/BR * BL6 .34 D1
Tower Ct *EDGW/EG* BL7 ....16 C8
  TOT/BURYW * BL8 ....24 C4
Tower Gv *LEIGH* WN7 ....67 G6
Towers Av *BOLS/LL* BL3 ......35 K8
Towers Cl *POY/DIS* SK12 ....122 B7
Tower Sq *BRUN/LGST * M13 ...87M6
Towers Rd *POY/DIS* SK12 ....122 B6
Towers St *OLDE* OL4 ....60 A3
Tower St *DUK* SK16 ....91 G3
  EDGW/EG BL7 ....16 C8
  HEY OL10 ....40 F2
  HYDE SK14 ....102 A3
Towey Cl *GTN* M18 ....89 G6
Towncliffe Wk *HULME * M15 ...87 G6
Towncroft *DTN/ASHW* M34 .....90 C8
Towncroft Av *MDTN* M24 ......57 J2
Towncroft La *BOL* BL1 ....35 H4
Townend St *HYDE* SK14 ......102 B2
Townfield *URM* M41 ....95 L3
Townfield Av *AIMK* WN4 ......78 E2
Townfield Gdns *ALT* WA14 ...108 A7
Townfield Rd *ALT* WA14 .....108 A7
Townfields *AIMK* WN4 ....78 D1
Town Fields Cl *BURY* BL9 .....4 F6
Townfield St *OLDE* OL4 ......59 L5
Townfield Wk *HULME * M15 ....87 G6
Town Fold *MPL/ROM* SK6 ....114 C5
Town Gate Dr *URM* M41 ....94 F2
Town Hall La *CMANW* M2 ....6 F5
Town House Rd *LIT* OL15 .....20 C6
Towns Av *DTN/ASHW* M34 ....101 G3
  DUK SK16 ....90 F4
  GLSP SK13 ....104 A6
Townley Fold *HYDE* SK14 .....91 L6
Townley Rd *MILN* OL16 ....29 J6
Townley St *CHH* M8 ....72 C7
  MDTN M24 ....57 K3
  OP/CLY * M11 ....88 C4
Townley Ter *MILN * SK6 .....114 D6
Town Mdw *MILN* OL16 ....10 D5
Town Mill Brow *WHIT* OL12 ...10 A3
Townrow St *HEY * OL10 ....41 H2
Townscliffe La *MPL/ROM* SK6 114 A5
Townsend Rd *SWIN* M27 ....70 C3
Townsfield Rd *WHTN* BL5 .....50 B5
Townside Rw *BURY* BL9 ....4 F6
Townsley Gv *AUL* OL6 ....76 B7
Townson Dr *LEIGH* WN7 ....81 J3
Townton St *MPL/ROM* SK6 ....114 E5
Towton St *BKLY* M9 ....73 H4
Towyn Av *ORD* M5 ....86 D2
Toxhead Cl *HOR/BR* BL6 ......33 K1
Toxteth St *OP/CLY* M11 ......89 H5
Tracey St *CHH* M8 ....72 C7
Tracks La *WGNW/BIL/O* WN5 ...62 A1
Traders Av *URM* M41 ....85 H6
Trafalgar Av *DTN/ASHW* M34 .89M1
  POY/DIS SK12 ....129 L1
Trafalgar Gv *BRO* * M7 ......72 A7
Trafalgar Pl *DID/WITH* M20 ..98 D8
Trafalgar Rd *SALE* M33 ......96 F3
  SLFD M6 ....85 K1
  WGN WN1 ....14 F1
Trafalgar Sq *AULW* OL7 ......90 C3
Trafalgar St *AULW* OL7 ......90 C3
  BRO M7 ....72 B7
  OLD OL1 ....11 H3
  ROCH * OL11 ....9 G2
Trafford Av *URM* M41 ....96 B1
Trafford Bank Rd
  *OLDTF/WHR * M16 ....86 F7
Trafford Bvd *URM* M41 ....84 F6
Trafford Dr *HALE/TIMP* WA15 108 E4
  LHULT M38 ....52 E7
Trafford Gv *FWTH* BL4 ....53 H3
  STRET M32 ....97 H1
Trafford Park Rd *TRPK* M17 ..85 L4
Trafford Pl *HULME* M15 ......87 G8
  WILM/AE * SK9 ....127 H6
Trafford Rd *ECC* M30 ....85 G4
  ORD M5 ....86 D6
  WGNE/HIN WN2 ....48 F7
  WILM/AE SK9 ....126 E3
Trafford St *CSLFD* M3 ....6 D7
  FWTH BL4 ....53 J7
  OLDS OL8 ....9 H8
  ROCH OL11 ....9 G2
Trafford Wharf Rd *TRPK* M17 .85M5
Tragan Cl *EDGY/DAV* SK3 .....12 A6
Tragan Dr *OFTN* SK2 ....113 G6
Trail St *SLFD* M6 ....86 B2
Tram St *OP/CLY* M11 ....88 F5
Tramway Rd *IRL* M44 ....94 D3
Tranmere Cl *GTN* M18 ....88 E7
Tranmere Dr *WILM/AE* SK9 ..127 J1
Tranmere Rd *EDGY/DAV* SK3 ..12 A6
Transvaal St *OP/CLY* M11 ....89 G3

Travers St *HOR/BR* BL6 ......34 A3
Travis Brow *STKP* SK4 ....12 E4
Travis St *CMANE* M1 ....7 L6
  HYDE SK14 ....102 B2
  MILN OL16 ....29 L8
  ROY/SHW OL2 ....43 L5
Trawden Av *BOL* BL1 ....35M2
Trawden Dr *BURY* BL9 ....35 H4
Trawden Gn *OFTN* SK2 ....113 C8
Traylen Wy *WHIT* OL12 ....27 K3
Trecastell Cl *WGN* WN1 .....15M2
Tredcroft St *GLSP* SK13 ....104 F4
Tredgold St *HOR/BR* BL6 ....33M2
Tree Av *DROY* M43 ....89 K1
Tree Cl *BOL* BL1 ....60 A4
Treelands Wk *ORD* M5 ....86 E6
Treen Rd *TYLD* M29 ....67M4
Tree Tops *BOLE* BL2 ....22 F6
Treetops Av *RAMS* BL0 ....24 D1
Treetops Cl *OL3 * OL3 ....61 J3
Trefoil Wy *LIT* OL15 ....20 A6
Tregaer Fold *MDTN* M24 ......56 B2
Tregaron Gv *WGNE/HIN* WN2 ..65 K1
Trenam Pl *ORD* M5 ....86 E2
Trenant Rd *SLFD* M6 ....71 G7
Trenchard Dr *WYTH/NTH* M22 119 H5
Trencherbone *RAD* M26 ......38 B7
Trencherfield Mi
  *WGNS/IIMK * WN3 ....14 E6
Trengrove St *WHIT* OL12 ....27M3
Trent Av *CHAD* OL9 ....58 B4
  HEY OL10 ....40 D1
  MILN OL16 ....29 K6
Trent Bridge Wk
  OLDTF/WHR M16 ....97 K1
Trent Cl *BRAM/HZG* SK7 ....120 E6
  RDSH SK5 ....100 F7
Trent Ct *HULME * M15 ....87 G6
  WALK M28 ....68 E2
Trent Dr *BURY* BL9 ....25 J4
  WALK M28 ....68 E2
Trentham Av *FWTH* BL4 ....52 F3
  HTNM SK4 ....111 J1
Trentham Cl *FWTH* BL4 ....52 F3
Trentham Gv *NEWH/MOS* M40 ..73 K3
Trentham Lawns *SLFD* M6 ....71 K8
Trentham Rd *OLDTF/WHR* M16 .97 K1
Trentham St *FWTH* BL4 ....52 F3
  HULME M15 ....86 F5
  SWIN M27 ....70 B3
Trent Rd *AIMK* WN4 ....64 B7
  ROY/SHW OL2 ....43 K4
  WGNW/BIL/O WN5 ....46 F5
Trent St *MILN* OL16 ....11 L3
Tresco Av *STRET* M32 ....97 H3
Trescott Ms *WGNNW/ST* WN6 ..14 E6
Trevarrick Ct *HOR/BR* BL6 ...34 B2
Trevelyan Dr *WGNW/BIL/O* WN5 62 A3
Trevelyan St *ECC* M30 ....85 K2
Trevor Av *SALE* M33 ....108 C2
Trevor Dr *NEWH/MOS* M40 ....74 B2
Trevor Gv *STKP* SK1 ....13M6
Trevor Rd *ECC* M30 ....84 E1
  SWIN M27 ....70 B6
  URM M41 ....95 J1
Trevor St *OP/CLY* M11 ....89 H5
  ROCH OL11 ....41 L1
The Triangle *HALE/TIMP* WA15 108 E5
Tribune Av *ALT* WA14 ....107 L5
Trident Rd *ECC* M30 ....84 C5
Trillo Av *BOLE* BL2 ....3 K7
Trimdon Cl *OP/CLY* M11 ......88 E2
Trimingham Dr *TOT/BURYW* BL8 25 C6
Trimley Av *NEWH/MOS* M40 ...73 C7
Trinity Av *SALE* M33 ....97 G8
Trinity Buildings *MOSL * OL5 .77 G2
Trinity Cl *DUK* SK16 ....91 H4
Trinity Crs *AUL* OL6 ....90 D1
Trinity Gdns *AIMK* WN4 ......63 J8
  EDGY/DAV SK3 ....121 H1
Trinity Gn *RAMS* BL0 ....24 D1
Trinity Rd *SALE* M33 ....96 F8
Trinity St *BOLS/LL* BL3 ......2 D7
  BURY BL9 ....5 H5
  MDTN * M24 ....57 J4
  MPL/ROM * SK6 ....114 C6
  OLD OL1 ....9 J2
  STLY SK15 ....91 K3
Trinity Wy *CSLFD* M3 ....6 C4
Trippier Rd *ECC* M30 ....84 C4
Tripps Ms *DID/WITH* M20 .....98 C8
Triscombe Wy *OLDTF/WHR* M16 98 B1
Tristam Gv *BRUN/LGST* M13 ..87M6
Trojan Gdns *BRO* M7 ....72 A7
Troon Cl *BOLS/LL* BL3 ....51 J1
  BRAM/HZG SK7 ....121 J5
Troon Dr *CHD/CHDH* SK8 ....119 L3
Troon Rd *NTHM/RTH* M23 ....109 J6
Trough Ga *OLDS* OL8 ....75 G2
Troutbeck Av *ANC* M4 ....7M3
  NEWLW WA12 ....78 B8
Troutbeck Cl *RAMS* BL0 ......23 L2
  TYLD M29 ....67 K5
Troutbeck Ri *WGNW/BIL/O* WN5 46 F6
  CHD/CHDH SK8 ....119 K1
  HALE/TIMP WA15 ....109 C7
Troutbeck Wy *ROCH* OL11 .....27 L8
Trowbridge Dr *NEWH/MOS* M40 73M3
Trowbridge Rd
  DTN/ASHW M34 ....101 K3
Trows La *ROCH* OL11 ....42 A3
Trowtree Av *WGTN/LGST* M12 .88 B6
Troydale Dr *NEWH/MOS* M40 ..73 K6
Troy Wk *ORD * M5 ....86 E5
Trumpet St *CMANE* M1 ....6 E7
Truro Av *AUL* OL6 ....76 A5
  RDSH SK5 ....100 B5
  STRET M32 ....97 H2
Truro Cl *BRAM/HZG* SK7 ....121 H5
  TOT/BURYW BL8 ....4 C2
Truro Dr *SALE* M33 ....96 B6
Truro Rd *CHAD* OL9 ....58 D3
  TYLD M29 ....67M5
Trust Rd *GTN* M18 ....99M1
Tucker's Hill Brow
  WGNE/HIN WN2 ....32 A3
Tudbury Wy *CSLFD* M3 ....6 B2
Tudor Av *BKLY* M9 ....73 H3
  BOL BL1 ....35M2
  CHAD OL9 ....74 A1
  FWTH BL4 ....53 G8
  STLY SK15 ....92 A1
Tudor Cl *MOSL* OL5 ....77 H3

  RDSH SK5 ....100 B5
  WHIT OL12 ....71M1
Tudor Gn *WILM/AE* SK9 ......127 J3
  WGNS/IIMK WN3 ....63 H2
Tudor Hall St *ROCH* OL11 ...41M2
Tudor Rd *WILM/AE* SK9 ......127 J3
Tudor St *BOLS/LL * BL3 ......35M8
  MDTN M24 ....57 L4
  OLDS OL8 ....8 F8
  ROY/SHW OL2 ....43 L5
Tuffley Rd *NTHM/RTH* M23 ..109 K8
Tugford Cl *OLDTF/WHR* M16 ..98 B1
Tuley St *OP/CLY* M11 ....88 C5
Tulip Av *FWTH* BL4 ....52 D3
  FWTH BL4 ....53 J7
Tulip Cl *CHAD* OL9 ....58 B5
  EDGY/DAV SK3 ....112 A4
  SALE M33 ....95M8
Tulip Dr *HALE/TIMP* WA15 ..108 C6
  WGNNW/ST WN6 ....47 J1
Tulip Gv *WHIT* OL12 ....28 B1
Tulip Rd *PART* M31 ....106 B2
  RNFD/HAY WA11 ....78 C6
Tully Pl *BRO* M7 ....72 B8
Tully St *BRO* M7 ....72 B6
Tully St South *BRO* M7 .....72 B6
Tulpen Sq *CHAD* OL9 ....8 A4
Tulworth Rd *POY/DIS* SK12 ..121M8
Tumblewood Dr
  CHD/CHDH SK8 ....111 H8
Tunbridge Sq *ORD* M5 ....86 D7
Tunshill La *MILN* OL16 .....29M5
Tunshill Rd *NTHM/RTH* M23 .109 H3
Tuns Rd *OLDS* OL8 ....75 L2
Tunstall La *WGNW/BIL/O* WN5 .47 G7
Tunstall Rd *OLDE* OL4 ....59M6
Tunstall St *HTNM* SK4 ....13 H1
  OP/CLY * M11 ....89 J3
Tunstead Av *DID/WITH* M20 ..98 C6
Tunstead La *UPML* OL3 ......61M7
Turbary Wk *MILN* OL16 ....29 C6
Turf Cl *ROY/SHW* OL2 ....59 H1
Turf Hill Rd *MILN* OL16 .....11 K9
Turf House Cl *LIT * OL15 ....20 A5
Turfland Av *ROY/SHW* OL2 ...59 H1
Turf La *CHAD* OL9 ....74 D1
  ROY/SHW OL2 ....59 H1
Turf Lea Rd *MPL/ROM* SK6 ..123 K3
Turf Park Rd *ROY/SHW* OL2 ..59 H1
Turf Pit La *OLDE* OL4 ....60 B1
Turf St *RAD* M26 ....54 C1
Turf Ter *LIT* OL15 ....20 B3
Turfton Rd *ROY/SHW* OL2 ....59 J1
Turks Rd *RAD* M26 ....38 A7
Turk St *BOL* BL1 ....35M4
Turley St *CHH* M8 ....72 E6
Turnberry *BOLS/LL* BL3 ......51 J1
Turnberry Cl *TYLD* M29 .....67M4
Turnberry Dr *WILM/AE* SK9 .127 H4
Turnberry Rd *CHD/CHDH* SK8 119 L3
Turnbull Av *PWCH* M25 ......55M5
Turnbull Rd *BRUN/LGST* M13 .99 J2
  GTN M18 ....100 C1
Turnbury Cl *SALE* M33 ....96 B6
Turnbury Rd *WYTH/NTH* M22 .110 B7
Turncliff Crs *MPL/ROM* SK6 114 A5
Turncroft La *STKP* SK1 .....13M5
Turnditch Cl *WGNNW/ST* WN6 .31 K8
Turnell Wy *WALK* M28 ....69 K7
Turner Av *FAIL* M35 ....74 B6
  IRL M44 ....94 D1
  WGNE/HIN WN2 ....65 L1
Turner Bridge Rd *BOLE* BL2 ...3 L2
Turner Dr *URM* M41 ....96 C2
Turnerford Cl *EDGW/EG* BL7 .22 B3
Turner Gdns *HYDE* SK14 .....91 H8
Turner La *AUL* OL6 ....75 L8
  HYDE SK14 ....91 J8
  MPL/ROM SK6 ....101 J6
Turner's Pl *WHIT* OL12 .....28 B1
Turner St *ANC* M4 ....7 H3
  AUL OL6 ....75 L8
  BOL BL1 ....3 H2
  BRO M7 ....72 B5
  DTN/ASHW M34 ....90 C7
  GTN M18 ....89 G7
  LEIGH WN7 ....66 D4
  OLDE OL4 ....60 B4
  OLDTF/WHR M16 ....86 F6
  OP/CLY M11 ....88 F3
  WGN WN1 ....15 H3
  WGNE/HIN WN2 ....49 G6
  WHIT OL12 ....28 B3
  WHTN BL5 ....50 B7
Turners Yd *WGNW/BIL/O * WN5 46 B6
Turnfield Cl *MILN* OL16 .....29 G1
Turnfield Rd *CHD/CHDH* SK8 119 L1
Turnhill Rd *MILN* OL16 ......42 E1
Turnill Dr *AIMK* WN4 ....78 E2
Turnlee Cl *GLSP* SK13 ......104 F5
Turnlee Dr *GLSP* SK13 ......104 F5
Turnlee Rd *GLSP* SK13 ......104 F5
Turn Moss Rd *STRET* M32 ....97 G3
Turnough Rd *MILN* OL16 .....29 J5
The Turnpike *MPL/ROM* SK6 .114 A5
Turnpike Gn *SLFD * M6 ....86 C1
Turnpike Wk *OP/CLY* M11 ....88 C3
Turn Rd *RAMS* BL0 ....17 G4
Turnstone Av *NEWLW* WA12 ...78 F8
Turnstone Cl *LEIGH* WN7 ....66 D6
Turnstone Rd *BOLE* BL2 ......3 G7
  OFTN SK2 ....113 K7
Turn St *AUL* OL6 ....75M8
Turret Hall Dr *GOL/RIS/CU* WA3 80 B4
Turriff Gv *WGNE/HIN* WN2 ...48 D3
Turton Cl *HEY* OL10 ....40 D2
  TOT/BURYW BL8 ....38 D4
Turton Hts *BOLE* BL2 ....22 E6
Turton La *PWCH* M25 ....55 J7
Turton Rd *BOLE* BL2 ....22 F6
  TOT/BURYW BL8 ....23 K2
  TOT/BURYW BL8 ....24 B4
Turton St *BOL* BL1 ....2 E5
  GOL/RIS/CU WA3 ....79 K4
  OP/CLY * M11 ....89 H3
Turves Rd *CHD/CHDH* SK8 ...120 B3
Tuscan Rd *DID/WITH* M20 ...110 A4
Tuscany Vw *BRO* M7 ....71 J4
Tutbury St *ANC* M4 ....88 A3
Tuxford Wk *NEWH/MOS* M40 ...73 G7
Tweedale Av *BKLY* M9 ....56 F7
Tweedale St *ROCH* OL11 .....10 D7
Tweedale Wy *CHAD* OL9 ....74 D1
Tweed Cl *ALT* WA14 ....107M6
  OLDS OL8 ....9 H8

Tweedle Hill Rd BKLY M9 56 E8
Tweed St LEIGH WN7 66 E8
Tweenbrook Av
NTHM/RTH M23 118 C1
Tweesdale Cl WHTF M45 55 L3
Twelve Yards Rd ECC M30 84 A5
IRL M44 82 F8
Twigworth Rd WYTH/NTH M22 118 E2
Twillbrook Dr CSLFD * M3 6 D1
Twinegate WHIT OL12 28 B1
Twining Brook Rd
CHD/CHDH SK8 120 D1
Twining Rd TRPK M17 85 H4
Twinnies Rd WILM/AE SK9 126 F3
Twin St HEY OL10 41 H3
Twirl Hill Rd AUL OL6 76 B3
Twisse Rd BOLE BL2 37 J5
Twiss Green Dr
GOL/RIS/CU WA3 81 H8
Twiss Green La GOL/RIS/CU WA3 81 G8
Twist Av GOL/RIS/CU WA3 79 M4
Twist La LEIGH WN7 66 A7
Twoacre Av WYTH/NTH M22 109 M7
Two Acre Dr ROY/SHW OL2 43 J4
Two Acre La OLDE OL4 60 D2
Two Bridges Rd MILN OL16 43 L1
Two Brooks La TOT/BURYW BL8 23 L2
Two Trees La DTN/ASHW M34 101 K3
Twyford Cl DID/WITH M20 110 C1
Tybyrne Cl WALK M28 68 C5
Tydden St OLDS OL8 75 J1
Tydeman Wk MILN * OL16 29 K7
Tyldesley Ar WGN * WN1 15 G3
Tyldesley Old Rd ATH M46 67 G2
Tyldesley Pas ATH M46 67 J3
Tyldesley Rd ATH M46 67 G2
Tyldesley St RUSH/FAL M14 98 D1
Tyler St WILM/AE SK9 130 D3
Tymm St NEWH/MOS M40 73 M4
Tyndall Av NEWH/MOS M40 73 K3
Tyndall St OLDE OL4 59 M6
Tyne Ct WALK M28 68 F1
Tynedale Cl RDSH SK5 100 B7
Tynesbank WALK M28 68 F2
Tynesbank Cottages
WALK * M28 68 F1
Tyne St OLDE OL4 59 M5
Tynwald St OLDE OL4 59 M5
Tyrer Av WGNS/IIMK WN3 14 A9
Tyrol Wk OP/CLY M11 88 C4
Tyrone Cl NTHM/RTH M23 109 G4
Tyrone Dr ROCH OL11 27 J7
Tyro St OLDS * OL8 75 J1
Tyrrell Gv HYDE SK14 102 D3
Tyrrel Rd RDSH SK5 100 C3
Tysoe Gdns CSLFD M3 6 B2
Tyson St CHH M8 72 C4
Tytherington Dr RDSH SK5 100 A3

U

Uganda St BOLS/LL BL3 51 M2
Ukraine Rd BRO M7 71 K6
Uldale Dr MDTN M24 57 H3
Ullesthorpe WHIT OL12 10 D3
Ulleswater Cl BOLS/LL BL3 53 J1
Ulleswater St BOL BL1 36 C2
Ullswater Av AULW OL7 75 K8
ROY/SHW OL2 43 G6
WGNW/BIL/O WN5 46 C5
WHIT OL12 27 M3
Ullswater Dr BURY * BL9 39 H5
FWTH BL4 52 B5
MDTN M24 57 J1
WGNE/HIN WN2 48 E5
Ullswater Gv HEY OL10 41 G4
Ullswater Rd GOL/RIS/CU WA3 79 M3
STKP SK1 112 E5
TYLD M29 67 K5
URM M41 84 B8
WILM/AE SK9 119 L8
WYTH/NTH M22 118 D2
Ullswater St LEIGH WN7 66 B7
Ullswater Ter STLY SK15 76 D8
Ulster Av ROCH OL11 10 D9
Ulundi St RAD M26 54 D1
Ulverston Av CHAD OL9 58 D6
DID/WITH M20 98 C5
Ulverston Rd WGNS/IIMK WN3 63 J1
Umberton Rd WHTN BL5 51 J5
Uncouth Rd MILN OL16 29 H5
Underhill MPL/ROM SK6 113 M2
Underhill Rd OLD OL1 9 H1
Underhill Wk NEWH/MOS M40 73 L8
Under La CHAD OL9 74 E1
OLDE OL4 60 E8
Underwood WHIT OL12 10 D4
Underwood Cl GTN M18 89 J6
Underwood Rd HYDE SK14 103 G1
WILM/AE SK9 130 F3
Underwood St DUK SK16 90 E4
Underwood Wy ROY/SHW OL2 44 A4
Undsworth Ct HEY * OL10 41 G2
Unicorn St ECC M30 84 E4
Union Ar BURY BL9 4 F4
Union Buildings BOL * BL1 2 F6
Union Ct BOL * BL1 36 D2
Union Rd AUL OL6 75 M8
BOL BL1 36 D2
MPL/ROM * SK6 114 C6
NM/HAY SK22 124 D5
WHIT OL12 19 M8
Union St ANC M4 7 H3
AUL OL6 75 L8
BURY BL9 4 F4
CHAD OL9 58 E8
EDGW/EG BL7 22 A2
GLSP SK13 104 F4
GTN M18 89 H6
HYDE SK14 102 B2
LEIGH WN7 66 C7
MDTN M24 57 K3
OLD OL1 9 J6
OLDE OL4 60 B6
RAMS BL0 17 C6
ROY/SHW OL2 43 G8
RUSH/FAL * M14 98 E1
SLFD M6 71 K8
STKP SK1 13 J7
SWIN M27 70 B4
TYLD M29 67 J3
WGNE/HIN WN2 48 D4
WGTN/LGST M12 7 M8
WHIT OL12 10 E2
WHIT OL12 18 D4
Union St West CHAD OL9 9 G7
Union Ter CHH * M8 72 C4
United Rd OLDTF/WHR M16 86 B7
Unity Cl HEY OL10 40 E3
Unity Crs HEY OL10 40 E3
Unity Dr BRO M7 72 B6
Unity St HEY OL10 40 E3
Unity Wy STKP SK1 13 L7
University Rd SLFD M6 86 E1
University Rd West ORD * M5 86 E2
Unsworth Av GOL/RIS/CU WA3 80 A3
TYLD M29 67 L4
Unsworth St LEIGH WN7 66 B5
RAD M26 38 C8
Unsworth Wy OLD OL1 9 H3
Unwin Av GTN M18 89 G8
Upavon Rd WYTH/NTH M22 119 H1
Upcast La WILM/AE SK9 130 A1
Upholland Rd
WGNW/BIL/O WN5 46 A8
Upland Dr AIMK WN4 64 A8
LHULT M38 52 C6
Upland Rd OLDS OL8 59 H8
The Uplands MOSL OL5 77 G3
Uplands MDTN M24 57 K5
Uplands Av RAD M26 54 F2
Uplands Rd GLSP SK13 105 G4
HYDE SK14 102 D6
URM M41 95 H4
Upper Brook St
BRUN/LGST M13 87 L6
STKP SK1 13 K5
Upper Camp St BRO M7 72 A7
Upper Chorlton Rd
OLDTF/WHR M16 97 M1
Upper Cleminson St CSLFD M3 6 A3
Upper Cliff Hl ROY/SHW OL2 43 M3
Upper Conran St BKLY M9 73 H4
Upper Cyrus St
NEWH/MOS M40 88 B2
Upper Dicconson St WGN WN1 15 G2
Upper Dover St OP/CLY M11 88 D3
Upper Downs ALT WA14 116 E1
Upper George St TYLD M29 67 K4
WHIT OL12 10 F1
Upper Gloucester St SLFD M6 86 D1
Upper Hayes Cl MILN OL16 11 L3
Upper Helena St
NEWH/MOS M40 88 B2
Upper Hibbert La
MPL/ROM SK6 114 C8
Upper Kent Rd RUSH/FAL M14 99 G1
Upper Kirby St ANC M4 7 M4
Upper Lees Dr WHTN BL5 50 D3
Upper Lloyd St RUSH/FAL M14 98 D1
Upper Md EDGW/EG BL7 22 C3
Upper Medlock St HULME M15 87 J6
Uppermill Dr BNG/LEV M19 111 G1
Upper Monsall St
NEWH/MOS M40 73 H6
Upper Moss La HULME M15 87 H6
Upper Park Rd BRO M7 72 A3
RUSH/FAL M14 87 M8
Upper Passmonds Gv
ROCH OL11 27 L4
Upper St Stephen St
WGNNW/ST WN6 14 D3
Upper Stone Dr MILN OL16 29 G6
Upper West Gv BRUN/LGST M13 88 A7
Upper Wharf St ORD M5 86 F3
Upper Wilton St PWCH M25 55 M8
Uppingham Dr RAMS BL0 17 B5
Upton ROCH OL11 10 D7
Upton Av CHD/CHDH SK8 120 C4
HTNM SK4 99 H8
Upton Cl GOL/RIS/CU WA3 80 A4
MDTN M24 57 K7
Upton Dr ALT WA14 108 B4
Upton La TYLD M29 67 M4
Upton Rd ATH M46 51 H8
Upton St CMANE M1 7 J6
Upton Wy TOT/BURYW BL8 24 C7
Upwood Rd GOL/RIS/CU WA3 80 A5
Urban Dr HALE/TIMP WA15 108 B8
Urban Rd HALE/TIMP WA15 108 B8
SALE M33 96 D8
Urmson St OLDS OL8 75 J1
Urmston Av NEWLW WA12 78 E7
Urmston La STRET M32 96 D3
Urmston Pk URM M41 96 B2
Urmston St LEIGH WN7 66 A7
Urwick Rd MPL/ROM SK6 113 L3
Usk Cl WHTF M45 55 M5
Uttley St BOL BL1 36 A2
ROCH OL11 27 M8
Uxbridge St AUL OL6 90 D1

V

Vaal St OLDS OL8 74 F1
Valance Cl WGTN/LGST M12 88 D6
Valdene Cl FWTH BL4 53 G5
Valdene Dr FWTH BL4 53 G5
WALK M28 69 G4
The Vale MOSL OL5 76 E3
WGNNW/ST WN6 30 A4
Vale Av BURY BL9 39 G5
HOR/BR BL6 33 K1
HYDE SK14 102 D1
RAD M26 53 M5
SALE M33 97 H7
SWIN M27 70 D3
URM M41 95 H3
Vale Cl BRAM/HZG SK7 113 H8
HTNM SK4 111 J2
MPL/ROM SK6 114 C2
WGNNW/ST WN6 30 B4
Vale Coppice HOR/BR BL6 33 K1
Vale Cottages LIT OL15 20 B7
Vale Crs CHD/CHDH SK8 120 B2
Vale Dr CHAD OL9 8 E6
PWCH M25 71 K2
Vale Edge RAD M26 38 D7
Vale Head WILM/AE SK9 127 H2
Vale House Dr GLSP SK13 93 K6
Vale La FAIL M35 74 D7
Valemount GLSP SK13 93 K7
Valencia Rd BRO M7 71 L6
Valentia Rd BKLY M9 57 G8
Valentines Rd ATH M46 66 D3
Valentine St FAIL M35 74 B5
OLDE OL4 59 M6
Valerie Wk HULME M15 6 F9
Vale Rd ALT WA14 116 D3
DROY M43 89 L1
HALE/TIMP WA15 108 D7
HTNM SK4 111 J3
MPL/ROM SK6 113 L4
ROY/SHW OL2 44 A6
STLY SK15 77 H6
WILM/AE SK9 126 C4
Vale Side MOSL OL5 76 F3
Vale St AULW OL7 75 K6
BOLE BL2 37 K5
EDGW/EG BL7 16 D8
HEY OL10 41 H2
MDTN M24 57 L4
OP/CLY M11 88 F2
Vale Top Av BKLY M9 73 H5
Valetta Cl RUSH/FAL M14 98 E3
Vale Vw ALT * WA14 116 E3
Valewood Av HTNM SK4 111 K3
Valiant Rd WGNW/BIL/O WN5 47 G4
Valletts La BOL BL1 35 M3
The Valley ATH M46 67 H1
Valley Av TOT/BURYW BL8 24 E8
Valley Cl CHD/CHDH SK8 120 A1
MOSL OL5 76 E2
Valley Dr WILM/AE SK9 127 G1
Valley Gv DTN/ASHW M34 101 L2
Valley Ml EDGW/EG * BL7 22 C4
Valley New Rd ROY/SHW OL2 59 H1
Valley Ri ROY/SHW OL2 43 K3
Valley Rd BRAM/HZG SK7 121 H3
CHD/CHDH SK8 120 A1
GLSP SK13 104 C4
HYDE SK14 103 H4
MDTN M24 57 L2
MPL/ROM SK6 101 G8
NM/HAY SK22 125 M2
ROCH OL11 28 B8
ROY/SHW OL2 59 H1
URM M41 84 A8
WGNW/BIL/O WN5 47 G7
Valley Rd South URM M41 94 F2
Valley Vw HYDE SK14 91 K8
Valley Wk OP/CLY M11 88 C3
Valley Wy STLY SK15 91 M3
Valpy Av BOLE BL2 36 E1
Vanbrugh Gv
WGNW/BIL/O WN5 46 E3
Vancouver Quay SALQ M50 86 C5
Vandyke Av SLFD M6 85 L1
Vandyke St ROCH OL11 27 J3
Vane St ECC M30 84 F2
Vannes Gv HYDE SK14 103 J1
Vantomme St BOL BL1 22 B8
Varden Gv EDGY/DAV SK3 112 A7
Varden Rd POY/DIS SK12 129 J1
Vardon Dr WILM/AE SK9 127 H6
Varey St GTN M18 89 G7
Varley Rd BOLS/LL BL3 35 K8
Varley St NEWH/MOS M40 73 G8
Varna St OP/CLY M11 89 G5
Vauban Dr SLFD M6 85 L1
Vaudrey Dr BRAM/HZG SK7 122 A2
CHD/CHDH SK8 120 C1
HALE/TIMP WA15 108 D4
Vaudrey La DTN/ASHW M34 101 K2
Vaudrey Rd MPL/ROM SK6 101 K7
Vaudrey St STLY SK15 91 K3
Vaughan Av NEWH/MOS M40 73 K4
Vaughan Gv OLDE OL4 60 C6
Vaughan Rd CCHDY M21 98 A4
HTNM SK4 112 A1
Vaughan St ECC M30 84 E1
ROY/SHW OL2 59 H1
WGTN/LGST M12 88 C5
Vauxhall Rd WGN WN1 15 J4
Vauxhall St NEWH/MOS M40 72 E8
Vauze Av HOR/BR BL6 33 G3
Vauze House Cl HOR/BR BL6 33 G2
Vavasour Ct MILN * OL16 11 J6
Vavasour St MILN OL16 11 K6
Vawdrey Dr NTHM/RTH M23 109 J2
Vaynor WHIT OL12 10 D2
Vega St CHH M8 72 B8
Velmere Av BKLY M9 56 D7
Velour Cl BRO M7 87 G1
CSLFD M3 6 A1
Vendale Av SWIN M27 70 A6
Venetia St NEWH/MOS * M40 73 M7
Venice St BOLS/LL BL3 35 M8
CMANE * M1 7 H7
Venlow Gdns CHD/CHDH SK8 120 D3
Ventnor Av BNG/LEV M19 99 M4
BOL BL1 36 C1
BURY BL9 55 J1
SALE M33 96 E6
Ventnor Cl DTN/ASHW M34 101 L4
Ventnor Rd DID/WITH M20 110 F1
HTNM SK4 12 A2
Ventnor St BKLY M9 73 G4
ROCH OL11 10 E8
SLFD M6 71 L7
Ventura Cl RUSH/FAL M14 98 D3
Venture Scout Wy BRO M7 72 C6
Venture Wy POY/DIS SK12 129 K1
Venwood Ct PWCH * M25 71 J2
Venwood Rd PWCH M25 71 J2
Verbena Av FWTH BL4 52 D3
Verbena Cl PART M31 106 C1
Verdant La ECC M30 84 C4
Verdant Wy MILN OL16 42 F1
Verda St WGNE/HIN WN2 64 D4
Verdon St ANC M4 7 G1
Verdun Av SLFD M6 85 L1
Verdun Crs ROCH OL11 27 M4
Verdun Rd ECC M30 69 L8
Verdure Av BOL BL1 35 H4
SALE M33 108 F3
Verdure Cl FAIL M35 74 E4
Vere St SALQ M50 86 C3
Verity Cl DID/WITH M20 98 E6
ROY/SHW OL2 59 G2
Vermont St BOL BL1 2 A2
Verne Av SWIN M27 70 B4
Verne Dr OLD OL1 44 B7
Verney Rd ROY/SHW OL2 59 H2
Vernham Wk BOLS/LL BL3 36 B8
Vernon Av ECC * M30 85 J2
STKP SK1 112 E2
STRET M32 97 G3
Vernon Cl CHD/CHDH SK8 120 A3
POY/DIS SK12 129 H2
Vernon Dr MPL/ROM SK6 113 M5
PWCH M25 71 K2
Vernon Gv SALE M33 109 H1
Vernon Pk HALE/TIMP WA15 108 D5
Vernon Rd BRO M7 71 M3
DROY M43 89 H2
MPL/ROM SK6 113 J1
POY/DIS SK12 129 J2
TOT/BURYW BL8 24 C3
Vernon St AUL OL6 75 M8
BKLY M9 73 H5
BOL BL1 2 C3
BRAM/HZG SK7 121 M1
BRO M7 72 A7
BURY BL9 4 F1
FWTH BL4 53 H4
HYDE SK14 102 B2
LEIGH WN7 66 C7
MOSL * OL5 76 F2
STKP * SK1 13 J3
Vernon Wk BOL BL1 2 D2
Verona Dr NEWH/MOS M40 73 M8
Veronica Rd DID/WITH M20 110 F1
Verrill Av NTHM/RTH M23 109 M3
Vesper St FAIL M35 74 D4
Vesta St ANC M4 7 M4
RAMS BL0 17 B6
Vestris Dr SLFD M6 85 L1
Viaduct Rd ALT WA14 108 A5
Viaduct St CSLFD M3 6 D2
EDGY/DAV SK3 13 G5
WGTN/LGST M12 88 B4
Vicarage Av CHD/CHDH SK8 120 D4
Vicarage Cl BURY BL9 25 H4
DUK SK16 91 H4
OLDE OL4 60 C5
SLFD M6 85 L1
WGNE/HIN WN2 64 D2
Vicarage Crs AUL OL6 76 A7
Vicarage Dr DUK SK16 91 H4
MILN OL16 28 F1
Vicarage Gdns EDGY/DAV * SK3 13 G7
HYDE SK14 102 B2
Vicarage Gv ECC M30 85 J2
Vicarage La ALT WA14 116 E3
MDTN M24 58 A5
NM/HAY SK22 125 M2
POY/DIS SK12 122 A7
WGNNW/ST WN6 30 D7
Vicarage Rd AIMK WN4 78 E2
AULW OL7 75 L7
EDGY/DAV SK3 112 B6
HOR/BR BL6 33 G2
IRL M44 94 D2
SWIN M27 70 B4
URM M41 84 E8
WALK M28 52 F8
WGNE/HIN WN2 64 E3
WGNW/BIL/O WN5 46 A8
Vicarage Rd North ROCH OL11 41 M3
Vicarage Rd South ROCH OL11 41 M3
Vicarage Rd West HOR/BR BL6 32 F2
Vicarage Sq LEIGH * WN7 66 C7
Vicarage St BOLS/LL BL3 2 B8
OLDS OL8 74 F2
RAD M26 54 D1
ROY/SHW OL2 43 L5
Vicarage Vw ROCH OL11 42 A3
Vicarage Wy ROY/SHW OL2 43 K6
Vicar's Dr MILN OL16 10 E5
Vicar's Ga MILN OL16 10 E5
Vicars Hall Gdns WALK M28 68 C7
Vicars Hall La WALK M28 68 B8
Vicars Rd CCHDY M21 97 K4
Vicars St ECC M30 85 J2
Vicker Cl SWIN M27 70 C2
Vicker Gv DID/WITH M20 98 C7
Vickerman St BOL BL1 36 A2
Vickers Rw FWTH BL4 52 E4
Vickers St BOLS/LL * BL3 2 B8
NEWH/MOS M40 88 B1
Victor Av BURY BL9 25 H8
Victor Cl WGNW/BIL/O WN5 47 G4
Victoria Av BKLY M9 56 F7
BNG/LEV M19 99 K4
BRAM/HZG * SK7 122 A1
CHD/CHDH SK8 120 C2
DID/WITH M20 110 D1
ECC M30 85 J1
GLSP SK13 93 K7
HALE/TIMP WA15 108 B5
MPL/ROM SK6 113 J1
SWIN M27 70 D4
WGNE/HIN WN2 65 H3
WGNNW/ST WN6 14 C1
WHTF M45 55 K4
Victoria Av East BKLY M9 57 J8
Victoria Bridge St CSLFD M3 6 E2
Victoria Cl BRAM/HZG SK7 120 F6
EDGY/DAV SK3 13 H8
WALK * M28 68 D6
WGNE/HIN WN2 32 E6
Victoria Ct AULW OL7 90 D3
FWTH BL4 52 F2
Victoria Crs ECC M30 85 J1
WGNNW/ST WN6 31 H4
Victoria Dr SALE M33 109 G1
Victoria Gdns HYDE SK14 91 J8
ROY/SHW * OL2 43 L5
Victoria Gv BOL BL1 35 M3
HTNM SK4 99 M7
RUSH/FAL M14 98 F5
Victoria La SWIN M27 70 A4
WHTF M45 55 J5
Victoria Ldg BRO * M7 71 M7
Victoria Ms BURY BL9 55 L2
Victoria Pk STKP * SK1 112 E4
Victoria Pl TRPK M17 86 C7
Victoria Rd AIMK WN4 63 G8
ALT WA14 116 F2
BOL BL1 35 G5
DUK SK16 90 F6
ECC M30 85 H1
FWTH BL4 53 K6
HALE/TIMP WA15 108 D6
HOR/BR BL6 33 M1
IRL M44 94 C3
NEWLW WA12 78 F8
OLDTF/WHR M16 98 A2
RUSH/FAL M14 98 E4
SALE M33 109 G1
STKP SK1 112 E3
STRET M32 97 G2
URM M41 95 L2
WGNE/HIN WN2 64 D3
WILM/AE SK9 126 E6
WYTH/NTH M22 110 A4
Victoria Sq ANC * M4 7 K2
BOL BL1 2 E5
Victoria Station Ap CSLFD M3 6 F2
Victoria St ALT WA14 108 A7
AULW OL7 90 D3
CHAD OL9 8 C3
CSLFD M3 6 F2
DTN/ASHW M34 101 H1
DUK SK16 91 G4
FAIL M35 74 A6
FWTH BL4 52 E3
GLSP SK13 104 F4
HEY OL10 41 H3
HOR/BR BL6 33 G2
HYDE SK14 91 J8
HYDE SK14 91 L7
LEIGH WN7 66 B6
LIT OL15 20 C7
MDTN M24 57 K4
NM/HAY SK22 124 D6
OLDE OL4 9 M6
OLDE OL4 60 B6
OLDS * OL8 75 J4
OP/CLY M11 88 F4
RAD M26 54 D1
RAMS BL0 17 B6
ROY/SHW OL2 43 L5
STLY SK15 77 G8
STLY SK15 91 J2
TOT/BURYW BL8 4 B4
TOT/BURYW BL8 24 B5
WALK M28 68 D6
WGNE/HIN WN2 64 D2
WGNW/BIL/O WN5 47 H6
WHIT * OL12 10 E1
WHIT * OL12 18 D4
WHTN BL5 50 C4
Victoria St East AULW OL7 90 D3
Victoria Ter ROY/SHW * OL2 43 G7
WGNE/HIN WN2 65 J4
WGTN/LGST M12 88 C8
Victoria Wk CHAD OL9 8 C1
Victoria Wy BRAM/HZG SK7 120 F6
LEIGH WN7 66 B5
Victor Mann St OP/CLY M11 89 K5
Victor St CSLFD M3 6 B3
HEY OL10 41 H4
NEWH/MOS M40 72 F8
OLDS OL8 74 E3
Victory Gv DTN/ASHW M34 89 M5
Victory Rd BOLS/LL BL3 37 K8
Victory St BOL * BL1 35 M4
RUSH/FAL M14 98 F1
Vienna Rd EDGY/DAV SK3 112 A6
Vienna Rd East EDGY/DAV SK3 112 A6
View Cl UPML OL3 45 M7
Viewlands Dr WILM/AE SK9 127 H2
View St BOLS/LL BL3 2 A9
Vigo Av BOLS/LL BL3 51 L1
Vigo St HEY OL10 41 H3
OLDE OL4 60 A7
WGNE/HIN WN2 48 C2
Viking Cl OP/CLY M11 88 C3
Viking St BOLS/LL BL3 36 D8
ROCH OL11 27 M4
Villa Av WGNNW/ST WN6 31 K8
The Village URM M41 95 J4
Village Ct TRPK M17 85 M6
Village St BRO M7 71 M7
Village Vw WGNW/BIL/O WN5 62 B7
Village Wy WILM/AE SK9 127 H3
Village Wy (Ashburton Rd East)
TRPK M17 85 L6
Villa Rd OLDS OL8 59 J8
Villdale Av OFTN SK2 112 F5
Villiers Ct WHTF * M45 55 K6
Villiers Dr OLDS OL8 9 G8
Villiers St AUL OL6 91 G2
BURY BL9 5 J2
HYDE SK14 102 C1
Vinca Gv BRO M7 72 A6
Vincent Av CCHDY M21 97 K3
OLDE OL4 59 M4
Vincent St BOL BL1 2 A6
BRO M7 72 A5
HYDE SK14 102 C3
MDTN M24 57 K2
MILN * OL16 11 H7
OP/CLY M11 88 F4
Vincent Wy WGNW/BIL/O WN5 47 G4
Vine Av SWIN M27 70 E4
Vine Cl ROY/SHW OL2 43 L5
SALE M33 95 M7
Vine Ct MILN * OL16 11 J5
STRET M32 97 G3
Vine Fold NEWH/MOS M40 74 C3
Vine Gv OFTN SK2 112 F6
WGNS/IIMK WN3 14 F5
Vine Pl ROCH OL11 10 F8
Vinery Gv DTN/ASHW M34 101 H1
Vine St BRAM/HZG SK7 122 A1
BRO M7 71 L4
CHAD OL9 74 E1
ECC M30 84 F3
OP/CLY M11 89 H5
RAMS BL0 17 A8
WGN WN1 15 J1
WGNE/HIN WN2 49 G6
Vineyard Cl WHIT OL12 19 K5
Vineyard St OLDE OL4 59 L5
Viola Cl WGNNW/ST WN6 31 G2
Viola St OP/CLY M11 89 G2
Violet Av FWTH BL4 52 D3
Violet St AIMK WN4 78 E2
GTN M18 89 J6
OFTN SK2 112 C6
WGNS/IIMK WN3 15 L8
Violet Wy MDTN M24 58 A5
Virgil St HULME M15 86 F6
Virginia Cha CHD/CHDH SK8 120 B4
Virginia Cl NTHM/RTH M23 109 G5
Virginia St BOLS/LL BL3 35 L8
ROCH * OL11 28 B8
Virginia Wy WGNW/BIL/O WN5 46 F4
Viscount Dr CHD/CHDH SK8 119 M5
MANAIR * M90 118 B5
Viscount Rd WGNW/BIL/O WN5 47 G4
Viscount St RUSH/FAL M14 98 F1
Vista Av NEWLW WA12 78 D8
Vista Rd NEWLW WA12 78 D8
Vista Wy NEWLW WA12 78 D8
Vivian St ROCH OL11 10 D9
Vixen Cl CCHDY M21 98 B5
Voltaire Av SLFD M6 85 L1
Vorlich Dr CHAD OL9 58 C4
Vulcan Dr WGN WN1 15 J5
Vulcan Rd WGNW/BIL/O WN5 47 G4
Vulcan St OLD OL1 59 L3
Vyner Gv SALE M33 96 C6

W

Waddicor Av AUL OL6 76 B6
Waddington Cl
GOL/RIS/CU * WA3 80 C4
TOT/BURYW BL8 38 B2
Waddington Fold MILN OL16 42 F2
Waddington Rd BOL BL1 35 K3
Waddington St CHAD OL9 8 D3
Wade Bank WHTN BL5 50 C4
Wadebridge Av
NTHM/RTH M23 109 G5
Wadebridge Dr
TOT/BURYW BL8 38 C2
Wadeford Cl ANC M4 7 M2
Wade Hill La OLDE OL4 61 H4
Wade Rw UPML OL3 61 L4

Wadesmill Wk BRUN/LGST * M13 ....7 J9
Wadeson Rd BRUN/LGST M13 .....7 K9
Wade St BOLS/LL BL3 ....52 C1
 MDTN M24 ....58 A6
Wade Wk OP/CLY M11 ....88 D4
Wadham Gdns MPL/ROM SK6 ...101 M7
Wadham Wy HALE/TIMP WA15 ...117 H3
Wadhurst Wk BRUN/LGST * M13 ...87 M7
Wadlow Cl CSLFD * M3 ....6 C1
Wadsley Dr BOL BL1 ....8 F2
Wadsworth Cl WILM/AE SK9 ....127 J1
Wadsworth Dr WGNNW/ST WN6 ...47 J2
Wadsworth Ms DROY M43 ....89 J3
Waggoners Ct SWIN M27 ....70 C5
Waggon Rd BOLE BL2 ....37 G4
 MOSL OL5 ....76 F4
Wagner St BOL BL1 ....36 A1
Wagstaffe Dr FAIL M35 ....74 C5
Wagstaff St MDTN M24 ....57 K3
Wagtail Cl WALK M28 ....69 G4
Waincliffe Av CCHDY M21 ....98 A8
Wainfleet Cl WGNS/IIMK WN3 ....63 K2
Waingap Crs WHIT OL12 ....18 E4
Waingap Ri WHIT OL12 ....18 E5
Waingap Vw WHIT OL12 ....18 E5
Wainhouse Brow
 NM/HAY SK22 ....125M1
Wainman St SLFD M6 ....71 L7
Wainscot Cl TYLD M29 ....67 L5
Wainwright Av
 DTN/ASHW M34 ....100 C1
Wainwright Cl OFTN SK2 ....13 M9
 OLDE OL4 ....60 D5
Wainwright Rd ALT WA14 ....107 L7
Wainwright St DUK SK16 ....91 G3
 OLDS OL8 ....9 H8
Waithlands Rd MILN OL16 ....11 K6
Wakefield Crs MPL/ROM SK6 ...113 K3
 WGNNW/ST WN6 ....47 J6
Wakefield Dr OLD OL1 ....58 F3
 SWIN M27 ....54 A8
Wakefield Ms EDGW/EG BL7 .....22 C5
Wakefield Rd STLY SK15 ....91 L2
 CHAD OL9 ....8 D1
 CMANE * M1 ....7 G8
 GOL/RIS/CU WA3 ....79 K5
Wakeling Rd DTN/ASHW M34 ...101 H4
Walcot Pl WGNS/IIMK WN3 ......63 K2
Walcott Cl BRUN/LGST M13 .....88 A7
Wald Av RUSH/FAL M14 ....99 H5
Waldeck St BOL BL1 ....35 M4
Walden Cl RUSH/FAL M14 ....98 D4
Walden Crs BRAM/HZG SK7 .....121 L1
Walderton Av NEWH/MOS M40 ...73 K6
Waldon Cl CHD/CHDH SK8 ......111 G7
Waldon Cl BOLS/LL BL3 ....35M8
 WGNE/HIN WN2 ....49 J8
Waldorf Cl WGNS/IIMK WN3 .....63 K2
Wales St OLD OL1 ....59M3
Walford Rd AIMK WN4 ....78 F1
The Walk ATH M46 ....67 G1
 MILN OL16 ....10 E4
Walkdale Brow GLSP SK13 .....104 E5
Walkden Av WGN WN1 ....14 F2
Walkden Av East WGN WN1 .....47 M2
Walkden Dr WALK M28 ....68 E1
Walkden Market Pl WALK * M28 ..69 G1
Walkdens Av ATH M46 ....69 G3
Walkden Rd WALK M28 ....68 C2
Walkden St WHIT OL12 ....10 E1
Walker Av BOLS/LL BL3 ....52 C1
 FAIL * M35 ....74 E6
 STLY SK15 ....91M2
 WHTF M45 ....55 K6
Walker Cl FWTH BL4 ....53 C4
 HYDE SK14 ....102 C2
Walker La HYDE SK14 ....102 C2
Walker Rd BKLY M9 ....57 H8
 CHAD OL9 ....9 K8
 ECC M30 ....69 K8
 IRL * M44 ....94 C3
Walkers Cl UPML OL3 ....61 L4
Walkers Ct FWTH BL4 ....53 C4
Walker's Cft CSLFD M3 ....6 F2
Walkers Dr LEIGH WN7 ....66 D6
Walker's La OLDE OL4 ....60 D6
Walker's Rd OLDS OL8 ....74 F2
Walker St BOL BL1 ....2 B6
 BURY BL9 ....5 L4
 DTN/ASHW M34 ....90 B8
 GLSP SK13 ....93 K7
 HEY OL10 ....40 F3
 MDTN M24 ....56 F5
 MILN OL16 ....11 H5
 OLDS OL8 ....8 E7
 RAD M26 ....54 F3
 STKP SK1 ....13 J4
 WHTF M45 ....50 B4
Walkerwood Dr STLY SK15 ......92 A2
Walkmill UPML OL3 ....61 J3
Walk Mill Rd NM/HAY SK22 ...125M1
Walk Mill Rd WHIT OL12 ....19 L8
The Walkway BOLS/LL BL3 ......35 J7
Wallace Av RUSH/FAL M14 ....99 G1
Wallace La WGN WN1 ....15 K1
Wallace St OLDS OL8 ....59 J8
Wallasey Av RUSH/FAL M14 .....98 D3
Wallbank Dr WHIT OL12 ....58 D8
Wallbank Rd BRAM/HZG SK7 ...121 J3
Wallbrook Av
 WGNW/BIL/O WN5 ....62 A3
Wallbrook Crs LHULT M38 ......52 D6
The Walled Gdn SWIN M27 ......70 A6
Waller Av RUSH/FAL M14 ....98 F4
Walley St BOL BL1 ....36 B1
Wallgarth Cl WGNS/IIMK WN3 ...63 G2
Wallgate WGN WN1 ....14 F5
Wallhead Rd MILN OL16 ....29 C5
Wall Hill Rd UPML OL3 ....61 H3
Wallingford Rd URM M41 ....119 L7
 WILM/AE SK9 ....119 L7
Wallis St CHAD OL9 ....58 D8
 NEWH/MOS * M40 ....73 M7
Wallness La SLFD M6 ....86 F1
Wallshaw Pl OLD * OL1 ....9M5
Wallshaw St OLD OL1 ....9M5
Walls St WGNE/HIN WN2 ....65M2
 OLDS OL8 ....9 J8
 SLFD M6 ....86 C2
 WGNNW/ST WN6 ....14 A1
Wall Wy GTN M18 ....89 H8
Wallwork Cl ROCH OL11 ....27 K1
Wallwork Rd TRPK M17 ....68 A6
Wallwork St OP/CLY M11 ....89 H4
 RDSH SK5 ....100 C2
Wallworth Av GTN M18 ....89 G7
Wally Sq BRO M7 ....72 B6
Walmer Dr BRAM/HZG SK7 .....121 J3
Walmer Rd WGNE/HIN WN2 .....49 K7

Walmersley Ct MPL/ROM * SK6 ..114 C6
Walmersley Old Rd BURY BL9 ...25 J4
Walmersley Rd BURY BL9 ....5 G2
 BURY BL9 ....25 H3
 NEWH/MOS M40 ....74 B2
Walmer St GTN M18 ....89 H6
 RUSH/FAL M14 ....98 E1
Walmer St East RUSH/FAL M14 ..98 F1
Walmesley Dr WGNS/IIMK WN3 ...14 F7
Walmesley Dr WGN/HIN WN2 .....48 E5
Walmesley Rd LEIGH WN7 ....66 B2
Walmesley St WGN WN1 ....15 H5
Walmley Gv BOLS/LL BL3 ....51M1
Walmsley Av LIT OL15 ....29 J1
Walmsley Gv URM M41 ....95M2
Walmsley St NEWLW WA12 ....79 G8
 RDSH SK5 ....112 C1
 STLY SK15 ....91 K4
 TOT/BURYW BL8 ....24 E8
Walney Rd WGNS/IIMK WN3 .....63 G2
 WYTH/NTH M22 ....110 A8
Walnut Av BURY BL9 ....5 L3
 OLDE OL4 ....60 A4
 WGN WN1 ....48 A2
Walnut Cl HYDE SK14 ....102 D2
 SWIN M27 ....54 A8
 WILM/AE SK9 ....127 J4
Walnut Gv LEIGH WN7 ....66 C4
Walnut Rd ECC M30 ....69 K8
 PART M31 ....106 A1
Walnut St BOL BL1 ....36 C1
 GTN M18 ....89 G6
Walnut Tree Rd EDGY/DAV SK3 .111 K5
Walnut Wk WHIT M32 ....96 F4
Walpole Av WGNS/IIMK WN3 ....63 J1
Walpole St MILN OL16 ....11 H5
Walsall St SLFD M6 ....71 K7
Walsden St OP/CLY M11 ....88 F2
Walsh Av BKLY M9 ....72 F2
Walshaw Brook Cl
 TOT/BURYW BL8 ....24 C8
Walshaw Dr SWIN M27 ....70 C5
Walshaw La TOT/BURYW BL8 ....24 C8
Walshaw Rd TOT/BURYW BL8 ...24 C8
Walsh St NEWLW WA12 ....78 F7
Walshe St BURY BL9 ....4 C5
Walsh St CHAD OL9 ....8 B7
 HOR/BR BL6 ....21 H8
Walsingham Av DID/WITH M20 ..98 C8
 MDTN M24 ....57 K7
Walter Scott Av WGN WN1 ......31 L8
Walter Scott St OLD OL1 ....59 L4
Walters Dr OLDS OL8 ....75 K1
Walters Green Crs
 GOL/RIS/CU WA3 ....79 K2
Walter St AIMK * WN4 ....64 A8
 BKLY M9 ....73 G4
 GTN M18 ....89 H6
 LEIGH WN7 ....65 L7
 OLD OL1 ....9 K6
 OLDTF/WHR M16 ....86 F8
 PWCH M25 ....55 J8
 RAD M26 ....39 G6
 WALK M28 ....69 G2
 WGNW/BIL/O WN5 ....47 G6
Waltham Av GOL/RIS/CU WA3 ....81M5
 WGNNW/ST WN6 ....47 J1
Waltham Dr CHD/CHDH SK8 ....120 D6
Waltham Rd OLDTF/WHR M16 ...98 B3
Waltham St OLDS OL8 ....59M8
Walthew House La
 WGNW/BIL/O WN5 ....46 E3
Walthew La WGNE/HIN WN2 .....64 D2
 WGNW/BIL/O WN5 ....47 G2
Walton Cl MDTN M24 ....56 F3
Walton Ct BOLS/LL BL3 ....36 C8
Walton Dr BURY BL9 ....25 H4
 MPL/ROM SK6 ....114 A5
Walton Hall Dr RDSH SK5 .....100 A3
Walton Houses FAIL * M35 ......74 C4
Walton Pl FWTH BL4 ....53 H5
Walton Rd ALT WA14 ....107 L7
 BKLY M9 ....57 G7
 SALE M33 ....108 C3
Walton St ATH * M46 ....51 H8
 AULW OL7 ....75 J7
 HEY OL10 ....41 G4
 MDTN * M24 ....57 K2
 STKP * SK1 ....13 K5
Walwyn Cl STRET M32 ....97 H3
Wanborough Cl LEIGH WN7 ......66 C5
Wandsworth Av OP/CLY M11 ....89 G2
Wansbeck Cl STRET M32 ....97 H3
Wansfell Wk ANC M4 ....88 A2
Wansford St RUSH/FAL M14 .....98 D1
Wanstead Av BKLY M9 ....73 K1
Wapping St BOL BL1 ....36 A1
Warbeck Cl RDSH SK5 ....100 D2
 WGNE/HIN WN2 ....65 H1
Warbeck Rd NEWH/MOS M40 ....74 A2
Warbreck Gv SALE M33 ....109 G1
Warburton Cl
 HALE/TIMP WA15 ......117M6
 MPL/ROM SK6 ....113 K3
Warburton Dr
 HALE/TIMP WA15 ......117M6
Warburton La LYMM WA13 .....106 A4
 PART M31 ....106 C1
Warburton Pl ATH M46 ....67 G1
Warburton Rd WILM/AE SK9 ...119M8
Warburton St BOL BL1 ....36 C2
 DID/WITH M20 ....110 E1
 ECC M30 ....85 H3
 ORD M5 ....86 E6
Warburton Wy
 HALE/TIMP WA15 ......108 F5
Warcock Rd OLDE OL4 ....59M5
Wardend Cl LHULT * M38 ....52 D6
Wardens Bank WHTN BL5 ....50 B7
Warden St NEWH/MOS M40 .....73 L6
Wardle St HULME M15 ....87 H6
Ward La POY/DIS SK12 ....124 A8
 UPML OL3 ....45M8
Wardle Brook Av HYDE SK14 ..103 G1
Wardle Cl RAD M26 ....38 B7
 STRET M32 ....97 H2
Wardle Edge WHIT OL12 ....28 E1
Wardle Fold WHIT OL12 ....19 K5
Wardle Gdns WHIT OL12 ....28 E1
Wardle Rd SALE M33 ....108 E1
 WHIT OL12 ....19 K7
Wardle St BOLE BL2 ....3 L2
 LIT * OL15 ....20 B6
 NEWH/MOS M40 ....88 B1
 OLDE OL4 ....59 L6
Wardley Av CCHDY M21 ....98 B4
 WALK M28 ....68 C2
Wardley Hall La WALK M28 .....69 K4
Wardley Hall Rd WALK M28 .....69 L3
Wardley Rd TYLD M29 ....68 A4

Wardley Sq TYLD M29 ....68 A4
Wardley St SWIN M27 ....70 C4
 WGNW/BIL/O WN5 ....46 E7
Wardlow Av GLSP SK13 ....104 A5
Wardlow Ms GLSP SK13 ....104 B3
Wardlow St BOLS/LL BL3 ....35 L8
Wardour St ATH M46 ....66 F7
Ward Rd DID/WITH M20 ....110 E1
 DROY M43 ....89 L3
Wardsend Wk HULME * M15 .....87 C6
Ward St BKLY M9 ....72 F2
 FAIL M35 ....74 B4
 HYDE SK14 ....102 B2
 MPL/ROM SK6 ....113 J1
 NEWH/MOS M40 ....73 J4
 OLD OL1 ....8 F2
 OLD OL1 ....13 L8
 STLY SK15 ....91 K4
 WGNE/HIN WN2 ....49 C5
Wareham Gv ECC M30 ....84 F1
Wareham St CHH * M8 ....72 E1
 WGNE/HIN WN2 ....67 J4
Wareing St TYLD M29 ....67 J4
Wareing Wy BOLS/LL BL3 ....2 C6
Wareings Yd ROCH OL11 ....28 D8
Warford Av POY/DIS SK12 .....129 L2
Warford St ANC M4 ....72 B8
Warham St WILM/AE SK9 ......126 F5
The Warke Av WALK M28 ....69 J6
Warley Cl CHD/CHDH SK8 .....111 H6
Warley Gv DUK SK16 ....90 F4
Warley Rd OLDTF/WHR M16 .....97 K1
Warley St LIT OL15 ....20 C6
Warlingham St TOT/BURYW BL8 ..38 E3
Warlow Crest UPML OL3 ....61 K8
Warlow Dr LEIGH WN7 ....66 A3
 UPML OL3 ....61 K8
Warmby Gdns OLDS * OL8 ......75 G3
Warmington Dr
 WGTN/LGST M12 ....88 B6
Warminster Gv
 WGNS/IIMK WN3 ....63 G2
Warmley Rd NTHM/RTH M23 ...109 G4
Warncliffe St WGNW/BIL/O WN5 ..47 G7
Warne Av DROY M43 ....89M2
Warnford Cl NEWH/MOS M40 ...74 A8
Warnford St WGN WN1 ....47M2
War Office Rd ROCH OL11 ......27 H6
Warren Av CHD/CHDH SK8 ....111 L7
Warren Bank BKLY M9 ....72 F1
Warren Bruce Rd TRPK M17 ....86 A6
Warren Cl ATH M46 ....51 H8
 BRAM/HZG SK7 ....120 F2
 DTN/ASHW M34 ....101 C2
 POY/DIS SK12 ....121 K8
Warren Dr HALE/TIMP WA15 ...117M5
 NEWLW WA12 ....79 J8
 SWIN M27 ....70 A7
Warrener St SALE M33 ....109 G1
Warren Hey WILM/AE SK9 .....127 J4
Warren La OLDS OL8 ....74 E4
Warren Lea MPL/ROM SK6 ....114 E2
 POY/DIS SK12 ....122 A7
Warren Rd CHD/CHDH SK8 ....120 C2
 EDGY/DAV SK3 ....112 B6
 TRPK M17 ....85 L6
 WALK M28 ....69 H1
Warren St BKLY M9 ....72 F2
 BRO * M7 ....72 C4
 STKP SK1 ....13 J3
 TOT/BURYW BL8 ....38 E3
Warre St AUL OL6 ....90 E1
Warrington Av WGN WN1 ....15 H4
Warrington Rd AIMK WN4 ......78 E2
 BKLY M9 ....56 F8
 LEIGH WN7 ....81 L2
 NEWLW WA12 ....79 K6
 WGNE/HIN WN2 ....64 D2
 WGNS/IIMK WN3 ....15 J8
 WGNS/IIMK WN3 ....47 J8
 WGNS/IIMK WN3 ....63 J2
Warrington St AUL OL6 ....90 E1
 OLDE OL4 ....60 B7
 STLY SK15 ....91 L3
Warsall Rd WYTH/NTH M22 ...110 B5
Warslow Dr SALE M33 ....109 H3
Warsop Av WYTH/NTH M22 ....110 B2
Warstead Wk BRUN/LGST * M13 ..87M7
Warth Fold Rd RAD M26 ....38 F6
Warth Rd BURY BL9 ....38 F5
Warton Cl BRAM/HZG SK7 .....121 J5
 TOT/BURYW BL8 ....38 C3
Warton Dr NTHM/RTH M23 ....109 K7
Warwick Av AIMK WN4 ....79 G2
 DID/WITH M20 ....98 C8
 DTN/ASHW M34 ....101 J3
 SWIN M27 ....70 A2
 WHTF M45 ....55 L5
Warwick Cl CHD/CHDH SK8 ...111 K8
 DUK SK16 ....90 F6
 GLSP SK13 ....105 J4
 HTNM SK4 ....99M8
 MDTN M24 ....57 K7
 ROY/SHW OL2 ....43 C5
 TOT/BURYW BL8 ....24 D3
 TOT/BURYW BL8 ....24 E8
 WHTF M45 ....55 K5
Warwick Ct MDTN * M24 ....57 K4
 OLDTF/WHR M16 ....97 K1
 HALE/TIMP WA15 ......117 C3
 SALE M33 ....97 C8
 URM M41 ....84 E8
 WGNE/HIN WN2 ....49 J6
Warwick Gdns BOLS/LL BL3 ....51 L2
Warwick Gv DTN/ASHW M34 ....89M4
Warwick Rd ATH M46 ....50 F7
 AUL OL6 ....75M7
 CCHDY M21 ....97 L3
 FAIL M35 ....74 C7
 HALE/TIMP WA15 ......117 C3
 HTNM SK4 ....12 C1
 IRL M44 ....94 A7
 MDTN M24 ....57 L7
 MPL/ROM SK6 ....113 J2
 OLDTF/WHR M16 ....86 C7
 RAD M26 ....38 C6
 STRET M32 ....97 C7
 WALK M28 ....68 F3
 WGNE/HIN * WN2 ......32 F7
Warwick Rd South
 OLDTF/WHR M16 ....97 K1
Warwick St ANC M4 ....7 J3
 BOL BL1 ....22 B8
 CHAD OL9 ....58 C8
 HULME M15 ....87 H6
 LEIGH WN7 ....82 A1
 OLDE OL4 ....9 K4
 PWCH M25 ....55 K8
 ROY/SHW OL2 ....43 K8
 STKP SK1 ....13 K2
 STLY * SK15 ....91 K2
 WGN WN1 ....15 G3

URM M41 ....95 L1
Wasdale Dr CHD/CHDH SK8 ....119 K1
 MDTN M24 ....57 K1
Wasdale Rd AIMK WN4 ....63 K4
Wasdale Ter STLY SK15 ....76 D8
Wasdale Wk OLD OL1 ....9 L3
Washacre WHTN BL5 ....50 C5
Washacre Cl WHTN BL5 ....50 C5
Wash Brook CHAD OL9 ....58 E8
Washbrook Av WALK M28 ....68 E3
Washbrook Dr STRET M32 ......96 E3
Washburn Cl WGNE/HIN WN2 ...15M2
Washington Ct BURY BL9 ....5 G2
Washington St BOLS/LL BL3 ....35M6
 CHAD OL9 ....8 D5
 OLD OL1 ....8 F2
Wash La BURY BL9 ....25 J3
 BURY BL9 ....5 L5
 LEIGH WN7 ....66 F7
Wash Lane Ter BURY BL9 ....5 L4
Wash Ter TOT/BURYW BL8 ......24 E7
Washway Rd SALE M33 ....108 B3
Washwood Cl LHULT * M38 ......52 E6
Wasnidge Wk HULME * M15 .....87 J7
Wasp Av ROCH OL11 ....42 D1
Wastdale Av BURY BL9 ....55 K1
Wastdale Rd NTHM/RTH M23 ..109 J8
Waste St OLD * OL1 ....9M4
Wastwater St OLD OL1 ....9M4
Watburn Rd NM/HAY SK22 ....124 F3
Watchgate Cl MDTN M24 ....57 G1
Waterbeck St WGN WN1 ....15M2
Waterbridge WALK M28 ....69 K7
Watercroft ROCH OL11 ....27 G3
Waterdale Cl WALK M28 ....68 E7
Waterdale Dr WHTF M45 ....55 K4
Water Dr WGNNW/ST WN6 ......31 L5
Waterfield Wy FAIL M35 ....74 D6
Waterfold La BURY BL9 ....5 L7
Waterfoot Cottages HYDE SK14 ..92 B8
Waterford Av DID/WITH M20 ..110 A1
 MPL/ROM SK6 ....114 B2
Waterfront Quay SALO M50 .....86 C5
Watergate DTN/ASHW M34 .....89M4
Water Ga UPML OL3 ....61 L4
Watergate La WHTN BL5 ....51M5
Water Grove Rd DUK SK16 .....91 L6
Waterhouse Cl WHIT OL12 ......19 K7
Waterhouse Rd GTN M18 ....89 H8
Waterhouse St WHIT OL12 .....10 D3
Water La DROY M43 ....89 H3
 FWTH BL4 ....53 H5
 HYDE SK14 ....93 G7
 MILN OL16 ....29 K7
 RAMS BLO 17 D2
 WILM/AE SK9 ....126 E5
Water Lane St RAD M26 ....54 C1
Waterloo Ct BURY BL9 ....4 D8
Waterloo Gdns AUL OL6 ....76 B7
Waterloo Pl STKP * SK1 ....13 K5
Waterloo Rd AUL OL6 ....75 L7
 BKLY M9 ....73 G4
 BRAM/HZG SK7 ....121 H3
 CHH M8 ....72 B8
 MPL/ROM SK6 ....114 B2
 POY/DIS SK12 ....129 L2
 STKP SK1 ....13 K5
 STLY SK15 ....91 K2
Waterloo St AUL OL6 ....76 A8
 BOL BL1 ....2 F4
 CHH M8 ....72 F4
 CMANE M1 ....7 G6
 OLD OL1 ....9 K6
 TOT/BURYW BL8 ....14 B1
Watermans Cl BKLY M9 ....73 J4
 HOR/BR BL6 ....21 C8
Waterman Vw MILN OL16 ....11 K8
Watermead Cl EDGY/DAV SK3 .112 B8
Watermede WGNW/BIL/O WN5 ..62 B1
Watermeetings La
 MPL/ROM SK6 ....114 B2
Watermill Cl MILN OL16 ....29 G6
Watermill Ct AULW OL7 ....75 K7
Watermillock Gdns BOL BL1 ....36 C5
Waterpark Rd BRO M7 ....72 B4
Water's Edge FWTH BL4 ....52 D2
 MPL/ROM SK6 ....114 C7
Watersedge Cl CHD/CHDH SK8 .120 D1
Waters Edge Fold OLD OL1 ....43M8
Watersfield Cl CHD/CHDH SK8 .120 B4
Watersheddings St OLDE OL4 ...60 A3
Waterside GLSP SK13 ....93 K7
 HYDE SK14 ....103 C2
 MPL/ROM SK6 ....114 C7
 TRPK M17 ....86 C6
 UPML OL3 ....61M8
Waterside Av MPL/ROM SK6 ...114 C7
Waterside Cl CCHDY M21 ....98 A8
 HYDE SK14 ....103 C2
 OLD OL1 ....43M8
 RAD M26 ....39M8
Waterside Ct URM * M41 ....95 G2
Waterside Dr WGNS/IIMK WN3 ..14 B7
Waterside La MILN OL16 ....11 K3
Waterside Rd BURY BL9 ....24 F2
 POY/DIS SK12 ....124 A5
Waterslea ECC M30 ....85 G3
Waterslea Dr BOL BL1 ....35 J5
Watersmead Cl BOL BL1 ....36 C2
Watersmead St BOL BL1 ....36 C2
Watersmeet STRET M32 ....85M8
Waterson Av NEWH/MOS M40 ...73 K5
Waters Reach POY/DIS SK12 ...122 C6
 TRPK M17 ....86 C6
 WGN WN1 ....15M4
Water St ATH M46 ....67 G1
 AUL OL6 ....90 E1
 BKLY M9 ....73 G4
 BOL BL1 ....2 F4
 CSLFD M3 ....6 B6
 DTN/ASHW M34 ....90 C7
 EDGW/EG BL7 ....22 C2
 GLSP SK13 ....105 H2
 HYDE SK14 ....102 A1
 MDTN M24 ....57 J1
 MILN OL16 ....10 E5
 NEWLW WA12 ....78 E7
 RAD M26 ....39 H8
 ROY/SHW OL2 ....43 K8
 STKP SK1 ....13 G5
 STLY * SK15 ....91 K2
 WGN WN1 ....15 G3

WHIT OL12 ....18 C4
Waterton Av MOSL OL5 ....76 E2
Waterton La MOSL OL5 ....76 E2
Waterview Cl MILN OL16 ....43 L1
Waterview Pk LEIGH WN7 ....66 B8
Waterworks Dr NEWLW WA12 ...79 H1
 OLDE OL4 ....60 D3
 UPML OL3 ....45 K6
Watford Av RUSH/FAL M14 .....98 E2
Watford Bridge Rd
 NM/HAY SK22 ....124 F3
Watford La NM/HAY SK22 ......124 E2
Watford Rd NM/HAY SK22 .....124 F3
Watkin Av GLSP SK13 ....93 H8
Watkin Cl BRUN/LGST M13 .....87 L6
Watkins Dr PWCH M25 ....72 B1
Watkin St CSLFD M3 ....87 C1
 HYDE SK14 ....91 K7
 MILN OL16 ....28 D8
 WGN WN1 ....15 C3
Watling St TOT/BURYW BL8 ....23 J2
 TOT/BURYW BL8 ....38 C3
Watlington Cl OLD OL1 ....60 A1
Watson Av AIMK WN4 ....78 F1
 GOL/RIS/CU WA3 ....79 J3
Watson Gdns WHIT OL12 ....18 E4
Watson Rd FWTH BL4 ....52 C4
Watson Sq STKP SK1 ....13 K5
Watson St CMANW M2 ....6 E7
 DTN/ASHW M34 ....101 J1
 ECC M30 ....84 F2
 OLDE OL4 ....59M4
 RAD M26 ....38 D8
 SWIN M27 ....70 C3
Watton Cl SWIN * M27 ....70 C2
Watts St CHAD OL9 ....8 B4
 HOR/BR BL6 ....33 L2
 OLDS OL8 ....75 G2
 WHIT OL12 ....10 F2
Waugh Av FAIL M35 ....74 C6
Wavell Dr BURY BL9 ....55 K3
Wavell Rd WYTH/NTH M22 ....118 F2
Waveney Dr ALT WA14 ....107M6
 WILM/AE SK9 ....127 H2
Waveney Rd ROY/SHW OL2 .....43 K4
 WYTH/NTH M22 ....110 B8
Waverley Av WHIT OL12 ....10 D2
Waverley Av RUSH/FAL M14 ....53 J6
 STRET M32 ....97 H1
Waverley Crs DROY M43 ....89 K1
Waverley Dr CHD/CHDH SK8 ..120 D6
Waverley Gv LEIGH * WN7 ......67 C6
Waverley Rd BKLY M9 ....73 J5
 BOL BL1 ....36 B1
 EDGY/DAV SK3 ....12 C8
 GOL/RIS/CU WA3 ....80 A3
 HTNM SK4 ....10 A4
 MDTN M24 ....57 K1
 SALE M33 ....96 F6
 SWIN M27 ....70 F5
 WALK M28 ....68 E5
 WGNE/HIN WN2 ....48 F7
Waverley Rd West
 NEWH/MOS M40 ....73 J6
Waverley St OLD OL1 ....59 L4
 ROCH OL11 ....41M3
Waverton Av HTNM SK4 ....100 A5
Waverton Rd RUSH/FAL M14 ...98 D3
Wavertree Av ATH M46 ....50 F4
Wavertree Rd BKLY M9 ....56 F8
Wayfarers Wy SWIN M27 ....70 B5
Wayfaring WHTN BL5 ....50 C4
Wayland Rd GTN M18 ....100 A1
Wayland Rd South RDSH SK5 ..100 A1
Wayne Cl DROY M43 ....74 E8
Wayne St OP/CLY M11 ....89 H4
Wayoh Cft EDGW/EG BL7 ....16 C6
Wayside Dr POY/DIS SK12 .....121 L8
Wayside Gdns BRAM/HZG SK7 ..122 C2
Wayside Gv WALK M28 ....53 H8
Weald Cl BRUN/LGST M13 ......87M6
Wealdstone Gv BOL * BL1 ......36 E2
Weardale Rd BKLY M9 ....56 E7
Wearhead Cl GOL/RIS/CU WA3 ..79 K5
Wearish La WHTN BL5 ....49M6
Weaste Av LHULT M38 ....52 E8
Weaste Dr SLFD M6 ....86 A1
Weaste La ORD M5 ....86 A3
Weaste Rd ORD M5 ....86 A3
Weatherall St North BRO M7 .....72 C5
Weatherley Cl OLDS OL8 ....75 J3
Weatherley Dr MPL/ROM SK6 ..114 A6
Weaver Av WALK M28 ....68 D2
Weaver Cl ALT WA14 ....116 E3
Weaver Ct HULME * M15 ....87 G6
Weaver Dr BURY BL9 ....25 J4
Weaver Gv LEIGH WN7 ....65M8
Weaverham Cl BRUN/LGST M13 .99 J1
 MDTN M24 ....57 J3
Weavers Ct BOLS/LL BL3 ....2 B8
 MDTN M24 ....57 J3
Weavers Gn FWTH BL4 ....53 J7
Weavers La BRAM/HZG SK7 ...120 F6
Weavers Rd MDTN M24 ....57 J3
Webb Gv HYDE SK14 ....103 H3
Webb La STKP SK1 ....13M5
Webb St HOR/BR BL6 ....33M2
 TOT/BURYW BL8 ....4 B3
Webdale Dr NEWH/MOS M40 ....73 K5
Weber Dr BOLS/LL * BL3 ....2 B9
Webster Gv PWCH M25 ....71 J2
Webster's St WGNE/HIN WN2 ...64 D2
Webster St BOLS/LL BL3 ....3 J9
 MOSL OL5 ....76 F2
 OLDS OL8 ....9 J8
Wedgewood Dr
 WGNNW/ST WN6 ....47 C1
Wedgewood St
 NEWH/MOS M40 ....73 J8
Wedgwood Rd SWIN M27 ......70 E2
Wedhurst St OLDE * OL4 ....59M5
Weedall Av ORD M5 ....86 D6
Weedon Av NEWLW WA12 ....78 E7
Weedon St MILN OL16 ....28 C3
Weeton Av BOLE BL2 ....37 J5
Weighbridge Ct IRL M44 ....94 E1
Weir Rd MILN OL16 ....29 H5
Weir St FAIL M35 ....74 B5
Welbeck Av CHAD OL9 ....74 A1
 LIT OL15 ....20 B6
 URM M41 ....96 B1
Welbeck Cl MILN OL16 ....29 H6
 WHTF M45 ....55 J2
Welbeck Gv BRO M7 ....72 B5
Welbeck Rd AIMK WN4 ....63 L7
 BOL BL1 ....35 K4
 ECC M30 ....70 B8
 HYDE SK14 ....102 C2

MILN OL16 ....28 E8
RDSH SK5 ....100 C4
WALK M28 ....69 L6
WGNS/IIMK WN3 ....63 H1
Welbeck St GTN M18 ....89 G6
Welbeck St South AUL OL6 ....90 D2
Welburn Av WYTH/NTH M22 ....119 G1
Welburn St ROCH OL11 ....10 F8
Welbury Rd NTHM/RTH M23 ....109 J3
Welby St BRUN/LGST M13 ....88 A8
Welch Hill St LEIGH WN7 ....66 B8
Welch Rd HYDE SK14 ....91 J8
Welcomb Cl MPL/ROM SK6 ....101 J8
Welcomb St OP/CLY M11 ....88 E5
Welcome Pde OLDS 75 M1
Welcroft St STKP SK1 ....13 K6
Weldon Av BOLS/LL BL3 ....51 K2
Weldon Crs EDGY/DAV SK3 ....112 B8
Weldon Dr BKLY M9 ....57 C7
Weldon Gv WN1 WN1 ....48 B2
Weldon Rd ALT WA14 ....107 M6
Weld Rd DID/WITH M20 ....99 G5
Welford Av RUSH/FAL M14 ....79 M5
Welford Cl WILM/AE SK9 ....127 J4
Welford Gn RDSH SK5 ....100 C7
Welford St CHH M8 ....56 C8
Welford St SLFD M6 ....71 L8
Welkin Rd MPL/ROM SK6 ....112 F1
Wellacre Av URM M41 ....95 G2
Welland Av HEY OL10 ....40 C1
Welland Cl HULME * M15 ....87 C6
Welland Cl HULME M15 ....87 C6
Welland Rd AIMK WN4 ....
ROY/SHW OL2 ....43 K4
WILM/AE SK9 ....127 H2
Welland St OP/CLY M11 ....89 G4
RDSH SK5 ....100 C3
Wellbank PWCH * M25 ....71 J1
STLY SK15 ....91 M4
Wellbank Av BOLS/LL BL3 ....51 L1
OLDS OL8 ....59 K8
Wellbank St TOT/BURYW BL8 ....24 C6
Wellbank Vw WHIT OL12 ....27 J2
Wellbrooke Cl AIMK WN4 ....78 F1
Wellens Wy MDTN M24 ....56 F5
Weller Av CCHDY M21 ....98 A5
POY/DIS SK12 ....129 H2
Weller Cl POY/DIS SK12 ....129 H2
Wellesbourne Dr
NTHM/RTH M23 ....109 J5
Wellesley Av GTN M18 ....89 C6
Wellesley Cl NEWLW WA12 ....78 E7
WGNW/BIL/O WN5 ....47 H4
Wellfield Cl BURY BL9 ....39 H6
Wellfield La HALE/TIMP WA15 ....108 F8
Wellfield Pl ROCH * OL11 ....11 G9
Wellfield Rd BOLS/LL BL3 ....35 M7
CHH M8 ....72 D4
GOL/RIS/CU WA3 ....81 H8
NTHM/RTH M23 ....109 K5
OFTN SK2 ....112 F6
WGNE/HIN WN2 ....49 K8
WGNNW/ST WN6 ....31 J8
Wellfield St ROCH OL11 ....11 G9
Well Ga GLSP SK13 ....105 H2
Wellgate Av BNG/LEV M19 ....99 L4
Wellgreen Cl HALE/TIMP WA15 ....117 L1
Well Green Ldg
HALE/TIMP WA15 ....117 L1
Well Gv WHTF M45 ....55 H1
Wellham Rd WGNS/IIMK WN3 ....63 L1
Wellhead Cl HULME * M15 ....87 J7
Wellhouse Dr BKLY M9 ....73 M1
Well-i-Hole Rd OLDS 61 J8
Welling Rd NEWH/MOS M40 ....74 B4
Welling St BOL BL1 ....3 J1
Wellington Av OLDTF/WHR M16 ....98 A2
Wellington Cl SALE M33 ....96 C7
Wellington Clough AULW OL7 ....75 J6
Wellington Ct OLDS * OL8 ....59 C8
Wellington Crs
OLDTF/WHR M16 ....97 M1
Wellington Dr TYLD M29 ....68 B3
Wellington Gv HULME M15 ....87 C6
OFTN SK2 ....13 J9
WGNS/IIMK WN3 ....15 J9
Wellington Ms EDGW/EG BL7 ....16 D8
Wellington Pl ALT WA14 ....116 F1
MILN OL16 ....11 H3
Wellington Rd ATH M46 ....51 J7
AUL OL6 ....90 E1
BRAM/HZG SK7 ....122 D4
BURY BL9 ....4 F7
CHH M8 ....72 E4
ECC M30 ....85 H2
EDGW/EG BL7 ....16 D8
HALE/TIMP WA15 ....108 C6
OLDS OL8 ....58 F8
OLDTF/WHR M16 ....98 B2
RUSH/FAL M14 ....98 F5
SWIN M27 ....70 C4
UPML OL3 ....61 K6
Wellington Rd North HTNM SK4 ....99 L5
Wellington Rd South OFTN SK2....13 J8
Wellington Sq TOT/BURYW BL8 ....38 E3
Wellington St AUL OL6 ....90 E2
BOLS/LL BL3.. ....2 B6
BRAM/HZG SK7 ....122 B1
CHAD OL9 ....8 A3
CSLFD M3 ....6 B2
DTN/ASHW M34 ....90 C6
FAIL * M35 ....74 D3
FWTH BL4 ....53 C4
GTN M18 ....89 C7
HYDE SK14 ....101 M1
LIT OL15 ....20 C7
MILN OL16 ....29 K6
OLDE OL4 ....9 J7
RAD M26 ....38 F8
STKP SK1 ....13 H5
STRET M32 ....96 F3
TOT/BURYW BL8 ....24 B1
TOT/BURYW BL8 ....4 B6
WGN WN1 ....15 J4
WHIT OL12 ....10 F1
BOLS/LL BL3 ....50 B2
Wellington St East BRO M7 ....72 A5
Wellington St West BRO M7 ....72 A4
Wellington Ter ORD M5 ....86 A2
Wellington Vls TOT/BURYW BL8 ....38 E3
Wellington Wk BOLS/LL BL3 ....2 C6
Well I' Th' La ROCH OL11 ....11 G9
Well La WHTF M45 ....55 J2
Well Md MPL/ROM SK6 ....113 H1
Wellmead Cl CHH M8 ....72 C7
Well Meadow HYDE SK14 ....91 G8
Well Meadow La UPML OL3 ....61 M4
Wellock St NEWH/MOS M40 ....73 J6

Well Rw HYDE SK14 ....103 K4
Wells Cl CHAD OL9 ....58 D3
PWCH M25 ....71 M2
WGNW/BIL/O WN5 ....62 A7
Wells Cl CHD/CHDH SK8 ....119 L5
MDTN M24 ....56 F5
OP/CLY M11 ....89 J4
TYLD M29 ....67 L4
Wells Ct DUK SK16 ....90 F6
Wells Dr DUK SK16 ....90 F6
HTNM * SK4 ....111 H2
NEWH/HIN M40 ....48 C2
Wells Pl WGN WN1 ....15 L3
Wells Rd OLD OL1 ....44 B7
Wells St BURY BL9 ....4 D7
Well St BOL BL1 ....2 F4
BOLE BL2 ....37 M3
HEY OL10 ....41 H5
MAY/SK22 ....124 D4
ROCH OL11 ....11 H7
TYLD M29 ....67 K4
Well St West RAMS * BLO 17 B7
Wellwood Dr NEWH/MOS M40 ....73 K5
Wellyhole St OLDE OL4 ....60 B8
Welman Wy HALE/TIMP WA15 ....108 C8
Welney Rd OLDTF/WHR M16 ....97 L1
Welshpool Cl NTHM/RTH M23 ....109 L2
Welsh Rw MCFLDN SK10 ....130 D6
Weltdown Gdns ROY/SHW OL2 ....43 J4
Welton Av DID/WITH M20 ....110 F2
Welton Cl LEIGH WN7 ....66 F7
WILM/AE SK9 ....126 D8
Welton Dr WILM/AE SK9 ....126 C8
Welwyn Cl URM M41 ....84 F7
Welwyn Dr SLFD M6 ....70 D7
Welwyn Wk NEWH/MOS M40 ....88 A2
Wembley Av RUSH/FAL M14 ....98 F4
Wembley Rd GTN M18 ....88 F8
Wembury St BKLY * M9 ....73 H5
Wembury St North BKLY M9 ....73 H4
Wemsley Gv BOLE BL2 ....36 E3
Wem St CHAD OL9 ....58 D8
Wemyss Av RDSH SK5 ....100 C3
Wendlebury Cl LEIGH WN7 ....81 H3
Wendlebury Gn ROY/SHW OL2 ....43 K7
Wendon Rd NTHM/RTH M23 ....109 L7
Wendover Dr BOLS/LL BL3 ....35 H7
Wendover Rd NTHM/RTH M23 ....108 F5
URM M41 ....95 M2
Wenfield Dr BKLY M9 ....73 K1
Wenlock Av AUL OL6 ....75 L7
Wenlock Cl HOR/BR BL6 ....21 C6
OFTN SK2 ....113 K6
Wenlock Gv WGNE/HIN WN2 ....49 G8
Wenlock Rd LEIGH WN7 ....81 H2
SALE M33 ....108 D2
WGNE/HIN * WN2 ....49 G9
Wenlock St SWIN M27 ....70 A4
WGNE/HIN * WN2 ....49 J8
Wenlock Wy WGNS/LGST M12 ....88 D6
Wenning Cl WHTF M45 ....55 M3
Wensley Av
CHD/CHDH SK8 ....110 F6
Wensleydale Cl BURY BL9 ....55 K1
NTHM/RTH M23 ....118 B1
ROY/SHW OL2 ....42 F7
Wensleydale Rd LEIGH WN7 ....66 F7
Wensley Dr BRAM/HZG SK7 ....121 M5
DID/WITH M20 ....98 E7
Wensley Rd BRO M7 ....71 K3
CHD/CHDH SK8 ....110 F6
GOL/RIS/CU WA3 ....80 B5
RDSH SK5 ....100 C8
Wensley Wy MILN OL16 ....11 L6
Wentbridge Rd BOL BL1 ....2 B3
Wentworth Av FWTH BL4 ....52 F5
GTN M18 ....89 H7
HALE/TIMP WA15 ....108 D6
HEY OL10 ....41 G4
IRL * M44 ....94 D1
SLFD M6 ....85 M1
TOT/BURYW BL8 ....24 E8
WHTF M45 ....55 J3
Wentworth Cl MDTN M24 ....57 H4
MPL/ROM SK6 ....114 C4
RAD M26 ....38 A8
Wentworth Dr BRAM/HZG SK7 ....121 J5
SALE M33 ....96 C7
Wentworth Rd AIMK WN4 ....63 J8
ECC M30 ....85 H1
RDSH SK5 ....100 C3
SWIN M27 ....70 A6
Wenworth Av URM M41 ....95 L3
RUSH/FAL M14 ....98 F5
Werneth Av HYDE SK14 ....102 C4
Werneth Cl BRAM/HZG * SK7 ....113 H8
DTN/ASHW M34 ....101 J2
Werneth Crs OLDS 58 F8
Werneth Hall Rd OLDS OL8.. ....8 E9
Werneth Hollow
MPL/ROM SK6 ....101 L6
Werneth Low Rd
MPL/ROM SK6 ....102 A8
Werneth Ri HYDE SK14 ....102 C5
Werneth Rd GLSP SK13 ....104 D5
HYDE SK14 ....102 C2
MPL/ROM SK6 ....101 L6
Werneth St DTN/ASHW M34 ....90 C7
STKP SK1 ....13 J5
Wescoe Cl WGNW/BIL/O WN5 ....46 B7
Wesley Av RNFD/HAY WA11 ....78 B5
WHTN BL5 ....50 B2
Wesley Ct WALK * M28 ....53 G8
Wesley Dr AUL OL6 ....76 A6
WALK M28 ....69 J4
Wesley Gv ORD M5 ....86 E4
Wesley Ms BOLE * BL2 ....3 J5
Wesley St ATH * M46 ....67 H1
BOLS/LL BL3 ....2 C9
BRAM/HZG SK7 ....122 A1
ECC M30 ....84 F2
EDGW/EG BL7 ....16 D8
FAIL M35 ....74 D3
FWTH BL4 ....53 C4
GLSP SK13 ....93 K7
GLSP SK13 ....105 H2
HEY OL10 ....40 F2
MILN OL16 ....11 H4
OP/CLY M11 ....88 D4
ROY/SHW OL2 ....43 L6
STKP SK1 ....13 K5
STRET M32 ....96 F3
SWIN M27 ....70 C4
TOT/BURYW BL8 ....24 C1
WGNW/BIL/O WN5 ....47 G8
WHIT * OL12 ....28 E1

WHTN BL5 ....50 B2
Wessenden Bank East
OFTN SK2 ....113 G7
Wessenden Bank West
OFTN SK2 ....113 G7
Wessex Cl WGN WN1 ....31 L3
Wessex Park Cl ROY/SHW OL2 ....43 L4
Wessex Rd WGNW/BIL/O WN5 ....47 G3
Westage Gdns NTHM/RTH M23 ....109 K5
West Ashton St SALQ M50 ....86 C4
West Av ALT WA14 ....107 K7
BNG/LEV M19 ....99 J5
CHD/CHDH SK8 ....119 L3
FWTH BL4 ....52 E4
GOL/RIS/CU WA3 ....79 L3
GTN * M18 ....89 H7
LEIGH WN7 ....81 M1
NEWH/MOS M40 ....74 A3
STLY SK15 ....91 K2
WALK M28 ....68 F1
WHTF M45 ....55 H1
West Bank OP/CLY M11 ....89 K5
WILM/AE SK9 ....130 D4
Westbank Rd DID/WITH M20 ....99 G7
HOR/BR BL6 ....35 G6
West Bank St ATH M46 ....67 H3
ORD M5 ....86 F4
Westbourne Av BOLS/LL BL3 ....52 D1
FWTH BL4 ....54 A7
LEIGH WN7 ....66 C5
WHTF M45 ....55 C3
Westbourne Gv BKLY M9 ....73 G4
DID/WITH M20 ....98 D6
RDSH SK5 ....100 C4
SALE M33 ....96 D8
Westbourne Pk URM M41 ....96 A1
Westbourne Range GTN M18 ....100 C1
Westbourne Rd
DTN/ASHW M34 ....101 H2
ECC M30 ....69 L8
RUSH/FAL M14 ....99 G4
URM M41 ....96 A2
Westbourne St WGN WN1 ....15 C5
Westbridge Ms WGN WN1 ....15 C5
West Bridgewater St
LEIGH WN7 ....66 C8
Westbrook Cl BOLE BL2 ....3 G7
ROCH OL11 ....42 A4
Westbrook Ct BOLE * BL2 ....3 G7
Westbrook Rd SWIN M27 ....70 B5
TRPK M17 ....85 M5
Westbrook Sq WGTN/LGST M12 ....88 D6
Westbrook St BOLE BL2 ....3 H7
Westbury Av SALE M33 ....107 M3
WGNS/IIMK WN3 ....63 C2
Westbury Cl TOT/BURYW BL8 ....38 D3
WHTN BL5 ....50 D3
Westbury Dr MPL/ROM SK6 ....114 B6
Westbury Rd CHH M8 ....72 D3
Westbury St AUL OL6 ....90 F1
HYDE SK14 ....90 F7
Westbury Wy ROY/SHW OL2 ....59 G2
Westby Cl BRAM/HZG SK7 ....121 J5
Westby Gv BOLE BL2 ....3 K3
West Canteen Rd TRPK M17 ....85 M8
West Central Dr SWIN M27 ....70 B6
West Charles St ORD M5 ....86 E3
West Church St HEY OL10 ....40 F2
Westcliffe Rd BOL BL1 ....22 C6
West Cl ATH M46 ....67 H3
Westcombe Dr TOT/BURYW BL8 ....24 F8
Westcott Cl BOLE BL2 ....23 H7
Westcott Dr WGNS/IIMK WN3 ....46 F8
Westcott Gv ROY/SHW OL2 ....43 K7
Westcourt Rd BOLS/LL BL3 ....52 A1
SALE M33 ....96 D7
Westcraig Av NEWH/MOS M40 ....73 M1
West Craven St ORD M5 ....86 E5
Westcroft Rd DID/WITH M20 ....99 C8
West Crown Av ORD M5 ....86 E4
Westdale Gdns BNG/LEV M19 ....99 K7
Westdean Crs BNG/LEV M19 ....99 J7
West Dean St ORD M5 ....86 F3
West Downs Rd
CHD/CHDH SK8 ....120 B1
West Dr BURY BL9 ....25 H7
CHD/CHDH SK8 ....110 D8
DROY M43 ....89 J3
GLSP SK13 ....93 H6
SLFD M6 ....71 H6
SWIN M27 ....70 E5
West Duke St ORD M5 ....6 A5
West Egerton St ORD M5 ....86 E3
West End Av CHD/CHDH SK8 ....110 D6
West End St CHAD OL9 ....8 F5
Westend St FWTH BL4 ....52 E4
Westerdale OLDE OL4 ....59 M6
Westerdale Cl TYLD M29 ....67 L4
Westerdale Dr BOLS/LL BL3 ....35 K7
ROY/SHW OL2 ....42 F7
Westerham Av ORD M5 ....86 D3
Westerham Cl TOT/BURYW BL8 ....24 E5
Wester Hill Rd OLDS OL8 ....75 K3
Westerling Wy OLDTF/WHR M16 ....98 B1
Western Access TRPK * M17 ....85 J4
Western Av SWIN M27 ....71 G2
Western Cir BNG/LEV M19 ....99 J6
Western Rd URM M41 ....95 H3
Western St GTN M18 ....89 H6
SLFD M6 ....86 B1
Westerton Ct BOLS/LL BL3 ....2 A8
Westfield AIMK WN4 ....63 K8
Westfield Av AIMK WN4 ....63 K8
MDTN M24 ....57 K5
Westfield Cl ROCH OL11 ....11 K8
Westfield Dr MPL/ROM SK6 ....101 M7
Westfield Gv DTN/ASHW M34 ....90 B7
WGN WN1 ....47 L1
Westfield Rd BOLS/LL BL3 ....51 L2
CCHDY M21 ....97 L3
CHD/CHDH SK8 ....120 B4
DROY M43 ....89 H2
Westfields HALE/TIMP WA15 ....117 H4
Westfield St BRO M7 ....72 A3
CHAD OL9 ....8 C2
Westgate HALE/TIMP WA15 ....117 G2
SALE M33 ....96 D8
URM M41 ....95 J3
WHIT OL12 ....18 C5
WILM/AE SK9 ....126 E7
Westgate Av BKLY * M9 ....72 F2
BOL BL1 ....35 M5
BURY BL9 ....4 D7
RAMS BLO 24 C2
Westgate Cl WHIT OL12 ....18 C5
Westgate Dr SWIN M27 ....70 C6
TYLD M29 ....67 M6
WGNW/BIL/O WN5 ....46 A7

Westgate Rd SLFD M6 ....70 E8
Westgate St AULW OL7 ....90 D3
West Gn MDTN M24 ....56 E5
West Gv BRUN/LGST M13 ....88 A7
MOSL SK15 ....76 F4
OLDE OL4 ....60 B8
WHTN BL5 ....50 B6
Westgrove Av BOL * BL1 ....22 B6
Westhead Av GOL/RIS/CU WA3 ....80 B4
West High St ORD M5 ....86 D2
Westholme Ct WILM/AE SK9 ....130 D2
Westholme Rd DID/WITH M20 ....98 E7
WHTF M45 ....55 M5
West Hope St ORD M5 ....86 E3
Westhulme Av OLD OL1 ....8 E1
Westhulme St OLD OL1 ....8 E1
Westhulme Wy OLD OL1 ....58 F3
Westinghouse Cl
WGNNW/ST WN6 ....14 C4
Westinghouse Rd TRPK M17 ....85 L6
West King St CSLFD M3 ....6 C2
Westlake Gv WGNE/HIN WN2 ....49 L8
Westland Av BOL BL1 ....35 K3
FWTH BL4 ....52 F6
STKP * SK1 ....112 E3
The Westlands SWIN M27 ....70 E6
Westlands WHTF M45 ....55 J6
West Lea DTN/ASHW M34 ....101 K1
Westlea Dr GTN M18 ....100 A1
Westleigh Dr PWCH M25 ....72 A1
Westleigh La LEIGH WN7 ....66 A2
Westleigh St BKLY M9 ....73 H3
Westlock WGNS/IIMK WN3 ....14 E8
Westmarsh Cl BOL BL1 ....2 D1
West Marwood St BRO M7 ....72 B6
Westmead WGNNW/ST WN6 ....31 H4
Westmead Dr CHH M8 ....72 B7
HALE/TIMP WA15 ....108 C5
West Meade BOLS/LL BL3 ....52 B2
CCHDY M21 ....97 K5
PWCH * M25 ....72 A2
SWIN M27 ....70 B6
Westmeade Rd WALK M28 ....52 F7
West Meadow RDSH SK5 ....100 D3
Westmere Dr BKLY M9 ....72 F6
Westminster Av AUL OL6 ....76 A5
FWTH BL4 ....52 F4
HTNM SK4 ....99 M2
OLDTF/WHR M16 ....97 M2
RAD M26 ....38 A9
ROY/SHW OL2 ....42 F6
WHTF M45 ....55 J3
Westminster Cl FWTH * SK5 ....100 F6
SALE M33 ....108 A1
Westminster Dr
CHD/CHDH SK8 ....120 D6
LEIGH WN7 ....67 H6
RNFD/HAY WA11 ....78 C5
WILM/AE SK9 ....126 D8
Westminster Rd BOL BL1 ....22 B7
ECC M30 ....85 H1
FAIL M35 ....74 E4
HALE/TIMP WA15 ....117 J1
URM M41 ....85 G8
WALK M28 ....69 G2
Westminster St BNG/LEV * M19 ....99 L3
BURY BL9 ....4 E7
FWTH BL4 ....52 F4
HULME * M15 ....86 F5
OLD OL1 ....59 L4
ROCH OL11 ....10 A7
SWIN M27 ....70 A3
WGNW/BIL/O * WN5 ....47 J6
Westminster Wy DUK SK16 ....90 F6
Westmoorland St WGN WN1 ....15 K7
Westmoreland Cl ALT WA14 ....116 D4
BURY BL9 ....39 H6
Westmorland Av AULW OL7 ....75 K8
DUK SK16 ....91 H4
Westmorland Cl BURY * SK5 ....100 F6
Westmorland Dr RDSH SK5 ....100 E6
WHIT OL12 ....19 L6
Westmorland Rd
DID/WITH M20 ....110 D2
ECC M30 ....70 D7
PART M31 ....106 B2
SALE M33 ....108 F2
TYLD M29 ....67 K2
URM M41 ....95 M3
West Mosley St CMANW M2 ....7 G4
West Mt WGN WN1 ....48 A2
WGNW/BIL/O WN5 ....46 C6
Westmount Cl NEWH/MOS M40 ....74 B8
West Oak Pl CHD/CHDH * SK8 ....120 B3
Weston Av MILN OL16 ....28 E8
NEWH/MOS M40 ....74 B3
SWIN M27 ....54 C8
URM M41 ....95 J3
Westonby Ct AIMK WN4 ....79 G1
Weston Dr CHD/CHDH SK8 ....112 A8
DTN/ASHW M34 ....101 K1
Weston Gv HTNM SK4 ....99 M6
WYTH/NTH M22 ....110 B4
Weston Pk WGNNW/ST WN6 ....47 G1
Weston Rd IRL M44 ....94 D2
WILM/AE SK9 ....127 H6
Weston St ATH M46 ....51 H8
BOLS/LL BL3.. ....36 C8
MILN OL16 ....29 J6
NEWH/MOS * M40 ....88 A2
RDSH * SK5 ....100 B8
Westover MPL/ROM SK6 ....113 K4
Westover Rd URM M41 ....95 M1
Westover St SWIN M27 ....70 B4
West Pk HYDE SK14 ....102 B5
West Pk Av DTN/ASHW M34 ....101 L2
POY/DIS SK12 ....121 J8
West Park Rd BRAM/HZG SK7 ....122 C4
STKP SK1 ....112 E2
West Park St BRO M7 ....86 E5
West Pl BNG/LEV M19 ....99 J5
Westray Crs SLFD * M6 ....86 B3
Westray Rd BRUN/LGST M13 ....99 H2
Westrees LEIGH WN7 ....66 D5
West Rd ALT WA14 ....116 D4
PWCH M25 ....55 J7
STRET M32 ....85 K8
West Rw PWCH M25 ....71 J3
West Starkey St HEY OL10 ....40 F1
West St AUL OL6 ....90 E3
BOL BL1 ....35 M5
CHAD OL9 ....8 B6
DUK SK16 ....90 E3
EDGY/DAV SK3 ....12 E5
FAIL M35 ....74 B5
FWTH BL4 ....53 H3

GLSP SK13 ....93 J5
HEY OL10 ....41 G2
HYDE * SK14 ....91 G7
MDTN M24 ....57 K2
MILN OL16 ....11 G9
OLD OL1 ....9 H5
OLDE OL4 ....60 B7
OP/CLY M11 ....88 D4
RAMS * BLO 17 B7
STLY SK15 ....91 J4
WGNE/HIN WN2 ....48 D4
WGNE/HIN WN2 ....65 L1
WGNNW/ST WN6 ....14 D2
West V RAD M26 ....38 D7
West Vale Rd HALE/TIMP WA15 ....108 C7
West Vw LIT OL15 ....20 D7
RAMS BLO 17 C2
WILM/AE * SK9 ....126 C5
West View Gv WHTF M45 ....55 H1
West View Rd WYTH/NTH M22 ....110 B4
Westville Gdns BNG/LEV M19 ....99 H1
West Wk EDGW/EG BL7 ....22 A2
Westward Ho MILN OL16 ....29 J6
Westward Rd WILM/AE SK9 ....126 D6
West Wy BOL BL1 ....35 M5
LHULT M38 ....52 D7
Westway BKLY M9 ....56 F5
DROY M43 ....89 K5
OLDE OL4 ....60 B7
ROY/SHW OL2 ....43 L6
Westwell Gv LEIGH WN7 ....66 B4
Westwell St LEIGH WN7 ....66 B4
Westwood Av BRO M7 ....72 B4
HALE/TIMP WA15 ....108 C5
HYDE SK14 ....102 C1
URM M41 ....96 C3
WALK M28 ....68 D2
Westwood Crs ECC M30 ....69 L8
Westwood Dr CHAD OL9 ....58 E2
SALE M33 ....108 E2
SWIN M27 ....70 B6
Westwood La WGNS/IIMK WN3 ....15 H9
Westwood Rd BOL BL1 ....35 M4
CHD/CHDH SK8 ....119 K4
OFTN SK2 ....112 E8
STRET M32 ....96 E2
WGNS/IIMK * WN3 ....15 J9
Westwood St RUSH/FAL M14 ....87 J8
Westwood Ter
WGNS/IIMK * WN3 ....15 K9
West Works Rd TRPK M17 ....85 M8
Westworth Cl BOL BL1 ....2 B2
Wetheral Cl WGNE/HIN WN2 ....65 M1
Wetheral Dr BOLS/LL BL3 ....52 B1
Wetherall St BNG/LEV M19 ....99 L3
Wetherby Cl NEWLW WA12 ....78 F7
Wetherby Dr BRAM/HZG * SK7 ....122 F7
ROY/SHW OL2 ....42 F7
Wetherby St OP/CLY M11 ....89 G2
Wexham Gdns WGNE/HIN WN2....64 D1
Weybourne Av BKLY M9 ....56 B6
Weybourne Dr MPL/ROM SK6 ....101 J8
WGNS/IIMK * WN3 ....15 K9
Weybourne Gv BOLE BL2 ....22 E8
Weybridge Rd ANC M4 ....7 M3
Weybrook Rd HTNM SK4 ....99 L5
Weycroft Cl BOLE BL2 ....37 K6
Wey Gates Dr
HALE/TIMP WA15 ....117 L6
Weyhill Rd NTHM/RTH M23 ....109 K8
Weylands Gv SLFD M6 ....70 D6
Weymouth Dr WGNE/HIN WN2 ....49 K8
Weymouth Rd AUL OL6 ....76 B6
ECC M30 ....84 E1
Weymouth St BOL BL1 ....36 B7
Weythorne Dr BOL BL1 ....22 C8
BURY BL9 ....38 D2
Whalley Av BNG/LEV M19 ....99 L2
BOL BL1 ....35 J1
CCHDY M21 ....97 M5
GOL/RIS/CU WA3 ....81 M5
LIT OL15 ....20 A1
OLDTF/WHR M16 ....98 A1
SALE M33 ....96 F2
URM M41 ....96 B1
Whalley Cl HALE/TIMP WA15 ....108 C4
MILN * OL16 ....29 H6
WGNS/IIMK WN3 ....55 J3
WHTF M45 ....55 J3
Whalley Dr TOT/BURYW BL8 ....38 C2
Whalley Gdns WHIT OL12 ....27 L3
Whalley Gv AUL OL6 ....75 M5
LEIGH WN7 ....66 A3
OLDTF/WHR M16 ....98 A1
Whalley Rd HALE/TIMP WA15 ....117 J2
HEY OL10 ....40 D2
MDTN M24 ....57 J1
OFTN SK2 ....112 F5
OLDTF/WHR M16 ....98 A1
RAMS BLO 17 L3
WHIT OL12 ....27 L3
Whalley St NEWH/MOS M40 ....88 A2
Wham Bar Dr HEY OL10 ....40 D2
Wham Bottom La WHIT OL12 ....18 D3
Wham La UPML OL3 ....45 G3
Wham St HEY OL10 ....40 D2
Wharf Cl CMANE M1 ....7 K5
Wharfedale WHTN BL5 ....50 C2
Wharfedale Av NEWH/MOS M40 ....73 K3
Wharfedale Rd RDSH SK5 ....100 D4
Wharf End TRPK M17 ....85 L7
Wharf Rd ALT WA14 ....108 A5
SALE M33 ....96 F7
Wharfside Av ECC M30 ....85 G2
Wharfside Wy (Trafford Park Rd)
TRPK M17 ....85 G3
Wharf St CHAD OL9 ....74 E1
DUK SK16 ....90 D3
HTNM SK4 ....13 H1
Wharmby Rd RNFD/HAY WA11 ....78 B2
Wharmton Ri OLDE OL4 ....61 G6
Wharmton Vw MOSL OL5 ....77 G1
UPML OL3 ....61 K6
Wharncliffe Cl GLSP SK13 ....93 H8
Wharncliffe St
WGNE/HIN * WN2 ....49 G7
Wharton Av CCHDY M21 ....98 A5
Wharton Hall Cl TYLD M29 ....67 H2
Wharton La LHULT M38 ....52 A8
Wharton Ldg ECC M30 ....69 L8
Wheat Cl BRUN/LGST M13 ....87 M7
Wheat Cft EDGY/DAV SK3 ....112 C7

Wheatcroft GLSP SK13 ....93 H8
Wheater's Crs BRO M7 ....71 M4
Wheater's St BRO M7 ....72 A8
Wheater's Ter BRO M7 ....72 A8
Wheatfield STLY SK15 ....92 B5
MPL/ROM SK6 ....101 K8
Wheatfield Crs ROY/SHW OL2 ....58 F1
Wheatfield St BOLE BL2 ....3 K8
Wheathill St ROCH OL11 ....28 D8
Wheatlea Rd WGNS/IIMK WN3 ....63 J3
Wheatley Av NEWLW WA12 ....78 F7
Wheatley Rd SWIN M27 ....70 A2
Wheatley Wk WGTN/LGST M12 ....88 C6
Wheatsheaf Wk
WGNNW/ST WN6 ....31 G3
Wheeldale OLDE OL4 ....60 A6
Wheeldale CI BOL BL1 ....36 B2
Wheelock CI WILM/AE SK9 ....127 H5
Wheelton CI TOT/BURYW BL8 ....38 C6
Wheelwright CI MPL/ROM SK6 ....114 C4
ROCH * OL11 ....27 L8
Wheelwright Dr MILN OL16 ....28 F1
Whelan Av BURY BL9 ....39 H5
Whelan CI BURY BL9 ....39 H5
Wheler St OP/CLY M11 ....89 G4
Whelley WGN WN1 ....48 B2
Whernside Av AUL OL6 ....75 M5
NEWH/MOS M40 ....73 K3
Whetmorhurst Rd
MPL/ROM SK6 ....115 H8
Whetstone Hill CI OLD OL1 ....59 M2
Whetstone Hill La OLD OL1 ....59 M3
Whetstone Hill Rd OLD OL1 ....59 L2
Whewell Av RAD M26 ....39 G7
Whickham Rd RUSH/FAL M14 ....98 E1
Whiley St BRUN/LGST M13 ....88 C8
Whimberry Dr STLY SK15 ....77 G7
Whimberry Rd OFTN SK2 ....113 K7
TYLD M29 ....67 M5
Whinberry Rd ALT WA14 ....107 L5
Whinberry Wy OLDE OL4 ....44 B8
Whinchat Av NEWLW WA12 ....78 F9
Whinchat CI GOL/RIS/CU WA3 ....80 B5
OFTN SK2 ....113 K8
Whinfell Dr WGNNW/ST WN6 ....56 E3
Whinfield CI WGNNW/ST WN6 ....14 C4
Whins Av FWTH BL4 ....52 B4
Whins Crest HOR/BR BL6 ....34 F5
Whinslee Dr HOR/BR BL6 ....34 F5
Whinstone Wy OLD OL1 ....58 B3
Whipp St HEY OL10 ....40 E1
Whirley CI HTNM SK4 ....100 A7
Whistlecroft Ct
WGNS/IIMK WN3 ....15 M8
Whistley St WGNE/HIN WN2 ....64 E1
Whiston Dr BOLE BL2 ....3 L7
Whiston Rd CHH M8 ....72 E4
Whitaker St MDTN M24 ....57 J4
Whitbeam CI WGNE/HIN WN2 ....65 H2
Whitbrook Wy MDTN M24 ....41 M7
Whitburn Av BRUN/LGST M13 ....99 H2
Whitburn CI AIMK WN4 ....63 G8
BOLS/LL BL3 ....35 H8
Whitburn Dr TOT/BURYW BL8 ....24 F7
Whitburn Rd NTHM/RTH M23 ....109 K8
Whitby Av HEY OL10 ....40 F1
OLDTF/WHR M16 ....98 A1
RUSH/FAL M14 ....99 H4
SLFD M6 ....85 M1
URM M41 ....96 B2
Whitby CI CHD/CHDH SK8 ....110 F6
POY/DIS SK12 ....121 L7
TOT/BURYW BL8 ....38 C2
Whitby Rd OLDS OL8 ....75 M1
RUSH/FAL M14 ....99 C4
ROCH OL11 ....11 G8
Whitchurch Dr
OLDTF/WHR M16 ....87 G7
Whitchurch Gdns BOL BL1 ....36 B2
Whitchurch Rd DID/WITH M20 ....98 C5
Whitchurch St BRO M7 ....87 H1
Whiteacre WGNNW/ST WN6 ....30 B2
Whiteacre Rd AUL OL6 ....76 A8
Whiteacres SWIN M27 ....69 M5
White Bank Av RDSH SK5 ....100 F8
White Bank Rd OLDS OL8 ....75 G3
Whitebarn Rd WILM/AE SK9 ....130 E4
Whitebeam CI
HALE/TIMP WA15 ....109 H7
MILN OL16 ....43 K1
SLFD M6 ....86 D1
Whitebeam Ct SLFD * M6 ....86 D1
Whitebeam Wk WHTN BL5 ....50 C2
White Birk CI TOT/BURYW BL8 ....24 C2
White Brook La UPML OL3 ....61 M4
Whitebrook Rd RUSH/FAL M14 ....98 E3
White Carr La BURY BL9 ....25 K3
Whitecarr Av NEWH/MOS M40 ....74 B3
Whitechapel St DID/WITH M20 ....110 E1
White City Wy OLDTF/WHR M16 ....86 D7
Whitecliff CI RUSH/FAL M14 ....98 F1
Whitecroft Av GOL/RIS/CU WA3 ....80 B3
ROY/SHW OL2 ....44 A5
Whitecroft Dr TOT/BURYW BL8 ....38 C2
Whitecroft Gdns BNG/LEV M19 ....99 H8
Whitecroft Rd BOL BL1 ....35 K3
Whitecroft St OLD OL1 ....59 M3
Whitefield HTNM SK4 ....112 A1
Whitefield Av ROCH OL11 ....27 J4
Whitefield Rd BURY BL9 ....39 H5
MPL/ROM SK6 ....114 C1
SALE M33 ....96 C7
Whitegate BOLS/LL BL3 ....50 F2
LIT OL15 ....19 M8
Whitegate Av CHAD OL9 ....58 C8
Whitegate Av NEWH/MOS M40 ....74 B3
Whitegate Dr BOL BL1 ....22 C7
ORD M5 ....86 A1
SWIN M27 ....70 E2
Whitegate La CHAD OL9 ....58 C8
Whitegate Pk URM M41 ....95 H2
Whitegate Rd CHAD OL9 ....74 A1
Whitegates CI
HALE/TIMP WA15 ....108 D2
Whitegates La OLDE OL4 ....60 E2
Whitegates Rd CHD/CHDH SK8 ....111 G7
MDTN M24 ....41 M8
Whitehall Av WGNE/HIN WN2 ....30 B4
Whitehall CI WILM/AE SK9 ....126 E7
Whitehall La BOL BL1 ....22 A6
HOR/BR BL6 ....33 G1
OLDE OL4 ....44 C8
Whitehall Rd DID/WITH M20 ....110 F1

SALE M33 ....108 E2
WGNS/IIMK WN3 ....15 K8
WHIT OL12 ....10 E1
White Hart Meadow MDTN M24 ....57 K2
White Hart La HYDE SK14 ....91 G8
Whitehaven Gdns
DID/WITH M20 ....110 D2
Whitehaven Rd
BRAM/HZG SK7 ....120 E7
Whitehead Crs RAD M26 ....53 L5
TOT/BURYW BL8 ....24 F7
Whitehead Rd CCHDY M21 ....97 J4
SWIN M27 ....70 E2
Whitehead St MILN * OL16 ....29 H6
ROY/SHW OL2 ....43 J4
WALK M28 ....53 G8
White Hill CI AUL OL6 ....18 E8
Whitehill Dr NEWH/MOS M40 ....73 K5
Whitehill St HTNM SK4 ....100 B8
Whitehill St West HTNM SK4 ....100 A8
Whiteholme Av CCHDY M21 ....98 A8
Whitehope CI BOLS/LL BL3 ....2 C7
White Horse CI HOR/BR BL6 ....21 C7
White Horse Gdns SWIN * M27 ....69 M6
White Horse Gv WHTN BL5 ....50 D2
White Horse Mdw MILN * OL16 ....42 F2
White House Av CHH M8 ....72 B1
White House CI OLDE OL4 ....59 M7
White House CI HEY OL10 ....41 G5
Whitehouse Dr
HALE/TIMP WA15 ....117 K4
NTHM/RTH M23 ....109 K7
Whitehouse La ALT WA14 ....107 C5
Whitehurst Rd HTNM SK4 ....99 J8
Whitekirk CI BRUN/LGST M13 ....87 L6
White Lady CI WALK M28 ....68 C1
Whitelake Av URM M41 ....95 J1
Whitelake Vw URM M41 ....95 H1
Whiteland Av BOLS/LL BL3 ....35 L7
Whitelands DUK SK16 ....90 F2
Whitelands Rd AUL OL6 ....90 F2
Whitelea Dr EDGY/DAV SK3 ....112 A7
Whitelees Rd LIT OL15 ....20 B7
Whitelegge St TOT/BURYW BL8 ....24 E8
Whiteley Dr MDTN M24 ....57 M5
Whiteley PI ALT WA14 ....108 A6
Whiteley St CHAD OL9 ....58 E8
OP/CLY M11 ....88 E2
White Lion Brow BOL BL1 ....2 C4
White Lodge AIMK WN4 ....64 A8
Whitelow Rd CCHDY M21 ....97 M4
HTNM SK4 ....111 K1
RAMS BL0 ....17 E7
Whitemead St DTN/ASHW M34 ....90 C5
Whitemoss WHIT * OL12 ....27 L2
White Moss Av CCHDY M21 ....97 M4
White Moss Rd BURY BL9 ....73 H1
White Moss Rd East BKLY M9 ....57 J8
Whiteoak CI MPL/ROM SK6 ....114 B5
Whiteoak Rd RUSH/FAL M14 ....98 F4
Whiteoak Vw BOLS/LL BL3 ....37 G7
White Rd NM/HAY SK22 ....124 C3
Whites Cft NEWH/MOS M40 ....70 C4
Whiteside Av WGNE/HIN WN2 ....49 G5
WGNNW/ST WN6 ....14 B1
Whiteside CI ORD M5 ....86 A2
Whiteside Fold WHIT OL12 ....27 K3
Whitesmead CI POY/DIS SK12 ....123 M7
Whitestone CI HOR/BR BL6 ....35 G6
Whitestone Wk
BRUN/LGST * M13 ....88 A7
White St HULME M15 ....87 G6
LEIGH WN7 ....66 F8
SLFD M6 ....86 B3
TOT/BURYW BL8 ....38 E3
WGNW/BIL/O WN5 ....46 B6
White Swallows Rd SWIN M27 ....70 D6
Whitethorn Av BNG/LEV M19 ....99 K5
OLDTF/WHR M16 ....98 A1
Whitethorn CI MPL/ROM SK6 ....114 B5
Whitewater Dr BRO M7 ....71 J5
Whiteway St BKLY M9 ....73 H5
Whitewell CI BURY BL9 ....39 G5
MILN OL16 ....11 L2
Whitewillow CI FAIL M35 ....74 D6
Whitewood CI AIMK WN4 ....63 K6
Whitfield Av GLSP SK13 ....104 F5
Whitfield Crs MILN OL16 ....43 L1
Whitfield Cross GLSP SK13 ....105 C5
Whitfield Dr MILN OL16 ....29 H7
Whitfield Ri ROY/SHW OL2 ....43 K3
Whitfield St CSLFD M3 ....87 K1
LEIGH WN7 ....66 F8
Whitford Wk NEWH/MOS M40 ....88 A1
Whiting Gv BOLS/LL BL3 ....35 H6
Whitland Av BOL BL1 ....35 J4
Whitland Dr OLDS OL8 ....74 E2
Whit La SLFD M6 ....71 J6
Whitledge Gn AIMK WN4 ....63 K7
Whitledge Rd AIMK WN4 ....63 K7
Whitle Rd NM/HAY SK22 ....124 E3
Whitley Crs WGN WN1 ....31 L8
WGNE/HIN WN2 ....64 E5
Whitley Gdns
HALE/TIMP WA15 ....108 E5
Whitley PI HALE/TIMP WA15 ....108 E5
Whitley Rd HTNM SK4 ....111 H1
NEWH/MOS M40 ....72 F8
Whitley St BOLS/LL BL3 ....53 G2
Whitlow Av ALT WA14 ....107 L4
GOL/RIS/CU WA3 ....79 J3
Whitman St BKLY M9 ....73 J4
Whitmore Av AUL OL6 ....76 A8
Whitnall St HYDE * SK14 ....91 G7
Whitnall St HYDE * SK14 ....91 G7
Whitsand Rd WYTH/NTH M22 ....110 B7
Whitsbury Av GTN M18 ....100 A1
WGNE/HIN WN2 ....49 G8
Whitstable CI CHAD OL9 ....8 B7
Whitstable Rd
NEWH/MOS * M40 ....73 M3
Whitsters Hollow BOL BL1 ....35 L1
Whitsundale WHTN BL5 ....50 B4
Whittaker Dr LIT OL15 ....29 J2
Whittaker La LIT OL15 ....20 E8
PWCH M25 ....55 M8
ROCH OL11 ....27 G3
Whittaker St CHAD OL9 ....8 A1
NEWH/MOS M40 ....73 K4
RAD M26 ....38 E8
ROCH * OL11 ....27 H3
WGTN/LGST M12 ....88 A4
Whittingham Dr RAMS BL0 ....17 C3
Whittingham Gv OLD * OL1 ....8 F7
Whittington St AULW OL7 ....90 D3
Whittlebank Rd NM/HAY SK22 ....124 D2
Whittle CI WGNS/IIMK WN3 ....63 H2
Whittle Dr ROY/SHW OL2 ....44 A4

WALK M28 ....53 G7
WALK M28 ....69 H1
Whittle Gv BOL BL1 ....35 L3
WALK M28 ....69 H1
Whittle HI EDGW/EG BL7 ....22 B1
Whittle La HEY OL10 ....39 L4
Whittles Av DTN/ASHW M34 ....101 K1
Whittle's Cft CMANE * M1 ....7 K5
Whittle St ANC * M4 ....7 J3
LIT OL15 ....20 A7
SWIN M27 ....70 B5
TOT/BURYW BL8 ....4 A2
WALK M28 ....69 H1
Whitwell Wy GTN M18 ....88 F7
Whitworth La RUSH/FAL M14 ....99 C3
Whitworth Rake WHIT OL12 ....18 E4
Whitworth Rd WHIT OL12 ....28 C2
Whitworth Sq WHIT OL12 ....18 E4
Whitworth St CMANE M1 ....7 H7
HOR/BR BL6 ....33 K2
MILN * OL16 ....28 F2
OP/CLY M11 ....29 J6
Whitworth St East OP/CLY M11 ....88 E5
Whitworth St West CMANE M1 ....6 E7
Whixhall Av WGTN/LGST M12 ....88 B6
Whoolden St FWTH BL4 ....52 F3
Whowell Fold BOL BL1 ....35 M1
Whowell St BOLS/LL BL3 ....2 C7
Wibbersley Pk URM * M41 ....95 J2
Wichbrook Rd WALK M28 ....68 C1
Wicheaves Crs WALK M28 ....68 C1
The Wicheries LHULT M38 ....68 C1
Wicken Bank HEY OL10 ....41 H5
Wickenby Dr SALE M33 ....96 D8
Wicken St OFTN SK2 ....112 F5
Wickentree Holt WHIT OL12 ....27 K2
Wickentree La FAIL M35 ....74 D3
Wicker La HALE/TIMP WA15 ....117 K4
Wicket Gv SWIN M27 ....54 B8
Wickliffe PI ROCH OL11 ....10 E6
Wickliffe St BOL * BL1 ....2 D3
Wicklow Av EDGY/DAV SK3 ....12 A8
Wicklow Dr WYTH/NTH M22 ....119 C2
Wicklow Gv OLDE OL4 ....75 H1
Widcombe Dr BOLS/LL BL3 ....37 J7
Widdop CI POY/DIS SK12 ....121 K8
RUSH/FAL M14 ....98 E4
Widdow's St LEIGH WN7 ....66 E8
Widdrington Dr WGN WN1 ....48 A2
Widecombe CI URM * M41 ....84 E8
Widgeon CI POY/DIS SK12 ....121 K8
RUSH/FAL M14 ....98 E4
Widgeon Rd ALT WA14 ....107 L4
Widnes St OP/CLY * M11 ....88 F5
Wiend WGN WN1 ....15 G4
Wigan Av WGN WN1 ....15 G1
WGN WN1 ....31 L7
Wigan Lower Rd
WGNNW/ST WN6 ....30 F8
Wigan Pier WGNS/IIMK * WN3 ....14 D8
Wigan Rd AIMK WN4 ....63 J6
ATH M46 ....66 C2
BOLS/LL BL3 ....35 K8
GOL/RIS/CU WA3 ....79 L1
LEIGH WN7 ....65 M5
WGNE/HIN WN2 ....48 C2
WGNNW/ST WN6 ....30 E7
WGNNW/ST WN6 ....31 J5
WGNW/BIL/O WN5 ....62 C5
WHTN BL5 ....49 K5
Wigan Sq WGN * WN1 ....14 F3
Wiggins Wk RUSH/FAL M14 ....98 F1
Wightman Av NEWLW WA12 ....78 F7
Wigley St WGTN/LGST M12 ....88 B5
Wigmore Rd CHH M8 ....72 E5
Wigmore St AUL OL6 ....76 A8
Wigsby Av NEWH/MOS M40 ....73 M3
Wigshaw CI LEIGH WN7 ....81 J3
Wigwam CI POY/DIS SK12 ....121 L8
Wike St TOT/BURYW BL8 ....4 B3
Wilbraham Rd CCHDY M21 ....97 L4
OLDTF/WHR M16 ....98 B3
WALK M28 ....69 C1
Wilbraham St LEIGH WN7 ....65 M7
WHTN BL5 ....50 C4
Wilburn St ORD M5 ....6 A6
Wilby Av BOLS/LL BL3 ....37 K7
Wilby CI TOT/BURYW * BL8 ....25 G7
Wilby St CHH M8 ....72 E6
Wilcock CI OLDTF/WHR M16 ....87 H8
Wilcock Rd RNFD/HAY WA11 ....78 C4
Wilcock St WGNS/IIMK WN3 ....14 C5
Wilcott Dr SALE M33 ....96 E7
Wilcott Rd CHD/CHDH SK8 ....110 D7
Wild Arum CI GOL/RIS/CU WA3 ....80 B4
Wildbank Cha STLY SK15 ....92 B5
Wildbrook CI LHULT M38 ....68 B1
Wildbrook Crs OLDS OL8 ....75 K1
Wildbrook Gv LHULT M38 ....68 B1
Wildbrook Rd LHULT M38 ....52 B8
Wildbrook Ter OLDS * OL8 ....75 K1
Wildcroft Av NEWH/MOS M40 ....73 K3
Wilderswood Av HOR/BR BL6 ....21 D8
Wilderswood CI DID/WITH M20 ....98 F7
Wilderswood Ct HOR/BR BL6 ....21 D8
Wilde St DTN/ASHW M34 ....101 J1
Wildhouse La LIT OL15 ....29 J1
Wilding St WGNS/IIMK WN3 ....15 K8
Wildman La FWTH BL4 ....52 C4
Wildmoor Av OLDE OL4 ....60 B8
Wilds Pas LEIGH * WN7 ....66 C8
Wilds PI RAMS * BL0 ....17 B7
Wild St BRAM/HZG * SK7 ....121 M2
DUK SK16 ....91 G4
HEY OL10 ....41 H2
MPL/ROM SK6 ....113 J2
OFTN SK2 ....112 D6
OLD OL1 ....9 M4
OLDE OL4 ....60 B6
ROY/SHW OL2 ....43 M6
Wildwood CI RAMS BL0 ....17 A8
Wilford Av SALE M33 ....108 D2
Wilfred Dr BURY BL9 ....5 K1
Wilfred Rd ECC M30 ....84 D4
WALK M28 ....69 C2
Wilfred St EDGW/EG * BL7 ....22 D5
NEWH/MOS M40 ....73 K4
WGNW/BIL/O WN5 ....47 J5
Wilfrid's PI WGNNW/ST WN6 ....31 J8
Wilfrid St SWIN M27 ....70 C4
Wilkesley Av WGNNW/ST WN6 ....31 J8
Wilkes St OLD OL1 ....60 A1
Wilkin Cft CHD/CHDH SK8 ....120 A3
Wilkins La WILM/AE SK9 ....119 C1
Wilkinson Av BOLS/LL BL3 ....37 K8
Wilkinson Rd BOL BL1 ....22 A7

HTNM SK4 ....13 C2
HTNM SK4 ....13 C2
LEIGH WN7 ....66 B7
MDTN M24 ....57 J4
SALE M33 ....97 C8
Wilkinson St AUL OL6 ....90 D1
HTNM SK4 ....13 C2
LEIGH WN7 ....66 B7
MDTN M24 ....57 J4
SALE M33 ....97 C8
Wilks Av WYTH/NTH M22 ....119 H2
Willand CI BOLE BL2 ....37 K6
Willand Dr BOLE BL2 ....37 K7
Willan Rd BKLY M9 ....56 F8
ECC M30 ....85 H2
Willard Av WGNW/BIL/O WN5 ....62 A1
Willard St BRAM/HZG * SK7 ....121 M1
Willaston CI CCHDY M21 ....97 K5
Willbutts La ROCH OL11 ....27 M4
Willdale CI OP/CLY M11 ....88 D2
Willdor Gv EDGY/DAV SK3 ....111 L6
Willenhall Rd NTHM/RTH M23 ....109 M2
Willerby Rd BRO M7 ....72 B7
Willesden Av BRUN/LGST M13 ....99 H1
Will Griffith Wk OP/CLY M11 ....88 D4
William Chadwick CI
NEWH/MOS M40 ....87 M1
William CI URM M41 ....95 M3
William Greenwood CI
HEY OL10 ....40 F2
William Henry St ROCH OL11 ....28 D8
William Jessop Ct CMANE M1 ....7 L5
William Kay CI HULME M15 ....87 H8
William Lister CI
NEWH/MOS * M40 ....74 A8
Williams Crs CHAD OL9 ....74 C1
Williamson Av MPL/ROM SK6 ....101 K8
RAD M26 ....38 C6
Williamson La DROY M43 ....89 L4
AUL OL6 ....90 C2
RDSH SK5 ....100 B5
Williamson's Yd OLD * OL1 ....59 L5
Williams Rd GTN M18 ....88 F7
NEWH/MOS M40 ....73 L5
GTN M18 ....88 F8
Williams St BOLS/LL BL3 ....53 L1
William St AULW OL7 ....90 C2
CSLFD M3 ....74 D3
DID/WITH M20 ....110 E1
FAIL M35 ....74 D3
HOR/BR BL6 ....33 K1
LEIGH WN7 ....66 D7
LIT OL15 ....20 B7
MDTN M24 ....57 L4
MILN OL16 ....19 L8
RAD M26 ....38 E8
RAMS BL0 ....17 C3
ROCH OL11 ....10 E7
STKP SK1 ....112 E5
William St AULW OL7 ....90 C2
CSLFD M3 ....7 K1
Williams Williamson ....
Willingcott CI TOT/BURYW BL8 ....24 F5
Willingdon Dr PWCH M25 ....56 C1
Willis Rd EDGY/DAV SK3 ....112 B6
Willis St BOLS/LL BL3 ....35 M8
Willock St BRO M7 ....72 B6
Willoughby Av DID/WITH M20 ....98 F8
Willoughby CI SALE M33 ....96 D7
Willow Av CHD/CHDH SK8 ....120 B2
MDTN M24 ....57 M5
NEWLW WA12 ....79 C8
RDSH SK5 ....100 C8
TYLD M29 ....67 K6
URM M41 ....96 B2
Willow Bank CHD/CHDH SK8 ....120 C6
OLDE OL4 ....60 B4
RUSH/FAL M14 ....98 F4
Willowbank RAD M26 ....54 D4
Willowbank Av BOLE BL2 ....3 K7
Willow Bank CI OFTN SK2 ....113 C5
Willowbrook Av
NEWH/MOS M40 ....73 K5
Willowbrook Dr
WGNNW/ST WN6 ....30 E5
Willow CI BOLS/LL BL3 ....35 L8
DUK SK16 ....91 J5
POY/DIS SK12 ....129 J1
Willow Ct MPL/ROM SK6 ....114 C7
SALE M33 ....97 H7
Willow Crs LEIGH WN7 ....66 B4
Willowdale Av CHD/CHDH SK8 ....119 K2
Willowdene CI EDGW/EG BL7 ....22 C4
NEWH/MOS M40 ....88 A1
Willow Dr SALE M33 ....108 D2
WGNE/HIN WN2 ....65 J1
WILM/AE SK9 ....127 H1
Willowfield Gv AIMK WN4 ....78 D2
Willowfield Rd OLDE OL4 ....60 A2
Willow Fold DROY M43 ....89 L4
Willow Gv AIMK WN4 ....64 B7
CHAD OL9 ....58 C8
DTN/ASHW M34 ....101 H1
GOL/RIS/CU WA3 ....79 K3
GTN * M18 ....89 H8
MPL/ROM SK6 ....114 C7
Willow Hill Rd CHH M8 ....72 D2
Willow Lawn CHD/CHDH * SK8 ....120 C2
Willow Ldg WGNE/HIN WN2 ....64 E3
Willowmead Wy WHIT OL12 ....27 K2
Willowmoss CI WALK M28 ....69 H3
Willow Ri LIT OL15 ....15 K8
Willow Rd ECC M30 ....69 K8
MPL/ROM SK6 ....123 H5
NEWLW WA12 ....79 C8
PART M31 ....106 B2
PWCH M25 ....55 K6
RNFD/HAY WA11 ....78 B5
UPML OL3 ....61 K5
WGNNW/ST WN6 ....31 J8
The Willows BOLE BL2 ....37 K7
CCHDY M21 ....97 K5
MOSL OL5 ....77 H3
PART M31 ....106 C1
Willows End STLY SK15 ....92 A1
Willows La BOLS/LL BL3 ....35 C8
MILN OL16 ....29 G6
Willow St ATH M46 ....50 F8
BURY BL9 ....5 L4
CHH M8 ....72 B8
HEY OL10 ....41 G2
OLD OL1 ....9 M4
OP/CLY M11 ....88 D2
SWIN M27 ....70 A7
WALK M28 ....69 H5
Willow Tree CI WGN WN1 ....31 L6
Willow Tree Ms CHD/CHDH SK8 ....119 K3
Willow Tree Rd ALT WA14 ....116 F2

Willow Wy BRAM/HZG SK7 ....120 E5
DID/WITH M20 ....110 E5
Willow Wood CI AUL OL6 ....91 H1
Wilma St BKLY M9 ....56 F8
Wilmans Wk GLSP SK13 ....93 K6
Wilmcote CI HOR/BR BL6 ....35 C6
Wilmcote Rd NEWH/MOS M40 ....72 F8
Wilmot Dr GOL/RIS/CU WA3 ....79 J3
Wilmot St BOL BL1 ....35 M1
Wilmott St HULME M15 ....6 F9
Wilmslow Av BOL BL1 ....22 B7
Wilmslow Old Rd
HALE/TIMP WA15 ....118 B6
MCFLDN SK10 ....131 K3
Wilmslow Park Rd
WILM/AE SK9 ....127 C5
Wilmslow Rd BRAM/HZG SK7 ....127 M8
CHD/CHDH SK8 ....111 C8
CHD/CHDH SK8 ....119 M1
CHD/CHDH SK8 ....119 M4
DID/WITH M20 ....98 E5
DID/WITH M20 ....110 F3
HALE/TIMP WA15 ....118 B6
MCFLDN SK10 ....127 L8
MCFLDN SK10 ....128 A6
MCFLDN SK10 ....131 M3
WILM/AE SK9 ....119 M7
WILM/AE SK9 ....130 C2
Wilmur Av BRO M7 ....72 B6
WHTF M45 ....55 K5
Wilpshire Av WGTN/LGST M12 ....99 L1
Wilsford CI GOL/RIS/CU WA3 ....79 L3
Wilsham Rd WGNW/BIL/O WN5 ....46 D7
Wilshaw Gv AULW OL7 ....75 L6
Wilshaw La AULW OL7 ....75 K7
Wilson Av HEY OL10 ....40 D7
SWIN M27 ....70 E2
WGNNW/ST WN6 ....47 L2
Wilson Crs AUL OL6 ....76 B8
Wilson Fold Av HOR/BR BL6 ....34 C3
Wilson Rd BKLY M9 ....73 C3
HTNM SK4 ....99 L8
Wilsons Pk NEWH/MOS * M40 ....73 H7
Wilson St BOL * BL1 ....2 E6
BRUN/LGST M13 ....87 M6
BURY BL9 ....5 H6
FWTH BL4 ....53 H4
HOR/BR BL6 ....21 A8
HYDE SK14 ....102 B2
OLDS OL8 ....59 H8
OP/CLY M11 ....88 C4
RAD M26 ....38 C6
STRET M32 ....86 B8
UPML OL3 ....61 K7
WHIT OL12 ....10 E2
Wilson Wy OLD OL1 ....9 J4
Wilsthorpe CI BNG/LEV M19 ....99 M6
Wilton Av CHD/CHDH SK8 ....119 L5
OLDTF/WHR M16 ....97 K1
PWCH M25 ....72 A2
SWIN M27 ....70 F5
WGNE/HIN WN2 ....48 C2
Wilton Ct DTN/ASHW M34 ....89 K8
Wilton Crs WILM/AE SK9 ....130 C2
Wilton Dr BURY BL9 ....39 K7
HALE/TIMP WA15 ....117 L4
Wilton Gdns RAD M26 ....38 F7
Wilton Gv DTN/ASHW M34 ....89 K8
HEY OL10 ....41 C3
Wilton La GOL/RIS/CU WA3 ....80 D7
Wilton Paddock
DTN/ASHW M34 ....89 K8
Wilton PI CSLFD M3 ....6 A3
Wilton Rd BOL BL1 ....22 B7
CCHDY M21 ....97 L4
CHH M8 ....72 D2
SLFD M6 ....70 B8
WGNNW/ST WN6 ....30 D6
Wilton St AIMK WN4 ....63 J6
BOL BL1 ....36 C1
CHAD OL9 ....74 E1
DTN/ASHW M34 ....90 B8
HEY OL10 ....40 F2
MDTN M24 ....56 E5
PWCH M25 ....55 M8
RDSH SK5 ....100 C8
WGN WN1 ....15 H6
WHTF M45 ....55 J5
Wilton Ter WHIT OL12 ....10 C2
Wiltshire Av RDSH SK5 ....100 F3
Wiltshire CI BURY BL9 ....5 H8
Wiltshire Dr GLSP SK13 ....105 C4
Wiltshire PI WGNW/BIL/O WN5 ....46 F6
Wiltshire Rd CHAD OL9 ....8 B7
FAIL M35 ....74 C6
PART M31 ....106 B2
Wiltshire St BRO M7 ....72 B6
Wimberry Hill Rd WHTN BL5 ....50 A1
Wimbledon Dr EDGY/DAV SK3 ....111 M6
ROCH OL11 ....10 B9
Wimbledon Rd FAIL M35 ....74 E4
Wimborne Av URM M41 ....85 C9
Wimborne CI CHD/CHDH SK8 ....111 M8
HOR/BR BL6 ....34 C3
Wimborne Rd
WGNW/BIL/O WN5 ....46 D4
Wimpole St AUL OL6 ....90 F1
OLD OL1 ....9 L2
Wimpory St OP/CLY M11 ....89 C5
Winbolt St OFTN SK2 ....112 F8
Winby St ROCH OL11 ....11 H9
Wincanton Av NTHM/RTH M23 ....109 J4
Wincanton Dr BOL BL1 ....22 A5
Wincanton Pk OLDE OL4 ....60 A6
Wince CI MDTN M24 ....57 M6
Wincham CI HULME M15 ....87 C6
Wincham Rd SALE M33 ....108 B2
Winchcombe CI LEIGH WN7 ....81 H3
Winchester Av AIMK WN4 ....78 D1
AUL OL6 ....76 A5
CHAD OL9 ....58 C3
DTN/ASHW M34 ....101 J3
HEY OL10 ....40 F4
PWCH M25 ....71 M2
TYLD M29 ....67 M5
Winchester CI ROCH OL11 ....27 J5
TOT/BURYW BL8 ....24 F5
WGNNW/ST WN6 ....46 C5
WILM/AE SK9 ....126 C7
Winchester Gv HTNM SK4 ....12 B2
SALE M33 ....96 A8
Winchester Rd WGNS/IIMK WN3 ....15 J8
Winchester Pk DID/WITH M20 ....110 C1
Winchester Rd DUK SK16 ....91 K5
ECC M30 ....70 D8
HALE/TIMP WA15 ....117 L3
RAD M26 ....38 A7
RNFD/HAY WA11 ....78 B3
URM M41 ....96 A1

WGNW/BIL/O WN5 ....62 A3
Winchester Wy BOLE BL2 .....37 G3
Wincle Av POY/DIS SK12 .....129 K2
Wincombe St RUSH/FAL M14 ..98 E2
Windale WALK M28 ....68 E1
Winder Dr ANC M4 ....7 M4
Windermere Av ATH M46 ......51 G7
　BOLS/LL BL3 ....37 K8
　DTN/ASHW M34 ....100 D2
　SALE M33 ....109 G1
　SWIN M27 ....70 D5
Windermere CI OP/CLY M11 ...88 C4
　PWCH M25 ....55 H7
　STRET M32 ....96 F1
Windermere Crs AULW * OL7 ..75 J8
Windermere Dr BURY BL9 .....59 H5
　RAMS BL0 ....17 C5
　WILM/AE SK9 ....130 C3
Windermere Gv WHTN WN7 .....66 B7
Windermere Rd FWTH BL4 .....52 B5
　HYDE SK14 ....90 F7
　LEIGH WN7 ....66 B7
　MDTN M24 ....56 F2
　MPL/ROM SK6 ....122 F3
　ROY/SHW OL2 ....43 C5
　STKP SK1 ....112 E5
　STLY SK15 ....91 K1
　URM * M41 ....95 M3
　WGNE/HIN WN2 ....48 D5
　WGNE/HIN WN2 ....49 H7
　WGNE/HIN WN2 ....64 E4
　WGNW/BIL/O WN5 ....46 C4
　WILM/AE SK9 ....119 L8
Windermere St BOL BL1 ......36 C1
　WGN WN1 ....15 K2
Winders Wy SLFD M6 ....71 L8
Windfields CI CHD/CHDH SK8 120 D1
Windgate Ri STLY SK15 ......77 G7
Windham St MILN OL16 ....28 F1
Windle Av CHH M8 ....72 C1
Windle Ct OFTN SK2 ....113 H7
Windlehurst Dr WALK M28 ....68 E5
Windlehurst Old Rd
　MPL/ROM SK6 ....123 H2
Windlehurst Rd MPL/ROM SK6 122 F4
Windleshaw St WGNS/IIMK WN3 ..15 K8
Windley St BOLE BL2 ....3 H2
Windmill Av ORD M5 ....86 E5
Windmill CI DTN/ASHW M34 ..100 D2
　WALK M28 ....52 F7
　WGN WN1 ....15 J3
Windmill Ct MILN OL16 ......11 J6
Windmill La RDSH SK5 ......100 D3
　TYLD M29 ....67 J8
Windmill La SALE * M33 ....109 J1
　WALK M28 ....52 F7
Windmill St CMANW M2 ....6 E6
　MILN OL16 ....11 J6
Windover CI BOLS/LL BL3 ....51 K5
Windover St BOLS/LL BL3 ....35 K8
The Windmill WHIT OL12 .....18 D8
Windrush Av RAMS BL0 ....24 D2
Windrush Dr BKLY M9 ....73 G5
　WHTN BL5 ....50 C3
Windsor Av BOLS/LL BL3 .....53 K1
　CHAD OL9 ....58 D8
　CHD/CHDH SK8 ....110 C7
　FAIL M35 ....74 E4
　HEY OL10 ....40 E2
　HTNM SK4 ....111 K1
　IRL M44 ....94 E1
　LHULT M38 ....52 E7
　SALE M33 ....96 E6
　SWIN M27 ....70 D2
　TYLD M29 ....67 K6
　URM M41 ....95 J2
　WHTF M45 ....55 K5
　WILM/AE SK9 ....126 D6
Windsor CI POY/DIS SK12 ...121 M8
　TOT/BURYW BL8 ....24 D3
Windsor Crs WGNE/HIN WN2 ...33 C7
Windsor Dr ALT WA14 ....116 B3
　ALT WA14 ....116 B3
　AULW OL7 ....75 J8
　DTN/ASHW M34 ....90 A3
　DUK SK16 ....91 J5
　HOR/BR BL6 ....34 B2
　MPL/ROM SK6 ....114 B7
　RNFD/HAY WA11 ....78 D5
　STLY SK15 ....91 K1
　TOT/BURYW BL8 ....38 E4
Windsor Gv AUL OL6 ....75 M5
　BOL BL1 ....35 M3
　CHD/CHDH SK8 ....120 B4
　MPL/ROM SK6 ....114 B2
　RAD M26 ....53 L5
　WGNE/HIN WN2 ....65 L1
Windsor Rd AIMK WN4 ....78 E2
　BKLY M9 ....73 H5
　BNG/LEV M19 ....99 J3
　BRAM/HZG SK7 ....122 E3
　DROY M43 ....89 G2
　DTN/ASHW M34 ....100 D1
　EDGW/EG BL7 ....22 D5
　GOL/RIS/CU WA3 ....79 M4
　HYDE SK14 ....102 A5
　LEIGH WN7 ....67 H6
　MPL/ROM SK6 ....112 F1
　NEWH/MOS M40 ....74 B8
　OLDS OL8 ....8 E8
　PWCH M25 ....72 B1
　WGNW/BIL/O WN5 ....62 C7
Windsor St ATH M46 ....67 H2
　FAIL M35 ....74 D4
　GTN M18 ....89 F8
　NEWH/MOS M40 ....74 B8
　OFTN SK2 ....112 D6
　OLD OL1 ....59 K3
　ORD M5 ....86 E3
　ROCH OL11 ....11 G9
　WGN WN1 ....15 J2
Windsor Ter MILN OL16 ......11 M4
Windybank BKLY M9 ....56 F7
Windy Bank Av
　GOL/RIS/CU WA3 ....80 B4
Windy Harbour La
　EDGW/EG BL7 ....22 E4
Windyhill Dr BOLS/LL BL3 ...51 K1
Winfell Dr NEWH/MOS M40 ....88 A1
Winfield Av DID/WITH M20 ...99 J3
Winfield Dr GTN M18 ....89 G6
Winfield Gv MPL/ROM SK6 ...114 E3
Winfield St HYDE SK14 .....102 C2
Winford St NEWH/MOS M40 ....73 H4
Wingate Av TOT/BURYW BL8 ...38 E2
Wingate Dr DID/WITH M20 ...110 F2
　HALE/TIMP WA15 ....108 D7

WHTF M45 ....55 H3
Wingates Gv WHTN BL5 ....50 A1
Wingates La WHTN BL5 ....34 B8
Wingates Rd WGN WN1 ....31 M7
Wingates Sq WHTN BL5 ....50 B1
Wingate St ROCH OL11 ....27 G3
Wingfield Av WILM/AE SK9 ..126 C6
Wingfield CI WGNNW/ST WN6 ..31 K8
Wingfield Dr SWIN M27 ......70 D6
Wingfield Gv GLSP SK13 ....105 J5
Wingfield St STRET M32 .....86 A8
Wings Gv HEY OL10 ....41 G5
Winhill Rd NM/HAY SK22 ....121 J8
Winifred Av BURY BL9 ....26 C8
Winifred Rd DID/WITH M20 ..110 E1
　FWTH BL4 ....52 D3
　NEWH/MOS M40 ....73 L5
　OFTN SK2 ....112 D7
　URM M41 ....95 M1
Winifred St ECC M30 ....84 E3
　HYDE SK14 ....102 B5
　RAMS BL0 ....17 B7
　WGNS/IIMK WN3 ....15 K8
　WHIT OL12 ....27 L3
Winmarith Dr
　HALE/TIMP WA15 ....117 M5
Winmarleigh CI
　TOT/BURYW BL8 ....38 C3
Winmarleigh Gdns LEIGH WN7 ..81 H1
Winnats CI GLSP SK13 ......105 J4
Winnie St NEWH/MOS M40 .....74 A3
Winning Hill CI GTN M18 ....89 G8
Winnington Gn OFTN SK2 ....113 C7
Winnington Rd MPL/ROM SK6 114 C4
Winnipeg Quay SALQ M50 .....86 F5
The Winnows DTN/ASHW M34 ..101 G1
Winscar Rd WGNE/HIN WN2 ....71 G8
Winscombe Dr NEWH/MOS M40 ..72 F8
Winser St CMANE M1 ....7 G7
Winsfield Rd BRAM/HZG SK7 121 M4
Winsford CI RNFD/HAY WA11 ..78 B4
Winsford Dr ROCH OL11 ......27 J7
Winsford Gv BOLS/LL BL3 ....35 J7
Winsford Rd RUSH/FAL M14 ...98 D3
Winskill Rd IRL M44 ....94 D5
Winslade CI BRAM/HZG SK7 ..121 J2
　OLDE OL4 ....60 A3
Winslade Ms FWTH BL4 ....53 G3
Winsley Rd NTHM/RTH M23 ...109 J2
Winslow Av POY/DIS SK14 ...103 J2
Winslow PI BNG/LEV M19 .....99 J6
Winslow Rd BOLS/LL BL3 .....50 F2
Winslow St OP/CLY M11 ......88 D4
Winsmoor Dr WGNE/HIN WN2 ...48 A7
Winstanley PI WGNS/IIMK WN3 ..15 K8
Winstanley Rd AIMK WN4 .....62 E5
　NEWH/MOS M40 ....88 A1
　SALE M33 ....96 C4
　WGNE/HIN WN2 ....64 C4
　WGNW/BIL/O WN5 ....62 C1
Winstanley St
　NEWH/MOS M40 ....14 A7
Winster Av BRO M7 ....71 L6
　DID/WITH M20 ....98 B8
　STRET M32 ....96 D1
Winster CI BOLE BL2 ....37 J3
　WHTF M45 ....55 L4
Winster Dr BOLE BL2 ....37 H3
　MDTN M24 ....57 H2
　WGNE/HIN WN2 ....64 C2
Winster Gv OFTN SK2 ....112 D6
Winster Rd ECC M30 ....84 E4
Winston Av BOLS/LL BL3 .....53 M1
　ROCH OL11 ....27 H6
Winston CI MPL/ROM SK6 ....114 A5
　RAD M26 ....38 B7
Winston Rd BKLY M9 ....73 J3
　SALE M33 ....96 C7
Winswell St OP/CLY M11 .....88 E2
Winterbottom Gv HYDE SK14 .103 J2
Winterbottom St CHAD OL9 ....8 F5
Winterburn Av BOLE BL2 .....22 E6
　CCHDY M21 ....97 H8
Winterdyne St BKLY M9 ......73 H3
Winterfield Dr BOLS/LL BL3 .51 K1
Winterford Av BRUN/LGST M13 ..88 A7
Winterford Rd CHH M8 ....72 C5
　MOSL OL5 ....77 H3
Winter Hey La HOR/BR BL6 ...33 L1
Wintermans Rd CCHDY M21 ....98 A3
Winterslow Av
　NTHM/RTH M23 ....109 G3
Winter St BOL BL1 ....36 A1
Winterton CI WHTN BL5 ......50 D3
Winterton Rd RDSH SK5 .....100 D3
Winthrop Av NEWH/MOS M40 ...73 K7
Winton Av DTN/ASHW M34 .....90 A5
　NEWH/MOS M40 ....74 A3
　WGNW/BIL/O WN5 ....47 G7
Winton CI BRAM/HZG SK7 ....120 E3
Winton Gn HOR/BR BL6 ....34 C4
Winton Gv BOLS/LL BL3 ......35 H8
Winton Rd ALT WA14 ....116 E2
　GOL/RIS/CU WA3 ....80 B7
　SLFD M6 ....71 G6
Winton St AUL OL6 ....90 L1
　LIT OL15 ....20 C7
　STLY SK15 ....91 L3
Winward St BOLS/LL * BL3 ...35 K8
　LEIGH WN7 ....65 L7
　WHTN BL5 ....50 B3
Winwick La GOL/RIS/CU WA3 ..80 B8
Winwood Rd DID/WITH M20 ...110 F4
Winwood Rd NM/HAY SK22 ....124 D5
Wirral CI SWIN * M27 ....70 D2
Wirral Crs EDGY/DAV SK3 ...111 K4
Wirral Dr WGNS/IIMK WN3 ....62 F2
Wirral St NTHM/RTH M23 ....109 J3
Wisbeck Rd BOLE BL2 ....3 M3
Wiseley St OP/CLY M11 ......88 B4
Wiseman Ter PWCH M25 ....55 M8
Wishaw Sq CCHDY M21 ....98 B6
Wisley CI RDSH SK5 ....100 C4
Wistaria Rd GTN M18 ....89 G7
Witham CI WHYTH/NTH M22 ...110 B7
Witham CI HEY OL10 ....40 D1
　WGNNW/ST WN6 ....31 H3
Witham St AUL OL6 ....76 B8
Withenfield Rd
　NTHM/RTH M23 ....109 J4
Withens Gn OFTN SK2 ....113 H6
Withington Av GOL/RIS/CU WA3 ..81 K8
Withington Dr TYLD M29 .....67 M5
Withington Gra WGNE/HIN WN2 ..48 E2
Withington Gn MDTN M24 .....41 M8

FWTH BL4 ....52 F6
　SALE M33 ....96 D6
Woodfield Ms HYDE * SK14 ..102 A4
　MIL/ROM SK6 ....101 L7
　OFTN SK2 ....112 F4
　CHD/CHDH SK8 ....120 D5
　CHH M8 ....72 D3
　MDTN M24 ....57 H6
　SLFD M6 ....71 G8
Woodfield St BOLS/LL BL3 ...52 D1
　WGNE/HIN WN2 ....48 D1
Wood Fold BOLE BL2 ....22 F6
Woodfold Av BNG/LEV M19 ....99 K2
Woodfold Rd FAIL M35 ....74 D4
Woodford Av DTN/ASHW M34 ...90 D8
　ECC M30 ....84 E2
　GOL/RIS/CU WA3 ....80 A5
　ROY/SHW OL2 ....44 A5
Woodford Dr SWIN M27 ....70 B2
Woodford Gdns
　DID/WITH M20 ....110 D2
Woodford Gv BOLS/LL BL3 ....35 M8
Woodford La MCFLDN SK10 ...128 A6
Woodford St BRAM/HZG SK7 ..121 F7
　POY/DIS SK12 ....121 K7
　WILM/AE SK9 ....127 M4
Woodford St WGNE/HIN WN2 ..49 H6
　WGNW/BIL/O WN5 ....46 E6
Wood Gdns NM/HAY SK22 ....125 L1
Woodgarth LEIGH * WN7 .....65 M7
Woodgarth Av NEWH/MOS M40 ..74 A7
Woodgarth Dr SWIN M27 .....70 B6
Woodgarth La WALK M28 .....69 J7
Woodgate Av BURY BL9 ......26 A8
　ROCH OL11 ....27 K6
Woodgate CI MPL/ROM SK6 ..113 J1
Woodgate Dr PWCH M25 ......55 M6
Woodgate Hill Rd BURY BL9 ..5 M2
Woodgate Rd OLDTF/WHR M16 ..98 B3
Woodgate St BOLS/LL BL3 ...52 D1
Woodgrange CI SLFD M6 .....86 B2
Woodgreen CI WGNE/HIN WN2 ..49 G8
Woodgreen Dr RAD M26 ......54 D4
Wood Gv DTN/ASHW M34 ......90 C8
　MPL/ROM SK6 ....101 K7
　WHTF M45 ....55 H1
Woodhall Av DID/WITH M20 ...98 D5
　WHTF M45 ....55 C6
Woodhall CI BOLE BL2 ....36 F1
　BRAM/HZG SK7 ....128 B1
　TOT/BURYW * BL8 ....37 L2
Woodhall Crs RDSH SK5 .....100 D8
Woodhall Rd RDSH SK5 ......100 D8
Woodhall St FAIL M35 ....74 C4
Woodham Rd CHH M8 ....72 D4
Woodham Rd NTHM/RTH M23 ..109 J3
Woodhead CI RAMS BL0 ....17 C8
Woodhead Dr
　HALE/TIMP WA15 ....117 H3
Woodhead Gv WGNS/IIMK WN3 ..63 L2
Woodhead Rd GLSP SK13 .....93 L5
　GLSP SK13 ....105 G1
　HALE/TIMP WA15 ....117 K2
Woodhead St OLDTF/WHR M16 ..87 H8
Wood Hey CI RAD M26 ....54 A1
Wood Hey Gv
　DTN/ASHW * M34 ....101 K2
　WHIT OL12 ....19 G8
Woodhey Rd RAMS BL0 ....24 D1
Woodheys HTNM SK4 ....111 J1
Woodheys Cottages
　GLSP * SK13 ....103 H8
Woodheys Dr SALE M33 .....108 A3
Woodheys Rd LIT OL15 ......29 K2
Woodhill CI MDTN M24 ......57 J2
　WGTN/LGST M12 ....88 E8
Woodhill Dr PWCH M25 ......71 L2
Woodhill Fold TOT/BURYW BL8 ..4 C2
Woodhill Gv PWCH M25 ......71 L1
Woodhill Rd TOT/BURYW BL8 ..4 B1
Woodhill St TOT/BURYW BL8 ..4 B1
Woodhill V TOT/BURYW BL8 ..4 B1
Woodhouse Dr
　WALK M28 ....47 H1
Woodhouse Knowl UPML OL3 ..45 H8
Woodhouse La ALT WA14 ....106 F8
　SALE M33 ....107 L3
　SALE M33 ....108 A2
　WGNNW/ST WN6 ....14 A1
　WHIT OL12 ....27 G1
Woodhouse La East
　HALE/TIMP WA15 ....108 D3
Woodhouse Rd ROY/SHW OL2 ..43 M3
　URM M41 ....84 C8
　WYTH/NTH M22 ....118 F4
Woodhouse St ATH M46 ......67 G2
　GTN M18 ....89 G7
　NEWH/MOS M40 ....73 J7
Woodhurst Dr WGNNW/ST WN6 ..31 G3
Wooding CI PART M31 ....94 D8
Woodlake Av CCHDY M21 .....97 M8
Woodland Av BOLS/LL BL3 ...52 E2
　BRAM/HZG SK7 ....122 A3
　GTN M18 ....89 H8
　WGNE/HIN WN2 ....49 G8
Woodland Crs PWCH M25 .....71 L2
Woodland Dr AIMK WN4 ......63 J4
　WGNNW/ST WN6 ....31 H2
Woodland Gv EDGW/EG BL7 ...22 C2
　WGN WN1 ....48 A2
Woodland Pk ROY/SHW OL2 ...42 G9
Woodland Rd BNG/LEV M19 ...99 K4
　GTN M18 ....89 H8
　HEY OL10 ....41 H1
　TYLD M29 ....67 L5
Woodlands FAIL M35 ....74 B8
　URM M41 ....95 M1
Woodlands Av CHD/CHDH SK8 120 C4
　ECC M30 ....84 C4
　IRL M44 ....94 D1
　LEIGH WN7 ....81 J1
　MPL/ROM SK6 ....101 K7
　ROCH OL11 ....27 G2
　STRET M32 ....97 C2
　SWIN M27 ....69 M6
　URM M41 ....94 F2
　WGNS/IIMK WN3 ....15 M8
　WHTF M45 ....55 H3
Woodlands CI CHD/CHDH SK8 120 C4
　GLSP SK13 ....93 J6
　HYDE SK14 ....103 J3
　STLY SK15 ....92 A5

WALK M28 ....69 H5
　MPL/ROM SK6 ....101 L7
　OFTN SK2 ....112 F4
　SLFD M6 ....71 G8
　STLY SK15 ....92 A5
　TOT/BURYW BL8 ....38 E1
Woodlands La
　HALE/TIMP WA15 ....108 B7
Woodlands Pk NEWLW * WA12 ..108 B7
Woodlands Park Rd
　GLSP SK13 ....113 G4
Woodlands Pkwy
　HALE/TIMP WA15 ....108 B7
Woodlands Rd ALT WA14 ....108 B6
　AUL OL6 ....76 B6
　CHH M8 ....72 D4
　HTNM SK4 ....111 G2
　MILN OL16 ....28 H7
　NM/HAY * SK22 ....124 C4
　OLDTF/WHR M16 ....98 B3
　RAMS BL0 ....17 D2
　SALE M33 ....96 F7
　STLY SK15 ....92 A5
　WALK M28 ....69 H5
　WILM/AE SK9 ....126 C3
　WILM/AE SK9 ....127 J1
Woodlands St CHH M8 ....72 C4
Woodlands St HEY OL10 .....41 G2
　WGTN/LGST M12 ....88 E7
　WHIT OL12 ....28 D2
Woodland Wy MDTN M24 ......57 J6
Wood La AULW OL7 ....75 L7
　HALE/TIMP WA15 ....108 D7
　MDTN M24 ....56 F6
　MPL/ROM SK6 ....114 A7
　NM/HAY SK22 ....124 C4
　PART M31 ....106 B1
　RAMS BL0 ....14 CH
Wood La East MCFLDN SK10 ..129 M4
Wood La North MCFLDN SK10 129 M4
Wood La South MCFLDN SK10 129 L5
Wood La West MCFLDN SK10 ..129 L4
Woodlark CI CSLFD * M3 .....6 B4
Woodlawn Ct OLDTF/WHR M16 ..97 M1
Woodlea CHAD OL9 ....58 A5
Woodlea Av DID/WITH M20 ...99 H6
Woodlea CI WALK M28 ....52 A5
Woodlea Gv GLSP SK13 .....104 E5
Woodleigh Dr DROY M43 .....74 F3
Woodleigh Rd OLDE OL4 .....60 D5
Woodleigh St BKLY M9 ......73 J3
Woodley Av RAD M26 ....54 E3
Woodley CI OFTN SK2 ....113 G5
Woodley Gv LEIGH WN7 ......66 K7
Woodman Dr BURY BL9 ....25 H6
Woodman St STKP SK1 ....13 H3
Woodmeadow Ct MOSL OL5 ....76 C3
Woodmere Dr BKLY M9 ....73 H1
Woodmount CI NM/HAY SK22 ..88 H1
Woodnewton CI GTN M18 .....88 F8
Woodnook Rd WGNNW/ST WN6 ..30 B4
Woodpark CI OLDS OL8 ......75 K1
Woodpecker PI WALK * M28 ..69 G4
Woodridge Dr BOLE BL2 .....36 E3
Wood Rd HALE/TIMP WA15 ...108 D3
　OLDTF/WHR M16 ....97 M1
Wood Road La BURY BL9 .....24 A4
Wood Rd North
　OLDTF/WHR M16 ....97 M1
Woodrow Wk WGTN/LGST M12 ..88 C6
Woodrow Wy IRL M44 ....94 C4
Woodroyd CI BRAM/HZG SK7 ..120 F3
Woodroyd Dr BURY BL9 ......27 J1
Woodruffe Gdns
　MPL/ROM SK6 ....113 K4
The Woods ALT WA14 ....108 B6
　OLDE OL4 ....60 F6
　ROCH OL11 ....27 M8
Woods Ct BOL BL1 ....2 F4
Woodseats La GLSP SK13 ...103 K5
Woodsend Cir URM M41 ......95 C1
Woodsend Crescent Rd
　URM M41 ....95 C2
Woodsend Rd URM M41 ....95 H3
Woodsend Rd South URM M41 ..95 H3
Woods Gv CHD/CHDH SK8 ....120 C5
Woodshaw Gv WALK M28 ......68 F4
Woodside MILN OL16 ....29 M7
　OLDE OL4 ....44 A4
Woodside Av AIMK WN4 ......63 K4
　BNG/LEV M19 ....99 J7
　WALK M28 ....69 J2
Woodside CI OLDE OL4 ......60 B6
Woodside Dr HYDE SK14 ....102 B3
　MPL/ROM SK6 ....125 C5
　SLFD M6 ....85 M1
Woodside La POY/DIS SK12 ..122 A8
　MPL/ROM SK6 ....125 G3
Woodside PI BOLS/LL * BL3 ..3 M8
Woodside Rd OLDTF/WHR M16 ..97 L2
　RNFD/HAY WA11 ....78 B5
Woodside Sq NM/HAY SK22 ..124 C5
Woodside St NM/HAY SK22 ...77 H6
Woodside Vw ATH M46 ....51 H7
Wood's La AIMK WN4 ....63 M8
　CHD/CHDH SK8 ....120 D5
　UPML OL3 ....61 K3
Woods Lea BOL BL1 ....35 J5
Woods Moor La EDGY/DAV SK3 112 D8
Woodsmoor Rd SWIN M27 .....70 A5
Wood Sorrel Wy
　GOL/RIS/CU WA3 ....80 B4
Wood Sq DROY M43 ....89 K4
　UPML OL3 ....61 L4
Woods Rd IRL M44 ....94 C4
Wood's St WGNS/IIMK WN3 ...14 E6
Woodstock Av CHD/CHDH SK8 120 C5
　RDSH SK5 ....100 C7
Woodstock CI HEY OL10 .....41 H2
　LEIGH WN7 ....81 J1
Woodstock Crs MPL/ROM SK6 101 K7
Woodstock Dr BOL BL1 ......35 J5
　SWIN M27 ....70 B6
　TOT/BURYW BL8 ....24 A5
Woodstock Rd ALT WA14 ....107 M4
　NEWH/MOS M40 ....73 M3
　OLDTF/WHR M16 ....97 L1
　WHIT OL12 ....27 M3

Withington La WGNE/HIN WN2 ..48 E2
Withington Rd CCHDY M21 ...98 A4
　OLDTF/WHR M16 ....98 A4
Withington St HEY * OL10 ...41 H4
　SLFD M6 ....85 H3
Withinlee Rd MCFLDN SK10 .131 M6
Withins Av RAD M26 ....38 F7
Withins CI BOLE BL2 ....37 H4
Withins Dr BOLE BL2 ....37 H4
Withins Gv BOLE BL2 ....37 H4
Withins La BOLE BL2 ....37 H3
　RAD M26 ....38 F7
Withins Rd OLDS OL8 ....74 E2
　RNFD/HAY WA11 ....78 B4
Withnell CI NEWH/MOS * WN6 ..14 A1
Withnell Dr TOT/BURYW BL8 ..38 D3
Withnell Rd DID/WITH M20 ..111 G1
Withycombe PI SLFD M6 .....71 K7
Withy Gv ANC M4 ....7 G4
Withypool CI OFTN SK2 ....112 E7
Withy Tree Gv
　DTN/ASHW * M34 ....101 K2
Witley Dr SALE M33 ....96 A6
Witley Rd MILN OL16 ....11 K5
Wittenburg Rd HTNM SK4 ....12 A2
Witterage CI WGTN/LGST * M12 ..88 C6
Woburn Abbey UPML * OL3 ...61 K3
Woburn Av BOLE BL2 ....36 F1
　LEIGH WN7 ....81 J1
Woburn CI MILN OL16 ....29 H6
　RNFD/HAY WA11 ....78 C5
Woburn Dr BURY BL9 ....39 J7
　HALE/TIMP WA15 ....117 K2
Woburn Rd OLDTF/WHR M16 ...97 K2
Woburn St OLDTF/WHR M16 ...98 C1
Woden's Av ORD M5 ....86 F5
Woden St ORD M5 ....86 F5
Woking Back Gdns BOL BL1 ..36 B3
Woking Rd CHD/CHDH SK8 ...120 C6
Woking Ter BOL * BL1 ......36 B3
Wolfenden St BOL BL1 ......36 B2
Wolfenden Ter BOL * BL1 ...36 B2
Wolford Dr TYLD M29 ....67 M3
Wolfreton Crs SWIN M27 ....70 D1
Wolfson Sq AIMK WN4 ....63 J8
Wolmer St AIMK WN4 ....63 K8
Wolseley PI DID/WITH M20 ..98 F8
Wolseley Rd SALE M33 ......96 F6
Wolseley St MILN OL16 .....29 L8
　TOT/BURYW BL8 ....38 E3
Wolsey CI AIMK WN4 ....63 K7
Wolsey Dr ALT WA14 ....116 C3
Wolsey St HEY OL10 ....40 F3
　RAD M26 ....54 D1
Wolstenholme Av BURY BL9 ..25 J6
Wolstenholme Coalpit La
　ROCH OL11 ....26 E2
Wolstenholme La ROCH OL11 ..26 F2
Wolstenvale CI MDTN M24 ...57 L3
Wolver CI LHULT * M38 .....52 E6
Wolverton Av OLDS OL8 .....75 C1
Wolverton Dr WILM/AE SK9 ..127 G3
Wolvesey ROCH * OL11 ......10 D7
Woodacre OLDTF/WHR M16 ....97 H1
Woodacres Ct WILM/AE SK9 .126 D6
Woodall CI SALE M33 ....97 G8
Woodark CI OLDE OL4 ....60 C7
Woodbank Av MPL/ROM SK6 ..113 H1
　STKP SK1 ....112 E4
Woodbank Ct URM * M41 .....95 L1
Woodbank Dr TOT/BURYW BL8 ..24 F8
Wood Bank Rd LIT OL15 .....29 K1
Woodbine Av IRL M44 ....94 A8
Woodbine Crs OFTN SK2 .....13 K9
Woodbine Rd BOLS/LL BL3 ...51 M1
Woodbine St MILN OL16 .....11 H8
Woodbine St East MILN OL16 11 J8
Woodbourne Rd HTNM SK4 ....99 M6
　NM/HAY SK22 ....124 C7
　SALE M33 ....108 D2
Woodbray Av BNG/LEV M19 ...99 H7
Woodbridge Av DTN/ASHW M34 ..90 E6
Woodbridge Gdns WHIT OL12 ..27 M2
Woodbridge Gv NTHM/RTH M23 109 H3
Woodbridge Rd URM M41 .....95 G1
Woodbrook Av OLDE OL4 .....60 E5
Woodbrook La OLDE OL4 .....60 E5
Woodbrook Rd OLDE OL4 .....60 D5
Woodbrook Rd WILM/AE SK9 ..130 E3
Woodburn Dr BOL BL1 ....35 L1
Woodburn Rd WYTH/NTH M22 ..110 A4
Woodbury Crs DUK * SK16 ...90 E5
Woodbury Rd EDGY/DAV SK3 ..12 A9
Woodchurch WGN WN1 ....15 M1
Woodchurch Wk CHAD * OL9 ...8 A7
Woodcock CI DROY M43 ......89 M1
　ROCH OL11 ....27 J5
Woodcock Dr WGNE/HIN WN2 ..64 E2
Woodcock Gv GLSP SK13 ....105 J3
Woodcock GLSP SK13 ....105 K3
Woodcock Sq WGN * WN1 .....14 F3
Woodcote Av BRAM/HZG SK7 .120 E3
Woodcote Rd ALT WA14 .....107 K3
　ALT WA14 ....108 A3
Woodcote Vw WILM/AE SK9 ..127 K3
Wood Cottage CI WALK M28 ..68 C1
Woodcourt WGNS/IIMK WN3 ...14 E8
Wood Crs OLDE OL4 ....76 B1
Woodcroft OFTN SK2 ....113 G6
　WGNNW/ST WN6 ....30 B6
Woodcroft Av BNG/LEV M19 ..99 M4
Wooddagger CI WGNE/HIN WN2 ..49 J7
Woodeaton CI ROY/SHW OL2 ..43 K8
Wooded CI BURY BL9 ....25 J7
Wood Edge CI BOLS/LL * BL3 52 F1
Wood End BRAM/HZG SK7 ....120 F2
Woodend ROY/SHW OL2 ....43 M3
Woodend Dr STLY SK15 ......92 A6
Woodend La HYDE SK14 .....101 M3
　STLY SK15 ....92 A5
　WHIT OL12 ....19 L6
Woodend Rd EDGY/DAV SK3 ..112 C8
　WYTH/NTH M22 ....110 A8
Woodend St OLD OL1 ....9 H1
　OLDE OL4 ....60 C7
Woodfield WYTH/NTH M22 ...118 F1
Woodfield Av HYDE SK14 ...102 A4
　MPL/ROM SK6 ....101 K8
　WHIT * OL12 ....28 D2
Woodfield CI GLSP SK13 ....93 J7
Woodfield Crs AIMK WN4 ....63 H2
　MPL/ROM SK6 ....113 J2
Woodfield Ct OFTN * SK2 ..112 D8
Woodfield Gv ECC M30 ......84 F3

Woodlands CI CHD/CHDH SK8 120 C4
　GLSP SK13 ....93 J6
　HYDE SK14 ....103 J3
　STLY SK15 ....92 A5

Index - featured places

...M1

...8

98 E3
54 A1
113 G1
66 F1   55 K1
95 F8
107 M5   94 C6
110 A3   100 B5
90 B6   22 D7
89 M5   127 F6
179 H6   110 A3
60 D4   120 D4
57 H7   101 M4
118 C7   121 H1
129 M3   98 C8
98 C8   93 G8
35 M3   59 D4
12 C8   97 M2
27 E5   70 E2
12 B7   70 A3
12 B8   111 K2
128 C4   67 C3
50 F8   60 E4
109 K6   116 F3
10 F3   122 C3
42 D1   24 D1
100 B7   90 D7
27 H6   49 D7
7 M4   116 F3
7 H1   72 B4
5 G5   78 H1
101 H1   75 B8
88 A4   106 D7
87 M6   75 G5
112 E6   49 G5

Bage Lane Industrial Estate
ATH M46 .... 50 F8

Baguley Hall Primary School
NTHM/RTH M23 .... 109 K6

Baillie Street Health Centre
MILN OL16 .... 10 F3

Balderstone (Community) School
ROCH OL11 .... 42 D1

Bamford Business Park
RDSH SK5 .... 100 B7

Bamford Primary School
ROCH OL11 .... 27 H6

Band on the Wall
ANC M4 .... 7 H2

Bankfield Trading Estate
RDSH SK5 .... 100 B8

Bank Meadow Primary School
WGTN/LGST M12 .... 88 A4

Banks Lane Primary School
STKP SK1 .... 112 E4

Bare Trees J & I School
CHAD OL9 .... 8 A2

Baring Street Industrial Estate
CMANE M1 .... 7 L7

Barlow Hall Primary School
CCHDY M21 .... 97 M7

Barlow Medical Centre
DID/WITH M20 .... 110 D1

The Barlow RC High School
CHD/CHDH SK8 .... 110 F2

Barrack Hill Primary School
MPL/ROM SK6 .... 113 K2

Barrington Medical Centre
ALT WA14 .... 108 A6

Barton Business Park
ECC M30 .... 84 F3

Barton Clough Primary School
STRET M32 .... 85 J8

Barton Moss Primary School
ECC M30 .... 84 C3

Bayley Industrial Estate
STLY SK15 .... 91 J3

BBC North
CMANE M1 .... 7 H8

Bealey Community Hospital
RAD M26 .... 39 G8

Bealey Industrial Estate
RAD M26 .... 39 G7

Beal Vale Primary School
ROY/SHW OL2 .... 43 L5

Beaumont Hospital
HOR/BR BL6 .... 34 E4

Beaumont Primary School
BOLE BL2 .... 35 H7

Beaver Road Primary School
DID/WITH M20 .... 110 E1

Bedford Hall Methodist Primary School
LEIGH WN7 .... 81 L1

Bedford High School
LEIGH WN7 .... 67 G8

Beech Hill Primary School
WGNW/ST WN6 .... 47 K1

Beech House School
ROCH OL11 .... 10 C7

Bee Fold Medical Centre
ATH M46 .... 66 E2

Bee Hive Industrial Estate
HOR/BR BL6 .... 34 B5

Beever Primary School
OLD OL1 .... 9 L3

Beis Rochel Girls School
CHH M8 .... 72 C3

Bel-Air Hotel
WGN WN1 .... 31 M8

Belfield Community Primary School
MILN OL16 .... 11 L2

Belfield Trading Estate
MILN OL16 .... 29 G3

Belfry House Hotel
WILM/AE SK9 .... 119 M6

Belle Green Industrial Estate
WGNE/HIN WN2 .... 48 D4

Belle Vue Regional Hockey Centre
WGNW/LGST M12 .... 88 D8

Belmore Hotel
SALE M33 .... 108 E2

Benchill Primary School
WYTH/NTH M22 .... 109 M6

Bentfield Industrial Units
CHAD OL9 .... 8 B6

Bentinck Street Industrial Estate
HULME M15 .... 6 A9

Bethesda School
CHD/CHDH SK8 .... 119 M1

Bickershaw CE Primary School
WGNE/HIN WN2 .... 65 J4

Billinge Chapel End Parish Council
WGNW/BIL/O WN5 .... 62 B7

Billinge Chapel End Primary School
WGNW/BIL/O WN5 .... 62 B8

Billinge Clinic
WGNW/BIL/O WN5 .... 62 A8

Billinge Hospital
WGNW/BIL/O WN5 .... 62 A2

Birches Health Centre
PWCH M25 .... 55 M6

The Birches School
DID/WITH M20 .... 98 C7

Birchfields Primary School
RUSH/FAL M14 .... 99 H3

Birch Industrial Estate
HEY OL10 .... 40 D6

Birchinley Manor Showground
MILN OL16 .... 29 J4

Birch Vale Industrial Estate
NM/HAY SK22 .... 125 J2

Birtenshaw Hall School
BOL BL1 .... 22 E6

Birtle View Special School
HEY OL10 .... 40 F1

Bishop Bilsborrow RC Primary School
OLDTF/WHR M16 .... 98 C2

Bishop Bridgeman CE Primary School
BOLS/LL BL3 .... 36 B8

B & J Leisure Centre
WILM/AE SK9 .... 126 E5

Blackbrook Trading Estate
BNG/LEV M19 .... 99 L4

Blackley Cemetery
BKLY M9 .... 56 D8

Blackley Crematorium
BKLY M9 .... 56 D8

Blackrod Church School
HOR/BR BL6 .... 32 F2

Blackrod Primary School
HOR/BR BL6 .... 33 H4

Blackshaw Lane CP School
ROY/SHW OL2 .... 43 K8

Blackshaw Primary School
BOLE BL2 .... 37 K6

Blessed Thomas Holford Secondary School
HALE/TIMP WA15 .... 108 B8

Blue Chip Business Park
ALT WA14 .... 107 L5

Blue Coat CE School
OLD OL1 .... 9 K4

Bnos Yisroel Schools
BRO M7 .... 72 B5

Boarshaw Industrial Estate
MDTN M24 .... 57 L4

Boarshaw Primary School
MDTN M24 .... 57 L1

Boarshurst Business Park
UPML OL3 .... 61 L6

Bodmin Road Clinic
SALE M33 .... 96 A7

Boggart Hole Clough Track
BKLY M9 .... 73 J2

Bollin CP School
ALT WA14 .... 116 D3

Bolshaw Primary School
CHD/CHDH SK8 .... 119 K5

Bolton Business Centre
BOLE BL2 .... 3 G6

Bolton Community College
BOLE BL2 .... 3 G7

Bolton Excel Leisure Centre
BOLE BL2 .... 3 G7

Bolton Gates Retail Park
BOL BL1 .... 2 F2

Bolton Golf Club
HOR/BR BL6 .... 34 D4

Bolton Institute
BOLS/LL BL3 .... 2 C7

Bolton Institute of HE
BOLS/LL BL3 .... 2 C7

Bolton Little Theatre
BOL BL1 .... 2 C5

Bolton Old Links Golf Club
BOL BL1 .... 35 G1

Bolton Open Golf Club
BOLE BL2 .... 37 G1

Bolton Parish CE Primary School
BOLE BL2 .... 3 J4

Bolton Road Industrial Estate
ATH M46 .... 67 G1
WHTN BL5 .... 50 C3

Bolton RUFC
BOL BL1 .... 2 A2

Bolton Running Track
HOR/BR BL6 .... 33 M5

Bolton School Boys Division
BOL BL1 .... 35 M5

Bolton School Girls Division
BOL BL1 .... 35 L5

Bolton Sports Arena
HOR/BR BL6 .... 33 M5

Bolton Trophy & Sports Centre
BOLE BL2 .... 3 L4

Bolton Wanderers FC (Reebok Stadium)
HOR/BR BL6 .... 34 A5

Bond Street Industrial Estate
WGTN/LGST M12 .... 7 L7

Bonholt Industrial Estate
TOT/BURYW BL8 .... 24 D8

Booth Hall Childrens Hospital
BKLY M9 .... 73 J1

Booth House Trading Estate
CHAD OL9 .... 8 D7

Boothstown Methodist School
WALK M28 .... 68 C6

The Borchardt Medical Centre
DID/WITH M20 .... 98 C6

Bornmore Industrial Centre
TOT/BURYW BL8 .... 38 E1

Borron Road Industrial Estate
NEWLW WA12 .... 78 F8

Boundary Industrial Estate
BOLE BL2 .... 37 K5

Boundary Trading Estate
ECC M30 .... 83 M8

Bowdon CE Primary School
ALT WA14 .... 116 E3

Bowdon Cricket Club
ALT WA14 .... 116 E3

Bowdon Preparatory School for Girls
ALT WA14 .... 116 E2

Bowdon RUFC
HALE/TIMP WA15 .... 108 F8

Bowdon Vale Cricket Club
ALT WA14 .... 116 E4

Bower Hotel
CHAD OL9 .... 74 C2

Bowker Bank Industrial Park
CHH M8 .... 72 E2

Bowker Vale Primary School
BKLY M9 .... 56 C8

Bowling Alley
BURY BL9 .... 39 L6
OLDTF/WHR M16 .... 86 D7
WGNS/IIMK WN3 .... 14 E5

Bowness Primary School
BOLS/LL BL3 .... 53 J1

Brabyns Recreation Centre
MPL/ROM SK6 .... 114 C5

Brabyns School
MPL/ROM SK6 .... 114 D5

Brackley Municipal Golf Club
LHULT M38 .... 52 B6

Bradley Fold Trading Estate
BOLE BL2 .... 37 M6

Bradley Green Primary School
HYDE SK14 .... 91 J6

Bradley Hall Trading Estate
WGNNW/ST WN6 .... 31 J5

Bradshaw Cricket Club
BOLE BL2 .... 22 F7

Bradshaw Hall J & I School
CHD/CHDH SK8 .... 120 A3

Bradshaw Trading Estate
MDTN M24 .... 58 A7

Bramall Hall
BRAM/HZG SK7 .... 120 F3

Bramall Park Golf Club
CHD/CHDH SK8 .... 120 E3

Bramall Park Lawn Tennis Club
BRAM/HZG SK7 .... 120 F2

Bramall Park Tennis Club
BRAM/HZG SK7 .... 120 F4

Bramhall Golf Club
BRAM/HZG SK7 .... 121 H6

Bramhall Health Centre
BRAM/HZG SK7 .... 121 G6

Bramhall High School
BRAM/HZG SK7 .... 121 H4

Bramhall Moor Industrial Estate
BRAM/HZG SK7 .... 121 K2

Bramhall Park Medical Centre
BRAM/HZG SK7 .... 121 G2

Bramhall Village Shopping Centre
BRAM/HZG SK7 .... 120 F1

Brandwood Primary School
BOLS/LL BL3 .... 35 M8

Branwood Preparatory School
ECC M30 .... 85 H1

Bredbury Green Primary School
MPL/ROM SK6 .... 113 J8

Bredbury Hall Hotel & Country Club
MPL/ROM SK6 .... 113 G2

Breeze Hill Comprehensive School
OLDE OL4 .... 60 A7

Breightmet FC
BOLE BL2 .... 37 J5

Breightmet Golf Club
BOLE BL2 .... 37 K3

Breightmet Industrial Estate
BOLE BL2 .... 37 J5

Brentwood Special School
ALT WA14 .... 108 B5

Bretnall Primary School
BRO M7 .... 72 A5

Bridgebank Industrial Estate
HOR/BR BL6 .... 33 J1

Bridge College
OFTN SK2 .... 113 G7

Bridge Hall Primary School
EDGY/DAV SK3 .... 112 A6

Bridge House Medical Centre
CHD/CHDH SK8 .... 120 D1

Bridge Mills Business Park
SLFD M6 .... 71 J7

Bridgeside Business Centre
MPL/ROM SK6 .... 101 G6

Bridge Trading Estate
TOT/BURYW BL8 .... 4 B4

Bridgewater Concert Hall
CMANW M2 .... 6 F7

Bridgewater Primary School
LHULT M38 .... 52 F8

Bridgewater School
WALK M28 .... 69 K6

Brighton Road Industrial Estate
HTNM SK4 .... 12 B5

Brimrod Primary School
ROCH OL11 .... 10 B9

Brindale Primary School
RDSH SK5 .... 100 F8

Brindle Heath Industrial Estate
SLFD M6 .... 71 J8

Brindle House Community Mental Health Centre
HYDE SK14 .... 102 A2

Brinksway Trading Estate
HTNM SK4 .... 12 D6

Brinnington Health Centre
RDSH SK5 .... 100 F7

Briscoe Lane J & I School
NEWH/MOS M40 .... 73 L7

Britannia Bridge Primary School
WGNS/IIMK WN3 .... 15 K7

Britannia Business Park
BOLE BL2 .... 36 E2

Britannia Mill Industrial Estate
HEY OL10 .... 40 E2

Broadbent Fold Primary School
DUK SK16 .... 91 K5

Broadbottom Primary School
HYDE SK14 .... 103 J4

Broadfield Industrial Estate
HEY OL10 .... 40 E3

Broadfield Primary School
OLDS OL8 .... 59 J8

Broadheath Primary School
ALT WA14 .... 107 M4

Broadhurst Primary School
NEWH/MOS M40 .... 73 H4

Broadoak Business Park
TRPK M17 .... 85 J5

Broad Oak High School
BURY BL9 .... 5 M4

Broadoak High School
PART M31 .... 106 B2

Broad Oak Primary School
DID/WITH M20 .... 110 E4

Broadoak Primary School
AUL OL6 .... 75 M6
SWIN M27 .... 69 M6

Broadoak Sports Centre
AUL OL6 .... 76 A6

Broadstone Hall Primary School
HTNM SK4 .... 100 A6

Broadwalk Primary School
SLFD M6 .... 86 D1

Broadway Business Park
CHAD OL9 .... 8 B3

Broadway Industrial Estate
HYDE SK14 .... 90 E7
ORD M5 .... 86 D4

Brookburn Primary School
CCHDY M21 .... 97 K5

Brookdale Golf Club
FAIL M35 .... 74 F7

Brooke Dean Community School
WILM/AE SK9 .... 119 M8

Brookfield Business Park
CHD/CHDH SK8 .... 111 J7

Brookfield High School
WGNE/HIN WN2 .... 49 H8

Brookfield Industrial Estate
GLSP SK13 .... 104 B1

Brookhead Junior School
CHD/CHDH SK8 .... 111 J7

Brooklands Primary School
SALE M33 .... 108 D2

Brook Mill Medical Centre
LEIGH WN7 .... 66 D7

Brooks Bar Medical Centre
OLDTF/WHR M16 .... 87 G8

Brookside Business Park
MDTN M24 .... 58 A6

Brookside Primary School
MPL/ROM SK6 .... 123 G6

Brookway High School
NTHM/RTH M23 .... 109 H4

Broomwood CP School
HALE/TIMP WA15 .... 109 G7

Broughton Baths
BRO M7 .... 72 A6

Broughton Cricket Club
BRO M7 .... 71 M6

Broughton Jewish Cassel-Fox Primary School
BRO M7 .... 72 A4

Brownhill Special School
WHIT OL12 .... 10 D1

Brownlow Business Centre
BOL BL1 .... 36 A3

Brownlow Fold Primary School
BOL BL1 .... 36 A3

Brunswick Health Centre
BRUN/LGST M13 .... 87 L6

Bruntwood Primary School
CHD/CHDH SK8 .... 120 A4

Buckley Road Industrial Estate
WHIT OL12 .... 28 E2

Buckstones Primary School
ROY/SHW OL2 .... 44 A4

Buckton Vale Primary School
STLY SK15 .... 77 J3

Buile Hill High School
SLFD M6 .... 71 G8

Bullough Moor Primary School
HEY OL10 .... 40 D3

Burgess Primary School
BKLY M9 .... 73 H5

Burnage High School For Boys
BNG/LEV M19 .... 99 J7

Burnage Rugby Club
HTNM SK4 .... 111 H3

Burnden Industrial Estate
BOLS/LL BL3 .... 36 E8

Burnley Brow Community School
CHAD OL9 .... 8 D1

Burrs Country Park
TOT/BURYW BL8 .... 25 G6

Bury Business Centre
BURY BL9 .... 5 J7

Bury Catholic Preparatory School
BURY BL9 .... 4 D8

Bury CE High School
BURY BL9 .... 4 C8

Bury Cemetery
BURY BL9 .... 39 J5

Bury College
BURY BL9 .... 4 E6

Bury County Court
BURY BL9 .... 4 D5

Bury FC (Gigg Lane)
BURY BL9 .... 39 J5

Bury Golf Club
BURY BL9 .... 39 K8

Bury Grammar School for Girls & Boys
BURY BL9 .... 4 C8

Bury Industrial Estate
BOLE BL2 .... 37 J4

Bury Market
BURY BL9 .... 4 F5

Bury Sports Club
BURY BL9 .... 4 D9

Business & Arts Centre
HTNM SK4 .... 100 A5

Business & Technology Centre
ECC M30 .... 84 F2

Butterstile Primary School
PWCH M25 .... 71 K2

Button Lane School
NTHM/RTH M23 .... 109 J2

Byrchall High School
AIMK WN4 .... 78 E3

Byron Street Infant Community School
ROY/SHW OL2 .... 43 H8

Cadishead Junior School
IRL M44 .... 94 A6

Cadishead Recreation Centre
IRL M44 .... 94 A7

Caius House School
URM M41 .... 95 M3

Caldershaw Primary School
WHIT OL12 .... 27 J3

Cale Green Primary School
EDGY/DAV SK3 .... 112 C5

Camberwell Park School
BKLY M9 .... 56 F6

Cambrian Business Park
BOLS/LL BL3 .... 2 C9

Cambridge Industrial Estate
 BRO M7 .... 72 B8
Cambridge Street
 Industrial Area
 BRO M7 .... 72 B8
Campanile Hotel
 ORD M5 .... 6 A7
Cams Lane Primary School
 RAD M26 .... 54 C1
Canalside Industrial Estate
 MILN OL16 .... 11 J8
Cannon Street Health Centre
 BOLS/LL BL3 .... 2 B8
Canon Burrows CE
 Primary School
 AULW OL7 .... 75 J7
Canon Johnson CE
 Primary School
 AULW OL7 .... 75 L8
Canon Slade School
 BOLE BL2 .... 22 E8
Canon Williamson CE
 High School
 ECC M30 .... 84 C3
Cansfield High School
 AIMK WN4 .... 63 K8
Canterbury Road J & I School
 URM M41 .... 96 A1
Capital Business Centre
 BRAM/HZG SK7 .... 120 F6
Cardinal Langley RC
 High School
 MDTN M24 .... 41 M8
Cariocca Business Park
 NEWH/MOS M40 .... 88 B1
 WGTN/LGST M12 .... 88 A6
Carlton Industrial Centre
 BOLE BL2 .... 3 G6
Carrbrook Industrial Estate
 STLY SK15 .... 77 K6
Carrington Business Park
 PART M31 .... 94 F6
Castlebrook High School
 BURY BL9 .... 55 M1
Castlefield Gallery
 CSLFD M3 .... 6 D7
Castle Hawk Golf Club
 ROCH OL11 .... 41 J8
Castle Hill Primary School
 BOL BL1 .... 36 E2
Castle Hill School
 RDSH SK5 .... 100 F6
Castle Leisure Centre
 BURY BL9 .... 4 D4
Castle Park Industrial Estate
 OLD OL1 .... 59 L5
Castleton Gabriels FC
 ROCH OL11 .... 41 L2
Castleton Primary School
 ROCH OL11 .... 42 A2
Castleton Swimming Pool
 ROCH OL11 .... 41 M1
Cathedral Visitor Centre
 CSLFD M3 .... 6 F3
Cavendish Industrial Estate
 AUL OL6 .... 90 D1
Cavendish Road
 Primary School
 DID/WITH M20 .... 98 D7
Central Art Gallery
 AUL OL6 .... 90 C2
Central Industrial Estate
 BOLS/LL BL3 .... 2 E9
 MDTN M24 .... 57 K4
Central Leisure Centre
 MILN OL16 .... 11 G4
Central Primary School
 DTN/ASHW M34 .... 101 H1
Central Retail Park
 ANC M4 .... 7 L4
Century Mill Industrial Estate
 FWTH BL4 .... 52 E4
Chadderton AFC
 CHAD OL9 .... 8 A3
Chadderton Cemetery
 CHAD OL9 .... 58 D4
Chadderton Hall Junior School
 CHAD OL9 .... 58 D2
Chadderton Industrial Estate
 MDTN M24 .... 57 M7
Chadderton Shopping Precinct
 CHAD OL9 .... 8 B4
Chadderton Sports Centre &
 Public Baths
 CHAD OL9 .... 8 B4
Chadderton Town Health Centre
 CHAD OL9 .... 8 A4
Chadkirk Industrial Estate
 MPL/ROM SK6 .... 113 L4
Chalfont Primary School
 BOL BL1 .... 36 C2
Chanters Industrial Estate
 ATH M46 .... 51 J7
 ATH M46 .... 67 J2
Chantlers Primary School
 TOT/BURYW BL8 .... 38 D2
Chapelfield Primary School
 RAD M26 .... 54 F3
Chapel Medical Centre
 IRL M44 .... 94 D2
Chapel Street Primary School
 BNG/LEV M19 .... 99 L3
Charleston Industrial Estate
 AULW OL7 .... 75 L8
Charlestown Health Centre
 BKLY M9 .... 73 K2
Charlestown Primary School
 BKLY M9 .... 73 L1
 SLFD M6 .... 71 L8
Charlesworth School
 GLSP SK13 .... 103 M6
Cheadle Catholic
 Primary School
 CHD/CHDH SK8 .... 120 A2
Cheadle Cricket Club
 CHD/CHDH SK8 .... 110 F7
Cheadle Golf Club
 CHD/CHDH SK8 .... 111 H8
Cheadle Heath Clinic
 EDGY/DAV SK3 .... 111 K4
Cheadle Heath Primary School
 EDGY/DAV SK3 .... 111 K5
Cheadle Heath Sports Centre
 CHD/CHDH SK8 .... 111 K6
Cheadle Hulme College
 CHD/CHDH SK8 .... 120 D5
Cheadle Hulme Medical Centre
 CHD/CHDH SK8 .... 120 C4

Cheadle Hulme
 Recreation Centre
 CHD/CHDH SK8 .... 120 D5
Cheadle Hulme School
 CHD/CHDH SK8 .... 120 C4
Cheadle Primary School
 CHD/CHDH SK8 .... 111 G6
Cheadle Royal Hospital
 CHD/CHDH SK8 .... 119 L3
Cheadle Royal
 Shopping Centre
 CHD/CHDH SK8 .... 119 M2
Cheadle Swimming &
 Recreation Centre
 CHD/CHDH SK8 .... 111 H8
Cheadle Town FC
 CHD/CHDH SK8 .... 111 H7
Cheetham CE
 Community School
 BRO M7 .... 72 C5
Cheetham Hill Cricket Club
 CHH M8 .... 72 B3
Cheethwood Community &
 Sports Centre
 CHH M8 .... 72 B5
Cheetwood Primary School
 CHH M8 .... 72 B8
Cherry Manor
 Primary School
 SALE M33 .... 107 M2
Cherry Tree Hospital
 OFTN SK2 .... 112 F7
Cherry Tree Primary School
 FWTH BL4 .... 52 B4
Chesham Industrial Estate
 BURY BL9 .... 25 K8
Chesham Primary School
 BURY BL9 .... 25 K7
Chester Court Hotel
 STRET M32 .... 86 C8
Chethams School of Music
 CSLFD M3 .... 6 E3
Chichester Business Centre
 MILN OL16 .... 11 H5
Child Health Clinic
 MDTN M24 .... 57 J3
Chinese Medical Centre
 CSLFD M3 .... 6 D6
Chorley New Road
 Primary School
 HOR/BR BL6 .... 33 M3
Chorlton-cum-Hardy CE
 Primary School
 CCHDY M21 .... 97 K4
Chorlton-cum-Hardy
 Cricket Club
 CCHDY M21 .... 97 L6
Chorlton-cum-Hardy Golf Club
 CCHDY M21 .... 97 M7
Chorlton Leisure Centre
 CCHDY M21 .... 97 L3
Chorlton Park Primary School
 CCHDY M21 .... 97 M5
Chorlton Shopping Centre
 CCHDY M21 .... 97 K3
Chorlton Water Park
 CCHDY M21 .... 97 M8
Chowbent Primary School
 ATH M46 .... 67 H1
Christchurch CE
 Primary School
 BOLE BL2 .... 37 M3
Christ Church CE
 Primary School
 CHAD OL9 .... 58 A1
 TOT/BURYW BL8 .... 24 C8
 UPML OL3 .... 45 G2
Christ Church Pennington CE
 Primary School
 LEIGH WN7 .... 66 C8
Christie Hospital & Holt Radium
 Institute
 DID/WITH M20 .... 98 E6
Christie Street Industrial Estate
 STKP SK1 .... 13 L8
Christs Church CE
 Primary School
 BOLE BL2 .... 37 J2
Christ the King RC
 Primary School
 WALK M28 .... 69 H2
Church Road Primary School
 BOL BL1 .... 35 K2
Church Street Industrial Estate
 MDTN M24 .... 57 K2
City Centre Campus
 CSLFD M3 .... 6 C4
City College Manchester
 DID/WITH M20 .... 98 C8
 NTHM/RTH M23 .... 109 G4
 NTHM/RTH M23 .... 109 M3
City Course Trading Estate
 OP/CLY M11 .... 88 D5
City Court Trading Estate
 ANC M4 .... 7 L7
City Park Business Village
 OLDTF/WHR M16 .... 86 E7
Claremont Primary School
 RUSH/FAL M14 .... 98 D1
Clarendon Cottage School
 ECC M30 .... 85 J1
Clarendon County
 Primary School
 BOLS/LL BL3 .... 2 D9
Clarendon Fields
 Primary School
 DUK SK16 .... 90 E4
Clarendon Industrial Estate
 HYDE SK14 .... 102 B1
Clarendon Road
 Primary School
 ECC M30 .... 85 J1
Clarendon Square
 Shopping Centre
 HYDE SK14 .... 102 A2
Clarke Industrial Estate
 STRET M32 .... 85 K7
Clarksfield Primary School
 OLDE OL4 .... 59 M6
Claypool Primary School
 HOR/BR BL6 .... 34 B3
Clayton Health Centre
 OP/CLY M11 .... 88 C2
Clayton Industrial Estate
 OP/CLY M11 .... 89 G5
Cleavley Athletics Track
 ECC M30 .... 84 D1
Cleggs Lane Industrial Site
 LHULT M38 .... 52 E6

Cleveland Preparatory School
 BOL BL1 .... 35 K5
Clifton Country Park
 SWIN M27 .... 54 B7
Clifton Industrial Estate
 SWIN M27 .... 70 F1
Clifton Primary School
 SWIN M27 .... 70 C1
Cloughside School
 PWCH M25 .... 55 J6
The Club Theatre
 ALT WA14 .... 116 A1
Cobden Mill Industrial Estate
 FWTH BL4 .... 52 E3
Coldhurst Community Centre
 OLD OL1 .... 9 G3
Coldhurst Industrial Estate
 OLD OL1 .... 9 H3
Coliseum Theatre
 OLD OL1 .... 9 L5
College Street Health Centre
 LEIGH WN7 .... 66 D7
Collegiate Medical Centre
 CHH M8 .... 72 D5
Collier Brook Industrial Estate
 ATH M46 .... 66 F1
Comfort Inn
 WGTN/LGST M12 .... 88 D6
Comfort Inn Hotel
 WGTN/LGST M12 .... 88 D6
Commonwealth House
 MANAIR M90 .... 118 D4
Comtech Business Park
 WHTN BL5 .... 50 C1
Concord Business Park
 WYTH/NTH M22 .... 118 E3
 WYTH/NTH M22 .... 119 E3
Coney Green High School
 RAD M26 .... 38 E8
Constellation Trading Estate
 RAD M26 .... 38 C6
Co-operative Museum
 WHIT OL12 .... 10 D3
Copley High School
 STLY SK15 .... 92 A2
Copper Beeches School
 SALE M33 .... 96 C8
Coppice Industrial Estate
 OLDS OL8 .... 8 E8
Coppice J & I School
 OLDS OL8 .... 59 H8
Copthorne Hotel
 SALQ M50 .... 86 D6
Cornbrook Estate
 HULME M15 .... 6 A8
Cornerhouse Cinema
 CMANE M1 .... 7 G7
Cornishway Industrial Estate
 WYTH/NTH M22 .... 118 F4
Cornwall Street
 Industrial Estate
 OP/CLY M11 .... 89 G3
Corpus Christi RC
 Primary School
 CHAD OL9 .... 58 E8
Corpus Christi with St Anne RC
 Primary School
 ANC M4 .... 88 A3
Corrie Primary School
 DTN/ASHW M34 .... 101 H3
Counthill School
 OLDE OL4 .... 60 A2
County End Business Centre
 OLDE OL4 .... 60 C5
County Hotel
 BRAM/HZG SK7 .... 121 G5
Courts of Justice
 CSLFD M3 .... 6 D5
Crab Lane Primary School
 BKLY M9 .... 56 E8
Craft Centre
 ANC M4 .... 7 H3
Craft Shops
 BOL BL1 .... 2 E3
Cravenwood Primary School
 CHH M8 .... 72 C4
Cresta Court Hotel
 ALT WA14 .... 108 A7
The Cricketer Sports Club
 WGNS/IIMK WN3 .... 14 D8
Cricket Street Business Centre
 WGNNW/ST WN6 .... 14 C4
Croft Industrial Estate
 BURY BL9 .... 39 K7
Cromer Industrial Estate
 MDTN M24 .... 57 L3
Cromford Business Park
 OLD OL1 .... 59 L4
Crompton Cricket Club
 ROY/SHW OL2 .... 43 L4
Crompton Fold Primary School
 BOLE BL2 .... 37 H5
Crompton Health Centre
 ROY/SHW OL2 .... 43 L6
Crompton House School
 ROY/SHW OL2 .... 43 L4
Crompton & Royton Golf Club
 ROY/SHW OL2 .... 43 J7
Crompton Swimming Pool
 ROY/SHW OL2 .... 43 L6
Cromwell High School &
 Astley Sports College
 DUK SK16 .... 91 H6
Cromwell House Community
 Mental Health Centre
 ECC M30 .... 85 G2
Cromwell Special School
 DTN/ASHW M34 .... 100 C2
Cronshaw Industrial Estate
 ROCH OL11 .... 11 G7
Crosland Industrial Estate
 MPL/ROM SK6 .... 101 H8
Crossacres J & I School
 WYTH/NTH M22 .... 110 C8
Crossgates Primary School
 MILN OL16 .... 29 K5
Crowcroft
 Park Primary School
 WGTN/LGST M12 .... 99 K1
Crown Business Centre
 FAIL M35 .... 74 C2
Crowne Plaza
 CMANW M2 .... 6 F6
Crown Industrial Estate
 ALT WA14 .... 108 B5
 ANC M4 .... 7 L2
Crown Royal Industrial Park
 STKP SK1 .... 13 K6
Crumpsall Lane Primary School
 CHH M8 .... 72 D3

Cuba Industrial Estate
 RAMS BL0 .... 17 C4
Culcheth Hall School
 ALT WA14 .... 116 E1
Curzon Ashton FC
 AULW OL7 .... 90 C2
Curzon Cinema
 URM M41 .... 95 L2
Cutgate Shopping Precinct
 WHIT OL12 .... 27 L3
Dagenham Road
 Industrial Estate
 RUSH/FAL M14 .... 98 F1
Daisy Nook Country Park
 OLDS OL8 .... 75 H5
Dale Grove Primary Centre
 (Bankside)
 HYDE SK14 .... 102 C3
Dale Grove Special School
 AULW OL7 .... 75 K7
The Dale Primary School
 MPL/ROM SK6 .... 114 A5
Dale Street Industrial Estate
 RAD M26 .... 54 D2
Dancehouse Theatre &
 Northern Ballet Scool
 CMANE M1 .... 7 G8
Dane Bank Primary School
 DTN/ASHW M34 .... 100 D2
Dane Road Industrial Estate
 SALE M33 .... 96 F7
Darnhill CP School
 HEY OL10 .... 40 C3
Davaar Medical Centre
 DUK SK16 .... 90 F4
Davenport Golf Club
 POY/DIS SK12 .... 122 D8
David Cuthbert
 Business Centre
 OP/CLY M11 .... 88 F5
David Medical Centre
 CCHDY M21 .... 97 M6
Davyhulme Park Golf Club
 URM M41 .... 84 C8
Deakins Business Park
 EDGW/EG BL7 .... 22 A2
Deane Golf Club
 BOLS/LL BL3 .... 35 K7
Deane Leisure Centre
 BOLS/LL BL3 .... 35 J8
Deanery CE High School
 WGN WN1 .... 14 E3
The Deane School
 BOLS/LL BL3 .... 35 J8
Den Lane Medical Centre
 BRAM/HZG SK7 .... 121 M4
Dean Row Community
 Junior School
 WILM/AE SK9 .... 127 J3
The Deans CP School
 SWIN M27 .... 70 B4
Deans Road Industrial Estate
 SWIN M27 .... 70 A4
Deanway Trading Estate
 WILM/AE SK9 .... 127 H1
Deeplish Primary School
 ROCH OL11 .... 10 F8
Delamere School
 URM M41 .... 95 G2
De la Salle Centre &
 Pendleton College
 SLFD M6 .... 85 M1
Delph Clinic
 UPML OL3 .... 45 H8
Delph & Dobcross Cricket Club
 UPML OL3 .... 45 J8
Delph Primary School
 UPML OL3 .... 45 H7
Delta Business Park
 DTN/ASHW M34 .... 90 B5
Demmings Infant School
 CHD/CHDH SK8 .... 111 J7
Dental Hospital
 HULME M15 .... 87 K6
Denton Cemetery
 DTN/ASHW M34 .... 101 J4
Denton Cricket & Sports Club
 DTN/ASHW M34 .... 90 B7
Denton Golf Club
 DTN/ASHW M34 .... 89 L8
Denton St Lawrence
 Cricket Club
 DTN/ASHW M34 .... 101 J3
Department of
 Clinical Psychology
 ROY/SHW OL2 .... 59 H2
Derby High School
 BURY BL9 .... 4 C9
Derby Shopping Centre
 BOLS/LL BL3 .... 2 A8
Derwent Street Trading Estate
 ORD M5 .... 86 F5
The Designer Outlet
 SALQ M50 .... 86 C5
De Vere White's Hotel
 HOR/BR BL6 .... 34 A5
Devonshire Road
 Primary School
 BOL BL1 .... 35 K4
Devonshire Street
 Industrial Estate
 WGTN/LGST M12 .... 88 A6
Dial Park Primary School
 OFTN SK2 .... 113 G8
Didsbury CE Primary School
 DID/WITH M20 .... 110 E1
Didsbury Cricket Club
 DID/WITH M20 .... 110 F3
Didsbury Golf Club
 WYTH/NTH M22 .... 110 C3
Didsbury Medical Centre
 DID/WITH M20 .... 98 D8
Didsbury Primary School
 HTNM SK4 .... 111 J2
Diggle School
 UPML OL3 .... 45 M7
Dinting CE Primary School
 GLSP SK13 .... 104 D3
Dinting Lane Industrial Estate
 GLSP SK13 .... 104 D3
Dinting Lodge
 Industrial Estate
 GLSP SK13 .... 104 C1
Dinting Vale Business Park
 GLSP SK13 .... 104 B2
Disley Golf Club
 POY/DIS SK12 .... 123 L5
Disley Primary School
 POY/DIS SK12 .... 123 M6

Dobson Park Industrial Estate
 WGNE/HIN WN2 .... 48 C6
Dodd Lane Industrial Estate
 WHTN BL5 .... 33 L8
Douglas Valley Business Park
 WGN WN1 .... 31 M7
Downall Green RC
 Primary School
 AIMK WN4 .... 63 H6
Downing Street
 Industrial Estate
 CMANE M1 .... 7 K8
Dowry Park Industrial Estate
 OLDE OL4 .... 60 B5
Dowson Primary School
 HYDE SK14 .... 102 B4
Droylsden AFC
 DROY M43 .... 89 K3
Droylsden High School for Girls
 DROY M43 .... 89 H2
Droylsden Sports Centre
 DROY M43 .... 89 H2
Droylsden Swimming Pool
 DROY M43 .... 89 K4
Ducie Athletics Ground
 Running Track
 GTN M18 .... 88 C3
Ducie High School
 RUSH/FAL M14 .... 87 K8
Ducie High School For Boys
 RUSH/FAL M14 .... 87 L8
Ducie Sports Centre
 RUSH/FAL M14 .... 87 L8
Duke of Norfolk CE
 Primary School
 GLSP SK13 .... 105 G3
Dukesgate Primary School
 LHULT M38 .... 52 D7
Dukinfield Crematorium
 DUK SK16 .... 91 G3
Dukinfield Golf Club
 DUK SK16 .... 91 K5
Dukinfield Joint Cemetery
 DUK SK16 .... 91 G3
Dunham Forest Golf &
 Country Club
 ALT WA14 .... 107 J8
Dunscar Golf Club
 EDGW/EG BL7 .... 22 A4
Dunscar Industrial Estate
 EDGW/EG BL7 .... 22 B5
Dunstan Medical Centre
 BOLE BL2 .... 3 L4
Durnford Medical Centre
 MDTN M24 .... 57 J3
Durn Street Industrial Estate
 LIT OL15 .... 20 D6
Eagley Infant School
 EDGW/EG BL7 .... 22 D4
Eagley Junior School
 EDGW/EG BL7 .... 22 E4
East Crompton St Georges CE
 Primary School
 ROY/SHW OL2 .... 43 M5
East Crompton St James CE
 Primary School
 ROY/SHW OL2 .... 43 L5
East Lancashire Railway
 BURY BL9 .... 25 G4
 HEY OL10 .... 40 F4
East Ward Primary School
 BURY BL9 .... 5 L4
Eatock Primary School
 WHTN BL5 .... 50 B6
Eaton Place Business Centre
 SALE M33 .... 96 D8
Eccles College
 ECC M30 .... 70 C8
Eccles Crematorium
 ECC M30 .... 84 C4
Eccles Health Centre
 ECC M30 .... 85 J2
Eccles Recreation Centre
 ECC M30 .... 85 J3
Eccleston Avenue
 RUSH/FAL M14 .... 98 D3
Eccles Town Hall
 ECC M30 .... 85 J2
Edenfield Cricket Club
 RAMS BL0 .... 17 E1
Edge Fold Industrial Estate
 FWTH BL4 .... 51 M3
Edgworth CE/Methodist
 Primary School
 EDGW/EG BL7 .... 16 D7
Edgworth Cricket Club
 EDGW/EG BL7 .... 16 E6
Egerton Cricket Club
 EDGW/EG BL7 .... 22 A1
Egerton & Dunscar
 Health Centre
 EDGW/EG BL7 .... 22 C4
Egerton House Hotel
 EDGW/EG BL7 .... 22 B2
Egerton Park Arts College
 DTN/ASHW M34 .... 90 B7
Egerton Park Community
 High School
 DTN/ASHW M34 .... 90 A8
Elk Mill Central Retail Park
 OLD OL1 .... 58 E1
Elladene Park
 CCHDY M21 .... 97 M4
Ellenbrook Primary School
 WALK M28 .... 68 E5
Ellesmere Golf Club
 WALK M28 .... 69 J3
Ellesmere Retail Park
 WALK M28 .... 68 F1
Ellesmere Shopping Centre
 LHULT M38 .... 68 F1
Elmridge Primary School
 HALE/TIMP WA15 .... 117 L4
Elms Medical Centre
 WHTF M45 .... 55 H3
Elm Wood Primary School
 MDTN M24 .... 57 M4
Elsinore Business Centre
 OLDTF/WHR M16 .... 86 D8
The Elton High School
 TOT/BURYW BL8 .... 38 D1
Elton Primary School
 TOT/BURYW BL8 .... 38 F1
Emmanuel Christian School
 WHIT OL12 .... 28 A3

Emmanuel Holcombe
Primary School
TOT/BURY BL8 .... 17 A6
Empress Business Centre
OLDTF/WHR M16 .... 86 F6
Empress Industrial Estate
WGNE/HIN WN2 .... 15 M5
English Martyrs RC
Primary School
RNFD/HAY WA11 .... 78 A5
NM/HAY SK22 .... 95 M2
Ensor Trading Estate
NM/HAY SK22 .... 124 E6
Enterprise Trading Estate
GTN M18 .... 89 H6
TRPK M17 .... 85 K4
Esplanade Arts &
Heritage Centre
MILN OL16 .... 10 D5
Etchells Primary School
CHD/CHDH SK8 .... 119 L3
Etherow Country Park
MPL/ROM SK6 .... 115 G1
Etherow Industrial Estate
HYDE SK14 .... 93 G8
Eton Hill Industrial Estate
RAD M26 .... 38 F7
Etrop Grange Hotel
& Restaurant
MANAIR M90 .... 118 D3
ETZ Chaim School
CHH M8 .... 72 B2
Europa Business Park
EDGY/DAV SK3 .... 111 L6
Europa Trading Estate
RAD M26 .... 53 L5
Ewing School
DID/WITH M20 .... 98 D7
Express by Holiday Inn
GTN M18 .... 89 H7
HOR/BR BL6 .... 33 M5
SALQ M50 .... 86 C5
Express Trading Estate
FWTH BL4 .... 53 G6
The Eye Clinic
CMANW M2 .... 6 F5
Fahay Industrial Estate
NEWH/MOS M40 .... 88 B2
Failsworth Health Centre
FAIL M35 .... 74 B5
Failsworth Industrial Estate
FAIL M35 .... 73 M6
Failsworth School (Upper)
FAIL M35 .... 74 D5
Failsworth Shopping Centre
FAIL M35 .... 74 C5
Fairfield General Hospital
BURY BL9 .... 26 B8
Fairfield Golf & Sailing Club
DTN/ASHW M34 .... 89 L5
Fairfield High School for Girls
DROY M43 .... 89 J4
Fairfield Primary School
BURY BL9 .... 40 A1
Fairfield Road
Primary School
DROY M43 .... 89 J4
Fairhill Industrial Estate
IRL M44 .... 94 C5
Fairview Medical Centre
URM M41 .... 95 L2
Fairway Primary School
OFTN SK2 .... 113 H6
Falcon Business Centre
CHAD OL9 .... 8 C2
Falinge Park High School
WHIT OL12 .... 10 B1
Fall Birch Hospital Lodge
HOR/BR BL6 .... 34 D3
Fallowfield Medical Centre
RUSH/FAL M14 .... 99 G4
Fallowfield Shopping Centre
RUSH/FAL M14 .... 99 H3
Farjo Medical Centre
CMANE M1 .... 7 H6
Farnworth Cemetery
FWTH BL4 .... 53 H3
Farnworth Little Theatre
FWTH BL4 .... 53 G4
Farnworth Park
Industrial Estate
FWTH BL4 .... 53 G3
Farnworth Social Circle
Cricket Club
FWTH BL4 .... 52 F5
Farrowdale House School
ROY/SHW OL2 .... 43 L6
Fiddlers Lane Primary School
IRL M44 .... 94 E1
Fieldhouse Cricket Club
ROCH OL11 .... 27 H6
Fieldhouse Industrial Estate
WHIT OL12 .... 28 C2
Firbank Primary School
ROY/SHW OL2 .... 43 G5
Firgrove Business Park
MILN OL16 .... 29 G4
Firs CP School
SALE M33 .... 96 A8
Firsdale Industrial Estate
LEIGH WN7 .... 65 M6
Fir Tree Primary School
RDSH SK5 .... 100 B2
Firwood Industrial Estate
BOLE BL2 .... 36 F2
Firwood Manor
Preparatory School
CHAD OL9 .... 8 A1
Firwood Special School
BOLE BL2 .... 36 F2
Fishbrook Industrial Estate
FWTH BL4 .... 53 J5
Fishpool Infant School
BURY BL9 .... 4 F1
Fishwicks Industrial Estate
RNFD/HAY WA11 .... 78 C4
Fitton Hill Shopping Precinct
OLDS OL8 .... 75 J1
Five Fold Industrial Park
CHAD OL9 .... 8 F6
Flixton Cricket Club
URM M41 .... 95 H1
Flixton FC
URM M41 .... 95 G1
Flixton Girls High School
URM M41 .... 95 K2
Flixton Health Clinic
URM M41 .... 95 G2
Flixton J & I School
URM M41 .... 95 J2

Flowery Field Primary School
HYDE SK14 .... 91 G8
Forest Gate Community
Primary School
PART M31 .... 106 A1
Forest Park Primary School
SALE M33 .... 96 D8
Forest School
HALE/TIMP WA15 .... 108 C6
Forge Industrial Estate
OLDE OL4 .... 59 L5
Forum Leisure Centre
WYTH/NTH M22 .... 118 E1
Fourways Trading Estate
TRPK M17 .... 85 K6
Fowler Industrial Estate
HOR/BR BL6 .... 33 M2
Foyer & Coops Business Centre
WGN WN1 .... 14 E4
Fred Longworth High School
TYLD M29 .... 67 H3
Freehold Community
Primary School
CHAD OL9 .... 8 C8
Freetown Business Park
BURY BL9 .... 5 H1
The Friars Primary School
CSLFD M3 .... 6 B1
Friezland Primary School
OLDE OL4 .... 61 H7
Fulshaw CE Primary School
WILM/AE SK9 .... 126 D6
Furness Vale Business Centre
CHF/WBR SK23 .... 124 F8
Furrow Community School
MDTN M24 .... 56 F1
Galleon Leisure Centre
DID/WITH M20 .... 110 F4
The Galleries Shopping Centre
WGN WN1 .... 14 F3
Gallery of Costume
RUSH/FAL M14 .... 98 F2
The Gallery
HALE/TIMP WA15 .... 116 F1
Gamesley Community
Primary School
GLSP SK13 .... 104 B2
Garrett Hall Primary School
TYLD M29 .... 68 A5
Garrick Playhouse
ALT WA14 .... 108 A6
Garrick Theatre
EDGY/DAV SK3 .... 13 H5
Garswood FC
AIMK WN4 .... 62 E7
Garswood Primary School
AIMK WN4 .... 62 E6
Gaskell Primary School
BOL BL1 .... 2 B2
The Gates Primary School
WHTN BL5 .... 50 C2
The Gates Shopping Centre
BOL BL1 .... 2 E4
Gateway Industrial Estate
CMANE M1 .... 7 K5
Gathurst Golf Club
WGNNW/ST WN6 .... 30 C7
Gatley Golf Club
CHD/CHDH SK8 .... 119 K1
Gatley Health Centre
CHD/CHDH SK8 .... 110 D6
Gatley Primary School
CHD/CHDH SK8 .... 110 D7
Gee Cross Holy Trinity CE
Primary School
HYDE SK14 .... 102 C4
Gee Cross Social & Sports Club
HYDE SK14 .... 102 B4
Geler Wood Country Park
ROCH OL11 .... 26 F6
George H Carnall
Leisure Centre
URM M41 .... 85 H8
George Tomlinson School
FWTH BL4 .... 53 H6
Georgian Health Centre
OLD OL1 .... 9 K5
Gidlow Cemetery
WGNNW/ST WN6 .... 31 K7
Gilded Hollins Primary School
LEIGH WN7 .... 80 F3
Gilnow Mill Industrial Estate
BOL BL1 .... 35 M6
Gilnow Primary School
BOL BL1 .... 35 M6
Glazebury CE Primary School
GOL/RIS/CU WA3 .... 81 M5
Glebe House School
MILN OL16 .... 10 D6
Glen Trading Estate
OLDE OL4 .... 60 A6
Globe Industrial Estate
RAD M26 .... 54 E1
Globe Lane Industrial Estate
DUK SK16 .... 90 E5
Globe Lane Primary School
DUK SK16 .... 90 E6
Glodwick Health Centre
OLDE OL4 .... 59 L6
Glodwick Infant School
OLDE OL4 .... 59 L7
Glossopdale Community College
GLSP SK13 .... 104 F2
Glossop & District Golf Club
GLSP SK13 .... 105 K4
Glossop RUFC
GLSP SK13 .... 104 B5
Glossop Victorian
Swimming Pool
GLSP SK13 .... 104 F2
Gloucester House
Medical Centre
URM M41 .... 96 A1
GMB National College
OLDTF/WHR M16 .... 97 M2
GMEX Centre
CMANW M2 .... 6 E7
Golborne Clinic
GOL/RIS/CU WA3 .... 79 L3
Golborne CP School
GOL/RIS/CU WA3 .... 79 K4
Golborne High School
GOL/RIS/CU WA3 .... 79 M3
Golden Tulip Hotel
TRPK M17 .... 86 C6
Gorrells Industrial Estate
ROCH OL11 .... 42 B1
Gorsefield Primary School
RAD M26 .... 38 D8

Gorse Hall Primary School
STLY SK15 .... 91 J3
Gorse Hill Health Centre
STRET M32 .... 97 H1
Gorse Hill Primary School
STRET M32 .... 86 B8
Gorsey Bank Primary School
WILM/AE SK9 .... 126 D5
Gorton Brook First School
WGTN/LGST M12 .... 88 D6
Gorton Industrial Estate
GTN M18 .... 88 F6
Gorton Medical Centre
GTN M18 .... 89 G7
Gorton Mount Primary School
GTN M18 .... 99 M1
Gorton Retail Market
GTN M18 .... 89 G7
Goshen Sports Centre
BURY BL9 .... 39 K6
Goyt Valley Industrial Estate
CHF/WBR SK23 .... 124 F8
Granada Studios
CSLFD M3 .... 6 C5
Grange Primary School
WILM/AE SK9 .... 119 L8
Grange School
CHAD OL9 .... 9 G4
RUSH/FAL M14 .... 99 C1
Grange Valley Primary School
RNFD/HAY WA11 .... 78 A7
Grasmere Street Health Centre
LEIGH WN7 .... 66 B6
Grasscroft Independent School
OLDE OL4 .... 60 F7
Great Lever & Farnworth
Golf Club
FWTH BL4 .... 52 A3
Great Moor Clinic
OFTN SK2 .... 112 F7
Great Moor Primary School
OFTN SK2 .... 112 E8
Greave Primary School
MPL/ROM SK6 .... 101 M8
Greenacres Primary School
OLDE OL4 .... 59 M5
Greenbank Industrial Estate
WCNE/HIN WN2 .... 65 K1
Greenbank Primary School
WHIT OL12 .... 28 C3
Greenbank School
CHD/CHDH SK8 .... 120 C3
Greenbrow Infant School
NTHM/RTH M23 .... 118 B1
Greencourts Business Park
WYTH/NTH M22 .... 119 J5
Green End Junior School
BNG/LEV M19 .... 99 H7
Greenfield Cricket Club
UPML OL3 .... 61 L7
Greenfield Primary School
HYDE SK14 .... 102 B3
UPML OL3 .... 61 L6
Green Fold Special School
FWTH BL4 .... 52 C4
Greengate Industrial Estate
MILN OL16 .... 57 M7
Greenheys Business Centre
HULME M15 .... 87 K7
Greenhill Primary School
OLDE OL4 .... 9 K8
TOT/BURYW BL8 .... 38 C3
Green Lane Industrial Estate
HTNM SK4 .... 12 D3
Greenmount Cricket Club
TOT/BURYW BL8 .... 24 C3
Greenmount Primary School
TOT/BURYW BL8 .... 24 B2
Greenpine Industrial Park
HOR/BR BL6 .... 34 A4
Green Room Theatre
CMANE M1 .... 6 F7
Greenside Primary School
DROY M43 .... 89 J2
Greenside Trading Centre
DROY M43 .... 89 K3
Greenwood Business Centre
ORD M5 .... 86 D3
Greenwood Primary School
ECC M30 .... 70 B8
Greswell Primary School
DTN/ASHW M34 .... 101 H2
Greyhound & Speedway Stadium
GTN M18 .... 88 E7
Greyland Medical Centre
PWCH M25 .... 55 L6
Griffin Business Centre
SLFD M6 .... 71 M7
Grosvenor Business Park
MPL/ROM SK6 .... 101 J6
Grosvenor Industrial Estate
AULW OL7 .... 90 D3
Grosvenor Road
Primary School
SWIN M27 .... 70 E6
Guardian Angels RC
Primary School
RAMS BL0 .... 17 A8
Guide Bridge Industrial Estate
DTN/ASHW M34 .... 90 B4
Guide Bridge Theatre
DTN/ASHW M34 .... 90 B4
Guide Bridge Trading Estate
DTN/ASHW M34 .... 90 B4
Guinness Road Trading Estate
TRPK M17 .... 85 J4
Hadfield Clinic
GLSP SK13 .... 93 K7
Hadfield Industrial Estate
GLSP SK13 .... 93 J6
Hadfield Infant School
GLSP SK13 .... 93 J8
Hadfield St Charles RC Primary
GLSP SK13 .... 93 H7
Hague Bar Primary School
NM/HAY SK22 .... 124 A4
Haigh Hall Country Park
WGNE/HIN WN2 .... 32 C6
Halebarns Cricket Club
HALE/TIMP WA15 .... 117 M6
Hale Barns Cricket Club
HALE/TIMP WA15 .... 118 A4
Hale Golf Club
HALE/TIMP WA15 .... 117 J5
Hale Preparatory School
HALE/TIMP WA15 .... 117 G1
Halfpenny Bridge
Industrial Estate
ROCH OL11 .... 11 G6

Hallgate Bus Station
WGN WN1 .... 14 F3
Halliwell Industrial Estate
BOL BL1 .... 36 A1
Hamer County Community
Primary School
WHIT OL12 .... 28 E2
Hampson Street Trading Estate
ORD M5 .... 6 A5
Handforth Health Centre
WILM/AE SK9 .... 127 H1
Hanover Business Park
ALT WA14 .... 107 L5
Harcourt Industrial Centre
WALK M28 .... 53 G7
Hardman Fold Special School
FAIL M35 .... 74 A5
Hardy Mill Primary School
BOLE BL2 .... 23 J8
Hare Hill (NT)
MCFLDN SK10 .... 131 K6
Harper Green School
FWTH BL4 .... 52 E3
Harphurey Business Centre
BKLY M9 .... 73 G3
Harp Industrial Estate
ROCH OL11 .... 42 A2
Harp Trading Estate
TRPK M17 .... 85 G4
Harpurhey Health Centre
BKLY M9 .... 73 G4
Harpur Mount Primary School
BKLY M9 .... 73 G4
Harrop Fold School
WALK M28 .... 68 E2
Harrytown Catholic
High School
MPL/ROM SK6 .... 113 K2
Hart Common Golf Club
WHTN BL5 .... 49 L5
Hartford Industrial Estate
CHAD OL9 .... 8 D7
Hartshead High School
AUL OL6 .... 76 B5
Harwood Golf Club (Bolton)
BOLE BL2 .... 23 K8
Harwood Health Centre
BOLE BL2 .... 23 G7
Harwood Meadows
Primary School
BOLE BL2 .... 37 J1
Harwood Park Primary School
HEY OL10 .... 41 G3
Haslam Park Primary School
BOLS/LL BL3 .... 35 L7
Haslemere Industrial Estate
AIMK WN4 .... 63 K4
Hathershaw Technology College
OLDS OL8 .... 75 J2
Hat Museum
EDGY/DAV SK3 .... 13 H5
Hattersley Health Clinic
HYDE SK14 .... 103 H2
Hattersley Industrial Estate
HYDE SK14 .... 103 H3
Hawkins Clinic
MILN OL16 .... 10 F5
Hawkley Brook Trading Estate
WGNS/IIMK WN3 .... 63 H2
Hawkley Hall High School
WGNS/IIMK WN3 .... 63 L1
Hawksley Industrial Estate
OLDS OL8 .... 74 F1
Hawthorns Special School
DTN/ASHW M34 .... 90 A7
Haydock Cricket Club
RNFD/HAY WA11 .... 78 A5
Haydock Lane Industrial Estate
RNFD/HAY WA11 .... 78 B5
Haydock Medical Centre
RNFD/HAY WA11 .... 78 A6
Haydock Park Golf Club
NEWLW WA12 .... 79 J7
Haydock Park Racecourse
NEWLW WA12 .... 78 F3
Hayfield Primary School
NM/HAY SK22 .... 125 L1
Hayward School
BOLS/LL BL3 .... 52 A2
Hayward Sports Centre
BOLS/LL BL3 .... 51 M2
Hazeldene Medical Centre
NEWH/MOS M40 .... 74 B3
Hazel Grove Clinic
BRAM/HZG SK7 .... 122 A1
Hazel Grove Golf Club
BRAM/HZG SK7 .... 122 D3
Hazel Grove High School
BRAM/HZG SK7 .... 121 L3
Hazel Grove Pools &
Fitness Centre
BRAM/HZG SK7 .... 121 J3
Hazel Grove Primary School
BRAM/HZG SK7 .... 122 A1
Hazel Grove Recreation Centre
BRAM/HZG SK7 .... 121 L4
Hazlehurst Primary School
RAMS BL0 .... 17 A8
Heald Green Medical Centre
CHD/CHDH SK8 .... 119 K4
Heald Place Primary School
RUSH/FAL M14 .... 98 E1
Healey Dell Nature Reserve
WHIT OL12 .... 18 C8
Healey Primary School
WHIT OL12 .... 28 B1
Heap Bridge Primary School
BURY BL9 .... 40 A3
Heathfield Primary School
BOLS/LL BL3 .... 51 K2
Heaton Cemetery
BOL BL1 .... 35 L6
Heaton Cricket Club
BOL BL1 .... 35 K2
Heaton Hall
PWCH M25 .... 55 M8
Heaton Medical Centre
BOL BL1 .... 35 J2
Heaton Moor Golf Club
HTNM SK4 .... 99 K7
Heaton Moor Medical Centre
HTNM SK4 .... 99 M7
Heaton Moor Rugby Union FC
HTNM SK4 .... 12 B1
Heaton Norris Health Centre
HTNM SK4 .... 12 F1
Heaton Park Golf Centre
PWCH M25 .... 56 B6
Heaton Special School
HTNM SK4 .... 99 L7

Hempshaw Business Centre
STKP SK1 .... 112 E5
Henshaw Society for the Blind
OLDTF/WHR M16 .... 86 D8
Hertford Industrial Estate
AULW OL7 .... 90 D3
Hesketh Fletcher CE
High School
ATH M46 .... 66 F2
Hewitt Business Park
WGNW/BIL/O WN5 .... 46 B8
Heybrook Primary School
WHIT OL12 .... 11 H1
Heyes Lane J & I School
HALE/TIMP WA15 .... 108 E4
The Heys Primary School
AUL OL6 .... 91 G1
Hey with Zion Primary School
OLDE OL4 .... 60 B5
Heywood Cemetery
ROCH OL11 .... 27 J8
Heywood Community
High School
HEY OL10 .... 40 C3
Heywood Industrial Park
HEY OL10 .... 40 D4
Heywood Sports Complex
HEY OL10 .... 40 E1
Higginshaw Sports Club
OLD OL1 .... 9 L3
Highbank Trading Estate
OP/CLY M11 .... 89 G5
Highbarn Junior School
ROY/SHW OL2 .... 43 H7
High Birch Special School
ROCH OL11 .... 27 L7
Higher Broughton
Health Centre
BRO M7 .... 72 B6
Higher Lane Primary School
WHTF M45 .... 55 H4
Higher Openshaw
Community School
OP/CLY M11 .... 89 G4
Highfield Cemetery
MPL/ROM SK6 .... 113 J2
Highfield CE Primary School
WGNS/IIMK WN3 .... 46 F8
Highfield Cricket Club
WGNS/IIMK WN3 .... 46 F8
Highfield Hospital
ROCH OL11 .... 10 C8
Highfield Primary School
FWTH BL4 .... 52 D4
URM M41 .... 96 C2
Highfield Secondary School
WALK M28 .... 68 C6
High Lane Medical Centre
MPL/ROM SK6 .... 123 G5
High Lane Primary School
MPL/ROM SK6 .... 123 G4
High Lawn Primary School
BOL BL1 .... 22 B6
Highlea Secondary School
WALK M28 .... 68 C4
High Lea Tution Service
DID/WITH M20 .... 98 F5
High Point Hotel
OLDS OL8 .... 8 F7
Hillcrest Grammar School
EDGY/DAV SK3 .... 112 C6
Hillgate Business Centre
STKP SK1 .... 13 K7
Hill Top Community
Primary School
ROCH OL11 .... 42 D9
Hill Top Community
Special School
OLDE OL4 .... 44 D8
Hilton Lane Primary School
WALK M28 .... 68 D1
Hindley All Saints CEP School
WGNE/HIN WN2 .... 49 H7
Hindley Business Centre
WGNE/HIN WN2 .... 49 G7
Hindley Green Primary School
WGNE/HIN WN2 .... 65 L2
Hindley Hall Golf Club
WGNE/HIN WN2 .... 49 G4
Hindley Leisure Centre
WGNE/HIN WN2 .... 49 J7
Hindley Primary School
WGNE/HIN WN2 .... 49 H7
Hindsford Primary School
ATH M46 .... 67 H3
HM Prison
CSLFD M3 .... 72 C8
WGNE/HIN WN2 .... 65 G2
Hodge Clough Infant School
OLD OL1 .... 60 A1
Hodge Clough Junior School
OLD OL1 .... 60 A1
Holcombe Brook
Primary School
RAMS BL0 .... 24 D2
Holcombe Brook Sports Club
RAMS BL0 .... 24 D1
Holden Clough Primary School
AUL OL6 .... 76 A5
Holden Road Trading Estate
LEIGH WN7 .... 66 D7
Holiday Inn
BOLS/LL BL3 .... 35 H8
RNFD/HAY WA11 .... 78 E4
Hollingworth High School
MILN OL16 .... 29 K6
Hollingworth Lake
Activity Centre
LIT OL15 .... 29 K2
Hollingworth Lake
Caravan Park
LIT OL15 .... 29 M3
Hollingworth Lake
Country Park
LIT OL15 .... 29 M2
Hollingworth Primary School
HYDE SK14 .... 92 F7
Hollin Primary School
MDTN M24 .... 57 K1
Hollins Grundy Primary School
BURY BL9 .... 39 K7
Hollins Industrial Park
GLSP SK13 .... 93 G3
Hollins Primary School
WGNE/HIN WN2 .... 49 K7
Hollinwood Business Centre
FAIL M35 .... 74 E4
Hollinwood Cemetery
OLDS OL8 .... 74 F3

Hollinwood Cricket Club
OLDS OL8 .... 74 F4

Holly Bank Industrial Estate
RAD M26 .... 54 C1

Holly Mount RC Primary School
TOT/BURYW BL8 .... 24 A3

Hollywood Bowl
HOR/BR BL6 .... 34 A4
NEWH/MOS M40 .... 74 A3

Holt Town Industrial Estate
NEWH/MOS M40 .... 88 B2

Holy Cross & All Saints RC Primary School
ECC M30 .... 85 G4

Holy Cross 6th Form College
BURY BL9 .... 4 E8

Holy Family Catholic Primary School
SALE M33 .... 97 H8

Holy Family RC Primary School
OLDS OL8 .... 75 G4
ROCH OL11 .... 42 D1
WGNE/HIN WN2 .... 64 D3

Holy Infant RC Primary School
BOL BL1 .... 22 B8

Holy Name RC Primary School
HULME M15 .... 87 K7

Holy Rosary RC Primary School
OLDS OL8 .... 75 J2

Holy Trinity CE Dobcross School
UPML OL3 .... 61 J2

Holy Trinity CE Primary School
AUL OL6 .... 90 D1
BKLY M9 .... 73 H4
BURY BL9 .... 4 F6
LIT OL15 .... 20 C7

Hong Sing Chinese Medical Centre
BRAM/HZG SK7 .... 122 A1

Hooley Bridge Industrial Estate
HEY OL10 .... 26 F8

Hope Hospital
SLFD M6 .... 85 L2

Hope Special School
WCNS/IIMK WN3 .... 63 J2

Hopwood Cottage
MDTN M24 .... 41 M6

Hopwood Hall College
MDTN M24 .... 41 L7

Hopwood Medical Centre
HEY OL10 .... 41 H3

Hopwood Primary School
HEY OL10 .... 41 H4

Horton Mill Primary School
OLDE OL4 .... 59 L6

Horwich Business Park
HOR/BR BL6 .... 33 L2

Horwich Leisure Centre
HOR/BR BL6 .... 33 M1

Horwich Parish CE Primary School
HOR/BR BL6 .... 21 C8

Hotel Ibis
CMANE M1 .... 7 G6

Hotel Smokies Park
OLDS OL8 .... 75 J4

Houldsworth Golf Club
RDSH SK5 .... 100 B4

Houldsworth Medical Centre
RDSH SK5 .... 100 C5

Howe Bridge Crematorium
LEIGH WN7 .... 66 C3

Howe Bridge Sports Centre
ATH M46 .... 66 E3

Hubert House Jewish Boys School
BRO M7 .... 72 A4

Hubert Jewish High School for Girls
BRO M7 .... 71 M4

Hulme Adult Education Centre
HULME M15 .... 87 H6

Hulme Arch
HULME M15 .... 87 J6

The Hulme Grammar School for Girls & Boys
OLDS OL8 .... 59 G8

Hulme Hall Grammar School
CHD/CHDH SK8 .... 120 C3

Hulton Hospital
BOLS/LL BL3 .... 51 K1

Hurstfield Industrial Estate
HTNM SK4 .... 100 B6

Hursthead Primary School
CHD/CHDH SK8 .... 120 E6

Hurst Knoll CE Primary School
AUL OL6 .... 75 M8

Hurst Methodist Junior School
AUL OL6 .... 76 A5

Hurst Mills Industrial Estate
GLSP SK13 .... 105 K3

Hyde Cricket Club
HYDE SK14 .... 102 C6

Hyde Leisure Pool
HYDE SK14 .... 102 B2

Hyde Technology School
HYDE SK14 .... 90 F8

Hyde United FC
HYDE SK14 .... 102 C2

IMAX Cinema
ANC M4 .... 7 G3

IMEX Business Park
BRUN/LGST M13 .... 99 J1

Imperial War Museum North
TRPK M17 .... 86 B5

Ince Clinic & Community Centre
WGNE/HIN WN2 .... 48 D5

Ince in Makerfield Primary School
WGNE/HIN WN2 .... 48 D5

Indoor Tennis Centre
OP/CLY M11 .... 88 C2

Industrial Hygiene Research Laboratories
MCFLDN SK10 .... 130 E8

Inland Revenue Office
CSLFD M3 .... 6 D4

Innes Special School
WHIT OL12 .... 27 M3

Innkeepers Lodge
WILM/AE SK9 .... 126 E8

Innkeeper's Lodge Warrington
GOL/RIS/CU WA3 .... 80 B6

Inscape House Special School
WALK M28 .... 69 H3

Institute of Islamic Higher Education
EDGW/EG BL7 .... 22 D4

The Instructor College
STKP SK1 .... 13 J5

International Convention Centre
CMANW M2 .... 6 E6

International Swimming Pool
WGN WN1 .... 15 G5

Irlam & Cadishead Community High School
IRL M44 .... 94 B5

Irlam County Primary School
IRL M44 .... 94 C3

Irlam Endowed Primary School
IRL M44 .... 94 D2

Irlam Industrial Estate
IRL M44 .... 94 B5

Irlam Swimming Pool
IRL M44 .... 94 D3

James Brindley Primary School
WALK M28 .... 68 F3

Jeff Joseph Sale Moor Technology College
SALE M33 .... 109 G2

Jewish Museum
CHH M8 .... 72 D8

Jewish Senior Boys School
BRO M7 .... 72 A5

The JJB Stadium (Wigan AFC & Wigan Warriors RLFC)
WGNW/BIL/O WN5 .... 47 H4

John Rylands Library
CSLFD M3 .... 6 E5

Johnson Fold Primary School
BOL BL1 .... 35 J1

John Street Medical Centre
GOL/RIS/CU WA3 .... 79 K4

Joseph Adamson Industrial Estate
HYDE SK14 .... 101 M2

Jumbles Country Park
EDGW/EG BL7 .... 23 G3

Jury's Inn
CMANE M1 .... 6 E7

Kaskenmoor Comprehensive School
OLDS OL8 .... 74 E3

Kayley Industrial Estate
AULW OL7 .... 90 C1

Kearsley West Primary School
FWTH BL4 .... 53 H5

Kenmore Medical Centre
WILM/AE SK9 .... 126 E6

Kentmere Primary School
WHIT OL12 .... 28 E1

Kenyon Business Park
BOLS/LL BL3 .... 2 D8

Kershaw Business Centre
BOLS/LL BL3 .... 2 B8

Kiely Business Park
BURY BL9 .... 5 H1

Kilhey Court Hotel
WGN WN1 .... 31 M2

King David Junior & High School
CHH M8 .... 72 C3

Kingfisher Community Special School
CHAD OL9 .... 58 C7

Kingsdown High School
WGNW/BIL/O WN5 .... 46 F5

Kingshill School
TYLD M29 .... 67 J4

Kings Road Primary School
OLDTF/WHR M16 .... 97 K1

King Street Remedial Clinic
DUK SK16 .... 90 E3

Kingsway CP School
URM M41 .... 85 H8

Kingsway Retail Park
MILN OL16 .... 29 G5

Kingsway School
CHD/CHDH SK8 .... 110 F8

Kingsway Secondary School
CHD/CHDH SK8 .... 110 F7

Kingsway West Business Park
MILN OL16 .... 11 K8
ROCH OL11 .... 11 G9

Kirkfield Hotel
NEWLW WA12 .... 79 H8

Kirkless Industrial Estate
WGNE/HIN WN2 .... 48 D2

Knoll Street Industrial Park
BRO M7 .... 72 A1

Knowsley Junior School
OLDE OL4 .... 60 D5

Kratos Industrial Estate
URM M41 .... 85 J7

Lacey Green Primary School
WILM/AE SK9 .... 126 E3

Lady Barn House School
CHD/CHDH SK8 .... 119 M1

Ladybarn Primary School
DID/WITH M20 .... 99 G6

Ladybridge Primary School
BOLS/LL BL3 .... 35 J7
CHD/CHDH SK8 .... 111 L8

Ladybrook Primary School
BRAM/HZG SK7 .... 121 H5

Ladysmith Shopping Centre
AUL OL6 .... 90 E1

Ladywell Hospital Lodge
SALQ M50 .... 85 K2

Ladywood Special School
BOLS/LL BL3 .... 37 L8

Lamberhead Green Primary School
WGNW/BIL/O WN5 .... 46 E5

Lamberhead Industrial Estate
WGNW/BIL/O WN5 .... 46 E7

Lancashire CCC (County Ground, Old Trafford)
OLDTF/WHR M16 .... 86 D4

Lancasterian School
DID/WITH M20 .... 98 D7

Lance Burn Health Centre
SLFD M6 .... 86 D2

Landgate Industrial Estate
AIMK WN4 .... 63 K4

Lane End Primary School
CHD/CHDH SK8 .... 120 C1

Langdon College
BRO M7 .... 72 B3

Langley Primary School
MDTN M24 .... 57 H1

Language College
STRET M32 .... 86 C8

Langworthy Clinic
SLFD M6 .... 86 C2

Langworthy Road Primary School
SLFD M6 .... 86 C1

La Pergola Hotel
UPML OL3 .... 44 E1

Lark Hill Primary School
EDGY/DAV SK3 .... 12 D6

Last Drop Hotel
EDGW/EG BL7 .... 22 D3

The Last Drop Village
EDGW/EG BL7 .... 22 D3

Lavenham Business Centre
CHAD OL9 .... 8 D7

Lawn Cemetery
ALT WA14 .... 107 G4

Lawnhurst Trading Estate
CHD/CHDH SK8 .... 111 L7

Leeds Street Industrial Estate
WGNS/IIMK WN3 .... 14 D5

Leigh Business Park
LEIGH WN7 .... 81 L1

Leigh CE Infant School
LEIGH WN7 .... 66 C7

Leigh CE Junior School
LEIGH WN7 .... 66 C7

Leigh Central J & I School
LEIGH WN7 .... 66 C7

Leigh College Community Sixth Form College
LEIGH WN7 .... 81 H1

Leigh County Court
LEIGH WN7 .... 66 C7

Leigh Cricket Club
LEIGH WN7 .... 81 H2

Leigh FC
LEIGH WN7 .... 66 B6

Leigh Golf Club
GOL/RIS/CU WA3 .... 81 C8

Leigh Infant & Primary School
HYDE SK14 .... 102 B2

Leigh Rangers ARLFC
LEIGH WN7 .... 67 C8

Leigh RUFC
LEIGH WN7 .... 81 H3

Leigh Street Primary School
HYDE SK14 .... 102 C2

Le Meridien Victoria & Albert Hotel
ORD M5 .... 6 B5

Lemon Park Industrial Estate
HEY OL10 .... 41 H3

Levenshulme Baths
BNG/LEV M19 .... 99 L3

Levenshulme Health Centre
BNG/LEV M19 .... 99 L3

Levenshulme High School For Girls
BNG/LEV M19 .... 99 K5

Levenshulme Trading Estate
BNG/LEV M19 .... 99 M2

Lever Edge Primary School
BOLS/LL BL3 .... 52 A2

Lever Park School
HOR/BR BL6 .... 33 M1

Library, Museum & Art Gallery
OLD OL1 .... 9 K6

Light Oaks Primary School
SLFD M6 .... 70 E8

Lily Lane J & I School
NEWH/MOS M40 .... 73 K4

Limehurst Primary School
OLDS OL8 .... 75 G4

Limeside Primary School
OLDS OL8 .... 74 F3

Lime Tree Primary School
SALE M33 .... 109 H1

Linden Road Primary School
DTN/ASHW M34 .... 101 K1

Lindow Primary School
WILM/AE SK9 .... 130 A1

Linguard Business Centre
MILN OL16 .... 11 G5

Linkway Industrial Estate
MDTN M24 .... 57 L1

Linnyshaw Industrial Estate
FWTH BL4 .... 53 H6

Lisburne School
OFTN SK2 .... 113 H1

Littleborough Cricket Club
LIT OL15 .... 20 C1

Littleborough Primary School
LIT OL15 .... 20 C5

Little Lever School
BOLS/LL BL3 .... 53 J1

Littlemoor Primary School
OLDE OL4 .... 59 M4

Littlemoss Business Park
DROY M43 .... 89 M1

Littlemoss High School
DROY M43 .... 74 F8

Little Theatre
TYLD M29 .... 67 J4

Livingstone Primary School
MOSL OL5 .... 76 E4

L & M Business Park
ALT WA14 .... 107 L6

Lobden Golf Club
WHIT OL12 .... 18 F5

Lockside Medical Centre
STLY SK15 .... 91 L2

Longdendale High School
HYDE SK14 .... 92 F7

Longdendale Recreation Centre
HYDE SK14 .... 103 J1

Longfield Shopping Centre
PWCH M25 .... 55 K7

Longford Park Special School
STRET M32 .... 97 J2

Longford Trading Estate
STRET M32 .... 97 G1

Longshoot Health Centre
WGN WN1 .... 15 J2

Longsight Cricket Club
WGTN/LGST M12 .... 99 K1

Longsight Health Centre
BRUN/LGST M13 .... 88 B3

Longsight Industrial Estate
WGTN/LGST M12 .... 88 C5

Longsight Shopping Centre
WGTN/LGST M12 .... 88 C3

Lords College
BOLS/LL BL3 .... 3 G7

Lord Street Primary School
HOR/BR BL6 .... 21 B8

Loreto Convent Grammar School
ALT WA14 .... 107 M7

Loreto Preparatory School
ALT WA14 .... 107 M8

Lostock College
STRET M32 .... 96 D1

Lostock Hall Primary School
POY/DIS SK12 .... 128 F1

Lostock Industrial Estate
HOR/BR BL6 .... 34 B5

Lostock Primary School
HOR/BR BL6 .... 34 F6

Lower Broughton Health Centre
BRO M7 .... 72 A8

Lowercroft Primary School
TOT/BURYW BL8 .... 38 B2

Lower Kersal Primary School
BRO M7 .... 71 L6

Lower Park Primary School
POY/DIS SK12 .... 121 L8

Lowerplace Primary School
MILN OL16 .... 28 E8

Lowes Park Golf Club
BURY BL9 .... 25 K6

Low Hall Primary School
WGNE/HIN WN2 .... 64 D1

The Lowry Hotel
CSLFD M3 .... 6 D3

The Lowry
SALQ M50 .... 86 B5

Lowton Business Park
GOL/RIS/CU WA3 .... 80 D4

Lowton High School
GOL/RIS/CU WA3 .... 80 E4

Lowton J & I School
GOL/RIS/CU WA3 .... 80 D5

Lowton St Marys CE Primary School
GOL/RIS/CU WA3 .... 80 D4

Lowton West Primary School
GOL/RIS/CU WA3 .... 79 M4

Ludworth Primary School
MPL/ROM SK6 .... 114 D4

Lum Head Primary School
CHD/CHDH SK8 .... 119 K1

The Lyceum Musical Theatre
OLD OL1 .... 9 J6

Lyme Community Primary School
NEWLW WA12 .... 78 C8

Lyndhurst Primary School
DUK SK16 .... 90 F3
OLDS OL8 .... 75 G1

Lyntown Trading Estate
ECC M30 .... 85 G2

Lyon Industrial Estate
ALT WA14 .... 107 L5

Lyon Road Industrial Estate
FWTH BL4 .... 53 H7

Mabs Cross Primary School
WGN WN1 .... 15 H1

Macdonald Road Medical Centre
IRL M44 .... 94 B4

Mackenzie Industrial Estate
CHD/CHDH SK8 .... 111 L6

Magda House Medical Centre
OFTN SK2 .... 113 C8

Malbern Industrial Estate
DTN/ASHW M34 .... 89 M8

The Mall Shopping Centre
ECC M30 .... 85 J2

Mancentral Trading Estate
ORD M5 .... 6 B4

Manchester Airport World Freight Terminal
MANAIR M90 .... 118 C6

Manchester Aquatics Centre
BRUN/LGST M13 .... 7 J9

Manchester (Barton) Airfield
ECC M30 .... 84 B5

Manchester Business Park
MANAIR M90 .... 118 E4

Manchester Business School
HULME M15 .... 87 K6

Manchester Cathedral
CSLFD M3 .... 6 F2

Manchester Central Library
CMANW M2 .... 6 F6

Manchester Centre for the Deaf
BRUN/LGST M13 .... 87 K6

Manchester Centre for Vision
BRUN/LGST M13 .... 87 L7

Manchester City Art Galleries
CMANE M1 .... 7 G5

Manchester City FC (City of Manchester Stadium)
OP/CLY M11 .... 88 C3

Manchester College of Arts & Technology
CMANE M1 .... 7 J4
OP/CLY M11 .... 88 E5

Manchester Conference Centre & Hotel
CMANE M1 .... 7 J7

The Manchester Crematorium
CCHDY M21 .... 97 M6

Manchester Golf Club
BKLY M9 .... 57 L8

Manchester Grammar School
RUSH/FAL M14 .... 99 H2

Manchester High School for Girls
RUSH/FAL M14 .... 98 F3

Manchester Industrial Centre
CSLFD M3 .... 6 B6

Manchester International Airport
MANAIR M90 .... 118 D7

Manchester Islamic High School
RUSH/FAL M14 .... 97 K4

Manchester Jewish Grammar School
PWCH M25 .... 71 L1

Manchester Junior Girls School
BRO M7 .... 72 A3

Manchester Metropolitan University
CMANE M1 .... 7 G8
DID/WITH M20 .... 110 C1
DID/WITH M20 .... 110 D3
OLDTF/WHR M16 .... 98 C2
RUSH/FAL M14 .... 87 M8
RUSH/FAL M14 .... 99 G2

Manchester Metropolitan University Institute of Education (Didsbury)
DID/WITH M20 .... 110 D2

Manchester Museum
BRUN/LGST M13 .... 87 L6

Manchester Preparatory School
DID/WITH M20 .... 98 E8

Manchester Road CP School
DROY M43 .... 89 H3

Manchester Royal Infirmary
BRUN/LGST M13 .... 87 M7

Manchester RUFC
CHD/CHDH SK8 .... 120 C6

Manchester School of Management
BRUN/LGST M13 .... 87 K6

Manchester Southern Cemetery
CCHDY M21 .... 98 A6

Manchester United FC (Old Trafford)
OLDTF/WHR M16 .... 86 C7

Manchester United Museum & Tour Centre
OLDTF/WHR M16 .... 86 B7

Manchester University
BRUN/LGST M13 .... 87 M7

Manchester Youth Theatre
HULME M15 .... 87 J7

Mandeley Health Centre
BOL BL1 .... 22 B6

Manley Park Infant School
OLDTF/WHR M16 .... 97 M3

Manley Park Junior School
OLDTF/WHR M16 .... 97 M3

Manor Golf Club
FWTH BL4 .... 53 L8

Manor Green Primary School
DTN/ASHW M34 .... 101 K4

Manor High School
SALE M33 .... 95 M7

Manor House Surgery
GLSP SK13 .... 105 G3

Manway Business Park
ALT WA14 .... 108 B5

The Maples Medical Centre
NTHM/RTH M23 .... 109 J8

Marcliffe Industrial Estate
BRAM/HZG SK7 .... 122 B3

Marjory Lees Health Centre
OLD OL1 .... 9 K4

Marketgate Shopping Centre
WGN WN1 .... 14 F3

Market Place Shopping Centre
BOL BL1 .... 2 E4

Market Street Athletics Track
BURY BL9 .... 4 F7

Market Street Medical Centre
WGNE/HIN WN2 .... 49 G6

Markland Hill Primary School
BOL BL1 .... 35 J4

Marland Fold Special School
OLDS OL8 .... 75 K3

Marland Hill Primary School
ROCH OL11 .... 27 M7

Marple Clinic
MPL/ROM SK6 .... 114 C6

Marple Golf Club
MPL/ROM SK6 .... 123 G1

Marple Hall School
MPL/ROM SK6 .... 113 M5

Marriott Hotel
HALE/TIMP WA15 .... 118 A5

Marriott Worsley Park Hotel & Country Club
WALK M28 .... 69 H5

Marsh Green County Primary School
WGNW/BIL/O WN5 .... 47 G4

Marsh Green Health Centre
WGNW/BIL/O WN5 .... 47 G3

Marsh Lane Trading Estate
NM/HAY SK22 .... 124 C3

Marsland Street Industrial Centre
BRAM/HZG SK7 .... 121 M2

Marston Bentley Industrial Estate
WGNE/HIN WN2 .... 48 E2

Martland Mill Business Park
WGNW/BIL/O WN5 .... 47 G2

Martland Mill Industrial Estate
WGNW/BIL/O WN5 .... 46 F2

Marus Bridge Health Centre
WGNS/IIMK WN3 .... 63 J2

Marus Bridge School
WGNS/IIMK WN3 .... 63 H2

Masefield Primary School
BOLS/LL BL3 .... 37 L8

Mason Street Industrial Estate
WGNS/IIMK WN3 .... 14 D5

Maternity & Child Welfare Clinic
WGNE/HIN WN2 .... 48 F7

Matthew Moss High School
ROCH OL11 .... 27 K8

Mauldeth Medical Centre
DID/WITH M20 .... 99 G5

Mauldeth Road Primary School
DID/WITH M20 .... 99 H5

Mayfield Industrial Park
IRL M44 .... 94 F1

Mayfield Primary School
OLD OL1 .... 59 L4

Maypole Farm Estate
PART M31 .... 95 G6

Maypole Industrial Estate
WGNE/HIN WN2 .... 64 F5

Meade Hill School
BKLY M9 .... 56 C8

Meadow Bank Primary School
ATH M46 .... 50 F8

Meadow Industrial Estate
FAIL M35 .... 74 A6
STKP SK1 .... 13 K1

The Meadows School
BKLY M9 .... 57 J8

Meadway Health Centre
SALE M33 .... 108 B2

Meanwood Primary School
WHIT OL12 .... 27 M3

Medlock Infant School
BRUN/LGST M13 .... 7 K9

Medlock Leisure Centre
DROY M43 .... 89 L1

Medlock Valley Community School
OLDS OL8 .... 75 K1

Melland High School
RDSH SK5 .... 100 A2

Mellor Primary School
MPL/ROM SK6 .... 115 H6

Mellor Sports Club
MPL/ROM SK6 .... 115 G6

Mellor & Townscliffe Golf Club
MPL/ROM SK6 .... 115 G7

MEN Arena
CSLFD M3 .... 6 F1
Mental Health Centre
BOLE BL2 .... 37 J3
Menzies Avant Hotel
OLDS OL8 .... 8 E8
Mere Oaks School
WGN WN1 .... 31 L7
Meridian Clinic
BURY BL9 .... 4 D5
Mersey Drive Primary School
WHTF M45 .... 55 M2
Mersey Road Industrial Estate
FAIL M35 .... 74 C3
Mersey Trading Estate
HTNM SK4 .... 111 J3
Mersey Vale Primary School
HTNM SK4 .... 111 K3
Merseyway Centre
STKP SK1 .... 13 H3
Mesne Lea Primary School
WALK M28 .... 69 H3
Methodist Cemetery
BOLE BL2 .... 23 H8
Metro Cinema
AUL OL6 .... 90 E2
Micklehurst All Saints
Primary School
MOSL OL5 .... 77 H3
Micklehurst Cricket Club
MOSL OL5 .... 77 H3
Middleton Cemetery
MDTN M24 .... 57 H4
Middleton Crematorium
MDTN M24 .... 57 M2
Middleton Cricket Club
MDTN M24 .... 57 J2
Middleton Parish
Church School
MDTN M24 .... 57 J2
Middleton Public Baths
MDTN M24 .... 57 K4
Middleton Shopping Centre
MDTN M24 .... 57 J4
Middleton Technology School
MDTN M24 .... 57 L4
Milking Green
Industrial Estate
OLDE OL4 .... 60 B7
Mill 5 Belgrave
Industrial Estate
OLDS OL8 .... 75 K1
Millbrook Business Centre
NTHM/RTH M23 .... 109 H6
Millbrook Industrial Estate
NTHM/RTH M23 .... 109 H6
Millbrook Primary School
STLY SK15 .... 77 H1
WGNNW/ST WN6 .... 30 E6
Mill Gate Shopping Centre
BURY BL9 .... 4 F5
Millingford Industrial Estate
GOL/RIS/CU WA3 .... 79 L4
Mills Hill Primary School
CHAD OL9 .... 58 B4
Mill Street Industrial Estate
BOL BL1 .... 3 G4
Millwood Primary
Special School
BURY BL9 .... 39 J5
Milnrow Cricket Club
MILN OL16 .... 29 J5
Milnrow Health Centre
MILN OL16 .... 29 J6
Milnrow Parish CE
Primary School
MILN OL16 .... 29 J6
Milo Industrial Park
DROY M43 .... 89 L2
Milton St Johns CE
Primary School
MOSL OL5 .... 76 F2
Minden Medical Centre
BURY BL9 .... 5 G4
Moat House School
HTNM SK4 .... 112 B1
Monde Trading Estate
TRPK M17 .... 85 K6
Montague Business Park
OLDTF/WHR M16 .... 86 D8
Monton Bowling Club
ECC M30 .... 70 B8
Monton Cricket Club
ECC M30 .... 70 B8
Monton Medical Centre
ECC M30 .... 69 M8
Montrose School
WGNW/BIL/O WN5 .... 47 G5
Moor Allerton School
DID/WITH M20 .... 98 C8
Moorfield Community
Primary School
IRL M44 .... 94 D1
Moorfield Primary School
BRAM/HZG SK7 .... 121 L3
Moorgate Primary School
BOLE BL2 .... 3 K2
Moorgate Retail Park
BURY BL9 .... 5 G3
Moorhey Industrial Estate
OLDE OL4 .... 59 L6
Moorhouse Primary School
MILN OL16 .... 29 H6
Moorlands Junior School
SALE M33 .... 97 H7
Moor Lane Bus Station
BOL BL1 .... 2 D5
Moorside High School
SWIN M27 .... 70 A5
Moorside Leisure Centre
SWIN M27 .... 70 A5
Moorside Primary School
SWIN M27 .... 70 A5
Moravian College
DROY M43 .... 89 K4
Mornington High School
WGNE/HIN WN2 .... 49 J7
Morris Green Business Park
BOLS/LL BL3 .... 35 M4
Moses Gate Country Park
FWTH BL4 .... 53 H2
Moss Field Community Primary
School
HEY OL10 .... 40 F1
Mossfield County
Primary School
SWIN M27 .... 70 C3
Moss Hey Primary School
BRAM/HZG SK7 .... 120 E7

Moss Industrial Estate
LEIGH WN7 .... 80 E3
LEIGH WN7 .... 11 K8
Moss Lane Industrial Estate
ROY/SHW OL2 .... 59 K1
Mossley AFC
MOSL OL5 .... 76 F3
Mossley Health Centre
MOSL OL5 .... 76 F3
Mossley Hollins High School
MOSL OL5 .... 77 H3
Moss Park Junior School
STRET M32 .... 96 E2
Moss Side Health Centre
RUSH/FAL M14 .... 87 K8
Moss Side Leisure Centre
HULME M15 .... 87 J7
Moss View Primary School
PART M31 .... 106 D1
Moston Fields Primary School
NEWH/MOS M40 .... 73 K3
Moston Indoor Market
NEWH/MOS M40 .... 73 J4
Moston Lane Primary School
BKLY M9 .... 73 H4
Mottram CE Primary School
HYDE SK14 .... 103 K1
Mottram Hall Golf Club
MCFLDN SK10 .... 128 B8
Mottram St Andrew
Primary School
MCFLDN SK10 .... 131 L2
Mount Carmel RC
Junior School
BKLY M9 .... 73 G2
Mount Carmel RC
Primary School
BKLY M9 .... 73 G3
Mountheath Industrial Park
PWCH M25 .... 71 L3
Mount Pleasant
Business Centre
OLDE OL4 .... 59 L5
Mount St Joseph Business &
Enterprise College
BOLS/LL BL3 .... 52 C2
The Museum of Science &
Industry in Manches
CSLFD M3 .... 6 B6
Museum of the
Manchester Regiment
AUL OL6 .... 90 E1
Museum of Trade Union History
CMANE M1 .... 7 G6
Museum of Transport
CMH M8 .... 72 E6
Mytham Primary School
BOLS/LL BL3 .... 53 L1
Nasmyth Business Centre
ECC M30 .... 84 F2
National Cycling Centre
(Velodrome)
OP/CLY M11 .... 88 D2
National Industrial Estate
AULW OL7 .... 90 D2
National Squash Centre
OP/CLY M11 .... 88 C2
National Trading Estate
BRAM/HZG SK7 .... 121 L1
Natural History Museum
OLDS OL8 .... 8 D9
Navigation Primary School
ALT WA14 .... 108 A6
Navigation Trading Estate
NEWH/MOS M40 .... 73 K7
Nelson Business Centre
DTN/ASHW M34 .... 90 C8
Nether Alderley
Primary School
MCFLDN SK10 .... 130 D6
Neville Street
Industrial Estate
CHAD OL9 .... 8 C5
Nevill Road J & I School
BRAM/HZG SK7 .... 121 G2
Newall Green High School
NTHM/RTH M23 .... 109 J8
Newall Green Primary School
NTHM/RTH M23 .... 109 L8
New Ardwick Sports Centre
BRUN/LGST M13 .... 88 C4
New Barn Infant School
ROY/SHW OL2 .... 43 K6
Newby Road Industrial Estate
BRAM/HZG SK7 .... 121 M2
New Croft High School
SLFD M6 .... 86 C1
Newhaven Business Park
ECC M30 .... 85 H3
Newhey Community
Primary School
MILN OL16 .... 29 K8
New Kingsway Health Centre
DID/WITH M20 .... 99 G8
Newlands Medical Centre
BOL BL1 .... 35 K5
New Mills CP School
NM/HAY SK22 .... 124 D4
New Mills FC
NM/HAY SK22 .... 124 F4
New Mills Golf Club
NM/HAY SK22 .... 124 C3
New Mills Leisure Centre &
Swimming Pool
NM/HAY SK22 .... 124 E4
New Mills School
NM/HAY SK22 .... 124 E4
New Moston Primary School
NEWH/MOS M40 .... 74 B2
New Museum
OLD OL1 .... 9 H3
New North Manchester
Golf Club
MDTN M24 .... 57 G4
Newspaper Offices
BOL BL1 .... 2 F4
Newton Bank
Preparatory School
NEWLW WA12 .... 79 H8
Newton Business Park
HYDE SK14 .... 91 K7
Newton Health Clinic
NEWLW WA12 .... 78 E8
Newton-le-Willows
Community High School
NEWLW WA12 .... 79 G7
Newton-le-Willows Sports Club
NEWLW WA12 .... 78 F8
Newton Moor Industrial Estate
HYDE SK14 .... 91 H7

Newton Street Police Museum
CMANE M1 .... 7 J4
Newton Westpark
Primary School
LEIGH WN7 .... 65 M4
Newtown Primary School
NM/HAY SK22 .... 124 D6
Nicholas Varley
Community School
NEWH/MOS M40 .... 73 H8
Nicholls Sixth Form Centre
WGTN/LGST M12 .... 88 A5
Nicol Mere School
AIMK WN4 .... 63 K7
Norbury Hall Primary School
BRAM/HZG SK7 .... 122 A3
Norden Community
Primary School
WHIT OL12 .... 27 J2
Norden Cricket Club
WHIT OL12 .... 27 H2
Norley Hall Cricket Club
WGNW/BIL/O WN5 .... 46 E5
Norris Bank Medical Centre
HTNM SK4 .... 12 C4
Norris Bank Primary School
HTNM SK4 .... 12 B1
Nortex Business Centre
BOL BL1 .... 35 M4
North Area Sixth Form College
HTNM SK4 .... 99 L6
Northbank Industrial Park
IRL M44 .... 94 B6
IRL M44 .... 94 D4
North Cestrian
Grammar School
ALT WA14 .... 107 M7
North Chadderton School
(Upper)
CHAD OL9 .... 58 C3
North Cheshire Jewish
Primary School
CHD/CHDH SK8 .... 119 K2
Northenden Golf Club
WYTH/NTH M22 .... 110 B2
Northenden Primary School
WYTH/NTH M22 .... 110 A3
Northern A & O
Medical Centre
BURY BL9 .... 4 F4
Northern Cemetery
SWIN M27 .... 71 J5
Northern Moor Clinic
NTHM/RTH M23 .... 109 J3
North Grecian Street
Primary School
BRO M7 .... 71 M6
North Heaton Primary School
HTNM SK4 .... 99 M6
North Manchester Community
School for Girls
BKLY M9 .... 73 K2
North Manchester
General Hospital
CHH M8 .... 72 F3
North Manchester High School
for Boys
BKLY M9 .... 73 L1
North Quarry Business Park
WGNNW/ST WN6 .... 30 A3
North Quays Business Park
ALT WA14 .... 108 B3
North Reddish Health Centre
RDSH SK5 .... 100 B3
North Reddish Infant School
RDSH SK5 .... 100 C3
North Walkden Primary School
WALK M28 .... 52 F7
Norton Grange Hotel
ROCH OL11 .... 41 M5
Novotel
WALK M28 .... 69 H7
Novotel Hotel
CMANE M1 .... 6 F6
Nugent House School
WGNW/BIL/O WN5 .... 62 A8
Oakenclough Primary School
WILM/AE SK9 .... 127 H3
Oakenrod Primary School
ROCH OL11 .... 10 A5
Oakfield Primary School
HYDE SK14 .... 91 H7
Oakfield Trading Estate
HALE/TIMP WA15 .... 108 B7
Oakgrove School
SALE M33 .... 119 L5
Oakhill Trading Estate
LHULT M38 .... 52 E7
Oaklands Infant School
WILM/AE SK9 .... 127 J3
Oakleigh Medical Centre
CHH M8 .... 72 E3
The Oaks Business Park
NTHM/RTH M23 .... 109 G5
The Oaks Primary School
BOL BL1 .... 22 C6
Oakwood High School
CCHDY M21 .... 97 L7
CCHDY M21 .... 97 M5
SLFD M6 .... 70 F7
Octagon Theatre
BOL BL1 .... 2 E5
Odeon Cinema
CMANE M1 .... 6 F6
ROCH OL11 .... 28 B8
Offerton Green Clinic
OFTN SK2 .... 113 J7
Offerton Hall Primary School
OFTN SK2 .... 113 H6
Offerton Health Centre
STKP SK1 .... 112 E4
Offerton High School
OFTN SK2 .... 113 H5
Offerton Industrial Estate
STKP SK1 .... 112 F4
The Old Bell Inn
UPML OL3 .... 45 J8
Old Boston Trading Estate
RNFD/HAY WA11 .... 78 D4
Old Hall Clinic
MDTN M24 .... 110 E6
Old Hall Drive Primary School
GTN M18 .... 89 G8
Old Hall Primary School
TOT/BURYW BL8 .... 24 E5
Oldham 6th Form College
STLY SK15 .... 91 K2
Oldham Art Gallery
OLD OL1 .... 9 K6

Oldham Athletic FC
(Boundary Park)
ROY/SHW OL2 .... 59 G2
Oldham Broadway
Business Park
CHAD OL9 .... 58 B4
Oldham Business Centre
OLD OL1 .... 9 H7
Oldham Central Ind Park
OLD OL1 .... 9 M3
Oldham Central Trading Park
OLD OL1 .... 9 M2
Oldham College
CHAD OL9 .... 8 F5
Oldham County Court
OLD OL1 .... 9 G4
Oldham Crematorium
OLDS OL8 .... 74 F3
Oldham Cricket Club
OLD OL1 .... 59 M3
Oldham Golf Club
OLDE OL4 .... 60 C8
Oldham RUFC
OLDS OL8 .... 75 J4
Oldham Sports Centre
OLD OL1 .... 9 J5
Oldham Theatre Workshop
ROY/SHW OL2 .... 43 G8
Oldham West Business Centre
CHAD OL9 .... 8 A5
Old Mill Hotel & Leisure Centre
RAMS BL0 .... 17 B5
Old Moat J & I School
DID/WITH M20 .... 98 D5
Old Rectory Hotel
DTN/ASHW M34 .... 101 K1
Old Trafford Community School
OLDTF/WHR M16 .... 86 F7
Oldwood Primary School
WYTH/NTH M22 .... 118 D2
Olympia Trading Estate
HULME M15 .... 6 D8
Olympic House
MANAIR M90 .... 118 C5
The Open University
CCHDY M21 .... 97 L3
Opera House
CSLFD M3 .... 6 D5
The Operating Theatre
STRET M32 .... 97 H1
Orchard House Day Hospital
ROY/SHW OL2 .... 43 H8
Orchard Industrial Estate
SLFD M6 .... 71 K8
Orchard Trading Estate
SLFD M6 .... 71 J7
Ordsall Hall Museum
ORD M5 .... 86 E6
Ordsall Health Centre
ORD M5 .... 86 E4
Ordsall Recreation Centre
ORD M5 .... 86 D5
Oriel Bank High School
EDGY/DAV SK3 .... 112 C7
Oriental Arch
CMANE M1 .... 7 G5
Orion Business Park
CHD/CHDH SK8 .... 111 M7
Orion Trading Estate
TRPK M17 .... 85 K4
Orrell Clinic
WGNW/BIL/O WN5 .... 46 B5
Orrell Newfold C P School
WGNW/BIL/O WN5 .... 46 A8
Orrell RUFC
WGNW/BIL/O WN5 .... 46 B7
Orrell Water Park
WGNW/BIL/O WN5 .... 46 B8
Orrismere Primary School
CHD/CHDH SK8 .... 120 C1
Ortenbrook School
PART M31 .... 106 B2
Osborne Trading Estate
CHAD OL9 .... 8 D3
Oswald Road Primary School
CCHDY M21 .... 97 K3
Oulder Hill Community School
ROCH OL11 .... 27 L5
Our Lady & St Anselms RC
Primary School
WHIT OL12 .... 18 D2
Our Lady & St Pauls RC
Primary School
HEY OL10 .... 40 C3
Our Lady & the Lancashire
Martyrs RC Primary School
WALK M28 .... 68 D2
Our Lady of Grace RC
Primary School
PWCH M25 .... 55 K6
Our Lady of Lourdes RC
Primary School
FWTH BL4 .... 52 D4
PART M31 .... 106 B1
TOT/BURYW BL8 .... 24 F6
Our Lady of the Rosary RC
Primary School
LEIGH WN7 .... 65 L7
Our Lady RC Primary School
WGNE/HIN WN2 .... 32 F7
Our Ladys Catholic
Primary School
EDGY/DAV SK3 .... 13 G7
Our Ladys RC High School
ROY/SHW OL2 .... 59 G1
Our Ladys RC Primary School
OLDE OL4 .... 60 B1
OLDTF/WHR M16 .... 98 A1
Our Ladys RC School
BKLY M9 .... 57 G6
Overdale Crematorium
BOL BL1 .... 35 K6
Overdale School
MPL/ROM SK6 .... 113 J3
Overhead Walkway
MANAIR M90 .... 118 C5
Owl Business Centre
OLDE OL4 .... 60 A6
Oxford Grove Primary School
BOL BL1 .... 35 M3
Padfield Primary School
GLSP SK13 .... 93 L7
Pagefield Industrial Estate
WGNNW/ST WN6 .... 14 A2
Palace Cinema
STLY SK15 .... 91 K2
Palace Hotel
CMANE M1 .... 7 G7
Palace Theatre
CMANE M1 .... 7 G7

Palm Business Centre
CHAD OL9 .... 8 A5
Paragon Business Park
HOR/BR BL6 .... 34 A4
Paragon Industrial Estate
LIT OL15 .... 29 J1
Parish Church CE Junior School
OLD OL1 .... 9 J3
Park Business Centre
WGNE/HIN WN2 .... 49 G8
Park Dean Special School
OLDE OL4 .... 75 L2
Parker International Estate
DUK SK16 .... 90 E5
Parkfield Industrial Estate
MDTN M24 .... 57 H4
Parkfield Primary School
MDTN M24 .... 57 H3
Park Industrial Estate
AIMK WN4 .... 78 B1
Parklands High School
WYTH/NTH M22 .... 118 E1
Parklee Primary School
ATH M46 .... 66 F2
Park Mill Industrial Estate
MOSL OL5 .... 61 G8
Park Parade Industrial Estate
AULW OL7 .... 90 D2
Park Road CP School
ALT WA14 .... 108 B4
SALE M33 .... 96 D6
Park School
NTHM/RTH M23 .... 109 J4
Parkside Industrial Estate
ROY/SHW OL2 .... 43 H8
Parkview Centre
OLDS OL8 .... 9 K8
Park View Primary School
PWCH M25 .... 71 L1
Parkway Business Centre
OLDTF/WHR M16 .... 98 C3
Parkway Four Industrial Estate
TRPK M17 .... 85 K5
Parkway Trading Estate
STRET M32 .... 85 K7
Parochial CE Primary School
AUL OL6 .... 90 F1
Parrenthorn High School
PWCH M25 .... 56 A4
Parsonage Retail Park
LEIGH WN7 .... 66 B6
Partington CP School
PART M31 .... 106 C1
Partington Health Centre
PART M31 .... 106 C1
Partington Shopping Centre
PART M31 .... 106 C1
Partington Sports Centre
PART M31 .... 106 C2
Patricroft CE School
ECC M30 .... 84 F2
Peacefield Primary School
MPL/ROM SK6 .... 114 B7
Peacock County
Primary School
GTN M18 .... 88 F6
Peacock Primary School
HULME M15 .... 6 C9
Pearlbrook Industrial Estate
HOR/BR BL6 .... 33 L1
Pear New Mill
Industrial Estate
MPL/ROM SK6 .... 112 F2
Peel Brow Primary School
RAMS BL0 .... 17 D6
The Peel Centre
STKP SK1 .... 13 L3
Peel Hall County
Primary School
LHULT M38 .... 68 C1
Peel Health Centre
BURY BL9 .... 4 F6
Peel Moat Recreation Centre
HTNM SK4 .... 99 L2
Peerglow Industrial Estate
ALT WA14 .... 108 C3
Pemberton Business Centre
WGNW/BIL/O WN5 .... 46 F6
Pemberton Clinic
WGNW/BIL/O WN5 .... 47 G6
Pemberton Primary School
WGNW/BIL/O WN5 .... 46 F6
Pendleton College
SLFD M6 .... 71 G8
Pendleton Medical Centre
SLFD M6 .... 86 D2
Pennant Industrial Estate
OLD OL1 .... 59 L4
Pennine Business Park
HEY OL10 .... 40 E4
Pennington Flash
Country Park
LEIGH WN7 .... 80 F2
Pepper Mill Business Park
WGN WN1 .... 15 H5
Peterloo Medical Centre
MDTN M24 .... 57 H4
Philips High School
WHTF M45 .... 55 H4
Phoenix Industrial Estate
FAIL M35 .... 74 D4
Phoenix Medical Centre
STKP SK1 .... 13 K7
Phoenix Park Industrial Estate
HEY OL10 .... 41 J4
Piccadilly Trading Estate
ANC M4 .... 7 M6
CMANE M1 .... 7 J5
Pictor Special School
SALE M33 .... 96 C8
Pike Fold Primary School
BKLY M9 .... 72 F1
Pikes Lane Primary School
BOLS/LL BL3 .... 2 A7
Pike View Medical Centre
HOR/BR BL6 .... 21 B8
Pilot Industrial Estate
BOLS/LL BL3 .... 36 E8
Pilsworth Industrial Estate
BURY BL9 .... 39 G3
Pinfold J & I School
HYDE SK14 .... 103 H3
Pinnacle Business Centre
HTNM SK4 .... 13 H1
Pioneer Industrial Estate
WGNW/BIL/O WN5 .... 47 H5
Piper Hill School
NTHM/RTH M23 .... 109 J2
Plantation Industrial Estate
AUL OL6 .... 90 F2

Plant Hill High School
  BKLY M9 .... 56 F8
Plasman Industrial Centre
  BNG/LEV M19........................ 99 K3
Platt Bridge Clinic
  WGNE/HIN WN2 .... 64 D2
Players Theatre
  UPML OL3 .... 45 J8
Playhouse Theatre
  ORD M5 .... 86 D2
Plodder Lane Primary School
  FWTH BL4 .... 52 E3
Plymouth Court
  Business Centre
  BRUN/LGST M13 .... 87 M7
Plymouth Grove
  Primary School
  BRUN/LGST M13 .... 88 B7
The Point Retail Park
  MILN OL16 .... 11 G4
Poland Industrial Estate
  ANC M4 .... 7 L2
Portland Basin Museum
  AULW OL7 .... 90 D3
Portland Industrial Estate
  BURY BL9 .... 25 K8
Portwood Trading Estate
  STKP SK1 .... 13 M2
Potters House School
  BURY BL9 .... 25 J6
Pownall Green Primary School
  BRAM/HZG SK7 .... 121 G5
Pownall Hall School
  WILM/AE SK9 .... 126 D4
Poynton Clinic
  POY/DIS SK12 .... 122 A8
Poynton High School
  POY/DIS SK12........................ 129 K1
Poynton Leisure Centre
  POY/DIS SK12........................ 129 K2
Poynton Sports Club
  POY/DIS SK12........................ 122 A8
Premier Lodge
  AIMK WN4 .... 78 E2
  ALT WA14 .... 108 A6
  ALT WA14 .... 108 B3
  CMANW M2 .... 6 F6
  CSLFD M3 .... 6 E3
  HYDE SK14 .... 103 H1
  MDTN M24 .... 56 E5
  STKP SK1 .... 13 K4
  SWIN M27 .... 70 B5
  SWIN M27 .... 70 F5
  WGNNW/ST WN6 .... 30 C1
  WILM/AE SK9 .... 126 C5
  WILM/AE SK9 .... 127 H1
  WILM/AE SK9 .... 130 D4
Premier Lodge (City South)
  HULME M15 .... 6 E9
Prestwich Community
  High School
  PWCH M25 .... 55 L7
Prestwich Golf Club
  PWCH M25 .... 71 K3
Prestwich Health Centre
  PWCH M25 .... 55 K7
Prestwich Hospital
  PWCH M25 .... 55 J7
Prestwich Industrial Estate
  ATH M46 .... 50 E8
Prestwich Preparatory School
  PWCH M25 .... 55 M7
Priestnall School
  HTNM SK4 .... 111 J1
Prince of Wales Business Park
  OLD OL1 .... 59 M4
The Printworks
  Leisure Complex
  ANC M4 .... 7 G2
Priorslegh Medical Centre
  POY/DIS SK12........................ 122 A8
Propps Hall Primary School
  FAIL M35 .... 74 B6
Prospect House Medical Centre
  WGNW/BIL/O WN5 .... 46 D6
Prospect Industrial Estate
  WGNE/HIN WN2 .... 49 G7
Prospect Vale Primary School
  CHD/CHDH SK8 .... 119 K3
Pump House People's History
  Museum *CSLFD* M3 .... 6 D4
Python Industrial Estate
  LIT OL15 .... 20 D6
The Quadrangle
  Business Centre
  WGNE/HIN WN2...................... 49 L8
Quality Hotel
  ALT WA14 .... 116 F2
  WGN WN1 .... 15 H3
Quarry Bank Mill &
  Styal Estate NT
  WILM/AE SK9 .... 126 C2
Queen Elizabeth Hall
  OLD OL1 .... 9 H5
Queen Elizabeths High School
  MDTN M24 .... 41 J3
Queensgate Primary School
  BRAM/HZG SK7 .... 121 G8
Queens Road Primary School
  CHD/CHDH SK8 .... 120 C1
Queen Street Primary School
  FWTH BL4 .... 53 G4
Queensway Primary School
  ROCH OL11 .... 42 C1
Rack House Primary School
  NTHM/RTH M23........................ 109 K3
Radcliffe Borough AFC
  RAD M26 .... 38 B8
Radcliffe Cricket Club
  RAD M26 .... 38 B8
Radcliffe High School
  RAD M26 .... 54 C1
Radcliffe Junior School
  RAD M26 .... 38 B8
Radclyffe Athletics Centre
  CHAD OL9 .... 58 C5
Radclyffe Primary School
  ORD M5 .... 86 D5
The Radclyffe School (Upper)
  CHAD OL9 .... 58 C5
Radisson SAS Hotel
  MANAIR M90 .... 118 D5
Raikes Clough
  Industrial Estate
  BOLS/LL BL3 .... 37 F8
Raikes Lane Industrial Estate
  BOLS/LL BL3 .... 36 E8
Railway Street
  Industrial Estate
  GTN M18 .... 88 F6

Ralph Williams Clinic
  WHIT OL12 .... 28 F1
Ramillies Hall School
  CHD/CHDH SK8 .... 120 E2
Ramsbottom Cemetery
  RAMS BL0 .... 17 A8
Ramsbottom Cottage Hospital
  RAMS BL0 .... 17 C7
Ramsbottom Health Centre
  RAMS BL0 .... 17 B5
Ramsbottom Swimming Pool
  RAMS BL0 .... 17 C5
Rassbottom Industrial Estate
  STLY SK15 .... 91 J2
Ravensbury Primary School
  OP/CLY M11 .... 88 D1
Ravensfield Industrial Estate
  DUK SK16 .... 90 D3
Ravenside Retail Park
  BOLS/LL BL3 .... 2 F7
Rectory CE Primary School
  AIMK WN4 .... 63 G7
Reddish Vale Golf Club
  RDSH SK5 .... 100 D6
Reddish Vale School
  RDSH SK5 .... 100 C5
Red Lane Community School
  BOLE BL2 .... 37 J3
Red Rose Retail Centre
  ORD M5 .... 86 E3
Reebok Museum
  HOR/BR BL6 .... 34 A4
Regal Industrial Estate
  WGTN/LGST M12 .... 88 C5
Regent Cinema
  MPL/ROM SK6 .... 114 C6
Regent Park Golf Course
  HOR/BR BL6 .... 34 E5
Regent Trading Estate
  CSLFD M3 .... 6 A4
The Regimental Museum of XX
  Lancashire Fusiliers
  TOT/BURYW BL8 .... 38 E3
Reliance Trading Estate
  NEWH/MOS M40 .... 73 M5
Ribble Drive Primary School
  WHTF M45 .... 55 K3
Richmond J & I School
  CHAD OL9 .... 8 F6
Richmond Medical Centre
  AUL OL6 .... 90 F1
Richmond Park
  Athletics Stadium
  AULW OL7 .... 75 H8
Richmond Park School
  WGTN/LGST M12 .... 88 B7
The Ridge College
  MPL/ROM SK6 .... 114 B7
Ridge Danyers College
  CHD/CHDH SK8 .... 120 A1
Ridge Hill Primary &
  Infant School
  STLY SK15 .... 91 J1
Ridgmont Cemetery
  HOR/BR BL6 .... 34 A1
Ringway Golf Club
  HALE/TIMP WA15 .... 117 L3
Ringway Primary School
  WYTH/NTH M22........................ 118 F4
Ringway Trading Estate
  WYTH/NTH M22........................ 119 G4
Ripon Avenue School
  BURY BL9 .... 55 J1
Riverside Business Park
  WILM/AE SK9 .... 126 F5
Rivington & Blackrod
  High School
  HOR/BR BL6 .... 21 B4
Rivington Country Park
  HOR/BR BL6 .... 21 A4
R L Hughes Primary School
  AIMK WN4 .... 78 D1
Roaches Industrial Estate
  MOSL OL5 .... 61 H8
Robin Park Arena
  WGNW/BIL/O WN5 .... 14 A4
Robin Park Sports Centre
  WGNW/BIL/O WN5 .... 47 J4
Rochdale AFC
  (Spotland Stadium)
  ROCH OL11 .... 27 M4
Rochdale Cemetery
  ROCH OL11 .... 27 L5
Rochdale Crematorium
  ROCH OL11 .... 27 L5
Rochdale Cricket, Lacrosse &
  Squash Club
  ROCH OL11 .... 10 A4
Rochdale Curtain Theatre
  ROCH OL11 .... 10 D7
Rochdale Golf Club
  ROCH OL11 .... 27 K4
Rochdale Healthcare
  WHIT OL12 .... 19 M7
Rochdale Healthcare NHS Trust
  LIT OL15 .... 20 B7
Rochdale Industrial Centre
  ROCH OL11 .... 10 A6
Rochdale Infirmary
  WHIT OL12 .... 10 E1
Roe Cross Industrial Park
  HYDE SK14 .... 92 D7
Roker Industrial Estate
  OLD OL1 .... 59 L4
Rolls Crescent Primary School
  HULME M15 .... 87 H7
Roman Fort
  CSLFD M3 .... 6 C7
Romiley Golf Club
  MPL/ROM SK6 .... 114 A1
Romiley Health Centre
  MPL/ROM SK6 .... 113 M2
Romiley Primary School
  MPL/ROM SK6 .... 114 A2
Roscoe Fold Primary School
  BOLE BL2 .... 37 H4
Rose Bridge High School
  WGN WN1 .... 15 M3
Rosedale Shopping Centre
  NEWH/MOS M40 .... 73 M1
Rosehill Methodist
  Community School
  AUL OL6 .... 76 B7
Rose Hill Primary School
  MPL/ROM SK6 .... 114 B6
Ross Business Centre
  WGNW/BIL/O WN5 .... 47 G7
Roundthorn Industrial Estate
  NTHM/RTH M23........................ 109 H5
  NTHM/RTH M23........................ 109 H7

Roundwood School
  WYTH/NTH M22...................... 109 M5
Roxy Cinema
  OLDS OL8 .... 74 D3
Royal Albert Edward Infirmary
  WGN WN1 .... 47 M2
Royal Bolton Hospital
  FWTH BL4 .... 52 C3
Royal Exchange Clinic
  CMANW M2 .... 6 F4
Royal Exchange Shopping Centre
  ANC M4 .... 6 F3
  MILN OL16 .... 10 D4
Royal Exchange
  Theatre Company
  CMANW M2 .... 6 F4
Royal Manchester
  Childrens Hospital
  SWIN M27 .... 70 E5
Royal Northern
  College of Music
  HULME M15 .... 87 K6
Royal Oak Industrial Estate
  STKP SK1 .... 13 K7
Royal Oak Primary School
  NTHM/RTH M23...................... 109 K5
Royal Oldham Hospital
  OLD OL1 .... 8 F1
Royal Pennine Trading Estate
  ROCH OL11 .... 41 L1
Royce Trading Estate
  TRPK M17 .... 85 J5
Royle Pennine Trading Estate
  ROCH OL11 .... 42 A1
Royton and Crompton
  Comprehensive School
  ROY/SHW OL2 .... 43 K8
Royton Medical Centre
  ROY/SHW OL2 .... 43 G8
Royton Public Baths
  ROY/SHW OL2 .... 43 H8
Rugby Road Industrial Estate
  WHIT OL12 .... 11 C1
Runworth School
  BOLS/LL BL3 .... 35 J7
Rushcroft Primary School
  ROY/SHW OL2 .... 43 L4
Russell Scott Primary School
  DTN/ASHW M34...................... 90 B8
Rycroft Park Sports Club
  CHD/CHDH SK8 .... 120 B3
Rydings Special School
  WHIT OL12 .... 19 J8
Ryecroft Business Park
  AULW OL7 .... 90 C3
The Ryleys School
  WILM/AE SK9 .... 130 C3
Sacred Heart Catholic
  Primary School
  WGNE/HIN WN2...................... 65 L1
Sacred Heart RC Infant School
  GTN M18 .... 88 F8
Sacred Heart RC Primary School
  ATH M46 .... 67 H3
  LEIGH WN7 .... 66 B7
  MILN OL16 .... 11 L6
  NTHM/RTH M23........................ 109 J6
  OLD OL1 .... 59 M2
  WGNNW/ST WN6 .... 47 J2
  WHTN BL5 .... 50 C3
Saddleworth Business Centre
  UPML OL3 .... 45 J8
Saddleworth Golf Club
  UPML OL3 .... 61 K4
Saddleworth Museum &
  Art Gallery
  UPML OL3 .... 61 L4
Saddleworth Preparatory School
  OLDE OL4 .... 60 F4
Saddleworth School
  UPML OL3 .... 61 L3
Saddleworth Swimming Pool
  UPML OL3 .... 61 L5
St Aelreds RC
  Technology College
  NEWLW WA12 .... 79 C8
St Agnes CE Primary School
  BRUN/LGST M13 .... 99 J1
  OLDE OL4 .... 60 D7
St Aidans Catholic
  Primary School
  NTHM/RTH M23........................ 109 L3
St Aidans CE Primary School
  WGNW/BIL/O WN5 .... 62 B7
St Aidans RC Primary School
  WGNS/IIMK WN3 .... 63 G2
St Alphonsus RC Primary School
  OLDTF/WHR M16 .... 87 G7
St Ambrose Barlow RC
  High School
  SWIN M27 .... 70 C5
St Ambrose Barlow RC
  Primary School
  TYLD M29 .... 67 K7
St Ambrose College
  HALE/TIMP WA15 .... 117 K3
St Ambrose Preparatory School
  HALE/TIMP WA15 .... 117 K4
St Ambrose RC Primary School
  CCHDY M21 .... 98 A8
  EDGY/DAV SK3 .... 112 A7
St Andrew RC Primary School
  BOLE BL2 .... 37 H4
St Andrews CE Junior School
  GLSP SK13 .... 93 J8
St Andrews CE Primary School
  BNG/LEV M19........................ 99 L4
  RAD M26 .... 38 B6
  RAMS BL0 .... 17 B7
  WALK M28 .... 68 D7
  WGNNW/ST WN6 .... 47 J2
  WHTN BL5 .... 51 K4
St Andrews CE School
  ECC M30 .... 85 H3
St Andrews Medical Centre
  ECC M30 .... 85 H2
St Andrews Methodist
  Primary School
  WALK M28 .... 68 E1
St Andrew's VC CE
  Primary School
  WHIT OL12 .... 19 M8
St Annes CE (aided)
  Primary School
  SALE M33 .... 96 F8
St Annes CE Primary School
  OLDE OL4 .... 60 F6
  ROY/SHW OL2 .... 59 H1
  WGNNW/ST WN6 .... 47 G1

St Annes Ear Nose &
  Throat Hospital
  ALT WA14 .... 116 E1
St Annes Primary School
  DTN/ASHW M34...................... 90 D8
St Annes RC High School
  HTNM SK4 .... 100 A8
St Annes RC Primary School
  CHH M8 .... 72 D4
  DTN/ASHW M34...................... 89 K5
  OLDE OL4 .... 59 M5
St Anns J & I School
  STRET M32 .... 97 G2
St Anthonys RC Primary School
  WYTH/NTH M22...................... 118 F3
St Antonys RC High School
  URM M41 .... 96 C2
St Augustine of Canterbury
  RC School
  OLDS OL8 .... 75 G1
St Augustines CE
  Primary School
  NEWH/MOS M40 .... 73 H7
  SWIN M27 .... 70 E4
St Barnabas Primary School
  OP/CLY M11 .... 88 E4
St Bartholomews CE
  Primary School
  WHIT OL12 .... 18 D4
St Bede CE Primary School
  BOLS/LL BL3 .... 51 M2
St Bedes College
  OLDTF/WHR M16 .... 98 B1
St Benedict's Catholic
  Primary School
  WILM/AE SK9 .... 127 J1
St Benedicts RC Primary School
  WGNE/HIN WN2...................... 48 F6
  WILM/AE SK9 .... 120 A8
St Bernadettes Catholic
  Primary School
  WGNNW/ST WN6 .... 30 D6
St Bernadettes RC
  Primary School
  RDSH SK5 .... 100 E8
  WHTF M45 .... 55 J2
St Bernard RC Primary School
  BOLS/LL BL3 .... 35 H7
St Bernards RC Primary School
  BNG/LEV M19........................ 99 J6
St Boniface RC Primary School
  BRO M7 .... 71 M6
St Brendan RC Primary School
  BOLE BL2 .... 23 H7
St Brigids RC Primary School
  OP/CLY M11 .... 88 D3
St Catharines CE Primary School
  WGN WN1 .... 15 K4
St Catherine CE Primary School
  HOR/BR BL6 .... 33 L1
St Catherines
  Preparatory School
  MPL/ROM SK6 .... 114 E5
St Catherines RC
  Primary School
  DID/WITH M20 .... 110 F1
  GOL/RIS/CU WA3 .... 80 B5
St Chads CE Junior School
  BURY BL9 .... 4 F9
St Chads CE Primary School
  UPML OL3 .... 61 M3
St Chads RC Primary School
  CHH M8 .... 72 D7
St Charles RC Primary School
  SWIN M27 .... 70 A4
St Christophers RC
  Primary School
  AUL OL6 .... 76 B6
  MPL/ROM SK6 .... 113 K2
St Chrysostoms CE
  Primary School
  BRUN/LGST M13 .... 87 M7
St Clares RC Primary School
  BKLY M9 .... 56 F7
St Clement (Egerton) CE
  Primary School
  ORD M5 .... 86 E5
St Clements CE Primary School
  OP/CLY M11 .... 89 H5
St Columba RC Primary School
  BOLE BL2 .... 22 E8
St Cuthberts RC High School
  MILN OL16 .... 42 E3
St Cuthberts RC Primary School
  DID/WITH M20 .... 98 F7
  WGNW/BIL/O WN5 .... 47 G6
St Damians RC High School
  AUL OL6 .... 76 B5
St Davids CE Primary School
  WGNE/HIN WN2...................... 32 E5
St Dunstans RC Primary School
  NEWH/MOS M40 .... 73 K4
St Edmund Arrowsmith
  Catholic High School
  AIMK WN4 .... 78 D2
St Edmunds RC Primary School
  LHULT M38 .... 52 E8
  NEWH/MOS M40 .... 73 H6
St Edwards Catholic
  Primary School
  WGNW/BIL/O WN5 .... 47 J5
St Edwards CE Primary School
  ROCH OL11 .... 41 L2
St Edwards RC Primary School
  OLDE OL4 .... 60 B5
  RUSH/FAL M14 .... 98 E2
St Elisabeths CE Primary School
  RDSH SK5 .... 100 A4
St Elizabeth RC Primary School
  WYTH/NTH M22...................... 119 G2
St Ethelbert RC Primary School
  BOLS/LL BL3 .... 35 L7
St Gabriels CE Primary School
  MDTN M24 .... 57 M5
St Gabriels Medical Centre
  PWCH M25 .... 72 A2
St Gabriels RC High School
  BURY BL9 .... 4 B6
St Gabriels RC Primary School
  LEIGH WN7 .... 67 H5
  ROCH OL11 .... 42 A3
St Georges CE Infant School
  OFTN SK2 .... 112 C6
St Georges Central CE
  Primary School
  TYLD M29 .... 67 K3
St Georges CE Primary School
  ATH M46 .... 50 E8
  MOSL OL5 .... 76 D3
  NM/HAY SK22 .... 124 E4

St Georges CE (aided)
  Primary School
  HYDE SK14 .... 102 A3
St Georges RC
  Secondary School
  WALK M28 .... 68 F2
St Gilberts RC Primary School
  ECC M30 .... 84 D2
St Gregory RC Primary School
  FWTH BL4 .... 53 H4
St Herberts RC Primary School
  CHAD OL9 .... 58 D5
St Hilarys School
  WILM/AE SK9 .... 130 D3
St Hildas CE Primary School
  OLD OL1 .... 9 G3
  OLDTF/WHR M16 .... 97 L1
  PWCH M25 .... 55 M8
St Hugh of Lincoln
  Primary School
  STRET M32 .... 96 C1
St Hughs CE Primary School
  OLDE OL4 .... 60 A8
St Hughs RC Primary School
  HALE/TIMP WA15 .... 108 C5
St James CE Primary School
  AUL OL6 .... 90 F1
  GTN M18 .... 88 F8
  RUSH/FAL M14 .... 99 G2
  WGNS/IIMK WN3 .... 14 A9
  WHIT OL12 .... 19 K6
St James CE School
  GLSP SK13 .... 104 E4
St James CP School
  WGNW/BIL/O WN5 .... 46 A8
St James (Daisy Hill) CE Primary
  School
  WHTN BL5 .... 50 C7
St James Primary School
  RNFD/HAY WA11 .... 78 B6
St James RC High School
  CHD/CHDH SK8 .... 120 B5
St James RC Primary School
  HYDE SK14 .... 103 G2
St James Secondary School
  FWTH BL4 .... 52 D4
St James's RC School
  SLFD M6 .... 86 C1
St John Baptist's VA RC School
  ROCH OL11 .... 10 F6
St John Bosco RC
  Primary School
  BKLY M9 .... 57 K8
St John CE Primary School
  FWTH BL4 .... 53 H4
St John Fisher Catholic
  High School
  WGNNW/ST WN6 .... 47 J1
St John Fisher RC
  Primary School
  DTN/ASHW M34...................... 101 L3
St John Fisher &
  St Thomas More
  RC Primary School
  WYTH/NTH M22...................... 110 A8
St John RC Primary School
  EDGW/EG BL7 .... 22 C5
St John Rigby RC
  6th Form College
  WGNW/BIL/O WN5 .... 46 C2
St Johns Cathedral
  CSLFD M3 .... 6 A3
St Johns CE Infant School
  FAIL M35 .... 74 C4
  LEIGH WN7 .... 66 C6
St Johns CE J & I School
  WGNE/HIN WN2...................... 48 C1
  WGNE/HIN WN2...................... 48 D2
St Johns CE Junior School
  FAIL M35 .... 74 C5
St Johns CE Primary School
  BURY BL9 .... 25 H8
  DUK SK16 .... 91 H4
  HTNM SK4 .... 111 H2
  MDTN M24 .... 42 B6
  RAD M26 .... 54 D3
  SLFD M6 .... 70 F6
  WGNW/BIL/O WN5 .... 46 E6
St Johns Industrial Estate
  OLDE OL4 .... 60 B6
St Johns Medical Centre
  ALT WA14 .... 116 E1
St Johns Mosley Common CE
  Primary School
  WALK M28 .... 68 C4
St Johns Primary School
  IRL M44 .... 94 D1
St Johns RC Primary School
  CCHDY M21 .... 97 K3
St John Vianney School
  HTNM SK4 .... 12 A3
St John Vianney Upper School
  OLDTF/WHR M16 .... 97 L2
St Joseph RC Primary School
  BOL BL1 .... 35 M2
St Josephs Catholic
  Primary School
  WGNNW/ST WN6 .... 30 C1
St Josephs RC High School
  HEY OL10 .... 40 F4
St Josephs RC Primary &
  Nursery School
  RDSH SK5 .... 100 B4
St Josephs RC Primary School
  BOL BL1 .... 35 M3
  BRUN/LGST M13 .... 88 B2
  HEY OL10 .... 40 F3
  LEIGH WN7 .... 66 E6
  LHULT M38 .... 52 D7
  MOSL OL5 .... 76 F3
  ORD M5 .... 86 E4
  RAMS BL0 .... 17 B6
  ROY/SHW OL2 .... 43 K7
  SALE M33 .... 96 E8
  STKP SK1 .... 13 J4
St Josephs RC School
  HOR/BR BL6 .... 34 B3
St Josephs & St Bedes RC
  Primary School
  BURY BL9 .... 25 L8
St Judes Catholic
  Primary School
  WGNS/IIMK WN3 .... 47 J7
St Judes CE Primary School
  ANC M4 .... 7 L3
St Kentigerns Catholic School
  RUSH/FAL M14 .... 98 D3

St Lukes CE Primary School
  CHAD OL9 .... 58 D5
  GLSP SK13 .... 104 F3
  HEY OL10 .... 41 G1
  ORD M5 .... 86 A3
  WGTN/LGST M12 .... 88 B7
  GOL/RIS/CU WA3 .... 80 B5
St Lukes RC Primary School
  SLFD M6 .... 70 F7
St Malachys RC Primary School
  NEWH/MOS M40 .... 72 F7
St Margaret Marys RC School
  NEWH/MOS M40 .... 74 A1
St Margarets CE Primary School
  HEY OL10 .... 40 D3
  OLDS OL8 .... 74 F2
  OLDTF/WHR M16 .... 98 A2
  PWCH M25 .... 55 M4
St Margarets RC
  Primary School
  GLSP SK13 .... 104 A4
St Margarets Ward RC
  Primary School
  SALE M33 .... 107 M2
St Marie's RC Primary School
  BURY BL9 .... 4 F6
St Maries RC Primary School
  WGNNW/ST WN6 .... 31 H2
St Marks CE Primary School
  MPL/ROM SK6 .... 101 K8
  NEWH/MOS M40 .... 88 A1
  WALK M28 .... 69 J6
  WGNW/BIL/O WN5 .... 47 J5
St Marks RC Primary School
  SWIN M27 .... 70 D2
St Martins School
  SALE M33 .... 96 B7
St Mary CE Primary School
  BOLS/LL BL3 .... 35 J8
St Mary RC Primary School
  HOR/BR BL6 .... 34 A2
St Mary's Catholic Cemetery
  WALK M28 .... 69 L4
St Marys Catholic Junior School
  NEWLW WA12 .... 78 E8
St Marys Catholic School
  NEWLW WA12 .... 78 F8
St Marys CE Primary School
  DROY M43 .... 89 L3
  NEWH/MOS M40 .... 73 M3
  OLDTF/WHR M16 .... 87 H8
St Mary's CE Primary School
  PWCH M25 .... 55 K8
St Marys CE Primary School
  RDSH SK5 .... 100 D8
St Mary's CE Primary School
  ROCH OL11 .... 28 D8
St Marys CE Primary School
  ROY/SHW OL2 .... 43 J4
  TOT/BURYW BL8 .... 23 L2
  UPML OL3 .... 61 M8
  URM M41 .... 84 E8
St Marys CP School
  GLSP SK13 .... 105 G4
St Mary's Hospital
  BRUN/LGST M13 .... 87 M8
St Marys Medical Centre
  OLD OL1 .... 9 K5
St Marys RC High School
  TYLD M29 .... 67 K8
St Marys RC Primary School
  AUL OL6 .... 76 A8
  BNG/LEV M19 .... 99 K4
  DTN/ASHW M34 .... 101 H1
  DUK SK16 .... 91 H6
St Mary's RC Primary School
  ECC M30 .... 85 H3
St Marys RC Primary School
  FAIL M35 .... 74 B6
  HTNM SK4 .... 13 G2
St Mary's RC Primary School
  LIT OL15 .... 20 B7
St Marys RC Primary School
  MDTN M24 .... 57 H2
  MPL/ROM SK6 .... 114 D5
  NM/HAY SK22 .... 124 D4
  RAD M26 .... 38 D8
  SWIN M27 .... 70 C4
  WGNW/BIL/O WN5 .... 62 A8
St Marys & St Johns RC
  Primary School
  WGN WN1 .... 15 H2
St Matthew CE Primary School
  BOL BL1 .... 2 D1
  BOL BL1 .... 36 B3
  BOLS/LL BL3 .... 53 K1
St Matthews CE Infant School
  OLD OL1 .... 58 C2
St Matthews CE Primary School
  EDGY/DAV SK3 .... 13 G7
  STRET M32 .... 96 F4
St Matthews RC High School
  NEWH/MOS M40 .... 73 M2
St Maxentius CE
  Primary School
  BOLE BL2 .... 23 G7
St Michael CE Primary School
  BOLS/LL BL3 .... 52 F1
St Michaels CE Primary School
  HEY OL10 .... 26 F8
  MDTN M24 .... 57 K7
St Michaels CE School
  URM M41 .... 95 J3
St Michaels Primary School
  ATH M46 .... 66 E2
St Michaels RC Primary School
  WHTF M45 .... 55 L4
St Monicas RC High School
  PWCH M25 .... 71 M1
St Monicas RC Primary School
  URM M41 .... 95 G3
St Nathaniels CE
  Primary School
  WGNE/HIN WN2 .... 64 C1
St Osmund RC Primary School
  BOLE BL2 .... 37 G5
St Oswalds RC J & I School
  AIMK WN4 .... 78 C1
St Patrick's High School
  ECC M30 .... 84 C2
St Patricks RC Primary School
  ANC M4 .... 87 M1
  OLDS OL8 .... 8 F7
  WGN WN1 .... 15 J4
St Patricks VA RC
  Primary School
  WHIT OL12 .... 28 D3
St Paul CE Primary School
  BOL BL1 .... 36 C1

St Pauls Catholic High School
  NTHM/RTH M23 .... 109 L8
St Pauls Catholic
  Primary School
  POY/DIS SK12 .... 129 J2
St Paul's Cemetery
  BOL BL1 .... 35 M2
St Pauls CE Primary School
  BRO M7 .... 71 L4
  BURY BL9 .... 5 K1
  DID/WITH M20 .... 98 E6
  RAMS BL0 .... 17 C5
  RDSH SK5 .... 100 E8
  ROY/SHW OL2 .... 58 F1
  STLY SK15 .... 91 M2
  WALK M28 .... 69 H2
  WGNS/IIMK WN3 .... 63 J1
St Pauls New Windsor CE
  Primary School
  ORD M5 .... 86 E3
St Pauls Peel CE
  Primary School
  LHULT M38 .... 52 C7
St Pauls RC Primary School
  HYDE SK14 .... 91 J8
St Pauls Trading Estate
  STLY SK15 .... 91 M2
St Peter CE Primary School
  FWTH BL4 .... 53 G5
St Peter & Paul RC
  Primary School
  BOLS/LL BL3 .... 2 D8
St Peter & St John
  Primary School
  CSLFD M3 .... 6 B2
St Peters Catholic High School
  WGNW/BIL/O WN5 .... 46 C5
St Peters Catholic
  Primary School
  BRAM/HZG SK7 .... 121 M3
  STLY SK15 .... 91 L3
St Peters CE Infant School
  LEIGH WN7 .... 65 M7
St Peters CE Junior School
  LEIGH WN7 .... 65 M7
St Peters CE Primary School
  AIMK WN4 .... 63 J6
  AULW OL7 .... 90 D4
  BURY BL9 .... 39 H6
  NEWLW WA12 .... 79 G8
  SWIN M27 .... 70 B4
  WGNE/HIN WN2 .... 48 F7
St Peters Primary School
  NTHM/RTH M23 .... 118 C1
St Peters RC High School &
  Lower School
  GTN M18 .... 100 A2
St Peter's RC High School
  Upper School
  DROY M43 .... 89 H4
St Peters RC Primary School
  MDTN M24 .... 57 K5
St Peters VC CE Primary School
  MILN OL16 .... 11 K9
St Philip Howard RC School
  GLSP SK13 .... 104 E3
St Philips CE Primary School
  ATH M46 .... 67 H1
St Philips RC Primary School
  BRO M7 .... 71 M3
  OFTN SK2 .... 113 H6
St Philips School
  CSLFD M3 .... 6 A4
St Phillips CE Primary School
  HULME M15 .... 87 J6
St Raphaels Catholic
  Primary School
  STLY SK15 .... 77 H7
St Richards RC Primary School
  ATH M46 .... 50 F8
St's Aidan & Oswalds RC
  Primary School
  ROY/SHW OL2 .... 59 G1
St Saviour Primary School
  RAD M26 .... 53 M5
St Sebastians RC
  Primary School
  SLFD M6 .... 71 K7
St Simon & Jude CE
  Primary School
  BOLS/LL BL3 .... 52 C1
St Simons Catholic
  Primary School
  BRAM/HZG SK7 .... 122 A1
St Stephen & All Martyrs CE
  Primary School
  BOLE BL2 .... 3 L7
St Stephen CE Primary School
  FWTH BL4 .... 53 K6
St Stephens & All Martyrs
  Infant School
  OLD OL1 .... 9 K3
St Stephens CE
  Primary School
  BRAM/HZG SK7 .... 113 J8
  DTN/ASHW M34 .... 90 B4
  TOT/BURYW BL8 .... 38 E3
  TYLD M29 .... 67 L6
  WGN WN1 .... 48 B2
St Stephen's RC School
  DROY M43 .... 89 K2
St Teresa RC Primary School
  BOLS/LL BL3 .... 53 K1
St Teresas RC Primary School
  IRL M44 .... 94 B4
  STRET M32 .... 97 K1
St Thomas Aquinas RC
  High School
  CCHDY M21 .... 97 M5
St Thomas CE Primary School
  AIMK WN4 .... 78 F1
  BOL BL1 .... 36 A2
  BURY BL9 .... 5 K6
  GOL/RIS/CU WA3 .... 79 L3
  HTNM SK4 .... 99 H6
  LEIGH WN7 .... 66 E8
  OLD OL1 .... 9 G8
  OLDS OL8 .... 9 G8
  STKP SK1 .... 13 K6
  WHTN BL5 .... 50 B7
St Thomas Hospital
  EDGY/DAV SK3 .... 13 H8
St Thomas Leesfield CE
  Primary School
  OLDE OL4 .... 60 B7
St Thomas More
  Catholic High School
  WGNW/BIL/O WN5 .... 14 A6

St Thomas More RC
  High School
  DTN/ASHW M34 .... 101 J2
St Thomas More RC
  Primary School
  MDTN M24 .... 57 K7
St Thomas of Canterbury
  Catholic Primary School
  BOL BL1 .... 35 K4
St Thomas Primary School
  CHH M8 .... 72 F4
St Thomas RC Primary School
  BRO M7 .... 72 B6
St Thomas VA CE Primary School
  MILN OL16 .... 29 L8
St Vincent RC Infant School
  HALE/TIMP WA15 .... 108 B7
St Vincents RC Primary School
  WHIT OL16 .... 27 K3
St Wilfrids CE Primary School
  NEWH/MOS M40 .... 74 A7
  WCNNW/ST WN6 .... 31 J3
  WYTH/NTH M22 .... 110 B4
St Wilfrids RC Primary School
  HULME M15 .... 87 H6
St William RC Primary School
  BOLS/LL BL3 .... 52 B1
St Williams RC Primary School
  WGNE/HIN WN2 .... 48 C5
St Willibrords RC
  Primary School
  OP/CLY M11 .... 88 F1
St Winifreds RC
  Primary School
  HTNM SK4 .... 111 K2
Sale Cricket Club
  SALE M33 .... 97 G7
Sale Golf Club
  SALE M33 .... 97 J7
Sale Grammar School
  SALE M33 .... 108 C1
Sale Leisure Centre
  SALE M33 .... 96 F7
Salford City Reds RLFC
  (The Willows)
  ORD M5 .... 86 A2
Salford College
  ECC M30 .... 84 D2
  ORD M5 .... 86 D5
  SLFD M6 .... 71 L8
  WALK M28 .... 69 G3
Salford County Court
  ORD M5 .... 86 D3
Salford Medical Centre
  SLFD M6 .... 86 B1
Salford Museum & Art Gallery
  ORD M5 .... 86 F2
Salford University
  Business Park
  SLFD M6 .... 71 L8
Samuel Laycock
  Special School
  STLY SK15 .... 76 C8
Sandilands Primary School
  NTHM/RTH M23 .... 108 F4
Saviour CE Primary School
  NEWH/MOS M40 .... 72 F7
Savoy Cinema
  HTNM SK4 .... 111 K1
Saxon Hall Leisure Centre
  MILN OL16 .... 11 L3
Saxon Holme Hotel
  HTNM SK4 .... 100 A8
Scholes Shopping Precinct
  WGN WN1 .... 15 J3
School Street Industrial Estate
  BRAM/HZG SK7 .... 122 A2
Scot Lane End CE
  Primary School
  HOR/BR BL6 .... 33 H4
Scot Lane Industrial Estate
  HOR/BR BL6 .... 33 H6
Scot Lane Primary School
  WGNW/BIL/O WN5 .... 47 J5
Seaford Industrial Estate
  SLFD M6 .... 71 L8
Sedgley Park Primary School
  PWCH M25 .... 72 A2
Sedgley Park RUFC
  WHTF M45 .... 55 G6
Sedgley Park Trading Estate
  PWCH M25 .... 71 L3
Seedley Primary School
  SLFD M6 .... 86 B2
Seminar Centre
  CMANW M2 .... 6 E6
Sett Valley Medical Centre
  NM/HAY SK22 .... 124 E4
Seven Brooks Medical Centre
  ATH M46 .... 67 G1
Severnside Trading Estate
  TRPK M17 .... 85 L7
Seymour Park Primary School
  OLDTF/WHR M16 .... 86 E8
Seymour Road Primary School
  OP/CLY M11 .... 89 G3
Shakerley CE Primary School
  TYLD M29 .... 67 K2
Shandon Clinic (Europe)
  HULME M15 .... 87 K7
Sharples Primary School
  BOL BL1 .... 22 D7
Shawclough Primary School
  WHIT OL12 .... 28 B1
Shawclough Trading Estate
  WHIT OL12 .... 28 A1
Shawgrove School
  DID/WITH M20 .... 98 C6
Shaw Heath Health Centre
  EDGY/DAV SK3 .... 13 H8
Shay Lane Medical Centre
  HALE/TIMP WA15 .... 117 L3
Shepherd Cross
  Industrial Estate
  BOL BL1 .... 35 M2
Shepley North Industrial Estate
  DTN/ASHW M34 .... 90 D5
Shepley South Industrial Estate
  DTN/ASHW M34 .... 90 D6
Sherborne Trading Estate
  CHH M8 .... 72 C7
Sherwood Business Park
  ROCH OL11 .... 42 A2
Shevington County
  Primary School
  WGNNW/ST WN6 .... 30 C6
Shevington Vale
  Primary School
  WGNNW/ST WN6 .... 30 B4

Shire Hill Hospital
  GLSP SK13 .... 105 H1
Shiv Lodge Medical Centre
  BRUN/LGST M13 .... 99 J1
The Shopping Centre
  CHD/CHDH SK8 .... 120 C2
Showcase Cinemas Belle Vue
  WGTN/LGST M12 .... 88 E7
Siddal Moor Sports College
  HEY OL10 .... 41 G5
Simmondley Primary School
  GLSP SK13 .... 104 D4
Slough Industrial Estate
  ORD M5 .... 86 F4
Smallbridge Health Centre
  WHIT OL16 .... 28 F1
Smallbridge Industrial Park
  MILN OL16 .... 28 E2
Smedleylane Junior School
  CHH M8 .... 72 E6
Smithills School
  BOL BL1 .... 35 L1
Smithy Bridge Primary School
  LIT OL15 .... 29 J1
The Smithy Surgery
  HYDE SK14 .... 93 G7
Snipe Retail Park
  DTN/ASHW M34 .... 90 A4
South Chadderton School
  CHAD OL9 .... 74 C2
Southern Cross School
  CCHDY M21 .... 97 M7
South Failsworth
  Primary School
  FAIL M35 .... 74 B7
Southfield Industrial Estate
  TRPK M17 .... 85 M7
Southfields School
  SALE M33 .... 108 C1
Southgate Industrial Estate
  HEY OL10 .... 41 J3
South Lancashire
  Industrial Estate
  AIMK WN4 .... 63 L6
Southlink Business Park
  OLDE OL4 .... 9 M6
South Manchester High School
  WYTH/NTH M22 .... 118 F1
Southmoor Business Park
  NTHM/RTH M23 .... 109 H5
Southmoor Industrial Estate
  NTHM/RTH M23 .... 109 H6
South Oldham Business Park
  CHAD OL9 .... 8 D2
South Reddish Medical Centre
  RDSH SK5 .... 100 C8
Southside Industrial Park
  ATH M46 .... 50 E8
South Trafford College
  ALT WA14 .... 108 A4
South West Manchester
  Cricket Club
  CCHDY M21 .... 97 M3
Sovereign Business Park
  WGN WN1 .... 15 J6
Spa Road Industrial Estate
  BOL BL1 .... 2 B5
Sparrow Hill Community School
  MILN OL16 .... 10 E5
Spindle Point Primary School
  FWTH BL4 .... 53 L7
The Spindles Shopping Centre
  OLD OL1 .... 9 H6
Spinning Gate Shopping Centre
  LEIGH WN7 .... 66 C7
Sport City
  OP/CLY M11 .... 88 C2
Sports Injury Centre
  MDTN M24 .... 57 K5
Spotland Bridge
  Industrial Centre
  ROCH OL11 .... 10 A2
Spotland Primary School
  WHIT OL12 .... 10 B2
Springbank Industrial Estate
  WGNE/HIN WN2 .... 64 C1
Spring Brook Special School
  CHAD OL9 .... 58 C5
Springfield Business Centre
  CSLFD M3 .... 6 E1
Springfield Hotel
  MPL/ROM SK6 .... 114 C5
Springfield House
  Medical Centre
  OLD OL1 .... 59 M4
Springfield Industrial Estate
  FAIL M35 .... 74 B4
Springfield Park Golf Club
  ROCH OL11 .... 27 K7
Springfield Primary School
  SALE M33 .... 96 E8
Springhead Community
  Infant & First School
  OLDE OL4 .... 60 C6
Springhill High School
  MILN OL16 .... 11 L9
Springside County
  Primary School
  BURY BL9 .... 25 H5
Spring View Cricket Club
  WGNE/HIN WN2 .... 15 J6
Springwood Primary School
  MPL/ROM SK6 .... 114 B1
Springwood School
  SWIN M27 .... 70 D6
Spurley Hey High School
  GTN M18 .... 99 L2
Stag Industrial Estate
  ALT WA14 .... 107 L6
Stakehill Industrial Estate
  MDTN M24 .... 42 A8
Stalybridge Celtic AFC
  STLY SK15 .... 91 M4
Stalybridge Cricket Club
  STLY SK15 .... 91 H4
Stalybridge Millbrook
  Cricket Club
  STLY SK15 .... 77 G8
Stalybridge St Pauls
  Cricket Club
  DUK SK16 .... 91 J5
Stalyhill Infants School
  STLY SK15 .... 92 B5
Stalyhill Junior School
  STLY SK15 .... 92 A5
Staly Industrial Estate
  STLY SK15 .... 91 L2
Stamford Golf Club
  MOSL OL5 .... 77 H5

Stamford High School
  AUL OL6 .... 76 B8
Stamford Park J & I School
  HALE/TIMP WA15 .... 117 G1
Standish Clinic
  WGNNW/ST WN6 .... 31 H4
Standish Community
  High School
  WGNNW/ST WN6 .... 30 F2
Standish Court Golf Club
  WGNNW/ST WN6 .... 31 J3
Standish Cricket Club
  WGNNW/ST WN6 .... 31 H4
Stanley Green Industrial Estate
  CHD/CHDH SK8 .... 120 A6
  CHD/CHDH SK8 .... 120 A8
Stanley Green Retail Park
  CHD/CHDH SK8 .... 120 B6
Stanley Grove Primary School
  WGTN/LGST M12 .... 88 C8
Stanley Road Primary School
  CHAD OL9 .... 58 E8
Stanneylands Hotel
  WILM/AE SK9 .... 126 F2
Stansfield Hall CE Free
  Primary School
  LIT OL15 .... 20 D4
Stansfield Road J & I School
  FAIL M35 .... 74 D4
Star Industrial Estate
  OLDS OL8 .... 9 J8
Station Approach
  Business Estate
  ROCH OL11 .... 10 E7
Staveleigh Medical Centre
  STLY SK15 .... 91 K2
Stella Maris School
  HTNM SK4 .... 111 H2
Stepping Hill Hospital
  OFTN SK2 .... 112 E8
Stirling Industrial Estate
  HOR/BR BL6 .... 33 M2
Stockport Air Raid Shelter
  STKP SK1 .... 13 H4
Stockport Bus Station
  EDGY/DAV SK3 .... 13 G5
Stockport College of FE & HE
  EDGY/DAV SK3 .... 13 H7
Stockport County Court
  STKP SK1 .... 13 H5
Stockport County FC &
  Sale Sharks RUFC
  (Edgeley Park)
  EDGY/DAV SK3 .... 13 G9
Stockport Crematorium
  OFTN SK2 .... 13 M9
Stockport Cricket Club
  EDGY/DAV SK3 .... 112 E8
Stockport Golf Club
  OFTN SK2 .... 113 L7
Stockport Grammar School
  OFTN SK2 .... 112 D7
Stockport Mega Bowl
  EDGY/DAV SK3 .... 13 H6
Stockport RUFC
  BRAM/HZG SK7 .... 121 J4
Stockport School
  OFTN SK2 .... 112 E7
Stockport Trading Estate
  HTNM SK4 .... 12 A5
Stone Hill Industrial Estate
  FWTH BL4 .... 52 F5
Stoneleigh Primary School
  OLD OL1 .... 59 L2
The Strand Medical Centre
  ROCH OL11 .... 42 C2
Stretford Grammar School
  STRET M32 .... 97 H3
Stretford High School
  STRET M32 .... 86 C8
Stretford Leisure Centre
  STRET M32 .... 86 C8
Stretford Memorial Hospital
  OLDTF/WHR M16 .... 97 L1
Stubbins Primary School
  RAMS BL0 .... 17 D3
Students Union Building
  CMANE M1 .... 7 H9
Styal Golf Club
  WILM/AE SK9 .... 119 J7
Styal Primary School
  WILM/AE SK9 .... 119 G8
Sudden Health Centre
  ROCH OL11 .... 27 M8
Sudell Street Trading Estate
  ANC M4 .... 7 K1
Sugden Sports Centre
  CMANE M1 .... 7 H9
Summersales Industrial Estate
  WGNS/IIMK WN3 .... 46 E8
Summerseat Methodist
  Primary School
  BURY BL9 .... 25 G2
Summervale Primary School
  OLDS OL8 .... 8 F7
Summerville Primary School
  SLFD M6 .... 71 G7
Sunning Hill Primary School
  BOLS/LL BL3 .... 36 A8
Sunnybank Clinic
  BURY BL9 .... 55 K1
Sunny Bank Primary School
  BURY BL9 .... 55 K1
Sunset Business Centre
  FWTH BL4 .... 53 M7
Swan Lane Medical Centre
  BOLS/LL BL3 .... 36 A8
Swan Meadow
  Industrial Estate
  WGNS/IIMK WN3 .... 14 C2
Swinton Cemetery
  SWIN M27 .... 70 A5
The Swinton County
  High School
  SWIN M27 .... 70 B3
Swinton Cricket Club
  SWIN M27 .... 70 D5
Swinton Industrial Estate
  SWIN M27 .... 70 C5
Swinton Leisure Centre
  SWIN M27 .... 70 C4
Swinton Park Golf Club
  SWIN M27 .... 70 A4
Tameside Business
  Development Centre
  DTN/ASHW M34 .... 100 F1
Tameside Business Park
  DUK SK16 .... 90 E5
Tameside College
  HYDE SK14 .... 91 H8

Tameside College of Technology
AUL OL6 .... 91 G1
HYDE SK14 .... 102 A5
Tameside County Court
AUL OL6 .... 90 F2
Tameside General Hospital
AUL OL6 .... 76 C8
Tame Valley Primary School
MPL/ROM SK6 .... 100 F5
Tandle Hill Country Park
ROY/SHW OL2 .... 42 D6
Tanfield Special School
WGNE/HIN WN2 .... 49 J7
Tashbar School
BRO M7 .... 72 B3
Tavistock Industrial Estate
OP/CLY M11 .... 89 G6
Taylors Sports Club
ECC M30 .... 85 H3
Temple Primary School
CHH M8 .... 72 E6
Ten Acres Sports Complex
NEWH/MOS M40 .... 73 K7
Tennis Club
WILM/AE SK9 .... 126 B8
Terminal 1
MANAIR M90 .... 118 D6
Terminal 2
MANAIR M90 .... 118 C4
Terminal 3
MANAIR M90 .... 118 E6
Thames Industrial Estate
WGTN/LGST M12 .... 88 A5
Thames Trading Centre
IRL M44 .... 94 C5
Thomasson Memorial
Special School
BOL BL1 .... 35 L5
Thorn Grove Primary School
CHD/CHDH SK8 .... 120 C6
Thornham Cricket Club
MDTN M24 .... 42 A5
Thornham St James CE
Primary School
ROY/SHW OL2 .... 43 G4
Thornleigh Salesian College
BOL BL1 .... 22 A8
Thornsett Primary School
NM/HAY SK22 .... 125 G1
Thornsett Trading Estate
NM/HAY SK22 .... 125 G2
Thorp Primary School
ROY/SHW OL2 .... 42 F7
Three Sisters
AIMK WN4 .... 63 M5
Times Retail Park
HEY OL10 .... 40 F2
Timperley Health Centre
HALE/TIMP WA15 .... 108 D5
Tithe Barn Primary School
HTNM SK4 .... 111 K1
Tonacliffe Primary School
WHIT OL12 .... 18 D6
Tonge Bridge Industrial Estate
BOLE BL2 .... 3 J3
Tonge Cricket Club
BOLE BL2 .... 36 F1
Tonge Fold Health Centre
BOLE BL2 .... 3 L5
Tonge Moor Health Centre
BOLE BL2 .... 36 F3
Tonge Moor Primary School
BOLE BL2 .... 3 K1
Tootal Drive County
Primary School
SLFD M6 .... 85 M2
Top O'th'brow Primary School
BOLE BL2 .... 37 H2
Torkington Primary School
BRAM/HZG SK7 .... 122 C2
Tottington Health Centre
TOT/BURYW BL8 .... 24 B5
Tottington High School
TOT/BURYW BL8 .... 24 C6
Tottington Primary School
TOT/BURYW BL8 .... 24 C7
Tower (Remains of)
RAD M26 .... 55 G1
Towers Business Park
DID/WITH M20 .... 98 B8
DID/WITH M20 .... 110 E3
Townfield Industrial Estate
OLDE OL4 .... 59 L5
Towngate Business Centre
LHULT M38 .... 52 B7
Town Hall & Albert Halls
BOL BL1 .... 2 E5
Town Square Shopping Centre
OLD OL1 .... 9 J5
Trafalgar Business Park
BRO M7 .... 72 B8
Trafford Athletics Track
STRET M32 .... 97 J3
Trafford Centre
TRPK M17 .... 85 G6
Trafford Centre Leisure Complex
TRPK M17 .... 84 E6
Trafford FC
URM M41 .... 95 K3
Trafford General Hospital
URM M41 .... 95 K1
Trafford Healthcare
SALE M33 .... 109 G3
Trafford Retail Park
URM M41 .... 84 F7
Trafford Water Sports Centre
SALE M33 .... 97 H6
Trans Pennine Trading Estate
ROCH OL11 .... 42 A1
Travel Inn
CHAD OL9 .... 74 B2
CHD/CHDH SK8 .... 119 L2
CMANE M1 .... 7 G6
DTN/ASHW M34 .... 100 F1
GOL/RIS/CU WA3 .... 79 L5
MILN OL16 .... 28 K8
OFTN SK2 .... 112 D6
PWCH M25 .... 55 K7
SALE M33 .... 96 A6
TRPK M17 .... 85 G6
WGNS/IIMK WN3 .... 63 J3
WGNW/BIL/O WN5 .... 46 C5
Travel Inn Hotel
SALQ M50 .... 86 D5
Travelodge
CHAD OL9 .... 58 B8
CSLFD M3 .... 6 E3
RNFD/HAY WA11 .... 78 B4
Trent Industrial Estate
ROY/SHW OL2 .... 43 L4

The Triangle
ANC M4 .... 6 F3
Trinity CE High School
HULME M15 .... 87 K6
Trinity Retail Park
BOLE BL2 .... 3 H7
Trinity School
STLY SK15 .... 91 J3
Tudor Industrial Estate
DUK SK16 .... 90 D5
Tulketh Street
Industrial Estate
NEWH/MOS M40 .... 73 J4
Tunshill Golf Club
MILN OL16 .... 29 M6
Turton Golf Club
EDGW/EG BL7 .... 22 D2
Turton High School
EDGW/EG BL7 .... 22 E5
Turton Leisure Centre
EDGW/EG BL7 .... 22 D2
Turton Tower
EDGW/EG BL7 .... 22 F1
Tweed Street
Industrial Estate
LEIGH WN7 .... 66 E8
Twelve Apostles RC
Primary School
LEIGH WN7 .... 66 A4
Twiss Green Primary School
GOL/RIS/CU WA3 .... 81 H8
Two Porches School
ATH M46 .... 67 G1
Two Trees High School
DTN/ASHW M34 .... 101 L3
Tyldesley Cemetery
TYLD M29 .... 68 A4
Tyldesley Primary School
TYLD M29 .... 67 L5
Tyldesley Swimming Pool
TYLD M29 .... 67 H3
Tyntesfield CP School
SALE M33 .... 108 B3
UCI Cinema
TRPK M17 .... 85 G6
UGC Cinema
BOL BL1 .... 36 D1
DID/WITH M20 .... 111 G3
WGNW/BIL/O WN5 .... 47 J4
EDGY/DAV SK3 .... 13 H6
UMIST
CMANE M1 .... 7 J7
Union Mill Industrial Estate
MOSL OL5 .... 77 G1
United Trading Estate
OLDTF/WHR M16 .... 86 C7
University College Salford
CSLFD M3 .... 6 A2
University of Manchester
BRUN/LGST M13 .... 87 L6
ECC M30 .... 84 A6
RUSH/FAL M14 .... 99 G2
University of Manchester
Institute of Science &
Technology
BRUN/LGST M13 .... 7 J9
University of Salford
ORD M5 .... 86 F2
Unsworth Medical Centre
BURY BL9 .... 55 M1
Unsworth Primary School
BURY BL9 .... 55 K2
Urbis
ANC M4 .... 6 F2
Urmston Grammar School
URM M41 .... 95 M1
Urmston J & I School
URM M41 .... 95 L2
Urmston Leisure Centre
URM M41 .... 95 L2
Urmston Town FC
URM M41 .... 95 J3
Vaishali Medical Centre
CCHDY M21 .... 97 L3
Vale Park Industrial Estate
CHH M8 .... 72 F5
The Valley Leisure Centre
BOL BL1 .... 36 F1
Valley Special School
BRAM/HZG SK7 .... 120 E7
Varley Street Clinic
NEWH/MOS M40 .... 73 G8
Varna Street Primary School
OP/CLY M11 .... 89 G6
Vaughan Street
Industrial Estate
WGTN/LGST M12 .... 88 C5
Vauxhall Industrial Estate
RDSH SK5 .... 100 B6
RDSH SK5 .... 100 C8
Vernon Industrial Estate
STKP SK1 .... 13 M1
STKP SK1 .... 13 M2
The Vernon Infant School
POY/DIS SK12 .... 129 J1
The Vernon Junior School
POY/DIS SK12 .... 129 J1
Vernon Park Museum
STKP SK1 .... 112 C2
Vernon Park Primary School
STKP SK1 .... 13 L4
Vernon Road Medical Centre
TOT/BURYW BL8 .... 24 D3
Victoria Avenue
Primary School
BKLY M9 .... 57 G7
Victoria Industrial Estate
ANC M4 .... 88 A3
LEIGH WN7 .... 66 B6
Victoria Medical Centre
URM M41 .... 96 A2
Victoria Park Infant School
STRET M32 .... 97 G2
Victoria Park Junior School
STRET M32 .... 97 G2
Victoria Trading Estate
CHAD OL9 .... 74 E1
Victory Trading Estate
BOLS/LL BL3 .... 3 G9
Village Medical Centre
LIT OL15 .... 20 C7
VIP Centre Industrial Estate
OLD OL1 .... 59 M3
Wadeson Junior School
BRUN/LGST M13 .... 7 L9
Wadsworth Industrial Park
BOLS/LL BL3 .... 36 B8
Walkden High School
WALK M28 .... 69 H2

Walmersley Golf Club
BURY BL9 .... 25 L4
Walmsley CE Primary School
EDGW/EG BL7 .... 22 B3
Walshaw Sports Club
TOT/BURYW BL8 .... 24 C7
Walton Park Leisure Centre
SALE M33 .... 108 D2
Wardle High School
WHIT OL12 .... 19 L7
Wardley Industrial Estate
WALK M28 .... 69 M3
Warner Village Cinema
BURY BL9 .... 39 L6
HOR/BR BL6 .... 34 B4
SALQ M50 .... 86 C5
Warren Wood Primary School
OFTN SK2 .... 113 K7
Warrington Road
Industrial Estate
WGNS/IIMK WN3 .... 47 H7
Warth Park Industrial Estate
BURY BL9 .... 38 F5
Washacre Primary School
WHTN BL5 .... 50 C5
Washway Road Medical Centre
SALE M33 .... 96 D8
The Watergate Clinic
MILN OL16 .... 10 F4
Waterloo Industrial Park
BOL BL1 .... 3 G2
STKP SK1 .... 13 K5
Waterloo Primary School
AULW OL7 .... 75 J7
The Water Place
BOL BL1 .... 2 E6
Waters Edge Business Park
ORD M5 .... 86 E6
Watersheddings
Primary School
OLD OL1 .... 59 M3
Waterside Business Park
GLSP SK13 .... 93 J6
The Waterside Hotel
DID/WITH M20 .... 110 F4
Waterside Industrial Park
BOLS/LL BL3 .... 52 F1
Waterside Trading Estate
LEIGH WN7 .... 66 E8
Watersports Centre
SALQ M50 .... 86 C5
Watford Bridge
Industrial Estate
NM/HAY SK22 .... 124 E3
Waybridge Industrial Estate
ORD M5 .... 86 A4
Weaste Trading Estate
ORD M5 .... 86 A2
Webster Primary School
RUSH/FAL M14 .... 87 K8
Welfare Clinic
MDTN M24 .... 57 G2
Welkin Road Industrial Estate
STKP SK1 .... 112 E1
Wellacre High School for Boys
URM M41 .... 95 G3
Wellfield Junior School
SALE M33 .... 96 C6
Wellfield Medical Centre
CHH M8 .... 72 C4
Well Green Primary School
HALE/TIMP WA15 .... 117 J1
Wellington Road
Industrial Estate
AUL OL6 .... 90 D1
Wellington School
HALE/TIMP WA15 .... 108 C6
Wentworth High School
ECC M30 .... 70 C8
Werneth Cricket Bowling &
Tennis Club
OLDS OL8 .... 8 F9
Werneth Golf Club
OLDS OL8 .... 75 H3
Werneth J & I School
OLDS OL8 .... 59 G8
Werneth Low Golf Club
HYDE SK14 .... 102 E6
Werneth Private
Preparatory School
OLDS OL8 .... 8 E8
Werneth School
MPL/ROM SK6 .... 113 J2
Wesley Methodist
Primary School
RAD M26 .... 38 B7
Westbrook Trading Estate
TRPK M17 .... 86 A5
Westbury Street
Industrial Estate
HYDE SK14 .... 90 F7
West Croft Industrial Estate
MDTN M24 .... 56 F7
West End Medical Centre
AULW OL7 .... 90 C7
West End Primary School
AULW OL7 .... 90 C2
DTN/ASHW M34 .... 100 D1
West End Trading Estate
SWIN M27 .... 70 C3
Westenlea Clinic
DTN/ASHW M34 .... 90 B7
West Gorton Medical Centre
WGTN/LGST M12 .... 88 C6
West Hill School
STLY SK15 .... 91 J2
Westhoughton Clinic
WHTN BL5 .... 50 B4
Westhoughton Cricket Club
WHTN BL5 .... 50 B4
Westhoughton Golf Club
WHTN BL5 .... 50 A3
Westhoughton High School
WHTN BL5 .... 50 C4
Westhoughton Industrial Estate
WHTN BL5 .... 50 B2
Westhoughton Parochial CE
Primary School
WHTN BL5 .... 50 B4
Westhoughton Primary School
WHTN BL5 .... 50 C3
Westinghouse Industrial Estate
TRPK M17 .... 86 A7
Westleigh Cricket Club
LEIGH WN7 .... 66 A3
Westleigh High School
LEIGH WN7 .... 66 A3
Westleigh Methodist
Primary School
LEIGH WN7 .... 66 A4

Westleigh St Pauls
Primary School
LEIGH WN7 .... 66 B4
West Liverpool Street
Primary School
SLFD M6 .... 86 C2
Westmorland Primary School
RDSH SK5 .... 100 F6
West One Retail Park
SALQ M50 .... 85 K3
Westpoint Medical Centre
BNG/LEV M19 .... 99 J3
Westwood Business Centre
CHAD OL9 .... 8 E6
Westwood Cemetery
WGNS/IIMK WN3 .... 15 H9
Westwood Industrial Estate
CHAD OL9 .... 8 D5
Westwood Park Primary School
ECC M30 .... 84 E1
Westwood Primary School
CHAD OL9 .... 8 D6
Westwood Trading Estate
MPL/ROM SK6 .... 114 A7
Whalley Range FC
CCHDY M21 .... 98 A3
Whalley Range High School
OLDTF/WHR M16 .... 98 C4
Wharfside Business Centre
TRPK M17 .... 86 C6
Wharton Primary School
LHULT M38 .... 52 B6
Wheatfield Industrial Estate
ROY/SHW OL2 .... 59 G1
Wheatlea Industrial Estate
WGNS/IIMK WN3 .... 63 J2
Wheatsheaf Industrial Estate
SWIN M27 .... 70 E3
Wheatsheaf Shopping Centre
MILN OL16 .... 10 F3
Whelley Hospital
WGN WN1 .... 48 B2
White City Retail Park
OLDTF/WHR M16 .... 86 D7
Whitefield Community
Primary School
WHTF M45 .... 55 K4
Whitefield Golf Club
WHTF M45 .... 55 H5
Whitefield Medical Centre
WHTF M45 .... 55 H4
Whitegate End Primary School
CHAD OL9 .... 74 B1
Whitehill Industrial Estate
HTNM SK4 .... 100 B7
Whitehill Primary School
HTNM SK4 .... 100 B8
White Swan Industrial Estate
OLD OL1 .... 59 M4
Whitley Road Medical Centre
NEWH/MOS M40 .... 72 F8
Whittaker Golf Club
LIT OL15 .... 20 E8
Whittaker Moss
Primary School
ROCH OL11 .... 27 G3
The Whitworth Art Gallery
BRUN/LGST M13 .... 87 L8
Whitworth Community
High School
WHIT OL12 .... 18 D3
Whitworth Football &
Cricket Club
WHIT OL12 .... 18 D3
Whitworth Park School
RUSH/FAL M14 .... 87 K8
Whitworth Swimming Pool
WHIT OL12 .... 18 E2
The Wiend Centre
WGN WN1 .... 15 G4
Wigan Athletic FC (JJB Stadium)
WGNW/BIL/O WN5 .... 14 A3
Wigan Borough Cemetery
WGNS/IIMK WN3 .... 48 A7
Wigan Crematorium
WGNS/IIMK WN3 .... 48 A8
Wigan Golf Club
CHLY/EC PR7 .... 32 A2
Wigan Little Theatre
WGN WN1 .... 15 H3
Wigan Magistrates Court
WGN WN1 .... 15 H5
Wigan Pier
WGNS/IIMK WN3 .... 14 D6
Wigan RUFC
WGN WN1 .... 32 A7
Wigan Warriors RLFC (JJB Stadium)
WGNW/BIL/O WN5 .... 14 A3
Wilbraham Primary School
RUSH/FAL M14 .... 98 D3
Wild Bank Community School
STLY SK15 .... 92 A2
Willan Industrial Estate
ORD M5 .... 86 C3
William Andrews
Swimming Baths
DUK SK16 .... 91 G5
William Hulmes
Grammar School
OLDTF/WHR M16 .... 98 C3
William Roet Flixton Golf Club
URM M41 .... 95 K4
William Wroe Municipal
Golf Course
URM M41 .... 95 K2
Willow Bank Hotel
RUSH/FAL M14 .... 98 F4
Willow Grove Cemetery
RDSH SK5 .... 100 D7
Willow Grove School
AIMK WN4 .... 64 B7
The Willows Primary School
HALE/TIMP WA15 .... 108 C6
WYTH/NTH M22 .... 118 E2
Wilmslow Albion FC
WILM/AE SK9 .... 126 E1
Wilmslow Health Centre
WILM/AE SK9 .... 126 E6
Wilmslow High School
WILM/AE SK9 .... 126 F6
Wilmslow Leisure Centre
WILM/AE SK9 .... 126 D6
Wilmslow Preparatory School
WILM/AE SK9 .... 126 F5
Wilmslow RFC
WILM/AE SK9 .... 126 D3
Wilmslow Road
Medical Centre
RUSH/FAL M14 .... 98 F1
WILM/AE SK9 .... 119 M8

Wind in the Willows Hotel
GLSP SK13 .... 105 J4
Windmill Lane
Industrial Estate
DTN/ASHW M34 .... 100 F2
Wingates Industrial Estate
WHTN BL5 .... 50 A1
Winstanley College
WGNW/BIL/O WN5 .... 62 B1
Winstanley Medical Centre
WGNS/IIMK WN3 .... 63 G1
Winstanley Primary School
WGNS/IIMK WN3 .... 62 F2
Withington Bowling Club
RUSH/FAL M14 .... 98 F5
Withington Girls School
RUSH/FAL M14 .... 98 E4
Withington Golf Club
DID/WITH M20 .... 110 C2
Withington Hospital
DID/WITH M20 .... 98 C6
Withington Swimming Baths
DID/WITH M20 .... 98 E6
Withins High School
BOLE BL2 .... 37 H2
Wolfenden Primary School
BOL BL1 .... 36 B2
Woodbank Cricket Club
TOT/BURYW BL8 .... 25 G8
Woodbank Park Athletics Track
STKP SK1 .... 112 F3
Woodbank Primary School
TOT/BURYW BL8 .... 25 G8
Woodend Mills Industrial Estate
OLDE OL4 .... 60 C7
Woodfield Primary School
WGN WN1 .... 31 M8
Woodfields Retail Park
BURY BL9 .... 4 E3
Wood Fold Primary School
WGNNW/ST N6 .... 31 G4
Woodford Aerodrome
BRAM/HZG SK7 .... 128 D3
Woodford Cricket Club
BRAM/HZG SK7 .... 128 B2
Woodhey High School
RAMS BL0 .... 24 D1
Woodheys Primary School
SALE M33 .... 108 B2
Woodhouse Primary School
URM M41 .... 84 D8
Woodhouses Voluntary
Primary School
FAIL M35 .... 74 F6
Woodlands Hospital
WALK M28 .... 52 D8
Woodlands Industrial Estate
NEWLW WA12 .... 78 F6
Woodley Health Centre
MPL/ROM SK6 .... 101 K7
Woodley Primary School
MPL/ROM SK6 .... 101 L7
Woodley Sports Centre
MPL/ROM SK6 .... 101 K6
Woodsend Primary School
URM M41 .... 94 F1
Woods Hospital
GLSP SK13 .... 104 E1
Woodside School
WYTH/NTH M22 .... 110 C8
Woolfold Industrial Estate
TOT/BURYW BL8 .... 24 E8
Woolworths Sports Club
ROCH OL11 .... 41 M1
Worsley Business Park
TYLD M29 .... 68 C4
Worsley Golf Club
ECC M30 .... 69 M8
Worsley Mesnes
Primary School
WGNS/IIMK WN3 .... 47 K8
Worsley Road Industrial Estate
FWTH BL4 .... 52 F6
Worsley Trading Estate
LHULT M38 .... 52 B7
Worthington Lakes
Business Park
WGN WN1 .... 31 M4
Worthington Primary School
SALE M33 .... 97 J3
Worth Primary School
POY/DIS SK12 .... 129 K1
Wrightington Hospital
WGNNW/ST WN6 .... 30 B3
Wrightington Hotel &
Country Club
WGNNW/ST WN6 .... 30 C1
Wright Robinson Sports
College
GTN M18 .... 89 J6
The Wycliffe Hotel
EDGY/DAV SK3 .... 12 C8
Wythenshawe Hall
Country Park
NTHM/RTH M23 .... 109 L4
Wythenshawe Hospital
NTHM/RTH M23 .... 109 J8
Wythenshawe Park Track
NTHM/RTH M23 .... 109 K4
Xaverian Sixth Form College
RUSH/FAL M14 .... 98 F1
Yeargate Industrial Estate
BURY BL9 .... 40 A2
Yew Tree J & I School
CHAD OL9 .... 58 C8
Yew Tree Primary School
DUK SK16 .... 91 H6
Yew Tree Trading Estate
RNFD/HAY WA11 .... 78 A4
York House Hotel
SALQ M50 .... 90 D2
Y Sport & Leisure Centre
CSLFD M3 .... 6 C6

The Post Office is a registered trademark of Post Office Ltd. in the UK and other countries.

Schools address data provided by Education Direct.

Petrol station information supplied by Johnsons

One-way street data provided by © Tele Atlas N.V.   Tele Atlas

Garden centre information provided by:

Garden Centre Association   Britains best garden centres

Wyevale Garden Centre